J. Bucher

A Kannada-English School-Dictionary Chiefly Based on the Labours of the Reverend Doctor F. Kittel

J. Bucher

A Kannada-English School-Dictionary Chiefly Based on the Labours of the Reverend Doctor F. Kittel

ISBN/EAN: 9783337859473

Printed in Europe, USA, Canada, Australia, Japan

Cover: Foto ©Thomas Meinert / pixelio.de

More available books at **www.hansebooks.com**

A

KANNAḌA-ENGLISH

SCHOOL-DICTIONARY

CHIEFLY BASED ON THE LABOURS OF THE

REV. DR. F. KITTEL

BY THE

Rev. J. BUCHER.

ಕನ್ನಡ ಮತ್ತು ಇಂಗ್ಲಿಷ್

ಶಾಲಾನಿಘಂಟು

MANGALORE
BASEL MISSION BOOK & TRACT DEPOSITORY
1899

PRINTED AT THE BASEL MISSION PRESS, MANGALORE.

PREFACE.

The present work is designed to form a companion volume to the well known and much appreciated English-Canarese School-Dictionary, compiled by the Rev. F. Ziegler. The publication of a Kannaḍa-English School-Dictionary has for a long time been a deep-felt desideratum, as the two smaller editions hitherto extant have but insufficiently served their purpose. The stupendous work of the Rev. Dr. Kittel, the eminent lexicographer of the Kannaḍa language, whose unremitting labours have set a permanent literary monument to the language, standing out in bold features of historical, etymological and philological, critical researches for guidance and instruction to *litterateurs* striving after Kannaḍa embellishment and scholarship, held out promising inducements and marked facilities to undertake this work which is chiefly based upon it.

Plan and arrangement: To add to the usefulness of the work and to facilitate its use, I deemed it fit to indicate the principles that have been adopted in arranging the matter and when launching on new methods I have attempted rather to err on the side of cautious adherence than on the side of hasty innovation.

I. Orthography: *a.* **Obsolete Letters.** These are ಱ and ೞ, now universally represented by ರ and ಳ, and have been put in parantheses immediately after the words in which they occur to give an insight into their different origin and meaning.

N. B. The double consonant ಕ್ಷ has been brought to its proper place and is invariably to be looked up under the letter ಕ್.

b. **Sonnĕ.** The method of using **bindu** or **sonnĕ** indiscriminately before classified (*vargíya*) and unclassified (*avargíya*) letters sanctioned by former lexicographers, grammarians and time-honoured practice, has uniformily been adopted, though at variance with the laws of etymology. These laws have not seldom to give way to usage and well-established practice. But, though this convenient mode of representing by **sonnĕ** the letters ṇ, n and m, when followed by consonants of their own class, and the nasals ṅ, and ń has been adhered to, the alphabetical order of words has been maintained uninfringed. Words in which the sonnĕ occurs, appear now in their proper place in the alphabet. This may at the beginning occasion a little embarrassment to those who are accustomed to look up this class of words at the head of each letter, but all difficulty will with practice disappear.

c. **Orthography proper** is yet a neglected field of study. The colloquial language, legitimately abounding with provincial peculiarities, dialectical whimsicalities and vulgar inelegancies, must ever differ from the written language. The *lingua litera* should possess a uniform system of spelling, which it has in some respects not yet accepted, but approving of various spellings as authors think fit. The four short vowels ă, ĕ, ĭ, ŭ, for instance promiscuously interchange in words like: ಮದುವೆ, ಮದವೆ, ಮದಿವೆ, ಮದವೆ, ಮದುಮೆ, *etc.* ....or ಕಿತ್ತಳಿ, ಕಿತ್ತಳೆ, ಕಿತ್ತಿಳಿ, ಕಿತ್ತೆಳೆ, *etc.* ....or ಅಂಗಳ, -ಳು, -ಳಿ, -ಳೆ, *etc.* ...or ಅಪಿಮು, ಅಪೀಮು, ಅಪಮು, ಅಫು, *etc.* ...or ಚಗತಿ, ಚಗ^ತಿ, ಚಿಗ^ತಿ, ಚಿಗೆ^ತಿ, *etc.* As most of these forms occur in books, newspapers and documents, they demand the same attention of being embodied in the vocabulary which is a mere encumbrance to the student. Hence a standard orthography is greatly desired.

II. Compounds. This class of words is very numerous in the Kannaḍa language and materially contributes to its copiousness. The largest number of compounds has been received from the ductile, flexible and infinitely copious Saṁskṛita language, so peculiarly adapted to form numberless compounds. All compounds, irrespective of their origin, whether of pure Kannaḍa, of Saṁskṛita, of Tadbhava or of any other tongue, have been treated alike, and subordinated to leading words—a hyphen denoting the division of the members of the compound. Many compounds and especially Kannaḍa compounds, as ಇಮ್ಮಡಿ,

ಚಿನ್ನಬಟ್ಟು, ಚಿಂಬಳಿ, etc., had in many instances to be introduced as independent words when the euphonic changes effected in combining the separate parts would involve too great a task to recognise them. Both **Samskrita** noun-compounds, as of ಅಗ್ನಿ, ಆತ್ಮ, ಕರ್ಮ, ನೀತಿ, etc., as well as adjectival and adverbial compounds, as of ಅತಿ, ಪರ, ಅಷ್ಟ, ಸು, etc., have been treated in this manner, provided the phonetic changes caused by the sandhi of the two words remained unmodified. Where a phonetic change or an elision or a permutation of letters took place the compound was treated as a separate word.

III. Derivatives: *a.* **Unusual Derivatives.** It should be borne in mind that there is, logically speaking, a vast class of derivatives formed by adding to a primary root etymological terminations, inflectional affixes, *etc.*, . . .*e. g.* ಪು added to ನೆನೆ=ನೆನಪು, ಹೊಳೆ=ಹೊಳಪು; or ಸು added to ನೆನೆ=ನೆನಸು, ತಿಳಿ=ತಿಳಿಸು; or ಇಕೆ added to ನಂಬು=ನಂಬಿಕೆ, ಅಂಜು=ಅಂಜಿಕೆ, ಉಡು=ಉಡಿಕೆ; or ಮೆ added to ತಾಳು=(ತಾಳುಮೆ) ತಾಳ್ಮೆ, ಬಲ=ಬಲ್ಮೆ; etc. These being difficult to trace to their original constituent parts have, of course, been considered as underived and treated accordingly.

b. **Proper derivatives** of *abstract* and *personal* nouns, where no hazy uncertainty is felt, terminating in -ತನ, -ತ್ವ, -ತೆ, -ವಂತ, -ಗಾರ, -ಗಾರ್ತಿ, -ಖೋರ, -ಇಷ್ಟ, -ದಾರ, *etc.* have consistently been added on to the primary word. In incorporating these derivatives the same method has been employed as with the compound.

Verbal Derivatives of unfrequent occurrence terminating in -ಇಸು, as ಕೋಪಿಸು, ಸಂತೋಷಿಸು, ಸ್ನೇಹಿಸು, *etc.* have been exhibited under the primary words ಕೋಪ, ಸಂತೋಷ, ಸ್ನೇಹ, *etc.*, however with the alteration of writing the whole word in full to avoid ambiguity and confusion. Verbs of great importance and frequent usage, as: ಇಳಿಸು, ಕಲಿಸು, ನಡಿಸು, ಬೋಧಿಸು, *etc.*, have been introduced as independent words.

IV. Homonyms, of which the Kannaḍa language embosoms a good number, have occasionally been split up under two or three heads, when they obviously and intelligibly belong to different roots bearing the characteristics of distinct derivation.

Homonymous roots involving the sense of a noun, of a verb and even eventually of an adverb, as ಕುಟ್ಟು, ತಪ್ಪು, ನೆಟ್ಟನೆ, ತೊದಕು, ಹೊರ, *etc.* have been treated under one head with their respective grammatical signs.

V. Grammatical significations. For a School-Dictionary it is a most important feature to indicate the **parts of speech,** the determination of which cannot be left to the discretion of the pupil. The abbreviated grammatical signs have been added after the Kannaḍa word. The treatment of the **Saṁskṛita** different verbal derivations that have not yet assumed a definite part of speech in Kannaḍa has been made subject to the same method adopted by reliable Saṁskṛita lexicographers. The abbreviation for *"causative verb"*, with which the Kannaḍa language can be marvellously enriched, has been expelled as fallen into disuse and where necessary substituted by "*v. t.*" The grammatical signs are only added to the *leading word* and not to compounds or derivatives being in most cases self-evident.

VI. English equivalents. Special attention has been paid to the rendering of the English equivalents. Brevity and conciseness have systematically been aimed at in order to give a ready-made coin. Considerable pains have also been taken to contract and condense the equivalents into as few groups as practicable to facilitate comprehension. Another effort has been made while arranging the several meanings in order to indicate their actual growth and development, beginning, if possible, with the primitive meaning suggested by etymology. It has also been found recommendable not to adduce too many English equivalents to facilitate the choice of the most appropriate one.

VII. Origin of words. The Kannaḍa language is one of the principle representatives of the Dravidian language-family in South-India spoken by upwards of 10 millions. It is however to be remembered that the language, as in fact all languages, being in constant transition and permutation, does not only comprise Dravidian elements but has absorbed various alien ingredients. The most prominent and at the same time formative and constructive factor in the language is the *Dravidian* which forms the solid groundwork determining the declensional and conjugational and other inflections and supplying the more common, homely and familiar words, as ಬರು, ಕೇಳು, ನೋಡು, ಹೋಗು; ಒಳ್ಳೆ, ಕೆಟ್ಟ, ಚಲೋ; ಮನೆ, ಕೆಲಸ; ಮೇಲೆ, ಕೆಳಗೆ, *etc.* Next we have the **Saṁskṛita** element which has had a great influence upon the language in enriching its vocabulary, in augmenting its synonyms and in ennobling its composition. The introduction of Saṁskṛita words dates back to the contact of the Dravidians with the Aryans and supplied the language with almost all its abstract, religious and scientific terms. The Dravidian words are for every day events and natural feelings, while the Saṁskṛita are elegant, dignified and artificial, fitted for rhetoric, subtle disputation and the profound expressions of philosophy. Many have retained their unaltered Saṁskṛita form, whereas others have changed so as to suit the Kannaḍa tongue. The latter class are called Tadbhavas. Next we have a good number of **Hindustâni** and **Mahraṭi** words, chiefly relating to feudalism *and* militia, whose introduction is due to the Moghul and Mahratta conquests of Kannaḍa districts. Some few Portuguese expressions have found their way into the language too, as ಇಂಗ್ರೇಜಿ, ತುಬೀನು, *etc.* from the Portuguese period. Finally the **English** language has also commenced to contribute its mite mainly relating to education, jurisprudence and revenue. Some have already become home-words and, as time advances and a smattering of mispronounced English diffuses into the masses, it is but natural that this process of assimilation continues at even a more extensive rate.

To bring out this feature conspicuously it has been thought desirable to mark with the initials of the respective language the words migrated from. The carrying out of this principle has sometimes met with considerable difficulty with regard to words, doubtless of Saṁskṛitic origin, but which had come into Kannaḍa through the medium of another Indian language, as **s.** ದಶರಾತ್ರಿ = **h.** ದಸರಾ = **k.** ದಸರೆ; **s.** ಮರ್ಕಟ = **m.** ಮಂಕಡ = **k.** ಮಂಗ; **s.** ಕರ್ಪಟ = **h.** ಕಪ್ಡಾ = **k.** ಕಪಡೆ. In such cases the greatest probability has always carried the decision, as no comparative philological studies could be made. It has been the compiler's aim to attain to utmost accuracy with pure Kannaḍa and pure Saṁskṛita words, whereas with Tadbhavas such an exactitude was unattainable.

As ancient classical literature is extensively read in schools and colleges a considerable number of obsolete and obolescent words principally occurring in Jaimini Bhârata and other poetical works prescribed have been inserted and marked by the letters **a. k.**

VIII. Fusion of elements. The foreign words that have come into the language do not stand by themselves as an independent class but have become Kannaḍasised subject to Kannaḍa laws and analogies. But, notwithstanding this metamorphosis the borrowed words, taken as a class, have a peculiar character which separates them even to the feeling of an uneducated Kannaḍa man from the Dravidian stock, thus giving to the language a somewhat heterogeneous aspect. But a still more serious disadvantage is the necessity of expressing new ideas either with the help of Saṁskṛita or English. The expressiveness and suggestiveness of these terms are hidden from those who are unacquainted with Saṁskṛita and English, and thus the language suffers in its power of quickening and originating thought.

IX. Conclusion. To secure the greatest possible accuracy and perfection the manuscript copy was, before its print, placed into the hands of R. Ry. Bh. Shiva Rau, the experienced and learned corrector of the Basel Mission Press, whose thorough acquaintance with the great work of Dr. Kittel in having carried it through the press has enabled him to make some valuable suggestions and not a few additions, for whose liberal services the author is under great obligation. My thanks are also due to the Kanarese Pandit B. Rama Krishnaya, Munshi of the G. M. High School Mangalore, who assisted in reading the proof-sheets, and also to Mr. T. Maben, Assistant Teacher, G. M.

High School, for a list of legal terms. The printer and publisher deserve also a vote of thanks.

In conclusion the author desires to express his profound admiration for the supreme Kannaḍa scholarship of Dr. Kittel's work.

Though the compiler is more sensible of the deficiencies and shortcomings of this work than any other person can be, he does not hesitate to confidently commend it to the public, for whom it will prove both instructive and useful, and he will be amply rewarded for his night-labours bestowed upon it by its appreciative and extensive use.

Hints and suggestions for improvement and enhanced efficiency will readily and thankfully be received.

Mangalore, January 1899.

J. Bucher.

List of Abbreviations.

a. = adjective.
abl. = ablative.
acc. = accusative.
ad. = adverb.
a. k. = ancient Kannaḍa.
arith. = arithmetic.
chr., *christ.* = Christian.
cf. = confer, compare.
conj. = conjunction.
Cpd. = compound or *Cpds.* compounds.
dat. = dative.
decl. = declension.
dem. = demonstrative.
dupl., *dpl.* = a couple of words used to make the idea more impressive, *as:* ಕಾರಸ್ಥೋಳ, ಮಾತುಕಥೆ, *etc.*
e. = English.
e. g. = *exempli gratia* (for example).
esp. = especially.
etc. = *et caetera* (and so on).
f. = words of foreign derivation, *i. e.* Tamil, Telugu, Malayalam, Portuguese, Latin, Greek, *etc.*
f. = feminine.
fig. = figuratively.
fr. = from.
fut. = future.
gen. = genitive.
g., *gram.* = grammar.
h. = Hindustani, Persian, and Arabic.
hon. = honorific.
i. e. = *id est* (that is).
imp. = imperative.
int. = interjection.
inter. = interrogative.
lit. = literally.
loc. = locative.
k. = (pure) Kannaḍa.
m. = Mahratti words.
N. = Name; proper name.
n. = noun.
neg. = negative.
P. p. = Past participle (*P. ps.* = Past participles).
pl. = plural.
pref. = prefix.
prep. = preposition.
pres. = present.
pro. = pronoun.
q. v. = *quod vide* (which see).
reit. = reiteration, *i. e.* a couple of words, the first of which is rendered more impressive and powerful by the second one which is however meaningless by itself, *e. g.* ಅಡ್ಡಿಸಡ್ಡಿ, ಆಳುಗೀಳು, *etc.*
rep. = repetition, *i. e.* the act of repeating the same word twice or thrice, *e. g.* ಎಂತೆಂತ, ಎಲ್ಲೆಲ್ಲಿ, ಒಬ್ಬೊಬ್ಬ, ಎರಡೆರಡು, ದೊಡ್ಡ ದೊಡ್ಡ, ಸಣ್ಣ ಸಣ್ಣ, *etc.*
s. = (pure) Saṁskṛita.
s. = *sub*, under.
sing. = singular.
tb. = tadbhava.
v. i. = verb intransitive.
v. t. = verb transitive.
= equal (in meaning).
& = and.
-. = hyphen, indicating that the principal word is to be prefixed in the case of compounds and derivatives.

A

KANNAḌA-ENGLISH

SCHOOL-DICTIONARY.

ಕನ್ನಡ ಮತ್ತು ಇಂಗ್ಲಿಷ್

ಶಾಲಾನಿಘಂಟು.

ಅ. The first letter of the alphabet. 2, a short vowel inherent in every consonant. 3, a termination denoting etymological functions in declensions and conjugations, *as a. 1st pers. pl. imp.* ಹೋಗುವ, *b. gen. sing.* ನೀರ, *etc.* 4, a negative prefix to nouns derived from Sanskrit, *as* ಅಯೋಗ್ಯ unworthy (*fr.* ಯೋಗ್ಯ). Before a vowel ಅ becomes ಅನ್; thus ಅ-ಅಂತ = ಅನಂತ endless.

ಅಂ. A termination used in declension and conjugation in ancient Canarese. 2, *cop. conj.* both, and, also.

ಅಂಶ, ಅಂಶೆ s. *n.* A part, share, portion. 2, a fraction (*arith.*). 3, a degree of latitude or longitude. -ಚಕ್ರ. An astrological diagram.

ಅಂಶಕ s. *n.* A part. 2, a kinsman, coheir.

ಅಂಶಾಂಶ s. *n.* A part of a portion; a [sub-division.

ಅಂಶು (= ಅಂಸು 2) s. *n.* A ray of light. 2, the sun. 3, light, splendour. 4, a point. -ಜಾಲ. A collection of rays. -ಧರ. The sun. -ಮತ್ಫಲೆ. The plantain. -ಮಾಲಿ, -ಹಸ್ತ. The sun. -ಮಾಲೆ. Halo.

ಅಂಶುಕ s. *n.* Cloth, dress. 2, fine cloth.

ಅಂಸ s. *n.* The shoulder, shoulder-blade. -ಕೂಟ. A bull's hump.

ಅಂಸಲ s. *a.* Strong, stout, lusty.

ಅಃ k. *int.* expressing admiration, contempt or jest.

ಅಕ s. *n.* Pain, trouble; sin.

ಅಕಚ s. *a.* Bald-headed.

ಅಕಟ, ಅಕಟಕಟ, ಅಕಟಾ k. *int.* Alas! oh!

ಅಕಟವಿಕಟ k. *a.* Frightful. 2, adverse, contrary.

ಅಕಟಾಯಿಸು k. *v. i.* To become warped (leather).

ಅಕರ s. *a.* Handless, maimed.

ಅಕರ್ತವ್ಯ s. *a.* Not to be done, improper.

ಅಕರ್ಮ s. *a.* Without work. *n.* Crime. -ಕ. Neuter or intransitive (verb, *g.*).

ಅಕಲಂಕ s. *a.* Stainless, spotless, pure.

ಅಕಲ್ಮಷ s. *n.* Purity, innocency.

ಅಕಸಾಲ, ಅಕಸಾಲಿಗ, ಅಕಸಾಲೆ f. n. A gold or silver smith.

ಅಕಸ್ಮಾತ್, ಅಕಸ್ಮಾತ, ಅಕಸ್ಮಾತ್ತು s. *ad.* By chance, suddenly, unexpectedly.

ಅಕಳಸಕಳ k. n. Excessive tickling. *a.* Too much. 2, disrespectful.

ಅಕಾರ s. n. The letter ಅ.

ಅಕಾರಣ s. *a.* Causeless.

ಅಕಾರತು h. *a.* Vain, useless.

ಅಕಾರಾಂತ s. n. A term with final ಅ.

ಅಕಾರ್ಯ s. n. An improper act.

ಅಕಾಲ s. n. Inauspicious time. *a.* Unseasonable. -ಫಲ. Fruit out of season. -ಮರಣ. Untimely death.

ಅಕಿಂಚನ s. *a.* Very poor.

ಅಕುಟಿಲ s. *a.* Not crooked, upright, honest.

ಅಕುಪ್ಯ s. n. Gold, silver.

ಅಕೂಪಾರ s. n. The ocean. 2, the king of tortoises supposed to uphold the world; a big tortoise.

ಅಕೃತ್ಯ s. *a.* Undone. 2, criminal. *n.* What ought not to be done. 2, a crime.

ಅಕೃಷ್ಣಕರ್ಮ s. *a.* Guiltless.

ಅಕೋ = ಅಗೋ.

ಅಕ್ಕ k. n. An elder sister. -ತಂಗಿಯರು. Elder and younger sisters.

ಅಕ್ಕಚ್ಚಿ, ಅಕ್ಕಮ್ಮ k. n. An affectionate mode of addressing an elder sister.

ಅಕ್ಕಜ k. n. Wonder, surprise. 2, envy. *a.* Wonderful, curious.

ಅಕ್ಕಟ. = ಅಕಟ.

ಅಕ್ಕಡಿ, ಅಕ್ಕಡೆ k. n. A furrow between two others of a main crop.

ಅಕ್ಕಡಿತಕ್ಕಡಿ n. Deceit in words, *etc.*

ಅಕ್ಕಣೆ k. n. The close adhesion of the woof and warp in the web of a loom.

ಅಕ್ಕದಾಮ, ಅಕ್ಕಮಾಲೆ. *tb. of* ಅಕ್ಷಮಾಲೆ.

ಅಕ್ಕಬ k. n. Wonder, surprise.

ಅಕ್ಕಮ್ಮ. = ಅಕ್ಕಚ್ಚಿ *q. v.*

ಅಕ್ಕರ (*tb. of* ಅಕ್ಷರ) n. A letter of the alphabet.

ಅಕ್ಕರ, ಅಕ್ಕರತೆ, ಅಕ್ಕರಿಕೆ, ಅಕ್ಕರು (ರ=ಱ) k. n. Attachment, affection, love.

ಅಕ್ಕರೆ, ಅಕ್ಕರು (ರ=ಱ) k. n. Necessity. 2, occasion; need, want. 3, desire.

ಅಕ್ಕಲಕರೆ k. n. *Anthemis pyrethrum,* used for coughs, asthma, *etc.*

ಅಕ್ಕಲು. = ಹಕ್ಕಲು.

ಅಕ್ಕಸ k. n. Love, passion.

ಅಕ್ಕಸಾಲಿಗ. = ಅಕಸಾಲಿಗ, *q. v.*

ಅಕ್ಕಸಾಲೆ f. n. The workshop of a goldsmith. 2, a goldsmith.

ಅಕ್ಕಳಿಸು, ಅಕ್ಕುಳಿಸು k. *v. i.* The muscles of the stomach to contract from hunger. 2, to fear. 3, to flinch.

ಅಕ್ಕಾಡು a. k. *v. i.* To ooze, flow, run down, as tears, *etc.*

ಅಕ್ಕಿ k. n. Raw rice deprived of its husk; -ಗಚ್ಚು. Rice-water; *for cpds. see* ಎಲಕ್ಕಿ, ಕುಸಲಕ್ಕಿ, ಸಣ್ಣಕ್ಕಿ, ದಪ್ಪಕ್ಕಿ, *etc.*

ಅಕ್ಕಿಸು a. k. *v. t.* To digest.

ಅಕ್ಕು, ಅಕ್ಕುಂ a. k. *v. i.* To subdue. 2, to seize. 3, *fut. of* ಆಗು, it will become.

ಅಕ್ಕುಡಿಸು a. k. *v. i.* To become small.

ಅಕ್ಕುಳಿಸು. = ಅಕ್ಕಳಿಸು.

ಅಕ್ಕೆ *past gerund of* ಅಕ್ಕು. May it become.

ಅಕ್ರಮ s. n. Confusion, irregularity; sin.

ಅಕ್ರೂರ *a.* Gentle. *n.* Kṛishṇa's uncle and friend.

ಅಕ್ರೋಡ (*tb. of* ಅಕ್ಷೋಟ) n. A large, nut-bearing tree.

ಅಕ್ಷ s. n. A die for gambling. 2, the axle of a wheel. 3, the eye. 4, an organ of sense. 5, knowledge. 6, the soul. 7, a lawsuit. -ತೃತೀಯ. N. of a festival. -ಮಾಲೆ. A rosary.

ಅಕ್ಷತ, ಅಕ್ಷತೆ, ಅಕ್ಷಂತೆ s. *a.* Not crushed, whole. *n.* Raw rice generally mixed with turmeric and used for religious ceremonies.

ಅಕ್ಷಯ s. *a.* Imperishable, inexhaustible. -ಪಾತ್ರ. An inexhaustible vessel. 2, the 60th year of the Hindu cycle.

ಅಕ್ಷರ s. n. A letter of the alphabet. 2, eternal beatitude. 3, penance. 4, the sky.

ಅಕ್ಷಿ s. n. The eye. -ರೋಗ. Eye-disease. -ರೋಮ. Eyelash.

ಅಕ್ಷೌಹಿಣಿ s. n. A large army consisting of elephants, chariots, horse and foot.

ಅಖ್ k. *int.* expressing abhorrence or disgust.

ಅಖಂಡ s. a. Undivided; entire, whole.

ಅಖಂಡನ s. n. Non-refutation. 2, time.

ಅಖಂಡಿತ s. a. Unbroken. 2, continuous. 3, unrefuted.

ಅಖಾತ s. a. Not dug. n. A natural pond.

ಅಖಾದ್ಯ s. a. Uneatable, unfit to be eaten.

ಅಖಿನ್ನ s. a. Not distressed, not wearied.

ಅಖಿಲ s. a. Without a gap; entire, whole, all.

ಅಗ s. a. Not moving. n. A tree; a mountain.

ಅಗಚು k. v. t. To press firmly, compress, squeeze down.

ಅಗಜಾತೆ s. n. Pârvatî, the daughter of Himâlaya.

ಅಗಡು k. n. Viciousness, meanness. a. Wild, untamed. -ತನ. Mischievousness.

ಅಗಣಿ (*tb. of* ಅರ್ಗಲ) n. A wooden bolt to fasten a native door.

ಅಗಣಿತ s. a. Uncounted. 2, innumerable.

ಅಗತ, ಅಗತೆ k. n. The act of digging.

ಅಗತ್ಯ s. n. Necessity, want, need. a. Wanted, necessary. -ವಾಗಿ. Necessarily, urgently, positively.

ಅಗದ s. a. Free from disease, healthy. n. A medicine. ಅಗದಂಕಾರ. A physician.

ಅಗದಿ m. a. Altogether, wholly; quite.

ಅಗಧರ s. n. The mountain supporter, Vishṇu.

ಅಗಪೆ k. n. A ladle of cocoanut shell.

ಅಗಭೇದಿ s. n. The mountain-splitter: Indra. 2, a hatchet.

ಅಗಮ s. a. Not going. n. A tree. 2, a mountain.

ಅಗಮ್ಯ s. a. Inaccessible, unattainable.

ಅಗರು 1. k. n. Dandruff.

ಅಗರು 2. s. n. The balsam tree which yields Bdellium, *Amyris agallocha*. -ಗಂಧ. A yellow fragrant wood.

ಅಗಲ k. n. Expansion, space, extent. 2, width, breadth. 3, far distance. a. Broad.

ಅಗಲಿಕೆ k. n. Separation.

ಅಗಲಿಸು (*fr.* ಅಗಲು) k. v. t. To remove. 2, to separate, disunite.

ಅಗಲು k. v. i. To separate from, quit, part, leave. n. = ಅಗಲ.

ಅಗಲ್ಚು (= ಅಗಲಿಸು) k. v. t. To spread out; to abandon.

ಅಗಸ, ಅಗಸಿಗ k. n. A washerman. -ಗಿತ್ತಿ, ಅಗಸತಿ. A washerwoman.

ಅಗಸಾಲ, ಅಗಸಾಲಿಗ. = ಅಕಸಾಲ, *etc. q. v.*

ಅಗಸೆ 1, -ಬಾಗಲು k. n. A town-gate; the gate of a fort.

ಅಗಸೆ 2. (*tb. of* ಅತಸಿ) n. Common flax, *Linum usitatissimum*. 2, (*tb. of* ಅಗಸ್ತ್ಯ) a tree with scarlet flowers, *Sesbana grandiflora*. -ಎಣ್ಣೆ. Lin-seed oil. -ಹೂ. Lin-flower.

ಅಗಸ್ತ್ಯ s. n. N. of a ṛishi, son of Mitra and Varuṇa by Urvaśî. 2, the regent of the star Canopus.

ಅಗಳತ, ಅಗಳತೆ, ಅಗಳ್ತೆ (ಳ = ೞ) k. n. A fort ditch, trench, moat.

ಅಗಳಾಡಿಸು k. v. t. To cause to swing; to wave. ಅಗಳಾಡು v. i. To swing, shake.

ಅಗಳಿ (ಳ = ೞ). = ಅಗುಳಿ.

ಅಗಳು 1. k. n. A grain of boiled rice. 2, food.

ಅಗಳು 2. (ಳ = ೞ) k. v. t. & i. To dig, burrow. 2, to tear off. n. A fort ditch, moat.

ಅಗಾಡಿ h. n. The front, van. ad. In front.

ಅಗಾಧ s. n. A hole, chasm. a. Deep, bottomless, unfathomable.

ಅಗಾಧಿಪ s. n. The high mountain Mahâmêru.

ಅಗಿ k. v. t. To dig, burrow. 2, to chew, champ. v. i. to tremble, shake, fear. 2, to be glad.

ಅಗಿಣಿ k. n. Water (a word only used by educated Lingaits).

ಅಗಿಲು (= ಅಗರು 2, q. v.) s. n. Fragrance.

ಅಗಿಸು k. v. t. To cause to dig.

ಅಗುಚು. = ಅಗಚು, q. v.

ಅಗುಂದಲೆ k. n. Extensiveness, greatness. a. Great.

ಅಗುರು s. a. Not heavy, light. n. A fragrant aloe wood, *agallochum*.

ಅಗುರ್ಬು, ಅಗುರ್ವು k. n. Terror, amazement.

ಅಗುರ್ವಿಸು k. v. t. To terrify.

ಅಗುಲು k. v. t. To shake, move. v. i. To become loose.

ಅಗುಸೆ. = ಅಗಸೆ, q. v.

ಅಗುಳಿ (ಳ = ೞ) (tb. of ಅರ್ಗಲ) n. A bolt, a bar for locking a door.

ಅಗುಳು 1. = ಅಗಳು.

ಅಗುಳು 2. (ಳು = ೞು) k. v. t. To dig.

ಅಗೆ 1. = ಅಗಿ k. v. t. To dig. See ಅಗಿ.

ಅಗೆ 2. k. n. A seedling; a germ, bud, shoot; *cf.* ಮೊಳಕೆ. 2, a suffix to form adverbs, *e. g.* ನೆಟ್ಟಗೆ, ಸುಮ್ಮಗೆ. -ಕಟ್ಟು, -ಮಾಡು. To raise seedlings.

ಅಗೋ (= ಅಕೋ) k. *int.* Lo! behold!

ಅಗೋಚರ s. a. Invisible, imperceptible; wondrous.

ಅಗ್ಗ 1. (*tb. of* ಅರ್ಘ) n. Cheapness. a. Cheap; low, mean.

ಅಗ್ಗ 2. *tb. of* ಅಗ್ರ *q. v.*

ಅಗ್ಗಲಿಸು = ಅಗ್ಗಳಿಸು, *q. v.*

ಅಗ್ಗವಣಿ (= ಅಗಿಣಿ) k. n. Water. 2, an offering of water.

ಅಗ್ಗಳಿಕೆ k. n. Greatness; great power.

ಅಗ್ಗಳಿಸು (= ಅಗ್ಗಲಿಸು) k. v. t. & i. To be or become pre-eminent; to make great efforts; to excel.

ಅಗ್ಗಳೆ k. n. A powerful man.

ಅಗ್ಗಿ (*tb. of* ಅಗ್ನಿ). n. Fire.

ಅಗ್ಗಿಟಿಗೆ, ಅಗಿಷ್ಟಿಕೆ, ಅಗ್ಗಿಷ್ಟಿಕೆ (*tb. of* ಅಗ್ನಿಷ್ಟು, *etc.*) n. A potsherd used as a fire-pan or chafing dish.

ಅಗ್ನಿ s. n. Fire. 2, the god of fire, Agni. 3, the guardian of the south-east. 4, bile. 5, gold. -ಕಣ, -ಕಿಡಿ, -ಬಿಂದು. A spark. -ಕಾರ್ಯ. Feeding the sacrificial fire with ghee. -ಕಾಷ್ಠ. Firewood; *Agallochum*. -ಕುಂಡ. A firehole. -ಚಿತ್. One who arranges a sacrificial fire-place. -ಜ್ವಾಲೆ. Flame of fire; a plant bearing red blossoms used by dyers. -ತಾರೆ. The Pleiades. -ದೀಪನ. Stimulating digestion. -ದೇವಿ. The Pleiades. -ನಯನ, -ನೇತ್ರ. Śiva with an eye of fire. -ಫಲ. A diamond. -ಬಾಣ. A fiery arrow; a rocket. -ಬಾಧ. Damaging with fire. -ಭೂ. Born of fire; Śiva's son. -ಮಥನ, -ಮಂಥ. Production of fire by friction. -ಮಂಥ. The tree *Premna spinosa*. -ಮಾಂದ್ಯ. Languor of the digestive power. -ಮಿತ್ರ. The fire's friend: the wind. -ಮುಖ. A deity; Brahmâ. -ಮುಖಿ. The marking nut. -ರಕ್ಷಣೆ. Preservation of the sacred fire. -ವರ್ಣ. N. of a prince. -ಶಿಖ. Having a crest of fire; saffron; safflower; a lamp; a rocket; an arrow. -ಶಿಖೆ. A flame; the plant *Gloriosa superba*. -ಷ್ಟೋಮ. Praise of Agni; a peculiar sacrifice in spring. -ಸಂಸ್ಕಾರ. The consecration of fire; any rite in which the application of fire is essential. -ಸಖ. The wind. -ಸ್ತಂಭನ. The (magical) quenching of fire. -ಹೋತ್ರ. An oblation to Agni. -ಹೋತ್ರಿ. Practising the agni-hôtra; maintaining the sacrificial fire; one who has prepared the sacrificial fire-place. ಅಗ್ನೀಧ್ರ. The priest who kindles the fire.

ಅಗ್ನ್ಯುತ್ಪಾತ s. n. A meteor, comet.

ಅಗ್ರ 1. k. n. The thrush, a sore mouth.

ಅಗ್ರ 2. (= ಅಗ್ಗ 2) s. n. A top, point, summit. 2, the front. 3, the beginning. 4, excess. 5, praise. 6, a multitude.

7. aim, resting place. *a.* Prominent, excellent, best, chief, first. -ಗಣ್ಯ. Foremost, principal. -ಜ, -ಜನ್ಮ. First-born; an elder brother; a Brâhmaṇa. -ಣಿ. Foremost, excellent. -ತಃ. In front of. -ತಾಂಬೂಲ. The first present of betel leaf at an assembly. -ಪೂಜೆ. The first act of reverence rendered to the principal man at assemblies. -ಬಲ. An advance-force. -ಮಾಂಸ. The heart. -ಸಾಲೆ. The cooking hall of a temple. -ಹಾರ. Villages assigned to Brâhmaṇas for their maintenance. -ಹಾರಿಕ. A man belonging to an agrahâra.

ಅಗ್ರಾಮ್ಯ s. *a.* Not rustic. -ತೆ. Unvulgarity.

ಅಗ್ರಾಹ್ಯ s. *a.* Unacceptable, inadmissible.

ಅಗ್ರಿಮ s. *a.* Foremost. 2, best. 3, elder, eldest.

ಅಗ್ರಿಯ, ಅಗ್ರೀಯ s. *a.* Principal, best. *n.* An elder brother.

ಅಗ್ರೇದಿಧಿಷು s. *n.* A man who marries a widow at his first marriage.

ಅಗ್ರೇಶ್ವರ s. *n.* The supreme lord.

ಅಗ್ರೇಸರ s. *a.* Preceding. 2, best. *n.* A leader, headman.

ಅಗ್ರೋದಕ s. *n.* Water used for the worship of an idol.

ಅಗ್ರ್ಯ s. *a.* Foremost, first; best. 2, intent.

ಅಘ s. *n.* Sin, crime. 2, pain. 3, passion.

ಅಘಟನ s. *a.* Difficult, impossible.

ಅಘಟಿತ s. *a.* Not happened. 2, improbable, unlikely. *n.* Any wonder.

ಅಘನ s. *a.* Liquid, not dense.

ಅಘಮರ್ಷಣ s. *a.* Expiatory. *n.* A daily expiatory prayer, reciting a particular passage from the Vêdas.

ಅಘಾಟ s. *n.* A wonder; excess.

ಅಘೋರ s. *a.* Not terrific. 2, terrible. *n.* A euphemistic title of Śiva.

ಅಂಕ s. *n.* A hook. 2, the lap, thigh. 3, the side or flank. 4, the body. 5, a mark. 6, a numerical figure. 7, a fault. 8, a war. 9, proximity. 10, place. -ಡೊಂಕು. Excessive crookedness. -ಮಾಲೆ. A list of titles. -ವೀರ. A valiant man.

ಅಂಕಗಣಿತ s. *n.* Arithmetic.

ಅಂಕಣ f. *n.* The space between two pillars or beams.

ಅಂಕನ s. *n.* Marking, stamping.

ಅಂಕಿತ s. *a.* Marked. *n.* A sign, signature. 2, a word. 3, a dedication. -ನಾಮ. A proper name.

ಅಂಕಿಸು s. *v. t.* To mark, look at.

ಅಂಕುರ s. *n.* A sprout, shoot. 2, hair. 3, blood. ಅಂಕುರಿಸು. To sprout; to rise; to happen.

ಅಂಕುಶ (*tb.* ಅಂಕುಸ) s. *n.* A hook, esp. for driving an elephant.

ಅಂಕೆ 1. k. *n.* An order, command; control; restraint, check. 2, (= ಆನಿಕೆ) leaning against; a lever. 3, trust.

ಅಂಕೆ 2. *n.* (*tb. of* ಅಂಕ). A numerical figure; an account.

ಅಂಕೋಠ, ಅಂಕೋಲ, (-ಲು -ಲೆ) s. *n.* The plant *Alangium hexapetalum.*

ಅಂಗ 1. a. k. *n.* Way, manner, mode.

ಅಂಗ 2. s. *n.* A limb, member. 2, the body. 3, the mind. 4, an expedient. 5, a verse-line. 6, N. of Bengal proper. *int.* Indeed, true; please. -ಚಿತ್ತ. The heart's wish. -ಚೇಷ್ಟೆ. Gestures of the body. -ನ್ಯಾಸ. Ceremony of touching certain parts of the body. -ಪರೀಕ್ಷೆ, -ಶೋಧನೆ. Anatomy. -ಪ್ರದಕ್ಷಿಣ. Rolling one's body round a temple. -ರಕ್ಷ, -ರಕ್ಷಣೆ, -ರಕ್ಷೆ. Protection of the body; also an amulet. -ರಕ್ಷಕ. A body-guard. -ರಾಗ. Unguents for the body; perfuming the body. -ವಸ್ತ್ರ. A small cloth; an upper garment. -ವಿಕಾರ. Change of bodily appearance; fainting. -ವಿಕ್ಷೇಪ, -ಹಾರ. Gesticulation. -ಸಂಸ್ಕಾರ. Embellishment of body. -ಹೀನ. Mutilated; incorporeal. -ಹೀನತೆ. Mutilation.

ಅಂಗಜ s. n. (born from the body) The god of love, Kâma. 2, love, passion. 3, a son. 4, blood.

ಅಂಗಜನ್ಮ s. n. Kâma. ಅಂಗಜನ್ಮಾಂತಕ. The destroyer of Kâma, Śiva.

ಅಂಗಜಾತ s. = ಅಂಗಜ, p. v.

ಅಂಗಡಿ k. n. A shop, stall. -ಬೀದಿ. A market-street. -ಯವ, -ಕಾರ, -ಗಾರ. A shopkeeper. -ಮನೆ. A house with a shop. -ಮೂಲಿಕೆ. A shop drug. -ಸರಕು. The goods of a shop. -ಹಚ್ಚು, -ಹಾಕು. To open a shop.

ಅಂಗಣ (tb. of ಅಂಕಣ) n. A court, a yard, esp. in front of a house; an area.

ಅಂಗತ, ಅಂಗತ್ತ (= ಅಂಗಾತ) k. ad. Flatways, on the back.

ಅಂಗದ s. n. A bracelet worn on the upper arm. N. of a son of Vâli.

ಅಂಗನೆ, ಅಂಗನಾ s. n. A woman, female.

ಅಂಗರ. tb. of ಅಂಗಾರ, q. v.

ಅಂಗರೇಖು h. n. A long coat.

ಅಂಗಲ, ಅಂಗಲು, ಅಂಗಂಗಲು k. a. Separate, apart.

ಅಂಗಲಾಚು (-ಚಿದ) k. v. i. To weep, grieve, lament. ಅಂಗಲಾಪು. Grief.

ಅಂಗವಣೆ m. n. Habitude; power, vigour.

ಅಂಗವಿಸು a. k. v. i. To come together, meet, crowd. v. t. To lay hold of, seize.

ಅಂಗಳ, (-ಳು), ಅಂಗುಳ, (-ಳಿ, -ಳೆ) k. n. The palate of the mouth. 2, (tb. of ಅಂಕಣ) a courtyard.

ಅಂಗಾಂಗಿ s. n. Limb and limb related to another.

ಅಂಗಾತ k. = ಅಂಗತ etc., q. v.

ಅಂಗಾರ (= ಅಂಗರ) k. n. Charcoal. 2, Mars.

ಅಂಗಾರಕ (= ಅಂಗಾರ 1-2) s. n. 3, a sectarian mark made with charred wood. -ಧಾನಿಕೆ. A portable fire-place. -ವಾರ. Tuesday.

ಅಂಗಾಲು k. n. The sole of the foot.

ಅಂಗಿ s. n. A coat, frock, jacket.

ಅಂಗೀ s. n. Assent. -ಕರಣ, -ಕಾರ. Assenting, agreeing, accepting; acceptance.

ಅಂಗೀಕರಿಸು s. v. t. To agree to; to accept, adopt.

ಅಂಗುಟ. tb. of ಅಂಗುಷ್ಠ, q. v.

ಅಂಗುಲ (-ಲಿ) s. n. A finger. 2, the thumb. 3, a finger's breadth. ಅಂಗುಲಿತ್ರಾಣ. A finger-protector, used whilst shooting arrows. ಅಂಗುಲಿದರ್ಶನ. Pointing at with the finger. ಅಂಗುಲಿಮೋಟನ. Cracking the fingers.

ಅಂಗುಲೀಯ s. n. A finger-ring.

ಅಂಗುಷ್ಠ s. n. The thumb. 2, the great toe.

ಅಂಗುಸ್ತಾನಿ m. n. A thimble.

ಅಂಗುಳ, -ಳಿ, -ಳೆ. = ಅಂಗಳ etc.

ಅಂಗೂರ h. n. The grape.

ಅಂಗೆಯ್, ಅಂಗೈ k. n. The palm of the hand.

ಅಂಗೋಪಾಂಗ s. n. The body and its members.

ಅಂಗೋಸ್ತ್ರ. tb. of ಅಂಗವಸ್ತ್ರ, q. v.

ಅಂಘ್ರಿ s. n. A foot. 2, the root of a tree. -ಜ. The foot-born; a Śûdra.

ಅಚಂಡ s. a. Gentle, tractable.

ಅಚತುರ s. a. Not dexterous (f. ಅಚತುರೆ).

ಅಚಪಲ s. a. Unmoveable, steady. -ತೆ. Steadiness.

ಅಚರ s. a. Immoveable.

ಅಚಲ s. a. Immoveable, fixed. 2, eternal. n. A mountain; the earth. 2, an ascetic.

ಅಚಲೆ s. n. The earth.

ಅಚಾತುರ್ಯ s. n. Want of ability.

ಅಚಿಚಿ k. n. Impurity, filth.

ಅಚಿಂತ್ಯ s. a. Incomprehensible.

ಅಚಿರ s. a. Not long, short, brief; recent. -ದ್ಯುತಿ, ಅಚಿರಾಂಶು. Lightning.

ಅಚೀತ s. a. Unconscious; very poor.

ಅಚೇತನ s. n. Unconsciousness. a. Insensible, fainting.

ಅಚೈತನ್ಯ s. n. Unconsciousness; ignorance; matter.

ಅಚ್ಚ 1. (= ಅಚ್ಚು 1, *q. v.*) k. *a.* -ಕಟ್ಟು (= ಅಚ್ಚುಕಟ್ಟು). Proper boundary; suitable order, size, *etc.*

ಅಚ್ಚ 2. (*tb. of* ಅಚ್ಛ) *a.* Pure, clear; unmixed, real. 2, = ಅಚ್ಚು. -ಗನ್ನಡ. Pure Kannaḍa. -ನೀರು. Pure and fresh water. ಅಚ್ಚಪ್ಪ, ಅಚ್ಚಯ್ಯ. N.

ಅಚ್ಚಗ a. k. *n.* Bewilderment.

ಅಚ್ಚಡ (*tb. of* ಪ್ರಚ್ಛದ. = ಪಚ್ಚಡ, ವಚ್ಚಡ) *n.* A stout cotton cloth to cover at night.

ಅಚ್ಚತೆ. *tb. of* ಅಕ್ಷತ, *q. v.*

ಅಚ್ಚಯ. *tb. of* ಅಕ್ಷಯ, *q. v.*

ಅಚ್ಚರ. *tb. of* ಅಕ್ಷರ, *q. v.*

ಅಚ್ಚರಿ (*tb. of* ಆಶ್ಚರ್ಯ) *n.* Wonder, surprise.

ಅಚ್ಚಾಪಿಚ್ಚಿ, ಅಚ್ಚಾಪೆಚ್ಚಿ m. *ad.* Unmeaningly; foully (in eating).

ಅಚ್ಚಾಳು k. *n.* A firm, strong man. ಅಚ್ಚಾಳಿಕೆ. Firmness of a man.

ಅಚ್ಚಿ 1. k. *n.* Bread (used only by young children). 2, mother; a Malayâḷa woman. 3, a pap.

ಅಚ್ಚಿ 2. *tb. of* ಅಕ್ಷಿ, *q. v.*

ಅಚ್ಚಿಕೆ k. *n.* Paying unjustly.

ಅಚ್ಚಿಗ. *tb. of* ಅರ್ಚಕ.

ಅಚ್ಚು 1. (= ಅಚ್ಚ) k. *n.* Firmness; (bodily) strength. 2, a well-defined boundary. 3, a mould; an impression. 4, a type, stamp. 5, a weaver's reed. -ಅಕ್ಷರ, ಅಚ್ಚಕ್ಷರ. A printed letter. -ಕಟ್ಟು. = ಅಚ್ಚಕಟ್ಟು. -ಕೂಟ. A printing press. -ಬೆಲ್ಲ. A cake of jaggory. -ಭಕ್ತಿ. Firm devotion. -ಹಾಕು. To print, seal. -ಒತ್ತು. To seal, impress firmly.

ಅಚ್ಚು 2. k. *v. t.* To pay unjustly, *as* rent for failed crop. *n.* Intimacy, love. 2, (*tb. of* ಅಕ್ಷ) a die; an axle. 3, the soul.

ಅಚ್ಚು 3. f. *n.* A Pegu pony.

ಅಚ್ಚುಳಾಯ್ತು, ಅಚ್ಚುಳಾಯ್ಲು a. k. *n.* An attendant, guard.

ಅಚ್ಚೆ (= ಹಚ್ಚೆ) k. *n.* Tattooing, scarifying.

ಅಚ್ಚೇರು k. *n.* Half a seer.

ಅಚ್ಛ (= ಅಚ್ಚ) s. *a.* Pure, clear, transparent. -ಭಲ್ಲ. A white bear.

ಅಚ್ಛಿದ್ರ s. *a.* Unbroken, uninjured. 2, new. 3, defectless.

ಅಚ್ಛಿನ್ನ s. *a.* Uncut, uninjured; inseparable.

ಅಚ್ಯುತ s. *a.* Firm, imperishable. *n.* Vishṇu. -ತ್ವ. Permanence.

ಅಜ s. *a.* Unborn. *n.* Brahmâ. 2, Vishṇu. 3, Śiva. 4, the sun. 5, rain. 6, a driver, leader. 7, a ram; a he-goat. 8, the sign *Aries*.

ಅಜಕವ, ಅಜಕಾವ, ಅಜಗವ s. *n.* Śiva's bow.

ಅಜಗರ s. *n.* A huge serpent, *Boa constrictor*.

ಅಜಂಠ s. *a.* Not sewed, as a cloth.

ಅಜನ s. *a.* Unpeopled. *n.* A desert. 2, an insignificant person. 3, driving.

ಅಜನ್ಯ s. *a.* Unfit to be born. *n.* A phenomenon foreboding evil.

ಅಜಬಾಬು h. *n.* Goods and chattels, tools, baggage.

ಅಜಮಾಸು h. *n.* Rough calculation. *ad.* About.

ಅಜಮೋದ, ಅಜಮೋದೆ s. *n.* Bishop's weed, *Ligusticum ajwaen*. 2, common carraway, *Carum carui*.

ಅಜಯ s. *a.* Unconquerable, invincible. *n.* Defeat. 2, Vishṇu.

ಅಜರ 1. (= ಅಜುರ) a. k. *a.* The Indigo [plant.

ಅಜರ 2. s. *a.* Ageless, undecaying.

ಅಜರ್ಯ s. *a.* Indigestible; undecaying. *n.* Friendship.

ಅಜಶೃಂಗಿ s. *n.* Goat's horn: the shrub *Odina wodier*.

ಅಜಸ್ರ s. *a.* Not to be injured. 2, continual.

ಅಜಾಗರ s. *a.* Not awake. *n.* A common weed, *Eclipta alba*.

ಅಜಾಗರೂಕತೆ s. *n.* The state of being not wakeful. 2, carelessness.

ಅಜಾಗಲಸ್ತನ s. *n.* Nipple pending from the neck of goats. 2, a useless object.

ಅಜಾಗ್ರತೆ. = ಅಜಾಗರೂಕತೆ.

ಅಜಾಜಿ s. n. Cumin seed.

ಅಜಾಣಿ (tb. of ಅಜ್ಞಾನ) n. A foolish man.

ಅಜಾಂಡ s. n. Brahmâ's egg: the universe.

ಅಜಾತ s. a. Unborn, not existent. -ಶತ್ರು. One who has no enemies.

ಅಜಾಮುಲ, ಅಜಾಮೋದ. = ಅಜಮೋದ, q. v.

ಅಜಿಗಿಜಿ k. n. Ground lime.

ಅಜಿತ s. a. Unconquerable. 2, unsurpassed. n. Vishṇu.

ಅಜಿನ s. n. The skin. 2, the skin of an antelope. -ಪತ್ರ. A bat. -ಯೋನಿ. An antelope, a deer.

ಅಜಿರ s. a. Agile, quick. n. A court, yard. 2, an object of sense. 3, air.

ಅಜಿವಾನ h. n. Bishop's weed.

ಅಜಿಹ್ಮ s. a. Not crooked, straight. n. A fish; a frog.

ಅಜೀರ್ಣ s. a. Undigested. n. Indigestion.

ಅಜುರ. = ಅಜರ, q. v.

ಅಜೆ s. n. Nature. 2, illusion.

ಅಜೇಯ s. a. Invincible.

ಅಜ್ಜ 1. k. n. Opportunity. 2, the dry filaments.

ಅಜ್ಜ 2. (tb. of ಆರ್ಯ) n. A grandfather.

ಅಜ್ಜಿ (tb. of ಆರ್ಯಾ) n. A grandmother. -ಕಥೆ. An idle story.

ಅಜ್ಜಿಗೆ, ಅಜ್ಜುಗೆ (tb. of ಅರ್ಜಕ). n. A great-flowered jasmine.

ಅಜ್ಜುಗುಜ್ಜು k. n. The state of being thin and small. -ಪ್ರಾಯ. The age of debility.

ಅಜ್ಞ s. a. Not knowing; ignorant. 2, foolish. -ತೆ. Ignorance.

ಅಜ್ಞಾನ s. n. Ignorance. 2, mâyâ. -ತನ. Ignorance.

ಅಜ್ಞಾನಿ s. a. Ignorant, unwise. n. A stupid person.

ಅಂಚಲ, ಅಂಚಳ s. n. The end or border of a cloth.

ಅಂಚಿತ s. a. Bent. 2, honoured. 3, manifest, pure; beautiful.

ಅಂಚು 1. (= ಹಂಚು q. v.) k. v. t. To divide. 2, (= ಹೊಂಚು, q. v.) to lurk.

ಅಂಚು 2. (tb. of ಅಂತು) n. Edge, border, brim, selvage, skirt; bank, shore; side. -ಕಟ್ಟು. To construct a bank; to form a selvage.

ಅಂಚೆ 1. k. n. A postal road; a stage; the post (= ಟಪಾಲು). -ಕಚೇರಿ, -ಕಟ್ಟೆ. A post office. -ದಾರ. A postal officer. -ಯವ. A post runner.

ಅಂಚೆ 2. (= ಅಚೆ) ad. In that side. n. (tb. of ಹಂಸ) A swan. -ತುಪ್ಪಳ. Goose-down.

ಅಂಜನ s. n. Anointing. 2, a black collyrium applied to the eye-lashes. 3, magic ointment. 4, ink. 5, night. -ಕ್ರಿಯೆ. Anointing.

ಅಂಜನಿಕೆ s. n. A species of lizard. 2, a small mouse.

ಅಂಜಲಿ (= ಅಂಜುಲಿ) s. n. The cavity formed by hollowing the palms together; when raised towards the forehead it is a salutation to superiors. 2, a measure of corn. -ಪುಟ. = ಅಂಜಲಿ, No. 1.

ಅಂಜಿಕೆ k. n. Fear.

ಅಂಜಿಸು k. v. t. To frighten.

ಅಂಜು (= ಅಳರು) k. v. i. To fear, feel anxiety; to be afraid of. n. Fear. -ಕುಳಿ, -ಗುಳಿ. A coward.

ಅಂಜುಲಿ. = ಅಂಜಲಿ q. v.

ಅಂಜೂರ h. n. A fig; a fig-tree.

ಅಟ 1, ಅಟೆ k. n. Motion; play; speech. -ಮಟ. Trickery, fraud; escape. -ಮಟಿಸು, -ಮರಿಸು. To play tricks, deceive.

ಅಟ 2. m. n. Obstruction; a bar, lever. -ಕಟ. Weariness. -ಗೋಲು. A pole for lifting sacks.

ಅಟಕಾಯಿಸು h. v. t. To stop, hinder, check.

ಅಟಕಾವು, ಅಟಕ h. n. Obstruction, restraint.

ಅಟಕಿಸು. = ಅಟಕಾಯಿಸು, q. v.

ಅಟರುಷ, ಅಟರೂಷ f. n. The shrub *Justicia adhatoda*.

ಅಟವಣೆ, ಅಟ್ಟವಣೆ f. n. Addition and subtraction. 2, revenue.

ಅಟವಿ (= ಅಡವಿ) s. n. A wood, forest.

ಅಟೋಪ, ಅಟೋಪು f. n. Control, power.

ಅಟ್ಟ s. a. High, lofty; n. A garret or upper loft in a house. 2, a tower, buttress. 3, a scaffold. -ಹಾಸ = ಅಟ್ಟಾಸ. A loud laughter; a pomp, parade. 4, (fr. ಅಡು) cooked.

ಅಟ್ಟವೆ (= ಅಟ್ಟ) s. n. A structure of poles put on stones. 2, tb. of ಅಷ್ಟಮಿ, q. v.

ಅಟ್ಟಳೆ. tb. of ಅಟ್ಟಾಲ q. v.

ಅಟ್ಟಾಲ, ಅಟ್ಟಾಲಕ s. n. An apartment on the roof. 2, a palace. 3, a bastion.

ಅಟ್ಟಾಸ (tb. of ಅಟ್ಟಹಾಸ) n. see s. ಅಟ್ಟ.

ಅಟ್ಟಿಸು k. v. t. To take possession of. 2, to cause to pursue. 3, to cause to evaporate or to be wasted.

ಅಟ್ಟು k. v. t. To keep close to, follow. 2, to pursue, chase, drive away. 3, to send. 4, to put. v. i. To evaporate; to be wasted. n. Closeness. 2, putting. -ಕುಳಿ, -ಗುಣಿ. N. of a game in which cowries are put from hole to hole on a wooden board.

ಅಟ್ಟುಂಬಳಿ k. n. Gifts to the bride and bridegroom.

ಅಟ್ಟುಳಿ a. k. n. A crowd, multitude. 2, annoyance.

ಅಟ್ಟೆ k. n. A headless trunk. 2, a sole, sandal; skin, bark. 3, a leech.

ಅಟ್ಲು k. n. Mud. 2, (tb. of ಅಟ್ಟಾಲ) a stand on poles.

ಅಡ k. n. = ಅಡ್ಡ 1. -ಗಟ್ಟು. = ಅಡ್ಡಗಟ್ಟು.

ಅಡಕ k. n. Compacture. 2, piling, storing; a pile. 3, hiding one's self. 4, becoming obedient. 5, abridgment. -ಗೊಳಿಸು. To compress.

ಅಡಕು (= ಅಳ್ಕು) k. v. t. To press, as cotton. 2, to pile, as pots, grass, etc. 3, to put. 4, to subdue, control.

ಅಡಕೆ (= ಅಡಿಕೆ) k. n. The areca palm; its nut.

ಅಡಕೊತ್ತು, -ಗತ್ತರಿ k. n. A betel-nut cutter.

ಅಡಗಣಿಸು k. v. t. To thwart, obstruct.

ಅಡಗಿಸು k. v. t. To cause to hide; to conceal, hide. 2, to suppress. 3, to appease.

ಅಡಗು (= ಅಡಂಗು) k. v. i. To conceal one's self; to disappear. 2, to be quenched, humbled, contained in. 3, to crouch. n. (a. k.) Flesh, meat (= ಮಾಂಸ). 2, becomingness, agreeableness.

ಅಡಗೆ (= ಅಡಿಗೆ etc.) k. n. Cooking.

ಅಡಂಗು (= ಅಡಗು q. v.) a. k. n. A fort.

ಅಡಚಣೆ f. n. Difficulty, distress.

ಅಡಚು (cf. ಅಗಚು, ಅಡಕು, ಅಣಚು, etc.) k. v. t. To pack up, close; to stuff, press down; to humble. 2, to hush, silence. 3, to rap, cuff. [clothes.

ಅಡಡಿ k. n. Clothes to be washed; hired

ಅಡಪ (= ಹಡಪ) k. n. A barber's dressing case; a betel-pouch. -ವಳ (-ವಳ್ಳ). One who carries a betel-pouch.

ಅಡವು (= ಅಡಪು) k. n. A pledge, pawn.

ಅಡಬಡ k. ad. Rashly, e. g. -ತಿನ್ನು.

ಅಡಬಳ a. k. n. A cook. 2, flesh.

ಅಡಂಬರ (tb. of. ಆಡಂಬರ) n. Ostentation, display.

ಅಡಯಾಳ k. n. A mark, sign.

ಅಡರಾಟ k. n. A scuffle. 2, vying, rivalry.

ಅಡರು k. v. t. To climb, mount; to pounce upon, rush at. v. i. To be united with; to appear; to amass. n. An attack; an attempt. ಅಡರಿಸು. To cause to ascend, etc.

ಅಡರ್ಚು k. v. t. To bring together; to set in readiness.

ಅಡಲು k. v. i. To be shaken; to be afraid; to grieve. n. Tremor; confusion; fear. 2, mud.

ಅಡವಿ (tb. of ಅಟವಿ) n. A forest, wood, jungle. -ಗಿಚ್ಚು. Fire in forests. -ಪಾಲು. A miserable lot. -ಬೀಳು. To go astray.

ಅಡವು (= ಅಡಪು) k. n. Suitableness; closeness, thickness. 2, a pawn, pledge, deposit. 3, An impediment.

ಅಡಸಟ್ಟಿ h. n. Estimate, computation.

ಅಡಸಲ, ಅಡಸಾಲ. tb. of ಅಟರುಷ q. v.

ಅಡಸು (= ಅಡಚು) k. v. t. To attack, trouble. 2, to enter. 3, to put into, stuff into. 4, to hold firmly; to cover. v. i. To be stern; to be filled in.

ಅಡಹು k. a. see ಅಡವು No. 2.

ಅಡಾಡಿ k. n. Rashness, haste. ad. Quickly.

ಅಡಾಣೆ f. n. Unremunerated and forced labour or service. 2, a foreigner.

ಅಡಾಯಿಸು f. v. t. To stop, arrest; to put before (cf. ಅಡ್ಡಯಿಸು).

ಅಡಾಯುಧ k-s. n. A scimitar.

ಅಡಾವುಡಿ k. n. Alarm, uproar, quarrel, (riot.

ಅಡಿ (= ಅಂ) k. n. The foot; the measure of a foot. (ಅಡಿಗಳ ಮೇಲೆ ಬೀಳು, to fall down at the feet; ಅಡಿಕೆಡು, to become slow). 2, a verse-line. 3, a step, pace. (ಅಡಿಗಡಿಗೆ, from step to step; ಅಡಿಯಿಡು, to step, walk). 4, the bottom of any thing. (-ಕಾಣು, to see the bottom; -ತುಂಡು, the lower piece of anything; -ಪಟ್ಟಿ, a door-sill). 5, (= ಅಡು) cooking.

ಅಡಿಕೆ (= ಅಡಿಗೆ) k. n. Cooking. 2, (= ಅಡಕೆ, q. v.) the areca palm.

ಅಡಿಗಬ್ಬು k. n. Firewood.

ಅಡಿಗಲ್ಲು k. n. An anvil.

ಅಡಿಗೆ (= ಅಡಗೆ) k. n. Cooking, boiling; maturing; dinner. -ಮನೆ, -ಸಾಲೆ. A kitchen. -ಒಲೆ. A fire-place. -ಮಾಡು. To cook. -ಮಾಡುವವ, -ಯವ. A male cook. -ಯಾಗು. To be cooked. -ಸಾಮಾನ. Cooking utensils.

ಅಡಿಮೆ a. k. n. Slavery.

ಅಡಿಯ k. n. A slave.

ಅಡಿವಿ. = ಅಡವಿ, q. v.

ಅಡು k. v. t. To cook, boil, dress; to prepare a meal; to mature. n. Cooking, etc. -ಗಬ್ಬು. Fuel. -ಕೂಳು. Boiled rice. -ಗೂಲಚ್ಚ, -ಗೋಲಚ್ಚ. A woman who cooks for strangers. -ಬಾಣಲೆ. A frying pan.

ಅಡುಕು. = ಅಡಕು, q. v.

ಅಡುಸು k. n. Clay, mud.

ಅಡೆ 1. (= ಒಡೆ) a. k. If; when, e. g. ಕೇಳಿಸ ಸುವಡೆ, ಕೊಡುವಡೆ, etc.

ಅಡೆ 2. (=ಪಡೆ) k. v.t. To obtain, get, have; to shut up, enclose, confine. 2, (= ಅಣೆ) to strike, throw. v. i. To be enclosed, barred. n. A wood on which artisans put their working articles. 2, a sticky mass of tamarind, sugar, etc. 3, cowdung. 4, a thin cake of rice flour. 5, the border of a cloth. 6, a. k. Trust. -ಗಲ್ಲು. An anvil. -ಹಬ್ಬ. Cake-feast.

ಅಡ್ಡ 1. (= ಅಡ) k. n. The state of being across; obstacle. a. Crosswise, horizontal. -ಕಟ್ಟು. To fasten across; to thwart, stop, arrest. -ಕಟ್ಟು, -ಕಟ್ಟೆ. A dam in rice-fields. -ಕಸಬು, -ಕಸಬಿ. A profession contrary to custom. -ಕಾಲು. The leg put crosswise, as obstacle. -ಕಾವಲಿ, -ಕಾಲುವೆ. A by-channel. -ಕಾವಡಿ. A kâvaḍi carried on the neck. -ಕೀಲಿ. A transverse bolt. -ಕೂಸು. A child carried in the arms. -ಕೈ. The hand placed transversely. -ಕೆಲಸ. Extra work. -ಕೋಲು. A transverse bar. -ಕಟ್ಟಿಗೆ. A wooden cross bar. -ಅಗಲ. Distance across, width. -ಗೀಚು. To cross out. -ಗೀಟು, -ಗೆರೆ. A cross line. -ಕೊಂಬು. A cross branch. -ಗೋಡೆ. A partition or curtain wall. ಅಡ್ಡಂಕೆ. A figure written from left to right; the total. -ಬಾಟು. A shelter. -ಚೌಕ. An oblong frame; the Linga box. -ಅಂಘು, ಅಡ್ಡಂಘು. The breadth of the foot. -ಅಣೆ, ಅಡ್ಡಣೆ. The woof that crosses the warp in a loom. -ತಲೆ, -ದಲೆ. An ill-formed head. -ತಾಕು. To touch, thwart, interfere with. -ತಿಡ್ಡ, -ತಿಡ್ಡಿ, ಅಡ್ಡಾತಿಡ್ಡಿ. Awkwardness, clumsiness; awkwardly. -ತಿರುವು. To turn aside. -ತೊಡರು. To thwart, interfere. -ದಂಡಿ, -ದಂಡಿಗೆ. A scale beam; a bamboo pole across a palankeen to carry it. -ದಟ್ಟಿ.

A slit bamboo put crosswise. -ತೊಲೆ. A transverse beam. -ನಗೆ. A half-suppressed laugh. -ನಾಮ. A surname; a secterian crossmark on the forehead of Smârtas. -ನಾಲಿಗೆ. A lying or opposing tongue. -ನಿಲುವು. Breadth and height. -ನುಡಿ. Contradiction. -ಪಂಕ್ತಿ. A side-row of people at dinner. -ಪಟ್ಟಿ. The upper or lower part of a door-frame. -ಪಲ್ಲಕಿ. A palankeen carried crosswise. -ಬರು. To come in the way. -ಬೀಳು. To fall across; to prostrate. -ಮರ. A cross bar. -ಮಾತು. Gainsaying; an evasion. -ಮಾರ್ಗ. A cross way, by-path. -ಮುಡಿ. A knot of hair. -ವಾಗು. To be cross; -ವಾಗಿ, transversely, across, broadwise. -ಇಡು, -ವಿಡು. To oppose. -ಸಾಲು. (=-ಪಂಕ್ತಿ). A transverse line or furrow. -ಸುಳಿ. To pass by. -ಹಚ್ಚು. To apply horizontally, as sectarian mark. -ಹಾಕು. To put crosswise; to put before for obtaining a blessing or pardon. -ಹಾದಿ. =-ಮಾರ್ಗ. -ಹಾಯು. To pass by; to thwart. -ಹೆಸರು. =-ನಾಮ. -ಆಡು, ಅಡ್ಡಾಡು. To walk about, promenade. -ಆಸು, ಅಡ್ಡಾಸು. To recline, lean on. -ಇಕ್ಕು. To put across or before. ಅಡ್ಡೆಸಗು. To make hostile efforts. ಅಡ್ಡೇಟು. A shot beside the mark. ಅಡ್ಡೊಕ್ಕಲು. A new tenant, fresh comer. ಅಡ್ಡೋಟ. An indirect course.

ಅಡ್ಡ 2. k. n. Seven duḍḍus, two aṇas and four pies. 2, a weight $=\frac{1}{18}$th of a varaha.

ಅಡ್ಡಗಿಸು. = ಅಡ್ಡಯಿಸು, q. v.

ಅಡ್ಡಣಿಗೆ k. n. A three-legged stand.

ಅಡ್ಡನೆ (= ಅಡನೆ) k. ad. Across, transversely.

ಅಡ್ಡಯಿಸು (= ಅಡ್ಡಗಿಸು) k. v. t. To move obliquely. 2, to obstruct. 3, to intervene, conceal.

ಅಡ್ಡಲು k. n. An obstacle. ad. Across. ಅಡ್ಡಲಾಗು (-ಆಗು). To become an obstacle; to oppose.

ಅಡ್ಡವಿಸು (= ಅಡ್ಡಯಿಸು) a. k. v. t. To obstruct.

ಅಡ್ಡಾತಿಡ್ಡಿ. = ಅಡ್ಡತಿಡ್ಡಿ, q. v.

ಅಡ್ಡಾನ k. a. Broad.

ಅಡ್ಡಿ k. n. An obstacle; opposition; delay. -ಮಾಡು. To oppose, hinder.

ಅಡ್ಡಿಕೆ k. n. A necklace.

ಅಡ್ಡೆ k. n. A bamboo by which one or two persons carry burdens suspended from its midst or both ends. -ಹೊರು. To carry it.

ಅಡ್ನಾಡಿ (= ಅಡನಾಡಿ). k. n. A perverse or stubborn person.

ಅಡ್ಲಿಗೆ k. n. A flat basket or earthen vessel.

ಅಡ್ಲು k. n. Mud.

ಅಣ k. A suffix used in the formation of a verbal noun, or 1st pers. pl. imperat., e. g. ಮಾಡುವಣ, ನಡೆಯುವಣ.

ಅಣಂ (= ಅಣಂ) a. k. ad. Whatsoever, howsoever. a. Small.

ಅಣಕ k. n. Mockery, derision. 2, (= ಅಡಕ) closeness, firmness.

ಅಣಕಿಸು k. v. t. To mock, deride.

ಅಣಗಿಸು. = ಅಡಗಿಸು, q. v.

ಅಣಗು. = ಅಡಗು, q. v.

ಅಣಜಾಣ k. n. A very clever man.

ಅಣಬೆ k. n. A pitcher or water jar.

ಅಣಬೆ, ಅಣಂಬೆ k. n. A mushroom.

ಅಣಲು k. n. The under part of the mouth. 2, a squirrel.

ಅಣಸು k. n. A ferrule. 2, a throng.

ಅಣಾ (= ಆಣೆ) h. n. An anna.

ಅಣಿ (=ಅಡಗು) k. n. Joining together of threads in a loom. 2, fitness, beauty; order. 3, an array, a body of soldiers. -ಕಟ್ಟು. To join a certain number of threads, etc. -ತುಳಿ. To move the loom's treadle.

ಅಣಿಗೆ (= ಹಣಿಗೆ) k. n. A comb.

ಅಣಿಮ s. n. Minuteness. 2, the power of becoming an atom.

ಅಣಿಯುರ a. k. n. Fitness, nicety; greatness.

ಅಣಿಲೆ k. n. (= ಅಳಲೆ) Ink-nut, *Terminalia chebula.*

ಅಣು s. a. Minute. n. An atom. 2, Śiva.

ಅಣುಗ k. n. A son. ಅಣುಗಿ, ಅಣುಗೆ. A daughter.

ಅಣುಂಕು a. k. v. t. To humble; to ruin, destroy.

ಅಣೆ 1. k. *int. used in calling a woman:* ho! ho!

ಅಣೆ 2. (= ಅಣು) k. v. i. To touch, come in contact. 2, to be quenched. v. t. To strike, push. 2, to embrace. n. Approach. 2, a dam, dike. -ಕಟ್ಟು, -ಕಟ್ಟೆ. A dam.

ಅಂಟರಳೆ (= ಅಂಟುವಾಳ) f. n. The soap-nut tree.

ಅಂಟರಿಕೆ k. n. A prickly climbing shrub, *Acacia intsia.*

ಅಂಟರಿಸು k. v. t. To evaporate.

ಅಂಟು k. v. i. To come in contact with, touch; to be contagious v. t. To touch; to embrace. 2, (= ಅಟ್ಟು No. 1) to follow, pursue. n. Contagion; impurity. 2, gum, paste. 3, a grafted branch; a young plant. -ರೋಗ. A contagious disease.

ಅಂಡ s. n. An egg (ಮೊಟ್ಟೆ). -ಜ. Egg-born; a bird; a fish, *etc.*

ಅಂದಲೆ a. k. v. t. To oppress, trouble, hurt. n. Oppression, trouble.

ಅಂಡಿಸು k. v. i. To go near; to resort to.

ಅಂಡು k. n. An approach. 2, a buttock.

ಅಂಡೆ k. n. A vessel made of bamboo. 2, (a. k.) nearness, vicinity.

ಅಣ್ಣ k. n. An elder brother; an elderly male. 2, an affectionate mode of addressing boys, *as* ಅಣ್ಣಾ! *f.* ಅಣ್ಣಿ. -ತಮ್ಮಂದಿರು. Brothers.

ಅಣ್ಣಾಲಿಗೆ k. n. The uvula.

ಅಣ್ಣೆ k. n. Excellence, purity. -ಪಾಲು. Pure milk. -ಕಲ್ಲು. A pebble tossed in play; a hail stone.

ಅಣ್ಪಿತ a. k. n. Friendship.

ಅತಂತ್ರ s. a. Unrestrained; useless, waste.

ಅತರ್ಕ್ಯ s. a. Invincible.

ಅತಲ s. n. N. of a hell. (*lit.* bottomless).

ಅತಲಕುತಲ k. n. Tumult, confusion.

ಅತಸಿ s. n. Common flax, *Linum usitatissimum.*

ಅತಿ s. *ad.* Over, beyond. 2, exceedingly, much, very. 3, surpassing. -ಕರ್ಮ. A great sin. -ಕರ್ಮಿ. A great sinner. -ಕಾಟ. Great trouble. -ಕಾಟಕ. A very troublesome man. -ಕಾಯ. Gigantic; a son of Râvaṇa. -ಕೊಂಕು. Very crooked. -ಕ್ರಮ. -ಕ್ರಮಣ. Going over, transgression, trespass; surpassing; neglect; imposition. -ಕ್ರಮಿಸು. To surpass; trespass; to let pass away; to become excessive. -ಗಳೆ, -ಕಳೆ. To disregard, contemn; to deny; to spend (time). -ಗ್ರಾಹಕ. Smart. -ಜಡ. Very cold; very stupid. -ಜವ. Great speed. -ಜಾಗರ. Very wakeful; the black curlew. -ದಪ್ಪ. Very thick. -ದಾಹ. Great heat; great thirst. -ದುಃಖ. Great affliction. -ನಿಷ್ಠುರ. Very fierce. -ಪಾತ. Lapse; transgression. -ಪಾಪ. A heinous sin. -ಬಂಧನ. Close confinement. -ಬಲ. Very strong. -ವೇಗ. Very swift. -ಮಧುರ. Very sweet. -ಮಾತ್ರ. Beyond measure, excessive. -ಯಾಶೆ. = ಅತ್ಯಾಶೆ. -ಯುದ್ಧ. A great fight. -ರಸ. Full of juice or essence; rich in poetical taste; a sweet cake. -ರಿಕ್ತ. -ರೇಕ. Excessive. -ರೂಢ. Commonly known. -ವಾದ. Talkativeness. -ವಾಸ. Fast on the day before performing the Śrâddha. -ವೇಳೆ. Excessive. -ಶಯ. Excellence; surprise; trouble; superior, abundant, wonderful. -ಶಯಿಸು. To become great; to wonder. -ಸಣ್ಣ. Minute. -ಸರ್ಜನ. Liberality; a gift. -ಸಾರ. Great charm; diarrhoea, dysentery. -ಸೂಕ್ಷ್ಮ. Very fine, minute. -ಸ್ವಲ್ಪ.

Very little. -ಹಾಸ. Great laughter. -ಜಡತ್ವ. Great stupidity.

ಅತಿಥಿ s. n. An invited guest. -ಪೂಜನ. Hospitality. -ಸತ್ಕಾರ. Civilities to guests.

ಅತೀತ s. a. Gone by, past; gone beyond. 2, passed away. 3, having neglected. -ಕಾಲ. Past time. -ಕ್ರಿಯೆ. A neglected business.

ಅತೀಂದ್ರಿಯ s. a. Going beyond the senses. n. The mind.

ಅತೀವ s. ad. Exceedingly, very.

ಅತೀವ್ರ s. a. Not sharp, blunt. 2, slow.

ಅತುಕು a. k. v. t. To join, cement. v. i. To be joined, united.

ಅತುಲ s. a. Unequalled.

ಅತುಷಾರ s. a. Not cold or dewy.

ಅತುಷ್ಟಿ s. n. Dissatisfaction.

ಅತ್ತ, ಅತ್ತಲು k. ad. In that direction or place, aside; beyond. -ಕಡೆ. = ಅತ್ತ. ಅತ್ತತ್ತಲು, etc. Far beyond. ಅತ್ತಣ. Of that side or place. ಅತ್ತಿತ್ತ. Here and there.

ಅತ್ತರು f. n. Attar of roses; perfume, essence.

ಅತ್ತರಿ k. n. A carpenter's plane.

ಅತ್ತಿ k. n. The red-wooded fig-tree, *Ficus racemosa.*

ಅತ್ತಿಗೆ (*tb. of* ಅತ್ತಿಕೆ) n. An elder brother's wife.

ಅತ್ತು k. (*p. p. of* ಅಳು) Having wept.

ಅತ್ತೆ s. n. A mother-in-law. 2, (= ಸೋದರತ್ತೆ) a father's sister.

ಅತ್ಯಧಮ s. a. Exceedingly low or mean.

ಅತ್ಯಂತ s. a. Beyond limit; excessive. 2, endless. 3, absolute. -ದುಃಖ. Very great affliction.

ಅತ್ಯಯ s. n. Going over or beyond; surpassing. 2, death; sin. 3, danger; distress.

ಅತ್ಯರ್ಥ s. a. Excessive.

ಅತ್ಯಾಶೆ s. n. Extravagant desire or hope.

ಅತ್ಯಾಶ್ಚರ್ಯ s. n. A great marvel.

ಅತ್ಯುತ್ತಮ s. a. Exceedingly good.

ಅತ್ಯುನ್ನತ s. a. Very high.

ಅತ್ಯುಷ್ಣ s. a. Very hot.

ಅತ್ರಿ s. n. N. of a ṛishi and a star in the Great Bear. -ಜಾತ. Born from Atri: the moon.

ಅಥ s. An auspicious particle, used in stuti, maṅgala, *etc.* *ad.* Now, then; what? how? moreover; rather; but; else.

ಅಥರ್ವ s. n. The fourth vêda.

ಅಥವಾ s. ad. Or.

ಅದ k. *The termination of the relative negative participle, as* ಮಾಡದ, ತಿನ್ನದ.

ಅದಕು (= ಅಗಚು, ಅದಪು, ಅಮಕು *etc.*) k. v. t. To press, squeeze, cram. 2, to be bruised. n. A bruise in a metal vessel.

ಅದಟ a. k. n. A very firm or persevering man.

ಅದಟು a. k. v. t. To scold, reprimand; to subdue. v. i. (= ಅದರು) To tremble. n. Self-will; boldness; pride.

ಅದದಿ h. a. Of counting or numeration.

ಅದನಾ h. a. Low, mean, vulgar.

ಅದಪು (= ಅದಕು) k. v. t. To squeeze. 2, (a. k.) to upbraid, reprove.

ಅದಬು h. n. Respect, regard.

ಅದರು (= ಅದಟು) k. v. i. To tremble. n. Trembling, tremor. -ಗುಂಡಿಗೆ. Faint-heartedness. -ಬೆದರು. Shaking and quaking. -ವಾಯು. The palsy. ಅದರಿಸು. To make shake.

ಅದರ್ಶನ s. n. Non-vision, disappearance. a. Invisible.

ಅದಲಾಬದಲು, ಅದಲುಬದಲು f. n. Exchanging.

ಅದಲು. = ಅದರು.

ಅದಾತಾರ (*tb. of* ಅದಾತೃ) a. Not giving. n. A miser.

ಅದಾನು (3rd. *pers. sing. pres. of* ಆಗು) k. He may be. ಅದಾನೆ. He is.

ಅದಾಲತು h. n. Justice; a court of justice.

ಅದಾವತಿ h. n. Enmity, hatred.

ಅದಿತಿ s. n. The mother of the gods. 2, the earth.

ಅದಿಮು. = ಅದಳು, q. v.

ಅದಿರು (= ಅದರು) k. v. i. To tremble, shiver, fear.

ಅದಿರ್ಗಂತಿ, ಅದಿಮುರ್ಗತ್ತಿ k. n. The creeper *Gaertnera racemosa.*

ಅದಿರ್ಪು a. k. n. Trembling, fear.

ಅದೀಪನ s. a. Indigestive. n. Bad digestion.

ಅದು k. *pro.* That, it. 2, the affix of the 3rd person singular neuter of the negative mood; *as* ಮಾಡದು, ಹೋಗದು, ಹುಟ್ಟದು.

ಅದುಕು. = ಅತುಕು, k. q. v.

ಅದುಗು k. v. i. To become soft by pressing. ಅದುಗಿಸು. To make soft by pressing.

ಅದುಗೋ (= ಅಕೋ) k. *int.* Lo! behold!

ಅದುರು (= ಅದರು) k. v. i. To tremble. n. Native metal. 2, dandruff.

ಅದುಹು a. k. v. i. To be perplexed.

ಅದೃಢ s. a. Unstable. 2, irresolute.

ಅದೃಶ್ಯ s. a. Invisible; not fit to be seen.

ಅದೃಷ್ಟ s. a. Unseen, invisible; unknown. n. Unforeseen danger; destiny, fate. -ವಂತ, -ಶಾಲಿ. A lucky (or unlucky) man.

ಅದೆ 1. k. A termination of the negative participle, *as* ತಿನ್ನದೆ, ಉಣ್ಣದೆ.

ಅದೆ 2. *int.* Lo! look there. v. i. It is, there is, ಅದೇ. That very thing.

ಅದೋ k. *int.* Ah! oh!

ಅದ್ಗಲೆ, ಅದ್ವಗಲೆ k. n. An anvil.

ಅದ್ದಿಕೆ k. n. Immersion, dipping; dying clothes.

ಅದ್ದು k. v. t. To immerse, dip; to dye. 2, = ಅದು, *as in* ದೂರವಾದದ್ದು ಬೇಕಾದದ್ದು, ಹೊಡೆದದ್ದು *etc.*

ಅದ್ದಿ f. a. Acting. -ಕೆಲಸ. Acting work.

ಅದ್ಭುತ s. a. Wonderful. n. A marvel, wonder; surprise.

ಅದ್ಯ *ad.* Now, to-day. -ತನ. Referring to to-day. --ಭೂತ. The aorist (imperfect).

ಅದ್ವಯ s. a. Not two, without a second, unique. n. Non-duality. 2, identity.

ಅದ್ರಿ s. n. A stone; a mountain. 2, a tree. 3, the sun. -ಕನ್ಯೆ, -ಜೆ. Pârvati. -ಕೀಲೆ. The earth. -ತಟಿ. Tableland. -ಭೇದನ. Indra. -ರಾಜ. Himâlaya. -ಸಾರ. Iron.

ಅದ್ವೈತ s. a. Destitute of duality, unique. n. The doctrine of the identity of the Brahma and the universe; pantheism.

ಅಧನ s. a. Destitute of wealth or property.

ಅಧಮ s. a. Lowest. 2, vile, bad.

ಅಧರ s. a. Lower. 2. low, vile. n. The lower lip; the lip.

ಅಧರ್ಮ s. n. Unrighteousness, irreligion; wickedness. ಅಧರ್ಮಿ. An unrighteous or wicked man.

ಅಧಿ s. *ad.* Above; over and above; besides; upon.

ಅಧಿಕ s. a. Additional; abundant; intercalated. 2, surpassing, superior; excellent. n. Abundance. -ತರ. Very much. -ಮಾಸ. An intercalar month.

ಅಧಿಕರಣ s. n. Supremacy. 2, a receptacle. 3, a topic. 4, a category. 5, the locative case. ಅಧಿಕರಿಸು. To aim at; to master.

ಅಧಿಕಾಧಿಕ s. a. Over and above, very much.

ಅಧಿಕಾರ s. n. Authority; government, rule, right. 2, privilege. 3, the use of royal insignia, royalty. 4, an office. -ಕೊಡು. To empower. -ಸ್ಥ, ಅಧಿಕಾರಿ. A man in authority; an officer.

ಅಧಿಗತ s. a. Found, obtained. 2, learned.

ಅಧಿದೇವತೆ, ಅಧಿದೇವಿ, ಅಧಿದೈವತ s. n. A presiding deity.

ಅಧಿನಾಯಕ, ಅಧಿಪ, ಅಧಿಪತಿ s. n. A ruler.

ಅಧಿರಾಜ s. n. A supreme king.

ಅಧಿರೋಹಿಣಿ s. n. A ladder.

ಅಧಿವಾಸ s. n. An abode, house.

ಅಧಿಷ್ಠಾನ s. n. Standing by, abiding. 2, an abode; a basis, site; a settlement. 3, authority. ಅಧಿಷ್ಠಿಸು. To govern.

ಅಧೀನ s. a. Subject to, dependent upon.

ಅಧೀಶ s. n. A lord, master. -ತ್ವ. Authority, power.

ಅಧೃಷ್ಟ s. a. Not bold, modest.

ಅಧೇಲಿ f. n. A half-rupee.

ಅಧೈರ್ಯ s. n. Want of courage, timidity. -ಗೊಳ್ಳು. To become timid.

ಅಧೋಗತಿ s. n. Downward movement; perdition.

ಅಧೋಭಾಗ s. n. The lower part.

ಅಧೋಮುಖ s. ad. Bending the head; upside down.

ಅಧೋಲೋಕ s. n. The lower world.

ಅಧ್ಯಕ್ಷ s. a. Observable, supervising. n. An inspector. -ತನ. Superintendence.

ಅಧ್ಯಯನ s. n. Reading, esp. the Vêdas.

ಅಧ್ಯಾತ್ಮ s. n. The supreme soul.

ಅಧ್ಯಾಪಕ s. n. A teacher.

ಅಧ್ಯಾಪನ s. n. Instruction, esp. on the Vêdas.

ಅಧ್ಯಾಯ s. n. A lesson, chapter. 2, a reader.

ಅಧ್ರುವ s. a. Unfixed; uncertain.

ಅಧ್ವ s. n. A road. 2, time. 3, sky.

ಅಧ್ವರ s. n. A sacrifice.

ಅಧ್ವಾನ s. a. Devoid of sound. n. A wilderness. 3. misfortune.

ಅನ್. = ಅನ್ನು, ಅಂತ, ಅಂದರೆ, q. v.

ಅನ s. n. Breath.

ಅನಕ, ಅನಕಾ k. prep. Till, until. 2, meanwhile.

ಅನಘ s. a. Sinless, faultless.

ಅನಂಗ s. a. Incorporeal. n. Kâma. 2, the ether.

ಅನಚ್ಛ s. a. Unclear, turbid.

ಅನಡುಹ, ಅನಡ್ವಾಹ s. n. A bull. ಅನಡುಹಿ, ಅನಡ್ವಾಹಿ. A cow.

ಅನತಿಶಯ s. a. Not great, small.

ಅನದ್ಯತನಭೂತ s. n. The pluperfect tense (g.).

ಅನನುಕೂಲ s. a. Adverse, unfavourable.

ಅನಂತ s. a. Endless, infinite, eternal. n. Vishṇu, Kṛishṇa or Śiva. 2, the sky. 3, the earth. 4, the snake king. -ತ್ವ. Eternity; boundlessness.

ಅನಂತರ s. a. Having no interval. 2, following, next. ad. Afterwards. ಅನಂತರದಲ್ಲಿ, afterwards.

ಅನನ್ಯ s. a. Not different. 2, unique. 3, fixed on one object.

ಅನಪಕಾರಿ s. a. Harmless, innocuous.

ಅನಪರಾಧಿ s. a. Innocent. n. An innocent man.

ಅನರ್ಗಲ s. a. Unfettered, free; haughty.

ಅನರ್ಘ್ಯ s. a. Priceless.

ಅನರ್ಥ s. a. Worthless, useless; unhappy. 2, meaningless. n. Nonsense.

ಅನಲ, ಅನಲು s. n. Fire; the god of fire. 2, digestive power.

ಅನವದ್ಯ s. a. Irreproachable, faultless.

ಅನವಧಾನ s. a. Inattentive. n. -ತೆ. Inattention.

ಅನವಧಿ s. a. Unlimited.

ಅನವರತ s. a. Incessant.

ಅನವಸರ s. a. Having no leisure.

ಅನವು (= ಅನು) k. n. Suitable place, room.

ಅನಶನ s. n. Fasting.

ಅನಸೂಯೆ s. n. Unenviousness, freedom from spite. 2, the wife of Atri.

ಅನಹಿತ s. n. Disadvantage, loss.

ಅನಾಕಾರ s. a. Shapeless; deformed.

ಅನಾಚಾರ s. a. Regardless of custom, unprincipled. n. Irreligion; incivility.

ಅನಾಥ s. a. Fatherless, helpless, poor. -ನಾಥ. A friend of the friendless. ಅನಾಥೆ. A widow, helpless woman.

ಅನಾದರ, ಅನಾದರಣೆ s. n. Disrespect, slight.

ಅನಾದಿ s. a. Without beginning, eternal. n. Heaven. -ವಾರ್ತೆ. Tradition.

ಅನಾದೃತ s. a. Disrespected, despised.

ಅನಾದ್ಯ s. a. Having no beginning.

ಅನಾಧಾರತೆ s. n. The state of having no support.

ಅನಾಮಕ, ಅನಾಮಿಕ s. a. Nameless; infamous.

ಅನಾಮಿಕೆ, ಅನಾಮೆ s. n. The ring-finger.

ಅನಾಯಕ s. a. Without a leader. ad. Disorderly.

ಅನಾಯಾಸ s. n. Absence of exertion, ease. a. Easy.

ಅನಾರ್ಯ s. a. Not-respectable; vulgar; un-Aryan.

ಅನಾವೃಷ್ಟಿ s. n. Want of rain, drought.

ಅನಾಸು f. n. The pine-apple, *Ananas sativus.*

ಅನಿಚ್ಛೆ s. n. Absence of desire; indifference.

ಅನಿತು (= ಅನಿತ್ತು) a. k. *pro. (remote)* That much; that time; so much; so many. a. All, the whole. ಅನಿಬರು. All persons.

ಅನಿತ್ಯ s. a. Not everlasting; transient, unstable.

ಅನಿಮಿತ್ತ, ಅನಿಮಿತ್ಯ s. a. Causeless, groundless.

ಅನಿಮಿಷ s. a. Not winking, vigilant. n. Not a moment. 2, a god.

ಅನಿಯಮಿತ s. a. Lawless; irregular.

ಅನಿಲ s. n. Wind or air; the deity of wind.

ಅನಿವಾರ a. Refractory; excessive.

ಅನಿವಾರ್ಯ a. Inavertible. n. Calamity.

ಅನಿಶ s. a. Nightless; sleepless; continuous.

ಅನಿಷ್ಟ s. a. Unwished, disagreeable. n. Ill-luck; crime; hatred.

ಅನಿಸು k. v. t. To cause to say.

ಅನೀತಿ s. n. Injustice, immorality. -ವಂತ. An unjust man.

ಅನೀಶ s. n. One who has no protector or superior. a. Powerless.

ಅನು 1. k. n. (*cf.* ಅನವು, ಅನುವು) Fitness; propriety; loveliness. 2, worth. 3, readiness (*cf.* ಅನುವಾಗು). 4, success. 5, scheme, device. 6, accommodation. 7, occurrence; opportunity, leisure. -ಗೊಳಿಸು. To make ready, prepare. -ವಾಗು. To be ready or fit; an occasion to happen.

ಅನು 2. = ಅನ್ನು, *q. v.*

ಅನು 3. s. ad. Afterwards, then. *prep.* Along; with; severally, each by each; towards; like; according to.

ಅನುಕಂಪ s. n. Sympathy, compassion, tenderness.

ಅನುಕರಣ s. n. Imitation; resemblance. -ಪದ, -ಶಬ್ದ. An imitative word. ಅನುಕರಿಸು. To imitate. 2, to accept. 3, to make ready.

ಅನುಕರ್ಷ s. n. Attraction.

ಅನುಕೂಲ s. a. Favourable, agreeable. n. (=-ತೆ) Good-will; suitableness of circumstances, convenience; favour, help. -ಮಾಡು, ಅನುಕೂಲಿಸು. To be favourable; to help. -ಬೀಳು. To agree; to obtain.

ಅನುಕ್ರಮ s. n. Succession, method.

ಅನುಕ್ರಮಣ s. n. Methodical arrangement.

ಅನುಕ್ರಮಣಿಕೆ s. n. A table of contents; a preface.

ಅನುಗ s. a. Going after. n. A companion; a servant.

ಅನುಗತ s. a. Gone after. n. A follower.

ಅನುಗತಿ s. n. Succession, order.

ಅನುಗಮನ s. a. Following. n. Sati.

ಅನುಗಾಮಿ s. n. A follower, companion.

ಅನುಗುಣ s. a. Congenial with. -ತ್ವ. Congeniality.

ಅನುಗ್ರಹ s. n. Conferring benefits, favour, kindness; aid. -ಹೊಂದು, -ಪಡೆ. To gain favour.

ಅನುಗ್ರಹಿಸು s. v. t. To favour, grant, vouchsafe.

ಅನುಚಿತ s. a. Improper; wrong.

ಅನುಜ, ಅನುಜಾತ s. a. After-born. n. A younger brother.

ಅನುಜೀವಿ s. a. Living on (others). n. A dependent.

ಅನುಜ್ಞೆ s. *n.* Assent, permission; leave to depart. 2, an order.

ಅನುತಾಪ s. *n.* Repentance. 2, sorrow. ಅನುತಾಪಿ. Penitent.

ಅನುತ್ತಮ s. *a.* Highest; best, excellent.

ಅನುತ್ತರ s. *a.* Highest; best, excellent. 2, low, inferior. 3, silent, without any reply.

ಅನುದಿನ s. *ad.* Every day, daily.

ಅನುನಯ s. *n.* Salutation, courtesy. 2, entreaty. 3, conduct; discipline.

ಅನುಪತ್ಯ s. *n.* Absence of the means of subsistence; need.

ಅನುಪಪತ್ತಿ s. *n.* Non-accomplishment; insufficiency.

ಅನುಪಪನ್ನ s. *a.* Non-accomplished; deficient.

ಅನುಪಮ s. *a.* Incomparable, peerless; [best.

ಅನುಪಲ್ಲವಿ s. *n.* The response in a chorus.

ಅನುಪ್ರಾಸ s. *n.* Alliteration.

ಅನುಬಂಧ s. *n.* Binding, connection. 2, an uninterrupted series. 3, consequence, result. 4, motive. 5, an indicatory letter. 6, commencement. -ಕ್ರಿಯೆ. An auxiliary verb (*as* ಕೊಳ್ಳು *in* ಕಂಡುಕೊಳ್ಳು).

ಅನುಬಿಂಬ s. *n.* A reflection. ಅನುಬಿಂಬಿಸು. *v. i.* To be reflected.

ಅನುಭವ s. *n.* Knowledge from observation, enjoyment, experience. 2, apprehension, understanding. -ಮಾಡಿ ಕೊಳ್ಳು. To make one's self acquainted with.

ಅನುಭವಿಸು s. *v. t.* To experience: to enjoy, suffer, undergo.

ಅನುಭಾವ s. *n.* Dignity, authority. 2, resolution.

ಅನುಭೋಗ s. *n.* Enjoyment. 2, experience, undergoing.

ಅನುಭೋಗಿಸು s. *v. t.* To enjoy. 2, to experience.

ಅನುಮತ s. *a.* Approved; permitted, allowed. *n.* = ಅನುಮತಿ.

ಅನುಮತಿ (= ಅನುಮತ *n.*) s. *n.* Assent, permission; approbation.

ಅನುಮತಿಸು s. *v. t.* To assent, agree. 2, to persuade.

ಅನುಮಾನ s. *n.* Hesitation, doubt, suspicion. 2, inference *(in logic)*. -ಬೀಳು, -ಪಡು. To doubt, *etc.*

ಅನುಮಾನಿಸು s. *v. t.* To doubt, hesitate; to suspect.

ಅನುಮೇಯ s. *a.* Inferable. ಅನುಮೇಯಿಸು. To infer.

ಅನುಮೋದ s. *n.* Pleasure from sympathy; assent, acceptance. ಅನುಮೋದಿಸು *v. i.* To feel sympathetic joy; to assent.

ಅನುಯೋಗ s. *n.* A question. 2, reproof.

ಅನುಯೋಜನ s. *n.* A question. 2, attachment. ಅನುಯೋಜಿಸು *v. i.* To attach, join.

ಅನುರಕ್ತಿ, ಅನುರಾಗ s. *n.* Affection, love, devotion. ಅನುರಕ್ತಿಸು, ಅನುರಾಗಿಸು *v. t. v. i.* To love; to be fond of.

ಅನುರಾಧೆ s. *n.* The seventeenth lunar mansion.

ಅನುಲಾಪ s. *n.* Tautology. ಅನುಲಾಪಿಸು *v. t.* To repeat the same word.

ಅನುಲೇಪನ s. *n.* Ointment; anointing. ಅನುಲೇಪಿಸು *v. t.* To anoint.

ಅನುವರ್ತನ s. *n.* Following; concurring. 2, compliance, obedience. 3, continuance. 4, consequence. ಅನುವರ್ತಿಸು *v. t.* To refer or apply. 2, to follow.

ಅನುವಾದ s. *n.* Repetition; confirmation. 2, slander. ಅನುವಾದಿಸು *v. i.* To reason, argue.

ಅನುವು (= ಅನು), -ತನುವು k. *n.* Preparation for setting out. 2, refreshment.

ಅನುವೃತ್ತಿ s. *n.* Complying with. 2, reverting to. 3, imitating; conformity.

ಅನುವೇಸು. = ಅನ್ವಯಿಸು *s.* ಅನ್ವಯ.

ಅನುಶಯ s. *n.* Close connection. 2, evil result. 3, repentance. 4, wrath.

ಅನುಶಾಸನ s. *n.* Regulating; instruction, direction.

ಅನುಷ್ಠಾನ s. *n.* Undertaking; performance, practice, business. ಅನುಷ್ಠಿಸು *v. t.* To perform.

ಅನುಸಂಧಾನ s. n. Investigation. 2, plan, scheme. ಅನುಸಂಧಿಸು v. t. To join, connect; to meet.

ಅನುಸರಣೆ, ಅನುಸಾರ s. n. Following, imitating. 2, conformity to. ಅನುಸಾರವಾಗಿ. According to.

ಅನುಸರಿಸು s. v. t. To act in like manner; to follow.

ಅನುಸಾರಿ s. n. A follower.

ಅನುಸಾರಿಣಿ s. n. (lit. She who follows) N. of the second string of a lute.

ಅನುಸ್ವಾರ s. n. After-sound; the nasal sound represented by ಂ (g.).

ಅನೂಕ s. n. The spine. 2, race. 3, temperament.

ಅನೂನ s. a. Undiminished, not less; whole.

ಅನೂರು s. a. Thighless. n. Aruṇa; the dawn.

ಅನೃಜು s. a. Not straight. 2, wicked.

ಅನೃತ s. a. Untrue. n. Falsehood, lie. 2, agriculture.

ಅನೆ k. Suffix to form adverbs, as ಚಟ್ಟನೆ, ಉಸಿಕನೆ, ಸುಮ್ಮನೆ.

ಅನೆಯ, ಅನೇ k. Suffix to denote ordinals, as ಮೊದಲನೇ, ಎರಡನೇ, ಮೂರನೇ, etc.

ಅನೇಕ s. a. Not one, many, several. -ವಿಧ. In different ways, various. -ಆವರ್ತಿ. Many times.

ಅಂತ 1. (= ಅಂಥ, q. v.) k. ad. Such, such a one. 2, p. p. of ಅನ್ನು.

ಅಂತ 2. s. n. End, limit, boundary. 2, completion; death, decay. 3, a final syllable (g.). 4, certainty. 5, disposition. 6, nearness. 7, inside.

ಅಂತಃ (= ಅಂತರ್) s. ad. Within, in the middle. 2, between. -ಕರಣ. The inner organ, the heart, conscience, soul. 2, (fig.) favour, love, mercy (= ದಯ, ಪ್ರೀತಿ). -ಕರಣಪಡು. To have mercy. -ಕರಣಶುದ್ಧ. A man whose mind is pure. -ಕಲಹ. Inner strife. -ಪುರ. The inner or female apartment, gynaeceum. -ಶುದ್ಧಿ. Inward purity. -ಸಾರ. Having internal essence.

ಅಂತಃಸ್ಥ (cf. ಅಂತಸ್ಸು) s. a. Being amidst. n. A semi-vowel.

ಅಂತಕ s. a. Making an end. n. Death, Yama.

ಅಂತಸ್ಸು. See s. ಅಂತು.

ಅಂತರ್. = ಅಂತಃ, q. v.

ಅಂತರ s. a. Inner, interior. 2, near; related. 3, distant; different. 4, surpassing. n. The interior. 2, the soul (ಅಂತರಾತ್ಮ). 3, interval; distance; difference. 4, a variety. 5, period of time; occasion. 6, respect. 7, a surety. 8, great height. 9, obstacle (ಅಂತರಾಯ). 10, at the end of cpds. different, another, as ದೇಶಾಂತರ, another country; ಜನ್ಮಾಂತರ, ಮಾನಸಾಂತರ, ಲೋಕಾಂತರ, etc. ಅಂತರಾತ್ಮ. The soul.

ಅಂತರಂಗ s. n. The inner part; mind, heart. 2, secrecy.

ಅಂತರಗಂಗೆ s. n. A water-plant, Pistia stratiotes.

ಅಂತರಂತರ s. a. Leaving a proper distance when sitting at meals, or space between hills, etc.

ಅಂತರಾಂತರ s. n. The inner soul. 2, difference.

ಅಂತರಾಯ s. n. Obstacle, impediment.

ಅಂತರಾಲ s. n. Intermediate space or time.

ಅಂತರಿಕ್ಷ s. n. Atmosphere, sky.

ಅಂತರಿಸು s. v. t. To leave a space between. 2, to put off. v. i. To disappear.

ಅಂತರಿಂದೆ (ರಿ = ಱ) k. prep. Afterwards.

ಅಂತರಿಂದ್ರಿಯ k. n. An internal organ; manas, buddhi, ahaṅkâra and čhitta.

ಅಂತರ್ಗತ s. a. Included in. 2, hidden; forgotten.

ಅಂತರ್ಧಾನ s. n. Disappearance.

ಅಂತರ್ಭೂತ s. a. Internal, inner.

ಅಂತರ್ಮಂದಿರ, ಅಂತರ್ಗೃಹ s. n. An inner apartment.

ಅಂತರ್ಮುಖ s. n. Continual attention of the mind.

ಅಂತರ್ಯಗ s. *n.* The interior. 2, a hidden thought.

ಅಂತರ್ಯಾಮಿ s. *n.* The supreme soul.

ಅಂತಸ್ತಾಪ s. *n.* Inward heat; distress.

ಅಂತಸ್ತು *(tb. of* ಅಂತಸ್ಥ) *a.* Being between. *n.* A story of a building. 2, degree of rank.

ಅಂತಸ್ಥ s. *n.* A secret.

ಅಂತಹ a. k. = ಅಂತು, *q. v.*

ಅಂತಾ (= ಅಂಥ, *q. v.*) *ad.* Such. 2, = ಅನ್ನುತ್ತಾ. [*etc.* (*g.*).

ಅಂತಾನೆ, ಅಂತಿ, *etc.* = ಅನ್ನುತ್ತಾನೆ, ಅನ್ನುತ್ತಿ,

ಅಂತಿಕ s. *ad.* Near. *n.* Vicinity. 2, end.

ಅಂತು k. *ad.* In that manner, thus, so. *n.* The whole, total. ಅಂತಪ್ಪ, ಅಂತಹ. Such, such a one. ಅಂತಿಂತು (= ಅಂತು-ಇಂತು). Either so or thus, at any rate. ಅಂತೂ. And so; as for, *as* ಹೊಸವು ಅಂತೂ ತೋರಲಿಲ್ಲ, as for new ones they did not appear.

ಅಂತುಟು. = ಅನಿತು.

ಅಂತೆ 1., ಅಂತೇ k. *ad.* Even so; just like; just as (ಹಾಂಗೆ).

ಅಂತೆ 2. k. *d. v.* It is said; *see s.* ಅನ್ನು.

ಅಂತ್ಯ s. *a.* Last; final. 2, lowest. *n.* The end. -ಜ, -ಜನ್ಮ. Lowest born; a Śûdra.

ಅಂತ್ಯೇಷ್ಟಿ s. *n.* Funeral ceremonies.

ಅಂತ್ರ *tb. of* ಅಂತರ, *q. v. as* ದೇಶಾಂತ್ರ, ಮುಖಾಂತ್ರ, *etc.* 2, entrail, gut.

ಅಂಥ, ಅಂಥಾ (= ಅಂತಾ) k. *ad.* Such, of that kind, *as* ತಕ್ಕಂಥ, ಹುಟ್ಟಿದಂಥಾ, ಇರುವಂಥಾದ್ದು, *etc.* ಅಂಥಂಥಾ. Such and such.

ಅಂದ (= ಅನು 1) k. *n.* Fitness; beauty. 2, manner. 3, nature; faculty. 4, true state. -ಗೆಡಿಸು. To spoil, ruin. -ಗೆಡು. To become ugly. -ಗೇಡಿ. An ugly creature. -ಗೊಳಿಸು. To cause to look nice. -ಪಡೆ. To be beautiful. -ಗಾರ. A handsome man; *f.* -ಗಾರಳು, -ಗಾತಿ.

ಅಂದಣ, ಅಂದಳ *(tb. of* ಆಂದೋಲ) *n.* A litter, palankeen.

ಅಂದರೆ *(fr.* ಅನ್ನು) k. If one says; that is to say. ಸಂಧಿ ಅಂದರೇನು what is sandhi?

ಅಂದಾಜು h. *n.* Proportion; estimate. ಕಟ್ಟು. To make an estimate.

ಅಂದಿಪ್ಪನಾರು k. *n.* An evergreen tree, *Carallia integerrima.*

ಅಂದಿಹುಳ k. *n.* A small insect that infests grain.

ಅಂದು 1. k. *ad.* At that time, then. ಚಿಕ್ಕಂದು. Childhood. ಅಂದಿನಿಂದ. Since then. ಅಂದಿಗೆ. Then. ಅಂದೆಂದು. Always.

ಅಂದು 2. k. *v. t.* To suffer; to get at; to obtain. *v. i.* To reach, arrive.

ಅಂದುಕ s. *n.* A chain, fetter. 2, an anklet.

ಅಂದುಗು k. *n.* The clearing nut plant, *Strychnos potatorum.*

ಅಂದ್ರೆ. = ಅಂದರೆ, *q. v.*

ಅಂಧ s. *a.* Blind. *n.* Darkness. 2, turbid water. ಅಂಧಾದರಬಾರು h. A bad government.

ಅಂಧಕ s. *a.* Blind. *n.* A blind man. 2, darkness. 3, water.

ಅಂಧಕಾರ s. *n.* Darkness. -ಕವಿ, -ಮುಚ್ಚಿಕೊಳ್ಳು. Darkness to cover.

ಅಂಧ್ರ f. *n.* The Telugu country; a Telugu man.

ಅನ್ನ 1. (= ಅನ್ನೆ) a. k. *ad.* That time; meanwhile. -ಬರ, -ಬರೆ. So long as, until.

ಅನ್ನ 2. s. *n.* Food, *esp.* boiled rice. 2, the sun; water. -ಋಣ. One's allotment to eat rice. -ಕಂಟಕ. One who hinders another's living. -ಕುದಿಸು, -ಬೇಸು. To boil rice. -ಗತ. Depending on food. -ಛತ್ರ. A building in which food is distributed. -ದಾತ, -ದಾನಿ. A giver of food. -ದಾನ. Giving of food. -ದ್ವೇಷ. Want of appetite. -ಪಚನೆ. Digestion. -ಪದಾರ್ಥ. Rice and curry. -ಪಾನ. Meat and drink. -ಪ್ರಾಶನ. The ceremony of putting rice into a child's mouth for the first time. -ಭೇದಿ. Green vitriol. -ವಸ್ತ್ರ. Food and clothing. -ಶಾಂತಿ. Feeding the hungry. ಅನ್ನಾಭಾವ. Want of food. -ಹಾಕು, -ಇಕ್ಕು, -ಬಡಿಸು. To serve up rice at a meal. -ಸೇರು,

-ಹೋಗು. To have an appetite. ಅನ್ನಾ ರ್ಥಿ. A beggar.

ಅನ್ನು k. v. i. To say, speak, name. ಅನ್ನಿಸು. To cause to say, *etc.* ಅನ್ನಿಸಿಕೊಳ್ಳು. To be called, to pass for. (*P. ps.* ಅಂದು, ಅಂತ, ಅಂತಾ, having said, *for which often* ಎಂದು, *etc. are used*). *The verb* ಅನ್ನು, *like* ಎನ್ನು, *is used to introduce words and sentences, as* ಎಲ್ಲಿಗೆ ಹೋಗಲಿ ಅಂತ ಕೇಳಿದನು, he asked "where shall I go?" ಅಂತೆ. Having said, it is said. ಅಂದರೆ. That is to say *(explanatory)*. ಅನ್ನುವಿಕೆ. Saying.

ಅನ್ನೆ (= ಅನ್ನ 1) a. k. *ad.* Meanwhile, until. 2, truly, certainly.

ಅನ್ಯ, ಅನ್ಯಕ s. *a.* Other, another, different; foreign. -ಜಾತಿ. Another caste. -ದೇಶ. A foreign country. -ಪಾಕ. Cooked by others. -ಭಾವ. The mind of another. -ಭಾಷೆ. Another language.

ಅನ್ಯತರ s. *a.* Either of the two.

ಅನ್ಯತ್ರ s. *ad.* Elsewhere.

ಅನ್ಯಥಾ s. *ad.* Otherwise; in a different manner.

ಅನ್ಯಾಯ s. *n.* Unlawfulness, injustice. -ಗಾರ. An unjust man.

ಅನ್ಯೋನ್ಯ s. *a.* Mutual. *n.* Reciprocity. 2, intimacy, friendship, amity. -ಭಾವ. Mutual affection. -ವಾಗು. To become reconciled. -ಸಲ್ಲಾಪ. Conversation. -ಸ್ನೇಹ. Mutual friendship.

ಅನ್ವಯ s. *n.* Succession; connection. 2, race, family. 3, grammatical construction of a sentence *(g.)*. 4, drift, purport. ಅನ್ವಯಿಸು. To construe; to arrange words in order.

ಅನ್ವರ್ಥ s. *a.* Intelligible, clear. -ನಾಮ. A word of self-evident meaning.

ಅನ್ವವಾಯ s. *n.* Family, race.

ಅನ್ವಾಹಿತ s. *a.* Deposited. 2, renewed, as a sacred fire.

ಅನ್ವಿತ s. *a.* Connected; understood.

ಅನ್ವೇಷಣ s. *n.* Searching, investigation.

ಅಪ 1. = ಅಪ್ಪ.

ಅಪ 2. s. *ad.* Away. 2, negatively, contradictorily. 3, without.

ಅಪಕಾರ s. *n.* Wrong, offence, harm. 2, wickedness. ಅಪಕಾರಿ. An offender.

ಅಪಕೀರ್ತಿ s. *n.* Reproach. 2, disgrace, infamy. -ಹೊಂದು. To be disgraced. -ತಂದುಕೊಳ್ಳು. To incur disgrace.

ಅಪಕೃತ್ಯ s. *n.* A wrong act; damage, injury.

ಅಪಕ್ರಮ s. *n.* Going away. 2, flight. 3, (= ಅಕ್ರಮ) disorder.

ಅಪಕ್ವ s. *a.* Uncooked, raw. 2, unripe.

ಅಪಖ್ಯಾತಿ s. *n.* Injured reputation, disgrace.

ಅಪಗತ s. *a.* Gone, departed. 2, deceased. ಅಪಗತಿ. Low condition.

ಅಪಚಾರ s. *n.* Improper conduct; offence, mistake. 2, defect.

ಅಪಚಿತಿ s. *n.* Honour, respect. 2, loss. 3, expense.

ಅಪಜಯ s. *n.* Defeat, reverse, loss. -ಪಡಿಸು. To defeat. -ಹೊಂದು. To be defeated.

ಅಪಜ್ಞಾನ s. *n.* Concealment of knowledge.

ಅಪತ್ನೀಕ s. *a.* Wifeless. *n.* A widower.

ಅಪತ್ಯ s. *n.* Offspring, a child.

ಅಪಥ್ಯ s. *a.* Unfit, unwholesome. *n.* Bad diet. 2, a lie.

ಅಪದೂರು (ರು = ಱು) k. *n.* Slander, calumny; disgrace. -ಇಡು, -ಮಾಡು, -ಹಾಕು. To calumniate. -ಪಡು. To be disgraced.

ಅಪದೆಸೆ (*tb. of* ಅಪದಶೆ) *n.* A low miserable state.

ಅಪದೇಶ s. *n.* A pretence. 2, a butt, mark. 3, fame. 4, quarter.

ಅಪಧ್ವಂಸ s. *n.* Falling away; degradation.

ಅಪನಂಬಿಕೆ, ಅಪನಂಬಿಗೆ, ಅಪನಂಬುಗೆ k. *n.* Distrust, mistrust; unbelief.

ಅಪನಿಂದೆ s. *n.* Abuse, reproach. -ಹೊರಿಸು. To accuse falsely.

ಅಪಪ್ರಯೋಗ s. *n.* Misapplication.

ಅಪಭ್ರಂಶ s. *n.* Incorrect language.

ಅಪಮಾನ (= ಅವಮಾನ) s. n. Disrespect, dishonour, disgrace. -ಮಾಡು. To disgrace.

ಅಪಮೃತ್ಯು s. n. A sudden or violent death. 2, a minor death, i.e. a desperate sickness.

ಅಪರ s. a. Hinder, later. 2, following. 3, other. 4, different; distant. n. The hind foot of an elephant. 2, the future. 3, the west.

ಅಪರಂಜಿ f. n. Pure gold.

ಅಪರಪಕ್ಷ s. n. The latter or dark half of the month. 2, the other side, defendant.

ಅಪರರಾತ್ರಿ, ಅಪರಾತ್ರಿ s. n. The latter half of the night.

ಅಪರಾಜಿತ s. a. Unconquered. n. Vishṇu; [Šiva.

ಅಪರಾದ್ಧ s. a. Sinned; guilty.

ಅಪರಾಧ s. n. Offence, crime, 2, penalty, punishment. 3, fault, mistake. -ಕ್ಷಮಿಸಿಬಿಡು. To pardon an aparâdha. -ಕೊಡು. To pay a fine. -ಮಾಡು. To commit an aparâdha. -ಹೊರು. To charge an aparâdha upon.

ಅಪರಾಧಸ್ಥ, ಅಪರಾಧಿ s. n. A guilty person, criminal.

ಅಪರಾಹ್ಣ n. The afternoon.

ಅಪರಿಮಿತ s. a. Unmeasured, unlimited.

ಅಪರೂಪ (tb. ಅಪುರೂಪ) s. a. Ugly. 2, uncommon, rare.

ಅಪಲಾಪ s. n. Denial, abnegation; hiding. 2, an outcry. ಅಪಲಾಪಿಸು. To deny; to cry out.

ಅಪವಾದ s. n. Evil speaking, blame. 2, refutation. 3, exception.

ಅಪವಿತ್ರ s. a. Impure, unclean.

ಅಪಶಕುನ s. n. A bad omen.

ಅಪಶಬ್ದ s. n. A harsh word. 2, incorrect language.

ಅಪಸದ s. n. An outcaste.

ಅಪಸರ, tb. of ಅಪಸ್ವರ, q. v.

ಅಪಸಾಕ್ಷಿ s. n. False witness.

ಅಪಸಿದ್ಧಾಂತ s. n. An erroneous conclusion.

ಅಪಸ್ಮಾರ s. n. Forgetfulness; unconsciousness. 2, epilepsy.

ಅಪಸ್ವರ s. n. An unmusical sound. 2, a hoarse voice.

ಅಪಹರಣ s. n. Taking away; stealing.

ಅಪಹರಿಸು s. v. t. To take away; to rob, plunder.

ಅಪಹಾರ s. n. Taking away. 2, stealing. ಮಾನಾಪಹಾರ. Defamation.

ಅಪಹಾಸ್ಯ s. n. Ridicule, scorn, mockery. -ಮಾಡು. To mock at.

ಅಪಾಂಗ s. a. Deformed. n. The outer corner of the eye. 2, a sectarian mark.

ಅಪಾತ್ಯಯ s. n. Concealment of knowledge. [ment.

ಅಪಾತ್ರ s. a. Unworthy, unfit.

ಅಪಾದಾನ s. n. The ablative case (g.).

ಅಪಾಪೋಲಿ k. a. Stray, as cattle; disorderly, as a man; ill-done.

ಅಪಾಯ s. n. Going away. 2, destruction. 3, evil. 4, peril, danger.

ಅಪಾರ s. a. Shoreless, unbounded; immense.

ಅಪಾರ್ಥ s. a. Unmeaning. n. False argu-

ಅಪಾಶ್ರಯ s. n. A refuge. 2, a fence, hedge. a. Helpless.

ಅಪಿ s. prep. On; near to. ad. Moreover. 2, though. 3, certainly. 4, perhaps.

ಅಪಿಧಾನ s. n. Covering. 2, a cover.

ಅಪುತ್ರ s. a. Sonless.

ಅಪುನರ್ಭವ s. n. Exemption from further transmigration (= ಮುಕ್ತಿ).

ಅಪುಷ್ಪ s. a. Not flowering.

ಅಪೂಪ s. n. A cake of flour, etc.

ಅಪೂರ್ವ s. a. Unprecedented. 2, extraordinary, wonderful, unparalleled.

ಅಪೇಕ್ಷಿಸು s. v. t. To desire, wish for; to expect.

ಅಪೇಕ್ಷೆ s. n. Desire, wish; hope. -ಹುಟ್ಟಿಸು. To excite desire, etc.

ಅಪೋಹ s. n. Removal of doubt. 2, arguing.

ಅಪ್ಪ 1. (pr. part. of ಆಗು. = ಆಗುವ) a. k. Becoming; being, e. g. ಪ್ರಿಯವಪ

ನುಡಿ. ಅಪ್ಪಂತೆ. As well as possible. ಅಪ್ಪಂಥವ. An agreeable or fit man. ಅಪ್ಪುದು. = ಆಗುವದು.

ಅಪ್ಪ 2. k. n. Father; cf. ಚಿಕ್ಕಪ್ಪ, ದೊಡ್ಡಪ್ಪ, *etc.* 2, *an affix to proper name, as* ಪೊನ್ನಪ್ಪ. 3, (*tb. of* ಅಪೂಪ) a rice cake.

ಅಪ್ಪಟ f. a. Pure, unmixed.

ಅಪ್ಪಟೆ k. n. Flatness.

ಅಪ್ಪಣೆ (*tb. of* ಆಜ್ಞಾಪನ) n. Order, command, law. 2, permission, leave. -ಕೇಳು. To ask permission. -ಕೊಡು. To give permission; to order. -ತಕ್ಕೊಳ್ಳು, -ಹೊಂದು. To take leave. -ಮಾಡು. To order.

ಅಪ್ಪನ (*tb. of* ಅರ್ಪಣ) n. Tax; rent.

ಅಪ್ಪಯಿಸು k. v. t. To embrace; to seize eagerly.

ಅಪ್ಪರಿಸು k. v. t. To lift up and throw [down.

ಅಪ್ಪಳಿಸು k. v. t. To strike against; to slap. 2, = ಅಪ್ಪರಿಸು.

ಅಪ್ಪಿಗೆ (= ಅಪ್ಪುಗೆ) k. n. Joining, cementing. 2, a patch.

ಅಪ್ಪು 1. k. v. t. To join, unite. 2, to embrace. n. An embrace (ಆಲಿಂಗನ). ಅಪ್ಪಿಕೊಳ್ಳು. To embrace, clasp. ಅಪ್ಪಿಕೊಳುಹ, ಅಪ್ಪಿಕೊಳ್ಳುವಿಕೆ. An embrace.

ಅಪ್ಪು 2. (*tb. of* ಅಪ್) n. Water.

ಅಪ್ಪುಗೆ, ಅಪ್ಪುವಿಕೆ k. n. An embrace.

ಅಪ್ರಕಾಶ s. a. Not shining; hidden.

ಅಪ್ರತಿ, ಅಪ್ರತಿಮ s. a. Unequalled, incomparable.

ಅಪ್ರತಿಷ್ಠೆ s. n. Instability. 2, ill-fame, dishonour. -ಮಾಡು. To disgrace.

ಅಪ್ರತೀತಿ s. n. Unjust imputation.

ಅಪ್ರತ್ಯಕ್ಷ s. a. Invisible, imperceptible.

ಅಪ್ರಬುದ್ಧ s. a. Stupid, dull.

ಅಪ್ರಮಾಣ s. a. Unlimited; unproved, unauthorised; dishonest. n. A lie.

ಅಪ್ರಮಾಣಿಕ (= ಅಪ್ರಾಮಾಣಿಕ) s. a. Unproved, unwarranted; unworthy of being believed. -ತೆ. Untruthfulness, dishonesty.

ಅಪ್ರಮೇಯ s. a. Unfathomable, inscru- [table.

ಅಪ್ರಯೋಜಕ s. a. Unserviceable, useless.

ಅಪ್ರಸಿದ್ಧ s. a. Unknown, obscure. ಅಪ್ರಸಿದ್ಧಿ. n. The state of being unknown, obscurity.

ಅಪ್ರಸ್ತುತ s. a. Unpraised; irrelevant; unsuitable; accidental.

ಅಪ್ರಾಮಾಣಿಕ. = ಅಪ್ರಮಾಣಿಕ, q. v.

ಅಪ್ರಿಯ s. a. Disagreeable, disliked.

ಅಪ್ರೀತಿ s. n. Want of love, disaffection; dislike.

ಅಪ್ರೌಢ s. a. Modest; unlearned. -ತೆ. Ignorance.

ಅಪ್ಸರ, ಅಪ್ಸರಸ್, ಅಪ್ಸರಸಿ, ಅಪ್ಸರೆ s. n. A celestial nymph.

ಅಫಲ s. a. Unfruitful. 2, barren, useless.

ಅಫಿನಿ, ಅಫಿಮು, ಅಫೀಮು, ಅಫು h. n. Opium. -ಖೋರ. An opium eater.

ಅಬಕಾರಿ. = ಅಬುಕಾರಿ, q. v.

ಅಬಕ್ಕನೆ k. ad. Hastily.

ಅಬದ್ಧ s. a. Unbound. 2, wrong. n. A lie, falsehood. -ಖೋರ, -ಗಾರ. A liar. -ಭಾಷಣ. Lying. -ಸಾಕ್ಷಿ. False witness.

ಅಬಂದರ, ಅಬಂದರೆ (*tb. of* ಅಭದ್ರ) n. Disorder, confusion; waste.

ಅಬಲ s. a. Weak, feeble. n. Weakness. ಅಬಲೆ. A woman.

ಅಬಾಡು f. a. Valueless, futile. n. Tare in weighing. ಅಬಾತ, -ಮನುಷ್ಯ. A man of monstrous circumference. -ಅಂಗಿ. A very wide jacket. -ಕಟ್ಟು, -ತೂಕ ಮಾಡು. To tare.

ಅಬಾಸ, ಅಬಾಸು f. n. Incongruity. 2, disagreeableness (= ಅಸಹ್ಯ).

ಅಬುಕಾರಿ (=ಅಬಕಾರಿ) h. n. Revenue derived from intoxicating liquors.

ಅಬುಜ. *tb. of* ಅಬ್ಜ, q. v.

ಅಬ್ಜ (*tb.* ಅಬುಜ) s. a. Born in water. n. The moon. 2, a lotus. 3, a pearl. -ಕರ. A lotus-like hand. -ಗರ್ಭ, -ಜ, -ಭವ. Offspring of the lotus: Brahmâ. -ಬಂಧು, -ಸಖ. The sun. -ವಾಸಿನಿ. Lakshmî. -ವೈರಿ, ಅಬ್ಜಾರಿ, ಅಬ್ಜಾಹಿತ. The moon.

ಅಬ್ದ s. n. A cloud. 2, a year. -ತುಲ್ಲು. The grass *Cyperus rotundus.*

ಅಬ್ಧಿ s. n. The ocean. 2, pure knowledge (ಶೀವಲಜ್ಞಾನ). 3, right behaviour (ನೀತಿ). -ಜ, -ನಂದನ. The moon. -ಶಯನ, -ಶಾಯಿ. Vishṇu.

ಅಬ್ಬ, ಅಬ್ಬಬ್ಬ, ಅಬ್ಬಾ k. int. Ha! 2, ah, alas!

ಅಬ್ಬರ, ಅಬ್ಬರಣೆ k. n. A loud cry; sound, report; noise. 2, desire.

ಅಬ್ಬರಿಸು k. v. i. To cry aloud; to bark, howl. 2, to desire.

ಅಬ್ಬಳಿಕೆ k. n. Eructation or belching.

ಅಬ್ಬ್ಬುಜಿ k. n. Soot; mould.

ಅಬ್ಬೆ k. n. A plant from which pens are made. 2, (tb. of ಅಂಬೆ) mother.

ಅಬ್ರು h. n. Honour, reputation.

ಅಭಕ್ತ s. a. Undevout; unbelieving.

ಅಭಂಗ s. a. Not breaking; without destruction.

ಅಭಯ s. a. Unfearful, fearless. n. Fearlessness, peace, safety. -ಈ, -ಕೊಡು. To give assurance of security. -ದಾತ, -ಪ್ರದಾನ. Giving safety.

ಅಭವ s. a. Unborn.

ಅಭಾಗ್ಯ s. a. Unfortunate, poor; wretched.

ಅಭಾಜನ s. a. Improper. n. Impropriety.

ಅಭಾವ s. n. Non-existence, absence. 2, omission. 3, death. -ಕ್ರಿಯೆ. The negative mood (g.).

ಅಭಿ s. ad. On. 2, towards. 3, in presence of. 4, intensely.

ಅಭಿಖ್ಯ, ಅಭಿಖ್ಯೆ s. n. A name; a word, [term.

ಅಭಿಗಮನ s. n. Coming near. 2, adoration (of idols) at noon.

ಅಭಿಘಾತ s. n. Attack; injury, loss.

ಅಭಿಘಾರ s. n. Ghee put on food or oblation.

ಅಭಿಚರ s. n. A servant.

ಅಭಿಚಾರ s. n. Incantation, sorcery.

ಅಭಿಜನ s. n. Race, family, ancestors. 2, fame; a badge of honour.

ಅಭಿಜಾತ s. a. Well-born, noble. 2, proper. 3, learned.

ಅಭಿಜಿತ್ s. a. Victorious. n. Midday.

ಅಭಿಜ್ಞ s. a. Knowing, clever. -ತೆ, ಅಭಿಜ್ಞಾನ. Knowledge.

ಅಭಿಧಾನ, ಅಭಿಧೆ s. n. A name. 2, speech; a word. 3, sense, meaning. 4, a vocabulary.

ಅಭಿನಯ s. n. Indication of a passion by look or gesture. 2, dramatic representation. ಅಭಿನಯಿಸು. To represent dramatically; to imitate.

ಅಭಿನವ s. a. Quite new; fresh, young. ಅಭಿನವಿಸು. To become new.

ಅಭಿನಿವೇಶ s. n. Inclination, attachment. 2, determination.

ಅಭಿನ್ನ s. a. Unbroken, undivided. 2, unaltered; identical.

ಅಭಿಪ್ರಾಯ s. n. Aim, purpose, intention, opinion; meaning. -ಮಾಡು. To interpret.

ಅಭಿಮತ s. a. Assented to. 2, wished. n. Desire, wish. ಅಭಿಮತಿಸು. To assent to, approve of.

ಅಭಿಮಂತ್ರಣ s. n. Calling, inviting. 2, consecrating by a formula (ಮಂತ್ರ). ಅಭಿಮಂತ್ರಿಸು. To consecrate; to charm.

ಅಭಿಮನ್ಯು s. n. A son of Arjuna.

ಅಭಿಮಾನ s. n. Conceit, pride. 2, noble feeling; affection, love; self-respect. -ಹಿಡಿ. To love. -ಗಿತ್ತಿ. A proud female.

ಅಭಿಮಾನಿ s. n. A person of noble feelings. a. Proud.

ಅಭಿಮಾನಿಸು s. v. t. To honour; to love; to shelter, protect.

ಅಭಿಮುಖ s. a. Facing, fronting. 2, approaching.

ಅಭಿಯೋಗ s. n. Application; exertion. 2, an attack; fight; a charge.

ಅಭಿರಾಮ s. a. Pleasing, delightful, beautiful.

ಅಭಿರುಚಿ s. n. Desire, taste, pleasure.

ಅಭಿರೂಪ s. a. Pleasing, handsome.

ಅಭಿಲಾಷ, ಅಭಿಲಾಷೆ s. n. Desire, wish. ಅಭಿಲಾಷಿಸು. To desire, wish.

ಅಭಿವಂದನ, ಅಭಿವಾದ, ಅಭಿವಾದನ s. n. Respectful salutation. ಅಭಿವಂದಿಸು. To salute respectfully.

ಅಭಿವೃದ್ಧಿ s. n. Increase; prosperity, success; progress.

ಅಭಿಶಾಪ s. n. Curse; calumny.

ಅಭಿಷಂಗ s. n. Union. 2, attachment. 3, debt. 4, a curse.

ಅಭಿಷಿಕ್ತ s. a. Sprinkled over; inaugurated, enthroned.

ಅಭಿಷೇಕ s. n. Sprinkling over; consecration, inauguration. 2, the liquid used for sprinkling. 3, purifying an idol with ablutions. ಪಟ್ಟಾಭಿಷೇಕ. Coronation of a king. -ಮಾಡು, ಅಭಿಷೇಕಿಸು. To sprinkle over; to inaugurate

ಅಭಿಸರಣ s. a. Going towards; dispersion; following.

ಅಭಿಹತಿ s. n. A stroke; injury.

ಅಭಿಹಾರ s. n. Seizing, robbing. 2, an attack. 3, reversion. 4, exertion.

ಅಭೀಕ್ಷಿಸು s. v. i. To look towards.

ಅಭೀಷ್ಟ s. a. Wished, desired. 2, acceptable. -ಸಿದ್ಧಿ. Gaining of a desired object.

ಅಭೇದ s. n. Absence of difference; identity.

ಅಭೇದ್ಯ s. a. Impenetrable; indivisible.

ಅಭ್ಯಂಗ,. ಅಭ್ಯಂಗನ, ಅಭ್ಯಂಜನ s. n. Smearing the body with unctuous substances. 2, an unguent.

ಅಭ್ಯನುಜ್ಞೆ s. n. Permission; order.

ಅಭ್ಯಂತರ s. n. The interior. 2, an obstacle, impediment. -ಮಾಡು, ಅಭ್ಯಂತರಿಸು. To hinder.

ಅಭ್ಯರ್ಚನ s. n. Worship, reverence.

ಅಭ್ಯಸ್ತ s. a. Practised; studied.

ಅಭ್ಯಾಗತ s. a. Come, arrived. n. An uninvited guest.

ಅಭ್ಯಾಗಮ s. n. Arrival; visit.

ಅಭ್ಯಾಸ s. n. Use, habit. 2, study, learning. 3, practice, exercise. -ನಡಿಸು, ಅಭ್ಯಾಸಿಸು. To study, practise. *cpds.:* ವಿದ್ಯಾಭ್ಯಾಸ, ಶರೀರಾಭ್ಯಾಸ.

ಅಭ್ಯಾಸಿ s. n. A student.

ಅಭ್ಯುತ್ಥಾನ, ಅಭ್ಯುದಯ s. n. Rising, elevation; increase, prosperity.

ಅಭ್ರ s. n. A cloud. 2, sky, atmosphere. 3, the eye. 4, talc, mica. -ಕೇಶ. N. of Śiva. -ಗರ್ಜನೆ. Thunder. -ಮಣಿ. Heaven's gem: the sun, moon. -ಮಾಲೆ. Succession of clouds.

ಅಭ್ರಕ s. n. The sedge *Cyperus rotandus*. 2, talc, mica.

ಅಮಕು. = ಅದಕು, ಅಮುಗು.

ಅಮಕ್ಕಳ k. n. Tumult.

ಅಮಗ k. n. A fit opportunity; festive occasion. 2, season.

ಅಮಗು (= ಅಮುಕು) k. v. t. To squeeze, *etc.*

ಅಮಂಗಲ s. a. Inauspicious, unlucky. -ಕರ. Causing ill-luck. -ಕಾರಿ. One who causes ill-luck. -ಹಾರಿ. One who averts ill-luck. ಅಮಂಗಲೆ. A widow.

ಅಮಂಗುರ k. n. A medicinal shrub, *Physalis flexuosa*.

ಅಮಟೆ (*tb. of* ಅಂಬಷ್ಠೆ), -ಕಾಯಿ. n. A hog-plum.

ಅಮತ s. a. Unfelt, imperceptible.

ಅಮತಿ s. n. Unconsciousness; ignorance.

ಅಮನುಷ್ಯ s. a. Not human. n. A demon.

ಅಮಮ k. *int. of surprise and pain:* Ha! alas!

ಅಮರ s. a. Immortal. n. A god. 2, quicksilver. -ದಬಳ್ಳಿ. A shrubby creeper. -ಕೋಶ. N. of the Saṁskṛita dictionary by Amarasiṁha. -ಗಂಗೆ, -ನದಿ. The celestial Ganges. -ತ್ವ. Immortality. -ಪತಿ. Indra. -ಲೋಕ. Heaven. ಅಮರಿ, ಅಮರೆ. A female deity.

ಅಮರಾದ್ರಿ s. n. The mountain of the gods: Mêru.

ಅಮರಾವತಿ s. n. The abode of the gods.

ಅಮರಿಕೆ, ಅಮರ್ಕೆ k. n. Fitness, suitableness.

ಅಮರು k. v. i. To be closely united; to be linked to. 2, to arise, appear. 3, to be fit; to fit. 4, to fall upon; to climb. 5, to embrace. ಅಮರಿಸು. To cause to join; to prepare; to reprove.

ಅಮರ್ಚು (=ಅಮರಿಸು) k. *v. t.* To join. 2, to apply. 3, to put on. 4, to seize. 5, to prepare; to perform. ಅಮರ್ಚಿಸು. To cause to join.

ಅಮರ್ತ್ಯ s. *a.* Immortal. *n.* A god.

ಅಮರ್ದು (*tb. of* ಅಮೃತ, *q. v.*) *n.* Ambrosia. ಅಮ್ಮರ್ದುಣಿ. A god. -ಗದಿರ. The moon.

ಅಮರ್ಯಾದೆ s. *n.* Disrespect, rudeness, impropriety.

ಅಮರ್ಷ s. *n.* Non-endurance. 2, impatience; passion.

ಅಮಲ್, ಅಮಲು 1. h. *n.* Intoxication, drunkenness. -ಆಗು, -ಏರು, -ಹತ್ತು. To be drunk. -ಗಾರ. A drunkard.

ಅಮಲ್, ಅಮಲು 2. h. *n.* Business. 2, rule, reign. 3, an office. 4, collection of revenue. -ದಾರ. A native revenue collector.

ಅಮಲ s. *a.* Stainless, clean. *n.* Talc. -ತೆ, -ತ್ವ. Stainlessness.

ಅಮಲಿನ s. *a.* Stainless.

ಅಮವಾಲು h. *a.* Unclaimed, heirless. -ಜಿಂದಿಗೆ. An unclaimed property of a person dying without heirs which reverts to the government.

ಅಮವಾಸೆ. *tb. of.* ಅಮಾವಾಸ್ಯೆ, *q. v.*

ಅಮಳ (*tb. of* ಯಮಲ) *n.* A pair, twin.

ಅಮಾಂಸ s. *a.* Without flesh; feeble, thin.

ಅಮಾತ್ಯ s. *n.* A minister, counsellor.

ಅಮಾನತು h. *n.* A deposit, charge. 2, suspension.

ಅಮಾನಿ h. *n.* What is in charge of a collector on the part of government in opposition to that which is rented out to tenants of the soil.

ಅಮಾನುಷ s. *a.* Inhuman; monstrous.

ಅಮಾರ್ಗ s. *a.* Pathless. *n.* A wrong road. 2, a bad man.

ಅಮಾವಾಸೆ, ಅಮಾಸೆ. *tb. of* ಅಮಾವಾಸ್ಯೆ.

ಅಮಾವಾಸ್ಯೆ s. *n.* The first day of the first quarter on which the moon is invisible.

ಅಮಿತ s. *a.* Unmeasured, boundless, infinite.

ಅಮಿತ್ರ s. *n.* An enemy.

ಅಮೀನ h. *n.* A petty revenue officer. 2, the lowest executive officer of a civil court.

ಅಮುಕು, ಅಮುಗು, ಅಮುಚು (= ಅದಕು) k. *v. t.* To press down.

ಅಮೂಲ್ಯ s. *a.* Priceless, precious, inestimable.

ಅಮೃಣಾಲ s. *n.* The root of a fragrant grass, *Kaskas.*

ಅಮೃತ (*tb.* ಅಮರ್ದು, *q. v.*) s. *a.* Immortal. *n.* Immortality. 2, ambrosia, food of the gods. 3, anything sweet, *e. g.* water, milk, juice of sôma. 4, quicksilver. 5, a ray. 6, N. of several plants. -ಕರ. The moon; a physician. -ತ್ವ. Immortality. -ಫಲ. The custard-apple. -ಬಳ್ಳಿ. The heart-leaved moonseed. ಅಮೃತಾಂಧ. A deity.

ಅಮೇಧ್ಯ s. *a.* Impure; unholy. *n.* Excrement, faeces.

ಅಮೇಯ s. *a.* Immeasurable.

ಅಮೋಘ s. *a.* Unfailing; efficacious; productive.

ಅಮೋಲಿಕ (*tb. of* ಅಮೌಲ್ಯಕ) *a.* Invaluable, excellent.

ಅಮೌಲ್ಯ s. *a.* Priceless; excellent, invaluable.

ಅಂಪಕ k. *n.* An entertainment given to friends at their departure.

ಅಂಬ. = ಅನ್ನುವ, *p. p. of* ಅನ್ನು, *q. v.*

ಅಂಬಕ s. *n.* An eye.

ಅಂಬಕಳ (*tb. of* ಅಮ್ಲ) *n.* A kind of pap mixed with buttermilk.

ಅಂಬಟೆ. = ಅಮಟೆ, *q. v.*

ಅಂಬರ s. *n.* Clothes, apparel. 2, the sky, atmosphere. 3, cotton. 4, talc. 5, a perfume, *Ambergris.* -ಮಣಿ. The sun. ರಕ್ತಾಂಬರ. A purple cloth.

ಅಂಬರೀಷ s. *n.* A frying-pan. 2, the sun. 3, Śiva, Vishṇu. 4, war. 5, remorse.

ಅಂಬಲ k. *n.* A public hall.

ಅಂಬಲಿ (*tb. of* ಆಮ್ಲ. = ಅಂಬಕಳ, *q. v.*) *n.* A kind of porridge.

ಅಂಬಾ s. *n.* The cry of a cow.

ಅಂಬಾಡಿಯೆಲೆ k. *n.* A whitish and fragrant kind of betel leaf.

ಅಂಬಾರ h. *n.* A heap of thrashed straw. -ಖಾನೆ. A granary.

ಅಂಬಾರಿ h. *n.* A howdah on an elephant.

ಅಂಬಾತೆ k. *n.* A kind of insect. ಅಂದಾ ರುಣ್ಣಿ. An insect infesting cattle.

ಅಂಬಿ k. *n.* A boat. -ಗಾರ. = ಅಂಬಿಗ, *q. v.*

ಅಂಬಿಕಾ, ಅಂಬಿಕೆ s. *n.* A mother. 2, Durgâ.

ಅಂಬಿಗ, ಅಂಬಿಗಾರ k. *n.* A boatman.

ಅಂಬಿಲ. = ಅಂಬಲಿ, *q. v.*

ಅಂಬು 1. k. *n.* An arrow. -ಗಾರ. An archer. ಅಂಬಿನ ಹೆಡೆ, ಅಂಬಿನ ಹೊದೆ. A quiver. ಬಿಲ್ಲಂಬು. A bow and arrow.

ಅಂಬು 2. a. k. *v. i.* To dry, fade.

ಅಂಬು 3. s. *n.* Water. -ಚರ. Aquatic. -ಜ. Water-born: a lotus. -ಜಮಿತ್ರ. The sun. -ಜೋದ್ಭವ. Brahmâ. -ದ, -ಧರ. A cloud. -ನಿಧಿ, -ರಾಶಿ. The ocean. -ವಾಹ. A cloud. -ಸರಣಿ. The bed of a stream.

ಅಂಬುಗರಿಕೆ k. *n.* The creeping bent grass, *Agrostis stolorufera.*

ಅಂಬುಧಿ s. *n.* The ocean.

ಅಂಬೆ 1. (= ಅಮ್ಮಾ) s. *n.* A mother. 2, Durgâ.

ಅಂಬೆ 2. = ಅಂಬಾ, *q. v.*

ಅಂಬೆ 3. = ಆಮ್ಲ. -ಹಳದಿ. Scented turmeric.

ಅಂಬೆಗಾಲು 4. k. *n.* The crawling knees. ಅಂಬೆಗಾಲಾಡು, ಅಂಬೆಗಾಲಿಕ್ಕು, ಅಂಬೆಗಾಲಿಡು. To crawl on hands and knees.

ಅಂಭ, ಅಂಭಸ್ s. *n.* Water.

ಅಂಭೋಜ, ಅಂಭೋಜಾತ, ಅಂಭೋರುಹ s. *n.* A lotus.

ಅಂಭೋಧಿ, ಅಂಭೋನಿಧಿ s. *n.* The ocean.

ಅಮ್ಮ (*tb. of* ಅಂಬೆ) *n.* A mother. 2, a respectful title for females (*as* ಅಮ್ಮನ ವರು); a respectable woman. 3, a grandmother. 4, a village goddess (Durgâ). 5, the smallpox. *See* ಚಿಕ್ಕಮ್ಮ, ದೊಡ್ಡಮ್ಮ, ಕಲ್ಲಮ್ಮ. ಅಮ್ಮಗಳು. Widows. ಅಮ್ಮಣ್ಣಿ. An affectionate name for a female; a coward. ಅಮ್ಮನ ಬೇನೆ. Cholera.

ಅಮ್ಮಮ್ಮಾ, ಅಮ್ಮಲಾಲಾ (= ಅಮಲ, *q. v.*) *int. of pain or weariness:* Ah! alas!

ಅಮ್ಮಣ್ಣಿ k. *n.* A nipple, teat.

ಅಮ್ಮಾಲೆ k. *n.* A game of throwing hand-balls in the air.

ಅಮ್ಮು a. k. *v. i.* To be able; to wish, desire. *n.* Desire.

ಅಮ್ಲ s. *n.* Sourness, acidity. 2, vinegar.

ಅಮ್ಲಾನ s. *n.* The globe amaranth, *Gomphraena globosa.*

ಅಮ್ಲಿ, ಅಮ್ಲಿಕೆ s. *n.* The tamarind tree, *Tamarindus indica.*

ಅಯ್ 1. ಅಯ್ಯ k. *n.* Sir. -ಗಳು. A schoolmaster.

ಅಯ್ 2. (= ಅಯ್ದು 2) k. *a.* Five. -ನೂರು. Five hundred. -ಮಡಿ, -ವಡಿ. Five fold. -ವಣ್ಣ. Five colours. -ವತ್ತು. Fifty. -ಸಾಸಿರ. Five thousand. -ಸರ. A five fold string (of pearls).

ಅಯನ s. *n.* Going. 2, road, path. 3, half a solar year. ಅಯನಿಸು. To move, as the sun.

ಅಯಸ್ s. *n.* Iron; steel; metal.

ಅಯಾನ s. *a.* Not moving; stopping. 2, without a vehicle.

ಅಯಿದು k. *a.* Five.

ಅಯಿನು h. *a.* Original, principal, prime.

ಅಯಿಂದಾ h. *ad.* Hereafter; in future.

ಅಯಿಬು h. *n.* A flaw, fault, defect.

ಅಯಿರೆ (*tb. of* ಅಚಿರಾ). *n.* A wife whose husband is alive.

ಅಯಿಲು (= ಅರುಲು, *q. v.*) k. *n.* Bewilderment, madness.

ಅಯಿರಾವತ. = ಐರಾವತ.

ಅಯಿವಜು h. *n.* Property, wealth; cash, money.

ಅಯುಕ್ತ s. *a.* Unfit, unsuitable, improper.

ಅಯುತ f. *n.* A myriad.

ಅಯೋಗ್ಯ s. *a.* Unfit, unsuitable, unworthy. -ತನ, -ತೆ. Unfitness, disqualification; unworthiness.

ಅಯೋಧ್ಯ s. *n.* Oude, the capital of Râma.

ಅಯ್ಕಲ್ a. k. *n.* Cold, coldness; frost; snow. 2, the cold season.

ಅಯ್ತು (*fr.* ಆಹುದು- ಎ 3) = ಆದೆ. k. It certainly is, it is.

ಅಯ್ದು 1. k. *v. i.* To go to; to join. 2, to approach (ಬರು). 3, to obtain (-ಹೊಂದು). ಅಯ್ದಿಸು. To cause to go to, *etc.* ಅಯ್ದೆ. Exceedingly, greatly, then, even.

ಅಯ್ದು 2. (= ಅಯಿದು) k. *a.* Five. -ವರೆ. Five and a half. -ರಸ. Five liquids.

ಅಯ್ಯ s. *n.* A master, sir. 2, a father. 3, a Jangama. 4, a teacher. -ತನ. The state of being an Ayya or Jangama. -ಂಗಾರ. An epithet of respect among Śrîvaishṇavas. *cpds.* ಅಕ್ಕಯ್ಯ, ಅಣ್ಣಯ್ಯ, ಅಪ್ಪಯ್ಯ, ಅಮ್ಮಯ್ಯ, ಮಾವಯ್ಯ, ಭಾವಯ್ಯ.

ಅಯ್ಯಯೋ, ಅಯ್ಯೋ k. *int. of grief:* Alas! 2, *of surprise:* Aha!

ಅಯ್ರಾಣಿ f. *n.* A small vessel or vase used at weddings.

ಅಯ್ರು f. *n.* A disease of the eye.

ಅಯ್ವತ್ತು k. *see* ಅಯ್.

ಅಯ್ನು (= ಅನಿತು, *q. v.*) a. k. *ad.* That much.

ಅರ 1. (= ಅರ್ಗ) k. *n.* A file.

ಅರ 2. (= ಅರೆ 2) k. *a.* A half. -ಕಾಲೊತ್ತು. The half ರ when written as ೯. -ಕ್ಷಣ. Half a moment. -ಗಣ್ಣು. A purblind eye. -ಗಾಯ. A slight wound. -ಗಾವು. Slight heat. -ಗೋಡೆ. A low wall. -ಗೋರು. Half of the produce of a field. -ಚಲ್ಲಣ. Breeches covering the buttocks. -ತಾವು. Half a sheet of paper. -ದಲೆ. Half the head. -ಪಾವು. Three rupees' weight. -ಮಣ. Half a maund. -ಮನಸ್ಸು. Reluctance. -ಮರೆ. Partial screening; want of sincerity. -ವಾಸಿ. One half. -ಸೇರು. Half a sêr.

ಅರ 3. *abbrev. of* ಅರಸು, *q. v.* -ಗಿಣಿ. A parrakeet. -ನೆಲ್ಲಿ. The country gooseberry. -ಮಗ. A king's son. -ಮನೆ. A palace; a court. -ಸ್ಥಾನ. A royal council.

ಅರಕ k. *n.* Washing rice. 2, the state of broken or injured, *as* a tile. ಅರ ಕಂಚಟ್ಟು. A brass basin.

ಅರಕು h. *n.* Spirit, juice, essence; toddy.

ಅರಕೆ k. *n.* The half.

ಅರಗು 1. k. *n.* A border, margin. 2, vicinity.

ಅರಗು 2. k. *v. i.* To decay; to be digested.

ಅರಗು 3. (*tb. of* ಲಾಕ್ಷೆ) *n.* Gumlac; sealing-wax. ಅರಗಿನ ಕಡ್ಡಿ. A stick of lac. ಅರಗಿನ ಮಸಿ, -ಶಾಯಿ. A superior ink made from lac, *etc.* ಮುದ್ರೆ-. Sealing wax.

ಅರಚನೆ s. *n.* Disorder.

ಅರಚು (ರ = ಱ). = ಅರಿಚು.

ಅರಟೆ k. *n.* = ಹರಟೆ. 2, a reel.

ಅರಡು (= ಪರಡು) k. *v. i.* To be extended, *etc.*

ಅರಣ k. *n.* A nuptial present.

ಅರಣಿ s. *n.* The wood of the *Ficus religiosa* used for kindling fire by attrition.

ಅರಣೆ (= ರಾಣೆ) k. *n.* A greenish kind of lizard.

ಅರಣ್ಯ s. *n.* A wood, forest, wilderness (= ಕಾಡು, ವನ, ಅಡವಿ).

ಅರತ 1. k. *n.* The act of grinding.

ಅರತ 2. s. *a.* Indifferent to.

ಅರತ್ನಿ s. *n.* The elbow. 2, a cubit.

ಅರದ s. *a.* Toothless.

ಅರದಳ, ಅರದಾಳ, ಅರಿದಳ, ಅರಿದಾಳ (*tb. of* ಹರಿತಾಳ). *n.* Yellow orpiment.

ಅರದೇಶಿಪರದೇಶಿ s. *n.* A mendicant, pilgrim.

ಅರನಾರಿ k. *n.* Paralysis; *also* -ಬೇನೆ. 2, one-sidedness.

ಅರಬ, ಅರಬಿ f. *n.* An Arab. -ಸ್ಥಾನ, -ದೇಶ. Arabia. ಅರಬಿ. Arabian.

ಅರಬು (ರ = ಱ). k. *n.* Drought, famine.

ಅರಮನೆ (*see* s. ಅರ 2) *n.* A palace; a court. 2, government.

ಅರಮಾಯಿಷಿ, ಪರಮಾಯಿಷಿ h. *n.* A gift of rare value.

ಅರಮೆ a. k. *ad.* To some extent; here and there. [aha!

ಅರರೆ s. *int. of wonder:* Well done!

ಅರಲು, ಅರಳು k. *v. i.* To expand, open (*as* flowers). *n.* A flower. -ಅರಲ ಮಾಡು, ಅರಲಿಸು. To cause to blossom. -ವಡಿಗ, -ವಡಿಗ. A florist.

ಅರವ, ಅರವು k. *n.* Tamil. -ಭಾಷೆ. The T. language. -ದೇಶ. The T. country. -ಗಿತ್ತಿ. A Tamil woman.

ಅರವಟಿಕೆ, ಅರವಟಿಗೆ, ಅರವಟ್ಟಿಗೆ, ಅರಹೊಟ್ಟಿಗೆ (ರ=ಱ) k. *n.* A shed on the roadside in which water, buttermilk, *etc.* are distributed gratis. ಅರವಟ್ಟಿಗ. A of founder an aravaṭigĕ.

ಅರವತ್ತು (ರ=ಱ) k. *a.* Sixty.

ಅರವಾಸಿ, ಅರವಾಶಿ. *See* s. ಅರ 2.

ಅರವಿಂದ s. *n.* A lotus. -ನೇತ್ರೆ. A lotus-eyed woman. -ಬಂಧು, -ಸಖ. The sun.

ಅರವು (ರ=ಱ) k. *n.* Knowledge.

ಅರವೆ (ರ=ಱ) k. *n.* Indigestion. 2, cloth.

ಅರಸ, ಅರಸು (*tb. of* ರಾಜ) *n.* A king, lord. ಅರಸತಿ. A queen. -ಧರ್ಮ. A king's duty. -ಗುಣ, -ಮಗ, *etc.* -ತನ. Kingship, royalty. -ಹುಣ್ಣು. A carbuncle.

ಅರಸಿ (*tb. of* ರಾಜ್ಞಿ) *n.* A queen.

ಅರಸಿನ, ಅರಸಿಣ (*tb. of* ಹರಿದ್ರಾ) *n.* Turmeric.

ಅರಸು (ರ=ಱ) k. *v. t.* To inquire after, seek, search. *n.* Research, enquiry.

ಅರಸೆಮರ. = ಅರಳಿ, *q. v.*

ಅರಳ k. *n.* Amazement, perplexity.

ಅರಳಿ (= ಅರಸೆಮರ) k. *n.* The poplar-leaved fig-tree, *Ficus religiosa.*

ಅರಳು (= ಅರಲು, *q. v.*) k. *v. i.* To bloom. *n.* A flower. 2, parched grain.

ಅರಳೆ 1. k. *n.* Dressed cotton. 2, a post, pillar.

ಅರಳೆ 2. (= ಅಣಿಲೆ) k. *n.* The gall nut, *Terminalia chebula.*

ಅರಳೆಲೆ k. *n.* A forehead ornament for young children. 2, a fig leaf.

ಅರಾಜಕ s. *a.* Anarchical.

ಅರಾತಿ s. *n.* An enemy, foe.

ಅರಾಲ s. *a.* Bent, crooked, curved.

ಅರಿ 1. (= ಹರಿ) k. *v. t.* To cut or lop off. *n.* Cutting off, gnawing.

ಅರಿ 2. (= ಅರೆ) k. *v. t.* To grind on a slab. -ಸು. To cause to grind.

ಅರಿ 3. k. *n.* A mass of unthrashed corn. 2, excess in corn measure. 3, a disease of the eye (-ಗಣ್ಣು).

ಅರಿ 4. (ರಿ = ಱಿ) k. *v. i. & t.* To learn to know; to know, understand. *P. ps.* ಅರಿದು, ಅರಿತು. ಅರಿಯದಿರು, ಅರಿಯದೆ ಹೋಗು. To be ignorant of. ಅರಿಯದವ > < ಅರಿದವ, ಅರಿತವ. ಅರಿಸು. To make known, inform.

ಅರಿ 5. s. *n.* An enemy.

ಅರಿಕೆ, ಅರಿತ, ಅರಿಹ, ಅರಿಹು (ರಿ = ಱಿ) k. *n.* Knowledge; understanding; information. ಅರಿಕೆ ಮಾಡು. To inform.

ಅರಿಚು (ರಿ = ಱಿ) a. k. *v. i.* To bawl, scream. [tree.

ಅರಿಟಾಳ (*tb. of* ಅರಿಷ್ಟ) *n.* The soapnut

ಅರಿತ್ರ s. *n.* An oar; a rudder.

ಅರಿದು a. k. *a.* Impossible, inexplicable.

ಅರಿಮೆ (ರಿ = ಱಿ). = ಅರಿಕೆ, *q. v.*

ಅರಿಲ್ (ರ = ಱ) a. k. *n.* A star. 2, mud.

ಅರಿವು. = ಅರಿಕೆ, *q. v.*

ಅರಿವೆ, ಅರಿವಿ (ರಿ = ಱಿ). = ಅರವೆ.

ಅರಿಷ್ಟ s. *a.* Unhurt. *n.* Good or bad luck, misfortune. 2, buttermilk. 3, the neem tree. 4, the soap-nut tree, *Sapindus trifoliatus.* ಕಷ್ಟಾರಿಷ್ಟ. A very heavy calamity.

ಅರಿಸಮಾಸ s. *n.* An unsuitable composition of words.

ಅರಿಸಿನ. = ಅರಸಿನ, *q. v.*

ಅರಿಸು k. *v. t.* To cause to cut off. 2, to cause to grind. 3, (ರಿ = ಱಿ) to inform.

ಅರಿಸೆ (*tb. of* ಅರ್ಶಸ್) *n.* Piles.

ಅರು 1. (ರು=ಱು) = ಆರು. k. *a.* Six. -ವಡಿ. Six-fold. -ವತ್ತು. Sixty.

ಅರು 2. (ರು=ಱು) a. k. *v. i.* To be cut asunder; to cease.

ಅರುಗು. = ಅರಗು 1, *q. v.*

ಅರುಚಿ s. *n.* Aversion, dislike; disgust.

ಅರುಚು. = ಅರಿಚು, *q. v.*

ಅರುಣ s. *a.* Yellow, ruddy. *n.* Aruṇa, the dawn. 2, a ray. -ಸಾರಥಿ. The sun. ಅರುಣೋದಯ. Sunrise.

ಅರುಂಧತಿ s. *n.* N. of the wife of Vasishṭha. 2, N. of a star. -ನಾಥ. Vasishṭha.

ಅರುಪು (ರ=ಱ;) *see s.* ಅರಿ 4) a. k. *v. t.* To make known.

ಅರುಬುತ. *tb. of* ಅದ್ಭುತ, *q. v.*

ಅರುಮೆ a. k. *n.* Love, affection.

ಅರುಂಬು a. k. *n.* A flower-bud.

ಅರುಲು (ರು=ಱು) k. *n.* Mud. -ಗದ್ದೆ. A muddy paddy-field.

ಅರುಲುಮರುಲು, ಅರುಳುಮರುಳು k. *n.* Bewilderment, dotage.

ಅರುವು (ರು=ಱು.=ಅರಿವೆ) k. *n.* Knowledge. -ಮರುವು. Silliness, dotage.

ಅರುಹು (ರ=ಱ) k. *v. t.* To make known. *n.* Knowledge.

ಅರೂಪ s. *a.* Formless; ugly.

ಅರೆ 1. k. *v. t.* To grind, pulverize. 2, (ರೆ=ಱೆ) to strike, beat. *n.* The plant *Grislea tomentosa.* 2, a. k. stone, rock. 3, the back. -ಯಟ್ಟು. To pursue.

ಅರೆ 2. (= ಅರ *q. v.*) k. *n.* A half. 2, a little. -ಗಡಿ. To cut into halves. -ಗಣ್ಬು. A loose knot of hair. -ಗುಂಡಿಗೆ. Half-heartedness, timidity. -ಗೆಲಸ. Unfinished work. -ದೆರೆ. To open half. -ನುಡಿ. Indistinct utterance. -ನೋಟ. A leer, side glance. -ಪಾಲು. Half a part. -ಬೇವು. The Persian lilac. -ಬಿರಿ. To be half opened, *as* a flower. -ಮರುಳ. A half-mad man. -ಮನೆ. Hesitation, doubt. -ಮೈ. Half the body. -ಮಾದಲು ಗಿಡ, -ಮಾವಳದ ಗಿಡ. A spinous shrub, *Randia dumetorum.* -ವರಿಸು. To leave unfinished. -ವೆರೆ. The half moon.

ಅರೋಗ s. *n.* Health. ಅರೋಗಿ. A healthy person.

ಅರೋಚಕ, ಅರೋಚಿಕೆ s. *n.* Want of appetite; disgust, indigestion. *a.* Insipid.

ಅರ್ಕ s. *n.* Radiance. 2, the sun. 3, crystal. 4, Indra. 5, swallow wort, *Calotropis gigantea.* -ವಾರ. Sunday.

ಅರ್ಕೆ k. *n.* Weeping, lamentation.

ಅರ್ಗಲ, ಅರ್ಗಲೆ (*tb.* ಅಗಳ್) s. *n.* An impediment; a bolt, lock.

ಅರ್ಗಳ a. k. *n.* Greatness; a great man.

ಅರ್ಘ s. *n.* Price, cost. 2, an offering to gods, *etc.*

ಅರ್ಘ್ಯ s. *a.* Valuable; venerable. *n.* A reverential offering to gods or venerable men.

ಅರ್ಚ s. *n.* Invocation, worship. -ಕ. A worshipper. -ನೆ. Worship, homage. ಅರ್ಚಿಸು. To worship.

ಅರ್ಚಿಸ್ s. *n.* Flame. 2, shine, lustre.

ಅರ್ಚು (= ಅರಿಚು, *q. v.*) k. *v. i.* To cry aloud.

ಅರ್ಜಿ, (ಅರ್ಜು) h. *n.* A written petition. -ಬರೆಯು, -ಹಾಕು, -ಕೊಡು, -ಮಾಡು, *etc.* To petition. -ದಾರ. A petitioner.

ಅರ್ಜಿಸು s. *v. t.* To acquire, gain.

ಅರ್ಜುನ s. *a.* White. *n.* Silver. 2, the tree *Terminalia arjuna.* 3, the son of Indra and Kuntî.

ಅರ್ಣ s. *a.* Moving. *n.* Water. -ವ. The ocean.

ಅರ್ತಿ k. *n.* Love; desire. 2, pleasure, fun. -ಗೆಡಿಸು. To spoil a wish. -ಕಾರ. A man of pleasure. -ಸು. To be pleased with.

ಅರ್ತೊಲೆ (*fr.* ಅರೆ-ತೊಲೆ) k. *n.* The weight of half a rupee.

ಅರ್ಥ s. *n.* Aim, purpose; cause, reason. 2, meaning. 3, advantage, utility. 4, a request. 5, manner, sort. 6, wealth. -ಕಾರಿ. Useful. -ಕೊಡು. To mean; to confer riches. -ನಿಶ್ಚಯ. Ascertainment. -ವಂತ. A man of property. -ವಾದ. Explanatory remark.

-ವಿಸು. To explain, expound. -ಶಾಸ್ತ್ರ. The science of polity. -ಶ್ಲೇಷ. Pun. -ಹೀನ. Meaningless; poor; failing. -ಹೇಳು. To interpret. ಅರ್ಥಾಂತರ. A different meaning. ಅರ್ಥಾಪತ್ತಿ. An inference.

ಅರ್ಥಿ s. *a.* Desiring. *n.* A beggar. 2, a plaintiff. -ತ್ವ. Entreaty. -ಸು. To desire; to ask for.

ಅರ್ಧ s. *a.* Half, halved. *n.* A half. -ಆಣೆ. Half an Anna. -ಗೋಲ. A hemisphere. -ಚಂದ್ರ. A crescent. -ದೃಷ್ಟಿ. Purblind. -ರಾತ್ರಿ. Midnight. -ವಿರಾಮ. A semicolon. ಅರ್ಧಾಂಗ. Half the body. -ಯಿಸು, ಅರ್ಧಿಸು. To halve.

ಅರ್ನ (= ಅರ) k. *n.* A file.

ಅರ್ನೂರು. = ಅರುನೂರು, *q. v.*

ಅರ್ಪಣ s. *n.* Placing upon. 2, offering, delivering, consigning. ಅರ್ಪಿಸು. To offer, deliver, consign.

ಅರ್ಬಿ a. k. *n.* A torrent checked in its course. ಅರ್ಬಿಸು. To roar.

ಅರ್ಬು k. *n.* Crying. ಅರ್ಬಾಟ. Crying aloud.

ಅರ್ಬುದ s. *n.* A serpent. 2, a hundred millions. 3, swelling, polypus.

ಅರ್ಭಕ s. *a.* Small, weak. *n.* A child; the young of any animal.

ಅರ್ಲು (= ಅರುಲು, *q. v.*) k. *n.* Mud, clay.

ಅರ್ವ s. *a.* Vile, low. *n.* A horse. -ತಿ. A mare.

ಅರ್ವತ್ತು. *See s.* ಅರು.

ಅರ್ಶಸ್ s. *n.* Piles.

ಅರ್ಹ s. *a.* Deserving, worthy. 2, proper, fit. *n.* A Jaina saint. -ಣೆ. Worship. -ತ್. Venerable; a Jaina saint.

ಅಲ್ a. k. *n.* That place, direction, *as in* ಅತ್ತಲ್ (ಅತ್ತ-ಅಲ್), ಎತ್ತಲ್ (ಎತ್ತ-ಅಲ್). 2, state or condition, in verbal nouns, *as* ಉಣಲ್, ಬಯ್ಯಲ್. *v. i.* To be fit, right or sufficient.

ಅಲ (= ಅಲಾ) k. *int. of assent:* Indeed; *of surprise:* ah!

ಅಲಕ s. *n.* A curl, hair-lock.

ಅಲಕಾಪುರ s. *n.* Kubêra's residence.

ಅಲಕು. = ಅಲಗು, ಅಲುಗು, *q. v.*

ಅಲಕ್ತಕ s. *n.* Red lac.

ಅಲಕ್ಷಣ s. *n.* An inauspicious sign. *a.* Unfortunate. ಅಲಕ್ಷಿತ. Unseen; unobserved.

ಅಲಕ್ಷಿಸು s. *v. t.* To disregard, slight.

ಅಲಕ್ಷ್ಯ s. *n.* Disregard, contempt. *a.* Insignificant.

ಅಲಗರ್ದ s. *n.* A water-snake.

ಅಲಗು (= ಅಲಕು) k. *v. i.* To move about; to be agitated. *n.* The blade of a knife, sword, *etc.*

ಅಲಘು s. *a.* Not light; weighty; solemn.

ಅಲಂಕರಣ s. *n.* Adorning.

ಅಲಂಕರಿಸು s. *v. t.* To ornament, decorate.

ಅಲಂಕಾರ s. *n.* Ornament. 2, elegance. 3, a rhetorical expression. -ಶಾಸ್ತ್ರ. A text-book of rhetoric. -ಮಾಡು. = ಅಲಂಕರಿಸು, *q. v.* ಅಲಂಕೃತ. Ornamented.

ಅಲಂಗ f. *n.* A rampart.

ಅಲಂಘ್ಯ s. *a.* Insurmountable, inviolable.

ಅಲತಗೆ, ಅಲತಿಗೆ (*tb. of* ಅಲಕ್ತಕ) *n.* Lac, used as red ink.

ಅಲಪು, ಅಲಪಟೆ k. *n.* Weariness, fatigue.

ಅಲಬು k. *n.* N. of different species of *Alysicarpus.*

ಅಲಭ್ಯ s. *a.* Unattainable. 2, rare, (casual.

ಅಲಂಪು a. k. *n.* Beauty; ornament; pleasure.

ಅಲರು (= ಅರಲು, *q. v.*) k. *v. i.* To spread; to open, blossom, bloom. *P. p.* ಅಲರ್ದು. *n.* A flower, bloom. ಅಲರ್ಗಣ್ಣು. A flower-like eye. -ತೋರಣ. A festoon of flowers. -ವಕ್ಕಿ. The large black bee. ಅಲರ್ವಸೆ. A bed of flowers. -ಬಳ್ಳಿ. A flowering creeper. ಅಲರಿಸು, ಅಲರ್ಚು. To cause to blossom.

ಅಲಲ್ ಹಿಸಾಬು h. *n.* Pay given beforehand.

ಅಲವಿಕೆ, ಅಲವು (=ಅಲಪು) k. n. Fatigue, weariness.

ಅಲಸ s. a. Lazy, idle, weary, faint. -ತ್ವ. Idleness.

ಅಲಸಂದಿ, ಅಲಸಂದಿಗೆ k. n. A species of pulse, *Vigna catjang*.

ಅಲಸಿಕೆ, ಅಲಸು k. n. Fatigue; idleness. -ಆಗು, -ಪಡು. To be tired.

ಅಲಸು k. v. i. To become weary, tired, vexed. v. t. To shake, agitate, *as* in water. n. Weariness; idleness. -ಗಾರ. A lazy man.

ಅಲಾತ s. n. A fire brand. 2, a rope, cord.

ಅಲಾಬು h. n. Mahammadans' Moharam festival. 2, the bottle-gourd.

ಅಲಾಯಿದ, ಅಲಾಹಿದ h. a. Distinct, apart.

ಅಲಾಯಿಬಲಾಯಿ h. n. An affectionate greeting, embrace.

ಅಲಿ (=ಅಲ್ಲಿ) k. *ad.* There, *as* ತುಪ್ಪದಲಿ, ಸಭೆಯಲಿ, ನಿಮ್ಮಲಿ. v. i. =ಅಲಿಂ. Must, may. 2, *pr. imper. as* ಆಗಲಿ, ಇರಲಿ, ಉಣ್ಣಲಿ, ತಕ್ಕೊಳ್ಳಲಿ, ತರಲಿ, ಸಾರಲಿ.

ಅಲಿಕ s. n. The forehead.

ಅಲಿಗಿನ ಗಿಡ k. n. An aquatic plant, *Aeshynomene aspera*.

ಅಲಿಂಗ s. a. Genderless (*g.*).

ಅಲಿಂದ s. n. A terrace before a house-door.

ಅಲುಕು, ಅಲುಗು, ಅಲುಂಗು k. v. i. To be agitated, shaky or loose; to shake. ಅಲುಗಾಡು. To shake, tremble. ಅಲುಕಿಸು, ಅಲುಂಗಿಸು v. t. To skake.

ಅಲುಗೋಜಿ h. n. A whistle, pipe.

ಅಲುಬು a. k. v. t. To wash with water.

ಅಲೆ k. v. i. To move about, shake. 2, to roam, wander; to dangle. v. t. To shake. n. A wave, billow.

ಅಲೇಖ s. n. A blank book. 2, a deity.

ಅಲೇಮಾನಿ f. n. Allemagne, Germany, Europe. -ಕತ್ತಿ. A dragoon sword. -ತುರುಪು. A dragoon troop.

ಅಲೊಡಂ, ಅಲೊಡನೆ a. k. *conj.* When; *as*, ಬರಲೊಡಂ, ಪ್ರಕಟಿಸಲೊಡನೆ.

ಅಲೋಕ s. n. Not the world; the spiritual world.

ಅಲೌಕಿಕ s. a. Not worldly; not secular, unusual. -ತನ. Unworldliness; unusualness.

ಅಲ್ಕಾಬು h. n. A title; titles, honors.

ಅಲ್ಪ s. a. Small; little; insignificant; mean. -ತನ. Smallness. -ದಿನ. A few days. -ಪ್ರಾಣ. An unaspirated letter. -ಬುದ್ಧಿ. Weak-mindedness. -ಮತಿ. Weak-minded, stupid. -ವೃಷ್ಟಿ. Small rain. -ಸ್ವಲ್ಪ. Rather little. ಅಲ್ಪಾಯುಷ್ಯ. A short life. ಅಲ್ಪಿಷ್ಟ. Very small.

ಅಲ್ಮೈರ f. n. An almira, a chest of drawers, wardrobe.

ಅಲ್ಲ 1. (*fr.* ಅಲ್[6] No. 2, *q. v.*) k *ad.* Not, no; *its opposite is* ಹೌದು. -ಗಳೆ. To reject, deny. ಅಲ್ಲವೆ *int.* Is it not? ಅಲ್ಲದ. Being not good, fit. -ವನು. A useless or bad man. ಅಲ್ಲದೆ. Besides, except, unless. ಇದಲ್ಲದೆ. Moreover. ಅಲ್ಲೆನ್ನು. To deny.

ಅಲ್ಲ 2. k. n. Green ginger.

ಅಲ್ಲಕಲ್ಲೋಲ (=ಅಲ್ಲೋಲಕಲ್ಲೋಲ) k. n. Great agitation (*as* of water or mind), confusion, disorder, tumult.

ಅಲ್ಲಗಳೆ k. v. t. To deny, reject, refuse.

ಅಲ್ಲಣೆ, ಅಲ್ಲಣಿಗೆ a. k. n. Mirth, merry-making, jest.

ಅಲ್ಲರ k. n. Separation of lovers or friends.

ಅಲ್ಲರಿ k. n. Trouble, disturbance, harass.

ಅಲ್ಲಾಟ, ಅಲ್ಲಾಟಿಕೆ k. n. Moving about.

ಅಲ್ಲಾಡು k. v. i. To move, shake, swing; to be loose. ಅಲ್ಲಾಡಿಸು. v. t. To shake, move about.

ಅಲ್ಲಿ (=ಅಲಿ) k. *ad.* There, in that place. -ಹೋಗು. Go there. ಅಲ್ಲಲ್ಲಿ. Here and there. ಅಲ್ಲಿಗಲ್ಲಿಗೆ. Here and there. -ತನಕ. So far as that place; till then. 2, *used to form the loc., as* ಮನೆಯಲ್ಲಿ, *etc.* 3, *also added to rel. part., as* ಹೋಗುವಲ್ಲಿ, ಇದ್ದಲ್ಲಿ, *etc.*

ಅಲ್ಲಿಗಾರಿಗ k. n. A washerman.

ಅಲ್ಲು k. v. t. To join, knit, plait, braid.

ಅಲ್ಲೋಲಕಲ್ಲೋಲ. = ಅಲ್ಲಕಲ್ಲೋಲ, q. v.

ಅವ 1., ಅವನು k. pro. He, that man; f. ಅವಳು; pl. ಅವರು. ಅವರಿಬ್ಬರು. Both of them.

ಅವ 2. s. ad. Off, away, down *(implying disrespect)*.

ಅವಕಾಶ s. n. Place; opportunity, leisure; interval.

ಅವಕೃಪೆ s. n. Displeasure, disfavour.

ಅವಕ್ರ s. a. Not crooked; upright, straight.

ಅವಗಡ f. n. An obstruction; jeopardy. 2, inaccessibility. 3, monstrosity. 4, impossibility. ಅವಗಡಿಸು. To depress, slight, suppress. 2, to hurry, hasten, become impetuous.

ಅವಗಣಿತ s. a. Disregarded, despised.

ಅವಗತ s. a. Gone near. 2, known, understood. ಅವಗತಿ. Knowledge.

ಅವಗಮನ s. n. Understanding, comprehension.

ಅವಗಾಹ, ಅವಗಾಹನ s. n. Diving into; bathing. 2, comprehension. ಅವಗಾಹಿಸು, ಅವಗಹಿಸು. To dive into; to enter into; to comprehend.

ಅವಗುಣ s. n. A vice; an evil effect.

ಅವಗ್ರಹ, ಅವಗ್ರಾಹ s. n. Separation. 2, obstacle. 3, drought. ಅವಗ್ರಹಿಸು. To lay hold on, attain.

ಅವಘಾತ s. n. Striking, killing. 2, a violent blow.

ಅವಚು (= ಅಗಚು, ಅದಕು) k. v. t. To press; to confine, embrace. 2, to hide.

ಅವಚ್ಛಿನ್ನ s. a. Cut off, broken. 2, predicated.

ಅವಚ್ಛೇದ s. n. Any thing cut off; portion. 2, distinction. 3, discrimination.

ಅವಜ್ಞತೆ s. n. Negligence.

ಅವಜ್ಞೆ s. n. Disregard, disrespect, contempt.

ಅವತಂಸ s. n. A garland of flowers. 2, a crest.

ಅವತರಣ s. n. Descending. 2, annotation. ಅವತರಣಿಕೆ. = ಅವತಾರಿಕೆ.

ಅವತರಿಸು s. v. i. To descend; to become incarnate.

ಅವತಾರ s. n. Descent. 2, incarnation. -ಎತ್ತು, -ತಕ್ಕೊಳ್ಳು. To become incarnate.

ಅವತಾರಿಕೆ s. n. A preamble or preface.

ಅವತೆ. tb. of ಅವಸ್ಥೆ, q. v.

ಅವದಶೆ s. n. Misfortune.

ಅವದಾತ s. a. White. 2, pure; beautiful.

ಅವದಾನ s. n. A great act, achievement.

ಅವದೂರು, = ಅಪದೂರು, q. v.

ಅವದ್ಯ s. a. Low, inferior; disagreeable.

ಅವಧರಿಸು s. v. t. To think upon, listen to.

ಅವಧಾನ s. n. Attention; care; devotion. ಅವಧಾನಿ. Attentive, careful; a title. ಅವಧಾನಿಸು. To mind, pay attention.

ಅವಧಾರಣ (-ಣೆ) s. n. Affirmation; emphasis. ಅವಧಾರಿಸು. To ascertain.

ಅವಧಿ s. n. A limit; period, time. 2, opportunity. 3, engagement. 4, extremity; misfortune.

ಅವಧೂತ s. a. Shaken off; rejected, separated from worldliness. n. A virakta.

ಅವಧ್ಯ s. a. Inviolable.

ಅವನ s. n. Favour. 2, joy. 3, satisfaction. -ತಿ. Prostration.

ಅವನಿ s. n. The earth. -ಜೆ, -ಸುತೆ. Sitâ. -ಧರ. A mountain. -ಪ, -ಪತಿ, -ಪಾಲಕ, ಅವನೀಶ. A king. -ರುಹ. A tree.

ಅವಪಥ್ಯ s. n. An error in diet.

ಅವಭೃಥ s. a. Removing. n. Purification by bathing, *as* after sacrifice or marriage.

ಅವಮತಿ s. n. Dislike, disregard.

ಅವಮನ್ನಣೆ (tb. of ಅವಮಾನನೆ). = ಅವಮರ್ಯಾದೆ.

ಅವಮರ್ಯಾದೆ s. n. Incivility, disrespect.

ಅವಮಾನ (= ಅಪಮಾನ) s. n. Disrespect, dishonour. -ಮಾಡು, -ಪಡಿಸು. To treat contemptuously.

ಅವಯುವ s. n. A limb, member; part. -ಸಂಬಂಧ. The relation of membership.

ಅವಯೋಗ s. n. An inauspicious omen.

ಅವರ 1. s. a. Inferior, low; posterior, following. -ಜ. A younger brother.

ಅವರ 2. k. pro. Their.

ಅವರೂಪಿತ s. a. Misshapen, deformed.

ಅವರೆ (tb. of ಅಮರೆ) n. A species of pulse, *Phaseolus radiatus.*

ಅವರೋಧ s. n. Obstruction. 2, seraglio of a palace.

ಅವರೋಹ s. n. A shoot of a plant, a pendent branch. 2, the climbing of a creeper.

ಅವರ್ಗ s. n. A non-class. a. Unclassified. ಅವರ್ಗೀಯ. Not belonging to the classified consonants (g.).

ಅವರ್ಜ f. n. A day book, ledger.

ಅವರ್ಷಣ s. n. Drought.

ಅವಲಕ್ಕಿ k. n. Rice scalded, dried, fried, and flattened by beating it in a mortar.

ಅವಲಕ್ಷಣ s. n. An unlucky sign.

ಅವಲಗ್ನ s. a. Hanging down. n. The waist.

ಅವಲಂಬ, ಅವಲಂಬನೆ s. n. Resting on; dependence, support; a prop, stay. ಅವಲಂಬಿಸು. v. t. To hang on; to depend on. ಅವಲಂಬಿತ. Supported.

ಅವಲೀಲೆ s. n. Sport, play. ad. Easily, readily.

ಅವಲು k. n. Pounding in a mortar; cf. ಅವಲಕ್ಕಿ.

ಅವಲೋಕ, ಅವಲೋಕನ s. n. Seeing, looking. 2, sight (ನೋಟ). 3, observation. ಅವಲೋಕಿಸು. To look at (ನೋಡು).

ಅವಶ s. a. Uncontrolled. 2, necessary.

ಅವಶಕುನ. = ಅಪಶಕುನ, q. v.

ಅವಶಾತ್ (fr. ಅವಶ) ad. Unawares, suddenly.

ಅವಶಿಷ್ಟ s. a. Left, remaining. n. Remainder.

ಅವಶ್ಯ s. a. Inevitable. n. Necessity, urgency. ad. Necessarily, certainly. -ಬೀಳು. To become necessary.

ಅವಷ್ಟಂಭ s. n. Relying on. 2, self-confidence. 3, a pillar. ಅವಷ್ಟಂಭಿಸು. To lean upon.

ಅವಸರ s. n. Occasion, opportunity. 2, haste, speed, urgency, hurry. -ಪಡಬೇಡ. Don't be in a hurry. ಹಟ್ಟವಸರ. Great hurry. ಅವಸರಿಸು. To make haste, be eager.

ಅವಸಾನ s. n. Conclusion, termination, end; death; limit.

ಅವಸಾಯ s. n. Conclusion; certainty. 2, remainder.

ಅವಸ್ಥೆ s. n. State, condition (as: ಬಾಲ್ಯಾವಸ್ಥೆ, childhood; ಯೌವನಾವಸ್ಥೆ, manhood; ವೃದ್ಧಾವಸ್ಥೆ, old age). 3, trouble, strait. -ಬೀಳು. To come into troubles.

ಅವಹೇಲ, ಅವಹೇಲನ s. n. Disrespect, contempt.

ಅವಳಿ, (tb. of ಯಮಲಿ) ಅವಳಿಜವಳಿ. n. A pair. -ಮಕ್ಕಳು. Twins.

ಅವಳು k. pro. She.

ಅವಾಕ್ಷರ s. n. A mispronunciation.

ಅವಾಚಿ s. n. The south.

ಅವಾಚ್ಯ s. a. Improper to be uttered; obscene.

ಅವಾಜು f. n. Voice, sound; report.

ಅವಾಂತರ s. a. Intermediate. n. Incursion; havoc.

ಅವಾಯಿ f. n. A report or rumour. 2, bustle; alarm.

ಅವಾರ s. n. The near bank of a river.

ಅವಿ 1. k. v. t. To hide, conceal. 2, (= ಅಳಿ) v. i. To rot, perish; to go out, be extinguished.

ಅವಿ 2. s. n. A sheep. 2, the sun. 3, a mountain.

ಅವಿಕಲ s. a. Perfect, entire. 2, consistent.

ಅವಿಘ್ನ s. a. Unhindered. n. Safety.

ಅವಿಚಾರ, ಅವಿಚಾರಣೆ s. n. Inconsideration, inadvertance, promptitude. ಅವಿಚಾರಿ. Inconsiderate; an indiscriminate person. ಅವಿಚಾರಿತನಿರ್ಣಯ. Prejudice.

ಅವಿಚಾಲಿತ s. a. Unshaken, unmoved.

ಅವಿಚು (= ಅವಿಸು, ಅವುಚು) k. v. t. To hide, conceal.

ಅವಿಚ್ಛಿನ್ನ, ಅವಿಚ್ಛೇದ s. a. Unseparated, undivided; entire, incessant.

ಅವಿದ್ಯ s. a. Unwise, foolish. ಅವಿದ್ಯೆ. n. Ignorance. 2, illusion.

ಅವಿಧಿ s. n. Irregularity. 2, misfortune, trouble.

ಅವಿಧೇಯ s. a. Disobedient. -ತ್ವ. Disobedience.

ಅವಿಭಕ್ತ s. a. Undivided, joint.

ಅವಿಭಾಗ s. a. Undivided. n. Undivided condition.

ಅವಿಮುಕ್ತ s. a. Unloosed. n. N. of a tîrtha near Benares.

ಅವಿರಲ, ಅವಿರಳ s. a. Close; thick, compact. 2, not rare.

ಅವಿರುದ್ಧ s. a. Unobstructed; proper, consistent with.

ಅವಿಲಂಬ, ಅವಿಲಂಬನ s. a. Not delaying, quick.

ಅವಿವೇಕ s. n. Want of discrimination; ignorance; indiscretion. ಅವಿವೇಕಿ. Inconsiderate; short-sighted.

ಅವಿಶೇಷ s. a. Uniform, alike. n. Uniformity, equability.

ಅವಿಶ್ವಾಸ s. n. Distrust, unbelief (= ಅಪನಂಬುಗೆ, q. v.). ಅವಿಶ್ವಾಸಿ. An unbeliever, infidel.

ಅವಿಸು. = ಅವಿಚು.

ಅವಿಹಿತ s. a. Unprescribed. 2, improper.

ಅವೀರೆ s. n. A woman who has neither husband nor son.

ಅವು, ಅವುಗಳು k. pro. They; pl. of ಅದು.

ಅವುಕು, ಅವುಗು, ಅವುಂಕು (=ಅದಳು, ಅವಚು) k. v. t. To press, squeeze. ಅವುಕಿಸು. To cause to press, etc.

ಅವುಚು. =ಅವಿಚು. 2, to hold firmly.

ಅವುಡಲ, ಅವುಡಲು (tb. of ಆಮಂಡ) n. The castor-oil plant, *Ricinus communis*.

ಅವುಡು k. v. i. To chew, champ. n. The jaw. 2, the lower lip.

ಅವುತಣ (= ಔತಣ) k. n. An invitation to dinner. 2, a festive dinner.

ಅವುತೆ k. n. A coat of mail.

ಅವೆ k. pl. of ಅದೆ. (They) are. *Cpds.:* ಆಗುತ್ತವೆ, ಕಾಣುತ್ತವೆ, *etc.*

ಅವೇದ್ಯ s. a. Unascertainable.

ಅವೈದಿಕ s. a. Not vêdic. n. A man not versed in the vêda.

ಅವ್ಯಕ್ತ s. a. Indistinct, imperceptible. 2, inarticulate. n. The soul.

ಅವ್ಯಥೆ s. n. Ease, happiness (= ಸುಖ).

ಅವ್ಯಯ s. a. Unchangeable, imperishable. n. An indeclinable word, a particle. 2, heaven. -ಕ್ರಿಯಾಪದ. A form of verb used for all genders, numbers, and tenses.

ಅವ್ಯವಸ್ಥೆ s. n. Disorder, confusion.

ಅವ್ಯವಹಿತ s. a. Adjoining, contiguous. -ಪೂರ್ವಕಾಲ. The time just past.

ಅವ್ಯಾಪಾರ s. n. Recess from work.

ಅವ್ಯಾಪ್ಯ s. a. Peculiar. 2, not pervading.

ಅವ್ವ, ಅವ್ವೆ (tb. of ಅಂಬೆ) n. A mother. 2, a feminine title of respect and love. 3, an elderly woman. ಅವ್ವಪ್ಪಚ್ಚಿಯಾಟ. A kind of children's sport.

ಅವ್ವವ್ವ. = ಅಮ್ಮಮ್ಮ, q. v.

ಅವ್ವಳಿಸು a. k. v. i. To jump up or upon.

ಅವ್ವಾ k. Imitation of the note of the cuckoo.

ಅಶಕ್ತ s. a. Unable, incompetent; weak. -ತನ, -ತೆ, ಅಶಕ್ತಿ. Inability, weakness.

ಅಶಕ್ಯ s. a. Impossible.

ಅಶನ s. n. Eating. 2, food.

ಅಶನಾರ್ಥ s. n. Maintenance, ration.

ಅಶನಾರ್ಥಿ s. n. One who is desirous of or asks for food.

ಅಶರೀರ s. a. Bodiless. n. The sky. 2, Kâma. -ವಾಕ್ಯ, -ವಾಣಿ. An oracle, voice from heaven.

ಅಶಾಸ್ತ್ರ, ಅಶಾಸ್ತ್ರೀಯ s. a. Unscriptural, heterodox.

ಅಶಿಕ್ಷಿತ s. a. Untrained, unlearnt.

ಅಶೀತಿ s. a. Eighty.

ಅಶುಚಿ s. a. Impure. n. Impurity; *also* -ತ್ವ. [Impurity.

ಅಶುದ್ಧ s. a. Impure; incorrect. ಅಶುದ್ಧಿ.

ಅಶುಭ s. a. Inauspicious. n. Ill-luck.

ಅಶೇಷ s. a. Without remainder, entire. 2, infinite, endless.

ಅಶೋಕ s. a. Sorrowless. n. A deity. 2, the tree *Jonesia asoka*.

ಅಶೋಧಿತ s. a. Unpurified, unrevised; unrefined.

ಅಶೋಭಿತ s. a. Not beautiful. [ness.

ಅಶೋಭೆ s. n. Absence of beauty, comeli-

ಅಶೌಚ s. n. Impurity.

ಅಶ್ಮ s. n. A stone. 2, a cloud. -ಕಾರಕ. A stone mason. -ಗರ್ಭ. An emerald. -ರಿ. The disease of the gravel. -ಸಾರ. Iron.

ಅಶ್ಮಾರೋಪಣ s. n. A ceremony at marriages.

ಅಶ್ರದ್ಧೆ s. n. Unbelief, distrust. 2, dislike.

ಅಶ್ರಾಂತ s. a. Unwearied; continual.

ಅಶ್ರು s. n. A tear.

ಅಶ್ರುತ s. a. Unheard; inaudible.

ಅಶ್ಲೀಲ s. a. Ugly; vulgar.

ಅಶ್ವ s. n. A horse. -ಗಂಧ, -ಗಂಧಿ. The plant *Physalis flexuosa*. -ತರ. A mule. -ಪಾಲ. A groom. -ಮೇಧ. The horse-sacrifice. -ರಥ. A carriage drawn by horses. -ರಾಜ. A royal horse. -ಲಕ್ಷ್ಮೀ. Richness in horses. -ವೈದ್ಯ. A veterinary surgeon. -ಶಾಲೆ. A stable. ಅಶ್ವಾರೋಹ. A horseman. ಅಶ್ವೆ. A mare.

ಅಶ್ವತ್ಥ s. n. The holy fig-tree. *Ficus religiosa*.

ಅಶ್ವತ್ಥಾಮ s. n. N. of Drôṇa's son.

ಅಶ್ವಿನಿ s. n. A goddess, mother of the twin sons. 2, the first of the 28 nakshatras. [rank.

ಅಷರಾಫ್ h. n. Noblemen, persons of

ಅಷ್ಟ s. a. Eight. -ಕ. Eightfold. -ಕಷ್ಟ. The eight troubles; much trouble. -ಕೋಣ, -ದಲ. An octagon. -ಗಂಧ. The eight perfumes. -ತಾಲ. A mode of beating time in music. -ದಿಕ್ಕು, -ದಿಕ್. The eight cardinal points of the compass. -ಪದಿ. N. of a Kannaḍa metre; N. of a poem. -ಪಾದ. Spider. -ಭಾಗ್ಯ. The eight requisites to the regal state, *as:* ರಾಜ್ಯ, ಭಂಡಾರ, ಸೈನ್ಯ, ಆನೆ, ಕುದುರೆ, ಛತ್ರ, ಚಾಮರ, ಆಂದೋಲನ. -ಭೋಗ. The eight pleasures, *as:* ಮನೆ, ವಸ್ತ್ರ, ಆಭರಣ, *etc.* -ಮ. The eighth. -ಮದ. The eight kinds of pride, viz. of ಅನ್ನ, ಅರ್ಥ, ವಿದ್ಯೆ, ಕುಲ, ರೂಪ, *etc.* -ಮೂರ್ತಿ. Eight-formed: Śiva. -ವಸು. Eight demigods, *as:* ಅಪ, ಧ್ರುವ, ಸೋಮ, ಅನಿಲ, ಅನಲ, *etc.* -ವಿಧಪೂಜೆ. Worship of an idol with eight things: ಗಂಧ, ದೀಪ, ಧೂಪ, *etc.* -ವಿವಾಹ. The eight kinds of marriage. ಅಷ್ಟಾಂಗ. Eight parts of the body for performing obeisance *as:* hands, breast, forehead, eyes, throat and middle of the back. ಅಷ್ಟಾಂಗಯೋಗ. The eight stations of yôga, *as:* ಯಮ, ನಿಯಮ, ಆಸನ, ಪ್ರಾಣಾಯಾಮ, ಪ್ರತ್ಯಾಹಾರ, ಧಾರಣ, ಧ್ಯಾನ, ಸಮಾಧಿ.

ಅಷ್ಟಮಿ s. n. The eighth lunar day of either fortnight.

ಅಷ್ಟಾರ್ಚನೆ s. n. Eight daily observances to the household gods, *as:* ಸ್ನಾನ, ವಸ್ತ್ರಾಭರಣ, ಗಂಧ, ಅಕ್ಷತೆ, ಪುಷ್ಪ, ಧೂಪ, ದೀಪ, ನೈವೇದ್ಯ.

ಅಷ್ಟಾದಶ s. a. Eighteen. -ಜಾತಿ. Eighteen castes. -ಪರ್ವ. Eighteen books of Mahâbhârata. -ಪುರಾಣ. The eighteen Purâṇas. ಅಷ್ಟಾಪದ. A spider. ಅಷ್ಟಾವಕ್ರ. Greatly deformed, ugly; N. of a saint. ಅಷ್ಟಾವಿಧಾನ. Eight kinds of service to an idol after the pûjĕ.

ಅಷ್ಟು k. n. That measure. *pro.* That much, so much. ಅಷ್ಟರೊಳಗೆ, ಅಷ್ಟರೊಳು. Meanwhile. ಅಷ್ಟರು. So many persons. ಅದಷ್ಟು, ಹೇಳಿದಷ್ಟು, ಎರಡಷ್ಟು, *etc.* ಅಷ್ಟೇ. Even that much. -ಒಂದು, ಅಷ್ಟೊಂದು. At all events, a little. ಅಷ್ಟೋತ್ತರಶತಕ. One hundred and eight.

ಅಸ್ಥಿ s. n. Seed; a kernel, stone.

ಅಸ a. k. n. Slenderness, weakness. 2, fitness; order; strength. -ವಲ್ಲ

ದಪ. An energetic man. -ಗೊರೆ, -ವಳಿ. Strength to fail, be exhausted. -ವಸ. Haste, speed.

ಅಸಂಶಯು s. n. Doubtlessness, certainty.

ಅಸಂಸ್ಕಾರ s. n. The state of being uninitiated.

ಅಸಂಹ್ಯ. tb. of ಅಸಹ್ಯ.

ಅಸಂಹಿಸು. = ಅಸಹಿಸು, q. v.

ಅಸಗ k. n. A washerman. 2, N. of a Kannaḍa author.

ಅಸಂಖ್ಯ. ಅಸಂಖ್ಯಾತ, ಅಸಂಖ್ಯೇಯು s. a. Innumerable.

ಅಸಂಗತಿ s. n. Non-attachment. 2, impropriety, incongruity. a. Not attached.

ಅಸಂಗತ s. a. Unassociated. 2, uneven. 3, inconsistent. 4, imperishable.

ಅಸಡ k. n. A stupid man. ಅಸಡಿ. A stupid woman. [ಮರೆ, etc.

ಅಸಡು k. n. Stupidity, stubbornness. -ಕು

ಅಸಡ್ಡಾಳ (tb. of ಅಶ್ರದ್ಧೆ) n. Contemptibleness; ugliness.

ಅಸಡ್ಡೆ (tb. of ಅಶ್ರದ್ಧೆ) n. Dislike, contempt, scorn. -ಮಾಡು. To despise, slight.

ಅಸತಿ s. n. An unfaithful wife.

ಅಸತ್ಯ s. a. Untrue. n. Untruth; falsehood.

ಅಸದಳ (tb. of ಅಸಾಧ್ಯ) n. Impossibility.

ಅಸಂತುಷ್ಟ s. a. Displeased, not content. ಅಸಂತುಷ್ಟಿ. Discontent.

ಅಸಂತೃಪ್ತಿ s. n. Dissatisfaction; discontent. [tent.

ಅಸಂತೋಷ s. n. Displeasure, discon-

ಅಸಂದರ್ಭ s. n. Hinderance, inconvenience. [vulgar.

ಅಸಭ್ಯ s. a. Unfit for an assembly,

ಅಸಮ s. a. Unequal, uneven. 2, odd.

ಅಸಮಯ s. n. Unfit time.

ಅಸಮರ್ಥ s. a. Powerless, feeble; incompetent.

ಅಸಮಶರ s. n. The five-arrowed: Kâma.

ಅಸಮಾಧಾನ s. n. Displeasure; discontent; indisposition. [equalled.

ಅಸಮಾನ s. a. Unequal, unlike; un-

ಅಸಮಾನಗಿರಿ h. n. A ceiling cloth. 2, an ornamental brush of peacock's feathers.

ಅಸಮಾಪ್ತ s. a. Unfinished, incomplete. -ಕ್ರಿಯೆ. A participle (g.), as, ಹೋಗಿ, ನಡೆದು, etc.

ಅಸಂಪೂರ್ಣ s. a. Incomplete, imperfect.

ಅಸಂಬಂಧ s. n. Non-connection.

ಅಸಂಭವ s. a. Inconsistent, improbable, unlikely. n. An extraordinary event.

ಅಸಂಭಾವ್ಯ s. a. Incomprehensible. -ತ್ವ. Incomprehensibleness. [from.

ಅಸಮ್ಮತ s. a. Disapproved, differing

ಅಸಮ್ಮತಿ s. n. Dissent, disapproval.

ಅಸಯ್ಯ. tb. of ಅಸಹ್ಯ, q. v.

ಅಸಲು h. a. Original; legitimate, wellborn; exactly copied. n. The principal; an original.

ಅಸಹಾಯ s. a. Friendless, lonely.

ಅಸಹಿಸು s. v. i. To be intolerant; to be disgusted with.

ಅಸಹ್ಯ s. a. Unbearable, disgustful. n. Disgust. -ಪಡು. To be disgusted.

ಅಸಾಧಾರಣ s. a. Uncommon; peculiar; distinguished.

ಅಸಾಧ್ಯ (= ಅಸದಳ) s. a. Impossible; incurable.

ಅಸಿ 1. k. int. of disgust: Fy!

ಅಸಿ 2. k. v. t. To scatter, disperse. v. i. To shake, move. n. That which is laid on the ground. 2, (a. k.) thinness. -ಕಲ್ಲು. The lower stone for grinding curry-stuff. -ದು. That is thin. -ನಡು. A tender waist. -ಪೂ. A delicate flower. -ಬೆರಳು. A thin finger.

ಅಸಿ 3. s. n. A sword, knife. -ಪತ್ರ. The blade of a sword. [glio.

ಅಸಿಕ್ನಿ s. n. A female servant in a sera-

ಅಸು s. n. Life. -ಈ, -ಕೊಡು. To give life. -ಬಿಡು, -ವಳಿ. To give up one's life, die. -ಧಾರಣ. Existence. -ಲಾಭ. Escaping with life.

ಅಸುಂಬು k. v. t. To shake, agitate.

ಅಸುರ್ a. k. v. i. To feel disgusted; to be impatient. n. Fatigue.

ಅಸುರ s. n. The sun. 2, a demon, an Asura. -ರಿಪು, -ವೈರಿ, -ಹರ, ಅಸುರಾರಿ. Vishṇu, Kṛishṇa.

ಅಸೂಯು, ಅಸೂಯೆ s. n. Displeasure. 2, envy, jealousy. 3, aversion. -ಪಡು. To bear malice.

ಅಸೆ. = ಅಸಿ.

ಅಸೌಖ್ಯ s. n. Ailment, indisposition; [disease.

ಅಸೌಮ್ಯ s. a. Ugly; disagreeable. -ಸ್ವರ. Having a croaking voice.

ಅಸ್ತ s. a. Disappeared. n. Sunset. -ಮನ, -ಮಯ, -ಮಾನ. Disappearance; setting, as a heavenly body, sunset. -ವ್ಯಸ್ತ. Disordered. ಅಸ್ತಮಿಸು. To set.

ಅಸ್ತರು, ಅಸ್ತಿ h. n. Lining of a garment.

ಅಸ್ತಿಭಾರ, ಅಸ್ತಿವಾರ s. n. A foundation.

ಅಸ್ತು s. int. Be it so, let it be.

ಅಸ್ತ್ರ s. n. A missile weapon. 2, a bow. -ಗೃಹ. An arsenal. -ಜೀವ. A soldier. ಅಸ್ತ್ರಿ. A bowman.

ಅಸ್ಥಿ s. n. A bone. -ಗತ. Seated in the bones. -ಪಂಜರ. A skeleton. -ಪಾತ್ರ. An urn. -ಶೇಷ. A skeleton. -ಸ್ರಾವ. A kind of consumption.

ಅಸ್ಥಿರ s. a. Unsteady; uncertain. -ತ್ವ. Unsteadiness.

ಅಸ್ಪಷ್ಟ s. a. Indistinct.

ಅಸ್ರು (= ಅಶ್ರು) s. a. A tear. 2, water. 3, an eye. 4, blood.

ಅಸ್ವತಂತ್ರ s. a. Dependant, subject.

ಅಸ್ವಭಾವಿಕ s. a. Unnatural.

ಅಸ್ವರ s. a. Indistinct; having a disagreeable voice. n. A consonant (g.).

ಅಸ್ವಸ್ಥ s. n. Illness, sickness, ailment.

ಅಸ್ವಾರಸ್ಯ s. a. Sapless, insipid.

ಅಸ್ವಾರ್ಥ s. n. Disinterestedness; generosity.

ಅಹ (= ಅಪ್ಪ q. v., ಆಗುವ). a. k. ಅಹುದು, ಹೌದು. Yes. ಅಹುದಾಗು. To be yes or true. ಅಹುದೆನ್ನು. To say yes; to assent, affirm. [thus.

ಅಹಗೆ (= ಹಾಗೆ) a. k. ad. That manner;

ಅಹಂಕಾರ, ಅಹಂಕೃತಿ, ಅಹಂಕ್ರಿಯೆ s. n. The sense of self; egotism, pride, haughtiness. ಅಹಂಕರಿಸು. To be egotistic or proud. ಅಹಂಕಾರವಂತ, ಅಹಂಕಾರಿ. A proud man. [manner.

ಅಹಂಗೆ (= ಹಾಗೆ, q. v.) a. k. ad. That

ಅಹನಿ (Dual: day and night) s. n. A day. ಅಹನ್ಯಹನಿ. Day by day, daily.

ಅಹಮ್ s. pron. I. -ಅಹಮಿಕೆ. Conceit. -ಭಾವ. High notion of one's own superiority. -ಮತಿ. Conceit.

ಅಹರ್, ಅಹಸ್ s. n. A day. ಅಹರ್ನಿಶ. Day and night.

ಅಹಲೆಕಾರ h. n. A public servant.

ಅಹವಾಲು h. n. State, circumstances, condition.

ಅಹಷಾಂ h. n. Attendance, retinue. 2, a number of coolies.

ಅಹಹ, ಅಹಹಾ s. int. of joy or sorrow.

ಅಹಿ s. n. A serpent. 2, the demon Vṛitra. -ಕಟಕ. A number of serpents. -ಕಾಂತ, -ಪ, -ಪತಿ. The lord of serpents: Śêsha. -ಭೂಷಣ. Śiva. -ಶಯ್ಯೆ. A couch of snakes.

ಅಹಿತ s. a. Not beneficial, unfriendly. n. An enemy; damage. -ಕರ. Adverse; unwholesome. -ತ್ವ. Enmity.

ಅಹುದು. See s. ಅಹ.

ಅಹೇತು s. n. Causelessness. -ಕ. Cause- [less.

ಅಹೋರಾತ್ರ, ಅಹೋರಾತ್ರಿ s. n. Day and night, from sunrise to sunrise.

ಅಳ a. k. n. Contact; nearness. 2, fitness; propriety; comeliness. 3, power, strength. 4, possibility. -ವಡಿಕೆ. Joining; bringing about. -ವಡಿಸು. To join; to tie; to attach; to bring about. -ವಡು. To be closely joined; to be at hand. -ವಳಿ. To be depressed, to faint.

ಅಳಕ k. a. Neither thick nor thin (fluids).

ಅಳಕು k. v. i. To fear. 2, (= ಅಳುಕು) to prick, throb. 3, (= ಅಲುಕು) to move about. n. Fear. 2, the pricking of a thorn. ಅಳಕಿಸು. To frighten. ಅಳಕ್ಯಾಡು. To shake as water, to bubble

ಅಳಟು (ಳ = ೞ) k. v. i. To be in anguish.

ಅಳತೆ k. n. Measure; extent; measurement. -ಮಾಡು. To measure.

ಅಳರು (ರು = ಱು) a. k. v. i. To fear. n. Fear, anguish. ಅಳರಿಸು. To frighten.

ಅಳಲು (ಳ = ೞ) a. k. v. i. To grieve, be afflicted. n. Grief, sorrow, affliction. ಅಳಲಿಸು. To grieve, harass.

ಅಳಲೆ k. n. A squirrel. 2, = ಅಣಿಲೆ, q. v.

ಅಳವಿ (= ಅಳ, q. v.) a. k. n. Nearness. 2, strength. 3, combat. 4, trust.

ಅಳವು k. n. Measure. -ಗೋಲು. A measuring rod.

ಅಳವೆ (ಳ = ೞ) k. n. The bar; the ebbing of the tide in a river-mouth.

ಅಳವೇಲಿ. = ಅಳುವೇರಿ, ಅೞುವೇರಿ, q. v.

ಅಳಸು k. v. t. To measure or cause to be measured. 2, (= ಅಳಿಸು) to efface.

ಅಳಿ (ಳಿ = ೞಿ) k. v. i. To be ruined; to perish, decay; to disappear; to die. v. t. To ruin. 2, (= ಅಳೆ) to measure. n. Ruin; waste; damage. 2, remainder of liquids. 3, a void, nought (expressed by the sign 6̄). -ಕಣ್ಣು. A bad eye. -ಗಬ್ಬ. Miserable poetry. -ಗವಿ, -ಗಬ್ಬಿಗ. A bad poet. -ಜಪ. Useless prayers. -ಯಾಸೆ. Vain hope.

ಅಳಿಕಿಸು k. v. t. To oppose; to harass. 2, to frighten. 3, (ಳಿ = ೞಿ) to efface, erase.

ಅಳಿಗೆ k. n. An earthen vessel.

ಅಳಿಪು 1. a. k. v. i. To be addicted to; to long for. n. Desire, attachment, love.

ಅಳಿಪು 2. (ಳಿ = ೞಿ) k. v. t. To destroy. v. i. To be destroyed. n. Ruin, destruction; death.

ಅಳಿಯ k. n. A son-in-law, a nephew. -ಸಂತಾನ. The law of inheritance according to which a man's property descends to his sister's son. -ತನ. Being an ಅಳಿಯ.

ಅಳಿಲು (= ಅಳಲೆ) k. n. A squirrel.

ಅಳಿಸು (ಳಿ = ೞಿ) k. v. t. To ruin, destroy; to kill.

ಅಳು (ಳು = ೞು) k. v. i. To weep, cry. -ವಿಕೆ, -ವು. Weeping. -ಗೂಸು. A cross child. -ಕುಳಿ, -ಬುರುಕ. A crying or fretful person; f. -ಬುರುಕಿ. ಅಳಿಸು. To make weep.

ಅಳುಕಿಸು. = ಅಳಿಕಿಸು.

ಅಳುಕು, ಅಳ್ಕು k. v. i. To fear, be afraid. n. Fear.

ಅಳುಗು (ಳು = ೞು) a. k. v. i. To decay. v. t. To love.

ಅಳುಂಬ a. k. n. Excess; greatness; excellence.

ಅಳುಲು (= ಅಣಿಲು) k. n. A squirrel.

ಅಳುವೇರಿ. = ಅಳವೇರಿ, q. v.

ಅಳೆ (= ಅಳ No. 3) k. v. t. To measure. n. Measure. 2, buttermilk. -ದು ಕೊಡು. To measure out. -ದು ತುಂಬಿಕೊಡು. To give heaped measure. -ದು ಹಾಕು. To ponder. -ಯುಂಬ. A Gŏlla.

ಅಳ್ಕಜ (ಳ್ಕ = ೞ್ಕ) k. n. Envy, jealousy. -ಕಾರ. An envious man.

ಅಳ್ಕನೆ k. ad. Suddenly.

ಅಳ್ಕರು (ಳ್ಕರು = ೞ್ಕಱು) a. k. v. t. To love. 2, to fear. n. Love.

ಅಳ್ಕು 1. = ಅಳುಕು.

ಅಳ್ಕು 2. (ಳ್ಕು = ೞ್ಕು) a. k. v. i. To be worn out, digested. n. The state of being worn out or digested.

ಅಳ್ಕೆ k. n. An embrace. 2, (ಳ್ಕೆ = ೞ್ಕೆ) weeping. 3, boiling.

ಅಳ್ಗು (ಳ್ಗು = ೞ್ಗು) k. v. i. To be dissolved; to decay.

ಅಳ್ತಿ (ಳ್ತಿ = ೞ್ತಿ. = ಅರ್ತಿ) k. n. Love. 2, pleasure. -ವಡು. To feel love. -ಕಾರ. A lover.

ಅಳ್ದು (ಳ್ದು = ೞ್ದು) a. k. v. i. To wither, fade. 2, to die. 3, (= ಅದ್ದು) to dip.

ಅಳ್ಳು k. n. Shaking, trembling. ಅಳ್ಳಾಡು (= ಅಲ್ಲಾಡು). To move, shake, tremble.

ಅಳ್ಳೆ k. n. What is shaking. 2, the sides of the abdomen; the weak spot; tenderness. 3, the flank of an animal. -ಗೊಬ್ಬು. Feebleness. -ಗೊಂಬು. A slender branch.

ಆ

ಆ. 1. k. The second letter of the alphabet. 2, *a remote pronominal adjective:* That; those, *as:* ಆ ಮನುಷ್ಯ. That man. ಆ ಕಡೆ. That side. ಆ ಕಾರಣ. Therefore. ಆ ಕ್ಷಣ. Instantly. ಆ ಬಗ್ಗೆ. On that account. ಆ ಬಳಿಕ. Thereafter. ಆ ಮೇಲೆ. Afterward. ಆ ವರೆಗೆ. Until then. ಆವಾಗ. Then. 3, *a final particle in friendly conversation, as:* ಪಾ, ರಾಮಾ! ಮಕ್ಕಳಿರಾ! 4, *an interrogative affix, as:* ಬಂದಿರಾ? ಹೋಗುತ್ತೀರಾ?

ಆ 2. s. *ad.* From. 2, towards. 3, all around. 4, till, as far as.

ಆಂ (= ನಾ, ನಾನು) a. k. *pro.* I.

ಆಃ k. *int. of surprise and sorrow.*

ಆಕರ s. *n.* A multitude. 2, a mine. 3, a place.

ಆಕರಣ, ಆಕರಣೆ s. *n.* Calling; a challenge. ಆಕರಿಸು. To accept; to challenge.

ಆಕರ್ಣನ s. *n.* Hearing, listening. ಆಕರ್ಣಿಸು. To hear, listen (*cf.* ಆಲಿಸು, ಕೇಳು).

ಆಕರ್ಷ s. *n.* Drawing, attraction towards one's self (= ಆಕರ್ಷಣ). 2, a die or dice; playing with dice, *etc.* 3, temptation, allurement. -ಕ. A magnet. ಆಕರ್ಷಿಸು. To attract, draw.

ಆಕಸ್ಮಿಕ s. *a.* Sudden. *ad.* Suddenly; instantly.

ಆಕಳ, ಆಕಳು k. *n.* A cow. -ಕರ. A cow's calf. -ಮಂದೆ. A herd of cattle. -ಹಟ್ಟಿ. A cowpen.

ಆಕಳಾಸ k. *n.* Disgust.

ಆಕಳಿಕೆ (= ಆಕುಳಿಕೆ) k. *n.* Yawning, gaping. ಆಕಳಿಸು *v. i.* To yawn, gape.

ಆಕಾಂಕ್ಷೆ s. *n.* Desire, wish. 2, requiring of a word to complete the sense. 3, suspicion. ಆಕಾಂಕ್ಷಿಸು. To desire, wish.

ಆಕಾರ s. *n.* Form, shape. 2, a hint, sign. 3, the vowel ಆ. -ಪೂಜೆ. = ಮೂರ್ತಿಪೂಜೆ. -ಗುಪ್ತಿ, -ಗೋಪನ. Dissimulation.

ಆಕಾರಣ s. *n.* Calling; challenging.

ಆಕಾಶ (*tb.* ಆಕಾಸ, ಆಗಸ) s. *n.* The sky or atmosphere; an empty space. 2, the ether. -ಗಂಗೆ. A cascade. -ಗೂಡು, -ದೀಪ. A lamp hung on a pole. -ಬಾಣ. A sky-rocket. -ಬಿಲ್ಲು. The rainbow. -ವಾಣಿ. An aerial voice.

ಆಕಾಸ. *tb. of* ಆಕಾಶ, *q. v.*

ಆಕೀರ್ಣ s. *a.* Scattered; crowded; confused.

ಆಕು a. k. *n.* A leaf; a herb, filament. -ರಾಯಿ. A file.

ಆಕುಂಚನ s. *n.* Bending; contraction; curving. ಆಕುಂಚಿತ. Bent, contracted.

ಆಕುಲ, ಆಕುಲಿತ s. *a.* Filled with, full; confused, bewildered.

ಆಕುಳಿಕೆ. = ಆಕಳಿಕೆ, *q. v.*

ಆಕೃತಿ s. *n.* Form, shape. 2, the body. 3, tribe, species.

ಆಕೆ 1. k. *pro.* That woman, she. 2, she, the married wife (*hon.*).

ಆಕೆ 2. a. k. *n.* Power, valour. -ವಾಳ. A valiant man.

ಆಕ್ರಂದನ s. *n.* Lamentation, weeping. ಆಕ್ರಂದಿಸು. To weep, lament.

ಆಕ್ರಮಣ s. *n.* Approaching. 2, attacking; seizing, grasping. 3, overpowering.

ಆಕ್ರಮಿಸು s. *v. t.* To seize, grasp. *v. i.* [To rise.

ಆಕ್ರಾಂತ s. *a.* Possessed, obtained. 2, subjected, overpowered. *Cpds.:* ದುಃಖಾಕ್ರಾಂತ; ಮಂದಾಕ್ರಾಂತ, *etc.*

ಆಕ್ರೋಶ s. *n.* Calling aloud. 2, reviling, abusing.

ಆಕ್ಷೇಪ s. *n.* Tossing. 2, abuse, taunt; reproach. 3, objection, doubt. -ಮಾಡು, ಆಕ್ಷೇಪಿಸು. To reproach; to object.

ಆಖರಿ h. *n.* The end. ಆಖರು. = ಆಖೈರು.

ಆಖಾತ s. *n.* A natural pond.

ಆಖು s. *n.* A rat, mouse. -ಗ, -ರಥ, -ವಾಹನ. Gaṇêśa.

ಆಖೇಟ s. n. Chase, hunting. 2, fright.

ಆಖೈರು h. a. Last, final. n. The end.

ಆಖ್ಯ s. a. Named. 2, making known. n. = ಆಖ್ಯೆ.

ಆಖ್ಯಾತ s. a. Made known; famous. 2, conjugated. n. A verb, predicate (g.). -ಪದ. An inflected verb (g.). -ವಿಭಕ್ತಿ. An affix of conjugation (g.).

ಆಖ್ಯಾತಿ s. n. Fame, name. -ಸು. To make known.

ಆಖ್ಯಾನ s. n. Saying. 2, a tale. 3, a word.

ಆಖ್ಯೆ s. n. An appellation; fame; a name.

ಆಗ, ಆಗಲು, ಆಗ್ಗೆ k. ad. That time; then. ಆಗಾಗ, ಆಗಾಗ್ಗೆ, ಆಗಿಂದಾಗ್ಗೆ. From time to time, occasionally. ಆಗಿನ. Of that time.

ಆಗಡ a. k. n. Sport, fun, mockery. -ಕಾರ. A scoffer, teaser.

ಆಗಡು (= ಆಗ) a. k. ad. Then.

ಆಗತ s. a. Come, received. -ಸ್ವಾಗತ. Reciption, welcome. ಆಗತಿ. Arrival; return; income; chance.

ಆಗಮ s. n. Arrival. 2, precept; a work on sacred science. 3, an augment (g.). 4, knowledge, science. -ನ. Coming. ಆಗಮಾಮ್ನಾಯ. The śâstras and vêdas. ಆಗಮಿಸು. To arrive.

ಆಗರ (tb. of ಆಗಾರ) n. An abode, asylum. 2, a garden. 3, a saltpan.

ಆಗಲ್, ಆಗಲು. = ಆಗ, q. v.

ಆಗಲಿ. See s. ಆಗು.

ಆಗಸ (tb. of ಆಕಾಶ). -ಮಣಿ. The sun.

ಆಗಳು (= ಆಗ) a. k. ad. Always. 2, that time.

ಆಗಾಗ, ಆಗಾಗ್ಗೆ. See s. ಆಗ.

ಆಗಾಶ್ಯ s. n. Pretence of agony or injury.

ಆಗಾಮಿ s. a. Coming; future. -ಕ್ರಿಯೆ. The future tense (g.). ಆಗಾಮಿಕ. Relating to future.

ಆಗಾರ (= ಆಗರ) s. n. A house, dwelling.

ಆಗು k. v. i. To come into being. 2, to take place, happen. 3, to grow. 4, to become. 5, to be. 6, to be done or finished. 7, to come under. 8, to be suitable, fit; to agree. 9, to be possible; to be related. ಅವನು ನನಗೆ ಏನೂ ಆಗುವದಿಲ್ಲ, he is not related to me. ಆದದ್ದು ಆಯಿತು, what is done is done. ಆಗಗೊಡು. To allow to happen. ಆಗದ. Not coming about, impossible. ಆಗದವನು. An unfriendly man; ಕೆಲಸಕ್ಕೆ ಆಗದವನು, an incompetent man. ಆಗದು. It is unfit or forbidden, as: ಮಾತಲಾಗದು. ಆಗಲಿ. (3rd. pr. sing. imp.) May become or be; be it (so) (ಹಾಗಾಗಲಿ, be it so). Rep. to express: whether—or, either- or, as: ಇದಾಗಲಿ ಅದಾಗಲಿ, either this or that; ಬಡವರಾಗಲಿ ಐಶ್ವರ್ಯವಂತರಾಗಲಿ, whether poor or rich. ಆಗುವ (pr. p.). Possible, practicable. ಆಗುವಂತೆ ಮಾಡು, ಆಗುವ ಹಾಗೆ ಮಾಡು. To accomplish, bring about. ಆಗಿ. (p. p.) Having become, happened, being finished, etc.: 1, affixed to adjectives or nouns it is used to form adverbs, as: ಚನ್ನಾಗಿ, ಮೃದುವಾಗಿ, ಸಲುವಾಗಿ, ಸಂತೋಷವಾಗಿ, etc. 2, it is used to convey the idea of "voluntarily", "of itself", as: ಅವನಾಗಿ or ತಾನಾಗಿ ಬಂದನು, he came of his own accord. 3, with the Dative it signifies: for, on account of, in behalf of, as: ನಿನಗಾಗಿ, ತಂದೆಯ ಮಾತಿಗಾಗಿ, ಮಾಡುವದಕ್ಕಾಗಿ, ಮಾಡಿದಕ್ಕಾಗಿ, ಮಾತದಕ್ಕಾಗಿ, ಇದ್ದದ್ದಕ್ಕಾಗಿ. 4, it signifies a state or quality, as: ಆಭರಣವಾಗಿರುವ ಬಂಗಾರ; ಬಹಳ ಅಧಿಕವಾಗಿರುವದು. ಆಗಿಹೋಗು. To be finished; to die. ಆದರೂ (ಆದಡೆಯು, ಆದೊಡೆಯು). Though; soever. ಆದರೆ. If it be, if so. ಆಗು is also used to form a kind of passive, as: ಹೇಳೋಣವಾಯಿತು; ಕೊಡೋಣವಾಯಿತು. ಆಗಿಸು. To bring about, perform. ಆಗುವಿಕೆ. Becoming, happening.

ಆಗೆ k. ad. In, into.

ಆಗೆ = ಆಗ, q. v.

ಆಗ್ನೇಯ s. a. Relating to fire. n. The south-east quarter.

ಆಗ್ಯೆ (= ಆಗ, q. v.) k. ad. Then. ಆಗಿಂದಾಗ್ಯೆ. From time to time. ಆಗ್ಯೂ. Also, then; notwithstanding, though, *as*, ಮಾಡಿದಾಗ್ಯೂ. Though he did it.

ಆಗ್ರಹ s. n. Seizing. 2, earnest solicitation. 3, violence (ಬಲಾತ್ಕಾರ). 4, anger. ಆಗ್ರಹಿಸು. To become angry.

ಆಘ್ರಾಣ s. n. Smelling. ಆಘ್ರಾಣಿಸು. To smell.

ಆಂಗಿರಸ s. n. Bṛihaspati. 2, the 6th year in the cycle of sixty.

ಆಚಂದ್ರಾರ್ಕ s. a. As long as moon and sun endure.

ಆಚಮನ s. n. Rinsing the mouth or sipping water at a religious ceremony.

ಆಚರಣೆ s. n. Observing. 2, conduct, practice; performance. -ಮಾಡು, ಆಚರಿಸು. To perform, observe.

ಆಚಾರ s. n. Conduct; good behaviour. 2, an established rule of conduct; custom, usage, practice. *Cpds.:* ವ್ರತಾಚಾರ, ಕುಲಾಚಾರ, ದೇಶಾಚಾರ, ಲೋಕಾಚಾರ, *etc.*

ಆಚಾರಿ (*tb. of* ಆಚಾರ್ಯ) n. A title assumed by Brahmin cooks, idol-makers, smiths, artificers, house-pûjâris, *etc.*

ಆಚಾರ್ಯ s. n. A spiritual guide. 2, a conductor of religious ceremonies. 3, a title of learned men.

ಆಚೆ k. *ad.* That side; beyond. 2, after, afterwards, *as:* ಆಚೆಯ ಹೊಲ, ಆಚೆಬೀದಿ. -ಕಡೆ. That side.

ಆಚ್ಛಾದನ s. n. Covering, concealing; a covering. ಆಚ್ಛಾದಿಸು. To cover, conceal.

ಆಜ s. n. Relating to goats. -ಕ. A flock of goats.

ಆಜಿ s. n. Going, running. 2, war, battle. 3, level ground.

ಆಜೀವ, ಆಜನ್ಮ s. n. Livelihood. *ad.* As long as life endures.

ಆಜ್ಞಾಪನ s. n. Ordering. ಆಜ್ಞಾಪಿಸು. To order, command.

ಆಜ್ಞೆ (*tb.* ಆಣೆ) s. n. An order, command. 2, permission. 3, verdict, punishment. -ನಿರ್ಣಯ. A penal decree. -ಕೊಡು. To order; to allow. -ತಕ್ಕೊಳ್ಳು. To take leave. -ಮಾಡು. To order; to condemn, punish. -ಮೀರು. To transgress a command. ಆಜ್ಞಾಧಾರಕ. Obedient.

ಆಟ k. n. Motion. 2, play, sport, amusement, jest. 3, a dance, stage performance; gambling. 4, sound. *Cpds.:* ಕಳ್ಳಾಟ, ಕೊಂಡಾಟ, ಕೋಲಾಟ, ತೋಳಾಟ, ನೀರಾಟ, ಹುಡುಗಾಟ, ಹೋರಾಟ. -ಆಡು. To play; to act, perform. -ಕಾತಿ, -ಗಾತಿ. A dancing girl. -ಗಾರ, -ಗುಳಿ, -ಂಗುಳಿ. A player; a gambler. -ಪಾಟ. *dupl.* -ವಿಕ. A player; an actor; a cheat; (s.) a woodman.

ಆಟಂಕ s. n. Obstruction, obstacle. ಆಟಂಕಿಸು. To hinder.

ಆಟಾಳಿ k. n. A person given to play.

ಆಟಾಳು f. n. An extra servant.

ಆಟಿ k. n. A player. -ಕೆ, -ಗೆ (*cf.* ಆಡಿಕೆ). Play. ಆಟಿಸು. To long for, desire.

ಆಟು k. n. Motion; play. (f.) *a.* Minor; extra.

ಆಟೋಪ s. n. Ostentation, pomp. 2, control, power.

ಆಡಂಗಿ k. n. A female.

ಆಡಂಬರ s. n. A drum. 2, roaring. 3, thunder. 4, pomp, display. 5, expanse; a heap.

ಆಡಳಿತ, ಆಡಳಿತೆ k. n. Administration, management.

ಆಡಿ k. n. That moves or plays. ಆಡಿಕೆ. A holding, motion; play; a holiday. ಆಡಿಗ. An actor. -ತನ. Moving, playing.

ಆಡು 1. k. *v. i.* To be in motion; to wag, wave, shake. 2, to play, sport. 3, to dance, act. 4, to speak, utter, sound. 5, to abuse. *Cpds.:* ಅಲ್ಲಾಡು, ಈಡಾಡು, ಕುಣಿದಾಡು, ಕೊಂಡಾಡು, ತಿರಿಗಾಡು, ಬೀಸಾಡು, ಹೊರಳಾಡು, ಹೋರಾಡು, *etc.* n. Motion. -ಕಳಿ. A playful person. -ವಿಕೆ, -ಹ, ಆಡಿಕೆ. Moving, playing. ಆಡಿಸು. To cause to move, play, dance, *etc.*

ಆಡು 2. k. n. A he-goat. -ನೆಲ್ಲಿಗಿಡ. A herb, *Phyllanthus madraspatensis.*

6

-ಮುಟ್ಟದ ಗಿತ, -ಸೋಗೆ-. A shrub, *Justicia adhatoda.*

ಆಡೇಲು k. n. A screech owl.

ಆಢಕ s. n. A measure of grain.

ಆಢಕಿ s. n. A kind of pulse.

ಆಢ್ಯ s. a. Rich, wealthy. n. Arrogance.

ಆಣ್ (= ಆಳ್) k. a. Male. n. Priority.

ಆಣತಿ 1. k. n. Singing, praising.

ಆಣತಿ 2. (*tb. of* ಆಜ್ಞಪ್ತಿ) n. An order, command.

ಆಣಿ 1. k. n. Roundness. 2, excellency, preciousness. -ಮುತ್ತು. A costly pearl.

ಆಣಿ 2. s. n. The linch-pin; a nail. 2, a limit. -ಕಲ್ಲು. The base of a pillar. -ಕಾರ. A nail-maker.

ಆಣಿಸು k. v. i. To crack or burst.

ಆಣಿಕಲ್ಲು k. n. A hailstone.

ಆಣೆ 1. (*tb. of* ಆಜ್ಞೆ) n. Command. 2, oath. -ಇಡು, -ಕಟ್ಟು, -ಮಾಡು, -ಹಾಕು. To swear. -ಬಿಡಿಸು. To free from an oath. ದೇವರಾಣೆ. By God. ಮಗನಾಣೆ. By my son.

ಆಣೆ 2. k. n. A crack. -ಬಿಡು. To crack, burst.

ಆಂಡಿ k. n. A Šaiva religious mendicant.

ಆಣ್ಮ, ಆಣ್ಮ (*fr.* ಆಣ್) a. k. n. A ruler, lord, master.

ಆತ, ಆತಂ k. *dem. pro.* That man, he.

ಆತಂಕ (= ಅಟಂಕ) s. n. Obstacle, hindrance (ಅಡ್ಡಿ). 2, disease. 3, fear. ಆತಂಕಿಸು. To hinder.

ಆತತಾಯಿ s. n. An assailant, felon, murderer.

ಆತಪ s. n. Sunshine. ಆತಪ್ತ a. Heated.

ಆತಪತ್ರ s. n. A parasol.

ಆತಿಥ್ಯ s. n. Hospitality. 2, a guest. -ಕೊಡು, -ಮಾಡು. To entertain a guest.

ಆತೀರ್ಣ s. a. Crossed, passed over.

ಆತು, = ಅಂತು k. p. p. *of* ಅನು, q. v.

ಆತುರ s. n. Longing for. 2, excitement; haste. -ತೆ. Desire. -ಪಡು, -ಬೀಳು, -ಪಡಸು. To be hasty. ಆತುರಿಸು. To feel desire.

ಆತುಷ್ಟಿ s. n. Complete satisfaction.

ಆತೆ, ಆತೆಹುಳ k. n. A cockroach.

ಆತ್ಮ s. n. The soul. 2, the self. 3, nature, character. 4, intellect; mind. 5, the soul of the universe. 6, effort. 7, wind, air. -ಕ. (*in cpds.*) Having the nature of. -ಘಾತಕ. Suicide. -ಜ, -ಜಾತ, -ಭವ. A son. -ಜೆ, -ಜಾತೆ, -ಭವೆ. A daughter. -ಜ್ಞ. Self-knowing; a sage. -ದ್ರೋಹಿ. Fretful, miserable. -ನಿವೇದನ, ಆತ್ಮಾರ್ಪಣ. Offering one's self as a sacrifice. -ನೇಪದ. The middle voice of a verb (*g.*). -ಭೂ. Self-born; Brahmâ. -ವಂಚಕ. Self-deceiver. -ವಂಚನೆ. Self-delusion. -ವಿದ್. Self-knowing; a sage. -ಸ್ತುತಿ. Self-praise. ಆತ್ಮಾರ್ಥ. One's own sake; reflexive (*g.*). *Cpds:* ಪರಮಾತ್ಮ, ಜೀವಾತ್ಮ, ಪುಣ್ಯಾತ್ಮ, ಪಾಪಾತ್ಮ, ದುರಾತ್ಮ, *etc.*

ಆತ್ಮಿಕ (= ಆತ್ಮಕ, q. v.) s. a. Having the nature of.

ಆತ್ಮೀಯ s. a. Own, relating to self.

ಆತ್ರೇಯ s. n. Durvâsa. 2, the moon.

ಆದ k. (*rel. p. p. of* ಆಗು, *q. v.*). *Affixed to nouns it converts them into adjectives, as:* ಭಾರವಾದ, heavy; ವಿಸ್ತಾರವಾದ, extensive, *etc.* -ಕಾರಣ, -ದರಿಂದ. Therefore. ಆದಾನು. He may become. ಆದೀತು. It may be; yes.

ಆದರ, ಆದರಣೆ s. n. Reverence, homage. 2, kind treatment, kindness; consolation. ಆದರಿಗ. A helper in trouble. ಆದರಿಸು. To respect; to treat kindly.

ಆದರೂ (*fr.* ಆಗು) k. *conj.* Either, or. 2, any. (ಯಾರಾದರೂ, any one; ಏನಾದರೂ, something; ಎಲ್ಲಾದರೂ, anywhere). 3, at least (ಈಗಲಾದರೂ, at least now). 4, though (ಮಾಡಿದರೂ, though he did).

ಆದರೆ (*fr.* ಆಗು) *cond. conj.* If, if it be (ಹಾಗಾದರೆ, if it be so). 2, but.

ಆದರ್ಶ s. n. A mirror. -ನ. Showing; a mirror.

ಆದಲೆ (*fr.* ಅ-ತಲೆ) k. n. Forehead; front.

ಆದಾಯ s. n. Gain, income, profit; advantage.

ಆದಿ s. n. Beginning. a. First, prior. (ಅನಾದಿ, without beginning; ಅನಾದಿಯಿಂದ, from eternity). con. And so on, etc. -ಕಾರಣ. A primary cause. -ದೇವ. The creator. -ಶೇಷ. The sovereign of the serpent race. Cpds: ಅನಾದಿ, ಯುಗಾದಿ, ದಿನಾದಿ, ಜಗದಾದಿ.

ಆದಿತ್ಯ s. n. The sun. -ವಾರ. Sunday.

ಆದಿಮ s. a. First, prior, original.

ಆದೀಕ s. n. Profit, gain, income.

ಆದು. = ಆಯ್ದು. P. p. of ಆಯು, q. v.

ಆದೇಯ s. n. A gift.

ಆದೇಶ s. n. Information. 2, precept. 3, an order. 4, a substitute.

ಆದ್ಯ s. a. First, initial. -ಕವಿ. N. of Vâlmîki.

ಆಧಾನ s. n. Placing, depositing. 2, a deposit, pledge; a surety. 3, a receptacle.

ಆಧಾರ s. n. Support, aid. 2, authority, sanction, foundation. 3, a receptacle. -ಸ್ಥ, ಆಧಾರಿ. A man of property. -ವಿಲ್ಲದವನು, ನಿರಾಧಾರಿ, a destitute man.

ಆಧಿ s. n. Location. 2, a deposit. 3, thought; care; anxiety; cf. ವ್ಯಾಧಿ.

ಆಧಿಕ್ಯ s. n. Excess, abundance; superiority.

ಆಧಿಪತ್ಯ s. n. Supremacy, authority.

ಆಧೀನ s. a. Subjected, dependent. n. Subjection, control, charge. Cpds: ಸ್ವಾಧೀನ, ಪರಾಧೀನ, ದೈವಾಧೀನ.

ಆನ. = ಅದ. Rel. p. p. of ಆನು, q. v.

ಆನಕ s. n. A large drum beaten at one end. 2, a tambourine.

ಆನತ s. a. Bent, bowed; humbled, submissive.

ಆನನ s. n. The mouth; face.

ಆನಂದ s. n. Happiness, joy, delight. 2, the 48th year of the cycle. -ಕರ, -ಕಾರಕ. Gladdening. -ಜಲ. Tears of joy. -ಪಡು. To rejoice. -ಭೈರವಿ. A kind of tune. ಆನಂದಿಸು. To rejoice.

ಆನಮ s. n. Bending. ಆನಮಿಸು. To salute reverently.

ಆನಿಕಲ್ಲು (= ಆಣೆಕಲ್ಲು) k. n. A hailstone.

ಆನು k. v. t. To touch, join. 2, to rest on; to recline on; to lean. 3, to lay hold of, put on; to receive; to bear, endure. v. i. To be slow. (P. p. ಆತು). ಆತುಉರಿ. To burn slowly. ಆನಿಸು. To cause to touch, etc. n. = ಆನಿಕೆ. Leaning on.

ಆನುಕೂಲ್ಯ s. n. Suitableness, conformity.

ಆನುಗುಣ್ಯ s. n. Congeniality.

ಆನೆ 1. k. n. An elephant (= ಗಜ, ಕರಿ, ನಾಗ). Cpds: ಕಾಡಾನೆ, ನೀರಾನೆ, ಬೆಳ್ಳಾನೆ, ಹೆಣ್ಣಾನೆ, etc. -ಕಾಲು. The Cochin leg, elephantiasis. -ಕಾಸು, -ದುಡ್ಡು. An old copper coin so called. -ಗಜ್ಜು. A troublesome kind of itch. -ದಂತ. Ivory. -ಬಾಗಲು. The entrance gate of a palace. -ಮಯ್ಲಿ. A bad kind of small-pox. -ಮುಸುಡಿನ ನೆಗಳು. The long-nosed alligator. -ಮೆಟ್ಟು. The foot-print of an elephant. -ಗುಲಿ. An elephant-killer. -ಹಳ್ಳ, -ಗೊಳ್ಳ. A pit for catching wild elephants.

ಆನೆ 2. (= ಹಾನೆ) He is. 2, aff. for 3rd pers. sing. masc. present; as: ಇರುತ್ತಾನೆ, ಬರುತ್ತಾನೆ, etc.

ಆಂತರ್ಯ (fr. ಅಂತರ) s. n. The inside, heart; the mind; secrecy.

ಆಂತು (= ಆತು) k. P. p. of ಆನು, q. v.

ಆಂತ್ರ s. n. The bowels, entrails. -ವಾಯು, -ವೃದ್ಧಿ. Ingual hernia, rupture.

ಆಂದೆಗ (= ಅಡೀಲು) k. n. The white screech owl.

ಆಂದೋಲ, ಆಂದೋಲನ s. n. Swinging.

ಆಂದೋಲಿಕ s. n. A palankeen (ಪಾಲಕಿ).

ಆಂಧಸಿಕ s. n. A cook.

ಆಂಧ್ರ s. n. Tĕlugu. -ದೇಶ. T. country.

ಆಪ 1. k. Rel. pres. p. of ಆರ್. Being strong, able or possible. -ನಿತು, ಆಪಷ್ಟು. As much as possible. ಆಪುದು. It will be possible.

ಆಪ 2. s. n. Water.

ಆಪಗೆ s. n. A river, stream.

ಆಪಣ s. n. A shop. 2, a market. ಆಪಣಿಕ. A shop-keeper, merchant.

ಆಪತು, ಆಪತ್ತು, ಆಪದ (tb. of ಆಪದ್) n. Trouble; misfortune, calamity, distress. -ಪಡು, -ಬೀಳು. To be in distress. ಆಪತ್ಕಾಲ. A time of trouble. ಆಪದ್ಧರ್ಮ. Practice allowable in time of distress.

ಆಪನ್ನ s. a. Gained, acquired. 2, distressed.

ಆಪಾತ s. n. Rushing on; throwing down; happening. 2, the instant.

ಆಪಾದ, ಆಪಾದನ s. n. Accusation; punishment. ಆಪಾದಿಸು. To charge, punish.

ಆಪಾನ s. n. A drinking-party.

ಆಪು k. n. An object to lean upon, refuge, protection. 2, a kind of bulrush, *Typha elephantina*.

ಆಪೂರ್ಣ s. a. Full. -ತೆ. Fulness.

ಆಪೇಕ್ಷಿಕ s. a. Expecting, wishing. ಆಪೇಕ್ಷಿತ a. Wished.

ಆಪೇಕ್ಷೆ. = ಅಪೇಕ್ಷೆ.

ಆಪೋಶನ s. n. Sipping of water at the beginning and end of meals.

ಆಪ್ತ s. a. Obtained, reached; apt, fit. 2, trustworthy. n. A friend.

ಆಪ್ತಾಗಿರಿ f. n. An ornamental umbrella borne over râjas.

ಆಪ್ತಿ s. n. Reaching; obtaining; aptitude.

ಆಪ್ಯ s. a. Watery; consisting of water. 2, obtainable.

ಆಪ್ಯಾಯನ s. a. Causing fulness; satisfying. n. Satisfaction, pleasure.

ಆಪ್ಲವ, ಅಪ್ಲವನ s. n. Bathing, ablution. -ವ್ರತಿ. A Brâhmaṇa who has taken the bath after his period of study.

ಆಬರು, ಆಬುರು, ಆಬ್ರು h. n. Honour, character, renown. -ಗೇಡಿ. A man without honour or character.

ಆಬಾದು h. a. Flourishing, cultivated.

ಆಬಾಸ (tb. of ಆಭಾಸ) n. Fallacy; failure, defect.

ಆಬ್ದಿಕ s. a. Annual, yearly.

ಆಭರಣ s. n. An ornament.

ಆಭಾವ s. n. Manner, mode.

ಆಭಾಷಣ s. n. Addressing, speaking.

ಆಭಾಸ s. n. Splendour, light; appearance; reflection.

ಆಭೀರ s. n. A cowherd.

ಆಭ್ಯಂತರ (fr. ಅಭ್ಯಂತರ, q. v.) s. a. Internal. n. Obstacle.

ಆಮ 1. s. a. Raw; uncooked; unripe. n. Constipation; passing unhealthy excretions (mucus); sickness. -ರಕ್ತ, -ಶಂಕೆ. Dysentery. -ಸೋಲು. A sour sauce or seasoning made of tamarind.

ಆಮ 2. k. n. A potter's kiln.

ಆಮದು h. n. Coming; income; import.

ಆಮಂತ್ರ, ಆಮಂತ್ರಣ s. n. Welcome. 2, invitation.

ಆಮಯ s. n. Sickness, disease.

ಆಮಲಕ s. n. The plant *Emblic myrobalan* (= ನೆಲ್ಲಿ).

ಆಮವಡೆ (tb. of ಆಮವಟಿ) n. A kind of cake made of split pulse mixed with spices, fried in ghee or oil and soaked in curds.

ಆಮಾತ್ಯ s. n. A minister, counsellor.

ಆಮಾಶಯ s. n. The stomach.

ಆಮಿಷ s. n. Flesh. 2, a bribe. 3, a gift. 4, desire.

ಆಮಿಾನ. = ಅಮಿಾನ, q. v.

ಆಮಿಾಲ h. n. A native revenue officer.

ಆಮುಷ್ಮಿಕ s. a. Belonging to the other world.

ಆಮೂಲ s. ad. By the root, entirely.

ಆಮೆ k. n. A tortoise, turtle.

ಆಮೋದ s. a. Gladdening. n. Pleasure, joy. 2, fragrance. ಆಮೋದಿಸು. To be glad; to smell at.

ಆಂಬರ (tb. ಅಮ್ಲ) n. Pepper water with tamarind.

ಆಂಬೋಡೆ See ಆಮವಡೆ.

ಆಮ್ಲ, ಆಮ್ಲಿಕೆ s. n. The tamarind tree. 2, sourness, acidity.

ಆಯ 1. s. k. n. The inside; the vital part of the body. 2, detail, particulars. -ಕಟ್ಟು. Structure of tenderness.

ಆಯ 2. k. n. Measure, dimension, extent; rule, order; fitness. 2, craftiness, deceit. -ಕಟ್ಟು. Properness, suitableness; measure, extent. -ಗಾರ. A clever man. -ಕಟ್ಟುಗಾರ. A man who does his work properly.

ಆಯ 3. s. n. Revenue. 2, profit. -ಸಾಮ್ಯ, -ಸ್ವಾಮ್ಯ. Corn given by the villagers to the hereditary servants of the village as their established fees of office. -ಗಾರ. A hereditary village servant.

ಆಯತ 1., ಆಯತ್ತ 1. k. n. Fitness. 2, readiness. 3, ease. [diffuse.

ಆಯತ 2. s. a. Checked. 2, extended;

ಆಯತನ s. n. A place, seat, home. 2, an altar. 3, a temple.

ಆಯತ್ತ 2. s. a. Dependent on. 2, docile.

ಆಯಾಸ s. n. Effort, exertion; trouble. 2, fatigue. -ಗೊಳ್ಳು, -ಪಾಗು, -ಪಡು. To become weary.

ಆಯಿ 1. h. n. A mother.

ಆಯಿ 2, ಆಯು 1. k. n. Collecting. v. t. To collect, gather; to select. P. p. ಆದು. -ಕೆ, -ವಿಕೆ. Selecting. ಆದುಕೊಳ್ಳು. To select for one's self. ಆಯಿಸು. To cause to choose. -ಕುಳಿ. A beggar.

ಆಯಿತು, ಆಯಿತ್ತು k. (*3rd pers. sing. past t. of* ಆಗು). It became, it is done, *etc.*

ಆಯು 2., ಆಯುಷ್ಯ, ಆಯುಸ್ s. n. Life; age, duration of life. -ವಂತ, ಆಯುಷ್ಮಂತ. Long-lived. ಆಯುರಾರೋಗ್ಯ. Long life and health. ಆಯುರ್ದಾಯ. The term of life. -ಹೀನ, ಆಯುಹೀನ. Short-lived.

ಆಯುಧ s. n. A weapon. 2, a tool. -ಶಾಲೆ. An arsenal. -ಪಾಣಿ, -ಧಾರಿ, -ಸ್ಥ, ಆಯುಧಿಕ. A soldier. -ಧರಿಸು. To arm.

ಆಯುರ್ವೇದ s. n. Medicine. ಆಯುರ್ವೇದಿ. A physician.

ಆರ (*Inf. of* ಆರ್ *to be filled, teem*) k. *aff.* To the full, *as:* ಕಣ್ಣಾರ, ಕಿವಿಯಾರ, ಮನಸ್ಸಾರ, *etc.* -ಗಾಡು. A perfect wild; a place never cultivated.

ಆರಡಿ a. k. n. Publicity; infamy, scandal.

ಆರಣ್ಯ s. a. Relating to a forest. n. A forest. -ಕ. A woodman.

ಆರತಿ, ಆರ್ತಿ (*tb. of* ಆರಾತ್ರಿಕ) n. The ceremony of waving (around an idol or person) a burning lamp. *Cpds:* ದೀಪಾರತಿ, ಧೂಪಾರತಿ, ಮಂಗಳಾರತಿ. -ಎತ್ತು, -ಬೆಳಗು, -ಮಾಡು. Ârati to wave. -ಕೊಡು. Â. to offer.

ಆರಬ್ಧ s. a. Begun. n. Beginning. ಆರಭ್ಯ. Beginning from.

ಆರಂಬ, ಆರಂಬು k. n. Tillage, cultivation. -ಗಾರ. A cultivator, farmer.

ಆರಂಭ s. n. Beginning, commencement. 2, effort. -ವಾಗು, ಆರಂಭಿಸು. To begin.

ಆರಯಿಸು, ಆರೈಸು k. v. t. To expect, look for, take care of.

ಆರಯು, ಆರಯ್ಯು k. v. t. To search; to investigate, consider; to look to; to nourish. ಆರಯ್ಕೆ. Searching; fostering.

ಆರವಾರ k. n. Bawling. 2, (f.) a mortgage with possession.

ಆರಾಟ (ರ = ಱ) a. k. n. The anxiety of a sick man.

ಆರಾತಿ s. n. An enemy.

ಆರಾಧಕ s. n. A worshipper.

ಆರಾಧನೆ s. n. Service, worship. ಆರಾಧಿಸು. To worship, adore (ಪೂಜಿಸು).

ಆರಾಧ್ಯ s. a. To be worshipped or served. n. A class of Śaiva Brâhmaṇas.

ಆರಾಮ s. n. Repose. 2, pleasure. 3, a grove, garden.

ಆರಿಕೆ k. n. The Indian millet, *Panicum italicum.*

ಆರಿದ್ರ. *tb. of* ಆರ್ದ್ರಾ.

ಆರಿಸು k. v. t. To collect, gather; to pick out, choose. 2, (ರ = ಱ) to quench, allay; to heal.

ಆರು 1. k. n. Fullness, abundance. *ad.* Fully. *Cpds:* ನೂರಾರು, ಸಾವಿರಾರು.

ಆರು. 2. = ಯಾರು.

ಆರು 3. k. n. A pair of oxen yoked to the plough. 2, a frame put on the neck of cattle. *v. i.* To cry aloud. -ಹೂಡು, -ಕಟ್ಟು. To yoke oxen to a plough.

ಆರು 4. (ರು=ಱು) k. *v. i.* To go out, be extinguished. 2, to grow cool. 3, to dry. 4, to heal. ಆರಿಹೋಗು. To dry up, *etc.* ಆರಬಿಡು, ಆರಿಡು, ಆರಿಕ್ಕು. To put out to dry.

ಆರು 5. (ರು=ಱು) k. *a.* Six. ಆರಡಿ. Six feet: the dark blue bee. ಆರನೆಯ. Sixth. *Cpds.:* -ಗಂಟು, -ದಳ, -ದಾಡೆ, -ನೂರು, -ರುತು, -ವರ್ಣ, -ಸಾವಿರ, *etc.*

ಆರೂಢ s. *a.* Mounted, ascended.

ಆರೆ 1. k. *n.* A shrub, *Bauhinia racemosa.*

ಆರೆ 2. f. *n.* A shoemaker's knife. 2, Mahratta. -ಕಾರ. A Mahratta man.

ಆರೆ 3. = ಆರ. 2, *pl. of* ಆನೆ 1.

ಆರೋಗಣೆ k. *n.* Eating; a meal (= ಭೋಜನ). -ಮಾಡು, ಆರೋಗಿಸು. To eat.

ಆರೋಗ್ಯ s. *n.* Health. *a.* Wholesome. -ಗೊಳಿಸು. To make healthy. -ಕರ, -ಕಾರಕ. Healthy, wholesome.

ಆರೋಪ, ಆರೋಪಣ s. *n.* An accusation, charge. ಆರೋಪಿ. An accused person. -ತರು, ಆರೋಪಿಸು. To apply, ascribe; to accuse.

ಆರೋಹ, ಆರೋಹಣ s. *n.* Rising, mounting, ascending; a ladder. ಆರೋಹಿಸು. To ascend.

ಆರ್ಭು k. *v. i.* To cry aloud. 2, (=ಆರಿಸು No. 2) to quench.

ಆರ್ಜನೆ s. *n.* Acquiring. ಆರ್ಜಿಸು. To acquire.

ಆರ್ಜವ s. *n.* Honesty, rectitude. 2, flattery.

ಆರ್ತ s. *a.* Afflicted, distressed; unhappy; full of desire. -ವ. Seasonable. -ಸ್ವರ. Cry of pain.

ಆರ್ತಿ s. *n.* Pain, sickness. 2, desire. 3, = ಆರತಿ, *q. v.*

ಆರ್ದ್ರ s. *a.* Wet, moist; fresh; soft. -ಕ. Green ginger. -ಕ. Green ginger. -ಗೊಳಿಸು. To moisten. -ತ್ವ. -ಭಾವ. Moisture.

ಆರ್ದ್ರ s. *n.* The sixth lunar mansion.

ಆರ್ಭ a. k. *n.* Might, force, valour (ಪರಾಕ್ರಮ).

ಆರ್ಭು, ಆರ್ಭಟ k. *n.* Crying aloud, roaring. ಆರ್ಭಟಿಸು, ಆರ್ಭಡಿಸು. To cry aloud.

ಆರ್ಯ s. *n.* A respectable, venerable man, an Ârya. 2, a man of good family. 3, an elder. ಆರ್ಯಾವರ್ತ. The abode of the Âryas, the country between the Himâlaya and the Vindhya mountains.

ಆರ್ಷ s. *n.* A certain form of marriage. ಆರ್ಷೇಯ. Venerable; very ancient.

ಆಲ k. *n.* The Banian, *Ficus indica;* ಆಲದ ಮರ. 2, the red water-lily. 3, (s.) animal poison.

ಆಲಂಬ, ಆಲಂಬನೆ s. *n.* Depending on. 2, support; assistance. -ಮಾಡು, ಆಲಂಬಿಸು. To lean upon; support. -ಕೊಡು. To give support. -ಹಚ್ಚಿಕೊಳ್ಳು. To patronize. ಆಲಂಬಿತ. Supported.

ಆಲಂಭ s. *n.* Seizing; killing.

ಆಲಯ s. *n.* An abode, house; an asylum. *Cpds.:* ದೇವಾಲಯ, ಹಿಮಾಲಯ, *etc.*

ಆಲಯಿಸು, ಆಲಿಯ್ಸು k. *v. i.* & *t.* To listen, attend to, mind.

ಆಲವಾಲ s. *n.* A trench for water round the foot of a tree.

ಆಲಸ್ಯ s. *n.* Idleness, indolence; weariness, languor. -ಗಾರ. A lazy man; sickly man. -ತನ. = ಆಲಸ್ಯ. -ವಾಗು. To be slow. -ಮಾಡು. To delay.

ಆಲಾಪ, ಆಲಾಪನೆ s. *n.* Speech, conversation. 2, lamentation. 3, the prelude in music. ಆಲಾಪಿಸು. To converse; to lament.

ಆಲಿ 1. k. *n.* The pupil of the eye. 2, an inflammation of the eye. -ಕಲ್ಲು. (=ಆಣೆಕಲ್ಲು) A hailstone.

ಆಲಿ 2. s. *n.* A bee. 2, a female friend. 3, desire. 4, a line. 5, a bridge; dike.

ಆಲಿಂಗನ s. *n.* Embracing, clasping; an embrace. -ಮಾಡು, ಆಲಿಂಗಿಸು. To embrace.

ಆಲಿಸು. = ಆಲಯಿಸು, *q. v.*

ಆಲು s. *n.* A small water-jar. 2, an esculent root, *Arum campanulatum.*

3, one who possesses, *as:* ಕರುಣಾಲು, ದಯಾಲು. -ಗಡ್ಡೆ. A potato.

ಆಲೆ k. *n.* A sugar-cane mill. 2, the lobe of the ear.

ಆಲೋಕ, ಆಲೋಕನ s. *n.* Looking; sight, aspect. 2, light, lustre. ಆಲೋಕಿಸು. To behold. ಆಲೋಕಿತ. Seen.

ಆಲೋಚನೆ s. *n.* Thought; opinion; intention; counsel. -ಮಾಡು, ಆಲೋಚಿಸು. To think, consider. -ಕೊಡು, -ಹೇಳು. To give one's opinion.

ಆಲೋಡನ s. *n.* Mixing; stirring. 2, acquaintance, experience.

ಆವ, ಆವಂ (= ಯಾವ) a. k. *pro.* What? which? ಆವನಾನೊಬ್ಬ. Whoever. ಆವಲ್ಲಿ (= ಎಲ್ಲಿ). Where? ಆವಾಗ. When? ಆವುದಾನೊಂದು. Whatsoever. ಆವುದು. What?

ಆವಗಂ a. k. *ad.* Whenever, always. 2, further.

ಆವರಣ s. *a.* Covering; veiling; enclosing. *n.* A fence, railing; a bolt. ಆವರಿಸು. To cover, conceal, enclose.

ಆವರಿ. = ಆವಿ 1, *q. v.*

ಆವರ್ಜಾ, ಆವರ್ಜೆ h. *n.* A head in the ledger.

ಆವರ್ತ s. *n.* Turning, revolving. 2, a whirlpool.

ಆವರ್ತನ s. *n.* Turning, repeating.

ಆವರ್ತಿ s. *n.* A turn, time. -ಮಾಡು. To repeat, as a lesson.

ಆವಲಿ, ಆವಳಿ s. *n.* A row, range, line. 2, a series. 3, a heap.

ಆವಶ್ಯಕ s. *a.* Necessary, inevitable. *n.* Need.

ಆವಾಗ (*fr.* ಆವ) k. *ad.* When.

ಆವಾಪ s. *n.* Scattering. 2, a trench for water at the root of a tree (= ಆಲವಾಲ). 3, a bracelet.

ಆವಾಸ s. *n.* An abode, dwelling.

ಆವಾಹನ s. *n.* Inviting; invoking a deity to occupy an image.

ಆವಿ (= ಆವರಿ) k. *n.* Steam, vapour; heat. 2, a potter's kiln.

ಆವಿರ್ಭವ s. *n.* Becoming manifest. ಆವಿರ್ಭವಿಸು. To be manifest; to be born.

ಆವಿರ್ಭೂತ s. *a.* Become visible.

ಆವು k. *n.* A cow. *pro.* We.

ಆವುತಿ. *tb. of* ಆಹುತಿ, *q. v.*

ಆವೃತ s. *a.* Enclosed, covered. ಆವೃತಿ. Covering. 2, an edition, *as* of a book.

ಆವೃತ್ತ s. *a.* Turned round, averted.

ಆವೃತ್ತಿ s. *n.* Repetition. 2, revolution. 3, an edition, *as,* of a book.

ಆವೆ (= ಆಮೆ) k. *n.* A turtle, tortoise. -ಚಿಪ್ಪು. A tortoise shell.

ಆವೇಗ s. *n.* Hurry; agitation.

ಆವೇಶ s. *n.* Entering, taking possession of. 2, demoniacal frenzy; excitement. 3, pride. -ತುಂಬು, -ಬರು, -ಆಗು. To be possessed by a demon.

ಆವೇಷ s. *n.* Pervading; visiting.

ಆವೇಷ್ಟನ s. *n.* Surrounding, wrapping; a wrapper; an enclosure. ಆವೇಷ್ಟಿಸು. To surround, wrap.

ಆಶ. *tb. of* ಆಸೆ, *q. v.*

ಆಶಂಸನ s. *n.* Wishing. 2, declaring. ಆಶಂಸೆ. Wish, desire, hope; declaration.

ಆಶಯ s. *n.* A resting place; an asylum; a receptacle. 2, meaning, intention. 3, will. 4, property.

ಆಶಾಪಾಶ, ಆಶಾಬಂಧ s. *n.* The snare of lust.

ಆಶಾಭಂಗ s. *n.* Disappointment.

ಆಶಿಸು s. *v. t.* To desire, wish. 2, to bless.

ಆಶೀರ್ವಚನ, ಆಶೀರ್ವಾದ s. *n.* A blessing, benediction. -ಕೊಡು, -ಮಾಡು, ಆಶೀರ್ವದಿಸು. To bless.

ಆಶು s. *a.* Quick, fast. *n.* Haste. -ಗ. The wind; the sun.

ಆಶೆ s. *n.* Wish, desire; expectation, hope. -ಗೊಳ್ಳು, -ಪಡು, -ಮಾಡು. To desire. -ಕೊಡು, -ತೋರಿಸು. To hold out hopes. -ಕೆಡಿಸು. To disappoint. -ನಿಂತು ಹೋಗು. To despair.

ಆಶೌಚ (*fr.* ಅಶುಚಿ) s. *n.* Impurity.

ಆಶ್ಚರ್ಯ s. *a.* Curious, marvellous. *n.* Wonder; surprise, astonishment.

-ಗೊಳ್ಳು, -ಪಡು. To be surprised. -ಕರ. Surprising.

ಆಶ್ಮ (fr. ಅಶ್ಮ) s. a. Stony, made of stone.

ಆಶ್ರಮ s. n. A hermitage. 2, one of the four religious orders, i. e. ಬ್ರಹ್ಮಚಾರಿ, ಗೃಹಸ್ಥ, ವಾನಪ್ರಸ್ಥ, ಸನ್ಯಾಸಿ.

ಆಶ್ರಯ (tb. ಆಸರ, ಆಸರೆ) s. n. Depending on; a support, shelter, refuge; protection. -ಕೊಡು. To afford help. -ಗೊಳ್ಳು. To have recourse to for shelter. ಆಶ್ರಯಿಸು. To join; to obtain; to follow; to approach for protection.

ಆಶ್ರವ s. n. Stream, flow. 2, distress. 3, a promise. a. Obedient, compliant.

ಆಶ್ರಿತ s. a. Resorting to; having sought the protection of; protected; being dependant on. n. A dependant.

ಆಶ್ಲೇಷ s. n. An embrace. 2, N. of the 9th lunar mansion.

ಆಶ್ವಯುಜ, ಆಶ್ವಿನ, ಆಶ್ವೀಜ s. n. The 7th lunar month (September-October).

ಆಶ್ವಾಸ s. n. Breathing. 2, encouraging, consolation; also -ನ. 3, a chapter of a book. ಆಶ್ವಾಸಿಸು. To breathe; to comfort.

ಆಷಾಢ s. n. The 4th lunar month (June-July). 2, an ascetic's staff. -ಭೂತಿ. A cheat, scamp.

ಆಷಾಗ್ರಿ (tb. ಆಸಡಿ) s. n. The plant *Asparagus racemosus*.

ಆಸಕ್ತ s. a. Devotedly attached to. 2, zealously pursuing.

ಆಸಕ್ತಿ s. n. Attachment; diligence, zeal. ಆಸಕ್ತಿಯಿಂದಿರು. To be ardently devoted to.

ಆಸಡಿ, tb. of ಆಷಾಢಿ, q. v.

ಆಸನ s. n. Sitting; sitting as devotees in peculiar postures. 2, a seat, stool, chair. *Cpds.:* ಕೂರ್ಮಾಸನ, ಗರುಡಾಸನ, ಪದ್ಮಾಸನ, ಸಿಂಹಾಸನ, *etc.*

ಆಸನ್ನ s. a. Sat down; closely united; near.

ಆಸಪಾಕ (tb. of ಆಸ್ಯಪಾಕ) n. Aphthous [disease.

ಆಸಪ್ರಾಸ s. n. Gasping, panting.

ಆಸರ, ಆಸರೆ. tb. of ಆಶ್ರಯ, q. v.

ಆಸರು (ರು = ಱು) k. v. i. To be weary or fatigued. P. p. ಆಸತ್ತು. n. Weariness, fatigue. -ಬೇಸರ. *dupl.* Fatigue. -ಪಡು. To be tired. ಆಸಗಳೆ. To remove fatigue, to rest.

ಆಸವ s. n. Distilling. 2, spirituous liquor.

ಆಸಾದನ s. n. Laying down; meeting with; obtaining.

ಆಸಾಮಿ h. n. A person or individual.

ಆಸಾರ s. n. Incursion. 2, a heavy fall of rain. 3, provision, food. -ಮಳೆ. A kind of hail.

ಆಸು k. n. The sâl tree, *Shorea robusta.*

ಆಸುರ 1. a. k. n. Increase, abundance; strength. 2, annoyance, trouble.

ಆಸುರ 2. (fr. ಅಸುರ) s. a. Relating to evil spirits. n. A form of marriage.

ಆಸೆ (tb. of ಆಶೆ, q. v.) -ಗೆಯ್ಯು. To shelter, protect. -ಗೊಳ್ಳಿಸು. To allure. -ಬಡಕತನ. Avarice. -ಮಾಡು. To desire. -ಗಾರ, -ಬಡಕ. A covetous man.

ಆಸೇವನ, ಆಸೇವೆ s. n. Attending to; assiduous practice; commerce.

ಆಸ್ತರಣ s. n. Spreading. 2, a carpet. 3, a layer.

ಆಸ್ತಿ s. n. Property, wealth. -ಪಾಸ್ತಿ. *redl.* -ಕ. A believer in God and another world, a theist; a man of property; pious, faithful. -ಕ್ಯ. Theism. -ಗಾರ, -ವಂತ. A man of property.

ಆಸ್ಥಾನ s. n. Place, site. 2, an assembly. ಆಸ್ಥಾನಿಕ. A courtier.

ಆಸ್ಥೆ s. n. An assembly. 2, care. 3, effort. 4, condition.

ಆಸ್ಪತ್ರೆ f. n. The English "hospital".

ಆಸ್ಪದ s. n. Place. 2, position. 3, business. 4, basis, occasion, opportunity. -ಕೊಡು. To allow.

ಆಸ್ಫೋಟ, ಆಸ್ಫೋಟನ s. n. Moving to and fro, flapping; clapping the arms; knocking, as at a door. ಆಸ್ಫೋಟನಿ. A gimlet.

ಆಸ್ಯ s. n. The mouth; the face. -ಪಾಕ. (= ಆಸಪಾಕ) Sore mouth. ಆಸ್ಯಾಸವ. Spittle, saliva.

ಆಸ್ವಾದ, ಆಸ್ವಾದನ s. n. Tasting, eating; flavour. ಆಸ್ವಾದಿಸು. To taste; to enjoy.

ಆಹ್‌ k. int. of dislike: Fy!

ಆಹತ s. a. Struck. 2, multiplied. 3, known. n. New cloth. 2, a drum. -ಲಕ್ಷಣ. Noted for good qualities.

ಆಹರ, ಆಹರಣ s. n. Bringing, fetching. 2, seizing; robbing. ಆಹರಿಸು. To take away, rob.

ಆಹವ s. n. Summoning; challenging. 2, war, battle. 3, sacrifice. ಆಹವಂಗೊಡು. To challenge. ಆಹವಿ. A warrior.

ಆಹಾ s. int. of surprise, pity or sorrow.

ಆಹಾರ s. n. Taking food. 2, food. -ತಕ್ಕೊಳ್ಳು. To take food. -ಪಚನ. Digestion. -ಸಂಭವ. The chyle. ಆಹಾರಿಸು. To eat.

ಆಹುತಿ (tb. ಅವುತಿ) s. n. Oblations offering; an oblation to the deities. -ಈ, -ಕೊಡು. To offer an oblation. -ತಕ್ಕೊಳ್ಳು. To receive an offering.

ಆಹೂತಿ s. n. Calling; summoning.

ಆಹೋ k. int. of wonder or surprise.

ಆಹ್ನಿಕ s. a. Daily. n. A religious ceremony to be performed every day.

ಆಹ್ಲಾದ (tb. ಅಹಲ್ಲಾದ) s. n. Joy, delight. -ಕರ, -ಕಾರಿ. Gladdening. -ವಾಗು. To be glad. -ಪಡಿಸು. To make glad.

ಆಳ (ಳ = ಡ) k. n. Depth. 2, humiliation. -ನೋಡು, -ಹಿಡಿ. To sound the depth. -ಪಳ್ಳ, -ಹಳ್ಳ. A deep tank.

ಆಳವೇರಿ. = ಅಳುವೇರಿ.

ಆಳಂಬೆ k. n. A mushroom.

ಆಳವಾಳ. = ಆಲವಾಲ, q. v.

ಆಳಿ 1. k. An affix for forming nouns, as ಓಪಾಳಿ, ಜೂಪಾಳಿ, ಮಾತಾಳಿ, ಕೇಡಾಳಿ; etc.

ಆಳಿ 2. (ಳ = ಡ) a. k. n. Depth. 2, craftiness, trickery. -ಕೊಡು. To deceive. -ಕೊಳುಹ. Deceit.

ಆಳಿ 3. (ಳ = ಡ) a. k. n. Contempt, disgrace. -ಗೊಳ್‌. To despise.

ಆಳಿಕೆ k. n. Rule; reign.

ಆಳಿದಾಳಿ (ಳ = ಡ) k. n. Tumult, noise.

ಆಳಿಂದಕಿ (= ಅಳಿಲು) k. n. A squirrel.

ಆಳು 1. k. v. t. To get. 2, to hold. 3, to govern, rule, manage. P. p. ಆಳ್ದು. ಆಳಿಸು. To cause to rule. -ತನ, -ವಿಕೆ, ಆಳ್ತನ. Ruling, reign; service. ಆಳ್ದ, ಆಳ್ವ. A ruler, master.

ಆಳು 2. k. n. A servant; a soldier; a messenger. 2, a grown up person in general. Cpds.: ಕಾಲಾಳು, ಬಿಲ್ಲಾಳು, ಕೂಲಿಯಾಳು, etc. -ಕೆಲಸ. Drudgery; work done by servants. -ಮಗ. A servant. ಆಳ್ವಲ್ಮೆ. Manly strength.

ಆಳು 3. (ಳು = ಡು) a. k. v. i. To sink in a fluid; to immerse, dive; to be deep.

ಆಳುವೇರಿ (= ಅಳವೇರಿ, ಅಳುವೇರಿ, ಆಳವೇರಿ) k. n. A merlon of a fort.

ಇ

ಇ. k. The third letter of the alphabet. 2, the final of many Kannaḍa nominal bases, verbal themes, etc., as: ಗಾಳಿ, ಕನ್ನಡಿ, ನುಡಿ, ಉರಿ, ಇಲ್ಲಿ, ಅಲ್ಲಿ, etc. 3, a prox. pro. adj. as in ಇಗೋ, ಇದು, ಇವ, etc. 4, the termination of the p. p. (gerund) of verbs ending in ಉ, as: ಎತ್ತಿ, ಮುತ್ತಿ, ಸಾರಿಸಿ, ಅಂಜಿಸಿ, etc. 5, an auxiliary letter to form the dative, as: ಅವನಿಗೆ ಅವರಿಗೆ, etc. 6, a termination for the 2nd pers. pl. imperat., as: ಇರಿ, ಮಾಡಿ, ಹೋಗಿ, etc. 7, an affix to form feminines, as: ಗಾತಿ, ಗಿತ್ತಿ, ಹೆಂಡತಿ, etc.

ಇಂ k. An auxiliary syllable to form the genitive, dative, locative singular, preceding their final ಅ, ಗೆ, ಒಳ್‌ or ಅಲ್ಲಿ

respectively, as: ಗುರುವಿನ, ಗೋವಿನ; ಲೇಸಿಂಗೆ, ಗುರುವಿಂಗೆ; ಮಾತಿನೊಳ್, ಕರ್ತೃವಿನೊಳ್, ಗುರುವಿನಲ್ಲಿ, ಊರಿನಲ್ಲಿ; *and to form the instrumental sing. and plur., either following the shorter or the common longer form of the genitive, as:* ರೂಪಿನಿಂದ, ಕಾಲಿನಿಂದ, ವಿದ್ವಾಂಸರಿಂದ, *etc.*

ಇಕ್ (= ಇಚ್, ಇತ್, ಇಮ್, *etc.*) a. k. Two. ಇಕ್ಕಟ್ಟು. Two ways or parties; narrowness, strait; dilemma. ಇಕ್ಕಟ್ಟುಮುಕ್ಕಟ್ಟು. Many difficulties. ಇಕ್ಕಡೆ, ಇಕ್ಕೆಲ. Both sides. ಇಕ್ಕಣ್ಣು. Both eyes. ಇಕ್ಕರೆ. Both banks. ಇಕ್ಕಾಲು. Both legs. ಇಕ್ಕೆಯ್. Both arms.

ಇಕಾರ s. The letter ಇ.

ಇಕೆ 1. k. *An affix for the formation of neuter nouns, as:* ಹುಡುಗಾಟಿಕೆ, ಬುದ್ಧಿವಂತಿಕೆ, ಹೆಚ್ಚಿಕೆ, *etc.*

ಇಕೆ 2. (= ಇಕ್ಕೆ) k. *An affix to form the dative of the infinitive with final* ಅಲು, *as:* ಮಾಡಲಿಕೆ, ಹೋಗಲಿಕೆ, ಹೇಳಲಿಕೆ *etc.*

ಇಕೊ, ಇಕೋ, ಇಗೋ k. *int.* Look here! lo! behold!

ಇಕ್ಕಟ್ಟು (*see s.* ಇಕ್). k. *n.* Strait, dilemma. ಇಕ್ಕಟ್ಟಿನ ಸ್ಥಳ. A narrow passage. ಇಕ್ಕಟ್ಟಾಗು. To be strait.

ಇಕ್ಕರಿಸು k. *v. i.* To sound. *v. t.* To kill.

ಇಕ್ಕಳ (ಳ=ೞ) k. *n.* Tongs, pincers.

ಇಕ್ಕು k. *v. t.* To put, place; to beat; to serve, *as* food; to give, *as* money, alms, *etc.;* to abandon; to be put. 2, to kill. ಇಕ್ಕಿಡು, ಇಕ್ಕಿರಿಸು. To put aside, lay by. ಇಕ್ಕಿಸು. To cause to put, *etc.* ಇಕ್ಕುಹ. Putting, *etc.*

ಇಕ್ಕೆ 1. k. *n.* Abiding; an abode, a place of rest or refuge (= ಆಶ್ರಯ).

ಇಕ್ಕೆ 2. (= ಇಕೆ 2) k. *An affix of infinitive, as:* ಮಾಡಲಿಕ್ಕೆ, ಹೋಗಲಿಕ್ಕೆ, *etc.*

ಇಕ್ಕೇರಿ k. *n.* The residence of the kings of Bidanûr. -ವರಹ. A gold coin of that name.

ಇಕ್ಕೋ. = ಇಕೋ, *etc. q. v.*

ಇಕ್ಷು s. *n.* The sugar-cane; *also* -ದಂಡ. -ರಸ. Sugar-cane juice. -ಶರಾಸನ. Kâma.

ಇಕ್ಷ್ವಾಕು s. *n.* A bitter gourd. 2, N. of the first king of the solar dynasty.

ಇಗ k. *An affix to form masculines, as:* ಗಾಣಿಗ, ದಾಂಡಿಗ, ದಾಳಿಗ, ಹೂವಡಿಗ.

ಇಗರು k. *v. i.* To be evaporated, dried up. 2, to shoot, sprout. *n.* A sprout, germ. 2, the gums.

ಇಗರ್ಜಿ (= ಇಂಗ್ರೇಜಿ No. 2) f. *n.* A church.

ಇಗೋ. = ಇಕೋ *etc., q. v.*

ಇಂ, ಇಮ್ k. *n.* Sweetness; agreeableness. ಇಂಗಡಲ್. The sea of milk. ಇಂಗೋಲು. The sugar-cane.

ಇಂಕಾರು h. *n.* Refusal, denial, abnegation, disdain; *also* ಇನ್ಕಾರು. -ಮಾಡು, ಇಂಕರಿಸು. To deny, refuse.

ಇಂಕ್ರ k. *n.* A little.

ಇಂಗಡ (*tb. of* ವಿಘಟ. = ವಿಂಗಡ, *q. v.*) s. *n.* Separateness. ಇಂಗಡಿಸು. To separate.

ಇಂಗಲಿಕ, ಇಂಗಲೀಕ, ಇಂಗುಲಿಕ (*tb. of* ಹಿಂಗುಲ) *n.* Vermilion.

ಇಂಗಳ (*tb. of* ಅಂಗಾರ) *n.* Heated charcoal; fire. -ಗಣ್ಣ. Śiva. ಇಂಗಳಂಗೊಳ್ಳು. To catch fire.

ಇಂಗಿತ s. *n.* A hint, sign. 2, aim, intention, covert purpose. -ಜ್ಞ. Understanding signs, *etc.*

ಇಂಗು 1. k. *v. i.* To be imbibed; to soak into. 2, to dry up. 3, to boil away. 4, to give. ಇಂಗಿಸು. To evaporate; to cause to give.

ಇಂಗು 2. (*tb. of* ಹಿಂಗು) *n.* A perennial plant, *Ferula asafoetida.* -ಹಚ್ಚು, -ಹಾಕು. To deceive.

ಇಂಗ್ರೇಜಿ, ಇಂಗ್ಲೀಷು f. *n.* English. 2, (= ಇಗರ್ಜಿ) an "église", a Roman Catholic church.

ಇಜ a. k. *An affix to form masculines denoting* "born of", *as,* ಅಲರಿಜ (flower-born), Brahmâ.

ಇಚ್ಚ. = ಇಚ್ಛೆ. ಇಚ್ಚರಾಶಿ. A random figure, the third term in the rule of three.

ಇಚ್ಚಕ, ಇಚ್ಚಗ (*tb. of* ಇಚ್ಛಕ) *n.* Coaxing; flattery. 2, a flatterer. -ತನ. Flattering. -ಮಾಡು. To flatter, coax.

ಇಚ್ಚಯಿಸು (tb. of ಇಚ್ಛಯಿಸು) v. t. To desire, wish, covet.

ಇಚ್ಚೆ (tb. of ಇಚ್ಛೆ, q. v.). -ಗೊಳಿಸು. To allure. -ಕಾರ, -ಗಾರ. One who wishes or wills; a willing man; f. -ಗಾತಿ. -ತೀರು. A wish to be gratified.

ಇಚ್ಛೆ (tb. ಇಚ್ಚೆ) s. n. Wish, desire; inclination. 2, a question in mathematics. ಇಚ್ಛಾನುಸಾರ. According to one's wish. ಇಚ್ಛಾಪೂರ್ತಿ. Full gratification of one's desires.

ಇಜ್ k. a. Two. -ಜತೆ, -ಜೊತೆ, -ಜೋಡು. Unlikeness, dissimilarity, oddness.

ಇಜಾಫೆ h. n. Increase, augmentation.

ಇಜಾರ, ಇಜಾರು h. n. Trowsers, breeches.

ಇಜಾರೆ h. n. A contract, monopoly. ಇಜಾರದಾರ. A contractor, monopolist.

ಇಟಕು (=ಇಡಕು) k. n. Narrowness, straitness. v. t. To come within reach.

ಇಟ್ಟಣೆ, ಇಟ್ಟಳ a. k. n. A crowd, throng; abundance. 2, hindrance, strait. ಇಟ್ಟಣಿಸು, ಇಟ್ಟಳಿಸು. To be close, crowded; to throng.

ಇಟ್ಟಿ, ಇಟ್ಟಂಗಿ k. n. The vomit-nut tree, *Strychnos nux vomica*. 2, (tb. of ಯಷ್ಟಿ) a spear, lance.

ಇಟ್ಟಿಗೆ (tb. of ಇಷ್ಟಕ) n. A brick. -ಅಚ್ಚು. A brick mould. -ಗೂಡು, -ಬಟ್ಟಿ. A brick kiln. -ಮಾಡು. Brick to make. -ಯವ. A brick-maker.

ಇಟ್ಟೆಡೆ, ಇಟ್ಟೆಡೆ k. n. Narrowness; a strait, obstacle.

ಇಡಕು k. v. t. To pinch; to press, beat, cuff. n. (= ಇಟಕು, q. v.) Narrowness; trouble.

ಇಡರು (= ಎಡರು) k. n. Hindrance, obstacle. 2, trouble. 3, enmity. v. i. (ರು = ಱು) To stumble.

ಇಡಿ k. v. i. To be close, heaped; to crowd; to abound. 2, to be powdered; to crumble. v. t. To pound. n. The state of being close. 2, the whole. 3, a collection, mass. 4, cement. -ಗಂಟು. A treasure. -ಸು. To cause to powder; to cause to put, erect, etc.

ಇಡು k. v. t. To put down; to throw. 2, to put, place; to give, as a name; to set, plant. 3, to put on; to lay by, keep; to preserve. 4, *at the end of certain words:* to produce, make, etc. n. (= ಇಡುವಿಕೆ). Putting; planting. ಇಟ್ಟುಕೊಳ್ಳು. To take into one's employ; to lay by, *as* money, *etc.;* to put on, keep. *Cpds.:* ಆಣೆಯಿಡು, to adjure; ಕೂಗಿಡು, to cry; ತೂಗಿಡು, to amass; ಮನಸ್ಸಿಡು, to mind; ಮೊರೆಯಿಡು, to invoke; ಮುದ್ದಿಡು, to kiss; ಆನಿಡು, to prop.

ಇಡುಕು, ಇಡುಗು (= ಇಡಕು) k. n. Narrowness. 2, a cattle-disease. 3, freedom. v. t. To unloose, set free. ಇಡುಕಿರು. A throng, crowd. -ಮುಡುಕು, ಇಡುಮುಡುಕು. A narrow curve or passage. -ತೊಡಗು. Full of difficulties.

ಇಡುಗೆ k. n. Putting on. 2, an ornament.

ಇಡುವು k. n. A crack, hole.

ಇಡೆ 1. = ಎಡೆ 1, q. v.

ಇಡೆ 2. f. n. The earth. 2, heaven. 3, an oblation, food. 4, a cow. 5, speech.

ಇಡ್ಡಲಿ, ಇಡ್ಡಲಿಗೆ, ಇಡ್ಡಳಿಗೆ k. n. A kind of sour pudding.

ಇಣಚಿ k. n. A squirrel.

ಇಣೆ, ಇಣಿ k. n. An ox's hump.

ಇಂಡೆ a. k. n. A crack; a piece, lump. 2, a wreath, garland.

ಇತ್ k. a. Two. ಇತ್ತಟ್ಟು. Both sides. ಇತ್ತಡಿ. Both banks. ಇತ್ತಂಡ. Both portions. ಇತ್ತರ. Two lines, both sides. ಇತ್ತಲೆ Two or both heads.

ಇತಬಾರಿ h. a. Trustworthy.

ಇತರ s. a. Other, different. 2, low, vulgar. -ತ್ರ. At an other place. ಇತರೇತರ. Mutual. ಇತರೇತರಕ್ರಿಯೆ. An action of two or more persons.

ಇತಿ 1. ಇತ್ತಿ k. *An affix to form feminines, as:* ಬಾಣತಿ, ಮುದಲಿಗಿತ್ತಿ, ಒಕ್ಕಲಗಿತ್ತಿ, *etc.*

ಇತಿ 2. s. *conj.* Therefore. 2, in conclusion, here ends. -ವ. Thus indeed.

ಇತಿಹಾಸ s. n. A legend, traditional account. -ಕಾರ. A historian, narrator.

ಇತು k. *A termination of the third pers. sing. neuter of the imperfect, as:* ಮಾಡಿತು, ಮುರಿಯಿತು, ಹೇಳಿತು, *etc.*

ಇತ್ತ (*prox. of* ಅತ್ತ) k. *ad.* This side; in this direction or place; after this, further; *also* ಇತ್ತಲು. -ಅತ್ತ. To and fro. -ಕಡೆ. This side. ಇತ್ತಿತ್ತ. *rep.* Nearer; in course of time. -ಲಾಗಿ, -ಲಾಗೆ. To this side; afterwards, lately, recently.

ಇತ್ತು k. *P. p. of* ಈ. Having given. 2, it was.

ಇತ್ಯರ್ಥ s. *n.* The whole matter; settlement, decision.

ಇತ್ಯಾದಿ s. *ad.* And so on, etc.

ಇದ, ಇದಕೊ, ಇದಿಗೋ k. *int.* Lo! look here!

ಇದಿರು (= ಎದುರು, *q. v.*) k. *n.* That which is opposite; the front; opposition. ಇದಿರಾಗು. To face. ಇದಿರಿಕ್ಕು, ಇದಿರಿಡು. To put in front; to oppose. ಇದಿರುತ್ತರ. Contradiction. -ನೋಡು. To look straight; to expect. ಇದಿರೊಡ್ಡಣ. The hostile army. ಇದಿರೊಡ್ಡು. To oppose. ಇದಿರ್ಗೊಳ್ಳು. To come to meet out of respect or love.

ಇದಿರಿಸು (= ಎದುರಿಸು), ಇದಿರ್ಚು k. *v. t.* To face; to oppose, withstand.

ಇದು k. *prox. dem. pro.* This, it.

ಇದುರು. = ಇದಿರು. -ವಾದಿ. A defendant. -ವಾದಿಸು. To contradict; to contend.

ಇದೆ k. *3rd pers. sing. pres. neut. of* ಇರು. It is, there is. 2, lo! just now.

ಇದ್ದಲಿ, ಇದ್ದಲು k. *n.* Charcoal.

ಇದ್ದು, (ಇರ್ದು) k. *P. p. of* ಇರು, to be. *By means of* ಇದ್ದು *a subjunctive mood is formed, as:* ಇದ್ದರೆ, if. ಇದ್ದಕಿದ್ದಹಾಗೆ. Just as it was; without any apparent cause.

ಇನ್ (= ಇಕ್ *etc.*) k. *n.* Two. 2, sweetness. ಇನ್ನೂರು. Two hundred.

ಇನ s. *n.* A master, king. 2, the sun. 3, a husband. -ಕುಮಾರ. Saturn; Yama; Karṇa; Sugrîva. -ರಿಪು. Râhu.

ಇನಾಮು, ಇನಾಮು h. *n.* A present, gift; a grant in general. ಇನಾಮತಿ. Land assigned either in favour or charity, or in compensation of the duties of hereditary office. -ದಾರ. A holder of an inâm.

ಇನಾಯತು h. *n.* Favour, grace; a grant. -ನಾಮೆ. A letter of favour.

ಇನಿ a. k. *n.* Sweetness; loveliness. ಇನಿದು. That is sweet; ambrosia.

ಇನಿತು, ಇನಿಸು (= ಇಷ್ಟು) k. *prox. dem. pro.* This much, this measure. 2, all this or these. 3, a little, a trifle. ಇನಿಬರು. So many persons (as these).

ಇಂತ 1, ಇಂತಾ. k. *An affix of comparison.* Than, *as:* ಇದಕ್ಕಿಂತ, ಮುಂಚೆಗಿಂತ, *etc.*

ಇಂತ 2, ಇಂತಹ. = ಇಂಥ.

ಇಂತೆ, ಇಂತು k. *ad.* Thus, so; in this manner; (*at the end of letters:*) in conclusion, *as:* ಇಂತಿ ಚಿನ್ನಹ, ಇಂತಿ ಸಲಾಂ. ಇಂತಪ್ಪ, ಇಂತಹ. = ಇಂಥ. Being of this kind, such. ಇಂತಿಷ್ಟು. So and so many or much; very much.

ಇಂಥ, ಇಂಥಾ (= ಇಂತಹ) k. *ad.* Such, like this, of this kind. ಇಂಥಿಂಥ. Such and such.

ಇಂದ (= ಇಂ) k. *An affix to form the instr. or abl. case, as:* ಅವನಿಂದ, ನನ್ನಿಂದ, ಮನುಷ್ಯರಿಂದ, ನನ್ನ ದೆಸೆಯಿಂದ, *etc.*

ಇಂದಿರ (*tb. of* ಇಂದ್ರ, *q.v.*). ಇಂದಿರಾ, ಇಂದಿರೆ. Lakshmî.

ಇಂದೀವರ s. *n.* The blue lotus.

ಇಂದು 1. k. *ad.* This time; to-day. ಇಂದಿಗೆ. For to-day. -ತನಕ, -ವರೆಗೆ. Till to-day. ಇಂದಿನಿಂದ. From to-day.

ಇಂದು 2. s. *n.* The moon. -ಕಳೆ, -ರೇಖೆ. A digit of the moon. -ಕಾಂತ. The lunar gem. -ಜನಕ. The ocean. -ಮಂಡಲ. The disk of the moon. -ವಾರ. Monday.

ಇಂದ್ರ (*tb.* ಇಂದಿರ) s. *n.* Indra, the deity of svarga, and the regent of the East quarter. 2, a prince. *a.* Best, excellent. -ಕೀಲ. N. of a mountain. -ಕೋಶ. A platform, terrace. -ಗೋಪ. The cochineal insect; the firefly. -ಜಾಲ. Indra's net: deception, fraud, trick; jugglery. -ಜಿತ್. Conqueror of Indra!

a son of Râvaṇa. -ಧನುಸ್, -ಚಾಪ. A rainbow. -ನೀಲ. A sapphire. -ಪುರ, -ಲೋಕ. Heaven. ಇಂದ್ರಾಣಿ. Indra's wife.

ಇಂದ್ರಿಯ s. n. Relating to Indra. 2, power; faculty. 3, an organ of sense. -ನಿಗ್ರಹ. Restraint of the organs of sense. -ನಿಗ್ರಹ ಮಾಡು. To restrain them. -ನಿಗ್ರಹಿ. One who restrains them. *Cpds.*: ಜ್ಞಾನೇಂದ್ರಿಯ, ಕರ್ಮೇಂದ್ರಿಯ, *etc.*

ಇಂಧನ s. n. Kindling. 2, fuel.

ಇನ್ನು k. *ad.* Further, yet, still; moreover; hereafter. *n.* The current time. ಇನ್ನಷ್ಟು. So much more. ಇನ್ನಿಲ್ಲ. No more, no longer; not yet. -ಮುಂದೆ, -ಮೇಲೆ. Henceforth, hereafter. ಇನ್ನೆಲ್ಲಿ. Where else? ಇನ್ನೊಂದು. Another thing. ಇನ್ನೊಬ್ಬ. Another man. ಇನ್ನೊಮ್ಮೆ. Once more, again.

ಇಪ್ಪ a. k. (= ಇರುವ) *Pres. rel. part. of* ಇರು. Being, *etc.*

ಇಪ್ಪತ್ತು k. *a.* Twenty. *Cpds.* ಇಪ್ಪತ್ತೊಂದು, ಇಪ್ಪತ್ತೆರಡು. *etc.*

ಇಪ್ಪೆ, ಇಪ್ಪೆಯ ಮರ k. n. The tree *Bassia latifolia.*

ಇಬ್ (= ಇರ್). k. *a.* Two. ಇಬ್ಬಗೆ. Two divisions. ಇಬ್ಬಂದಿ. Mongrel: of low descent; double-tongued. ಇಬ್ಬರು. Two persons. ಇಬ್ಬಳ. Two baḷas. ಇಬ್ಬಾಯಿ. Two mouths, double edge. ಇಬ್ಬಿಬ್ಬರು. Two and two persons.

ಇಬಡಿ, ಇಬ್ಬಡಿ k. n. A kind of blackwood tree.

ಇಬನಿ, ಇಬ್ಬನಿ k. n. Fog, mist, dew.

ಇಬ್ಭಾಗ (*fr.* ಇದ್-ಭಾಗ). k. n. Two parts.

ಇಭ s. n. An elephant. -ಪುರ. = ಹಸ್ತಿನಾಪುರ.

ಇಮ್ 1. (= ಇನ್) k. *a.* Sweet. ಇಮ್ಮಾವು. A sweet mango. ಇಮ್ಮೊರೆ. An entreaty in sweet, humble words.

ಇಮ್ 2. k. *a.* Two. ಇಮ್ಮಡಿ, ಇರ್ಮಡಿ. Two fold, double. ಇಮ್ಮಡಿ ಮಾಡು, ಇಮ್ಮಡಿಸು. To double. ಇಮ್ಮಿಗಿಲ್. Twice as much. ಇಮ್ಮೆಯ್. Two sides, *as* of a cloth.

ಇಮರು, ಇಮಿರು, ಇಮುರು k. *v. i.* To evaporate, dry up; to wane, waste away.

ಇಮಾರತು h. n. An edifice; a palace.

ಇಮೆ a. k. n. The eyelid.

ಇಂಪು, ಇಮ್ಮು k. n. Sweetness; agreeableness, pleasantness. -ಪಡೆ. To become nice. ಇಂಪಾಗಿ, ಇಮ್ಮನೆ. Sweetly (ಕಿವಿಗಿಂಪಾಗಿ, melodiously).

ಇಂಬ k. n. Expansion, width, breadth.

ಇಂಬು 1. k. n. A resting place; a home; a place; space, room (ಆಶ್ರಯ). ಇಂಬಾಗು. To become a shelter; to give room. -ಗೊಡು. To give place; to afford shelter. -ಗೊಳಿಸು. To place.

ಇಂಬು 2. (= ಎಂಬು) k. n. A saying, word.

ಇಮ್ಮನೆ k. *ad.* In a sweet, agreeable or proper manner.

ಇಮ್ಮು (= ಇಮ್ 1, ಇಂಪು, *q. v.*) k. n. Sweetness; ambrosia.

ಇಮ್ಮೆ k. *a.* Twice.

ಇಯತ್ತೆ f. n. Quantity.

ಇರಕು, ಇರುಕು, ಇರುಂಕು (ರ = ಱ) k. *v. i.* To be compressed, squeezed. (= ಇರಕಿಸು) *v. t.* To press, squeeze. *n.* The state of being squeezed. 2, butting.

ಇರಚಲು (ರ = ಱ) k. n. A driving rain.

ಇರಟು. = ಇರಳು, *q. v.*

ಇರವಂತಿಗೆ k. n. A kind of jasmine, *Jasminum sambac.*

ಇರವು a. k. n. Being; staying; support; condition, system.

ಇರಸಾಲು h. n. A remittance to the treasury.

ಇರಸು, ಇರಿಚು k. n. An iron axle-tree.

ಇರಳು (= ಇರುಳು, *q. v.*) k. n. Night.

ಇರಾದಾ, ಇರಾದೆ h. n. Purpose, design, intention; accord.

ಇರಿ 1. k. *A honorific affix, employed in addressing a superior, as:* ಬೇಡಿರಿ, ಹೋದಿರಿ, ಸಾಕಿರಿ, *etc.* 2, *an affix of the 2nd pers. pl. past, fut., imper., and neg., as:* ಮಾಡಿದಿರಿ, ಮಾಡುವಿರಿ, ಮಾಡದಿರಿ, ಮಾಡಿರಿ, *etc.*

ಇರಿ 2. (ರಿ = ಱಿ) k. *v. t.* To beat, strike; to pierce, stab; to butt; to kill. 2, to fling. -ದಾಡು. To stab mutually. ಇರತ, ಇರಿತ, ಇರಿವು. Piercing, stabbing, *etc.*

ಇರಿಚಲು. = ಇರಚಲು, *q. v.*

ಇರಿವೆ, ಇರುವೆ ಇರುಂಬೆ, ಇರುಪೆ, (ರು = ಱು) k. *n.* An ant. -ಗೂಡು, -ಹುತ್ತು. An ant hill.

ಇರಿಸಿಲು (ರಿ = ಱಿ) k. *n.* A pit-fall to catch elephants, *etc.*

ಇರಿಸು k. *v. t.* To cause to be or to stay; to place, put, deposit.

ಇರು k. *v. i.* To be; to exist; to remain, stay; to hesitate, delay. *n.* (ರು = ಱು). Goring, butting. *P. p.* ಇರ್ದು (= ಇದ್ದು, *q. v.*). ಇರಗೊಡು. To allow to be. ಇರಬೇಡ. Do not be! *With a dative or locative case, it expresses possession, as:* ನನಗೆ ಮನೆ ಇದೆ, I have a house. ಇರಲು. Being, remaining. ಇರುವಿಕೆ, ಇರುಹ. Being, existing, *etc.* ಇರ ಇರುತ್ತ, ಇರುತ್ತಿರುತ್ತ. In course of time, gradually.

ಇರುಕು (= ಇರಕು, *etc. q. v.* ರು = ಱು) k. *v. t.* To compress, *etc.* *n.* A narrow place, thicket.

ಇರುಬು (ರು = ಱು). = ಇರಿಸಿಲು.

ಇರುಬೆ (ರು = ಱು) k. *n.* A throng, crowd.

ಇರುವಾಯಿಕಟ್ಟು (*fr.* ಎರಡು ಬಾಯಿ ಕಟ್ಟು) k. *n.* Constipation and stoppage of urine.

ಇರುವಾರ k. *n.* Two shares: both the landlord's and cultivator's share of the produce.

ಇರುಳು (= ಇರಳು) k. *n.* Night. ಇರುಳರಸು. The moon. -ತಳವಾರ. A night-watchman. -ಹಗಲು. Night and day. -ಹೊತ್ತು. Night time.

ಇರ್ (= ಇಱ್) k. *a.* Two. ಇರ್ಕಟ್ಟು = ಇಕ್ಕಟ್ಟು, *q. v.* ಇರ್ಕಾಲು = ಇಕ್ಕಾಲು, *q. v.* ಇರ್ಕಿವಿ. Both ears. ಇರ್ಕೆಯ್ (= ಇಕ್ಕೆಯ್). Both hands. ಇರ್ತಲೆ (= ಇತ್ತಲೆ). Two heads; two generations. -ತಲೆಗೊಜ್ಜ, -ತಲೆಗೊಬ್ಬ. A grandfather. ಇರ್ಬಲ. Both forces. ಇರ್ಬಾಳಿ. The second cultivation. ಇರ್ಬೇನೆ. A complicated disease. -ಮಡಿ = ಇಮ್ಮಡಿ *s.* ಇಮ್, *q. v.*

ಇರ್ಕಿಸು (= ಇಕ್ಕಿಸು) k. *v. t.* To cause to put; to cause to kill.

ಇರ್ಕು (= ಇಕ್ಕು) k. *v. t.* To put down. 2, to destroy. *n.* Killing, destroying.

ಇರ್ಮೆ a. k. *n.* Loveliness, desire, charm. *a.* (= ಇಮ್ಮೆ) Twice.

ಇರ್ವಾರು (= ಉರ್ವಾರು) *n.* A sort of cucumber.

ಇಲಾಖೆ h. *n.* A claim; a village under a township. 2, department; district; presidency.

ಇಲಾಚಿ h. *n.* Cardamoms.

ಇಲಾಜು h. *n.* A remedy; a resource; a means. -ಮಾಡು. To attempt.

ಇಲಾಲು h. *n.* A large torch.

ಇಲಿ k. *n.* A rat; a mouse. -ಕಿವಿ. Rat-ear: a small-leafed vegetable. -ಪಾಷಾಣ. Rat's bane, arsenic. -ಬಲೆ, -ಬೋನು. A rat-trap. -ಯಾಲ, -ವಾಲ. An aquatic plant, *Salvinea cucullata.*

ಇಲಿಕು k. *v. i.* To be squeezed, bruised.

ಇಲಿಚಿ k. *n.* The jujube tree.

ಇಲಿಮಿಂಚಿ k. *n.* A lemon, the lemon tree.

ಇಲುಕು k. *n.* Cramp, sprain.

ಇಲೆ (ಇಲಾ), ಇಳೆ s. *n.* The earth. 2, a cow. 3, speech. 4, Budha's wife. ಇಲಾತಲ. Earth's surface. ಇಲಾಧಿಪ, ಇಲಾಧೀಶ, ಇಲೇಶ. A king. ಇಲಾಪುತ್ರ. The planet Mars; a Śûdra. ಇಲಾಪುತ್ರಿ. Sîtâ.

ಇಲ್ಲ k. (*fr. defective verb* ಇಲ್, to be) *Third person of the neg. mood, used for all persons, genders, and numbers:* It, he, she is not or exists not, *etc.;* there does not occur or come. 2, not; no, *as:* ಗುರುವಿಲ್ಲ, ಮಗನಿಲ್ಲ, ಹಿತವರಿಲ್ಲ, ಸವಿಯಿಲ್ಲ; ಮಾಡುವದಿಲ್ಲ, ಬೇಕಾಗಿಲ್ಲ, ನೋಡಿಲ್ಲ or ನೋಡಲಿಲ್ಲ; ಬಂದಿದ್ದಿಲ್ಲ, ಮಾತಾಡಲಿಕ್ಕಿಲ್ಲ, *etc.* ಇಲ್ಲದೆ. *Part. neg.* Not being, not existing, without. ಇಲ್ಲದ. *Rel. part. neg.* ಇಲ್ಲದತನ. Nothingness, poorness. ಇಲ್ಲದವನು. A poor man. ಇಲ್ಲದ ಹಾಗೆ ಮಾಡು. To destroy. ಇಲ್ಲದಾಗು, ಇಲ್ಲವಾಗು, ಇಲ್ಲಾಗು. To cease to exist, fail, disappear. ಇಲ್ಲವೆ, ಇಲ್ಲವೇ. Is there not? or not? or. ಇಲ್ಲವೇ ಇಲ್ಲ. Certainly not. ಇಲ್ಲವೋ, ಇಲ್ಲೋ. Or not? is it not? ಇಲ್ಲೆನ್ನು. To say no.

ಇಲ್ಲಣ k. n. Soot.

ಇಲ್ಲದೆ, ಇಲ್ಲವೆ, ಇಲ್ಲಾ. *See s.* ಇಲ್ಲ.

ಇಲ್ಲಾಮಲ್ಲಿ k. n. A tell-tale; backbiting. -ತನ. Scandal.

ಇಲ್ಲಿ k. *ad.* In this place, here; this place (*opp. of* ಅಲ್ಲಿ). -ಗಲ್ಲಿಗೆ. From here to there. -ತನಕ. So far as this, up to this. -ದ, -ಯವನು. A man of this place.

ಇವ k. *prox. dem. pro.* This man, he; *also* -ನು. -ಳು. This woman, she. ಈತ *and* ಈಕೆ *are used as substitutes for* ಇವ *and* ಇವಳು *respectively when speaking of a respectable person; cf.* ಈತ *and* ಈಕೆ.

ಇವು, ಇವುಗಳು k. *pl. of* ಇದು, *q. v.*

ಇವೆ k. *pl. of* ಇದೆ.

ಇಷಾರೆ f. n. A sign or signal; a hint.

ಇಷು s. n. An arrow. -ಧಿ. A quiver.

ಇಷ್ಟ s. a. Wished, desired; agreeable; dear, beloved. n. Wish, desire; love. 2, a husband. 3, sacrificing. -ಕಾರಿ. A person who confers what is desired or agreeable. -ಗಂಧ. Fragrant; a fragrant substance. -ದೇವತೆ. A tutelary deity. -ಮಿತ್ರರು. Friends and acquaintances, beloved friends. -ಶಿಷ್ಟರು. Dear good people. -ಸಿದ್ಧಿ, ಇಷ್ಟಾಪೂರ್ತಿ. The fulfilment of one's desire. ಇಷ್ಟಾರ್ಥ. Anything desired or agreeable.

ಇಷ್ಟು (= ಇನಿತು) k. *prox. dem. n. & pro.* This much, so much as this; thus much or many, *etc.* ಇಷ್ಟಷ್ಟು. This much and that much. ಅವನ ಕಷ್ಟ ಇಷ್ಟಷ್ಟಲ್ಲ, his trouble is excessive. ಇಷ್ಟೊತ್ತು, *etc.* ಇಷ್ಟೊಂದು. So much as this; little; much.

ಇಸಕೊಳ್ಳು k. v. t. To take. *imp.* ಇಸಕೋ!

ಇಸಬು h. n. An itch which attacks the wrists. -ಗೋಲು. An annual plant, fleawort.

ಇಸಮು h. n. A name; an individual. -ವಾರ. Name by name. -ವಾರಪಟ್ಟಿ. An individual account. [an era.

ಇಸವಿ h. a. Christian. n. The Christi-

ಇಸು 1. (= ಎಸು, *q. v.*) k. v. t. To throw, shoot, as an arrow.

ಇಸು 2. k. *Affix joined 1, to Saṁskṛita, tadbhava (and Hindusthâni) themes to form verbs, and 2, to Kannaḍa themes to form (transitive or) causative verbs, as:* ಅಂಗೀಕರಿಸು, ಅನುಕರಿಸು, ಬದಲಾಯಿಸು, ಭಾವಿಸು, ಭಾಗಿಸು, ಪಾಲಿಸು, ಪರಿಹರಿಸು, ರಕ್ಷಿಸು, ಪೂಜಿಸು, ನಡೆಯಿಸು, ನೋಯಿಸು, ಮೇಯಿಸು, ಮಾಡಿಸು, ಆಡಿಸು, ಮುತ್ತಿಸು, ಕಾಣಿಸು, ತರಿಸು, ಬರಿಸು, ರಂಗಿಸು, *etc.*

ಇಸ್ತಕಬಾಲು h. n. Reception, meeting and receiving a visitor.

ಇಸ್ತಿಹಾರ್ h. n. Proclamation. -ನಾಮೆ. A written notice; advertisement.

ಇಸ್ತ್ರೀ h. n. A smoothing iron; ironing.

ಇಸ್ವಿ. = ಇಸವಿ.

ಇಸ್ಸಿ k. *int.* Fie! ಇಸ್ಸಿಸ್ಸಿ. *rep.*

ಇಹ 1. (= ಇಪ್ಪ, ಇರುವ, *etc. pres. rel. p. of* ಇರು, to be). a. k. n. Being; stay. ಇಹದು. = ಇರುವದು, ಇಪ್ಪದು, *etc.*

ಇಹ 2. s. *ad.* Here; at this time. n. The present state, present world. -ಪರ. Earth and heaven. -ಲೋಕ. This world.

ಇಹಗೆ, ಇಹಂಗೆ (= ಹೀಗೆ, *etc., q. v.*) a. k. *ad.* In this manner, thus.

ಇಳ (ಳ = ೞ) k. n. Coming down, descending. -ತರ. A going down, declining, *as* in age; subsiding, *as* anger, disease, *etc.*; reduction; a slope. -ವರೆ, -ವಾರೆ. A slope. -ಹೊತ್ತು. Midday to sunset.

ಇಳಕು (ಳ = ೞ) k. v. t. To cause to go down, to lower. v. i. To go down, incline. ಇಳಕಲ, ಇಳಕಲು. Sloping, a sloping ground.

ಇಳತ, ಇಳಿತ (ಳ=ಐ) k. n. Descending, descent. 2, ebb.

ಇಳಿ (ಳ=ಐ) k. v. i. To come down, descend, alight; to set, as the sun; to become less; to subside; to be abated, as anger; to be dispelled; to slope. -ಜಾರು. A declivity, slope; to slip down. -ದಾರವಾರ, -ಭೋಗ್ಯ. A mortgage with possession. -ಬೀಳು. To fall downwards; to fly away. -ಯಲಿಕ್ಕು. To suspend. -ಬಿಡು. To let down. -ಮುಳುಗು. To dive completely. -ಯುವಿಕೆ. Descending. -ತ. Descent etc.; fading; degraded condition. -ಗೊಳ್ಳು. To humble one's self.

ಇಳಿಚು, ಇಳಿಸು 1. (ಳ=ಐ) k. v. t. To cause to descend; to let down, lower; to take down, etc.; to dispel.

ಇಳಿಸು (ಳ=ಐ) 2. k. n. Stopping, thwarting. -ನೂಂಕು. To thwart, oppose.

ಇಳೆ (= ಇಲೆ) s. n. The earth (ಭೂಮಿ). 2, water (ಜಲ). 3, food (ಅನ್ನ). 4, sound (ಶಬ್ದ).

ಈ. The fourth letter of the alphabet. 2, contraction of ಇಯು: (1) in the acc. sing., as: ಜಾಡೀ ಹೇಳು, ಗಾಳೀ ತಕ್ಕೊಳ್ಳು; (2) in the gen. sing., as: ನೆಲ್ಲೀ ಕಾಯಿ, ತಾಯಿಇ ಮೊಲೆ; (3) in the loc. sing., as: ಹಂತೀಲಿ, ಹಾದೀಲಿ. 3, contraction of ಇಯಿ: (1) in the imperat., as: ನಡೀರಿ! ಹೊಡೀರಿ! (2) in the third pers. sing. impf., as: ಮುಗೀತು, ಮುರೀತು.

ಈ 2. dem. pro. (substitute of ಇದು). This; these. -ದಾರಿ, -ಸಾರಿ. This time. ಈ ಕಾರಣ. This cause, on this account. ಈ ತರ, ಈ ಪ್ರಕಾರ, ಈ ಬಗ್ಗೆ, ಈ ರೀತಿ, ಈ ಮೇರೆ. In this manner. ಈ ವರಿಗೆ, -ವರೆಗೆ. Till now, thus far. ಈವಾಗ. Now, this time. ಈವೊತ್ತು, -ಹೊತ್ತು. Today.

ಈ 3. k. v. t. To give, bestow; to allow. P.p. ಇತ್ತ. v. i. (=ಈಯು, ಈನ್, q. v.) To bring forth. ಈಯಲಾಗು. To be brought forth;. ಈಯಿಸು. To cause to give; to cause to bring forth.

ಈಕಾರ s. The letter ಈ.

ಈಕೆ k. hon. pro. This woman, she; cf. ಇವಳು.

ಈಕ್ಷಕ s. n. A spectator, beholder.

ಈಕ್ಷಣ s. n. Seeing; sight. 2, the eye. ಈಕ್ಷಣಿಕ. A male fortune-teller; f. ಈಕ್ಷಣಿಕೆ.

ಈಕ್ಷಿತ s. n. Looking.

ಈಕ್ಷಿತ s. a. Seen, regarded, considered.

ಈಕ್ಷಿಸು s. v. t. & i. To see, behold, look at; to consider. -ವಿಕೆ. Seeing.

ಈಕ್ಷೆ s. n. Sight, viewing.

ಈಗ, ಈಗಡು, ಈಗಲು, ಈಗಳ್ k. ad. Now; at this time. ಈಗಲೂ. Also now. ಈಗಲೇ. Just now. Cpds.: ಈಗಿನಷ್ಟು, ಈಗಿನವರು, etc. ಈಗ್ಗೆ. For the present; now. ಈಗ್ಯೂ. Still now.

ಈಚಲ, ಈಚಲು 1, ಈಚಲೆ, ಈಚಿಲ k. n. The wild date tree. -ನೀರು. Toddy. -ಗಾರ. A toddy-drawer or -seller; f. -ಗಾತಿ.

ಈಚಲು 2. k. n. The white ant when winged.

ಈಚು 1. k. n. Dryness, saplessness, witheredness. -ಹೋಗು. To become sapless.

ಈಚು 2. (tb. of ಈಷೆ) n. The pole or shaft of a plough, cart, etc. -ಕಯ್. The staff or handle in the shaft of a plough.

ಈಚೆ k. ad. This side; on this side. ಈಚಿಗೆ, ಈಚೆಗೆ. To this side; afterwards, later.

ಈಜು, ಈಜಾಡು (=ಈಸು) k. v. i. To swim. n. Swimming; also ಈಜಾಟ.

ಈಟಂಗಿ. = ಇಟ್ಟಿಗೆ, q. v.

ಈಟಿ f. n. A lance, spear, javelin.

ಈಟು. = ಇಷ್ಟು, q. v.

ಈಡಿ k. n. Toddy. -ಗ. A man of the toddy-drawers' caste; f. -ಗಿತ್ತಿ.

ಈಡಿತ s. a. Praised.

ಈಡು 1. (fr. ಇಡು) k. n. Putting, throwing. ಈಡಾಗು. To be exposed to; to become an object for, to incur. ಈಡಾಡು. To scatter, disperse, expose.

ಈಡು 2. k. n. Increase; strength; means. 2, proportion; a prop, support; fitness; equality; an equivalent, compensation; a pawn, pledge, security. -ಕಾರ, -ಗಾರ. A powerful man. ಈಡಾಗು. To become equal; to suffice; to become bail or bondsman. -ಇಡು, -ಕಟ್ಟು, -ಹಾಕು. To pledge. -ಜೋಡು. A good match. -ಮಾಡು. To make equal.

ಈಡೇರು (fr. ಈಡು-ಏರು) k. v. i. To be fulfilled. ಈಡೇರಿಸು. To fulfil.

ಈಂಟು a. k. v. t. To drink, sip.

ಈತ k. hon. pro. This person, he. Rel. past part. of ಈ 3, v. i.

ಈತಿ s. n. Calamity from rain, drought, locusts, etc.

ಈತು k. An affix for 3rd pers. sing. neut. pres. of uncertainty or possibility, as: ಬಂದೀತು, ಬಿಟ್ಟೀತು.

ಈದು k. P. p. of ಈ 3, v. i. and ಈನ್, q. v. -ಎಕೆ. Bringing forth.

ಈನು (=ಈ 3, v. i.) k. v. i. To bring forth young, yean, cub.

ಈಪಿ k. n. The dung of flies; a nit.

ಈಪ್ಸೆ s. n. Desire, wish. ಈಪ್ಸಿತ. Desired.

ಈಬು f. n. Difference.

ಈಯು. = ಈ, q. v.

ಈರ್ (=ಇರ್, etc.) k. a. Two. ಈರಡಿ. Two feet. ಈರಯ್ದು. Ten. ಈರಯ್ದುಸಾಸಿರ. Ten thousand. ಈರಾರು. Twelve. ಈರಾರು ರಾಶಿ. The twelve signs of the zodiac. ಈರೇಳು. Fourteen.

ಈರು k. v. t. To pull. 2, to comb ou nits. n. A nit. 2, (ರು=ಱು) the gums.

ಈರಣಿಗೆ k. n. A comb for removing nits.

ಈರುಳ್ಳಿ (=ನೀರುಳ್ಳಿ) k. n. An onion.

ಈರ್ಷೆ, ಈರ್ಷ್ಯೆ s. n. Envy, spite, malice.

ಈಲಿ f. n. A sort of weapon: a short sword, a cudgel.

ಈಲು k. n. Attachment, as that of animals or children.

ಈವರು (ರು=ಱು) a. k. ad. A little while ago.

ಈವಾಗ (=ಈಗ) k. ad. Now, at this time.

ಈಶ s. n. An owner, lord, master. 2, Śiva (ಈಶ್ವರ). -ತ್ವ. Supremacy.

ಈಶಾನ s. n. Śiva; the regent of the north-east quarter. 2, the sun. ಈಶಾನ್ಯ. The north-east quarter.

ಈಶ್ವರ (tb. ಈಸರ) s. n. A lord. 2, Śiva. 3, the 11th year of the cycle. 4, the universal soul. -ಬಳ್ಳಿ, -ಬೇರು. A twining shrub, Indian birthwort. ಈಶ್ವರಿ, ಈಶ್ವರೆ. Durgâ. ಈಶ್ವರೇಶ್ವರ. The lord of lords: Śiva.

ಈಷಣ s. n. Desire, wish. -ತ್ರಯ. The three dominant desires: ದಾರೇಷಣ, ಪುತ್ರೇಷಣ, ವಿತ್ತೇಷಣ, the desire after a wife, a son and riches.

ಈಷತ್ s. ad. Slightly. n. A little. ಈಷದ್ಭೇದ. A slight difference.

ಈಷೆ (tb. ಈಚು, ಈಸು) s. n. The pole or shaft of a plough or carriage.

ಈಸರ. tb. of ಈಶ್ವರ, q. v.

ಈಸು 1. (=ಈಜು) k. v. i. To swim. n. Swimming. ಈಸಗಲಿಸು. To teach to swim. ಈಸಾಡು.= ಈಸು. -ಕುಂಬಳಕಾಯಿ. A dried pumpkin used in swimming.

ಈಸು 2, ಈಯಿಸು (fr. ಈ) k. v. t. To cause to give. 2, to yield, allow. 3, to cause to calve. ಈಸಿಕೊಳ್ಳು. To take.

ಈಸು 3. (=ಇನಿತು, q. v.) k. pro. So much as this, this much.

ಈಸು 4. *tb. of* ಈಷೆ, *q. v.*

ಈಹ, ಈಹೆ s. *n.* Effort, exertion; wish, desire.

ಈಹಾಮೃಗ s. *n.* A wolf.

ಈಳಿಗೆ (*tb. of* ಈಲಿಕ) *n.* A sickle. 2, a blade set in a stock for slitting up vegetables. -ಕತ್ತಿ, -ಮಣೆ. The stock wherein the blade is set.

ಈಳಿಗೆ (ಳ = ಱ) k. *n.* Disentanglement, freedom.

ಈಳೆ k. *n.* An orange, *etc.; cf.* ಕಿತ್ತೀಳೆ, ದೊಡ್ಡೀಳೆ.

ಉ

ಉ. The fifth letter of the alphabet. 2, *the final of many Kannaḍa words, as:* ಕರು, ಕಾವು, ಕಳವು; ಕೊಡು, ನೋಡು; ಎರಡು, *etc.* 3, *an auxiliary letter added to words ending in a consonant in classical language, as:* ಬಿಲ್ಲು, ಕಲ್ಲು, ಹೇಳು, ಕೇಳು, *etc.* 4, *an auxiliary letter to form tadbhavas, as:* ರಜ್ಜು, ತೇಜಸ್ಸು, ಮನಸ್ಸು, *etc.* 5, *an auxiliary to form the nominative of nouns ending in* ಇ *or* ಎ, *as:* ಸಭೆಯು, ವಿದ್ಯೆಯು, ಗಿಳಿಯು, ಹೇಡಿಯು, *etc.*

ಉಂ 1. k. *conj.* = ಅಂ.

ಉಂ 2. k. *int. of displeasure.*

ಉಃ k. *int. of joy*: hey! ah!

ಉಕ k. *An affix to form masc. nouns, as:* ಕಟ್ಟುಕ, ತಟ್ಟುಕ, *etc.*

ಉಕಾರ s. *n.* The letter ಉ.

ಉಕ್ಕಡ k. *n.* The outermost part of a town or village. 2, an entrenchment about a camp; a match; a guard-house. 3, a piece of rope tied to the end of a well-rope, for fastening the vessel.

ಉಕ್ಕಂದ k. *n.* Swell: abundance. 2, a narrow board or piece of bamboo tied between two beams used for hanging clothes, *etc.* on.

ಉಕ್ಕಿವ, ಉಕ್ಕೆವ k. *n.* Cunning, fraud.

ಉಕ್ಕು 1. k. *v. i.* To rise, swell, *as* the sea; to come up in boiling; to foam; to boil, *as* rage; to be elated. *n.* Rising. 2, spume, froth. 3, pride. 4, power. -ಇಳಿ. To lose one's power. -ಎಕೆ. Rising. ಉಕ್ಕೇರು. To rise up, effervesce.

ಉಕ್ಕು 2. k. *n.* Steel. -ಸುಣ್ಣ. Ashes of calcined iron.

ಉಕ್ಕೆ k. *n.* Ploughing. 2, remainder. -ಹೊಡೆ. To plough.

ಉಕ್ತಿ s. *n.* Speech; a word, expression. -ಸು. To speak.

ಉಕ್ಷ s. *n.* An ox, bull. -ಗ. One who rides on an ox: Śiva. -ಪತಿ, -ರಾಜ. Śiva.

ಉಖೆ s. *n.* A pot, caldron.

ಉಗನಿಬಳ್ಳಿ k. *n.* A shrubby creeper, the heart-leaved moonseed, *Cocculus cordifolius.* 2, the creeper *Lettsomia aggregata.*

ಉಗಮ (*tb. of* ಉದ್ಗಮ) *n.* Source, origin.

ಉಗರಿಸು k. *v. i.* To gasp, breathe hard.

ಉಗಾದಿ. *tb. of* ಯುಗಾದಿ, *q. v.*

ಉಗಿ 1. k. *v. t.* To pull, draw off or out. 2, to hurt, rend, slit, break. 3, to fear. *n.* Pulling.

ಉಗಿ 2. (= ಉಗುಳು) k. *v. i.* To spit, spirt out.

ಉಗಿ 3. k. *n.* Steam; vapour or reek. -ಕಾವು. The heat of steam. -ಕಾಸು. To warm by steam. -ಕೊಡು. To foment. -ಯಂತ್ರ. A steam-engine.

ಉಗು k. *v. i.* To become loose; to flow, trickle; to be shed; to let loose; to throw. ಉಗಿಸು. To let loose, spill.

ಉಗುರ್, ಉಗುರು k. *n.* A nail; a claw. -ಕಣ್ಣು. The quick of a finger-nail.

-ನಂಜು. Poison caused by scratching. -ಬೆಚ್ಚಗೆ. Luke-warm. -ಸುತ್ತು. A whitlow. ಉಗುರಿಸು. To scratch asunder.

ಉಗುಳು (ಳು=ಬು) k. v. i. To spit out; to sputter. n. Spittle, saliva. ಉಗುಳಿಸು. To cause to spit. -ರೋಗ. Salivation.

ಉಗ್ಗ k. n. A rope or cord attached to anything, as a handle.

ಉಗ್ಗಡ, ಉಗ್ಗಡಣೆ a. k. n. Repeated sounds, as in dancing or music; noise, clamour. ಉಗ್ಗಡಿಸು. To sound; to cry out, proclaim.

ಉಗ್ಗಾರ. tb. of ಉದ್ಗಾರ, q. v.

ಉಗ್ಗಿ k. = ಹುಗ್ಗಿ.

ಉಗ್ಗು k. v. i. To stammer, falter in speaking. v. t. To throw as water. n. Stammering.

ಉಗ್ರ s. a. Terrific. 2, cruel. 3, hot, sharp. 4, angry. n. Śiva. *Cpds.*: -ಕೋಪ, -ಬಿಸಲು, -ಬುದ್ಧಿ, -ಶಕ್ತಿ, *etc.* -ಗಂಧ. Bishop's seed; carroway. -ತೆ. Violence, passion, anger. -ಶಾಸನ. A severe command. -ಸೇನ. N. of Kamsa's father.

ಉಗ್ರಾಣ k. n. A storehouse, granary; a treasury.

ಉಗ್ರಾಣಿ, ಉಗ್ರಾಣಿಕ k. n. A store-keeper. 2, a village-peon.

ಉಘೆ k. *int.* Hurra! huzza!

ಉಂಚೆ k. n. The warp spread and starched.

ಉಂಚಿಸು k. v. t. To consider; to observe.

ಉಂಗುಟ. tb. of ಅಂಗುಷ್ಠ, q. v.

ಉಂಗರ, ಉಂಗುರ k. n. A ring. -ಗೂದಲು. A ringlet. -ಬೆರಳು. The ring-finger. ಮುದ್ರೆಯುಂಗುರ. A seal-ring.

ಉಚಾಯಿಸು s. v. i. To go beyond; to overstep; to transgress; to pass or elapse, *as* time, *etc.*

ಉಚಿತ s. a. Delightful, agreeable. 2, usual. 3, right, proper, convenient, suitable. n. A gift, present. -ಜ್ಞ. Knowing what is proper. -ವಾಗಿ. Gratuitously.

ಉಚ್ಚ (= ಉದ್ದ) s. a. High, lofty, elevated; tall; deep. n. The apex of a planet's orbit.

ಉಚ್ಚರಣೆ s. n. Uttering; pronunciation.

ಉಚ್ಚರಿಸು s. v. i. & v. t. To utter, pronounce, speak.

ಉಚ್ಚಲಿಸು, ಉಚ್ಚಳಿಸು k. v. i. To come forth, proceed. 2, to separate. 3, to penetrate. 4, to run over, *as* water.

ಉಚ್ಚಾಟನ s. n. Scaring; expelling, removing by means of magical incantations.

ಉಚ್ಚಾಪತಿ f. n. Taking of goods upon credit. -ಆಗಿ. On credit.

ಉಚ್ಚಾರ, ಉಚ್ಚಾರಣೆ s. n. Utterance, pronunciation, articulation.

ಉಚ್ಚಿ k. n. The top or crown of the head. -ಬಾಯಿ. The fontanel.

ಉಚ್ಚಿಕೆ s. n. Diarrhoea.

ಉಚ್ಚು k. v. t. To pull out, draw, *as* a sword. 2, to untie, loosen. v. i. To become loose; to fly off, as an arrow. 2, to become free. 3, to be purged. n. Looseness, *etc.* -ಗಂಟು. A loose knot. ಉಚ್ಚಿ ಬಿಡು, ಉಚ್ಚಿ ಹಾಕು. To strip off. ಉಚ್ಚಾಗು, ಉಚ್ಚಿ ಬರು, ಉಚ್ಚಿ ಬೀಳು. To become loose.

ಉಚ್ಚೆ k. n. Urine. -ಕಟ್ಟು. Stoppage of urine. -ಚೀಲ. The bladder. -ಜಾಡ್ಯ, -ಪೀಡೆ, -ರೋಗ. A urinary disease, diabetes. -ಬಿಡು, -ಹೊಯ್ಯು. To void urine.

ಉಚ್ಚೈಃಶ್ರವಸ್ s. n. Indra's horse.

ಉಚ್ಚೈರ್ಘೋಷ s. n. Neighing.

ಉಚ್ಛಿಷ್ಟ s. a. Left, rejected. n. Leavings, orts; remainder.

ಉಚ್ಛೋಷಣ s. n. Drying up, making dry.

ಉಚ್ಛ್ವಾಸ s. n. Breathing, breath.

ಉಜಾಡು h. a. Desolate, depopulated.

ಉಜೂರು h. n. Deference, respect.

ಉಜ್ಜಯಿನಿ s. n. N. of a city in Mâlava, Oujein.

ಉಜ್ಜು k. v. t. To rub. n. Rubbing. -ಕಂಬಳಿ. A kind of blanket. -ಕಲ್ಲು. A smoothing stone. -ಕೊರಡು, -ಗೊರಡು. A carpenter's plane.

ಉಜ್ಜುಗ. tb. of ಉದ್ಯೋಗ, q. v.

ಉಜ್ಜ್ವಲ s. a. Blazing up; bright, clear; beautiful, lovely. -ತೆ. Splendour. ಉಜ್ವಲಿಸು. To flame, shine.

ಉಂಚ 1. k. n. A bamboo basket used for covering poultry.

ಉಂಚ 2. = ಉಚ್ಚ.

ಉಟ s. n. Leaves, grass, etc. used in thatching. -ಜ. A hut made of leaves.

ಉಟಾಯಿಸು f. v. t. To raise.

ಉಟ್ಟಿ k. n. A net-work sling for suspending pots, etc. 2, (= ಹುಟ್ಟಿ) a honeycomb.

ಉಟ್ಟು 1. k. n. An anchor. 2, (= ಹುಟ್ಟು) a paddle.

ಉಟ್ಟು 2. = ಹುಟ್ಟು k. 2, P. p. of ಉಡು, q. v.

ಉಟ್ಲಾಟ, ಉಟ್ಲುಬಡಿ k. n. A play in which any eatables or vessels containing them are suspended and swung and persons attempt to get them.

ಉಡ = ಉಡಿ 2. k. -ದಾರ (= ಉಡಿದಾರ). A waist-string or zone; a woman's girdle.

ಉಡಗಿಸು. = ಉಡುಗಿಸು.

ಉಡಗು. = ಉಡುಗು.

ಉಡಚು k. n. A venereal boil.

ಉಡಪು k. n. Clothes, garments.

ಉಡಾಫೆ h. n. Denial, rejection, scorn.

ಉಡಾಯಿಸು h. v. t. To reject contemptuously.

ಉಡಾಸ h. n. Causing to fly or wave. -ಪಾವಡ, -ರುಮಾಲು. A silk cloth used as a fan in ceremonial processions.

ಉಡಿ 1. k. v. i. To be shattered to pieces; to crush, bruise; to pull asunder, as dough; to twist, as a wick.

ಉಡಿ 2. k. n. A pouch made by females (or males) by folding the front part of their garment for putting in eatables, money, etc. 2, the hip, waist (-ದಾರ, -ನೂಲು. = ಉಡದಾರ, q. v.). 3, (= ಉಡಿಕೆ) a garment. 4, a kind of disease.

ಉಡಿಕೆ, ಉಡಿಗೆ k. n. Putting on clothes, wearing, clothing; raiment. -ತೊಡಿಗೆ. Apparel and ornaments.

ಉಡಿಲು. = ಉಡಿ 2, q. v.

ಉಡು 1. k. v. t. To wrap round the waist; to put on the lower garment, as the sîrĕ, dôtra, etc. P. p. ಉಟ್ಟು. n. (= ಉಡಿ) The waist. 2, a garment, clothes. -ಗೆರೆ, -ಗೊರೆ. A present of sîrĕ, etc. to the bride and bridegroom at the celebration of their marriage or on any auspicious occasion. -ದಾರ. = ಉಡದಾರ.

ಉಡು 2. k. n. An iguana, *Lacerta monitor.*

ಉಡು 3. s. n. A star. 2, water. -ಪ, -ಪತಿ, -ರಾಜ. The moon.

ಉಡುಕಿಸು k. v. t. To straighten, tighten, compress; to vex.

ಉಡುಗು (= ಉಡಗು) k. v. i. To shrink, shrivel; to abate; to fade; to disappear; to desist; to stop; to remove; to leave, quit. v. t. To sweep. ಉಡುಗಿಸು. To cause to shrink, sweep, etc.

ಉಡುಗೆ. = ಉಡಿಕೆ, q. v.

ಉಡುತೆ k. n. A squirrel.

ಉಡುಪ s. n. The moon (s. ಉಡು 3). 2, a raft, float. 3, the bird called câtaka. 4, a serpent.

ಉಡುಪು. = ಉಡಪು, q. v.

ಉಡುರು k. n. The bellowing of an ox or a bull.

ಉಡುವೆ k. n. A jungle.

ಉಡೆ (= ಉಡಿ 2, q. v.) k. n. The waist.

ಉಡ್ಡಿ k. n. Any set of three, as marbles, seeds, etc. with a fourth set on the top. -ಇಕ್ಕು, -ಇಡು, -ಹಾಕು. To set thus.

ಉಣಾತಿ a. a. Inferior, lower.

ಉಣಿ, (ಉಣಿಗ) k. n. A person who feeds on. -ಕೆ. Taking a meal. -ಸು. A meal,

ಉಂಟು 1. k. (*Third pers. sing. of the pres. of* ಉಳ್⁴ *to be*) There is; it is *etc.* 2, that exists. 3, *with the dative it expresses possession (as:* ಅವನಿಗುಂಟು, he has). *n.* Existence. ಉಂಟಾಗು. To become; to happen; to be born; to accrue to. ಉಂಟಾಗುವಿಕೆ. Becoming, *etc.* -ಮಾಡು. To cause to be, to create, produce. -ಮಾಡುವಿಕೆ. Creating.

ಉಂಟು. 2. k. = ಉರುಟು. ಉಂಟಾಡು. To roll.

ಉಂಡಲಿಗೆ k. *n.* A kind of rice cake.

ಉಂಡಿಗ s. *n.* A single, solitary man.

ಉಂಡಿಗೆ k. *n.* A stamp. 2, a pass, a ticket for free passage.

ಉಂಡು k. *P. p. of* ಉಣ್ಣು, *q. v.*

ಉಂಡೆ k. *n.* A ball of anything, *as* of raw sugar, tamarind, *etc.* -ಗಟ್ಟು. To form a ball.

ಉಣ್ಣ k. *n.* Taking a meal; a meal. 2, a tick.

ಉಣ್ಣು k. *v. t.* To eat a meal (*or* ûṭa), *as* anna (kûḷ), hôḷigê, *etc.* 2, to enjoy, as riches. *P. p.* ಉಂಡು. ಉಣ್ಣ ಬಡಿಸು, ಉಣ್ಣಲಿಕ್ಕು, ಉಣ್ಣಲಿಡು. To serve up a meal. ಉಂಡಾಡಿ, -ಗ. A glutton. ಉಣ್ಣ ವಳಿಯದು. Much, further; in vain. ಮೊಲೆಯುಣ್ಣು. To suck.

ಉಣ್ಣೆ (*tb. of* ಊರ್ಣ) *n.* Wool.

ಉಣ್ಮು s. k. *v. i.* To go up; to break forth; to issue.

ಉತಾರು s. *n.* Subsiding; alleviation; diminution; descent; cheapness.

ಉತಾವಳಿ f. *n.* Haste, impatience.

ಉತ್ಕಟ s. *a.* Excessive; important, supĕrior, high. 2, proud. 3, mad, furious. 4, difficult. *n.* Eagerness; affliction.

ಉತ್ಕಂಠಿತ s. *a.* Desiring, longing for; distressed.

ಉತ್ಕಂಠೆ s. *n.* Longing; regretting; anxiety, regret.

ಉತ್ಕರ್ಷ s. *a.* Raising; drawing out. *n.* Excellence. 2, joy; pleasure.

ಉತ್ಕಲಿಕೆ s. *n.* Longing for. 2, fear. 3, a wave.

ಉತ್ಕೃಷ್ಟ s. *a.* Excellent, eminent, superior. -ತೆ. Excellence.

ಉತ್ಕ್ರಮ, ಉತ್ಕ್ರಮಣ s. *n.* Going out or astray; transgression. ಉತ್ಕ್ರಮಿಸು. To depart, *as* life; to exceed, transgress, *as* an order.

ಉತ್ತ, ಉತ್ತಾ, ಉತ್ತಂ k. *A termination of the pres. participle, as:* ನಡಗುತ್ತ, ಬಿಟ್ಟಿಸುತ್ತ, ನೋಡುತ್ತಾ, ಬರುತ್ತಂ, *etc.*

ಉತ್ತ, ಉತ್ತಲ್ k. *ad.* To or in the middle side or direction; *cf.* ಅತ್ತ *and* ಇತ್ತ.

ಉತ್ತಂಡ s. *n.* A gold necklace worn by women.

ಉತ್ತತ್ತಿ. = ಉತ್ತುತ್ತೆ, *q. v.*

ಉತ್ತಮ s. *a.* Uppermost; chief, best, excellent. *n.* The first person *(g.)*. -ಪುರುಷ. An excellent man; the first person *(g.)*. -ಶ್ಲೋಕ. A man well spoken of. ಉತ್ತಮಾಂಗ. The head. ಉತ್ತಮಾಧಮ. Good and bad. ಉತ್ತಮಿಕೆ. Excellence, superiority. ಉತ್ತಮೋತ್ತಮ. The very best.

ಉತ್ತರ 1. s. *a.* Higher, upper. 2, superior, excellent. 3, northern. 4, left; posterior. 5, subsequent, following, latter. *n.* An answer, reply; a mandate. 2, a defence, rejoinder. 3, future consequence. -ಆಡು, -ಕೊಡು, -ಈ, -ಹೇಳು. To give an answer. -ನಿಲ್ಲಿಸು. To silence. -ದಿಕ್ಕು. The northern direction. -ಕರ್ಮ, -ಕ್ರಿಯೆ. Funeral rites. -ಕಾಶಿ. Benares. -ಧ್ರುವ. The north pole. -ಪಕ್ಷ. A defendant; the dark half of the month. -ಪೂಜೆ. Worship at the close of a ceremony. -ವಾದಿ. A defendant. ಉತ್ತರಾಧಿಕಾರಿ. A successor; an heir. ಉತ್ತರಾಯಣ. The summer solstice. ಉತ್ತರೋತ್ತರ. More and more; success; welfare. ಉತ್ತರಿಸು. To answer; to order.

ಉತ್ತರ 2. s. *a.* Crossing over; coming out, escaping from. -ಣ. Crossing over.

ಉತ್ತರಣಿ k. *n.* A common weed, *Achyranthes aspera.*

ಉತ್ತರಾಜಿ s. *a.* Relating to the north. -ವೋಲೆ. A female's ear-ornament.

ಉತ್ತರಾಭಾದ್ರ s. n. The twenty-sixth lunar mansion.

ಉತ್ತರಾಷಾಢ s. n. The twenty-first lunar mansion.

ಉತ್ತರಿಸು s. v. t. To cross; to come out; to escape; cf. ಉತ್ತರ 2.

ಉತ್ತರೀಯ, -ಕ s. ಉತ್ತರಿಗೆ (its tb.) n. An upper garment.

ಉತ್ತರೆ s. n. The north. 2, the twelfth lunar mansion. 3, N. of Virâṭa's daughter.

ಉತ್ತಾನ s. a. Lying on the back. 2, shallow. -ಪಾದ. N. of a star; N. of a king.

ಉತ್ತಾ.= ಉತ್ತ, etc., q. v.

ಉತ್ತಾರ s. n. Rescuing. 2, remission; giving back. 3, land given rent-free by government to an individual (śânabhôga, gauḍa, etc.) as a reward for services.

ಉತ್ತಾಲ, ಉತ್ತಾಳ s. a. Formidable; arduous, difficult; speedy; high, tall.

ಉತ್ತೀರ್ಣ s. a. Crossed; rescued, liberated, released.

ಉತ್ತು (= ಉತುರ್). P. p. of ಉರು, q. v. 2, p. p. of ಉಳು.

ಉತ್ತುತ್ತೆ (= ಉತ್ತತ್ತಿ) k. n. Dried dates.

ಉತ್ತೆ k. An affix for forming third pers. sing. neut. as: ಆಗುತ್ತೆ (= ಆಗುತ್ತದೆ), ಇರುತ್ತೆ (= ಇರುತ್ತದೆ), etc.

ಉತ್ತೇಜಕ s. a. Stimulating, stimulant.

ಉತ್ತೇಜನ s. n. Incitement; an incentive, inducement, stimulant.

ಉತ್ಥಾನ s. n. Rising; resurrection. 2, manly exertion. 3, starting on an expedition. 4, a courtyard (ಅಂಗಳ). 5, joy. -ದ್ವಾದಶಿ. A feast of the 12th day in the month of ಕಾರ್ತಿಕ.

ಉತ್ಪತ್ತಿ s. n. Birth, production, origin; produce, profit. -ಸ್ಥಾನ. The source of anything.

ಉತ್ಪಥ s. n. Error, evil. 2, the air, sky.

ಉತ್ಪನ್ನ s. a. Born, produced. n. Produce, profit. -ತೆ. Origin; production.

ಉತ್ಪಲ s. n. The blue lotus, Nymphaea caerulea. -ಮಾಲೆ. N. of a vṛitta. -ಮಿತ್ರ. The moon.

ಉತ್ಪಾತ s. n. A portent, prodigy or phenomenon; any public calamity, as earthquake, eclipse, etc. -ಕ. Perverse.

ಉತ್ಪಾದ s. n. Coming forth, producing. -ನ. Bringing forth.

ಉತ್ಪಾದಿಸು s. v. i. To produce.

ಉತ್ಪ್ರೇಕ್ಷೆ s. n. Overlooking; indifference. 2, a simile; comparison.

ಉತ್ಸರ್ಗ s. n. Emission. 2, excretion. 3, quitting. 4, gift. 5, a general precept.

ಉತ್ಸರ್ಜನ s. n. Letting loose, quitting; gift.

ಉತ್ಸರ್ಜಿಸು s. v. t. To let loose; to quit, abandon.

ಉತ್ಸವ s. n. Elevation. 2, joy. 3, a festival; a festive procession. 4, a libation. ಉತ್ಸವಿಸು. To make merry, be glad. Cpds.: ದೀಪೋತ್ಸವ, ರಥೋತ್ಸವ.

ಉತ್ಸಹ (tb. of ಉತ್ಸಾಹ, q. v.) n. A feast, a festive procession.

ಉತ್ಸಾಹ s. n. Effort, perseverence, energy. 2, joy, happiness. 3, heroism. -ಧ್ವನಿ. A sound of delight. ಉತ್ಸಾಹಿ. Active, persevering; a happy person. ಉತ್ಸಾಹಿಸು. To rejoice.

ಉತ್ಸುಕ s. a. Restless. 2, eager. 3, longing for. 4, regretting for. n. Ardent desire. -ತೆ. Zeal; affection; regret.

ಉದ, ಉದಕ s. n. Water. ಉದಜ. The lotus.

ಉದಧಿ s. n. A reservoir for water; the ocean.

ಉದಯ s. n. Rising. 2, the eastern mountain behind which the sun is supposed to rise. 3, light. 4, creation, production. 5, becoming visible. -ಕಾಲ. The time of sunrise. -ರಾಗ. The dawn; a morning carol. ಉದಯಾಚಲ, ಉದಯಾದ್ರಿ. = ಉದಯ No. 2.

ಉದಯಾದಿತ್ಯ. The rising sun. ಉದಯಿಸು. To rise; to be born.

ಉದರ s. n. The belly, womb. -ನಿರ್ವಾಹ. Sustenance of life. -ಪೂರ. Till the belly is full. -ಪೋಷಣೆ. Feeding the belly. -ಶೂಲೆ. The colic.

ಉದರಿ s. n. Having a belly. 2, = ಉದ್ದರಿ.

ಉದರಿಸು k. v. t. To cause to fall or drop down.

ಉದರು, ಉದುರು k. v. i. To fall, drop down. n. Falling. 2, the state of boiled rice or pulse not sticking to one another.

ಉದಾತ್ತ s. a. Elevated, high. 2, generous; illustrious. -ಚರಿತ. A man of noble behaviour.

ಉದಾನ s. n. Breathing upwards. -ವಾಯು. The vital air which rises up the throat and passes into the head.

ಉದಾರ s. a. Lofty, exalted; generous, liberal; proper, right. -ತನ, -ತೆ. Liberality, generosity. -ಶೀಲ. Generous-minded. ಉದಾರಿ. A liberal, generous person.

ಉದಾರು h. n. Debt; credit; cf. ಉದ್ದರಿ.

ಉದಾಸ s. n. Indifference, apathy.

ಉದಾಸೀನ s. a. Indifferent, neutral. 2, despised. n. Indifference; contempt, disregard. -ಮಾಡು. To disregard, disrespect.

ಉದಾಹರಣೆ s. n. Saying, declaration. 2, an example, illustration, instance. 3, a reply. 4, an opposite argument. ಉದಾಹರಿಸು. To declare, explain.

ಉದಿತ s. a. Bound. 2, said, spoken. 3, sprung up, born.

ಉದಿಸು. = ಉದಯಿಸು.

ಉದು a. k. dem. pro. (cf. ಅದು, ಇದು) This (between the two).

ಉದಿರು, ಉದುರು (= ಉದರು, q. v.) k. v. i. To fall down, drop, as fruits or leaves. ಉದುರಿಸು, ಉದಿರ್ಚು. = ಉದರಿಸು.

ಉದೋ k. int. Behold (what is between the two)! ho! halloo!

ಉದ್ಗಮ (= ಉಗಮ) s. n. Rising; source; origin; production; a flower. -ಮಂಜರಿ. A flower bunch. -ಮಾಲೆ. A flower-wreath. ಉದ್ಗಮಿಸು. To rise; to ascend; to be born.

ಉದ್ಗಾರ s. n. Spitting out, vomiting. 2, eructation. 3, an ejaculation; an interjection. -ವಾಚಕಚಿಹ್ನ. The sign of exclamation.

ಉದ್ಘಟ s. n. A kind of vessel. -ನ. Unfastening; revealing.

ಉದ್ಘಾಟ s. n. Watch or guard-house. -ಕ. An opener; a key. -ನ. (= ಉದ್ಘಟನ). Opening, revealing; raising. lifting up.

ಉದ್ಘೋಷಣ s. n. Crying out; sounding. ಉದ್ಘೋಷಿಸು. To cry out, sound.

ಉದ್ದ (tb. of ಊರ್ಧ್ವ) n. Height; tallness; length; depth. a. Long; tall. ಉದ್ದಗಲ. Length or height and breadth. Cpds.: -ಕಾಲು, -ಕೂದಲು, -ಗಿತ, -ದಾವಿ, etc. -ಮಲಗು. To lie down lengthwise. ಉದ್ದಳತೆ. Height; length. ಉದ್ವರುಟು. Very proud behaviour.

ಉದ್ದಂಡ s. a. Having a raised staff. 2, powerful, violent; proud. -ತನ. Pride.

ಉದ್ದನ, ಉದ್ದನ್ನ s. a. High, tall. -ಗೋಣು. A long neck.

ಉದ್ದಮಿ. = ಉದ್ದಿಮಿ, q. v.

ಉದ್ದರಿ. = ಉದ್ದಿರಿ, q. v.

ಉದ್ದಿ k. n. A low ridge in a field for irrigation purposes. -ಗೆ. The pole of a carriage.

ಉದ್ದಿರಿ, ಉದ್ರಿ (tb. of ಉದ್ಧಾರ) n. Credit, purchase on credit. -ಕೊಡು. To give on credit.

ಉದ್ದಮಿ, ಉದ್ದಿಮಿ, ಉದ್ದಿಮೆ (tb. of ಉದ್ಯಮ) n. Business, profession. -ಗಾರ, -ದಾರ. A trader; a farmer.

ಉದ್ದಿಶ್ಯ s. prep. Aiming at; with regard to, on account of.

ಉದ್ದೀಪ, -ನ s. n. Inflaming, exciting; animating; stimulating.

ಉದ್ದೀಪ್ತ s. a. Lighted; shining; inflamed.

ಉದ್ದು 1. (= ಉಜ್ಜು, q. v.) k. v. t. To rub.

ಉದ್ದು 2. k. n. A common pulse, *Phaseolus mungo; also* ಉದ್ದಿನ ಬೀಜ.

ಉದ್ದೇಶ s. n. Object, motive; purpose, meaning, intention. 2, an assignment; a previous statement. ಉದ್ದೇಶಿಸು. To aim at, intend.

ಉದ್ಧಟ s. a. Rude, impudent. n. Rudeness.

ಉದ್ಧರಣ s. n. Raising, lifting. 2, delivering, rescuing. 3, final emancipation.

ಉದ್ಧರಿಸು s. v. t. To lift up. 2, to rescue, deliver, save, release.

ಉದ್ಧರ್ಷ s. n. Great joy; a festival.

ಉದ್ಧಾರ s. n. Raising. 2, deliverance, redemption. 3, obligation. -ಕ. A deliverer. -ಮಾಡು. = ಉದ್ಧರಿಸು.

ಉದ್ಧೂತ s. a. Roused up. 2, exalted, high.

ಉದ್ಧೃತ s. a. Drawn up. 2, raised, elevated.

ಉದ್ಭವ s. n. Birth, production, origin; existence; manifestation. ಉದ್ಭವಿಸು. To be born; to exist.

ಉದ್ಭಾಸ s. n. Radiance, splendour.

ಉದ್ಭಿಜ್ಜ s. a. Sprouting, germinating. n. A plant or vegetable. -ಕೋಟಿ. The vegetable kingdom.

ಉದ್ಭಿನ್ನ s. a. Opened, budded. 2, different.

ಉದ್ಭ್ರಮ s. n. Whirling; agitation, anxiety. ಉದ್ಭ್ರಮಿಸು. To be perplexed.

ಉದ್ಯಮ (*tb.* ಉದ್ದಮ, *etc.*) s. n. Undertaking; exertion; business.

ಉದ್ಯಮಿ s. a. Active, diligent. -ಸು. To undertake anything.

ಉದ್ಯಾನ s. n. A garden, park. 2, motive, purpose. -ವನ. A beautiful garden.

ಉದ್ಯಾಪನ s. n. Accomplishing. 2, the concluding ceremony of any religious observance.

ಉದ್ಯುಕ್ತ s. a. Zealously active.

ಉದ್ಯೋಗ s. n. Business; an occupation, profession; an office, situation. 2, exertion. -ನಡಿಸು. To follow a profession. -ಮಾಡು. To work; to execise an office. -ಪರ್ವ. N. of the fifth book of the Mahâbhârata. -ಸ್ಥ. A man of profession; an official. ಉದ್ಯೋಗಿ. Active, diligent; a person in office. ಉದ್ಯೋಗಿಸು. To undertake anything; to be busy.

ಉದ್ರ s. n. An otter.

ಉದ್ರಿ. = ಉದ್ಧರಿ, *q. v.*

ಉದ್ರೇಕ s. n. Excess, increase, abundance. 2, enjoyment. 3, forwardness. ಉದ್ರೇಕಿಸು. To be excited.

ಉದ್ವರ್ತ, -ನ s. n. Going up, 2, rubbing and cleansing the body with unguents.

ಉದ್ವಹನ s. n. Lifting up. 2, carrying. 3, leading home, marrying.

ಉದ್ವಾರ್ಚನೆ s. n. Concluding ceremonies of an idol-worship.

ಉದ್ವಾಹನ s. n. That which raises. ಉದ್ವಾಹಿಕ. Matrimonial. ಉದ್ವಾಹಿಸು. To marry.

ಉದ್ವೇಗ s. n. Rashness; agitation; anxiety, fear. ಉದ್ವೇಗಿಸು. To go swiftly.

ಉನಿ k. v. i. To be soaked; to soak. -ಯು ಹಾಕು, ಉನಿಸು. To soak.

ಉನಿತು a. k. a. So much as this.

ಉಂತು k. ad. In this (intermediate) manner.

ಉಂದು k. ad. This (or at this intermediate) time.

ಉನ್ನತ s. a. Raised; elevated, high; eminent. n. Elevation, altitude. -ತ್ವ, -ತೆ. Height; sublimity, greatness; eminence; majesty. ಉನ್ನತೋನ್ನತ. Very high, the highest.

ಉನ್ನರು. = ಹುನ್ನರು.

ಉನ್ನಿಸು a. k. v. i. To think, consider.

ಉನ್ಮತ್ತ 1, ಉನ್ಮದ s. a. Intoxicated; mad, furious. 2, haughty, arrogant. ಉನ್ಮತ್ತತೆ, ಉನ್ಮಾದ. Madness; intoxication; pride.

ಉನ್ಮತ್ತ 2. s. n. The thorn-apple, *Datura* [*metel.*

ಉನ್ಮನ, -ಸ್ s. a. Excited in mind, longing for.

ಉನ್ಮಾದ s. n. Madness, extravagance, arrogance.

ಉನ್ಮೀಲನ s. n. Winking; awaking; expanding.

ಉಪ s. ad. Under; inferior; towards; on; near to; with; etc. 2, *prefixed to verbs or nouns it denotes approach, vicinity or inferiority, as:* -ಕ್ರಮ, -ಗ್ರಾಮ, -ಪುರಾಣ, *etc.*

ಉಪಕಥೆ s. n. A short story related in a long one.

ಉಪಕರಣ s. n. Helping. 2, an implement, instrument; a means.

ಉಪಕಾರ, s. n. Help, assistance; benefit; a favour, kindness; *also* ಉಪಕೃತಿ. -ಅರಿ, -ನೆನಸು, -ಸ್ಮರಿಸು. To be grateful. -ಮಾಡು, ಉಪಕರಿಸು. To benefit, help; to do a favour. -ಸ್ಮರಣೆ. Gratitude. -ಹೊರಿಸು. To put under obligation, to oblige. ಉಪಕಾರಿ. Gracious; a benefactor. ಉಪಕಾರಿಕೆ. A protectress; a palace.

ಉಪಕ್ರಮ s. n. Approach. 2, commencement. 3, a design. 4, a means. ಉಪಕ್ರಮಿಸು. To commence.

ಉಪಕ್ಷಮ s. n. Patience, forbearance.

ಉಪಗತ s. a. Gone to, approached; occurred; granted.

ಉಪಗೃಹ s. n. An inner apartment.

ಉಪಗ್ರಹ s. n. Confinement. 2, a minor planet.

ಉಪಘಾತ s. n. Injury, damage, hurt.

ಉಪಚಯ s. n. Collecting; accumulation; quantity, heap.

ಉಪಚರಣ, ಉಪಚಾರ s. n. Service; attendance; homage; attention, courtesy, civility. 2, pretext, metaphor. 3, physicking. ಉಪಚಾರಿ. Serving; a polite person. ಉಪಚರಿಸು. To wait on, to treat kindly.

ಉಪಜೀವನ s. n. Living; subsistence, livelihood; maintenance. -ಸಾಗಿಸು. To maintain one's existence. ಉಪಜೀವಕ. Living upon; a dependant. ಉಪಜೀವಿಸು. To live upon; to get one's livelihood; to live.

ಉಪಟಳ (*tb. of* ಉಪದ್ರ.) n. Annoyance, trouble.

ಉಪತಾಪ s. n. Heat. 2, pain, trouble. 3, disease. ಉಪತಾಪಿಸು. To feel pain; to be sorrowful.

ಉಪದೇಶ s. n. Instruction; teaching; information; advice; initiation in a mantra. -ಕ, ಉಪದೇಶಿ. A teacher; a spiritual guide. -ಕೊಡು, -ಮಾಡು, ಉಪದೇಶಿಸು. To instruct, teach, advise. -ತಕ್ಕೊಳ್ಳು. To take advice.

ಉಪದ್ರ (*tb. of* ಉಪದ್ರವ) n. A calamity, disaster; trouble; annoyance; a disease or affliction; a national distress. -ಕೊಡು, -ಮಾಡು, -ಪಡಿಸು. To trouble, afflict.

ಉಪಧೆ s. n. Imposition, fraud. 2, a penultimate letter *(g.)*.

ಉಪನಗರ s. n. A suburb.

ಉಪನಯನ s. n. Investiture with a thread to be worn over the left shoulder and under the right.

ಉಪನಿಷದ್ s. n. The knowledge of Brahmâ as the only existent. 2, the sections of the vêdas which treat of this knowledge.

ಉಪನೇತ್ರ s. n. Spectacles.

ಉಪನ್ಯಾಸ s. n. A statement, suggestion. 2, an introduction. 3, lecturing.

ಉಪಪತ್ತಿ s. n. Production; gaining; a theory; proof; means.

ಉಪಪನ್ನ s. a. Produced; gained; proved; suited to the occasion.

ಉಪಪಾತಕ s. n. A sin in the second degree, *as* killing a cow, *etc.*

ಉಪಭೋಗ s. n. Enjoyment; use. 2, pleasure. ಉಪಭೋಗಿಸು. To enjoy, *etc.*

ಉಪಮಾನ s. n. Comparison; analogy; illustration; a simile.

ಉಪಮೆ s. n. Resemblance, similarity; a simile; comparison. ಉಪಮಿಸು. To compare.

ಉಪಯುಕ್ತ s. a. Adapted, suitable; convenient; useful. -ತನ. A proper behaviour.

ಉಪಯೋಗ s. n. Application; use, service; utility. ಉಪಯೋಗಿಸು. To make use of, to use.

ಉಪರತಿ s. n. Ceasing, stopping; refraining from sensual enjoyment.

ಉಪರಿ s. ad. Above; upon; besides; beyond; after.

ಉಪರೋಧ s. n. Hindering; obstruction; impediment. -ಕ. One who hinders, etc. ಉಪರೋಧಿಸು. To hinder, etc.

ಉಪಲಬ್ಧ s. a. Obtained; perceived; well known.

ಉಪವನ s. n. A grove, garden in the suburbs.

ಉಪವಾಸ s. n. A fast, fasting. -ಇರು, -ಬೀಳು, -ಮಾಡು. To fast. ಉಪವಾಸಿ. One who fasts.

ಉಪವಿಶೇಷಣ s. n. A word used to modify an adjective, an adverb (g.).

ಉಪವೀತ s. n. The sacrificial thread worn by the three first classes.

ಉಪವೇದ s. n. Writings subordinate to the vêdas, as on medicine, music, etc.

ಉಪಶಮ, ಉಪಶಮನ s. n. Calmness, composure; patience. 2, quieting; appeasing. 3, anodyne. ಉಪಶಮಿಸು. To abate, become calm or refreshed; to take rest. -ಮಾಡು. To calm, appease.

ಉಪಶಾಂತಿ s. n. Calmness, composure, tranquillity.

ಉಪಸರ್ಗ s. n. Connection; nearness. 2, trouble, misfortune. 3, a calamity. 4, a preposition; a prefix (g.).

ಉಪಸರ್ಪಣೆ s. n. Approaching (for help). ಉಪಸರ್ಪಿಸು. To approach; to have recourse to.

ಉಪಸಾಗರ s. n. A bay.

ಉಪಸ್ಥಿತ s. ad. Approached, near, at hand.

ಉಪಹತಿ s. n. Destruction; vexation; disturbance; infatuation.

ಉಪಹಾರ s. n. An oblation; a tribute, present, gift.

ಉಪಾಕರ್ಮ s. n. A ceremony performed once a year before reciting the vêdas.

ಉಪಾಗಮ s. n. Approach; agreement. 2, a minor âgama.

ಉಪಾದಾನ s. n. Abstraction; withdrawing the organs of sense and perception from the outer world. 2, material cause. -ಕಾರಣ. Immediate or proximate cause.

ಉಪಾಧಿ s. n. Virtuous reflection. 2, deception, disguise. 3, a peculiarity. 4, an attribute, epithet. 5, the natural character of species, quality or action.

ಉಪಾಧ್ಯ s. n. Teacher. 2, a priest that conducts the ceremonies, etc.

ಉಪಾಧ್ಯಾಯ s. n. A schoolmaster; a preceptor. ಉಪಾಧ್ಯಾಯಿ, ಉಪಾಧ್ಯಾಯೆ. A female teacher; a teacher's wife.

ಉಪಾಯ s. n. A means, expedient, way, scheme, stratagem. -ಗಾರ, -ಶಾಲಿ. A schemer; an expert. -ಹೇಳು. To point out means. -ಕಲ್ಪಿಸು, -ಮಾಡು. To devise, contrive.

ಉಪಾಸ. tb. of ಉಪವಾಸ, q. v. ಉಪಾಸಿ. = ಉಪವಾಸಿ.

ಉಪಾಸನೆ s. n. Service, worship, adoration. -ಮಾಡು, ಉಪಾಸಿಸು. To worship.

ಉಪಾಸ್ತಿ s. n. Worship; meditation.

ಉಪೇಕ್ಷೆ s. n. Disregard, neglect; indifference. ಉಪೇಕ್ಷಿಸು. To disregard, disdain, neglect.

ಉಪೇಂದ್ರ s. n. Vishṇu or Kṛishṇa. 2, a king. 3, N. of a man.

ಉಪೋದ್ಘಾತ s. n. An example. 2, a beginning. 3, analysis.

ಉಪೋಷಣ, -ಷ್ಯ s. n. A fast, fasting.

ಉಪ್ಪಡ k. n. Salted and dried vegetables.

ಉಪ್ಪರ (tb. of ಉಪರಿ) n. Height, loftiness.

ಉಪ್ಪರಿಗೆ (tb. of ಉಪಕಾರಿಕೆ) n. A palace; an upstair house; the upper story of a house. -ಮನೆ. An upstair house.

ಉಪ್ಪರಿಸು k. v. i. To rise, *as* the soul; to jump up. *v. t.* To extend, increase, spread.

ಉಪ್ಪಲಿಗ k. n. One of the salt-maker's caste.

ಉಪ್ಪಲಿಗೆ k. n. A small tree, *Macaranga indica*.

ಉಪ್ಪಾರ (ರ=ಱ) k. n. A bricklayer, stone-mason. 2, a salt-maker; *f.* -ತಿ. ಉಪ್ಪಾರಿಕೆ. The business of a bricklayer or a salt-maker.

ಉಪ್ಪು k. n. Salt. 2, doting affection. 3, a game at which the women play. ಉಪ್ಪಗಟಿ. A thorny climbing shrub *Monetia*. ಉಪ್ಪಿನ ಕಟ್ಟೆ. A salt pan or depôt. ಉಪ್ಪಿನ ಕಲ್ಲು. Rock-salt. ಉಪ್ಪಿನ ಕಾಯಿ. Pickles. -ಕಾರ. Salt and other spicery. -ಗಡ್ಲೆ. Bengal gram parched and seathed in salt. ಉಪ್ಪಿಟ್ಟು. A kind of cake with various ingredients. -ಉಣ್ಣು, -ತಿನ್ನು. To be in one's employ. -ಮಡಿ. A salt—bed. -ಮಣ್ಣು. Salt earth. ಉಪ್ಪೂಡು. To salt.

ಉಬ್ಬಟೆ a.k. n. Swelling; elation; power; boldness, heroism. 2, crying aloud.

ಉಬ್ಬಣೆ k. n. A wooden beam for locking a door. 2, a kind of weapon; a club.

ಉಬ್ಬರ k. n. Swelling; increase; abundance. ಉಬ್ಬರಿಸು. To swell, be swollen; to rise; to be full; to be elated; to be joyful.

ಉಬ್ಬಲು (=ಉಮ್ಮಿ, ಉಯ್) k. n. The husk of paddy. 2, fallen hair or wool.

ಉಬ್ಬಸ, ಉಬ್ಬುಸ k. n. Asthma. 2, fretfulness, envy. 3, difficulty, trouble. -ಪಡು, -ಬೀಳು. To become asthmatic.

ಉಬ್ಬಳಿಕೆ k. n. Nausea, qualm, eructation. ಉಬ್ಬಳಿಸು. To nauseate.

ಉಬ್ಬು k. v. i. To swell; to rise; to be puffed up. *n.* The state of being swollen; elation; pride. 2, crying. -ವಿಕೆ, ಉಬ್ಬಿಕೆ. Swelling. -ಗುಂದು. Pride to fade. -ಗೊಬ್ಬು. Excessive pride. -ತಗ್ಗು. Hill and dale; unevenness. -ಹೊಳೆ. A swollen river. ಉಬ್ಬಿಸು. To cause to swell, *etc.*

ಉಬ್ಬೆ k. n. Heat; steam. 2, rain. -ಗೆ ಹಾಕು. To expose to steam. -ಮನೆ. A washerman's hut where dirty clothes are steamed.

ಉಬ್ಬೆಗ (*tb. of* ಉದ್ವೇಗ) n. Anxiety, fear, distress.

ಉಭಯ s. a. Both. -ಕರ್ತೃಕ. Two agents. -ತರು, -ತ್ರರು. Persons of both sides, both persons. -ತ್ರ. In both places or times. -ಪಾರ್ಶ್ವ. Both sides. -ಭಾಷೆ. Both languages: Samskṛita and Kannaḍa. -ಲಿಂಗ. A word of common gender. -ಲೋಕ. This and the other world. ಉಭಯಾನುಮತ. Mutually agreed to or accepted. ಉಭಯಾನುಮತಿ. Mutual agreement.

ಉಮಾ, ಉಮೆ s. n. Lin, flax, *Linum usitatissimum*. 2, Śiva's wife. ಉಮಾಪತಿ, ಉಮೆಯೊಡೆಯ. Śiva.

ಉಮೇದ, ಉಮೇದು h. n. Confidence, assurance; aptitude, inclination. -ವಾರ. A candidate, volunteer. -ವಾರಿ. Expectancy, volunteering.

ಉಂಬಳಿ, ಉಂಬುಳಿ (ಳಿ=ೞಿ) k. n. An enjoyment-gift: the rent-free grant of a land. -ಗಾರ. The holder of an umbaḷi.

ಉಂಬು k. *A vulgar form of* ಉಣ್ಣು, *q. v.*

ಉಮ್ಮತ್ತ. *tb. of* ಉನ್ಮತ್ತ, *q. v.*

ಉಮ್ಮಲು k. n. Phlegm, mucus. 2, difficult breathing.

ಉಮ್ಮಳ (*tb. of* ಉಷ್ಮನ್) n. Heat; grief, trouble, anxiety. ಉಮ್ಮಳಿಕೆ. Heat; distress, anxiety; fatigue. ಉಮ್ಮಳಿಸು. To be hot; to grieve, be distressed.

ಉಮ್ಮಿ, ಉಯ್. = ಉಬ್ಬಲು, *q. v.*

ಉಮ್ಮಿಗೆ, ಉಮ್ಮುಗೆ k. n. Milky grains of wheat or barley fried for eating.

ಉಮ್ಮೆ k. n. A stone used to remove juice. 2, (*tb. of* ಊಷ್ಮ) heat, steam.

ಉಯ್ k. v. t. To restrain, check, bind.

ಉಯ್ಯಾಲು, ಉಯ್ಯಾಲು, ಉಯ್ಯಾಲೆ k. n. A swing. ಉಯ್ಯಾಲೋತ್ಸವ. A festival at which the idol of Vishṇu is swung.

ಉರ (*tb.* *of* ಉರಸ್) *n.* The breast.

ಉರಗ s. *n.* A snake. -ಭೋಜ. A mungoose; a peacock. -ಶಯನ. Vishṇu. -ಪತಿ, ಉರಗೇಂದ್ರ. The king of snakes.

ಉರಟ. = ಉರಟು.

ಉರಟಣೆ k. *n.* Rolling-play: a play of a newly married couple.

ಉರಟಾ h. *a.* Inverse, upside down. -ಯಿಸು. To reject, deceive.

ಉರಟು (=ಉರುಟು) k. *v. i.* To roll. *n.* Coarseness, *as* of cloth, thread, hair, *etc.*, thickness. -ತೊಗಲು. A coarse skin. -ನೂಲು. Stout thread.

ಉರತ (=ಉರುತ) k. *n.* Burning; irritation.

ಉರಪು (=ಉರುಪು) k. *v. i.* To inflame, burn. *n.* Burning.

ಉರಲು 1. (=ಉರುಲು) k. *n.* A running knot; a noose, snare. 2, rolling, crumbling. -ಗಡ್ಡೆ. The potato.

ಉರಲು 2, ಉರವಲ k. *n.* Fuel.

ಉರವಣೆ k. *n.* Crying aloud.

ಉರವಣೆ k. *n.* Haste, rashness; impulse, urgency. ಉರವಣಿಸು. To act hastily or presumptuously.

ಉರಳಿ k. *n.* A ball, *as* of dough, *etc.* 2, a bulb. 3, a round vessel.

ಉರಳು. = ಉರುಳು, *q. v.*

ಉರಿ 1. k. *v. i.* To burn, blaze, glow; to burn from rage, envy, fever, *etc.* *n.* Burning; flame, blaze, *etc.* -ಆರಿಸು, -ಕೆಡಿಸು, -ನಂದಿಸು. To quench a flame. -ಕಜ್ಜಿ. A burning itch. -ಕಿಡಿ. A glowing spark. -ಕೆ, -ತ. Burning. -ಕೆಂಡ. A burning coal. -ಗಣ್ಣು. An inflamed eye. -ಗಿಚ್ಚು, -ಬೆಂಕಿ. A flaming fire. -ಚೇಳು. A reddish kind of scorpion. -ನಂಜು. Morbid humours of the body. -ನಾಲಗೆ. A fiery tongue. -ಮಾರಿ. The furious Durga; a passionate woman. -ಬತ್ತಿ, -ವತ್ತಿ. A burning wick. -ಮೂತ್ರ, -ಯುಚ್ಚೆ. Morbidly heated urine; strangury, gravel. -ಮಾತು, -ವಾತು. A sharp word. -ಹಚ್ಚು, -ಹತ್ತಿಸು. To kindle a fire. -ಪು, -ಸು. To cause to burn.

ಉರಿ 2. (ರಿ = ಱಿ) k. *n.* A coarse network for suspending pots and other vessels.

ಉರು 1. s. *a.* Great, much, excessive, eminent, precious. -ತರ. Greater, wider.

ಉರು 2. (ರು = ಱು) a. k. *v. i.* To be; to stay, stop; to hesitate; to come about.

ಉರುಕ (ರು = ಱು) k. *n.* Standing, stopping.

ಉರುಗು 1. k. *n.* Passion, anger.

ಉರುಗು 2. (ರು = ಱು) a. k. *v. i.* To be crooked, distorted. *n.* Crookedness. -ಕಾಲು. A crooked leg. -ಬಾಯಿ. A wry face. -ಬೆರಳು. A crooked finger.

ಉರುಟು (=ಉರಟು) k. *v. i.* To go beyond; to be overbearing. 2, to roll. *n.* Pride. 2, coarseness, *as* of cloth, *etc.* 3, rolling; roundness; a plain ring. ಉರುಟಾಣೆ. = ಉರಟಣೆ, *q. v.*

ಉರುತ, ಉರುಪು. = ಉರತ, ಉರಪು.

ಉರುಬು (ರು = ಱು) k. *n.* Violence; rapidity; force.

ಉರುಬೆ, ಉರುವು (ರು = ಱು) k. *n.* Mass, multitude, excess; excellence.

ಉರುಲು (= ಉರಲು) k. *n.* A noose, snare, gin. -ಹಾಕಿಕೊಳ್ಳು. To hang one's self.

ಉರುವಣೆ. = ಉರವಣೆ, *q. v.*

ಉರುಸು h. *n.* Offerings at the shrine of a Muhammadan saint.

ಉರುಳು k. *v. i.* To roll; to be turned over; to revolve. *n.* Rolling. 2, a noose. ಉರುಳಾಡು. To roll about. ಉರುಳಿಸು. To cause to roll, *etc.* -ಸೇವೆ. A religious vow or penance which consists in rolling one's self round a temple.

ಉರೆ (ರೆ = ಱೆ) k. *ad.* Abundantly, well, nicely, fully; much. *n.* Abundance.

ಉರೇ k. *int.* Bravo! well done!

ಉರ್ಕ. = ಉಕ್ಕು, *q. v.*

ಉರ್ಚು. = ಉಚ್ಚು, *q. v.*

ಉರ್ಜು. = ಉಜ್ಜು, *q. v.*

ಉರ್ಬು. = ಉಬ್ಬು, *q. v.*

ಉರ್ಳು. = ಉರುಳು, *q. v.*

ಉಲಕು k. v. i. To start up, as a tiger. 2, to flash on the mind; painful thoughts to arise. 3, to be sprained. n. A sprain.

ಉಲಿ k. v. i. To sound; to cry, utter, speak. n. A sound; a cry. -ಪ, -ಪು, -ಹು. A sound; a cry.

ಉಲಿಪೆ. = ಉಲುಫೆ, q. v.

ಉಲುಕು, ಉಲ್ಕು. = ಉಲಕು, q. v.

ಉಲುಟು. = ಉರುಳು, q. v.

ಉಲುಫೆ (= ಉಲಿಪೆ) h. n. Gratuitous supplies or presents given to great persons on a journey.

ಉಲೂಕ s. n. An owl.

ಉಲ್ಕ, ಉಲ್ಕೆ s. n. A flame; a meteor. 2, a firebrand. ಉಲ್ಕಾಪಾತ. Falling of a star.

ಉಲ್ಲಂಗಿ k. n. A snipe.

ಉಲ್ಲಂಘನೆ s. n. Passing over; transgression. ಉಲ್ಲಂಘಿಸು. To cross; to transgress.

ಉಲ್ಲಟ, ಉಲ್ಲಟಪಲ್ಲಟ (= ಉರಟಾ) f. a. Inverse, upside down, topsyturvy, out of order.

ಉಲ್ಲಸ. = ಉಲ್ಲಾಸ, q. v. ಉಲ್ಲಸಿಸು. = ಉಲ್ಲಾಸಿಸು.

ಉಲ್ಲಾಪ s. n. An outcry. 2, change of voice in grief, sickness, etc.

ಉಲ್ಲಾಸ s. n. Sport, joy, delight. -ಗಾರ. A gay man. ಉಲ್ಲಾಸಿಸು (=ಉಲ್ಲಸಿಸು). To delight, be merry.

ಉಲ್ಲಿ k. ad. In this intermediate place.

ಉಲ್ಲೇಖ, ಉಲ್ಲೇಖನ s. n. Scraping; writing, description. ಉಲ್ಲೇಖಿಸು. To write.

ಉಲ್ಹಾಸ. tb. of ಉಲ್ಲಾಸ. q. v.

ಉವ k. *An affix of the present rel. part. of the future, and of the imp., as* ಸಾಯುವ, ಬರುವ, ಕೇಳುವ. *ad.* This (intermediate) man.

ಉಶನಸ (*tb. of* ಉಶನಸ್) n. The planet Venus. 2, Śukra.

ಉಶ್ವಾಸ (*tb. of* ಉಚ್ಛ್ವಾಸ) n. Breathing; inhaling; breath. -ನಿಶ್ವಾಸ. Inhaling and exhaling.

ಉಷ, ಉಷಸ್ s. n. Morning light, dawn. ಉಷಃಕಾಲ. The dawn, daybreak.

ಉಷ್ಟ್ರ s. n. A camel. 2, an "ostrich". ಉಷ್ಟ್ರಿ, -ಕೆ. A she-camel.

ಉಷ್ಣ s. a. Hot, warm. 2, passionate; sharp. n. Heat, warmth; *also* -ತೆ. -ಉದಕ, ಉಷ್ಣೋದಕ. Hot water.

ಉಸಲಿ h. n. Boiled pulse seasoned with salt, chilli, *etc.*

ಉಸಬು, ಉಸುಕು, ಉಸುಬು k. n. Sand.

ಉಸಲು. = ಉಸುರು, q. v.

ಉಸಾಬರಿ f. n. Business, affair.

ಉಸುರು k. v. i. To speak, say; (to breathe). n. Breath; life. 2, taking breath. ಉಸುರಾಡಿಸು, ಉಸುರಿಕ್ಕು, ಉಸುರಿಡು, ಉಸುರುಗರೆ, ಉಸುರ್ವಿಡು. To breathe. -ಕಟ್ಟು, -ಹಿಡಿ. To hold the breath. -ಕಟ್ಟಿಸು. To choke. -ಕಳೆ, -ಬಿಡು. To exhale; to expire.

ಉಹೂ k. *int.* A sound used by cattle drivers in calling their cattle. *ad.* No, no!

ಉಳ್ k. v. t. To have, possess. v. i. To be. *Pres. rel. past* ಉಳ್ಳ. Being; possessing; *affixed to nouns it turns them into adjectives, as:* ಕೆಲಸವುಳ್ಳ, employed; ಬುದ್ಧಿಯುಳ್ಳ, wise; ಜ್ವರವುಳ್ಳ, feverish; ಪ್ರೀತಿಯುಳ್ಳ, lovely; *etc.*

ಉಳ (ಳ = ಐ) (= ಉಳಿ 2) k. n. Remaining, remnant. -ಕೊಳ್ಳು. To remain, stop; to escape. -ಗಡೆ, -ಪಡಿ, -ವು, -ಹು. The remainder. -ಕೆ. Remaining.

ಉಳಿ 1. k. v. i. To conceal one's self. n. A thief. 2, a chisel; an awl. 3, hiding; an ambush; a hunter's hut.

ಉಳಿ 2. (ಳ = ಐ) k. v. i. To leave, quit. 2. to be left, to remain. 3, to be left out. 4, to be saved. 5, to remain behind. *P. p.* ಉಳಿದು, ಉಳಿತು. n. Remaining, remnant. -ಕೆ. Remainder. -ಗ. A bird of omen. -ಪು, -ಸು. To spare, save, keep alive.

ಉಳು (ಳು = ಱು) k. v. t. To plough, P. p. ಉತ್ತು. ಉತ್ತಭೂಮಿ, ploughed land. -ಕ, -ಮೆ, -ವಿಕೆ. Ploughing.

ಉಳುಗು (ಳು = ಱು) k. v. t. To be attached. ಉಳ್ಗೆ. Attachment.

ಉಳ್ಳು k. v. i. To shine; to blaze. n. A shining substance, a meteor. 2, = ಉಲ್ಕ.

ಉಳ್ಳಿ k. n. A bulb; an onion. Cpds.: ಕಾರುಳ್ಳಿ, ನೀರುಳ್ಳಿ, ಬೆಳ್ಳುಳ್ಳಿ. -ಗಡ್ಡೆ. An onion.

ಊ

ಊ. The sixth letter of the alphabet. 2, *a copulative conjunction signifying:* and; and...and; also; at any rate; even; though. ಎಲ್ಲಿಯೂ, everywhere; ಎಂದೂ, always.

ಊಕಾರ s. The letter ಊ.

ಊಕೆ, ಊಂಕೆ k. n. The warp of a loom spread and starched.

ಊಚ, ಊಚು (*tb. of* ಉಚ್ಚ) a. Superior, costly. -ಅರಿವೆ. Costly cloth. -ನೀಚ. Superior and inferior.

ಊಜಿ k. n. An insect that infests grain.

ಊಟ (*fr.* ಉಣ್ಣು) k. n. A meal; taking a meal. -ಕೂಟ. A dinner party. -ಕೊಡು. To give a dinner. -ಕ್ಕೆ ಕರೆ. To invite to a meal. -ಗೀಟ. *reit.* -ಮಾಡು. To take a meal. -ಮಾಡಿಸು. To give a meal. -ಗಾರ. A great eater; *f.* -ಗಾರಳು, -ಗಾತಿ.

ಊಟು h. n. Rising. -ಬೈಸು. Rising and sitting down, *as* on haunches in quick succession.

ಊಟೆ k. n. A natural spring of water.

ಊಡು k. v. t. To give to eat, make eat. 2, to join, yoke. 2, to smear. v. i. To eat. ಊಡಿಸು. To cause to eat; *cf.* ಊಟ.

ಊತ (*fr.* ಊದು) k. n. Firmness.

ಊದ, ಊದು h. n. Frankincense. -ಬತ್ತಿ, -ಕಡ್ಡಿ. A stick covered with frankincense, pastille.

ಊದರೆ k. n. A kind of corn-tares, *Paspalum pilosum.*

ಊದಾ, ಊದಿ h. n. Lilac, sky-blue.

ಊದು k. v. t. To blow. 2, to refine metal. v. i. To be puffed up; to swell. n. Blowing; swollen state; *also:* ಊದಲು, ಊದಿಕೆ. -ಗೊಳವೆ, -ಗೋವಿ. A blow-pipe. -ಗಲ್ಲ. A swollen cheek. -ಗಾಲು. A swollen leg. ಊದಿ ಹೇಳು. To say distinctly.

ಊನ s. a. Lessened, deficient; maimed; defective. n. A defect, maim; deduction; *also* -ತೆ. -ಮಾಡು. To maim or injure.

ಊಬಲು = ಉಬ್ಬಲು, *q. v.*

ಊಬು k. n. The awn of barley. -ಹುಲ್ಲು. A common fodder grass.

ಊಮೆ k. n. A dumb man; a taciturn man.

ಊರು 1. k. n. A village; a town. -ಬಾಗಲು, ಊರಗಸೆ. A town gate. ಊರವ, ಊರಿನವ. A villager, townsman; *f.* ಊರವಳು. ಊರಾಳು. A villager; village-people. -ಕಟ್ಟೆ. A raised seat round a tree in front of a village. -ಕೇರಿ, -ಗೇರಿ. A village street. -ಜನರು, -ಮಂದಿ. Townsfolk. -ಹತ್ತಿರ. The neighbourhood of a village. -ಗ. A rustic, vulgar man. -ಗನುಡಿ. A vulgar expression.

ಊರು 2. (ರು = ಱು) v. t. To lean on, *as* a stick. 2, to put down, fix, set firmly; to plant (ಬೇರೂರು, to root). v. i. To be, exist; to settle; to stay. 2, to leak out, to spring, *as* water. 3, to be soaked. n. Leaning, *etc.* -ಕೋಲು. A walking stick. ಕಾಲೂರಿ ನಿಂತುಕೊಳ್ಳು. To stand firmly. ಊರಿಸು. To cause to lean on, penetrate, *etc.*; to steep, soak.

ಊರ್ಜ s. n. Power, energy; effort. ಊರ್ಜಿತ. Powerful; well established; mighty, excellent; much.

ಊರ್ಧ್ವ s. a. High, raised up. n. Elevation. -ಗತಿ. Going upwards, ascent; môksha. -ಪುಂಡ್ರ. A perpendicular line on the forehead of a Vaishṇava. -ಲೋಕ. Heaven. -ಶ್ವಾಸ. Expiration.

ಊರ್ಮಿ s. n. A wave. 2, a fold in a garment. -ಳೆ. Janaka's daughter and wife of Lakshmaṇa.

ಊಷ, ಊಷರ s. n. Salt ground.

ಊಷ್ಮ s. n. Heat; steam; passion.

ಊಸರವಳ್ಳಿ, ಊಸರುಳ್ಳಿ k. n. A kind of lizard, the Indian monitor.

ಊಹೆ (tb. of ಊಹ) n. A guess, conjecture. 2, reasoning; reflection. -ಮಾಡು, ಊಹಿಸು. To suppose, reason, infer.

ಊಳಿಗ (ಳ = ಐ') k. n. Work, business; service. -ದವ, ಊಳಿಗಿ. A male servant. -ಗಿತ್ತಿ. A female servant. -ತನ. Service.

ಊಳು a. k. v. i. To call; to cry out; to howl (p.p. ಊಳ್ದು, ಊಳಿ). n. A howl.

ಋ

ಋ. The seventh letter of the alphabet.

ಋಕಾರ s. The letter ಋ.

ಋಕ್ಕು. tb. of ಋಚ್, q. v.

ಋಗ್ವೇದ s. n. The ṛigvêda, the first of the four vêdas.

ಋಚ್ (tb. ಋಕ್ಕು) n. The ṛigvêda. 2, a verse of the ṛigvêda.

ಋಜು s. a. Straight; right; honest, upright. -ವೀರ. An honest hero.

ಋಣ s. n. Guilt. 2, debt; obligation. -ಕೊಡು. To lend money. -ತೀರಿಸು, -ಪರಿಹರಿಸು. To pay a debt. -ಮಾಡು. To borrow. -ಹೊರು. To incur debt. -ಗಾರ. A debtor. -ಬಾಧೆ. The trouble from debt. -ಮುಕ್ತ. Released from debt. -ಮುಕ್ತಿ, -ಮೋಕ್ಷ. Discharge of a debt. -ಸ್ಥ. A creditor; a debtor. ಋಣಾನುಬಂಧ. The connection of indebtedness in some preceding birth for certain sufferings or enjoyments.

ಋತ s. a. True, right. n. Truth. 2, gleaning. 3, an ascetic. 4, the sun, moon. 5, water.

ಋತು s. n. A period; an epoch; a period or season consisting of two months: ವಸಂತ, ಗ್ರೀಷ್ಮ, ವರ್ಷ, ಶರದ್, ಹೇಮಂತ, ಶಿಶಿರ. -ವೃತ್ತಿ. A year.

ಋತ್ವಿಜ್ s. n. A priest who officiates at sacrifices.

ಋದ್ಧಿ s. n. Growth; prosperity, welfare. 2, excellence; cf. ವೃದ್ಧಿ, q. v.

ಋಭುಕ್ಷ s. n. Indra.

ಋಶ್ಯ s. n. The white-footed antelope.

ಋಷಭ. = ವೃಷಭ, q. v.

ಋಷಿ s. n. An inspired poet, sage, saint, hermit; seven principal ṛishis are enumerated, see ಸಪ್ತರ್ಷಿ. 2, the seven principal stars of the great bear.

ಋಷ್ಯ (= ಋಶ್ಯ) s. n. The white-footed antelope. -ಮೂಕ. A mountain in the Dekhan, known as the temporary abode of Râma with Sugrîva. -ಶೃಂಗ. N. of a personage in the first book of the Râmâyaṇa.

ಋ ಌ ೡ

The eighth, ninth and tenth letters of the alphabet. No words begin with these letters, and the use of them is extremely rare.

ಎ

ಎ. The eleventh letter of the alphabet. 2, the final *(a) of nouns, (b) of verbs, and (c) of adverbs, as:* ಆನೆ, ಎಡೆ, ಒಲೆ; ತೆಗೆ, ತೊಳೆ, ಪಡೆ; ಮತ್ತೆ, ಮೇಲೆ, ಮೆಲ್ಲನೆ, ಒಳಗೆ, ಕೆಳಗೆ, *etc.* 3, *a particle of emphasis or vocative, as:* ನಾಲ್ಕೆ, ಆತನೆ, ತಾನೆ; ಕೇಳಿರೆ, ಕರೆಯಿರೆ, *etc.*; ದೇವರೆ, ಶಾಮನೆ, ಮಗನೆ, *etc.* 4, *a particle used in doubtful questions; as,* ಬಂದರಾಯಿತೆ? ಸಾಕೆ? 5, *termination of the 1st a. p. sing. of the future and impf. and of the neg. verb, as:* ಮಾಡುವೆ (= ಮಾಡುವೆನು); ಮಾಡಿದೆ (= ಮಾಡಿದೆನು); ಮಾಡೆ (= ಮಾಡೆನು).

ಎಂ a. k. *A termination of the 1st p. sing. pres. fut. and impf. and of the neg. verb, as:* ಬಾಳ್ದಪೆಂ, ಬಾಳ್ದಿಂ, ಬಾಳ್വೆಂ, ಬಾಳೆಂ.

ಎಕತ್ಯಾರು h. n. Authority, control, power.

ಎಕರಾರು h. n. A confession; a deposition.

ಎಕಾರ s. n. The letter ಎ.

ಎಕ್ಕ. *tb. of* ಏಕ. -ಟಿ. Alone, in private; a single person. -ಟಿಕರೆ. To call aside. -ತಾಳ. = ಏಕತಾಲ, *q. v.*

ಎಕ್ಕಟಿಗ k. n. A superior, noble man.

ಎಕ್ಕಟಿ k. n. Greatness; wonder.

ಎಕ್ಕಡ, ಎಕ್ಕವಡ f. n. A kind of leathern sandal.

ಎಕ್ಕತಾಳ k. n. Ridicule, mockery, jest. -ಮಾಡು. To mock, jest.

ಎಕ್ಕರಿಸು k. v. t. To mock, deride, make faces at.

ಎಕ್ಕಲ a. k. n. A wild hog. *a.* High, tall, huge.

ಎಕ್ಕಸಕ್ಕ, ಎಕ್ಕಸೆಕ್ಕ k. n. Confusion, doubt. 2, ridicule, mockery.

ಎಕ್ಕಿ k. n. A piece of timber forming one side of a cot-frame.

ಎಕ್ಕು k. v. t. To divide; to dress cotton, to card wool. *v. i.* To come up, stand on tiptoe. 2, to purge. ಎಕ್ಕಿಸು. To cause to dress cotton, *etc.*

ಎಕ್ಕೆ (*tb. of* ಅರ್ಕ) n. The swallow-wort, *Calotropis gigantea. Cpds.:* -ಕಾಯಿ, -ಗಿಡ, -ನಾರು, -ಹಾಲು.

ಎಗಚಿ k. n. The jujube tree, *Zizyphus jujuba.*

ಎಗರು k. v. i. To rise; to fly; to jump. 2, to fly away; to be spent, *as* money. to wear off, *as* gilt, paint, *etc.;* to be ruined, *as* commerce. ಎಗರಿಸು. To cause to rise, *etc.;* to pilfer.

ಎಗು k. n. Rising; embarkation. -ಮತಿ. Dues for embarking.

ಎಗ್ಗ, ಎಗ್ಗು ಳ a. k. n. A rude, rustic, low man. -ತನ. Rudeness; stupidity.

ಎಗ್ಗಳ. = ವೆಗ್ಗಳ.

ಎಗ್ಗು k. n. Shame. 2, disgrace; blame; harm. -ಳ. A bashful person. -ಳತನ. Bashfulness. -ಹಿಡಿ. To find fault with.

ಎಂಗಿ k. n. A stupid, silly person. 2, fraud, deceit. -ನಾಣ್ಯ. A counterfeit coin.

ಎಚಿ k. v. t. To shoot arrows; to expel, *as* water through a syringe.

ಎಚ್ಚತ್ತು k. *P. p. of* ಎಚ್ಚರು, *q. v.*

ಎಚ್ಚರ, ಎಚ್ಚರಿಕೆ (ರ = ಱ) k. n. Wakefulness; watchfulness, caution, precaution, care. -ಗೇಡಿ. An inattentive or negligent person. -ಗೇಡಿತನ. Inattention, negligence. -ಗೊಳಿಸು. To awaken. -ಗೊಳ್ಳು. To be awake; to make provision. -ತಪ್ಪು, -ಮರೆ. To lose one's self. ಎಚ್ಚರದಿಂದ ಇರು. To be watchful. -ವಡು. To be cautious. -ಆಗು, -ವಾಗು. To be awake. -ಕೊಡು. To call attention; to give caution.

ಎಚ್ಚರು (ರು = ಱು) k. *v. i.* To awake. ಎಚ್ಚರಿಸು. To awaken, wake; to caution, forewarn; to put in mind.

ಎಜಮಾನ. = ಯಜಮಾನ, *q. v.*

ಎಜ್ಜ (*tb. of* ವೇಧ) *n.* A bore, hole.

ಎಂಜಲ, ಎಂಜಲು k. *n.* Food or drink which has come in contact with the mouth and regarded as impure; spittle, saliva. -ಮಾತು. A past word; repeating another's words. -ಹುಳ. An insect living in orts. -ಮಾಡು, ಎಂಜಲಿಸು. To defile.

ಎಟಕು k. *v. i.* To come within reach. 2, to be sufficient. ಎಟಕಿನೋಡು. To peep standing on tiptoe. ಎಟಕಿಸು. To stand on tiptoe to reach anything.

ಎಟ್ಟ k. *n.* A bush-harrow. ಎಟ್ಟಾ ಹೊಡೆ. To roll or flatten sown field.

ಎಟ್ಟ k. *n.* An obstinate person. -ತನ. Obstinacy.

ಎಟ್ಟು k. *v. i.* To be accessible. *n.* A blow.

ಎಡ 1. (= ಎಡೆ) k. *n.* Place, ground. -ತಾಕು. To go and come frequently, to frequent.

ಎಡ 2. k. *n.* The left, the left side. *Cpds.*: -ಗಡೆ, -ಗಣ್ಣು, -ಗಾಲು, -ಗಿವಿ, -ಮಗ್ಗಲು, -ಹೆಗಲು, *etc.* -ಬಲ. Left and right. -ಮುರಿ. To turn to the left. -ಚ. A left-handed man.

ಎಡ 3. (= ಎಡೆ) k. *n.* Place between, interval; inferiority. -ಕುಂಟೆ. A smaller kind of weeding machine. -ತಡೆ. An obstacle. -ತರ. A middling sort; mediocrity. -ವಟ್ಟು, -ವಟ್ಟು. Bad state or character; stupidity.

ಎಡತಂ k. *n.* Difficulty, especially in speaking.

ಎಡರಾಳಿ k. *n.* A foe, adversary.

ಎಡರು 1. k. *n.* Strait, trouble. 2, an impediment, obstacle.

ಎಡರು 2. (ರು = ಱು) a. k. *n.* Poverty; ruin. 2, crookedness. *v. i.* To be crooked, to be dishonest. 2, to stumble, trip.

ಎಡವು, ಎಡಹು (*cf.* ಎಡರು 2, *v. i.*) k. *v. i.* To stumble, trip, to strike with the foot against.

ಎಡೆ 1. (= ಎಡ) k. *n.* A place, spot; ground. 2, room; interval, distance. 3, inferiority. -ಗ. A good-for-nothing man. -ಬಿಡದೆ. Uninterruptedly. -ಕಟ್ಟು. A small dam. -ಗೆಡೆ. To fall down. -ಗೆಡೆಗೆ. *rep.* Here and there. -ಗೊಡು. To give way, submit. -ಗೊಳ್ಳು. To take place, occur; to come to a stand; to obtain; to resort to. -ಪ್ರಾಯ, -ಹರೆಯ. The middle age. -ಆಡು, -ಯಾಡು. To move, wander, roam. -ಉಡುಗು, -ಯುಡುಗು. To leave room; to stop, cease. -ಒತ್ತು, -ಯೊತ್ತು. To compress, squeeze. -ಸೆಳೆ. The inner velocity of a river. -ಹೊತ್ತು. The time between sunrise and sunset.

ಎಡೆ 2. (*tb. of* ಇಡೆ) *n.* An offering; meal. 2, the leaf, *etc.* on which food is placed. -ಇಕ್ಕು, -ಇಡು, -ಕೊಡು, -ಮಾಡು, -ಹಾಕು. To present food to a deity or man.

ಎಡ್ಡ k. *n.* A cheat, liar. 2, (= ದಡ್ಡ) a stupid man. -ತನ. Falsehood; stupidity. -ತಿ. A stupid woman. ಎಡ್ಡಿಸು. To abuse; to mock; to cheat. ಎಡ್ಡು. Cheating; stupidity.

ಎಣಿಕೆ k. *n.* Counting, reckoning. 2, thinking; thought; notice, observation; opinion. -ಗೈಗೂಡು. Thinking to succeed. -ಗೆಯ್. To think, *etc.*

ಎಣಿಸು k. *v. t.* To add together, to count; to reckon; to estimate; to consider; to compare. *v. i.* To think of. ಎಣಿಸಿ ನೋಡು. To number.

ಎಣೆ 1. k. *n.* A couple, pair; connexion; fellowship; equality, similarity; a match. -ಕಳೆ, -ಗಳೆ. To become loose. -ಗಂಟು. A woman's braid of hair. -ಗೊಳ್ಳು. To become equal; to face. -ವಕ್ಕಿ, -ವಕ್ಕಿ. The ruddy goose.

ಎಣೆ 2. = ಹೆಣೆ.

ಎಂಟು 1. k. n. Arrogance.

ಎಂಟು 2. k. a. Eight. ಎಂಟನೆ. Eighth. ಎಂಟಾನೆಂಟು. About eight. ಎಂಟೂವರೆ. Eight and a half. ಎಂಟೆಂಟು. Eight and eight; eight times eight. -ದಿಕ್ಕು, -ದೆಸೆ. The eight points of the compass. -ಕೋಣ, -ಮೂಲೆ. An octagon.

ಎಣ್ಣಿಸು. = ಎಣಿಸು, q. v.

ಎಣ್ಣು k. v. i. To count; to think.

ಎಣ್ಣೆ k. n. Oil. -ಕಾಸು. To heat oil. -ಗೆಂಪು. Dark brown. -ತೆಗೆ. To extract oil. -ಬಿಡು, -ಹಾಕು, -ಹೊಯ್ಯು. To pour oil; to spoil as another's affairs. -ಹಚ್ಚಿಕೊಳ್ಳು. To anoint one's self with oil. -ಗಾಣ. An oil-mill. -ಗಸಿ, -ಕದಳು. The sediment of oil.

ಎಣ್ಬರು k. pro. Eight persons.

ಎತ್ತ 1, ಎತ್ತಲು k. ad. Where? which place or direction? -ಕಡೆ. Whither? ಎತ್ತಲುಂ. Everywhere. ಎತ್ತಾನುಂ. In whatsoever direction; occasionally. ಎತ್ತೆತ್ತಲುಂ. Everywhere.

ಎತ್ತ 2. (cf. ಎತ್ತು) k. n. Lifting up. 2, undertaking; finding out an item in an account. 3, deceit, cunning. -ಗಡೆ. A means, device; a trick.

ಎತ್ತರ, ಎತ್ತರು k. n. Height; tallness. -ಗದ್ದೆ. An elevated rice-field.

ಎತ್ತು 1. k. v. t. To lift, raise, take up; to collect, as money, alms, etc.; to assume, as a form (avatâra); to mention, as the name of another. n. =ಎತ್ತ 2. ಎತ್ತಿಕೆ. Lifting, etc. ಎತ್ತಿ ಬರೆ. To copy, as a manuscript. ಎತ್ತಿಕೊಂಡು ಹೋಗು. To take away. ಎತ್ತಿ ಹೋಗು. To go to attack. ಮೇಲೆತ್ತು, ಮೇಲಕ್ಕೆತ್ತು. To lift up. ಎತ್ತಿಸು. To cause to raise, etc. -ಗಡೆ. = ಎತ್ತಗಡೆ. -ಗಲ್ಲು. Lift-stone. -ಬಾಡಿಗೆ. Rent that is raised. -ಒಲೆ, ಎತ್ತೊಲೆ. A moveable stove. -ಎಕೆ. Lifting, raising, etc.

ಎತ್ತು 2. k. n. An ox, bullock. Cpds.: -ಗಾಡಿ, -ಭಂಡಿ, -ಸವಾರಿ, etc. -ನಾಲಿಗೆ. Bullock's tongue, *Trichodesma indicum*.

ಎತ್ತುವಳಿ k. n. Collecting money.

ಎತ್ನ. tb. of ಯತ್ನ, q. v.

ಎದರು, ಎದಿರು, ಎದುರು (= ಇದಿರು, q. v.) k. n. The front; that which is opposite. -ಆಡು, ಎದುರಾಡು. To outbid; to contradict. ಎದುರಾಯಿಸು. To oppose, contradict. ಎದುರಾಳಿ. An antagonist. -ಗೊಳ್ಳು, ಎದುಗೊಳ್ಳು, -ಬರು. To meet. -ನುಡಿ, -ಮಾತು, -ಎದುರುತ್ತರ. A contradiction. -ಬೀಳು, ಎದುರ್ಗಂಡಿಸು. To contradict. -ವ್ಯಾಜ್ಯ. A counter-claim. ಎದುರ್ಚೀಟು, ಎದುರ್ಪಡಿ. A document given by the purchaser of land stipulating to give it back on repayment of the purchase money within a definite term; a counterpart. ಎದುರ್ಪಳ್ಳಿ. A note of hand given for another that is lost; the counterpart of a deed or lease.

ಎದೆ k. n. The chest, breast; courage. -ಆರು. The breast to become dry; courage to be quenched. -ಒಡೆ. The heart to break: courage to fail. -ಕರಗು. The heart to melt. -ಕ, -ಕೊಡು. To become courageous. -ಕುಂದು, -ಗುಂದು, -ಗೆಡು. Courage to fail. -ಗುಂಡಿಗೆ. The pit of the stomach. -ಗೊಟ್ಟು ನಿಲ್ಲು. To stand boldly. -ಕಿಚ್ಚು, -ಗಿಚ್ಚು. Heartache. -ಗಾರ. A bold man. -ಗುದಿ. The heart to be agitated; violent mental agitation, fear. -ಗುಂದು. Courage to fail. -ಗೆಡಿಸು. To dishearten. -ಗೊಯಿಕ, -ಬಡಕ. A man who disheartens another. -ಮುರಿ. To labour to weariness, fag hard. -ಉರಿ, -ಯುರಿ. The heart-burn. -ಪೊಡಕ. A coward. -ಹಾರು. The heart to palpitate.

ಎದ್ದು k. P. p. of ಏಳು.

ಎನಿತು, ಎನಿತ್ತು a. k. pro. How much? how many?

ಎನಿಬರು a. k. *pro.* How many persons?

ಎನು k. *aff. The common form of* ಎಂ *for the 1st pers. sing. past., fut., and neg., as:* ಮಾಡಿದೆನು, ಮಾಡುವೆನು, ಮಾಡೆನು.

ಎಂತ 1. = ಅಂತ, *q. v. A common p. p. of* ಎನ್ನು, *q. v.*

ಎಂತ 2, ಎಂತಹ, ಎಂತಾ. = ಎಂಥ, *q. v.*

ಎಂತು k. *pro.* In what manner or way? how? ಎಂತುಂ. By all means.

ಎಂತುಟು, = ಎನಿತು, *q. v.*

ಎಂಥ, ಎಂಥಾ (=ಎಂತ 2) k. *pro.* What kind or sort? *int.* What a kind! how! *as:* ಎಂಥ ದೊಡ್ಡ ಮನೆ! ನೋಡು, ದೇವರು ಎಂಥಾ ಜ್ಞಾನಿಯು, ಎಂಥಾ ಸಮರ್ಥನು, ಎಂಥಾ ಒಳ್ಳೆಯವನು!

ಎಂದು 1. k. (*p. p. of* ಎನ್ನು) Having said. *Used to introduce a sentence, when it is equivalent to* "that", *as:* ಬಂದರು ಎಂದು ಹೇಳಿದನು, he said "they came". ಎಲ್ಲಿ ಹೋಗಲಿ ಎಂದು ಕೇಳಿದ್ದನು, "where shall I go?" he asked.

ಎಂದು 2. k. *ad.* What time? when? ಎಂದೂ, ಎಂದಿಗೂ, ಎಂದೆಂದಿಗೂ. For ever and ever, always, continually. ಎಂದಿಗಾದರೂ. At any time soever, once. ಎಂದಿನಂತೆ, ಎಂದಿನವೊಲ್, ಎಂದಿನ ಹಾಗೆ. As usual. ಎಂದುಂ, ಎಂದೂ. Ever, always.

ಎನ್ನ (= ನನ್ನ) a. k. *pro.* Of me, my. ಎನ್ನದು. Mine.

ಎನ್ನು (= ಅನ್ನು) k. *v. t.* To say, speak; to call. *P. ps.* ಎಂದು, ಎಂತ; *pres. p.* ಎಂಬ. ಎಂದರೆ, (ಎಂದೊಡೆ). = ಅಂದರೆ.

ಎಪ್ಪತ್ತು k. *a.* Seventy. ಎಪ್ಪತ್ನಾಲ್ಕು, ಎಪ್ಪತ್ತನಾಲ್ಕು. 74.

ಎಬಡ k. *n.* A foolish, silly man. -ತನ. Silliness.

ಎಬ್ಬಿಸು k. *v. t.* To rouse, awaken; to lift up; to raise; to enliven, give life. ಕೋಪವೆಬ್ಬಿಸು. To provoke.

ಎಬ್ಬು a. k. *v. i.* To rise. ಎಬ್ಬಟ್ಟು. To follww, pursue; to harass.

ಎಮ 1. (= ಎಮ್ಮ, *q. v.*) k. *int.* Well, indeed.

ಎಮ 2. k. *pro.* Our. ಎಮಗೆ. To us. ಎಮತು. Ours.

ಎಮಕೆ, ಎಮಿಕೆ k. *n.* A bone. 2, an ear-ornament.

ಎಮೆ, ಎವೆ k. *n.* An eyelash, eyelid. -ಇಕ್ಕು. To shut the eyelids.

ಎಂಬು k. *v. t.* To say. -ಎಕೆ. Saying. ಎಂಬ, -ವ. (*pres. rel. part. of* ಎನ್ನು). That is or are called. ಎಂಬುದಾಗಿ (ಎಂಬುದು-ಆಗಿ) *used as* ಎಂದು, *q. v.*

ಎಂಬತ್ತು k. *a.* Eighty.

ಎಮ್ಮ k. *pro.* Of us, our. ಎಮ್ಮದು. Ours.

ಎಮ್ಮೆ k. *n.* A female buffalo. -ಚೇಳು. A large black scorpion. -ಬಳ್ಳಿ. The plant *Convolvulus argenteus.* -ಹೋರಿ (-ಪೋರಿ). A male buffalo-calf.

ಎಯ್ಯು a. k. *n.* A porcupine. -ಮುಳ್ಳು. A porcupine quill.

ಎರಕ k. *n.* Any metal infusion; molten state. -ಹೊಯಿ. To pour melted metal into a mould, to cast.

ಎರಕೆ (ರ = ಱ) k. *n.* A wing; a fin; an arm.

ಎರಗು (ರ = ಱ) k. *v. i.* To bow; to make obeisance to; to alight, perch; to fall upon; to join; to accrue to. *n.* A bow, an obeisance.

ಎರಚು (ರ = ಱ) k. *v. t.* To sprinkle; to scatter; to strew; to sow. -ಎಕೆ. Strewing.

ಎರಡು k. *a.* Two. ಎರಡಕ್ಕೆ ಹೋಗು. To go to void excrement. -ಆಗು, ಎರಡಾಗು. To become separated. -ನಾಲಿಗೆಯವ. A double tongued, deceitful man, liar. -ನುಡಿ. To speak two things: to be insincere. -ಬಗೆ. To play tricks, act deceitfully; two ways. -ಮಾಡು. To split. -ವರೆ. Two and a half. -ಹೊತ್ತು. Morning and evening. ಎರಡೆರಡು. Two and two, two times two. ಎರಡೂ. Both.

ಎರಲ್, ಎರಲು (= ಹೆರಳ್) a. k. *n.* 2, wind, air. 3, playing.

ಎರಲೆ, ಎರಳೆ k. *n.* An antelope, deer.

ಎರವು k. *n.* An object of desire; a thing borrowed, *as* a book, *etc.*; a loan. 2, difference; damaging; deficiency; harm. -ಇಕ್ಕು, ಎರವಿಕ್ಕು. To grant an object of desire; to lend. -ಬೇಡು. To ask a loan. -ಮುಟ್ಟು ತಕ್ಕೊಳ್ಳು. To borrow.

ಎರುಬು k. *n.* Dung, muck.

ಎರೆ 1. k. *n.* A dark-brown colour. 2, black grease for wheels. 3, black soil (=-ನೆಲ, -ಭೂಮಿ, -ಮಣ್ಣು, -ಹೊಲ). 4, a worm that lives in orts; a bait. 5, food for animals. 6, = ಜೆಗೆ.

ಎರೆ 2. a. k. *v. t.* To beg, ask, solicit. -ವ. A beggar.

ಎರೆ 3. (ರೆ = ಱೆ) k. *v. t.* To pour out; to cast, *as* metal; to cover with water. *v. i.* To bathe. *n.* Pouring. 2, a master; *f.* ಎರತಿ. ಎರೆಯಪ್ಪ. A sweet pancake.

ಎರ್ದೆ. = ಎದೆ, *q. v.*

ಎಲಚಿ k. *n.* The jujube. -ಬಳ್ಳಿ. The bottle-gourd.

ಎಲಬು, ಎಲುಬು, ಎಲುವು k. *n.* A bone.

ಎಲರು a. k. *n.* Wind, air; breath. -ಉಣಿ, ಎಲರುಣಿ. Air-eater: a serpent.

ಎಲವ k. *n.* The silk-cotton tree, *Bombax heptaphyllum.*

ಎಲವೋ k. *int. (strong, rough)* Ho! o! oh!

ಎಲು, ಎಲುಬು, ಎಲುವು. = ಎಲಬು, *q. v.*

ಎಲಾ, ಎಲೇ k. *int. (familiar and friendly)* O! oh!

ಎಲೆ k. *n.* A leaf; the blade of a knife. 2, the betel leaf; a leaf-plate. ಎಲೆಯ ಮೇಲೆ ಕೂತಿರು. To sit at dinner. -ಅಡಿಕೆ, ಎಲಡಿಕೆ. Betel leaf and areca nut. ಎಲಡಿಕೆ ಹಾಕಿಕೊಳ್ಳು. To chew ĕlaḍikĕ -ಗಾರ. A betel-seller; *f.* -ಗಾತಿ. -ಕಾವು. A fomentation with a heated leaf. -ಕಳ್ಳಿ, -ಗಳ್ಳಿ. A thorny and milky shrub, *Euphorbia nivulia.* -ತುಂಬು, -ತೊಟ್ಟು. The stem of a leaf. -ತೋಟ. A betel garden. -ನಾಗರ. A small dangerous snake found on leaves. -ಬಿಡು. To sprout. -ಮಿಡತೆ. A green locust. -ವಸ್ತ್ರ. A coloured handkerchief. -ವನಿ, -ಹನಿ. A drop on a leaf.

ಎಲೋ k. *int.* O! *etc.*

ಎಲ್ಲ, ಎಲ್ಲವು, ಎಲ್ಲಾ k. *n.* All; everything; the whole. ಎಲ್ಲಮ್ಮ. N. of a goddess. ಎಲ್ಲರೂ. All persons. ಎಲ್ಲವೂ. All things. ಎಲ್ಲಾಗಳ್. Always.

ಎಲ್ಲಿ k. *ad.* In what place? where? whither? -ಯವ. A man of what place? -ಯದು. A thing of what place? -ಯಾದರೂ. Wheresoever; everywhere.

ಎಲ್ಲೆ k. *n.* A limit, boundary; *also* -ಕಟ್ಟು. -ಕಲ್ಲು. A boundary stone.

ಎವು k. *Termination of the first pers. pl. of past, fut., and neg., as:* ಕೇಳಿದೆವು, ಕೇಳುವೆವು, ಕೇಳೆವು.

ಎವೆ. = ಎಮೆ, *q. v.*

ಎಷ್ಟು (= ಎನಿತು) k. *inter. pro.* How much? how many? ಎಷ್ಟಂತ. To what extent? ಎಷ್ಟರ, ಎಷ್ಟರಲ್ಲಿ, ಎಷ್ಟರೊಳಗೆ, ಎಷ್ಟಕ್ಕೆ, *etc.* -ಮಟ್ಟಿಗೆ, ಎಷ್ಟರ ಮಟ್ಟಿಗೆ. To what extent? how long or far? ಎಷ್ಟೋ. How (very) many (one does not know).

ಎಸಕ (*fr.* ಎಸೆ) a. k. *n.* Shine, splendour, beauty; form; delight.

ಎಸಗು a. k. *v. t.* To engage in, undertake; to do, perform; to commence.

ಎಸಗೆ, ಎಸಿಗೆ (*fr.* ಎಸೆ 1) k. *n.* A throw, shot.

ಎಸರು k. *n.* The boiling water in a cooking pot; the water strained from boiled vegetables, *etc.;* pepper water.

ಎಸಳು k. *n.* A flower-leaf, petal; a small twig with leaves.

ಎಸಳೆ k. *n.* N. of a jungle tree.

ಎಸು, ಎಸೆ 1. k. *v. t.* To shoot an arrow; to throw. *P. ps.* ಎಸದು, ಎಸೆದು, ಎಸ್ತು. *n.* A shot; a throw; *also* ಎಸುಗೆ.

ಎಸೆ 2. k. *v. i.* To shine; to be brilliant, beautiful, distinguished; to appear; to become manifest.

ಎಹಗೆ, ಎಹಂಗೆ (= ಹ್ಯಾಗೆ, ಹ್ಯಾಂಗೆ) a. k. *ad.* In what manner? how?

ಎಳ 1. = ಎಳೆ, *q. v.*

ಎಳ 2, ಎಳತು, ಎಳದು k. *P. ps. of* ಎಳೆ, *q. v.* That is tender, young, *etc.*

ಎಳಗ k. *n.* A species of sheep; the ram used by boys for riding.

ಎಳಚಿ. = ಎಲಚಿ, *q. v.*

ಎಳದು, ಎಳೆದು k. *n.* Unsteadiness, fickleness. *ad.* Unsteadily.

ಎಳಸು a. k. v. i. To desire, long for; to take pleasure in. n. Desire, *etc.*

ಎಳೆ 1. (= ಎಳ) k. n. Tenderness; youth; weakness; moderation; lightness in colour, *etc.* a. Tender, young, *etc.* -ಗಂಡಿ, -ಗಂದು, -ಗಂದೆ. A newly calved cow, a milch cow. -ಗಾಯಿ. A tender fruit. -ಗಾಳಿ. Gentle wind. -ಗೂಸು. A tender infant. -ಕೆಂಪು, -ಗೆಂಪು. A light red, the colour of the dawn. -ಜೊನ್ನ. Faint moonshine. -ತನ. Tenderness; youth. -ತಳಿರ್, -ದಳಿರ್. Tender foliage. -ನಗೆ. A smile. -ನಾರು. A tender fine fibre. -ನೀರು. The water of a tender cocoanut. -ಪ್ರಾಯ. Youth. -ಬಣ್ಣ. A faint colour. -ಬಿಸಿಲು, -ವಿಸಿಲು. A morning or evening, sunshine. -ಮಾವು. A tender mango. -ಯುವ. A young man; a boy. -ಯುಳು. A young woman; a girl. -ಹುಲ್ಲು. Tender grass.

ಎಳೆ 2. (ಳೆ = ಱ) k. v. t. To pull, draw, drag; to seize, take forcibly. *P. ps.* ಎಳೆದು, ಎಳತು, ಎಳದು. ಎಳಕೊಳ್ಳು. To pull towards one's self; to lay hold of; to absorb. ಎಳದಾಡು. To pull mutually. ಎಳವು. Pulling, drawing; spasm, cramp. ಎಳಸು, ಎಳೆಸು. To cause to drag; to put off; to thwart.

ಎಳೆ 3. (ಳೆ = ಱ) k. n. Thread. ಎಳೆಯನ್ನು ತೆಗೆ. To spin.

ಎಳ್ಬು k. v. i. To go upwards, rise.

ಎಳ್ಳು k. n. The gingely-oil seed of *Sesamum indicum*. ಎಳ್ಳಗಸೆ. A blackish kind of linseed. -ಚಟ್ನಿ. A chatney of sesamum. -ನೀರು. Sesamum seeds and water offered to departed ancestors. -ಬೆಲ್ಲ. A mixture of sesamum and jaggory given as an auspicious present. -ಎಣ್ಣೆ, ಎಳ್ಳೆಣ್ಣೆ, -ತೈಲ. Sesamum oil. -ರೇವಡಿ. A sweetmeat of sesamum and sugar. -ಹುಗ್ಗಿ. A dish of milk, rice, and sesamum.

ಏ

ಏ. The twelfth letter of the alphabet. 2, *a particle of emphasis, as:* ಶಂಕರನು ನೀವೇ! ಒಮ್ಮೆಲೇ; ತಪ್ಪದೇ ಬಾ; ನಮ್ಮ ಹಿತದ ಸಲುವಾಗಿಯೇ. 3, *a contraction of* ಎಯ *a, in the genitive, as:* ಮನೇ ಬಾಗಲು, ಸಾಲೇ ಮನೆ; *b. in the locative, as:* ಕಡೇಲಿ, *etc.*; c, *in the affix* ಅನೆಯ, *as:* ಎರಡನೇ ಪುಸ್ತಕ; *d, in the infinitive, as:* ಕರೇ ಕಳುಹಿಸು. 4, = ಏನು, *etc.*, *q. v.* ಏಗೆಯ್ಯು. What to do? ಏವೇಳು. What to say?

ಏಕ s. a. One, alone, solitary. 2, unique, pre-eminent. 3, one of two or more. -ಕಾಲ. The same time. -ಗೃಹಕೃತ್ಯ. An undivided family. -ಚಕ್ರವರ್ತಿ, -ಛತ್ರಾಧಿಪತಿ. A supreme sovereign. -ಜಾತಿ. Once-born; a Śûdra. -ತರ. One of two or many. -ತಾಲ. Keeping time, harmony. -ತ್ರ. In one place, together. -ತ್ವ. Oneness, unity. -ದಾ. At once. -ದೇಶಿ. Of one or the same country. -ದೇಹ. Having only one body; closely united in friendship. -ಪತ್ನಿ. Only one wife. -ಮತಿ, -ಮನಸ್ಸು. One mind; unanimous. -ಮತ್ಯ. Concord. -ರಸ. Perfect assimilation. -ವಚನ. The singular number (*g.*). -ವಾಕ್ಯತೆ. Agreement of meaning. -ಸಪ್ತತಿ. 71. -ಸ್ಥ. Standing together; unanimous. -ಸ್ಥಾನ. The place of a unit. ಏಕಾ ಏಕಿ. Suddenly, all at once. ಏಕಾಕಿ. Alone, solitary. ಏಕಾಕ್ಷರ. A monosyllable. ಏಕಾಕ್ಷ. One-eyed; a crow. ಏಕಾಗ್ರ. Intent upon one object. ಏಕಾಂಗಿ. Of one member; solitary, alone. ಏಕಾದಶ. Eleven; the eleventh. ಏಕಾದಶಿ. The eleventh day of the waxing or waning moon on which Brâhmaṇas use to wake and fast. ಏಕಾಧಿಪತಿ. A sole monarch; an astrological term. ಏಕಾಂತ. A lonely place, solitude; secrecy; a secret; alone, secret, hidden. ಏಕಾಂತವಾಸ. A hermitage; a harem. ಏಕಾಬ್ದ. A heifer one year old. ಏಕಾರ್ಥ. One meaning; synonym. ಏಕಾಶ್ರಯ. The protection of one deity only. ಏಕಾಹ. The period of one day; a ceremony performed on the eleventh day in the course of funeral rites.

ಏಕಾರ s. *n.* The letter ಏ.

ಏಕೀನಿ h. *n.* Honesty, uprightness.

ಏಕೀಭಾವ s. *n.* Becoming one; association. ಏಕೀಭವಿಸು. To become one.

ಏಕೂನು f. *n.* Sum total.

ಏಕೋದ್ದಿಷ್ಟ s. *n.* The śrâddha performed for one deceased individual.

ಏಟು k. *n.* A blow; a throw. 2, a kind of gambling with dice. -ಗಾರ. A shooter. -ಕೊಡು, -ಬಡಿ, -ಹೊಡಿ. To strike a blow.

ಏಡಿ k. *n.* A crab. 2, a coward.

ಏಡಿಸು k. *v. i.* To speak ill; to mock.

ಏಣ s. *n.* A kind of deer or antelope; *f.* ಏಣಿ.

ಏಣಿ k. *n.* A ladder. -ದೀವಟಿಗೆ. A number of flambeaux fixed on a horizontal ladder and carried in a procession or before persons of distinction. -ಏರು, -ಹತ್ತು. To mount a ladder.

ಏಣು k. *n.* An edge, border.

ಏತ (*fr.* ಏರು) k. *n.* Ascent; rise. 2, a lever for raising water, picotta. 3, an instrument for pounding rice. -ಕೋಲು. The bamboo by which the bucket hangs.

ಏತಕೆ. = ಯಾತಕೆ, *see s.* ಏನು.

ಏತಾದೃಶ s. *ad.* Such like; of this kind, similar.

ಏದು k. *n.* A porcupine. *v. i.* To pant.

ಏನಿಕೆ k. *pro.* Some, a few.

ಏನು k. *inter. pro.* What? *dat.* ಏತಕ್ಕೆ; *instr.* ಏತರಿಂದ; *gen.* ಏತರ, *etc.* ಏನಾಗು. To become what? ಏನಾದರೂ, ಏನಾನುಂ. Whatsoever it may be; anything. ಏನಿಲ್ಲನ್ನು. To say it is nothing. ಏನೊ. O what?

ಏನೆ k. *aff. for the 1st pers. sing. pres., e. g.* ತರುತ್ತೇನೆ, ಮುಗಿಸುತ್ತೇನೆ, ನಡೆಯುತ್ತೇನೆ, *etc.*

ಏಬ್ರಾಸಿ. = ಏದ್ರಾಸಿ, *q. v.*

ಏಯ್. = ಏಸು, *q. v.*

ಏರಂಡ s. *n.* The castor-oil plant, *Palma Christi.*

ಏರಿ k. *n.* A raised bank, the bank of a tank, *etc.; also* ಕಟ್ಟೆ.

ಏರು 1. (= ಆರು) k. *n.* A pair of oxen yoked to the plough. -ಕಂದಾಯ, -ಸುಂಕ. Plough-tax.

ಏರು 2. (ರು = ಱು) k. *v. t.* To ascend; mount, climb. *v. i.* To rise; to increase. *P. p.* ಏರಿ. ಏರುತ್ತ, ಏರುವಿಕೆ, ಏರಿಕೆ. Rising, mounting, *etc.* ಏರ ಕಟ್ಟು. To tie on high, hang down. ಏರುಬ್ಬಸ. Hard breathing. ಏರಹಾಕು. To pile. ಏರಹೊತ್ತು. The time from sunrise to midday. ವಿಷವೇರು. Poison to take effect. ಏರಿಸು. To raise; to place upon, *etc.* ಏರಿ ಬರು. To ascend.

ಏರ್ಪಡು k. *v. i.* To be arranged, settled, fixed, established. ಏರ್ಪಡಿಸು. To arrange, to set in order. ಏರ್ಪಾಟು, ಏರ್ಪಾಡು. Arrangement; decision.

ಏಲಕ್ಕಿ f. *n.* Large cardamoms. -ಗಿಡ. The cardamom plant.

ಏಲಾಂ h. *n.* An auction, public sale.

ಏಲು k. *v. i.* To hang, dangle. ಏಲಾಡು. To swing.

ಏವ k. *n.* Disgust, dislike; ugliness.

ಏವಂ s. *ad.* Thus; certainly; even.

ಏವು k. *pl. of* ಏನು.

ಏವೆ k. *pl. of* ಏನೆ.

ಏಷಣ s. *n.* Seeking; wish, desire.

ಏಸಿಕೆ. = ಹೇಸಿಕೆ, *q. v.*

ಏಸು 1. k. v. t. To throw. n. A throw, shot. ಏಸಾಡು. To shoot arrows.

ಏಸು 2. (= ಎನಿತು) k. pro. What quantity? etc.

ಏಳಿಸು (= ಏಡಿಸು) k. v. t. To censure, reprove; to throw into shade. ಏಳಿದ. Contempt, blame.

ಏಳಿಗೆ, ಏಳ್ಗೆ (ಳ = ಱ) k. n. Rising; growth, increase; greatness, magnificence, glory; haughtiness.

ಏಳು 1. (ಳು = ೞು) k. v. i. To stand up, to get up, rise. P.p. ಎದ್ದು. ಎದ್ದುಹೋಗು. Get up and go away. ಏಳಿಸು. To raise. -ಏಕೆ, ಏಳ್ವಿಕೆ. Rising. ಏಳುತ್ತ ಬೀಳುತ್ತ. Rising and falling. ಏಳೇಳು, ಎದ್ದೇಳು. Rise, rise! arise.

ಏಳು 2. (ಳು = ೞು) k. a. Seven. ಏಳನೆ. Seventh. ಏಳೆಂಟು. Seven or eight; seven times eight. ಏಳೆಳೆಕಟ್ಟಾಣಿ. A necklace of gold beads composed of seven strings.

ಐ

ಐ. The thirteenth letter of the alphabet. *The initial ಐ in Kannaḍa words has arisen from ಅಯ್, ಅಯಿ, and those words may also be looked up under this spelling.*

ಐ s. int., as: ಐಸಾಕು. O! enough.

ಐಕಮತ್ಯ s. n. Unanimity, agreement.

ಐಕಾರ s. n. The letter ಐ.

ಐಕ್ಯ s. n. Oneness, unity; harmony; identity. -ಭಾವ. Oneness.

ಐಗಳು (= ಅಯ್ಗಳು) k. n. A Jaṅgama. 2, a school-master.

ಐತರು (= ಅಯ್ತರು) k. v. i. To come, approach.

ಐತಿಹ್ಯ s. n. Oral tradition, a legend, tale.

ಐದು 1. (= ಅಯ್ದು, q. v.) k. a. Five.

ಐದು 2. (= ಅಯ್ದು) k. v. i. To join; to draw near; to reach, obtain, get.

ಐದುತನ. = ಅಯ್ದೆತನ, q. v.

ಐನಾ k. n. A mirror; spectacles.

ಐನೋರು (= ಅಯ್ನೋರು) k. n. A school-master. 2, a respectful mode of addressing a Brâhmaṇa.

ಐರದಾಳಿ (= ಅಯ್ರದಾಳಿ) k. n. The marriage badge tied round a female's neck.

ಐರಾಣಿ. = ಅಯ್ರಾಣಿ, q. v.

ಐರಾವತ s. n. Indra's male elephant; f. ಐರಾವತಿ.

ಐಲವಿಲ s. n. Kuvêra.

ಐವಜಿ h. ad. Instead of.

ಐವಜು h. n. Property, wealth: cash or goods.

ಐವತ್ತು (= ಅಯ್ವತ್ತು) k. n. Fifty.

ಐಶ್ವರ್ಯ s. n. Power, might; wealth, riches, opulence. -ವಂತ. A rich man; f. -ವಂತೆ.

ಐಸಿರಿ. tb. of ಐಶ್ವರ್ಯ, q. v.

ಐಸು. = ಅಯಿಸು, q. v.

ಐಹಿಕ (fr. ಇಹ) s. a. Relating to this world; temporal, secular.

ಒ

ಒ. The fourteenth letter of the alphabet. 2, *a particle employed in common as well as doubtful questions, e. g.* ಅನೆಯೊ? 3, *in admonition and calling, as:* ಸ್ನಾನ ಮಾಡಿರೊ! ಬಾರೊ! ಒ ಕಾಳಪ್ಪ!

ಒಂಯಿ k. *n.* The cry of buffaloes.

ಒಕ್ k. *a.* One. 2, *short p. p. of* ಒಗೆ. ಒಕ್ಕಟ್ಟು. One bond; unanimity, concord, harmony. ಒಕ್ಕಣ್ಣ. A one-eyed man. ಒಕ್ಕೊಡು. To throw, cast away; to wash and give.

ಒಕಾರ k. *n.* The letter ಒ.

ಒಕ್ಕಣಿಕೆ, ಒಕ್ಕಣೆ s. *n.* The honorific address at the top of a letter, *etc.* 2, style of composition. ಒಕ್ಕಣಿಸು. To tell, say; to describe.

ಒಕ್ಕರಿಸು k. *v. i.* To spit out, vomit. 2, to retire.

ಒಕ್ಕಲ, ಒಕ್ಕಲಮಗ, ಒಕ್ಕಲಿಗ k. *n.* A farmer, husbandman; *f.* ಒಕ್ಕಲಿಗಿತಿ, ಒಕ್ಕಲಿತಿ.

ಒಕ್ಕಲಿಕ್ಕು k. *v. t.* To thrash down, destroy; to trouble greatly.

ಒಕ್ಕಲು k. *n.* Residing, tenancy; a home; residence. 2, a tenant, farmer; a subject. ಒಕ್ಕಲಾಗು. To become a tenant, *etc.* -ತನ. Husbandry, farming. ಒಕ್ಕಲ ಮನೆ, ಒಕ್ಕಲಡಿ. A tenant's house; a farmhouse.

ಒಕ್ಕು k. *v. t.* To tread out corn; to thrash. *n.* Thrashing. 2, an omen. -ಗೋಲು. A thrashing stick.

ಒಕ್ಕೆರೆ (*tb. of* ಪುಷ್ಕರ) *n.* A pond.

ಒಕ್ಕುಳಿಸು k. *v. i.* To belch.

ಒಗಟು, ಒಗಟೆ k. *n.* A riddle, enigma.

ಒಗಡಿಕೆ (= ಓಕರಿಕೆ) k. *n.* Vomiting.

ಒಗಡಿಸು. = ಒಕ್ಕರಿಸು, *q. v.*

ಒಗತ k. *n.* Washing. 2, throwing.

ಒಗತನ k. *n.* The harmonious life of husband and wife and their management of household affairs; the affairs of life.

ಒಗದು. = ಒಗೆದು, *p. p. of* ಒಗೆ.

ಒಗರು k. *n.* An astringent taste.

ಒಗಿ. = ಒಗೆ 2, *q. v.*

ಒಗು a. k. *n.* Running over, excess. 2, (= ಪೊಗು) to enter. -ಮಿಗೆ. Abundance.

ಒಗೆ 1. a. k. *v. i.* To come forth, be born, originate.

ಒಗೆ 2. k. *v. t.* To beat wet clothes on a stone for cleaning them, to wash. 2, to throw. *P. ps.* ಒಗೆದು, ಒಗದು.

ಒಗ್ಗ k. *n.* A follower of the mailâra linga.

ಒಗ್ಗರ k. *n.* A heap, mass.

ಒಗ್ಗರಣೆ k. *n.* A kind of seasoning. ಒಗ್ಗರಿಸು. To season, spice.

ಒಗ್ಗು k. *v. i.* To become one, unite with. 2, to agree with one's constitution, *as* water, *etc.* 3, (= ಬೊಗ್ಗು) to bow; to be submissive. *v. t.* To join. *n.* An assemblage, heap, mass.

ಒಂಚೆ k. *n.* A hook. 2, a gold armlet worn by females.

ಒಜ್ಜತ a. k. *n.* Equality, harmony; agreeableness; pleasure.

ಒಜ್ಜಯ, ಒಜ್ಜೆಯ a. k. *n.* Disgrace; impropriety; contempt.

ಒಜನ h. *n.* Gravity; dignity, influence.

ಒಜ್ಜರ a. k. *n.* A spring, fountain.

ಒಜ್ಜೆ (= ವಜ್ಜೆ) f. *n.* A weight, load, burden.

ಒಟ (= ವಟ) m. *int.* An imitative sound. --ಮಾತಾಡು, -ಗುಟ್ಟು. To talk much; to prate, gabble.

ಒಟಾರ f. *n.* The compound round a house.

ಒಟ್ಟ (= ವಟ್ಟ) h. *n.* Discount.

ಒಟ್ಟಜೆ, ಒಟ್ಟಲು k. *n.* A heap, mass, abundance.

ಒಟ್ಟಯಿಸು, ಒಟ್ಟಯ್ಸು. = ಒಟ್ಟೈಸು, *q. v.*

ಒಟ್ಟು k. *v. t.* To make one join; to put together, pile up. *v. i.* To come together, assemble; to become a mass, be united. *n.* Union; a heap, pile; sum total. 2, the close adhering of a lump of clay. ಒಟ್ಟಿಗೆ (*dat.*), ಒಟ್ಟಾರೆ, all together, on the whole. -ಆಗು, -ಕೂಡು. To come together, convene; to become one in mind. -ಆಗಿರು. To be united, *as* a family. -ಕೂಡಿಸು, -ಮಾಡು. To join together; to add up. -ಸೇರಿಕೆ. The whole amount. -ಲೆಕ್ಕ. Sum total. ಒಟ್ಟಿಕೆ. Heaping.

ಒಟ್ಟೆ k. *n.* A crack, hole. -ಬೀಳು. To be cracked, to get a hole.

ಒಟ್ಟೈಸು, ಒಟ್ಟೆಸು k. *v. t.* To collect, join; to heap together; to convene. *v. i.* To become one; to come together.

ಒಡ k. *n.* Union; being together, company. -ಗೂಡು. To join, be united with; to be obtained; to happen; to obtain. ಒಡಗೂಡಿಸು. To cause to be united with, *etc.* -ಗೂಟ. Close union. -ಹುಟ್ಟು. To be born by the same parents; birth as brothers and sisters; brothers or sisters. -ಬಡು. = ಒಡಂಬಡು.

ಒಡಕ, ಒಡಕು k. *n.* The state of being cracked or broken; a fracture, crack; disunion. -ಧ್ವನಿ. A broken voice. -ಬಾಯವ. One who cannot keep secrets.

ಒಡಕಲ k. *n.* Broken state; broken paddy or split pulse with chaff or husk.

ಒಡತಿ k. *n.* A mistress.

ಒಡದು. = ಒಡೆದು. *P. p. of* ಒಡೆ.

ಒಡನೆ (*fr.* ಒಡ) k. *prep.* With; together with. *ad.* Forthwith, immediately. ಒಡನಾಟ. Company, intercourse. ಒಡನಾಡಿ. A companion, friend. ಒಡನಾಡಿತನ. Companionship, friendship. ಒಡನಾಡು. To associate with. ಒಡನೊಡನೆ. All at once, *etc.*

ಒಡಂಬಡು (= ಒಡಬಡು) k. *v. i.* To agree, assent; to consent; to covenant. ಒಡಂಬಡಿಸು. To cause to agree; to persuade, convince. ಒಡಂಬಡಿಕೆ, ಒಡಂಬಡಿಕೆ. A covenant, agreement, bond, treaty, compact.

ಒಡರಿಸು, ಒಡರ್ಚು k. *v. t.* To join; to put to. *v. i.* To enter into, engage in, undertake, begin; to perform; to endeavour, try.

ಒಡಲು k. *n.* The body; the belly, stomach. ಒಡಲುರಿ. Burning of the belly; internal grief.

ಒಡವೆ, ಒಡಿವೆ k. *n.* A thing, substance, possession; a jewel; property, wealth.

ಒಡಿ 1. ಒಡೆ 1. k. *v. i.* To be broken, to crack, burst; to break forth, *as* a bud, *etc.*; to bud; to turn, *as* milk; to fail, *as* courage; to branch off. 2, to trickle through, ooze, sink. *v. t.* To break. -ಗಟ್ಟು, -ಯಕಟ್ಟು. To strain off, filter through a cloth. -ಗಲಸು. To break; to destroy; a broken mass. -ಬಡಿ, -ಮುರಿ. To bruise. -ಸು. To cause to break, *etc.*

ಒಡಿ 2. k. *n.* Heat.

ಒಡೆ 3. a. k. *aff.* If; when; to; *as:* ಉಳ್ಳೊಡೆ, ಬಂದೊಡೆ; ರಾಜನೊಡೆ.

ಒಡೆ 3. k. *n.* Possession, ownership; rule, sway; *also* -ತನ. -ಯ. An owner; a lord, master; a chief, leader; a ruler, king. -ಯರೊಡೆಯ. Lord of lords.

ಒಡ್ಡ 1. k. *n.* A class of people who cut stones, dig tanks and wells and speak a Tĕlugu patois.

ಒಡ್ಡ 2, ಒಡ್ಡಣ 1. k. *n.* A pile, heap. 2, an assembly; an army.

ಒಡ್ಡಣ 2. = ಒಡ್ಯಾಣ.

ಒಡ್ಡಂತಿ (*tb. of* ವರ್ಧಂತಿ, *q. v.*) *n.* A birthday festivity.

ಒಡ್ಡು k. *v. t.* To place, put, lay; to fix, set; to catch; to array. 2, to oppose, resist. 3, (= ಒಟ್ಟು) to heap up. *n.* A heap, pile, mass; a bank; a large gathering; a stake at play; host, army. ಒಡ್ಡಿಸು. To cause to place, *etc.* -ಓಲಗ, ಒಡ್ಡೋಲಗ. A great assembly, a royal audience, darbâr.

ಒಡ್ಯಾಣ k. *n.* A gold or silver belt or zone.

ಒಣ k. a. Dry. 2, sapless, profitless, empty; false. -ಆ. An emaciated man. -ಕೆಲಸ. Useless business. -ಗಾಯಿ. Dry fruit. -ಮಾತು. A senseless word. -ಮೋರೆ. A sad countenance. -ರಗಳೆ, -ಹರಟೆ. Useless talk. -ಸಂಶಯ. Groundless suspicion. -ಹೆಮ್ಮೆ. Vain pride.

ಒಣಗು k. v. i. To dry, become dry; to wither. ಒಣಗಿಲು. Dryness. ಒಣಗಿಸು. To dry.

ಒಂಟಿ 1. k. a. One, single, alone. *Cpds.:* -ದೋತ್ರ, -ಗಣ್ಣು, -ತೋಳು, *etc.* -ಎಲುವಿನವ, ಒಂಟೆಲುವಿನವ. A man of mere bones, a weak man. -ಗ. A single man. -ಗತನ, -ತನ. Loneliness, solitude. -ಗಿತ್ತಿ. A solitary woman.

ಒಂಟಿ 2. k. n. A gold earring.

ಒಂಟು k. v. i. To agree with one's health, *as* water.

ಒಂಟೆ (*tb. of* ಉಷ್ಟ್ರ) n. A camel.

ಒಂಡು k. n. Sediment, deposit, dregs; mud in rivers, tanks, *etc.*; turbidness.

ಒತ್ತಟ್ಟ k. n. The nightmare.

ಒತ್ತಟ್ಟು k. n. One side. *ad.* Aside.

ಒತ್ತಡ, ಒತ್ತಲ k. n. Fomentation.

ಒತ್ತರ k. n. Impetuousness; force; speed. 2, one layer or division. ಒತ್ತರಿಸು. To increase; to be or become lofty, haughty, impetuous, quick. v. t. To join closely; to subdue.

ಒತ್ತಾಯ k. n. Force, violence, compulsion; impetus.

ಒತ್ತಾಸೆ k. n. Help, assistance. -ಗಾರ. A helper, assistant.

ಒತ್ತು k. v. t. To press, squeeze; to shampoo; to press down; to impress, *as* a seal; to overpower; to trouble; to use unusual force or power, *as* in speaking, calling, *etc.*; to stress, emphasize. 2, to foment. v. i. To give way, step aside. n. Closeness; thickness; a pile; vicinity; pressure. 2, an under letter. ಒತ್ತಿಕೆ. Pressing. ಒತ್ತಿಸು. To cause to press, *etc.* ಒತ್ತಕ್ಷರ, ಒತ್ತಕ್ಷರ. A double consonant. -ಗೊಡು. To prop. -ಉಂಗರ, ಒತ್ತುಂಗರ. A thin finger-ring or toe-ring to tighten other rings.

ಒತ್ತೆ k. n. A pledge, pawn. 2, a single or one of a pair. -ಈ, -ಕೊಡು, -ಹಾಕು, -ಇರಿಸು, ಒತ್ತಿಡು. To pledge, pawn. -ಬಿಡಿಸು. To redeem a pawn. -ತಕ್ಕೊಳ್ಳು. To take a pawn.

ಒತ್ತೆರ k. n. One kind or sort.

ಒದಗು k. v. i. To come to hand, be got; to be effected; to be ready for; to be at hand; to be of use; to thrive, increase. 2, to give way, step aside. n. That is at hand. ಒದಗಿಸು. To cause to be obtained, to make ready, *etc.;* to fulfil.

ಒದಡು k. n. The lip.

ಒದರು (ರು=ಱು) k. v. i. To shake; to cry aloud, shout, shriek, howl; to shake, move to and fro. n. Shaking, *etc.* -ವಿಕೆ, ಒದರಾಟ. Crying with great noise. -ಆಡು, ಒದರಾಡು. To shout with great noise. ಒದರಿಸು. To cause to shout, howl, *etc.*

ಒದವು. = ಒದಗು, *q. v.* 2, to gain, obtain.

ಒದಿ, ಒದೆ k. v. t. To kick; to spur. *P. ps.* ಒದೆದು, ಒದದು, ಒದ್ದು. ಒದ್ದಿಕೆ. A kick. ಒದ್ದಾಟ. Mutual kicking; kicking in pain; struggle, trouble, hardship. ಒದ್ದಾಡು. To kick mutually; to kick in pain; to struggle in difficulty or distress.

ಒಡ್ಡಿಕೆ k. n. Union, concord, friendship.

ಒದ್ದೆ k. n. Wetness, dampness; moisture. a. Damp. wet. *Cpds.:* -ತಲೆ, -ನೆಲ, -ಬಟ್ಟೆ.

ಒನ್ k. a. One. -ದೆಸೆ. One direction.

ಒನಕೆ, ಒನಿಕೆ k. n. A large wooden pestle.

ಒನಪು = ಒಲಪು, *q. v.*

ಒನೆ k. v. t. To winnow, fan corn. ಒನಲಿ. A sieve.

ಒಂತು k. n. A turn, rotation, time. 2, a share. -ಗೊಳ್ಳು, -ಸಾಧಿಸು. To take one's turn. -ತಪ್ಪು, -ಬಿಡು. To miss one's turn. -ತೀರಿಸು. To finish one's turn. ಒಂತಿನವ. One who takes his turn.

ಒಂದಿಕೆ, ಒಂದಿಗೆ k. *prep.* Together with. ಅವನೊಂದಿಗೆ, *etc.*

ಒಂದು 1. (= ಹೊಂದು) k. *v. i.* To be one or united; to be linked to; to come to meet; to be fit, suitable. *v. t.* To obtain; to get; to use. ಒಂದಿಸು. To join; to place or fix on; to grant.

ಒಂದು 2. (ಒನ್) k. *a.* One; a, an; a certain thing. ಒಂದಕ್ಕೆ ಹೋಗು. To go to make water. ಒಂದನೆಯ. First. ಒಂದರೆ, ಒಂದೂವರೆ. One or one and a half. ಒಂದರಂತೆ. Like one; at the rate of one, per one. -ಆಗು, ಒಂದಾಗು. To become one; to unite. ಒಂದಾನೊಂದು. Some or other; a certain—; once upon a time. ಒಂದಿನಿತು, ಒಂದಿಷ್ಟು. A little. -ಗೂಡು. To be joined. -ತರ, -ಪ್ರಕಾರ, -ಬಗೆ. One sort or mode, an unusual manner. -ಬಾರಿ, -ಸಲ, -ಸಾರಿ, ಒಂದಾವರ್ತಿ. One time; once. -ಮಾಡು. To join, unite. -ವೇಳೆ. One time, once; perhaps. -ಹೊತ್ತು, ಒಪ್ಪೊತ್ತು. From morning till midday, or from midday till evening. ಒಂದೂ ಮುಕ್ಕಾಲು. One and three-fourths. -ಇಲ್ಲ, ಒಂದೂ ಇಲ್ಲ. Nothing. ಒಂದೆ. One only. -ಎರಡು, ಒಂದೆರಡು. One or two; a few. -ಎಲಗ, ಒಂದೆಲಗ. A herb, *Hydrocotile asiatica.* ಒಂದೊಂದು. *rep.* One — the other; one another; separate; own; each by itself.

ಒಪ್ಪ k. *n.* Fitness, properness, neatness, elegance; beauty; lustre, polish; correctness. -ಮಾಡು. To bestow the last honours (on a deceased person). -ಇಡು, -ಎಡು, -ಇಕ್ಕು, -ಎಕ್ಕು. To embellish, polish. -ಹಾಕು. To sign.

ಒಪ್ಪಂದ k. *n.* An agreement; a contract; a treaty; a covenant. -ಮಾಡು. To make an agreement, *etc.*

ಒಪ್ಪಯಿಸು. = ಒಪ್ಪಿಸು, *q. v.*

ಒಪ್ಪಾನೆ k. *n.* Fitness, propriety. *ad.* Fitly.

ಒಪ್ಪಿಕೆ, ಒಪ್ಪಿಗೆ, ಒಪ್ಪಿತ k. *n.* Consent, agreement; admission. ಒಪ್ಪಿತ ಹಾಕು. To sign.

ಒಪ್ಪಿಸು k. *v. t.* To deliver over, give in charge, commit, to give. 2, to deliver. 3, to prevail on. ಒಪ್ಪಿಸಿಕೊಳ್ಳು. To take over a charge; to comply with. ಒಪ್ಪಿಸಿ ಕೊಡು. To give over a charge, *as:* ಲೆಕ್ಕ-, ಪಾಠ-, ಉದ್ಯೋಗ-, *etc.*

ಒಪ್ಪು k. *v. i.* To suit, be fit, proper, agreeable. 2, to agree to, assent, consent; to admit. 3, to be manifested. *n.* Fitness; consent; beauty; elegance. ಒಪ್ಪಂತೆ. In a suitable manner. -ಆಚಾರ, ಒಪ್ಪಾಚಾರ. An agreement. -ಗೊಳಿಸು. To persuade. -ಎಸೆ, ಒಪ್ಪೆಸೆ. To appear to great advantage. -ಇಕೆ. Aggreeing, *etc.*; *cf.* ಒಪ್ಪಿಕೆ.

ಒಬ್ಬ k. *a.* One *(m. or f.)*; a, an. *n.* A certain man. ಒಬ್ಬನೆ. Only one; he alone. ಒಬ್ಬರು. Some; *the honorific plural*; somebody. ಒಬ್ಬರೊಬ್ಬರು. These —the others, one another; these and others; every, each; *also* ಒಬ್ಬರನ್ನೊಬ್ಬರು, ಒಬ್ಬರಿಗೊಬ್ಬರು. ಒಬ್ಬಳು, ಒಬ್ಬಾಕೆ. One woman; a woman. ಒಬ್ಬಾನೊಬ್ಬ. A certain (man or woman). ಒಬ್ಬೊಬ್ಬ. *rep.* Every or each (man or woman). ಒಬ್ಬೊಬ್ಬರು. They mutually; every one or each of them; they one by one. ಒಬ್ಬಂಟಿಗ, ಒಬ್ಬಟಿಗ. A single solitary man.

ಒಬ್ಬಟ್ಟು k. *n.* A sweet cake, hôḷigĕ.

ಒಬ್ಬಿ. = ಒಮ್ಮೆ, *q. v.*

ಒಬ್ಬೆ k. *n.* A bush, thicket.

ಒಮ್ k. *a.* One. ಒಂಬತ್ತು. Nine. ಒಮ್ಮನ. One mind, unanimity.

ಒಮ್ಮೆ k. *ad.* Once; one time or turn; together. ಒಮ್ಮೆಗೆ. All at once. ಒಮ್ಮೊಂದೊಮ್ಮೆ. Suddenly; at some time or other; sometimes. ಒಮ್ಮೆಲೆ. Together. ಒಮ್ಮೊಮ್ಮೆ. *rep.* Now and then, occasionally; by turns.

ಒಯ್, ಒಯಿ, ಒಯ್ಯು (= ವಯ್ಯು, *q. v.*) k. *v. t.* To carry off; to conduct, convey. *P. p.* ಒಯ್ದು. ಒಯ್ತು. Conveying, *etc.*

ಒಯ್ಯಾಳಿ, ಒಯ್ಯ್ಯಾಳಿ (= ವಯ್ಯಾಳಿ, *tb. of* ವಾಹ್ಯಾಳಿ) *n.* A ride on horseback. -ಗ. A rider on horseback. -ಬಯಲು. A plain used for horse-races.

ಒಯ್ಯನೆ k. *ad.* Slowly; gently; leisurely.

ಒಯ್ಯಾರ (= ವಯ್ಯಾರ, *tb. of* ವಿಕಾರ) *n.* Parade, coquetry. 2, beauty, grace. -ಗಾತಿ, -ಗಿತ್ತಿ. A coquette. -ಗಾರ, ಒಯ್ಯಾರಿ. A showy man. -ತನ. Showiness. -ಮಾಡು. To be dandy or foppish.

ಒಯ್ಯು. = ಒಯ್, *q. v.*

ಒರಗು (ರ = ಱ) k. *v. i.* To be bent; to recline, lean upon; to lie or fall down; to rest. *n.* A bend. 2, a cushion. ಒರಗಿಸು. To cause to recline.

ಒರಟು (= ಉರಟು, *q. v.*) k. *n.* Pride, gruffness. 2, coarseness. ಒರಟ. A rough man. ಒರಟಾಡು. To speak gruffly.

ಒರತೆ (ರ = ಱ) k. *n.* A spring, fountain; a flow; a fluid.

ಒರಲು 1. = ಒರಳು, *q. v.*

ಒರಲು 2, ಒಲರ್ (ರ = ಱ) a. k. *v. i.* To cry out or scream from pain, *etc.* *n.* An outcry, scream. ಒರಲಿಸು. To cause to cry out, *etc.*

ಒರಲೆ (ರ = ಱ) k. *n.* Soreness with watery humour. -ಗಣ್ಣಿನವ. A blear-eyed man. -ಗಾಲು. A foot affected with elephantiasis.

ಒರಸು, ಒರಿಸು k. *v. t.* To rub gently, stroke; to scour, brush; to wipe; to rub off or out; to blot out, efface. 2, to annoy; to crush. 3, to separate by friction, *as* grain from the ears. *n.* Rubbing; friction. 2, teasing; destroying.

ಒರಳು (= ಒರಲು) k. *n.* A large mortar. ಕಲ್ಲು-. A stone mortar.

ಒರುಷ. = ವರುಷ, *q. v.*

ಒರೆ 1. k. *v. t.* To rub, smear. 2, to rub on a touch-stone. 3, to try, examine; 4, to grind, make thin. 5, to draw, pull. *v. i.* To come in contact, to touch. 2, to sound; to utter, speak. *n.* Rubbing, *etc.* 2, a word, an expression. -ಗಲ್ಲು. A touch-stone. -ಗಲ್ಲಿಗೆ ಹಚ್ಚು. To apply to a touch-stone.

ಒರೆ (ರೆ = ಱೆ) 2. k. *v. i.* To ooze, spring, drip, flow; to be wet, moist.

ಒರೆ (ರೆ = ಱೆ) 3. k. *n.* A sheath, scabbard. -ಗಳೆ, -ಕೀಳು, -ತೆಗೆ. To draw a sword. -ಗಾರ. A sheathmaker. -ಗೊಳಿಸು. To sheath.

ಒರ್ಬ, ಒರ್ವ. = ಒಬ್ಬ, *q. v.*

ಒರ್ಮೆ. = ಒಮ್ಮೆ, *q. v.*

ಒಲಪು k. *n.* Affectation in walking; foppishness, coquetry. -ಗಾರ. A fop, dandy. -ಗಾರಳು, -ಗಾತಿ. A coquette.

ಒಲವು (= ಒಲುಮೆ, ಒಲ್ಮೆ) k. *n.* Pleasure; kindness, favour. ಈಶ್ವರನ-. The grace of God. -ಎತ್ತು, ಒಲವೆತ್ತು. To be pleased.

ಒಲಸೆ. = ವಲಸೆ, *q. v.*

ಒಲಿ k. *v. i.* To be pleased, favourable; to like, love; to be apt, fit. -ಮೆ, ಒಲುಮೆ (= ಒಲವು, ಒಲ್ಮೆ). Pleasure; affection, love, favour; royal protection. -ಸು. To please.

ಒಲೆ 1. k. *v. i.* To swing; to shake, tremble; to move. 2, to hang or bend to one side, *as* a wall, *etc.* *v. t.* To shake. ಒಲೆದಾಡು. To swing or move about.

ಒಲೆ 2. k. *n.* A fire-place, furnace, an oven, hearth. -ಗುಂಡು. The three stones of which an ŏlĕ consists. -ಇಡು, -ಮಾಡು, -ಹಾಕು, -ಹೂಡು. To form an ŏlĕ. -ಹೊತ್ತಿಸು. To kindle a fire. -ಗೆ ಬೆಂಕಿ ಹಾಕು. To put fire into an ŏlĕ.

ಒಲ್ಮೆ. = ಒಲಿಮೆ *s.* ಒಲಿ, *q. v.*

ಒಲ್ಲಿ k. *n.* A small dôtra.

ಒಲ್ಲು k. (*d. v.* To will; to like, love). ಒಲ್ಲೆ. *1st pers. s. neg., as:* ಮಾಡಲೊಲ್ಲೆ, ಹೋಗಲೊಲ್ಲೆ, I will not do *etc.* *Neg. part.* ಒಲ್ಲದೆ. ಯಾಕಾಗವೊಲ್ಲದು. (*vlg.* ಯಾಕಾಗವಲ್ಲದು). Why not?

ಒಸಗೆ k. *n*. Joy; feast, festival. 2, speech, news. -ಕಳುಹಿಸು. To send news.

ಒಸಡಿ, ಒಸಡು k. *n*. The gums.

ಒಸರು (*cf.* ಒರೆ 2) k. *v. i*. To ooze, trickle, flow gently. *n*. Oozing, *etc*. ಒಸರ್ಗಲ್. A kind of crystal. -ನೀರು. Trickling water.

ಒಸಿ (= ವಸಿ) f. *n*. A little.

ಒಳ್ 1. (= ಉಳ್) k. *n*. That is true, good, nice, *etc*. *Its final is doubled before a following vowel*. ಒಳ್ಗುಣ. A good quality. -ತೊಲೆ, -ದೊಲೆ. A beautiful beam. -ನುಡಿ, -ಮಾತು. A true, good word. -ಮುತ್ತು. A real pearl. -ಬೆಳಗು, -ವೆಳಗು. Beautiful lustre. -ಎಣ್ಣೆ, ಒಳ್ಳೆಣ್ಣೆ. Good, eatable oil.

ಒಳ್ (= ಒಳ, *q. v.*) 2. k. *prep*. In, into, among, at, with; *as:* ದೇವರೊಳ್, ಮನೆಯೊಳ್, ಕಿವಿಯೊಳ್, ನೀರೊಳ್, ದಿನದೊಳ್, *etc*. -ಅಂಕೆ, ಒಳಂಕೆ. Control. -ಅಟ್ಟೆ. ಒಳಟ್ಟೆ. The inner sole of a shoe.

ಒಳ k. *n*. The inside. *a*. Inner, subordinate. -ಕಲಮು. A subordinate paragraph. -ಕೈಯ್. The palm of the hand. -ಗಡೆ. The inner side, inside; meanwhile; afterwards, later. -ಗುಟ್ಟು. A secret. -ಗುಡಿ. The inner part of a temple. -ಡೊಂಕು. Bending inward, concave. -ದಾರಿ. A bye-path. -ದೇಶ, -ನಾಡು, -ಸೀಮೆ. An inland country. -ಪಡು. To yield, to be subject to; to be merged. -ಪಡಿಸು. To make subordinate; to inclose; to seduce. -ಭಾಗ. An inner part; a subdivision. -ಮೈ. The inner side, *as* of a cloth. -ಸಂಚು. A plot, intrigue. -ಸಂಚುಗಾರ. An intriguer, plotter. -ಸಾಲ. A secret debt. -ಸೆರಗು. The tail end of a woman's cloth. -ಹೊಟ್ಟೆ. The inside of the belly; the stomach. ಒಳಾಯ. Intermediate space.

ಒಳಗು k. *n*. The inside, inner part. *prep*. (= ಒಳಗೆ, *q. v.*) Within, in, into. -ಆಗು, ಒಳಗಾಗು. To get into the power of; to submit one's self; to be subject; to incur. ಒಳಗಿಂದೊಳಗೆ. Secretly, privately. -ಗೊಡು, -ದೋರು. To give out a secret.

ಒಳಗೆ (= ಒಳಗು) k. *prep*. Inside, within, in, into; *as:* ಉಡಿಯೊಳಗೆ, ನೆಲದೊಳಗೆ, ನೀರೊಳಗೆ, *etc*. -ಇರು, ಒಳಗಿರು. To be inside or in. -ಸೇರು. To go inside; to sink, *as* an eye. ಒಳಗೊಳಗೆ. *rep*.

ಒಳವು k. *n*. The inside; a secret. 2, control.

ಒಳಿತು, ಒಳ್ಳಿತು k. *n*. That is good, nice, handsome, excellent, well. ಒಳಿತಾಗಿ ಮಾಡು. To do a thing well.

ಒಳ್ಳಿದ k. *n*. A good, nice man.

ಒಳ್ಳೆ k. *n*. Goodness, handsomeness, *etc*. (*see* ಒಳಿತು). *a*. Good, nice, fine, excellent, proper; *gen*. ಒಳ್ಳೆಯ *or* ಒಳ್ಳೇ. *Cpds.:* -ಕೆಲಸ, -ಗುಣ, -ನಡತೆ. -ದು. = ಒಳಿತು, *q. v.* ಒಳ್ಳೇದು. Very good, well. -ಯವನು. A good man. -ತನ. Goodness, good conduct, propriety, *etc*.

ಓ

ಓ. The fifteenth letter of the alphabet. 2, *a contraction of* ಉವ; *as:* ಆಗೋದು, ಹೋಗೋದು, ಹೂಡೋದು, ಬಿತ್ತೋದು, *etc*. 3, *interrog. affix, as:* ಮುತ್ತಿದನೋ? ಬಿದ್ದನೋ? ಹೋಗುತ್ತೀಯೋ? ಇದ್ದಾಳೋ? *etc*. 4, *int. of admiration, etc., as in* ಎಂಥಾ ಕೆಟ್ಟವನೋ, ನೀನು! ಮಂಗಗಳು ಎಷ್ಟೋ ಕೆಲಸ ಮಾಡುತ್ತವೆ! 5, *int*. ಓ ಓ (= ಓಹೋ), o, oh! 6, *int. of calling, as:* ಓ ತಮ್ಮಾ, ಓ ದೇವರೆ. *v. i*. To be attached to, fond of. *P. p*. ಓತು. ಓವಂ. A beloved man, husband; *f*. ಓವಳ್.

ಓಕರಿ k. n. Vomiting. -ಸು (= ಒಕ್ಕರಿಸು, etc). To vomit, retch, spit out; to emit. -ಕೆ. Vomiting.

ಓಕಳಿ, ಓಕುಳಿ k. n. A red liquid of turmeric and chunam sprinkled upon persons at the hôḷi feast or other auspicious occasions. -ಆಡು. To sprinkle the ôkuḷi on one another.

ಓಕಾರ s. n. The letter ಓ.

ಓಗಟು = ಒಗಟು, q. v.

ಓಗರ k. n. Boiled rice; also ಓಗರದ ಗಂಟು. Cpds.: ಮೇಲೋಗರ, ಹಾಲೋಗರ. etc.

ಓಘ s. n. A stream, current. 2, a heap, multitude.

ಓಂಕಾರ s. n. The mystic syllable ôm.

ಓಜ k. n. A teacher, guru. 2, a carpenter, blacksmith.

ಓಜಸ್, ಓಜಸ್ಸು s. n. Strength, energy. 2, light, splendour. 3, manifestation.

ಓಜೆ a. k. n. A row, line, range; regularity, order.

ಓಟ (fr. ಓಡು) k. n. Running; a run, race; speed. -ಗಾರ. A runner, racer; f. -ಗಾರಳು, -ಗಾತಿ.

ಓಟೆ 1. k. n. The tree *Garcinia pictoria*. 2, a jungle reed. 3, a crack, hole.

ಓಟೆ 2. f. n. A half of a cocoa-nut shell. 2, the shell, as of the wood-apple, almonds, etc.

ಓಡ k. n. A boat, ferry boat. -ಗಾರ. A boatman.

ಓಡು 1. k. n. A fragment, potsherd; an earthen pan; the skull.

ಓಡು 2. k. v. i. To run; to flee. ಓಡಿ ಹೋಗು. To go quickly, decamp. ಓಡಾಟ, ಓಡ್ಯಾಟ. Running about. ಓಡಾಡು, ಓಡ್ಯಾಡು. To run about, skip. ಓಡಾಟ. Running about. ಓಡಿಸು. To cause to run; to drive away. ಓಡಿಸಿಬಿಡು. To drive off. -ವಿಕೆ, ಓಡಿಕೆ. Running.

ಓಡೆ k. n. An earthen hoop used for walling the inside of wells; a large store-vessel. 2, a fried cake.

ಓಣ k. A verbal affix, as: ಹೋಗೋಣ, ನಡೆಯೋಣ. 2, aff. of verbal nouns, as: ಬೊಗಳೋಣ, ಗುಣುಗುಟ್ಟೋಣ, ನಮ್ಮ ಆಡೋಣವು. 3, aff. of the 1st p. pl. imp., as: ಓಡೋಣ! ಹೋಗೋಣ! ನೋಡೋಣ! etc. Let us run! etc.

ಓಣಿ k. n. A line, row. 2, a lane, alley.

ಓತಿ k. n. A kind of lizard or chameleon, blood-sucker.

ಓದು (of ಓದು) k. n. Reading, study.

ಓದು k. v. t. To read; to recite; to study. ಓದಿಕೆ, -ವಿಕೆ. Reading, etc. ಓದಕಲಿ. To learn to read. ಓದಗೊಡು, ಓದಗೊಡಿಸು. To let read. ಓದಿ ಬಿಡು. To read off. ಓದಬರು. To be able to read. ಓದುವ ಹುಡುಗ. A pupil. ಓದಿಸು. To cause to read; to instruct. ಓದಾಳಿ. A reader; a learned man.

ಓನಾಮ s. n. The name or mantra that begins with ಓ, i. e. ಓ ನಮಃ ಶಿವಾಯ. 2, a N. of the alphabet.

ಓಪಾದಿ k. n. Likeness, similarity.

ಓಮ, ಓಮು, ಓವ, ಓವು k. n. Bishop's weed, *Ligusticum ajwaen*.

ಓಯಿ k. int. O! ho! hallo!

ಓರ (= ಓರೆ, q. v.) k. n. Declivity, sloping. 2, side, edge, margin.

ಓರಗಿತ್ತಿ (= ವಾರಗಿತ್ತಿ) k. n. A husband's brother's wife.

ಓರಗೆ k. n. Equality; similarity; a match. -ಯವ. A man of the same age.

ಓರಡಿ k. n. Sloping, declivity; variance.

ಓರಣ a. k. n. A line, row. ಓರಣಿಸು. To be or put in a row.

ಓರು k. n. A hole. v. i. To think; ponder; to consider.

ಓರೆ k. n. Leaning, sloping, bending; declivity; crookedness. a. Slant, oblique, crooked. -ಕೋರೆ. reit. -ಗಟ್ಟು. A tie bending to one side; a way of tying the turban. -ಗಣ್ಣು. A squint-eye; a side-glance. -ಚಪ್ಪರ. A pent-roof. Other cpds.: -ತಲೆ, -ಕೈ, -ಮೂಗು, -ಮೋರೆ, etc. -ಯಾಗು. To become crooked.

ಓಲಗ (= ವಾಲಗ) f. n. Service, homage, an assembly; an audience; a durbar. 2, a haut-boy. -ಈ, -ಕೊಡು. To hold a public levee, to pay homage. -ಶಾಲೆ. A hall of audience.

ಓಲಗಿಸು, ಓಲಯ್ಸು, ಓಲವಿಸು f. v. t. To serve; to assemble, to bring together.

ಓಲಾಟ k. n. Affection, friendship. 2, swinging.

ಓಲಾಡು k. v. t. To love. v. i. To sport in water; to swim, bathe.

ಓಲು k. n. A bail, security, pledge; a hostage. -ಆಗು, ಓಲಾಗು. To become bail. -ಇಕ್ಕು, -ಇರಿಸು, -ಕೊಡು, ಓಲಿಡು. To give as a pledge, security, or hostage. -ಗಾರ. A bondsman; f. -ಗಾತಿ.

ಓಲೆ k. n. A leaf of a palmyra-tree, a oadjan leaf used to write on with an iron style. 2, an ear-ornament of gold or of palm-leaves. -ಚಂದ್ರಿಕೆ. A coil of palm-leaf. -ಚವಳುಂಬು. A pendent of an ôlĕ ear-ring. -ತಿರಗಣಿ. The screw of an ear-ring. -ಪುಸ್ತಕ. A book of oadjan leaves. -ಭಾಗ್ಯ. A female's good fortune to wear an ôlĕ as a sign of her husband being alive. ಓಲೆಯ ಮರ. The palmyra tree.

ಓಲೆಕಾರ k. n. A government servant who carries letters, etc., a porter.

ಓಷಧಿ s. n. A plant, herb. 2, an annual plant.

ಓಷ್ಠ s. n. A lip. ಓಷ್ಠ್ಯ. A labial.

ಓಸರ k. a. Sloping, slanting. n. An unsatisfactorily balanced burden.

ಓಸರಿಸು k. v. i. To go to one side; to turn aside; to give way, yield; to go away; to hesitate.

ಓಸ್ಕರ (a. k. ಓಸುಗ) k. n. Cause, reason sake. prep. On account of. ಕಟ್ಟುವದಕ್ಕೋಸ್ಕರ, ನನಗೋಸ್ಕರ, ಒಳ್ಳೇದಕ್ಕೋಸ್ಕರ.

ಓಹೋ, ಓಹೋಹೋ k. int. of wonder, admiration, etc. Ho! stop! oho!

ಓಳಿ (= ಓಣಿ) k. n. A continuous line; a row; succession.

ಔ

ಔ. The sixteenth letter of the alphabet. *In Kannaḍa words it is another form of* ಅವು, *or of* ಅವ (*as:* ಅವುಡಲ= ಔಡಲ, ಅವುತಣ= ಔತಣ, ತವರು= ತೌರು), *and therefore for all Kannaḍa and Tadbhava words with initial* ಔ *not* [illegible]*nd below see under initial* ಅವ *or* ಅವು.

ಔಕಾರ s. n. The letter ಔ.

ಔಕು (= ಅವುಕು) k. v. t. To press down, squeeze, shampoo.

ಔಗು (= ಅವುಗು) k. v. t. To yield to pressure, as a ripe fruit.

ಔಚಿತ್ಯ (fr. ಉಚಿತ) s. n. Fitness, propriety; pleasure, delight.

ಔಜಸ s. n. Lustre, shine; gold.

ಔಟು. = ಅವುಟು, q. v.

ಔಡಲ (= ಅವುಡಲ, tb. of ಅಮಂಡ) n. The castor-oil plant.

ಔತಣ (= ಅವುತಣ) k. n. A festive dinner 2, an invitation to dinner. -ಮಾಡು. To make a feast.

ಔತುಕೊಳ್ಳು (= ಅವುತುಕೊಳ್ಳು, fr. ಅವಿ) k. v. t. To hide one's self.

ಔತ್ಸುಕ್ಯ (fr. ಉತ್ಸುಕ) s. n. Anxiety, uneasiness; eagerness, zeal.

ಔದಾರ್ಯ (fr. ಉದಾರ) s. n. Generosity, nobility, greatness.

ಔದಾಸೀನ್ಯ (fr. ಉದಾಸೀನ) s. n. Indifference, apathy.

ಔನ್ನತ್ಯ (fr. ಉನ್ನತ) s. n. Height; greatness; haughtiness.

ಔಪಾಸನ (*fr.* ಉಪಾಸನ) s. *n.* A kind of adoration of Agni. *a.* Devotional.

ಔರ (= ಹಪುರ) k. *n.* Lightness.

ಔರಸ s. *a.* Legitimate. *n.* A legitimate son.

ಔಷಧ s. *n.* Medicine, drug; a herb. -ಕೊಡು. To administer medicine. -ಮಾಡು. To prepare medicine, apply remedies.

ಔಷ್ಟ್ರಕ s. *n.* A herd of camels.

ಂ ಃ

The seventeenth and eighteenth letters of the alphabet. *The first is generally called* anusvâra *or* sŏunĕ, *and the second called visarga, is found only in Saṁskṛita words. There is no word beginning with either of these letters.*

ಕ್

ಕ್. The nineteenth letter of the alphabet. ಕ. The letter ಕ್ pronounced with the short a.

ಕ, ಕಂ s. *n.* Brahmâ. 2, the soul. 3, the sun. 4, the head. 5, water. 6, pleasure.

ಕಂಯಿ. = ಕಹಿ, *q. v.*

ಕಂಸ s. *n.* Brass. 2, a metal vessel, a goblet. 3, a king of Mathurâ killed by Kṛishṇa. 4, a bracket; an arc.

ಕಂಸಾಳ (*tb. of* ಕಾಂಸ್ಯತಾಲ) *n.* A gong; a triangle. -ಕ. A gold- or silversmith; *f.* -ಗಿತ್ತಿ.

ಕಕಾರ s. *n.* The letter ಕ.

ಕಕುದ s. *n.* A peak, summit. 2, a bull's hump. *a.* Pre-eminent, chief.

ಕಕುಭ s. *n.* A region, quarter. 2, the tree *Terminalia arjuna.* *a.* Chief, pre-eminent.

ಕಕುಲತೆ, ಕಕುಲಾತೆ k. *n.* Love; compassion; vain desire.

ಕಕ್ಕ f. *n.* A father's younger brother.

ಕಕ್ಕಡ f. *n.* A piece of twisted cloth dipped in oil, lighted, and used as a light.

ಕಕ್ಕಡೆ k. *n.* N. of a weapon.

ಕಕ್ಕಬಿಕ್ಕರಿ, ಕಕ್ಕರಿಬಿಕ್ಕರಿ k. *n.* Crookedness.

ಕಕ್ಕಲಾತೆ. = ಕಕುಲತೆ, *q. v.*

ಕಕ್ಕಸ 1. k. *n.* Trouble (heavy breathing, *etc.*) arising from an overloaded stomach, from running, *etc.*

ಕಕ್ಕಸ 2. *tb. of* ಕರ್ಕಶ, *q. v.* -ಗಾರ. A cruel man; *f.* -ಗಾತಿ.

ಕಕ್ಕಸು (= ಕಕ್ಕೋಸು) f. *n.* A cac-hus: a privy.

ಕಕ್ಕಾಬಿಕ್ಕ k. *n.* An affrighted or timid man. -ರಿ, ಕಕ್ಕಾಬಿಕ್ಕಿ, ಕಕ್ಕಾಬಿಕ್ಕು. Fear, alarm.

ಕಕ್ಕಿ (*cf.* ಕಕ್ಕ) s. *n.* A mother's younger sister; uncle's wife; step-mother.

ಕಕ್ಕು 1. (= ಕಡಿಕು) a. k. *n.* A notch, dent; the rough or toothed part of a millstone, file or saw; roughness; sharpness. 2, a splinter, shiver.

ಕಕ್ಕು 2. k. *v. i.* To vomit. *n.* Vomiting. ಕಕ್ಕಿಸು. To cause to vomit.

ಕಕ್ಕುಬಿಕ್ಕು. = ಕಕ್ಕಾಬಿಕ್ಕರಿ, *q. v.*

ಕಕ್ಕೆ k. *n.* The pudding-pipe tree, *Cassia fistula.*

ಕಕ್ಕೋಲ s. n. N. of a plant bearing a berry containing waxy and aromatic substance; a perfume made of its berries; *also* -ಕ.

ಕಕ್ಕೋಸು. = ಕಕ್ಕಸು, *q. v.*

ಕಕ್ಷ (= ಕಚ್ಛ) s. n. The hem of a garment tucked into the waist-band. 2, a girdle. 3, the armpit; *also* -ಮೂಲ. 4, a forest. 5, an objection or reply in argument. -ಪಾಲ. A bag carried under the armpit.

ಕಕ್ಷಿ s. n. One party as opposed to another; objection, contention. -ಗಾರ. A party (in a civil or criminal case).

ಕಗ (= ಕಡು, *q. v.*) k. n. Hardness; strength, *etc.* -ಗಂಟು (= ಕಡುಗಂಟು). A fast knot that cannot be easily untied; a hard knot in wood. -ಗತ್ತಲೆ. Thick darkness. -ಕಲ್ಲು, ಕಗ್ಗಲ್ಲು. A very hard stone. -ಕಾಡು, ಕಗ್ಗಾಡು. An impervious jungle. -ಕಾಯಿ, ಕಗ್ಗಾಯಿ. An unripe fruit. -ಕಾರು, ಕಗ್ಗಾರು. Great dryness, drought. -ಕಾಲ, -ಕಗ್ಗಾಲ. Famine. -ಕುಂಬಳ, ಕಗ್ಗುಂಬಳ. A hard gourd.

ಕಗ್ಗ k. n. A long, tedious speech or literary composition.

ಕಂ (= ಕಣ್ಣು) k. n. The eye. -ಕಣ. An eye-drop, tear. -ಕಡೆ, ಕಂಗಡೆ. A side-glance, leer. -ಕಾಣು, -ಗಾಣು. To perceive. -ಕೆಡು, ಕಂಗೆಡು. To be blinded, confused, vexed; to be afraid. -ಗೆಡಿಸು. To blind, bewilder, confuse.

ಕಂಕಣ, ಕಂಕಳ s. n. An ornament of the wrist, bracelet. 2, a waist-tie. 3, a crest, trinket. -ಕಾರ. Borax. -ಗ್ರಹಣ. A partial eclipse. -ಬದ್ಧ. A man tying a kaṅkaṇa round his wrist for any auspicious rites.

ಕಂಕರೆ h. n. Gravel, a pebble.

ಕಂಕಳು. = ಕಂಕುಳ, *q. v.*

ಕಂಕಾಲ s. n. A skeleton. -ಧರ. Who carries the backbone of Vishṇu: Śiva.

ಕಂಕಿ k. n. An ear of corn stripped of its grain. -ಬಡಿ. To thrash out corn.

ಕಂಕುಳ (ಳ = ೞ) k. n. The armpit.

ಕಂಗಳ, ಕಂಗಾಳ k. n. A blind man.

ಕಂಗಾರು k. n. Displeasure, anger.

ಕಂಗಾಲ್ h. a. Poor; poverty-stricken; weak. ಕಂಗಾಲು. A pauper. -ತನ. Pauperism, wretchedness.

ಕಂಗು. = ಕಂಗಾರು, *q. v.* 2, the heart-pea. 3, the Indian millet -ಆಗು, ಕಂಗಾಗು. To become angry or annoyed.

ಕಂಗೆಡು, *see s.* ಕಂ.

ಕಂಗೋರೆ m. n. An ornamental cordon, groove, *etc.*

ಕಚ s. n. The hair of the head. 2, matted hair. 3, a binding, a band.

ಕಚಕ್ಕನೆ k. *ad.* Smartly, forcibly. 2, with the sound of treading or anything falling into mud.

ಕಚಪ್ಪ k. n. A dish of boiled vegetables or fruits seasoned with salt, pepper, *etc.*

ಕಚರಾ h. n. Rubbish, dirt, straw. -ಕೆಲಸ. Worthless business. -ತೆರಿಗೆ. Municipal tax.

ಕಚೇರಿ (= ಕಚ್ಚೇರಿ) h. n. A hall of audience, a court for administration of public business; an office. -ಮಾಡು. To open a court or office for business. *Cpds.*: -ಕೆಲಸ, -ಚಾಕರಿ, -ಉದ್ಯೋಗ.

ಕಚೋರ f. n. The long Zedoary, *Curcuma zerumbet.*

ಕಚ್ಚಡ (= ಕಚ್ಚರ) h. n. Filth, rubbish.

ಕಚ್ಚಡಿ k. n. A kind of vegetable dish.

ಕಚ್ಚಳಿ (ಳ = ೞ) a. k. n. An honorary arm-ring.

ಕಚ್ಚಾ h. a. Unripe, green; raw; rude, rough; tender; minor, less. -ಸೇರು. A seer of only 20 or 24 rupees' weight. -ಕೆಲಸ. A clumsy affair. -ಮನುಷ್ಯ. A mean man. -ಲೆಕ್ಕ. A rough account.

ಕಚ್ಚು k. *v. t.* To bite; to sting. 2, to gripe, ache, *as* the stomach. *v. i.* To join. *n.* Biting; a bite, an incision; a notch; a wound. 2, washing; water in which rice has been washed.

-ಆಟ, ಕಚ್ಚಾಟ. Quarrel. -ಆಡು, ಕಚ್ಚಾಡು. To bite one another, as dogs; to quarrel. -ಕಚ್ಚಿಸು. To cause to bite.

ಕಚ್ಚೂರ f. n. A leafless plant, *Kaempferia galanga*.

ಕಚ್ಚೆ (tb. of ಕಕ್ಷ & ಕಚ್ಛ) n. The hem of a garment tucked into the waistband. 2, a female's cloth. 3, a girdle.

ಕಚ್ಚೇರಿ. = ಕಚೇರಿ, q. v.

ಕಚ್ಛ (= ಕಚ್ಚೆ no. 1) s. n. 2, marshy ground. 3, the bank of a river. 4, a tree. -ಶುದ್ಧಿ. Chasteness.

ಕಚ್ಛೋರ. = ಕಚೋರ, q. v.

ಕಜಾಕ್ h. n. The sash worn by peons or sepoys.

ಕಜೂರ (= ಖರ್ಜೂರ) f. n. The date fruit.

ಕಜ್ಜ. tb. of ಕಾರ್ಯ, q. v.=ಕೆಲಸ, ಉದ್ಯೋಗ.

ಕಜ್ಜಲ s. n. Lamp-black; a collyrium.

ಕಜ್ಜಾಯ f. n. Bread. 2, a kind of sweet cake.

ಕಜ್ಜಿ (tb. of ಖರ್ಜು) n. Scab (the disease), itch. -ಟುರುಕ. One infected with the itch and always scratching it; f. -ಟುರುಕಿ. -ಹುಳ. Parasite in the itch.

ಕಂಚಾ k. n. A marble. -ಆಡು. To play marbles.

ಕಂಚಿ 1. k. n. A kind of bitter and sour orange.

ಕಂಚಿ 2. (tb. of ಕಾಂಚಿ) n. The town Conjeveram. -ಮೇಕೆ. A small white goat.

ಕಂಚಿನಿ h. n. A dancing girl.

ಕಂಚಿವಾಳ s. n. The mountain ebony, *Bauhinia variegata*.

ಕಂಚು (tb. of ಕಾಂಸ್ಯ) n. White brass, bell-metal; a vessel made of it. -ಮಿಂಚಾಗು. To appear or come suddenly or like a flash. -ಉರಳಿ, -ರಳಿ. A round vessel of ಕಂಚು.

ಕಂಚುಕ s. n. A bodice, jacket; an armour.

ಕಂಜ s. a. Water-born. n. A lotus. 2, Brahmâ. -ಗರ್ಭ, -ನಾಭ, -ಲೋಚನ, ಕಂಜೋದರ. Vishṇu. -ಜ, -ಭವ, -ಉದಯ, ಕಂಜೋದಯ. Brahmâ. -ವೈರಿ. The moon. -ಸಖ, ಕಂಜಾಪ್ತ. The sun.

ಕಟ 1. (= ಕಡೆ) k. n. End; corner. -ಬಾಯಿ, -ವಾಯಿ. The two corners of the mouth; a cheeck.

ಕಟ 2. s. n. A twist of straw; a mat. 2, time, season. 3, the hip. 4, the temples of an elephant. 5, excess.

ಕಟಕ 1. k. n. A butcher.

ಕಟಕ 2. (tb. ಕಡಗ) s. n. A bracelet, anklet. 2, the side of a hill; tableland. 3, an army. 4, the ocean. 5, a tusk.

ಕಟಕಟಾ. = ಅಕಟ, q. v. .

ಕಟಕಟಿ, ಕಟಕಟೆ 1. k. n. Trouble, annoyance; grievance, distress.

ಕಟಕಟೆ 2. k. n. A railing, balustrade.

ಕಟಕರೋಣಿ, ಕಟಂಬರೆ s. n. The medicinal plant *Helleborus niger*.

ಕಟಕಿ k. n. Irony; derision. 2, a shrew.

ಕಟಕು 1. k. n. A sort of white or reddish clay. 2, dryness, crispness, as of bread.

ಕಟಕು 2. (tb. of ಕಟಕ) n. An ear-ring set with precious stones or pearls.

ಕಟಪಿಟಿ (= ಕಟಕಟ) k. n. Annoyance; teasing. 2, gabble.

ಕಟಾಕ್ಷ s. n. A side-glance. 2, kind regard, favour. ಕಟಾಕ್ಷಿಸು. To look at, to favour, regard.

ಕಟಾಂಜನ s. n. A railing to lean against.

ಕಟಾಯಿಸು h. v. t. To reap, as corn. 2, to deduct; to finish. ಕಟಾವು. Cutting, reaping.

ಕಟಾರಿ (= ಕಠಾರಿ) h. n. A sort of dagger.

ಕಟಾಹ (= ಕಡಾಯಿ) s. n. A boiler for oil or butter; a frying pan. 2, a hemisphere. 3, nearness. 4, opportunity, season.

ಕಟಿ 1, ಕಟೆ k. v. t. To cut a stone with a chisel. 2, to keep the mind awake.

ಕಟಿ 2. s. n. The hip, loins. -ಬಂಧ. A girdle; a zone of the earth. -ವಾತ.

Lumbago. -ಸೂತ್ರ. A waist-band worn by females.

ಕಟಿಕ. = ಕಟಿಕ, q. v.

ಕಟು, ಕಟುಕ s. a. Pungent; strong-scented; biting; bitter; fierce. 2, disagreeable. n. A pungent taste. -ಕರೋಹಿಣಿ. = ಕಟುಕರೋಹಿಣಿ, q. v.

ಕಟೋರ h. n. A bowl or cup.

ಕಟ್ಟ (= ಕಟ 1, ಕಡೆ 1) k. n. End. -ಕಡೆ. The farthest end; at the very end. -ಉತ್ತರ, ಕಟ್ಟುತ್ತರ. A final answer.

ಕಟ್ಟಡ, ಕಟ್ಟಣ k. n. A building.

ಕಟ್ಟಲೆ, ಕಟ್ಟಳೆ (fr. ಕಟ್ಟು) k. n. An order, command, rule; rate; a case. 2, a weight used by goldsmiths or jewellers. 3, thick butter-milk. -ಚೀಲ. A bag for keeping weights, etc. -ಮಾಡು. To order. ದಿನ-. Daily.

ಕಟ್ಟಿಗೆ (tb. of ಕಾಷ್ಠಿಕೆ) n. Wood or timber; fuel; a stick. -ಗಿಟ್ಟಿಗೆ. redi. -ಗಾರ, -ಯವ. A wood-seller. -ಗುಣ, -ಮನಸ್ಸು. A hard heart; obstinacy. -ಕಡಿ. To cut wood.

ಕಟ್ಟು 1. (= ಕಡು, q. v.) k. n. Intensity; excess, etc. ಕಟ್ಟಡವಿ, ಕಟ್ಟರಣ್ಯ. A thick jungle. ಕಟ್ಟಂಬಲಿ. A thick kind of porridge. ಕಟ್ಟಲೆ, ಕಟ್ಟಳೆ, see separately. ಕಟ್ಟಾಜ್ಞೆ. A strict order. ಕಟ್ಟಾಯ. A firm resolution. ಕಟ್ಟಾಳು. A strong man. ಕಟ್ಟಾಳ್ತನ. Great valor. ಕಟ್ಟುತ್ತರ. A strict order. ಕಟ್ಟುತ್ತಾರ. Remission of land-revenue on account of loss by failure of rain, etc. -ಮಸ್ತಿ. Excessive pride. -ದುಸ್ತು. Strength. -ಉಲುಹು, ಕಟ್ಟುಲುಹು. A great noise. -ಹುಳಿ. A strong acid. -ಊಳಿಗ, ಕಟ್ಟೂಳಿಗ. A hard task.

ಕಟ್ಟು 2. k. v. t. To bind, tie; to affix; to yoke; to construct, build, form; to dam in, as water; to shut up, as a door; to lay by, deposit, as money; to restrain; to apply to; to determine, as price; to collect; to obtain; to bewitch, charm. v. i. To be checked, stopped, formed. (ಕಟ್ಟಿಕೊಳ್ಳು. To embrace. ಪುಣ್ಯ ಕಟ್ಟಿಕೊಳ್ಳು. To obtain merit. ಕಟ್ಟಿಕೊಂಡು ಹೋಗು. To conduct away with one's self. ಕಟ್ಟಿಹಾಕು. = ಕಟ್ಟು 1, v. t. ಕಟ್ಟಿಸು. To cause to bind, etc. -ಐಕೆ. Tying). n. Binding, fastening; restraint. 2, a band, tie; a boundary. 3, a pack, bundle. 4, a frame. 5, build, form. 6, a regulation, rule. 7, a fiction. 8, bewitching. Cpds.: ಇಕ್ಕಟ್ಟು, ಕಣ್ಣುಕಟ್ಟು, ಚೌಕಟ್ಟು, ತಲೆಕಟ್ಟು, ನಡುಕಟ್ಟು, ನೆಲೆಗಟ್ಟು, ಮಣಿಕಟ್ಟು, etc. ಕಟ್ಟಡಕ. A binding written agreement. ಕಟ್ಟನ್ನ. Boiled rice tied up for a journey. ಕಟ್ಟಾಗು. To become a rule; to stop; to be shut, as school. ಕಟ್ಟಾಗಿ. Rightly, positively. ಕಟ್ಟಾಣಿ, ಕಠಾಣಿ. A necklace of small gold beads. -ಕಥೆ. A fiction. -ಮಾಡು. To bind, tie; to restrain; to regulate; order. -ಮುಟ್ಟು. Great embarrassment, strength. -ವಾಸ. A wrapper or cover. -ಶಬ್ದ. A fictitious term. -ಕಟ್ಟೊಡೆ. To break a rule; an association to be dissolved. -ಕ. A man who ties; a fiction.

ಕಟ್ಟು 3. k. n. Soup of any pulse. ಕಟ್ಟನ್ನ. Boiled rice mixed with it (cf. s. ಕಟ್ಟು). -ರಸ, -ಸಾರು. Such soup seasoned with salt, pepper, etc.

ಕಟ್ಟೆ k. n. A structure; a guard-house. 2, a dam, dike. 3, a bridge. 4, a basin round the foot of a tree (= ಆಲವಾಲ, q. v.). 5, a pond. Cpds.: ಅಣೆ-, ಟಪಾಲ-, ನೀರ-, ಸುಂಕದ-, etc.

ಕಟ್ಲೆ. = ಕಟ್ಟಳೆ, q. v. 2, a law-suit, case.

ಕಠಾರಿ. = ಕಟಾರಿ, q. v.

ಕಠಿಣ, ಕಠಿನ s. a. Hard; stiff, inflexible; violent; cruel, harsh. -ತೆ, -ತ್ವ. Hardness; cruelty. -ಹೃದಯ. A hard heart; hard-hearted, cruel. -ಬುದ್ಧಿ, -ಮನಸ್ಸು. A cruel disposition. -ರೋಗ. A dangerous sickness. -ಮಾಡು. To harden; to vex.

ಕಠೋರ s. a. Hard; stiff; sharp; cruel. 2, full. -ತನ. Hardness, severity. Cpds.: -ಮಾತು, -ವಾಕ್ಯ, -ಶಬ್ದ.

ಕಡ 1. k. n. A debt. 2, a loan. -ಬೀಳು. To incur debt. -ಗಾರ. A debtor.

ಕಡ 2. k. n. A ferry, ford.

ಕಡ 3. (=ಕಡೆ) k. n. End, corner.

ಕಡ 4. (=ಕಡು) k. n. Churning. 2, cutting. -ಗೋಲು. A churning stick. -ಕತ್ತಿ, -ಗತ್ತಿ. A chopper-bill; a small crescent knife.

ಕಡಗು, ಕಡಂಗು k. n. A channel leading water to a tree; a ditch.

ಕಡಜ k. n. A wasp, hornet.

ಕಡತ (cf. ಕಡಿ) k. n. A book made of folded cloth covered with charcoal paste. 2, cutting; a cut, incision.

ಕಡದು (fr. ಕಡಿ) k. a. Steep; upright. 2, hard, rough, severe, firm. n. Steepness; uprightness; hardness, etc. -ಗಾರ. A powerful man; a harsh man.

ಕಡದು. P. p. of ಕಡಿ or ಕಡೆ.

ಕಡಂದುರು. =ಕಡಜ, q. v.

ಕಡಬು, ಕಡವ k. n. A species of deer.

ಕಡಬು, ಕಡುಬು k. n. A cake boiled in steam.

ಕಡಮೆ. = ಕಡಿಮೆ, q. v.

ಕಡಲು k. n. The sea; an ocean. -ಅಣುಗ, ಕಡಲಣುಗ. The moon. -ತೆರೆ. A wave of the sea. -ನಾಲಿಗೆ. Cuttle-fish bone.

ಕಡಲೆ. = ಕಡ್ಲೆ, q. v.

ಕಡವಸ. =ಕಡಾಸು, q. v.

ಕಡವೆ (=ಕಡಬು) k. n. An elk; the Indian stag.

ಕಡಸು k. n. A young cow or buffalo not yet calved.

ಕಡಾಕಡಿ (=ಖಡಾಖಡಿ) f. n. Strictness; accuracy.

ಕಡಾಣ.=ಕಡಿವಾಣ, q. v.

ಕಡಾಯಿ (tb. of ಕಟಾಹ) n. A large, round boiler.

ಕಡಾವಿಗೆ, ಕಡಾವು s. n. Wooden shoes. 2, a lathe; turning.

ಕಡಾಸು k. n. A skin (to sit or lie on); also ಕಡಾಸನ.

ಕಡಿ k. v. t. To bite, bite or cut off; to sting, as a bee; to pain, as the stomach; to gnash, as the teeth. 2, to cut, hack; to chop; to dig, as a well; to pull. v. i. To itch, as the body. P. ps. ಕಡ, ಕಡದು, ಕಡಿದು. ಕಡ ದಾಟ. Altercation. ಕಡದಾಡು. To cut down; to fight, wrangle. ಕಡಿ, ಕಡಿತ, ಕಡತ. A cut, bite; a chip, piece, bit; a potsherd; an oblong roll of cotton thread. -ತಲೆ. A leather-shield. -ಮೆಟ್ಟು. The impression of a horse's hoof. -ಯಕ್ಕಿ. Grits of rice.

ಕಡಿಮೆ (= ಕಡಮೆ) k. n. Deficiency; want, defect; inferiority. -ಮಾಡು. To make less, decrease. -ಯಾಗು. To become less. -ಬೀಳು. To fall short. ಹೆಚ್ಚು-. More or less; difference.

ಕಡಿವಾಣ, ಕಡಿಯಾಣ, ಕಡಿಯಣ k. n. A bit, bridle. -ಹಾಕು. To bridle. -ಎಳೆ, -ಬಿಗಿಹಿಡಿ. To pull in the reins.

ಕಡು (=ಕಟ್ಟು) k. n. Firmness; intensity; vehemence; swiftness; abundance, excess. ad. Greatly; swiftly. -ಕಷ್ಟ. Great trouble. -ಕಳ್ಳ. A great thief. -ಕೇಡು. A heavy loss. -ಕೋಪ, -ಗೋಪ. Great wrath. -ಕತ್ತಲೆ, -ಗತ್ತಲೆ. Great darkness. -ಗಲಿ. A great hero. -ಗಾಸಿ. Great trouble. -ಕುದುರೆ, -ಗುದುರೆ. A swift horse. -ಗೇಡಿ. A very mischievous person. -ಚಳಿ. Severe cold. -ನಾಲಿಗೆ. A talkative tongue. -ನೋವು. Acute pain. -ಪಾತಕ, -ಪಾಪ. A heinous sin. -ಪಾಪಿ. A notorious sinner. -ಮೂರ್ಖ. A big fool. -ವೇಗ. Great swiftness. -ಶೋಕ. Great grief. -ಹೆಡ್ಡ. A very stupid man.

ಕಡುಕು k. n. A cut, piece; a bit; a headless trunk.

ಕಡುಪು k. n. Force, vehemence; severity; pride; great valor.

ಕಡುಬು. =ಕಡಬು, q. v.

ಕಡೆ 1. (=ಕಟ 1) k. n. End, termination; limit; direction; place. a. Last, low, ulterior; inferior. -ಗಣಿಸು. To look upon as inferior, slight; to end. -ಗಾಣಿಸು. To finish, accomplish. -ಗೂ. To the very last; totally. -ಗೆ. Aside; towards; in the end, at last, finally. ಕಡೆಗೆ ತೆಗೆ. To rescue. -ಗೆ ಹೋಗು. To go last; to go aside. -ತನಕ. Until the end. -ನೋಟ. A side glance. -ದಾಟಿಸು, -ಹಾಯಿಸು. To cause to pass by, through or over; to save. -ಗೂಸು, -ಹುಟ್ಟು. The youngest child. ಕಡೇಲಿ. *A common form of* ಕಡೆಯಲ್ಲಿ. ಎಡಗಡೆ. The left side. ಬಲಗಡೆ. The right side.

ಕಡೆ 2. k. *v. t.* To churn; to stir; to rub together, *as* two pieces of wood to excite fire. 2, to turn in a lathe. 3, to pass over; to get through. *v. i.* To fall down, sink. ಮೊಸರು-. To churn curds. *n.* Churning. -ಗೋಲು.= ಕಡಗೋಲು *s.* ಕಡ 4. -ಹಲು. Turning a lathe; *also* ಕಡಾವು.

ಕಡ್ಡ k. *n.* A clown, blockhead; an unpolite man. 2, a pitfall to catch elephants. -ಮಾಡು. To make a dolt of one. ಕಡ್ಡಾಟ. Obstinacy, pertinacity; stupidity.

ಕಡ್ಡಾಯ k. *n.* Force, compulsion, exaction. -ಗಾರ. An outrageous man. -ಮಾಡು. To force, constrain.

ಕಡ್ಡಿ (*tb. of* ಕಾಷ್ಠ) *n.* A small stick, fibre of a leaf or a bit of a haulm. -ಅರಗು, -ಯರಗು. Stick lac; a stick of sealing wax.

ಕಡ್ಲೆ (= ಕಡಲೆ) k. *n.* The Bengal gram or chicken-pea, *Cicer arietinum.*

ಕಣ್ (= ಕಣ್ಣು, *q. v.*) k. *n.* The eye; a mesh. -ಕಾಡಿಗೆ, -ಕಪ್ಪು. A collyrium for the eye. -ಕುಣಿ. The socket of the eye. -ಕುಣಿಕೆ. The inner or outer corner of the eye. -ಗೆಡಿಸು, ಕಂಗೆಡಿಸು. To blind, bewilder, confuse. -ಚಲ್ಲ. A smile of the eye. -ಜಾಡೆ. A faint notice. ಕಣ್ಣಾರ, ಕಣ್ಣಾರೆ. Distinctly, clearly. ಕಣ್ಣಿಡು. To fix the eyes. ಕಣ್ಣೀರು. Tears. ಕಣ್ಣುಬ್ಬು. An eye-brow. ಕಣ್ಣುರಿ. Smarting of the eye; envy. ಕಣ್ಣೆಮೆ, ಕಣ್ಣೆವೆ. An eye-lash, eyelid. -ಪರೆ. A web or film of the eye. -ದೆರೆ, -ಬಿಡು. To open the eyes. -ಮುಚ್ಚು. To shut the eyes. -ಸನ್ನೆ, -ಸಯ್ಗೆ. A wink.

ಕಣ 1. s. *n.* A grain, single seed; a particle, a granule; an atom. 2, a drop, spark. *a.* Small.

ಕಣ 2. k. *n.* A piece of cloth for a female's bodice, *as* ರವಕೇ-.

ಕಣ 3. (*tb. of* ಖಲ) *n.* A thrashing floor; a battle-field; a misty halo round the moon.

ಕಣಕ k. *n.* Dough, especially of wheaten flour.

ಕಣಕಪ್ಪಡಿ (= ಕಣುಕಪ್ಪಟೆ) k. *n.* A flittermouse, bat.

ಕಣಗಲ, ಕಣಗಿಲ k. *n.* A shrub yielding Tapioca, the bitter *cassava* plant.

ಕಣಗಿಲೆ k. *n.* Fragrant oleander, *Nerium odorum.*

ಕಣಜ s. *n.* A corn-bin, *i. e.* a cylindrical structure for storing grain, a granary, barn. -ಹುಳ. A wasp. -ಹಾಕು. To store grain.

ಕಣವೆ (=ಕಣಿಮೆ, ಕಣಿವೆ) k. *n.* A hill-pass, gap, ditch.

ಕಣಾ k. *int.* Lo! indeed!

ಕಣಿ 1. k. *n.* Sight, spectacle; ominous sight; divination, sooth. -ಕೇಳು. To ask for a divination. -ಹೇಳು. To divine. -ಗಾರ. A fortune teller; *f.* -ಗಾತಿ.

ಕಣಿ 2. k. *n.* A knot, tie. 2, a stone.

ಕಣಿ 3. (*tb. of* ಖನಿ) *n.* A ditch; a mine.

ಕಣಿ 4. f. *n.* An atom; grits; a trifle.

ಕಣಿಕೆ k. *n.* The stalk of the great millet deprived of its ear.

ಕಣಿಮೆ, ಕಣಿವೆ. = ಕಣಮೆ, *q. v.*

ಕಣುಕಪ್ಪಟೆ. = ಕಣಕಪ್ಪಡಿ, *q. v.*

ಕಣೆ k. *n.* A stick; an arrow. 2, a wooden roller of an oil-mill.

ಕಂಟ (*tb. of* ಕಂಠ) *n.* An iron style for writing on palm-leaves. 2, the neck of a vessel.

ಕಂಟಕ s. *n.* A thorn; the point of a needle. 2, a foe. 3, annoyance, obstacle; danger. 4, a hunter. -ಫಲ. A jack fruit. ಕಂಟಕಿ. An awn; a troublesome woman.

ಕಂಟಕಾರಿ, -ಕೆ. s. n. A sort of prickly nightshade, *Solanum jacquini*.

ಕಂಟಲೆ, ಕಂಟ್ಲೆ k. n. A double bag carried across a beast.

ಕಂಟಿ s. n. A species of *Solanum*. 2, the *Acacia catechu*. 3, any thorny shrub. 4, a kind of gold ornament for the breast. *a.* Thorny; annoying.

ಕಂಟು k. n. An offset in the wall of a well or at the foot of a wall; a flight of stairs leading to a well.

ಕಂಠ (*tb.* ಕಂಟು) s. n. The throat. 2, the neck of a vessel. 3, an iron style for writing. 4, guttural sound. 5, the body. -ಪಾಠ. Learning by heart. -ಮಾಲೆ. A necklace. -ಲಗ್ನ. Embracing. -ಶೋಷ. Vain talk. -ಸೂತ್ರ. The thread worn by wives round their neck; the sacrificial thread. ಕಂಠೋಷ್ಠ್ಯ. The vowels ಒ, ಓ, and ಔ.

ಕಂಠಿ s. n. A collar; a necklace. ಕಂಠೀರವ. Roaring from the throat; a lion. ಕಂಠೀರವರಾಯ. N. of a Mysore king. ಕಂಠೀರವರಾಯನ ಹಣ. A gold fanam (4 ⅜ Anas).

ಕಂಡ 1. k. n. Flesh, meat.

ಕಂಡ 2. (*p. a. of* ಕಾಣು). Seen; he saw.

ಕಂಡ 3. (*tb. of* ಖಂಡ, *q. v.*) -ತುಂಡು ಮಾತಾಡು. To speak so that further argument becomes futile. -ಸಕ್ಕರೆ. Sugar-candy.

ಕಂಡನೆ k. n. Final settlement, treaty. *Cpds.*: -ಪತ್ರ, -ಹಣ, *etc.*

ಕಂಡಲಿ k. n. A kind of bill-hook or cleaver.

ಕಂಡಿ 1. k. n. A chink; a hole; an opening, gap.

ಕಂಡಿ 2. f. n. A measure of capacity and weight. 2, a certain timber-measure.

ಕಂಡಿಕೆ k. n. A ball of thread put into the weaver's shuttle. 2, (*fr.* ಕಡಿ) a piece.

ಕಂಡಿತ (= ಖಂಡಿತ, *fr.* ಕಡು) k. n. Firmness, positiveness, strictness, certainty. -ಮಾತು. A decisive word.

ಕಂಡಿಸು (= ಖಂಡಿಸು) k. *v. t.* To settle, *as* the price of a thing.

ಕಂಡು k. *P. p. of* ಕಾಣು, *q. v.*

ಕಂಡುಗ k. n. A measure of capacity equal to twenty kŏḷagas.

ಕಂಡೆಯ k. n. A kind of sword. 2, large extent.

ಕಂಡೋಲ f. n. A basket for holding grain; a store-room. 2, a weight from 20 to 28 maunds.

ಕಣ್ಣ k. n. A rope, cord; a neck-rope.

ಕಣ್ಣೀರು k. n. Tears. -ಸೋರು. Tears to flow. -ಇಡು, -ತರು, -ಸುರಿಸು. Tears to shed. *See s.* ಕಣ್.

ಕಣ್ಣು (= ಕಣ್, *q. v.*) k. n. The eye; an eye-like knot in sticks, *etc.*; a small hole, an orifice; a mesh. -ಕಟ್ಟು. To shut or bewitch the eyes; to deceive; jugglery. -ಕಟ್ಟನವ. A juggler. -ಕಾಣು. The eye to see. -ಕೆಂಪು. To assume an angry look. ಕಣ್ಗೆಸುರು. An evil eye. -ಕುಕ್ಕು. The eye to be dazzled, *as* by the rays of the sun. -ಗತ್ತಲೆ. Fainting, swoon. -ಗುಡ್ಡೆ. The eye-ball. -ಗೊಂಬೆ. The pupil of the eye. -ನೋವು, -ಬೇನೆ. Pain of the eye. -ಪಿಚ್ಚು, -ಪಿಸರು, -ಪಿಳ್ಳೆ. Rheum of the eye. -ಮಂಜು, -ಮಬ್ಬು. Dimness of sight. -ಮುಚ್ಚಾಲೆ. A kind of blindman's buff. -ಸನ್ನೆ. A sign made with the eye, a wink. -ಹುಬ್ಬು. The eyebrow. -ಹುಬ್ಬು ಗಂಟು ಹಾಕಿಕೊಳ್ಳು. To frown. -ಹೂವು. A white spot on the eye-ball. -ಹೋಗು. To lose the eye-sight. -ಎತ್ತು, ಕಣ್ಣೆತ್ತು. To lift up the eyes. -ಮರೆ ಮಾಡು. To hide from view. -ಹೊಡೆ. To twinkle the eye.

ಕಣ್ಣುಕಪ್ಪಟಿ. = ಕಣಕಪ್ಪಟಿ, *q. v.*

ಕಣ್ಣೆ k. n. A clot, lump, *as* of jaggory, flesh, *etc.*

ಕತಕ s. n. The clearing nut tree, *Strychnos potatorum*.

ಕತಬೆ h. n. A writ of agreement, written bond.

ಕತಬೆಗ (= ಕದಬೆಗ) h. n. Strife, contention; controversy.

ಕತಿ (= ಖತಿ) k. n. Anger, wrath.

ಕತ್ತರಿ (= ಕತ್ರಿ, tb. of ಕರ್ತರಿ) n. Scissors, shears; a rat-trap. -ಗಳ್ಳ. A pick-pocket. -ಭಾವುಲಿ. A gold ornament worn near the top of the ear. -ಸು. To cut with scissors; to cut; to shear; to pick, steal.

ಕತ್ತಲೆ (ಕತ್ತಲು) k. n. Darkness. ಮುಂಗತ್ತಲೆ. Darkness after sunset. ಹಿಂಗತ್ತಲೆ. Darkness before dawn. -ಆಗು. To be dark.

ಕತ್ತಾಳೆ k. n. The Barbadoes aloe. 2, the small aloe.

ಕತ್ತಿ (tb. of ಕತ್ರಿ) n. A knife; a razor; a sword. -ಕಟ್ಟು. To gird on one's sword; to be hostile. -ಮತ. A religion established by the sword or force. -ಸಾಧಕ, -ಸಾಧನ. Sword exercise. ಬಿಚ್ಚು-. A naked sword. -ಬಿಚ್ಚು. To draw a sword. -ದುಡುಕು, -ತಿವಿ. To pierce with a sword.

ಕತ್ತು 1. k. n. The neck, throat. -ಕೊಯ್ಯು. To cut the throat.

ಕತ್ತು 2. k. v. t. To inflame, kindle.

ಕತ್ತು 3. h. n. Writ; a writing. 2, a kind of hand-writing.

ಕತ್ತೂರಿ. tb. of ಕಸ್ತೂರಿ, q. v.

ಕತ್ತೆ k. n. An ass, donkey. -ಕಿರುಬ, -ಕಿರುಬ. The hyæna; a kind of deer.

ಕತ್ರಿ. = ಕತ್ತರಿ, q. v.

ಕಥನ s. n. Telling, relating; narration, tale. ಕಥಿಕ. A story-teller.

ಕಥೆ s. n. A speech; a tale, story; narrative. 2, affair. -ಹೇಳು, ಕಥಿಸು. To relate a story. ಕಥಾಂತರ. The course of a story or conversation.

ಕದ k. n. The leaf of a door; a door.

ಕದಕದ k. int. Ha! ha! ha! -ನಗು. To laugh loudly. ಕದಕದಿಸು. To shake, be agitated.

ಕದಡು k. v. i. To be shaken, stirred' troubled; to become turbid, muddy, impure. v. t. To stir. n. Turbidness; mud. 2, commotion, tumult.

ಕದನ s. n. War, fight. -ಗಲಿ. A hero in battle.

ಕದಂಬ (= ಕದಂಬ) s. n. The tree *Nauclea cadamba*. 2, a multitude. 3, mustard seed, turmeric.

ಕದರು k. n. A spindle. 2, lustre.

ಕದಬೆಗ. = ಕತಬೆಗ, q. v.

ಕದಲಿ s. n. The plantain tree or banana, *Musa sapientum*. 2, a flag, banner. 3, Śiva. 4, an elephant.

ಕದಲು (= ಕದಡು, q. v.) k. v. i. To move, shake. ಕದಲಾಡು. To move about, shake, be unsteady. ಕದಲಿಕೆ. Motion. ಕದಲಿಸು. To cause to move or shake; to cause to become turbid.

ಕದಿ k. v. t. To steal. P. p. ಕದ್ದು. -ಕ, -ಗ. A thief; f. -ಕಿ.

ಕದಿರು, ಕದರು k. n. A spike of corn, ear. 2, a spindle. 3, splendour.

ಕದೀಮು h. a. Old, ancient. ಕದೀಮು. An old servant, veteran. ಕದೀಮಿ. Long standing.

ಕದುಬು a. k. v. t. To press; to distress, trouble.

ಕದುರು. = ಕದರು, q. v.

ಕದೆ a. k. v. i. To join, approach.

ಕದ್ದು k. P. p. of ಕದಿ.

ಕದ್ರು s. a. Brown, tawny. n. N. of Kaśyapa's wife.

ಕನ್ k. n. Blackness. ಕನ್ನಡ. The black country: Kannaḍa (Canarese), the country and its language; Canara, the Carnatic. ಕನ್ನಡಭಾಷೆ. Canarese language.

ಕನಸು k. n. A dream. -ವರಿಕೆ. Talking in one's sleep. -ವರಿಸು. To talk in sleep.

ಕನಕ s. n. Gold. 2, the thorn-apple, *Datura metel* and *fastuosa*. 3, a N. -ದಾಸ. N. of a Vaishṇava devotee who composed many dâsapadas.

-ವೃಷ್ಟಿ. A shower of gold. ಕನಕಾಭಿಷೇಕ. Honouring a venerable person by pouring gold-coins on his feet or head.

ಕನಡಿ. = ಕನ್ನಡಿ, *q. v.*

ಕನಡಕ k. *n.* A pair of spectacles.

ಕನರು k. *n.* A disagreeable smell, *as* that of burning oil.

ಕನಲು k. *v. i.* To chafe, be angry. *n.* Anger.

ಕನಸು (= ಕನ) k. *n.* A dream, vision. -ಕಾಣು, -ಕಂಡುಕೊಳ್ಳು, -ಬೀಳು. To dream.

ಕನಿ k. *n.* Tender-heartedness; pity, kindness. -ಕರ. Pity, compassion. -ಕರ ಪಡು, -ಕರಿಸು. To have compassion on.

ಕನಿಷ್ಠ s. *n.* The smallest or least, the last or worst; inferior, base. 2, the youngest. -ಕೆ, ಕನಿಷ್ಠೆ. The little finger.

ಕಂತ, ಕಂತು h. *n.* A fixed term of payment, instalment (ವಾಯಿದೆ).

ಕಂತು 1. k. *v. i.* To set, *as* the sun, *etc.* ಕಂತಿಸು. To extinguish.

ಕಂತು 2. s. *a.* Happy. *n.* The heart. 2, a granary.

ಕಂತೆ k. *n.* A bundle, *as* of straw, *etc.*

ಕಂಥೆ s. *n.* A rag, patched garment; a thick cloth made of quilted rags.

ಕಂದ 1. k. *n.* A young child; a term of endearment for grown-up children.

ಕಂದ 2. s. *n.* A bulbous or esculent root, bulb. 2, a lump, swelling. 3, a kind of metre. -ಮೂಲ. A radish and other esculent roots.

ಕಂದಕ h. *n.* A ditch, trench.

ಕಂದರ s. *n.* A cave, glen; a valley.

ಕಂದಲು k. *n.* A small earthen water-vessel.

ಕಂದಾಚಾರ h. *n.* Military; police.

ಕಂದಾಯ h. *n.* Tribute; tax, land-tax. 2, a space of four months.

ಕಂದಿ k. *n.* A cow that has calved. *a.* Dust-coloured.

ಕಂದಿಕೆ k. *n.* Fading, faded state.

ಕಂದು 1. k. *v. i.* To be burnt or scorched; to turn black, *as* the body. 2, to wan, fade, wither, wane. *n.* Discoloration by scorching; blackness; want of lustre. 2, lowness of spirits, sorrow. -ಕುಂದು. Stains and deficiencies. -ಬೆಳ್ಳಿ. Impure silver.

ಕಂದು 2. k. *n.* A calf. 2, young plantain trees. 3, the foetus of beasts.

ಕಂದು 3. f. *n.* An iron plate for baking cakes.

ಕಂದೋಟಿ h. *n.* A money-bag, purse.

ಕನ್ನ k. *n.* A hole made by burglars in a house-wall. -ಕಳವು, -ಜೋರಿ. Burglary. -ಗತ್ತರಿ. A burglar's instrument. -ಗಾರ, ಕನ್ನೋಜ. A burglar. -ಕೊರೆ, -ಹಾಕು. To break a hole in a wall for burglary.

ಕನ್ನಡ. = ಕನ್, *q. v.*

ಕನ್ನಡಿ (= ಕನಡಿ) k. *n.* A looking-glass, mirror; a pair of spectacles.

ಕನ್ನಡಿಗ k. *n.* A man of Kannaḍa country; *f.* ಕನ್ನಡಗಿತಿ.

ಕನ್ನಡಿಸು k. *v. t.* To translate into Kannaḍa. 2, to mirror.

ಕನ್ನಿಕೆ, ಕನ್ಯಕೆ. = ಕನ್ಯೆ, *q. v.*

ಕನ್ನೆ. *tb. of* ಕನ್ಯೆ, *q. v.*

ಕನ್ಯೆ s. *n.* A girl, maiden, virgin. 2, the sign of the zodiac *Virgo.* -ತನ. Maidenhood. ಕನ್ಯಾಕುಮಾರಿ. Cape Comorin. ಕನ್ಯಾದಾನ. Giving a girl in marriage. ಕನ್ಯಾವ್ರತ. A vow of virginity.

ಕಪಟ s. *n.* Fraud, deceit, hypocrisy, disguise, dissimulation. -ಗಾರ, -ಸ್ಥ, ಕಪಟಿ. A deceitful man, hypocrite. -ತನ, -ತ್ವ. Deceitfulness. -ವೇಷ. Disguise. ನಿಷ್ಕಪಟ. Sincerity.

ಕಪಡ h. *n.* An article of apparel, cloth.

ಕಪನಿ f. *n.* A sort of cloak dyed with kâvi and worn by liṅgâyita priests or ascetics.

ಕಪಲಿ, ಕಪಿಲೆ k. *n.* An apparatus for raising water, consisting of pulley, rope and leathern bucket, worked by oxen. -ಬಾನಿ. The leathern bucket. -ಹೊಡೆ, -ಕಟ್ಟು. To draw water.

ಕವಾಟ s. n. The leaf of a door; a door. 2, an almira.

ಕಪಾಲ s. n. The skull. 2, a cup, jar, pot; a lid. 3, a potsherd.

ಕಪಿ s. n. A monkey. -ಮುಷ್ಟಿ. A firm grasp. -ಮುಷ್ಟಿಗಾರ. An obstinate fellow.

ಕಪಿತ್ಥ s. n. The wood-apple tree, *Feronia elephantum*.

ಕಪಿಲ s. n. Brown, tawny. n. N. of a ṛishi, the founder of the sâṅkhya philosophy. ಕಪಿಲೆ. A brown coloured cow.

ಕಪಿಶ s. a. Brown. n. Incense.

ಕಪೋತ k. n. A dove, pigeon.

ಕಪೋಲ s. n. A cheek.

ಕಪ್ಪ 1. k. n. Tribute; *also* -ಕಾಣಿಕೆ.

ಕಪ್ಪ 2. k. n. A ring of wire for the wrist or feet.

ಕಪ್ಪಡ (*tb. of* ಕರ್ಪಟ) n. A tattered cloth.

ಕಪ್ಪರ (*tb. of* ಕರ್ಪರ) n. A large potsherd.

ಕಪ್ಪು 1. k. v. t. To dig. n. A hole in the ground, pit. -ಕುಳಿ. A hole for catching elephants.

ಕಪ್ಪು 2. k. n. Blackness; the black colour; collyrium. a. Black.

ಕಪ್ಪು 3. = ಕಪ್ಪ 1, q. v.

ಕಪ್ಪುರ. *tb. of* ಕರ್ಪೂರ, q. v.

ಕಪ್ಪೆ k. n. A frog. -ಕಣ್ಣು. Very large eyes. -ಕುರು. A frog-shaped boil. -ಚಿಪ್ಪು. A bivalve shell. -ಹುಣ್ಣು. A spreading sore in the palm of the hand or sole of the foot.

ಕಫ s. n. Phlegm.

ಕಬ್ k. n. Blackness. 2, a stone. ಕಬ್ಬಕ್ಕಿ. A rose-finch. ಕಬ್ಬಸುರಿ. The wave-leafed fig-tree, *Ficus infectoria*.

ಕಬಕ್ಕನೆ k. ad. In a snatching manner. -ಕಚ್ಚು. To bite snatchingly, *as* a dog. -ನುಂಗು. To gulp quickly, *as* beasts.

ಕಬಂಧ s. n. Water. 2, a cloud. 3, a headless trunk.

ಕಬರ h. n. A Muhammadan tomb.

ಕಬರಿ s. n. A knot of braided hair.

ಕಬರು h. n. News, information. 2, attention. -ದಾರ. A careful or strict man. -ದಾರ್. Take care! mind! -ದಾರಿ. Carefulness, strictness.

ಕಬಲ (*tb. of* ಕವಲ) n. A mouthful; a bolus, pill. ಕಬಲಿಸು. To eat, devour.

ಕಬಾತ f. n. A bullock or horse-load of grass, *etc.* ಕಬಾಡಿ, -ಗ. A person who brings and sells it; a milk-man.

ಕಬೂಲು h. n. Agreeing to; consent. agreement; *also* ಕಬೂಲಿ. -ಆಗು. To consent.

ಕಬೋಜಿ k. n. A blind man.

ಕಬ್ಬ. *tb. of* ಕಾವ್ಯ, q. v.

ಕಬ್ಬಕ್ಕಿ k. n. A rose-finch, starling; *see* s. ಕಬ್.

ಕಬ್ಬಿಗ (*tb. of* ಕವಿ) n. A poet.

ಕಬ್ಬಿಣ, ಕಬ್ಬುನ k. n. Iron. -ಕಿಟ್ಟ. Rust of iron, dross.

ಕಬ್ಬು k. n. Sugarcane. ಕಬ್ಬಿನ ಹಾಲು. Juice of sugarcane.

ಕಮಟು, ಕಮುಟು h. n. Rancidity, smell of burnt oil or ghee.

ಕಮಂಡಲ, ಕಮಂಡಲು s. n. An ascetic's water-pot.

ಕಮನೀಯ s. a. Desirable; lovely, pleasing.

ಕಮರು k. v. i. To be burnt, scorched. n. Scorchedness; the disagreeable smell arising from burnt oil, *etc.; also* ಕಮರಿಕೆ, -ಗೆ.

ಕಮಲ s. n. The lotus, *Nelumbium speciosum*. 2, water. 3, the moon. -ಅಕ್ಷ, ಕಮಲಾಕ್ಷ. Vishṇu; lotus seed. -ನಾಭ, ಕಮಲೇಶ. Vishṇu. -ಗರ್ಭ, -ಜ, -ಭವ, ಕಮಲೋದ್ಭವ. Brahmâ. -ಬಾಂಧವ, -ಮಿತ್ರ, -ಸಖ. The sun. -ವೈರಿ. The moon. ಕಮಲಾಲಯೆ, ಕಮಲೆ. Lakshmî.

ಕಮಾನು h. n. A bow; an arch, a vault; a spring, *as* of a watch; a fiddle-stick.

ಕಮಾಯಿಷಿ m. n. Collection of the revenues. -ದಾರ. A sea-custom superintendent; a toll-collector.

ಕಂಪ, ಕಂಪನ, ಕಂಪಾಯಮಾನ s. n. Trembling, tremor, quaking. ಕಂಪಿಸು. To tremble, *etc.*

ಕಂಪು k. n. A bad smell. 2, fragrance.

ಕಂಬ. tb. of ಕಂಭ, q. v.

ಕಂಬನಿ k. n. An eye-drop: tear. -ತೊಡೆ. To wipe tears. -ಇಡು, -ಇಕ್ಕು, -ಗರಿ, -ಸುರಿ. To shed tears, weep.

ಕಂಬಲ, ಕಂಬಳಿ s. n. A blanket, cumley. 2, a dew-lap. -ಹುಳ. A caterpillar.

ಕಂಬಳ k. n. Daily hire or wages. -ಗಾರ. A day-labourer.

ಕಂಬಿ k. n. Wire, an iron band; a bar, rail; the bridge of the nose. 2, a stripe running parallel with the border of a cloth. 3, a thick bamboo laid across the shoulder for carrying burdens. 4, a club, mace. -ಗ. A mace bearer, doorkeeper. -ಕಾರ. A kambi bearer. -ಯಚ್ಚು, ಕಂಬಚ್ಚು. A plate with holes for drawing wire.

ಕಂಭ (tb. of ಸ್ತಂಭ) n. A post, pillar. -ಪೂಜೆ. Worship paid to the first pillar when erecting a building.

ಕಮ್ಮಗಾರ. = ಕಮ್ಮಾರ, q. v.

ಕಮ್ಮಗೆ, ಕಮ್ಮನೆ k. ad. Fragrantly, deliciously.

ಕಮ್ಮಟ k. n. Coinage; mint. ಕಮ್ಮಟಿ. A coiner.

ಕಮ್ಮರು h. n. The loins, waist. -ಬಂದ. A waistband, belt.

ಕಮ್ಮಾರ (tb. of ಕರ್ಮಕಾರ) n. A blacksmith. -ಸಾಲೆ. The workshop of a blacksmith.

ಕಮ್ಮಿ h. n. Deficiency. -ಜಾಸ್ತಿ. More or less.

ಕಮ್ಮು k. n. Fragrance. v. i. Breath to be fragrant.

ಕಯ್ 1. (= ಕೆಯ್) k. v. t. To do.

ಕಯ್ 2. (= ಕೆಯ್, ಕೈ) k. n. The hand.

ಕಯ್ 3, ಕಯಿ (ಕಹಿ, q. v.) k. n. Bitterness; also ಕಯ್ಪು. -ಬೇವು. Neem or margosa tree; also ಬೇವು.

ಕರ 1. k. P. p. of ಕರೆ. -ಕೊಳ್ಳು. = ಕರೆದು ಕೊಳ್ಳು. -ಕೊಂಡುಬರು. To bring along with one's self. -ಕೊಂಡು ಹೋಗು. To conduct away with one's self. -ತರು. To calland bring.

ಕರ 2. s. n. Doing, making (ಕೃತ್ಯ). 2, the hand (ಹಸ್ತ, ಕೆಯ್). 3, the elephant's trunk. 4, tax; royal revenue. 5, a ray of light. 6, a cloud.

ಕರಕರೆ k. n. Grief, trouble; worrying, annoyance. -ಮಾಡು. To vex. ಕರಕರಿಸು. To feel remorse; to be grieved.

ಕರಕು k. n. Cinder; the crust formed on cooking pots. 2, calcined drugs.

ಕರಗ (tb. of ಕರಕ) n. A kind of water-jar.

ಕರಗಸ (=ಗರಗಸ, tb. of ಕ್ರಕಚ) n. A saw. -ದ ಹಲ್ಲು. The teeth of a saw.

ಕರಗು k. v. i. To be dissolved; to melt; to melt away; to become softened to pity or love; to wane, as the body; to pine away for grief; to languish. ಕರಗಿಸು. To cause to be dissolved; to melt.

ಕರಜಿಕಾಯಿ k. n. A small pancake.

ಕರಟ s. n. The shell of a cocoanut.

ಕರಟಕ s. n. A crow. 2, N. of a jackal in the Hitôpadêśa; a backbiter.

ಕರಡ k. n. Dried fodder-grass.

ಕರಡಿ k. n. A bear. -ಮರಿ. A bear's cub.

ಕರಡಿಗೆ (tb. of ಕರಂಡಕ) n. A basket or covered box; a casket or small box of metal or wood.

ಕರಡು 1. k. a. Rough, uneven, hard; waste, useless. -ಕಾಗದ. A waste paper. -ಬರೆ. To write roughly. -ಮುತ್ತು. Rough, inferior pearl.

ಕರಡು 2. f. a. Rough, as an account. n. A day-book; scrawling; a scrawl.

ಕರಣ s. n. Making; causing. 2, an instrument, means. 3, an organ of sense; also ಕರಣೇಂದ್ರಿಯ. 4, cause, motive. 5, a scribe. 6, a rhythm; dramatic action.

ಕರಣಿ s. n. Doing. 2, = ಕರಣಿಕ. 3, a mason's trowel; also ಕರಣಿಕೆ.

ಕರಣಿಕ, ಕರಣೀಕ s. n. A writer; a village clerk; the head native official of a district collector's office.

ಕರಣೆ 1. k. n. A clot, lump. 2, a ball made of iron filings, and rice flour and rubbed on tambours to make them sound well.

ಕರಣೆ 2. h. n. The large brass trumpet which sounds the bass.

ಕರಂಡ, ಕರಂಡಕ. = ಕರಡಿಗೆ, q. v.

ಕರತಲ s. n. The palm of the hand.

ಕರತಾಲ, -ಳ s. n. A cymbal. 2, beating time by clapping the hands.

ಕರದು. P. p. of ಕರೆ 1.

ಕರಪೀಠ s. n. A flat piece of wood for cripples to rest their hands on.

ಕರಬೂಜು h. n. The musk-melon.

ಕರರುಹ s. n. A finger-nail.

ಕರವೀರ s. n. A fragrant oleander.

ಕರಸು = ಕರಿಸು, s. ಕರಿ, q. v.

ಕರಹ k. n. Calling, inviting.

ಕರಳು. = ಕರುಳು, q. v.

ಕರಾಚೂರಿ f. n. A sword. 2, a man of positive speech. ಕರಾಚೂರು. Positiveness.

ಕರಾಡಿ s. n. A class of Brâhmaṇas.

ಕರಾರ, ಕರಾರು h. n. A promise; an agreement. -ನಾಮೆ. A written contract.

ಕರಾಲ, ಕರಾಳ s. a. Great, large. 2, formidable, dreadful. 3, crooked.

ಕರಾಲಂಬನ, ಕರಾವಲಂಬನ s. n. A helping hand; helping; support.

ಕರಾವಳಿ k. n. The seacoast region or that of the banks of a river.

ಕರಿ 1. s. v. i. To be scorched, burnt. 2, to fry, roast. 3, to dig. P. ps. ಕರಿದು, ಕರಿತು. ಕರಿಸು. To cause to fry or roast.

ಕರಿ 2. (= ಕರ್ರ) k. n. Blackness; a dark-blue colour. 2, charcoal. Gen. ಕರಿಯ or ಕರೀ. -ಕ, -ಗ. A black man; f. -ಕಿ, -ಗಿ. -ಜಾಲಿ. A thorny shrub with fragrant flowers, *Acacia farnesiana*; the babool tree, *Acacia arabica*. -ಜಗೆ. A disease of the cotton plant. -ಜೀರಿಗೆ. A potherb, *Nigella sativa*. -ತುಂಬೆ. The Malabar cat-mint, *Anisomeles malabarica*. -ತುಳಸಿ. A small shrub, the holy basil, *Ocimum sanctum*. -ದಿವಸ. An unpropitious day. -ದು. That is black. -ನೆಕ್ಕಿ. A wild shrub, *Gendarusa vulgaris*. -ಬೇವು. The curry-leaf tree, *Murraya koenigii*. -ಮಣಿ. A black bead worn by married women. -ಮರ. The ebony tree. -ಯುತ್ರಾಣಿಗಿಡ. A Jamaican plant, *Stachytarpheta jamaicensis*. -ಯುಪ್ಪು. A kind of black sea-salt. -ಹತ್ತಿ. The American cotton-plant. -ಹರಿ. To tear (i. e. do away with) unpropitiousness.

ಕರಿ 3. s. n. An elephant. -ಮುಖ, -ವದನ. Gaṇêśa.

ಕರಿ 4. (= ಕಱ) k. n. Vegetables of any kind. 2, flesh, curry.

ಕರಿ 5. = ಕರೆ, q. v.

ಕರಿತು P. p. of ಕರಿ 1, q. v.

ಕರಿಕೆ (ರಿ = ಱ) k. n. The Huriallee [grass.

ಕರೀರ s. n. A tender shoot of bamboo. 2, a thorny shrub, *Capparis aphylla*.

ಕರು 1. k. n. Embossed work, bass-relief; a puppet.

ಕರು 2. (ರು = ಱು) k. n. A calf; also ಕರ.

ಕರುಣ, ಕರುಣೆ s. n. Pity; compassion, mercy. 2, favour; pardon. a. Merciful. -ವಂತ. Compassionate, pitiable; a compassionate man. ಕರುಣಾತ್ಮ. Pitiful. -ಕರ, ಕರುಣಾಳು. A person who possesses pity; compassionate. ಕರುಣಾಕರ, ಕರುಣಾಬ್ಧಿ, ಕರುಣಾಂಬು, ಕರುಣಾಶರನಿಧಿ, ಕರುಣಾಸಾಗರ, ಕರುಣಾಸಮುದ್ರ, ಕರುಣಾಸಿಂಧು. An ocean of mercy. ಕರುಣಿಸು. To be merciful, to show mercy to.

ಕರುಳು k. n. An entrail; the bowels. 2, love, pity. -ತೋರಿಸು. To be openhearted; to show mercy. -ಎಳೆ. Bowels to yearn. -ಕಟ್ಟು. To restrain the bowels.

ಕರುಬು, ಕರುಂಬು (ರು = ಱು) k. v. t. To envy. n. Envy.

ಕರೆ 1. k. v. t. To call, invite; to sound. P. ps. ಕರೆದು, ಕರದು. -ಕಳಿಸು, -ಕಳುಹಿಸು.

To send one person to call another. ಕರಸು, ಕರಿಸು, ಕರೆಯಿಸು, ಕರೆಸು. To cause to call, send for. -ಯುವಿಕೆ. Calling.

ಕರೆ 2. k. n. A bank, shore; a boundary. 2, the border of a cloth or blanket. 3, a cow-house.

ಕರೆ 3. (= ಕರಿ, q. v.) k. n. Blackness; a dark-blue colour; also ಕರ್ರಗೆ. Cpds.: -ಬೆಕ್ಕು, -ಕರಡಿ, -ಕೂದಲು, -ಚಿಕ್ಕಿ, -ಜಿಗರಿ, -ತೋಳ, -ಬಣ್ಣ, -ಮಜ್ಜೆ, -ಮುದ್ದು, -ಮೆಣಸು, -ಹಲ್ಲಿ, etc. -ವ್ವ. The black dame: a household-goddess.

ಕರೆ 4. (ರೆ = ಱೆ) k. v. t. To milk; to cause to flow, to rain; to give milk.

ಕರೋಡ h. n. A crore, lakh.

ಕರ್ಕಟ, ಕರ್ಕಾಟಕ s. n. A crab: the sign Cancer.

ಕರ್ಕಶ s. a. Hard, firm. 2, rough, harsh, severe, violent; unkind. -ತೆ. Hardness, harshness.

ಕರ್ಕೋಟಕ s. n. N. of a serpent; also -ಕ.

ಕರ್ಜೆ. = ಕಱುಬ, ಖರ್ಜು, q. v.

ಕರ್ಜಿಕಾಯಿ. = ಕರಜಿಕಾಯಿ, q. v.

ಕರ್ಜೂರ (= ಕರ್ಜೂರ) f. n. The fruit of the date tree.

ಕರ್ಣ s. n. The ear. 2, a helm, rudder. 3, the sun. 4, N. of a hero. -ಗತ. Come to the ear. -ಪಿಶಾಚಿ. A demon forced to communicate by whispering in the ear. -ಶೂಲೆ. Ear-ache. ಕರ್ಣೇಂದ್ರಿಯ. The organ of hearing.

ಕರ್ಣಾಟ (= ಕನ್ನಡ) s. n. The Karṇâṭa country. -ಕ. Belonging to K.; the K. language; (also -ಭಾಷೆ); the Karṇâṭa man. -ಕೋವಿ. A matchlock. -ವ್ಯಾಕರಣ. A grammar of K. language. -ದೇಶ. K. country. -ಧಾತು. A K. verbal root.

ಕರ್ಣಿ, ಕರ್ಣಿಕೆ. tb. of ಕರಣಿ, ಕರಣಿಕ, q. v.

ಕರ್ತ. tb. of ಕರ್ತೃ, q. v.

ಕರ್ತರಿ (= ಕತ್ತರಿ, ಕತ್ರಿ, q. v.) s. n. Scissors.

ಕರ್ತವ್ಯ s. a. Fit to be done. n. Obligation, duty, task.

ಕರ್ತೃ s. n. A doer, author, agent; a creator; a master. 2, an agent, the active noun, subject (g.). -ತ್ವ. Agency.

ಕರ್ಪಾಸ s. n. Cotton.

ಕರ್ಪುರ, ಕರ್ಪೂರ s. n. Camphor. -ಬಳ್ಳಿ. Thick-leaved lavender, *Lavendula carnosa*. -ಶಿಲಾಜತು, -ಶಿಲಾಧಾತು. A crystallized gypsum.

ಕರ್ಮ s. n. An act, action; performance, business; duty. 2, the accusative; the objective noun (g.); the idea of the passive voice (g.). 3, any religious action. 4, sin. -ಕಾರ. An artisan, mechanic. -ಗತಿ. Fate. -ಠ. Skilful in work; scrupulously exact in performance of a religious rite. -ದೋಷ. Sin, vice. -ಧಾರಯ. N. of a class of compounds. -ಮಾರ್ಗ. The way of works. -ವಿಪಾಕ. The consequences of actions. -ಸಾಕ್ಷಿ. The sun. -ಸಿದ್ಧಿ. Success. ಕರ್ಮಾಂತರ. Funeral rites. ಕರ್ಮಿ. Acting; a sinner. ಕರ್ಮಿಷ್ಠ. Very active; very sinful. ಕರ್ಮೇಂದ್ರಿಯ. The organ of action.

ಕರ್ಮಣಿ s. n. A verb in the passive voice (g.).

ಕರ್ಷ, ಕರ್ಷಣ s. n. Drawing, dragging.

ಕರ್ಳು. = ಕರುಳು, q. v.

ಕಲ್ (= ಕಲ್ಲು) k. n. A stone. -ಕುಟಿಗ. A mason. -ತೊಟ್ಟಿ. A stone-trough. -ನಾರು. The bastard aloe. -ಪಣೆ. A stone quarry. -ಮಳೆ. Hail.

ಕಲ s. a. Dumb. n. Gold. 2, a musical time; a melodious tone, as humming, etc. -ಕಂಠ. The cuckoo (ಕೋಗಿಲೆ); a bee; a swan; a pleasing tone. -ಕಲ. A confused noise. -ಕಲಾಟ. Twittering of birds. -ರವ. A low sweet tone.

ಕಲಕೆ, ಕಲ್ಕ k. n. Mixture; a mixture of unboiled ingredients; infusion (med.).

ಕಲಕಾಲ k. n. A very long time. ad. At all times, permanently.

ಕಲಕು k. v. i. To be agitated, shaken, turbid, etc. v. t. To agitate, shake; to stir up, disturb. n. Turbidness.

-ಮಾಡು, ಕಲಕಾಡು. To make turbid. ಕಲಕಿಸು. To disturb, stir.

ಕಲಂಕ s. n. A stain, spot, mark. 2, a fault, blemish. 3, fierceness.

ಕಲಗಚ್ಚು k. n. The water in which raw rice and other vegetables have been washed and mixed with strained rice-water, *etc.* and given to cattle.

ಕಲಂಗಡಿ f. n. The water-melon.

ಕಲತ್ರ s. n. A wife.

ಕಲಬತ್ತು h. n. A mortar and pestle.

ಕಲಬೆರಕೆ k. n. Mixture, *as* of cold and hot water.

ಕಲಮ f. n. White rice growing in deep water.

ಕಲಮು, ಕಲಂ h. n. A reed pen; a painter's brush. 2, a paragraph; a distinct head, item. 3, a graft. -ದಾನಿ. A standish.

ಕಲಲು h. n. Ruin, loss.

ಕಲಶ s. n. A water-vessel, jar, pitcher, vase. 2, an ornamental or rounded pinnacle on the top of a temple; a dome. -ಪೂಜೆ. The rite of worshipping a water-pot. -ಪ್ರತಿಷ್ಠೆ. The rite of fixing a dome on the top of a temple, *etc.* -ಸ್ಥಾಪನೆ. A rite preliminary to ಕಲಶಪೂಜೆ.

ಕಲಸು k. v. t. To mix, mingle. n. Mixed state. ಕಲಸನ್ನ. Boiled rice mixed with tamarind, chillies, salt, *etc.*

ಕಲಹ s. n. Quarrel, strife; war, battle. ಕಲಹಿಸು. To quarrel.

ಕಲಹಂಸ s. n. A kind of goose or swan.

ಕಲಾಕಾಂತ s. n. The moon.

ಕಲಾಕೌಶಲ್ಯ s. n. Cleverness in the elegant arts, *as* singing, dancing, *etc.*

ಕಲಾಪ s. n. Quarrel, contention. 2, a collection. 3, an ornament. 4, a quiver.

ಕಲಾಬತು h. n. Silken thread covered with gold or silver.

ಕಲಾಯ, ಕಲಾಯಿ h. n. The tinning of brass and other vessels. -ಗಾರ. A tinner of vessels.

ಕಲಾಲ h. n. A distiller or vendor of spirituous liquors.

ಕಲಾಸಿ h. n. A seaman, lascar.

ಕಲಿ 1. k. v. t. To learn, study. v. i. To be mixed; to come together, to meet. *P. p.* ಕಲಿತು. n. A learned man. -ಕೆ, -ತ. Learning, skill. ಕಲಿಸು. To teach; to mix; *also* ಕಲಸು, *q. v.*

ಕಲಿ 2. s. n. A warrior, hero. 2, the fourth age of the world, the age of sin; *also* -ಯುಗ. -ತನ. Valor, heroism. -ಕಾಲ. A time of sin and misery, the age of vice.

ಕಲಿತು. *P. p. of* ಕಲಿ, *q. v.*

ಕಲುಷ s. a. Turbid, muddy. n. Sin.

ಕಲೆ 1. k. n. The scar; a stain, taint.

ಕಲೆ 2, ಕಲಾ s. n. A small part; a sixteenth of the moon's orb. 2, a measure of time. 3, a fine art (there are 64). 4, skill. 5, grace, lustre.

ಕಲ್ಕ s. n. Dirt, filth; a kind of paste. 2, sin; pride.

ಕಲ್ಕಿ s. n. N. of Vishṇu in his tenth and last avatâra yet to come.

ಕಲ್ಪ s. n. A precept, injunction. 2, one of the six vêdâṅgas which prescribes rituals. 3, a day of Brahmâ or the period of a thousand yugas. -ತರು, -ದ್ರುಮ, -ವೃಕ್ಷ. One of the trees (-ಲತೆ, a creeper) of svarga granting all desires.

ಕಲ್ಪನೆ s. n. Making; fabrication, invention. 2, a fancy, idea; an imagination. ಕಲ್ಪಿತ. Fabricated, artificial, invented.

ಕಲ್ಪಿಸು s. v. t. To make; to fabricate, invent; to assume, feign; to give a precept.

ಕಲ್ಮಷ s. n. A stain; a blemish; sin; dirt.

ಕಲ್ಯಾಣ s. a. Beautiful; happy, auspicious, lucky. n. Good fortune, prosperity, welfare. 2, a marriage festival. ಕಲ್ಯಾಣಿ. Sarasvatî; Pârvatî;

Lakshmī; N. of a tune. -ಸಾಯಿ. A kind of sweetmeat.

ಕಲ್ಲಂಗಡಲೆ k. n. A shrubby plant, *Sida rhombiafolia*.

ಕಲ್ಲಂಗಡಿ. = ಕಲಂಗಡಿ, *q. v.*

ಕಲ್ಲಿ k. n. A kind of coarse net-work; a bag made of it.

ಕಲ್ಲು k. n. A stone. -ಅಣಬೆ, ಕಲ್ಲಣಬೆ. A mushroom growing in rocks. -ಇದ್ದಲಿ. Mineral coal. -ಕಣಿ, ಕಲ್ಲಕಣಿ. A quarry. -ಕುಟಿಗ. A stone-cutter or mason. -ಗುಂಡು. A boulder. -ನಾರು (=ಕಲ್ನಾರು). Asbestus. -ಬಂಡೆ. A rock. -ಬಾಳೆ. A wild plantain tree. -ಮಳೆ. Hail. -ಮುಳ್ಳು. Stones and thorns. -ಮೆಟ್ಟು. Stone steps. -ಸಕ್ಕರೆ. Sugar-candy. -ಸುಂಟಿ. Wild ginger. -ಸುಣ್ಣ. Stone-lime. -ಹಾಕು. To throw a stone down; to destroy another's business. -ಹೂವು. Lichen on stones. -ಎದೆ, ಕಲ್ಲೆದೆ. A stone-like or firm heart. ಕಲ್ಲೆದೆಯವ. A man who has an unfeeling heart. -ಎಸೆ, ಕಲ್ಲೆಸೆ. To throw stones, *also* -ಬಗೆ, -ಹೊಡೆ; a stone's throw. -ಒತ್ತು, ಕಲ್ಲೊತ್ತು. Stone pressure; a kind of hard boil on the heel.

ಕಲ್ಲೋಲ s. n. A surge, billow, wave.

ಕವ k. *An imitative sound of anger.* - - ಮಾಡು. To scold.

ಕವಚ s. n. Armour, coat of mail; a jacket. 2, an amulet.

ಕವಚು. = ಕವಿಚು, *q. v.*

ಕವಟ (*tb. of* ಕಪಟ) -ಕಂಟಕ. An ugly-looking puppet of dough. -ಗಂಟಕ. A great cheat.

ಕವಡಿ, ಕವಡೆ (*tb. of* ಕಪರ್ದ) n. A cowrie.

ಕವಡಿಕೆ k. n. An ornamental, stitched binding of a dôtra.

ಕವಡು k. n. A bifurcation. -ಮಾತು. A word out of place.

ಕವಣೆ k. n. A sling for throwing stones. -ಕಲ್ಲು ಹೊಡಿ, - - ಎಸೆ. To sling a stone.

ಕವದಿ. = ಕವುದಿ, *q. v.*

ಕವನ s. n. Composing; a poetical composition; a fancy. -ಗಾರ. A poet.

ಕವಲ, ಕವಳ (= ಕಬಲ) s. n. A mouthful, morsel; bolus. 2, a gargle.

ಕವಲು k. v. i. To become forked, to branch off. n. A forked branch or stick; divided state; a couple, pair. -ಬಡೆ, ಕವಲೊಡೆ. To get branches.

ಕವಲೆ. *tb. of* ಕಪಿಲೆ, *q. v.*

ಕವಳ k. n. A swoon. 2, = ಕವಳೆ. 3, = ಕವಳಗೆ 2.

ಕವಳಗೆ 1. (*tb. of* ಕಪಾಲಿಕೆ) n. Śiva's alms-pot, a skull. 2, a metal vessel.

ಕವಳಗೆ 2. f. n. A pack or bundle of betel or plantain-leaves. -ಮನೆ. A house with a gable-roof.

ಕವಳೆ f. n. A spinous shrub, bearing black eatable berries, *Corissa carandas*.

ಕವಾಟ. = ಕಪಾಟ, *q. v.*

ಕವಾಡ. = ಕಬಾಡ, *q. v.* ಕವಾಡಿಗ. A cowherd; *f.* -ಗಿತ್ತಿ.

ಕವಾತು, ಕವಾಯಿತು h. n. Military manoeuvres; parade.

ಕವಿ 1, k. v. t. & v. i. To come upon; to attack; to cover, overspread. (*P. ps.* ಕವಿ, ಕವಿ, ಕವಿದು). n. A rush. -ಚು, -ಸು. To put upon.

ಕವಿ 2. s. n. A wise man; a poet. 2, Śukra. 3, water. -ಕೌಶಲ. The cleverness of a poet. -ತೆ, -ತ್ವ. Poesy, poetic style. -ರಾಜ, ಕವೀಶ್ವರ. A very eminent poet. ನರ-. A taught poet. ವರ-. A born poet.

ಕವಿಚು k. v. i. To be turned upside down, to be upset.

ಕವಿಯ s. n. The bit of a bridle.

ಕವಿಲೆ. *tb. of* ಕಪಿಲೆ, *q. v.*

ಕವುಂಕುಳು. = ಕಂಕುಳ, *q. v.*

ಕವುಜು, ಕವುಜುಗ f. n. The wood or the oriental partridge.

ಕವುದಿ k. n. A quilted cover for the night; quilted rags.

ಕವ್ಯ s. n. An oblation of food ot ancestors.

ಕಶೆ s. n. A whip; a string, rope.

ಕಶ್ಮಲ s. n. Consternation, alarm; fainting. a. Foul, dirty.

ಕಶ್ಯಪ s. n. A tortoise. 2, N. of a ṛishi.

ಕಷಾಯ s. a. Astringent. 2, fragrant. n. An infusion, decoction of medicinal herbs. -ಕಾಸು. To decoct.

ಕಷ್ಟ s. n. Trouble, misery, woe. 2, bodily exertion, toil, hard work. 3, difficulty. a. Bad, evil; severe. -ಕೊಡು. To give trouble. -ಪಡು. To suffer trouble. -ಪಡಿಸು. To afflict, annoy. -ಮಾಡಿಸಿಕೊಳ್ಳು. To get one's self shaved. -ಮಾಡು. To toil; to shave. -ಸಹಿಸು, -ಸೋಸು. Patiently to bear trouble. ಕಷ್ಟಾಳು. Painstaking.

ಕಸ 1. k. n. Rubbish, sweepings, offscourings; impurities in the body; a weed. -ಕಣ್ಣು. An inflamed eye. -ಗುಡಿಸು, -ಹೊಡೆ. To sweep. -ಕಿಲು, -ಬರಿಗೆ, -ಬರಲು. A broom. -ದವ. A scavenger.

ಕಸ 2. k. P. p. of ಕಸಿ. -ಕೊಳ್ಳು. To take away by force, snatch away.

ಕಸಕಸೆ h. n. Poppy-seed. -ಗಿಡ. The opium poppy, *Papaver somniferum.*

ಕಸಗಾಯಿ k. n. A hard, unripe fruit.

ಕಸಬು h. n. Business, trade, profession.

ಕಸಬೆ h. n. The chief town of a district or tâluk; *also* ಕಸಬಾ.

ಕಸರು 1. k. n. Astringency. 2, unripeness. 3, bad humours in the body. 4, dust.

ಕಸರು 2. h. n. Deficiency, defect; profit or loss on the exchange of coins.

ಕಸವಿಸಿ, ಕಸಿವಿಸಿ k. n. Uneasiness, as in the bowels; disquiet.

ಕಸಾಬ, ಕಸಾಯ, ಕಸಾಯಿ h. n. A butcher.

ಕಸಾರಿಕೆ f. n. Indisposition.

ಕಸಿ 1. k. v. i. To slip down from; to fall. 2, to ooze, trickle. n. Fine rain, drizzling.

ಕಸಿ 2. h. a. Pruned, castrated. n. Pruning, castration. -ಮಾಡು. To prune, castrate.

ಕಸುಗಾಯಿ. = ಕಸಗಾಯಿ, q. v.

ಕಸುವು f. n. Strength, power; the nutrimental principle, *as* of soils, *etc.*

ಕಸೂತಿ h. n. Embroidery. -ತೆಗೆ, -ಹಾಕು. To embroider.

ಕಸೆ f. n. The tie of an angi, *etc.* -ಹಾವಡೆ. A petticoat with strings attached.

ಕಸ್ತಿ h. n. Violence, force, annoyance.

ಕಸ್ತು h. n. Cares, trouble; fuss, ado. -ಗಾರ. A painstaker. -ತಗಾದೆ. A peremptory demand for payment.

ಕಸ್ತೂರಿ s. n. Musk. 2, a scented mark put on the forehead. -ಅರಿಸಿನ. A kind of scented turmeric. -ಕಡ್ಡಿ. A stick covered with musk. -ಗೊಬ್ಬಳಿ. A kind of Acacia with fragrant flowers. -ಮೃಗ. The musk-deer.

ಕಹಳೆ *(tb. of* ಕಹಲೆ) n. A metal trumpet.

ಕಹಿ k. n. Bitterness; *also* -ವು. -ಗಿಡ. A bitter shrub. -ಪಲ್ಯ. Bitter greens. -ಸೋರೆ. A kind of bitter gourd.

ಕಳ 1. k. a. *Sound in weeping.* 2, *a sound in boiling, as of rice.* 3, *sound indicating agitation.* -ಕಳ. *rep.* -ಕಳನೆ ಅಳು. To weep and sob. -ವಳ. Agitation; distress, anxiety. -ವಳಗೊಳ್ಳು, -ವಳಪಡು, -ವಳಿಸು. To be agitated; to grieve, to be anxious, perplexed.

ಕಳ 2. (= ಕಳ್ಳ) k. n. A thief, rogue. 2, a battle field.

ಕಳ 3. *P. p. of* ಕಳೆ, *q. v.* -ಕೊಳ್ಳು. To put off, let drop; to spend; to lose; to get rid of; to break, *as* a promise (ಮಾತು); to give up, *as* a friendship (ಸ್ನೇಹ).

ಕಳ 4. (*tb. of* ಖಲ) n. A threshing floor.

ಕಳಂಕ. = ಕಲಂಕ, *q. v.*

ಕಳಚು s. v. t. To put off, let drop. 2, to shake off; to pull off. v. i. To become loose.

ಕಳತ (ಳ = ಱ) k. n. Purging.

ಕಳತ್ರ. = ಕಲತ್ರ, *q. v.*

ಕಳದು. *P. p. of* ಕಳೆ, *q. v.*

ಕಳಮು. = ಕಲಮು, *q. v.*

ಕಳವು k. *n.* Theft.

ಕಳವೆ h. *a.* Rejected, adulterated; base (*as* coin, fruits, *etc.*).

ಕಳಸ. *tb. of* ಕಲಶ, *q. v.*

ಕಳಸಿಗೆ f. *n.* A water-pot. 2, a corn-measure equal to ⅓ of a muḍi.

ಕಳಹು. = ಕಳುಹಿಸು, *q. v.*

ಕಳಿ (ಳಿ = ೞಿ) 1. k. *v. t. & v. i.* To end, die. 2, to loosen; to remove. 3, to purge. *n.* A great distance. 2, sour gruel.

ಕಳಿ 2. k. *v. i.* To ripen well. (*P. p.* ಕಳಿತು). *n.* Ripeness. -ಹಣ್ಣು. A ripe fruit.

ಕಳಿಂಗ f. *n.* A cunning, bad man.

ಕಳಿಲೆ (*tb. of* ಕರೀರ) *n.* A tender bamboo shoot used for pickles.

ಕಳಿಸು, ಕಳಿಹಿಸು, ಕಳುಹಿಸು, ಕಳುಹು k. *v. t.* To send, despatch, delegate; to dismiss. ಕಳುಹಿಸಿ ತರಿಸು. To send for. ಹೇಳಿ-. To send word. ಕರೇ-. To send one to call another.

ಕಳು a. k. *v. t.* To steal.

ಕಳೆ (= ಕಳಿ) k. *v. t.* To throw away; to abandon, leave; to reject, pull off; to leave out; to get rid of; to subtract, deduct; to spend, *as* time or money; to draw out, *as* a sword; to remove, do away with, destroy; to extinguish, *as* a lamp; to lose. *v. i.* To become loose; to go, pass, be spent. (*P. ps.* ಕಳ, ಕಳದು, ಕಳೆದು). *n.* Removal. -ನಗ. The yoke fastened round the neck of the bullocks. -ದ ಕೀಲು. The pegs used to fasten the yoke.

ಕಳೆ 2. k. *n.* Weed. -ಕೀಳು, -ತೆಗಿ. To weed.

ಕಳೆ 3. (*tb. of* ಕಲಾ) *n.* Shine, lustre; a ray; beauty. 2, the fine arts. 3, a part; a digit. 4, the number sixteen. -ಗಳೆ. To lose one's lustre. -ಗುಂದು, -ಕೆಡು. Lustre to fade.

ಕಳ್ಳ (= ಕಳ 2) k. *n.* A thief; a rogue, bad fellow; *f.* -ತಿ, ಕಳ್ಳಿ. -ಕಾಗದ, -ಚೀಟು, -ಪತ್ರ. A forged document. -ಕಿಂಡಿ. A hole made by burglars. -ಕುಣಿ. The hollow above the chest between the larynx and trachea. -ಗಂಟು. A sham-bundle; a puzzle-knot. -ಜನ. Thieves. -ದನ. Thievish straying cattle. -ದಾರಿ. A thieves' path. -ಮಾತು. A lie. -ರುಜು. A forged signature. -ವೇಷ. A disguise. -ಸಾಕ್ಷಿ. False witness. -ಹುಂಡಿ. A forged cheque. -ಹೊನ್ನು. A counterfeit coin. -ಉಸುಬು, ಕಳ್ಳುಸುಬು. Quicksand. -ಆಟ, ಕಳ್ಳಾಟ, -ತನ. Thievishness; theft.

ಕಳ್ಳಿ k. *n.* The milk-hedge, *Euphorbia tirukalli*. 2, a wicked person.

ಕಳ್ಳು k. *n.* Toddy.

ಕಾ. = ಕಾಯು, *q. v.*

ಕಾಂಸ್ಯ s. *n.* White brass, bell-metal, any amalgam of zinc and copper.

ಕಾಕ (*tb.* ಕಾಗೆ) s. *n.* A crow. 2, an impudent fellow. 3, N. of a râkshasa. -ಜ್ವರ. A quartan ague. -ಪಕ್ಷ. Three or five locks of hair left over the temples at the time of tonsure. -ಬಲಿ. Offering of food to crows. -ಬುದ್ಧಿ. Insolent notions. -ಭಾಜನ. The crow's portion; waste, ruin.

ಕಾಕಂಬಿ, ಕಾಕವಿ f. *n.* Molasses.

ಕಾಕಮಾರಿ s. *n.* A twining shrub, *Cocculi indici*.

ಕಾಕಲಿ s. *n.* A soft, sweet sound.

ಕಾಕಾ (= ಕಕ್ಕ) h. *n.* A paternal uncle.

ಕಾಕಿ (= ಕಾಗಿ) s. *n.* A (female) crow. -ಗಿಡ. A common spinous shrub, *Canthium parviflorum*.

ಕಾಕು 1. k. *n.* Overheat, excitement, tiredness from the effects of sun, trouble, *etc.* 2, sharp smell, *as* of onion.

ಕಾಕು 2. s. *n.* Change of voice, *as* in fear, anger, grief, *etc.* 2, sarcasm; perversity. 3, stress. 4, patois. -ಮತಿ. A perverse mind. -ಮಾತು. A perverse word.

ಕಾಕುದ s. *n.* The palate.

ಕಾಕುರುಳು k. *n.* Dry cowdung of forests.

ಕಾಕೋದರ s. n. A serpent. -ಶಾಯಿ. Vishṇu.

ಕಾಗಡಿ k. n. = ಕಾವಡಿ. 2, a kind of cradle.

ಕಾಗದ h. n. Paper; a letter, note, document. -ಪತ್ರ. Letters and notes, correspondence. -ಬರೆ. To write a letter. -ತಲಪು A letter to arrive. -ಹಚ್ಚು. To affix a public notice.

ಕಾಗಿ, ಕಾಗೆ (tb. of ಕಾಕ) n. A crow. -ಗಣ್ಣು. Small eyes, as those of a crow. -ಬಣ್ಣ. A black colour. -ಬಂಗಾರ. Talc mineral. -ರೋಗ. A disease (consumption) by which the face becomes black.

ಕಾಗುಣಿತ k. n. Spelling, putting letters together.

ಕಾಂಕೆ (= ಕಾಕು) k. n. Heat of any kind.

ಕಾಂಕ್ಷೆ s. n. Wish, desire. 2, a disease of the eyes. -ತೀರಿಸಿಕೊಳ್ಳು. To fulfill one's desire. ಕಾಂಕ್ಷಿಸು. To desire, wish.

ಕಾಚ (= ಕಾಜು, ಗಾಜು) s. n. Glass; alkaline ashes. 2, a sling for suspending things. -ಲವಣ. A medicinal salt. -ಹುಲ್ಲು. A fragrant grass.

ಕಾಚಿ. = ಕಾಮುಂಚ. -ಗಿಡ. The plant *Solanum indicum*. -ಹುಲ್ಲು. = ಕಾಂಚಿಹುಲ್ಲು.

ಕಾಚು k. n. Cashoo, catechu, solidified juice of *Acacia catechu*.

ಕಾಜವಾರ (= ಕಾಸರ್ಕ) k. n. The tree bearing the *nux vomica*.

ಕಾಜಿ h. n. A Muhammadan priest; a judge.

ಕಾಜು. tb. of ಕಾಚ, q. v.

ಕಾಂಚನ s. n. Gold. 2, a tree with fragrant blossoms, *Mesua ferrea*.

ಕಾಂಚಿ s. n. A girdle, a woman's zone.

ಕಾಂಚಿ ಹುಲ್ಲು (cf. ಕಾಚಿಹುಲ್ಲು) k. n. Lemon grass, *Andropogon shoenanthus*.

ಕಾಂಚಿವಾಳ. = ಕಂಚಿವಾಳ, q. v.

ಕಾಂಜಿರ k. n. = ಕಾಜವಾರ, q. v. 2, a species of gourd.

ಕಾಟ (fr. ಕಾಡು 1) k. n. Trouble, annoyance, plague. 2, a forester. 3, a strong smell, as that of tobacco, chillies, etc. -ಆಚಾರ, ಕಾಟಾಚಾರ. Good behaviour to avoid annoyance. -ಕ. A forester or fowler; a troublesome man (f. ಕಾಟಕಿ); trouble. -ಕತನ. Annoyance.

ಕಾಟಕಾಯ, ಕಾಟಕಾಯಿ, ಕಾಟಗಾಯ k. n. Plundering, marauding, pillaging.

ಕಾಟು k. n. A bite, cut.

ಕಾಟಿ k. n. A kind of fermented pap of jôḷa or râgi.

ಕಾಠಿಣ್ಯ s. n. Hardness; firmness; severity.

ಕಾಡ. = ಕಾಡು 2, q. v. Cpds.: -ಗಿಡ್ಡ, -ಎಮ್ಮೆ, -ಕೋಣ, -ನಾಯಿ, -ನೊಣ, -ಬಸವಣ್ಣ, etc.

ಕಾಡಿ f. n. A blade of grass, a bit of straw, etc.; a stick. -ಕಾರ. Caustic.

ಕಾಡಿಗ k. n. A troublesome man. 2, a duck.

ಕಾಡಿಗೆ h. n. Lampblack; a collyrium prepared from it. -ಜೋಳ. A blackish jôḷa. -ಬಣ್ಣ. Black colour.

ಕಾಡು 1. k. v. t. To treat harshly; to give trouble; to tease; to plague. ಕಾಡಿಸು. To trouble, plague.

ಕಾಡು 2. (= ಕಾತ) k. n. A forest; a jungle. a. Wild. Cpds.: -ಕುದುರೆ, -ಕುರಿ, -ಕುರುಬ, -ಕೋಣ, -ಗತ್ತೆ, -ಗಿಡ್ಡ, -ಗೆಣಸು, -ಜನ, -ನಾಯಿ, -ನೊಣ, -ಬೆಕ್ಕು, -ಬೆಳ್ಳುಳ್ಳಿ, -ಮನುಷ್ಯ, -ಮೃಗ, -ರೋಗ, -ಹಂದಿ, -ಹಾಗಲ, -ಹೆಸರು, etc. Wild or jungle—, etc.

ಕಾಡೆ 1. f. n. A decoction.

ಕಾಡೆ 2. (tb. of ಕಾಂಡ) n. A stalk.

ಕಾಣ k. n. One who does not see. 2, a crow. a. One-eyed.

ಕಾಣಿ 1. k. n. A sixty-fourth fractional part ($\frac{1}{64}$) of any coin (cpds.: ಅರೆ-, ಗಿಡ್ಡಗಾಣಿ, ದುಗ್ಗಾಣಿ, ಮುಕ್ಕಾಣಿ). 2, gift; property; hereditary right. ಕಾಣಾಚಿ. Hereditary right to lands, etc.

ಕಾಣಿ 2. s. n. Unevenness of scales. 2, that which is put to counterpoise. -ಕಟ್ಟು. To make scales even. -ತೂಕ. A weight put to balance scales.

ಕಾಣಿಕೆ k. n. A present, gift. 2, sight. -ಕೊಡು. To make presents. -ಇಟ್ಟು ಕೈ ಮುಗಿ. To give a present and worship.

ಕಾಣಿಸು k. v. t. To show. 2, to show one's self. v. i. To become visible; to appear.

ಕಾಣು k. v. t. To see, regard, perceive. v. i. To appear; to be apparent. P. p. ಕಂಡು. ಕಾಣಗೊಡು. To let appear. ಕಾಣಬರು, ಕಂಡುಬರು. To appear, come in sight. ಕಾಣೆ (for f.), ಕಾಣೋ (for male) emph. See! lo! ಕಂಡು ಹೋಗು. To visit. ಕಂಡು ನೋಡು. To examine. ಕಂಡು ಮಾಡು. To imitate. ಕಂಡು ಮಾತಾಡು. To have an interview with. ಕಾಣುವಿಕೆ, ಕಾಣ್ಕೆ. Seeing; appearing. ಕಾಣಿಕೆ, ಕಾಣ್ಕೆ. Sight; a present, gift. ಕಾಣ್ಕೆ. Great valour.

ಕಾಂಡ s. n. A stalk, stem. 2, an arrow. 3, a part; the section of a book. 4, a bundle. 5, season. 6, water. -ಪಟ. A curtain, screen.

ಕಾಂಡಾಲ s. n. A granary constructed of bamboos.

ಕಾಂಡಿಗೆ s. n. N. of a plant; a kind of a gourd, *Cucumis utilissimus.*

ಕಾತರ, ಕಾತಳ s. a. Confused, agitated, perplexed. 2, timid, afraid. n. Confusion, perplexity; *also* ಕಾತರತೆ. 2, alarm, fright; ಕಾತರಿಸು. To be agitated, perplexed.

ಕಾತರಿ (ಖಾತರಿ) h. n. Assurance; guarantee.

ಕಾತಿ a. k. n. Coir; cord made of it. 2, anger.

ಕಾತು. = ಕಾಯ್ದು, P. p. of ಕಾಯು.

ಕಾದಲ್, ಕಾದಲ್ಕೆ a. k. n. Affection, love. ಕಾದಲ. A dear man; a paramour. ಕಾದಲೆ. A sweetheart.

ಕಾದು 1, ಕಾದಾಡು k. v. t. To war, fight. ಕಾದಾಟ. A fight, quarrel.

ಕಾದು 2. P. p. of ಕಾ & ಕಾಯು.

ಕಾನ h. n. Ear. -ದಾವಲಿ. An ear ornament.

ಕಾನನ s. n. A wood, forest.

ಕಾನೂನು h. n. A rule, regulation.

ಕಾಂತ s. a. Dear, beloved; beautiful; agreeable. n. A lover, husband. 2, a stone. 3, a house. 4, the moon. ಕಾಂತೆ. A lovely woman, wife.

ಕಾಂತಾರ s. n. A forest. 2, a difficult road. 3, a kind of sugarcane; *also* -ಕ.

ಕಾಂತಿ s. n. Wish; loveliness, beauty; splendour, lustre; personal decoration. -ತಪ್ಪು, -ಮುಚ್ಚು. Lustre to be obscured. -ಗುಂದು. Lustre to decrease.

ಕಾಪಟ್ಯ (fr. ಕಪಟ) s. n. Dishonesty, fraud.

ಕಾಪಾಡು, *see s.* ಕಾಪು.

ಕಾಪಾಲ s. a. Relating to the skull. ಕಾಪಾಲಿಕ. A religious mendicant; Śiva's worshipper.

ಕಾಪಿ 1. h. n. Coffee. -ಗಿಡ. The coffee-tree.

ಕಾಪಿ 2. f. n. N. of a tune.

ಕಾಪಿ 3. f. n. A copy.

ಕಾಪು k. n. Guarding, preserving, protection. 2, a preservative ceremony on the 7th day after a child's birth. ಕಾಪಾಡಿಸು. To make watch or guard. ಕಾಪಾಡು. To guard, protect, take care of, defend, nourish. ಕಾಪಾಡುವಿಕೆ. = ಕಾಪು.

ಕಾಮ s. n. Wish, desire; love; lust. 2, the god of love. -ನ ಬಿಲ್ಲು. The rainbow. -ನ ಸುಡುವದು. The burning of an effigy of Kâma at his annual festival. -ನ ಹುಣ್ಣಿಮೆ. Kâma's annual festival, the hôḷi. -ಕರ. Following one's own inclinations. -ಕಸ್ತೂರಿ. Sweet Basil. -ಕ್ರೋಧ ಲೋಭ ಮೋಹ ಮದ ಮತ್ಸರ. The six vices. -ಜನಕ. Vishṇu or Kṛishṇa. -ಧೇನು. The cow of plenty. -ಪತ್ನಿ. Rati the wife of Kâma. -ಬಾಣ. The (five) arrows of Kâma. -ವಿಕಾರ. Unnatural desire. ಕಾಮಾಕ್ಷಿ. Durgâ; a kind of lute. -ಆತುರ, ಕಾಮಾತುರ. Excited by lust. -ವೈರಿ, ಕಾಮಾರಿ. Śiva. ಕಾಮಿ. Lustful; a libidinous man. ಕಾಮಿತ. Wished, desired; a wish, desire. ಕಾಮಿತಾರ್ಥ. A desired object. ಕಾಮಿನಿ. A loving woman; a woman in general. ಕಾಮಿಸು. To wish, desire. ಕಾಮ್ಯ. Desirable; agreeable; optional. ಕಾವ್ಯಾರ್ಥ. An advantage desired from observances or rites.

ಕಾಮಗಾರಿ f. n. Work; workmanship. -ಶಿಕ್ಷೆ. Imprisonment with hard labour.

ಕಾಮಂಚಿ k. n. The lemon grass, *Andropogon schoenanthus.*

ಕಾಮಣಿ, ಕಾಮಲೆ, ಕಾಮಿಲೆ k. n. A kind of [jaundice.

ಕಾಮಾಟಿ f. n. Labour (for wages). 2, a day-labourer; *also* ಕಾಮಾಟಿ.

ಕಾಯ s. n. The body. 2, a multitude. -ಜ. -ಜಾತ. A son; Kâma.

ಕಾಯಂ h. a. Fixed, permanent, confirmed. -ಮಾಡು. To confirm.

ಕಾಯಕ s. n. Work, profession; pursuit; rite. *a.* Relating to the body.

ಕಾಯದೆ, ಕಾಯಿದೆ h. n. A rule, regulation.

ಕಾಯಿ 1. = ಕಾಯು, *q. v.*

ಕಾಯಿ 2. k. n. An unripe fruit in hard or nearly full-grown state; any nut, pod. 2, hardness, callosity. -ಆಗು, ಕಾಯಾಗು. Fruit to grow. -ಕಟ್ಟು, -ಗಟ್ಟು. To form or become hard, *as* a boil. -ಕಸರು, -ಕಸಿ. Various vegetables. -ಪಲ್ಯ, -ಪಲ್ಯೆ, -ಸೊಪ್ಪು. Pod and leaf vegetables. -ಬಿಡು. To get fruits. -ಹಾಲು. The milk of a cocoanut.

ಕಾಯಿಲೆ h. n. Sickness.

ಕಾಯಿಸು k. v. t. To boil, make hot; *also* ಕಾಸು. 2, to watch.

ಕಾಯು 1. (= ಕಾ, ಕಾಯಿ, *q. v.*) k. v. t. To guard, protect; to take care of; to tend; to watch; to keep in check. *v. i.* To wait. *P. ps.* ಕಾದು, ಕಾಯ್ದು.

ಕಾಯು 2. k. v. i. To grow hot, be heated; to become angry. *P. ps.* ಕಾದು, ಕಾಯ್ದು.

ಕಾಯ್ಪು (= ಕಾವು) k. n. Heat. 2, wrath.

ಕಾರ್ k. a. Black. n. Blackness. 2, rainy season. -ಗತ್ತಲೆ, -ಪೊಬ್ಬು. Sable darkness. -ಮುಗಿಲು. A black cloud. -ಇರುಳು, ಕಾರಿರುಳು. A dark night. -ಎಳ್ಳು, ಕಾರೆಳ್ಳು. A mole.

ಕಾರ 1. (*tb. of* ಕ್ಷಾರ) n. Pungency, hotness of taste; a pungent, hot substance. 2, an alkali, *as* soda or potash. 3, wrath. -ಸಾಯಿ. A kind of vermicelli

ಕಾರ 2. s. n. Making, causing. 2, a maker, doer. 3, *a term used to designate the sound of a letter, as* ಅಕಾರ, ಇಕಾರ, *etc.*

ಕಾರಕ s. a. Making. n. An agent. -ಪದ. A noun on which the case of an adjective depends *(g.)*.

ಕಾರಕೂನ h. n. A clerk; a tollman.

ಕಾರಖಾನೆ, ಕಾರ್ಖಾನೆ h. n. A manufactory, work-shop.

ಕಾರಗೃಹ, ಕಾರಾಗೃಹ s. n. A jail.

ಕಾರಂಜಿ f. n. A playing fountain.

ಕಾರಣ s. n. Cause; reason; motive, origin; a means. 2, agency, instrumentality. 3, need of. *ad.* For, on account of. -ಪುರುಷ. A deity; a great man. -ಬೀಳು. To be necessary. ಕಾರಣಿಕ. Causal, investigating the cause; an examiner; performance.

ಕಾರಣಿ k. n. The red stripes or painting upon the walls of a house.

ಕಾರಭಾರ h. n. Business, affairs; government. -ಮಾಡು. To manage. ಕಾರಭಾರಿ. A superintendent, manager.

ಕಾರವಿ h. n. A kind of red cotton cloth.

ಕಾರಿ 1. k. n. A backwater; an arm of the sea. 2, a ford.

ಕಾರಿ 2. s. n. Making, causing, *etc.* 2, an artist, artificer, actor. -ಕೆ. A female who does; a doing, a business; a comment, gloss.

ಕಾರೀಕ f. n. The dried date-fruit.

ಕಾರು 1. k. n. Blackness. -ಗತ್ತಲೆ. Sable darkness.

ಕಾರು 2. = ಕಾರ್. -ಹುಣ್ಣಿವೆ. A feast in the third month. -ಹುಲ್ಲು. Grass in the rainy season. -ಗದ್ದೆ. Wet cultivation. -ಬೆಳೆ. The wet-season crop.

ಕಾರು 3. (ರು = ಱು) k. v. i. To vomit. n. Vomiting. ಕಾರಿಕೆ. Vomiting. ಕಾರಿಸು. To cause to vomit.

ಕಾರುಣ್ಯ s. n. Compassion, kindness. -ನಿಧಿ. A treasure of compassion. -ಸಾಗರ. An ocean of compassion.

ಕಾರುಬಾರು. = ಕಾರಭಾರ, q. v.

ಕಾರೆ 1. k. n. The spinous shrub *Webera tetandra*. *Cpds.*: -ಗಿಡ, -ಮುಳ್ಳು, -ಹಣ್ಣು.

ಕಾರೆ 2. f. n. Confinement; a prison (*cf.* ಕಾರಗೃಹ). 2, pain. 3, a gold collar.

ಕಾರೆ 3. *tb. of* ಕಾರ್ಯ, q. v. -ಗಾರ. A workman. -ಗಾರಿಕೆ. Workmanship.

ಕಾರ್ಖಾನೆ. = ಕಾರಖಾನೆ, q. v.

ಕಾರ್ಗತ್ತಲೆ, *see s.* ಕಾರು 1.

ಕಾರ್ತಿಕ s. n. N. of the 8th lunar month (October-November).

ಕಾರ್ಪಣ್ಯ (*fr.* ಕೃಪಣ) s. n. Poverty; imbecility; pity; parsimony, niggardliness. -ಪಡು. To be in distress.

ಕಾರ್ಪಾಸ s. a. Made of cotton. n. Cotton; cotton-cloth.

ಕಾರ್ಯ (= ಕಾರೆ) s. n. Affair, business, act. 2, object, purpose. 3, cause, origin. -ವಾಸಿ. A good state of affairs. -ಭಾಗ. A division of a work; plot, intrigue. -ಸಾಧಿಸು. To accomplish a business. -ಸಿದ್ಧಿ. Success, fulfilment of an object. -ಸಿದ್ಧಿಸು. Work to be accomplished.

ಕಾಲ s. n. Time, the proper time. 2, a period of time, season, life-time. 3, death, Yama. 4, fate. 5, power. 6, tense of a verb. -ಕಳೆ. To spend time. -ಕ್ಷೇಪ. Spending the time; delay; livelihood. -ಕೂಟ. Deadly poison. -ಖಂಡ. The liver. -ಗಣನ. Calculation of time. -ಗಣನವಿದ್ಯೆ. Astronomy. -ಗತಿ. The lapse of time. -ಚಕ್ರ. The wheel of time; vicissitude of life. -ಜ್ಞ. An astrologer. -ಜ್ಞಾನ. Knowledge of time or futurity. -ಜ್ಞಾನ ಹೇಳು. To foretell. -ಜ್ಞಾನಿ. A prophet. -ತ್ರಯ. The three times: past, present, and future, or morning, noon and evening. -ತುಂಬು. Time to be fulfilled; death to come. -ದರ್ಶಿ. A seer. -ಪುರುಷ, -ಮೂರ್ತಿ. Time personified. -ಭೈರವ, -ರುದ್ರ. A terrible form of Śiva. -ಮಾನ. Measurement of time. -ವಶ, ಕಾಲಾಧೀನ. Subject to time or death. -ವಾಚಕ. A term expressing time. -ಹರಣ. Passing away time; delay. ಕಾಲಾನುಕಾಲ. From season to season; once. ಕಾಲಾನುಸಾರ, ಕಾಲಾನುಸರಣೆ. Conformity to the times. ಕಾಲಾಂತರ. Interval; period; process of time. ಕಾಲಾವಧಿ. Fixed time; the end of a year.

ಕಾಲಾಟ, ಕಾಲಾಡಿ, -ಡಿಸು, *see s.* ಕಾಲು.

ಕಾಲಿ (= ಕಾಳೆ) s. n. Blackness. 2, Durga; *also* ಕಾಲಿಕಾದೇವಿ. -ದಾಸ. N. of a celebrated poet.

ಕಾಲಿಂಗ (=ಕಳಿಂಗ) s. n. N. of a country or people. 2, the black snake.

ಕಾಲಿಂದಿ s. n. The river Yamuna. 2, fem. name.

ಕಾಲಿವೆ, ಕಾಲುವೆ k. n. A water-course, channel.

ಕಾಲು k. n. The foot, leg. 2, a strand or lock of hair. -ಅಟ್ಟ, ಕಾಲಟ್ಟ. A bench. ಕಾಲಾಡು. To take a walk; *caus.* ಕಾಲಾಡಿಸು. -ಆಡಿ, ಕಾಲಾಡಿ. A fast walker; a wanderer, roamer. -ಆಳು, ಕಾಲಾಳು. A foot-soldier. -ಇಕ್ಕು, -ಇಡು, -ಊರು, ಕಾಲಿಕ್ಕು, ಕಾಲಿಡು, ಕಾಲೂರು. To take a step; to walk. -ಕಟ್ಟು, ಕಾಲ್ಗಟ್ಟು. To tie the leg; to embrace one's feet; a shackle; marriage. -ಕಡಗ. A plain anklet. -ಕುಪ್ಪಸ, -ಕುಬುಸ. Trowsers. -ಉಂಗರ, ಕಾಲುಂಗರ. A ring worn on the second toe. -ಗಡ. A ford. -ಚೀಲ. Stockings. -ತೆಗೆ, ಕಾಲ್ತೆಗೆ. To retreat, flee. -ದಾರಿ, -ವಟ್ಟೆ. A footpath. -ದೂಳು. Dust of the feet: an evil (*as* belly-ache) supposed to have occasioned from contact with one's feet-dust. -ನಡಿಗೆ, -ನಡೆ. Walking on foot. -ಬಲ. Foot-soldiers. -ಬೀಳು. To fall at one's feet. -ಮಡಿ. To bend the leg, *i. e.* to make water; urine. -ಮರೆ, -ಮೆಟ್ಟು. A sandal or shoe. -ಮಾಡು. To make for, begin. -ಸರಪಣಿ. A chain ornament worn above the ankles.

ಕಾಲು 2. k. *n.* A quarter or fourth part.

ಕಾಲುವೆ. = ಕಾಲಿವೆ, *q. v.*

ಕಾಲುಷ್ಯ (*fr.* ಕಲುಷ) s. *n.* Foulness, filth; sin. 2, want of harmony.

ಕಾಲೋಚಿತ s. *a.* Opportune, in season, suitable to the time. *n.* A suitable time.

ಕಾವಂಚಿ k. *n.* The lemon grass, *Andropogon schoenanthus.*

ಕಾವಡಿ k. *n.* A bamboo pole with slings at each end for carrying burdens across the shoulder.

ಕಾವಣಿ a. k. *n.* A shed, pandal.

ಕಾವಂದ h. *n.* Lord, master, owner.

ಕಾವರ a. k. *n.* Passion, anger, wrath.

ಕಾವಲ, ಕಾವಲು k. *n.* Guarding, watching; a guard, watch; custody. 2, a pasture ground. -ಗಾರ, -ದವ, -ವ. A guard, sentinel.

ಕಾವಲಿ k. *n.* A frying or baking pan.

ಕಾವಲೆ. = ಕಾಲಿವೆ, *q. v.*

ಕಾವಳ k. *n.* Darkness.

ಕಾವಿ k. *n.* A red earth or ochre.

ಕಾವು 1. (= ಕಾಯ್ಪು, *etc.*) k. *n.* Heat; glow. 2, cauterization. -ಕೊಡು, -ಹಾಕು. To cauterize, foment.

ಕಾವು 2. k. *n.* A stalk, stem; a handle.

ಕಾವೆ h. *n.* Ringing and turning of a horse whilst at full speed. -ತಿರುಗಿಸು. To longe a horse.

ಕಾವೇರಿ s. *n.* N. of a river; N. of a fem.

ಕಾವ್ಯ (*fr.* ಕವಿ) s. *n.* Poetry; a poetical composition. -ಕರ್ತಾರ, -ಕರ್ತೃ. A poet. -ರಚನೆ. Composition of a piece of poetry.

ಕಾಶಿ (= ಕಾಸಿ) s. *n.* Benares. 2, N. of a people. ದಕ್ಷಿಣ-. Hampe near Bellary. ಉತ್ತರ-. Benares. -ಕಾಗದ. Good white paper. -ತಾಲಿ. A marriage badge attached to a female's necklace. -ಪಟ್ಟೆ. Fine silk. -ಭಾಗೀರಥಿ. Water brought from Benares.

ಕಾಶ್ಮೀರ s. *n.* N. of a country. 2, saffron.

ಕಾಷಾಯ s. *a.* Red. *n.* A red cloth; *also* -ವಸನ.

ಕಾಷ್ಠ s. *n.* A piece of wood, a stick; dry wood. 2, a blockhead. -ವ್ಯಸನ. Vain grief. ಕಾಷ್ಠಿಕೆ. = ಕಟ್ಟಿಗೆ.

ಕಾಷ್ಠೆ s. *n.* A region of the world. 2, place, site. 3, a measure of time. 4, excellence.

ಕಾಸ s. *n.* Cough, catarrh. 2, asthma. -ಮರ್ದ. A cough-medicine, *Cassia sophora.*

ಕಾಸಗಾರ, ಕಾಸದಾರ, ಕಾಸ್ತಾರ h. *n.* A [groom.

ಕಾಸಗಿ h. *a.* Private, not public; own.

ಕಾಸರ, ಕಾಸರ್ಕ, ಕಾಸುರಕ (= ಕಾಜವಾರ. *tb.* *of* ಕಾರಸ್ಕರ) *n.* The tree *Strychnos nux vomica.*

ಕಾಸಾ h. *a.* Good, fine; legitimate; own.

ಕಾಸಿ 1. = ಕಾಶಿ, *q. v.* -ದಾವಳಿ. A soft woollen dâvaḷi.

ಕಾಸಿ 2. (*tb. of* ಕಾಶಾ) *n.* A cloth for girding the loins.

ಕಾಸು 1. (= ಕಾಯಿಸು) k. *v. t.* To warm, make hot; to boil; to bake *as* bread, *etc.*

ಕಾಸು 2. k. *n.* The smallest copper coin, a cash; a coin in general.

ಕಾಳ s. *a.* Black. -ಗತ್ತಲೆ. Sable darkness. -ಜೀರಿಗೆ. Black cummin. -ರಾತ್ರಿ. A dark night.

ಕಾಳಗ k. *n.* Fight, battle, war.

ಕಾಳಂಜಿ k. *n.* A spittoon. 2, a vessel from which scented water is sprinkled.

ಕಾಳಿ (= ಕಾಲಿ) s. *n.* Durgâ. -ಅಮ್ಮ, ಕಾಳಮ್ಮ. N. -ನಾಥ. Śiva.

ಕಾಳಿಂಗ s. *n.* The black cobra, *Naga tripudians.*

ಕಾಳಜ, ಕಾಳಿಜ f. *n.* The liver. 2. the breast, heart.

ಕಾಳು (ಳು = ಱು) k. *n.* A corn, single grain; seed; a pea; a bean. 2, (= ಕಾಡು) a forest, *etc.* -ಆಗು, ಕಾಳಾಗು. To be ruined; to become troublesome or hostile. -ಭೈರವ. A ferocious Bhairava.

ಕಿಕ್ಕರಿಸು k. *v. t.* To make small, to reduce. *v. i.* To be closely united or thickset, *as* fruits or leaves on a tree.

ಕಿಕ್ಕಿರಿ k. v. i. To be close together, dense. n. A crowd, throng.

ಕಿಗ್ಗಟ್ಟು k. n. A small tie or band.

ಕಿಂಕರ s. n. A servant, slave. -ತೆ, -ತ್ವ. Servitude; destitution.

ಕಿಚ, ಕಿಚಿ k. *An imitative sound.* -ಗುಟ್ಟು, -ಅನ್ನು. To chirp, chatter.

ಕಿಚಡಿ, ಕಿಚ್ಚಡಿ h. n. A mixture of boiled rice and pulse.

ಕಿಚ್ಚು k. n. Fire. -ಮೋರೆ. A wrathful countenance. ಹೊಟ್ಟೆ-. Envy.

ಕಿಂಚಿತ s. a. Somewhat. 2, a little.

ಕಿಟಕಿ, ಕೆಟಿಕಿ, ಕಿಡಕಿ h. n. A window; a wicket. -ಬಾಗಲು. The window-opening. -ಬಾವಲಿ. An ear-ornament. -ತೆರೆ. To open a window.

ಕಿಟ್ಟ 1. k. n. A gajuga (*Molucca bean*).

ಕಿಟ್ಟ 2. s. n. Secretion; excrement; dross of iron; rust, *etc.*; cowdung kept in a pit.

ಕಿಟ್ಟ k. n. A kind of torture in which the hand, ear, or nose is pressed between two sticks.

ಕಿಡಿ k. n. A spark. -ಕಿಡಿ. *rep.* -ಕಿಡಿಯಾಗು. To be enraged. -ಗಣ್ಣು. A fiery, red eye. -ಬೆಂಕಿ. A little fire.

ಕಿಡಿಗೇಡಿ k. n. A mischievous boy. -ತನ. Mischievousness.

ಕಿಣಿ k. *An imitative sound.* -ಎನ್ನು, -ಗುಟ್ಟು. To tinkle, tingle.

ಕಿಂಡಿ k. n. A chink, gap, cleft.

ಕಿತಾಬು h. n. A title. 2, a book.

ಕಿತ್ತಡಿ k. n. An ascetic, a ṛishi.

ಕಿತ್ತಳೆ, -ಹಣ್ಣು k. n. An orange.

ಕಿತ್ತಾ h. n. A time, turn. -ವಾರ. In fragments.

ಕಿತ್ತಾಟ (= ಕಚ್ಚಾಟ) k. n. Strife, quarrel.

ಕಿತ್ತಾನ್, ಕಿಂತಾನ್ h. n. Canvas, linen.

ಕಿತ್ತು k. v. t. To pluck out. 2, *p. p. of* ಕೀಳು.

ಕಿನಕಾಪು, ಕಿನಕಾಬು h. n. Silk stuff interwoven with gold or silver thread, brocade.

ಕಿನಾರ, ಕಿನಾರೆ h. n. Edge, border.

ಕಿನ್ನರ s. n. A human figure with a horse's head; a demigod serving Kuvêra. -ಪತಿ. Kuvêra.

ಕಿನ್ನರಿ s. n. A lute. 2, *f. of* ಕಿನ್ನರ.

ಕಿಫಾಯತಿ m. n. Profit, gain.

ಕಿಬ್ಬೆರಳು, ಕಿಬ್ಬೊಟ್ಟೆ k. n. The little finger.

ಕಿಂಪುರುಷ. = ಕಿನ್ನರ, *q. v.*

ಕಿಮ್ಮತು h. n. Price, value.

ಕಿರಣ s. n. A ray of light.

ಕಿರದು (ರ = ಱ), *see s.* ಕಿರಿ 2, *q. v.*

ಕಿರಬ, ಕಿರಬು (ರ = ಱ) k. n. A hyena; a leopard.

ಕಿರಮಂಜಿ f. n. Cochineal; cochineal colour.

ಕಿರಾಣಿ m. n. Grocery, *as* sugar, spices, *etc.*

ಕಿರಾತ s. n. N. of a savage tribe inhabiting woods and mountains.

ಕಿರಾಯ h. n. Rent, hire, fare.

ಕಿರಿ 1. k. v. i. To grin.

ಕಿರಿ 2. (ರ = ಱ) = ಕಿರು 1. k. a. Small, little, short, young trifling; junior. -ಕುಲ = ಕಿರುಕುಲ. *Cpds.*: -ಗಂಟೆ, -ಗಣ್ಣು, -ಗಿವಿ, -ಗೂದಲು, -ಗೆಯ್, -ತಂಗಿ, -ತಮ್ಮ. -ದು, ಕಿರದು, ಕಿರ್ದು. A small insignificant affair or state. -ನುಡಿ. To use mean language; a disrespectful word. -ನೆಲ್ಲಿಗಿಡ. The plant *Flacourtia cataphracta.* -ನೋಟ. A leer. -ಬೆರಳು, -ಬೊಟ್ಟು. The little finger. -ಯನು. A young man, a junior; *f.* ಕಿರಿಯಳು. -ಮಗ. The youngest son. -ಹೊಟ್ಟೆ. The abdomen.

ಕಿರಿಕಿಜೋಡು (ರಿ = ಱಿ) k. n. A pair of creaking shoes.

ಕಿರಿಕಿರಿ h. n. Annoyance, trouble.

ಕಿರಿಗೆ (ರಿ = ಱಿ) k. n. A small sîrĕ worn by girls.

ಕಿರಿದು, *see s.* ಕಿರಿ.

ಕಿರಿಯಾತು f. n. A kind of gentian, *Agathotes chirayta.*

ಕಿರೀಟ s. n. A diadem, crown, tiara. ನವರತ್ನ-. A crown of nine sorts of gems.

ಕಿರು 1. = ಕಿರಿ, *q. v.* -ಕಸಲೆ, -ಕುಸಾಲೆ A kind of potherb. -ಕುಲ, ಕಿರಕುಳ. A low or inferior caste or kind. -ಗತ್ತಲೆ. Slight darkness. -ಗತ್ತಿ. A short sword. -ಗೊರಳು. A short neck. -ದೊಡೆ. The shank, lower or upper part of the leg. -ನಗೆ. A smile. -ನಾಲಿಗೆ. The uvula. -ಬೆರಳು. = ಕಿರಿಬೆರಳು, *s.* ಕಿರಿ. -ತುರುಚಿ. A plant that stings like a nettle, *Tragia cannabina.*

ಕಿರು 2. (ರು = ಱು) k. *An imitative sound.* -ಗುಟ್ಟು. To cry, scream; to creak, *as* a door.

ಕಿರ್ದಿ h. *n.* An account of receipts and disbursements.

ಕಿಲಬು. = ಕಿಲುಬು, *q. v.*

ಕಿಲ, ಕಿಲಿ k. *int. An imitative sound.* --ನಗು. To titter from pleasure.

ಕಿಲುಬು, ಕಿಲುವು (= ಕಿಲಬು) k. *n.* Rust; verdigris. *v. t.* To get corroded or covered with verdigris.

ಕಿಲ್ಬಿಷ s. *n.* Fault, offence, sin; disease.

ಕಿಲ್ಲೆ h. *n.* A fort. -ದಾರ. The commander of a fort.

ಕಿವಚು k. *v. t.* To crush and squeeze with the hand.

ಕಿವಡು k. *n.* Deafness; *also* -ತನ. ಕಿವಡ. A deaf man; *f.* ಕಿವಡಿ.

ಕಿವಿ k. *n.* The ear (ಕರ್ಣ, ಶ್ರೋತ್ರ, ಶ್ರವಣ); the touch-hole of a cannon; a handle, *as* of a frying pan. -ಕೊಡು. To listen, pay attention to. -ಕೊಟ್ಟು ಕೇಳು. To hear attentively. -ತೂತು. A perforation in the auricle. -ತೂತು ಮಾಡು. To bore the ear. -ತೆರೆ. To open the ears. -ಮಾತು. A whispered word. -ಮುಚ್ಚು. To shut the ears. -ಯ ಮೇಲೆ ಇಡು, -ಯ ಮೇಲೆ ಹಾಕು. To make known, to communicate. -ಯಾರೆ. Attentively. -ಹರಕ. A man whose auricle is rent; *f.* -ಹರಕಿ. -ಹಿಂಡು, -ತಿರಿಗಿಸು. To twist the ear.

ಕಿವುಡು. = ಕಿವಡು, *q. v.*

ಕಿಸ k. *n.* Putting astride; grinning. -ಗಾಲು. The legs put astride (in walking). -ಬಾಯಿ. A grinning mouth. -ಬಾಯ. A grinner, simpleton.

ಕಿಸಕ್ಕನೆ k. *ad.* Suddenly, unawares. 2, sneeringly.

ಕಿಸಮು h. *n.* Kind, sort. -ವಾರು. Sorted.

ಕಿಸಿ k. *v. t.* To put astride. *v. i.* To grin.

ಕಿಸು k. *n.* Redness; a dark-red colour. 2, = ಕಿಸ, *q. v.*

ಕಿಸುರು k. *v. i.* To be disagreeable. *n.* Disagreeableness, disgustfulness; strife, quarrel.

ಕಿಸೆ h. *n.* A pocket.

ಕಿಸ್ತಿ, ಕಿಸ್ತು h. *n.* An instalment; payment by instalments, *as* of assessment. -ಬಂದಿ. Settlement of revenue by instalments. -ಬಾಕಿ. Arrears of instalments.

ಕಿಳರು a. k. *v. i.* To neigh.

ಕೀ 1. k. *int. An imitative sound.* ಕೀ ಕೀ. The cry of certain birds. -ಹಕ್ಕಿ. The curlew.

ಕೀ 2. k. *v. i.* To become pus.

ಕೀಚಕ s. *n.* A hollow bamboo whistling in the wind. 2, a chief of Virâṭarâja's army.

ಕೀಟ, ಕೀಟಕ s. *n.* A worm, insect. ಕೀಟಕತನ. Mischief-making.

ಕೀಟಲೆ k. *n.* Mischief-making trouble.

ಕೀನಾಶ s. *a.* Poor, wretched; small, little. 2, sick.

ಕೀರ k. *n.* The mungoose. 2, (f.) a parrot. 3, (*tb. of* ಕ್ಷೀರ) milk.

ಕೀರು 1. (ರು = ಱು) k. *v. i.* To scream. 2, to rage, fume. *v. t.* To scrape, scratch.

ಕೀರು 2. f. *n.* A dish composed of rice, wheat, *etc.*

ಕೀರ್ತನೆ s. *n.* A praise, song of praise; eulogium. 2, fame, glory.

ಕೀರ್ತಿ s. *n.* Fame, glory, renown, report. 2, praise, worship. -ಗಳಿಸು. To acquire fame. -ವಂತ. A famous man. -ಪಡಿಸು, -ಸು. To praise, laud.

ಕೀಲ. = ಕೀಲು, *q. v.*

ಕೀಲಕ s. *n.* A pin, bolt, wedge, *etc.* 2, the forty-second year in the Hindu cycle.

ಕೀಲಿ s. n. A lock; the spring of a watch. -ಕೆಯ್. The key of a lock. -ತೆಗೆ. To unlock.

ಕೀಲು (tb. of ಕೀಲ) n. A pin, peg, bolt, bar, wedge, joint, etc. 2, device, contrivance; a secret. ಕೀಲಿಸು. To bind, fasten, fix, pin.

ಕೀವು (fr. ಕೀ) k. n. Pus, matter of a sore.

ಕೀಸು a. k. v. t. To make thin, scrape. 2, to pull out or off. n. Scraping, scratching. 2, a coil of palm leaf put in the ear-hole.

ಕೀಳು 1. (ಳು=ಱು) k. n. Lowness, meanness. 2, a low, inferior, base, mean man. 3, a veranda. -ಜಾತಿ. A low caste. -ಮನುಷ್ಯ, ಕೀಳ. A low man. -ತನ. Lowness, inferiority. -ತರ. An inferior kind. -ಮೇಲು. Evil and good. -ಮಾತು, -ನುಡಿ. A low, improper word.

ಕೀಳು 2. k. v. t. To pull out; to pluck out or up; to uproot, eradicate. P. p. ಕಿತ್ತು.

ಕು s. *A particle implying inferiority, wickedness, etc.*

ಕುಕಿಲು k. n. The cuckoo. v. i. To cry as a cuckoo.

ಕುಕೂಲ s. n. A smoking fire.

ಕುಕ್ಕಡಿ f. n. The quantity of thread spun in one ball. 2, the ball-like swelling produced on the upper arm from being struck. -ಏಳು. To swell thus.

ಕುಕ್ಕರಿಸು k. v. t. To put down with violence or destroy, as vessels; 2, to squat.

ಕುಕ್ಕಿಬಳ್ಳಿ k. n. A creeper running wild, *Passiflora foetida*.

ಕುಕ್ಕು 1. k. v. t. To peck; to strike in a pecking manner; to hack, dig up. 2, (fig.) to urge. 3, to beat gently, as a cloth in washing. v. i. To wink, be dazzled by the sunlight, etc.

ಕುಕ್ಕು 2. k. n. A heron, crane. 2, shaking.

ಕುಕ್ಕುಟ s. n. A cock. ಕುಕ್ಕುಟಿ. A hen. ಕುಕ್ಕುಟಾಸನ. A certain posture of an ascetic during religious meditation.

ಕುಕ್ಕುರ s. n. A dog. 2, a vegetable perfume.

ಕುಕ್ಕೆ k. n. A small basket.

ಕುಕ್ಕೋಟ k. n. Trot, as of a horse.

ಕುಕ್ಷಿ s. n. A cavity. 2, the belly. ಕುಕ್ಷಂಭರಿ. Selfish, greedy.

ಕುಗ್ಗು k. v. i. To become low, be depressed; to crouch; to decrease; to cease or stop, as voice or speech. ಕುಗ್ಗಿಸು. To cause to be depressed, etc.

ಕುಗ್ರಾಮ s. n. A hamlet. -ವಾಸಿ. A petty villager.

ಕುಂಕುಮ s. n. Saffron, *Crocus sativus*. 2, crimsoned saffron-powder applied by married women to their foreheads; a kind of cosmetic. -ಕೇಸರ. The saffron flower.

ಕುಂಕೆ k. n. The nape of the neck. 2, the shoulder.

ಕುಂಗು.=ಕುಗ್ಗು, q. v.

ಕುಚ s. n. The female breast; a nipple.

ಕುಚಾಳಿ f. n. A bad disposition; jeering, mockery.

ಕುಚು k. n. Whispering. - -ಮಾತಾಡು. To whisper.

ಕುಚೇಷ್ಟೆ s. n. An evil design, wicked contrivance; reviling and defaming; wild tricks.

ಕುಚೋದ್ಯ s. n. Ridicule, derision, mockery; an evil thought. -ಗಾರ. A mocker, reviler.

ಕುಚ್ಚಿತ. tb. of ಕುತ್ಸಿತ, q. v.

ಕುಚ್ಚು 1. k. v. t. To boil. -ಅಕ್ಕಿ. Rice made from paddy slightly boiled and dried.

ಕುಚ್ಚು 2. (tb. of ಕೂರ್ಚ.=ಕುಂಚ, q. v.) n. A bunch, bundle, cluster; a tassel; a brush.

ಕುಜ s. a. Earth-born, low-born. n. The earth's son: the planet Mars. -ವಾರ. Tuesday.

ಕುಜ್ಜಿ k. n. An unripe jack-fruit.

ಕುಂಚ (=ಕುಚ್ಚು 2) s. n. A bunch, cluster, tassel; a brush used by weavers; *also* ಕುಂಚಿಗೆ.

ಕುಂಚಿ s. n. A hooded cloak for children.

ಕುಂಚಿಗೆ (*tb. of* ಕೂರ್ಚಕ) n. A brush used by weavers for cleaning the warp.

ಕುಂಜ s. n. A place overgrown with creepers; a bower.

ಕುಂಜರ s. n. An elephant. *a.* Pre-eminent, excellent.

ಕುಟಂಕ (*tb.* ಕೊಟ್ಟಿಗೆ) n. A roof; hut.

ಕುಟರು (*tb.* ಗುಡಾರ) n. A tent.

ಕುಟಾಯಿಸು h. v. t. To mix.

ಕುಟಿ s. A curve. 2, a hut. 3, a nosegay.

ಕುಟಿಕ, ಕುಟಿಗ k. *aff.* One who beats, *etc. Cpds.:* ಕಲ್ಲು-, ಮರ-, ಚೆಂಬು-, *etc.*

ಕುಟಿಲ s. a. Bent, crooked, curved. 2, curly. 3, dishonest, fraudulent. *n.* Insincerity, dishonesty. -ತನ, -ತೆ, -ತ್ವ. Dishonesty.

ಕುಟೀರ s. n. A hut, cottage.

ಕುಟುಕು k. v. t. To gulp, swallow. 2, to sting. *n.* A draught, morsel.

ಕುಟುಂಬ s. n. A household, family; a wife. -ಸ್ಥ. A housefather. ಕುಟುಂಬಿ. A householder; *f.* ಕುಟುಂಬಿನಿ.

ಕುಟ್ಟಣ k. n. A metal mortar to pound betel-nuts.

ಕುಟ್ಟಣಿ, ಕುಟ್ಟನಿ (=ಕುಂಟಣಿ) s. n. A bawd, procuress.

ಕುಟ್ಟು k. v. t. To beat, strike, pound, bruise. 2, to throw. 3, to prick, ache. 4, (*at the end of cpds.*) to utter, *etc.*, to do (*as:* ಗುಣುಗುಟ್ಟು, ಬುಸುಗುಟ್ಟು, ಸೊಪ್ಪುಗುಟ್ಟು, *etc.*). *n.* A blow; a piercing pain in the bowels. -ವಿಕೆ, ಕುಟ್ಟುಕೆ. Beating.

ಕುಟ್ಟೆ k. n. Decay, the state of being pulverised by wood-worms.

ಕುಠಾರ, ಕುಠಾರಿ s. n. An axe. -ಧರ. Gaṇapati; Paraśurâma.

ಕುಡ k. n. A staff-like iron roller for clearing cotton from the seed. 2, a cauterising iron. 3, a stick of sealing wax.

ಕುಡಕ, ಕುಡಿಕ k. n. A drinker, drunkard.

ಕುಡತ, ಕುಡಿತ k. n. Drinking; a draught.

ಕುಡತಾ, ಕುಡತಿ f. n. A jacket.

ಕುಡತೆ, ಕುಡಿತೆ k. n. The hollowed palm of the hand. 2, a liquid measure in S. C. = $\frac{1}{2}$ sheer.

ಕುಡವ s. n. A measure of capacity = $\frac{1}{4}$ ಪ್ರಸ್ಥ.

ಕುಡಿ 1. k. v. t. & i. To drink; to inhale. *n.* Drinking. -ಸು. To cause to drink. -ನೀರು. Drinking water.

ಕುಡಿ 2. k. n. A point, top; a bamboo shoot, the end of a lamp's wick; the lash of a whip; the point of a flame. 2, a flag. -ನೋಟ. A side glance. -ಮೀಸೆ. A mustache with pointed extremities. -ಸೆರಗು. The extreme point of a cloth.

ಕುಡಿಕೆ k. n. A small vessel; an inkstand, bottle, *etc.* -ಬಿರುಸು. A kind of firework.

ಕುಡು 1. (= ಕೊಡು) a. k. v. t. To give, *etc.*

ಕುಡು 2. k. n. Croockedness. -ಗಲು, -ಗೋಲು. A sickle. -ಮಿಂಚು. A zigzag lightning.

ಕುಡುಕು k. v. t. To wash (a cloth) gently. 2, to peck.

ಕುಡುಪು k. n. A stick for beating drums, *etc.;* a fiddle-stick.

ಕುಣತ (= ಕುಣಿತ) k. n. Dancing.

ಕುಣಿ 1. k. n. A hole, a pit; a grave-pit. -ಗಣ್ಣು. A sunken eye. -ನರಿ. A fox.

ಕುಣಿ 2, ಕುಣಿಯು, ಕುಣಿದಾಡು k. v. t. To dance; to jump, frisk, hop. -ತ, -ದಾಟ, -ಯುವಿಕೆ. Dancing.

ಕುಣಿ 3. s. a. Crooked-armed; having a withered or crippled arm. -ಕ. A cripple.

ಕುಣಿಕೆ k. n. A loop, noose; a clasp; a link; knot. 2, a hollow, cavity. 3, a finger. 4, a corner.

ಕುಣಿತ, ಕುಣಿಹ. = ಕುಣತ, *q. v.*

ಕುಂಟ k. n. A cripple, lame man; f. ಕುಂಟಿ. 2, tb. of ಕುಂಠ. -ಗಾಲು. A lame foot. -ಣಿಕೆ. Hopping. -ಣಿಕೆಯಾಟ. A hop-scotch.

ಕುಂಟಣಿ (tb. of ಕುಟ್ಟಿಣಿ, q. v.) k. n. A procurer, whoremaster; also -ಗ; f. -ಗಿತ್ತಿ.

ಕುಂಟು k. n. Lameness; hopping; a hop. v. t. To limp, halt, hop.

ಕುಂಟೆ k. n. An instrument for levelling ploughed ground and removing noxious weeds. 2, the web-beam in a loom. 3, a pool, pond. 4, a broom-stick.

ಕುಂಠ s. a. Blunt, dull; indolent, weak; foolish; cf. ಕುಂಟ. ಕುಂಠಿತ. Blunted; lazy, stupid; confounded.

ಕುಂಡ s. n. A pit. 2, a pot. 3, a pool, pond. 4, a son born in adultery; also -ಗೋಳಕ.

ಕುಂಡರು. = ಕುಂಡ್ರು, q. v. ಕುಂಡರಬೀಳು. To fall or sink down.

ಕುಂಡಲ s. n. An ear-ring, also one worn as a badge of honour by Paṇḍitas, etc.; brackets. 2, an astrological diagram; also ಗ್ರಹ-. -ಪಂಡಿತ. A scholar who wears a pair of such a badge.

ಕುಂಡಲಿ s. a. Circular, spiral. n. A snake. 2, the herb *Mollugs cerviana*.

ಕುಂಡೆ k. n. Buttocks; the posteriors; the bottom of a vessel. -ಚಣ್ಣ. Tight breeches.

ಕುಂಡ್ರು (= ಕುಂಡರು, ಕೂಡ್ರು, etc.) k. v. i. To sit down. ಕುಂಡ್ರಿಸು. = ಕುಳ್ಳಿರಿಸು.

ಕುತನಿ, ಕುತನಿ, ಕುತ್ತನಿ h. n. Satin.

ಕುತಂತ್ರ s. n. A wicked design. -ಗಾರ. A man of wicked devices.

ಕುತರ್ಕ s. n. Fallacious argument, fallacy, sophism.

ಕುತು f. n. A leathern oil-bottle.

ಕುತುಕ f. n. Eagerness; desire; curiosity.

ಕುತುಬಿ h. n. The Muhammadan Friday sermon and blessing.

ಕುತೂಹಲ s. n. Eagerness; curiosity; desire. 2, sport, amusement.

ಕುತ್ತ k. n. Defect, deficiency; fault; sickness; trouble; adversity, danger. ಕುತ್ತಿ. A sickly female.

ಕುತ್ತಿಗೆ k. n. The throat; the neck.

ಕುತ್ತು k. v. t. To beat, strike, bruise; to push. n. A stroke; that is small. -ಅಡಿ, ಕುತ್ತಡಿ. A small foot. -ಗೆ. Striking. ಕುತ್ತಿಸು. To cause to beat.

ಕುತ್ಸಿತ s. a. Reviled, despised; contemptible, vile.

ಕುದಕಲು. = ಕುಚ್ಚು, q. v.

ಕುದರು, ಕುದುರು k. n. Low ground; a hollow; the bed of a stream.

ಕುದರೆ. = ಕುದುರೆ, q. v.

ಕುದಿ k. v. i. To boil, bubble up. 2, to suffer pain, to grieve (P. ps. ಕುದಿದು, ಕುದ್ದು). n. Boiling; grief. ಕುದಿಸು, -ಸು. To boil, etc.

ಕುದುಕು a. k. v. i. To trot. n. Trotting.

ಕುದುರು k. v. i. To recover from illness, be set, arranged, etc.; to come to hand; to fit; to become quiet, firm; to prosper, succeed. n. Settlement; symmetry; health, family. 2, a garden-bed. 3, a rim of a mortar. -ಪಾಟು. Success, as of a business. -ಮಾಡು. To fix, establish.

ಕುದುರೆ k. n. A horse. 2, the cock of a gun. 3, a knight at chess. -ಕಿವಿಗನ ಮರ. The tree *Terminalia tomentosa*. -ಗಾರ, -ಯುವ. A horsekeeper. -ಬಾಲ. The hair of a horse's tail. -ಮಸಾಲೆ. A perennial fodder plant, the *Lucerne* grass. -ಮುಖ. N. of a sanitarium on the Western Ghauts. -ಮುಸುಡಿನ ಗಳು. A kind of crocodile. -ರಾಹುತ. A horseman. -ಏರು, -ಹತ್ತು. To mount a horse.

ಕುದೆ a. k. n. A fetter.

ಕುದ್ದಾಲ (tb. ಗುದ್ದಲಿ) s. n. A hoe, a kind of spade. 2, mountain ebony.

ಕುದ್ದು. P. p. of ಕುದಿ, q. v.

ಕುದ್ರಿಗೇಡಿತನ k. n. Envy.

ಕುನಸು h. n. Rancour, spite.

ಕುನಿ a. k. v. i. To bend, bow, stoop.

n. A curved ground. -ಚೀಲ. A sack, bag. -ಪ್ಪ. Crookedness; insolence.

ಕುಂತಲ s. n. Hair; *cf.* ಕೂದಲು. 2, a mode of dressing the hair. 3, N. of a country.

ಕುಂತಿ s. n. N. of the daughter of the Yâdava prince Śûra and mother of the Pâṇḍavas.

ಕುಂತು. = ಕುಳಿತು, ಕೂತು, *etc.* (*P. p. of* ಕುಳಿರು). Having sat down.

ಕುಂದ 1. k. n. A pillar of bricks, *etc.*

ಕುಂದ 2. s. n. A kind of jasmine. 2, Olibanum, a resin. 3, one of Kubêra's treasures.

ಕುಂದಕ k. n. Defect; hindrance.

ಕುಂದಣ k. n. Setting a precious stone with gold. 2, fine gold.

ಕುಂದಣಿಗೆ, ಕುಂದಳಿಗೆ k. n. The rim of a mortar.

ಕುಂದು k. n. To become lean; to wane, decrease, fail, sink; to faint, cease. *n.* Decrease, deficiency; defect, want; fault; emaciation; grief. -ಇಡು, -ತರು, ಕುಂದಿಡು. To find fault with. ಕುಂದು ವಿಕೆ, ಕುಂದುಹ. Decreasing, decline. ಕುಂದಿಸು. To cause to decrease, *etc.*

ಕುನ್ನಿ k. n. A cub, puppy, *etc.*; a young dog.

ಕುಪಿತ s. a. Provoked, angry. *n.* Anger. -ಮತಿ. A passionate person.

ಕುಪ್ಪಟಿ, ಕುಪ್ಪಡಿಗೆ k. n. A portable furnace.

ಕುಪ್ಪರಿಸು. = ಕುಪ್ಪಳಿಸು, *q. v.*

ಕುಪ್ಪಸ (*tb. of* ಕೂರ್ಪಾಸ) *n.* A bodice; a jacket; a cuirass.

ಕುಪ್ಪಳಿಸು k. v. i. To heap; to be numerous; to jump over. 2, to be injured or scalded; to blister. *v. t.* To amass, heap.

ಕುಪ್ಪಿ (*tb. of* ಕೂಪಿ) *n.* A vial, flask, bottle.

ಕುಪ್ಪು k. v. t. To heap, lay up. *v. i.* (= ಕುಪ್ಪಳಿಸು) To leap, jump. *n.* A kind of disease. ಕುಪ್ಪಿಸು. To cause (an animal) to jump; to jump with joined feet.

ಕುಪ್ಪೆ k. n. A pile, heap; a dunghill.

ಕುಬಕು k. v. t. To dig up the ground slightly.

ಕುಬುದ್ಧಿ s. n. Evil-mindedness.

ಕುಬುಸ, ಕುಬ್ಸ. = ಕುಪ್ಪಸ, *q. v.*

ಕುಬೇರ. = ಕುವೇರ, *q. v.*

ಕುಬೋಧಕ s. n. A bad teacher. ಕುಬೋಧನೆ. Bad instruction.

ಕುಬ್ಜ s. a. Hump-backed; dwarfish; *f.* ಕುಬ್ಜೆ.

ಕುಮಕಿ, ಕುಮಕು, ಕುಮ್ಮಕು h. n. Help; assistance.

ಕುಮತಿ s. n. Evil-mindedness; weak intellect.

ಕುಮರಿ k. n. A piece of forest land cleared of its trees and cultivated for one or two years only.

ಕುಮಾರ s. n. A boy, youth, son. 2, the heir apparent. 3, Skanda, the god of war. -ಗುರು. Śiva. -ವಾಲ್ಮೀಕಿ. The author of Kannaḍa Râmâyaṇa. -ವ್ಯಾಸ. The author of Kannaḍa Bhârata. -ಸ್ವಾಮಿ. Skanda.

ಕುಮಾರಿ, ಕುಮಾರತೆ, ಕುಮಾರ್ತೆ s. n. A young girl, maiden; a daughter. ಕುಮಾರೀಭೂತಿರ. Cape Comorin.

ಕುಮುಕು. = ಕುಮಕಿ, *q. v.*

ಕುಮುಟು k. n. Nauseousness; mustiness, damp smell.

ಕುಮುದ s. n. The white water-lily, *Nymphaea esculenta.* 2, the blue lotus. 3, the elephant of the south-west quarter. 4, the moon. 5, camphor. *a.* Brown, tawny. -ಗಡ್ಡೆ. A fragrant garden flower, *Kaemferia rotunda.* -ಪ್ರಿಯ, -ಬಂಧು, -ಬಾಂಧವ, ಕುಮುದಿನೀ ಕಾಂತ. The moon. -ವೈರಿ, ಕುಮುದಾರಿ. The sun.

ಕುಂಪಣಿ f. n. Company.

ಕುಂಬಳ (*tb. of* ಕೂಷ್ಮಾಂಡ) *n.* The pumpkin gourd. -ಕಾಯಿ. A pumpkin. -ಬಳ್ಳಿ. The pumpkin-creeper.

ಕುಂಬಾರ (ರ = ಐ) (*tb. of* ಕುಂಭಕಾರ) *n.* A potter; *f.* -ಗಿತ್ತಿ, -ತಿ, -ಮಾಳಿ. -ತಿಗರಿ.

A potter's wheel. -ತನ, ಕುಂಬಾರಿಕೆ. The business of a potter.

ಕುಂಬು k. n. Bowing down; an obeisance. 2, decay.

ಕುಂಟೆ k. n. A wall on a roof that serves for a balustrade.

ಕುಂಭ s. n. A water-jar, pot; the sign of the zodiac *Aquarius*. 2, N. of a demon. 3, a grain measure. -ಕ. Stopping the breath in yôga. -ಕರ್ಣ. N. of a râkshasa. -ಕಾರ. A potter. -ಕೋಣ. N. of a town in Tanjore.

ಕುಂಭಿನಿ s. n. The earth.

ಕುಂಭೀಪಾಕ s. n. A hell in which the wicked are baked like potter's vessels, *etc.*

ಕುಮ್ಮು k. v. t. To beat with a pestle, pound. n. Pounding.

ಕುಯಿಲು k. n. Cutting, reaping. 2, a tenon. -ಆಳು, ಕುಯಿಲಾಳು. A reaper.

ಕುಯುಕ್ತಿ s. n. A wicked device.

ಕುರಗ f. n. An instrument of goldsmiths, *etc.*; a sort of anvil.

ಕುರಂಗ s. n. An antelope, deer.

ಕುರಚು (ರ=ಱ). = ಕುರುಚು, q. v.

ಕುರಂಜಿ (*tb. of* ಕುರುವಿಂದ) n. The corundum-stone, *Spatum adamanticum*, used for cutting diamonds.

ಕುರಟಿಕೆ, ಕುರಟಿಗೆ. = ಕುರುಟಿಕೆ, q. v.

ಕುರಡ. = ಕುರುಡ, q. v.

ಕುರಬ. = ಕುರುಬ, q. v.

ಕುರರ s. n. An osprey; f. ಕುರರಿ.

ಕುರಾನು. = ಖುರಾನು, q. v.

ಕುರಿ 1. (ರಿ=ಱಿ) k. n. A mark; aim; an object of aim. v. t. To mark; to take note of, regard, mind. *P. p.* ಕುರಿತು *(used as a particle)*. With a view to, respecting, regarding, *etc.* ಕುರಿಪು. A mark, *etc.*

ಕುರಿ 2. (ರಿ=ಱಿ) k. n. A sheep, ram. -ಕೂದಲು, -ತುಪ್ಪಟ್ಟ. Wool. -ಕಾವ, -ಗಾವ. A shepherd. -ಗಿಡ. A creeper said to be an antidote for snake-bites. -ತನ. A sheepish disposition. -ಮಂದೆ, -ಹಿಂಡು. A flock of sheep. -ಮರಿ. A lamb. -ಹಟ್ಟಿ. A sheepfold.

ಕುರಿಚಿ (=ಕುರ್ಚಿ) h. n. A chair.

ಕುರಿತು, *see s.* ಕುರಿ 1, q. v.

ಕುರು 1. k. n. A protuberance on the body; a boil. 2, smallness.

ಕುರು 2. s. n. The ancestor of the Pâṇḍus and Dhṛitarâshṭra. -ಕ್ಷೇತ್ರ. N. of the field of battle between the Kurus and Pâṇḍus near Delhi. -ವೈರಿ. Bhîma.

ಕುರುಗಣೆ (ರು=ಱು) k. n. The state of being diminished. 2, the serum of the ear, ear-wax.

ಕುರುಚು (ರು = ಱು) (=ಕುರಚು) k. n. Smallness; dwarfishness. a. Small, dwarfish.

ಕುರುಜು k. n. An artificial frame-work used to put idols in, *etc.*

ಕುರುಟಿಕೆ, ಕುರುಟಿಗೆ h. n. A plant used as medicine for the eyes, *Odina wodier*.

ಕುರುಡ (=ಕುರಡ) k. a. Blind. n. A blind man; f. ಕುರುಡಿ. -ತನ, ಕುರುಡು. Blindness. ಕುರುಡು ಬೀಳು. To become blind.

ಕುರುಂದ. = ಕುರಂಜಿ, q. v.

ಕುರುಪು (ರು = ಱು) k. n. A mark, sign; a characteristic; acquaintance. -ಇಡು, ಕುರುಪಿಡು. To mark, define; to consider.

ಕುರುಬ (ರು = ಱು) k. n. A shepherd. 2, a foolish man; f. -ತಿ, -ಗಿತ್ತಿ. -ನ ಗಡ್ಡೆ. A perennial creeping plant, *Lepidagathis cristata*. -ತನ. The profession of a shepherd; foolishness.

ಕುರುಂಬ (ರು = ಱು) k. n. A caste of mountaineers; f. ಕುರುಂಬಿತಿ.

ಕುರುಬೆ k. n. A tender, young cocoanut.

ಕುರುವಕ s. n. A crimson sort of amaranth. 2, a species of barleria. 3, the red cedar.

ಕುರುವಿಂದ (=ಕುರಂಜಿ, q. v.) s. n. The fragrant grass, *Cyperus rotundus*. 2, vermillion. 3, the corundum-stone.

ಕುರುಹು (ರು=ಱು) (=ಕುರುಪು) k. n. A sign, mark, *etc.*

ಕುರುಳು, ಕುರುಳ್ k. n. A curl or lock of hair. 2, a cake of dried cow-dung.

ಕುರೂಪ s. a. Ugly, deformed. n. Ugliness. ಕುರೂಪಿ. An ugly person.

ಕುರ್ಚಿ (=ಕುರಿಚಿ) h. n. A chair.

ಕುರ್ಚಿಗೆ k. n. A weeding hook.

ಕುಲ s. n. A race, family, tribe, caste. 2, a crowd, herd, troop, multitude. 3, a noble family. 4, a house. -ಕ. =-ಜ. -ಕರ್ಣಿ. A village clerk or accountant. -ಕ್ಷಯ. Extinction of a race or caste. -ಕಾಯಕ.=-ವೃತ್ತಿ. -ಗೆಡಕ. A spoiler of caste; one whose caste is spoiled, *also* -ಗೇಡಿ; a bad rude fellow. -ಗೆಡು. Caste to be spoiled. -ಗೇಡಿತನ. The act of spoiling caste; an act disgraceful to one's family. -ಗೋತ್ರ. Caste and family. -ಜ. Well-born; ancestral. -ದೇವತೆ, -ದೈವ. The tutelar deity of a caste or family. -ಧರ್ಮ, ಕುಲಾಚಾರ. Duty peculiar to a race or caste. -ನಾರಿ, -ಸ್ತ್ರೀ. A woman of a good family. -ಪುತ್ರ. A son of a noble family. -ಭ್ರಷ್ಟ. An outcast. -ವಿಹೀನ, -ಹೀನ. A man of low birth. -ವೃತ್ತಿ. Caste professsion. -ಶ್ರೇಷ್ಠ. Eminent by birth. -ಸಂಬಂಧ. Family connection. -ಸ್ಥ. Belonging to a good family; *f.* -ಸ್ಥೆ. ಕುಲಾಚಾರ. The established practices of caste. ಕುಲೋದ್ಧಾರಕ. A man who elevates a race or family.

ಕುಲಕು. =ಕುಲುಕು, *q. v.*

ಕುಲಾಯ, ಕುಲಾಯಿ, ಕುಲಾವಿ h. n. A little cap.

ಕುಲಾಯಿಸು h. v. t. To open, expand, to increase; *also* ಖುಲಾಯಿಸು.

ಕುಲಾಲ s. n. A potter; *f.* ಕುಲಾಲಿ. -ಚಕ್ರ. A potter's wheel.

ಕುಲಾಸ. = ಖುಲಾಸ, *q. v.*

ಕುಲಿಕು. = ಕುಲುಕು, *q. v.*

ಕುಲಿಮೆ. = ಕುಲುಮೆ, *q. v.*

ಕುಲೀನ s. a. Of high descent, well-born.

ಕುಲುಕು k. v. i. To shake, *as* a vessel, body or voice. n. Shaking; a shake; trotting. ಕುಲುಕಿಸು. To cause to shake; to agitate. -ಗಾತಿ. A coquette. ಕುಲುಕೋಟ. Trottings, trut.

ಕುಲುಮೆ, ಕುಲ್ಮೆ k. n. A fire-pit or furnace.

ಕುಲ್ಲ h. n. A male buffalo.

ಕುಲ್ಮಾಷ s. n. Sour gruel. 2, a sort of phaseolus. 3, a species of dolichos, *Dolichos biflorus.*

ಕುಲ್ಯ s. n. A canal. 2, a ditch; a dyke. 3, a river. 4, a bad habit. a. Of a good family, well-born.

ಕುಲ್ಲಾ h. a. Expanded, opened; *also* ಖುಲ್ಲಾ.

ಕುಲ್ಲು h. n. The whole.

ಕುವರ 1. *tb. of* ಕುಮಾರ, *q. v.*

ಕುವರ 2. k. n. A potter. 2, a veil.

ಕುವಲಯ s. n. Any water-lily.

ಕುವಾಕ್, ಕುವಾಚ್ s. n. Speaking ill of any one.

ಕುವಿಂದ, -ಕ s. n. A weaver.

ಕುವೇರ (=ಕುಬೇರ) s. n. The god of wealth and regent of the north.

ಕುವ್ವೆ. = ಕೂವೆ, *q. v.*

ಕುಶ s. n. The sacrificial grass. 2, a son of Râmačandra. ಕುಶಾಗ್ರ. Point of kuša-grass. ಕುಶಾಗ್ರಬುದ್ಧಿ, -ಮತಿ. Acumen; shrewd, intelligent.

ಕುಶಲ s. a. Right, proper; prosperous; clever, expert. n. Cleverness. 2, well-being. 3, virtue. -ಗಾರ. A clever man; *f.* -ಗಾತಿ, ಕುಶಲಿ. -ತನ, -ತೆ. Cleverness, ability. -ಪ್ರಶ್ನೆ. A friendly enquiry after one's welfare.

ಕುಶಾಲು h. n. Ease; fun, frolic, pleasure. -ಪಿರಂಗಿ. Salute firing. -ಮಾಡು. To rejoice.

ಕುಶಿ, ಕುಷಿ h. n. Pleasure; will.

ಕುಶಿನಿ f. n. Kitchen. -ಗಾರ. A cook.

ಕುಷ್ಕಿ h. n. Dry land not artificially irrigated.

ಕುಷ್ಠ s. n. Leprosy; *also* -ರೋಗ.

ಕುಸಕು. = ಕುಸುಕು, *q. v.*

ಕುಸಕುಸು k. *n.* Whispering. -ಮಾತಾಡು, ಕುಸುಗುಟ್ಟು. To whisper.

ಕುಸಂಧಿ s. *n.* An improper union of letters. 2, an unlucky conjunction of stars. 3, a narrow space.

ಕುಸಿ k. *v. i.* To bend, stoop; to sink, give way, to tumble. *n.* Bending, sinking. 2, the peg or pin of a door. -ಬೀಳು. To give way as a wall, *etc.*

ಕುಸುಕು k. *v. t.* To strike. 2, (= ಕುಕ್ಕು) to wash by slightly beating.

ಕುಸುಬು k. *v. t.* To wash (= ಒಗಿ) clothes by beating them on a stone.

ಕುಸುಮ s. *n.* A flower. -ಷಟ್ಪದಿ. N. of a metre.

ಕುಸುಂಬರಿ (= ಕೋಸಂಬರಿ) f. *n.* Raw fruits, *etc.* preserved as a seasoning.

ಕುಸುಂಬೆ (*tb. of* ಕುಸುಂಭ) *n.* Dried flowers of safflower. 2, the red dye prepared from them. -ದುಪ್ಪಟಿ. A deep red cloth. -ಬಣ್ಣ. A deep red colour.

ಕುಸುಂಭ (= ಕುಸುಂಬೆ) s. *n.* The safflower *Carthamus tinctorius.* 2, a student's water-pot.

ಕುಸುರಿ, ಕುಸುರು k. *n.* The pulp or soft part of some vegetables and fruits. 2, the sticky filament of flowers. -ಗಾಯಿ. A very young unripe fruit.

ಕುಸ್ತಿ h. *n.* Wrestling. -ಬಿಡು. To set on to wrestle. -ಯಾಡು, -ಹಿಡಿ. To wrestle.

ಕುಸ್ತುಂಬರಿ, ಕುಸ್ತುಂಬರು. = ಕೊತ್ತುಂಬರಿ, *q. v.*

ಕುಹಕ (= ಕುಯುಕ) s. *n.* A cheat, rogue; a juggler, (*f.* ಕುಹಕಿ); deception, legerdemain.

ಕುಳ 1. (= ಕುಲ, *q. v.*) s. *n.* Family, race. 2, a tenant. 3, a tax-payer. -ವಾಡಿ. An inferior village-servant. -ವಾಡಿಕೆ, -ವಾಡಿತನ. The business of a kuḷavâḍi. -ವಾರು. A settlement made with the farmers individually.

ಕುಳ 2. (ಳ = ಱ) k. *n.* Confusion. 2, a ploughshare; a cauterizing iron.

ಕುಳಿ 1. k. *n.* *An affix for the formation of nouns, as:* ಬಡ-, ಮರು-, *etc.*

ಕುಳಿ 2. (ಳಿ = ಱಿ) k. *n.* A hollow; a hole; a pit. *v. t.* To dig, make a hole.

ಕುಳಿತು (*P. p. of* ಕುಳಿರು) k. Seated, sat down. -ಕೊಳ್ಳು. To sit down.

ಕುಳಿರು 1. (= ಕುಂಡ್ರು, ಕುಳ್ಳಿರು, ಕೂಡ್ರು) k. *v. i.* To sit down, squat; to stoop.

ಕುಳಿರು 2. k. *n.* Coolness, coldness; cold; snow. ಕುಳಿರ್ಗಾಳಿ. A cool wind. ಕುಳಿರ್ವೆಟ್ಟು. The snow-mountain: Himâlaya.

ಕುಳ್ಳ k. *n.* A dwarf; *f.* ಕುಳ್ಳಿ.

ಕುಳ್ಳಿತು. = ಕುಳಿತು, *q. v.*

ಕುಳ್ಳಿರು (= ಕುಳಿರು) k. *v. i.* To sit down. ಕುಳ್ಳಿರಿಸು. To cause to sit down.

ಕುಳ್ಳು k. *n.* A cake of dried cow-dung. 2, shortness. -ತಾಳಿ. A pile of kuḷḷu for cooking. -ದಾನ. A stack of kuḷḷu.

ಕೂಕಣಿ, ಕೂಗಟಿ, ಕೂಗಣಿ k. *n.* Ear-wax.

ಕೂಗು k. *v. i.* To cry aloud, to cry out (*also* -ಹಾಕು, ಕೂಗಾಡು, ಕೂಗಿಡು). *n.* A cry, clamour, shout. ಕೂಗಳತೆ. The distance at which a loud cry can be heard. -ವಿಕೆ. Crying aloud.

ಕೂಚು 1. k. *n.* A post in a wall for the support of beams. 2, smallness. -ಗಿಡ. A small, stunted tree.

ಕೂಚು 2. h. *n.* March or decampment of troops or people.

ಕೂಜ (= ಕೂಜೆ) h. *n.* An earthen water-jug; a goglet.

ಕೂಟ 1. (*fr.* ಕೂಡು) k. *n.* A junction; union; an assembly, crowd; a quantity; company. -ಕೂಡು. To assemble.

ಕೂಟ 2. s. *n.* The summit of a mountain; any prominence. 2, a plot; fraud, conspiracy. 3, an astrological term.

ಕೂಟಸ್ಥ s. *n.* The male representative of a family. 2, eternally the same, *as* space, soul, *etc.*

ಕೂಡ, ಕೂಡಾ (*inf. of* ಕೂಡು) k. *prep.* Together with, along with; with. 2, also, likewise. -ಇಡು, ಕೂಡಿಡು. To heap, pile up.

ಕೂಡಲು, ಕೂಡ್ಲು k. n. A junction; confluence. ಕೂಡಲೆ, ಕೂಡ್ಲೆ. At the very moment; forthwith.

ಕೂಡಿಕೆ k. n. Joining; meeting. 2, marrying a widow. -ಗಂಡ. A man who has married a widow. -ಹೆಂಡತಿ. A remarried widow.

ಕೂಡಿಸು k. v. t. To join; to mix; to add; to amass. -ವಿಕೆ. Adding; addition.

ಕೂಡು k. v. i. To join, unite; to meet, come together; to be possible; to take place. 2, to be fit. v. t. To join, add, *as* numbers. ಕೂಡ, *inf.* ಕೂಡ ಬೀಳು. To be accumulated. -ಹಾಕು. To heap up. ಕೂಡಿ ಬರು. To come together; to prosper, *as* a business; to assemble and come to a place; to astrologically agree, *as* the horoscopes.

ಕೂಡೆ k. *prep.* With, together with; at the same time; further, also. -ಕೂಡೆ. Mutually, all together.

ಕೂಡ್ರು (= ಕುಳ್ಳಿರು) k. v. i. To sit down. ಕೂಡ್ರಿಸು. To cause to sit down.

ಕೂಡ್ಲೆ. = ಕೂಡಲೆ, q. v.

ಕೂತು k. *P. p. of* ಕುಳಿರು, q. v.

ಕೂದಲು k. n. Hair of the head or body.

ಕೂನು k. v. i. To bend, stoop. n. A hump. 2, a mark, sign. ಕೂನ. A hump-backed man; *f.* ಕೂನಿ.

ಕೂಪ s. n. A hole; a well. 2, a mast.

ಕೂರಿಗೆ (ರ=ಱ) k. n. A sowing machine.

ಕೂರು 1. k. n. Sharpness; acuteness; *also* ಕೂರಿಕೆ. ಕೂರಾಳು. A brave soldier. ಕೂರಿದ. A sharp, acute or brave man.

ಕೂರು 2. k. n. A tenon.

ಕೂರು 3. k. v. i. To mind, be attached to, to love. ಕೂರ್ಪ, ಕೂರ್ಪವನು. A lover; beloved man; a husband. ಕೂರ್ಪು. Love.

ಕೂರು 4. k. v. i. To sit down.

ಕೂರೆ (ರೆ=ಱೆ) k. n. A kind of cloth-louse.

ಕೂರ್ಚ s. n. A bunch, bundle. 2, the space between the eyebrows. 3, the beard, mustaches. -ಕ, ಕೂರ್ಚಿಕೆ. A brush.

ಕೂರ್ಪಾಸ. = ಕುಪ್ಪಸ, q. v.

ಕೂರ್ಮ s. n. A tortoise, turtle. 2, the second incarnation of Vishṇu; *also* ಕೂರ್ಮಾವತಾರ. -ಪುರಾಣ. The purâṇa of the said incarnation. ಕೂರ್ಮಾಸನ. A stool in the form of a tortoise back.

ಕೂರ್ಮೆ s. k. n. Attachment, love.

ಕೂಲಂಕಷ, ಕೂಲಂಕುಷ s. n. The whole, from first to last.

ಕೂಲಿ k. n. Hire, wages, esp. daily cooly. 2, a day-labourer, a cooly. -ಕೆಲಸ. Daily labour. -ಮಾಡು, -ಕೆಲಸ ಮಾಡು. To work as a day-labourer. -ಕಾರ, -ಯವ, -ಯಾಳು. A cooly; *f.* -ಕಾತಿ, -ಯವಳು, -ಯಾಳಿ.

ಕೂಲು 1. k. v. i. To fall down; to be overturned, ruined. ಕೂಲಿಸು. To cause to fall.

ಕೂಲು 2. k. n. A tenon. 2, a sloping flight of stairs leading down to the water of a tank.

ಕೂವ (*tb. of* ಕೂಪ). n. A mast; *also* -ಕಂಬ.

ಕೂವೆ (= ಕುವ್ವೆ) k. n. The East-Indian arrowroot, *Curcuma angustifolia.*

ಕೂಷ್ಮಾಂಡ s. n. The pumpkin gourd.

ಕೂಸು k. n. An infant, babe. ಕೂಸಾಟ. Children's play. ಕೂಸಾಡು. To play like children. ಕೂಸಾಡಿಸು. To amuse a child. -ತನ. Childhood. ಕೂಸಾಳು. A weak, useless person.

ಕೂಳ (ಳ=ೞ) k. n. A vulgar, rude, stupid, vile man; *f.* ಕೂಳಿ. *a.* Vulgar, *etc.* -ತನ. Rudeness, meanness.

ಕೂಳಿ, ಕೂಳೆ 1. k. n. A basket for fishing.

ಕೂಳು (ಳು=ೞು) (*tb. of* ಕೂರು) n. Boiled rice, food. -ಬಕ್ಕ, -ಬೊಕ್ಕ, ಕೂಳ್ವಣಿಗ. A glutton. -ಸೀರೆ. Food and clothing.

ಕೂಳೆ 2. k. n. The stump of jôḷa; stubble in general.

ಕೃಚ್ಛ್ರ s. n. Distress. 2, difficulty. 3,

pain. *a.* Bad, miserable. -ಮೂತ್ರಪ್ರವೃತ್ತಿ. Difficulty in the evacuations.

ಕೃತ s. *a.* Done, made, wrought. *n.* Deed, action, accomplishment. 2, the first of the four yugas of the world. 3, a kind action, benefit. -ಕ. Made, artificial; simulated, false; hypocrisy. -ಕೃತ್ಯ. Contented, satisfied. -ಘ್ನ. Ungrateful. -ಘ್ನತೆ. Ingratitude. -ಜ್ಞ. Grateful. -ಜ್ಞತೆ, -ಜ್ಞತ್ವ. Gratitude. -ಯುಗ. = ಕೃತ No. 2. -ವರ್ಮ, -ಹಸ್ತ. Dexterous, skilful. ಕೃತಾಕೃತ. Done and not done. ಕೃತಾರ್ಥ. Successful; satisfied; clever.

ಕೃತಿ s. *n.* Doing, action; a literary work, poem. -ಪತಿ. An author, a poet.

ಕೃತ್ತಿ s. *n.* Hide, skin. 2, the birch tree.

ಕೃತ್ತಿಕೆ s. *n.* The third lunar mansion containing six stars called the *Pleiades*.

ಕೃತ್ಯ s. *a.* To be done, proper. *n.* Action, act, deed; business, duty.

ಕೃತ್ಯೆ s. *n.* An act, deed. 2, a female deity.

ಕೃತ್ರಿಮ s. *a.* Artificial. 2, false, deceitful. *n.* Guile, deceit. 2, bewitchment, witchcraft. ಕೃತ್ರಿಮಿ. A deceitful person.

ಕೃದಂತ s. *n.* A word ending with a ಕೃತ್ affix.

ಕೃಪಣ s. *n.* Pitiable, miserable, poor. 2, avaricious. -ತನ, -ತ್ವ. Wretchedness; avarice.

ಕೃಪಾ s. *n.* Pity, tenderness, compassion, mercifulness; kindness; *also* ಕೃಪೆ. -ಕಟಾಕ್ಷ, -ದೃಷ್ಟಿ. A kind look, the eye of favour. -ನಿಧಿ, -ಸಾಗರ. An ocean of tenderness. -ಳು. Compassionate, merciful. -ಹೀನ. Pitiless.

ಕೃಮಿ (= ಕ್ರಿಮಿ) s. *n.* A worm, insect. 2, a spider. -ಘ್ನ. A vermifuge, *Erycibe paniculata*.

ಕೃಶ s. *a.* Lean, emaciated, thin, slender.

ಕೃಷಿ s. *n.* Agriculture, husbandry. -ಕ, ಕೃಷೀವಲ. A husbandman.

ಕೃಷ್ಟ. *tb.* of ಕೃಷ್ಣ, *q. v.*

ಕೃಷ್ಣ (= ಕೃಷ್ಟ, ಕ್ರಿಷ್ಣ) s. *a.* Black; wicked. *n.* The dark half of the lunar month. 2, one of the incarnations of Vishṇu. 3, a crow. 4, the black antelope. 5, Indra. 6, a river so called. -ಕರ್ಮ. An evil deed; criminal. -ಜಯಂತಿ. Kṛishṇa's birthday. -ಪಕ್ಷ. = ಕೃಷ್ಣ *n.* No. 1. -ಪಾಡ್ಯ. The first day of the moon's wane. -ವಕ್ತ್ರ. Black-faced. -ಸನ್ನಿ. A disease in which the tongue turns black. -ಸರ್ಪ. The black cobra. -ಹೃದಯ. A wicked disposition. ಕೃಷ್ಣಾಗರು. A black variety of *Agallochum* or aloe wood. ಕೃಷ್ಣಾಜಿನ. The skin of the black antelope. ಕೃಷ್ಣಾವತಾರ. An incarnation of Kṛishṇa.

ಕೆ (= ಅಕೆ, ಅಕ್ಕೆ, ಅಗೆ, ಇಕೆ, ಇಕ್ಕೆ, *etc.*) k. *A suffix to form the dative sing., as:* ವನಕೆ, ಮರಕ್ಕೆ, *etc.* 2, *a nominal or pronominal suffix, as:* ಬಾಳಿಕೆ, ಮಡಿಕೆ, ಹರಿಕೆ, ಅಕೆ, ಈಕೆ, *etc.*

ಕೆಕ್ಕರಬಳ್ಳಿ k. *n.* The melon vine. ಕೆಕ್ಕರಿಕೆ. The musk-melon.

ಕೆಕ್ಕಸ k. *n.* Insult, insulting language.

ಕೆಕ್ಕಳಿಸು k. *v. i.* To be excited from fear.

ಕೆಂ, ಕೆಂಬ್ (= ಕೆತ್, ಕೆನ್, ಕೆಮ್) k. *n.* Redness. *a.* Red. -ಕಣ್. Red or fiery eye. -ಕಿಡಿ. A red spark. -ಗುಡಿ. The red sprout: coral. -ಗೆಂಡ. A shining live coal.

ಕೆಚ್ಚನೆ (= ಕೆಂ, *q. v.*) k. *ad.* Redly. *n.* Redness.

ಕೆಚ್ಚಲ, ಕೆಚ್ಚಲು k. *n.* The udder of beasts.

ಕೆಚ್ಚು 1. k. *v. t.* To join the ends of two threads by twisting them with the fingers. *n.* The knot formed by twisting.

ಕೆಚ್ಚು 2. k. *n.* Core, the heart of a tree; essence, strength. 2, pride. -ಗಟ್ಟು. To become strong. ಕೆಚ್ಚಡಕೆ. Pieces of hard areca nuts.

ಕೆಂ, ಕೆಣ್ಣ್ k. n. Redness; *also* -ಚಗೆ, -ಚನೆ, -ಚು. ಕೆಂಚ. A red or brown man; *f.* ಕೆಂಚಿ. -ಚಗ -ಚಗೆ. A kind of red ant.

ಕೆಟ್ಟ *(past rel. part. of* ಕೆಡು) k. a. Wicked, bad; foul, rotten. 2, mischievous, injurious. 3, abominable. 4, fierce. -ತನ. A bad, wicked disposition.

ಕೆಟ್ಟು. *P. p. of* ಕೆಡು, *q. v.*

ಕೆಡಕ k. n. A mischief-maker; a bad, wicked, mean man; *f.* ಕೆಡಕಿ. -ತನ. A bad, depraved nature or conduct.

ಕೆಡಕು k. n. Corruption; ruin; foulness; evil. -ತನ. = ಕೆಡಕತನ.

ಕೆಡವು (= ಕೆಡಹು, ಕೆಡಪು) k. v. t. To make fall down; to fell; to throw to the ground; to pull down.

ಕೆಡಪು. = ಕೆಡವು, *q. v.* 2, to pierce through, *as* a hole.

ಕೆಡಹು. = ಕೆಡವು, *q. v.*

ಕೆಡಿಸು *(fr.* ಕೆಡು) k. v. t. To destroy, ruin; to spoil; to deflower; to extinguish, *as* a lamp. *Cpds.:* ಎಡೆ-, ಕಾಲ್-, ಗತಿ-, ನಡೆ-, *etc.*

ಕೆಡು k. v. i. To be ruined, spoiled; to become foul, bad, vicious, vile, low; to be extinguished. *P. p.* ಕೆಟ್ಟು. *Cpds.:* ಗತಿ-, ದೆಸೆ-, ನೆಲೆ-, ಮತಿ-, *etc.* ಕೆಟ್ಟುಹೋಗು. = ಕೆಡು. -ಕು = ಕೆಡಕು, *q. v.* -ವಿಕೆ, -ಹ. Ruin, destruction.

ಕೆಡೆ a. k. v. i. To fall down, drop, sink. v. t. To let fall. n. The act of dropping (words) thoughtlessly. -ನುಡಿ. To speak thoughtlessly; a thoughtless word or speech.

ಕೆಣಕು k. v. t. To irritate or provoke. ಕೆಣಕಾಟ. Provocation. ಕೆಣಕಿಸು. To cause provocation.

ಕೆಂಡ k. n. A live coal. -ಗಣ್ಣು. A fiery or red eye. -ರೊಟ್ಟಿ. Bread baked on coals. -ಸಂಪಿಗೆ. A red sort of sampigĕ. -ಸೇವೆ. The ceremony of walking over burning coals.

ಕೆತ್ತನೆ (= ಕೆತ್ತಿಕೆ, ಕೆತ್ತಿಗೆ) k. n. The act of setting, *as* precious stones, *etc.;* engraving.

ಕೆತ್ತು k. v. t. To chisel, carve, engrave, cut; to scrape; to chip, *as* grass, plank, *etc.;* to make thin. 2, to enclose; set, *as* precious stones. ಕೆತ್ತಿಸು. To cause to carve, engrave. ಕೆತ್ತಿಕೆ, ಕೆತ್ತಿಗೆ. The act of setting, engraving, carving, *etc.* ಕೆತ್ತಿಗೆ ಸರಪಣಿ. A chain set with precious stones.

ಕೆತ್ತೆ k. n. A chip, paring.

ಕೆದಕು k. v. t. To stir, scratch.

ಕೆದರು (ರು = ಱು) k. v. i. To scatter, be scattered about; to disperse; to swing about; to scratch, *as* fowls, dogs, *etc.*

ಕೆನ್ (= ಕೆಂ, *q. v.*) Red. *Cpds.:* -ದಾವರೆ, -ದಾಳೆ, -ನಾಲಿಗೆ, -ನೀರು, -ನೆತ್ತರು, -ನೆಯ್ದಿಲೆ, -ನೆಲ, *etc.*

ಕೆನೆ k. n. The cream of milk. 2, beauty. -ಕಟ್ಟು. Cream to set. -ಗಂಜಿ. The scum of boiled rice. -ಮೊಸರು. Creamy curds.

ಕೆಂದು (= ಕೆನ್) k. n. Redness.

ಕೆನ್ನೆ k. n. The upper cheek.

ಕೆಮ್ (= ಕೆನ್, *etc., q. v.*) k. a. Red. *Cpds.:* -ಬಟ್ಟೆ, -ಬಣ್ಣ, -ಬೆಳಗು, -ಮಣ್ಣು, -ಮ್ಮೋರೆ, *etc.*

ಕೆಂಪಗೆ k. a. Red. ad. Redly.

ಕೆಂಪು k. n. Redness; red colour; a ruby; *also* -ಕಲ್ಲು. -ಕುಂಟಾಲಗಿಡ. A medicinal shrub, *Gomphia angustifolia.* -ಗೋರಟೆ. The red species of Barleria. -ಜಂಬುನೇರಲು. The fruit of the tree *Eugenia malaccensis.* -ನೆಲಗುಂಬಳ. A water-plant, *Polygonum glabrum.* -ಬಂಗದ ಬಳ್ಳಿ. The creeping plant, *Ipomaea biloba.* -ಬಸಳೆ. The vegetable *Basella rubra.* -ಮಂದಾರ. The red flower of *Bauhinia variegata.* -ಲಾವಗೆ. The rock bush-quail, *Perdicula argoondah.* -ಹುಲಿಗಿಡ. A small shrub, *Phyllanthus rhamnoides.*

ಕೆಂಬಾರ k. n. The redness of evening.

ಕೆಮ್ಮು k. n. A cough; coughing; *also* ಕೆಮ್ಮಲು. v. i. To cough. ಕೆಮ್ಮಿಸು. To cause to cough.

ಕೆಯ್. = ಕೈ, *q. v. and its cpds.* -ತ, -ತೆ, -ಮೆ. An act, performance; deceit, fraud.

ಕೆಯ್ದು. = ಕೈದು. -ಕಾರ. A soldier.

ಕೆಯಿ. (= ಕೈ, *q. v.*) k. *n.* A field.

ಕೆರ 1. ಕೆರವು k. *n.* A leather sandal; a shoe.

ಕೆರ 2. = ಕೆರದು. *P. p. of* ಕೆರೆ *in* ಕೆರಕೊಳ್ಳು.

ಕೆರಕು k. *n.* Roughness (*as* of stone). 2, scab.

ಕೆರಂಟು a. k. *v. i.* To scratch.

ಕೆರಸೆ (= ಗೆರಸೆ) k. *n.* A flat bamboo basket.

ಕೆರಳು k. *v. i.* To cry, shout. 2, to become angry. 3, to increase, *as* pain, *etc.*; to spread, *as* a sore.

ಕೆರೆ 1. k. *v. t.* To scratch, scrape. 2, to shave.

ಕೆರೆ 2. (ರ = ಱ) k. *n.* A tank. -ಕಟ್ಟೆ. The bank of a tank. -ಯೊಡಲು. The inner part of a tank. -ಕಾಲುವೆ. The channel of a tank. -ತೂಬು. The sluice of a tank. -ಹಾವು. A water snake.

ಕೆಲ 1. a. k. *n.* Side; vicinity; the right or left side. -ಕೆಲ. *rep.* Both sides. -ಸಾಗು (-ಆಗು). To go aside. -ಸಾರು. To get out of the way, retire.

ಕೆಲ 2. k. *a.* Some, several, a few. -ಬರು, -ವರು. Some or a few persons. -ವು, -ಹು. Some or a few things.

ಕೆಲಸ k. *n.* Work; occupation; business; affair; employment; act; use. -ಕ್ಕೆ ಬರು, -ಕ್ಕೆ ಬೀಳು. To come to work; to be serviceable. -ಗಳ್ಳ. A lazy man; *f.* -ಗಳ್ಳತಿ, -ಗಳ್ಳಿ. -ತಕ್ಕೊಳ್ಳು. To exact work. -ಹೇಳು. To order a work.

ಕೆಲಸಿ k. *n.* A barber and hair-dresser; *also* -ಗ. 2, a person who works.

ಕೆಲೆ k. *v. i.* To cry for joy. 2, to cry out abusively. -ತ. Abusive vociferation.

ಕೆಲ್ಲ k. *n.* A shiver, splinter.

ಕೆಸರು (ರು=ಱು) k. *n.* Wet soil; mud, mire. -ಗಲ್ಲು. A foundation stone. ಕೆಸರಿಗೆ. The drain of a bathroom.

ಕೆಸವು k. *n.* A mushroom.

ಕೆಸು k. *n.* A stemless plant with large leaves and eatable tubers, the *Cocco, Arum colocasia.*

ಕೆಳ (= ಕೆಳಗು, *q. v.*) k. *a.* Lower. -ಗಡೆ, -ತಟ್ಟು. The lower side; downwards, beneath. -ತನಕ. To the bottom. -ತುಟಿ. The lower lip. -ದವಡೆ. The molars of the lower jaw. -ಭಾಗ. The lower part. -ಹೊಟ್ಟೆ. The abdomen, pelvis.

ಕೆಳಗು, ಕೆಳಗೆ (= ಕೆಳ) k. *n.* The state of being under, below, down or inferior; the bottom. *ad.* Under, down. *Decl.* ಕೆಳಗಿನಿಂದ, ಕೆಳಕ್ಕೆ, ಕೆಳಗಿನ, *etc.* ಕೆಳಗಿಡು. To lay down. ಕೆಳಗಿಳಿ. To descend. -ಬೀಳು. To fall to the ground. -ಮೇಲು ಮಾಡು. To make the lower side upper; to turn. -ಮೇಲೆ. Topsyturvy.

ಕೆಳದಿ (= ಗೆಳತಿ) k. *n.* A female companion.

ಕೆಳರ್ (ಕೆರಳು) a. k. *v. i.* To gape; to open, expand; to blossom. 2, to cry out; to dispute, wrangle.

ಕೆಳೆ (= ಗೆಳೆ) a. k. *n.* Union; friendship; a companion, friend. -ಯ. A male companion. -ತನ. Companionship.

ಕೇಕರ s. *a.* Squint-eyed. *n.* A leer.

ಕೇಕರಿಸು k. *v. i.* To hawk in spitting. ಕೇಕರಿಕೆ. Hawking in spitting.

ಕೇಕು, ಕೇಗು k. *v. i.* To cry as a peacock. *n.* The cry of a peacock.

ಕೇಡಿ k. *n.* One who ruins or is ruined; *also* -ಗ, ಕೇಡುಗ. *Cpds.*: ಕುಲ-, ತಿಳಿ-, ದಾಯ್-, ಬುದ್ಧಿ-, ಮತಿ-, ವಿಚಾರ-, ವ್ರತ-, *etc.* -ಗತನ, -ತನ. Destructiveness, impairedness.

ಕೇಡು k. *n.* Ruin, destruction; mischief; disaster; loss. -ಗಾಲ. A disastrous period. ಕೇಡಾಳಿ. A mischief-maker.

ಕೇಣ k. *n.* Envy, grudge; anger. 2, deliberation. -ಕಾರ. A grudger. -ಸರ. Envy; stubbornness

ಕೇತಕಿ s. *n.* The fragrant screw-pine, *Pandanus odoratissimus.*

ಕೇತನ s. *n.* Summons, invitation; *also* ಕೇತ. 2, business. 3, a place. 4, splendour.

ಕೇತು s. n. A ray of light; brightness. 2, a comet. 3, the descending node. 4, a flag.

ಕೇವಗೆ, ಕೇದಿಗೆ. tb. of ಕೇತಕಿ, q. v.

ಕೇದಾರ s. n. A field; a park. 2, a temple. 3, the body. -ಗೌಳ. N. of a tune.

ಕೇಂದ್ರ s. n. The centre of a circle. 2, a planet's distance from the first point of its orbit.

ಕೇಪಲ k. n. A shrub with red or white flowers, *Ixora coccinea*.

ಕೇಪು f. n. A periodical supply of merchandise.

ಕೇರ m. n. Rubbish, refuse, *etc.* a. Inferior. -ಮಾವು. An inferior mango.

ಕೇರಲ, ಕೇರಳ s. n. The Malabar country.

ಕೇರಿ k. n. A street, lane.

ಕೇರು 1. k. n. The tree *Semecarpus anacardium*, which produces the marking nut. -ಬೀಜ. The marking-nut.

ಕೇರು 2. (ರು = ಱು) k. v. t. To winnow.

ಕೇರೆ k. n. The rat-snake, *Ptyas mucosus; also* -ಹಾವು.

ಕೇಲು k. n. A large earthen water-jar.

ಕೇವಲ s. a. Alone, only, mere. 2, entire, whole, all. 3, pure, unmingled.

ಕೇಶ s. n. The hair of the head. -ಮಾರ್ಜನಿ. A comb. ಕೇಶಿ, ಕೇಶಿಕ. Having much hair.

ಕೇಶವ s. n. Kṛishṇa, Vishṇu. 2, N. of the author of the Šabdamaṇidarpaṇa; *also* ಕೇಶಿರಾಜ.

ಕೇಸರ s. n. The filament of flowers. 2, the plant *Mimusops elengi*. 3, saffron. 4, the mane of a horse or lion.

ಕೇಸರ-ಈ-ಹಿಂದ್ h. n. The empress of Hindusthân, title of Queen Victoria.

ಕೇಸರಿ s. a. Having a mane. 2, saffron coloured. n. A lion. 2, a horse. -ಭತ್ತ. A kind of paddy. -ಭಾತು. Rice seasoned with saffron, sugar, *etc.*

ಕೇಸು a. k. n. Redness. ಕೇಸಕ್ಕಿ. A red kind of rice. ಕೇಸುರಿ. A red flame. ಕೇಸುಳ್ಳಿ. An onion.

ಕೇಳಿ (ಳ = ೞ) a. k. n. A line, series; a group.

ಕೇಳು k. v. i. To hear; to listen to; to heed, mind. v. t. To hear, mind. 2, to ask, beg; to demand. *P. p.* ಕೇಳಿ, ಕೇಳ್ದು. -ವಿಕೆ, ಕೇಳಿಕೆ. Hearing; asking; hearsay. ಕೇಳಿಸು. To cause to hear or listen; to be heard; to hear; to sound.

ಕೈ (=ಕೆಯ್) k. n. The hand (ಹಸ್ತ). 2, an elephant's trunk. 3, a branch, spathe. 4, a staff; a handle; a key. 5, means, instrumentality. 6, handiness. ಕೈಯ *is used for the genitive or dative;* ಕೈಯಿಂದ *instrumental, and* ಕೈಯಲ್ಲಿ, *locative or dative, as:* ನನ್ನ ಕೈಯ ಕೆಳಗೆ, under me; ಅವನ ಕೈಯ ಹೇಳು, tell him; ಅವನ ಕೈಯಿಂದಾಯಿತು, it was done by him; ಅವನ ಕೈಯಲ್ಲಿ ಹೇಳಿದೆ, I told him; ನಿನ್ನ ಕೈಯಲ್ಲಿ ಏನದೆ? what have you got? *etc.* -ಕಟ್ಟು. A kind of ornamental bracelet. -ಕರಣ. A medical treatment. -ಕಷ್ಟ, -ಕೆಲಸ. Handicraft. -ಕಾಗದ. A note of hand; a bond. -ಕಾಲು. Hands and feet. -ಕಾಲು ಕಟ್ಟಿ ಕೊಳ್ಳು. To make obeisance. -ಕಾಲು ಬೀಳು. To fall to one's feet. -ಕೂಲಿ. Working as a day-labourer; wages for such work. -ಕೂಲಿಗಾರ. A day-labourer. -ಕೂಸು. A child in arms. -ಕೆಳಗೆ. Under one's control or authority. -ಕೊಡಲಿ. A small axe. -ಕೊಡು. To help; to deceive. -ಕೊಳ್ಳು. To seize; to receive, obtain, accept, adopt; to undertake; to mind (ಸ್ವೀಕರಿಸು, ಅಂಗೀಕರಿಸು, *etc.*). -ಕೋಲು. A walking stick. -ಕೆಲಸ. Hand-stock. -ಗಡ. A temporary loan given without bond or interest. -ಗಂಟು. A purse of money for one's own use. -ಗತ್ತಿ. A small knife. -ಗಡಕ. A male pilferer; *f.* -ಗಡಕಿ. -ಗಾಣಿಕೆ. A present given with the hand. -ಗಾಯು. To protect. -ಗಾರ. A clever man. -ಗಾರಿಕೆ. The arts of industry, manufacture. -ಗುದ್ದಲಿ. A small hoe. -ಗುರುತು. A person's signature. -ಗೂಡಿಸು. To accomplish. -ಗೂಡಿ ಬರು, -ಗೂಡು. To be obtained; to succeed. -ಗೆಡು. To lose, be defeated. -ಗೊಡು. To give the hand; to stretch the hand for help or promise. -ಚಪ್ಪರ. A shrine wherein idols are carried about. -ಚಪ್ಪಳಿ, -ಚಪ್ಪಳೆ. Clapping the hands. -ಚಳಕ. Dexterity, sleight of hand. -ಚಳಕು. Cramp in the hand. -ಚಾಚು. To stretch out the hand. -ಚಿಟಿಕೆ, -ಚಿಟುಕು. A snap with the fingers. -ಚೀಟು. A note of hand. -ಚೀಲ. A glove; a small bag. -ಜೋಡಿಸು, -ಮುಗಿ. To join the hands in greeting. -ತಟ್ಟು. To clap the hands; to touch pieces of money in counting; to beckon. -ತಪ್ಪು. A mistake; a slip of the pen; to fall from the hand. -ತಾಳ. A kind of cymbal. -ತಾಳು. An instrument to move the inner latch of a door from out-side. -ತುತ್ತು. A handful of food. -ತೊಡಿಗೆ. Ornaments of the hand. -ದಸ್ತು. A deal of cards for games. -ದುಡುಕು. To grasp; to thrust the hand into; seizing. -ದೊಡ್ಡದು ಮಾಡು. To be liberal in giving alms. -ನೀಡು. To stretch out the hand. -ನೀರು. Water poured over the hands of the marrying couple. -ನೆರವು. Help, assistance. -ಪಾವಡ. A handkerchief; *also* -ವಟ್ಟ, -ವಸ್ತ್ರ. -ಪಿಡಿ. A handle; a looking glass; a handbook. -ಬಟ್ಟಲು. A small cup; a scoop. -ಬದಲು. A loan (of money). -ಬರಹ. Handwriting. -ಬಳೆ. A bracelet. -ಬಾಚಿ. A small adze. -ಬಾಳು. A sickle. -ಬಿಡು. To let loose one's hand; to cease to assist; to desert. -ಮಗ್ಗ. A hand-loom. -ಮರೆ. To be confounded or amazed; an attitude in dancing. -ಮಸಕು. Black dirt on the hand; a slow poison. -ಮಾಟ. A hand-gesture. -ಮಾಡು. To make signs with the hand; to rebel; to brandish; to bargain. -ಮಾರು. A fathom; offering of goods for sale at the doors. -ಮಿಗು. To become excessive. -ಮೀರು. To exceed, surpass, go beyond; to get out of one's power. -ಮುಟ್ಟು. To touch with the hand; small utensils. -ಮುರಿ. The hand to break; *fig.* a plain bracelet, *also* -ಮುರಿಗೆ. -ಯಕ್ಷರ (-ಅಕ್ಷರ). Writ, hand-writing; signature. -ಯಾಡಿಸು. To move with the hand; to rub gently; to stroke. -ಯಾರೆ. With full and open hands; with a prompt hand. -ಯಾರೈಕೆ. Nursing with one's own hand, supporting by one's own means. -ಯಾಸೆ (-ಆಸೆ). Bribery; a bribe. -ಯಾಳು (-ಆಳು). An assistant, servant. -ಯೆಣ್ಣೆ. Oil extracted by hand. -ಯೆತ್ತು. To raise the open hand. -ಯೊಡ್ಡು (-ಒಡ್ಡು). To hold out the open hands to receive anything. -ಲಾಗು (-ಆಗು). To be produced by the hand; to be practicable; to be able, useful. -ವಶ. Actual possession. -ವಶವಾಗು. To come into one's power or possession. -ವಾರ. A pair of compasses; praise, eulogy. -ವಾರಿಸು. To praise. -ಬೀಸು. To swing the arms when walking. -ಸನ್ನೆ. A sign made with the hand. -ಸಾಗು. To be possible. -ಸಾಲೆ. A veranda. -ಸೂರೆ. Spoil, plunder. -ಸೆರೆ. Arrest, captivity. -ಸೊಡರು. A small lamp. -ಹಚ್ಚು, -ಹಾಕು. To put the hand to. -ಗೆ ಬರು. To be obtained; to become useful. -ಯಲ್ಲಿ. In the hand, *etc.* -ಯೊಳಗೆ. In or into the power; under the control.

ಕೈ 2. k. *n.* Bitterness.

ಕೈಕೊಳ್ಳು *see s.* ಕೈ.

ಕೈಂಕರ್ಯ (*fr.* ಕಿಂಕರ) s. *n.* Service; servitude.

ಕೈದಿ h. *n.* A prisoner.

ಕೈದು 1. k. *n.* A weapon.

ಕೈದು 2. h. *n.* Imprisonment; restraint; arrest. -ಖಾನೆ. A prison. -ಮಾಡು. To put a stop to; to arrest.

ಕೈಫಿಯತು h. *n.* Statement; an affair, case; a suit, plaint.

ಕೈಲಾಸ s. n. N. of a mountain in the Himâlaya range, the seat of Kuvêra and paradise of Šiva. -ಗತ. A lost debt. -ವಾಸಿ. A deceased worshipper of Šiva.

ಕೈವಲ್ಯ (fr. ಕೇವಲ) s. n. Perfect exemption from further transmigration, absorption in the supreme soul. 2, pureness.

ಕೊಕ್ಕರಿಬಿಕ್ಕರಿ (= ಕಕ್ಕರಬಿಕ್ಕರಿ) k. n. Crookedness, as in writing.

ಕೊಕ್ಕರಿಸು k. v. i. To chuckle, giggle. 2, (fr. ಕುಚು) to shrink, shrug as from cold, fear, etc. 3, to menace, abuse.

ಕೊಕ್ಕರೆ k. n. A crane.

ಕೊಕ್ಕು (fr. ಕೊಂಕು) k. n. The beak or bill.

ಕೊಕ್ಕೆ k. n. Crookedness; a crook; a hook. -ಕೋಲು. A hook; a walking stick with a bent handle. -ಮನುಷ್ಯ. A perverse man. -ಮೊಳೆ. A hooked nail.

ಕೊಗ್ಗ (= ಕೊಂಗ) k. n. Crookedness. 2, a man with uncouth voice.

ಕೊಗ್ಗಿ, ಕೊಗ್ಗಲಿ, ಕೊಗ್ಗೆ k. n. A very common under-shrub, *Tephrosia purpurea*.

ಕೊಂಕಣ k. n. The Concan country of the western coast. -ಸ್ಥ, ಕೊಂಕಣಿ, ಕೊಂಕಣಿಗ. A Concan Brâhmaṇa.

ಕೊಂಕು k. v. i. To be bent, crooked, curved, deformed; to become perverse, untrue, etc. n. Crookedness, etc. -ಕೊರತೆ. Wrongs and defects. -ಗುರುಳು, -ಗೂದಲು. Curled hair. -ನುಡಿ. An altered voice or speech.

ಕೊಂಕುಳು (= ಕಂಕುಳು) k. n. The armpit.

ಕೊಂಗ. = ಕೊಗ್ಗ, q. v. -ಮಂಗ. A buffoon. -ತನ. Buffoonery.

ಕೊಂಬೆ (= ಕೊಂಬೆ) k. n. The branch of a tree.

ಕೊಚ್ಚಿ k. n. Cochin on the Malabar coast.

ಕೊಚ್ಚು 1. k. v. t. To sift flour on a small fan. 2, (= ಕೊಚುರ) to cut up, to chop. n. Cuttings, chips. 2, powder, dust. ಕೊಚ್ಚಿಕೆ. The act of cutting.

ಕೊಚ್ಚು 2. k. v. i. To speak much, prattle, brag.

ಕೊಚ್ಚೆ k. n. Mud, mire.

ಕೊಜ್ಜ h. n. A eunuch.

ಕೊಂಚ k. n. A little; littleness; inferiority. -ದವ. An insignificant man.

ಕೊಟಾರ (= ಕೊಟ್ಟಾರ) k. n. A threshing floor.

ಕೊಟಿಗೆ. = ಕೊಟ್ಟಿಗೆ, q. v.

ಕೊಟ್ಟ 1. (= ಗೊಟ್ಟ) k. n. A bamboo tube. 2, an extremity. -ಕೊನೆ. The extreme point.

ಕೊಟ್ಟ 2. f. n. A fort. -ಗಾರ. A man of a fort.

ಕೊಟ್ಟಗೆ (= ಕೊಟಿಗೆ, ಕೊಟ್ಟಿಗೆ. tb. of ಕುಟುಂಬ) n. A stall, out-house; a barn, room, etc.

ಕೊಟ್ಟಣ (fr. ಕುಟ್ಟು) k. n. Beating the husk from paddy, etc.

ಕೊಟ್ಟಾರ (tb. of ಕೋಷ್ಠಾಗಾರ) n. A threshing floor. ಕೊಟ್ಟಾರಿ. The officer in charge of a granary; a steward.

ಕೊಟ್ಟಿ h. a. False, counterfeit, forged; vicious, bad. -ಕತಬಿ. A forged bond. -ನಡತೆ. A bad conduct. -ರೂಪಾಯಿ. A counterfeit rupee.

ಕೊಟ್ಟಿಗೆ. = ಕೊಟ್ಟಗೆ, q. v.

ಕೊಟ್ಟು 1. P. p. of ಕೊಡು.

ಕೊಟ್ಟು 2. k. n. A point; a nipple; a crest, a head-ornament.

ಕೊಟ್ಟೆ k. n. The stone or kernel of fruit.

ಕೊಠಡಿ h. n. A chamber, room.

ಕೊಡ (tb. of ಕುಟ) n. A pitcher, pot. -ಪಾನ. A kŏḍa of copper or brass.

ಕೊಡಕೆ, ಕೊಡಂಕೆ a. k. n. The ear. -ಮುರು. An ear-ring.

ಕೊಡಗು k. n. The Coorg country. -ಕತ್ತಿ. A Coorg-knife, a broad sword. ಕೊಡಗ. A Coorg man.

ಕೊಡಗೆ k. n. A gift, grant.

ಕೊಡಚಿಗಿಡ k. n. A large prickly shrub, *Zizyphus xylopyrus*.

ಕೊಡಚು k. v. t. To remove, rub off, *as* ear-wax or impurities.

ಕೊಡತ k. n. The pain of a sore. 2, severe itching. 3, a stick tied to a dog's neck.

ಕೊಡತಿ (*f*. ಕುಡು) k. n. A wooden hammer.

ಕೊಡವು, ಕೊಸವು k. v. t. To scatter or throw about; to shake.

ಕೊಡಲಿ (= ಕೊಡ್ಲಿ. *tb. of* ಕುಠಾರ) n. An axe, hatchet.

ಕೊಡಸಿಗೆ k. n. The small tree *Cluytia collina*. 2, (*tb. of* ಕುಟಜಕ) the medicinal tree *Wrightia antidysenterica*.

ಕೊಡಿ k. n. Strength, stoutness. -ಕಲ್ಲು. Stone-like firmness in one's health.

ಕೊಡಿಗೆ. = ಕೊಡಗೆ, *q. v.* -ಮಾನ್ಯ. Land free of rent.

ಕೊಡು (*cf*. ಕುಡು) k. v. t. To give; to present, bestow, grant. *P. p.* ಕೊಟ್ಟು. ಕೊಡು *is often added to other verbs without altering their meaning, as:* ಕಳುಹಿಸಿಕೊಡು. = ಕಳುಹಿಸು; ವಿಭಾಗಿಸಿಕೊಡು. = ವಿಭಾಗಿಸು, *etc. Affixed to infinitive forms of other verbs it denotes* to allow, permit, *as:* ಮಾಡಗೊಡು, ಬರಗೊಡು, to allow to do, come, *etc.* ಕೊಡಿಸು. To cause to give. ಕೊಡು, -ವಿಕೆ. Giving. -ಕೊಳ್ಳುವದು. Giving and receiving.

ಕೊಡೆ k. n. An umbrella; a parasol. v. t. To hollow, scrape, scoop. 2, to ache.

ಕೊಡ್ಡ k. n. A stupid man, a clown.

ಕೊಡ್ಗಿ. = ಕೊಡಲಿ, *q. v.*

ಕೊಣ (= ಕೊಳ) k. n. A pond, tank.

ಕೊಣತ k. n. A club swung in the hands for exercise.

ಕೊಣಬಿಗೆ k. n. A round wooden dish to knead dough *etc.* in.

ಕೊಂಡ 1. k. n. A hill, mountain. -ಮುಸುಡಿ. A large black-faced monkey.

ಕೊಂಡ 2. *tb. of* ಕುಂಡ, *q. v.* -ಹಬ್ಬ. A feast in honour of Vîrabhadra.

ಕೊಂಡಾಡು (*see s.* ಕೊಳ್ಳು) k. v. t. To applaud, praise, glorify.

ಕೊಂಗಿ k. n. A hook; the link of a padlock. 2, the sting of a scorpion. -ಸು. To slander, defame.

ಕೊಂಡು. *P. p. of* ಕೊಳ್ಳು, *q. v.*

ಕೊಂಡೆ k. n. A chaplet of pearls. 2, a tassel.

ಕೊಂಡೆಗ, ಕೊಂಡೆಯ k. n. Calumny, slander, defamation. 2, a slanderer, defamer; *also* -ಗಾರ; *f.* ಕೊಂಡೆಗಿತ್ತಿ.

ಕೊತ್ವಾಲ h. n. The chief officer of a town police. 2, the overseer of a travellers' bangalow.

ಕೊತ್ತಳ k. n. A bulwark, bastion.

ಕೊತ್ತಿ k. n. A cat.

ಕೊತ್ತು k. v. t. To chop, mince. n. A bunch, cluster. 2, a mark for a liquid measure.

ಕೊತ್ತುಂಬರಿ (*tb. of* ಕುಸ್ತುಂಬುರಿ) n. Coriander seed.

ಕೊದಲು k. v. i. To hesitate in speaking, to stammer; to mutter. n. Stammering.

ಕೊನರು a. k. v. i. To sprout; to arise, extend. n. A shoot, sprout; the film of a lotus.

ಕೊನೆ k. v. i. To succeed in an object. n. An extremity; a point; a top; an end; a branch. *Cpds.:* ಮರದ-, ಪಾದದ-, ತುಟಿಯ-, ಬಿಲ್ಲಿನ-, *etc.* -ಗಾಣಿಸು. To accomplish. -ಗಾಣು. To be accomplished.

ಕೊಂತ (*tb. of* ಕುಂತ) n. A spear, lance. -ಕಾರ. A spearman.

ಕೊಂದು. *P. p. of* ಕೊಲ್ಲು, *q. v.*

ಕೊಂದೆ k. n. The tree *Cassia fistula.*

ಕೊಪ್ಪ, ಕೊಪ್ಪಲ k. n. A hamlet, village; *affixed to village-names.*

ಕೊಪ್ಪರಿಗೆ (*tb. of* ಖರ್ಪರ) n. A metal boiler.

ಕೊಪ್ಪು k. n. The notched extremity of a bow or horn. 2, a woman's knot of hair. 3, an ear-ornament.

ಕೊಪ್ಪೆ k. n. The hood made of a cumbly.

ಕೊಬರಿ, ಕೊಬ್ಬರಿ k. n. The kernel of the cocoanut. -ಚಟ್ನಿ. A kind of chutney. -ತುಪ್ಪ. Congealed cocoanut oil. -ಬಟ್ಟಲು.

Half of a cocoanut kernel. -ಎಣ್ಣೆ. Cocoanut oil.

ಕೊಬ್ಬು k. v. i. To grow fat, thick, *etc.*; to be rank, luxuriant; to become proud, insolent. *n.* Fat; luxuriance; pride. ಕೊಬ್ಬಿಗ. A proud man.

ಕೊಮೆ k. v. i. To begin to burn, *as* fire or anger.

ಕೊಂಪೆ 1. k. n. A small bundle or load of thorny twigs. 2, a thorn bush.

ಕೊಂಪೆ 2. k. n. A small hamlet; *cf.* ಕೊಪ್ಪ.

ಕೊಂಬು 1. k. v. t. To seize, take. ಕೊಂಬ.= ಕೊಳ್ಳುವ, *q. v.* ಕೊಂಬೋಣ. Taking.

ಕೊಂಬು 2. k. n. A horn of animals; a tusk. 2, ಉ or its embodied form ು 3, a branch of a tree; *also* ಕೊಂಬೆ.

ಕೊಂಬೆ k. n. A branch.

ಕೊಮ್ಮೆ k. n. A corn-bin. 2, hog-weed, *Boerhavia procumbens.*

ಕೊಯಿ, ಕೊಯ್ಯು k. v. t. To cut; to pluck, *as* fruit, *etc.* v. i. To crop, reap. *P. ps.* ಕೊಯಿದು, ಕೊಯ್ದು. ಕೊಯಿಕ. A cutter. ಕೊಯಿಕತನ, ಕೊಯಿತ. Cutting. -ಲು. Reaping, plucking. ಕೊಯಿಸು. To cause to cut.

ಕೊರ 1. k. n. *The sound produced by hoarseness;* the pur, *as* of a cat (*see* ಕೊತ್ತಿ). -ಎನ್ನು, -ಗುಟ್ಟು. To pur.

ಕೊರ 2. (ರ=ಱ. *cf.* ಕೊರೆ 1) k. n. Cutting. -ಕಲ್ಲು. A rugged stone.

ಕೊರಕಲು (ರ=ಱ) k. n. A cut, channel, the bed of a stream. ಕೊರಕು. To bite.

ಕೊರಗಣೆ k. n. Sorrow.

ಕೊರಗು k. v. i. To become sapless; to shrivel; to wane; to sorrow. *n.* Sorrow. ಕೊರಗಿಸು. To cause to be sapless.

ಕೊರಚ (ರ=ಱ) k. n. A thievish wandering hill-tribe.

ಕೊರಚು, ಕೊರಚಾಡು (ರ=ಱ) k. v. t. To upbraid, revile; to speak much and uselessly. ಕೊರಚಾಟ. Upbraiding; mocking; reviling; useless talk.

ಕೊರಟು k. n. The state of being stunted or checked in growth. -ಬೀಳು. To get stunted.

ಕೊರಡು k. n. The trunk of a lopped tree; a stump, lop. 2, a clod-crusher.

ಕೊರಡೆ (ರ=ಱ) f. n. A whip.

ಕೊರತೆ (ರ=ಱ) k. n. Deficiency; want; loss; defect; fault. -ಪಡು. To feel a want; to be poor. -ಬರು, -ಬೀಳು. Deficiency or loss to come about.

ಕೊರನಾರಿಗಡ್ಡೆ k. n. A kind of sedge, *Cyperus hexastachyus.*

ಕೊರಪ k. n. A curry-comb.

ಕೊರಲು.=ಕೊರಳು, *q. v.*

ಕೊರಲೆ (ರ=ಱ) k. n. A kind of millet, *Panicum italicum.* 2, a kind of ant.

ಕೊರವ (ರ=ಱ) k. n. A man of a tribe so called who make baskets, mats, *etc.; f.* -ತಿ, *and* ಕೊರವಂಜಿ, who is also a fortune-teller.

ಕೊರಳು k. n. The throat; the neck; voice. -ಕಟ್ಟಿಕೊಳ್ಳು. To embrace one's neck from love. -ಕೊಯಿಕ. A cut-throat. -ಪಟ್ಟಿ. A collar.

ಕೊರಿ, ಕೊರೆ 1. (ರಿ, ರೆ=ಱಿ, ಱೆ) k. v. t. To cut, *as* wood, letters, *etc.*; to break, bore, *as* a hole; to excavate, *as* running water the soil; to pierce *as* cold. 2, to diminish. 3, to whirl, rave. *n.* Cutting; a cut off piece. -ತ, ಕೊರತ. Cutting; piercing of cold.

ಕೊರಿಪಿರಿ f. n. Annoyance, trouble.

ಕೊರೆ 2. (ರೆ=ಱೆ) k. n. Smallness, deficiency, defect. 2, rest, remainder. 3, a rambler. *P. p.* -ದು, ಕೊರದು. -ದಿನ. A day of absence. -ಪ್ರಾಣ. The point of death. -ಸಂಬಳ. The rest of pay.

ಕೊಲಿಕೆ k. n. A clasp, hook, *etc.*

ಕೊಲಿಮೆ, ಕೊಲುಮೆ.=ಕುಲಿಮೆ. k. n. A forge.

ಕೊಲು.=ಕೊಲ್ಲು, *q. v.*

ಕೊಲೆ k. n. Killing, murder, slaughter. -ಗ, -ಗಡಿಕ, -ಗೆಡುಕ, -ಗಾರ. A murderer. -ಪಾತಕ. Manslaughter.

ಕೊಲ್ಲಟಿಗ k. n. A pole-dancer, rope-dancer; *f.* ಕೊಲ್ಲಟಗಿತ್ತಿ.

ಕೊಲ್ಲಣಿಗೆ a. k. n. Playing, play, performance.

ಕೊಲ್ಲಾರ, ಕೊಲ್ಲಾರಿ, ಕೊಲ್ಲಾರು k. n. A cart drawn by oxen.

ಕೊಲ್ಲಿ k. n. A bend, curve; a nook; a gulf, bay. ಕೊಲ್ಲೆ. Bend.

ಕೊಲ್ಲು k. v. t. To kill, slay, murder. P. p. ಕೊಂದು. -ವಿಕೆ. Killing. -ವವ, -ಳ. A murderer.

ಕೊಸರು k. v. i. To spread, *as* a sore; to become overbearing; to disentangle one's self forcibly from another's hold. v. t. To desire; to demand an article gratis or into the bargain. n. Anything given to boot in buying.

ಕೊಳ (=ಕೊಣ) k. n. A pond.

ಕೊಳಕು (ಳ=ೞ) k. n. The state of decay, rottenness, putridity. ಕೊಳಕ. A dirty man; a decrepit man; f. ಕೊಳಕಿ. -ಮಂಡಲ, -ಹಾವು. The chain viper. -ತನ. Filthiness.

ಕೊಳಕೆ, ಕೊಳ್ಕೆ k. n. The third crop of rice.

ಕೊಳಗ 1. k. n. A measure of grain = 4 baḷḷas. 2, a large metal vessel.

ಕೊಳಗ 2. k. n. The hoof of a beast.

ಕೊಳಗುಳಿಕೆ, ಕೊಳವಳಿಕೆ k. n. A spiny herb *Barleria longifolia.*

ಕೊಳಚೆ, ಕೊಳಚಿ (ಳ=ೞ) (*cf.* ಕೊಳಕು) k. n. The state of being impure, stinking, muddy, *etc.*; soft mud.

ಕೊಳತು. =ಕೊಳೆತು (ಳ=ೞ). P. p. of ಕೊಳೆ.

ಕೊಳಲು (ಳ=ೞ) k. n. A flute, fife.

ಕೊಳವಿ, ಕೊಳವೆ (ಳ=ೞ) k. n. A tube, blow-pipe.

ಕೊಳಸು. =ಕೊಳೆಸು, q. v.

ಕೊಳು. =ಕೊಳ್ಳು, q. v.

ಕೊಳೆ (ಳೆ=ೞೆ) k. v. i. To wear out, *as* cloth; to decay, rot, spoil; to spoil, become putrid; to wither; to become lean. P. ps. ಕೊಳೆತು, ಕೊಳತು. n. Dirt; impurity; mud; bodily excretion; hinderance, detention. -ಹಾಕು. To rot; to detain. ಕೊಳಸು, ಕೊಳೆಸು. To cause to rot.

ಕೊಳ್ಳ k. n. A depth, the cleft of a rock, cave, *etc.*

ಕೊಳ್ಳಿ k. n. A fire-brand. -ದೆವ್ವ, -ಪಿಶಾಚ. An *ignis fatuus.*

ಕೊಳ್ಳು k. v. t. To seize; to take; to accept; to take for one's own use or benefit; to obtain; to buy; to undertake. P. p. ಕೊಂಡು. *Imp. sing.* ಕೋ. *Pres. part.* ಕೊಳ್ಳುತ್ತ, ಕೋತ. ಕೊಳ್ಳು *as the second member of a compound:* to get, obtain, acquire, hold on, *as: rel. pr. part.* ಬರ-, ಮಾಡ-. ಕೊಂಡು-. To buy. ಕೊಂಡು ಬರು. To bring. ಕೊಂಡು ಹೋಗು. To take away. ಕೊಂಡಾಟ. Praise. ಕೊಂಡಾಡು. To praise, reverence. ಕೊಳ್ಳುವಿಕೆ. Taking, *etc.*

ಕೊಳ್ಳೆ k. n. Pillage, plunder. -ಗಾರ. A plunderer.

ಕೋ k. *An imp. sing. of* ಕೊಳ್ಳು.

ಕೋಕನದ s. n. The red lotus.

ಕೋಕಿಲ. =ಕೋಗಿಲೆ, q. v.

ಕೋಗಿಲೆ (*tb. of* ಕೋಕಿಲ) n. The Indian cuckoo, *Cuculus indicus.* -ಯ ಗಿಡ. A plant of which the leaves are used for plates, *etc.*

ಕೋಗೀರು h. n. A cushion used as a saddle.

ಕೋಚು (=ಕೋಸು) k. n. -ಭಟ್ಟ. A foolish, stupid bhaṭṭa; a N.

ಕೋಟ s. n. Crookedness. 2, a shed, hut. 3, a fort. -ಡಿ. A room; *also* ಕೊಟ್ಟಡಿ.

ಕೋಟರ s. n. The hollow of a tree.

ಕೋಟಲೆ k. n. Trouble, affliction, pain. -ಪಡು. To suffer pain. ಕೋಟಲಿಗ. A troublesome man.

ಕೋಟಿ s. n. A crore or ten millions. 2, the point or extreme part. 3, the edge of a sword. 4, an angle. 5, a countless number. -ಪಾತ್ರ. A rudder. ಕೋಟೀರ. A crest. ಕೋಟೀಶ. A harrow. ಕೋಟ್ಯನುಕೋಟಿ, ಕೋಟ್ಯಂತರ. Countless.

ಕೋಟೆ (*tb. of* ಕೋಟ) n. A wall round a town, rampart; a fort. -ತೆನೆ,

-ಕೊಂಬೆ. The battlements of a fort. -ಗಸ್ತು. A fort patrole. -ಗಾವಲು. A fort-guard.

ಕೋಟ್ಟಾರ f. n. A stronghold of thieves. 2, the steps of a pond.

ಕೋಠಿ f. n. A granary; a factory, warehouse.

ಕೋಡಗ k. n. A monkey, ape. -ಚೇಷ್ಟೆ. An apish trick.

ಕೋಡಂಗಿ k. n. An apish man; a buffoon. -ತನ. Buffoonery.

ಕೋಡಬಳೆ k. n. A kind of fried cake in the form of a ring.

ಕೋಡಿ 1. k. n. An outlet or weir of a tank. -ಕಟ್ಟು. To stop the outlet. -ಕಡಿ. To open the outlet.

ಕೋಡಿ 2. k. n. Deficiency, defect, want. 2, number 20.

ಕೋಡಿ 3. k. n. A kind of a flag with an image of a demi-god set up on a post before a temple. -ಹಬ್ಬ. A festival in connection with it.

ಕೋಡು 1. a. k. v. i. To be cool. 2, to fear. 3, to shrink. n. Coldness. 2, fear. 3, shrinking.

ಕೋಡು 2. k. n. A horn of animals; a tusk. 2, the peak of a hill. 3, a branch. -ಕಳ್ಳಿ. The milkhedge. -ಗಲ್ಲು. The peak of a hill. -ಮುರುಕಬಳ್ಳಿ. The creeper *Cynanchum pauciflorum.*

ಕೋಡೆ k. n. West wind; the hot season. -ಗದ್ದೆ. A field yielding crop in the hot season.

ಕೋಣ 1. k. n. A male buffalo. 2, a foolish man. -ದ ಬಳ್ಳಿ. A leafless, shrubby creeper, *Sarcostemma intermedium.* -ತಿದ್ದು, -ಸಾಧಕ ಮಾಡು. To train a buffalo.

ಕೋಣ 2. s. n. An angle, a corner.

ಕೋಣೆ k. n. An inner apartment or chamber, room. 2, a kitchen.

ಕೋತ k. n. N. of a low-caste tribe on the Nilagiri. 2, (f.) deficiency, reduction. -ಗಿರಿ. N. of one of the Nilagiri hills.

ಕೋತಂಬರಿ (*tb. of* ಕುಸ್ತುಂಬುರಿ) n. Coriander.

ಕೋತಲು h. n. Saving, laying up. -ಸಂಬಳ. An extra pay.

ಕೋತಿ k. n. A monkey, ape. -ಚೇಷ್ಟೆ. A monkey's trick.

ಕೋತು m. n. Farming, tenanting. 2, (= ಬಾರಕೋತು) barracks.

ಕೋದಂಡ k. n. A rope for punishment, suspended in schools, on which a boy is tied up with his hands clasped and which he is not permitted to loose.

ಕೋನ (*tb. of* ಕೋಣ 2) n. An angle, corner. ಕೋನೇರಿ, ಕೋನೇರು. A stone built tank with steps on all sides.

ಕೋಪ s. n. Passion, wrath, anger. -ಗಾರ. A passionate man; *f.* -ಗಾತಿ. ಕೋಪಿಷ್ಠ. Very passionate; an irascible man; *f.* ಕೋಪಿಷ್ಠಳು. -ಶಾಂತ ಮಾಡು. To pacify, appease. ಕೋಪಿಸು. To become angry. ಕೋಪೋದ್ರೇಕ. Excess of passion.

ಕೋಮಟಿ k. n. A Vaiśya shopkeeper. 2, a miser; *also* -ಗ; *f.* -ಗಿತ್ತಿ. -ತನ. A Kômaṭi's profession; covetousness.

ಕೋಮಲ s. a. Tender, soft; sweet; pleasing. -ತೆ. Softness, *etc.*

ಕೋಯಷ್ಟಿ s. n. The lapwing; the paddy bird.

ಕೋರ. = ಖೋರ, *q. v.*

ಕೋರಕ s. n. A bud.

ಕೋರಂಗಿ s. n. Small cardamoms.

ಕೋರಂಬು f. n. A frontlet of idols.

ಕೋರಯಿಸು k. v. i. To be dazzled.

ಕೋರಾ f. n. Unbleached cotton cloth. *a.* New. ಕೋರಾನ್ನ. Undressed corn.

ಕೋರಿ (ರ=ಱ) k. n. A rag; a worn out blanket. -ಸೆಟ್ಟಿ. A Lingâyta hawker or tradesman. -ಹಣ್ಣು. A ripe mulberry. -ಹುಳ. A caterpillar.

ಕೋರಿಕೆ (ರ=ಱ) k. n. Wish, desire, longing, hope. -ಈಡೇರು, -ತೀರು, -ನೆರವೇರು. A wish to be gratified.

ಕೋರು 1. (ರು=ಱು) k. v. t. To wish, desire, hope.

ಕೋರು 2. (*fr.* ಕೊರೆ) k. *n.* A part, portion, share in cultivation, *etc.*

ಕೋರೆ 1. k. *n.* Crookedness; perverseness. -ಪಟ. A small flag.

ಕೋರೆ 2. (ರೆ = ಱೆ, *fr.* ಕೊರೆ) k. *n.* Cutting; sharpness. 2, a tusk; a long tooth, fang. -ದಾಡೆ, -ಹಲ್ಲು. A pointed tooth. -ಮೀಸೆ. Pointed whiskers. -ರುಮಾಲು. A turban with pointed foldings.

ಕೋರ್ಟು f. *n.* A court.

ಕೋಲ k. *n.* Decoration; figure, form, *as* of masks, dresses, *etc.*, as used in devil dances. 2, public procession.

ಕೋಲಾರ k. *n.* Colar. -ತಟ್ಟು. A country pony.

ಕೋಲಾಹಲ s. *n.* A loud noise; an uproar.

ಕೋಲಿ k. *n.* A stubble of jôḷa.

ಕೋಲು k. *n.* A stick, staff, rod; a measure of length. ಕೋಲರಗು. A stick of sealing wax. ಕೋಲಾಟ. A children's play with alternate motions and mutually striking small sticks. ಕೋಲಾಡು. To play as above. -ಊರು. To lean on a stick. -ಕುದುರೆ. A stick on which boys ride; a crutch. -ಗಳ್ಳಿ. A species of leafless milk-hedge.

ಕೋಲುಕಾರ k. *n.* A peon.

ಕೋವ a. k. *n.* A potter.

ಕೋವಿ k. *n.* A tube. 2, a gun, matchlock. -ಹಾರಿಸು. To shoot.

ಕೋವಿದ s. *a.* Skilled, experienced, wise; *f.* ಕೋವಿದೆ.

ಕೋವೆ 1. k. *n.* Dyspepsy. 2, a boil on the head of children. 3, the climbing plant *Bryonia grandis* with red fruit. 4, a crucible.

ಕೋವೆ 2. h. *n.* A kind of condensed milk.

ಕೋಶ, ಕೋಷ s. *n.* A case; a sheath, scabbard; a pod. 2, a storehouse, treasury. 3, a vocabulary, dictionary; *cf.* ಅಮರ-. -ಗೃಹ. A treasury.

ಕೋಷ್ಠ s. *n.* The intestines. 2, an apartment; a granary. 3, (= ಕುಷ್ಠ) leprosy. 4, a square, *as* in tables of calculation; *also* ಕೋಷ್ಠಕ.

ಕೋಸಂಬರಿ. = ಕೋಸುಂಬರಿ, *q. v.*

ಕೋಸು 1. k. *n.* The state of being crooked or curved, *as* that of a wall, road, *etc.* -ಗಣ್ಣು. A squint eye.

ಕೋಸು 2. h. *n.* Cabbage. 2, (*tb. of* ಕ್ರೋಶ) a distance of 3 miles.

ಕೋಸುಂಬರಿ f. *n.* Raw fruit, *etc.*, preserved *as* a seasoning.

ಕೋಳ k. *n.* Stocks for criminals.

ಕೋಳಿ (ಳಿ = ಱಿ) k. *n.* A cock; a hen; a fowl in general. -ಕಟ್ಟು. To set cocks a fighting. -ಕೋಡು. Calicut. -ಗರಿ. A quill. -ಗೂಡು. A hen's nest. -ತತ್ತಿ. A fowl's egg. -ಹುಂಜ. A cock.

ಕೋಳು k. *n.* Seizure; pillage; calumny.

ಕೋಳೆ (ಳೆ = ಱೆ) k. *n.* Thick phlegm.

ಕೌ. *For words beginning with this letter and not found below, see under* ಕವ *or* ಕವು.

ಕೌಂಗು (*tb. of* ಕ್ರಮುಕ) *n.* The betel-nut tree, *Areca catechu.*

ಕೌಟಿಲ್ಯ s. *n.* Crookedness; falsehood; deceit, *etc.*; *also* ಕೌಟಿಲ್ಯತೆ.

ಕೌಂಡನ್ಯ, ಕೌಂಡಿನ್ಯ s. *n.* N. of a sage; N. of a grammarian.

ಕೌತುಕ (*fr.* ಕುತುಕ) s. *n.* Curiosity; a wonder; surprise, astonishment. 2, eagerness. 3, joy, pleasure; sport, gaity.

ಕೌತೂಹಲ (*fr.* ಕುತೂಹಲ) s. *n.* Eagerness, vehemence; curiosity.

ಕೌಂತೇಯ (*fr.* ಕುಂತಿ) s. *n.* N. of Sahadêva, Yudhishṭhira, Bhîma, and Arjuna.

ಕೌಪೀನ s. *n.* A small piece of cloth worn over the privities. 2, a wrong act.

ಕೌಮಾರ (*fr.* ಕುಮಾರ) s. *a.* Juvenile. *n.* Childhood.

ಕೌಮುದಿ (*fr.* ಕುಮುದ) s. *n.* Moonlight.

ಕೌರವ s. *n.* A descendant of Kuru.

ಕೌಲಿಕ (*fr.* ಕುಲ) s. *a.* Belonging to a family; ancestral. *n.* A heretic, impostor. 2, (= ಕೌಲೀನ) rumour, report.

ಕೌಲೀನ s. *a.* Belonging to a noble family. *n.* A good report.

ಕೌಲು h. *n.* Agreement. 2, safeguard to pass, *as* granted to an enemy. 3, stipulated tribute. -ಕರಾರು. An agreement.

ಕೌಶಲ (*fr.* ಕುಶಲ) s. *n.* Well-being, happiness. 2, skilfulness, cleverness.

ಕೌಶಿಕ s. *n.* Indra. 2, N. of Viśvâmitra. 3, a snake-catcher. 4, an owl.

ಕೌಸಲ್ಯೆ s. *n.* The wife of Daśaratha and mother of Râma.

ಕೌಸ್ತುಭ s. *n.* The jewel suspended on Vishṇu's or Kṛishṇa's breast.

ಕೌಳಿಕ (*tb. of* ಕೌಟಿಕ) *n.* A butcher. 2, deceit.

ಕ್ಕೆ k. *A dative affix, as:* ದನಕ್ಕೆ, ಮರಕ್ಕೆ, ಅದಕ್ಕೆ, *etc.*

ಕ್ಯಾಕರಿಸು. = ಕೇಕರಿಸು, *q. v.*

ಕ್ರತು s. *n.* Sacrifice, offering. -ಧ್ವಂಸಿ. Śiva. -ಪುರುಷ. Vishṇu.

ಕ್ರಂದನ s. *n.* Crying out, calling. 2, weeping.

ಕ್ರಮ s. *n.* A step; the foot. 2, order, series; regular course. 3, method, manner. 4, a sacred precept. -ಣ. Going, proceeding, advancing. *Cpds.:* ಅತಿ-, ಅನು-, ಕಾಲ-, *etc.* -ತಪ್ಪು. Order to be missed. ಕ್ರಮಿಸು. To go, walk; to cross.

ಕ್ರಮಾಗತ s. *a.* Descended regularly or lineally.

ಕ್ರಮೇಣ s. *a.* By degrees, gradually, in order.

ಕ್ರಯ s. *n.* Price, value. 2, buying. -ಇಡು, -ಕಟ್ಟು. To fix a price. -ಕೊಡು. To pay for. -ಬೀಳು. Price to fetch; to cost. -ವಿಕ್ರಯ. Trade, traffic. -ಚೀಟು, -ಶಾಸನ. A deed of sale. ಕ್ರಯಿಕ. A purchaser.

ಕ್ರವ್ಯ s. *n.* Raw flesh. ಕ್ರವ್ಯಾದ. Carnivorous; a râkshasa.

ಕ್ರಾಂತಿ s. *n.* Going; the sun's course on the globe; the ecliptic; *also* -ಚಕ್ರ, -ವೃತ್ತ.

ಕ್ರಿಮಿ (=ಕೃಮಿ) s. *n.* An insect, worm. -ಜ. Produced by worms: silk.

ಕ್ರಿಯಾತ್ಮಕ s. *a.* Having the nature of a verb.

ಕ್ರಿಯಾ (ಕ್ರಿಯೆ) s. *n.* Action, work, business; an act. 2, time, tense; a verb. 3, a literary work. 4, bodily action. 5, a religious ceremony. 6, expiation. 7, a means; an instrument. -ಪದ. A verb. -ಫಲ. Consequence of acts. -ಮಾಲೆ. The conjugation of a verb. -ಅರ್ಥ. The meaning of a verb. -ವಂತ. An active man; a truthful man. -ವಾಚಕ. A verbal noun. -ವಿಭಕ್ತಿ. An inflection of the persons of a tense. -ವಿಶೇಷಣ. That which defines an action: an adverb. -ಸಮಾಸ. A verbal compound.

ಕ್ರಿಷ್ಣ, ಕ್ರಿಷ್ಟಣ. *tb. of* ಕೃಷ್ಣ, *q. v.*

ಕ್ರಿಸ್ತ *n.* Christ. -ಶಕ. The era of Christ. ಕ್ರಿಸ್ತಿ. Christian. ಕ್ರಿಸ್ತಿಯ. A Protestant Christian; *f.* -ಳು.

ಕ್ರೀಡೆ s. *n.* Play, sport, amusement. ಕ್ರೀಡಿಸು. To play, sport. ಕ್ರೀಡಾವನ. A pleasure garden, park.

ಕ್ರುಪೆ. *tb. of* ಕೃಪೆ, *q. v.*

ಕ್ರೂಜಿ f. *n.* A cross. -ಗೆ ಜಡಿ, ಕ್ರೂಜಸು. To crucify.

ಕ್ರೂರ s. *a.* Cruel, fierce, pitiless; hot; sharp; harsh, terrible. *n.* A scoundrel. -ಕರ್ಮಿ. A person who performs pitiless deeds. -ಚಿತ್ತ. A cruel-minded man. -ತನ, -ತ್ವ. Cruelty.

ಕ್ರೇತವ್ಯ, ಕ್ರೇಯ s. *a.* Purchasable.

ಕ್ರೈಸ್ತ f. *n.* A Christian. *a.* Christian. -ತ್ವ, -ಧರ್ಮ. Christianity.

ಕ್ರೋಡ s. *n.* The chest, breast, bosom. 2, Saturn. -ರೂಪಿ. Vishṇu. ಕ್ರೋಡೀಕರಿಸು. To abridge, write briefly.

ಕ್ರೋಧ s. *n.* Anger, wrath, passion.

ಕ್ರೋಧನ s. *n.* The fifty-ninth year of the cycle.

ಕ್ರೋಧಿ s. *a.* Angry, passionate. *n.* The thirty-eighth year of the cycle.

ಕ್ರೋಶ s. *n.* Calling out; a cry, shout. 2, a measure of distance, a kos, $\frac{1}{4}$ yôjana.

ಕ್ರೌಂಚ s. n. A curlew. 2, a mountain in the Himâlaya. 3, one of the divisions of the world.

ಕ್ರೌರ್ಯ (fr. ಕ್ರೂರ) s. n. Cruelty, fierceness.

ಕ್ಲಿಷ್ಟ s. a. Fatigued, tired. 2, put to shame. 3, contradictory.

ಕ್ಲೀಬ s. a. Idle, slothful; mean, miserly. n. The neuter gender.

ಕ್ಲುಪ್ತ (tb. of ಕ್ಲೃಪ್ತ), a. Arranged; fixed.

ಕ್ಲೇಶ s. n. Affliction, pain; distress. -ಪಡು. To suffer pain, to grieve.

ಕ್ವಚಿತ್ s. ad. Anywhere; somewhere. 2, sometimes. 3, very little.

ಕ್ಷಕಾರ s. n. The syllable ಕ್ಷ.

ಕ್ಷಣ s. n. A moment. 2, a measure of time equal to 4 minutes or ⅘ second. 3, leisure. 4, season. -ದ. Leisure-giving; night. -ಪ್ರಭೆ. Lightning. -ಭಂಗುರ. Transient, perishable. ಕ್ಷಣಾರ್ಧ. Half a moment. ಕ್ಷಣಿಕ. Momentory, transient.

ಕ್ಷತ್ರ, ಕ್ಷತ್ರಿಯ s. n. A man of the military caste, Kshatriya; f. ಕ್ಷತ್ರಿಯೆ.

ಕ್ಷಪಣ s. n. Fasting. 2, A Buddha or Jaina mendicant.

ಕ್ಷಮ s. a. Patient, enduring, putting up with. 2, adequate, competent.

ಕ್ಷಮಿಸು s. v. t. To endure, bear patiently; to put up with; to pardon, forgive. ಪಾಪ ಕ್ಷಮಿಸಿ ಬಿಡು. To pardon sin.

ಕ್ಷಮೆ (ಕ್ಷಮಾ) s. n. Patience, forbearance, indul- gence, long-suffering; pardon, forgiveness.

ಕ್ಷಯ s. n. Wane, decrease, diminution, consumption; loss, destruction. 2, pulmonary consumption. 3, sixtieth year of the cycle. -ತಿಥಿ. A lunar day beginning after sunrise and ending before that of the next. -ಪಕ್ಷ. The fortnight of the waning moon. -ರೋಗ. Consumption in general. ಕ್ಷಯಿಸು. To wane, decrease.

ಕ್ಷರ s. a. Perishable.

ಕ್ಷಾಂತ s. a. Enduring, patient. ಕ್ಷಾಂತಿ. Patience, forbearance.

ಕ್ಷಾಮ s. a. Scorched; emaciated, wasted, thin. n. Emaciation, debility; famine.

ಕ್ಷಾರ s. a. Salty, biting, acid, pungent. n. Salt, any saline substance, alkali; soda, nitre, saltpetre; essence.

ಕ್ಷಾಲ, ಕ್ಷಾಲನ s. n. Washing. ಕ್ಷಾಲಿತ. Washed, cleansed.

ಕ್ಷಿತಿ s. n. An abode. 2, the earth; a field. 3, decrease, wane, loss. ಕ್ಷಿತ. Decreased, wasted. -ಕಾಂತ, -ನಾಥ, -ಪ, -ಪತಿ, -ಪಾಲ, -ರಮಣ, ಕ್ಷಿತೀಶ. A king.

ಕ್ಷಿಪ್ರ s. a. Quick, swift, speedy.

ಕ್ಷೀಣ s. a. Wasted, worn away; emaciated, thin, slender; miserable. -ತ್ವ. Wasting, diminution, decay.

ಕ್ಷೀರ s. n. Milk. 2, water. -ಜ. Curds. -ನೀರ. Milk and water. -ಸ. Essence of milk. -ಸಮುದ್ರ, ಕ್ಷೀರಾಬ್ಧಿ. The sea of milk. ಕ್ಷೀರಾಗಾರ. A dairy. ಕ್ಷೀರಾಗಾರಿ. A dairy-man.

ಕ್ಷುದ್ರ s. a. Small, little. 2, poor, miserable. 3, low, vile. 4, avaricious, niggardly. n. A fault; slander. -ಕ, -ಗಾರ. A slanderer. ಕ್ಷುದ್ರಿ. A slanderous person.

ಕ್ಷುಧೆ (ಕ್ಷುಧಾ) s. n. Hunger. ಕ್ಷುಧಾರ್ತ, ಕ್ಷುಧಿತ. Hungry.

ಕ್ಷುರ s. n. A razor. -ಕ, -ಮರ್ದಿ, ಕ್ಷುರಿ. A barber.

ಕ್ಷುಲ್ಲಕ (=ಕ್ಷುದ್ರ, ಕ್ಷುದ್ರಕ) s. a. Little; thin. 2, poor, indigent. 3, avaricious. n. A man of the lowest extraction.

ಕ್ಷೇತ್ರ s. n. A field. 2, place, country; a place of pilgrimage. 3, the body. 4, a diagram. -ಜೀವ. A husbandman. -ಜ್ಞ. Experienced, skilful; the soul. -ಪಾಲ. A deity protecting the fields: Bhairava. -ಫಲ. Area; quotient.

ಕ್ಷೇಪ s. n. Casting; pushing; depressing; passing away. Cpds.: ಕಾಲ-, ನಿ-, ಸಂ-.

ಕ್ಷೇಮ s. n. Well-being, weal, happiness; health. -ಕರ. Promoting well-being. -ಸಮಾಚಾರ. News regarding a person's welfare.

ಕ್ಷೋಣಿ s. n. The earth; a field. 2, a certain high number. -ಪತಿ. A king.

ಕ್ಷೋಭ s. n. Agitation, commotion, disturbance, emotion, alarm.

ಕ್ಷೌರ (*fr.* ಕ್ಷುರ) s. n. Shaving. -ಮಾಡಿಸಿಕೊಳ್ಳು. To get one's self shaved. -ಕತ್ತಿ. A razor. -ಕ. A barber.

ಖ

ಖ. The twentieth letter of the alphabet.

ಖ s. n. The sky. 2, an organ of sense (ಇಂದ್ರಿಯ). 3, perception (ಬುದ್ಧಿ). 4, mind (ಮನಸ್). -ಗ, -ಚರ. Moving in the air: the sun; a bird; an arrow. -ಗಪತಿ, -ಗೇಶ್ವರ. Garuḍa. -ಗೋಲ. The celestial sphere; astronomy.

ಖಚಿತ s. *a.* Bound; inlaid, studded. 2, joined. 3, positive, true.

ಖಜ s. n. Stirring, churning. 2, a ladle. -ಕ. An awning, canopy.

ಖಜಾಕೆ s. n. A ladle, spoon.

ಖಜಾನೆ h. n. A treasury; treasure. ಖಜಾಂಚಿ. A cashkeeper.

ಖಜ್ಜಾ h. n. Quarrelling. -ಖೋರ. A quarrelsome man.

ಖಟ್ವ, ಖಟ್ವೆ s. n. A bedstead, cot. 2, a hammock.

ಖಡ್ಗ s. n. A sword. 2, a rhinoceros; *also* -ಮೃಗ. ಖಡ್ಗಾಖಡಿ, *etc.* Sword to sword; a sword-fight; *also* ಖಡಾಖಡಿ.

ಖಂಡ (= ಕಂಡ) s. *a.* Broken, divided. *n.* A fragment, part, piece; a section. 2, a division of the terrestrial globe.

ಖಂಡಣೆ, ಖಂಡನ s. n. Dividing, reducing to pieces; refuting.

ಖಂಡಿತ 1. (=ಕಂಡಿತ, *q. v.*) k. n. Firmness, strictness, certainty.

ಖಂಡಿತ 2. s. *a.* Cut, taken to pieces; refuted.

ಖಂಡಿಸು s. *v. t.* To break, crush, cut; to disappoint, *etc.*; to refute (in argument).

ಖತಾವಣಿ m. n. The paper on which the items of the day-book are abstracted.

ಖತಿ (= ಕತಿ) k. n. Anger, wrath, rage.

ಖದಿರ s. n. The tree *Acacia catechu;* its resin called *catechu.*

ಖದ್ಯೋತ s. n. A fire-fly; the sun.

ಖನಕ s. n. A digger, miner; a house-breaker. 2, a rat.

ಖನನ s. n. Digging; burying.

ಖನಿ (= ಕಣಿ) s. n. A mine, quarry. -ಜ. A mineral. -ತ್ರ. A spade.

ಖಪುರ s. n. The betel-nut tree, *Areca catechu.* 2, the mouth. 3, a buffalo. 4, disgrace.

ಖರ s. *a.* Hard, sharp, pungent. *n.* The twenty-fifth year of the cycle. 2, an ass. 3, N. of a râkshasa. -ಕರ. Hot-rayed; the sun. -ಶಾಣ. A grindstone; a sharp saw.

ಖರಡೆ h. n. A foul copy; a day-book; a scrawl; *also* ಕರಡು.

ಖರಾರು h. n. A currycomb.

ಖರೀದಿ h. n. A purchase; price, cost.

ಖರೆ 1. f. *a.* True, correct. -ಹೇಳು. To speak truly.

ಖರೆ 2. s. n. The grass *Andropogon serratus.*

ಖರ್ಚು (=ಕರ್ಚು, *q. v.*) h. n. Expenditure, expense, costs. -ವೆಚ್ಚ. *dupl.* -ದಾರ. A spendthrift. -ಬೀಳು, -ಹಿಡಿ. To cost money.

ಖರ್ಜು s. n. Itch, scab.

ಖರ್ಜೂರ (= ಕಜ್ಜೂರ, *etc.*) s. n. The date-tree, *Phoenix dactylifera.*

ಖರ್ವ s. a. Maimed; short, low. n. A dwarf. 2, ten thousand millions.

ಖರ್ಜೂರ (= ಕರ್ಜೂರ) s. n. The water-melon.

ಖಲ s. n. A rogue, scoundrel. 2, a threshing floor. 3, sediment, dregs. 4, contest, battle. 5, a mortar. a. Low, base. -ಕರಣ. Threshing corn. -ತಿ. Bald-headed. -ಪು. A sweeper.

ಖಲ್ಲ s. n. A leaf or paper rolled into a cup.

ಖಳ. = ಖಲ, q. v.

ಖಳಿಲನೆ (ಳ = ಱ) k. ad. Loudly, roughly.

ಖಾಡ. = ಖಡ್ಗ, q. v. ಖಾಡಾಖಾಡಿ. A wrestling match.

ಖಾಣೆ h. n. Food; fodder.

ಖಾತರಿ. = ಕಾತರಿ, q. v.

ಖಾತೆ 1. s. n. An artificial pond.

ಖಾತೆ 2. f. n. An account on the day-book. 2, province, department.

ಖಾದನ s. n. Eating; food. ಖಾದಿತ. Eaten.

ಖಾದಿ f. n. A thick cotton-stuff.

ಖಾನ h. n. A prince, chief; a title borne by Mohammadan nobles.

ಖಾನೆ h. n. A place, house, *as in* ಕಾರಖಾನೆ, ಮೇಜುವಾನೆ. 2, a sliding box, drawer. -ಸುಮಾರಿ. A census of the population.

ಖಾಮುಖಾ h. ad. Positively, certainly.

ಖಾರಿ f. n. A measure of capacity equivalent to about three bushels.

ಖಾಲಿ h. a. Empty, vacant. 2, unemployed. 3, useless. -ಆಗು. To become vacant; to be disappointed.

ಖಾಸಾ. = ಕಾಸಾ, q. v. -ಸ್ವಾರಿ. The equipage or procession of a chieftain; the chieftain in person.

ಖಿಜಮತ h. n. Service, attendance.

ಖಿನ್ನ s. a. Depressed, distressed, wearied.

ಖಿಲ s. n. A piece of waste land. 2. a supplement. 3, anything empty or fruitless.

ಖಿಲಾತು h. n. A robe of honour.

ಖುದ f. n. God.

ಖುದ್ದು h. a. Own; in person; self.

ಖುರ (= ಕುರ) f. n. A hoof.

ಖುರಾಕು f. n. Rich, nutritive diet.

ಖುರಾನು (= ಕುರಾನ) h. n. The Koran.

ಖುರ್ದುಬುರ್ದು h. n. Embezzlement.

ಖುನ್ನಾಸ, ಖುನ್ನೀಸು h. n. Obeisance, reverence.

ಖುಲಾಸ h. n. Openness; emptiness; evidence; clearness; freedom. a. Open.

ಖುಲ್ಲ s. a. Small, low, mean; wicked. 2, (h.) = ಕುಲ್ಲಾ. -ತನ. Meanness.

ಖುಷಾಮತು f. n. Flattery, fawning.

ಖುಷಾಲು. = ಕುಶಾಲು, q. v.

ಖುಷಿ. = ಕುಶಿ, q. v.

ಖೂನ h. n. An indication, sign.

ಖೂನಿ h. n. Murder. -ಖೋರ, -ಗಾರ. A murderer.

ಖೂಬು h. ad. Well, finely; copiously.

ಖೇಚರ (*fr.* ಖ) s. a. Moving in the air. n. A bird; a deity.

ಖೇಡೆಯ, ಖೇಡ್ಯ s. n. A shield.

ಖೇದ s. n. Sorrow, grief, distress, despondency. -ಗೊಳ್ಳು, ಖೇದಿಸು. To feel grieved.

ಖೇಪು s. n. A single time, turn.

ಖೇಲ s. n. Moving to and fro; *also* -ನ. ಖೇಲೆ. Play, sport.

ಖೋಡಿ s. n. An evil disposition; a vice; a mean, miserable wretch. a. Ill-disposed, having a bad habit. -ತನ. An evil disposition.

ಖ್ಯಾತ s. a. Well known, famous; *also* ಪ್ರ-. ಖ್ಯಾತಿ. Fame, celebrity, glory.

ಗ

ಗ. The twenty-first letter of the alphabet.

ಗ 1. k. *An affix to form words denoting time, as:* ಆಗ, ಈಗ, *etc.* 2, *an affix to form masculine nouns, as:* ಹುಡುಗ, ದಾರಿಗ, ಮಗ, *etc.*

ಗ 2. s. *a.* Going, moving.

ಗಕಾರ s. *n.* The letter ಗ.

ಗಕ್ಕನೆ k. *ad.* Quickly, suddenly.

ಗಗನ s. *n.* The sky, atmosphere. -ಮಣಿ. The sun. -ಚರ. A bird; a planet.

ಗಗ್ಗರ k. *n.* A hollow silver ornament filled with pebbles for jingling.

ಗಗ್ಗರಿ k. *n.* A hollow ring of brass containing bits of metal, *etc.* to produce a jingling noise.

ಗಂಗಡೊವಲು f. *n.* The dewlap of an ox or bull.

ಗಂಗಾ (= ಗಂಗೆ, *q. v.*) s. *n.* The Ganges. -ಜಮುನಾ. The Ganges and Yamuna rivers; a cloth with different coloured border on each side. -ದೇವಿ. A water-goddess. -ಧರ, -ಧರೇಶ್ವರ, -ಧೀಶ, -ವತಂಸ. Śiva. -ನಂದನ, -ಪುತ್ರ, -ಸುತ. Bhîshma. -ಯಾತ್ರೆ. Pilgrimage to the Ganges. -ಸ್ನಾನ. Bathing in the Ganges. ಗಂಗೋದಕ. Ganges water.

ಗಂಗಾಳ s. *n.* A circular metal vessel for holding water, *etc.* 2, a metal plate for eating from.

ಗಂಗೆ s. *n.* The river Ganges. 2, Satyavati, the boatman's daughter who became Bhîshma's mother. -ದೊಗಲು. = ಗಂಗಡೊವಲು.

ಗಚ್ಚಿ h. *n.* A chunammed floor. -ಎಣ್ಣೆ. Varnish.

ಗಚ್ಚು h. *n.* Mortar, plaster, cement.

ಗಜ 1. s. *n.* An elephant. 2, N. of a râkshasa. -ಕರ್ಣ. Ringworm. -ದಂತ. Elephant's tusk. -ನಗರಿ, -ಪುರ. Delhi. -ಪ್ರಾಸ. A kind of alliteration. -ಮುಖ, -ವದನ, ಗಜಾನನ. Gaṇêśa. -ಲಕ್ಷ್ಮಿ. A picture of Lakshmî with elephants on her sides. -ವೈರಿ, ಗಜಾರಿ. A lion. ಗಜೇಂದ್ರ. A large stately elephant.

ಗಜ 2. h. *n.* A measure of three feet; a yard. 2, a ramrod.

ಗಜಗ. = ಗಜುಗ, *q. v.*

ಗಜನಿ k. *n.* Poor rice lands.

ಗಜರು (ರು = ಱು) a. k. *v. t.* To roar; to scold. *n.* A loud sound or speech.

ಗಜಾಲು f. *n.* Loud idle talk. -ಗಾರ. A chatterer; *f.* -ಗಾತಿ.

ಗಜಿಬಿಜಿ k. *n.* Confusion, disorder, intricacy. -ಬರಹ. An illegible writing. -ಮಾರ್ಗ. A rough road. -ಮಾಡು. To confuse.

ಗಜುಗ, ಗಜ್ಜಿಗ, ಗಜ್ಜುಗ k. *n.* A prickly climbing shrub, the Molucca bean, *Guilandina bonducella.* 2, a protuberance from the eye-ball.

ಗಜ್ಜರಿ f. *n.* A sweet carrot.

ಗಜ್ಜಿ. = ಕಜ್ಜಿ, *q. v.*

ಗಜ್ಜೆ. = ಗೆಜ್ಜೆ, *q. v.*

ಗಂಜ f. *n.* A store-room, treasury. 2, a mine.

ಗಂಜಲ, ಗಂಜಳ k. *n.* The urine of cattle, *etc.* -ದ ಹುಲ್ಲು. A species of coarse grass, *Eleusine indica.*

ಗಂಜಿ (*tb. of* ಕಾಂಜಿ) *n.* Conjee, rice gruel; starch. -ಕಸ. A creeping plant, *Indigofera linifolia.* -ಬಟ್ಟೆ. A starched cloth. -ರಟ್ಟು. A cloth used in straining boiled rice.

ಗಂಜೀಫ h. *n.* A pack of round cards.

ಗಂಜು f. *n.* A set of round vessels that are put one within another in the form of a cone.

ಗಟಕ (*tb. of* ಘಟಕ) *n.* A powerful, able man.

ಗಟ್ಟ k. *n.* A ghaut, mountain-range.

ಗಟ್ಟಣೆ (*tb. of* ಘಟ್ಟನ) *n.* Beating down, *as* roads; loading a gun.

ಗಟ್ಟಿ k. *n.* Firmness; hardness; the state of (fluids, *etc.*) being thick, solid; strength, ability. 2, a lump. 3, an ingot. 4, smartness, fineness. 5, a strong, smart person. *a.* Firm, strong, solid. -ಆಳು. A strong, able person. -ಕೆಲಸ. A strong work. -ಗ. A strong, energetic man. -ಮೊಸರು. Thick curds. -ಹಾಲು. Thick milk. -ವಳ್ತಿ. A toilet woman.

ಗಟ್ಟಿಸು (= ಘಟ್ಟಿಸು) f. *v. t.* To strike, beat. 2, (k.) to make effort (to speak loud).

ಗಟ್ಟು (=ಗಡ್ಡು) f. *n.* A bundle, ream of paper.

ಗಡ 1. = ಗಡು, *q. v.*

ಗಡ 2. h. *n.* A small fort. 2, a liquid measure.

ಗಡ 3. k. *int. expressing quick motion or disorder.* -ಗಡ. Quickly (used of walking, reading, eating, *etc.*). -ಗಡ ಎನ್ನು. To rattle, *as* thunder, carts, *etc.* -ಬಡ, -ಬಡಿ, -ಬಿಡಿ. Bustle, confusion, tumult, ado.

ಗಡ 4. = ಗಡು, *q. v.*

ಗಡಗಂಚಿ h. *n.* A stand, shelf.

ಗಡಂಗ h. *n.* A godown, store-room; a spirit-shop.

ಗಡಚು. =ಗಡುಸು, *q. v.*

ಗಡಣ a. k. *n.* A mass, heap; a multitude. ಗಡಣಿಸು. To join, heap, pile.

ಗಡಣೆ (*tb. of* ಗಣನೆ) *n.* Reckoning; meaning, sense. -ಗೊಳ್ಳು. To regard, care for, *etc.*

ಗಡತರ (=ಗಡುತರ) k. *n.* Massiveness, stoutness, strength. *a.* Massive, *etc.*

ಗಡದ, ಗಡದು f. *a.* Thick, *as* darkness; sound, deep, *as* sleep, study, *etc.*

ಗಡಪು h. *n.* Disappearance, hiding.

ಗಡವು. = ಗಡು, *q. v.*

ಗಡಸರಿ k. *n.* A stout, robust person.

ಗಡಾಯಿಸು f. *v. t.* To hide or fix firmly in the earth.

ಗಡಾರಿ h. *n.* An iron crow-bar.

ಗಡಿ 1. (=ಗಡ) k. *n.* A term, limit; a frontier; a place. -ಕಲ್ಲು. A boundary-stone. -ಕಿಲ್ಲೆ, -ಕೋಟೆ, -ದುರ್ಗ. A hill fort. -ಪಾರು ಮಾಡು. To banish.

ಗಡಿ 2. (*tb. of* ಘಟಿ) *n.* An hour of 24 minutes; a gong.

ಗಡಿಗೆ (*tb. of* ಘಟಿಕಾ) *n.* An earthen vessel.

ಗಡಿಬಿಡಿ (*see s.* ಗಡ 3) k. *n.* Confusion; vexation.

ಗಡಿಯಾರ, ಗಡಿಯಾಲ h. *n.* An hour-glass; a gong; a watch, clock.

ಗಡು k. *n.* A limit; a period, term, instalment; *also* -ಬು, -ವು.

ಗಡುತರ. =ಗಡತರ, *q. v.*

ಗಡುದು. =ಗಡದ, *q. v.*

ಗಡುಸು (=ಗಡಚು) k. *n.* Hardness, brittleness, *as* of iron; difficulty, *as* of work; heaviness, *as* of rain.

ಗಡೆ 1. k. *n.* A bamboo pole. 2, match; comparison. -ಕಾರ. A man who carries a pole with a flag; an oarsman.

ಗಡೆ 2. (*tb. of* ಘಟಿ) *n.* A wheel for raising water.

ಗಡ್ಡ k. *n.* The beard; the chin. -ಇಡು, -ಬಿಡಿಸು, -ಬೆಳಸು. To let the beard grow. -ಬೋಳಿಸು. To have the beard shaved.

ಗಡ್ಡಿ. = ಗಟ್ಟಿ, *q. v.*

ಗಡ್ಡೆ k. *n.* A mass; a lump, clump. 2, any bulbous root. 3, the root of the ear. 4, an island; *also* ನಡು-. -ಕಟ್ಟು. To freeze, congeal; to grow in clumps, *as* grass. ಗೆಣಸಿನ-. A sweet potato. ಮೊಸರಿನ-. A clot of curdled milk.

ಗಣ s. *n.* A flock, multitude, troop, tribe. 2, a body of troops equal to 27 chariots, 27 elephants, 81 horses and 135 foot. 3, the attendants of Śiva. 4, a syllable foot in prosody. 5, a number. 6, a group of lunar mansions. -ಕ, ಗಣಿಕ. An arithmetician; an accountant; an astrologer; *f.* -ಕೆ, -ಕಿ. -ನೆ. Reckoning, counting; esteeming.

-ಪತಿ, ಗಣಾಧಿಪ, ಗಣಾಧೀಶ. Gaṇêśa; Śiva. -ಯಿಸು, ಗಣಿಸು. To count, reckon; to consider, regard.

ಗಣಾಜಿಲೆ k. n. Hogweed, *Boerhavia procumbens.* 2, the chicken-pox.

ಗಣಿಲು (=ಗಣಿಕೆ) k. n. A knuckle of the fingers; a knot or joint in a cane.

ಗಣಾರ್ಚನೆ s. n. The homage paid by the Liṅgavantas to the Jaṅgamas.

ಗಣಿಕೆ (=ಗಣಿಲು) k. n. A knot, joint. -ಹುಣ್ಣು. A sore on the finger joints.

ಗಣಿತ s. n. Calculating, the science of computation, arithmetic. *a.* Counted. -ಗಾರ, -ಜ್ಞ. An astrologer. -ವಿದ್ಯೆ, -ಶಾಸ್ತ್ರ. The science of computation, comprising arithmetic, algebra and geometry. ಗಣಿತಿಸು, ಗಣಿಬಿಸು. To count; to consider.

ಗಣೆ k. n. The stalk of an onion.

ಗಣೆಗಾರ k. n. A boatman; a tumbler.

ಗಣೇಶ, ಗಣೇಶ್ವರ s. n. Pârvati's son Gaṇêśa.

ಗಂಟಡಿ h. n. A small bundle, parcel.

ಗಂಟಲ, ಗಂಟಲು, ಗಂಟ್ಲು k. n. The throat.

ಗಂಟಿ k. n. A kind of small gold earring.

ಗಂಟು (*tb.* of ಗ್ರಂಥಿ) n. The knot or joint of a reed, bamboo or a cane. 2, a knot. 3, a bundle, parcel. 4, money, wealth; capital in trade. 5, swelling and hardening of the veins. ಗಂಟಾಸೆ. The desire of becoming rich. -ಗಳ್ಳ. One who falsely assumes the appearance of poverty; one who does not return a loan. -ಗೊಯ್ಕ. A pick-pocket. -ತುಂಬೆ. The herb *Leucas urticaefolia.* -ಬಾರಂಗಿ. An under-shrub, *Clerodendron serratum.* -ಬೀಳು. To get knotted; close connection to spring up; union or harmony to take place; to run counter to; to attack. -ಮೋರೆ. A frowning look or countenance. -ವ್ಯಾಜ್ಯ. A difficult lawsuit. -ಹಾಕು. To make a knot; to knit, *as* the eye-brows; to employ capital.

ಗಂಟೆ (*tb.* of ಘಂಟೆ) n. An English hour. -ಬಾರಿಸು, -ಹೊಡೆ. To ring a bell.

ಗಂಟ್ಲು. =ಗಂಟಲು, *q. v.*

ಗಂಡ 1. k. n. A strong, male person; a husband (*pl.* ಗಂಡರು, ಗಂಡಂದಿರು). 2, (=ಗಂಡು)strength, greatness. -ಕ, -ಮೃಗ. A rhinoceros. -ಗಲಿ. A strong hero. -ಗೂಸು, ಗಂಡುಗೂಸು. A male person. -ಮೆಣಸು. The Pimento tree, *Eugenia acris.* -ಹೆಂಡರು, -ಹೆಂಡತಿಯರು. Husband and wife.

ಗಂಡ 2. s. n. The cheek. 2, a boil. 3, the force of any disease, rain, wind, *etc.*; the baneful influence of a star (*cf.* ಗಂಡಾಂತರ). *a.* Chief, best, excellent. -ಮಾಲೆ, ಗಂಡಾಮಾಲೆ. Scrofula of the throat. -ಸ್ಥಲ. The temples of an elephant.

ಗಂಡಸ, ಗಂಡಸು k. n. A male person. -ತನ. Virility. -ಮಕ್ಕಳು. Male persons.

ಗಂಡಾಗುಂಡಿ h. n. Impudence; audacity.

ಗಂಡಾಂತರ s. n. Danger, peril, jeopardy (*cf. s.* ಗಂಡ 2).

ಗಂಡಾಮಾಲೆ. *See s.* ಗಂಡ 2, *q. v.*

ಗಂಡು k. n. Strength; manliness; firmness; bravery. 2, the male sex; a male. *a.* Male, manly. ಗಂಡಕ್ಷರ. An aspirate. ಗಂಡಾಡು. A he-goat. ಗಂಡಾಳು. A male cooly. -ಕೆಲಸ. A superior work. -ಕೇಪಲ. The shrub *Memecylon amplexicaule.* -ಗೊಳ್ಳು. To become impetuous. -ಬಿದರು. A solid bamboo. -ಗತನ. Manliness, valour. *Other cpds.:* -ಗೂಸು, -ಗೋಗಿಲೆ, -ಜಾತಿ, -ಜಂಕೆ, -ಪಶು, -ಮಕ್ಕಳು, -ಮರಿ, -ಮೃಗ, -ಸಿಂಹ, -ಹುಳ, -ಹುಡುಗ. A boy.

ಗಂಡೂಷ s. n. Rinsing the mouth.

ಗಣ್ಣ h. n. A division of paddy land.

ಗಣ್ಯ s. a. Calculable, numerable; worthy of esteem.

ಗತ s. a. Gone, departed; past; disappeared; arrived at; gone to any state; belonging to; relating to. -ಗೋಷ್ಠಿ. Stale words; indefinite postponement, *as* of a law-suit. ಗತಾನುಗತಿಕ. Successive, in rotation; following custom, imitating. ಗತಾರ್ಥ. Unmeaning, nonsensical; deprived of an object.

ಗತಿ s. *n.* Going, motion; gait; march, progress. 2, a path, way; refuge, resource; an expedient, means; course of events, condition; happiness. 3, the diurnal motion of a planet in its orbit. 4, transmigration. 5, deliberation; knowledge. 6, sin, vice. -ಗೆಡು. Progress, state, *etc.* to be destroyed. -ಗೆಡಿಸು. To destroy the course, condition, *etc.*; to check. -ಗೇಡಿ. A person destroying his own or others welfare. -ಗೇಡು. Ruin of welfare, *etc.* -ಸು. To go; to die; to pass, *as* time. -ವಿಹೀನ, -ಹೀನ. Remediless; forlorn. ಸದ್ಗತಿ. Good fortune; heaven. ದುರ್ಗತಿ. Misfortune, poverty; hell.

ಗತ್ತು (*tb. of* ಗತಿ) *n.* Beating time in music for dancers. -ಗಾರ. A time-server.

ಗತ್ಯಂತರ s. *n.* Another remedy or resource; a way of avoiding.

ಗದ 1. s. *n.* Speaking, speech.

ಗದ 2. s. *n.* Disease, sickness.

ಗದ 3. k. *n.* Shaking, quick motion. -ಗದ ನಡುಗು, -ಗದನೆ ನಡುಗು (*v. i.*). To shake, tremble violently; *also* -ಗದಿಸು.

ಗದಗು k. *n.* The smell of cattle urine, burning chillies, *etc.*

ಗದರು (ರು = ಱು) k. *v. i.* To thunder, roar, cry; to menace; to exhort earnestly. ಗದರಿಸು. To exhort earnestly; to scare, frighten. ಗದರಿಕೆ. Reproof, exhortation.

ಗದಾ, ಗದೆ s. *n.* A mace, club. ಗದಾಧರ. Kṛishṇa.

ಗದು k. *n.* A swelling, tumour.

ಗದ್ಗದ, ಗದ್ಗದಿಕೆ s. *n.* Stammering; indistinct utterance, *as* sobbing, *etc.*

ಗದ್ದ k. *n.* The chin.

ಗದ್ದರಿಸು = ಗದರಿಸು, *q. v. v. i.* To thunder, roar.

ಗದ್ದಲ k. *n.* Noise; din.

ಗದ್ದಿಗೆ, ಗದ್ದುಗೆ k. *n.* A throne; a seat; a tomb monument of Jaṅgamas. 2, a basis.

ಗದ್ದೆ k. *n.* A field, paddy-land. -ತೆವರು, -ಬದ. A ridge between rice-fields. -ಮುರಿ. A paddy-field. -ಮುರಿರುಮಾಲೆ. A turban-cloth with square stripes.

ಗದ್ಯ s. *a.* To be spoken. *n.* Prose. -ಪದ್ಯ. Prose and verse.

ಗದ್ಯಾಣ s. *n.* A silver weight equal to about a farthing. 2, a small gold coin.

ಗನ. *tb. of* ಘನ, *q. v.*

ಗಂತು s. *n.* A way, course. 2, moving about.

ಗಂದ. *tb. of* ಗಂಧ, *q. v.* -ವಟ್ಟಿಗೆ, -ಪಟ್ಟಿಗೆ. The cross bars fastening the planks of a door. -ಪುಡಿ, -ಹುಡಿ. Perfumed powder. -ಗಂದಿಗ. A perfume-seller; an oculist.

ಗಂಧ (= ಗಂದ) s. *n.* Smell, odour. 2, a perfume. 3, sandal-wood. 4, arrogance. -ದ ಎಣ್ಣೆ. Sandal oil. -ಕಚೋರ. Zedoary, *Curcuma zedoaria*. -ಬೇವು. The curry leaf-tree, *Murraya koenigii*. -ಮೆಣಸು. Cubeb, *Piper cubeba*. -ಸರಕು. Spicery, perfumery, scented drugs. -ಕಸ್ತೂರಿ. Scented musk. -ದ ತೈಲ. Sandal oil. -ನ. Fragrance; perseverance; manifestation; intimation. -ಫಲಿ. A medicinal plant and perfume. -ಮಾಲ್ಯ. A fragrant garland. -ಮೂಷಿ, -ಮೂಷಿಕೆ. The musk rat. -ರಸ. Myrrh. -ವತಿ. The earth; a kind of perfume. -ವಾಹ. The wind. -ವೀಡ. Black salt. ಗಂಧಾಕ್ಷತೆ. The pigment called akshatĕ and sandal-paste.

ಗಂಧಕ s. *n.* Sulphur. -ದ್ರುತಿ. Sulphuric acid. -ಶುದ್ಧಿ. Prepared sulphur.

ಗಂಧರ್ವ s. *n.* A celestial musician. 2, a singer. 3, a ghost. 4, a kind of deer. -ವಿವಾಹ. A marriage on mutual agreement of the parties.

ಗಪಚಿಪ್ h. *a.* Silent, still. *int.* Silence!

ಗಪಗಪ, ಗಪಗಪನೆ, ಗಪ್ಪಗಪ್ಪ, *etc.* k. *ad.* Quickly, greedily.

ಗಪ್ಪನೆ (= ಕಪ್ಪನೆ) k. *ad.* Suddenly, all at once. -ಹಿಡಿ. To seize suddenly.

ಗಪ್ಪಿ h. *n.* A lie, falsehood.

ಗಪ್ಪು h. *n.* Deceit; falsehood. 2, invisibleness. 3, stillness, muteness.

ಗಬಗಬ. = ಗಪಗಪ, *etc.*, *q. v.*

ಗಬ್ಬ. *tb. of* ಗರ್ಭ, *q. v.* -ವಾಗು. To become pregnant (used of cattle).

ಗಬ್ಬಿ (*tb. of* ಗರ್ವ) *a.* Proud, haughty.

ಗಬ್ಬು k. *n.* A bad smell, stench.

ಗಭೀರ (= ಗಂಭೀರ) s. *a.* Deep; profound, grave, solemn.

ಗಮ 1. k. *n.* Strong scent, fragrance. -ಗಮ ನಾರು, -ಗಮಿಸು. To smell sweetly.

ಗಮ 2. s. *n.* Going; march. 2, flightiness; thoughtlessness, rashness.

ಗಮಕ s. *a.* Making clear. *n.* An evidence. 2, a kind of consecutive compound. 3, = ಗಮ 2, No. 2, loftiness; exertion.

ಗಮನ 1. k. *n.* Odour, fragrance.

ಗಮನ 2. s. *a.* Going, walking; march. ಗಮನಿಸು, ಗಮಿಸು. To go; to walk.

ಗಂಪೆ k. *n.* A basket.

ಗಂಭೀರ (= ಗಭೀರ, *q. v.*) s. *a.* Deep; solemn. -ತೆ. Depth; profoundness, sagacity.

ಗಮ್ಮತ್ತು h. *n.* Game, play; amusement, fun.

ಗಮ್ಮನೆ k. *ad.* Quickly.

ಗಮ್ಯ s. *a.* Accessible; attainable; intelligible, suitable.

ಗಯ, ಗಯೆ s. *n.* N. of a place of pilgrimage in Behar. ಗಯಾವಳ. A begging Brâhmaṇa at Gayâ; an extortioner. ಗಯಾಳ. A weak-minded or vain man. ಗಯ್ಯಾಳಿ. A shrew, scold, vixen.

ಗರ 1. s. *n.* A drink; poison, venom. 2, an astrological division of the day; *see* ಗರಜವಾಕರಣ.

ಗರ 2. (*tb. of* ಗ್ರಹ, *q. v.*) *n.* A planet; an evil spirit. -ಬಡೆ, -ಹೊಡೆ. An evil spirit to smite any one. -ವಟಿಗೆ, -ವಟ್ಟಿಗೆ. Possession, frenzy, torment. -ವಟಿಸು. To become possessed with an evil spirit; to rave, wander. -ಹಿಡಿ. An evil spirit to seize.

ಗರಕು k. *n.* Unevenness, roughness.

ಗರಗ, ಗರುಗ k. *n.* A common weed, *Eclipta alba.*

ಗರಗತ್ತಿ k. *n.* The tree *Ficus asperrima.*

ಗರಗರ (ರ = ಱ) k. *ad.* Whirlingly, smartingly, quickly. -ನೆ ತಿರುಗು. To turn around, *as* a millstone, *etc.*

ಗರಗರಿಕೆ a. k. *n.* Pleasantness; beauty.

ಗರಗಸ (*tb. of* ಕ್ರಕಚ) *n.* A saw. -ದ ಮರ. A tree with rough leaves, *Ficus conglomerata.*

ಗರಗು (ರ=ಱ=ಗರುಗು) k. *n.* The state of being scorched by heat. *a.* Fragile, brittle, dry, *as* flowers, leaves, *etc.*

ಗರಜವಾಕರಣ, ಗರಜೆ s. *n.* The fifth of the eleven astrological divisions of the day.

ಗರಜು h. *n.* Need, necessity; pressing business.

ಗರಡಿ. = ಗರುಡಿ, *q. v.*

ಗರತಿ (*tb. of* ಗೃಹತಿ) *n.* A decent and reputable woman.

ಗರಮ h. *a.* Hot. *n.* Heat. ಗರಮಿ. Heat.

ಗರಲ s. *n.* Poison, venom. -ಗ್ರೀವ, -ಧರ, ಗರಲಾಶನ. Śiva. -ಪೂರ. A serpent.

ಗರಸು (= ಗರುಸು) k. *n.* Gravel.

ಗರಸೆ k. *n.* A measure (of salt) equal to 400 marakâls.

ಗರಾಣದಾರ h. *n.* A respectable man.

ಗರಿ (ರಿ = ಱಿ) k. *n.* A feather; a wing; the feather-like leaf of a palm, *etc.* -ಗಟ್ಟು. To get strength; to improve. -ಮರ. The two side-portions of a wheel of an idol-car.

ಗರಿಕೆ. = ಕರಿಕೆ, *q. v.*

ಗರಿಮ, ಗರಿಮೆ, ಗರಿಮೆ s. *n.* Heaviness, weight. 2, dignity, worth.

ಗರೀಬ h. a. Poor.

ಗರೀಯಸ್ (fr. ಗುರು) s. a. Heavier; dearer.

ಗರುಡ s. n. The feathered vehicle of Vishṇu; an eagle, kite. 2, a building shaped like Garuḍa. 3, a military array. -ಕಂಬ, -ಗಂಬ. A pillar before a temple on which at festivals an image of Garuḍa or Nandi is set up. -ಪಾತಾಳ. A medicinal herb, *Ophiorrhiza mungos,* said to be an antidote to snake-bites. -ಪುರಾಣ. N. of a small purâṇa by Garuḍa. -ಫಲ. The tree *Hydnocarpus venenata.* -ವಾಹನ. A kind of idol-conveyance.

ಗರುಡಿ (= ಗರಡಿ) k. n. An abode. 2, a fencing-school, gymnasium; *also* -ಮನೆ. -ಸಾಧಕ, -ಸಾಧನೆ. Gymnastic exercises.

ಗರುವಲಿ (= ಗಾಳಿ) a. k. n. Wind.

ಗರುಸು. = ಗರಸು, q. v.

ಗರ್ರನೆ k. n. A sound in loud belching or in creaking.

ಗರ್ಗರಿ (tb. of ಘರ್ಘರಿ) n. A churn. -ಗಿಡ. A medicinal herb, *Wedelia calendulacea.*

ಗರ್ಜನೆ s. n. Roaring; rumbling. 2, wrath; reproach. -ಮಾಡು, ಗರ್ಜಿಸು. To roar.

ಗರ್ಜೆ k. n. N. of a tree of which the sour fruits are used for pickles.

ಗರ್ತೆ. = ಗರತಿ, q. v.

ಗರ್ದಭ s. n. An ass.

ಗರ್ಧನೆ s. n. Greediness.

ಗರ್ಭ (= ಗಬ್ಬ) s. n. The womb. 2, an embryo. 3, a child. 4, the inside, interior. -ಗುಡಿ, -ಗೃಹ. A lying-in chamber; the sanctuary of a temple. -ಧರಿಸು. To conceive. -ಧಾರಣ. Pregnancy, gestation. -ವತಿ. A pregnant female. -ಶ್ರೀಮಂತ. Born to riches and honour. -ಸಂಸ್ಕಾರ. A purificatory rite observed by pregnant females. ಗರ್ಭಿಣಿ. Pregnant; a pregnant woman. ಗರ್ಭಿತ. Pregnant; inclosed. ಗರ್ಭೀಕರಿಸು. To inclose, comprise.

ಗರ್ವ (= ಗಬ್ಬ) s. n. Pride, arrogance, conceit. -ಹೀನ. Prideless. ಗರ್ವಿ. Proud, haughty. ಗರ್ವಿಷ್ಠ. Most haughty. ಗರ್ವಿಸು. To become proud.

ಗರ್ವು. tb. of ಗರ್ವ, q. v.

ಗಲಗಲ (= ಕಲಕಲ) s. n. Clamour, confused chatter. -ಮಾಡು. To chatter loudly.

ಗಲಗು 1. k. n. A kind of reed for pens.

ಗಲಗು 2. k. n. Loud chatter.

ಗಲತಿ. = ಗಲ್ಲತ್ತು, q. v.

ಗಲಬರಿಕೆ k. n. Rinsing. ಗಲಬರಿಸು. To rinse.

ಗಲಬಿಲಿ. = ಗಲಿಬಿಲಿ, q. v.

ಗಲಟೆ f. n. Hubbub, uproar; clamour.

ಗಲಮಿಾಸೆ h. n. Mustaches curling over the cheeks.

ಗಲಸಾಧನೆ s. n. A kind of jugglery consisting in swallowing stones, *etc.*

ಗಲಿಬಿಲಿ k. n. Disorder, confusion.

ಗಲೀಜು h. a. Dirty, filthy.

ಗಲುಹು k. n. Tinkling, jingling.

ಗಲೇಫ h. n. A case, *as* of a pillow, sofa, *etc.*

ಗಲ್ಪಟ್ಟಿ s. n. A wrapper round the throat, neck-tie.

ಗಲ್ಲ k. n. The cheek. -ತಗ್ಗು. A dimple in the cheek. [ಗಲತಿ.

ಗಲ್ಲತ್ತು h. a. Astray; misplaced; *also*

ಗಲ್ಲಾ h. n. Corn. 2, = ಗಲ್ಲೆ, q. v.

ಗಲ್ಲಿ s. n. A lane, alley.

ಗಲ್ಲಿಸು k. v. t. To shake, *as* the boiled contents of a pot, *etc.*, or *as* corn, *etc.*, on a fan. 2, to trouble, annoy. *v. i.* To be troubled, *etc.*

ಗಲ್ಲು f. n. Hanging, *as* a culprit. ಗಲ್ಲಾಗು. To be hanged. ಗಲ್ಲಿಗೆ ಕೊಡು, -ಹಾಕು. To hang on the gallows. ಗಲ್ಲಿನ ಶಿಕ್ಷೆ. Punishment by hanging. -ಮರ. A gallows.

ಗಲ್ಲೆ k. n. A lump, clot. 2, (= ಗಲ್ಲಾ) a money-hole in the shop of shroffs and dealers.

ಗವ k. n. Smart itching. -ಗವ ಎನ್ನು. To itch very much.

ಗವಡ. = ಗವುಡ, q. v.

ಗವನ k. n. Attention, care, heed. ಗವ ನಿಸು. To heed, mind.

ಗವಯ s. n. A species of ox, the Gayal.

ಗವರಿಗ (ರ = ಱ) a. k. n. A basket-maker.

ಗವಲು. = ಗವುಲು, q. v.

ಗವಸಣೆ, -ಕೆ, -ಗೆ k. n. A cover, wrapper, case, sack.

ಗವಳಿ 1. = ಗವುಳಿ, q. v.

ಗವಳಿ 2. ಗವಳಿಗ (= ಗೌಳಿಗ, ಗೋವಳಿಗ. tb. of ಗೋಪಾಲಿ, -ಳ) n. A man of the cow-herd caste; f. ಗವಳಗಿತ್ತಿ.

ಗವಾಕ್ಷ s. n. A small round-window; an air-hole.

ಗವಾರ h. a. Rustic, clownish.

ಗವಿ k. n. A cave, cell. 2, covering. -ಸು. To heed, pay attention.

ಗವುಜಿ k. n. Noise, hubbub.

ಗವುಡ (= ಗೌಡ) s. n. The chief officer of a village. 2, a title of honour among peasants; f. -ಗಿತ್ತಿ, -ಸಾನಿ. -ತನ, ಗವುಡಿಕೆ. A Gavuḍa's business. ಗವುಡಿ. A maid-servant.

ಗವುಲಿ f. n. A flour-paste made into threads and cut into small bits.

ಗವುಲು (= ಗವಲು) k. n. A fetid smell.

ಗವುಳಿ k. n. The house lizard.

ಗವ್ಯ s. a. Belonging to a cow: milk, cheese, butter, urine and dung; also ಪಂಚ-.

ಗಸಗಸ k. n. A sound like quick rubbing. -ತಿಕ್ಕು. To rub, as the teeth, clothes on a stone, etc.

ಗಸಣೆ k. n. Care, concern, grief.

ಗಸಿ k. n. The sediment or dregs of oil, melted butter, or pickles.

ಗಸ್ತು h. n. A patrol, going the rounds; also -ಪಹರೆ.

ಗಹಗಹ k. n. The sound of laughter. ಗಹಗಹಿಸು. To laugh merrily. ಗಹಗ ಹಿಕೆ. Hilarity.

ಗಹನ s. a. Deep, dense; inaccessible. 2, difficult of comprehension, profound. n. A thicket; a wood. 2, a mystery, secret.

ಗಹ್ವರ s. a. Deep. 2, contiguous. n. A thicket. 2, an abyss; a cave. 3, a deep secret. 4, a jungle. 5, hypocrisy.

ಗಳ 1. (= ಗಲ) s. n. The neck, throat. -ದೊಡಿಗೆ. A neck-ornament. -ಗಾಳ. A hook for the throat.

ಗಳ 2. (= ಗಱ) k. n. Quick motion. -ಗಳನೆ. Quickly.

ಗಳಪು (ಳ = ೞ) k. v. i. To chatter, prate. n. Idle talk. ಗಳಪ. A loquacious, lying man. ಗಳಪತ್ತ. Idle prattle.

ಗಳಗೆ, ಗಳಿಗೆ 1. (tb. of ಘಟಿಕೆ) n. A high bamboo-basket for storing corn.

ಗಳಂತಿಗೆ f. n. An inner chamber.

ಗಳಿಕೆ (ಳ = ೞ) f. n. Acquirement, acquisition; gain.

ಗಳಿಗೆ 2. (tb. of ಘಟಿಕೆ) n. A fold, as of cloth.

ಗಳಿಗೆ 3. (ಳ = ೞ) (tb. of ಘಟಿಕೆ) n. A period of twenty-four minutes; a short time.

ಗಳಿಸು (tb. of ಘಟಿಸು) v. t. To procure; to acquire, obtain, gain.

ಗಳು k. An affix of the plural, as: ಮನೆ-, ಮರ-, ಕಾಲು-, ಇವು-, etc.

ಗಳೆ (ಳೆ = ೞೆ) k. n. A bamboo rod; a pole, staff; a churning stick.

ಗಳೇವು h. n. A complete agricultural apparatus; a set of implements.

ಗಾಗಳ k. n. Noise; hubbub.

ಗಾಂಗೇಯ (fr. ಗಂಗಾ) s. a. Belonging to the Ganges. n. Karṇa. 2, Bhīshma.

ಗಾಜು (tb. of ಕಾಚ, q. v.) n. Glass.

ಗಾಂಜಿ (= ಗಂಜ) s. n. The dried heads of the hemp-plant. -ಗಿಡ. The hemp-plant, Cannabis sativa.

ಗಾಟ, ಗಾಟು (= ಕಾಟು) k. n. A sharp, strong smell as of tobacco, burnt chillies, etc.

ಗಾಡಿ m. n. A load-cart; a carriage. -ಚಟ್ಟು. The inner seat of a cart. -ನತ್ತು.

A round nose-ring. -ಗಾರ, -ಯವ. A cart-driver.

ಗಾಡಿಗ (= ಗಾರುಡಿಗ) s. n. A juggler.

ಗಾಢ s. a. Hidden or absorbed in. 2, tight, close, firm, compact; deep, sound, *as* sleep; intense. 3, excessive, much. -ನಿದ್ರೆ. A sound sleep. ಗಾಢಾಂಧಕಾರ. Thick darkness.

ಗಾಣ k. n. An oil-mill; a sugarcane-mill. 2, (= ಗಾಳ) a hook; a fish-hook. -ಆಡಿಸು. To work a mill.

ಗಾಣಿಗ k. n. An oil-miller; *f.* ಗಾಣಿಗಿತ್ತಿ.

ಗಾಂಡಿವ, ಗಾಂಡೀವ s. n. Arjuna's bow. ಗಾಂಡಿವಿ, ಗಾಂಡೀವಿ. Arjuna.

ಗಾಂಡು m. n. The posteriors. -ಗುಡಿಗೆ. A bump with the knee upon a boy's posteriors; an aching fever. [ಘಾತ.

ಗಾತ (*tb. of* ಘಾತ) n. Depth. 2, *tb. of*

ಗಾತರ, ಗಾತ್ರ 1. (= ಗಡತರ, *q. v.*) k. n. Stoutness; thickness.

ಗಾತಿ (= ಗಾತಿ) s. *A fem. affix of nouns, as:* ರಚ್ಚೆ-, ಕೋಪ-, ಜಗಳ-, ವಿನೋದ-, *etc.*

ಗಾತ್ರ 2. s. n. A limb of the body. 2, the body. [proverb.

ಗಾಥೆ (= ಗಾದೆ) s. n. A song; a saying,

ಗಾದರಿ k. n. The mark left by a whip, by the bite of a musquito, *etc.*

ಗಾದಿ h. n. Cushion. 2, the seat of an eminent personage.

ಗಾದೆ (*tb. of* ಗಾಥೆ) n. A saying, proverb; *also* -ಮಾತು. [*cf.* ಆ-.

ಗಾಧ s. a. Fordable, shallow. n. Bottom.

ಗಾನ s. n. Singing; a song.

ಗಾಂಧಾರ s. n. The third of the seven primary notes of music. 2, Candahar and its people.

ಗಾಂಧಾರಿ s. n. N. of the wife of Dhṛitarâshṭra. 2, N. of a râga.

ಗಾಬರ, ಗಾಬರಿ (= ಘಾಬರ) h. a. Overcome by terror, grief, *etc.* n. Terror, consternation.

ಗಾಬು k. n. Fear, alarm.

ಗಾಂಪ k. n. A rustic, simpleton. -ತನ. The behaviour of a rustic. ಗಾಂಪು. Stupidity.

ಗಾಂಭೀರ್ಯ s. n. Deepness, profundity, earnestness, sagacity.

ಗಾಯ (= ಘಾಯ) k. n. A hit, bruise, wound. 2, (*tb. of* ಗಾಲ) straining, sifting.

ಗಾಯಕ s. n. A singer, musician.

ಗಾಯತ್ರಿ s. n. A song. 2, N. of a type of metres. 3, the vedic verse repeated by every Brâhmaṇa.

ಗಾಯನ s. n. Singing; song. -ಗಾರ. A singer, musician.

ಗಾರ s. *A masc. affix of nouns denoting agency, profession, etc., as:* ಕಂಚು-, ಕುದುರೆ-, *etc.*

ಗಾರಡ, ಗಾರಡಿ. *tb. of* ಗಾರುಡ, *q. v.*

ಗಾರಣ a. k. n. Tale-bearing, calumniating.

ಗಾರಿಗೆ k. n. A flat cake made of wheat or black gram and fried in ghee or oil. ಗಾರಿಸು. To fry.

ಗಾರು k. n. A sharp eruption on the body from internal heat. -ಬೊಕ್ಕೆ. A rash.

ಗಾರುಡ (*fr.* ಗರುಡ) s. a. Relating to garuḍa. n. A charm against poison. 2, jugglery. -ತನ, ಗಾರುಡಿ. Jugglery. ಗಾರುಡಿಗ. A conjurer, juggler; a poison doctor.

ಗಾರೆ m. n. Lime, plaster, mortar. -ಕೆಲಸ. A plastering work. -ಗಾರ. A plasterer.

ಗಾರ್ದಭ s. a. Asinine. n. An ass.

ಗಾಲ (= ಗಾಯ No. 2) s. n. Flowing; straining; swallowing.

ಗಾಲಿ k. n. A wheel.

ಗಾಲಿತ s. a. Strained, sifted. [hurry.

ಗಾಲುಮೇಲು m. n. Disorder; commotion;

ಗಾವದ, ಗಾವುದ (*tb. of* ಗವ್ಯೂತ) n. An Indian league.

ಗಾಸಿ (= ಘಾಸಿ) k. n. Trouble, annoyance, fatigue; pain.

ಗಾಳ k. n. A fish-hook.

ಗಾಳಿ (= ಘಾಳಿ, *q. v.*) k. n. Wind, air; emptiness; a demon. *Cpds.*: ಎಳೆ-, ತಂ-, ಬಿರು-, ಬಿಸು-, ಸುಟ್ಟುರ-, *etc.* -ಗಂಟು

A mass of lies. -ತಕ್ಕೊಳ್ಳು. To take an airing. -ಪಟ. A paper kite. -ಪೂಜೆ. Demon worship. -ಬಿಡು. Wind to begin to blow. -ಮಾತು. An empty word; abuse, slur. -ಸುದ್ದಿ. A false report. -ಹಾಕು. To fan.

ಗಾಳಿಸು s. v. t. To strain; to sift.

ಗಿಚ್ಚಿ k. n. Pegging one top into another. -ಹೊಡೆ. To peg likewise.

ಗಿಜಿ k. *A sound denoting confusion.* -ಗಿಜಿ. The state of being crowded. -ಗುಟ್ಟು. To be crowded. -ಬಿಜಿ. The chirping of birds; confusion, disorder.

ಗಿಂಜು k. n. Being full of seeds and disagreeable taste.

ಗಿಟಕ, ಗಿಟಕು k. n. The kernel of the cocoanut when still in the nut.

ಗಿಟ್ಟು (=ಈಟ್ಟು) k. v. i. To be obtained. 2, to be closely pressed. ಗಿಟ್ಟದವ. A useless man.

ಗಿಡ k. n. A plant; a small tree, shrub. -ಗಡ್ಡೆ, -ಗಂಟಿ. *dupl.* -ಮೂಲಿಕೆ. Medicinal plants and roots; a herbal medicine.

ಗಿಡಗ, ಗಿಡುಗ k. n. A hawk; a falcon.

ಗಿಡಿ k. v. t. To devour by mouthfuls. n. An imitative sound. -ಬಿಡಿ. A small drum like an hour-glass.

ಗಿಡು. =ಗಿಡ, q. v.

ಗಿಡ್ಡ k. n. A short, small man; a dwarf. -ನೆ. Short, small. *Cpds.:* -ಕಾಲು, -ಕೈ. -ನಾಯಿ, *etc.*

ಗಿಡ್ಡು k. n. Shortness, smallness.

ಗಿಣಿ (=ಗಿಳಿ) k. n. A parrot. -ಮೂಗು. A parrot's beak; a Roman nose.

ಗಿಂಟಿ k. n. Gingham, stout cloth.

ಗಿಂಡಿ k. n. A small round water-vessel with or without a spout.

ಗಿಣ್ಣ, ಗಿಣ್ಣು 1. k. n. The milk of a lately calved cow or buffalo.

ಗಿಣ್ಣೆ k. n. A cancerous disease destroying toes and fingers.

ಗಿಣ್ಣು 2. (=ಗೆಣ್ಣು) k. n. A knot, joint, *as* of a sugarcane, finger, *etc.*

ಗಿತ್ತಿ k. *A fem. affix of nouns, as:* ಕುಟಿಲ-, ಕುಂಬಾರ-, ಡೊಂಬರ-, *etc.*

ಗಿದ್ದ k. n. A quarter (¼). -ಕಾಣಿ. ¼ of a kâṇi. -ನ. The fourth part of a sŏligĕ.

ಗಿರ. =ಗಿದ್ದ. -ಕಾಲು. 1/16 part. -ಪಾವು. ¼ part of a measuring seer.

ಗಿರಕು (ರ=ಱ) k. n. Being close, strait, narrow.

ಗಿರಕೆ, ಗಿರಿಕೆ k. n. The ankle.

ಗಿರಣಿ f. n. A cotton-press.

ಗಿರದಿ f. n. A round cushion.

ಗಿರಬ್ದಾರಿ h. n. Distress, penury; fate.

ಗಿರಾಕಿ h. n. A buyer; a customer. *a.* Saleable.

ಗಿರಾಸತಿ (*tb. of* ಗೃಹಗತಿ) n. One's private affairs.

ಗಿರಾಯಿಸು. =ಗೇರಾಯಿಸು, *q. v.*

ಗಿರಿ 1. s. n. A mountain, hill. *a.* Respectable, venerable. -ಕರ್ಣಿಕೆ. A species of Achyranthes. -ಜಾ, -ಜಾತೆ, -ಜೆ, -ಸುತೆ. Mountain-born: Pârvati. -ಧರ. Kṛishṇa; Vishṇu in the form of a tortoise. -ರಾಜ. The Himâlaya. -ಶೃಂಗ. A mountain peak.

ಗಿರಿ 2. h. *Aff. denoting office, business or profession, as:* ದಿವಾನ-, ಸಿಪಾಯಿ-, ಮುನಿಷಿ-.

ಗಿರಿ 3. (ರಿ=ಱಿ) k. n. Whirling, buzzing. -ಗಿಟ್ಟಿ. A kind of rattle-box. -ಗಿರಿತಿರುಗು. To turn round with speed.

ಗಿರು (ರು=ಱು) k. n. Creaking. -ಗಟಿ. A sort of castanets; a child's turning rattle. -ಗುಟ್ಟು. To creak, *as* a door.

ಗಿರ್ರನೆ k. *ad.* Quickly, speedily; with a whirl.

ಗಿಲಕು k. n. Tinkling, rattling, *etc.*; a jingle. -ಗಿಲಕು. *rep.* The sound emitted by the gejje.

ಗಿಲಾಯ, ಗಿಲಾಯಿ h. n. A plaster of lime, water and sand.

ಗಿಲಿ k. n. Fear. -ಹಿಡಿ. To be afraid.

ಗಿಲಿಕೆ k. n. A child's rattle-box.

ಗಿಲಿಬಿಲಿ. =ಗಲಿಬಿಲಿ, *q. v.*

ಗಿಲ್ಲಾ h. n. A complaint; slander.

ಗಿಳಿ (= ಗಿಣಿ) k. n. A parrot.

ಗೀಂಕಾರ k. n. The roaring of an elephant; *also* ಘೀಂಕಾರ.

ಗೀಚಲುಬಾಚಲು (= ಗೀಚುಬಾಚು) k. n. Scrawl, scribble.

ಗೀಚು, ಗೀಜು, ಗೀರು k. v. t. To scrape; to scratch, scrawl; to draw lines with a pen; to erase. v. i. To scribble. n. A scratch; scrawling; a furrow. -ಬಾಚು. = ಗೀಚಲು ಬಾಚಲು, q. v.

ಗೀಜಗ, ಗೀಜುಗ k. n. The bottle-bird, *Ploceus baya*.

ಗೀಟು (= ಗೀರು, q. v.) k. n. A line, stroke.

ಗೀತ, ಗೀತೆ s. n. A song, hymn. ಗೀತಿ. Singing; a song. 2, the Bhagavadgîtâ.

ಗೀಮು k. n. A house, abode.

ಗೀರು (= ಗೀಟು, ಗೀಚು, q. v.) k. v. t. To scrape or rub off, *as* butter; to draw. *as* lines. n. A scratch; a line, streak, stripe, groove. ಗೀರ ಚಿಪ್ಪು, -ಸಿಂಪಿ. A striped shell. -ಗಂಧ. Sandal streaks on the body. -ನಾಮ. A sectarian line of gôpi on the forehead. -ಬಳೆ. A fluted gold bracelet.

ಗೀರ್ವಾಣ s. n. A god, deity. -ಭಾಷೆ. Samskṛita.

ಗುಂಯಿ k. n. Whizzing, buzzing. -ಗುಂಯಿ. *rep. The sound of some insects.*

ಗುಕ್ಕು 1. k. v. t. To draw a deep breath whilst speaking. ಗುಕ್ಕಿ ಮಾತಾಡು. To falter in speaking.

ಗುಕ್ಕು 2. k. n. An inarticulate sound. 2, a mouthful. 3, palpitation of the heart.

ಗುಗ್ಗರಿ k. n. Grain boiled and seasoned. 2, shrinking. 3, = ಗುಗ್ಗುರಿ. -ಕಸ. An annual weed, *Hedyotis aspera*. -ಗೊಳಲು. A mode of punishing boys by tying the hands round the knees in a sitting posture and fixing a stick between them.

ಗುಗ್ಗಳ (= ಗುಗ್ಗುಳು) s. n. The fragrant gum bdellium; a powder made of it.

ಗುಗ್ಗುರಿ k. n. Curling, bristling, *as* the hair of the body. 2, = ಗುಗ್ಗರಿ. -ಗೊಳ್ಳು. To become erect, horripilate, bristle.

ಗುಗ್ಗುಳು, ಗುಗ್ಗುಳ. = ಗುಗ್ಗಳ, q. v. 2, the tree *Amyris agallochum*. 3, *Morunga hyperanthera.*

ಗುಂಗಾಡ, ಗುಂಗಾಡಿ, ಗುಂಗಾಣ k. n. A musquito.

ಗುಂಗಿ k. n. A large black bee; *also* -ಹುಳ.

ಗುಂಗು k. n. The husk of paddy.

ಗುಂಗುರು 1. k. n. Curling. -ಕೂದಲು. = ಉಂಗುರ ಕೂದಲು. Curled hair.

ಗುಂಗುರು 2. k. n. An eye-fly. 2, a musquito, gnat.

ಗುಚ್ಛ s. n. A bundle, tassel, bunch, *as* of flowers; a cluster. 2, a bush. 3, a necklace of 32 strings.

ಗುಜರಾಥ (= ಗುಜ್ಜರಾಷ್ಟ್ರ. *tb. of* ಗುರ್ಜರರಾಷ್ಟ್ರ) n. The district of Gujarât. ಗುಜರಾಥಿ. An inhabitant or language of Gujarât.

ಗುಜರಾನು h. n. Livelihood, subsistence.

ಗುಜರಿ (= ಗುಜ್ಜರಿ) f. n. The evening market.

ಗುಜಸ್ತ h. a. Past, *as* a year, *etc.*

ಗುಜುಗುಜು k. n. *A sound in whispering;* whispering. -ಮಾತಾಡು, ಗುಜುಗುಜಿಸು. To whisper.

ಗುಜುರು, ಗುಜ್ಜ 1. a. k. n. Shortness, smallness.

ಗುಜ್ಜ 2. k. n. A dwarf.

ಗುಜ್ಜರಾಷ್ಟ್ರ. = ಗುಜರಾಥ, q. v. -ಪಟ್ಟೆ. Fine cloth from Gujarât.

ಗುಜ್ಜರಿ. = ಗುಜರಿ, q. v.

ಗುಜ್ಜಾರಿ k. n. A dwarf; f. ಗುಜ್ಜಿ.

ಗುಜ್ಜು k. n. A small perpendicular post, to raise short beams; a queen-post. 2, shortness, smallness.

ಗುಂಜಾಯಿಷಿ h. n. Illicit profit; excess of the area of the land under assessment.

ಗುಂಜಾಲಾಡು s. n. A sweetmeat of Bengal gram-dough formed like Abrus seeds.

ಗುಂಜಿ s. n. The seed of *Abrus precatorius; also* ಗುಂಜು.

ಗುಂಜು k. v. i. To be entangled, *as* thread. 2, to pull, contract, *as* muscles. *n.* Particles of cotton sticking to one's cloth; nap. 2, the coir of cocoanuts.

ಗುಟಕು, ಗುಟುಕು k. *n.* A single gulp or draught of any liquid. ಗುಟುಕರಿಸು. To drink in a single gulp. ಗುಟುಗುಟು ಕುಡಿ, ಗುಟುಕಿಸು. To drink in gulps. ಗುಟುಕ್ಕನೆ. With a single gulp.

ಗುಟುಗರೆ k. *v. i.* To grunt, bellow, *as* a bull.

ಗುಟಿಕೆ s. *n.* A pill, bolus.

ಗುಟ್ಟ. = ಗುತ್ತ, *q. v.*

ಗುಟ್ಟಿ k. *n.* A mixture of medicine for babies.

ಗುಟ್ಟು k. *n.* A secret; a hidden thought; one's private affairs.

ಗುಡ s. *n.* A ball, globe. 2, molasses, jaggory. -ಪಾನ. A beverage made of jaggory, *etc.*

ಗುಡಸಲು, ಗುಡುಸಲು, *etc.* k. *n.* A hut with a thatched roof.

ಗುಡಸು k. *n.* A round thing. 2, (=ಗುಡಿಸು) the round mark ' used for the vowel ಾ, and the round mark ‿ used for the vowel ು.

ಗುಡಾಕು f. *n.* A preparation of tobacco for smoking or snuff.

ಗುಡಾಣ k. *n.* A large water-vessel, caldron.

ಗುಡಾರ s. *n.* A tent. 2, a thick coarse cloth.

ಗುಡಿ 1. (=ಗುಡಸು No 1) k. *n.* A circle; a halo. 2, a mass, cluster. -ಕಟ್ಟು. A halo to form round the sun or moon; to form a ring; to come together, *as* people.

ಗುಡಿ 2. (*tb. of* ಕುಟಿ) *n.* A house; a temple. -ಗಟ್ಟು. A group of houses. -ಗಾರ. A turner and cabinet-maker.

ಗುಡಿಗೆ h. *n.* Breeches. -ಚಣ್ಣ. A sort of breeches.

ಗುಡಿಸು k. *v. t.* To sweep. 2, to heap up. ಗುಡಿಸಲು, ಗುಡಿಸಿಲು. Sweeping.

ಗುಡುಗು 1. k. *v. i.* To run when playing at tip-cat or ball. ಗುಡುಗಾಡು. To run about.

ಗುಡುಗು 2. k. *v. i.* To thunder. *n.* Thunder, roar, *etc.*

ಗುಡುಗುಡಿ m. *n.* A smoking pipe; a hubble-bubble.

ಗುಡುಗುಡಿಸು k. *v. i.* To grumble; to roar; to growl, grunt.

ಗುಡುಸಲು. = ಗುಡಸಲು, *q. v.*

ಗುಡ್ಡ 1. k. *n.* A boy, pupil; a dwarf. 2, shortness.

ಗುಡ್ಡ 2. k. *n.* A mountain; a hill. -ಗಾಡು. *dpl.* -ಗಾಡುಜನ. Jungle-people. -ದ ಗೋಟೀ ಮರ. A shrub, *Alangium lamarkii.* -ಪನ್ನೇರಳು. A small tree, *Eugenia zeilanica.* -ರಂಜಿಮರ. The tree *Elacocarpus serratus.*

ಗುಡ್ಡು k. *n.* The eye-ball. 2, an egg, spawn. 3, shortness, smallness.

ಗುಡ್ಡೆ k. *n.* A heap, pile. 2, a piece of cloth used by men.

ಗುಣ s. *n.* A cord, string. 2, quality, property. 3, the three fundamental qualities: satva, rajas, tamas. 4, a good quality, virtue, merit, excellence; wisdom; energy; dignity; goodness; temperance; recovery from sickness; favourable issue; benefit. 5, political wisdom. 6, flavour, taste. 7, multiplication. 8, a secondary gradation of a vowel, the vowels a, ê, ô. 9, joy. 10, protection. 11, *at the end of a compound:* fold, times. -ಕ. (*math.*) Multiplier. -ಕರ, -ಕಾರ. Profitable. -ಗ್ರಾಹಿ. One who appreciates good qualities. -ಜ್ಞ. A scholar. -ತ್ವ. Dependence; virtue. -ದೋಷ. Virtue and vice. -ಧರ್ಮ. The virtue or duty incidental to certain qualities, *as:* clemency is the virtue of royalty. -ನ. (*math.*) Multiplication. -ನಾಮ. A name that expresses the nature of a thing, person, *etc.* -ನಿಧಿ. An ocean of virtues. -ಮಣಿ.

A jewel of virtues. -ಯಿಸು. = ಗುಣಿಸು. -ವಚನ, -ವಾಚಕ. (*g.*) An adjective. -ವಂತ. A good man; *f.* -ವಂತೆ. -ಶ್ರೇಷ್ಠ. Pre-eminent in virtues. ಗುಣಾಕಾರ. (*math.*) Multiplication. ಗುಣಿ. Endowed with good qualities. ಗುಣಿತ. (*math.*) Multiplied; multiplication.

ಗುಣಿ (= ಕುಣಿ) k. *n.* A hole, pit. -ಗಣ್ಣು. A sunken eye. -ಗಲ್ಲ. A sunken cheek.

ಗುಣಿಸು s. *v. t.* To multiply; to enumerate; to calculate.

ಗುಣಿಕೆ. *tb. of* ಗುಟಿಕೆ, *q. v.*

ಗುಣುಗುಟ್ಟು k. *v. i.* To murmur, grumble, mutter.

ಗುಂಟ 1. k. *n.* Proximity. *ad.* Near; along, *as* ದಾರಿ-, ಮನೆ-.

ಗುಂಟ 2. (= ಗೂಟ) k. *n.* A peg, plug.

ಗುಂಟೆ f. *n.* The $\frac{1}{40}$ part of an acre.

ಗುಂಡ (= ಗುಂಡಿ, ಗುಂಡು) k. *n.* Roundness, hollowness and deepness. 2, a N.; a servant. -ಬಾವಿ. A temporary well sunk in the dry bed of a stream. -ಬಟ್ಟಲು. A small round and deep metal vessel. -ಗೆ. Of a round, globular form. -ಲಿಗೆ. A round water-vessel.

ಗುಂಡಾಂತರ k. *n.* A foundation. -ಮಾಡು. To lay a foundation; to ruin completely.

ಗುಂಡಿ (=ಗುಂಡ) k. *n.* A hole, pit, hollow. 2, = ಗುಂಡಿಗೆ, *q. v.* 3, a large round vessel. -ಕಾಯಿ. The physical heart.

ಗುಂಡಿಗೆ k. *n.* The pit of the stomach. 2, the thorax, heart; courage.

ಗುಂಡು 1. a. k. *n.* A heap, mass; a crowd, *etc.*

ಗುಂಡು 2. k. *n.* Anything round, *as* a boulder; a stone for grinding or constructing an ôlĕ; a globe; a ball, marble; a bullet, cannon ball. -ಅರ, ಗುಂಡರ. A round file. -ಕಲ್ಲು. A grinding stone. -ಮಲ್ಲಿಗೆ. A kind of jasmine. -ಮುಳುಗ. A diving water-bird. -ಬಾರಿಸು, -ಹೊಡೆ. To shoot a bullet; to fire a gun.

ಗುಣ್ಯ s. *a.* Endowed with qualities. *n.* The multiplicand.

ಗುತ್ತ k. *n.* Closeness; tightness. -ಬಳೆ. A tight bracelet. -ನೆ. Closely, tightly.

ಗುತ್ತಾ, ಗುತ್ತೆ. = ಗುತ್ತಿಗೆ, *q. v.*

ಗುತ್ತಿ a. k. *n.* A bunch or cluster of flowers. 2, a bush.

ಗುತ್ತಿಗೆ, ಗುತ್ತ k. *n.* An exclusive right of sale, farm, monopoly. 2, rental on land.

ಗುದಗ k. *n.* A fat, stout man; *f.* ಗುದಗಿ. 2, a prop behind a door to keep it shut.

ಗುದಗೆ. = ಗುದಿಗೆ, *q. v.*

ಗುದಿ 1. k. *n.* A rope for the feet used in climbing palm trees. 2, a bunch.

ಗುದಿ 2. k. *v. i.* To jump; to stamp.

ಗುದಿಗೆ, ಗುದುಗೆ (= ಗುದಗೆ) k. *n.* A club, cudgel.

ಗುದ್ದಲಿ, ಗುದ್ಲಿ (*tb. of* ಕುದ್ದಾಲ) *n.* A kind of pickaxe, hoe.

ಗುದ್ದಿ k. *n.* A clog tied to the neck of cattle.

ಗುದ್ದು 1. k. *n.* A hole, *as* of a mouse, snake, fox, *etc.*

ಗುದ್ದು 2. k. *v. t.* To strike with the fist, fist, cuff, box; to pound. *n.* A blow with the fist. ಗುದ್ದಾಟ. Fisticuffs. ಗುದ್ದಾಡು. To box. -ಮೊಳ. A short cubit. -ವಿಕೆ. Fisting; pounding.

ಗುನಿ k. *n.* A small crest on the grain of jôḷa. 2, the husk of paddy.

ಗುನ್ನ k. *n.* Smallness. 2, a raised spot. ಗುನ್ನಾನೆ. A dwarfish elephant.

ಗುನ್ನಾಂಪಟ್ಟಿ k. *n.* Paper gilt with tinsel.

ಗುಪ್ತ s. *a.* Concealed, hidden, secret. 2, guarded, preserved. -ಚ. A spy. ಗುಪ್ತಿ. Concealment; protection; a sword-stick.

ಗುಪ್ಪನೆ k. *ad.* Silently.

ಗುಬರು, ಗುಬುರು k. *n.* Thickness, *as* of a foliage. 2, veiling, covering. -ಕಟ್ಟು, -ಗಟ್ಟು. To become thick in foliage; a cover over the head; a cloak.

ಗುಬಾರು k. *n.* Noise of a crowd. 2, a swelling.

ಗುಬ್ಬಿ 1. k. n. A knob, protuberance. 2, a button. -ಮೊಳೆ. A stout nail with a pommelled head.

ಗುಬ್ಬಿ 2. k. n. A sparrow; *also* ಗುಬ್ಬಚ್ಚಿ, -ಬೆ ಳಸೆ. A small grass whose seeds stick to one's clothes, *Lappago aliena*. -ಹುಲ್ಲು. A common grass, *Sporobolus diander*.

ಗುಮಗುಮಾಯಿಸು k. v. t. To send forth a fragrant odour; *also* ಗುಮುಗುಮು ಅನ್ನು.

ಗುಮಟ, ಗುಮ್ಮಟ h. n. A copula or dome. 2, a huge figure of stone, representing a Jaina saint.

ಗುಮರಿ f. n. Fight of children.

ಗುಮಸ್ತ. = ಗುಮಾಸ್ತ, *q. v.*

ಗುಮಾನ h. n. Heed, care, consideration; suspicion, surmise. ಗುಮಾನಿ. Suspicious; suspected.

ಗುಮಾಸ್ತ h. n. An agent, deputy; an accountant. -ಗಿರಿ. The post of a gumâsta.

ಗುಂಪು k. n. A mass, heap, crowd, number. -ಕೂಡು, -ಗೊಳ್ಳು. To assemble.

ಗುಂಫ s. a. Stringing together; arranging. -ನ. Winding, arranging. ಗುಂಫಿತ. Strung together; arranged.

ಗುಂಬ 1. k. n. Mysteriousness, obscurity. 2, reservedness.

ಗುಂಬ 2. (*tb. of* ಕುಂಭ) n. A pot. 2, the nave of a wheel.

ಗುಮ್ಮ k. n. A bugbear, devil.

ಗುಮ್ಮಟ. = ಗುಮಟ, *q. v.*

ಗುಮ್ಮನ. = ಗುಂಬ 1., *q. v.* -ಗುಸುಕ. *dupl.* Reservedness; a reserved man; *f.* -ಗುಸುಕಿ.

ಗುಮ್ಮನೆ k. *ad.* Quickly.

ಗುಮ್ಮು k. v. t. To cuff, box; to strike. *v. i.* To push one's self along, *as* a baby. *n.* A push forward, *as* in swimming. 2, recoil. ಗುಮ್ಮಿಕ್ಕು. To recoil.

ಗುಮ್ಮುಟ. = ಗುಮಟ, *q. v.*

ಗುರಕೆ (ರ = ಱ) k. n. Snoring; growling. ಗುರಕಾಯಿಸು. To growl, snarl at, *as* a dog, *etc.*; to turn upon one in anger.

ಗುರತು (ರ = ಱ). = ಗುರುತ.

ಗುರಾಣಿ s. n. A shield.

ಗುರಿ (ರಿ = ಱಿ) k. n. An aim. 2, a mark, butt. -ಕಾರ. A man skilled in archery; a headman. -ಇಡು, -ನೋಡು, -ಹಿಡಿ. To take aim. -ತಾಕು. To hit the mark. -ಯಾಗು. To become the butt of; to fall into, *as* into sin; to be stricken, *as* with sorrow. -ಹೊಡೆ. To aim and shoot; to hit the mark.

ಗುರು 1. s. a. Heavy, weighty; venerable. *n.* Any venerable person; a religious teacher. 2, Bṛihaspati (Jupiter), the preceptor of the gods. -ಕುಲವಾಸ. Stay in the house of gurus. -ಕುಲವಾಸಿ. A disciple, pupil. -ತರ. Heavier, larger, more important. -ತ್ವ. Weight; dignity; worth; a teachership. -ದಕ್ಷಿಣೆ. A present to a teacher. -ಭಕ್ತಿ. Devotedness to one's teacher. -ಮಠ. A guru's residence. -ಮಂತ್ರ. The counsel of a guru. -ಮೂರ್ತಿ. The visible shape of a teacher; N. -ವಾರ. Thursday. -ಶೇಷ. The orts of a guru's meal. -ಶೇಷಪ್ರಸಾದ. Distribution of the orts of a guru's meal to his devotees. -ಹಸ್ತ. A Liṅgavanta. -ಹಿರಿಯರು. *dpl.* Preceptors and ancestors.

ಗುರು 2. (ರು = ಱು) k. n. A sound in snoring or purring; *also* ಗುರುಕು. -ಗುಟ್ಟು, -ಗುರಿಸು, -ಗುರೆನ್ನು. To snore; to pur. -ಗುಮ್ಮನೆ. Silently.

ಗುರುಕು. = ಗುರಕೆ, *q. v.*

ಗುರುಗಂಜಿ (= ಗುಲಗಂಜಿ) k. n. The creeper *Abrus precotorius*, wild liquorice and its seeds.

ಗುರುತ, ಗುರುತು (ರ = ಱ) k. n. A mark, sign; a characteristic mark; any sign used by illiterate persons for their signature. 2, knowledge. ಗುರುತಿನವ. A male acquaintance. ಗುರುತಿಲ್ಲದವ. An unacquainted man, a stranger. -ಹಚ್ಚು. To point out; to note, record. -ನೋಡು, -ಹಿಡಿ. To notice the peculiar features of a person or thing; to recognise. -ಹೇಳು. To tell the peculiar feature of a person or thing.

ಗುರ್ರುಗುಟ್ಟು (=ಗುರಕಾಯಿಸು s. ಗುರಕೆ) k. v. i. To growl, snarl, as dogs, etc.

ಗುರ್ತು. = ಗುರುತು, q. v.

ಗುಲ್ಗೆ k. n. The camboge tree, Garcinia pictoria.

ಗುಜರ್ರಾತ s. n. Gujarât. -ಪಟ್ಟೆ. Woven silk or fine cloth from G.

ಗುರ್ವಿ, ಗುರ್ವಿಣಿ s. n. A pregnant woman.

ಗುಲಗಂಜಿ. = ಗುರುಗಂಜಿ, q. v.

ಗುಲಾಬಿ h. n. A rose; also -ಹೂ. a. Rose-coloured. -ಗಿಡ. A rose bush. -ಬಣ್ಣ. Rose colour.

ಗುಲಾಮ h. n. A slave, menial. -ತನ. Slavery, bondage.

ಗುಲಾಲು m. n. The red powder which the Hindus throw about at the hôḷi feast.

ಗುಲ್ಮ s. n. A shrub, bush; a thicket. 2, a disease of the spleen. 3, a body of troops consisting of 9 elephants, 9 chariots, 27 horses, and 45 foot. -ವೃದ್ಧಿ. Ague-cake-

ಗುಲ್ಲು k. n. A loud noise, hubbub.

ಗುಸಗುಸ. = ಕುಸಕುಸ, q. v.

ಗುಹೆ (=ಗವಿ) s. n. A cave, cavern.

ಗುಹ್ಯ s. a. Private, secret. n. A secret, mystery.

ಗುಳ 1. = ಗುಡ, q. v.

ಗುಳ 2. (ಳ=ಱ) k. n. A horse's or elephant's trappings. 2, (=ಕುಳ) a bar of iron.

ಗುಳ k. affix for the formation of nouns, as ಅಟ್ಟು, ಬಂಡು-.

ಗುಳಿಕ (tb. of ಕುಲಿಕ) n. N. of Kêtu.

ಗುಳಿಗೆ (tb. of ಗುಟಿಕೆ, q. v.) n. A ball, pill, bolus.

ಗುಳುಗುಳು k. n. The murmuring sound produced by rippling water.

ಗುಳೆ, ಗುಳ್ಯ k. n. People leaving a place en masse from invasion or famine. -ತೆಗೆ, -ಹೋಗು. People to remove en masse, etc. -ಗುಳೇದಗುಡ್ಡ. N. of a place in the Bijapur district.

ಗುಳ್ಳ k. n. A stout herb, Solanum ferox. 2, a round kind of brinjal.

ಗುಳ್ಳೆ, ಗುಳ್ಳೆ k. n. A bubble; a blister; a small round shell.

ಗೂಗಿ, ಗೂಗೆ (= ಗೂಬೆ) k. n. An owl.

ಗೂಟ (= ಗೂಂಟ) k. n. A peg, pin.

ಗೂಡು k. n. A nest; a dove-cot; a fowl-house; a recess, niche; a cage, trap; the pit of the stomach; the hollow in bones; a frame.

ಗೂಡೆ k. n. A basket.

ಗೂಢ s. a. Covered, hidden; invisible; secret, private; occult. -ಚಾರ, -ಪುರುಷ. A spy. ಗೂಢಾಂಗ. A tortoise.

ಗೂಂಟ. = ಗೂಟ, q. v.

ಗೂದೆ 1. k. n. The love-apple or tomato.

ಗೂದೆ 2. k. n. Prolapsus of the anus.

ಗೂನು k. n. A hump. -ಬೆನ್ನು. A hump-back. ಗೂನ. A man with a hump; f. ಗೂನಿ.

ಗೂಬೆ (=ಗೂಗಿ, etc.) k. n. An owl. -ಗಣ್ಣು. A rolling eye, or one of deficient sight. -ಬಾಳು. An idle life; longivity.

ಗೂರಲು, ಗೂರು k. n. An asthmatic disease; also ಗೂರುಬ್ಬಸ.

ಗೂರು (ರು = ಱು) k. v. t. To root up the earth with horns.

ಗೂರ್ಮಿಸು a. k. v. i. To murmur or roar, as the water; to sound.

ಗೂಳಿ k. n. A bull 2, a big louse. -ಬಸವ, -ಹೋರಿ. A bull allowed to roam at liberty and dedicated to a deity.

ಗೂಳೆ. = ಗುಳೆ, q. v.

ಗೃಂಜನ s. n. Garlic.

ಗೃಧ್ರ s. a. Greedy. n. A vulture.

ಗೃಹ s. n. A house. -ಕಲಹ. Domestic dissensions. -ಕೃತ್ಯ. Domestic duties, household matters. -ಕ್ಷಯ. The ruin of a house. -ಛಿದ್ರ. A family folly; a private foible. -ಪತಿ, -ಮೇಧಿ. A householder, a Brâhmaṇa who is married and settled. -ಪ್ರವೇಶ. The ceremony of occupying a newly built house; a female's first entrance into her husband's house. -ಮಾತೆ. A mother-in-law. -ಮೇಧ. A domestic sacrifice. -ಶಾಂತಿ. Purificatory ceremonies of a house. -ಸ್ಥ, ಗೃಹಾಧಿಪ. A householder; a gentleman, patrician. -ಸ್ಥಾಶ್ರಮ. The second of the four religious stages of a Brâhmaṇa. -ಸ್ಥಿಕೆ. Politeness, gentlemanliness. -ಸ್ಥೆ. A housewife; a matron. ಗೃಹಾವಗ್ರಹಣಿ. The threshold. ಗೃಹಿಣಿ. The mistress of a house; a wife.

ಗೃಹ್ಯ, ಗೃಹ್ಯಕ s. a. Domestic; domesticated, tame. -ಸೂತ್ರ. A class of ritual works containing directions for domestic ceremonies.

ಗೆ k. *A suffix for the dative, as:* ಅರಸಿಗೆ, ನಾಳಿಗೆ, ಅತಗೆ, ಅಳೆಗೆ, *etc.*

ಗೆಜ್ಜೆ (= ಗಜ್ಜೆ) k. n. A spherical jingling bell. 2, the groin. -ಗೋಲು. A stick to which gĕjjĕs are attached, used in music or by post-runners. -ಹುಲ್ಲು. A common grass, *Andropogon aciculatus.* -ಗಾರ. A maker of small bells.

ಗೆಡ್ಡೆ (= ಗಡ್ಡೆ, q. v.) k. n. Any bulbous root.

ಗೆಣತಿ k. n. A female companion; *also* ಗೆಣೆಗಾತಿ.

ಗೆಣಸು, ಗೆಣಸು k. n. A bulbous root: a species of *Yam dioscorea;* the sweet potato, *Batatas edulis.*

ಗೆಣೆತನ, ಗೆಣೆತನ, ಗೆಳೆತನ k. n. Companionship, friendship.

ಗೆಣ್ಣು. = ಗಿಣ್ಣು, q. v.

ಗೆದಲು (= ಗೆದ್ದಲೆ, q. v.) k. n. The white ant, termite.

ಗೆದಿ (= ಗೆಲಿ) k. v. t. To conquer; to gain.

ಗೆದ್ದಲು. = ಗೆದಲು, q. v.

ಗೆದ್ದು. = ಗೆಲಿದು, ಗೆಲ್ದು. P. p. of ಗೆದಿ, ಗೆಲ್ಲು.

ಗೆಯಿ, ಗೆಯು k. v. t. To perform, do; to prepare; to work, till. *Cpds.:* ಕೆಲಸಂ-, ಕ್ಷೇಮ-, ನಿದ್ರೆ-, ಪುಣ್ಯಂ-, ಮುದ್ದು-, *etc.* -ಸು. To cause to perform, *etc.* ಗೆಯ್ಮೊಕ್ಕಲಿಗ. A husbandman.

ಗೆರಸೆ, ಗೆರಿಸೆ (= ಕೆರಸೆ, q. v.) k. n. A basket.

ಗೆರೆ k. n. A scratch; a line; a streak. -ಹಾಕು. To rule; to mark; to draw a line over.

ಗೆಲವು, ಗೆಲುವು k. n. Gain; victory. 2, a happy, sprightly air. -ಸೋಲು. Gain and loss.

ಗೆಲಿ, ಗೆಲು, ಗೆಲ್ಲು k. v. t. To win, gain, to overcome, conquer; to triumph. *P. p.* ಗೆಲ್ದು, ಗೆದ್ದು, ಗೆಲುಮೊಗ. A winning countenance. ಗೆಲುಗೆ, ಗೆಲುವಿಕೆ. Winning. ಗೆಲಸು, ಗೆಲ್ಲಿಸು. To cause to win, *etc.*

ಗೆಳತಿ (= ಕೆಳದಿ, *etc.*) k. n. A female friend.

ಗೆಳೆ (= ಕೆಳೆ, q. v.) k. n. A friend, companion. -ತನ. Friendship, companionship, *etc.*

ಗೇ k. v. t. To perform, *etc.* *P. p.* ಗೇದು.

ಗೇಣಿ k. n. Rent, contract. -ಚೀಟು. A lease. ಮೂಲ-. A permanent lease. ಸಾಲ-. Annual lease. ವಾಯಿದೆ-. A lease for a fixed time.

ಗೇಣು k. n. A span. -ಹೊಟ್ಟೆ. The stomach that is only a span in length or breadth.

ಗೇಂಡ, ಗೇಂಡಾಮೃಗ f. n. Rhinoceros.

ಗೇನ. *tb. of* ಜ್ಞಾನ, q. v.

ಗೇಟೆ k. n. A morbid swelling. -ಮೋರೆ. A swollen face. -ಹೊಟ್ಟೆ. A swollen belly.

ಗೇಮೆ k. n. Work. -ಕರಾರು. A labour contract.

ಗೇಯು. = ಗೆಯ್ಯು, q. v.

ಗೇರಾಯಿಸು h. v. t. To surround, hem in.

ಗೇರಿ f. n. Giddiness.

ಗೇರು 1. k. n. *A phlegmatic sound produced in the chest.*

ಗೇರು 2. k. n. The marking-nut tree; the cashew-nut tree. -ಬೀಜ. The marking nut, *Semecarpus anacardium;* the cashew-nut tree.

ಗೇಲಿ k. n. Ridicule, derision. -ಮಾಡು. To ridicule.

ಗೈ. = ಗೆಯಿ, *etc., as:* ನಿದ್ದೆಗೈ, to sleep. ಯೋಚನೆಗೈ, to reflect, *etc.*

ಗೈರ, ಗೈರು h. *pref.* Dis-, un-, extra, out of. -ಖರ್ಚು. Extra expense. -ಮಾಮೂ

ಲು. That is against custom or usage. -ವಾಜಬಿ. Unreasonable, improper. -ವಿಲೆ. Out of order; lost. -ಹಾಜರು. Absent.

ಗೊಂಗಡಿ h. n. A cloak or blanket worn over the head and face. 2, a cumbly.

ಗೊಂಗೆ a. k. n. A mass, heap. 2, the large grey babbler.

ಗೊಜಗು k. v. i. To speak indistinctly. n. Indistinct speech.

ಗೊಜ್ಜಲು k. n. Mud, mire.

ಗೊಜ್ಜು k. n. A thick mess of boiled brinjals, mangoes, *etc.* mixed with tamarind, chillies, *etc.* 2, acidity, sourness.

ಗೊಜ್ಜೆ k. n. Putridity; mud, mire.

ಗೊಂಚಲು k. n. A bunch, cluster, *as:* ಹೂವಿನ-, ಹಣ್ಣಿನ-, ಮುತ್ತುಗಳ-, ಕಾಯಿ-, *etc.*

ಗೊಟಕು. = ಗುಟುಕು, *etc., q. v.*

ಗೊಟರು k. n. A hole, hollow. -ಬೀಳು. A hollow to be formed.

ಗೊಟ್ಟ k. n. A bamboo tube for administering food or medicine to cattle. 2, a mango-stone. 3, a corner.

ಗೊಟ್ಟು k. n. Scarcity. 2, dryness. 3, obstinacy. -ಕಾಲ. Drought.

ಗೊಡಗು. = ಗೊಟರು, *q. v.*

ಗೊಡವೆ k. n. Connexion; intercourse; concern with, care about.

ಗೊಡ್ಡು (*cf.* ಗೊಟ್ಟು) k. n. Barrenness, sterility; saplessness. -ಆಕಳು. A barren cow. -ಆಟ, ಗೊಡ್ಡಾಟ. Nonsense. -ಕೆಲಸ. Useless work. -ಮರ. A barren tree. -ಮಾತು. A vain word. -ಸಾರು. A broth without strength. -ಹರಟೆ. Useless talk.

ಗೊಣಗು k. v. i. To nasalize. n. Nasalization. 2, grumbling, murmuring. ಗೊಣಗ. One who nasalizes; *f.* ಗೊಣಗಿ.

ಗೊಣಸು k. n. A link of a chain. 2, a loop. 3, a bunch of 5 pearls.

ಗೊಂಡೆ k. n. A cluster; a tuft; a tassel. 2, a thickset state. 3, an amaranth, *Gomphrena globosa*. ಗೊಂಡಾರಣ್ಯ. An impervious jungle.

ಗೊಣ್ಣೆ k. n. Mucus of the nose. 2, a blot of ink.

ಗೊತ್ತು (= ಗುರುತು, *q. v.*) k. n. A mark, sign, token. 2, knowledge, acquaintance. 3, appointment, regulation, order; a place of resort or shelter. -ಗಾರ. A male acquaintance; a person of distinction; a headman. -ಮಾಡು, -ಹಚ್ಚು, -ಹತ್ತಿಸು. To find out. ಗೊತ್ತಾಗು. To be known; to be found out.

ಗೊದಕು, ಗೊದಗು k. n. Mud, mire.

ಗೊದಗೊದ k. n. Thickness, *as* of ambali, *etc.*

ಗೊದಮು k. n. A bat used in leading the course of an idol-car.

ಗೊದ್ದ k. n. A large black ant.

ಗೊದ್ದೆ k. n. Pig's dung.

ಗೊನೆ k. n. A cluster or bunch of fruit, *as* of cocoanuts, plantains, mangoes, *etc.*

ಗೊಂದಣ, ಗೊಂದಣೆ a. k. n. A mass; an assemblage; a crowd, throng. ಗೊಂದಣಿಸು. To assemble, *etc;* to be plentiful.

ಗೊಂದಲ f. n. Confusion; bustle; tumult.

ಗೊಂದಿ k. n. An alley, lane. 2, a strait.

ಗೊಬ್ಬರ k. n. Manure. 2, the measles.

ಗೊಂಬೆ (= ಬೊಂಬೆ) k. n. An image, idol; a puppet, doll; the pupil of the eye. -ಮದುವೆ. A sham-marriage made by children with dolls.

ಗೊರಕು (ರ = ಱ) k. n. Snoring.

ಗೊರಗು k. n. A kind of hood made of leaves or grass.

ಗೊರಜೆ k. n. N. of a plant. -ಪಲ್ಯ. A common potherb, *Digera arvensis*.

ಗೊರಲೆ (ರ = ಱ) k. n. A kind of termites.

ಗೊರವ k. n. A class of Śaiva beggars; *f.* -ತಿ, ಗೊರವಿತಿ.

ಗೊರವಂಕ k. n. The common Maina, *Acridotheres tristis*.

ಗೊರವಿ k. n. An evergreen tree which makes good torches, *Ixora parviflora*.

ಗೊರಸು, ಗೊರಿಸೆ, ಗೊರುಸು k. n. A hoof.

ಗೊಲೆ k. n. The notched extremity of a bow. 2, a cluster.

ಗೊಲ್ಲ (tb. of ಗೋಪಾಲ) n. A cowherd; f. -ತಿ. 2, an assistant cashkeeper.

ಗೊಳಗೊಳಕೆ k. n. The yellow thistle, *Argemone mexicana*.

ಗೊಳಲಿ k. n. Husk, chaff. 2, the rind of a tamarind fruit.

ಗೋ (= ಗೋವು) s. n. A cow. 2, a bull. 3, a ray of light (ಕಿರಣ). 4, heaven. 5, the earth. 6, water. 7, Sarasvatî. -ಕರ್ಣ. A cow's ear; a place of pilgrimage in North Kanara. -ಕುಲ. A herd of kine; a cow-house; a village on the river Yamunâ, Kṛishṇa's residence. -ಕುಲಾಷ್ಟಮಿ. The birthday of Kṛishṇa. -ಕ್ಷುರ. The plant *Asteracantha longifolia*. -ಜಾತಿ. Cattle; cattle-like nature. -ದಾನ. Gift of a cow. -ಧನ. Property in cattle. -ಪಥ. A cattle path. -ಪುಚ್ಛ. A cow's tail; a necklace of 2 or more strings. -ಮಯ. Cowdung. -ಮಾಂಸ. Beef. -ಮಾರಿ. A disease of cattle. -ಮುಖ. A cow's mouth; a round platter with a snout used for placing idols on. -ಮುಖವ್ಯಾಘ್ರ. "A wolf in sheep's clothing." -ಮೇಧ. Sacrifice of a cow. -ರಕ್ಷ, -ರಕ್ಷಕ. A cowherd. -ರಸ. Cow's milk; buttermilk. -ಶಾಲೆ. A cowpen. -ವತ್ಸ. A calf.

ಗೋಗರೆ k. v. t. To beg loudly. n. Bellowing sound of a bull-frog.

ಗೋಚರ s. n. Range (*lit.* field for cattle). a. Being within range or reach of, accessible, attainable, perceivable by the mind, sense, or the eye. -ವಾಗು, ಗೋಚರಿಸು. To become perceptable; to appear.

ಗೋಚೆ f. n. A cloth to cover the privities.

ಗೋಜು k. n. Interference, entanglement. 2, intercourse. 3, embarrassment, trouble.

ಗೋಟು 1. k. n. Fringe, ribbon, edging, trimming. 2, a stunted tamarind fruit. 3, the state of being full grown, but hard; *as* ಗೋಟಡಿಕೆ. A hard, inferior kind of areca nut.

ಗೋಟು 2. h. n. The border or hem of a garment. 2, a cloak of broadcloth.

ಗೋಡು k. n. Sediment from the bottom of wells, tanks, *etc.*

ಗೋಡೆ (tb. of ಕುಡ್ಯ) n. A wall. -ಗನ್ನ. A hole made by burglars in a wall. ಹಾಳು-. A dilapidated wall.

ಗೋಣ k. n. = ಗೋಣು. 2, a man with a neck. -ಗೊಯ್ಕ. A cut-throat; f. -ಗೊಯ್ಕೆ.

ಗೋಣಿ 1. k. n. A sack, pack-sack; *also* -ಚೀಲ. 2, a confluent kind of small-pox; *also* -ದಡಾರ. -ಚೀಲ, -ತಟ್ಟು. Sackcloth.

ಗೋಣಿ 2. (= ಗೋಳಿ) k. n. The tree called *Ficus elastica*.

ಗೋಣು k. n. The nape, neck, throat. -ಗೊಯ್ಕ. A cut-throat. -ಮುರಿದು ಬೀಳು. To drop the head and fall, *as* in dying.

ಗೋತ 1. k. n. The fetid urine of cattle.

ಗೋತ 2. k. n. A ruinous business; loss. -ಹಾಕು. To die.

ಗೋತ್ರ s. n. A cow-pen. 2, family, race, lineage; kin; offspring. 2, the family-name. -ಜ. A relation.

ಗೋದಣ, ಗೋದಲಿ, ಗೋದಲೆ k. n. A crib for cattle.

ಗೋದಾವರಿ s. n. The Godavery river.

ಗೋದಿ (tb. of ಗೋಧೂಮ) n. Wheat, *Triticum vulgare*. -ಕಾಳು. A grain of wheat; wheat. -ನಾಗರ. *Naga tripudians*. -ರವೆ, -ಸಜ್ಜಿಗೆ. Granulated wheaten flour, rolong. -ಹಿಟ್ಟು. Wheaten flour.

ಗೋಧೂಳಿ s. n. Dust raised by cattle on the road when coming home. 2, evening twilight. -ಲಗ್ನ. Marriage performed at gôdhûli.

ಗೋಧಿ s. n. The forehead. 2, an iguana.

ಗೋಧಿಕೆ, ಗೋಧೆ s. n. A large kind of lizard; an iguana.

ಗೋನಾಳಿ s. k. n. The throat, neck.

ಗೋಂದ, ಗೋಂದು h. n. Gum.

ಗೋಪ s. n. A cowherd. 2, the head of a district; a king. 3, Kṛishṇa. -ತಿ. A bull. -ನ. Guarding, protection. -ವಾಹನ. Indra's vehicle: Airâvata; Brahmâ's vehicle: the haṁsa; Vishṇu's vehicle: Garuḍa. -ಸ್ತ್ರೀ. A herd's-woman.

ಗೋಪಾಲ (= ಗೋವ, q. v.) s. n. A cowherd; a caste of Vaishṇava mendicants. 2, alms. 3, a N. -ಪುಟ್ಟಿ. A mendicant's bamboo basket.

ಗೋಪಿ s. n. A cowherd's wife, Kṛishṇa's foster-mother; a milkmaid. -ಚಂದನ. A species of white clay used by Vaishṇavas for making sectarian marks.

ಗೋಪು (tb. of ಗೋಪ) n. N. 2, a neck-ornament.

ಗೋಪುರ s. n. A town-gate, gate; a tower over the gate of a city or temple.

ಗೋಪ್ಯ s. a. Secret, hidden.

ಗೋಮನಾಳಿ, ಗೋಮಾಳೆ, etc. k. n. The neck or throat with Adam's apple.

ಗೋಮಯ s. n. Cowdung.

ಗೋಮಾಂತಕ s. n. Goa.

ಗೋಮು f. n. A bad mark in a horse.

ಗೋಮೇದಕ, ಗೋಮೇದಿಕ s. n. A precious stone of a reddish colour.

ಕೋರಟೆ, ಗೋರಂಟ, ಗೋರಂಟೆ (tb. of ಕುರುಂಟ) n. The prickly flower-plant *Lawsonia spinosa*.

ಗೋರಾ h. a. White; of fair complexion.

ಗೋರಿ 1. h. n. A grave, tomb.

ಗೋರಿ 2. k. n. Drawing together; attracting, decoy. 2, a kind of rake. -ಕಾಯಿ. *Dolichos fabaeformis*.

ಗೋರು 1. k. v. t. To draw; to gather pile; to fish with a net, etc. 2, to scratch. n. Drawing, etc. -ಮಣೆ. A kind of rake.

ಗೋರು 2. f. n. Trouble, annoyance.

ಗೋರೆ k. n. A shovel.

ಗೋರೋಚನ (tb. ಗೋರೋಜನ) s. n. A yellow pigment prepared from the urine or bile of a cow or found in its head.

ಗೋಲ (= ಗೋಲು, ಗೋಳ) s. n. A ball, globe, circle, sphere. -ರಸ. Gum-myrrh. ಗೋಲಾಕಾರ. Globular. ಗೋಲಾರ್ಧ. A hemisphere.

ಗೋಲಕ h. n. A money-box, till. 2, a ball.

ಗೋಲಕೊಂಡ s. n. Goloonda near Hydrabad.

ಗೋಲಿ s. n. A small ball. -ಕಲ್ಲು. A marble.

ಗೋಲು (tb. of ಗೋಲ, q. v.) n. A circle, ring; a globe. ಗೋಲುಂಗರ. A plain finger-ring.

ಗೋವಗಿಡ k. n. The guava tree, *Psidium guatava*.

ಗೋವರ್ಧನ s. n. A hill in Vṛindâvana.

ಗೋವಳ. tb. of ಗೋಪಾಲ, q. v.

ಗೋವಿಂದ s. n. A chief-herdsman. 2, Kṛishṇa; Vishṇu.

ಗೋವು. = ಗೋ, q. v.

ಗೋವೆ s. n. Goa.

ಗೋಷಾ h. n. A veil, cover used by Mohammadan women when appearing in public.

ಗೋಷ್ಟಿ m. n. A word; a story.

ಗೋಷ್ಠ s. n. A cow-pen.

ಗೋಷ್ಠಿ s. n. An assembly. 2, a conversation, discourse.

ಗೋಷ್ವಾರೆ h. n. An abstract, summary.

ಗೋಸಾಯಿ, ಗೋಸಾವಿ. tb. of ಗೋಸ್ವಾಮಿ, q. v.

ಗೋಸುಂಟೆ k. n. A chameleon.

ಗೋಸ್ಕರ. = ಓಸ್ಕರ, q. v.

ಗೋಸ್ವಾಮಿ (= ಗೋಸಾಯಿ) s. n. The master of cows. 2, a religious mendicant.

ಗೋಳ (tb. of ಗೋಲ, q. v.) n. A ball; a globe. 2, (k.) clamour, tumult.

ಗೋಳಾಡು k. v. t. To bewail, lament. ಗೋಳಾಟ. Lamentation, weeping. ಗೋಳಿಡು. = ಗೋಳಾಡು.

ಗೋಳಿ k. *n.* Any kind of fig tree which bears no apparent flowers; the banyan tree, *Ficus bengalensis*. 2, a small potherb of the genus *Portulaca*. -ಹಕ್ಕಿ. A teal, water-duck.

ಗೌಡ 1. (= ಗವುಡ, *q. v.*) k. *n.* The headman of a village; *f.* -ಗಿತ್ತಿ.

ಗೌಡ 2. s. *n.* Sweetmeats. 2, the district of Gaur in Bengal. -ಮಾರ್ಗ, -ರೀತಿ. The gauḍa style. -ಬಂಗಾಳಿ. Trickery.

ಗೌಣ s. *a.* Subordinate, secondary.

ಗೌತಮ s. *n.* N. of Buddha or Sâkyamuni, the founder of the Buddhist sect.

ಗೌರಮ್ಮ, ಗೌರವ್ವ s. & k. *n.* Pârvati.

ಗೌರವ (*fr.* ಗುರು) s. *a.* Relating to a guru. *n.* Weight, gravity. 2, importance. 3, dignity, respectability.

ಗೌರಿ s. *n.* A virgin. 2, Pârvati. 3, a yellow pigment. -ಕಾಂತ, -ಪತಿ. Śiva. -ಪಾಷಾಣ. A kind of mineral. -ಪುತ್ರ. Gaṇapati.

ಗೌಲಿ (= ಗವುಲಿ, *q. v.*) f. *n.* A paste of wheaten flour cut into threads.

ಗೌಳಿ (= ಗವಳಿ, ಗವಳಿಗ) k. *n.* A milkman.

ಗ್ನಾನ. *tb. of* ಜ್ಞಾನ, *q. v.*

ಗ್ರಂಥ s. *n.* Binding. 2, a book or composition in prose or verse; a code; a religious treatise. 3, wealth. 4, great knowledge. -ಕರ್ತ, -ಕಾರ. An author. -ಲಿಪಿ. One of the characters used in writing.

ಗ್ರಂಥಿ s. *n.* A knot; a tie; a joint, gland.

ಗ್ರಸ್ತ s. *a.* Devoured, eaten; seized. 2, imperfectly pronounced.

ಗ್ರಹ s. *n.* A planet. 2, an imp, evil spirit, demon. -ಚಾರ. The bad influence of unpropitious stars; fate, destiny. -ಪತಿ. The sun. -ಪೀಡೆ, -ಬಾಧೆ. Trouble from unpropitious stars or demons. -ಮಾಲೆ. The planets. -ಶಾಂತಿ. Propitiation of the planets by offerings.

ಗ್ರಹಣ s. *n.* Seizing; taking, accepting. 2, seizure of the sun or moon: an eclipse. 3, understanding, comprehension.

ಗ್ರಹಣಿ s. *n.* Diarrhœa, dysentery. 2, rickets; marasmus.

ಗ್ರಹಸ್ತ. *tb. of* ಗೃಹಸ್ಥ, *q. v.*

ಗ್ರಹಿಕೆ s. *n.* Understanding, comprehension.

ಗ್ರಹಿಸು s. *v. t.* To accept, acknowledge; to comprehend, understand.

ಗ್ರಾಚಾರ. *tb. of* ಗ್ರಹಚಾರ *s.* ಗ್ರಹ, *q. v.*

ಗ್ರಾಮ s. *n.* A village. 2, a multitude: collection. -ಕೀಟಕ. Village vermin; a mischief-maker. -ಣಿ. The headman of a village. -ದೇವತೆ. The deity of a village. -ಮುನಸೀಫ. A Gavuḍa, a village-munsif. -ವಾಸಿ. A villager; tame. -ಶಾಂತಿ. Purification of a village from infesting devils, *etc.* -ಸ್ಥ. A villager.

ಗ್ರಾಮ್ಯ s. *a.* Rustic; vulgar, coarse, rude. *n.* A villager; an uneducated man. -ಪಶು. A domestic beast. -ಭಾಷೆ. A vulgar dialect. -ಶಬ್ದ. A vulgar term.

ಗ್ರಾಸ s. *n.* A mouthful, morsel. 2, food, nourishment. ಗ್ರಾಸೋಪಾಯ. Means of subsistence.

ಗ್ರಾಹಕ s. *a.* Seizing, receiving, accepting, perceiving. -ಶಕ್ತಿ. The faculty of comprehension.

ಗ್ರಾಹಿ s. *a.* Seizing, accepting, *etc.*; holding; perceiving.

ಗ್ರಾಹ್ಯ s. *a.* Perceivable; acceptable; comprehensible.

ಗ್ರೀಷ್ಮ, -ಕಾಲ s. *n.* The hot season from the middle of May to the middle of July; heat, warmth.

ಘ್

ಘ್. The twenty-second letter of the alphabet.

ಘಕಾರ s. n. The letter ಘ.

ಘಟ s. a. Coming to, reaching, joining. n. Collection. 2, a troop of elephants. 3, the body. 4, an earthen water-vessel. -ಸರ್ಪ. A large serpent.

ಘಟಕ s. a. Strong, powerful; forming a constituent part. n. A manager between parties.

ಘಟನೆ s. n. Joining, junction; arranging, effecting; effort, exertion; accomplishment, success.

ಘಟಿ s. n. A small water-jar. 2, a period of 24 minutes. 3, a gong. 4, a sinking cup for measuring time. -ಯಂತ್ರ. A machine for raising water.

ಘಟಿಕೆ (= ಗಳಿಗೆ 3, q. v.) s. n. A period of 24 minutes.

ಘಟಿತ s. a. Joined, united; planned, devised; occurred. ಘಟಿತಾರ್ಥ. Practicableness.

ಘಟಿಸು (= ಗಳಿಸು, q. v.) s. v. i. To be gained; to happen, etc.; also ಘಟಿಯಿಸು.

ಘಟೆ s. n. Effort, endeavour. 2, an assemblage, collection.

ಘಟ್ಟ (= ಗಟ್ಟ, q. v.) k. n. A range of mountains, ghaut, defile. ಸೋಪಾನ-. A staircase.

ಘಟ್ಟಣೆ s. n. Beating down, as a road; folding by beating gently.

ಘಟ್ಟನ (= ಘಟ್ಟಣೆ) s. n. Touching; rubbing, beating, striking; compressing; practice.

ಘಟ್ಟಿ (= ಗಟ್ಟಿ, q. v.) k. a. Firm. 2, loud. 3, solid. 4, able, clever. -ಗ. A strong, able man. -ತನ. Strength, energy, ability.

ಘಟ್ಟಿಸು. = ಗಟ್ಟಿಸು, q. v.

ಘಡಾ (tb. of ಘಟ) n. A drum formed of an earthen vessel.

ಘಡಾಯಿಸು. = ಗಡಾಯಿಸು, q. v.

ಘಡಾರಿ. = ಗಡಾರಿ, q. v.

ಘಡಿಯಾರ, ಘಡಿಯಾಲ. = ಗಡಿಯಾರ, q. v.

ಘಂಟಾ, ಘಂಟೆ (= ಗಂಟೆ) s. n. A bell; a gong. ಘಂಟಾಕರ್ಣ. An attendant on Śiva. ಘಂಟಾನಾದ, ಘಂಟಾರವ. The sound of a bell.

ಘನ s. a. Compact, solid, hard, dense, full; large, great, much; auspicious. n. Any compact substance. 2, respect, honour, dignity; greatness. 2, an assemblage; solidity. -ಅಳತೆ. A cubic measure. -ತರ. Uncommonly hard, thick, great, etc. -ತೆ, -ತ್ವ. Firmness, solidity; greatness, excellence. ಘನೀಭೂತ. Thickened, compact. -ರಸ. Water; a decoction; camphor.

ಘವು. = ಗವು 1, q. v.

ಘರಟ್ಟ s. n. A grindstone.

ಘರ್ಮ (= ಗರವು) s. n. Heat; sunshine; the hot season. 2, sweat, perspiration; also -ಜಲ.

ಘರ್ಷಣ s. n. Rubbing; grinding; friction; furbishing.

ಘಳಿಗೆ. = ಗಳಿಗೆ 2, 3, q. v.

ಘಳಿಲ್, ಘಳಿಲನೆ (ಳಿ=ಱ) a. k. ad. Quickly.

ಘಾಟ, ಘಾಟೆ s. n. The nape of the neck.

ಘಾಡಾ h. a. Thick, coarse, as cloth.

ಘಾತ s. n. Striking; wounding, killing. 2, destruction, ruin; a blow. -ಕ. Killing, felonious; a murderer; f. -ಕಿ. -ನ. Killing, striking. ವಿಶ್ವಾಸ-. Breach of trust; ಘಾತಿ. Killing; a killer. ಘಾತಿಸು. To strike; to slay, etc.

ಘಾತುಕ s. a. Killing, destructive, mischievous.

ಘಾಬರಿ. = ಗಾಬರಿ, q. v.

ಘಾಯ (= ಗಾಯ, q. v.) k. n. A wound. -ವಾಗು. To be wounded.

ಘಾರಿಗೆ. = ಗಾರಿಗೆ, q. v.

ಘಾಸಿ (=ಗಾಸಿ, *q. v.*) k. *n.* Harass, distress; fatigue; pain, hurt.

ಘಾಳಿ (= ಗಾಳಿ, *q. v.*) k. *n.* Wind, air. ಬಿರು-. A hurricane. ತಂ-. A cool breeze. -ತಕ್ಕೊಳ್ಳು, -ತಿನ್ನು. To take an airing. -ವಾರ್ತೆ, -ಸುದ್ದಿ. A false report; a rumour.

ಘೀಂಕಾರ (=ಗೀಂಕಾರ, *q. v.*) k. *n.* The roaring of an elephant.

ಘುಟಿಕೆ s. *n.* The ankle.

ಘೃಣೆ, ಘೃಣೆ s. *n.* Heat; ardour; tenderness; disgust.

ಘೃತ s. *n.* Clarified butter, ghee.

ಘೇರು f. *n.* A circumference.

ಘೋರ s. *a.* Terrific, frightful, terrible, awful, vehement. -ತರ. Very terrible. -ಮೂರ್ತಿ. Bhairava.

ಘೋಷ s. *n.* Sound, noise, cry, roar. 2, a station of herdsmen. -ಣೆ. Speaking loud; crying. -ವರ್ಣ, ಘೋಷಾಕ್ಷರ. A sonant letter. ಘೋಷಿಸು. To make a great noise; to cry out, proclaim.

ಘ್ರಾಣ s. *n.* Smell, odour; the nose. -ತರ್ಪಣ. Fragrant substance; a perfume. ಘ್ರಾಣಿಸು. To smell. ಘ್ರಾಣೇಂದ್ರಿಯ. The organ of smell.

ಙ

ಙ. The twenty-third letter of the alphabet. *No words begin with it.*

ಚ

ಚ. The twenty-fourth letter of the alphabet.

ಚಕಚಕ (=ಝಗಝಗ) s. *ad.* Glitteringly.

ಚಕಡಾ (*tb. of* ಶಕಟ). = ಚಕ್ಕಡಿ, *q. v.*

ಚಕಮುಕಿ, ಚಕ್ಕಮುಕ್ಕಿ h. *n.* A flint and steel for striking fire. -ಹತ್ತಿ. Silk-cotton tinder.

ಚಕಾರ s. *n.* The letter ಚ. -ಶಬ್ದ. A word.

ಚಕಿತ s. *a.* Shaking; afraid, timid.

ಚಕೋತ (*tb. of* ಚಕ್ರವರ್ತಿ), ಚಕೋತು. = ಚಕ್ಕೋತ, *q. v.*

ಚಕೋರ s. *n.* The bartavelle or Greek partridge. 2, = ಚಕ್ಕೋತ.

ಚಕ್ಕಚೌಕ (= ಚಚ್ಚೌಕ) *tb. a.* Square.

ಚಕ್ಕಡಿ (=ಚಕಡಾ. *tb. of* ಶಕಟ) *n.* A cart; a travelling cart.

ಚಕ್ಕನೆ a. k. *ad.* Quickly, suddenly.

ಚಕ್ಕಂದ k. *n.* Idle talk; happiness, pleasure.

ಚಕ್ಕರ. *tb. of* ಚಕ್ರ, *q. v.*

ಚಕ್ಕಲಗುಳಿ, ಚಕ್ಕಳಗುಳಿ k. *n.* Tickling another. -ಮಾಡು. To tickle.

ಚಕ್ಕಲಿ, ಚಕ್ಕುಲಿ (*tb. of* ಶಷ್ಕುಲಿ) *n.* A cake made in the form of a ring and fried in ghee or oil.

ಚಕ್ಕವಕ್ಕಿ. = ಚಕ್ರವಾಕ s. ಚಕ್ರ, *q. v.*

ಚಕ್ಕಳ 1. k. *n.* A cot or seat of cane or bamboo. -ಬಕ್ಕಳ, -ಮುಕ್ಕಳಿ. Sitting cross-legged.

ಚಕ್ಕಳ 2. f. *n.* Skin, leather.

ಚಕ್ಕುಬಂದಿ h. *n.* Defining of the boundaries of an estate; jurisdiction.

ಚಕ್ಕೆ (= ಚೆಕ್ಕೆ, ಸಕ್ಕೆ. *tb. of* ಶಲ್ಕ) *n.* A chip of wood or of stone.

ಚಕ್ಕೋತ, ಚಕ್ಕೋತು (= ಚಕೋತ, *etc. tb. of* ಚಕ್ರವರ್ತಿ) *n.* The pumplemose or shaddock, *Citrus decumana.* 2, an esculent vegetable, goose-foot.

ಚಕ್ರ (=ಚಕ್ಕರ) s. n. A wheel. 2, a potter's wheel. 3, a discus. 4, a circle, diagram. 5, a plaything for children. 6, a realm; rule. 7, a circuit. 8, a multitude; a form of military array. 9, the horizon. 10, an ancient coin; a quarter rupee. -ಧರ, -ಪಾಣಿ. Vishṇu or Kṛishṇa. -ಪಕ್ಷಿ. =-ವಾಕ. -ವರ್ತಿ. A sovereign, emperor. -ವರ್ತಿನಿ. An empress. -ವರ್ತಿಸೊಪ್ಪು. The pot-herb, *Chenopodium album*, the goose-foot. -ವಾಕ. The ruddy goose. ಚಕ್ರಾಂಗ. A gander. ಚಕ್ರಾಂಗಿ A goose.

ಚಕ್ಲಿ k. n. A cultivated tree, the Manilla tamarind, *Pithecolobum dulce*.

ಚಕ್ಷು s. n. The eye. -ರಿಂದ್ರಿಯ. The sense of seeing.

ಚಗಚೆ (=ಚೊಗಚೆ) k. n. The plant *Cassia tora*.

ಚಂಗ. = ಚಂಗ್ಗ, q. v.

ಚಂಗದಿರ. = ಚೆಂಗದಿರ, q. v.

ಚಂಗನೆ k. ad. In bounds, with agility.

ಚಂಗಲಕೋಷ್ಟ k. n. A sort of Costus.

ಚಂಗು 1. k. n. A jump, leap, *etc.*; agility. v. i. To jump, *etc.* -ಚಂಗನೆ ಹಾರು. To jump with agility.

ಚಂಗು 2. h. n. A Jew's harp.

ಚಂಗೂಲಿ k. n. A day-labourer.

ಚಂಗ್ಗ (=ಚಂಗ) k. n. Crookedness, perverseness. -ಮಂಗ್ಗತನ. Apish pranks, frolics, sport.

ಚಚ್ಚರ (=ಜೆಚ್ಚರ) k. n. Haste. 2, wakefulness, care.

ಚಚ್ಚು. = ಜೆಚ್ಚು, q. v.

ಚಚ್ಚೌಕ (=ಚಕ್ಕಚೌಕ, q. v.) f. a. Square.

ಚಜ್ಜಿ k. n. A kind of grain, *Holcus spicatus*.

ಚಂಚಲ s. a. Shaking; unsteady; fickle, capricious. n. The wind. -ತನ, -ತ್ವ. Unsteadiness, fickleness. -ಮನಸ್ಸು. Fickle-mindedness.

ಚಂಚಲಿ k. n. A small cultivated tree, *Flacourtia catafracta*.

ಚಂಚಲೆ s. n. Lightning; fortune.

ಚಂಚಿ m. n. A bag with pockets for betel, *etc.*

ಚಂಚು s. n. The beak of a bird.

ಚಂಜಿ. = ಸಂಜೆ, q. v.

ಚಟ s. n. A taste, taking; an acquired liking or fondness; an ill-habit. -ತೀರಿಸಿ ಕೊಳ್ಳು. To eradicate a habit.

ಚಟಕ k. n. A ceremony in honor of the departed ancestors; *also* -ಶ್ರಾದ್ಧ. 2, a sparrow; *f.* ಚಟಕಿ.

ಚಟಕಾಯಿಸು (=ಚಟಾಯಿಸು) h. v. t. To cut or knock off, cut short.

ಚಟಕು. = ಚಟುಕು, q. v.

ಚಟಕ್ಕನೆ k. ad. All at once, suddenly.

ಚಟಪಟ k. n. A snapping or crashing sound. 2, (f.) fretting and grieving. ad. Quickly.

ಚಟಪಟಿಕೆ f. n. Quickness, smartness, sharpness, briskness.

ಚಟಾಕು h. n. The sixteenth part of a pakkâ sêr.

ಚಟಾಯಿಸು. = ಚಟಕಾಯಿಸು, q. v.

ಚಟಿಗೆ (*cf.* ಚಟ್ಟಿ) k. n. A small earthen pot with a broad mouth.

ಚಟುವಟಿಕೆ. = ಚಟಪಟಿಕೆ, q. v.

ಚಟ್ಟ 1. (=ಚಟ್ಟು) k. n. Flatness. 2, the frame or bottom of a cart, bedstead, chair, *etc.* 3, a bier or litter.

ಚಟ್ಟ 2. k. n. Order, regulation (*in law*); neatness, fineness.

ಚಟ್ಟನೆ k. ad. Suddenly, all at once.

ಚಟ್ಟಿ (= ಚಟ್ಟಿ) k. n. An earthen pot.

ಚಟ್ಟು 1. =ಚಟ್ಟ 1, q. v. 2, (=ಚತ್ತು) the flat cloth-cover over a palankeen. 3, the seedless pod of beans, *etc.*

ಚಟ್ಟು 2. k. n. Impurity. 2, destruction. -ಮಾಡು. To kill; to ruin.

ಚಟ್ಟು 3. k. n. The dried fruit of nĕlli.

ಚಟ್ಟಿ k. n. Flatness, levelness. 2, European dress. -ಕಾರ. A man dressed in European fashion; a Eurasian.

ಚಟ್ಣಿ h. n. A seasoning prepared of chopped chillies, *etc.*; chutney.

ಚಡತಿ h. n. Jealousy.

ಚಢಾಯಿಸು h. v. t. To tighten, fasten. 2, to increase, raise; to lay on; to lash.

ಚಡಾವು h. n. Ascent, rise; increase, *as* of assessment, value, *etc.* 2, a kind of shoes.

ಚಡಿ 1. f. n. A dovetail (*in carpentry*).

ಚಡಿ 2. h. n. A cane. 2, a staircase.

ಚಡುಪುಡನೆ k. *ad.* Quickly, rapidly.

ಚಡ್ಡಿ k. n. Breeches reaching to the thighs.

ಚಣಕ s. n. The chick-pea, Bengal gram. 2, = ಚಡ್ಡಿ, *q. v.*

ಚಣಿಗೆ k. n. A sort of pulse or lentil, *Cicer lens*.

ಚಂಡ s. *a.* Hot, fiery; passionate, wrathful; impetuous; mischievous. *n.* Heat; passion. 2, Śiva; N. of a demon.

ಚಂಡವಾಳ f. n. Earnest money, a handsel.

ಚಂಡಾಲ s. n. An outcaste; a man of the lowest and most despised of the mixed tribes.

ಚಂಡಿ 1. s. n. A passionate and violent female. 2, an obstinate or mischievous man. 3, obstinacy, *etc.* 4, Durgâ; N. of a female. -ಕಾ, -ಕೆ. Durgâ. -ತನ. Obstinacy. -ಸು. To be obstinate or angry.

ಚಂಡಿ 2. (= ತಂಡಿ) k. n. Wetness. *a.* Wet, moist.

ಚಂಡಿಕೆ k. n. A tuft; a crest; a tuft of hair left on the head at the tonsure. -ಬಿಡು. To leave a tuft on the head.

ಚಂಡು 1. (= ಚೆಂಡು) k. n. A ball to play with; a bunch or cluster of flowers. ಚಂಡಾಡು. To play at ball. -ಮಲ್ಲಿಗೆ. A variety of jasmine. -ಹೂವು. A flower like marigold, *a Chrysanthemum*.

ಚಂಡು 2. k. n. The nape of the neck, neck.

ಚಂಡೆ s. n. Durgâ; *also* ಚಂಡಿ, -ಕೆ. 2, a certain perfume. ಚಂಡೇಶ, ಚಂಡೇಶ್ವರ. Śiva.

ಚಣ್ಣ k. n. Short breeches.

ಚತುಃ.=ಚತುರ 1. -ಪದ, -ಪಾದ. A quadruped.

ಚತುರ 1. s. *a.* Four. -ಕಳ್ಳಿ. The triangular spurge, *Euphorbia antiquarum*. -ಧಿಪತಿ. A commander of four districts or of constituents of an army. -ಶ್ರ. Quadrangular; a square; a boundary. ಚತುರಾನನ, ಚತುರಾಸ್ಯ. Four-faced: Brahmâ. ಚತುರೋಪಾಯ. The four expedients or means of success. ಚತುರಂಗ. Four-membered: chess. ಚತುರಂಗಬಲ, ಚತುರ್ಬಲ. A complete army comprising elephants, chariots, cavalry and infantry.

ಚತುರ 2. (= ಚದರ, ಚದುರ, *etc.*) s. *a.* Dexterous, clever, ingenious. 2, charming. *n.* Skilfulness, dexterity; shrewdness. *also* -ತೆ, -ತನ.

ಚತುರ್ಥ s. *a.* Fourth; the fourth. ಚತುರ್ಥೀ. The fourth case, the dative; the fourth day in a lunar fortnight.

ಚತುರ್ದಶ s. *a.* Fourteen. ಚತುರ್ದಶಿ. The fourteenth day in a lunar fortnight.

ಚತುರ್ದಿಶೆ s. n. The four points of the compass.

ಚತುರ್ಭುಜ s. *a.* Four-armed. *n.* Vishṇu, Kṛishṇa.

ಚತುರ್ಮುಖ s. n. Brahmâ; Śiva.

ಚತುರ್ಯುಗ s. n. The four yugas or ages of the world.

ಚತುರ್ವರ್ಣ s. n. The four castes.

ಚತುರ್ವಿಂಶತಿ s. *a.* Twenty-four.

ಚತುರ್ವಿಧ s. *a.* Four-fold.

ಚತುರ್ವೇದ s. n. The four vêdas.

ಚತುಷ್ಟಯ s. *a.* Four-fold. *n.* An aggregate of four.

ಚತುಷ್ಕೋಣ s. *a.* Square, quadrangular. *n.* A square.

ಚತುಷ್ಪದ, ಚತುಷ್ಪಾದ್, ಚತುಷ್ಪಾದ s. *a.* Four-footed. *n.* A quadruped.

ಚತ್ತರಿಗೆ *tb. of* ಛತ್ರಿಕೆ. = ಛತ್ರಿ, *q. v.*

ಚತ್ತು m. *n.* A ceiling; a covering in general.

ಚತ್ರಿ, -ಗೆ (*tb. of* ಛತ್ರಿ) *n.* An umbrella, parasol.

ಚತ್ವರ s. *n.* A quadrangular place.

ಚತ್ವಾರಿ s. *n.* Four. ಚತ್ವಾರಿಂಶತ. Forty.

ಚದರ (*tb. of* ಚತುರ) *a.* Square.

ಚದರು (ರು=ಱು) k. *v. i. & t.* To scatter, disperse. ಚದರಿಸು. *v. t.* To scatter, disperse.

ಚದುರ. *tb. of* ಚತುರ, *q. v.*

ಚಂದ 1. (*tb. of* ಛಂದ) *a.* Pleasing, beautiful, lovely. *n.* Fitness, niceness; beauty. 2, appearance, shape, form; manner. -ಗೆಡು. Beauty to be gone. -ಗೇಡಿ. A mannerless person.

ಚಂದ 2. (*tb. of* ಚಂದ್ರ) *n.* The moon; *also* -ಪ್ಪ, -ಮಾಮ.

ಚಂದನ, ಚಂದಲ s. *n.* Sandal, *Sirium myrtifolium:* either the tree, the wood, or its preparation.

ಚಂದಿ f. *n.* A gable-wall.

ಚಂದಿರ. *tb. of* ಚಂದ್ರ, *q. v.*

ಚಂದ್ರ 1. s. *a.* Glittering, excellent. *n.* The moon. 2, gold. 3, the red colour. 4, camphor. 5, excellence. -ಕಾಂತ. The moon-stone, a fabulous gem. -ಕಾಂತಿ. Moonlight; the moon-flower, *Ipomaea grandiflora.* -ಕೋಲು. A head-ornament of gold. -ಗ್ರಹಣ. An eclipse of the moon. -ಜ್ಯೋತಿ. Moonlight; a kind of firework. -ತಾರಾ ಬಲ. Propitiousness of the moon and stars. -ಬಿಂಬ, -ಮಂಡಲ. The lunar disk. -ಭಾಗೆ. The Chenab river. -ಲೋಕ. The sphere of the moon. -ವಂಶ. The lunar race of kings. -ಶಾಲೆ. An upper room. -ಸೂರ್ಯ. Moon and sun. -ಹಾರ. A necklace of moonlike gold beads. -ಹಾಸ. N. of a prince.

ಚಂದ್ರ 2. k. *n.* Red lead, *minium.* -ಕಾಳಿ ಸೀರೆ, -ಗಾವಿಸೀರೆ. A kind of sīrĕ. -ಬಾಳೆ. A reddish kind of plantain. -ಮಾವು. A reddish kind of mango.

ಚಂದ್ರಿಕೆ s. *n.* Moonlight; elucidation. 2, a coil of written palm-leaf.

ಚಂದ್ರೋದಯ s. *n.* Moon-rise. -ಮಾತ್ರೆ. A cooling bolus.

ಚನ್ನ k. *n.* A beautiful, handsome man. 2, N.; *also* -ಪ್ಪ, -ಯ್ಯ. -ಪಟ್ಟ. Madras. -ಬಸವ. N.; son of Basava's sister. -ಬಸವಪುರಾಣ. A poetical Kannaḍa work about Čannabasava.

ಚನ್ನಾಗಿ k. *ad.* Nicely, well; *see s.* ಚನ್ನು.

ಚನ್ನಿಗ k. *n.* A handsome, fine man; *f.* -ಳು.

ಚನ್ನು k. *n.* Beauty, grace, niceness; excellence. *Cpds.:* ಚನ್ನಭಕ್ತಿ, ಚನ್ನಮಗ, ಚನ್ನ ಮಾತು, *etc.* ಚನ್ನಾಗಿ. Nicely, well, properly; correctly.

ಚನ್ನೆ k. *n.* A beautiful female. ಚನ್ನಕ್ಕ, ಚನ್ನವ್ವ. N.

ಚಪ್ h. *int.* Hush! silent!

ಚಪಟಿ. = ಚಪ್ಪಟಿ, *q. v.*

ಚಪಲ s. *a.* Moving to and fro, wavering unsteady, fickle; wanton. 2, active quick, agile, swift. 3, inconsiderate 4, momentary. -ತನ, -ತೆ, -ತ್ವ. Fickleness; inconstancy; smartness. ಚಪಲೆ. A fickle woman; lightning.

ಚಪಾಟಿ m. *n.* A slap. -ಬಡಿ. To slap with open hands.

ಚಪಾತಿ h. *n.* A hand-made cake.

ಚಪಾಯಿಸು h. *v. t.* To hide.

ಚಪಾವಣೆ, ಚಪಾವು h. *n.* Hiding, concealment.

ಚಪ್ಪಗೆ k. *n.* Insipidness, tastelessness. *ad.* Insipidly.

ಚಪ್ಪಟೆ 1. k. *n.* Flatness. *a.* Flat. -ಮೂಗು. A flat nose. -ಕಲ್ಲು. A flat stone.

ಚಪ್ಪಟೆ 2. (= ಚಪಾಟಿ) h. *n.* A smart slap. -ಬಡಿ, -ಹೊಡೆ. To slap with the palm.

ಚಪ್ಪಡಿ (*cf.* ಚಪ್ಪಟೆ 1) k. *n.* A large flat stone. 2, a dodge, trick. -ಎಳೆ, -ಹಾಕು. To drag or put a flat stone (on another's business): to ruin.

ಚಪ್ಪರ (= ಚಪ್ರ) k. *n.* A shed. 2, a court-yard. 3, a thatched or tiled roof. 4, a trellis. 5, the canopy of a bedstead. *Cpds.:* ಮದಿವೆ-, ಬಿಸಲು-, ಹುಲ್ಲು-, ಹಂಚಿನ-, *etc.* -ಮಂಚ. A canopied bedstead. -ಮನೆ. A shed. -ಹಾಕು. To put up a thatch.

ಚಪ್ಪರಣೆ k. *n.* A smacking of the lips used by peasants to stop their cattle.

ಚಪ್ಪರಿಸು 1. k. *v. i.* To chuckle or cluck to an animal. 2, to smack the lips; to chew with a noise. 3, to chirp.

ಚಪ್ಪರಿಸು 2. (= ಚಪ್ಪಳಿಸು) k. *v. t.* To slap, pat.

ಚಪ್ಪಲಿ h. *n.* A shoe or sandal.

ಚಪ್ಪಳಿ. = ಚಪ್ಪಟೆ 2, *q. v.*

ಚಪ್ಪಾಳೆ k. *n.* Clapping the hands. -ತಿಕ್ಕು, ಚಪ್ಪಳಿಕ್ಕು. To clap the hands.

ಚಪ್ಪೆ 1. k. *n.* The hip-bone. 2, insipidness.

ಚಪ್ಪೆ 2. f. *n.* An impression, seal, stamp.

ಚಪ್ರ. = ಚಪ್ಪರ, *q. v.*

ಚಬಕು, ಚಬುಕು h. *n.* A horse-whip. -ಹೊಡೆ, -ತಳೆ. To whip. -ಮರ. The Casuarina tree.

ಚಮಕಾಯಿಸು, ಚಮಕಿಸು f. *v. t.* To lash soundly; to frighten, rebuke. 2, to make to flash or brandish.

ಚಮಟಿಕೆ, ಚಮಟಿಗೆ. = ಚಮ್ಮಟಿಗೆ, *q. v.*

ಚಮಡ h. *n.* The skin.

ಚಮತ್ಕಾರ, ಚಮತ್ಕೃತಿ, s. *n.* Astonishment, surprise; a show, spectacle; a wonder; skilfulness, cleverness. 2, wit, eloquence. -ದ ಒಕ್ಕಣೆ. Ambiguous style.

ಚಮರ s. *n.* The yak or *bos grunniens.* 2, the chowry or long brush made of the yak's tail; *also* ಚಮರಿ.

ಚಮು, ಚಮೂ s. *n.* An army. 2, a division of an army consisting of 129 elephants, 129 cars, 2187 horses, and 3685 foot. -ಪ, -ಪತಿ. A general.

ಚಮ್ಚ h. *n.* A spoon.

ಚಂಪಕ s. *n.* A yellow fragrant flower, *Michelia champaca.*

ಚಂಬು (= ಚೆಂಬು, *q. v.*) k. *n.* Copper. 2, a globular vessel used for drinking; *cf.* ತಂಬಿಗೆ. -ಕುಟಿಗ. A coppersmith.

ಚಮ್ಮಟಿಗೆ (= ಚಮುಟಿಕೆ. *tb. of* ಚರ್ಮಪಟ್ಟಿಕೆ, ಚರ್ಮಯಷ್ಟಿಕೆ) 3. a whip. 2, a sledge-hammer. 3, a leather backgammon board; *also* ಚಮ್ಮಟ್ಟಿಗೆ.

ಚಮ್ಮಾರ (*tb. of* ಚರ್ಮಕಾರ) *n.* A shoemaker; a worker in leather.

ಚರ 1. k. *An imitative sound.* -ಕ್ಕನೆ. With the sound of ಚರ. ಚರಚರ. *rep.* The sound of scratching with the nails or with a pen, *etc.* ಚರಚರನೆ. With the sound of ಚರಚರ.

ಚರ 2. s. *a.* Moving, walking; movable; living. *n.* Locomotive, any animal. 2, a spy; *cf.* ಚಾರ. ಚರನುಡಿ (*i. e.* ಚರರ ನುಡಿ). News brought by spies. -ಕ. A wanderer; a spy; witchcraft. -ಆಸ್ತಿ, -ಸೊತ್ತು. Movable property. -ಬಂಡವಲ. Live stock; capital employed in business. -ಯಿಸು. To walk about.

ಚರಣ s. *n.* Moving. 2, a foot. 3, a sect, school. 4, a verse-line. -ತಲ. The sole. -ಯುಗ. Both the feet.

ಚರಂತಿ s. *n.* A jaṅgama who has taken the vow of celibacy.

ಚರಬಾಗಿಸು s. & k. *v. i.* To go away (*used in liṅgavanta maṭhas*).

ಚರಬಿ (= ಚೆರ್ಬಿ) h. *n.* Fat, suet.

ಚರಮ s. *a.* Last, final, ultimate; western.

ಚರವಿಗೆ, ಚರಿವಿಗೆ k. *n.* A large copper or brass pot for carrying water.

ಚರಾಚರ s. *a.* Movable and immovable. *n.* Animals and plants; all created things.

ಚರಾಯಿ f. *n.* Pasture; pasture-ground.

ಚರಿಗೆ. = ಚರವಿಗೆ, *q. v.*

ಚರಿತ s. *n.* Going, course; conduct, practice; deeds; story. ಚರಿತಾರ್ಥ. Attaining one's object, successful. *n.* Accomplishment; welfare.

ಚರಿತ್ರ s. *n.* Walk, behaviour; exploits; story, history or account of one's deeds, *etc.*; nature, disposition. -ಗಾರ. A historian.

ಚರಿತ್ರ್ಯ. = ಚರಿತ್ರ, *q. v.*

ಚರಿಸು (*cf.* ಚರ) s. *v. i.* To move about; to walk; to wander, roam; to behave; to set about.

ಚರು s. *n.* A caldron, pan, pot. 2, (=ಚರುವು) an oblation of rice, *etc.* to the gods or manes.

ಚರುಗ k. *n.* An offering to Dômavva.

ಚರುವು. = ಚರು No. 2, *q. v.*

ಚರ್ಚೆ s. *n.* Reflection, consideration. 2, investigation, reasoning, inquiry, logic. 3, a word. 4, idle slander; ridicule. 5, a quarrel, dispute. 6, perfuming the body. ಚರ್ಚಿಸು. To consider; to investigate; to discuss.

ಚರ್ಮ s. *n.* Skin, leather, hide, bark, *etc.* 2, a shield. -ಕಾರ. A shoemaker. -ಚಕ್ಷು. The material, physical eye. -ಪಟ್ಟಿಕೆ. = ಚಮ್ಮಟ್ಟಿಗೆ, *q. v.*

ಚರ್ಯೆ s. *n.* Going; behaviour, conduct; practice; occupation.

ಚರ್ವಣ s. *n.* Chewing, masticating; solid food.

ಚಲ 1. s. *a.* Moving, stirring; unsteady; movable. *n.* Agitation.

ಚಲ 2. (*tb. of* ಛಲ) *n.* Firmness of character, resoluteness, obstinacy, self-will. -ಗಾರ. An obstinate man; A resolute speaker; an obstinate person.

ಚಲನ, ಚಲನೆ s. *a.* Moving; wandering. *n.* Going away; setting out, departing.

ಚಲಮೆ, ಚಲಿಮೆ s. *n.* A small pit; a spring of water or a fountain head, brook.

ಚಲಾಯಿಸು (*fr.* ಚಲ). *v. t.* To make go, to execute. *v. i.* To go beyond; to be finished.

ಚಲಾವಣೆ, ಚಲಾವಣಿ f. *a.* Current, *as* coin, *etc.* *n.* Currency; practice.

ಚಲಿತ s. *n.* Moving; trembling, marching.

ಚಲಿಸು s. *v. t.* To move; to stir; to tremble; to go astray; to start.

ಚಲುವಿಕೆ, ಚಲುವು (= ಚೆಲುವು, ಚಲ್ವು) k. *n.* Beauty, handsomeness, elegance, grace; niceness. ಚಲುವ, ಚಲ್ವ. A handsome man; *f.* ಚಲುವಿ, ಚಲುವೆ, ಚಲುವತಿ.

ಚಲೊ, ಚಲೋ k. *a.* Beautiful, nice, elegant; *also* ಚೆಲೊ. ಚಲೋದು. That is nice, well, *etc.* *Cpds.:* -ಬುದ್ಧಿ, -ಮನಸ್ಸು. -ಭಕ್ತಿ, -ಗುಣ, -ನಡತೆ, -ಮಾತು, *etc.*

ಚಲ್ಲ 1. k. *n.* Fun, amusement, pleasure; smile. ಚಲ್ಲವಾಡು. To sport, gambol. ಚಲ್ಲಾಟ. Sport, fun. ಚಲ್ಲಾಟವಾಡು.= ಚಲ್ಲವಾಡು. -ವತ್ತ. A jocose man; a man who gets his living by coaxing.

ಚಲ್ಲ 2. (*inf. of* ಚಲ್ಲು. *q. v.*). -ಬಡಿ. To drive off, disperse, scatter. ಚಲ್ಲಾಪಲ್ಲಿ, ಚಲ್ಲಾ ಪಿಲ್ಲಿ. Disorderly, confusedly.

ಚಲ್ಲನ್ f. *n.* A challan, voucher; an invoice.

ಚಲ್ಲಣ (= ಚಣ್ಣ) k. *n.* Breeches of different length.

ಚಲ್ಲಾಟ. *see s.* ಚಲ್ಲ 1 *and s.* ಚಲ್ಲು 1.

ಚಲ್ಲು 1. (= ಚೆಲ್ಲು, *q. v.*) k. *v. t.* To scatter about; to pour out, spill, *as* milk; to squander; to throw away; to sow, *as* seed. ಚಲ್ಲಾಟ. Throwing about. ಚಲ್ಲಾಡು. To throw about. ಚಲ್ಲಿಬಿಡು. To spill, throw away. ಚಲ್ಲಿಹೋಗು. To be spilt.

ಚಲ್ಲು 2. k. *n.* An idle person, a gadabout. -ತನ. Idleness.

ಚಲ್ವ, ಚಲ್ವಿಕೆ, ಚಲ್ವು. = ಚಲುವ, ಚಲುವಿಕೆ, *q. v.*

ಚವಕಿ (= ಚೌಕಿ) h. *n.* A low seat, stool. 2, a guard-house; a maṭha; the inner veranda of a house.

ಚವಡಿಕೆ (= ಚೌಡಿಕೆ. *tb. of* ಚಮುಂಡಿಕೆ) *n.* A kind of lute.

ಚವರ. = ಚಮರ, *q. v.*

ಚವರಿ (= ಚೌರಿ) s. *n.* A kind of head-ornament made of the hair of the yak's tail.

ಚವಲ f. *n.* Two Aṇas; *cf.* ಚವುಲಿ.

ಚವುಕ. = ಚೌಕ, *q. v.* 2, cheap.

ಚವುಕಸಿ (= ಚೌಕಸಿ) h. *n.* Careful inquiry; investigation.

ಚವುಕಳಿ (*fr. tb.* ಚೌಕ) *n.* An ear-ring with four pearls. 2, a chequered cloth.

ಚವುಕಾರ f. *n.* Soap.

ಚವುಡಿ, ಚವುಂಡಿ (*tb. of* ಚಾಮುಂಡಿ) *n.* N. of a female demon worshipped by Śûdras.

ಚವುತಿ. *tb. of* ಚತುರ್ಥೀ. = ಚೌತಿ, *q. v.*

ಚವುದರಿ (= ಚೌದರಿ) f. *n.* A village officer. 2, the officer of a royal guard.

ಚವುಲ. = ಚವಲ, *q. v.* 2, = ಚೌಲ.

ಚವುಳು (= ಚೌಳು) k. *n.* Brackishness. -ಉಪ್ಪು, ಚವುಳುಪ್ಪು, -ಕಾರ. Soda-saltpetre.

ಚಹಾ (= ಚಾ, ಚಾಹ) h. *n.* Tea.

ಚಹಾರೆ f. *n.* Features, complexion. 2, green fodder.

ಚಳಕ a. k. *n.* Expertness, dexterity, skill.

ಚಳಕು (= ಚಳುಕು) k. *n.* The cramp; rheumatic pains. *v. i.* To be painfully contracted, *as* a muscle of the body.

ಚಳತುಂಬು f. *n.* A kind of ear-drop.

ಚಳಿ 1. k. *v. i.* To become tired or fatigued; the feet to pain from walking. -ಸು. To cause to be fatigued; to trouble.

ಚಳಿ 2. k. *n.* Coldness, cold; chill, frost, snow, *etc.* -ಗಾಲ. The cold season. -ಜ್ವರ. Ague. -ನಾಡು. A cold country. -ಆಗು, -ಬೀಳು. To become cold. -ಹಿಡಿ. To catch cold.

ಚಳುಕು. = ಚಳಕು, *q. v.*

ಚಳೆ k. *v. i.* To abound, *as* fruits on a tree, *etc.* *n.* Sprinkling; *also* ಚಳೆಯ. -ಕೊಡು, -ಹಾಕು. To sprinkle.

ಚಳ್ಳು k. *n.* A long flexible twig. ಚಳ್ಳವರೆ. A cultivated pulse, *Dolichos lablab.*

ಚಳ್ಳೆ. (*tb. of* ಶೇಲು) *n.* The Sepistan plum of a gummy character; *also* -ಮರ.

ಚಾ. = ಚಹಾ, *q. v.*

ಚಾಕ್ e. *n.* Chalk.

ಚಾಕ f. *n.* Neat, tidy, trim. -ಚಕ್ಕ. Acuteness; agility, speed.

ಚಾಕರ h. *n.* A servant; *f.* -ಳು.

ಚಾಕರಿ h. *n.* Service; employment. -ಚಾಕರಿ. *reit.* -ಯವ. A servant; *f.* -ಯವಳು.

ಚಾಕು h. *n.* A penknife.

ಚಾಚು k. *v. t.* To stretch out, hold out, extend; *also* ಚಾಚಿಬಿಡು. ಚಾಚಿಸು. To cause to stretch out.

ಚಾಂಚಲ್ಯ (*fr.* ಚಂಚಲ) s. *n.* Fickleness, unsteadiness.

ಚಾಟಕ s. *n.* Jugglery; incantation; *also* -ಮಂತ್ರ, -ವಿದ್ಯೆ.

ಚಾಟಿ k. *n.* A whip.

ಚಾಟು 1. k. *n.* A refuge; a shelter.

ಚಾಟು 2. s. *n.* Pleasing discourse; flattery; clear speech. -ತನ. Agreeableness; flattery.

ಚಾಡಿ h. *n.* Slander, backbiting. -ಕಾರ, -ಖೋರ, -ಗ, -ಗಾರ, ಚಾಡ. A slanderer; a talebearer.

ಚಾಣ. = ಚಾನ, ಚೇಣ, *q. v.*

ಚಾಂಡಾಲ. = ಚಂಡಾಲ, *q. v.*

ಚಾತಕ s. *n.* The bird *Cuculus melanoleucus* (supposed to live upon rain-drops).

ಚಾತಾಳದವ k. *n.* A so-called Sarternee, a man of a Śûdra caste that worships Vishṇu.

ಚಾತುರ (*fr.* ಚತುರ) s. *a.* Dexterous, clever, ingenious. -ತನ, ಚಾತುರ್ಯ. Dexterity, cleverness, shrewdness; pleasantness.

ಚಾತುರ್ಥಿಕ (*fr.* ಚತುರ್ಥ). s. *a.* Quartan, *as* ague.

ಚಾದರ h. *n.* A cotton or silk sheet or a dôtra worked with gold or silver threads.

ಚಾನ (= ಚಾಣ) k. *n.* A small chisel.

ಚಾಂದಣೆ, ಚಾಂದನಿ h. *n.* An awning.

ಚಾಂದ್ರ (*fr.* ಚಂದ್ರ) s. *a.* Lunar. -ಮಾನ. Lunar measurement of time. -ಮಾಸ. A lunar month. -ಮಾನವರ್ಷ, -ಸಂವತ್ಸರ. The lunar year. ಚಾಂದ್ರಾಯಣ. An expiatory observance regulated by moon's phases.

ಚಾಪ 1. s. *n.* A bow. 2, a rainbow.

ಚಾಪ 2. = ಚಾಪೆ 2, *q. v.* 2, = ಚಾಪು 2, *q. v.*

ಚಾಪಲ, ಚಾಪಲ್ಯ (*fr.* ಚಪಲ) s. *n.* Mobility; unsteadiness; fickleness; agility.

ಚಾಪಿಸು h. *v. t.* To stamp; to print; *also* ಛಾಪಿಸು.

ಚಾಪು 1. k. *n.* Stretch, length, extent.

ಚಾಪು 2. h. *n.* The cock of a gun.

ಚಾಪೆ 1. k. *n.* A mat.

ಚಾಪೆ 2. (= ಚಾಪ) h. *n.* A stamp; a type; an impression. -ಖಾನೆ. A printing office.

ಚಾಮರ (= ಚಮರ) s. *n.* A chowry, the bushy tail of the *Bos grunniens* used as a fan.

ಚಾಮುಂಡಿ s. *n.* Durgâ; *also* ಚಾಮುಂಡೇಶ್ವರಿ.

ಚಾಯು (*tb. of* ಛಾಯೆ) *n.* Colour, shade, *etc.*; *also* ಚಾಯಿ. 2, the madder plant.

ಚಾರ 1. s. *n.* Course, motion. 2, a spy, messenger. 2, a prison. -ಚಿಪ್ಪಿ. A privy.

ಚಾರ 2. f. *n.* Green fodder of cattle.

ಚಾರ 3. (ರ = ಐ) k. *n.* A line, streak.

ಚಾರಣ s. *n.* Wandering; a strolling actor, bard; a celestial singer.

ಚಾರಿ s. *n.* Acting. 2, course. 3, a way, manner, method. 4, stratagem. 5, intention, mind. 6, cheapness.

ಚಾರಿತ್ರ s. *n.* Conduct, behaviour; a ceremony.

ಚಾರಿಸು k. *v. t.* To grind, triturate, *as* sandal; to mix by rubbing, *as* medicine.

ಚಾರು 1. s. *a.* Agreeable, lovely; beautiful.

ಚಾರು 2. (ರು = ಱು) k. *n.* Sap, juice; broth.

ಚಾರ್ಖಾನೆ f. *n.* A square. -ಸೀರೆ. A female's cloth with small coloured squares in it.

ಚಾರ್ಮಾಡಿ f. *n.* N. of a ghaut.

ಚಾರ್ವಾಕ s. *n.* An atheist or materialist; a sceptic.

ಚಾಲ s. *a.* Movable, changing. -ಗೇಣಿ. (Movable rent); rent for one year. -ತಿ, ಚಾಲ್ತಿ. That is in use; current.

ಚಾಲಕ್, ಚಾಲಾಕ್ h. *a.* Smart, dexterous, clever.

ಚಾಲನ s. *n.* Causing to move or pass through; sifting; making loose. ಚಾಲನಿ. A sieve, strainer.

ಚಾಲು (= ಚಾಲ, *q. v.*) s. *n.* Moving; custom, manner. 2, currency, *as* of a coin, order, *etc.* 3, a pace, *as* of a horse.

ಚಾವಡಿ h. *n.* A court; a village-hall; a veranda.

ಚಾವಣಿ h. *n.* Cantonments, temporary erections for troops. 2, a roof, roofing.

ಚಾವಿ h. *n.* A key. -ಕೊಡು. To wind, *as* a clock or watch.

ಚಾಳಕ f. *a.* Mischievous. *n.* A man full of tricks and pranks.

ಚಾಳಿ (*tb. of* ಚಾಲ) *n.* Conduct, practice, habit; a silly habit. -ಸು. To be fickle, *etc.* 2, to sift.

ಚಾಳಿಸು (*fr.* ಚಾಲ) *n.* Dimness of vision. 2, the age of 40. ಚಾಳೀಸು. A pair of spectacles.

ಛಿಃ (= ಛೀ, ಛೀ) k. *int.* Fie! for shame! pshaw!

ಚಿಕಣಿ h. *a.* Hard; thick, rich. -ಅಡಿಕೆ, -ಯಡಿಕೆ. A fine kind of betel-nut.

ಚಿಕಿತ್ಸೆ s. *n.* The science of medicine, therapeutics. ಚಿಕಿತ್ಸಕ. A physician.

ಚಿಕೀರ್ಷೆ s. *n.* Will, design.

ಚಿಕ್ಕ k. *a.* Little, small; young. -ಅಕ್ಕ, ಚಿಕ್ಕಕ್ಕ. A younger of the elder sisters. -ಅಣ್ಣ, ಚಿಕ್ಕಣ್ಣ. A younger of the elder brothers. -ತಂದೆ. = ಚಿಕ್ಕಪ್ಪ, *q. v.* -ತಮ್ಮ. The youngest brother. -ತಾಯಿ. An aunt; a step-mother. ಚಿಕ್ಕದು. That is small. ಚಿಕ್ಕಂದು. Childhood. ಚಿಕ್ಕಪ್ಪ. An uncle. -ಪ್ರಾಯ. Age between the 7th and 16th year. -ಮಕ್ಕಳು. Small, young children. -ಮಾತು. An insignificant word. ಚಿಕ್ಕಮ್ಮ, ಚಿಕ್ಕವ್ವ. = -ತಾಯಿ. -ತನ. = ಚಿಕ್ಕಂದು, *q. v.*

ಚಿಕ್ಕಣ k. *n.* A small bodice.

ಚಿಕ್ಕಣ್ಣ, ಚಿಕ್ಕಪ್ಪ, ಚಿಕ್ಕಮ್ಮ, ಚಿಕ್ಕವ್ವ. *see s.* [ಚಿಕ್ಕ.

ಚಿಕ್ಕಾಡು, ಚಿಕ್ಕಾಡಿ k. *n.* A flea.

ಚಿಕ್ಕಾಸು k. *n.* A small cash; a trifle.

ಚಿಕ್ಕೆ, ಚಿಕ್ಕೆ 1. k. n. A spot, speck, dot, *as* that of a cat, cloth, *etc.* 2, a star. 3, an aunt. -ಬೊಟ್ಟು. A black dot applied to the forehead between the eye-brows.

ಚಿಕ್ಕೆ 2. k. n. A flat-nosed woman. 2, a mouse. 3, a betel-nut.

ಚಿಗತು. = ಚಿಗಿತು. *P. p. of* ಚಿಗಿ.

ಚಿಗರಿ, ಚಿಗರೆ k. n. An antelope.

ಚಿಗರು. = ಚಿಗುರು, *q. v.*

ಚಿಗರೆ. = ಚಿಗರಿ, *q. v.*

ಚಿಗಳಿ k. n. A ball made of fried gingely oil-seed mixed with jaggory.

ಚಿಗಿ 1. k. *v. t.* To throw with the fingers.

ಚಿಗಿ 2. (=ಚಿಗುರು). k. *v. i.* To sprout, shoot. 2, (= ಜಿಗಿ) to jump.

ಚಿಗುರು (= ಚಿಗರು) k. *v. i.* To sprout, shoot; to bud, blossom. *n.* A sprout, shoot. ಚಿಗುರೆಲೆ. A young betel leaf; a fresh leaf.

ಚಿಟಕಾಯಿಸು h. *v. t.* To loosen a thorn in the flesh with a needle; to cause pain.

ಚಿಟಕಿ. = ಚಿಟಿಕೆ 1, 2, *q. v.*

ಚಿಟಕು (= ಚಿಟುಕು) k. n. Cracking of the finger-joints. 2, a quantity of thread wound upon a reel, a skein. -ಮುರಿ. To crack the finger-joints.

ಚಿಟಗುಟ್ಟು k. *v. i.* To throb, *as* the head.

ಚಿಟಿ k. n. Smallness, littleness. -ಕೊರಗು. The hind hoofs of cattle.

ಚಿಟಿಕೆ 1. k. n. A snap with finger and the thumb. 2, a little; a pinch, *as* of snuff; *also* ಚಿಟಿಕಿ. 3, a castenet. -ಹಾಕು. To snap with the fingers.

ಚಿಟಿಕೆ 2. k. n. Cauterising in any part of the body to cure particular diseases. -ಹಾಕು. To cauterise for that purpose.

ಚಿಟುಕು. = ಚಿಟಕು, *q. v.*

ಚಿಟ್ಟನೆ k. *ad.* With a scream.

ಚಿಟ್ಟಾಮುಟ್ಟಿ k. n. A perennial plant, *Pavonia zeylanica.*

ಚಿಟ್ಟು k. n. A measure of grain, equal to four sêru or soligĕ.

ಚಿಟ್ಟು (= ಚಿಟಿ) k. n. Smallness, shortness. 2, disgust. ಚಿಟ್ಟಿಲಿ. A small rat, a mouse. -ಹರಳು. A herbaceous shrub, *Sida cordifolia*; a small kind of castor-oil seed. ಚಿಟ್ಟೊಳಗ. A small work.

ಚಿಟ್ಠ h. n. A roll of lands under cultivation.

ಚಿಟ್ಟಿ (= ಚಿಟ್ಠಿ) h. n. A rough daybook.

ಚಿಡಾಯಿಸು f. *v. t.* To excite, provoke.

ಚಿಣಿ, ಚಿಣ್ಣ (= ಚಿಟಿ) k. n. Smallness. 2, the bat in the game of tip-cat; *also* -ಕೋಲು. -ಕೋಲಾಟ, -ಯಾಟ. The game of tip-cat.

ಚಿಣ್ಣ k. n. A little one, a boy.

ಚಿತಾ, ಚಿತಿ, ಚಿತೆ s. n. A funeral pile. ಚಿತಾಭಸ್ಮ. The ashes of a funeral pile.

ಚಿತ್ತ s. *a.* Perceived. *n.* Thought; intention, aim, wish, will. 2, the heart; the mind. -ಗೊಡು. To agree to. -ಭೇದ. Inconsistency of purpose or will. -ಭ್ರಮೆ, -ವಿಭ್ರಮೆ. Madness. -ವೃತ್ತಿ. Disposition of mind; feeling; the mind; the attention. -ಶುದ್ಧಿ. Purity of mind. ದೇವರ ಚಿತ್ತ. God's will.

ಚಿತ್ತಯಿಸು, ಚಿತ್ತಯ್ಸು, ಚಿತ್ತವಿಸು s. *v. t.* To attend to, notice, consider.

ಚಿತ್ತರ. *tb. of* ಚಿತ್ರ, *q. v.*

ಚಿತ್ತಾರ (*tb. of* ಚಿತ್ರಾಕಾರ) n. A portrait; any picture. ಚಿತ್ತಾರಿಗ. A painter.

ಚಿತ್ತಿನಿ s. n. An intelligent woman.

ಚಿತ್ತು h. n. A blot, obliteration, correction in writing.

ಚಿತ್ತೆ. *tb. of* ಚಿತ್ರೆ, *q. v.*

ಚಿತ್ರ (= ಚಿತ್ತರ) s. *a.* Perceptible; bright-coloured, variegated. *n.* An ornament. 2, a painting, picture, sketch. 3, variegated colour. 4, a wonder, marvel; *also* ವಿ- (ಅದ್ಭುತ, ಆಶ್ಚರ್ಯ). 5, a mark on the forehead. -ತೆಗೆ, -ಬರೆ. To draw a picture. -ಕ. A painter; a leopard or chita. -ಕಾಯ. A tiger, panther. -ಕಾರ, -ಗಾರ. A painter. -ಕೂಟ. N. of a hill. -ಗುಪ್ತ. N. of the recorder of the vices and virtues of mankind in Yama's world. -ಪಟ. A picture, painting. -ಭಾನು. The sixteenth year of the cycle of sixty. -ಮೂಲ, -ಮೂಲಿಕೆ. An under-shrub, the Ceylon leadwort. -ಲೇಖೆ. A portrait; N. of a daughter of king Vâṇa's minister. -ವಧೆ. Horrid torture. -ವಿಚಿತ್ರ. Variegated, multiform. ಚಿತ್ರಾಕಾರ. = ಚಿತ್ರಾರ.

ಚಿತ್ರಾನ್ನ s. n. Boiled rice mixed with various condiments.

ಚಿತ್ರಾಪುರ s. n. N. of a place in North [Kanara.

ಚಿತ್ರಾಸನ s. n. A square carpet of a variegated colour.

ಚಿತ್ರಿ, ಚಿತ್ರಿಕ s. n. A painter. ಚಿತ್ರಿತ. Variegated, painted. ಚಿತ್ರಿಸು. To draw; to paint.

ಚಿತ್ರೆ s. n. The fourteenth lunar mansion, *Spica virginis*. 2, a sort of cucumber, *Cucumis madraspatanus*.

ಚಿದಕು k. v. t. To peel the skin of soaked avarĕ pulse by squeezing. n. Peeling of the skin, *as* of soaked pulse.

ಚಿದಂಬರ s. n. N. of a place of pilgrimage.

ಚಿದಾನಂದ s. n. Intellectual happiness. -ಮೂರ್ತಿ, -ರೂಪ. Śiva.

ಚಿದ್ರೂಪ s. a. Intelligent, thoughtful, amiable, good-hearted. n. Kṛishṇa.

ಚಿನ k. n. Small pieces. -ಕಡಿ. To mince.

ಚಿನಾಯಿ s. a. Relating to or coming from China.

ಚಿನಿವಾರ, ಚಿನಿವಾಲ k. n. A money-changer; a jeweller.

ಚಿನುಕುರುಳಿ k. n. Soaked and germinated gram seasoned with salt and chillies and fried.

ಚಿಂತನ, ಚಿಂತನೆ s. n. Thinking, consideration, reflecting upon; anxious thought.

ಚಿಂತಾಕುಲ s. a. Anxious, solicitous.

ಚಿಂತಾಕ್ರಾಂತ s. a. Overcome by anxiety or care; f. ಚಿಂತಾಕ್ರಾಂತೆ.

ಚಿಂತಾಮಣಿ s. n. The philosopher's stone. 2, N. of a work in Kanarese. -ಪುಸ್ತಕ. A book on omens. -ಯಂತ್ರ. A talisman.

ಚಿಂತಾಲು h. n. Large scales for weigh- [ing.

ಚಿಂತಿತ s. a. Thought, reflected upon. n. Care; intention.

ಚಿಂತಿಸು s. v. t. To think about, reflect upon. v. i. To be anxious, sorrowful.

ಚಿಂತೆ (ಚಿಂತಾ) s. n. Sad or sorrowful thought, care, anxiety; reflection. ಚಿಂತೆ ಇಲ್ಲ. Never mind. -ಗೆಯ್ಯು, -ಗೊಳ್ಳು, -ಮಾಡು. To be anxious. -ಮಾಡು. To reflect, consider. ಚಿಂತ್ಯ. To be thought of, reflected.

ಚಿಂದಿ f. n. A shred, strip; a rag.

ಚಿನುಮಯ. = ಚಿನ್ಮಯ, q. v.

ಚಿನ್ನ k. n. Gold. 2, smallness. -ವರದ (= ಚಿನಿವಾರ, q. v.). A dealer in gold; a shroff..

ಚಿನ್ನಿವಾರ. = ಚಿನಿವಾರ, q. v.

ಚಿನ್ಹೆ, ಚಿನ್ಹ (tb. of ಚಿಹ್ನ) n. A sign, token, mark.

ಚಿನ್ಮಯ s. a. Full of knowledge. n. All-intelligence.

ಚಿಪ್ಪಿಗ 1. (tb. of ಶಿಲ್ಪಿಕ) n. An artisan, mechanic.

ಚಿಪ್ಪಿಗ 2. (= ಚಿಂಪಿಗ, fr. s. ಸಿವ್ to sew) n. A tailor.

ಚಿಪ್ಪು k. n. A shell, cockle, crust, hard covering; the skull. -ಗಟ್ಟು. The shell to form, *as* of a cocoanut.

ಚಿಬ್ಬಲ, ಚಿಬ್ಬಲು k. n. A bamboo lid.

ಚಿಬ್ಬು (tb. of ಸಿಧ್ಮ) n. A reddish or blackish spot on the body, freckle.

ಚಿಮಕು, ಚಿಮುಕಿಸು (= ಚಿಮಿಕಿಸು, ಚಿಮುಕಿಸು) k. v. t. To sprinkle.

ಚಿಮಟ, ಚಿಮಟಿಗೆ f. n. A pair of tweezers, pincers.

ಚಿಮಣಿ e. n. A chimney.

ಚಿಮಿಚಿಮಿಸು k. v. i. To prattle, *as* children. 2, welter, wallow.

ಚಿಮಿಕಿಸು, ಚಿಮುಕಿಸು. = ಚಿಮುಕಿಸು, q. v.

ಚಿಮುಟಿ f. n. Nippers. -ಕ್ಷೌರ. Plucking out hairs with nippers.

ಚಿಮುಟು k. v. i. To twinkle, wink. 2, (f.) to squeeze, pinch.

ಚಿಂಪಿಗ (= ಚಿಪ್ಪಿಗ, fr. s. ಶಿಪ್) n. A tailor.

ಚಿಮ್ಮು k. v. t. To propel with the finger. 2, to push forward; to cast, fling; to butt or toss with horns. 3, to squirt. 4, to break forth; to gush out; to fly off. 5, to brandish a weapon.

ಚಿಯೋನ್ f. n. Zion; the Church of God.

ಚಿರ s. a. Long, lasting a long time. -ಂಜೀವ, -ಜೀವಿ, -ಂಜೀವಿ. Long-lived; a term used in epistles when addressing or referring to a younger relative. -ತರ. Uncommonly long.

ಚಿರತೆ (ರ = ಱ) k. n. A cheeta or hunting leopard.

ಚಿರಾಕು h. n. A lamp.

ಚಿರಾಯಿತ (ರಾ = ಱಾ) k. n. A kind of gentian, *Agathotes chirayta.*

ಚಿರಾಯು s. a. Long-lived. n. A crow. ಚಿರಾಯು. For a long time; a long time.

ಚಿರ್ತ. = ಚಿರತೆ, q. v.

ಚಿಲಕ k. n. A hasp or small chain for fastening a door.

ಚಿಲವಾನ k. n. The odd money over a round sum.

ಚಿಲಿಕೆ k. n. Small pieces of wood used for building a flat roof. 2, the pot-herb *Hingtsha repens.*

ಚಿಲಿಮೆ h. n. The bowl of a hukka.

ಚಿಲ್ಮರಿ m. n. A very irritable person.

ಚಿಲ್ಮಿಷ (= ಕಿಲ್ಬಿಷ) s. n. Malice, roguery. -ಗಾರ. A mischievous fellow.

ಚಿಲ್ಲ 1. k. n. The clearing-nut tree, *Strychnos potatorum.*

ಚಿಲ್ಲ 2. f. a. Blear-eyed. n. The Bengal kite. -ಗಣ್ಣು. A bleared eye.

ಚಿಲ್ಲರ, ಚಿಲ್ಲರೆ (ರ = ಱ) k. n. Smallness, pettiness, trifling; cash under one rupee. -ಖರ್ಚು. Petty expenses. -ಜಿನಸು, -ಸಾಮಾನು. Sundry small articles of commerce, *as* grain, *etc.* -ಮಾತು. A trifling word. -ರೊಕ್ಕ. Small money, change.

ಚಿಲ್ಲಾ. = ಚಿಲ್ಲಾ, q. v. ಚಿಲ್ಲಾಪಿಲ್ಲಿ. = ಚಿಲ್ಲಾಪಿಲ್ಲಿ, q. v.

ಚಿಲ್ಲು k. n. A piece of wood holding a spindle.

ಚಿವಟು. = ಚಿಮುಟು, q. v.

ಚಿವರು. = ಚಿವುರು, q. v.

ಚಿವುಟು 1. k. v. t. To cut off, pluck off or pinch off with the nails.

ಚಿವುಟು 2. = ಚಿಮುಟು, q. v.

ಚಿವುರು (= ಚಿವರು) k. v. t. To scratch with the nails or claws. n. Scratching. -ಗಾಯ. A wound made by scratching.

ಚಿವ್ವು k. v. t. To shave or scrape; to peel or bark; to trim; to smooth or polish.

ಚೀ (= ಛೀ, q. v.) k. int. Fie! shame! ಚೀ ಚೀ. rep. Fie, fie!

ಚೀಟಿ, ಚೀಟು 1. h. n. Printed cotton, chintz. -ಪಾಟಿ. reit.

ಚೀಟಿ, ಚೀಟು 2. h. n. A chit, note; a bill, bond; a lot, ticket. ಅಂಗಡಿ-. A note to a shopkeeper. ಕಳ್ಳ-. A forged note of hand. ರಹದಾರಿ-. A passport. -ಹಾಕು. To cast lots.

ಚೀಡೆ k. n. A fried sweetmeat in the form of a marble.

ಚೀನ f. n. China; Chinese. 2, a kind of cloth. -ದೇಶ. China. ಚೀನಿ. Chinese. ಚೀನಿಕಾಯಿ. The squash-gourd. ಚೀನಿಸಕ್ಕರೆ. Granulated white sugar. ಚೀನಿಬೆಳ್ಳಿ. Pure silver without alloy.

ಚೀಪು 1. k. v. t. To suck.

ಚೀಪು 2. f. n. A piece of stone or wood used as a supporting prop.

ಚೀರಣಿ k. n. A small chisel.

ಚೀರು 1. = ಚಿವರು, q. v.

ಚೀರು 2. (ರು = ಱು) k. v. i. To scream, cry out. n. Screaming. 2, raging, fierceness.

ಚೀಲ k. n. A bag, sack.

ಚುಕಾಣಿ, ಚುಕ್ಕಾಣಿ h. n. The helm of a ship or boat.

ಚುಕಾಯಿಸು h. v. t. To settle, adjust; to fix, *as* the price; to discharge.

ಚುಕ್ಕಿ (*tb. of* ಶುಕ್ರ) *n.* Śukra, the planet Venus. 2, = ಚಿಕ್ಕೆ, *q. v.*

ಚುಕ್ಕೆ (= ಚಿಕ್ಕೆ) k. *n.* A small mark, dot, spot.

ಚುಂಗಡಿ k. *n.* Pettiness: small money, change; a trifling sum. 2, interest on money.

ಚುಂಗಾಣಿ k. *n.* A small smoking pipe.

ಚುಂಗು k. *n.* The end of a turban; a dangling tatter. 2, the fibrous tuft, *as* of a pealed cocoanut.

ಚುಚ್ಚು k. *v. t.* To insert. 2, to pierce into, *as* with a knife, thorn, *etc.*; to pierce or bore, *as* the ears. 3, to incite, *as* to quarrel. *n.* Piercing. ಚುಚ್ಚಿಸು. To cause to pierce.

ಚುಂಚ, ಚುಂಚು 1. k. *n.* A bird's beak. ಚುಂಚಿಲಿ. A musk-rat.

ಚುಂಚು 2. k. *a.* A projecting ledge on a house. 2, the hair curling round the forehead. 3, red or brown colour.

ಚುಟಕು h. *n.* Shortness, brevity.

ಚುಟಕ್ಕನೆ k. *ad.* Fiercely, painfully, *as* a scorpion stings.

ಚುಟ್ಟ, ಚುಟ್ಟಿ k. *n.* A cheeroot, cigar.

ಚುದ್ರ (*tb. of* ಕ್ಷುದ್ರ) *n.* Slander. -ತನ. Slandering.

ಚುನಾಬ್ h. *n.* Side. 2, majesty, excellency.

ಚುನಾಯಿಕೆ, ಚುನಾವಣೆ h. *n.* Choosing, selection.

ಚುನಾಯಿಸು h. *v. t.* To choose. 2, to plait, fold.

ಚುನ್ನ a. k. *n.* Blame, censure, abuse; scorn. -ನುಡಿ. A word of abuse. -ಮಾಡು. To blame, censure.

ಚುಮಚುಮ k. *rep. int.* With intense brilliancy, used of the rising of the sun. *n.* Throbbing or smarting sensation.

ಚುಂಬನ s. *n.* Kissing; a kiss. ಚುಂಬಕ. A loadstone.

ಚುಂಬಿಸು s. *v. t.* To touch lightly or softly.

ಚುರಚಿ. = ತುರಚಿ, *q. v.*

ಚುರುಕು (ರು=ಱು), ಚುರ್ಕು k. *n.* Quickness, speed, haste; heat; keenness, smartness, sharpness. 2, force, vehemence. 3, dearness. *a.* Quick, sharp. -ಬುದ್ಧಿ. Quick understanding. -ತನ. Keenness; smartness.

ಚುರುಚುರು k. *ad.* With violent smarting. -ಗುಟ್ಟು, -ಎನ್ನು. To smart violently.

ಚುಲಕ, ಚುಲುಕು k. *n.* Lightness of temper or conduct, levity; *also* -ಬುದ್ಧಿ, -ತನ.

ಚುಳಿಕೆ k. *n.* A stout stick to beat cotton with.

ಚೂಟಿ k. *n.* Aim. 2, a device; scheme, expedient; *also* ಚೂಟು. -ಗಾರ. A contriver, schemer.

ಚೂಡ, ಚೂಡಾ, ಚೂಡೆ s. *n.* A single look or tuft of hair left on the head at tonsure. 2, a crest, plume. 3, a kind of bracelet. ಚೂಡಾಕರ್ಮ. The rite of tonsure. ಚೂಡಾಮಣಿ. A jewel worn in a crest; any person or thing pre-eminently excellent.

ಚೂಣಿ a. k. *n.* The foremost part, front, van.

ಚೂಪು a. k. *n.* Sight; a look, glance; the eye. 2, pointedness, *as* of a pen.

ಚೂರಣ. *tb. of* ಚೂರ್ಣ, *q. v.*

ಚೂರಿ (*tb. of* ಛೂರಿ) *n.* A penknife; a knife; a table-knife.

ಚೂರು 1. k. *n.* A frame thrown over houses to form the roof.

ಚೂರು 2. k. *n.* A part, portion, piece, fragment. ಚೂರಡಿಕೆ. Betel-nut in small bits. -ಚೂರು. *rep.* Bits and pieces.

ಚೂರುಮುರಿ (=ತುರುಮುರಿ) f. *n.* Cleaned rice, soaked and parched.

ಚೂರ್ಣ (= ಸುಣ್ಣ) s. *n.* Powder, dust, crumbs. 2, chunam or lime. 3, = ಸೂರ್ಣ. *a.* Powdered, pulverised.

ಚೂರ್ಣಿಕೆ s. *n.* A kind of easy prose.

ಚೂಲಿಕೆ s. *n.* The comb or crest of a cock. 2, the front.

ಚೆಕ್ಕು. = ಚಕ್ಕು, *q. v.* 2, an oil-press, sugar-mill.

ಚೆಕ್ಕೆ. = ಚಕ್ಕೆ, q. v.

ಚೆಂಗು (= ಚಂಗು, q. v.) k. v. i. To jump, skip, caper; to run away. n. A jump.

ಚೆಚ್ಚರ (= ಚಚ್ಚರ, q. v.) k. n. Quickness. 2, certainty. 3, carefulness. ಚೆಚ್ಚರಿಗ. A zealously active man.

ಚೆಚ್ಚು (= ಚಚ್ಚು, q. v.) k. v. t. To crush, grind, etc.

ಚೆಟ್ಟ. = ಚಟ್ಟ 2, q. v.

ಚೆಟ್ಟೆ k. n. A hen-sparrow. 2, = ಚಟ್ಟಿ.

ಚೆಟ್ಟು. = ಚಟ್ಟು, q. v.

ಚೆಂಡಿಕೆ. = ಚಂಡಿಕೆ, q. v.

ಚೆಂಡು (= ಚಂಡು, q. v.) k. n. A play-ball.

ಚೆದರು = ಚದರು, q. v.

ಚೆಂದ. = ಚಂದ 1, q. v.

ಚೆಂದರ, ಚೆಂದಿರ. = ಚಂದ್ರ 1, q. v.

ಚೆನ್ನು. = ಚನ್ನು, q. v. ಚೆನ್ನಾಗಿ. = ಚನ್ನಾಗಿ.

ಚೆಂಬಿಗೆ (= ತಂಬಿಗೆ) k. n. A brass vessel, used for drinking water, etc.

ಚೆರಬಿ. = ಚರಬಿ, q. v.

ಚೆರಿಗೆ. = ಚರಿಗೆ, q. v.

ಚೆರ್ಚೆ (tb. of ಚರ್ಚೆ, q. v.) s. n. Ridicule, etc.

ಚೆರ್ಬಿ. = ಚರಬಿ, q. v.

ಚೆಲುವು, ಚೆಲೊ. = ಚಲುವು, ಚಲೊ, etc., q. v.

ಚೆಲ್ಲಾಟ. = ಚಲ್ಲಾಟ, q. v.

ಚೆಲ್ಲು (= ಚಲ್ಲು 1, q. v.) k. v. t. To scatter about, shed, spill, etc. ಚೆಲ್ಲಿಸು. To cause to scatter about, etc.

ಚೆಲ್ವ, ಚೆಲುವ. = ಚಲ್ವ, etc., q. v.

ಚೇಗು k. n. The heart or core of a tree; essence.

ಚೇಚೇ f. int. Fie! shame! 2, not so!

ಚೇಟ, ಚೇಟಕ s. n. A servant, slave; f. ಚೇಟಿ.

ಚೇಡೆ f. n. A goblin summoned to harrass people. -ಮಾಡು. To practise black-art.

ಚೇತನ (fr. ಚಿತ್) s. a. Conscious; intelligent; alive; living. n. The mind, soul; a living and sentient being. 2, power, strength.

ಚೇತನ್ಯ (tb. of ಚೈತನ್ಯ) n. Power.

ಚೇತರಿಸು (i. e. ಚೇತನಿಸು, fr. ಚೇತನ) v. i. To re- cover consciousness. ಚೇತರಿಕೆ. Con- sciousness, strength.

ಚೇತಸ್ s. n. Consciousness; intelligence; the mind, intellect.

ಚೇಪು k. n. A gush, as of milk.

ಚೇರ k. n. The Cêra or Koṅgu country.

ಚೇಲ s. n. Cloth; a garment.

ಚೇಷ್ಟೆ s. n. Gesture, grimaces; action; exertion. 2, mischievous tricks, derision. ಕು-. A ridiculous grimace. -ಗಾರ. A man full of tricks and pranks.

ಚೇಳು (ಳು = ಱು) k. n. A scorpion. -ಕೊಂಡಿಗಿಡ, -ಬಾಲದಗಿಡ. The Indian turnsole, *Heliotropium indicum*. -ಬಾಣ. A rocket resembling a scorpion in its movements. -ಕುಟುಕು, -ಬಡಿ. A scorpion to sting. -ಕೊಂಡಿ. A scorpion's sting.

ಚೈತನ್ಯ (= ಚೇತನ) s. n. Intelligence, consciousness; sensation, the soul. 2, power, strength. 3, N. of a Vaishṇava reformer. -ಸ್ಥ. A rich man.

ಚೈತ್ಯ (fr. ಚಿತಾ) s. a. Relating to a funeral pile. n. A monument, tombstone, temple. 2, (fr. ಚಿತ್) the mind.

ಚೈತ್ರ s. n. The first month of the lunar year (March-April).

ಚೊಕ್ಕ k. n. Niceness, elegance, beauty, charm, etc. 2, purity, cleanness. -ಊಟ. An excellent meal. -ಚಿನ್ನ. Pure gold. -ನೀರು. Pure water. -ಬೆಳ್ಳಿ. Pure silver.

ಚೊಕ್ಕಟ, -ಟು, ಚೊಕ್ಕಳಿಕೆ. = ಚೊಕ್ಕ, q. v.

ಚೊಗಟೆ k. n. The annual herb *Cassia occidentalis*.

ಚೊಂಗ (= ಚೊಂಚ, ಚೊಂಚು) k. n. Crookedness, perverseness. 2, a perverse man; f. ಚೊಂಗಿ. *Cpds.*: -ಕಾಲು, -ಗೆಯ್ಮೆ, etc.

ಚೊಚ್ಚಲು, ಚೊಚ್ಚಿಲು k. n. The first birth; the first offspring. -ಮಗ. A first-born son. -ಮಗಳು. A first-born daughter.

ಚೊಂಚ, ಚೊಂಚು. = ಚೊಂಗ, q. v.

ಚೊಟ್ಟ. = ಚೊಂಗ, q. v.

ಚೊಲ್ಲಣ. = ಚಲ್ಲಣ, *q. v.*

ಚೋಜಿಗ (= ಸೋಜಿಗ. *tb. of* ಚೋದ್ಯ) *n.* Surprise, wonder; a marvel, wonder.

ಚೋಟು k. *n.* A span. ಚೋಟಗಲ. A span's breadth. ಚೋಟಳತೆ. A span's measure. ಚೋಟುದ್ದ. A span's length. ಚೋಟೆತ್ತರ. A span's height.

ಚೋದ್ಯ (= ಚೋಜಿಗ, *etc.*) s. *n.* Surprise, astonishment, wonder.

ಚೋಪದಾರ f. *n.* A mace-bearer.

ಚೋರ s. *n.* A thief, robber. -ತನ, -ತ್ವ, ಚೋರಿ. Theft, robbery.

ಚೋಲ, -ಕ s. *n.* A short jacket; bodice.

ಚೋಲಿ s. *n.* A kind of chignon made of some hair of the čamari.

ಚೋಳ k. *n.* The coast of Coromandel; N. of its people. -ದೇಶ, -ಮಂಡಲ. The Čōḷa country.

ಚೌಕ (= ಚವುಕ. *tb. of* ಚತುಷ್ಕ) *a.* Four-sided, square. *n.* A four-sided linga-box. 2, a square handkerchief. 3, four rupees. 4, a square in a town where four roads meet; a square in the centre of a temple or house. 5, the number four on a die. 6, prolixity, worthlessness (*as in* ಚೌಕದ ಮಾತು).

ಚೌಕಟ್ಟು h. *n.* A frame.

ಚೌಕಶುದ್ಧ (*tb. of* ಚತುಷ್ಕ & s.) *n.* Whole square.

ಚೌಕಸಿ. = ಚವುಕಸಿ, *q. v.*

ಚೌಕಳಿ. = ಚವುಕಳಿ, *q. v.*

ಚೌಕಿ (= ಚವಕಿ, ಚವುಕಿ, *q. v.*) *n.* A group of four houses. 2, the square in the centre of a house.

ಚೌಕೀದಾರ h. *n.* A watchmaṇ.

ಚೌಕು. = ಚೌಕ, *q. v.* -ಳ. Four castes.

ಚೌತಿ (= ಚವುತಿ. *tb. of* ಚತುರ್ಥಿ) *n.* The fourth lunar day.

ಚೌದರಿ. = ಚವುದರಿ, *q. v.*

ಚೌಪದ (*tb. of* ಚತುಃಪದ) *n.* A class of metres.

ಚೌರ. *tb. of* ಕ್ಷೌರ, *q. v.*

ಚೌರಿ (= ಚವರಿ. *tb. of* ಚಾಮರ) *n.* A chowry.

ಚೌಲ s. *n.* The tonsure of a child. 2, (= ಚವಲ) a silver coin of two Aṇas.

ಚೌಳು. = ಚವುಳು, *q. v.*

ಛ

ಛ. The twenty-fifth letter of the alphabet.

ಛಕಾರ s. *n.* The syllable ಛ.

ಛಟ k. *int. An imitative sound.* -ಛಟ. *rep.* The sound of snapping or clashing.

ಛಡಾಛಡಿ h. *ad.* Quickly.

ಛತ್ರ 1. (= ಚತ್ರ) s. *n.* A parasol, umbrella. -ಕ. A mushroom. -ಪತಿ. A regal title.

ಛತ್ರ 2. s. *n.* A choultry, inn.

ಛದ, -ನ s. *n.* A covering. 2, a wing. 3, a leaf.

ಛದಿಸ್ s. *n.* A covering. 2, the thatch or roof of a house.

ಛದ್ಮನೆ s. *n.* Disguise, fraud, deceit, trick.

ಛಂದ. = ಚಂದ 1, *q. v.*

ಛಂದಸ್ಸು s. *n.* Metrical science, prosody. 2, the vedic hymns.

ಛರ್ದಿ h. *n.* Sickness, vomiting.

ಛಲ s. *n.* Fraud, deceit, deception, disguise; pretext; device. 2, (= ಚಲ 2) firmness. -ವಾದಿ. An obstinate man.

ಛವಿ s. *n.* Skin. 2, colour; beauty. 3, light, lustre.

ಛಾನಸ (*tb. of* ಛಾಂದಸ) *n.* Loitering, delay. -ಗಾರ. A loiterer.

ಛಾಂದಸ (*fr.* ಛಂದಸ್) *s. a.* Relating to prosody. *n.* A Brâhmaṇa conversant with the vêdas; *also* ಛಾಂದಸಿಕ.

ಛಾಯೆ, ಛಾಯಾ (= ಚಾಯೆ) *s. n.* Shade, shadow. 2, reflection. 3, a screen, protection, respect. 4, splendour. 5, faint appearance. ಛಾಯಾತನಯ, ಛಾಯಾನಂದನ. The son of ċhâyâ: the planet Saturn. ಛಾಯಾಯಂತ್ರ. Shadow-instrument: a sundial.

ಛಿದ್ರ *s. n.* A hole, slit, rent; a defect, flaw, fault. ಛಿದ್ರಾನ್ವೇಷಣ. Searching for faults.

ಛಿನ್ನ *s. a.* Cut; divided, torn, broken. -ಭಿನ್ನ, -ಛಿನ್ನ. Shattered, piecemeal.

ಛೂರಿ. = ಚೂರಿ, *q. v.*

ಛೇಕ *s. a.* Tame. 2, shrewd, clever. *n.* A kind of alliteration.

ಛೇದ *s. n.* Cutting; chopping; tearing off; a section, piece. 2, a divisor, denominator of a fraction; *also* -ನ. -ಮಾಡು, ಛೇದಿಸು. To cut, make an incision; to cut asunder.

ಜ್

ಜ್. The twenty-sixth letter of the alphabet.

ಜ *s. a.* Born. *n.* A son, *as:* ಅಗ್ರಜ, ಆತ್ಮಜ, ಇಂದ್ರಜ, ಉದ್ಭಿಜ, *etc.*

ಜಕಾತಿ h. *n.* Customs, excise.

ಜಕಾರ *s. n.* The letter ಜ.

ಜಕೇರೆ h. *n.* An old store or hoard.

ಜಕ್ಕ (*tb. of* ಯಕ್ಷ, *q. v.*). ಜಕ್ಕಣ, ಜಕ್ಕಪ್ಪ. N.; *f.* ಜಕ್ಕವ್ವ.

ಜಕ್ಕಣಿ. = ಜಕ್ಕಿಣಿ, *q. v.*

ಜಕ್ಕಲು k. *n.* Obsequiousness, fawning.

ಜಕ್ಕಿಣಿ (*tb. of* ಯಕ್ಷಿಣಿ) *n.* A woman who dies in the matron state and receives divine honours, *i. e.* sîrĉs are dedicated to her, *etc.*

ಜಕ್ಕಿಸು (= ಜಗ್ಗಿಸು) k. *v. t.* To pull with effort. 2, to press down. *v. i.* To be rude.

ಜಕ್ಕುಲಿ k. *v.* Ticklishness (*cf.* ಚಕ್ಕುಲಗುಳಿ). -ಸು. To amuse, divert; to jeer at, deride; to tickle; to touch; to play about.

ಜಗ 1. (= ಝಗ) *s. n.* Glittering; notoriety. -ಜಗ, -ಜಗನೆ. Sparkingly, brightly. -ಜಗಹೊಳೆ. To shine brilliantly. -ಜಗಿಸು. To glitter, shine.

ಜಗ 2. (*tb. of* ಜಗತ್) *n.* The world. -ಜ್ಜನ. Mankind. -ಜ್ಜ್ಯೋತಿ. The ligh. of the world: the sun. -ದೊಡೆಯ. The lord of the world. -ಬಂಟ. The greatest liar in the world; the most shameless man. -ಮೊಂಡ. The most stupid man in the world.

ಜಗತಿ, ಜಗತ್ತು (= ಜಗ) *s. n.* The world, universe. ಜಗತ್ಕರ್ತ, ಜಗತ್ಕರ್ತೃ. The creator of the world; Brahmâ. ಜಗತ್ತ್ರಯ. The three worlds: svarga, bhûmi, and pâtâḷa. ಜಗದೀಶ, ಜಗದೀಶ್ವರ. The Lord of the universe. ಜಗದ್ಗುರು. The guru of the world; Jesus Christ; an eminent guru. ಜಗದ್ರಕ್ಷಕ. The Saviour of the world: Christ. ಜಗನ್ನಾಥ. The Lord of the world: God; N. of a town near Cuttack. ಜಗನ್ನಾಯಕ. The governor of the world: God. ಜಗನ್ಮಾತೆ. Durgâ, Lakshmî.

ಜಗತಿ 1. = ಜಗಲಿ, *q. v.*

ಜಗತಿ 2. (= ಜಗತ್ತು) *s. n.* The earth. 2, the world, universe. 3, the king and his subjects. -ವಲಯ. Earth's circumference; the terrestrial globe.

ಜಗತ್ಯ. *tb. of* ಜಗತ್, *q. v.*

ಜಗಲಿ (= ಜಗತಿ) k. n. A raised, open veranda; a seat of mud, *etc.*

ಜಗಳ k. n. A quarrel, fight; war. -ಗಂಟ, ಗಾರ. A quarrelsome man; *f.* -ಗಾತಿ. -ತರು. To rouse a quarrel. -ತೆಗೆ. To pick a quarrel. -ಹುಟ್ಟು. To create a quarrel. ಜಗಳಾಡು, -ಮಾಡು. To quarrel.

ಜಗಳೆ (= ಜಾಗಟೆ) *tb.* n. A gong.

ಜಗಿ (= ಜಿಗಿ) k. *v. t.* To chew, *as* betel.

ಜಗುಳು (ಳು = ಱು) a. k. *v. i.* To go off; to slip; to drop down.

ಜಗ್ಗಿಸು. = ಜಕ್ಕಿಸು, *q. v.*

ಜಗ್ಗು 1. k. *v. i.* To bend down, *as* a tree with fruit; to sink, *as* a wall; to hang down. *n.* Bending.

ಜಗ್ಗು 2. k. *v. t.* To pull, drag, draw.

ಜಂಕಿಸು a. k. *v. t.* To scold, chide; to despise. *v. i.* To cry. ಜಂಕಣೆ. Scolding. ಜಂಕೆ. Crying out.

ಜಂಗಮ s. *a.* Movable; locomotive; living. *n.* A Liṅgavanta; *f.* -ಗಿತ್ತಿ. -ಪ್ರಸಾದ. Any favour from a Jaṅgama. -ಲಿಂಗ. A Jaṅgama; a liṅga worn by him.

ಜಂಗಲ, ಜಂಗಲು h. n. A forest, jungle.

ಜಂಗಾಲ್ 1. f. n. A platform with railings placed on two boats, used at ferries.

ಜಂಗಾಲ್ 2. h. n. Zangar, a greenish blue dye.

ಜಂಗು k. n. A bell worn by a Jaṅgama mendicant.

ಜಂಗುಳಿ k. n. A mass, assemblage, herd, *etc.*

ಜಂಗೆ k. n. A stride.

ಜಂಘೆ s. n. The shank or lower part of the leg; the leg. ಜಂಘಾನಿಲ. A swift wind. ಜಂಘಾಬಲ. Power of legs. ಜಂಘಾಲ. Running, fleet, swift; a runner, courier.

ಜಜ್ಜರಿತ. *tb.* of ಜರ್ಜರಿತ, *q. v.*

ಜಜ್ಜು k. *v. t.* To bruise, crush, squash. *n.* A bruise.

ಜಂಜರ h. *a.* General: consecutive, not specified or classified. -ನಂಬರ. Consecutive number. -ಬಂದಿ. Running numbers or papers.

ಜಂಜಡ, ಜಂಜಾಟ f. n. Trouble, bother, plague.

ಜಂಜಾಲು h. n. A swivel gun.

ಜಟಕಾಯಿಸು f. *v. t.* To scorn, treat scornfully; *also* ಜಟಕರಿಸು.

ಜಟಪಟ f. *ad.* Smartly, quick. ಜಟಪಟಿ, ಜಟಾಪಟಿ. Strife, scuffle; angry discussion.

ಜಟಾಜೂಟ s. n. A quantity of twisted hair.

ಜಟಾಮಾಂಸಿ s. n. A herb growing on the Himâlaya, the Indian spikenard.

ಜಟಾಯು s. n. N. of a fabulous vulture.

ಜಟಿ, ಜಟಾ (= ಜಡೆ, *q. v.*) s. n. Twisted and matted hair; a tress of hair. 2, a pendent root from the banyan. *etc.* 3, the fibrous root of trees. ಜಟಾಧಾರಿ. Wearing matted or braided hair.

ಜಟ್ಟಿ (= ಜೆಟ್ಟಿ) f. n. A professional wrestler. -ಮಲ್ಲ. *dpl.* An athlete among wrestlers. -ಕಾಳಗ, -ಕುಸ್ತಿ, -ಗುದ್ದಾಟ, -ಯುದ್ಧ. A wrestling match. -ಮುಳ್ಳು. Steel of boxers.

ಜಠರ s. n. The belly. *a.* Hard, firm. ಜಠರಾಗ್ನಿ. The gastric juice.

ಜಡ s. *a.* Cold, frigid, chilly. 2, slow, dull, apathetic, stupid; foolish. 3, hard, solid. *n.* Cold. 2, (= ಜಡ್ಡು) indisposition, illness. -ಕಾಲ. The cold season. -ಗುಣ. A sluggish disposition. -ಹೋಗು. To be difficult.

ಜಡಜ (= ಜಲಜ) s. *a.* Water-born. *n.* A lotus.

ಜಡತ (*fr.* ಜಡಿ) k. n. Beating, driving in, *as* a nail. -ಮಾಡು. To drive in, *etc.*

ಜಡತಿ f. n. A close and narrow search.

ಜಡತೆ, ಜಡತ್ವ s. n. Coldness; apathy; stupidity; inertness.

ಜಡಾಯಿಸು (= ಚಡಾಯಿಸು, *q. v.*) k. *v. t.* To drive in; to fasten or bolt, *as* a door.

ಜಡಿ 1. k. *v. t.* To threaten, menace; to frighten; to blame, chide; to urge on.

2, to wave, brandish, *as* a sword, *etc.* 3, to beat; to pound. 4, to beat into; to drive in, *as* a nail. -ಸು. To cause to beat.

ಜಡಿ 2. k. *n.* A long-continued, fine, small rain; *also* -ಮಳೆ.

ಜಡೀಭಾವ (*fr.* ಜಡ) s. *n.* Dulness, apathy, insensibility.

ಜಡುಪು f. *n.* A flap (attached to a paper kite).

ಜಡೆ. *tb. of* ಜಟೆ, *q. v.* -ಕಳ್ಳಿ. A kind of Euphorbia, triangular spurge. -ಕುಚ್ಚು. An ornament attached to a tress of hair of women. -ನಾಗರ, -ಬಿಲ್ಲೆ. Ornaments worn by women over their plaited hair.

ಜಡ್ಜಿ e. *n.* The judge.

ಜಡ್ಡು 1. (= ಜಡ್ಡ) k. *n.* A callous spot; a wart, scar. 2, the disagreeable smell of sheep's milk, *etc.*

ಜಡ್ಡು 2. (*tb. of* ಜಡ) *n.* Slight indisposition; sickness; dulness; *also* -ತನ. -ಬುದ್ಧಿ. A dull understanding.

ಜಂಟಿ h. *n.* Joining; meeting; partnership. -ಗಾರ. A partner. -ಪಟ್ಟಿ. Title-deeds in the name of two persons. -ಮಾಡು, -ಹಾಕು. To join, tie. -ಸು. To join; to annex.

ಜಂಡೆ h. *n.* A flag, banner.

ಜತನ (= ಯತನ. *tb. of* ಯತ್ನ) *n.* Care, heed.

ಜತಿ (*tb. of* ಯತಿ) *n.* An ascetic. 2, harmony in music.

ಜತೆ (= ಜತ್ತು, ಜೊತ್ತು. *tb. of* ಯುತಿ) *n.* Union; intercourse; company; a pair; a fellow. -ಗಾರ. A male companion; *f.* -ಗಾತಿ. -ಬೀಳು. To pair, accompany.

ಜತ್ತಕೆ a. k. *n.* Fraud, deceit, hypocrisy; disguise.

ಜತ್ತಿಗೆ. = ಜೊತ್ತಿಗೆ, *q. v.*

ಜತ್ತು (= ಜತೆ) *tb. n.* Intercourse, friendship.

ಜನ s. *n.* Man, mankind, people; a person in general. -ಜನಿತ. Known to all. -ತೆ. People, mankind; birth. -ನಾಥ, -ಪ, -ಪತಿ, -ರಮಣ. A king. -ರಂಜನ. Gratifying people. -ಪದ. A community, people; an empire. -ವಾರ್ತೆ. Rumour, report.

ಜನಕ s. *n.* A progenitor, father; Sitâ's father. -ಜೆ, -ತನಯೆ, ಜನಕಾತ್ಮಜೆ. Sitâ.

ಜನನ (= ಜನ್ಮ) s. *n.* Birth; production. 2, race, lineage. -ಪತ್ರ, -ಪತ್ರಿಕೆ. Horoscope. ಜನನಿ. A mother.

ಜನಮೇಜಯ s. *n.* N. of a king, Parikshit's son.

ಜನಾಂಗ s. *n.* A nation, tribe.

ಜನಾನಿ h. *a.* Made for women. *n.* A seraglio, harem.

ಜನಾಂತ s. *n.* An uninhabited place. 2, a region, country.

ಜನಾರ್ದನ s. *n.* Vishṇu, Kṛishṇa.

ಜನಿ 1. s. *n.* Birth, production. 2, a woman. 3, a daughter-in-law. -ತ. Born, begotten. -ಯಿಸು. To be born or produced.

ಜನಿ 2. k. *v. i.* To flow; to drop.

ಜನಿವಾರ (= ಜನ್ನಿವಾರ. *tb. of* ಯಜ್ಞೋಪವೀತ) *n.* The sacrificial thread.

ಜನೆ a. k. *n.* The yolk of an egg.

ಜಂತ. *tb. of* ದಂತ, *q. v.*

ಜಂತು s. *n.* A creature, living being. 2, any animal.

ಜಂತೆ f. *n.* A short small beam or rafter.

ಜಂತ್ರ. *tb. of* ಯಂತ್ರ, *q. v.*

ಜನ್ನ (*tb. of* ಯಜ್ಞ) *n.* A sacrifice.

ಜನ್ನಗೆ (*tb. of* ಯಾಜ್ಞಿಕ) *n.* That belongs to sacrifice.

ಜನ್ನಿವಾರ. = ಜನಿವಾರ, *q. v.*

ಜನ್ಮ (= ಜಲ್ಮ) s. *n.* Birth, production, origin; existence, life. -ಕೊಡು. To give birth to. -ತಕ್ಕೊಳ್ಳು, -ಎತ್ತು. To be born. -ದೇಶ. Native country. -ನಕ್ಷತ್ರ. The natal star. -ಪತ್ರ, -ಪತ್ರಿಕೆ. Horoscope. -ಪಾಪ. Original sin. -ಭೂಮಿ. Birthplace. -ರಾಶಿ. The sign of the zodiac that contains the natal star. ಜನ್ಮಿಸು. = ಜನಿಸು.

ಜನ್ಮಾಂತರ s. *n.* Another state of existence; transmigration.

ಜನ್ಮಿ s. n. A creature, man.

ಜನ್ಯ s. a. Born, produced. n. Rumour, report. 2, war, combat.

ಜಪ s. n. Muttering; muttering a vedic verse, names of a deity, charms, prayers. -ಮಾಡು, ಜಪಿಸು. To perform japa. -ಮಾಲಿಕೆ, -ಮಾಲೆ, -ಸರ. A rosary.

ಜಪ್ತಿ h. n. Seizure, confiscation, attachment *(law)*.

ಜಪ್ಪಿಸು f. v. i. To wait and watch patiently, to lurk.

ಜಬರ, ಜಬರು h. n. Powerful. -ದಸ್ತು. Oppression; force; violence.

ಜಬರಿಸು k. v. t. To chide, scold.

ಜಬಾಬು. = ಜವಾಬು, q. v.

ಜಬ್ಬಲ k. n. The state of being weak, infirm or frail from old age, *etc.*

ಜಬ್ಬು 1. (= ಜಬ್ಬಲ) k. n. Weakness; softness; slackness.

ಜಬ್ಬು 2. (= ಜಬರಿಸು) k. v. t. To scold, abuse. 2, to suck. n. Weakness; frailty; softness; slackness.

ಜಮಖಾನೆ h. n. A sitting carpet.

ಜಮದಗ್ನಿ s. n. Blazing fire. 2, N. of Paraśurâma's father.

ಜಮಾ (= ಜಮೆ) h. n. Receipts, income; collection. -ಖರ್ಚು. Receipts and disbursements. -ಬಂದಿ. Settlement of assessments. -ಯಿಸು. To assemble; to collect; to succeed, *as* a business. -ವಸೂಲು -ಬಾಕಿ. The collections and the outstanding balances.

ಜಮಾದಾರ h. n. A commander of a body of troops; the head peon.

ಜಮೀದಾರ (=ಜಮೀನುದಾರ) h. n. A zemindar, landholder.

ಜಮೀನು h. n. Land or ground. -ದಾರ. = ಜಮೀದಾರ, q. v. [ದಾರ, q. v.

ಜಮೆ. = ಜಮಾ, q. v. ಜಮೇದಾರ. = ಜಮಾ

ಜಂಪು f. n. Drowsiness, sleepiness.

ಜಂಪೆತಾಳ f. n. Slow time in music, *andante.*

ಜಂಬ (= ಡಬ್ಬು, ಡಂಭ. *tb. of* ದಂಭ) n. Ostentation, pomp. -ಗಾರ. A man of ostentation.

ಜಂಬರ k. n. Affair, business.

ಜಂಬೀರ s. n. A lemon.

ಜಂಬು 1. k. n. Length. 2, a kind of reed, *Typha angustifolia.*

ಜಂಬು 2. s. n. The rose apple, *Eugenia jambolana.* -ದ್ವೀಪ. The central division of the world, including India; India.

ಜಂಬುಕ s. n. A jackal.

ಜಂಬುಖಾನೆ. = ಜಮಖಾನೆ, q. v.

ಜಂಭ s. n. A lemon. 2, N. of a demon destroyed by Indra. 3, the jaws; a tooth, tusk.

ಜಯ s. n. Victory; conquest; winning. 2, the twenty-eighth year of the cycle. -ಜಯ. *rep.* Hurra! bravo! all hail! glory unto! -ಹೊಂದು. To gain victory. -ಘೋಷ, -ಧ್ವನಿ. A shout or cry of victory. -ಪತ್ರ. A record of victory. -ಮಂಗಲ. A cheer of victory. -ಲಕ್ಷ್ಮಿ, -ಶ್ರೀ. The goddess of victory. -ವಂತ, -ಶಾಲಿ, -ಶೀಲ. A conqueror. -ಸು. = ಜಯಿಸು, q. v.

ಜಯಂತಿ s. n. A flag, banner. 2, the day on which a deity assumed an incarnation. 3, the plant *Sesbania aegyptiaca.*

ಜಯಮಿನಿ. *tb. of* ಜೈಮಿನಿ, q. v.

ಜಯಸು, ಜಯಿಸು s. v. t. To conquer, defeat, overcome.

ಜರ 1. k. n. Sliding. -ಕುಂಡಿ, ಜರಗುಂಡಿ. Sliding on the posteriors, *as* children do.

ಜರ 2. *tb. of* ಜ್ವರ, q. v. ಚಳಿ-. Ague. -ಗಂಡೆ. Ague-cake.

ಜರ 3. h. n. Brocade. 2, a little, somewhat.

ಜರ 4. (= ಜರೆ 1) s. n. Growing old; decaying, wasting.

ಜರಗು (= ಜರುಗು) k. v. i. To slip, slide; to roll down *as* sand from a heap; to pass, elapse *as* time; to be done *as* a business. n. Loose texture *as* that of cloth. ಜರಗಿಸು. To cause to slide, to push or carry on *as* work.

ಜರಠ h. a. Worn out; old; hard, solid. 2, bent, drooping. 3, harsh, cruel. n. Old age. 2, mud, mire.

ಜರಗು k. n. Unsubstantiality; uselessness.

ಜರಡೆ (= ಜಲ್ಲಡೆ) k. n. A sieve.

ಜರಣ s. a. Waxing old. 2, promoting digestion. n. Cumin-seed.

ಜರತಾರ, ಜರತಾರೆ h. n. Silver wire covered with gold. ಜರತಾರಿ. Worked with jaratâra.

ಜರದು (= ಜರಿದು). P. p. of ಜರಿ 1.

ಜರಬು (= ಜರುಬು) h. n. Terribleness; awe.

ಜರಾಯು s. n. The womb. 2, the afterbirth. -ಜ. Born of the womb.

ಜರಿ 1. (= ಸರಿ) k. v. i. To slip or fall; to slide or slip down; to shrink back. 2, to fall away; to lose flesh. n. A ravine worn by a stream. -ಗಿಡ. A fern. ಹಿಂಜರಿ. To retreat, retire. ಮುಂಜರಿ. To advance.

ಜರಿ 2. h. n. Gold or silver threads. a. Worked with such threads. ಜರೀಪಟಕ. A laced belt; a grand flag.

ಜರಿ 3. (ರಿ = ಱ) k. n. A centipede.

ಜರಿ 4. (ರಿ = ಱ) = ಜರೆ 2, q. v.

ಜರೀಪ h. n. A giraffe.

ಜರೀಬು h. n. A land-measure. 2, measurement.

ಜರುಗು. = ಜರಗು, q. v.

ಜರುಚು (ರು = ಱು) k. v. i. To talk much, to be loquacious. n. Garrulity, vain talk.

ಜರುಬು. = ಜರಬು, q. v.

ಜರೂರು h. ad. Necessarily, urgently; at all events.

ಜರೆ 1. (= ಜರ 4, ಜರಾ) s. n. Old age; decrepitude, grey hair.

ಜರೆ 2. (ರೆ = ಱೆ) k. v. t. To rebuke, abuse; to disgrace, disdain, jeer at. P. ps. ಜರದು, ಜರೆದು.

ಜರ್ಜರ s. a. Old, infirm, decayed. 2, broken, shattered. ಜರ್ಜರಿತ (= ಜಜ್ಜರಿತ). Torn, broken in pieces; infirm. ಜರ್ಜರಿಸು. To become infirm.

ಜಬ್ಬು k. v. t. To scold, rebuke.

ಜಲ (= ಜಳ) s. n. Water (ಉದಕ, ನೀರು). 2, fraud, hypocrisy. -ಕ. Relating to water; a bath, bathing. -ಕಣ. A water-drop. -ಕಂಟಕ. A crocodile; danger from water. -ಕನ್ಯೆ. A water-nymph. -ಕ್ರೀಡೆ. Sporting in water; bathing for pleasure. -ಕ್ಷಾಲನ. Washing or cleansing with water. -ಗಾರ. One who searches for gold in drains, etc. -ಗ್ರಹ. A shark or crocodile. -ಚರ. Aquatic; a fish. -ಜ, -ಜಾತ. A lotus; a shell. -ಜಂತು. An aquatic animal. -ಜಾರಿ. The moon. -ತರಂಗ. A wave; harmonicon. -ದ, -ಧರ. A cloud; a fragrant grass, Cyperus rotundus. -ದಾರಿ. A drain, kennel. -ದ್ರೋಣಿ. A bucket. -ಧಿ, -ನಿಧಿ. The ocean. -ಪಕ್ಷಿ. A water-bird. -ಪತಿ. Varuṇa. -ಪದ್ಧತಿ. A water-course, a gutter. -ಪುಷ್ಪ. An aquatic flower; a fish. -ಪ್ರಲಯ. A deluge. -ಪ್ರವಾಹ. The current of water. -ಬುದುಬುದ. A water-bubble. -ಮಯ. Watery. -ಯಂತ್ರ. A syringe; a water-engine. -ರಾಶಿ. The ocean. -ರುಹ. A lotus. -ರುಹರಿಪು. The moon. -ವಾಯಸ. The diver-bird. -ಶಂಕೆ. Fear arising from water; making water. -ಶುಕ್ತಿ. A bivalve shell. -ಸಂಧಿ. Straits. -ಹರಿ. A small vessel with a channel for conveying water. ಜಲಾಧಾರ. A reservoir.

ಜಲದಿ (= ಜಲ್ದಿ) h. ad. Quickly.

ಜಲಾಯಿಸು s. v. t. To burn.

ಜಲಾಲಿ h. n. A sort of masquerade at the Moharam.

ಜಲಾವರ್ತ s. n. A whirlpool, eddy.

ಜಲಾಶಯ, ಜಲಾಶ್ರಯ (fr. ಜಲ) s. n. A lake or pond.

ಜಲೂಕೆ s. n. A leech.

ಜಲೋದರ s. n. Dropsy.

ಜಲ್ದಿ. = ಜಲದಿ, q. v.

ಜಲ್ಪ, ಜಲ್ಪನ s. n. Talk; chatter; discussion. ಜಲ್ಪಾಕ. Talkative; a chatterer; f. ಜಲ್ಪಾಕಿ.

ಜಲ್ಮ. tb. of ಜನ್ಮ, q. v.

ಜಲ್ಲಡಿ, ಜಲ್ಲಡೆ. = ಜರಡಿ, q. v.

ಜಲ್ಲನೆ k. ad. With a start.

ಜಲ್ಲಿ 1. (= ಜಲ್ಲೆ) k. n. A round bamboo basket used for storing corn.

ಜಲ್ಲಿ 2. k. n. Broken stone. 2, falsehood, lie. 3, tassels; hangings. -ಕೊಚ್ಚು, -ಹೊಡೆ. To lie.

ಜಲ್ಲಿಸು k. v. t. To sift.

ಜಲ್ಲು f. n. A boatman's pole. 2, the state of being torn, as cloth or leaves.

ಜಲ್ಲೆ k. n. A bamboo pole.

ಜವ 1. s. n. Speed, velocity, swiftness. -ಗೆಡು. Velocity to be impaired.

ಜವ 2. tb. of ಯಮ, q. v.

ಜವಕಾರ (tb. of ಯವಕ್ಷಾರ) n. Saltpetre.

ಜವನಿಕೆ (tb. of ಯವನಿಕೆ) n. A curtain, screen, veil.

ಜವಳಿ 1. k. n. Cloth of any kind. -ಕ, -ಕಾರ. A cloth-seller.

ಜವಳಿ 2. (tb. of ಯಮಲಿ) n. A pair; twins; sameness. -ನುಡಿ. Two words.

ಜವಳು. = ಜವುಗು, etc., q. v.

ಜವಾಜಿ, ಜವಾದಿ (= ಜವ್ವಾಜ) h. n. Civet. 2, musk. -ಬೆಕ್ಕು. A civet cat.

ಜವಾನ h. n. A peon.

ಜವಾಬು (= ಜಬಾಬು) h. n. An answer, reply. -ದಾರ. A responsible man. -ದಾರಿ. Responsibility.

ಜವಾರಿ f. a. Produced in one's own country, as cloth, wool, etc.

ಜವಾಹೀರು h. n. A jewel; jewelry.

ಜವಿ k. n. The hair of a horse's tail.

ಜವುಗು, ಜವುಳು (= ಜವಳು) k. n. Swampy ground, a swamp.

ಜವೆ. tb. of ಯವ, q. v. -ಗೋದಿ. Barley, *Hordeum vulgare.*

ಜವ್ವನ. tb. of ಯೌವನ, q. v.

ಜವ್ವಾಜಿ. = ಜವಾಜ, q. v.

ಜವ್ವಾಲೆ (= ಉಯ್ಯಾಲೆ, ಜೋಕಾಲೆ) f. n. A swing.

ಜಸ. tb. of ಯಶ, q. v.

ಜಹಗೀರು (= ಜಾಗೀರು) h. n. An assignment by government of lands or revenues. -ದಾರ. The holder of a jahagiru.

ಜಹಜು h. n. A ship.

ಜಹ್ನು s. n. N. of a king who adopted Ganges as his daughter. -ತನಯ, ಜಾಹ್ನವಿ. The Ganges.

ಜಳ s. n. Heat; hot vapour. -ಜಳ. Shining brightly.

ಜಳಕ (= ಜಲಕ, s. ಜಲ) s. n. A bath, bathing. -ಮಾಡು. To bathe.

ಜಳ್ಳು (= ಜರಡು, q. v.) k. n. Emptiness, hollowness. -ಕಾಳು. An empty grain of corn. -ಮಾತು. A vain word. -ಎಳ್ಳು, ಜಳ್ಳೆಳ್ಳು. Barren sesamum.

ಜಾ, ಜಾಕಾಯಿ. = ಜಾಜಿ, ಜಾಜಿಕಾಯಿ, q. v.

ಜಾಗ h. n. A place, spot, room.

ಜಾಗಟೆ (tb. of ಜಯಘಂಟೆ) n. A gong used by religious mendicants, in temples, etc.

ಜಾಗರ, ಜಾಗರಣ (= ಜಾಗ್ರತೆ) s. n. Waking, wakefulness; keeping a vigil.

ಜಾಗರೂಕ s. a. Wakeful. -ತೆ. Wakefulness.

ಜಾಗೀರು. = ಜಹಗೀರು, q. v.

ಜಾಗು a. k. n. Silence, taciturnity.

ಜಾಗ್ರತ s. a. Awake; attentive; also ಜಾಗೃತ. n. = ಜಾಗ್ರತೆ. -ಎಡು. To pay attention.

ಜಾಗ್ರತೆ s. n. Wakefulness; attention, carefulness. -ಗೊಳ್ಳು, -ತೆಕೊಳ್ಳು. To take care. -ಮಾಡು, -ಪಡು. To be attentive.

ಜಾಂಗಲಿಕ, ಜಾಂಗುಲಿಕ s. n. A snake-catcher, juggler.

ಜಾಜಿ (tb. of ಜಾತಿ) n. Nutmeg, mace. 2, *Jasminum grandiflorum.* -ಕಾಯಿ. Nutmeg. -ಪತ್ರೆ. Mace. -ಮಲ್ಲಿಗೆ, -ಹೂವು. Jasmine.

ಜಾಜು k. n. Red colour.

ಜಾಜ್ವಲ್ಯಮಾನ s. a. Shining, resplendent.

ಜಾಠರ s. a. Stomachic, abdominal.

ಜಾಡ (= ಜೇಡ) k. n. A weaver; f. -ಗಿತ್ತಿ, -ತ್ತಿ. 2, a spider; also -ಹುಳ. -ನ ಗೂಡು. A spider's nest.

ಜಾಡಣೆ (= ಝಾಡಣೆ) f. n. Shaking; sweeping; throwing; discharging; diarrhoea.

ಜಾಡಮಾಲಿ h. n. A sweeper.

ಜಾಡಾ h. n. A general clearance of accounts; also ಜಾಡೆ.

ಜಾಡಿ 1. h. n. A discharge; a flood; an outburst, as of tears, wrath, etc.

ಜಾಡಿ 2. k. n. A common cumbly.

ಜಾಡಿ 3. h. n. A jar.

ಜಾಡಿಸು f. v. t. To sweep; to dust. 2, to shake off, as dust from cloth, etc.; to jerk or throw out, as an arm, etc.; to purge. 3, to reprove.

ಜಾಡೆ k. n. The mark of a footstep, track, trace; wink, hint.

ಜಾಡ್ಯ (fr. ಜಡ) s. n. Coldness; apathy; indisposition, disease.

ಜಾಣ (tb. of ಜ್ಞಾನಿ) n. A skilful, knowing, or clever man; f. -ಳು, ಜಾಣೆ. -ತನ, ಜಾಣಿಮೆ, ಜಾಣ್ಮೆ. Cleverness; knowledge; understanding.

ಜಾತ s. a. Born, brought forth, produced; possessing; manifest. n. A son; birth; a creature; a race, kind, sort, species; a mass. -ಕ. A horoscope. -ಕರ್ಮ. A ceremony performed on the birth of a child.

ಜಾತಾಬಾಕಿ h. n. Balance, remainder after deductions.

ಜಾತಿ s. n. Birth. 2, lineage, race, family; tribe, caste. 3, kind, sort, species. 4, superior breed. 5, (= ಜಾಜಿ) nutmeg. 6, the great-flowered jasmine. ಉತ್ತಮ-, ಒಳ್ಳೇ-, ಮೇಲು-. A high caste; a good family. ಕೀಳು-, ಕೆಟ್ಟ-, ನೀಚ-, ಹೀನ-. A low caste. -ದ್ವೇಷ. Enmity with one's caste. -ಧರ್ಮ. The law or usage of caste. -ಭೇದ. A distinction of castes. -ಭ್ರಷ್ಟ. An outcast. -ವಂತ. Of high breed or rank. -ಸಂಕರ. A medley of castes. -ಹೀನ. = -ಭ್ರಷ್ಟ, q. v.

ಜಾತ್ಯ s. a. Belonging to a family, or caste; of noble descent.

ಜಾತ್ರೆ. tb. of ಯಾತ್ರೆ, q. v.

ಜಾದೂಗಿರಿ h. n. Magical arts.

ಜಾನಕೀ s. n. Sitâ, the wife of Râma. -ಪತಿ, -ರಮಣ. Râma.

ಜಾನು s. n. The knee.

ಜಾನ್ಹವಿ. = ಜಾಹ್ನವಿ, q. v.

ಜಾಪಾಳದ ಕಾಯಿ f. n. The croton-seed. ಜಾಪಾಳದ ಗಿಡ. *Croton tiglium* plant.

ಜಾಪ್ಯ (tb. of ಯಾಪ್ಯ) n. Loitering; laziness. 2, a sluggard, lazy man. a. To be muttered. -ಗಾರ. A sloth, sluggard.

ಜಾಬಿತೆ, ಜಾಬಿತಾ h. n. A passport; a memorandum; an inventary, catalogue.

ಜಾಬು (= ಜವಾಬು) h. n. An answer; a letter of correspondence.

ಜಾಮ. = ಜಾವ, q. v.

ಜಾಮಾತೃ s. n. A son-in-law.

ಜಾಮೀನ, ಜಾಮೀನು h. n. A bail, security; surety, sponsor. -ದಾರ, ಜಾಮೀನ್ದಾರ. A surety, bondsman. -ದಸ್ತಾವೇಜು. Surety-bond.

ಜಾಮೇಯ s. n. A sister's son.

ಜಾಂಬು f. n. A sort of goblet.

ಜಾಂಬವ s. a. Belonging to the jambu tree. 2, = ಜಾಂಬವಂತ.

ಜಾಂಬವಂತ s. n. N. of the chief of the bears. ಜಾಂಬವತಿ. His daughter.

ಜಾಯಮಾನ s. a. Being born.

ಜಾಯಾ s. n. Loss, injury, damage.

ಜಾಯಿ. = ಜಾಜ, q. v.

ಜಾಯು s. n. A medicament, medicine.

ಜಾರ s. n. A paramour; an adulterer. -ತ್ವ. Adultery. -ಪುರುಷ. = ಜಾರ. -ಸ್ತ್ರೀ, ಜಾರೆ. An adulteress, harlot.

ಜಾರಿ h. n. Relieving from a state of sequestration, as land. 2, currency. 3, enforcement, execution. -ಮಾಡು. To execute.

ಜಾರು (ರು=ಋ) k. v. i. To slip, slide. 2, to steal away; to withdraw, retire. 3, to go off; to run away. 4, to flow down. 5, to become loose, as a knot. n. Slipping; disappearance; a slide. -ವಿಕೆ. Sliding, etc.; flowing.

ಜಾಲ s. n. A net, snare; a web; a net-work. 2, a lattice, loophole. 3, deception, illusion; conjuring. 4, pride. 5, a pretext. 6, a multitude. 7, a cover, covering, film. 8, an unblown flower. 9, an organ of sense. 10, the sky. -ಗಾರ. (=ಜಲಗಾರ) A deceiver, conjurer; a fisherman; f. -ಗಾತಿ.

ಜಾಲಕ s. n. A woven texture; a web. 2, a loophole; cf. ಜಾಲಿಕೆ.

ಜಾಲರಿ h. n. Net-work, fringe.

ಜಾಲಾರಿ k. n. A tree yielding a kind of lac, *Shorea talura*.

ಜಾಲಿ 1. k. n. The thorny babool tree, *Acacia arabica*. 2, the thorny shrub, *Acacia farnesiana*.

ಜಾಲಿ 2. s. n. A species of cucumber, *Trichosanthes dioeca*. 2, a fisherman.

ಜಾಲಿಕ s. n. A fisherman. 2, a spider. 3, a conjurer, juggler. 4, = ಜಾಲಿಕೆ Nos. 1 & 2.

ಜಾಲಿಕೆ s. n. A net. 2, a chain-armour. 3, a leech. 4, woollen cloth; cf. ಜಾಲಕ. ಜಾಲಿಸು (=ಜಾಳಿಸು). To cleanse rice etc. by washing in water.

ಜಾವ (tb. of ಯಾಮ) n. A night-watch; the eighth part of a day; also ಜಾಮು.

ಜಾವಳ (tb. of ಸಾಮಾನ್ಯ) a. Common, vulgar; insignificant.

ಜಾವಿಗೆ f. n. The match of a matchlock.

ಜಾವು. = ಜಾವ, q. v.

ಜಾಸ್ತಿ h. n. Excess; oppression, force. a. More than, additional, extra.

ಜಾಹೀರಾತು h. n. Proclamation.

ಜಾಹೀರು h. a. Published; public. -ನಾಮೆ. A written proclamation.

ಜಾಹ್ನವಿ (fr. ಜಹ್ನು) s. n. The daughter of Jahnu: the Ganges.

ಜಾಳ. = ಜಾಲ, q. v. -ಅರಿವೆ. Cloth of a thin texture. -ಕ. = ಜಾಲಕ, q. v.

ಜಾಳಿಗೆ 1. (tb. of ಜಾಲಕ or ಜಾಲಿಕಾ) n. A net. 2, a lattice-window. 3, a purse. 4, an assemblage.

ಜಾಳಿಗೆ 2. (ಳ=ಱ) k. n. Cloth, raiment.

ಜಾಳು. = ಜರಡು, q. v. -ನುಡಿ, -ಮಾತು. An empty, vain speech.

ಜಿಗಟು (=ಜಿಬುಟು) k. n. Stickiness. 2, gum. 3, birdlime.

ಜಿಗಣೆ, ಜಿಗಣಿ, ಜಿಗಳೆ f. n. A leech.

ಜಿಗಿ 1. k. n. Thickness, viscidity. 2, a kind of blight or mildew falling on the cotton plant. 2, gum.

ಜಿಗಿ 2. k. v. i. To jump. 2, (=ಜಗಿ) to chew, as betelnut, bread, etc.

ಜಿಗುಪ್ಸೆ. tb. of ಜುಗುಪ್ಸೆ, q. v.

ಜಿಂಕೆ k. n. An antelope.

ಜಿಂಗಿ s. n. Intoxication. 2, the plant *Rubia munjista*, madder.

ಜಿಜ್ಞಾಸೆ s. n. Desire of knowing; inquiry, investigation.

ಜಿಟ್ಟೆ k. n. A grasshopper. 2, a sty.

ಜಿಡ್ಡಿ. = ಜಿಡ್ಡು, q. v.

ಜಿಡ್ಡು k. n. A greasy or oily substance. 2, rancidity.

ಜಿಣಗು, ಜಿಣುಗು. = ಜಿನಗು, q. v.

ಜಿತ 1. s. a. Subdued, overcome, won, -ಕಾಮ. One who has subdued desire, lust, etc., an ascetic; f. -ಕಾಮೆ. -ಶತ್ರು. One who has conquered his enemies. ಜಿತಾಕ್ಷ, ಜಿತೇಂದ್ರಿಯ. One who has conquered his passions.

ಜಿತ 2. (tb. of ಸ್ಥಿತ) a. Fixed, firm, stable. -ಪಡಿಸು. To make firm; to commit to memory. -ಪಡು. To become firm, to be mastered, as a lesson. -ಮಾಡು. = -ಪಡಿಸು. -ಬುದ್ಧಿ. A firm mind.

ಜಿದ್ದು h. n. Affront; contention. 2, spite, hatred.

ಜಿನ s. a. Victorious; steady; brave. n. A saint of the Bauddha sect; a

Jaina saint. -ಪ್ರಬುದ್ಧಿ. Jaina doctrine. -ಮುನಿ, -ಯತಿ. A Jaina saint, ascetic, monk.

ಜಿನಗು (= ಜಿಣಗು) k. n. Fineness, *as* of texture, thread, *etc.*

ಜಿನಸು (= ಜೀನಸು) h. n. An article; wares, goods.

ಜಿನಿಗಿಸು k. v. i. To become insensible; to faint. v. t. To liquefy, melt, *as* butter.

ಜಿನುಗು 1. = ಜಿನಗು, *q. v.*

ಜಿನುಗು 2. k. v. i. To drizzle. 2, to mutter, hum. 3, to melt, *as* butter, ghee, *etc.* n. Drizzling rain.

ಜಿಂದಗಿ, ಜಿಂದಿಗಿ h. n. Goods and chattels; one's estate, (movable) property.

ಜಿಪಣ, ಜಿಪುಣ (*tb. of* ಕೃಪಣ) n. A miserly, avaricious man; *f.* ಜಿಪುಣಿ.

ಜಿಬಟು. = ಜಿಗಟು, *q. v.*

ಜಿಬರು k. n. Rheum of the eye.

ಜಿಬಳ. = ಜಿಬ್ಬು. ಜಿಬಳಡಿಕೆ. Tender arecanut, cut into pieces, boiled and dried.

ಜಿಬ್ಬು k. n. Stickiness, sliminess.

ಜಿಮ್ಖಾನ f. & h. n. Gymkhana, an association for the competition in gymnastics and sports.

ಜಿಮ್ಮಿ k. n. A prickly tree, *Zanthoxylon rhetsa.*

ಜಿಮ್ಮೆ h. n. Charge, trust of a thing.

ಜಿರಾಯಿತು h. n. Land fit for agriculture. 2, cultivation.

ಜಿರಲೆ (ರ = ಱ) k. n. A centipede. 2, a cockroach. 3, a kind of earwig.

ಜಿಲಿಬಿಲಿ, ಜಿಲೇಬಿ h. n. A sort of sweetmeat.

ಜಿಲೇವು f. n. Glitter, gloss, shine.

ಜಿಲ್ಲಾ, ಜಿಲ್ಲೆ h. n. A district. -ದಾರ. The governor of a district.

ಜಿಲ್ಲು k. n. The sensation produced by touching cold water. ಜಿಲ್ಲೆನ್ನು. That sensation to be produced.

ಜಿಷ್ಣು s. a. Victorious, triumphant. n. An arhat. 2, Indra. 3, Vishṇu. 4, Śiva.

ಜಿಹ್ವೆ, ಜಿಹ್ವಾ s. n. The tongue. 2, the flame of fire. ಜಿಹ್ವಾಮೂಲ. The root of the tongue. ಜಿಹ್ವಾರವ. A word.

ಜೀಕಳಿ k. n. A squirt, syringe.

ಜೀಟು k. n. A prop, stay, *as* for a wall.

ಜೀತ (*tb. of* ಜೀವಿತ) n. Living; salary, wages; work. -ಗಾರ. A paid servant.

ಜೀನ 1. (*tb. of* ದೀನ) n. A niggardly, miserly man; *f.* ಜೀನಿ. a. Decayed, old. -ತನ. Niggardliness.

ಜೀನ 2. h. n. A saddle. -ಗಾರ. A saddler.

ಜೀನಸು. = ಜಿನಸು, *q. v.*

ಜೀನಿ, ಜೀನು. = ಜೀನ 2, *q. v.*

ಜೀಬಿ h. n. The area between the inner and outer walls.

ಜೀಯ f. n. Sir, master; a particle expressing assent.

ಜೀರಿಗೆ (*tb. of* ಜೀರಕ) n. The cumin seed. -ಮಾವು. A kind of fragrant mango. -ಸಣ್ಣಕ್ಕಿ, -ಸಾಲೆ. A superior kind of rice.

ಜೀರು (ರು = ಱು) k. n. Screaming; shrilling; *cf.* ಚೀರು. -ಜಂಜೆ. A kind of bee.

ಜೀರ್ಕೊಳವಿ (= ಜೀಕಳಿ) k. n. A syringe.

ಜೀರ್ಣ s. a. Grown old; worn out, consumed, digested. -ಕೋಶ. The stomach. -ವಸ್ತ್ರ. Old, tattered cloth. ಜೀರ್ಣಿಸು. To be digested. ಜೀರ್ಣೋದ್ಧಾರ. Repairing of what is worn out.

ಜೀವ s. a. Living. n. A living being, a creature. 2, existence, life. 3, (= ಜೀವಾತ್ಮ) the principle of life, the living soul. 4, (= -ನ) livelihood. 5, Bṛihaspati. 6, water. -ಕ. A servant; a usurer. -ಕಳೆ. The glow of life, life. -ಕೊಡು. To give up one's life. -ಗಳ್ಳ. A coward. -ತೆಗೆ. To kill. -ದ ಗೆಳೆಯ. A very dear friend. -ದ ಭಯ. Fear to lose one's life. -ದ ಮೇಲಿನ ಆಶೆ, -ದಾಶೆ. Love of one's life. -ದ ಹಂಗು. Obligation with regard to one's life. -ದಾನ. The gift of life. -ದಿಂದ ಇರು. To be alive. -ದಿಂದ ಉಳಿ. To remain alive. -ಧನ. Live stock, cattle. -ಮಾನ. Life-time, life. -ರಾಶಿ. The animal kingdom. -ಹಿಂಸೆ. Destroying life. -ಸ್ಥಾನ. A vital organ. ಜೀವಾಕ್ಷರ. A vowel.

ಜೀವತ್, ಜೀವಂತ s. a. Living, alive.

ಜೀವನ s. n. Life, existence; means of subsistence, livelihood. 2, water. -ವಾಹ. A cloud. ಜೀವನಾಂಶ, ಜೀವನಾರ್ಥ. Maintenance, livelihood. ಜೀವನೋಪಾಯ. Means of livelihood.

ಜೀವನ್ಮುಕ್ತಿ s. n. Liberation from further births and from ritual acts. ಜೀವನ್ಮುಕ್ತ. A man purified by knowledge of Brahma.

ಜೀವಾತ್ಮ. = ಜೀವ No. 3, q. v.

ಜೀವಾಳ (tb. of ಜೀವಲ) n. A vital member or organ. 2, a chip put in the mouthpiece of a musical pipe or drone. 3, substance, pith, essence.

ಜೀವಿ s. n. A living being. a. Living, alive. -ತ. Living; life, existence; wages. -ತ ಕಾಲ. Lifetime. -ಸು. To live, exist; to live by.

ಜುಕಾಯಿಸು h. v. i. To stoop, bend; to reel, stagger.

ಜುಗಾರು f. n. Gambling.

ಜುಗುಪ್ಸೆ s. n. Censure, reproach. 2, aversion, disgust.

ಜುಂಜು k. n. The comb of a cock.

ಜುಟ್ಟು k. n. The tuft of hair left on the crown of the head at tonsure; a crest, as of a cock. -ಬಿಡಿಸು. To produce a juṭṭu at tonsure.

ಜುಟ್ಲೆ k. n. A kind of pigeon.

ಜುಡುಪು h. n. A bush; a thicket.

ಜುಣುಗು k. v. i. To shrink, contract; to withdraw. n. Shrinkage.

ಜುಮಕಿ h. n. The pendant of an earring.

ಜುಮಲಾ. = ಜುಮ್ಲಾ, q. v.

ಜುಮ್ಮನೆ k. ad. Quickly. 2, with horripilation.

ಜುಮ್ಮಾಮಸೀದಿ h. n. A mosque that is visited on Fridays.

ಜುಮ್ಲಾ h. n. Amount, sum, total.

ಜುರಮಾನ, ಜುಲಮಾನ (= ಜುಲುಮಾನು, ಜುಲ್ಮಾನೆ) h. n. A fine, penalty, punishment.

ಜುಲಮೆ. = ಜುಲುಮೆ, q. v.

ಜುಲಾಬು h. n. A purgative; a purge. 2, diarrhoea.

ಜುಲಾಯಿ f. n. A weaver. 2, (e) July (7th month of the year).

ಜುಲಿಪೆ h. n. Small locks of hair kept on children's head as ornament.

ಜುಲುಮಾನು. = ಜುಲಮಾನ, q. v.

ಜುಲುಮೆ (= ಜುಲಮೆ, ಜುಲ್ಮಿ) h. n. Oppression, tyranny, injustice, compulsion.

ಜುಲ್ಮಾನೆ. = ಜುಲಮಾನ, q. v.

ಜುವ್ವಿಮರ k. n. The wavy-leafed fig-tree, *Ficus infectoria*.

ಜೂಗಳಿಸು (= ತೂಕಡಿಸು) k. v. i. To nod, doze; to move on or proceed slowly, as vehicles or work.

ಜೂಗು. = ತೂಗು, q. v. ಜೂಗಾಡು (= ತೂಗಾಡು). To waddle.

ಜೂಜು. (tb. of ದ್ಯೂತ) n. Gambling, game. ಜೂಜಾಡು. To gamble, game. -ಕಟ್ಟು. To wager. -ಗಾರ. A gambler.

ಜೂಟ 1. (tb. of ಜುಟಿತ) n. The matted or clotted hair of an ascetic. 2, bodily strength of children.

ಜೂಟ 2. h. n. A lie.

ಜೂಡಿ f. n. A favourable quit-rent on inâm lands.

ಜೂತಿ h. n. A shoe. 2, (f.) impulse, energy.

ಜೂನು e. n. June (6th month of the year).

ಜೂಪರ k. n. Thin, drizzling rain.

ಜೂಲು 1. k. n. A tatter. -ನಾಯಿ. A dog with long hair.

ಜೂಲು 2. h. n. A body-cloth of horses, etc.

ಜೂಳಿ k. n. The spout of a vessel.

ಜೆ s. a. Born (f.). n. A daughter, as ಆತ್ಮ-, etc.

ಜೆಗು. = ಜಗ್ಗು, q. v.

ಜೆಂಗಿ h. a. Relating to war. n. Petulance; dunning; besieging. -ಸರಂಜಾಮು. Arms and ammunition.

ಜಿಟ್ಟಿ. = ಜಟ್ಟಿ, q. v.

ಜಿಡೆ. = ಜಡೆ, q. v.

ಜಿನುಯೆರಿ e. n. January (1st month of the year).

ಜೀಗಟೆ. = ಜಾಗಟೆ, q. v.

ಜೀಡ. = ಜಾಡ, q. v.

ಜೇಡಿ k. n. A sort of pipe-clay, chalk.

ಜೇನು k. n. Honey; also -ತುಪ್ಪ. -ನೊಣ, -ಹುಳ. A honey-bee. -ಹುಟ್ಟು, -ಗೂಡು. A honey-comb. -ಮೇಣ. Wax.

ಜೇಬು h. n. A pocket.

ಜೇರು 1. h. a. Feeble; exhausted. n. Weakness, indisposition.

ಜೇರು 2. k. n. A wall. -ಗಂಡಿ, -ಗಿಂಡಿ. An embrasure for guns; a loophole. -ಮುತ್ತಿಗೆ. A close siege.

ಜೇವಣಿಗೆ k. n. Sweetness, pleasantness.

ಜೇಷ್ಠಮಧು s. n. Liquorice.

ಜೈನ (fr. ಜಿನ) s. n. A Jaina.

ಜೈಮಿನಿ s. n. N. of a ṛishi and philosopher. -ಭಾರತ. A Kannaḍa metrical translation of a Saṁskṛita poem.

ಜೊಟ್ಟು. = ಜರಡು, q. v.

ಜೊಂಡಿಗ k. n. A cockroach.

ಜೊಂಡು k. n. The scurf of the head, dandruff. 2, a filthy mass of scum floating on water. 3, the elephant-grass.

ಜೊತೆ (= ಜತೆ. tb. of ಯುತ) n. Union, company, pair. -ಗೊಳಿಸು. To join. -ಗಾರ. = ಜತೆಗಾರ, q. v.

ಜೊತ್ತು. = ಜತ್ತು, q. v.

ಜೊನ್ನವಕ್ಕಿ (tb. of ಜ್ಯೋತ್ಸ್ನಪಕ್ಷಿ) n. The Greek partridge.

ಜೊಂಪ a. k. n. A cluster, bunch.

ಜೊಂಪಿಸು a. k. v. t. To cause to tremble. v. i. To tremble; to be aroused. 2, to get intoxicated, stupefied.

ಜೊಂಪು a. k. n. Inebriation, stupor, paralisation.

ಜೊಲ್ಲು k. n. Saliva, slaver.

ಜೊಳ್ಳು (= ಜಳ್ಳು, q. v.) k. n. Emptiness.

ಜೋ k. int. Hush! ಜೋ ಜೋ. Hush, hush! used in lulling infants; cf. -ಗಳ.

ಜೋಕಾಲೆ. = ಜವ್ವಾಲೆ, q. v.

ಜೋಕು m. n. An affected manner of speaking, walking, dressing, etc.; a scheme, trick. -ಗಾರ. A man of affected manners; f. -ಗಾತಿ.

ಜೋಕೆ k. n. Attention, caution, care. 2, beauty, harmony. -ಮಾಡು. To take care, protect. -ಯಾಗಿರು. To be attentive, cautious; to be safe, well protected.

ಜೋಗ. tb. of ಯೋಗ, q. v. -ತಿ. A female beggar dedicated to Ellamma.

ಜೋಗಳ (= ಜೋಗುಳ) k. n. A lullaby.

ಜೋಗಿ. tb. of ಯೋಗಿ, q. v.

ಜೋಗು k. n. A waterfall. 2, benumbed sensation of a limb.

ಜೋಗುಳ. = ಜೋಗಳ, q. v.

ಜೋಡಣೆ f. n. Joining, junction; preparation; readiness.

ಜೋಡಿ f. n. A pair or couple. 2, a sheet of paper.

ಜೋಡಿಸು f. v. t. To join, unite; to put to; to collect.

ಜೋಡು f. n. Junction, union; company; a pair or couple; a match. 2, a pair of shoes. 3, a suit of armour. 4, close connection. ಜೋಡಕ್ಷರ. A double letter, diphthong.

ಜೋತಿ. tb. of ಜ್ಯೋತಿ, q. v.

ಜೋತಿಷ. = ಜ್ಯೋತಿಷ, q. v.

ಜೋತು. = ಜೋಲ್ದು. P. p. of ಜೋಲು, q. v.

ಜೋದ (tb. of ಯೋಧ್ಯ) n. An elephant-driver.

ಜೋನಿ k. n. Fluidity, as of jaggory; also -ಬೆಲ್ಲ. -ಗ. One of a Śûdra caste.

ಜೋಪಡಿ f. n. A hut; a cottage.

ಜೋಪಾನ f. n. Taking care of, looking after; fostering. -ಮಾಡು. To take care of.

ಜೋಬು, -ದ್ರ k. n. A dull, lazy man.

ಜೋಮಾಲೆ k. n. A gold necklace.

ಜೋಯಿಸ. *tb. of* ಜ್ಯೋತಿಷ, *q. v.*

ಜೋರಾವರಿ (= ಜೋರು 2, *q. v.*) h. *n.* Violence, force.

ಜೋರು 1. (= ಸೋರು) k. *v. i.* To trickle, drip, leak. *n.* Trickling; a flow. -ಗಟ್ಟು. To tie up in a cloth for straining, *as* curds. -ಹಾಕು. To strain, *as* soaked grain.

ಜೋರು 2. h. *n.* Strength; force; violence; stress; oppression, compulsion. -ವರಾತ. Dunning hard for payment.

ಜೋಲಿ 1. f. *n.* Concern; business, affair. 2, connexion, intercourse.

ಜೋಲಿ 2. f. *n.* Hanging, dangling; oscillation; evasion, delay. -ಮಾಡು. To delay. -ಗಾರ. A loiterer.

ಜೋಲು k. *v. i.* To hang down from; to move to and fro; to swing, oscillate, dangle; to droop; (*also* ಜೋಲಾಡು. *P. ps.* ಜೋಲ್ದು, ಜೋತು). *n.* Hanging down, slackness, looseness. -ಕಿವಿ. A long, flapping ear. -ಬಾವಲಿ. A kind of ear-ornament. -ಬೀಳು. To hang down, *etc.* -ಮುಖ. A downcast countenance. ಜೋಲ್ದುರುಬು. A loose tuft of hair.

ಜೋಳ (*tb. of* ಯವನಾಲ) *n.* One of the several species of millet. 2, (*tb. of* ಯುಗಲ) union; pair. -ವಾಳಿ. An associate; a partner.

ಜೋಳಿಗೆ (*tb. of* ಝೌಲಿಕ) *n.* A small bag for receiving alms; a wallet.

ಜ್ಞ s. *a.* Knowing; intelligent. -ತೆ, -ತ್ವ. Knowledge of.

ಜ್ಞಪ್ತಿ s. *n.* Knowing, understanding, apprehension.

ಜ್ಞಾತ s. *a.* Known, understood. -ಸಿದ್ಧಾಂತ. Versed in any science or śâstra.

ಜ್ಞಾತಿ s. *n.* A paternal relation; kinsman.

ಜ್ಞಾನ s. *n.* Knowledge; cognizance; intelligence; religious knowledge. -ಚಕ್ಷು, -ದೃಷ್ಟಿ. The eye of intelligence, intellectual vision. -ಮಂಟಪ. A prison (*ironically*). -ಮಾರ್ಗ. The path of wisdom. -ವಂತ. A wise man; *f.* -ವಂತೆ. -ವೃದ್ಧ. Advanced in knowledge.

ಜ್ಞಾನಿ s. *n.* A wise person, sage. 2, an astronomer or astrologer. -ತೆ. Knowledge, perception. -ಸು. To consider, reflect. ಜ್ಞಾನೇಂದ್ರಿಯ. An organ of perception; the skin, tongue, eye, ear, and nose.

ಜ್ಞಾಪಕ s. *n.* Bearing in mind, remembrance, recollection. ಜ್ಞಾಪಿಸು. To indicate, notify.

ಜ್ಞೇಯ s. *a.* Cognizable, perceptible.

ಜ್ಯೇಷ್ಠ s. *a.* Most excellent; oldest; elder-born. *n.* An elder brother. 2, the third lunar-month.

ಜ್ಯೇಷ್ಠೆ s. *n.* An elder sister. 2, the eighteenth lunar mansion.

ಜ್ಯೋತಿ (= ಜೋತಿ, ಜ್ಯೋತಿಸ್) s. *n.* Light; brightness, clearness. 2, fire. 3, a ray of light. 4, a star. 5, the eye. -ಶ್ಶಾಸ್ತ್ರ. The science of astronomy (or astrology).

ಜ್ಯೋತಿಷ (= ಜೋಯಿಸ, *q. v.*) s. *n.* Astronomy; astrology. 2, an astronomer, astrologer; *also* ಜ್ಯೋತಿಷಿಕ, ಜ್ಯೋತಿಷ್ಕ.

ಜ್ಯೋತಿಸ್. = ಜ್ಯೋತಿ, *q. v.*

ಜ್ಯೋತ್ಸ್ನಾ s. *n.* A moonlight night; *also* ಜ್ಯೋತ್ಸ್ನೆ. 2, a species of cucumber.

ಜ್ವರ s. *a.* Heated, inflamed. *n.* Fever. 2, mental pain, grief.

ಜ್ವಲ s. *n.* Flame, blaze. -ತ್. Burning, blazing. -ತ್ಪರ್ವತ. A volcano. -ನ. Shining, burning. ಜ್ವಲಿತ. Kindled, blazing. ಜ್ವಲಿಸು. To burn, flame.

ಜ್ವಾಲೆ, ಜ್ವಾಲಾ s. *n.* A blaze, flame. 2, fire. ಜ್ವಾಲಾಮುಖಿ. A volcano.

ಝ್

ಝ್. The twenty-seventh letter of the alphabet. *It occurs only in a limited number of Kannaḍa and Tadbhava words.*

ಝಕಾರ s. *n.* The letter ಝ.

ಝಗೆ f. *n.* A robe extending to the feet.

ಝಂಕಾರ (= ಝೇಂಕಾರ) s. *n.* Buzzing or humming, *as* of bees, *etc.*

ಝಂಝಾವಾತ s. *n.* A violent storm with rain.

ಝಣಝಣ s. *n.* The jingling or tinkling of ornaments; *also* -ತ್ಕಾರ, -ತ್ಕೃತಿ.

ಝಲ್ಲರಿ s. *n.* A sort of drum or cymbal. 2, a curl, lock of hair. 3, tassels, fringes; *cf.* ಜಾಲರಿ.

ಝಲ್ಲಿ k. *n.* Tassels, fringes, hangings.

ಝಷ s. *n.* A fish.

ಝಳಪಿಸು s. *v. t.* To make glitter or shine. 2, to brandish, *as* a sword.

ಝಾಯಿ s. *n.* A sort of drum; *also* ಜಾಯಿ.

ಝಿಂಟಿ s. *n.* The shrub *Barleria cristata.*

ಝಿಲ್ಲಿಕೆ, ಝಿಲ್ಲೀಕೆ, ಝೀರುಕೆ s. *n.* A cricket.

ಝೇಂಕಾರ. = ಝಂಕಾರ, *q. v.* ಝೇಂಕರಿಸು. To hum, buzz.

ಞ್

ಞ್. The twenty-eighth letter of the alphabet.

ಟ್

ಟ್. The twenty-ninth letter of the alphabet.

ಟಕಾಯಿಸು f. *v. t.* To put in mind, remind. 2, to deceive, cheat. *v. i.* To be exhausted.

ಟಕಾರ s. *n.* The letter ಟ.

ಟಕ್ಕ (= ಠಕ್ಕ) h. *n.* A cunning fellow, rogue.

ಟಕ್ಕಿಸು. = ಟಕಾಯಿಸು, *q. v.*

ಟಕ್ಕು (= ಠಕ್ಕು) f. *n.* Cunning, trickery, hypocrisy. -ತನ. Cunning, deceitful behaviour. -ಟವಳಿ. *dpl.*

ಟಗರು k. *n.* A ram.

ಟಂಕ s. *n.* A stone-mason's hammer. 2, pride, conceit. 3, a stamped coin. -ಶಾಲೆ. A mint.

ಟಂಕಣ s. *n.* Borax; *also* -ಕಾರ.

ಟಂಕಾರ, ಟಂಕೃತಿ s. *n.* Howling; a sound, clang; the twang of a bow-string.

ಟಂಕೆ k. *n.* A staff. 2, (s.) the leg.

ಟಂಗು h. *n.* A saddle girth. -ಹರಿ. To be reduced to poverty.

ಟಣಕಲಿ k. *n.* An aquatic plant, *Aeshynomene aspera.*

ಟಣಕ್ಕನೆ k. *ad.* With a bounce in leaping.

ಟಣಾಯಿಸು h. *v. t.* To stop, detain.

ಟಪಾಲು. = ಟಪ್ಪಾಲು, *q. v.*

ಟಪ್ಪಾ h. *n.* = ಟಪ್ಪೆ, *q. v.* 2, a variety in song.

ಟಪ್ಪಾಲು h. *n.* The post, mail. ಟಪ್ಪಾಲಿಗೆ ಹಾಕು. To post. ಟಪ್ಪಾಲಿನವ. The postman. -ಕಚ್ಚೇ. A post-office. ಟಪ್ಪಾಲ್ಗಾಡಿ. A post-coach.

ಟಪ್ಪೆ h. *n.* A stage; a halting place. -ಕುದುರೆ. A relay-horse.

ಟರಾಯಿಸು h. *v. t.* To settle, fix, decide.

ಟರಾವಣೆ, ಟರಾವು h. *n.* Settlement, decision.

ಟಲಾಯಿಸು f. *v. t.* To lead, *as* a horse. *v. i.* To walk about.

ಟಲಾಸು. = ತಲಾಸು, *q. v.*

ಟವಣೆ k. *n.* Simple and compound addition.

ಟವಳಿ m. *n.* Guile, trick, deceit. -ಗಾರ. A deceiver.

ಟವುಳಿ (= ಟೌಳಿ) k. *n.* Armour, mail.

ಟಾಕಣ h. *n.* A pony.

ಟಾಕಾ f. *n.* A stitch; *also* ಟಾಕು.

ಟಾಕು 1. f. *n.* The nib of a pen; a steel-pen. -ಹೊಡೆ. To nib a pen.

ಟಾಕು 2. k. *n.* A support; a vault. -ಗೂಡು. Arches with niches on the walls surrounding big temples.

ಟಾಕುಟೀಕು f. *ad.* Orderly, neatly. *n.* Neatness, order.

ಟಾಕೋಟಾಕು f. *ad.* Speedily.

ಟಾಣ, ಟಾಣಯು. = ಠಾಣಾ, *q. v.*

ಟಾವು (= ಠಾವು) f. *n.* A place; room; an abode. ಟಾವಿಕೆ. Knowledge, acquaintance with.

ಟಿಕಾಣೆ f. *n.* A place; spot; an abode; seat; destination. 2, means, opportunity.

ಟಿಟ್ಟಿಭ s. *n.* The bird *Parra jacana,* the lapwing.

ಟಿಪಾಯಿಸು h. *v. t.* To shuffle, *as* cards.

ಟಿಪ್ಪಣ, ಟಿಪ್ಪಣಿ f. *n.* A gloss, comment, commentary. 2, a note, memorandum. -ಗಾರ. A commentator.

ಟಿಸಲು k. *n.* A forked or lateral branch.

ಟೀಕು 1. s. *n.* A commentary; a gloss; *also* ಟೀಕಾ, ಟೀಕೆ. ಟೀಕಾಕಾರ. A commentator. ಟೀಕಿಸು. To explain, interpret.

ಟೀಕು 2. (= ಠೀಕು) h. *n.* Right, just, proper.

ಟೀಕೆ f. *n.* A necklace of gold wire. 2 a gem. 3, = ಟೀಕು 1.

ಟುಮುಕಿ f. *n.* A tom-tom.

ಟೆಕ್ಕೆ 1. k. *n.* A banner or standard.

ಟೆಕ್ಕೆ 2. (= ತೆಕ್ಕೆ) k. *n.* An embrace. 2, wood, *etc.* grasped in arms.

ಟೆಂಕ. = ಟಂಕ, *q. v.*

ಟೆಂಕಲು. = ತೆಂಕಲು, *q. v.*

ಟೆಪಾರಿಕೆ f. *n.* A lid. 2, striking off excess of grain in a measure.

ಟೊಂಕ k. *n.* The hip and loins; the waist.

ಟೊಂಗೆ (= ಕೊಂಗೆ) k. *n.* The branch of a tree.

ಟೊಣಪ f. *n.* A fat dolt, blockhead.

ಟೊಣಪೆ f. *n.* A cudgel, mace. 2, stoutness.

ಟೊಣೆ a. k. *v. t.* To cheat, deceive.

ಟೊಣ್ಣೆ f. *n.* A stout dull woman.

ಟೊಪ್ಪರ, ಟೊಪ್ಪಿ, ಟೊಪ್ಪಿಗೆ (= ತೋಪಿ, *q. v.*) f. *n.* A cap; a hat.

ಟೊಳ್ಳು (= ತೊಳ್ಳು) k. *n.* Hollowness, emptiness. -ಮಾತು. A vain speech. -ಮಾಡು, -ಕೊರೆ. To scoop out.

ಟೊಳ್ಳೆ k. *n.* A hollow, cavity; a fistula. 2, a perished eye-socket.

ಟೋಕು h. *a.* Whole or round, *as* a number; wholesale; *also* ತೋಕು.

ಟೋಪಿ. = ಟೊಪ್ಪಿ, *q. v.*

ಟೌಳಿ. = ಟವುಳಿ, *q. v.*

ಠ

ಠ. The thirtieth letter of the alphabet.

ಠಕಾರ s. n. The letter ಠ.

ಠಕ್ಕ. = ಟಕ್ಕ, q. v.

ಠಕ್ಕು. = ಟಕ್ಕು, q. v.

ಠಪ್ಪೆ h. n. A stamp.

ಠಾಕೂರ s. n. An object of reverence; an honorific title.

ಠಾಣ್ಯ, ಠಾಣೆ (*tb. of* ಸ್ಥಾನ) n. The head station of a district; an encampment; a police station; a garrison. -ಗೆ ಹಾಕು. To capture. -ದಾರ. The officer in charge of a ṭhâṇâ.

ಠಾವಿ. = ಠಾವಿಕೆ, s. ಠಾವು, q. v.

ಠಾವು. = ಠಾವು, q. v.

ಠಿಕಾಣಿ. = ಟಿಕಾಣಿ, q. v.

ಠೀಕು. = ಟೀಕು 2, q. v.

ಠೀವಿ f. n. Style, fashion; grandeur; ornament. 2, an air, manner.

ಠೇವಣಿ, ಠೇವು f. n. A stock (of money). 2, a deposit (*as* security).

ಡ

ಡ. The thirty-first letter of the alphabet.

ಡಕಾರ s. n. The letter ಡ.

ಡಕಾಯಿತಿ. = ಡಾಕಾಯಿತಿ, q. v.

ಡಕ್ಕೆ (*tb. of* ಢಕ್ಕೆ 2). = ಡಂಕ, q. v.

ಡಗೆ (= ದಗೆ) f. n. Deceit. 2, heat, sultriness.

ಡಂಕ (= ಡಕ್ಕೆ) s. n. A pretty large double drum.

ಡಂಗರ, ಡಂಗುರ f. n. A public proclamation by beat of tom-tom. -ಬಡಿ, -ಹೊಡೆ, -ಹೊಯ್. To proclaim by beat of tom-tom.

ಡಂಗುರುಚಾಟ k. n. A kind of 'hide and seek' play.

ಡಂಗೆ (= ದಂಗೆ) h. n. Tumult, uproar; dunning. -ಕೊಡುತುಕೊಳ್ಳು, -ಮಾಡು. To dun. -ಗಾರ. An uproarious man.

ಡಬಡ್ಡಾಳಿಕೆ h. n. Showiness, an empty display of greatness or authority; an imposing air.

ಡಬರಿ f. n. A cylindrical saucepan.

ಡಬಾಗೀ f. n. A pair of kettle-drums.

ಡಬೀರಿ h. n. A moonshee, writer.

ಡಬ್ಬ 1. = ಡಬ್ಬಿ, q. v.

ಡಬ್ಬ 2, ಡಬ್ಬನೆ k. *ad.* Suddenly, *used of vessels, etc. falling from above.*

ಡಬ್ಬಿ h. n. A small box, *as* a snuff-box, pill-box, offering-box, *etc.*

ಡಬ್ಬು 1. (= ದೊಬ್ಬು) k. v. t. To shove, push, thrust. 2, = ಡಬ್ಬ 2. ಡಬ್ಬುಗವಚು, ಡಬ್ಬುಹಾಕು. To put upside down.

ಡಬ್ಬು 2. f. n. A kind of drum.

ಡಬ್ಬು 3. f. n. Showiness, ostentation; bragging; falsehood, lie. 2, a dub or copper coin, four pies. -ಗಾರ. A showy man.

ಡಬ್ಬೆ h. n. A large tin box.

ಡಮರ s. n. A riot, tumult, turmoil; distress.

ಡಮರುಕ s. n. A kind of drum.

ಡಮಾಗೀ, ಡಮಾರ f. n. A pair of kettle-drums.

ಡೆಂಬ, ಡಂಭ (= ಡಂಬ. *tb. of* ದಂಭ) n. Pomp, ostentation, show. ಡಂಬಾಚಾರ. Vain display. -ಕ. Arrogance, pride; an ostentatious man; a deceiver. -ಗಾರ. A showy man.

ಡಯನ s. n. Flying in the air.

ಡರಕೆ, ಡರಕು (ರ=ಱ) k. n. A belch.

ಡಲಾಯಿತ h. *n.* A peon of a district office.

ಡವಕೆ a. k. *n.* A spittoon.

ಡವಣೆ f. *n.* A kind of drum shaped like an hour-glass.

ಡವಾಲಿ h. *n.* A peon's belt.

ಡವಿಗೆ k. *n.* A thick bamboo. 2, a skeleton's skull; *also* ಡವುಗೆ.

ಡವುಡು (= ದವುಡು) h. *n.* A race or run.

ಡವುಲು (= ಡೌಲು) h. *n.* Shape, form; way, manner; indications, appearance. 2, estimated revenue; probable produce. 3, a pompous air; empty display. -ಕೊಟ್ಟು. To brag, boast. -ಜಾಸ್ತಿ. Too high an estimate. -ದಾರ. An ostentatious man. -ಮಾಡು. To make a show.

ಡಾಕಾಯಿತಿ (= ಡಕಾಯಿತಿ) h. *n.* Dacoity, gang-robbery.

ಡಾಕಿಣೆ k. *n.* The sword of a female demon.

ಡಾಕಿನಿ k. *n.* A kind of female demon attending Kâli. 2, = ಡಾಕಿಣಿ, *q. v.*.

ಡಾಕು, ಡಾಗು h. *n.* A spot, stain; inoculated cow-pox. 2, an attack. 3, dawk, post-office.

ಡಾಗಿಲಿ a. k. *n.* An anvil.

ಡಾಗಿನೆ. = ದಾಗಿನೆ, *q. v.*

ಡಾಣ (= ದಾಣ. *tb. of* ಧಾನ್ಯ) *n.* Horse-gram.

ಡಾಣೆ, ಡಾಣೆ a. k. *n.* A staff, club.

ಡಾಬು 1. (*tb. of* ದಾಮ) *n.* A woman's girdle.

ಡಾಬು 2. k. *n.* Intimidation, menacing; awfulness; *also* -ಜರಬು.

ಡಾಮರ. = ಡಮರ, *q. v.* 2, dammer.

ಡಾಂಬಿಕ (*tb. of* ದಾಂಭಿಕ) *a.* Deceitful; proud.

ಡಾಲು (*tb. of* ಢಾಲ) *n.* A shield, buckler.

ಡಾವಣೆ (*tb. of* ದಾಮನಿ) *n.* A long rope for tying cattle in a row. -ಕಟ್ಟು. To tie cattle in a row.

ಡಾವರಿಸು a. k. *v. i.* To whirl about; to flicker, *as* flames; to rave.

ಡಾವು h. *n.* Spite, malice, hatred; revenge. 2, (= ಡಾವುರ) desire. -ತೀರಿಸು. To revenge one's self.

ಡಾವುರ (= ದಾವರ) f. *n.* Burning thirst; desire; need, want.

ಡಾವೆ. = ಡಾವು, *q. v.*

ಡಾಳ, ಡಾಳ f. *n.* Lustre; beauty; gracefulness. -ಯಿಸು, ಡಾಳಿಸು. To shine; to be beautiful.

ಡಾಳಿಮ, ಡಾಳಿಂಬ, ಡಾಳಿಂಬೆ. = ದಾಡಿಮ, *q. v.*

ಡಿಕ್ಕಾ, ಡಿಕ್ಕಿ k. *n.* A push, butt. ಡಿಕ್ಕಾಡಿಕ್ಕಿ, ಡಿಕ್ಕಾಮುಕ್ಕಿ. *dpl.* -ಕೊಡು, -ಹೊಡೆ. To butt.

ಡಿಂಗರ s. *n.* A servant, slave; *also* ಡಿಂಗರಿಗ. 2, a rogue. 3, a fat man.

ಡಿಂಡಿಮ s. *n.* A kind of small drum.

ಡಿಂಬ s. *n.* A scuffle, turmoil. 2, calamity arising from excessive rain, drought, locusts, *etc.* 3, a globe; an egg. 4, a child.

ಡಿಂಬು k. *n.* A lamp-stand.

ಡಿಂಭ s. *n.* A new-born child, young animal. 2, a fool.

ಡಿಳ್ಳ a. k. *n.* Tottering state, agitation of mind; fear.

ಡಿಲ್ಲಿ, ಡಿಳ್ಳಿ s. *n.* The town of Delhi.

ಡಿಲ, ಡಿಲಿ h. *a.* Loose, slack. *n.* Delay. -ಬಿಡು. To slacken; to delay.

ಡುಬರಿ (= ಡುಬ್ಬ, ಡುಬ್ಬು) k. *n.* The hump on a camel's back. 2, curvedness, roundness.

ಡುಬಾಯಿಸು f. *v. t.* To immerse; to ruin.

ಡುಬ್ಬ, ಡುಬ್ಬು. = ಡುಬರಿ, *q. v.*

ಡುರಕಿ (ರ = ಱ) k. *n.* The bellowing of bulls and oxen. -ಹಾಕು. To bellow.

ಡೆಂಕಣ, ಡೆಂಕಣೆ a. k. *n.* The flag-staff on a bastion.

ಡೆಂಕೆ. = ಡಂಕ, *q. v.*

ಡೆಂಡಣಿಸು f. *v. i.* To be overcome or stupefied, *as* by grief, terror, *etc.*

ಡೆಬ್ಬೆ (= ಡಬ್ಬೆ) k. *n.* A blow.

ಡೇಗೆ k. *n.* A hawk, falcon.

ಡೇರಾ, ಡೇರೆ h. *n.* A tent.

ಡೊಕ್ಕರ 1. a. k. *n.* Thumping, striking; a blow.

ಡೊಕ್ಕರ 2. = ಡೊಗರು, *q. v.*

ಡೊಕ್ಕರಿಸು k. *v. t.* To choke, stifle.

ಡೊಕ್ಕೆ k. *n.* The body. -ಯೆಲುಬು. A rib.

ಡೊಗರು (ರು=ಱು) k. *n.* A hollow, hole, *as* in a wall, *etc.*

ಡೊಗೆ k. *v. t.* To make a hole.

ಡೊಗ್ಗೆ k. *n.* Thickness, *as* of butter-milk.

ಡೊಂಕ, ಡೊಂಕು k. *n.* Crookedness; a bend, curve. -ಕಾಲು. A bent leg. -ಗೋಣು. A bent neck. -ತನ. = ಡೊಂಕ.

ಡೊಂಗರ f. *n.* A steep rock; a precipice.

ಡೊಣೆ k. *n.* A small pond in rocks. 2, a hollow, hole. 3, a quiver. -ಗಣ್ಣು. A sunken eye.

ಡೊಣ್ಣೆ k. *n.* A cudgel, club. 2, a chameleon. -ಕಾಟಿ. N. of several kinds of Agames. -ಮೂಗು. A huge nose. -ಮೆಣಸಿನ ಕಾಯಿ. A large kind of chilli. -ಹುಳ. An insect living in cowdung.

ಡೊಬ್ಬ. = ದೊಬ್ಬು, *q. v.*

ಡೊಂಬ, ಡೊಂಬರ f. *n.* A caste of tumblers; *f.* -ಗಿತ್ತಿ.

ಡೊಂಬಿ k. *n.* A mass, multitude, crowd; mob.

ಡೊಳ್ಳಾಸ a. k. *n.* Trick, fraud; a fantastic form.

ಡೊಳ್ಳು (= ಡೊಳ್ಳು) k. *n.* Hollowness; a huge belly; *also* -ಹೊಟ್ಟೆ. *a.* Hollow, huge. -ಗಾರ. A boaster. -ಮಾತು. An empty speech.

ಡೋಕಾ h. *n.* Danger, peril; injury; loss in trade. -ರಿ. One who cries out when he is not hurt.

ಡೋಣಿ (= ದೋಣಿ. *tb. of* ದ್ರೋಣಿ) *n.* A tub, trough, *etc.*; a boat.

ಡೋರ h. *n.* A man who colours leather.

ಡೋರಿಯ h. *n.* A sort of striped cloth.

ಡೋಲಿ h. *n.* A dooly or litter. -ತೊಟ್ಟಿಲು. A swinging cradle.

ಡೋಲು (*tb. of* ಢೋಲ) *n.* A large drum.

ಡಾಲು. = ಡವಲು, *q. v.*

ಢ್

ಢ್. The thirty-second letter of the alphabet.

ಢಕಾರ s. *n.* The letter ಢ.

ಢಕ್ಕಾಮುಕ್ಕಿ h. *n.* Shoving and cuffing; *also* ಢಕ್ಕಾಮುಕ್ಕ.

ಢಕ್ಕೆ 1. h. *n.* A sudden push; a shock; damage, harm. -ಪಡು, -ಬೀಳು. To receive a shock.

ಢಕ್ಕೆ 2. s. *n.* A double drum.

ಢಾಲ. = ಡಾಲು, *q. v.*

ಢಾಳು f. *n.* Cast, mould; way, style. ಢಾಳ. A clever fellow.

ಢೆಂಕಣ. = ಡೆಂಕಣ, *q. v.*

ಢೋಲ. = ಡೋಲು, *q. v.*

ಣ್

ಣ್. The thirty-third letter of the alphabet. *It stands as final in many Kannaḍa and some Tadbhava words, as:* ಉಣ್, ಕಣ್, ಕಾಣ್, ಗೇಣ್, ಜೇಣ್, *etc.*

ಣಕಾರ s. *n.* The letter ಣ.

ತ್

ತ್. The thirty-fourth letter of the alphabet.

ತಂಸೂಕು h. n. A note of hand, bond.

ತಕ್ (= ತೆಗೆದು). *P. p. of* ತೆಗೆ, *in* ತಕ್ಕೊಳ್ಳು, ತಕ್ಕೋ (= ತೆಗೆದುಕೊಳ್ಳು), *etc.*

ತಕತೆ. = ತಕ್ತೆ, *q. v.*

ತಕರಾರು, ತಕರೀರು h. n. Starting objections; making difficulties, contesting. -ಅರ್ಜಿ. An appeal; a counter-petition.

ತಕಶೀರು (= ತಕ್ಸೀರು) h. n. An offence, fault. -ಗಾರ. An offender.

ತಕಾರ s. n. The letter ತ.

ತಕಾವಿ h. n. Advances made to cultivators from the public treasury.

ತಕ್ಕ (*P. p. rel. of* ತಗು) k. a. Fit, proper; right, suitable, good; worthy, deserving. *n.* A good man, friend. ತಕ್ಕದು. That is fit, *etc.*; anything proper. ನೀನು ಹೋಗ ತಕ್ಕದು, you ought to go. ತಕ್ಕಂತೆ, ತಕ್ಕ ಹಾಗೆ. As is or was fit. -ನಿತು, -ಷ್ಟು. As much as is suitable.

ತಕ್ಕಡಿ f. n. A balance or pair of scales. -ಕಲ್ಲೆ, -ಕಲ್ಲು. Scale weights. -ಬಟ್ಟು, -ಬಿಲ್ಲೆ. The scale-pan.

ತಕ್ಕಳಿಸು k. v. t. To sprinkle, *as* water.

ತಕ್ಕಾಬಿಕ್ಕಿ h. n. Fraud, dishonest doings.

ತಕ್ಕಾಳಿ k. n. The tomato or love-apple, *Lycopersicum esculentum.*

ತಕ್ಕು a. k. n. Greatness, largeness. 2, love, affection, desire. -ವು. Fitness.

ತಕ್ಕೆ (= ಟಕ್ಕೆ 2) k. n. Embracing. 2, wood, *etc.* that can be once grasped with the arms. 3, joining; a mate. 4, an accumulation, heap. 5, a number of persons, *etc.* assembled together. [*etc.*

ತಕ್ಕೊಳ್ಳು (*fr.* ತಕ್, *q. v.*) *v. t.* To take,

ತಕ್ತೆ h. n. A tabular statement, *etc.*; an account, *as* of receipts, expenses, *etc.*

ತಕ್ಯ h. n. A pillow, cushion, pad.

ತಕ್ರ s. n. Buttermilk.

ತಕ್ಷಕ s. n. A cutter, carpenter; *also* ತಕ್ಷ. 2, the principal serpent of pâtâḷa.

ತಕ್ಷಣ *tb. of* ತತ್ಕ್ಷಣ, *q. v.*

ತಕ್ಸೀರು. = ತಕಶೀರು, *q. v.*

ತಗಚೆ k. n. The under-shrub *Cassia occidentalis.* 2, the Indian mulberry tree, *Morinda citrifolia.*

ತಗಡು f. n. A flat piece or sheet of metal; a metal plate.

ತಗಣೆ, ತಗಣಿ k. n. A bug. -ಬೀಳು. To have bugs.

ತಗರ (= ತವರ. *tb. of* ತಮರ) *n.* Tin.

ತಗರು (= ಟಗರು) k. n. A ram.

ತಗಲು, ತಗುಲು 1. k. *v. i.* To come in contact with; to touch, hit.

ತಗಲು, ತಗುಲು 2. f. n. Trick, fraud; *also* ದಗಲು. -ಗಾರ. A cheat.

ತಗಹು a. k. n. An obstacle. 2, connection; continuous line; order.

ತಗಾದೆ h. n. Urging for payment. 2, a claim, dispute; a suit.

ತಗು a. k. *v. i.* To be fit or proper; *see* ತಕ್ಕ.

ತಗುಳು a. k. *v. i.* To be joined together; to approach; to commence. *v. t.* To chase, pursue; to drive away; to push back.

ತಗುಳ್ಚು a. k. *v. t.* To join. 2, to get to. 3, to undertake; to employ. 4, to set on fire.

ತಗೆ a. k. *v. t.* To stop, arrest; to stun. *n.* Stopping.

ತಗ್ಯೀರು h. n. Dismissal.

ತಗ್ಗಿ 1. k. n. N. of a tree. 2, a large shrub, *Clorodendron phlomoides.*

ತಗ್ಗಿ 2. h. n. Thuggee; the practice of kidnapping.

ತಗ್ಗಿಸು k. *v. t.* To make low; to bow, *as* the head; to lessen; to appease.

ತಗ್ಗು k. v. i. To be low, depressed; to stoop; to be humble; to decrease; to be appeased, *etc.* n. Low ground; a declivity; a hole; a valley; decrease; scarcity. ತಗ್ಗಾಳು. A dwarf. -ಗದ್ದೆ. A low paddy-field. -ದವಸ. Dear grain. -ದಿಣ್ಣೆ. Dale and hill. -ನೆಲ, -ಭೂಮಿ. Low ground. -ಮುಗ್ಗು. Ups and downs.

ತಂಗದಿರು a. k. n. A cool ray. ತಂಗದಿರ. The moon.

ತಂಗಳು k. n. Any cold or stale food, *as* rice, bread, *etc.*; *also* ತಂಗಳನ್ನ.

ತಂಗಾಳಿ k. n. A cool breeze.

ತಂಗಿ k. n. A younger sister. 2, an epithet of endearment for a female younger than one's self.

ತಂಗು k. v. i. To stop; to stay, sojourn. n. Halt: a day's journey.

ತಂಗುಡ k. n. A horse's or elephant's trappings.

ತಂಗೇಡಿ k. n. The plant *Cassia auriculata.*

ತಜವಿಜಿ, ತಜವೀಜು h. n. Investigating; planning; arranging.

ತಂಜಾವೂರು k. n. Tanjore.

ತಟ s. n. A declivity. 2, a bank or shore. 3, a field. 4, the sky, horizon. -ಸ್ಥ. Standing still; awaiting intently; indifferent.

ತಟಕು k. n. A drop, *as* of water, *etc.*; a small quantity.

ತಟಕ್ಕನೆ k. ad. In drops. 2, quickly, suddenly.

ತಟಗುಟ್ಟು (*fr.* ತಟ, -ಕುಟ್ಟು) k. v. t. To hammer. v. i. To wander about.

ತಟವಟ k. n. Fraud, trickery. -ಗಾರ. A deceitful man, liar.

ತಟಾಯ್ (*i. e.* ತಟ್ಟಿಹಾಯ್) k. v. i. To pass by or over, *as* a river, *etc.* 2, to pass right through.

ತಟಾರನೆ. = ತಟಕ್ಕನೆ, *q. v.*

ತಟಿತ್ತು s. n. Lightning.

ತಟ್ಟ a. k. n. Flatness, levelness. 2, a thin, emaciated fellow.

ತಟ್ಟನೆ (= ತಟಕ್ಕನೆ, *q. v.*) k. *ad.* Suddenly, all at once.

ತಟ್ಟಿ (= ತಡಿಕೆ, *q. v.*) k. n. A frame-work of bamboos, plaited palm-leaves or straw; a tatty. 2, matting.

ತಟ್ಟು 1. k. v. t. To tap; to touch; to pat; to strike; to clap; to knock; to drive; to remove. n. A slap or pat; a blow. 2, (*fig.*) a blow, *as* of disease, danger, *etc.*; fatigue. 3, the measles. 4, flatness. -ಮುಟ್ಟು. A great strait or dilemma.

ತಟ್ಟು 2. k. n. Side; direction.

ತಟ್ಟು 3. h. n. A pony or tattoo.

ತಟ್ಟು 4. f. n. Sackcloth.

ತಟ್ಟೆ 1. (= ತಟ್ಟ, *etc.*) k. n. Flatness. 2, a flat, lid-like basket. 3, a platter, plate. 4, a flat, beanless pod.

ತಟ್ಟೆ 2. k. n. A bamboo split in two.

ತಟ್ರೆ k. n. A woman's shoe.

ತಡ (*cf.* ತಡವು, ತಡೆ) k. n. Check, obstacle. 2, delay. 3, perplexity, confusion. -ಗಟ್ಟು. To stop, *as* water; to charm, *as* snakes, *etc.* -ತ. Stopping, restraining; lasting, wearing well, *as* cloth. -ಪಡಿಸು. To impede; to perplex; to turn the wrong way. -ಮಾಡು. To delay; to be slow, loiter; to delude, perplex. -ವಾಗು. Delay to occur.

ತಡಕು k. v. t. To grope for, seek. ತಡಕಿಸು. To cause to seek.

ತಡಗಣೆ k. n. The pulse *Vigna catjang.*

ತಡಪು k. n. Hindrance. 2, a small cloth like apron.

ತಡವರಿಸು k. v. t. To grope; to seek.

ತಡವು k. v. t. To touch or rub gently. 2, (=ತಡವರಿಸು) to grope. 3, to stop. n. Delay.

ತಡವೆ k. n. A time, turn.

ತಡಸಲು f. n. A water-fall.

ತಡಸು a. k. v. i. To stay, wait. v. t. (=ತಡಿಸು) To stop, hinder. n. Impeding, hindering.

ತಡಹು k. n. Stop, cessation. v. t. To stroke.

ತಡಾಕು f. n. Smartness, shrewdness.

ತಡಿ 1. k. n. A thick staff, cudgel.

ತಡಿ 2. k. n. A saddle made of woollen or cotton cloth; a mattress.

ತಡಿ 3. k. a. Damp, wet. -ಪುಡಿ. Imperfectly moistened, as clay.

ತಡಿ 4. (tb. of ತಟ) n. A bank, shore.

ತಡಿಕೆ (=ತಟ್ಟಿ) k. n. A frame of bamboos, straw or leaves used as a screen, tatty, etc.

ತಡಿಸು k. v. t. To stop; to detain; to keep off.

ತಡೆ k. v. i. To delay, lose time; to loiter; to wait. 2, to last, as cloth. v. t. To stop; to detain, check; to endure, bear. n. (= ತಡ, q. v.) An obstacle, hindrance, impediment; a charm; delay. -ಕಟ್ಟು. = ತಡಗಟ್ಟು, s. ತಡ, q. v. -ಗಟ್ಟು. A dam. -ಹಾಕು. To stop; to raise objections.

ತಣಕಾಯಿಸು (fr. ತನು) h. v. t. To inquire after.

ತಣಲು k. n. Glowing coals.

ತಣಸು k. n. Coldness, coolness; wetness; also ತಣಿವು.

ತಣಿ k. v. i. To grow cool; to be refreshed; to be calmed or appeased. 2, to get feeble. (P. p. ತಣಿತು, ತಣಿದು). n. Shame, modesty. -ಸು. To cool, refresh, appease.

ತಣಿಪು, ತಣಿವು, ತಣುವು k. n. Coolness, calmness, appeasement; satiation.

ತಣ್ಣಾಳಿ. = ತಂಗಾಳಿ, q. v.

ತಂಟೆ h. n. A quarrel, dispute; trouble, annoyance. 2, connection; interference. -ಗಾರ, -ಖೋರ. A quarrelsome man. -ಮಾಡು. To annoy. -ಮಾರಿ. A troublesome person; also ತಂಟ್ಲಮಾರಿ.

ತಂಡ k. n. A mass; a multitude; a crowd; a party. ತಂಡೋಪತಂಡ. Crowds upon crowds.

ತಂಡಸ f. n. Pincers, tongs.

ತಂಡಿ (= ಥಂಡಿ) k. n. Cold; wetness.

ತಂಡುಲ s. n. Rice cleaned from the husk.

ತಂಡೆ k. n. A foot-ornament of women.

ತಂಡೇಲ f. n. The master of a boat, a tindal.

ತಣ್ಣ k. n. Coolness, cold. -ಗೆ, -ನೆ. Cold, cool; cooling; refreshing; calm.

ತಣ್ಣಸ. = ತಣಸು, q. v.

ತಣ್ಣೀರು k. n. Cool or cold water. -ತಳಿ. To sprinkle cold water.

ತಣ್ಣರಲು, ತಣ್ಣಲರು k. n. Cool breeze.

ತಣ್ಣೆಳಲು k. n. A cool shade.

ತಣ್ಪು. = ತಂಪು, q. v.

ತಣ್ಬಿಸಿಲು k. n. Assuaged sunshine or heat.

ತತ s. a. Extended, spread. n. A stringed musical instrument.

ತತಿ 1. s. n. Extent; a series, range; a crowd, troop.

ತತಿ 2. (tb. of ತತ್) n. A proper time or [season.

ತತ್ಕಾಲ s. n. That time; present time. ad. Directly, immediately.

ತತ್ಕ್ಷಣ s. n. The same moment. ad. Instantly, forthwith.

ತತ್ತರ 1. f. n. Trembling, shuddering. -ಗುಟ್ಟು, -ಗೊಳ್ಳು, ತತ್ತರಿಸು. To tremble.

ತತ್ತರ 2. (ರ = ಱ) a. k. n. Perplexity, confusion.

ತತ್ತಿ (= ತೆತ್ತಿ) k. n. An egg.

ತತ್ಪರ s. a. Intent upon, wholly devoted to. -ತೆ. Entire devotion.

ತತ್ಪುರುಷ s. n. The supreme soul. 2, a class of compounds (g.).

ತತ್ಪೂರ್ವ s. a. Prior, former.

ತತ್ರ s. ad. There, thither; therein; then.

ತತ್ವ s. n. The true or real state; reality, truth; essential nature; the very essence; a principle; Brahmâ. -ಜ್ಞ. Knowing the true nature of anything, understanding the principles of a science. -ಜ್ಞಾನ. Knowledge of the truth. -ಜ್ಞಾನಿ. A philosopher. -ಶಾಸ್ತ್ರ. Philosophy.

ತತ್ವಾರ s. *n.* Want, lack.

ತತ್ಸಮ s. *a.* The same with it. *n.* A word that exists in Kannaḍa as well as in Saṁskṛita.

ತಥಾ s. *ad.* So, thus. 2, it is so. -ಸ್ತು. May it be so.

ತಥ್ಯ s. *a.* True, genuine. *n.* Truth.

ತದಕು k. *v. t.* To strike, beat. *n.* Striking, beating.

ತದನಂತರ s. *a.* Next to that. *ad.* Thereupon, then.

ತದಲು, ತದ್ಲು k. *n.* A frame of thorns, *etc.*, used as a gate in a hedge.

ತದಾರಭ್ಯ s. *ad.* Thence, since then.

ತದಿಕು, ತದುಕು k. *n.* The gum olibanum tree, *Boswellia thurifera.*

ತದಿಗಿಣ k. *int. Sounds used in beating time in music.*

ತದಿಗೆ. *tb. of* ತೃತೀಯ, *q. v.*

ತದ್ದಿನ s. *n.* That day. 2, the day of mourning for deceased relations.

ತದ್ಧರ್ಮ s. *n.* That business; that religion.

ತದ್ಧಿತ s. *n. An affix to form nouns, or a noun formed by it;* a derivative noun (*g.*).

ತದ್ಭವ s. *n.* A word corrupted from Saṁskṛita or any other language.

ತದ್ವತ್ s. *ad.* So, in that manner; also, likewise.

ತನ k. *An affix for forming true Kannaḍa words, as:* ಒಕ್ಕಲು-, ಕಲಿ-, ಕಳ್ಳ-, ಬಡ-, ಮನೆ-, *etc.*

ತನಕ k. *prep.* Till, until, as far as.

ತನಕಿ h. *n.* Ascertaining; examination.

ತನಯ s. *n.* A son; *f.* ತನಯೆ. A daughter.

ತನಿ a. k. *v. i.* To thrive, develop. *P. p.* ತನಿದು. *n.* The state of having thriven, full, developed, matured, *etc.* -ಗಂಪು. A rich fragrance. -ಗಬ್ಬು. Juicy sugarcane. -ಬೆಲ್ಲ. Delicious jaggory. -ರಸ. Essence, excellent flavour. -ವೀರರಸ. Great heroism. -ಸುಖ. Great pleasure or joy. -ಸೊಬಗು. Great beauty. -ಹರಕೆ. Great blessing.

ತನು 1. s. *a.* Thin, slender; small; delicate. *n.* The body. 2, the skin. -ಜ, -ಜಾತ, -ಭವ. A son; *f.* -ಜಾತೆ, -ಜೆ. -ಮನಧನ. Body, mind, and property.

ತನು 2. = ತಂಪು, *q. v.*

ತನೆ k. *n.* Pregnancy of beasts.

ತಂತರ. *tb. of* ತಂತ್ರ, *q. v.*

ತಂತಿ (*tb. of* ತಂತ್ರಿ) *n.* A string, cord; a wire, *as* of a lute. -ಟಪ್ಪಾಲು. The telegraph. -ವಾದ್ಯ. A stringed instrument. -ವರ್ತಮಾನ. A telegram.

ತಂತು 1. (= ತಂದಿತು) k. *Third pers. singl. impf. of* ತರು.

ತಂತು 2. s. *n.* A thread, string, a filament; a wire. -ಕರಣ. Weaving, spinning. -ಪಟ. Cotton cloth. -ವಾದ್ಯ. Any stringed instrument. -ವಾಯ. A weaver; a spider; a loom. -ಹಾರುವ. A thread Brâhmaṇa.

ತಂತು 3. *tb. of* ತಂತ್ರ, *q. v.* -ಗಾರ. A cunning man.

ತಂತ್ರ s. *n.* A thread. 2, a loom; vesture. 3, a system; ritual. 4, an established doctrine. 5, magical and mystic formularies. 6, a charm. 7, a design; cunning, trick, intrigue, plot. 8, a curse; plotting. -ಗಾರ. (= ತಂತುಗಾರ) A cunning, crafty man. -ಬಂತ್ರ ಮಾಡು. To contaminate, adulterate.

ತಂತ್ರಿ s. *n.* = ತಂತಿ. 2, a pûjâri. -ಸು. To use an expedient.

ತಂದಲ್ a. k. *n.* Water-drops, spray.

ತಂದು. *P. p. of* ತರು, *q. v.*

ತಂದೆ k. *n.* Father. -ಗೆ ತಂದೆ. A paternal grandfather. -ತಾಯಿ. Father and mother. -ತಾಯಿಗಳು. Parents. -ವಾದಿ. Relationship by father's side.

ತಂದ್ರಿ s. *n.* Fatigue; sleepiness; exhaustion.

ತನ್ನ k. *pro. Gen. of* ತಾನು, *q. v.*; *dat.* ತನಗೆ; *acc.* ತನ್ನನ್ನು; *abl.* ತನ್ನಿಂದ.

ತನ್ನಿ k. *2nd pers. pl. imp. of* ತರು.

ತನ್ಮಧ್ಯ s. *ad.* Meanwhile.

ತಪ s. *n.* Heat; burning. 2, the hot season. 3, austerity, penance. 4, a demon. -ಗೆಯ್ಯು. To perform a penance. -ನ. Heating, burning; the sun; mental distress. ತಪೋಧನ. Rich in penance; ascetic, pious; an ascetic, devotee. ತಪೋಲೋಕ. One of the seven Hindu worlds inhabited by devotees.

ತಪಕ್ಕನೆ k. *ad.* All at once.

ತಪಟೆ f. *n.* A tambourine beaten with sticks.

ತಪರಾಖು h. *n.* A slap on the cheek.

ತಪಲೆ f. *n.* A round metallic cooking vessel.

ತಪಶೀಲು h. *n.* Details, minute description.

ತಪಶ್ಚರಣ, ತಪಶ್ಚರಣೆ, ತಪಶ್ಚರ್ಯೆ (*fr.* ತಪ) s. *n.* The practice of penance.

ತಪಸ್, ತಪಸ್ಸು (*fr.* ತಪ) s. *n.* Heat. 2, austerity, penance.

ತಪಸಿ 1., ತಪಸ್ವಿ (*tb. of* ತಪಸ್ವಿ) *n.* An ascetic, religious mendicant; *f.* -ನಿ.

ತಪಸಿ 2. f. *n.* The wild mangosteen, *Diospyros embryopteris*; *also* -ಗಿಡ. 2, the plant *Caesalpinia bonducella.*

ತಪಾಲು. = ಟಪಾಲು, *q. v.*

ತಪಿತ s. *a.* Heated, burnt.

ತಪಿಸು s. *v. i.* To be hot; to burn; to suffer pain.

ತಪ್ತ s. *a.* Heated, burnt, afflicted.

ತಪ್ಪ. = ತರುವ, ತರ್ಪ. *Pres. rel. part. of* ತರು.

ತಪ್ಪಟೆ. = ತಪಟೆ, *q. v.*

ತಪ್ಪನೆ k. *ad.* Quickly, all at once.

ತಪ್ಪಲ, ತಪ್ಪಲು k. *n.* The level ground on the top of a mountain; table-land.

ತಪ್ಪಲೆ. = ತಪಲೆ, *q. v.*

ತಪ್ಪಸಿಗಿಡ. = ತಪಸಿಗಿಡ, *q. v.*

ತಪ್ಪಿತ. = ತಪ್ಪು, *q. v.*

ತಪ್ಪಿಸು k. *v. t.* To cause to miss or pass by; to let slip; to avert; to evade; to avoid; to escape, *etc.*

ತಪ್ಪು k. *v. i.* To make a false step; to slip; to mistake or blunder; to be missed or lost; to fail; to disappear; to miss. *n.* Slipping, erring. 2, a slip, error, mistake, blunder; an impropriety; a fault, misdemeanour. ತಪ್ಪಡಿ. A false step. -ಒಪ್ಪಿಕೊಳ್ಳು. To acknowledge one's fault. -ಕಾಣಿಕೆ. A gift to make amends for a misdeed. -ಕೆಲಸ. A misdeed. -ಕ್ಷಮಿಸು, -ಸಯ್ರಿಸು. -ಸಹಿಸು. To overlook a fault. -ಗಂಟು. A wrong knot or connection. -ದಾರಿ. A wrong road. -ಬೀಳು. A mistake to occur. -ಮಾಡು. To make a mistake. -ತಿದ್ದು. To correct a mistake. -ಸಾಧಿಸು. To charge (a man) with a fault. -ಹಿಡಿ. To find fault with. -ಹೆಜ್ಜೆ. = ತಪ್ಪಡಿ. -ಹೊರಿಸು. To accuse (one) of a fault. -ವಿಕೆ. Erring, missing. ತಪ್ಪಿ ಹೋಗು. To be lost, *as* an employment; to go astray.

ತಫಾವತು h. *n.* Difference; deviation, variance, *as* of accounts; failure; shortcoming.

ತಬಕ, ತಬಕು h. *n.* A plate for betel-leaf, *etc.*

ತಬಟೆ. = ತಪಟೆ, *q. v.*

ತಬಲಕು h. *n.* A packet of papers. 2, a string which binds a packet.

ತಬೀಯತು h. *n.* Constitution; disposition.

ತಬೇಲಿ h. *n.* A stable.

ತಬ್ಬರಿಸು k. *v. i.* To be overcome by terror, grief, *etc.*; to be amazed. 2, to slip, stumble.

ತಬ್ಬಲಿ. = ತಬ್ಬಿಲಿ, *q. v.* -ಕೂಸು. An orphan, child. -ಕೆಲಸ. Vile action. -ಮನುಷ್ಯ, A vile man.

ತಬಿಬ್ಬು k. *n.* Bewilderment, maze.

ತಬ್ಬಿಲಿ (= ತಬ್ಬಲಿ) k. *n.* A child's bereavement of its mother or parents. 2, a wretched, mean or inferior person or thing.

ತಬ್ಬು k. *v. t.* To embrace. 2, to clasp in the arms, *as* a quantity of wood, *etc.* *n.* An embrace. -ಹುಲ್ಲು. An armful of grass. ತಬ್ಬಿಸು. To cause to embrace or clasp.

ತಬ್ದೀಲಿ h. *n.* Exchange, transfer; arrangement

ತಮ s. *aff. of superl.* Most.

ತಮ, ತಮಸ್. = ತಮಸ್ಸು, *q. v.*

ತಮಗೆ k. *pro.* (*dat. of* ತಾವು) To them.

ತಮತು, ತಮತ್ತು, ತಮ್ಮದು k. *pro.* Theirs; yours (*honorif.*).

ತಮರ. = ತವರ, *q. v.*

ತಮಸೂಕು h. *n.* A note of hand, bond.

ತಮಸ್ಸು (*tb. of* ತಮಸ್) *n.* Darkness, gloom. 2, mental darkness; sin; ignorance. 3, Râhu.

ತಮಾಮು h. *n.* The whole. *ad.* Wholly, entirely.

ತಮಾಷೆ h. *n.* A farce; tricks of conjurers; sport, fun; a pantomime. -ಗಾರ. A showman, buffoon.

ತಮಿಳ k. *n.* The Tamiḷ language; Tamiḷ.

ತಂಪು (= ತಣ್ಪು) k. *n.* Coolness, coldness; wetness; a cooling, gratifying or refreshing quality or thing. *a.* Cool. *ad.* Coolly. -ಮಾಡು, ತಂಪಿಸು. To cool: to extinguish, *as* fire or a light. -ಗಾಳಿ. A cool wind. ತಂಪಿನ ಮರ. A shady tree.

ತಂಬತ್ತಿಜಾಲಿ k. *n.* A shrub with long thorns and fragrant yellow flowers, *Acacia eburnea.*

ತಂಬಳ (ಳ = ೞ). = ತಮಿಳ, *q. v.*

ತಂಬಾಕೆ, ತಂಬಾಕು h. *n.* Tobacco.

ತಂಬಿ h. *n.* Chastisement, beating.

ತಂಬಿಗೆ. = ಚೆಂಬಿಗೆ, *q. v.*

ತಂಬಿಟ್ಟು k. *n.* The flour of fried rice mixed with milk or water, jaggory, *etc.*

ತಂಬು h. *n.* A tent.

ತಂಬುಲ. *tb. of* ತಾಂಬೂಲ, *q. v.*

ತಂಬುಳಿ k. *n.* Vegetables ground with cocoanut scrapings, mixed with curds, salted and seasoned to taste.

ತಂಬೂರ h. *n.* A kind of guitar with three to five strings; *also* ತಂಬೂರಿ.

ತಮ್ಮ 1. k. *pro.* (*gen. of* ತಾವು) Their; your (*honorif.*). -ದು. Theirs; yours. *Acc.* ತಮ್ಮನ್ನು; *instr.* ತಮ್ಮಿಂದ; *loc.* ತಮ್ಮಲ್ಲಿ.

ತಮ್ಮ 2. k. *n.* A younger brother; also a word of endearment; *pl.* ತಮ್ಮಂದ್ಯರು, ತಮ್ಮಂದಿರು.

ತಮ್ಮಟೆ (= ತವಟೆ, *q. v.*) k. *n.* A tambourine.

ತಮ್ಮಡಿ k. *n.* An attendant on an idol.

ತಮ್ಮೆ k. *n.* The lobe of the ear or gristle of the nose. -ಗಿಡ. A cultivated pulse, *Dolichos lablab.*

ತಯಾರ, ತಯಾರು h. *a.* Prepared, made ready, waiting to do, *etc.* ತಯಾರಿ. Readiness, preparation. -ಮಾಡು, ತಯಾರಿಸು. To make ready, prepare.

ತರ 1. (= ತರಹ, ತರಾ) h. *n.* Kind, manner, fashion; rank, class; sort; succession; order; equality. 2, a layer, stratum; a heap. -ಗತಿ. Classification; sort, kind; condition; grade, class. -ಗಾರ. A bricklayer. -ತರ. *rep.* Varieties. ಕೀಳ್-. Low rank, inferior sort. ಮೇಲ್-. High rank, good sort.

ತರ 2. k. *An imitative sound.* -ಗುಟ್ಟು. To tremble. -ತರ = ತರತರ.

ತರ 3. s. *aff. of comp. degree.* More; *as:* ಅಧಿಕ-, ಪ್ರಿಯ-, ಲಘು-, *etc.*

ತರ 4. s. *n.* Passing, crossing; *also* -ಣ.

ತರಕಲು (= ತರಕು, ತರಸು 2) k. *n.* Roughness, unsmoothness, unevenness; *as:* -ಕಂಬಳಿ, -ಕಲ್ಲು, -ನೆಲ, -ಮೈ, *etc.*

ತರಕಾರಿ h. *n.* Esculent vegetables.

ತರಕು. = ತರಕಲು, *q. v.*

ತರಗಸಿ k. *n.* *Cassia tora*; *cf.* ತಗಚೆ.

ತರಗು 1. (= ತಗ್ಗು) k. *n.* Diminishing; wastage. 2, customary deduction; brokerage, commission. ತರಗಿನಂಗಡಿ. A broker's shop.

ತರಗು 2. (ರ = ಱ) k. *n.* That which is dried: dry or dead leaves said to be eaten by ascetics. ತರಗೆಲೆ. A dry leaf.

ತರಂಗ s. *n.* A wave, billow, surge. ತರಂಗಿಣಿ. A river.

ತರಟ, ತರಟು a. k. *n.* Baldness. -ದಲೆ, -ಮಂಡೆ. A bald head.

ತರಣ s. a. Crossing over. ತರಣಿ. A float, boat; the sun; the plant *Aloe perfoliata;* a kind of rose.

ತರತರ, -ನೆ. k. *ad.* Tremblingly, quakingly. -ನಡುಗು. To tremble, quake.

ತರದೂದು h. *n.* Getting ready; improving; effort, labour, exertion.

ತರಪು k. *n.* An inferior stone like a diamond; *also* ತರಪು.

ತರಫ h. *n.* Side, direction; party; a division of a district.

ತರಬು (= ತರುಬು. ರ = ಱ) k. *v. i.* To stay, stop.

ತರಬೇತು h. *n.* Education, training.

ತರಲ s. *a.* Moving to and fro, unsteady, fickle. 2, liquid. 3, sparkling. *n.* A child, infant. 2, the central gem of a necklace. -ತೆ, -ತ್ವ. Unsteadiness. ತರಲೆ. Rice-gruel.

ತರವಾರ, ತರವಾರಿ (= ತಲವಾರ) f. *n.* A sword, scymitar.

ತರಸ s. *n.* Meat, flesh.

ತರಸು 1. = ತರಿಸು, *q. v.*

ತರಸು 2. (= ತರಕಲು) k. *n.* A field lying waste or fallow.

ತರಹ. = ತರ 1, *q. v.*

ತರಹರ k. *n.* The exercise of patience, forbearance; *also* ತರಹರಿಕೆ. ತರಹರಿಸು. To be patient; to bear patiently.

ತರಳ. = ತರಲ, *q. v.*

ತರಳು k. *n.* A ripe dried fruit, *as* a cocoanut.

ತರಳೆ (ರ = ಱ) h. *n.* A useless business. -ಮನುಷ್ಯ. A good-for-nothing man. -ಮಾತು. A useless word.

ತರಾ (= ತರ 1). -ತರ. *rep.* Various kinds or ways; differences of rank. -ವಳಿ. Various kinds.

ತರಾತುರಿ (*tb. of* ತ್ವರಾ-ತ್ವರಿ) *n.* Speed, haste.

ತರಾಸು (= ತ್ರಾಸು) h. *n.* A balance, scales.

ತರಿ 1. (= ತರಕಲು) k. *n.* Roughness; grit.

ತರಿ 2. (ರಿ = ಱಿ) k. *v. t.* To strip or cut off the leaves from a bough, *etc.*, to pluck; to cut. *v. i.* To be chafed or grazed. -ಸು. To cause to cut.

ತರಿಸು s. *v. i.* To cross over; to float, swim.

ತರು 1. k. *v. t.* To bring; to give. *P. p.* ತಂದು; *neut. sing. past* ತಂದಿತು, ತಂತು. *imper. 2nd. pers. sing.* ತಾ; *pl.* ತನ್ನಿ, ತರ್ರಿ. ತರಿಸು. To cause to lead or bring. -ವಳಿ. Bringing home, *as* a girl for marriage. -ವಿಕೆ. Bringing, fetching.

ತರು 2. (ರು = ಱು) a. k. *v. i.* To join; to approach; to engage in. *n.* The state of being joined, fit, or settled. -ವಾಯ, *q. v.*

ತರು 3. s *n.* A tree. -ಕುಟಿ. A squirrel. -ಬೊಡಲ್. The foot of a tree.

ತರುಣ 1. s. *a.* Young, tender, juvenile; fresh, lively. *n.* A young man; a boy; *f.* ತರುಣಿ. -ತೆ, -ತ್ವ. Tenderness, youth, juvenility.

ತರುಣ 2. (ರು = ಱು) k. *a.* Fit or proper time.

ತರುಪು. = ತರಪು, *q. v.*

ತರುಬು. = ತರಬು, *q. v.*

ತರುವಾಯ (*fr.* ತರು 2, *q. v.*) k. *ad.* Afterwards, subsequently.

ತರ್ಕ s. *n.* Supposition, conjecture. 2, reasoning, speculation. 3, deliberation; dispute, discussion. 4, doubt. 5, logic. 6, wish. 7, motive. -ಕ, ತಾರ್ಕಿಕ. A logician, disputant, reasoner. -ವಾದ. Disputation. -ವಿದ್ಯೆ, -ಶಾಸ್ತ್ರ. The science of logic. ತರ್ಕಿಸು. To reason; to speculate, dispute.

ತರ್ಜನ s. *n.* Threatening, pointing at in ridicule; putting to shame; wrath. ತರ್ಜನಿ. The forefinger. ತರ್ಜಿಸು. To threaten.

ತರ್ಜುಮೆ h. *n.* A translation; an abstract.

ತರ್ಪಣ s. *n.* Satisfying, pleasing; satisfaction; an oblation to the manes or gods; a libation. ತರ್ಪಿಸು. To please, satisfy; to offer an oblation to the manes or gods.

ತಲೆ (= ತರಳೆ) k. n. Idle talk.

ತರ್ಷ, ತರ್ಷಣ s. n. Thirst; desire.

ತಲ 1. (= ತಳ) s. n. A level surface. 2, the palm of the hand. 3, depth; the lower part, base; a pit, pond; the ground. 4, the palmyra tree. 5, cause, origin, motive. ತಲಾತಲ. One of the seven divisions of hell.

ತಲ 2. = ತರ 1, etc., q. v. -ತಲಾಂತರ (= ತಲ-ತಲ-ಅಂತರ). Generations upon generations. ತಲಾಂತರ. A generation.

ತಲಪು k. v. i. To reach, come to hand; to arrive. ತಲಪಿಸು. To cause to reach, etc.

ತಲಬು h. n. Pay, wages; a summons.

ತಲವಾರ (= ತರವಾರ) f. n. A sword.

ತಲಾರಿ. = ತಳವಾರ, q. v.

ತಲಾವು h. n. A tank.

ತಲಾಸು h. n. Search, quest. -ಮಾಡು. To make inquiry into; to get, obtain.

ತಲೆ k. n. The head; a generation; that which is uppermost or principal. -ಕಟ್ಟು. A head-tie; the head or top-dash of a letter; an adjoining field. -ಕೆಳಗು, -ಕೆಳಗೆ. The head downwards; topsyturvy. -ಕೊಟ್ಟಮಾರಿ. A brawler. -ಗಡಿ. To behead. -ಗಾಯು. To protect. -ಗಿಂಬು. A pillow. -ಗೆಡಹು (= ಗಡಿ). To decapitate. -ಗೇರು. To rise to the head, to affect it, as poison. -ಗೊಡು. To risk one's life in. -ಗೊಯ್ಯು. To decapitate. -ಗೊಯ್ಕ. A murderer; a ruffian; a cheat. -ತಿರುಗು. To become giddy. -ತೂಗು. To nod; a nod. -ದಿಂಬು. = -ಗಿಂಬು. -ದೋರು. To spring up, appear. -ನೋಯು, -ನಿಡಿ. The head to ache. -ನೋವು, -ನಿಡಿತ. The headache. -ಪಟ್ಟಿ. A piece of wood over a door. -ಪಟ್ಟು. An application for headache. -ಬಾಗಲು. The entrance door. -ಬುರುಡೆ. The skull. -ಬಿಲಗು. The ridge-pole. -ಬೇನೆ. = ತಲೆನೋವು. -ಬೇಸರ. Tiresomeness. -ಬೋಳಿಸು. To shave the head. -ಬೋಳಿಸಿಕೊಳ್ಳು, -ಮಾಡಿಸಿಕೊಳ್ಳು. To get the head shaved. -ಯ ಮೇಲೆ ಕೂಡ್ರು. To trouble; to be forward. -ಯ ಮೇಲೆ ಹೊತ್ತುಕೊಳ್ಳು. To take upon one's self. -ಯಾಳ. A chief, headman. -ಯಾರು. A kind of yoke for cattle. -ಯೆತ್ತು. To rise from a poor condition. -ಯೋಡು. The skull. -ದಾಗಿಸು. To bend the head, obey. -ಬಾಗು. The head to bend. -ಶೂಲೆ. = -ನೋವು. -ಹಂಚು. A ridge tile. -ಹಿಡಿ. To affect the head, as a strong smell, etc. -ಹೋಕ. A very dissolute man. -ಹೊರೆ. A load carried upon the head.

ತಲ್ಪ s. n. A bed; a couch. 2, an upper story.

ತಲ್ಲಣ, ತಲ್ಲಳ k. n. Agitation; alarm; fear; grief, etc. ತಲ್ಲಣಿಸು. To be agitated, alarmed; to be anxious about.

ತವ s. pro. Of thee, thine, thy.

ತವಕ s. n. Love; desire; eagerness; haste, hurry. ತವಕಿಸು. To be eager; to hasten.

ತವಕ್ಷೀರ (tb. of ತ್ವಕ್ಕ್ಷೀರ) n. Manna of bamboo. 2, an extract from wheat, etc.

ತವಟು (= ತವುಟು) k. v. t. To sift pounded grain, etc., on a bamboo fan.

ತವಡು, ತವುಡು k. n. Bran.

ತವರ, ತವರು 1. f. n. Tin.

ತವರು 2. k. n. The house of a woman's own people; also -ಮನೆ.

ತವಾಯಿ h. n. A fine; ill-luck, great trouble. 2, detention.

ತವು a. k. v. i. To decrease; to waste away; to perish. v. t. To diminish. n. Decrease; ruin. ತವಿಸು. To cause to decrease; to destroy.

ತವುಟು. = ತವಟು, q. v.

ತವುಟೆಗಿಡ k. n. The gooseberry bush, the red myrtle, *Rhodomyrtus tomentosa*.

ತವೆ 1. = ಸವೆ, q. v.

ತವೆ 2. a. k. ad. Abundantly, wholly, further.

ತವೆ 3. h. n. A metal lid of cooking vessels.

ತಸಕಲು, ತಸಕು f. *n.* Cheating, trickery.

ತಸದೀಕು (= ತಸ್ತೀಕು) h. *n.* A fixed allowance paid by government to a pagoda, mosque, *etc.*, in lieu of assumed lands.

ತಸಬೀರು h. *n.* A picture.

ತಸ್ಕರ s. *n.* A thief, robber; theft; *f.* [ತಸ್ಕರಿ.

ತಸ್ಕಲು. = ತಸಕಲು, *q. v.*

ತಸ್ತೀಕು. = ತಸದೀಕು, *q. v.*

ತಸ್ತು h. *n.* A metal water-vessel; an [ewer.

ತಹ 1. a. k. *Rel. pres. part. of* ತರು.

ತಹ 2. h *n.* Peace; agreement of opinion. -ನಾಮೆ. A written treaty, agreement.

ತಹಕೀಕು h. *a.* Correct, true.

ತಹತಹ k. *n.* Anxiety; distress; eager- [ness.

ತಹಶೀಲು (= ತಾಸೀಲು) h. *n.* Collection of the revenue. -ದಾರ. A Tahsildâr, a native collector, the head of a talook.

ತಳ (= ತಲ 1, *q. v.*) s. *n.* The bottom, *etc.*; the hand. -ಹಲ್ಲು. The lowest step, *as* of a ladder. ತಳಾರಿಸು. To dry what is at the bottom; to rest the feet after much walking.

ತಳಕು k. *n.* Shine, glitter, flash. 2, coquetry. 3, = ತಕ್ಕೆ. -ಹಾಕು. To tie two beasts together.

ತಳತಳ k. *n.* Brightness, gleam, glitter. -ಗುಟ್ಟು, ತಳತಳಿಸು. To glitter, flash, shine.

ತಳಪ, ತಳಪು k. *n.* Splendour, lustre, shine; a dye to colour the hair.

ತಳಮಳ, ತಳವಳ k. *n.* Agitation, alarm, fear. -ಗುಟ್ಟು, ತಳಮಳಿಸು. To be agitated, alarmed.

ತಳರ್ a. k. *v. i.* To move; to totter; to set out, depart. *n.* Moving; tottering.

ತಳವರ, ತಳವಾರ (*tb. of* ಸ್ಥಲವಾರ) *n.* A watchman, beadle. -ನ ಬಳ್ಳಿ. A climbing herb, *Vitis setosa.*

ತಳಹದಿ, ತಳಾದಿ f. *n.* The foundation of a building.

ತಳಿ 1. k. *v. t.* To strew, sprinkle. *n.* Strewing, sprinkling. ತಳಿಸು. To cause to sprinkle.

ತಳಿ 2. k. *v. i.* To shoot, sprout. 2, to unfold; to appear. *n.* A race, family; a stock or breed.

ತಳಿ 3. k. *n.* A fence; an asylum; a choultry for travellers.

ತಳಿ 4. (ಳಿ = ೞಿ) k. *n.* A clog, cudgel; a palisade.

ತಳಿಗೆ f. *n.* A metal plate turned up at the rim.

ತಳಿರು a. k. *v. i.* To sprout, put forth leaves. *n.* A young shoot, sprout. ತಳಿರ್ದುಟಿ. A bud-like lip. ತಳಿರ್ದೋರಣ. A festoon of young leaves. ತಳಿರ್ಬಿಡು. To put forth shoots. -ತಳಿರ್ವಸೆ. A bed of tender leaves

ತಳಿಸು (*cf. s.* ತಳಿ 1) k. *v. t.* To pound, beat.

ತಳುಗು (= ತಂಗು) k. *v. i.* To stay, halt.

ತಳುವು (= ತಡವು) a. k. *v. i.* To stay, delay; to be slow; to be bewildered. *n.* Stop, delay.

ತಳೆ 1. a. k. *v. t.* To hold; to bear; to carry, support; to obtain, get. *n.* A tie, halter, fetters.

ತಳೆ 2. (ಳೆ = ೞೆ) k. *n.* A parasol, an umbrella.

ತಳ್ತು k. *v. t.* To smear the body with an unguent. *n.* Anointing; lustre.

ತಳ್ಗು (ಳ್ಗು = ೞ್ಗು). = ತಗ್ಗು, *q. v.*

ತಳ್ವಂಕ a. k. *n.* Embarrassment, fear, *etc.*

ತಳ್ಳಿ k. *n.* Connexion; association, company; intimacy. 2, raising quarrels; slander, calumny. -ಕೋರ. A slanderer. -ಮಾಡು. To calumniate. -ಅರ್ಜಿ. An anonymous petition.

ತಳ್ಳು (= ತೆಳ್ಳು) k. *v. t.* To push, shove away, thrust, drive; to dismiss, reject. *n.* Pushing, *etc.*; dismissal; *also* -ವಡ, ತಳ್ಪಡ.

ತಾ 1, **ತಾಂ.** = ತಾನು, *q. v.*

ತಾ 2. k. *2nd pers. sing. imp. of* ತರು. Bring.

ತಾಕತ್ತು h. *n.* Power, strength.

ತಾಕೀದಿ, ತಾಕೀದು h. n. Injunction, direction. 2, a letter from a superior to a subordinate government officer.

ತಾಕು (= ತಾಗು) k. v. i. To join, touch. v. t. To come in contact with, to hit, strike or dash against; to collide with; to attack. n. Touching, hitting. -ತೋಕು. Wear and tear. ತಾಕಿಸು. To make touch, etc.

ತಾಕುಳ. = ತಾಗುಳ, q. v.

ತಾಗಾಯತಿ h. prep. Until; up to.

ತಾಗು. = ತಾಕು, q. v.

ತಾಗುದಿ a. k. n. An ambush, lurking place.

ತಾಗುಳ (= ತಾಕುಳ) a. k. n. Ardour, passion; formidableness.

ತಾಜಾ, ತಾಜೇ h. a. Fresh; green; new. -ಕಲಮ್. A fresh para; a postscript.

ತಾಜೀಮು h. n. Treating with ceremony and respect.

ತಾಟ h. n. A dining plate. 2, stiffness, tightness; pride; also ತಾಟಿ. -ಗಿತ್ತಿ. A quarrelsome, wicked woman.

ತಾಟಕಿ, ತಾಟಕೆ s. n. A female fiend; a vixen; a hideous woman. -ತನ. A wicked, quarrelsome disposition.

ತಾಟು 1. k. v. t. To strike against, touch, come in contact with. 2, to strike. n. Striking against, etc. -ಕೊಡು. To knock one against another.

ತಾಟು 2. f. n. The sloping frame of a roof.

ತಾಟು 3. = ತಾಟ, q. v.

ತಾಟು 4. h. n. Pomp; show. -ಗಾರ. A showy man. -ಮಾಡು. To make fine.

ತಾಡನ s. n. Beating, striking. ತಾಡಿಸು. To beat.

ತಾಣ. tb. of ಸ್ಥಾನ, q. v.

ತಾಂಡವ s. n. A wild dance, esp. of the god Śiva.

ತಾಂಡವಾಳ k. n. Cast iron; also ತಂಡವಾಳ.

ತಾತ (= ತಂದೆ) s. n. A father. 2, a grand-father.

ತಾತಾತೂತು k. a. Full of holes.

ತಾತಿ. = ತಾಯಿತಿ, q. v.

ತಾತ್ಕಾಲಿಕ (fr. ತತ್ಕಾಲ) s. a. Contemporary, instantly appearing; immediate.

ತಾತ್ಪರ್ಯ s. n. Aim, object, purpose, intent. 2, meaning, purport, drift. 3, explanation.

ತಾತ್ಸಾರ f. n. Slight, disrespect, contempt.

ತಾದೃಶ s. ad. Such like, such a one.

ತಾನ s. a. Drawn, stretched. n. Expanse; a thread; a tone; the key-note in music.

ತಾನು 1. k. pro. He, she, it, in the reflexive or reciprocal sense. pl. ತಾವು, ತಾನಾಗಿ. Of himself, etc., voluntarily.

ತಾನು 2. h. n. A web or piece of cloth.

ತಾಂತ್ರಿಕ s. a. Relating to tantras. n. A man versed in any science or system; a scholar.

ತಾಪ s. n. Heat; torment; distress. -ಜ್ವರ. A burning fever. -ತ್ರಯ. The three sorts of affliction, i. e. Ádhidaivika, Ádhibhautika and Ádhyátmika.

ತಾಪಾಳು k. n. A bar, bolt.

ತಾಪಿ s. a. Oppressed by heat. -ತ. Heated, distressed, pained.

ತಾಪಿಸು s. v. i. To be hot; to burn; to suffer pain. v. t. To warn, admonish.

ತಾಪು k. n. A pimp's house.

ತಾಪೆ h. n. A set of dancing girls and musicians.

ತಾಪ್ತಾ h. n. A kind of silk cloth.

ತಾಬೂತು h. n. A bier carried about at the Moharam by Muhammadans.

ತಾಬೆ h. n. Dependance; charge. -ದಾರ. A dependant.

ತಾಬೇಲು (= ತಾಂಬೇಲು) k. n. A turtle.

ತಾಮರೆ (= ತಾವರೆ) a. k. n. A lotus. 2, the ring-worm.

ತಾಮಸ (fr. ತಮಸ್) s. a. Of darkness. n. Slothfulness, slowness; darkness. 2, a villain. -ಗಾರ. A sloth, sluggard. ತಾಮಸಿ. Night; a vicious man.

ತಾಂಬಾಣ f. n. A metal dish.

ತಾಂಬೂಲ (= ತಂಬುಲ) s. n. A betel-leaf roll with its ingredients: betelnut, spices and lime. 2, the areca-nut.

ತಾಂಬೇಲು. = ತಾಬೇಲು, q. v.

ತಾಮ್ರ s. n. Copper. a. Coppery red. -ಭಸ್ಮ. Oxide of copper. -ಕುಟ್ಟಕ. A coppersmith. -ತಗಡು. Sheet-copper. -ಪರ್ಣಿ. N. of a river or a town. -ಮುಖಿ. A European.

ತಾಯಿ k. n. Mother. -ತಂದೆ. Mother and father; pl. -ತಂದೆಗಳು. Parents.

ತಾಯಿತಿ f. n. A small box or tube containing an amulet and worn on any part of the body.

ತಾರ್ k. v. t. *The base for the neg. of* ತರ್; *as* ತಾರ. (He) won't bring. ತಾರದ. Not brought, *etc.*

ತಾರ 1. f. n. A copper coin of 2 kâsu.

ತಾರ 2. s. a. Crossing, floating. 2, high, *as* a note in music. 3, clear; white; good, excellent. n. The ether, sky. 2, a mountain. 3, a star. 4, the pupil of the eye. ತಾರಾಬಲ. The influence of stars. ತಾರಾಮಂಡಲ. The starry region, zodiac; a large well; a kind of fire-work.

ತಾರ 3. h. n. Tare (in trade). -ತಕ್ಕಡಿ. Fraud, deceit. -ತಕ್ಕಡಿಗ. A deceiver.

ತಾರಕ s. n. One who helps another through a difficulty; a protector. 2, a star. 3, daitya; *also* ತಾರಕಾಸುರ.

ತಾರಣ s. n. One that enables to cross; crossing. 2, the 18th year of the cycle.

ತಾರತಮ್ಯ (*fr.* ತರ more, and ತಮ most) s. n. Gradation; discrimination.

ತಾರಯಿಸು, ತಾರವಿಸು f. v. t. To sing in soprano; to exercise the voice before singing.

ತಾರಸಿ h. n. Work done with bricks and gârĕ.

ತಾರಿ. = ತಾರೆ 2, q. v.

ತಾರೀಖು, ತಾರೀಕು h. n. A date.

ತಾರೀಫು h. n. Praise, applause. 2, fun.

ತಾರು (ರು = ಱು) k. v. i. To become dry; to wither, wane. n. Dryness. 2, a bunch of areca-nuts. -ಗದ. A double door. -ಮಾರು. Disorder, confusion.

ತಾರುಣ್ಯ s. n. Youth, youthfulness.

ತಾರೆ 1. = ತಾರ 2, q. v. 2, Vâli's wife. 3, Bṛihaspati's wife.

ತಾರೆ 2. (ರೆ = ಱೆ) k. n. A large timber tree, the *Beleric myrobalan.*

ತಾರ್ಕಣೆ s. n. Personal observation. 2, demonstration.

ತಾರ್ಕಿಕ (*fr.* ತರ್ಕ) s. n. A sophist; a disputant.

ತಾಲ 1. (= ತಾಳ) s. n. Clapping the hands. 2, beating time in music; musical time. 3, a cymbal. 4, a short span, the palm of the hand.

ತಾಲ 2. (= ತಾಲಿ 3, ತಾಳೆ 2) s. n. The palmyra tree, *Borassus flabelliformis.* -ಪತ್ರ. A palmyra leaf. -ಮಧು. Toddy.

ತಾಲವ್ಯ (*fr.* ತಾಲು). s. a. Palatal. ತಾಲವ್ಯಾಕ್ಷರ. A palatal letter.

ತಾಲಿ 1. (= ತಾಳಿ 3) k. n. A golden neck-ornament, *as* a marriage-badge.

ತಾಲಿ 2. (*tb. of* ಸ್ಥಾಲಿ) n. A kind of metal vessel.

ತಾಲಿ 3. (= ತಾಳೆ 2) s. a. The talipot or fan-palm, *Corypha taliera.* 2, = ತಾಲ 2.

ತಾಲೀಮು h. n. Gymnastic instruction; a gymnasium; *also* -ಖಾನೆ.

ತಾಲು s. n. The palate.

ತಾಲೂಕು h. n. A talook, division of a district.

ತಾವಡ k. n. A necklace of lotus beads.

ತಾವರೆ (= ತಾಮರೆ. *tb. of* ತಾಮರಸ) n. The lotus. *Cpds.*: ಅಡಿದಾವರೆ, ಕೆಂಪು-, ನೆಲ-, ಬಿಳಿ-, ಬೆಟ್ಟ-, ಮರ-, *etc.* -ಕಂದ. Brahmâ. -ಗಡ್ಡೆ. The bulbous root of a lotus. -ಗಣ್ಣ. Vishṇu. -ಮಣಿ. A lotus seed often used as a bead.

ತಾವು 1. k. *pro.* (*pl. of* ತಾನು) They. 2, you (*honorif.*).

ತಾವು 2. (= ಠಾವು, q. v.) k. n. A place, *etc.*

ತಾವು 3. h. n. A sheet of paper.

ತಾಸೀಲು. = ತಹಸೀಲು, *q. v.*

ತಾಸು h. *n.* An hour. -ಬಡಿ, -ಬಾರಿಸು. To strike the hour. -ಹೊತ್ತು. An hour's time.

ತಾಸೆ f. *n.* A flat drum. -ದವ. A drummer.

ತಾಳ. = ತಾಲ 1, No. 2, *etc.*, *q. v.* -ಗತಿ. A mode of beating time in music. -ಧರ. A time-keeper in a musical performance.

ತಾಳದ k. *n.* Boiled and seasoned vegetables.

ತಾಳಿ 1. k. *n.* A pile of dried cakes of cowdung.

ತಾಳಿ 2. (*tb. of* ತಾಲ 2) *n.* The palmyra tree, *Borassus flabelliformis.*

ತಾಳಿ 3. = ತಾಲಿ 1, *q. v.*

ತಾಳಿಕೆ. = ತಾಳಿಮೆ, *q. v.*

ತಾಳಿಮೆ k. *n.* Patient endurance; patience; forbearance; *also* ತಾಳ್ಮೆ.

ತಾಳಿಸು k. *v. t.* To season food. 2, to temper, sharpen.

ತಾಳು 1. k. *v. t.* To hold; to take, get; undergo. *v. i.* To suffer patiently, endure; to wait; to wear well; to bear with. *P. p.* ತಾಳಿ, ತಾಳ್ದು. ಕೋಪ-. To get angry; to suppress anger; to pardon.

ತಾಳು 2. (ಳು = ಱು) k. *n.* The bar or bolt of a door. 2, a corn-stalk. 3, the bottom.

ತಾಳುಮೆ. = ತಾಳಿಮೆ, *q. v.*

ತಾಳೆ 1. f. *n.* Tallying, agreement, *as* of accounts, *etc.* -ನೋಡು, -ಹಾಕು. To compare together. -ಬೀಳು. To agree with, tally.

ತಾಳೆ 2. = ತಾಲ 2, *q. v.* -ಮರ. = ತಾಳಿ 2. -ಯೋಲೆ, -ವಾಲೆ, -ವೋಲೆ. A hollow coil of palm leaf worn by married women into the lobe of their ears.

ತಾಳೆ 3. (ಳೆ = ಱೆ) k. *n.* The fragrant screwpine, *Pandanus odoratissimus.*

ತಾಳ್ಕೆ. = ತಾಳಿಮೆ, *etc.*, *q. v.*

ತಾಳ್ವಾರಿ (*fr.* ತಾಳು 2) k. *n.* The bottom of a tree or hill.

ತಿಕಡಿ, ತಿಕ್ಕಡಿ f. *n.* A mason's level; an instrument used in spinning thread.

ತಿಕ್ಕಲು k. *n.* Confused mind (*cf.* ದಿಗಿಲು). 2, stuttering, stammering. ತಿಕ್ಕಲಾಟ. Confused behaviour. -ತಿಕ್ಕಲಾಗಿ ಮಾತಾಡು. To stutter.

ತಿಕ್ಕು k. *v. t.* To rub, scour; to wipe. 2, to treat harshly, annoy. ತಿಕ್ಕ್ಯಾಟ, ತಿಕ್ಕಾಟ. Rubbing, scouring; annoying.

ತಿಕ್ತ s. *a.* Sharp; bitter. *n.* Pungency; bitterness. -ಕ. Bitter; the plant *Trichosanthes dioeca.*

ತಿಗಟು, ತಿಗಟೆ, ತಿಗಡು, ತಿಗುಡು k. *n.* Rind, bark.

ತಿಗಡಿ h. *n.* Fraud. -ಬಿಗಡಿ. *dpl.*

ತಿಗಡೆ (*tb. of* ತ್ರಿಪುಟಿ) *n.* Indian jalap. -ಬಳ್ಳಿ. Its creeper, *Ipomoea turpethum.*

ತಿಗಳ, ತಿಗುಳ k. *n.* A Tamil man, *esp.* an emigrant; *f.* -ಗಿತ್ತಿ, ತಿಗಳತಿ.

ತಿಗುರಿ k. *n.* A potter's wheel.

ತಿಗುರು (*cf.* ತಿಕ್ಕು) a. k. *v. t.* To rub; to annoy. *n.* An unguent, perfume.

ತಿಗ್ರಾಮುಗ್ರಾ k. *ad.* In a very rough manner.

ತಿಂಗಳು k. *n.* The moon; a month. ತಿಂಗಳವರೆ. A kind of avarĕ bearing every month. -ಬೆಳಕು. Moonlight.

ತಿಟ್ಟು k. *n.* Rising ground, hillock. 2, abuse. *v. t.* To abuse, scold.

ತಿಣಕು, ತಿಣುಕು k. *v. i.* To strain. 2, to undergo trouble. *v. t.* To press, to make violent efforts.

ತಿಂಡಿ k. *n.* Food. 2, itch. -ಕೋರ, -ಬಾಕ, -ಹೋಕ, -ಹೋತ. A glutton; *f.* -ಗಾತಿ. -ಇಡು, -ಹಾಕು. To set food before one.

ತಿಣ್ಣ a. k. *n.* Thickness; greatness; weight; excess.

ತಿತಿಕ್ಷೆ s. *n.* Forbearance, patience, resignation.

ತಿತ್ತಿ (= ತಿದಿ. *tb. of* ದೃತಿ) *n.* A leather bag. 2, bellows.

ತಿತ್ತಿರಿ s. *n.* The francoline partridge.

ತಿಥಿ s. *n.* A lunar day. 2, an annual ceremony performed by Brâhmaṇas for their deceased ancestors.

ತಿದಿ (= ತಿತ್ತಿ. *tb. of* ದೃತಿ) *n.* A pair of bellows. -ಊದು. To blow bellows.

ತಿದ್ದು k. *v. t.* To make straight; to correct, rectify, mend; to improve; to reform; to train; to break. 2, to settle a debt. *n.* Correction, *etc.* -ಪಡಿ, -ಪಾಟ, -ಪಾಟು. A corrected state, improvement. ತಿದ್ದಿದ. Corrected; trained, *as*: -ಕುದುರೆ, -ಎತ್ತು, -ಮನೆ. ತಿದ್ದಿಸು. To cause to correct, train, *etc.*

ತಿನಸ, ತಿನಸು 1, ತಿನಿಸು k. *n.* Food. -ಗೂಳಿ. A glutton.

ತಿನಸು 2. k. *n.* Irritation in the skin, itching; the itch; irritability.

ತಿನಸು 3, ತಿನಿಸು 2, ತಿನ್ನಿಸು (*cf.* ತಿನ್ನು) k. *v. t.* To make eat, feed.

ತಿನು. = ತಿನ್ನು, *q. v.* *P. p.* ತಿಂದು.

ತಿಂತಿಣಿ k. *n.* A crowd, multitude; a row. -ಸು. To be crowded.

ತಿಂದು. *P. p. of* ತಿನ್ನು.

ತಿನ್ನಾಳಿ k. *n.* A glutton, gourmand.

ತಿನ್ನು k. *v. t.* To eat, *as* things requiring biting. 2, to suffer or undergo, *as* blows, *etc.* 3, to take, *as* bribes. *P. p.* ತಿಂದು; *part. neg.* ತಿನ್ನದೆ; *rel. part.* ತಿನ್ನುವ, ತಿಂದ, ತಿಂಬ; *3rd pers. neut. sing. imp.* ತಿಂತು.

ತಿಪ್ಪಲಿ k. *n.* *Piper longum.*

ತಿಪ್ಪೆ (=ತಿಟ್ಟು, *q. v.*) k. *n.* A heap, hillock; a pile; a dung-hill. -ಕುಣಿ, -ಹಳ್ಳ. A dung-hole.

ತಿಬ್ಬಳಿ (= ತಿಳವಳಿಕೆ) k. *n.* Understanding, knowledge; sense.

ತಿಬ್ಬಿ h. *n.* A manner of stitching.

ತಿಬ್ಬು k. *n.* The string of a bow.

ತಿಮರ, ತಿಮರು, ತಿಮುರು k. *n.* Irritation in the skin, itching.

ತಿಮಿ 1. = ತಿವಿ, *q. v.*

ತಿಮಿ 2, ತಿಮಿಂಗಿಲ s. *n.* A large fabulous fish.

ತಿಮಿರ s. *n.* Darkness; dimness of the eyes. 2, ignorance. 3, sorrow. 4, Râhu. -ರಿಪು, -ವೈರಿ. The sun.

ತಿಮಿರು k. *v. t.* To rub and clean the skin.

ತಿಂಬು (= ತಿನ್ನು, *q. v.*) k. *In the pres. and fut., as:* ತಿಂಬುತ್ತದೆ, ತಿಂಬೋಣ, *etc.* -ವಿಕೆ. Eating.

ತಿರಕ. = ತಿರುಕ, *q. v.*

ತಿರಗಣಿ (= ತಿರುಗಣಿ, ತಿರುಗುಣಿ) k. *n.* Turning; a wheel for raising water; a windlass, roller; a screw.

ತಿರಗು. = ತಿರಿಗು, ತಿರುಗು, *q. v.*

ತಿರಪ, ತಿರಪೆ. = ತಿರುಪೆ, *q. v.*

ತಿರಸ್ಕರಿಸು s. *v. t.* To put aside, disrespect, disdain, scorn.

ತಿರಸ್ಕಾರ s. *n.* Setting aside; disregard, disdain, reproach, abuse.

ತಿರಳು (=ತಿರುಳು, ತಿಳಲು, *q. v.*) k. *n.* Pith, core; pulp; kernel; essence.

ತಿರಿ k. *v. i.* To turn round; to wander about. 2, to beg alms. ತಿರಿದುಣ್ಣು, ತಿರಿದುಂಬು. To live by alms.

ತಿರಿಗೆ k. *ad.* Again, once more. ತಿರಿ-. Again and again.

ತಿರಿಗಿಸು (= ತಿರಗಿಸು) k. *v. t.* To turn; to twist.

ತಿರಿಗು (= ತಿರುಗು, *q. v.*) k. *v. i.* To go round; to turn; to roll; to go back; to change or shift, *as* the wind; to cease, *as* a disease; to wander or ramble about. ತಿರಿಗಾಟ. Wandering about; *also* ತಿರಿಗಾಡುವಿಕೆ. ತಿರಿಗಾಡು. To walk or wander about. ತಿರಿಗಿಕೊಳ್ಳು. To turn round. ತಿರಿಗಿ ಬರು. To return. ತಿರಿಗಿ ಬೀಳು. To turn round and fall upon, to affront; to revolt. ತಿರಿಗಿ ಮಾತಾಡು. To contradict.

ತಿರಿಚು k. *v. t.* To twist, *as* a string, *etc.*, to wring off, *as* the neck of a bird.

ತಿರು 1. k. *n.* Turning; a bow-string. 2, (= ತಿರಪ, *etc.*) begging. -ಚೋಳಿ. A beggar; a mendicant's bowl. -ಮುರು. Turnings and windings; reverse order; deceit.

ತಿರು 2. (*tb. of* ಶ್ರೀ) *a.* Holy, sacred. -ಕೂಳು. Holy, *i. e.* sacrificial food. -ಚೂರ್ಣ. Coloured powders used for the sectarian mark by votaries of Vishṇu. -ಪತಿ. The town Tirupati in the Arcot district. -ಮಣ್ಣು. Sacred clay to make sectarian marks to the right and left of the forehead. -ಪರ್ವತ, -ಮಲೆ. The sacred hill with the Vaishṇava fane at Tirupati. -ಮಾಳಿಗೆ. A guru's house. -ಮುಡಿ. A holy tuft of hair at the back of the head. -ವಾಂಕೋಡು. Travancore.

ತಿರು 3. = ತೆರು, q. v.

ತಿರುಕ (= ತಿರಕ) k. n. A wanderer; a beggar.

ತಿರುಗಣೆ, ತಿರುಗುಣೆ. = ತಿರಗಣೆ, q. v.

ತಿರುಗು. = ತಿರಿಗು, q. v.

ತಿರುಪು k. n. A screw. 2, changing. ತಿರುಪಿನ ಓಲೆ. A gold ear-ornament with a screw. -ಹೂ, ತಿರುಪಿನ ಹೂ. A head-ornament with a screw.

ತಿರುಪೆ (= ತಿರಪ) k. n. Wandering about (for alms); begging; alms. -ಎತ್ತು, -ಬೇಡು. To beg.

ತಿರುವು k. v. t. To turn, as the head, key, screw, stone in a mortar. n. Turning; a bow-string.

ತಿರುಹು. = ತಿರುವು, q. v.

ತಿರುಳು. = ತಿರಳು, q. v.

ತಿರೋಹಿತ s. a. Covered, hidden, lost.

ತಿರ್ಯಗ್ s. a. Going horizontally. n. An amphibious animal; a bird. -ಪುಂಡ್ರ. A horizontal sectarial line on the forehead of a Śaiva. -ಜಂತು, -ಜೀವ. An animal. -ಯೋನಿ. The animal creation. -ಲೋಕ. The earth.

ತೀರ್ವೆ f. n. Assessment, duty, tax. -ದಾರ. A person paying assessment.

ತಿಲ s. n. The *Sesamum* plant and its seed. -ಘಾತಕ. An oilman.

ತಿಲಕ s. n. A freckle. 2, a sectarian or ornamental mark made on the forehead with coloured earth, *etc.*

ತಿಲೋನಿ s. n. A strong smelling annual herb, *Gynandropsis pentaphylla*.

ತಿಲ್ಲಾನ k. n. A series of sounds used in humming a tune.

ತಿವಿ (= ತಿಮಿ 1.) k. v. t. To strike with the fist, box. 2, to pierce, stab. n. Piercing, *etc.*; *also* -ತ. ತಿವಿಸು. To cause to strike.

ತಿಷ್ಠೆ s. n. Staying, standing. -ಮಾಡು. To stay, lodge.

ತಿಳ, ತಿಳು (= ತಿಳಿದು, ತಿಳಿದು). *P. p. of* ತಿಳಿ, *in* ತಿಳಕೊಳ್ಳು, ತಿಳುಕೊಳ್ಳು.

ತಿಳಲು. = ತಿರಳು, q. v.

ತಿಳಿ k. v. i. To become clear, pure. 2, to be plain or known. v. t. To know, understand, perceive, learn; to feel as pain. ನನಗೆ ತಿಳಿಯುತ್ತದೆ. I understand, know, *etc.*; ನನಗೆ ತಿಳಿಯಿತು. I understood, *etc.* -ಯಗೊಡು. To let know. -ಯಪಡಿಸು. To make known. -ಯಬರು. = ತಿಳಿ, No. 2. -ಯುವಿಕೆ, -ವಳಿಕೆ, -ವಿಕೆ, ತಿಳುವಳಿಕೆ, ತಿಳುವಿಕೆ. Knowledge; understanding, intelligence. -ಹೇಳು, -ಯ ಮಾಡು. = -ಸು, q. v.

ತಿಳಿ 2. k. n. Clearness, pureness. 2, knowledge, understanding; *also* -ವು. 3, clear substances, *as* conjee water, *etc.* -ಗೇಡಿ. A stupid person. -ಗೇಡಿತನ. Ignorance, stupidity. -ನಿದ್ರೆ. A light sleep. *Other cpds.*: -ನೀರು, -ಬಣ್ಣ, -ರಸ, -ಸುಣ್ಣ, *etc.*

ತಿಳಿಸು k. v. t. To make clear or known; to let know; to inform.

ತಿಳುಹು, ತಿಳುಹಿಸು k. v. t. To make known, to let know.

ತೀ k. n. Fire. v. t. To burn.

ತೀಕ್ಷ್ಣ s. a. Sharp; hot, pungent, fiery; harsh; zealous; energetic. n. Sharpness; heat; haste. 2, poison. -ಬುದ್ಧಿ. A keen mind.

ತೀಟೆ k. n. Itching; irritation; an itching desire, lust, lasciviousness. -ಕೆರೆ. To scratch an irritation in the skin. -ಜಗಳ. Useless quarrel. -ದಾಯಿ. A blabber. -ಹತ್ತು, -ಹಿಡಿ. To be affected with the itch.

ತೀಂಡು k. v. t. To press, squeeze, rub; to scour; to smear on, *as* unguents on the body; to sharpen; to rub out, *as* insects; to strike with the palm of the hand. v. i. To touch, *as* air. 2, to blow, *as* the wind.

ತೀನಿ k. n. Food; feeding. ತೀನಾಳಿ. A glutton.

ತೀರ 1. s. n. A shore, bank; margin, brink, edge.

ತೀರ 2, ತೀರಾ (fr. ತೀರು 1) k. ad. Fully, quite, very.

ತೀರಿಕೆ (= ತೀರ್ಕೆ) k. n. Conclusion, end; decision. 2, leisure. -ಮಾಡು. To finish, complete. ನ್ಯಾಯ-. The judgment.

ತೀರು 1. k. v. i. To be finished, come to an end; to end, cease; to be done, accomplished. 2, to cease to live, die. 3, to be paid, liquidated, settled. -ವಿಕೆ. End, termination. ತೀರಿಸು. To finish; to accomplish, carry out, execute; to fulfill, to settle, decide; to clear off, liquidate, pay, as: ಉಪಕಾರ-, ಕಾಂಕ್ಷೆ-, ದಾವೃ-, ಬಡ್ಡಿ-, ಮುಯ್ಯಕ್ಕೆ ಮುಯ್ಯ-, ನ್ಯಾಯ-, ನೀರಡಿಕೆ-, ವ್ಯಾಜ್ಯ-, ಸಾಲ-, ಸಿಟ್ಟು-, ಹಗೆ-. etc. ತೀರಿಸಿಬಿಡು, ತೀರಿಸಿ ಹಾಕು. To finish off. ತೀರಿತು. Ended. ತೀರದು. Can't be finished.

ತೀರು 2. k. n. Conclusion. 2, settlement. 3, finish; beauty; manner, mode; peculiar habit; also ತೀರ. -ಗಡೆ. End, completion. -ವಡಿ, -ಪಾಟು. Leisure, opportunity. -ಮಾನ. Conclusion; settlement, decision, sentence. -ಮಾನಿಸು. To finish, determine, decide.

ತೀರುವೆ k. n. Dues, fees, customs, tax.

ತೀರ್ಚು. = ತೀರಿಸು, q. v.

ತೀರ್ಥ s. n. A passage, ford. 2, a holy place in the vicinity of streams. 3, sacred water. 4, a sacred object; a school of philosophy. 5, a worthy person. 6, an ascetic. -ಕರ. A Jina. -ಪಾದ, -ರೂಪ. A title for a venerable man. -ಯಾತ್ರೆ. A pilgrimage. -ಶ್ರಾದ್ಧ. Funeral ceremonies observed at a place of pilgrimage.

ತೀರ್ಪು (fr. ತೀರು) k. n. Settlement, decision, sentence. -ಆಗು. To be decided.

ತೀರ್ವಿಕೆ (= ತೀರಿಕೆ) k. n. Ending, end.

ತೀರ್ವೆ. = ತೀರುವೆ, q. v.

ತೀವು a. k. v. i. To become full; to abound. v. t. To fill.

ತೀವ್ರ s. a. Strong, severe; fierce; sharp; rash, quick; excessive, much. -ಗೊಳ್ಳು, -ಪಡು. To be quick. -ತೆ, -ತ್ವ. Sharpness; severity; -ಬುದ್ಧಿ. A keen mind.

ತುಕಡಿ, ತುಕ್ಕಡಿ h. n. A bit; a bit of bread; detachment. 2, a district, province. -ದಾರ. The headman of a district.

ತುಕ್ಕು 1. a. k. v. i. To crowd, throng.

ತುಕ್ಕು 2. k. n. Rust of iron; canker.

ತುಂಗ 1. s. a. High, lofty, prominent, chief. -ಭದ್ರೆ. The river Tungabhadre in the Mysore territory.

ತುಂಗ 2, ತುಂಗೆ k. n. A species of grass. -ಗಡ್ಡೆ, -ಮುಸ್ತೆ. The bulb of *Cyperus rotundus*. -ಹುಲ್ಲು. The *Cyperus* grass.

ತುಚ್ಛ s. a. Trifling; contemptible; low, mean. ತುಚ್ಛೀಕಾರ. Contempt. -ತುಚ್ಛೀಕರಿಸು. To contemn, disdain.

ತುಟಾರ f. n. Inconsideration, indiscretion. ತುಟಾರಿಸು. To be indiscreet.

ತುಟಿ k. n. The lip. -ಜಾರಿದ ಮುತ್ತು. A slip of the tongue. ಗಡಸು-, ಹಂದಿ-, ದೊಡ್ಡ-. A large lip. -ಸೇವೆ. Lip-service, hypocrisy.

ತುಟ್ಟಿ (tb. of ತ್ರುಟಿ?) n. Dearness. a. Dear. ad. Dearly; at a high rate. -ಧಾರಣೆ. A high price. -ಸು. To decrease in, strength or power.

ತುಡಗ. = ತುಡುಗ, q. v.

ತುಡು (= ತೊಡು, q. v.) v. t. To join, put on as clothes; to cover.

ತುಡುಕು a. k. v. t. To grasp quickly, seize, snatch. n. Grasping quickly. -ಉಳಿ. A grasping thief; cf. ಕೈಡುಡುಕು.

ತುಡುಗ (= ತುಡಗ) k. n. A thief, rascal; f. ತುಡುಗಿ. -ಆವು, -ದನ. A thievish cow. -ತನ. Theft, thievishness. -ಬುದ್ಧಿ. A wicked mind.

ತುಡುಗು k. n. Theft, stealth, rascality; a stolen thing. -ಮಾಡು. To steal.

ತುಡುಪು k. n. An oar; a flat wooden spoon.

ತುಣಕ, ತುಣುಕು 1, ತುಣುಕು 1. a. k. n. A fragment, piece, bit. ಅರಿವೆ-, ರೊಟ್ಟಿ-, *etc.*

ತುಣುಕು 2, ತುಣುಕು 2. (= ತುಳಕು, ತುಳುಕು, *etc.*) k. v. i. To shake or be agitated, *as* water.

ತುಣಿ. = ತುಳಿ, *q. v.*

ತುಂಟ k. n. A mischievous, wicked, insolent, lewd man, rogue, *etc.*; *f.* ತುಂಟಿ. -ಕುದುರೆ. A wicked horse. -ಹುಡುಗ. A wicked boy. -ಕೆಲಸ. A mischievous business. -ತನ, ತುಂಟಾಟ. Wickedness, mischief, impudence; *also* ತುಂಟು. -ಬುಂಟ. *reit.*

ತುಂಡ s. n. A beak; a snout; the point of an instrument.

ತುಂಡಿ s. n. A beak; the mouth; the navel.

ತುಂಡಿಸು k. v. t. To cut or break into pieces, make piece-meal, *etc.*

ತುಂಡು k. n. A fragment, piece; a bit, a little. ತುಂಡಂಗಿ. A small jacket; a cockroach. -ಕಾಲು. A maimed leg. -ತುಂಡು. *rep.* -ದೊರೆ, -ಪಾಳೆಗಾರ. A petty chieftain. -ಮಾಡು. To cut into pieces. -ಬಟ್ಟೆ. A rag. -ತುಂಡಾಗಿ ಬೀಳು. To fall to pieces. -ತನ. = ತುಂಟತನ.

ತುತೂರಿ, ತುತ್ತೂರಿ f. n. A long trumpet. -ಊದು. To blow the trumpet.

ತುತ್ತ = ತುದಿ, *q. v.* -ತುದಿ. The very point.

ತುತ್ತ (*tb. of* ತುತ್ಥ) n. Blue vitriol, sulphate of copper.

ತುತ್ತು k. n. A mouthful of food; a morsel; food. *v. t.* To take by mouthfuls.

ತುದಾ (= ಸುದಾ?) s. *ad.* Or, perhaps, however.

ತುದಿ k. n. An extremity, end, point, top, tip. *Cpds.:* ಮೂಗಿನ-, ಮೊಲೆಯ-, ಬೆಟ್ಟದ-, ಸುಂಡಿಲ-, ಬಿಲ್ಲ-, ಕೆಲಸದ-, ಭುಜದ-, *etc.* -ಕಾಲ್. Tiptoe. -ಕುಂಡಿ. The hip, loins. -ಗಯ್ದು. To be hazardous. -ಗುಂಡು. A summit. -ಗೆ ಬರು. To be nearly ready. -ನಾಲಿಗೆ. The tip of the tongue. -ಬಾಲ. The end of a tail. -ಮುಟ್ಟ. To the end, completely. -ಮೂಗು. The tip of the nose. -ಮೊದಲು. The foremost point; the very beginning; beginning and end.

ತುಂತುರು (ರು=ಱು) k. n. Drizzling; spray; a drop. -ಮಳೆ. A fine, drizzling rain. -ಮಯ್ಯು. Vapour, fog. -ಹನಿ. Spray.

ತುಂದ s. n. The belly. ತುಂದಿ. Gorbellied; corpulent; *also* ತುಂದಿಕ, ತುಂದಿಲ.

ತುನ್ನ s. *a.* Hit, stung, hurt. -ವಾಯ. A tailor.

ತುಪರಿಬಳ್ಳಿ k. n. A creeping plant much cultivated, *Luffa aegyptiaca.*

ತುಪಾಕಿ h. n. A musket, matchlock, gun. -ಕುಂದ, -ಕಟ್ಟಿಗೆ. A gun-stock. -ಚಾಪು. A gun-lock. -ತೂತು. The touch-hole of a gun. -ಚಾಪಿನ ಕೀಲು. The trigger. -ಜಡಿ. To load a gun. -ಹಚ್ಚು, -ಹಾರಿಸು, -ಹೊಡೆ. To fire a gun. -ಚಾವಿಗೆ. The match of a matchlock.

ತುಪಾನು h. n. A storm, typhoon; slander, calumny. -ಹಾಕು, -ಹೊರಿಸು. To accuse falsely.

ತುಪ್ಪ k. n. Clarified butter, ghee. *Cpds.:* ಹೊಸ-, ಕಾಸಿದ-, ಕರಗಿಸಿದ-, ಜೇನ-, *etc.* -ಗೆಣಸು. A species of sweet potato. -ಹೀರೆ, ತುಪ್ಪೀರೆ. A kind of Luffa.

ತುಪ್ಪಟ, ತುಪ್ಪಳ k. n. A feather; the soft plumage or down of birds; the soft hair of rabbits, *etc.*

ತುಬಾಕಿ. = ತುಪಾಕಿ, *q. v.*

ತುಬ್ಬು k. v. t. To point out a thief. *v. i.* To be found out. *n.* Detection. -ಮಾಡು. To detect, find out.

ತುಮಕಿ k. n. The wild mangosteen tree, *Diospyros embryopteris; also* ತುಮರಿ.

ತುಮುಲ s. n. Uproar, tumult.

ತುಂಬ. = ತುಂಬಾ, *q. v.* s. ತುಂಬು.

ತುಂಬಿ 1. (= ದುಂಬಿ) k. n. A large black bee. *Cpds.:* ಎಳೆ-, ಕೆಂಪು-, ಮಾಲೆ-, *etc.*

ತುಂಬಿ 2. f. n. A kind of long gourd, *Lagenaria vulgaris.*

ತುಂಬಿ 3. = ತುಂಬೆ, *q. v.*

ತುಂಬು 1. k. v. i. To become full, be filled up; to abound; to get plump.

2, to possess, *as* a demon. *v. t.* To fill. *n.* Becoming full, *etc.* -ಯೌವನ. Blooming youth. ತುಂಬ, ತುಂಬಾ. Fully, all over, much. ತುಂಬಿಕೆ. Repletion, *etc.* ತುಂಬಿಸು. To fill; to cause to fill.

ತುಂಬು 2. k. *n.* The foot-stalk of a leaf, flower or fruit, stalk.

ತುಂಬು 3. (= ತೂಬು) a. k. *n.* A tube: the wheel-nave through which the axle passes. 2, an outlet, sluice; *also* ತೂಬು.

ತುಂಬುರ, ತುಂಬುರು 1. s. *n.* N. of a Gandharva.

ತುಂಬುರು 2. k. *n.* The wild mangosteen, *Diospyros embryopteris.*

ತುಂಬೆ k. *n.* The herb *Phlomis indica.* 2, the very common weed *Leucas linifolia.*

ತುಯ್ಯು k. *v. t.* To pull, draw, stretch. -ತ. Pulling.

ತುಯ್ಯಾಲು k. *n.* A dish of rice, milk and sugar.

ತುರ s. *a.* Quick, swift.

ತುರಕ. = ತುರುಕ, *q. v.*

ತುರಗ s. *a.* Going quickly. *n.* A horse.

ತುರಂಗ 1. = ತುರಗ, *q. v.* -ವಕ್ತ್ರ, -ವದನ. Horse-faced: a Kinnara.

ತುರಂಗ 2. f. *n.* A prison.

ತುರಂಗಿ s. *n.* A horseman, rider; a groom.

ತುರಚೆಗಿಡ (ರ = ಱ) k. *n.* An annual plant, stinging like nettles, cowhage.

ತುರಂಜಿ h. *n.* A tree so called. *a.* Excellent.

ತುರತ (*tb. of* ತ್ವರಿತ) *n.* Haste, urgency. *ad.* Quickly, soon.

ತುರಾಯ, ತುರಾಯಿ h. *n.* An ornament for the turban; a plume, crest; a tufted head of certain flowers. -ಮರ. A cypress.

ತುರಿ 1. (ರಿ = ಱಿ) k. *n.* Itching, scratching; the itch; lust. -ಕಜ್ಜಿ, -ಗಜ್ಜಿ. Scab, herpes. -ಕೆ. Itching, scratching. -ಕೆಗಿಡ. The Nilgiri nettle, *Urtica heterophylla.* -ಚು, -ಸು. To scratch, itch.

ತುರಿ 2. k. *n.* Grating. 2, scraping.

ತುರಿತ. = ತುರತ, *q. v.*

ತುರು (ರು = ಱು) a. k. *n.* A cow; kine. -ಪಳ್ಳಿ, -ಹಟ್ಟಿ. A cowpen. -ಮಂದೆ, -ಹಿಂಡು. A herd of kine. -ಗಾರ, -ವಳ. A cowherd; *f.* -ಗಾತಿ, -ವಳ್ತಿ.

ತುರುಕ (= ತುರಕ) h. *n.* A Turk; a Musulman. *a.* Turkish.

ತುರುಕು (ರು = ಱು) k. *v. t.* To force into, cram, stuff; *also* ತುರುಚು.

ತುರುಗ (ರು = ಱು) a. k. *n.* A throng, crowd; *also* ತುರುಗಲ್.

ತುರುಗು (ರು = ಱು) a. k. *v. i.* To be crammed, crowded, amassed. *n.* A throng, crowd.

ತುರುಪು e. *n.* A "troop"; a trump or winning card.

ತುರುಬು (ರು = ಱು) k. *v. t.* To tuck in, *as* flowers in the hair, *also* ತುರುಕು, *q. v.* *n.* The bundle of hair of the head.

ತುರುವು k. *v. t.* To scrape, bore, hollow, *as* fruits or kernel out of its shell. *n.* Grating, scraping.

ತುರುವೆ (ರು = ಱು) k. *n.* The country mallow, *Sida indica.*

ತುರುಷ್ಕ s. *n.* A Mahomedan; a foreigner. 2, olibanum, Indian incense.

ತುರುಸು. = ತುರಿಸು, *q. v.*

ತುರ್ತ. = ತುರತ, *q. v.*

ತುಲನ s. *n.* Lifting, raising; weighing

ತುಲಸಿ (= ತುಳಸಿ) s. *n.* A small shrub, the holy basil, *Ocymum sanctum.* -ಕಟ್ಟೆ. A square pedestal in which the holy basil is planted. -ಪೂಜೆ. Worship of the basil shrub. -ಮಾಲೆ. A garland of the basil shoots.

ತುಲೆ, ತುಲಾ (= ತೊಲೆ, ತೋಲ) s. *n.* A balance, scales. 2, weight. 3, the sign of the zodiac *Libra.* 4, equality. 5, the beam of a balance. 6, a rupee's weight. ತುಲಾಭಾರ. The weight of gold, jewels, *etc.*, against one's person and distributed to Brâhmaṇas.

ತುವರಿ. = ತೊಗರಿ, *q. v.*

ತುವಾಲ e. *n.* A towel.

ತುಷ s. *n.* The husk of grain.

ತುಷಾರ s. *a.* Cold, frigid, dewy. *n.* Cold, frost, dew.

ತುಷ್ಟ s. *a.* Satisfied, contented, glad, *etc.*

ತುಷ್ಟಿ s. *n.* Satisfaction; pleasure. -ಪಡಿಸು. To satisfy, gratify, appease. -ಪಡು. To be satisfied or contented.

ತುಸ, ತುಸು k. *n.* A little. -ತುಸ. *rep.*

ತುಹಿನ s. *n.* Mist, dew; cold. 2, moonlight. 3, camphor. -ಗಿರಿ. The Himâlaya.

ತುಳಕು, ತುಳುಕು (= ತುಣುಕು) k. *v. i.* To be agitated, to shake, as water, *etc.*; to be scattered in drops; to run over; *also* ತುಳಕಾಡು.

ತುಳಸಿ. = ತುಲಸಿ, *q. v.*

ತುಳಿ (ಳ = ೞ) k. *v. t.* To tread on, trample; to crush to pieces with the feet. 2, to annoy, harass. *v. i.* To be trodden down; to be abject. *P. ps.* ತುಳಿದು, ತುಳಿದು. *n.* Treading, trampling, *etc.*; *also* ತುಳಿದಾಟ.- ಗೆಂಡ. Walking on fire. ತುಳಿತ. Treading, *etc.*

ತುಳಿಲ್ (ಳ = ೞ) a. k. *n.* A salutation, obeisance. 2, valour. 3, work, servitude. ತುಳಿಲಾಳು. A valorous man. ತುಳಿಲ್ಗೊಳ್. To be valorous; to be a servant.

ತುಳು k. *n.* Tuḷu, N. of a country on the western coast of South-India. -ವ. Relating to Tuḷu; a Tuḷu man.

ತುಳುಕು. = ತುಳಕು, *q. v.*

ತುಳ್ಳು a. k. *v. i.* To roll; to jump; *also* ತುಳ್ಳಾಡು.

ತೂ k. *int. An imitative sound of spitting or of flouting.* -ತೂ. *Flouting with* fie! hoot! -ತೂ ಎನ್ನು. To say fie.

ತೂಕ (= ತೂಗು 2) k. *n.* Weight; worth; the weight of gold varaha. -ದ ಕಲ್ಲು. The measure of weight. -ಮಾಡು, -ಹಾಕು. To weigh. -ಮಾಡಿಸು. To get weighed.

ತೂಕು k. *n.* Weight. 2, nodding. ತೂಕಡಿಕೆ. Drowsiness, lassitude. ತೂಕಡಿಸು. To doze.

ತೂಗು 1. k. *v. t.* To weigh. 2, to swing or rock, *as* a cradle; to wag, *as* the head; to hang up. ತೂಗಾಡು. To hang down, swing; to rock, *as* a cradle; to waddle. ತೂಗಿ ನೋಡು. To weigh and examine. ತೂಗಿಸು. To cause to weigh, rock, *etc.*

ತೂಗು 2. (= ತೂಕ, ತೂಕು) k. *n.* Weighing; swinging, *etc.* ತೂಗಡಿಸು. = ತೂಕಡಿಸು. -ಕೋಲು. A kind of balance. -ದೀವಿಗೆ. A hanging lamp. -ಮಂಚ. A swinging cot. -ಮಣೆ. A swing. -ಮರ. A gallows. -ತಲೆ. A nodding head.

ತೂತು k. *n.* A hole. ತೂತಾಗು. To get a hole. -ಕೆಡವು. To pierce a hole through. -ಕೊರೆ, -ತೆಗೆ, -ಮಾಡು. To bore a hole. -ಬೀಳು. To become holed, be spoiled.

ತೂಪರೆ, ತೂಬರೆ k. *n.* The wild mangosteen tree.

ತೂಬು k. *n.* The nave of a wheel. 2, the sluice of a tank. 3, the hole of an axe, hoe, *etc.*, into which the handle goes. -ಮುಚ್ಚು. To shut up a flood-gate. -ತೆರೆ. To open it.

ತೂರು 1. (ರು = ಱು) k. *v. t.* To winnow. *v. i.* To be shaken off. 2, to run, bolt away. *n.* Winnowing.

ತೂರು 2. (ರು = ಱು) k. *v. i.* To enter; to go through a hole, *as* a thread, *etc.*; to penetrate. 2, to drizzle. *n.* Drizzling. 2, penetrating.

ತೂರ್ಣ s. *a.* Quick, fleet. *n.* Rapidity, quickness.

ತೂರ್ಯ s. *n.* A musical instrument. 2, a bugle.

ತೂಲ s. *n.* Cotton; the down of birds.

ತೂಳು a. k. *v. t.* To go off; to recoil. 2, to rush forward; to chase. 3, to originate. *n.* Attacking.

ತೃಣ s. n. Any gramineous plant; grass; a reed; straw. -ಕುಟಿ. A thatched hut. -ಗ್ರಾಹಿ. Amber. -ಧ್ವಜ. A bamboo. -ಪ್ರಾಯ. Worth a straw, worthless. -ರಾಜ. The palmyra tree; the cocoanut tree; bamboo; sugarcane.

ತೃತೀಯ s. n. The third. 2, chunam (being the third ingredient of tâmbûla). -ವಿಭಕ್ತಿ. The instrumental case. ತೃತೀಯೆ. The 3rd day of a lunar fortnight.

ತೃಪ್ತ s. a. Satisfied, contented, pleased.

ತೃಪ್ತಿ s. n. Satisfaction, contentment; pleasure; gratification. -ಗೊಳ್ಳು, -ಪಡು. To get satisfied, pleased. -ಪಡಿಸು, -ಮಾಡು. To satisfy, please.

ತೃಷಿತ, ತೃಷ್ಣಕ s. a. Thirsty.

ತೃಷೆ s. n. Thirst. 2, desire.

ತೆಕ್ಕನೆ a. k. ad. Greatly, very much.

ತೆಕ್ಕೆ, ತೆಕ್ಕೆ k. n. An embrace. 2, a coil. -ಬೀಳು. To clasp in the arms. -ಹಾಕು. To embrace.

ತೆಗದು, ತೆಗೆದು k. P. p. of ತೆಗಿ, ತೆಗೆ. ತೆಗದುಕೊಳ್ಳು. To take, receive. -ಹಾಕು. To put away, remove, dismiss.

ತೆಗಸು. = ತೆಗಿಸು, q. v.

ತೆಗಳ್ (ಳ್ = ಱ್) a. k. v. t. To rebuke; to blame, abuse. n. Blame, abuse.

ತೆಗಿ, ತೆಗೆ k. v. t. To take; to buy; to take away, steal; to seize; to exact; to put out; to prolong, as a note in music; to obtain; to open, as a door; to undertake; to pick up, as a quarrel; to assume, as a birth; to employ, as a grammatical form; to vaccinate (ಟುಯ್ಲ್ಲ-); to draw, as a line, map, etc. (ಗೆರೆ-); to bore, as a hole; to find out, as a means; to ask about; to dig, as a channel, etc. v. i. To be taken away; to become less; to disappear. 2, to retreat, flee. P. p. ತೆಗದು, ತೆಗೆದು. ತೆಗೆದುಕೊಂಡು ಬರು. To bring. ತೆಗೆದುಕೊಂಡು ಹೋಗು. To take away. ತೆಗೆದುಹಾಕು (see s. ತೆಗದು). To throw down; to raise as a siege. ತೆಗೆಯುಗೊಡು. To allow to take. ಹಿಂದಕ್ಕೆ-, ಹಿಂದೆಗೆ. To draw back, retreat, retire. ನಾಚಿಕೆ-. To dishonour one. -ಸು, -ಯಿಸು. To cause to take, etc.

ತೆಗೆ 2. k. v. t. To grind, as sandalwood on a stone.

ತೆಂಕ, ತೆಂಕಣ k. n. The south; also ತೆಂಕಲು, -ಗಾಳಿ, ತೆಂಗಾಳಿ. South wind. -ದೇಶ, etc. -ದಿಸೆ. The southern quarter.

ತೆಂಕು k. v. i. To float, swim.

ತೆಂಗಲೆ k. n. A certain Vaishṇava mode of putting the nâma.

ತೆಂಗು k. n. The cocoanut palm, Cocos nucifera. ತೆಂಗಿನ ಕಾಯಿ. A cocoanut. ತೆಂಗಿನ ಮರ. = ತೆಂಗು. ತೆಂಗಿನ ನಾರು. The coir or fibre of the cocoanut. Other cpds.: ತೆಂಗಿನ ಎಣ್ಣೆ, ತೆಂಗಿನ ಗಡ್ಡೆ, ತೆಂಗಿನ ಗರಿ, ತೆಂಗಿನ ಬೆಲ್ಲ, etc.

ತೆಂಟು a. k. v. t. To winnow.

ತೆಂಡೆ k. n. A small bundle, as of grass, etc. -ಸುತ್ತು. To tie together, as growing sugarcanes.

ತೆತ್ತಿ. = ತತ್ತಿ, q. v.

ತೆತ್ತಿಗ a. k. n. A servant. 2, a connection, friend.

ತೆತ್ತಿಸು a. k. v. t. To bring into close connection; to insert; to pierce through.

ತೆತ್ತು 1. P. p. of ತೆರು

ತೆತ್ತು 2. k. v. t. To twist. v. i. To be twisted, connected.

ತೆನಿಸು e. n. Tennis, a play in which a ball is kept in motion (ಚೆಂಡಾಟ).

ತೆನೆ k. n. A spike, ear of corn. 2, the coping of a wall; the top of a rampart, a merlon of a fort. -ಗಜ. The Indian millet.

ತೆಪ್ಪ k. n. A float, raft. -ತೇಲು. To float a raft. -ಒತ್ತು, -ನೂಕು. To push a raft.

ತೆಪ್ಪಗೆ, ತೆಪ್ಪನೆ k. ad. At leisure, at ease; well.

ತೆಪ್ಪರಿಸು (ರಿ = ಱಿ) k. v. i. To become conscious; to start up, awake (with ಕೊಳ್ಳು); also ತೆಪ್ಪರು.

ತೆರ 1. (ರ=ಐ) a. k. n. An opening, a way, course; manner, sort. ತೆರಂ. In a manner, *etc.*

ತೆರ 2. (ರ=ಐ) = ತೆರದು, ತೆರೆದು. *P. p. of* ತೆರೆ *in* ತೆರಕೊಳ್ಳು, to open.

ತೆರ 3. (ರ=ಐ). = ತೆರವು. *q. v.*

ತೆರಗೆ. = ತೆರಿಗೆ, *q. v.*

ತೆರಟು k. *v. t.* To tuck up (a garment when passing a river); to join, unite.

ತೆರಪು (ರ=ಐ) k. *n.* An opening, a gap; an interval; room, place. 2, cessation, *as* of rain. 3, leisure. 4, opportunity. 5, the state of being empty, *as* a house, box, *etc.* -ಗೊಳ್ಳು. To occupy more place; to leave room (for others).

ತೆರವು (ರ=ಐ). = ತೆರಪು, *q. v.* 2, the price paid for a wife; *also* ತೆರ. -ಮಾಡು. To empty.

ತೆರಳು 1. a. k. *v. i.* To move, stir; to tremble, quiver; to proceed; to set out, depart. ತೆರಳ್ಕೆ. Moving; quivering; setting out.

ತೆರಳು 2. a. k. *v. t.* To join; to assemble. ತೆರಳ್ಕೆ. A mass, multitude.

ತೆರಳೆ k. *n.* A round lump. 2, sap, pith. -ಯ ಹುಳ. A silk-worm; an insect in fruits.

ತೆರಿಗೆ (ರಿ=ಐ) k. *n.* Tribute, tax; *also* ತೆರಗೆ. -ಎತ್ತು. To levy taxes. -ಕಟ್ಟು. To impose a tax. -ಕಾಗದ. A written lease. -ಕೊಡು. To pay taxes. -ಬಿಡು. To free from taxes.

ತೆರಿ. = ತೆರೆ, *q. v.*

ತೆರಿಸು (ರಿ=ಐ) k. *v. t.* To cause to open, *etc.* 2, to cause to pay, *as* taxes, *etc.*

ತೆರು (ರ=ಐ) k. *v. t.* To pay. *P. p.* ತೆತ್ತು. -ವಿಕೆ. Paying.

ತೆರೆ 1. (ರೆ=ಐ) k. *v. i.* To be uncovered; to open. *v. t.* To open; to uncover; to unfold. *P. ps.* ತೆರದು, ತೆರಿದು, ತೆರೆದು. *n.* Opening; tribute, tax.

ತೆರೆ 2. k. *n.* A wave, billow. 2, a fold; a wrinkle. 3, a curtain, screen. -ಕೊನೆ. The crest of a wave. -ತೆಗೆ. To remove a curtain. -ಬಿಡು. To let down a curtain. -ಯುಲಿ. The roar of waves. -ಬಡಿ, -ಹೊಡಿ. The waves to beat.

ತೆಲಗು, ತೆಲುಗು k. *n.* Tĕlugu; the Tĕlugu language. ತೆಲುಗ, ತೆಲುಂಗ. A Tĕlugu man; *f.* ತೆಲಗಿತಿ, ತೆಲುಗಿತಿ, ತೆಲುಂಗಿತಿ.

ತೆಲಿಗ್ರಾಮು e. *n.* A telegram, a message by wire to a distance (ತಂತಿವರ್ತಮಾನ).

ತೆಲಿಗ್ರಾಫು e. *n.* Telegraph (ತಂತಿಟಪ್ಪಾಲು).

ತೆಲಿಫೋನು e. *n.* Telephone, an apparatus for transmitting sound to a distance.

ತೆಲ್ಲಟಿ a. k. *n.* A gift, present, *esp.* to the bride and bridegroom at their marriage; *also* ತಲ್ಲಟು.

ತೆವಟು. = ತವಟು, *q. v.*

ತೆವಡೆ k. *n.* A small dam in a field. 2, = ತಂಡೆ.

ತೆವರಿ, ತೆವರು k. *n.* A hillock; a balk. *v. t.* To rub; to tease. 2, to rob; steal.

ತೆವಲು, ತೆವುಲು (=ತಿಮುರ) k. *n.* An itching desire.

ತೆವಳು k. *v. i.* To creep along.

ತೆಳು (=ತಿಳಿ 2) k. *n.* Thinness, fineness, delicateness. -ಕಾಗದ. Thin paper. -ಗನ್ನಡ. Fine or perspicuous Kannaḍa. -ನೀರು. Clear water. -ಪು, -ವು. Thinness; watery state. -ಬಟ್ಟೆ. Fine cloth. -ಬಣ್ಣ. A light colour. -ವೆಲರ್. A gentle breeze.

ತೆಳ್ಳಗೆ, ತೆಳ್ಳನೆ k. *a.* Thin; delicate, *etc.* *ad.* Thinly, *etc.* *n.* Thinness.

ತೆಳ್ಳು. = ತಳ್ಳು, *q. v.*

ತೇ. = ತೇಯು, *q. v.*

ತೇಗು 1. k. *n.* The teak tree, *Tectona grandis.*

ತೇಗು 2. k. *v. i.* To belch. *n.* A belch. -ವಿಕೆ. Belching.

ತೇಜ s. *n.* Radiance, splendour, brilliance. 2, power, might, energy. 3, majesty, glory, fame. 4, the sun; *also* ತೇಜಸ್. -ಃಪುಂಜ. A mass of lustre; a learned or virtuous man. -ಸ್ವಿ. Brilliant; powerful. ತೇಜಿ. A horse. ತೇಜೋಮಯ. Full of light, energy, *etc.* ತೇಜೋವಂತ. A bright-faced man.

ತೇಟು h. n. Genuine, pure.

ತೇಟೆ k. n. Purity, clearness, *as* of water. -ಪಡಿಸು, -ಮಾಡು. To clear up.

ತೇಪೆ (= ತ್ಯಾಪೆ) k. n. A patch.

ತೇಮ (= ತೇವ, ತ್ಯಾವ) s. n. Wetness, damp; moisture. -ನ. Moistening; a sauce.

ತೇಮಾನ k. n. Loss in assaying metals. 2, waste from want of work.

ತೇಯು (= ತೇ, *q. v.*) k. v. t. To grind or macerate in water on a slab. *P. ps.* ತೇದು, ತೇಯ್ದು.

ತೇರು 1. k. n. A chariot; an idol car. ತೇರಾಟ. An idol car-festival. -ಎಳೆ, -ಹಿಡಿ. To draw a car in procession.

ತೇರು 2. k. v. i. To reach. 2, to be successful. 3, to recover from illness, *as:* ಸುಖ-, ರೋಗ-, ಕಷ್ಟ-. -ಗಡೆ. Success, *as* in an examination.

ತೇಲು k. v. i. To be afloat, to float. 2, to slip, glide off. 3, to become loose, *as* the roots of young plants. *P. ps.* ತೇಲಿ, ತೇಲ್ದು. ತೇಲಬಿಟ್ಟು. To suspend. ತೇಲಾಡು. To float about. ತೇಲಿಸು. To make float; to open the eyes wide, stare.

ತೇಲಿ (*tb. of* ತೈಲಿ) n. An oilman.

ತೇವ, ತೇವು (*tb. of* ತೇಮ) n. Wetness, moisture.

ತೇವುಳ k. n. A disease of falling off of the hair.

ತೈನಾತಿ h. a. Stipendiary; placed at the command of; assigned.

ತೈಲ s. n. Sesamum oil; oil in general. -ಪರ್ಣ. Sandal; turpentine. -ಪಾಕ. Any article of food fried in oil. -ತಿಕ್ಕು, -ಪೂಸು, -ಹಚ್ಚು. To apply oil, anoint. ತೈಲಿಕ. An oilman.

ತೈಲಿ h. n. A bag, purse. s. = ತೇಲಿ.

ತೊಕ್ಕು k. n. Fruits pounded and mixed with salt, chillies, *etc.*

ತೊಗಟು, ತೊಗಟೆ k. n. Bark, rind, peel; a pod.

ತೊಗರಿ (*tb. of* ತುವರಿ, *q. v.*) n. The pigeon-pea.

ತೊಗರು k. n. Red colour, scarlet.

ತೊಗಲು k. n. The skin; a hide, leather; peel, *as* of an orange. ತೊಗಲುಬಾವಲಿ. The flying fox. -ಬೊಂಬೆ. A leathern puppet. -ಸುಲಿ. To flay, skin.

ತೊಗೆ k. n. A dish of boiled split pulse.

ತೊಂಗಲ್ a. k. n. A cluster; a bundle, bunch, tassel; *also* ತೊಂಗೆ.

ತೊಂಗು k. v. i. To hang down, swing. 2, to stoop (*as in* ತೊಂಗಿ ನೋಡು).

ತೊಟ್ಟಿಲು (= ತೊಟ್ಲು) k. n. A cradle.

ತೊಟ್ಟಿ k. n. A trough, font, tub.

ತೊಟ್ಟು 1. *P. p. of* ತೊಡು, *q. v.*

ತೊಟ್ಟು 2. k. n. A nipple. 2, the foot-stalk of a fruit, flower or leaf.

ತೊಟ್ಟು 3. (= ತಟಕು) k. n. A drop.

ತೊಟ್ಟೆ k. n. A bees' empty cell.

ತೊಟ್ಲು. = ತೊಟ್ಟಿಲು, *q. v.*

ತೊಡಕು k. v. i. To get entangled, *as* thread, a horn in a tree, *etc.* 2, to engage, *as* in work. 3, to be in opposition. *v. t.* To commence (= ತೊಡಗು); to entangle; to hinder, interfere. *n.* Entanglement; impediment, hindrance; objection; perplexity. -ಬೀಳು. To become entangled; to be hindered. ತೊಡಕಾಗು. To be hindered, *as* work.

ತೊಡಗು (= ತೊಡಕು, *v. t.*) k. v. t. To engage, *as* in work; to begin; to undertake. *v. i.* To be begun. ತೊಡಗಿಸು. To cause to commence or undertake.

ತೊಡಂಬೆ a. k. n. A cluster; a bundle, bunch.

ತೊಡರು k. v. i. To be linked to, connected with, *etc.*; to join; to fall in with; to be arrested, checked; to be caught. *v. t.* To encircle, *as* creepers round a tree. *n.* Connection; a badge of honour; an impediment, a check.

ತೊಡರಿಸು, ತೊಡರ್ಚು k. v. t. To tie, link, insert, fasten, fix.

ತೊಡವು, ತೊಡಹು k. n. Apparel, clothing; an ornament. 2, the beginning; the bottom.

ತೊಡಸು k. v. t. To wipe away; to efface, destroy. 2, to cause to smear, *as* chunam, cowdung, *etc.*; *also* ತೊಡಿಸು, ತೊಡಯಿಸು, ತೊಡೆಯಿಸು.

ತೊಡಿಗೆ k. n. Apparel, clothing; an ornament.

ತೊಡು (= ತುಡು) k. v. t. To put on, *as* clothes, ornaments, *etc.* *P. p.* ತೊಟ್ಟು. ತೊಡಿಸು. To dress another; = ತೊಡಸು, *q. v.*

ತೊಡೆ 1. k. v. t. To smear, anoint, rub on, *as* oil, unguents; to whitewash. 2, to wipe, *as* tears. 3, to efface, destroy.

ತೊಡೆ 2. k. n. The thigh. -ವಾಳ. A bubo.

ತೊಣಚಿ, ತೊಣಚೆ k. n. A gadfly, dogfly.

ತೊಣೆ a. k. n. Likeness, equality.

ತೊಂಗಲು k. n. A chaplet of pearls. 2, (f.) = ಸುಂಡಲು, *q. v.*

ತೊಂಡು k. n. Insolence. 2, straying. 3, chatter, prate. -ಜುಲುಮಾನೆ. A fine for the trespass of stray cattle. -ದನ. Stray cattle. -ತನ. Strolling, straying.

ತೊಂಡೆ 1. k. n. A chameleon. 2, the upper part of a sugarcane.

ತೊಂಡೆ 2. (*tb. of* ತುಂಡಿ) n. The tiny gourd *Momordica monadelpha*. *Cpds.*: ಕಾಗೆ-, -ಕಾಯಿ, -ಬಳ್ಳಿ, ಹುಚ್ಚು-.

ತೊಂಡ್ಲು. = ತೊಂಡಲು, *q. v.*

ತೊತ್ತು k. n. A female servant; a mean woman. ತೊತ್ತಿನ ಮಗ. The son of a maid-servant.

ತೊದ k. n. A Tŏda of the Nilgiris.

ತೊದಲು k. v. i. To stammer, falter. n. Stammering; faltering; speaking indistinctly. 2, untruth. -ನುಡಿ, -ಮಾತು. Stammering speech. -ನಾಲಿಗೆ. A stammering tongue.

ತೊನೆ a. k. v. i. To swing, wave to and fro.

ತೊಂತು k. v. t. To wind one's self round. 2, to instigate one (to quarrel).

ತೊಂದರೆ, ತೊಂದ್ರೆ k. n. Intricacy, embarrassment; difficulty, trouble, vexation, impediment, drawback. -ಗೊಳ್ಳು, -ಪಡು, -ಬೀಳು. To get embarrassed, *etc.* -ಗೊಳಿಸು. To embarrass, *etc.* -ಕೆಲಸ, -ಕಾರ್ಯ. A troublesome affair.

ತೊನ್ನು k. n. Leprosy; white leprosy.

ತೊಪ್ಪಲು k. n. All small leaves of plants in general.

ತೊಪ್ಪೆ k. n. Fresh cow-dung.

ತೊಂಬತ್ತು k. a. Ninety.

ತೊಂಟೆ a. k. n. A cluster. 2, a host; multitude. 3, a large bamboo basket.

ತೊಯು, ತೊಯ್ಯು (= ತೋಯು) k. v. i. To become wet or moist. v. t. To moisten. *P. p.* ತೊಯಿದು. ತೊಯಿಸು, ತೊಯ್ಯಿಸು. To make wet; to steep in water.

ತೊರಡು (ರ = ಱ) k. n. A hook for taking down fruits from trees.

ತೊರಳೆ k. n. The spleen.

ತೊರೆ 1. k. v. i. Milk to form in the breast. a. Mature, ripe.

ತೊರೆ 2. (ರೆ = ಱೆ) k. v. t. To put away, quit, give up, reject. *P. ps.* ತೊರದು, ತೊರೆದು.

ತೊರೆ 3. (ರೆ = ಱೆ) k. n. A hollow, hole; a cave. 2, a stream, river. -ಮಾವು. A mango-tree near a river. -ಮುಂಕೆ. An undershrub, *Indigofera trita*.

ತೊರೆಯ k. n. A salt-maker.

ತೊಲಗು k. v. i. To go away, depart; to go aside; to retire; to be separated; to fail. ತೊಲಗಿ ಹೋಗು. To forsake. ತೊಲಗಿಸು. To separate, cause to go away.

ತೊಲೆ (*tb. of* ತುಲಾ) n. A beam of wood. 2, a balance. 3, a rupee's weight.

ತೊಳ (= ತೊಳದು, ತೊಳೆದು). *P. p. of* ತೊಳೆ, *in* ತೊಳಕೊಳ್ಳು.

ತೊಳಗು a. k. v. i. To shine, be bright. n. Splendour.

ತೊಳಲು (ಳ = ೞ) a. k. v. i. To move round. 2, to roam or wander about. 3, to get perplexed. v. t. To roll. n. Moving; roaming. ತೊಳಲಿ. Moving round. ತೊಳಲಿಕಲ್ಲು. A wooden hand-mill. ತೊಳಲಿಕೆ, ತೊಳಲುವಿಕೆ. Roaming or wandering about.

ತೊಳಸಲು k. n. Pounding. ತೊಳಸಲಕ್ಕಿ. Rice cleared of its bran.

ತೊಳಸು 1. k. v. t. To beat, pound, *as* rice so as to deprive it of its bran. 2, to box, fight. 3, to cause to wash; to get washed. *n.* Pounding; boxing. 2, entanglement

ತೊಳಸು 2. (ಳ=ೞ) k. v. t. To turn round. *v. i.* To nauseate. *n.* Revolving, rolling; wandering.

ತೊಳೆ, ತೊಳೆ 1. k. v. t. To wash. *P. ps.* ತೊಳದು, ತೊಳೆದು.

ತೊಳೆ 2. k. n. A hole. 2, one of the divisions in an orange, jack fruit, *etc.* -ಮಾಡು. -ಹಾಕು. To bore a hole.

ತೊಳ್ತು. = ತೊತ್ತು.

ತೊಳ್ತುಳ (ಳ್ತುಳ=ಟ್ತುಟ) a. k. n. Poor, miserable, dejected.

ತೊಳ್ಳೆ k. n. A hollow, hole, cavity. 2, deficit, debt.

ತೊೞ. = ತೋಯು, q. v.

ತೋಕೆ a. k. n. A tail.

ತೋಚು (= ತೋರು) k. v. i. To appear, seem, occur to the mind. ಹೀಗೆ ತೋಚುತ್ತದೆ. So it seems. ತೋಚಿಕೆ. Appearing, occurring to the mind.

ತೋಟ k. n. A garden. -ಗಾರ, ತೋಟಿಗ. A gardener, florist.

ತೋಟಿ k. n. An inferior village servant, sweeper, scavenger, *etc.* 2, a scuffle; a quarrel.

ತೋಟೆ h. n. A cartridge; *also* ತೊಗಟೆ.

ತೋಡ k. n. A kind of white rat that infests crops.

ತೋಡಿ k. n. N. of a tune.

ತೋಡು 1. k. v. t. To go out. *v. t.* To bale out water; to wind thread from one spool upon another. 2, to dig, excavate; to burrow. *n.* A water-course.

ತೋಡು 2. k. n. An expedient.

ತೋಡೆ h. n. A ring of gold, *etc.*, for the wrist or ankle.

ತೋಂಟ. = ತೋಟ, q. v.

ತೋತಾಯ f. n. A counterfeit; an imposter.

ತೋದು k. n. An expedient. 2, *p. p.* of ತೋ. -ಗಾರ. A man clever in expedients.

ತೋಪ, ತೋಫ. = ತೋಪು, q. v.

ತೋಪದೆ k. n. A carpenter's plane.

ತೋಪಿ. = ಟೊಪ್ಪಿ, q. v.

ತೋಪು k. n. A clump of trees, grove, wood.

ತೋಫು h. n. A cannon. -ಖಾನೆ. A depôt of artillery stores. -ಹಾರು. A gun to be fired. -ಸುಡು, -ಹಾರಿಸು. To fire a gun.

ತೋಬರಿ f. n. A horse's mouth-bag.

ತೋಯ s. n. Water. -ಜ. A lotus. -ಜನಾಭ, -ಜಾಕ್ಷ. Vishṇu. -ಜಮಿತ್ರ. The sun. -ಜಾರಿ. The moon. -ನಿಧಿ. The ocean. ತೋಯಾಶಯ. A lake.

ತೋಯು k. v. i. To become wet or moist. *P. p.* ತೋಯಿದು. ತೋಯಿಸು. To moisten, wet; to soak, steep.

ತೋರ k. n. Bigness, largeness, stoutness; greatness; a stout man. -ತಲೆ. A large head. -ಪನಿ, -ಹನಿ. A big drop. -ಹ, ತೋರಿಹ. Being large.

ತೋರಂಜಿ f. n. The pumplemose or shaddock tree, *Citrus decumana*.

ತೋರಣ s. n. A festoon suspended across gateways, streets, *etc.*

ತೋರಿಕೆ (ರಿ = ಱ) k. n. Appearance; sight. 2, conjecture, opinion. 3, exhibition; *also* ತೋಱಿಕೆ.

ತೋರು (ರು = ಱು) k. v. i. To appear, seem, be visible; to come into existence; to occur. *v. t.* To show, exhibit; to evince. *n.* Appearing, showing. ತೋರಭವು. A mortgage without possession. -ಬೆರಳು. The fore-finger. ತೋರಿಸು. To show; to evince. ತೋರಿಸಿ ಕೊಡು. To point out. ತೋರಿಸುವಿಕೆ. Showing. -ವಿಕೆ. = ತೋರಿಕೆ.

ತೋಲ s. n. Weight; a weight of gold or silver amounting to 210 grains. 2, (= ತೊಲೆ) a rupee's weight, a Tōla.

ತೋಲು k. *a.* Much, plenty. *n.* A way, road.

ತೋಲೆ k. *n.* A cataract.

ತೋವೆ. = ತೊಗೆ, *q. v.*

ತೋಷ s. *n.* Satisfaction, contentment; joy, pleasure; *also* -ಣ. ತೋಷಿಸು. To be delighted, pleased.

ತೋಷೇಖಾನೆ h. *n.* A treasury.

ತೋಸ್ತಾನು h. *n.* A leather pouch.

ತೋಸ್ತು e. *n.* A toast. ತೋಸ್ತಿನ ರೊಟ್ಟಿ. A toasted bread.

ತೋಹು a. k. *n.* Deceit; a lurking place; an ambush. 2, decoying. 3, a hedge; a thicket; a crowd.

ತೋಳ k. *n.* A wolf.

ತೋಳು k. *n.* The arm. -ಎತ್ತಿತೂಗು. To dandle a child in the arms. ತೋಳ ತೊಡಗೆ, -ಬಂದಿ. An arm-bracelet. -ಬಲ. Strength of the arm. -ಬೀಸು. To swing the arm.

ತೌ *For words with this initial see s.* ತವ *or* ತವು.

ತೌರು. = ತವರು, *q. v.*

ತ್ಯಕ್ತ s. *a.* Left, forsaken; thrown away.

ತ್ಯಜನ s. *n.* Leaving, abandoning.

ತ್ಯಜಿಸು s. *v. t.* To leave, quit, renounce; to dismiss; to shun.

ತ್ಯಾಗ 1. (= ತೇಗ) k. *n.* Teak.

ತ್ಯಾಗ 2. s. *n.* Abandoning, renouncing; resigning; gift, donation; generosity. -ಭೋಗ. Generosity and enjoyment. ತ್ಯಾಗಿ. Leaving; liberal; a donor; a hero.

ತ್ಯಾಜ್ಯ s. *a.* To be left, avoided, abandoned, shunned. *n.* An unlucky hour. 2, giving up, resigning.

ತ್ಯಾಪೆ. = ತೇಪೆ, *q. v.*

ತ್ಯಾವ. = ತೇವ, *q. v.* ತ್ಯಾವಿಸು. To moisten, *etc.*

ತ್ರಯ s. *a.* Triple, threefold. *n.* A triad. ತ್ರಯೋದಶ. Thirteenth. ತ್ರಯೋದಶಿ. The thirteenth day of the lunar fortnight.

ತ್ರಸ s. *a.* Movable, moving. *n.* Animals.

ತ್ರಸರ s. *n.* A weaver's shuttle.

ತ್ರಾಣ s. *n.* Protection, defence; help. 2, strength, vigour, might, ability. 3, capacity. -ಗುಂದು. Power to be impaired. -ಗುಂದಿಸು. To impair power. -ಗೊಳ್ಳು, -ಹೊಂದು. To become strong.

ತ್ರಾಣಿ One who is strong or powerful. ಸರ್ವತ್ರಾಣಿ. Almighty; the Almighty, God.

ತ್ರಾತ s. *a.* Protected, saved.

ತ್ರಾಸ s. *n.* Fear, anxiety; vexation, annoyance. -ಕೊಡು. To vex, harass. -ಗೊಳ್ಳು. To be vexed.

ತ್ರಾಸು (= ತರಾಸು) f. *n.* A balance. -ಮುಳ್ಳು. The needle of a scale beam.

ತ್ರಾಹಿ s. *int.* Protect! save!

ತ್ರಿ s. *a.* Three. -ಕರಣ (= ಕರಣತ್ರಯ). Mind, speech and action. -ಕರಣಶುದ್ಧಿ. Purity of mind, speech and action. -ಕಾಲ. Past, present and future; morning, noon and evening. -ಕೋಣ. Triangular; a triangle. -ಗುಣ. The three qualities of nature, *i. e.* satva, rajas and tamas; threefold, thrice. -ಜಗತ್. Heaven, earth and the lower region. -ತಯ. A triad. -ತಾಪ. = ತಾಪತ್ರಯ. -ದಂಡ. The triple staff of a mendicant Brâhmaṇa who has renounced the world. -ದರ್ಶಿ. Seeing the past, present and future, omniscient. -ದಶ. Thirty. -ದೋಷ. Disorder of the three humours of the body, vitiation of the bile, blood and phlegm. -ದೋಷಹರ. Removing the tridôsha. -ನಾಮ. = ಮೂರು ನಾಮ, *q. v.* -ಪಥ. The three paths; the sky, earth, and lower region. -ಗಾಮಿನಿ, -ಪಥೆ. The Ganges. -ಪದಿ. N. of a metre; a tripod. -ಪುಟ. Triangular; a musical tâla that requires three beatings. -ಪುಂಡ್ರ. A sectarian mark consisting of three lines made on different parts of the body by Śaivas and Vaishṇavas. -ಪುರ. Three strong cities. -ಪುರುಷ.

Brahmâ, Vishṇu and Śiva; three generations. -ಭುವನ. Heaven, earth and the lower region. -ಮತ. Three systems of religion: smârta or advaita, mâdhva or dvaita, râmânuja or viśishṭâdvaita. -ಮೂರ್ತಿ. The triad of Brahmâ, Vishṇu and Śiva. -ಯಂಬಕ. = ತ್ರ್ಯಂಬಕ. -ರತ್ನ. The three gems: Buddha, the law, and the congregation. -ರಾತ್ರಿ. Three nights. -ಲಿಂಗ. Having three genders: an adjective. -ಲೋಕ. = ತ್ರಿಭುವನ, *q. v.* -ವರ್ಗ. Three objects of life: religion or virtue, wealth, and pleasure. -ವಿದ್ಯೆ. The three branches of knowledge. -ವೇಣಿ. Triple braid; the junction of the Ganges, the Yamunâ and the Sarasvatî. -ಶೂಲ. A trident. -ಸಂಧಿಗ್ರಾಹಿ. One who understands and remembers a ślôka hearing it three times.

ತ್ರೇತಾ, ತ್ರೇತೆ s. *n.* A triad. 2, the second of the four ages of the world. ತ್ರೇತಾಗ್ನಿ. The three sacred fires collectively.

ತ್ರೈಕಾಲಿಕ (*fr.* ತ್ರಿಕಾಲ) s. *a.* Relating to the three times, *i. e.* past, present, and future.

ತ್ರೈರಾಶಿಕ s. *n.* The rule of three.

ತ್ರ್ಯಂಬಕ (= ತ್ರಿಯಂಬಕ) s. *a.* Triocular. *n.* Śiva. 2, N. of a town.

ತ್ರ್ಯಾಹಿಕ s. *a.* Tertian, quartan, *as* fever.

ತ್ವಕ್, ತ್ವಚ್ s. *n.* Skin. 2, bark, rind, husk.

ತ್ವಕ್ಕ್ಷೀರೆ (ತವಕ್ಷೀರ) f. *n.* Manna of bamboo, tabâshîr.

ತ್ವರಿತ s. *a.* Quick, swift, speedy.

ತ್ವರ (*tb. of* ತ್ವರೆ) *n.* Haste, speed, velocity. -ಪಡು. To be quick, hasty, *etc.*

ತ್ವಾಷ್ಟ್ರ s. *n.* A man of very dirty, nasty habits.

ಥ್. The thirty-fifth letter of the alphabet. *In Kannaḍa it occurs only in few words.*

ಥಕಾರ s. *n.* The letter ಥ.

ಥಟ್ಟು a. k. *n.* A mass, host, army. -ರಿ. (= -ಉರಿ) To blaze up.

ದ್. The thirty-sixth letter of the alphabet.

ದ. *The termination of the affirmative and negative relative participles, as:* ಕೇಳಿದ, ಮಾಡಿದ, ಹೇಳಿದ, ಹೋದ, ತಿರಿದ, *etc.;* ಕೇಳದ, ಮಾಡದ, ಹೇಳದ, ಹೋಗದ, ತಿರದ, *etc.*

ದಂಶ s. *n.* A bite, sting. 2, a tooth, 3, a gad-fly. -ಕ. Biting; any thing fit to be chewed, *as* pickles.

ದಂಷ್ಟ್ರ s. *n.* A large tooth, tusk, fang. ದಂಷ್ಟ್ರಾಯುಧ. A wild boar; a monkey.

ದಕಾರ s. *n.* The letter ದ.

ದಕ್ಕಣ, ದಕ್ಕಿಣ (*tb. of* ದಕ್ಷಿಣ) *n.* The south; the upper Dekhan.

ದಕ್ಕು k. *v. i.* To be obtained, got, acquired; to remain as in one's possession. 2, to remain; to be saved; to become well. *n.* Acquirement, possession; property. ನನಗೆ ದಕ್ಕಿತು. I have obtained it. -ಮಾಡಿಕೊಳ್ಳು. To obtain possession. ದಕ್ಕಿಸಿಕೊಳ್ಳು. To appropriate to one's self; to keep in one's stomach.

ದಕ್ಷ s. a. Skilful, able, intelligent. n. N. of a son of Brahmâ. 2, ability; fitness. -ಕನ್ಯೆ. Durgâ. -ತೆ. Cleverness, ability.

ದಕ್ಷಿಣ (= ದಕ್ಕಣ) s. a. Right, not left. 2, straightforward, sincere, upright. n. The south, country of the south, the Dekhan. -ಧ್ರುವ. The south-pole. ದಕ್ಷಿಣಾಯನ. The sun's progress south of the equator, winter solstice. ದಕ್ಷಿಣೋತ್ತರ. The south and the north; right and left.

ದಕ್ಷಿಣೆ (= ದಖಣಾ) s. n. The south. 2, (money) presents given to Brâhmaṇas. 3, a fee, gift.

ದಖಣ, ದಖ್ಖಣ, ದಖನ (tb. of ದಕ್ಷಿಣಾ) n. The upper Dekhan. ದಖಣಿ, ದಖನಿ. The Hindusthâni language.

ದಗಡಿ f. n. A rude woman.

ದಗಲು h. n. Trick, fraud. -ಬಾಜ. Roguery; a dishonest person; also ದಗಾಖೋರ.

ದಗಲೆ h. n. Armour, a coat of mail.

ದಗಾ, ದಗೆ h. n. Deceit, fraud; imposture. ದಗಾಖೋರ. A dishonest man. -ಖೋರತನ. Deceiving.

ದಗೆ f. n. Heat, glow.

ದಗ್ಗನೆ k. ad. With a blaze. -ಉರಿ. To burn brightly.

ದಗ್ಧ s. a. Burnt, scorched. -ಹಸ್ತ. A luckless man.

ದಂಗೆ (= ತಂಗೆ) h. n. Tumult and confusion, as of a mutiny. -ಏಳು. To become rebellious. -ಮಾಡು, -ಬೀಳು. To rebel.

ದಜ್ಜಿ k. n. Half of a split tamarind seed. -ಬಾರ. A kind of backgammon.

ದಟ್ಟ k. a. Thick, stout, robust; crowded together, thick-set, dense. n. Quilted rags. -ಕೂದಲು. Thick, bushy hair. -ಗೆ. Densely. -ಣೆ. The state of being thick, crowded together, close, etc. -ಯಿಸು, -ಯ್ಸು. To grow thick, close, dense. -ನ್ನ. Thick, dense, etc.

ದಟ್ಟಿ k. n. A waist-band; a sash.

ದಟ್ಟಿಸು k. v. t. To rub out, obliterate; to efface. 2, (f.) to scold, menace.

ದಟ್ಟು k. n. Stumbling. ದಟ್ಟಡಿ. A tottering, waddling step.

ದಡ 1. *A sound imitating the rattling of thunder, etc.; trembling, quivering, palpitation.* -ದಡ, -ಬಡ. *rep.* -ದತ, -ದತನೆ. In hurry and flurry. -ಬತ ಮಾತಾಡು. To speak rapidly.

ದಡ 2. (tb. of ತಟ) n. A bank, shore.

ದಡಂಬಡಿಕೆ k. n. Impetuousness, force.

ದಡಾರ (tb. of ದದ್ರು) n. Measles.

ದಡಿ 1. (= ದಂಡ) k. n. A staff; a cudgel. -ಗ. A clubman.

ದಡಿ 2. f. n. The border of a cloth.

ದಡೂತಿ f. n. Of close texture, as cloth. 2, respectability; wealth.

ದಡೆ h. n. A weight of ten sêrs and equal to ¼ of a maund. 2, a weight to counterbalance.

ದಡ್ಡ k. n. A blockhead; a stupid, ignorant man; f. -ಳು, ದಡ್ಡಿ. 2, a double consonant; also -ಕ್ಕರ. Cpds.: -ಕೆಲಸ, -ಗುಣ, -ಮಗ, etc. -ತನ. Stupidity, ignorance.

ದಡ್ಡಿ (= ತಡಿಕೆ) k. n. A tatty, screen. 2, a cage. 3, a stable.

ದತ್ರಂಟೆ k. n. A profligate woman.

ದಣ (= ದಣಿದ) k. P. p. of ದಣಿ, in ದಣಕೊಳ್ಳು.

ದಣವು k. n. Fatigue, weariness, exhaustion. -ಆರಿಸು, -ತೀರಿಸು. To take rest. -ಆಗಿರು. To be weary. -ಗೊಳ್ಳು. To be fatigued.

ದಣಿ 1. k. v. i. To be fatigued or tired. 2, to be satiated. ದಣಿಸು. To cause to be fatigued; to satiate.

ದಣಿ 2. tb. of ಧನಿ, q. v.

ದಣಿವು, ದಣು, ದಣುವು. = ದಣವು, q. v.

ದಂಟು k. n. A stalk. Cpds.: ಜೋಳದ-, ತಾವರೆಯ-, ಸೂರಣದ-, etc.

ದಂಡ (= ದಂಡು) s. n. A stick, staff, rod. 2, a stalk. 3, a staff or sceptre. 4, the oar of a boat. 5, punishment; a fine; imprisonment. 6, a form of military array; an army; *also* ದಂಡು. -ಕಟ್ಟು. To set a fine on. -ಕೊಡು. To pay a fine. -ಬೀಳು. A fine to be imposed upon. -ಕ. N. of a vṛitta; a pole. -ನೀತಿ. Administration of justice; ethics. -ಯಾತ್ರೆ. A bridal procession; conquest of a region. -ಪ್ರಣಮ, -ಪ್ರಣಾಮ, -ವತ್ಪ್ರಣಾಮ. A prostration of the body.

ದಂಡನ s. *n*. Beating, punishing, inflicting punishment; torment; *also* ದಂಡನೆ. -ಶರ್ತ. A penalty-clause in a document.

ದಂಡಿ 1. k. *n*. Greatness, might; abundance, excess. 2, anger. 3, cruelty.

ದಂಡಿ 2. s. *n*. A doorkeeper, porter. 2, a religious mendicant carrying a staff; an ascetic.

ದಂಡಿಗೆ (*tb. of* ದಂಡಿಕೆ) *n*. The beam of a balance. 2, a kind of palankeen.

ದಂಡಿಸು s. *v. t*. To punish, chastise; to mortify.

ದಂಡು (*tb. of* ದಂಡ) *n*. An army. -ಇಡು, -ಇಟ್ಟುಕೊಳ್ಳು. To keep an army. -ಕೂಡಿಸು. To assemble an army. -ಬಿಡು. To encamp an army. ದಂಡೆತ್ತು. To levy an army. ದಂಡಿಗೆ ಹೋಗು. To enlist in the army.

ದಂಡೆ 1. s. *n*. A string; a garland, wreath. 2, a kind of gymnastic exercise of the body.

ದಂಡೆ 2. (*tb. of* ತಟಿ) *n*. A bank, shore. -ಗುಂಟ. Along the shore.

ದಂಡೋರ. = ಡಂಗರ, *q. v.* -ಹಾಕಿಸು. To be proclaimed by beat of drum.

ದತ್ತ s. *a*. Given, granted, made over. -ಪುತ್ರ. An adopted son. ದತ್ತಾಪಹಾರ. The resumption of a gift. ವಾಗ್ದತ್ತ. A promise.

ದತ್ತೂರ, ದತ್ತೂರಿ (*tb. of* ಧತ್ತೂರ) *n*. The thorn-apple, *Datura alba*.

ದದ್ದು 1. k. *n*. Being cracked, *as* an earthen vessel.

ದದ್ದು 2. (*tb. of* ದದ್ರು) *n*. Cutaneous eruption, herpes, rash, ringworm.

ದಧಿ s. *n*. Curds. -ಫಲ. Wood-apple. -ಸಾರ. Butter.

ದನ (*tb. of* ಧನ) *n*. Cattle; a cow, bullock. -ಗಾಯುವವ. A herdsman. -ದ ಮಂದೆ, -ದ ಹಿಂಡು. A herd of cattle.

ದನಿ (*tb. of* ಧ್ವನಿ) *n*. A sound, voice. -ಗೊಡು, -ಗೊಳ್ಳು. To echo.

ದನು s. *a*. N. of Daksha's daughter and Kaśyapa's wife. -ಜ. A Dânava. -ಜಮಥನ, -ಜಹರ, -ಜಾರಿ. Kṛishṇa.

ದಂತ s. *n*. A tooth; a tusk, fang. 2, an elephant's tusk, ivory. 3, an elephant. -ದೋಲೆ. An ôlĕ of ivory. -ಧಾವನ. Cleaning the teeth. -ಮೂಲ. The root of a tooth. -ವಕ್ರ. N. of a Dânava. -ಶಠ. Acidity, sourness. -ಶಠೆ. Wood sorrel. -ಹೀನ. Toothless.

ದಂತಿ s. *a*. Having teeth. *n*. An elephant. 2, the croton plant, *Croton tiglium*; *also* -ಕೆ. -ಮುಖ. Gaṇapati.

ದಂತ್ಯ s. *a*. Dental, as a letter.

ದಂದಲೆ h. *n*. Vexation, chicanery.

ದಂದುಗ k. *n*. Intricacy; trouble, annoyance. -ಗೊಳ್ಳು, -ಪಡೆ (-ಬಡೆ). To fall into trouble.

ದಪ್ಪ k. *n*. Thickness; stoutness; coarseness. *Cpds.*: -ಕೈ, -ನೂಲು, -ನೇಯ್ಗೆ, -ಎಲೆ, -ತುಟಿ, *etc.* -ನೆ, -ನ್ನ. Thick; coarse.

ದಫನು h. *n*. Burial.

ದಫಾ, ದಫೇ h. *n*. Time, turn. 2, a party of peons. ದಫೇದಾರ. A head peon.

ದಫ್ತರ h. *n*. A record, register; a bundle of records. -ದಾರ. A head native revenue officer of a collectorate.

ದಬದಬ k. *n*. *A sound imitating the palpitation of the heart or any heavy fall.* -ಅನ್ನು. To palpitate. ದಬದ್ಧಬಿ. A waterfall.

ದಬಾದುಬಿ f. *n*. Unfair dealing, cheating.

ದಬಾಯಿಸು f. *v. t*. To force down; to menace; to slam, *as* a door.

ದಬ್ಬಣ, ದಬ್ಬಳ f. *n*. A pack-needle.

ದಬ್ಬು (= ದೊಬ್ಬು, ತೊಬ್ಬು) k. *v. t*. To push.

ದಬ್ಬೆ (= ಡಬ್ಬೆ) k. n. A slip, split, strip, esp. of bamboo. 2, (f.) a blow.

ದಮ s. a. Taming. n. Self-restraint, subduing the passions; also -ನ.

ದಮಡಿ (= ದಮ್ಮಡಿ) h. n. A kâsu, the fourth part of a duḍḍu. 2, a small tambourine.

ದಮನಕ s. n. N. of jackal.

ದಮಯಂತಿ s. n. N. of Nala's wife.

ದಮಾನು h. n. The large sail of a boat. a. Leeward.

ದಮಾಸು h. n. Damask. 2, a wooden leveller.

ದಮಿತ s. a. Subdued, conquered. -ಅಘ, ದಮಿತಾಘ. One whose sin is subdued.

ದಂಪತಿ s. n. The master of the house. 2, (dual) man and wife. -ಗಳನ್ನು ಕೂಡಿಸು. To join in marriage by repeating certain formulas.

ದಂಭ s. n. Arrogance, ostentation, pride. 2, deceit, fraud, hypocrisy. -ಕ. Arrogant, etc. ದಂಭಾಚಾರ, -ಶೀಲ. Arrogant, ostentatious behaviour.

ದಮ್ಮ. tb. of ಧರ್ಮ, q. v. ದಮ್ಮಯ್ಯ. Generous master!

ದಮ್ಮಡಿ. = ದಮಡಿ, q. v.

ದಮ್ಮು h. n. Breath; panting; asthma. -ಕಟ್ಟು, -ಹಿಡಿ. To suspend one's breath; breath to be choked.

ದಯೆ (tb. of ದಯಾ) n. Sympathy, compassion, tenderness, pity, mercy, clemency, love. -ಪಾಲಿಸು. To take pity on; to grant graciously. -ಮಾಡು. To be kind, considerate; to grant graciously. -ವಂತ. A compassionate man. ದಯಾಕಟಾಕ್ಷ. A side-glance full of mercy, kindness, etc. ದಯಾಧಾರ. A very compassionate man. ದಯಾಗುಣ. The quality of compassion, etc. ದಯಾರಸ. The feeling of compassion. ದಯಾಂಬುಧಿ, ದಯಾಸಮುದ್ರ, ದಯಾಬ್ಧಿ. Ocean of compassion. ದಯಾಲು, -ವು. Pitiful, merciful, kind, etc.

ದರ f. n. Rate, price.

ದರಕು k. n. Roughness; hoarseness.

ದರಖಾಸ್ತು h. n. An application, offer for a rent or farm.

ದರಗ h. n. A Mohammadan place of worship.

ದರಜಾಸ್ತಿ h. n. An extra tax.

ದರಜಿ (= ದರ್ಜಿ) h. n. A tailor.

ದರಣ (tb. of ಧರಣ) n. The weight and value of one-fourth of a varaha: 11 aṇês 8 kâsus.

ದರದು h. n. Care, regard; need.

ದರಬಾರ, ದರಬಾರು h. n. A royal court; a hall of audience; a levee-room. 2, the people assembled. 3, government, rule. 4, pomp, show.

ದರಮಹಾ h. n. Monthly pay. a. Monthly.

ದರವಾಜಾ h. n. A gate or door; a gateway.

ದರಿ s. n. A cave; a hole. 2, a valley.

ದರಿಂವಿಲ್ಲಾ h. ad. In this case; at this time; hereinafter.

ದರಿದ್ರ s. a. Poor, needy; distressed. n. A poor man; f. -ಳು. 2, poverty, want; also -ತನ, -ತ್ವ.

ದರಿಯಾಪ್ತಿ (= ದರ್ಯಾಫ್ತಿ) h. n. Investigation.

ದರುವು (tb. of ಧ್ರುವ) n. A song in peculiar metre.

ದರುಶನ. tb. of ದರ್ಶನ, q. v.

ದರೆ s. n. A cave. 2, barren soil. 3, a wall.

ದರೋಗ h. n. The chief native officer in the department of abkâri, salt, sandal, etc.

ದರೋಬಸ್ತು h. n. All without exception.

ದರ್ಜಾ, ದರ್ಜೆ h. n. Rank, order, grade.

ದರ್ಜಿ. = ದರಜಿ, q. v.

ದರ್ಪ s. n. Pride, arrogance. 2, boldness.

ದರ್ಪಣ s. n. A looking-glass, mirror.

ದರ್ಬಾರು. = ದರಬಾರು, q. v.

ದರ್ಭ, ದರ್ಭೆ s. n. The kuṡa grass, Poa cynosuroides.

ದರ್ಯಾಪ್ತಿ. = ದರಿಯಾಪ್ತಿ, *q. v.*

ದರ್ಶ **s. n.** Looking at, viewing; sight, view. -ಕ. A spectator; an exhibitor; a savant; showing, displaying. -ಕ ಸರ್ವನಾಮ. A demonstrative pronoun.

ದರ್ಶನ s. n. Seeing. 2, sight, vision, appearance, observation; perception. 3, exhibition. 4, a visit. 5, view, theory. 6, a system of philosophy. -ಕೊಡು. To favour one with a visit. -ತೆಗೆ, -ಮಾಡು. To visit.

ದರ್ಶಿ s. n. Seeing; showing; a seer, spectator; *f.* -ನಿ. -ತ. Seen; shown; apparent. -ಸು. To see.

ದಲ್ a. k. *ad.* Certainly, to be sure, indeed.

ದಲ. = ದಳ 3, *q. v.*

ದಲನ s. n. Splitting, breaking to pieces, bursting.

ದಲಾಲಿ, ದಲ್ಲಾಳಿ h. n. Brokerage; commission. 2, a broker. -ತನ. A broker's business.

ದವ s. n. Fire. 2, a wood on fire. 3, a forest conflagration; *also* ದವಾನಲ.

ದವಡು. = ದವುಡು, *q. v.*

ದವಡೆ k. n. The jaw bone, mandible. -ಹಲ್ಲು. The molars.

ದವತಿ, ದವುತಿ, ದೌತಿ h. n. An inkstand.

ದವನ (*tb. of* ದಮನ) n. The plant *Artemisia indica* and its flower.

ದವಸ (*tb. of* ಯವಸ) n. Corn, grain. -ಧಾನ್ಯ. *reit.*

ದವಳ s. n. A conch-shell used for blowing. 2, *tb. of* ಧವಲ, *q. v.*

ದವಾ h. n. Medicine. -ಖಾನೆ. A medicine-shop, dispensary.

ದವಾಲಿ. = ಡವಾಲಿ, *q. v.*

ದವುಡು (= ದವಡು, ದೌಡು) h. n. A race, run. 2, a military excursion, expedition.

ದಶ s. a. Ten. -ಕ. Tenfold; a decade. -ಕಂಠ, -ಗ್ರೀವ, -ಮುಖ, -ವದನ, -ಶಿರ. Râvaṇa. -ಗುಣ. Tenfold; penalty for not affixing a stamp to an official document. -ದಾನ. Ten gifts: cows, land, sesamum, gold, ghee, raiment, betel, grain, jaggory, daughters in marriage. -ದಿಕ್ಕು. The eight points of the compass and the earth and sky. -ಮ. Tenth. -ಮಾಂಶ. Decimal. -ಮಿ. The tenth lunar day. -ರಥ. N. of Râma's father. ದಶಾಂಶ. Ten parts; the tenth part. ದಶಾಂಗ. Ten members; an incense composed of ten ingredients. ದಶಾವತಾರ. The ten incarnations of Vishṇu. ದಶೇಂದ್ರಿಯ. The ten organs of perception and action.

ದಶೆ s. n. The skirt, edge or hem of a garment; the wick of a lamp. 2, age, period. 3, state or condition of life. 4, fate. ದಶಾವಂತ. A fortunate man. ದಶಾಹೀನ. An unfortunate man.

ದಸಕತ್ತು h. n. Hand-writing; signature.

ದಸಕು k. n. A thin, dust-like coating on certain grains, as jôḷa, râgi, *etc.*, a kind of husk.

ದಸನು e. n. A dozen, 12 pieces; *also* ಡಜನು.

ದಸಮಾಹೆ e. n. Ten months' pay given for twelve.

ದಸರ, ದಸರೆ (*tb. of* ದಶರಾತ್ರಿ) n. The tenth day of the śuklapaksha, of the seventh month (âśvina), the last day of the navarâtri; *also* -ಹಬ್ಬ.

ದಸಿ k. n. A stake; a wooden peg.

ದಸೆ. *tb. of* ದಶೆ, *q. v.*

ದಸ್ಖತ್ತು. = ದಸಕತ್ತು, *q. v.*

ದಸ್ತಾವೇಜು, ದಸ್ತೈವಜು h. n. A document; a bond.

ದಸ್ತು h. n. A quire of paper. 2, a pack of 3 cards. 3, money withheld by government to an official. .

ದಸ್ತೂರಿ h. n. Custom, fashion. 2, customary fees; postage; tax.

ದಹನ s. n. Consuming by fire, burning. 2, fire; Agni. -ಸಂಸ್ಕಾರ. The rites of cremation. ದಹಿಸು. To burn up.

ದಳ 1. (ಳ = ಐ) a. k. n. An army containing infantry, cavalry, elephants and chariots. -ಪತಿ, -ಮುಖ್ಯ, -ವಾಯಿ. A general. -ಮುಖ. The van of an army.

ದಳ 2. f. n. Thickness, solidity. -ಸರ. Thickness; compactness.

ದಳ 3. (=ದಲ) f. n. A leaf, petal. 2, a part, fragment.

ದಳಾಳಿ. =ದಲಾಲಿ, q. v.

ದಳಿ k. v. t. To seam. v. i. To become abundant, *as* fruits *etc.*; to spread, *as* small-pox, *etc.*

ದಾಕ್ತರು e. n. A doctor; European physician.

ದಾಕ್ಷಾಯಣಿ s. n. N. of any of the daughters of Daksha. -ಪುತ್ರ. Gaṇêśa.

ದಾಕ್ಷಿಣ್ಯ (*fr.* ದಕ್ಷಿಣಾ) s. n. Civility, courtesy, politeness; honesty, candour; obsequiousness. -ಗಾರ, -ವಂತ, -ಶಾಲಿ. An obsequious man.

ದಾಖಲಾತು h. n. Proof, documentary evidence.

ದಾಖಲು h. *a.* Entered, *as* into an account, *etc.* n. Entry of an item in an account or register. -ಮಾಡು. To enter, *as* a name into a register, *etc.*

ದಾಗಡಿಬಳ್ಳಿ k. n. A winding half shrubby plant, *Cocculus villosus.*

ದಾಗಿನ h. n. Jewels worn on the body; personal property.

ದಾಗುಜೂಜಿ h. n. Repairing, doing up.

ದಾಟಿಸು k. v. t. To make cross, *etc.*

ದಾಟು k. v. t. To cross, ford; to pass; to go beyond; to escape. v. i. To die; to expire or pass away, elapse, *as* time. n. Stepping, passing over, *etc.* -ಕಥೆ. A summary. -ಕಾಲು. A far-stepping foot. -ಹೊಲಿಗೆ. Sewing with long stitches.

ದಾಡಿ h. n. The beard.

ದಾಡಿಮ, ದಾಡಿಂಬ s. n. The pomegranate tree and its fruit, *Punica granatum.*

ದಾಡೆ (*tb. of* ದಂಷ್ಟ್ರ) n. A tusk; a fang; a molar. 2, a jawbone.

ದಾಣಿ (*tb. of* ಧಾನ್ಯ) n. Grain. 2, (=ದಾವಣಿ) a rope.

ದಾಣಾ f. n. Thickness, stoutness. -ದಡಿ. A very stout man; *cf.* ದಾಂಡಿಗ.

ದಾಂಟು. =ದಾಟು, q. v.

ದಾಂಡಿಗ f. n. A stout, strong man. -ತನ. Rudeness.

ದಾತ, ದಾತಾರ *tb. of* ದಾತೃ, q. v.

ದಾತೃ s. n. A giver, donor. -ತ್ವ. Liberality.

ದಾದ (*tb. of* ತಾತ, q. v.) n. A respectful term of address for an elderly man.

ದಾದಿ (*tb. of* ಧಾತ್ರಿ) n. A nurse.

ದಾನ s. n. Giving; a gift, present, donation. -ಈಯು, -ಮಾಡು. To make gifts, *etc.* -ಗುಣ. A liberal disposition. -ತೆ. Liberality. -ಧರ್ಮ. Almsgiving, charitable acts. -ಪತ್ರ, -ಶಾಸನ. A deed of gift. -ಪಾತ್ರ. A presented vessel; an object of charity. -ವಸ್ತ್ರ. A presented cloth. -ಶೀಲ, -ಶೂರ. A generous person.

ದಾನವ s. n. Danu's descendant; a giant.

ದಾನಿ s. n. A donor.

ದಾಂತ s. *a.* Subdued, enduring. 2, ending in ದ. ದಾಂತಿ. Self-restraint.

ದಾಂದಲೆ. =ದಂದಲೆ, q. v.

ದಾಪು k. n. Stretch, *etc.*; the measure of a stride. -ಹಾಕು. To measure by strides.

ದಾಬುಣಿಕಾರಿ f. n. A certain border of a cloth.

ದಾಬು. =ಡಾಬು 1, 2, q. v.

ದಾಮ (=ಡಾಬು 1, q. v.) s. n. A string, cord, thread. 2, a girdle. 3, a chaplet, wreath for the forehead. -ನಿ. =ದಾವಣಿ.

ದಾಮಾಷಾ h. n. Proportionate distribution, equitable allotment, dividends.

ದಾಮೋದರ s. *a.* Having a cord round the belly. n. Kṛishṇa.

ದಾಂಭಿಕ (*fr.* ದಂಭ) s. *a.* Deceitful; ostentatious, proud. n. Ostentatiousness; *also* ದಾಂಭಿಕ.

ದಾಯ s. n. A gift, present. 2, a part, partition. 3, share, inheritance, patrimony. 4, property. 5, a throw of dice. 6, an opportunity, fit moment; a means. -ಕ. A giver; heir, kinsman. -ವಿಭಾಗ. A portion of inheritance.

ದಾಯಾದಿ (*tb. of* ದಾಯಾದ್ಯ) *n.* A descendant from a male stock.

ದಾಯಿ (*tb. of* ಧಾತ್ರಿ) *n.* A wet nurse. 2, (*s.*) giving, granting.

ದಾಯಿಗ (*tb. of* ದಾಯಕ) *n.* A remote kinsman. 2, = ದಾಯಾದಿ.

ದಾರ 1. s. *n.* A rent, cleft, hole. 2, a wife. -ಕ. A child.

ದಾರ 2. *tb. of* ದ್ವಾರ, *q. v.*

ದಾರ 3. (*tb. of* ಧಾರ) *n.* A string, thread. 2, (*aff.*) holder, possessor, *as:* ಅಮಲ-, ದಾವಾ-, *etc.*

ದಾರಣೆ f. *n.* Rate, market price.

ದಾರಬಂದ, ದಾರವಂದ (*tb. of* ದ್ವಾರಬಂಧ) *n.* A doorframe. 2, the panel of a door.

ದಾರಿ k. *n.* A way, road, path. -ಕಟ್ಟು. To block up a way. -ಕೊಡು. To let pass. -ಗೊಳ್ಳು. To start; to make a way for one's self, *as* water. -ನಡೆ. To go on foot; to travel. -ನೋಡು. To look out for, wait for. -ಬಿಡು. To go out of the way. -ಹೋಕ. A stroller. -ಕಾರ, -ಗ. A traveller.

ದಾರಿದ್ರ್ಯ, ದಾರಿದ್ರ್ಯ s. *n.* Poverty, indigence, distress.

ದಾರು s. *n.* A piece of wood, timber. 2, = ದೇವದಾರು. -ಹಸ್ತ, -ಹಸ್ತಕ. A wooden spoon or ladle.

ದಾರುಣ s. *a.* Cruel, horrible; hard, rough. *n.* Cruelty, horror.

ದಾರೆ 1, -ಹುಳಿ k. *n.* The fruit of *Averrhoa carambola.*

ದಾರೆ 2, *tb. of* ಧಾರೆ, *q. v.*

ದಾರ್ಢ್ಯ s. *n.* Stability, strength, energy.

ದಾಲಚಿನ್ನಿ, ದಾಲ್ಚಿನಿ f. *n.* Cinnamon.

ದಾಲು h. *n.* Split pulse, dhâl.

ದಾವ 1. = ಯಾವ, *q. v.*

ದಾವ 2. (= ದವ) s. *n.* A forest conflagration; *also* ದಾವಾಗ್ನಿ, ದಾವಾನಲ. 2, a forest.

ದಾವಣಿ (*tb. of* ದಾಮನಿ) *n.* A rope for tying cattle.

ದಾವತಿ f. *n.* Labour, toil, exertion, trouble. -ಗೊಳ್ಳು, -ಪಡು. To toil, *etc.* -ಪಡಿಸು. To give trouble. -ಮಾಡು. To take pains.

ದಾವರ f. *n.* Thirst, desire; need, want; *also* ದಾವು.

ದಾವಾ, ದಾವೆ (= ದಾವು) h. *n.* Enmity, spite; a suit, complaint. -ಸೊತ್ತು. Property in litigation. -ದಾರ. A prosecutor; complainant, plaintiff.

ದಾಶ s. *n.* A fisherman. 2, a servant.

ದಾಶರಥಿ (*fr.* ದಶರಥ) s. *n.* Râma.

ದಾಷ್ಟೀಕ (*tb. of* ಧಾರ್ಷ್ಟ್ಯಕ) *n.* A bold and influential man; boldness. -ತನ. Boldness.

ದಾಸ s. *n.* A male servant, slave; a devotee; *f.* ದಾಸಿ. -ಗೆಲಸ. Servile work. -ಭಾವ. The attitude of a slave. -ಯ್ಯ. A (Vaishṇava) devotee; *f.* -ಗಿತ್ತಿ. ದಾಸರ ಪದಗಳು. Songs composed by Vaishṇava devotees. -ತ್ವ. Servitude, slavery.

ದಾಸಣಿ, ದಾಸವಾಣಿ, ದಾಸವಾಳ, *etc.* f. *n.* The shoe-flower or China rose, *Hibiscus rosa sinensis.*

ದಾಸರ, ದಾಸರಿ (*tb. of* ದಾಸೇರ) *n.* A Vaishṇava religious mendicant. -ಹಾವು. The boa.

ದಾಸೊಳ. = ದಾಸಣ, *q. v.*

ದಾಸಿ s. *n.* A female servant or slave.

ದಾಸೋಹ (*fr.* ದಾಸಃ ಅಹಂ I am a servant) s. *n.* Self-subjection; devotion.

ದಾಸ್ತಾನ (*cf.* ತೋಸ್ತಾನು) h. *n.* A deposit; reserve, stock.

ದಾಹ s. *n.* Burning; internal heat. 2, ardent desire. 3, thirst. -ಗೊಳ್ಳು. To become thirsty. -ನಿವಾರಣೆ, -ಶಮನ, -ಶಾಂತಿ. Quenching desire or thirst.

ದಾಳಾ, ದಾಳಿ (ಳ = ಡ. *tb. of* ಧಾಟಿ) *n.* An impetuous assault; an attack; a rush; an inroad. -ಇಡು. To make an assault; to rush up to. ದಾಳಾದಾಳಿ. A mutual assault.

ದಾಳಿಂಬ, ದಾಳಿಂಬೆ, *etc.* (*tb. of* ದಾಡಿಮ, *q. v.*) *n.* A pomegranate.

ದಿಕ್ಕು (*tb. of* ದಿಶ್) *n.* A point of the compass, direction. 2, refuge, protection, help. -ದಿಕ್ಕಿಗೆ. In every direction. ದಿಕ್ಕಿಲ್ಲದೆ. Refuge, *etc.*, not existing. ದಿಕ್ಕಿಲ್ಲದವ. A helpless man. ದಿಕ್ಕಾಪಾಲು. Dispersion in all directions; ruined condition. -ಚಕ್ರ, ದಿಕ್ಚಕ್ರ. The horizon; a mariner's compass.

ದಿಕ್ಪಾಲ, -ಕ *s. n.* The regent or guardian of one of the quarters of the world.

ದಿಗಂತ *s. n.* The visible horizon.

ದಿಗಂಬರ *s. a.* Sky-clothed, unclad, naked. *n.* A naked mendicant.

ದಿಗರು h. *ad.* Also, additionally. *a.* Another. -ಜವಾಬು. Another or contradictory answer.

ದಿಗಿಲು k. *n.* Consternation, horror, alarm, fear.

ದಿಗಿಸು a. k. *v. t.* To let down, lower.

ದಿಗುಲು. = ದಿಗಿಲು, *q. v.*

ದಿಗ್ಗಜ *s. n.* An elephant of one of the eight quarters of the compass.

ದಿಗ್ಗನೆ k. *ad.* Suddenly, all at once.

ದಿಗ್ದೇಶ *s. n.* Various regions, distant countries.

ದಿಗ್ಬಂಧನ *s. n.* A general charm to keep off all evils.

ದಿಗ್ಬಲಿ *s. n.* An offering to the regions of the sky.

ದಿಗ್ಭ್ರಮೆ, ದಿಗ್ಭ್ರಾಂತಿ *s. n.* Consternation.

ದಿಗ್ರೀ e. *n.* Degree. *n.* Division or interval marked on a thermometer or barometer; *also* ಡಿಗ್ರೀ.

ದಿಗ್ವಾಚಕ *s. n.* A term denoting direction.

ದಿಗ್ವಿಜಯ *s. n.* Universal conquest.

ದಿಂಕು a. k. *n.* A jump, leap. 2, gambol. ದಿಂಕಿಡು. To leap, jump.

ದಿಟ (*tb. of* ದಿಷ್ಟ) *n.* Truth. *ad.* Certainly, truly. -ಪುಟ. Courage, stout, robust. -ಮಾತು. A true word.

ದಿಟ್ಟ (*tb. of* ಧೃಷ್ಟ) *a.* Bold, courageous; strong, powerful. -ಗಾರ. A bold man. -ತನ. Boldness.

ದಿಟ್ಟಿ. *tb. of* ದೃಷ್ಟಿ, *q. v.* -ಕೊನೆ, -ಗೊನೆ. A side-glance. -ಗೊಳಿಸು. To appear. -ಸು. To see; to look at.

ದಿಡ (*tb. of* ದೃಢ) *a.* Firm, strong, *etc.* *n.* Firmness, strength.

ದಿಡ್ಡಿ f. *n.* A wicket; a sally-post; *also* -ಬಾಗಲು.

ದಿಣ್ಣು k. *n.* An eminence; a hillock.

ದಿಂಡಿಗ k. *n.* The tree *Anogeissus latifolia,* which yields a hard, white gum.

ದಿಂಡು k. *n.* A heap; a big stone; a bundle of wood or grass; a bale of cloth. 2, the handle of a plough; a log. 3, the trunk of a tree. 4, the centre of an orange; the core of a plantain tree. 5, thickness; strength; pride; nutritiousness. -ಆ. A stout man. -ಕೈ. A stout arm. -ಮೆಯ್ಯಿ. A stout, strong body. -ಗೊಳ್ಳು, -ಪಡು, -ಬೀಳು. To become stout.

ದಿಣ್ಣೆ (= ದಿನ್ನೆ, *q. v.*) k. *n.* An eminence; a bank.

ದಿತಿ *s. n.* N. of a daughter of Daksha, wife of Kaśyapa.

ದಿನ *s. n.* A day. -ಗಟ್ಲೆ. Daily. -ಕಳೆ, -ಗಳೆ. To spend a day. -ಕೂಲಿ. Daily hire. -ದಂತೆ, -ದ ಹಾಗೆ. As usual. -ದಿನ. *rep.* Daily. -ದಿನಕ್ಕೆ. Day by day, daily. -ಚರ್ಯೆ. The daily observance of rites; an official journal. -ಕರ, -ನಾಥ, -ಪ. The sun. -ಪ್ರತಿ. = ದಿನಂಪ್ರತಿ. -ಮಾನ. The length of a day. ದಿನಂಪ್ರತಿ. Daily. -ವಹಿ. A diary, day-book. -ವರ್ತಮಾನ, -ವಾರ್ತೆ, -ಸುದ್ದಿ. Daily news.

ದಿನಸಿ (= ಜಿನಸು) f. *n.* Grain; *also* ದಿನಸು, ದಿನುಸು.

ದಿನಾ *s. ad.* Daily; *also* -ಗ, -ಗಲು, -ಲು.

ದಿಬ್ಬ k. *n.* An eminence, a hillock; *cf.* ದಿಣ್ಣೆ.

ದಿನ್ನೆ. = ದಿಣ್ಣೆ, *q. v.* -ತಗ್ಗು. Hill and dale.

ದಿಬ್ಬಣ k. *n.* A nuptial procession. 2, a wooden stopple.

ದಿಮಾಕು h. *n.* Haughtiness, inflation; arrogance, pride.

ದಿಂಬು k. n. A pillow for the head; also ತಲೆ-. 2, the pericarp of a lotus.

ದಿಮ್ಮಗೆ, ದಿಮ್ಮನೆ k. ad. Strongly; loudly.

ದಿಮ್ಮಿ k. n. A log of wood. 2, a bulb.

ದಿಮ್ಮು 1. k. n. Giddiness. -ಹತ್ತು, -ಏರು. Giddiness to come over one.

ದಿಮ್ಮು 2. k. v. t. To push, shove.

ದಿವ s. n. Heaven; the sky, air. 2, day, a day. -ರಾತ್ರಿ. Day and night.

ದಿವಸ (= ದಿನ, q. v.) s. n. A day. -ಕಳೆ. = ದಿನಗಳೆ, q. v. -ಕ್ಕೆ ಹಾಕಳು. To procrastinate. -ದಿವಸ. rep. = ದಿನ ದಿನ. -ಹತ್ತು, -ಹಿಡಿ. Days to be required (it takes ... days). -ವ್ಯಾಪಾರ. = ದಿನಚರ್ಯೆ, q. v.

ದಿವಾಕರ s. n. The sun.

ದಿವಾಣ, ದಿವಾನ h. n. A minister or chief officer of state. 2, a royal hall; a court of justice. 3, the sarkâr; also ದಿವಾನು.

ದಿವಾನಾ h. a. Mad; foolish.

ದಿವಾಭೀತಿ s. n. A person timid by day. 2, an owl; a thief.

ದಿವಾರಾತ್ರ, ದಿವಾರಾತ್ರಿ s. n. Day and night.

ದಿವಾಳಿ 1. tb. of ದೀಪಾವಳಿ, q. v.

ದಿವಾಳಿ 2. f. n. Bankruptcy. -ಎತ್ತಿ ಹೋಗು, -ತೆಗೆ. To become bankrupt. -ಖೋರ. A spendthrift; a bankrupt.

ದಿವಿ s. n. Heavens, the sky. 2, a day. -ಜ. A deity. -ಜಪದ. Svarga. -ನಾಯಕ. Indra.

ದಿವ್ಯ s. a. Divine, heavenly; charming, beautiful. -ಕಳೆ. Divine lustre.

ದಿಶ್. = ದಿಕ್ಕು, q. v. ದಿಶಾಧಿಪ. = ದಿಕ್ಪಾಲ. The guardians are surarâja, agni, kâla, niruti, varuṇa, maruta, arthêśa, îśa.

ದಿಶ, ದಿಶೆ s. n. A quarter or point of the compass, direction, region.

ದಿಷ್ಟ s. a. Appointed, ordered; fixed. n. Assignment, decree; fate; aim.

ದಿಷ್ಟಿ (tb. of ದೃಷ್ಟಿ, q. v.) n. The eye; sight.

ದೀಕ್ಷೆ s. n. Preparation or consecration for a religious ceremony; initiation; dedication; devotion, e. g. ಪಿತೃ-, ಮಾತೃ-, ವಿವಾಹ-, ಶೈವ-, etc. ದೀಕ್ಷಿತ. Initiated, consecrated; a conductor of a sacrifice; a family N.

ದೀಟು k. n. Similarity, equality. 2, valuation. -ಆಗಿರು, -ಗೊಳ್ಳು, -ಪಡು, -ಬೀಳು. To be equal.

ದೀನ s. a. Afflicted; miserable. 2, dejected, downcast. 3, poor, indigent. 4, humble. -ಗುಣ. A humble disposition. -ತನ, -ತೆ, -ತ್ವ, -ಭಾವ. Humility. ದೀನೋದ್ಧಾರಿ. A deliverer of the humble.

ದೀಪ s. n. A lamp; a light. (2, tb. of ದ್ವೀಪ. -ದ್ರಾಕ್ಷೆ. Imported raisins). -ಕಚ್ಚು. = -ಹಚ್ಚು. -ಆರಿಸು, -ಕಂತಿಸು, -ಕಳೆ, -ತೆಗೆ, -ದೊಡ್ಡದು ಮಾಡು (superstition). To extinguish a lamp. -ದ ಕಡ್ಡಿ. A match. -ಹಚ್ಚು. To light a lamp. -ಕಂಬ. = -ಸ್ತಂಬ, q. v. -ದ ಮಲ್ಲಿ. A female image with a lamp-cup. -ದರ್ಶನ. Looking upon a lamp as in an adoring attitude. -ಸ್ತಂಬ. A lampstand. ದೀಪಾರತಿ. A kind of lighted ârati. ದೀಪಾವಳಿ (= ದಿವಾಳಿ, q. v.). A festival with nocturnal illuminations; also ದೀಪೋತ್ಸವ.

ದೀಪ್ತ s. a. Illuminated, bright. ದೀಪ್ತಿ. Brilliancy, light, lustre; a ray, flash.

ದೀರ್ಘ s. a. Long (as space or time). 2, long, as a vowel. -ಕಾಲ. A long time. -ಕೋತಿ. A cockle. -ತೆ. Length, longness. -ದರ್ಶಿ. Seeing far, wise; a seer. -ದೃಷ್ಟಿ. Far-seeing, far-sighted, shrewd; a sagacious man. -ದ್ವೇಷ. An old grudge. -ನಿದ್ರೆ, -ಶಯನ. Death. -ರೋಗ. A long illness. -ಶಾಂತಿ. Long-suffering, patience. ದೀರ್ಘಾಯು, ದೀರ್ಘಾಯುಷ್ಯ. Long life.

ದೀವಟಿ, ದೀವಟಿಗೆ (tb. of ದೀಪವಟಿಕೆ) n. A torch, flambeau. -ಗ, -ಯವ. A torch-bearer. -ಸಲಾಮು. An honouring ceremony performed every evening by waving lighted torches before a noble personage or an idol.

ದೀವಾಳಿ. tb. of ದೀಪಾವಳಿ, q. v.

ದೀವಿ. *tb. of* ದ್ವೀಪ, *q. v.* -ಹಲಸು. The breadfruit tree, *Artocarpus incisa.*

ದೀವಿಗೆ (*tb. of* ದೀಪಿಕೆ) *n.* A lamp. 2, brightness, brilliancy.

ದು k. *A termination of the p. p., as:* ಕುಡಿದು, ತಂದು, ನಡೆದು, ನೆನೆದು, ಕೊಂದು, *etc.* 2, *tb. of* ದ್ವಿ.

ದುಃ s. *pref.* Evil, bad, difficult, hard.

ದುಃಖ s. *n.* Unhappiness, pain, sorrow, grief, affliction, distress, misery; trouble, difficulty. -ಕೊಡು. To give trouble. -ಗೊಳ್ಳು, -ಪಡು. To be grieved, *etc.* -ಪಡಿಸು. To cause trouble, *etc.* -ಮಾಡು. To feel unhappy; to grieve, *etc.* -ಕರ. Causing pain, sorrow, *etc.* -ಜೀವಿ. Living in pain or distress. -ಶಮನ, -ಶಾಂತಿ. Allaying or cessation of pain, grief, *etc.*

ದುಃಖಿ s. *n.* Sorrowing, afflicted. -ತ. Pained, distressed. -ಸು. To be unhappy; to grieve.

ದುಃಶಬ್ದ s. *n.* A bad sound or word.

ದುಃಶೀಲ s. *a.* Badly disposed, ill-natured, reprobate.

ದುಃಸ್ಥಿತಿ s. *n.* Ill condition, unhappiness.

ದುಕಾನು h. *n.* A shop. -ದಾರ. A shopkeeper.

ದುಕೂಲ s. *n.* Woven silk, very fine cloth.

ದುಗತ, ದುಗುಡ (*tb. of* ದುರ್ಗತಿ) *n.* Grief, care, anxiety; uneasiness.

ದುಗ್ಗ. *tb. of* ದುರ್ಗ, *q. v.*

ದುಗ್ಗಾಣಿ (*fr.* ದು-ಕಾಣಿ) s. *n.* Two kâṇis, two kâsus.

ದುಗ್ಧ s. *n.* Milk; sap. ದುಗ್ಧಾಭಿಷೇಕ. Bathing with milk. ದುಗ್ಧಾಬ್ಧಿ. The sea of milk.

ದುಗ್ಧಿಕೆ s. *n.* A sort of *Asclepias.* 2, a kind of gourd.

ದುಗ್ಧಿ (*tb. of* ದುರ್ಬುದ್ಧಿ) *n.* Doubt, suspense. 2, ill will; envy.

ದುಡಕು. = ದುಡುಕು, *q. v.*

ದುಡಿ k. *v. i.* To labour, work, toil. 2, to throb and pain, *as* a boil. *v. t.* To acquire by one's labour. -ತ, -ಮೆ. Acquisition, gain. -ಮೆಗಾರ. An economist. -ಸು. To cause to labour.

ದುಡುಕು k. *v. t.* To act rashly, violently or wickedly. *n.* Rashness, insolence; *also* -ತನ. -ಬುದ್ಧಿ. A rash mind.

ದುಡುಮ್ k. *A sound of suddenly falling.* -ಪ್ರವೇಶ. Entering headlong upon a work. -ನೆ. Suddenly.

ದುಡುಮೆ. = ದುಡಿಮೆ, *see s.* ದುಡಿ. -ಗಾರ. An economist.

ದುಡ್ಡು k. *n.* A copper coin, $\frac{1}{3}$ of an Aṇa. 2, money. ದುಡ್ಡಾಶೆ. Covetousness.

ದುಂಟು k. *n.* Rocking, unevenness. ದುಂಟಾಡು. To rock, to be uneven, *as* a table, *etc.*

ದುಂಡಗೆ, ದುಂಡಿಗೆ k. *ad.* Roundly. *a.* Round. *n.* Roundness; *also* ದುಂಡನೆ, ದುಂಡನ್ನ, ದುಂಡಾನೆ.

ದುಂಡಿಗು k. *n.* A shrub from Brazil, used for hedges, *Jatropha curcas.*

ದುಂಡು k. *n.* Roundness. 2, a plain bracelet. ದುಂಡಿಸು. To round, move circularly.

ದುತ್ತಾರಿ h. *n.* Worked muslin.

ದುತ್ತೂರ, -ರಿ (*tb. of* ಧುತ್ತೂರ, *q. v.*) *n.* The thorn-apple.

ದುದ್ದು k. *n.* The pulpy mass of a cucumber or pumpkin which contains the seeds.

ದುಂದು k. *n.* Excessive expenditure, waste, prodigality. ದುಂದವುತನ. A sumptuous dinner without occasion. -ಮಾಡು. To squander. -ಗಾರ. A spendthrift, prodigal. -ಗಾರತನ, -ಗಾರಿಕೆ. Spendthriftness, prodigality.

ದುಂದುಭಿ s. *n.* The fifty-sixth year of the cycle. 2, a large kettle-drum.

ದುಪಟಿ, ದುಪ್ಪಟಿ, ದುಪ್ಪಟಿ (*tb. of* ದ್ವಿಪಟ್ಟಿಕಾ) *n.* A double cloth; a sheet.

ದುಬಾರಿ h. *a.* Double; excessive. -ಖರ್ಚು. Double expense. -ಪ್ರತಿ. A duplicate. -ತನ. Prodigality.

ದುಬಾಸಿ (*tb. of* ದ್ವಿಭಾಷಿ) *n.* An interpreter.

ದುಬ್ಬ k. *n.* A very stout man; *f.* ದುಬ್ಬಿ.

ದುಮುಕು, ದುಮ್ಮಿಕ್ಕು k. v. i. To leap or jump down.

ದುಂಬು k. n. Dust.

ದುಮ್ಮಾನ (tb. of ದುರ್ಮಾನ) n. Distress, sorrow, grief.

ದುಯುಮ್ h. a. Secondary, subordinate.

ದುರ್, ದುಶ್, ದುಷ್, ದುಸ್ (=ದುಃ) s. pref. Evil, bad, difficult, hard, etc.

ದುರ a. k. n. A battle, war.

ದುರಂಗಿ (tb. of ದ್ವಿರಂಗ) a. Double coloured, as cloth.

ದುರಂಜಿ f. n. The custard-apple, *Anona squamosa.*

ದುರದೃಷ್ಟ s. n. Bad luck, misfortune.

ದುರಬೀನು h. n. A telescope.

ದುರಭಿಪ್ರಾಯ s. n. An evil intention.

ದುರಭಿಮಾನ s. n. Offensive pride, presumption. ದುರಭಿಮಾನಿ. Disagreeably proud.

ದುರಭ್ಯಾಸ s. n. A bad practice or habit.

ದುರವಸ್ಥೆ s. n. A miserable condition; a bad situation.

ದುರಸ್ತು (=ದುರುಸ್ತು) h. a. Right, fit, in good order. -ಮಾಡು. To repair.

ದುರಹಂಕಾರ s. n. Offensive egotism, presumption.

ದುರಾಗ್ರಹ s. n. Foolish obstinacy. ದುರಾಗ್ರಹಿ. A head-strong person.

ದುರಾಚರಣೆ s. n. Bad behaviour, evil practices.

ದುರಾಚಾರ s. n. Bad conduct, wickedness. ದುರಾಚಾರಿ. Loose, licentious.

ದುರಾತ್ಮ s. n. A malevolent person; a rascal, scoundrel; f. ದುರಾತ್ಮಿಕೆ.

ದುರಾಲಭ s. a. Difficult of attainment.

ದುರಾಲೋಚನೆ s. a. A bad thought or intention.

ದುರಾಶೆ s. n. Bad hope or desire. 2, groundless hope. -ಗಾರ. A man of bad desire.

ದುರಿಚ್ಛೆ s. n. Bad desire.

ದುರಿತ s. n. Evil ways, sin. -ಹರ. Removing sin.

ದುರೀಷಣೆ s. n. A bad wish; curse.

ದುರುಕ್ತಿ s. n. Harsh, offensive speech; abuse.

ದುರುಸ್ತು.=ದುರಸ್ತು, q. v.

ದುರುಳ (tb. of ಧೂರ್ತ) n. A cunning, dishonest or wicked man; f. ದುರುಳೆ. -ತನ. Wickedness.

ದುರ್ಗ (=ದುಗ್ಗ) s. a. Difficult of access. n. A stronghold, fort. 2, a forest.

ದುರ್ಗತ s. a. Unfortunate, distressed, poor. ದುರ್ಗತಿ. Ill condition; misfortune; misery; hell.

ದುರ್ಗಂಧ s. n. A bad smell, stink.

ದುರ್ಗಮ s. a. Difficult of access or attainment.

ದುರ್ಗಾಷ್ಟಮಿ s. n. The eighth lunar day of the month of Âśvina, the birthday of Durgâ.

ದುರ್ಗಿ.=ದುರ್ಗೆ, q. v. -ಬೇನೆ. Cholera.

ದುರ್ಗುಣ s. a. An evil quality; a vicious propensity.

ದುರ್ಗೆ, ದುರ್ಗಾ s. n. Daughter of Himavat and wife of Śiva.

ದುರ್ಘಟ s. a. Difficult, unattainable.

ದುರ್ಜನ s. n. A bad man; a mischievous man, villain.

ದುರ್ಜಯ s. a. Invincible.

ದುರ್ದರ್ಶ s. a. Disagreeable to the sight; disgusting.

ದುರ್ದಶೆ s. n. A bad situation; misfortune, calamity; also ದುರ್ದೆಸೆ.

ದುರ್ದಿನ s. n. A dark, cloudy day; bad weather.

ದುರ್ದೈವ s. n. Hard fate, bad luck, unlucky destiny; misfortune; also -ಯೋಗ. 2, a bad deity.

ದುರ್ಧರ s. a. Difficult to be borne or suffered; irresistible; difficult, impracticable; dangerous.

ದುರ್ಧರ್ಷ s. a. Difficult of being assailed; inviolable; intolerable.

ದುರ್ನಡತೆ s.-k. n. Bad conduct.

ದುರ್ನಾಮ s. n. A bad name; piles.

ದುರ್ನಿಮಿತ್ತ s. n. A bad omen. 2, a foul pretext.

ದುರ್ನೀತಿ s. n. Bad conduct; impropriety; bad ethics.

ದುರ್ನೆವ (tb. of ದುರ್ನಿಘ) n. A bad excuse, poor pretence.

ದುರ್ಬಗೆ s.-k. n. Evil intention; wicked resolve.

ದುರ್ಬಲ s. a. Weak, feeble.

ದುರ್ಬೀನು = ದುರಬೀನು, q. v.

ದುರ್ಬುದ್ಧಿ s. n. Folly, silliness. 2, evil-mindedness.

ದುರ್ಬೋಧನೆ, ದುರ್ಬೋಧೆ s. n. Evil counsel; bad, harmful teaching.

ದುರ್ಭಯ s. n. Fear or painful apprehension of evil.

ದುರ್ಭರ s. a. Burdensome, intolerable.

ದುರ್ಭಾಗ್ಯ s. n. Ill luck, lucklessness.

ದುರ್ಭಾವ s. n. Ill will, hostile feeling, hatred.

ದುರ್ಭಾಷಣೆ, ದುರ್ಭಾಷೆ s. n. Bad, abusive speech, opprobrious language.

ದುರ್ಭಿಕ್ಷ s. n. Scarcity of provisions, dearth, famine. -ಬೀಳು. A famine etc. to come to pass.

ದುರ್ಮತ s. n. A bad opinion, doctrine, or tenet.

ದುರ್ಮತಿ s. n. Evil-mindedness, malignity; foolishness. 2, the fifty-fifth year of the cycle.

ದುರ್ಮನ, -ಸ್ s. n. A bad disposition, evil mind. 2, bad advice.

ದುರ್ಮರಣ s. n. Any violent or unnatural death.

ದುರ್ಮಾಂಸ s. n. Proud flesh that grows in a sore or wound.

ದುರ್ಮಾರ್ಗ s. n. Misconduct; offence; wickedness; also -ತನ. 2, a bad man.

ದುರ್ಮುಖಿ s. n. The thirtieth year of the cycle of sixty.

ದುರ್ಮೋಹ s. n. Bewildered, infatuated or enamoured state. 2, ignorance, folly.

ದುರ್ಯಶ s. n. Ill repute, dishonour.

ದುರ್ಯೋಧನ s. n. N. of the eldest son of Dhṛitarâshṭra.

ದುರ್ಲಕ್ಷಣ s. n. A bad sign or symptom; a bad character; a vice.

ದುರ್ಲಕ್ಷ್ಯ s. a. Difficult to be observed; disagreeable to sight. n. Inadvertence.

ದುರ್ಲಭ s. a. Difficult to be obtained; scarce, rare; excellent; dear.

ದುರ್ವಚನ s. n. A harsh expression; abusive language, insult.

ದುರ್ವಾಕ್ s. n. Evil speech; inelegant language.

ದುರ್ವಾರ s. a. Difficult to be repressed, irresistible.

ದುರ್ವಾರ್ತೆ s. n. Bad news, sad intelligence.

ದುರ್ವಾಸ, -ಸ್ s. n. N. of a ṛishi. a. Unclothed.

ದುರ್ವಾಸನೆ s. n. Bad smell, stink. 2, an evil recollection of past actions.

ದುರ್ವಿದಗ್ಧ s. a. Unskilled; stupid; wholly ignorant.

ದುರ್ವಿನೀತ s. a. Ill-trained; ill-mannered; stubborn.

ದುರ್ವಿವಾದ s. n. A bad contest at law.

ದುರ್ವಿಷಯ s. n. A bad thing or affair.

ದುರ್ವೃತ್ತ s. n. Bad conduct, mean practices. a. Vile, wicked.

ದುರ್ವೃತ್ತಿ s. n. Disreputable conduct, bad practices.

ದುರ್ವ್ಯಯ s. n. Useless expense.

ದುರ್ವ್ಯಸನ s. n. An evil habit; bad desire. ದುರ್ವ್ಯಸನಿ. A man of evil habits; f. ದುರ್ವ್ಯಸನೆ.

ದುರ್ವ್ಯಾಪಾರ s. n. Evil action or operation.

ದುವ್ವಾಳಿ f. n. Rapid course; a run. -ಸು. To make run.

ದುಶ್. = ದುರ್, q. v.

ದುಶ್ಚಾಲಿ s. n. A wicked, impious or immoral conduct. -ತನ. Wickedness, iniquity, immorality.

ದುಶ್ಚಿಹ್ನೆ s. n. An inauspicious sign; an ill omen.

ದುಶ್ಚೇಷ್ಟೆ s. n. Naughtiness.

ದುಶ್ಶಕುನ s. n. A bad omen.

ದುಶ್ಶಾಲು s.-f. n. Two shawls; a double shawl.

ದುಶ್ಶಾಸನ (=ದುಃಶಾಸನ) s. a. Intractable. n. N. of a son of Dhṛitarâshṭra.

ದುಷ್ಕರ್ಮ s. n. An evil act, crime. ದುಷ್ಕರ್ಮಿ. Sinful, wicked.

ದುಷ್ಕಾಮ s. n. Inordinate passion, lust, vice.

ದುಷ್ಕಾಲ s. n. An evil time on account of sin, famine, *etc.*

ದುಷ್ಕೃತ್ಯ s. n. A misdeed, sin, crime.

ದುಷ್ಟ s. a. Corrupt, bad, wicked, vicious, depraved, noxious. -ಗುಣ. A wicked disposition. -ತನ. Wickedness. -ಬುದ್ಧಿ. Evil-minded; an evil mind; a N. -ಮೃಗ. A wild beast. ದುಷ್ಟಾತ್ಮ. Of a bad nature, wicked; an evil spirit.

ದುಷ್ಪ್ರಯೋಗ s. n. Bad use, useless purpose; foul aim.

ದುಷ್ಫಲ s. n. A bad fruit or result.

ದುಸ್. = ದುರ್, *q. v.*

ದುಸರಿಬಳ್ಳಿ n. A winding half shrubby plant, *Cocculus villosus.*

ದುಸ್ತರ s. a. Impassable; invincible.

ದುಸ್ತು f. n. Dress; a suit of clothes.

ದುಸ್ಸಂಗ s. n. Bad inclination. 2, bad company. ದುಸ್ಸಂಗಿ. A person who associates with evil companions.

ದುಸ್ಸಂತತಿ s. n. A bad progeny or family.

ದುಸ್ಸಹ s. a. Intolerable, unbearable. -ವಾಸ. Bad association.

ದುಸ್ಸ್ವಪ್ನ s. n. An evil dream.

ದುಸ್ಸ್ವಭಾವ s. n. A bad disposition or nature.

ದುಹಿ (*tb. of* ದ್ವಿ) n. Discordance; hatred, ill-will.

ದುಹಿತೃ s. n. A daughter; *tb.* ದುಹಿತೆ.

ದುಹೇರ f. a. Doubled; double; *cf.* ದುಬಾರಿ.

ದೂಗು k. v. t. To push, thrust, shove away or aside, throw out of, *as* out of a village, caste, *etc.* ದೂಡಿಸು. To cause to push, *etc.*

ದೂಂಟು k. v. i. To walk on one leg, hop.

ದೂತ s. n. A messenger, envoy, ambassador; *f.* ದೂತಿ. -ಲಕ್ಷಣ. The characteristic mark of a messenger.

ದೂದಿ (*tb. of* ತೂಲ) n. Cleaned cotton. 2, silkcotton used as tinder.

ದೂಪ. *tb. of* ಧೂಪ, *q. v.*

ದೂಮರ (*tb. of* ಧೂಮ್ರ) n. Fine drizzling rain.

ದೂರ s. a. Distant, far from; remote. n. Distance, farness, remoteness; a long distance. ದೂರಕ್ಕೆ. To a distance; from afar. -ಮಾಡು. To remove. -ದರ್ಶಿ. Far-seeing, wise; a prophet. -ದೃಷ್ಟಿ. Far-sightedness, foresight, discernment.

ದೂರಿ h. n. An axle-tree.

ದೂರು (ರು = ಱು) k. v. t. To bear tales; to report evil of others; to blame, reproach, abuse; to slander. n. Blame, slander, calumny. -ಗೊಳ್ಳು. To get blamed, *etc.* -ಹೇಳು. To tell tales, slander, blame, *etc.* -ತರು, -ಹೊರು. To bring blame upon one's self.

ದೂರ್ವೆ, ದೂರ್ವಾ s. n. The grass *Panicum dactylon.*

ದೂಲ (*tb. of* ತುಲಾ) n. A beam of timber.

ದೂಷಕ s. a. Dishonouring; reviling; blaming. n. A reviler, seducer, abuser, blasphemer.

ದೂಷಣೆ s. n. Corrupting; contaminating; censuring, abusing; blame; guilt, sin. -ಮಾಡು. To abuse, blame, *etc.* -ಹೇಳು. To tell tales, *etc.* -ಹೊಂದು. To get blamed. ದೂಷಿಸು. To blame, censure, abuse, *etc.*

ದೂಷ್ಯ s. a. Censurable; condemnable; contemptible. n. Cloth; cotton, calico.

ದೂಸ, ದೂಸು (*tb. of* ದೂಷ್ಯ) n. Cloth. ದೂಸಿಗ. A cloth merchant. ದೂಸಿಗವಸರ. A cloth merchant's shop.

ದೂಸರು a. k. n. Reason, motive, cause; self-interest.

ದೂಳಿ, ದೂಳು (*tb. of* ಧೂಲಿ) n. Dust; powder; pollen. -ಮರ. A dust-board.

ದೃಕ್ಕು (*tb. of* ದೃಶ್) *n.* An eye; seeing. ದೃಕ್ಸಿದ್ಧಾಂತ. The science of astronomical observation. ದೃಗ್ಗಣಿತ. Calculations founded on observations of heavenly bodies.

ದೃಢ s. *a.* Firm, strong, solid; tenacious, compact. 2, confirmed, established; certain, reliable. 3, powerful, mighty. *n.* Truth. -ಚಿತ್ತ. A strong will. -ಗೊಳ್ಳು. To become firm. -ಪಡಿಸು. To strengthen, confirm. -ಬುದ್ಧಿ, -ಮನಸ್ಸು. A firm mind. ದೃಢಾಂಗ. Firm-bodied, stalwart; *also* ದೃಢಾಂಗಿ. ದೃಢೀಕರಣ. Making firm; confirmation; an act of becoming a member of the Church of Christ.

ದೃಶ (=ದೃಶ್) s. *a.* Seeing, viewing. *n.* The eye. ದೃಶ್ಯ. Visible; to be looked at; beautiful. -ಮಾಡು. To show. ದೃಶ್ಯಾ-. Visible and invisible.

ದೃಷ್ಟ s. *a.* Seen, beheld, observed; visible, apparent; decided; known.

ದೃಷ್ಟಾಂತ s. *n.* An example, illustration, instance, evidence. 2, a Śâstra: science.

ದೃಷ್ಟಿ (=ದಿಟ್ಟಿ, ದಿಷ್ಟಿ) s. *n.* Seeing. 2, sight; look, glance. 3, the eye. 4, intellect. -ಇಡು. To look or aim at; to look after. -ಕೊಡು. To pay attention to, *etc.* -ಗೆ ಬೀಳು. To appear. -ಗೋಚರ. The range of the sight, in sight, visible. -ದೋಷ. A blast from an evil eye. -ಸು. To see, look at.

ದೆಮ್ಮಾಖಿ f. *n.* Greatness, pomp.

ದೆಬ್ಬೆ. =ದಬ್ಬೆ, *q. v.*

ದೆವ್ವ (*tb. of* ದೈವ) *n.* A demon, evil spirit, phantom. -ಚೇಷ್ಟೆ. The grimaces of one who is possessed. -ತಿಂಡಿ. A glutton. -ಬಡಿ. A demon to strike (or possess) a person; *also* -ಹೊಡೆ. -ಬಿಡಿಸು. To exorcise. -ಸೋಕು. The touch of an evil spirit. -ಹಿಡಿ. A demon to possess a person.

ದೆಸೆಂಬರ e. *n.* December (12th month of the year).

ದೆಸೆ (*tb. of* ದಿಶೆ) *n.* A point of the compass. 2, (*tb. of* ದಶೆ) condition, state. 3, luck, *etc.* ಅವನ ದೆಸೆಯಿಂದ. On his account. -ಗಾರ, -ವಂತ. A fortunate man. -ಗೆಡು. Refuge *etc.* to be lost.

ದೇಗಲ, ದೇಗುಲ (*tb. of* ದೇವಕುಲ) *n.* A temple. ದೇಗುಲಿಗ. An attendant on an idol.

ದೇಟು, ದೇಂಟು f. *n.* A stem.

ದೇಢ h. *a.* One and a half.

ದೇಣೆ, ದೇಣಿ, ದೇಣೆ h. *n.* Money due, a debt. 2, mercantile transactions. ದೇಣಾಲೇಣ. Lending and borrowing; mercantile transaction. ದೇಣೆದಾರ. A debtor.

ದೇದೀಪ್ಯಮಾನ s. *a.* Brilliant, splendid.

ದೇವ s. *a.* Divine, celestial. *n.* A deity, god. 2, a king. 3, an honourific title; his majesty, his honour. ದೇವರು. Your honour; *pl.* ದೇವಗಳ್, ದೇವರು. *The pl. honourific form is used also of men; but when used of God the predicate is put in singl.* -ಕಣಿಗಿಲು. A white sort of oleander. -ಕಾರ್ಯ. Any act of worship, any religious rite. -ಕುಸುಮ. Cloves. -ಖಾತ, -ಖಾತಕ. A natural pond. -ಗಂಗೆ. The celestial Ganges. -ಗಣ. A class of nakshatras. -ತನ, -ತೆ, -ತ್ವ. Divinity; a deity, god. -ತರು. A celestial tree. -ತಾಯನ. A temple. -ತಾರ್ಚನೆ, ದೇವಾರಾಧನೆ. Divine worship. -ದತ್ತ. God-given; N. of the conch-shell of Arjuna; N. of any one. -ದಾಯ, -ಮಾನ್ಯ. Lands allotted rent-free to pagodas. -ದಾರ, -ದಾರು. A species of pine, *Pinus deodora.* -ದಾಸ. A servant of god; N.; *f.* -ದಾಸಿ. -ದೂತ. An angel. -ನಾಗರಿ. The character in which Samskṛita is usually written. -ನಾಳ. A kind of reed. -ಪೂಜೆ. Worship of gods. -ಭೂಮಿ, -ಲೋಕ. Heaven. -ಮಂದಿರ. =ದೇವಾಲಯ. -ಮಾದಳ. A large kind of citron. -ಮಾನುಷ. A divine man; a harmless fellow. -ಮಾರ್ಗ. The sky, ether.

-ಯಜ್ಞ. The hôma sacrifice. -ಯಾನ. The vehicle of a god. -ರಥ. The car of a deity. -ರಾಜ. Indra. -ಲಿಪಿ. A divine writing. -ವೈರಿ. A râkshasa. -ಸಭೆ. An assembly of gods. -ಸ್ತ್ರೀ. A celestial nymph; *also* ದೇವಾಂಗನೆ. -ಸ್ಥಾನ. A temple. ದೇವತಾಂಶ. A part of the deity; divine. ದೇವಾದ್ರಿ. Mount Mêru. ದೇವಾಧಿದೇವ. A god above all other gods. ದೇವಾಲಯ. A temple; church; heaven. -ಸ್ವ. Property endowed to the service of temples.

ದೇವಕಿ s. *n.* Kṛishṇa's mother.

ದೇವಡಿ f. *n.* A porch; the threshold; a house. -ಗ. An attendant upon an idol.

ದೇವನ s. *n.* Going, motion. 2, sport, play. 3, a die. 4, grief, sorrow.

ದೇವರ s. *n.* A husband's younger brother.

ದೇವರ್ಷಿ s. *n.* A heavenly ṛishi, *as* Nârada, Atri, *etc.*

ದೇವಲ, -ಕ s. *n.* An attendant on an idol.

ದೇವಾಂಗ s. *a.* N. of an emanation from Sadâśiva, held as the inventor of weaving. 2, a kind of cloth. -ದವರು. A class of Śaiva weavers.

ದೇವಿ 1. s. *n.* A goddess. 2, Durgâ. 3, a queen; a princess. 4, the small-pox. 5, *an honourific termination of fem. names.* -ಪಂಡಿತ. A vaccinator.

ದೇವಿ 2. h. *a.* Giving. ಲೇವಾ-. Borrowing and lending.

ದೇವೇಂದ್ರ s. *n.* The chief of the gods: Indra.

ದೇಶ s. *n.* A place; a side; a country, district. -ಕಾಲ. Place and time. -ಪರ್ಯಟನ, ದೇಶಾಟನ. Travelling abroad. -ಭಾಷೆ. The language of a country. -ಭ್ರಷ್ಟ. Expelled from a country. -ಭ್ರಷ್ಟತ್ವ. Expatriation. -ಸ್ಥ. Resident in a country; a class of Brâhmaṇas. ದೇಶಾಚಾರ. The customs and manners of a country. ದೇಶಾಧಿಪ, ದೇಶಾಧಿಪತಿ. The ruler of a country. ದೇಶಾಂತರ. Another or foreign country. ದೇಶಾಭಿಮಾನ. High opinion of one's country, patriotism. ದೇಶಾಭಿಮಾನಿ. A person who has this opinion; a patriot.

ದೇಶಾಯಿ. = ದೇಸಾಯಿ, *q. v.*

ದೇಶಾವರ, ದೇಶಾವಾರ s. *n.* Begging alms from country to country; foreign countries. 2, alms. 3, imports.

ದೇಶಿ s. *a.* Belonging to a country. *n.* The dialect of a country. 2, a certain râga. -ಕ. A guide; a teacher; a traveller; a stranger. ದೇಶೀಯ, ದೇಶ್ಯ. Local; provincial; native.

ದೇಸಾಯಿ f. *n.* The head of a district; an hereditary officer.

ದೇಸಿ (= ದೆಸಿ) a. k. *n.* Beauty, comeliness. -ಗಾರ. An artist; *f.* -ಕಾತಿ.

ದೇಸಿಗ. *tb. of* ದೇಶಿಕ, *q. v.*

ದೇಹ s. *n.* The body. -ತ್ಯಾಗ. Death. -ದಂಡನೆ. Mortification of the body; corporal punishment. -ಗುಣ, -ಧರ್ಮ. The constitution. -ಧಾರಿ. A living being; an individual. -ಶುದ್ಧಿ. Bodily purification. -ಸಾಧನೆ. Bodily exercise, *as* bathing, *etc.* ದೇಹಾಂತ. Death.

ದೇಹಿ s. *a.* Having a body, corporeal, embodied. *n.* A living man. 2, the soul.

ದೈತ್ಯ s. *n.* A demon, asura, râkshasa; *also* ದೈತೇಯ. -ಧ್ವಂಸಿ, -ವೈರಿ, ದೈತ್ಯಾರಿ. Vishṇu. -ಗುರು. Śukra.

ದೈನ್ಯ (*fr.* ದೀನ) s. *n.* Feebleness; depression, humbleness. -ಪಡು. To be low spirited; to be humble. -ವೃತ್ತಿ. Miserable subsistence; humble behaviour.

ದೈವ (*fr.* ದೇವ) s. *a.* Divine. *n.* A deity, god; *also* ದೈವತ. 2, destiny; fortune, fate. 3, property, wealth. 4, a demon or devil. -ಕ. Divine. -ಜ್ಞ. An astrologer. -ಪರ. Fatalistic. -ಗತಿ, -ಯೋಗ. Fortune, chance. -ಶಾಲಿ. A fortunate person. ದೈವಾಧೀನ. Depending on deity, subject to fate; death.

ದೈವಿಕ s. *a.* Divine, providential.

ದೈಹಿಕ s. *a.* Corporal.

ತೊಗೆ k. v. t. To dig or excavate with the nails, *etc.*

ದೊಡ್ಡ k. a. Large, big, stout, thick, great; extensive; important; chief; loud; old; *as:* -ಅಡವಿ, -ಕಲ್ಲು, -ಕೂಗು, -ಕೆಲಸ, -ತಪ್ಪು, -ತಾಳ್ಮೆ, -ದನ, -ದೊಣ್ಣೆ, -ದೊರೆ, -ನಾಯಿ, -ನೋಣ, -ಬೀದಿ, -ಬೆಟ್ಟ, -ಮನೆ, -ಮರ, -ಮಾತು, -ಹೊಟ್ಟೆ, *etc.* A large, big, *etc.* ದೊಡ್ಡಕ್ಕ. The elder of the elder sisters. ದೊಡ್ಡಣ್ಣ. The eldest of the elder brothers. ದೊಡ್ಡದು. A thing which is large. -ತಂದೆ. Father's elder brother; great aunt's husband. -ತಾಯಿ. Mother's elder sister; great uncle's wife. ದೊಡ್ಡಪ್ಪ. = -ತಂದೆ. -ನಡೆ. A fast walk. -ನಿದ್ರೆ. Long sleep; death. -ಮನಸ್ಸು. A generous mind; generosity. -ಮರದರಿಸಿನ. The tree turmeric. -ಮಾರ್ಗ. A high road. -ರಕ್ತಗಂಧಿ. The royal Gool-mohr, *Poinciana regia.* ದೊಡ್ಡವ. A great, noble, old, rich, tall, *etc.*, man; *f.* -ವಳು. ದೊಡ್ಡೊಕ್ಕಲು. A well-to-do inhabitant. -ತನ, -ತ್ವ, -ಸ್ತನ, -ಸ್ತಿಕೆ. Exalted position, greatness, dignity. ದೊಡ್ಡಿತು. That is large, *etc.*

ದೊಡ್ಡಿ k. n. A cow-pen, fold, stable; a stockade for impaling wild elephants; a settler's first house.

ದೊಡ್ಡೆ k. n. The bat used at tip-cat.

ದೊಣ್ಣೆ k. n. A cudgel, club, mace.

ದೊದ್ದೆ a. k. n. A mass; a crowd, mob; tumult. 2, indistinct speech.

ದೊಂದೆ k. n. A bundle of sticks, grass, *etc.*, used as a torch; *diminutive* ದೊಂದಿ.

ದೊನ್ನೆ k. n. A leaf-cup.

ದೊಬ್ಬು (= ತೊಬ್ಬು, *q. v.*) k. v. t. To shove, push, thrust, throw.

ದೊಂಬ (= ಡೊಂಬ, *q. v.*) f. n. A caste of tumblers, mountebank. -ಗಳು. A tumbler's pole. ದೊಂಬರಾಟ. Tumbling.

ದೊಂಬಿ k. n. A crowd, mob; riotous mob, affray, quarrel. -ಜಗಳ. A street quarrel. -ದಾಸರು. One of a company of stage players. -ಸಾಕ್ಷಿ. A confused testimony. -ಗಾರ. A rioter.

ದೊರಕಿಸು k. v. t. To cause to obtain, *etc.*

ದೊರಕು (= ದೊರೆ) k. v. i. To be obtained, gained or found; to accrue. *P. p.* ದೊರತು. *Used impersonally with the dative case, as:* ನಮಗೆ ದೊರಕುತ್ತದೆ. We get.

ದೊರಿ, ದೊರೆ 1. = ದೊರಕು, *q. v.* *P. ps.* ದೊರಿತು, ದೊರದು, ದೊರೆದು.

ದೊರೆ 2. a. k. n. Resemblance; likeness, equality; propriety. 2, gain, advantage, use.

ದೊರೆ 3. (*tb. of* ಧುರ್ಯ) n. A chief; a king; a master; a man of the ruling class; a gentleman. -ತನ. Kingship, government, rule. -ತನ ಮಾಡು. To rule. -ಸಾನಿ. A lady.

ದೋಟಿ k. n. A pole with a hook for plucking fruit, *etc.*

ದೋಣಿ (= ಡೋಣಿ. *tb. of* ದ್ರೋಣಿ) n. A boat.

ದೋತರ, ದೋತ್ರ f. n. A Hindu-male's garment worn around the waist or over the shoulder. -ಉಟ್ಟುಕೊಳ್ಳು. To wear such a garment. -ಹೊದ್ದುಕೊಳ್ಳು. To put on a garment.

ದೋಬಿ f. n. A washerman.

ದೋಮೆ k. n. A musquito; a gnat.

ದೋರ 1, ದೋರೆ 1. a. k. n. Full-grown or mature state. -ಗಾಯಿ. A full-grown fruit.

ದೋರ 2, ದೋರೆ 2. h. n. Thread. 2, a kind of bracelet.

ದೋಲ s. n. Swinging, rocking. 2, a swing.

ದೋಲಿ (= ಡೋಲಿ), ದೋಲೆ s. n. A swing; a litter, palanquin. ದೋಲೋತ್ಸವ. The ceremony of swinging an idol.

ದೋಷ s. n. Fault, vice, defect; a blemish; blame, reproach; badness, sin; morbid affection, disease; spots on the tongue foreboding death. -ಆಡು. To blame. -ಇಡು. To put fault or blame upon. -ಹಚ್ಚು. To lay or bring reproach upon; to find fault with. -ಕಾರಿ. An evil-doer. -ಗ್ರಾಹಿ. Fault-finding, censorious. -ಜ್ಞ. A discerning wise man; a physician. -ತ್ರಯ. Vitiation of the three humours *as* wind, bile, and phlegm. -ಹರಣ. Removing blemish. ದೋಷಾಕರ. The moon; faulty. ದೋಷಾರೋಪಣ. Accusation.

ದೋಷಿ s. *a.* Faulty, guilty, sinful. -ಸು. Morbid affection to arise, *as* in fever.

ದೋಷೆ s. *n.* Darkness, night. 2, the arm.

ದೋಸೆ k. *n.* A flat, spongy cake of rice-flour, uddu, *etc.*

ದೋಸ್ತಿ h. *n.* Friendship. -ಗಾರ. A friend.

ದೋಹದ, ದೋಹಳ s. *n.* A longing of a pregnant woman; any morbid desire.

ದೋಳು (= ಡೋಲು. *tb.* *of* ಢೋಲ) *n.* A drum.

ದೌತು. = ದವುತು, *q. v.*

ದೌತಿ (= ದವತಿ, *q. v.*) f. *n.* An inkstand.

ದೌತ್ಯ (*fr.* ದೂತ) s. *n.* The function of a messenger.

ದೌರಾತ್ಮ್ಯ (*fr.* ದುರಾತ್ಮ) s. *n.* Evil-mindedness, wickedness.

ದೌರ್ಬಲ್ಯ s. *n.* Weakness, infirmity.

ದೌರ್ಭಾಗ್ಯ (*fr.* ದುರ್ಭಾಗ್ಯ) s. *n.* Ill-luck, misfortune.

ದೌಲತು h. *n.* Wealth, affluence.

ದೌಷ್ಟ್ಯ (*fr.* ದುಷ್ಟ) s. *n.* Depravity, wickedness.

ದೌಹಿತ್ರ (*fr.* ದುಹಿತೃ) s. *n.* A daughter's son.

ದ್ಯಾವ. *tb.* *of* ದೇವ, *q. v.*

ದ್ಯು s. *n.* A day. 2, the sky. -ನದಿ. The celestial Ganges. -ಮುಖ. Dawn, morning.

ದ್ಯುತ್, ದ್ಯುತಿ s. *n.* Brightness, brilliancy, lustre, light.

ದ್ಯೂತ (= ಜೂಜು, *etc.*) s. *n.* Gambling. -ಕಾರ. A gambler.

ದ್ಯೋತ s. *n.* Shine, light, splendour. -ನ. Shining, enlightening; seeing. ದ್ಯೋತಿಸು. To shine; to appear.

ದ್ರಮು s. *n.* A dram; a dose of liquor.

ದ್ರವ s. *n.* Dripping, flowing; liquid; fluidity. 2, moisture; essence, juice. 3, melting from pity or tenderness.

ದ್ರವಿಡ s. *n.* N. of a people and district on the east coast of the Dekhan: Tamil. -ಭಾಷೆ. A family of languages in South-India, *as:* Tamil, Telugu, Kannaḍa, Malayâlam and Tuḷu.

ದ್ರವಿಸು s. *v. i.* To become liquid. *v. t.* To melt, *as* the mind.

ದ್ರವ್ಯ s. *n.* Substance, property, wealth, money. 2, a substance, thing. 3, the receptacle of properties, *etc.*, elementary substance. -ವಂತ, -ಸ್ಥ. A wealthy man. ದ್ರವ್ಯಾನುಕೂಲ. Help of money towards any business. ದ್ರವ್ಯಾಶೆ. Covetousness.

ದ್ರಾಕ್ಷೆ, ದ್ರಾಕ್ಷಿ s. *n.* The vine. 2, a grape, grapes. -ಚಪ್ಪರ. A vine-pandal. -ಪಾಕ. An accomplished style of diction in poetry. -ಬಳ್ಳಿ. The grape vine. -ರಸ. Grape juice. -ಸರಾಯಿ. Wine. -ಹಣ್ಣು. A ripe grape.

ದ್ರಾಬೆ (*tb.* *of* ದ್ರಾವ) *n.* A blockhead. 2, wretchedness, feebleness. 3, trash, rubbish. 4, a wretched and poor person.

ದ್ರಾವ s. *n.* Liquefaction, distilling. -ಕ. A drug prepared by distillation.

ದ್ರಾವಿಡ (*fr.* ದ್ರವಿಡ) s. *a.* Belonging to Draviḍa.

ದ್ರುತ s. *a.* Run, flown. 2, melted, liquid. 3, quick, swift.

ದ್ರುಪದ s. *n.* King of the Pâñcâlas and father of Draupadî.

ದ್ರೋಣ s. *n.* A trough, bucket, cup. 2, a measure of capacity, equal to 4 âḍhakas. 3, Drôṇâcârya, the teacher of the Kurus and Pâṇḍavas.

ದ್ರೋಣಿ (= ದೋಣಿ, *q. v.*) s. *n.* A boat. 2, a valley.

ದ್ರೋಹ s. *n.* Injury, mischief, treachery, treason; rebellion, wrong. ದ್ರೋಹಿ.

Spiteful, treacherous; a traitor, betrayer; *as:* ಗುರು-, ಪಿತೃ-, ಮಾತೃ-, ಮಿತ್ರ-, ಸ್ವಾಮಿ-, *etc.*

ದ್ರೌಪದಿ (*fr.* ದ್ರುಪದ) s. *n.* N. of the daughter of Drupada and wife of the five Pâṇḍu princes.

ದ್ವಂದ್ವ s. *n.* A pair, couple. 2, any pair of opposites, *as* right and wrong, heat and cold, *etc.* 3, strife, contest. 4, doubt, uncertainty. 5, a form of compound (*g.*). -ಯುದ್ಧ. A duel, single combat.

ದ್ವಯ s. *a.* Twofold, both, double. *n.* A pair.

ದ್ವಾದಶ s. *a.* Twelve. 2, the twelfth. ದ್ವಾದಶಿ. The twelfth day of a lunar fortnight.

ದ್ವಾಪರ, ದ್ವಾಪಾರ s. *n.* The third of the four yugas of the world. 2, doubt. 3, war.

ದ್ವಾರ s. *n.* A door, gate. 2, a way, means, medium. ದ್ವಾರಾ. By means of, through. -ಪಟ್ಟಿ. The threshold; the panel of a door. -ಪಾಲ, -ಪಾಲಕ. A door-keeper. -ಬಂಧ. A door-frame.

ದ್ವಾರಕಾಪುರ, ದ್ವಾರಕೆ, ದ್ವಾರಾವತಿ s. *n.* Dvârakâ, the capital of Kṛishṇa.

ದ್ವಿ s. *a.* Two. -ಕರ್ಮ. Two accusatives. -ಗು. A grammatical compound. -ಗುಣ. Two-fold, double. -ಗುಣಿಸು. To multiply by two. -ಜ. Twice-born; a man of the first three classes: a Brâhmaṇa, Kshatriya, or Vaiśya; a bird; a snake; a star; a house. -ಧಾಪಿ. = ದುದಾಪಿ, *q. v.* *Cpds.:* -ಮಾಸ, -ಮುಖ, *etc.*

ದ್ವಿತೀಯ s. *a.* Second. -ವಿವಾಹ. A second marriage. -ವಿಭಕ್ತಿ. The accusative. ದ್ವಿತೀಯೆ. The 2nd of the lunar fortnight.

ದ್ವಿತ್ವ s. *n.* Doubleness. 2, a pair, couple. 3, reduplication of a consonant.

ದ್ವಿಧಾ s. *ad.* In a two-fold manner. -ಗತಿ. Duplicity.

ದ್ವಿಪ s. *n.* An elephant (*lit. drinking twice*).

ದ್ವಿಪದ s. *n.* A biped. *a.* Two-footed.

ದ್ವಿಪದಿ s. *n.* A kind of metre.

ದ್ವಿರದ s. *n.* An elephant.

ದ್ವಿರುಕ್ತಿ s. *n.* Repetition, tautology.

ದ್ವಿಸ್ವಭಾವ s. *a.* Having a double nature.

ದ್ವೀಪ s. *n.* An island; a sandbank. ದ್ವೀಪಾಂತರ. A foreign island. ದ್ವೀಪಿ. A tiger, leopard.

ದ್ವೇಷ s. *n.* Hate, hatred, enmity; dislike. ದ್ವೇಷಿ. A hater, foe, enemy. ದ್ವೇಷಿಸು. To hate, dislike.

ದ್ವೈತ s. *n.* Duality, dualism. 2, dualism in philosophy, *as* of spirit and matter, *etc.*

ದ್ವೈಧ s. *n.* Duplicity. 2, disunion; dispute; doubt. ದ್ವೈಧೀಭಾವ. Duplicity, fraud, doubt.

ದ್ವೈಪಾಯನ s. *n.* The island-born Vyâsa.

ದ್ವ್ಯಾಹಿಕ s. *a.* Returning every second day, *as* fever.

ಧ್. The thirty-seventh letter of the alphabet. *In Kannaḍa it occurs only in a few dêśiya and tadbhava words.*

ಧಕಾರ s. *n.* The letter ಧ.

ಧಗ *f. n.* Fire, blaze. -ಧಗೆ. Blazing, flaming; being very brilliant, glittering much. -ಧಗನೆ. *rep.* With a fierce glow, *etc.* -ಧಗಿಸು. To burn fiercely.

ಧತ್ತೂರ (=ದತ್ತೂರ) s. *n.* The white thorn-apple, *Datura alba.*

ಧನ s. *n.* Property, wealth, riches, money. 2, wealth in cattle. -ಕ್ಷಯ.

Loss of property. ಧನಂಜಯ. Conquering wealth; fire; Arjuna. -ಪಾಲ. A guardian of treasure: Kubêra. -ಬಲ. Power of wealth. -ಮದ. Pride of wealth. -ಲಕ್ಷ್ಮಿ. Riches. -ಲೋಭ. Covetousness, avarice. -ವಂತ. A rich man. -ಹೀನ. Poor. ಧನಾಢ್ಯ. Wealthy.

ಧನಾಸರಿ s. n. N. of a tune.

ಧನಿ, -ಕ s. n. A rich man; an owner, master.

ಧನಿಷ್ಠೆ s. n. The twenty-third lunar mansion.

ಧನು, ಧನುರ್ (= ಧನುಸ್) s. n. A bow. 2, the sign *Sagittarius*. ಧನುರ್ಧಾರಿ. Bearing a bow: an archer. ಧನುರ್ಬಾಣ. A bow and arrow. ಧನುರ್ಮಾಸ. The solar 9th month. ಧನುರ್ವಾತ, ಧನುರ್ವಾಯು. Tetanus, a disease which bends the body like a bow. ಧನುರ್ವಿದ್ಯೆ. Archery. ಧನುರ್ವೇದ. The science of archery; N. of a treatise on archery.

ಧನುಸ್ (= ಧನು, *q. v.*) s. n. A bow. 2, the sign *Sagittarius*. 2, an arc.

ಧನ್ಯ s. a. Opulent, rich. 2, fortunate, happy, blest; lucky. -ತೆ. Opulence; good fortune. ಧನ್ಯೆ. A fortunate woman; *Emblic myrobalan*.

ಧನ್ಮಡಿ h. n. A rice-field; *also* ಧಾನ್ಮಡಿ.

ಧನ್ವಂತರಿ s. n. The sun. 2, N. of a celebrated physician.

ಧಮನ, ಧಮನಿ s. n. A reed, pipe, tube.

ಧಮ್ಮಿಲ್ಲ s. n. A braided and ornamented hair of a woman.

ಧರ s. n. Holding, bearing, wearing; having; sustaining. 2, a mountain. -ಣ. Bearing, holding; a support; a weight for gold.

ಧರಣಿ s. n. The earth; the ground. -ಜ, -ಜಾತ. A tree. -ತಲ. Earth's surface. -ಪ, -ಪತಿ, -ಪಾಲಕ, -ವರ, -ವಲ್ಲಭ, -ಈಶ, -ಈಶ್ವರ. A king. -ಧರ, -ಧ್ರ. The serpent śêsha; a mountain.

ಧರಾಧಿಪ, ಧರಾಧಿಪತಿ, ಧರಾಧೀಶ s. n. A king.

ಧರಿತ್ರಿ (= ಧರಣಿ, *q. v.*) s. n. The earth.

ಧರಿಸು s. v. t. To hold, bear, carry; to contain; to put on one's self, *as* clothes, *etc.*; to obtain, get. ಅವತಾರ-. To become incarnate. ಗರ್ಭ-. To become pregnant.

ಧರ್ಮ s. n. Ordinance, law; duty; right, justice; charity; liberality; a pious act. 2, usage, custom. 3, virtue, merit, good works; religion, piety. 4, almsgiving; alms; gift. 5, harmlessness. 6, sacrifice. 7, nature. 8, the god of justice: Yama. -ಕರ್ತ. The manager of a temple, almshouse, *etc.* -ಕೊಡು, -ಮಾಡು. To give alms. -ಬೇಡು. To ask for alms. -ಕಾರ್ಯ. Any pious act. -ಗ್ರಂಥ. A code of religious laws. -ತ್ಯಾಗ. Apostacy. -ತ್ಯಾಗಿ. An apostate. -ದೇವತೆ, -ದೇವಿ. Virtue personified as a woman. -ನಿಷ್ಠೆ. Devotion to religion or charity. -ಪತ್ನಿ. A lawful wife. -ಬುದ್ಧಿ. Virtuousness, charitable disposition. -ಮಾರ್ಗ. The path of virtue. -ಜ, -ಪುತ್ರ, -ರಾಜ, -ರಾಯ. Yudhishṭhira, Yama. -ವಂತ. A virtuous or pious man. -ಶಾಲೆ. A building for travellers; a poor-asylum; a school at which children are taught gratis. -ಶಾಸ್ತ್ರ. A code of law; jurisprudence. -ಶೀಲ. Virtuous, pious. -ಸತ್ರ. An alms-house. -ಸ್ಥಲ. N. of a place of pilgrimage in S. Canara. ಧರ್ಮಾತ್ಮ. A just and pious man. ಧರ್ಮಾಧಿಕಾರಿ. A judge; the almoner of a prince. ಧರ್ಮಾಧ್ಯಕ್ಷ. An administrator of laws, king. ಧರ್ಮಾರ್ಥ. In charity; as a gift, gratis (*esp. as* ಧರ್ಮಾರ್ಥವಾಗಿ).

ಧರ್ಮಿ s. a. Virtuous, religious, just. -ಷ್ಠ. Most pious, very virtuous, *etc.*

ಧವಲ, -ಳ s. a. White, dazzling. 2, beautiful. n. A kind of camphor. ಧವಳೆ. A white cow.

ಧಾಟಿ s. n. Assault.

ಧಾತ. *tb. of* ಧಾತೃ, *q. v.*

ಧಾತು s. n. Natural condition. 2, an element, primary substance, primitive matter, *as* earth, water, fire, air and ether or âkâśa. 3, an essential ingredient of the body, *as* blood, marrow, *etc.* 4, the organs of sense. 5, a mineral; a metal; an ore. 6, a grammatical root. 7, origin. 8, strength. 9, the pulse. 10, the tenth year of the cycle of sixty. -ಕುಂದು, -ಗುಂದು. Strength to decrease. -ನೋಡು. To feel the pulse. -ನಷ್ಟ, -ನಾಶನ. Loss of strength. -ಪಾಠ. A list of verbal themes. -ಪುಷ್ಟಿ. Nutrition or strength of the body. -ಲಕ್ಷಣ. The state of the pulse. -ವಾದ. Mineralogy.

ಧಾತೃ s. *n.* A founder, maker, creator. 2, Brahmâ.

ಧಾತ್ರಿ (= ದಾದಿ) s. *n.* A wet-nurse, foster-mother. 2, the earth. 3, *Emblic myrobalan.*

ಧಾನ್ಯ s. *n.* Corn, grain; rice. -ಧನ. Property in grain. ನವ-. Nine kinds of corn grown in India.

ಧಾಮ s. *n.* A house, home. 2, the body. 3, radiance, light. 4, dignity.

ಧಾರ (= ದಾರ) s. *n.* Holding. 2, a holder. 3, streaming down; flowing; a violent shower, gush. 4, a wave. 5, a hole. 6, a thread. -ಕ. A receptacle, box; a post. -ಣ. The act of holding, bearing, undergoing, preserving, protecting, assuming, *etc.*; keeping the mind collected, holding the breath suspended.

ಧಾರಣೆ (= ಧಾರಣ, *q. v.*) f. *n.* Rate, price. ಪೇಟೆ-. Market price.

ಧಾರಾಗೃಹೀತ s. *n.* A present received from the donor by pouring water over it; *also* ಧಾರಾದತ್ತ.

ಧಾರಾಳ s. *n.* Profusion; freedom from reserve; liberality, generosity. ಧಾರಾಳಿ. A liberal person. -ದ ಮಾತು, -ದ ನುಡಿ. Eloquence.

ಧಾರಿ s. *aff.* A person who holds, wears, *etc.*

ಧಾರುಣಿ (*tb.* of ಧಾರಿಣಿ) *n.* The earth.

ಧಾರೆ (= ಧಾರ) s. *n.* The dropping of any liquid; a stream of water; a shower. 2, the pace of a horse. 3, the sharp edge of a sword or any cutting instrument.

ಧಾರ್ಮಿಕ (*fr.* ಧರ್ಮ) s. *a.* Righteous, virtuous, religious. -ತನ. Righteousness.

ಧಾರ್ಷ್ಟ್ಯ (*fr.* ಧೃಷ್ಟ) s. *n.* Impudence, violence.

ಧಾವಕ s. *a.* Washing, cleansing. 2, running.

ಧಾವನ s. *n.* Rubbing off; cleansing. 2, running, flowing. 3, attack, assault.

ಧಾಷತ್ತು h. *n.* Boldness, courage, impudence. 2, dread, awe.

ಧಿಕ್ s. *int.* Fie! shame! -ಕರಿಸು. To reproach, censure; to treat scornfully. -ಕಾರ. Reproach, censure; disrespect.

ಧಿಷ್ಣ್ಯ s. *a.* Intelligent. *n.* a thoughtful man. 2, Brahmâ. 3, a star.

ಧೀ s. *n.* Thought; understanding, intellect. -ಮತ್ (*tb.* ಧೀಮನ, ಧೀಮಂತ). Intelligent, wise; an intelligent man.

ಧೀರ s. *a.* Firm, resolute, brave, daring. 2, intelligent, prudent; sensible. -ತನ, -ತೆ, -ತ್ವ. Firmness, energy, courage, resolution.

ಧೀವರ s. *n.* A very intelligent man. 2, a fisherman.

ಧೀಶ s. *n.* A very intelligent man.

ಧುನಿ s. *a.* Sounding, roaring. *n.* A river.

ಧುರ. = ದುರ, *q. v.*

ಧುರಂಧರ s. *a.* Bearing the yoke; laden with good qualities. *n.* A foreman, leader, chief. 2, a man of business.

ಧುರ್ಯ (= ದೊರೆ, *q. v.*) s. *a.* Able to bear a yoke. *n.* A beast of burden. 2, a leader, chief.

ಧೂಪ (= ದೂಪ) s. *n.* Incense, frankincense, perfume. -ದೀಪನೈವೇದ್ಯ. The three essential constituents of idol-worship: the burning of incense, the waving of lamps, and the offering of boiled rice, *etc.* ಧೂಪಾರತಿ, ಧೂಪಾತಿರ್. A censer. -ದ ಮರ. The white dammer tree, *Valeria indica.* -ಅರ್ಪಿಸು, -ತೋರು, -ಎತ್ತು, -ಹಾಕು. To offer incense. ಧೂಪಿಸು. To incense; to perfume.

ಧೂಮ s. n. Smoke, vapour. -ಕೇತು. A meteor; a comet. -ಪಾನ. Smoking tobacco. -ಉ. Smoky. -ಶಕಟ. A railway carriage.

ಧೂಮ್ರ s. a. Smoke-coloured, grey, dark-red; dark, obscure. -ಪತ್ರೆ. Tobacco. -ಪಾನ. = ಧೂಮಪಾನ, *q. v.*

ಧೂರ್ಜಟಿ s. n. Śiva.

ಧೂರ್ತ s. a. Cunning, crafty, subtle. n. A rogue, cheat. 2, a passionate man; *f.* ಧೂರ್ತೆ. -ತ್ವ. Passion, wrath.

ಧೂಲಿ, ಧೂಳಿ. = ದೂಳಿ, *q. v.*

ಧೃತರಾಷ್ಟ್ರ s. n. Dhṛitarâshṭra, the eldest blind-born son of Vyâsa and the father of Duryôdhana. 2, a blind man. 3, a kind of bird.

ಧೃತಿ s. n. Firmness, steadfastness, energy, courage. 2, pleasure. -ಗೆಡು. Courage to lose.

ಥೆರ್ಮೊಮಿಟರ್ e. n. Thermometer, an instrument for measuring temperature.

ಧೇನು s. n. A milch cow.

ಧೈರ್ಯ (*fr.* ಧೀರ) s. n. Firmness; steadiness, constancy. 2, fortitude, courage. -ಕುಗ್ಗು, -ಕುಂದು. Courage, *etc.*, to sink. -ಕೆಡು, -ಗೆಡು. Courage to lose. -ಗೊಳ್ಳು, -ತಾಳು, -ಪಡು, -ಮಾಡು. To be encouraged, to take courage. -ಗೊಳಿಸು, -ಪಡಿಸು. To encourage. -ಬಿಡು. To lose courage. -ಗಾರ, -ವಂತ, -ಶಾಲಿ, -ಸ್ಥ. A courageous man.

ಧೋರಣೆ s. n. A vehicle in general. 2, aim, bent, tendency; manner, style, course. ಧೋರಣಿ. A good style of composition; disregard, inattention. -ಗಾರ. An inattentive man.

ಧೌತ s. a. Washed, cleansed; bright, pure. -ವಸ್ತ್ರ. Washed cloth.

ಧ್ಯಾನ s. n. Meditation, thought, reflection; heed. 2, an abstract religious contemplation. -ದಲ್ಲಿ ಬರು. To come to the mind. -ದೊಳಗೆ ಇಡು. To consider, mind. -ಪರ. Absorbed in meditation. -ಯೋಗ. Profound meditation; meditation and abstraction. ಧ್ಯಾನಿಸು. To think of, contemplate, meditate, reflect upon; to counsel with one's self.

ಧ್ರುವ s. a. Firm, immovable, fixed; constant, eternal. n. The polar star; the north pole. 2, the introductory stanza of a poem. 3, N. of a king, the son of ಉತ್ತಾನಪಾದ. -ನಕ್ಷತ್ರ. The polar star. -ಲೋಕ. The region of the polar star. -ವೃತ್ತ. A polar circle, arctic and antarctic. -ಸ್ಥಾನ. An extremity of the earth's axis.

ಧ್ವಂಸ s. n. Destruction; loss.

ಧ್ವಜ s. n. A banner, flag, ensign. -ಸ್ತಂಭ. A flag-staff.

ಧ್ವಜಿನಿ s. n. A standard-bearer; an arm.

ಧ್ವನಿ s. n. Sound, echo, noise, tone; a voice; a word. 2, allusion, hint. -ಗೈಯ್ಯು, -ಗೊಡು, -ಮಾಡು. To sound, roar, *etc.* ಪ್ರತಿ-. An echo.

ಧ್ವಾಂಕ್ಷ s. n. A crow, crane.

ಧ್ವಾನ s. n. Sound, noise; humming.

ನ್

ನ್. The thirty-eighth letter of the alphabet.

ನಕಲಿ h. *n.* Ridicule, joking, jesting, satire; mimicry. *Cpds.*: -ಮಾತು, -ಚೇಷ್ಟೆ, -ಗಾರ, -ಯವ. A buffoon, mimic.

ನಕಲು h. *n.* A copy, transcript. -ತೆಗೆ, -ಮಾಡು. To copy.

ನಕಷಿ (= ನಕಾಷಿ, ನಕ್ಷೆ) h. *n.* Ornamental representation; engraving; embroidery. 2, a picture; a map, plan.

ನಕಾರ s. *n.* The letter ನ. 2, denying, denial. ನಕಾರಿಸು. To deny, decline.

ನಕಾರಿ f. *a.* Inferior, bad, useless.

ನಕಾಷಿ. = ನಕಷಿ, *q. v.* -ತೆಗೆ, -ಮಾಡು. To carve, engrave, *etc.*

ನಕುಲ s. *n.* The mungoose, *Viverra ichneumon.* 2, the fourth of the Pâṇḍu princes.

ನಕ್ಕಿ f. *n.* A ring of wire worn on fingers while playing upon a stringed instrument.

ನಕ್ಕು k. *v. t.* To lick; *also* ನೆಕ್ಕು. 2, *p. p. of* ನಗು.

ನಕ್ತ s. *n.* Night. 2, fasting on certain nights. -ಂಚರ. A thief; an owl; a cat; a goblin.

ನಕ್ರ s. *n.* A crocodile, alligator. -ಧ್ವಜ. Kṛishṇa's son Pradyumna.

ನಕ್ಷೆ (= ನಕಷಿ, *etc.*) h. *n.* A map, picture.

ನಕ್ಷತ್ರ s. *n.* A star. 2, a constellation, lunar mansion. -ಗತಿ. The motion of the lunar mansions. -ಬಾಣ. A sky-rocket. -ಮಂಡಲ, -ಲೋಕ. The firmament. ಜನ್ಮ-. The star on which a man is born, natal star.

ನಕ್ಷೆ. = ನಕ್ಷ, *q. v.*

ನಖ, ನಖರ s. *n.* A nail of a finger or of a toe; a claw, talon.

ನಗ 1. s. *n.* An ornament; an article; a piece. 2, a load of articles. 3, a ship.

ನಗ 2. s. *n.* A mountain. 2, a tree. -ಜಾತೆ, -ಜೆ. Pârvatî.

ನಗದಿ h. *n.* Ready money. *a.* Fiscal, financial. -ಗುಮಾಸ್ತ. A cashier.

ನಗದು h. *n.* Ready money or cash.

ನಗರ s. *n.* A town, city. -ವಾಸಿ. A citizen. -ಶೋಧಕ. A town-watchman. -ಶೋಧನ. Inspection of a town.

ನಗಾರ, ನಗಾರಿ h. *n.* A large kettle-drum. -ಖಾನೆ. A place where the instruments of a band are kept; a band-stand.

ನಗು k. *v. i.* To laugh, smile; to laugh at, deride; to open (*P. p.* ನಕ್ಕು). *n.* A laugh, smile; laughter; derision. -ಮೊಗ. A smiling face.

ನಗೆ (= ನಗು *n.*) k. *n.* A laugh, *etc.*; blooming, *etc.* -ಆಡು, ನಗಾಡು. To laugh. -ಗೇಡು. A laughing-stock. -ಮಾತು. A joke. -ಮುಖ, -ಮೋರೆ. = ನಗುಮೊಗ, *q. v.* -ಗಾರ. A joker, ridiculer.

ನಗ್ಗಲು. = ನೆಗ್ಗಲು, *q. v.*

ನಗ್ಗು k. *v. i.* To become bruised, *as* a metal vessel. *n.* A bruise in a metal vessel. -ಬೀಳು. To get bruised. ನಗ್ಗಿ ಹೋಗು. To go stooping.

ನಗ್ನ s. *a.* Naked, bare. *n.* Śiva; nakedness.

ನಚ್ಚು 1. (= ನೆಚ್ಚು, *q. v.*) k. *v. t.* To confide, trust, put confidence in, believe. 2, to desire, love. *n.* Confidence, trust, faith, belief. 2, desire, love. ನಚ್ಚಿಕೆ, ನೆಚ್ಚಗೆ (= ನೆಚ್ಚಿಕೆ, -ನೆಗೆ). Confiding, trust, *etc.*

ನಚ್ಚು 2. k. *n.* Doubt. -ಮಾತು. An unreliable word.

ನಜರಾಣೆ, -ಕೆ h. *n.* A forced tax levied on all the people, an unjust fine.

ನಜರು h. *n.* Favourable look, sight; a present to a superior. -ಕಾಣಿಕೆ. = ನಜರಾಣೆ, *q. v.* -ಬಂದಿ. Temporary confinement.

ನಜರೇತು f. n. Nazaret, native place of Jesus Christ in Palestine.

ನಜುಗು k. v. i. To squash, crush, bruise, *as* dry ginger, pepper, *etc.*

ನಜ್ಜು k. n. A crushed state. -ಗುಜ್ಜು. A completely crushed mass.

ನಂಜು 1. k. v. t. To take a little, eat a little of any thing as a relish.

ನಂಜು 2. k. n. Poison; impurity of the blood; paralysis of the brain. -ಗೊರಳ, ನಂಜುಂಡ, ನಂಜುಂಡೇಶ್ವರ, ನಂಜ. Śiva. -ಜೋಗಿ. A dealer in antidotes. -ರೋಗ. Paralysis of the brain.

ನಟ s. n. An actor, dancer, mime. 2, the tree *Colosanthes indica*. -ನೆ. A pantomime; a dance; hypocrisy. ನಟಿ. An actress; an actor. ನಟಯಿಸು, ನಟಿಸು. To dance, act.

ನಟಿಕೆ k. n. The cracking of the finger or other joints.

ನಟ್ಟ, ನಟ್ಟೆ k. a. Middle, central. ನಟ್ಟಡವಿ. The middle of a forest. -ನಡು, -ನಡುವೆ. The very middle. ನಟ್ಟಿರುಳು. Midnight. ನಟ್ಟೆಲುವು. The backbone.

ನಟ್ಟವಿಗ, ನಟ್ಟುಗಾರ, ನಟ್ಟುವ s. n. An actor. 2, a dancing-master; *f.* ನಟ್ಟುವಗಾತಿ, ನಟ್ಟವಿಗಿತ್ತಿ, ನಟ್ಟುವಿತಿ.

ನಟ್ಟು k. n. Grass, its wide spreading roots.

ನಡ 1. (= ನಡದು, ನಡೆದು) *P. p. of* ನಡೆ, *in* ನಡಕೊಳ್ಳು. 2, (= ನಡೆ) walking *etc.* -ಸು. = ನಡಿಸು.

ನಡ 2. = ನಡು, *q. v.* *Cpds.:* -ಕಟ್ಟು. = ನಡುಕಟ್ಟು, *q. v.* -ಗಂಭ, -ಪ್ರಾಯ, -ಬೀದಿ, -ಭಾಗ, -ರಾತ್ರೆ, -ಹಾದಿ, *etc.* -ನಡುವೆ. The very midst.

ನಡ 3, ನಡಕ k. n. Trembling.

ನಡಗು. = ನಡುಗು, *q. v.*

ನಡತೆ k. n. Walk, course, conduct, behaviour. -ವಂತ. A man of proper conduct; *f.* -ವಂತೆ.

ನಡವಡಿಕೆ, ನಡವಳಿ, ನಡವಳಿಕೆ, ನಡಾವಳಿ, ನಡವಳಿತ k. n. Conduct, behaviour; custom, usage. 2, proceedings.

ನಡವು. = ನಡು 1, *q. v.* ನಡವಂತರ. Interval, intervening time, middle space.

ನಡವೆ k. n. The house-floor opposite the entrance-door.

ನಡಾಂತರ. = ನಡವಂತರ s. ನಡವು, *q. v.*

ನಡಾವಳಿ. = ನಡವಡಿಕೆ, *etc., q. v.*

ನಡಿ (= ನಡೆ, *q. v.*) k. v. i. To walk, *etc.* -ಗೆ. Pace, walk. -ಸು. To cause to walk, proceed, go; to carry on; to manage; to treat; to carry out, fulfil, *as* a promise; *also* ನಡಯಿಸು.

ನಡು 1. (= ನಡ 2) k. n. The middle, centre; the waist; the flank of a horse, *etc.*; *also* -ವು. -ಕಟ್ಟು. A waist-band, girdle. -ಗಡ್ಡೆ. An island. *Cpds.:* -ಗುಡ್ಡ, -ತಲೆ, -ತಟು, -ತೊಟ್ಟಿ, -ದಟ್ಟಿ, -ನಾಡು, -ಬೀದಿ, -ಬೆಟ್ಟು, -ಬೆರಳು, -ಮನೆ, -ರಾಜ್ಯ, -ರಾತ್ರಿ, -ಹಗಲು, -ಹರೆಯ, *etc.* -ನಡುವೆ. The very midst. -ವೆ. Between. -ವಂತರ. = ನಡವಂತರ.

ನಡು 2. (= ನೆಡು, *q. v.*) k. v. t. To plant, fix firmly, *etc.*

ನಡುಕ k. n. Trembling, shivering; tremor; fear.

ನಡುಗು (= ನಡಗು) k. v. i. To tremble, shake, shiver, quake.

ನಡೆ (= ನಡಿ) k. v. i. To walk; to march; to go on, proceed; to go; to be current; to continue; to come to pass; to behave, conduct one's self; to succeed; to be obedient to. (*P. ps.* ನಡದು, ನಡೆದು.) -ದಾಡು. To walk about. *n.* Walking; going; walk; course; gait; march; going; conduct, behaviour; *also* ನಡತೆ. 2, cattle. -ಗೆಡಿಸು. To cause to stop. -ನಡೆಗೆ. At every step. -ನುಡಿ. Conduct and speech. -ಮಡಿ. A clean cloth to walk over. -ಮಾಡ. A self-moving chariot of the gods.

ನಂಟ (= ನೆಂಟ, *q. v.*) k. n. A relative, *etc.* -ತನ, -ಸ್ತಿಕೆ. Relationship; *also* ನಂಟು (= ನೆಂಟು, *q. v.*).

ನತ್ತು 1. (= ನೆತ್ತು) k. v. i. To stutter, stammer. ನತ್ತಿ ಮಾತಾಡು. To stammer.

ನತ್ತು 2. (= ನೊತ್ತು) f. n. A nose-jewel.

ನತ್ವ s. n. Doubt, suspicion, uncertainty.

ನದ s. n. A river (*personified as male*); *f.* ನದಿ. 2, sounding. ನದಿ. A river. -ಪ್ರವಾಹ. The current or flow of a river.

ನನ್. = ನಾನು. *Gen.* ನನ, ನನ್ನ, ನನ್. *Dat.* ನನಗೆ, ನನಿಗೆ. *Acc.* ನನ್ನ, ನನ್ನನು, ನನ್ನನ್ನು. *Loc.* ನನಲಿ, ನನಲ್ಲಿ, ನನ್ನಲ್ಲಿ.

ನನೆ 1. a. k. *v. i.* To become wet, moist. -ಸು, ನನಸು. To moisten.

ನನೆ 2. a. k. *n.* A flower-bud, opening bud. *v. i.* To bud. -ಗೊಂಬು. A branch with buds. -ಮೊಗ್ಗೆ. A bud and blossom.

ನಂದ s. *n.* Happiness, joy. 2, N. of a cowherd who was the foster-father of Kṛishṇa. -ಕ. Gladdening; the sword of Kṛishṇa.

ನಂದನ s. *n.* Gladdening. 2, a son. 3, a garden, grove; *also* -ವನ. 4, twenty-sixth year of the cycle of sixty. ನಂದನೆ. A daughter.

ನಂದಾದೀಪ, ನಂದಾದೀವಿಗೆ (*fr.* ನಂದದ ದೀಪ or ದೀವಿಗೆ) k.-s. *n.* An ever burning lamp; *cf.* ನಂದು.

ನಂದಿ s. *n.* Joy, delight. 2, Śiva's bull. *a.* Happy; gladdening. -ಬಟ್ಟಲುಗಿಡ. A shrub with fragrant white flowers, *Tabernaemontana coronaria.* -ಮಂಟಪ. A kind of angular diagram. -ವಾಹನ. Śiva.

ನಂದು (= ನೊಂದು, *q. v.*) *v. i.* To be extinguished, to go out, *etc.* 2, to disappear, vanish. ನಂದಿಸು. To extinguish, quench.

ನಂದೆ s. *n.* Delight, felicity, prosperity. 2, the first, sixth or eleventh day of a lunar fortnight.

ನನ್ನ k. *pro. Gen. of* ನನ್, ನಾನು.

ನನ್ನಿ k. *n.* Truth, certainty. 2, love, affection. -ಮಾಡು. To verify, prove.

ನಪುಂಸಕ s. *n.* A hermaphrodite, a eunuch. 2, the neuter gender; *also* -ಲಿಂಗ.

ನಪ್ಪೆ k. *n.* A bruise in a fruit or tree.

ನಫರ h. *n.* A mean wretch.

ನಫೆ h. *n.* Profit, gain. -ಬಡ್ಡಿ. (24 per cent.) interest.

ನಬೀ h. *n.* A prophet: the prophet Mahomed. ಇಸಾ-. Jesus Christ.

ನಭ, ನಭಸ್ s. *n.* The sky, atmosphere. -ಸಂಗಮು. A bird. ನಭೋಽಜನ. A god. ನಭೋಮಂಡಲ. The firmament, sky.

ನಮ್ k. *pro.* We. *Gen.* ನಮ್, ನಮ, ನಮ್ಮ. *Dat.* ನಮಗೆ. *Acc.* ನಮ್ಮನು, ನಮ್ಮನ್ನು. *Abl.* ನಮ್ಮಿಂದ. *Loc.* ನಮ್ಮಲಿ, ನಮ್ಮಲ್ಲಿ.

ನಮನ s. *n.* Bowing, obeisance.

ನಮಲು k. *v. t.* To chew, masticate, to chew the cud. *n.* Chewing the cud. -ಹಾಕು. To chew the cud.

ನಮಸ್ s. *n.* Bowing; a bow, salutation, obeisance. -ಕರಿಸು. To bow, make obeisance, adore. -ಕಾರ. Obeisance, reverence, adoration.

ನಮಾಜು h. *n.* Worship; divine service.

ನಮಿಸು s. *v. t.* To bow; to worship, adore.

ನಮೂದು h. *a.* Declared, shown, mentioned, recorded. -ಮಾಡು, ನಮೂದಿಸು. To record, mention, show.

ನಮೂನೆ h. *n.* A specimen, sample; a model; a copy.

ನಮೆ k. *v. i.* To grow lean or thin; to wear away; to become less; to be poor.

ನಂಬರ e. *n.* Number; a case, lawsuit. -ದ ಕಟ್ಟು. The proceedings of a lawsuit. ಮೂಲ-. An original suit.

ನಂಬಿಕೆ, ನಂಬಿಗೆ, ನಂಬುಗೆ k. *n.* Confidence, trust, fidelity, faith, belief; faithfulness. ನಂಬಿಗಸ್ತ. A faithful man. ನಂಬಿಗಸ್ತಿಕೆ. Faithfulness, trustworthiness. -ಉಳಿಸಿಕೊಳ್ಳು, -ಕಾದುಕೊಳ್ಳು. To remain faithful.

ನಂಬು k. *v. t.* To confide, trust, put confidence in, believe; to suppose. -ವಿಕೆ. = ನಂಬಿಕೆ. ನಂಬಿಸು. To cause to confide; to coax, persuade.

ನಂಬುಗೆ. = ನಂಬಿಕೆ, *q. v.*

ನಮ್ಮ k. *pro.* (*pl. of* ನನ್ನ) Our, ours.

ನಮ್ಮಕ h. n. Salt. -ಕೋಠಿ. A salt factory.

ನಮ್ರ s. a. Bent, bowed. 2, lowly, submissive, humble. -ತೆ, -ತ್ವ, -ಭಾವ. Meekness, humility.

ನಯ 1. k. n. Softness, fineness; mildness, gentleness; cheapness. -ಗಾರೆ. Smooth plaster. -ನುಡಿ, -ಮಾತು. A gentle word. -ಬಟ್ಟೆ. Fine cloth.

ನಯ 2. s. a. Guiding, leading. 2, fit, right, proper. n. Behaviour, conduct, way of life. 2, prudent conduct; reason. 3, polity, policy, political economy. 4, plan; principle. 5, opinion. 6, right, justice. -ಗುಣ. A proper quality. -ವಂತ, -ಶಾಲಿ. A prudent man.

ನಯನ s. n. Guiding. 2, the leading organ: the eye. -ಚ್ಛದ. An eyelid. -ಜಲ, -ವಾರಿ, ನಯನಾಶ್ರು, ನಯನೋದಕ. Tears. -ರೋಗ. An eye-disease. ಉಪ-. Investiture with the brahmanical thread.

ನರ 1. k. n. A sinew, nerve, muscle; a vein, artery. -ಹುಲಿ. = ನರೂಲಿ.

ನರ 2. s. n. A man. 2, Arjuna. -ಕವಿ, -ಗಬ್ಬಿಗ. A profane poet. -ದೇವ, -ನಾಥ, -ಪತಿ, -ಪಾಲ, -ವರ, ನರಾಧಿಪ. A king. -ಪ್ರೇತ. A ghost-like, lean man. -ಬಲಿ. A human sacrifice. -ಭಕ್ಷಕ. A cannibal. -ಮನುಷ್ಯ. A human being. -ಲೋಕ. The earth; mortals. -ಕೇಸರಿ, -ಸಿಂಗ, -ಸಿಂಹ, -ಹರಿ. Man-lion: Vishṇu in his fourth avatâra. -ಶ್ರೇಷ್ಠ. Best of men. -ಹತ್ಯೆ. Manslaughter. ನರೇಂದ್ರ. The lord of men, a king.

ನರಕ s. n. Hell, the Tartarus. 2, a mass of filth. 3, N. of a demon slain by Kṛishṇa; also ನರಕಾಸುರ. -ಕೂಪ. A pit of filth. -ಚತುರ್ದಶಿ. A festival in the month of Âśvina to commemorate the destruction of Narakâsura. -ಬಾಧೆ, -ಯಾತನೆ, -ವೇದನೆ. The pains of hell. ನರಕಾಧಿಪತಿ. Yama.

ನರಕು k. v. t. To bruise. v. i. To groan, etc.

ನರಟು k. v. i. To become stunted in growth. n. Stunted growth. 2, grumbling. -ಗಾರ. A discontented man, grumbler.

ನರಳು k. v. i. To groan, moan.

ನರಿ k. n. A jackal, fox. -ಕೂಗು. The howl of jackals. -ಚೆಂಡು. A perennial creeping plant, *Lepidagathis cristata*. -ಬಾಲದ ಹುಲ್ಲು. The plant *Hemionites cordifolia*; the common grass *Setaria glauca*. -ಬುದ್ಧಿ. Cunning.

ನರು (ರು = ಱು) a. k. n. Fragrance, scent; smell. -ಗಂಪು. Fragrance.

ನರುಗು k. n. Grey colour. -ಗಂಬಳಿ. A cumbly with white and black stripes.

ನರೂಲಿ k. n. A wart, mole; also ನರಹುಲಿ.

ನರೆ k. v. i. To become grey, as the hair. n. Grey hair; hoary age. *Cpds.*: -ಕಂಬಳಿ, -ಕುರಿ, -ಕೂದಲು, -ಗಡ್ಡ, -ಗೊಂಗಡಿ, -ತಲೆ, *etc.*

ನರ್ತಕ s. n. A dancer; f. ನರ್ತಕಿ.

ನರ್ತನ s. n. Dancing. ನರ್ತಿಸು. To dance.

ನರ್ಮ s. n. Sport, play, pastime; joke; wit. -ದಾ, -ದೆ. N. of a river. -ಸಖ, -ಸಚಿವ. An associate of a prince.

ನಲ್ a. k. n. Goodness, fairness; loveliness; dearness. *Cpds.*: -ಗುಟುಕು, -ಗುದುರೆ, -ಗೆಳೆಯ, -ನುಡಿ, *etc.* ನಲ್ಲ. A good, dear man; a friend; f. ನಲ್ಲಳು.

ನಲ 1. (= ನಲವು, ನಲಿ, ನಲಿವು, ನಲ್ಮೆ) a. k. n. Pleasure, delight.

ನಲ 2. s. n. A species of reed. 2, N. of a king and husband of Damayantî. -ಕೂಬರ. N. of a son of Kubêra.

ನಲಗು (= ನಲುಗು) k. v. i. To become rumpled, as cloth, paper, *etc.*; to become flabby by heat; to droop as vegetables, *etc.*; to grow faint or feeble from sickness, *etc.*

ನಲವು. = ನಲ 1, q. v.

ನಲಿ a. k. v. i. To rejoice; to be pleased; to be fond of. n. (= ನಲ 1) Pleasure; also -ವು. -ದಾಡು. To be greatly delighted.

ನಲಿನ s. n. A lotus; a water-lily. -ಗರ್ಭ, -ಜ. Brahmâ. -ಬಾಂಧವ, -ಮಿತ್ರ, -ಸಖ. The sun. -ವೈರಿ. The moon. ನಲಿನಿ. A lotus as *f.*; a pond abounding in lotuses.

ನಲುಗು. = ನಲಗು, *q. v.*

ನಲ್ಮೆ a. k. n. Fondness; goodness; welfare, prosperity.

ನಲ್ಲ (*fr.* ನಲ್) a. k. n. Goodness; beauty. 2, a good man. *Cpds.:* -ತೈಲ, -ಮುದ್ದು, -ರೂಪು, -ವಸ್ತು.

ನಲ್ವತ್ತು k. a. Forty; *also* ನಾಲ್ವತ್ತು.

ನಲ್ಸು. = ನಲ 1, *q. v.*

ನವ 1. s. a. New, fresh, modern. -ತ. Freshness; novelty; = ನೌತ.

ನವ 2. s. a. Nine. -ಕ. Consisting of nine. -ಖಂಡ. Nine fabulous continents. -ಗ್ರಹ. The nine planets, namely: Âditya, Sôma, Mangala, Budha, Bṛihaspati, Šukra, Šani, Râhu, and Kêtu. -ಗ್ರಹದಾನ. Nine-fold gifts to the nine planets. -ಗ್ರಹಶಾಂತಿ. Propitiation of the nine planets. -ಜ್ವರ. A fever continuing for nine days. -ದ್ವಾರ. The nine outlets of the body. -ಧಾನ್ಯ. The nine grains: gôdivĕ, bhatta, uddu, hĕsaru, kaḍalĕ, tŏgari, huraḷi, avarĕ and ĕḷḷu. -ಮ. The ninth. -ಮಾಲಿಕೆ. Arabian jasmine. -ಮಿ. The ninth day of the lunar fortnight. -ರಂಗ. The middle hall of a temple. -ರತ್ನ. The nine precious gems: vajra, vaiḍûrya, gômêdhika, pushyarâga, nîla, marakata, mâṇikya, vidruma, and mauktika. -ರಸ. The nine tastes or sentiments. -ರಾತ್ರಿ. Nine nights: a nine-days' feast of Durgâ, Indra, or Vishṇu. -ರಾಶಿಕ. The double rule of three: proportion (*arith.*). -ವಿಧ ಭಕ್ತಿ. Nine modes of devotion.

ನವಕರ. = ನವುಕರ.

ನವಂಬರ s. n. November (11th month of the year).

ನವಣೆ k. n. The Italian millet, *Panicum italicum.*

ನವನೀತ s. n. Fresh butter. -ಕ. Clarified butter.

ನವರು. = ನವುರು, *q. v.*

ನವಲು e. n. A novel; a peculiar style of writing. 2, novelty.

ನವಸಾಗರ s. n. Sal ammoniac.

ನವರು. = ನವುರು, *q. v.*

ನವಸಿಗ k. n. A tormenter, molester.

ನವಾಬ್ h. n. A Nabob.

ನವಾಯಿ h. n. Novelty: unusual beauty, grandeur. -ಕಾರ. A grandee. -ತ. Newly made: one of a class of Konkaṇi speaking Mohammadans.

ನವಾರ h. n. A broad tape.

ನವಿರು k. n. Hair. 2, = ನವುರು, *q. v.*

ನವಿಲು k. n. A peacock, pea-fowl; *also* ನವುಲು. -ಗರಿ. A peacock's feathers. -ಜುಟ್ಟು. A peacock's tuft.

ನವೀನ s. a. New, fresh; excellent.

ನವುಕರ (= ನೌಕರ) h. n. A servant; *also* ನವಕರ. ನವುಕರಿ. Service.

ನವುಬತ್ತು h. n. A large kettle-drum.

ನವುರು (= ನವರು) k. n. That which is soft, thin, small, *as* grass, hair, *etc.*

ನವುಲು k. n. The pea-fowl, *Pavo cristatus.*

ನವೆ 1. (= ನವೊ, *q. v.*) k. v. i. To become thin. *P. ps.* ನವದು, ನವೆದು.

ನವೆ 2. k. n. Itching; the itch. -ಯಾಗು, -ಹತ್ತು. To itch; to get itch.

ನಶಿಸು s. v. i. To vanish; to perish.

ನಶೀಬು. = ನಸೀಬು, *q. v.*

ನಶ್ವರ s. n. Perishing, vanishing; transient.

ನಷ್ಟ s. a. Lost; vanished; perished. *n.* Loss; damage; ruin, destruction. -ಜಾತಕ. The casting of a lost nativity. -ಜೀವಿ. A sufferer from loss; a lost life. -ದೃಷ್ಟಿ. A blind man. -ದ್ರವ್ಯ. A lost thing. -ಧನ. Lost riches. ನಷ್ಟೇಂದ್ರಿಯ. Loss of one's organs of sense; impotency.

ನಸರಿ k. n. A good kind of honey.

ನಸಿ 1. (= ನವೊ, *etc.*) k. v. i. To wear out, wane, wither, decay. 2, to faint.

3, to become poor. *P. ps.* ನಸದು, ನಸಿದು.

ನಸಿ 2. (*tb. of* ನಸ್ಯ. = ನಸೆ, *q. v.*) Snuff; *also* -ಪುಡಿ.

ನಸಿಕು, ನಸಿಗು (= ನಸುಕು) k. *n.* Dawn, twilight. ನಸಿಕಲೆ. Early in the morning.

ನಸೀಬು h. *n.* Fortune, lot.

ನಸೀಯತ್ತು h. *n.* Chastisement.

ನಸು a. k. *n.* Minuteness, smallness; a little; a trifle. -ಗತ್ತಲೆ. Early dawn. -ಗಾಳಿ. A light wind, breeze. -ಕುನ್ನಿ. A plant stinging like nettles; cowhage. -ಗೆಂಪು. A tawny colour. -ನಗು. To smile. -ನಗೆ. A smile. -ಬಿಳಿದು. Grey colour. -ಲಜ್ಜೆ. Modesty. -ಸಯ್ರಣೆ. A little patience.

ನಸುಕು. = ನಸಿಕು, *q. v.*

ನಸೂರಿ h. *n.* Slight fever. -ಬರು. To be feverish.

ನಸೆ s. *n.* The nose. 2, (= ನಸಿ 2) snuff; *also* -ಪುಡಿ. ನಸ್ಯ. Relating to the nose; snuff that produces sneezing.

ನಳ. = ನಲ, *q. v.*

ನಳನಳಿಕೆ a. k. *n.* Softness, tenderness, beauty. ನಳನಳಿಸು. To be soft, tender, nice, bright.

ನಳಿಗೆ (*tb. of* ನಲಕ) *n.* A tube.

ನಳಿನ. = ನಲಿನ, *q. v.*

ನಳ್ಳಿ k. *n.* A crab.

ನಾ k. *pro.* I; *also* ನಾಂ. 2, four. -ಗಾಲು. Four feet. -ಗಾಲೋಟ. A canter; a gallop.

ನಾಕ s. *n.* Heaven, the sky, atmosphere; the abode of the gods.

ನಾಕಾರಿ, ನಾಕಾರೆ. = ನಕಾರಿ, *q. v.*

ನಾಕಿ s. *n.* A deity, god. -ನಿಕರ. A multitude of gods.

ನಾಕು k. *a.* Four. 2, (f.) an ant-hill. -ಮಡಿ. Four-fold.

ನಾಕ್ರೈಸ್ತ h. f. *n.* A Non-christian, unbeliever.

ನಾಖುಷಿ h. *n.* Dissatisfaction, discontent; displeasure.

ನಾಕ್ಷತ್ರ s. *a.* Belonging to the stars, sidereal. -ಮಾಸ. Sidereal computation of time.

ನಾಗ s. *n.* A snake, *esp.* the *Cobra capella.* 2, a fabulous serpent-demon. 3, an elephant. 4, any great man. 5, fire; cloud, darkness. 6, water. 7, lead. -ಕನ್ಯೆ. A female of serpentine extraction. -ಕುಂಡಲ. Śiva. -ಕುಷ್ಠ. A kind of leprosy. -ಕೇಸರ. The tree *Mesua ferrea.* -ದಂತಿ. A species of sunflower; the Indian jalap. -ಪಂಚಮಿ. A feast on the 5th day of Śrâvaṇa for the worship of serpent-images. -ಪ್ರತಿಷ್ಠೆ. Placing a stone-image of cobra for worship. -ಬೆತ್ತ. A snake-coloured cane. -ಮಲ್ಲಿಗೆ. A tall, shrubby plant, *Rhinacanthus communis.* -ಮುರಿಗೆ. A serpentine bracelet. -ರತ್ನ. A jewel supposed to be found in the head of a cobra. -ಲೋಕ. The world of the serpent demons. -ವಂದಿಗೆ. A shelf, peg, hook. -ವರ್ಮ. N. of a Kannaḍa poet. -ವಾಸ. Abode of the Nâgas. -ಶಯನ, -ಶಾಯಿ. Vishṇu. -ವೇಣಿ. A woman with snake-like tresses. -ಸಂಪಿಗೆ. A middle-sized flower-tree, *Mesua ferrea.* -ಸ್ವರ. A kind of pipe used by snake-players.

ನಾಗರ 1. (= ನಾಗ, *q. v.*) s. *n.* A snake, *esp.* the cobra. 2, an ornament with the image of a cobra; *also* -ಹೆಡೆ ನಾಗರು. -ಕಾಟ. A disease of the skin; childlessness. -ಪಂಚಮಿ. = ನಾಗಪಂಚಮಿ. -ಹಾವು. The cobra.

ನಾಗರ 2. (*fr.* ನಗರ) s. *a.* Belonging to a town, civic; polite; clever. *n.* A citizen. 2, = ದೇವನಾಗರಿ, *q. v.* 3, dry ginger.

ನಾಗರಿಕ, ನಾಗರೀಕ s. *a.* Town-bred; polite; clever. *n.* A townsman; a citizen; a cockney.

ನಾಗವಲಿ (*tb. of* ನಾಗವಲ್ಲಿ) *n.* Betel-nut: the first chewing of betel-nut at a marriage.

ನಾಗವಲ್ಲಿ (=ನಾಗವಲಿ, *q. v.*) s. *n*. The betel creeper, *Piper betel*. -ಪಟ್ಟದ. A cloth given to the son-in-law on the last day of his marriage.

ನಾಗಾಶನ s. *n*. A peacock. 2, Garuḍa.

ನಾಗೇಂದ್ರ s. *n*. The serpent Śêsha.

ನಾಚಿಕೆ k. *n*. Bashfulness, shame, modesty, decorum; grace. -ಕೆಡು, -ಗೆಡು. Shame or modesty to be lost. -ಗೇಡಿ. A shameless person. -ಗೇಡಿತನ, -ಗೇಡು. Shamelessness, impudence. -ಗೊಳ್ಳು. To feel ashamed. -ಬಿಡು. To give up shame.

ನಾಚು 1. k. *v. i.* To become ashamed or embarrassed. ನಾಚಿಸು. To cause to be ashamed; to disgrace.

ನಾಚು 2. f. *n*. A nautch, dance, dancing. -ಮಾಡು. To dance, act.

ನಾಜರು f. *n*. The sheriff of a law-court.

ನಾಜೂಕು h. *a*. Delicate, soft, tender.

ನಾಟ h. *n*. A stem or beam of wood.

ನಾಟಕ s. *n*. A play, drama, dramatic representation. -ಧಾರಿ, -ಪುರುಷ. An actor, mime. -ಶಾಲೆ. A play-house, theatre.

ನಾಟಿ k. *n*. Young plants, *esp*. of rice, fit for transplanting. 2, transplanting. 3, (f.) a kind of râga.

ನಾಟು (=ನಡು) k. *v. i.* To get within, to be pierced or stuck into, *as* a thorn. *v. t.* To fix in the ground, plant; to pierce into. *n*. Planting; depth; *also* ನಾಟಿಕೆ. -ಕೋಲು. A planting stick. ನಾಟಿಸು. To make plant.

ನಾಟ್ಯ s. *n*. Dancing, or dramatic representation. -ಗಾರ. An actor. -ಗಾರೆ, -ಗಾತಿ. An actress. -ಮಂದಿರ, -ರಂಗ. A theatre.

ನಾಡದು k. *n*. & *ad*. The day after tomorrow; *also* ನಾಡಿದು.

ನಾಡಾಡಿ, -ಗ k. *n*. A rustic; a common person.

ನಾಡಿ s. *n*. The tubular stalk of any plant. 2, any tubular organ, *as* an artery, a vein, a nerve, *etc*. 3, any pipe or tube. 4, a fistulous sore. 5, the pulse. 6, a period of twenty-four minutes; *also* -ಕೆ. 7, a juggling trick. -ಆಡು, -ನಡೆ. The pulse to beat. -ನಿಲ್ಲು. The pulse to cease. -ನೋಡು. To feel the pulse. -ಪರೀಕ್ಷೆ. Examining the pulse.

ನಾಡಿಗ k. *n*. A village-superintendent. 2, one of a caste so called in Canara; *f*. -ಗಿತ್ತಿ. -ತನ. A nâḍiga's business.

ನಾಡು k. *n*. A province, district; the country. -ಗವುಡ. The headman of a village. -ನಾಡೆ. A common proverb. -ಶಾನಭೋಗ. The accountant of a village.

ನಾಡೆ a. k. *ad*. Further, moreover, much, excessively.

ನಾಣ್ (=ನಾಚಿಕೆ, *etc.*, *q. v.*) a. k. *n*. Bashfulness, shame, modesty, *etc*. 2, =ನಾಡು. ನಾಣಿಲಿ. Shameless; a shameless person. ನಾಣಿಲಿತನ. Shamelessness. -ಗೆಡಿಕ. A shameless man. -ಗೆಡಿಸು. To disgrace, reproach. -ನುಡಿ. Popular report, common talk.

ನಾಣ್ಯ 1. k. *n*. Fineness, goodness, good quality, *as* that of cloth, grain, *etc.*; honesty, truth. -ಸ್ಥ, -ವಂತ. A trustworthy man.

ನಾಣ್ಯ 2. f. *n*. A coin; money. -ಪರೀಕ್ಷೆ. Assaying money. -ವಟ್ಟ. The agio on money. -ವಾರು. The detailed account of various coins.

ನಾತ (=ನಾರು) k. *n*. Smell in general; a bad smell; stench. -ಗೊಳ್ಳು, -ಬರು, -ಹಿಡಿ. To smell; to stink.

ನಾತು. *P. p. of* ನಾರು, *q. v*.

ನಾಥ s. *n*. A protector; a master, ruler; a husband. -ವತ್. Dependent, subject.

ನಾದ s. *n*. A sound, a tone in general. 2, a note of music; *as:* ಘಂಟಾ-, ವೀಣಾ-, ಕೊಳಲು-, ಸಿಂಹ-, *etc*.

ನಾದನಿ (*tb. of* ನನಾಂದೃ) *n*. A husband's sister; a brother's wife.

ನಾದಾರಿ h. *n*. Insolvency, pauperism. ನಾದಾರು. Insolvent; a pauper.

ನಾದಿನಿ. = ನಾದನಿ, *q. v*.

ನಾದಿಸು s. v. i. To sound.

ನಾದು k. v. t. To knead, as dough, *etc.* v. i. To moisten, soak; to cool. ನಾದಿಸು. To knead.

ನಾದುರುಸ್ತಿ h. a. Out of order; unrepaired, unmended.

ನಾದೇಯ s. a. Aquatic. ನಾದೇಯಿ. A species of reed, *Calamus fasciculatus;* the orange-tree; the shoe-flower plant.

ನಾನಾ s. a. Of different kinds, various, manifold, diverse. *ad.* Variously, manifoldly. *Cpds.:* -ಕಾರ್ಯ, -ಕೆಲಸ, -ತರ, -ಪ್ರಕಾರ, -ಬಗೆ, -ರೀತಿ, -ವಿಧ, *etc.* -ರೂಪ. Various forms. ನಾನಾರ್ಥ. Homonymous; a homonym.

ನಾನು 1. k. *pro.* I.

ನಾನು 2. k. v. i. To get wet, moist, damp. *P. ps.* ನಾತು, ನಾದು.

ನಾನೂರು k. a. Four hundred.

ನಾಂದಿ s. n. Joy; prosperity. 2, eulogium or praise of a deity; a prayer recited at the opening of a religious ceremony or of a drama. -ಮುಖ, -ಶ್ರಾದ್ಧ. A commemorative offering to the manes before any joyous occasion, *as* marriage, *etc.*

ನಾಪಿತ s. n. A barber; *also* ನಾವಿಗ, ನಾಪಿಗ.

ನಾಭಿ s. n. The navel. 2, the nave of a wheel. 3, the centre, focus, middle. 4, a near relation.

ನಾಮ s. n. A name. 2, a noun. 3, the sectarian mark of Vaishṇavas. *ad.* By name. 2, possibly. -ಕೋಳಿ. The pigmy cormorant. -ದ ಬೇರು. The country sarsaparilla, *Hemidesmus indicus.* -ಕರಣ. The ceremony of naming a child. -ಧಾರಿ. A Vaishṇava; renowned. -ಧೇಯ. A name, title. -ಪದ, -ವಾಚಕ. A noun. -ಸ್ಮರಣ. Bearing in mind the name of a god. -ಹಾಕು. To put on the Vaishṇava marks; to cheat. ನಾಮಾಂಕಿತ. Renowned.

ನಾಮಂಜೂರು h. n. Disapproval. -ಮಾಡು. Disallow, disapprove.

ನಾಮರ್ದಿ h. n. Unmanliness, cowardice; [a coward.

ನಾಮಿ s. n. Bending. 2, a N. for all vowels, except ಅ and ಆ. -ಕ. Having a name.

ನಾಮೂಷಿ h. n. Disgrace, shame.

ನಾಮೆ h. n. A deed: letters patent.

ನಾಯ (*tb. of* ನ್ಯಾಯ) n. A lawsuit.

ನಾಯಕ s. a. Pre-eminent, chief. n. A guide, leader; a chief, head; a general, commander; a husband; *f.* ನಾಯಕಿ. -ತ್ವ. Leadership. -ವಾಡಿ. A chief, headman, *as* of a caste, village, *etc.*

ನಾಯಬ h. n. A deputy. -ಸಿರಸ್ತೇದಾರ. A native head clerk of a subordinate office.

ನಾಯಿ k. n. A dog. -ಕುನ್ನಿ, -ಮರಿ. A puppy, whelp. -ಕೊಡೆ. A mushroom. -ಕೆಮ್ಮು, -ಗೆಮ್ಮು. The hooping cough. -ತುಲಸಿ. The herb *Ocimum album.* -ಬದುಕು, -ಬಾಳು. A wretched, miserable existence. -ಬೆಳಗಿಣ. An annual herb, *Cleome viscosa.* -ಬೇಲ. The plant *Flacourtia sapida.* -ಬೊಗಳು, -ಕೂಗು. A dog to bark. -ಯುಳ್ಳಿ. A bulbous plant, *Scilla indica.*

ನಾಯಿಂದ (*tb. of* ನಾಪಿತ) n. A barber.

ನಾರಂಗ s. n. The orange tree; an orange.

ನಾರದ s. n. N. of a devarshi. -ವೀಣೆ. Nârada's lute: a kind of lute.

ನಾರಾಗೋರ k. n. A very meagre man.

ನಾರಾಚ s. n. A long arrow; a style to write with.

ನಾರಾಯಣ (*fr.* ನರ divine spirit and ಅಯನ pervading) s. n. Brahmâ. 2, Vishṇu, Kṛishṇa (*sometimes the deity who was before all worlds*). ನಾರಾಯಣಿ. Lakshmî; Durgâ.

ನಾರಿ 1. k. n. A bow-string.

ನಾರಿ 2. s. n. A woman, wife.

ನಾರಿಕೇರ, ನಾರಿಕೇಲ s. n. The cocoanut.

ನಾರು 1. k. n. A fibre: fibres of plants, strings in mangoes and other fruits.

2, cloth made of hemp, or linen; *also* -ಮಡಿ. -ಸೀರೆ. A female's linen garment. -ಕಟ್ಟು. Fibre-like pus to form in a sore. -ಗ. A dealer in fibres. -ಬೇರು. Fibres and roots. -ಹುಣ್ಣು. A guinea-worm.

ನಾರು 2. (ರು=ಱು) k. *n.* Smell. *v. i.* To smell; to stink. *P. ps.* ನಾರಿ, ನಾತು. -ವ ಬೇಳೆ, ನಾರಂಬೇಳೆ. A strong smelling herb, *Cleome pentaphylla.*

ನಾಲ 1. (=ನಾಳ) h. *n.* A horse or bullock-shoe. -ಗಾರ, -ಬಂದಿ. One who shoes a horse or bullock.

ನಾಲ 2. h. *n.* A drain, gutter.

ನಾಲಾಯಖು h. *a.* Unfit, ineligible. *n.* Demerit.

ನಾಲಿ (=ನಾಳಿ) s. *n.* A tubular stalk. 2, a tube. 3, a period of 24 minutes.

ನಾಲಿಗೆ k. *n.* The tongue. 2, the clapper of a bell. -ಕೆಡು. Appetite to be lost; a promise to fail. -ತಪ್ಪು. A promise to break; a slip of the tongue. -ತಿರುಗು. To be able to speak fluently. -ಪ್ರಮಾಣ. Confidence in one's words or promises. -ಬೀಳು. To become unable to utter. -ಉಳಿಸು. To keep one's promise. -ವಾಸಿ. Trustworthiness. -ಹೋಗು. =-ಬೀಳು.

ನಾಲಿಸು h. *n.* Complaint; censure, sneer, reprobation. -ಮಾಡು. To disapprove, disparage.

ನಾಲ್ಕು k. *a.* Four. ನಾಲ್ಕಡಿ. Four feet. ನಾಲ್ಕನೆ. Fourth. ನಾಲ್ಕಯಿದು. 9. ನಾಲ್ಕಷ್ಟು. Four times as much. ನಾಲ್ಕಾರು. Four or six; several, some. -ಕೆಲಸ. Every kind of work. -ಜನ, -ಜನರು. All persons, every body. -ಜಾತಿ, -ವರ್ಣ. The four castes. -ದಿಕ್ಕು, -ದೆಸೆ. The four points of the compass. -ಮಾಡು. To divide into four. -ಮಾತು. Some words. ನಾಲ್ಕೂಕಾಲು. 4¼. ನಾಲ್ವತ್ತು. Forty. ನಾಲ್ವರು. Four persons.

ನಾವಲಿಗ (*tb. of* ನಾಪಿತ) *n.* A barber.

ನಾವಾಡಿಗ f. *n.* A boatman; a helmsman.

ನಾವಾರ (=ನವಾರ) h. *n.* A broad tape.

ನಾವಿಕ s. *n.* A sailor; steersman, pilot.

ನಾವಿದ, ನಾವಿಂದ. *tb. of* ನಾಪಿತ, *q. v.*

ನಾವು k. *pro. pl. of* ನಾನು. We. *See its decl. s.* ನಮ್ಮ.

ನಾವೆ s. *n.* A boat, ship, vessel. ನಾವ್ಯ. Navigable.

ನಾಶ s. *n.* Destruction, annihilation, ruin, loss; death. -ಗೊಳಿಸು, -ಮಾಡು. To destroy, ruin, kill. -ಹೊಂದು. To be ruined. -ನ. Destroying, *etc.*; ruin.

ನಾಷ್ಟ h. *n.* Breakfast; luncheon.

ನಾಸ s. *n.* The nose. ನಾಸಿ. Snuff. ನಾಸಿಕ, ನಾಸೆ. A nose; a trunk.

ನಾಸ್ತ. = ನಾಷ್ಟ, *q. v.*

ನಾಸ್ತಿ s. It is not, there is not; non-existence. -ಕ. An atheist; an infidel. -ಕತನ, -ಕತೆ, -ಕತ್ವ, -ಕ್ಯ. Atheism; infidelity.

ನಾಳ (=ನಾಲ, *q. v.*) s. *n.* A pipe, tube. *etc.* 2, the clapper of a bell.

ನಾಳಿ. *tb. of* ನಾಡಿ, *q. v.*; *also* a water-channel; a weaver's shuttle.

ನಾಳೆ k. *ad.* To-morrow.

ನಿಃ. = ನಿರ್, ನಿಶ್, ನಿಷ್, ನಿಸ್, *q. v.*

ನಿಃಶಂಕ s. *n.* Fearless; without hesitation or fear. ನಿಃಶಂಕೆ. Boldness, confidence.

ನಿಃಶಬ್ದ s. *a.* Noiseless. *n.* Silence, calm.

ನಿಃಶೇಷ s. *a.* Without remainder; complete, entire.

ನಿಃಸಂಗ s. *a.* Unattached; indifferent; disinterested. *n.* Unattachment, indifference.

ನಿಃಸಂದೇಹ s. *a.* Doubtless, certain. *n.* Certainty.

ನಿಃಸಹಾಯ s. *a.* Helpless, unassisted.

ನಿಃಸಾರ s. *a.* Sapless, insipid; worthless.

ನಿಕಟ s. *a.* Near, proximate. *n.* Pith, sap.

ನಿಕರ s. *n.* A heap; a flock, multitude.

ನಿಕಾ h. *n.* A Mohammadan marriage.

ನಿಕಾಮ s. *n.* Wish, desire.

ನಿಕಾಯ s. n. A heap, set, flock. 2, a house, dwelling.

ನಿಕಾಲಸು h. a. Plain, blunt, open, *as* a person, speech, *etc.*

ನಿಕುಂಜ s. n. An arbour, thicket.

ನಿಕುರುಂಬ s. n. A flock, multitude.

ನಿಕೃತಿ s. n. Dishonest practice, deception, fraud.

ನಿಕೃಷ್ಟ s. a. Drawn down; low, base, vulgar.

ನಿಕೇತನ s. n. A house, dwelling.

ನಿಕ್ಕುವ a. k. n. Truth, certainty. *ad.* Truly, certainly.

ನಿಕ್ಷೇಪ s. n. Placing; a deposit, pledge, trust. 2, a hidden treasure. ನಿಕ್ಷೇಪಿಸು. To deposit; to bury.

ನಿಖಿಲ s. a. Complete, all, entire.

ನಿಗದಿ h. n. Fixing, *as* a hire, salary, *etc.*; decision. -ಮಾಡು. To fix; to decide.

ನಿಗಮ s. n. Insertion. 2, a passage of the vêdas. 3, the vêda; a sacred precept. *a.* Issued from; liberated, set free.

ನಿಗರ 1. (= ನಿಗುರು, q. v.) k. a. Straight, erect; *also* ನಿಗುರ. -ಗಿವಿ. An erect ear. ನಿಗರಿಕೆ. Straightness.

ನಿಗರ 2. (*tb. of* ನಿಕರ) n. The best of anything.

ನಿಗರು. = ನಿಗುರು, *q. v.*

ನಿಗರ್ವ (=ನಿರ್ಗರ್ವ) s. a. Prideless, humble. n. Humility. ನಿಗರ್ವಿ. A humble person.

ನಿಗಾ, ನಿಗಾವಾನಿ, ನಿಗಾವು h. n. Care in looking after; tending; regard to.

ನಿಗುರು k. v. i. To be stretched forth; to spread, expand; to become erect; to rise; to swell, become proud. n. Expansion. ನಿಗುರಿಸು. To stretch forth, *etc.*

ನಿಗೂಢ s. a. Hidden, secret; profound, obscure.

ನಿಗ್ರಾಹ್ಯ s. a. Punishable.

ನಿಗೇವಾನಿ. = ನಿಗಾ, *q. v.*

ನಿಗ್ಗರ (*tb. of* ನಿಗ್ರಹ) n. Coercion, compulsion.

ನಿಗ್ಗವ a. k. n. The tusks of an elephant: ivory.

ನಿಗ್ರಹ s. n. Keeping in check; coercion; restraint; subjugation; humbling; punishing. 2, rebuke, blame. 3, aversion; dislike; a mental pain. ನಿಗ್ರಹಿಸು. To restrain, subdue, keep in check; to punish. ನಿಗ್ರಹಿಸುವಿಕೆ. Keeping in check.

ನಿಘಂಟು s. n. A vocabulary, dictionary.

ನಿಘರ್ಷಣ s. n. Friction, grinding, trituration.

ನಿಚಯ s. n. A collection; a heap; assemblage.

ನಿಚ್ಚ. *tb. of* ನಿತ್ಯ, *q. v.*

ನಿಚ್ಚಣಿ, -ಕೆ, -ಗೆ (*tb. of* ನಿಃಶ್ರೇಣಿ) n. A ladder.

ನಿಚ್ಚಯ. *tb. of* ನಿಶ್ಚಯ, *q. v.*

ನಿಜ s. a. Innate. 2, own. 3, real, true, actual, genuine. n. Reality, truth. -ಗುಣ. A truthful man. -ಮಾರ್ಗ. The proper way. -ರೂಪ. One's own shape. -ಸಾಕ್ಷಿ. True evidence. -ಸ್ಥ. = ನಿಜಗುಣ. -ಮುಡಿ. A moorah of 42 sheers.

ನಿಜಾಮ h. n. Ruler: the title of the native sovereign of Hyderabad.

ನಿಟಿಲ s. n. The forehead.

ನಿಟ್ಟು *abbr. of* ನಿಡಿದು (*in* ನಿಡು, *q. v.*). -ಸುರು. A drawn out, deep sigh. --ಬಿಡು. To sigh deeply. ನಿಟ್ಟೆಲುವು. The spine. ನಿಟ್ಟೋಟ. A long run.

ನಿಡಿ 1. = ನಿಡು, *q. v.* -ದು. That which is long; length.

ನಿಡಿ 2. k. n. A strong stifling smell, *as* that of tobacco, cayenne pepper, *etc.* 2, scum, froth.

ನಿಡು a. k. n. Length; extensiveness; bigness. *Cpds.:* -ಕರ, -ಗವಸೆ, -ಗೊಂಬು, -ಗೋಡು, -ಗೋಲು, -ದಾಡೆ, -ಜಡೆ, -ನರ, -ನಿದ್ರೆ, -ಬತ್ತಳಿಕೆ, -ಬಲೆ, -ಬಾವಿ, -ಬೆರಳು, -ಬೊಟ್ಟೆ, -ಮೂಗು, -ಸರ, *etc.*

ನಿತ್ತು. = ನಿಂತು. *P. p. of* ನಿಲ್ಲು, *q. v.*

ನಿತ್ಯ s. a. Continual, perpetual; endless, eternal, everlasting; necessary, essential. -ಕಟ್ಟಳೆ. Daily observance. -ಕರ್ಮ. A daily rites. -ದಂತೆ. As usual. -ದರಿದ್ರ. An always poor man. -ತೆ, ತ್ವ. Eternity. -ದಾನ. Daily alms-giving. -ಶ್ರಾದ್ಧ. A daily śrâddha. ನಿತ್ಯಾತ್ಮ. The eternal soul.

ನಿತ್ರಾಣ (tb. of ನಿಸ್ತ್ರಾಣ) n. Weakness.

ನಿದರ್ಶನ s. n. An example or illustration. 2, a view, vision; omen.

ನಿದಾನ 1. s. n. A first cause. 2, end, termination. 3, pathology.

ನಿದಾನ 2. tb. of ನಿಧಾನ, q. v. -ವಂತ, -ಸ್ಥ, ನಿದಾನಿ. A patient man.

ನಿದೇಶ s. n. Command, instruction.

ನಿದ್ದೆ. tb. of ನಿದ್ರೆ, q. v. -ಗಣ್ಣು. Sleepy eyes. -ಮಾಡು. To sleep. -ಮೊಬ್ಬು. Drowsiness. -ಎಚ್ಚರು. To awake. -ಹತ್ತು. To be asleep. -ಹೋಗು. To fall asleep.

ನಿದ್ರೆ (= ನಿದ್ದೆ) s. n. Sleep; slumber. 2, sleepiness. -ಕೆಡು. Sleep to be spoiled. -ಗೆಯ್, -ಮಾಡು. To sleep. -ಹತ್ತು. = ನಿದ್ದೆಹತ್ತು. [ಧನ.

ನಿಧನ s. n. End. 2, death, loss. 3, = ನಿ

ನಿಧಾನ s. n. Laying aside. 2, a receptacle; a treasure, wealth. 3, a place of rest. 4, effort, work. 5, slowness, patience, pausing. -ಗೊಳ್ಳು. -ಪಡು, -ಬೀಳು, -ಮಾಡು, To consider, judge.

ನಿಧಿ s. n. A receptacle. 2, a treasure, wealth; a store. 3, the ocean.

ನಿನ್ k. pro. Thou; also ನೀನು. ನಿನ್ನ. Thy. ನಿನ್ನದು. Thine.

ನಿಂತು. = ನಿತ್ತು. P. p. of ನಿಲ್ಲು, q. v.

ನಿಂದಿರು. See s. ನಿಲ್ಲು, q. v.

ನಿಂದೆ s. n. Blame, censure, reproach, abuse, scorn. ನಿಂದಕ. A scorner. ನಿಂದಿಸು. To blame, abuse, etc.

ನಿಂದ್ಯ s. a. Blamable; despicable.

ನಿನ್ನ pro. Gen. of ನೀನು, q. v. Of thee, thine, thy. Acc. ನಿನ್ನನ್ನು. Dat. ನಿನಗೆ. Abl. ನಿನ್ನಿಂದ. Loc. ನಿನ್ನಲ್ಲಿ.

ನಿನ್ನೆ k. ad. Yesterday. Instr. -ಯಿಂದ. Dat. -ಗೆ. Gen. -ಯ, ನಿನ್ನಿನ.

ನಿಪಾತ s. n. Falling down; dying, death; ruined state. 2, putting down as irregular or exceptional, as a word in a compound; exception. 3, a particle (g.). -ಮಾಡು. To destroy.

ನಿಪುಣ s. a. Perfect; accurate. 2, clever, skilful. -ತನ, -ತೆ, -ತ್ವ. Skilfulness, cleverness.

ನಿಬದ್ಧ s. a. Bound; caught, fettered; confined. n. A fixed rule.

ನಿಬಂಧನೆ s. n. Binding; a rule, order.

ನಿಬಿಡ s. a. Thick, dense, tight. ನಿಬಿಡೀಕೃತ. Made close, dense, etc.

ನಿಬ್ಬಣ k. n. A marriage festival. ನಿಬ್ಬಣಿಗ. A bridegroom's companion.

ನಿಭಾಯಿಸು h. v. t. To endure, suffer, bear, succeed.

ನಿಮಗ್ನ s. a. Immersed; sunk in; depressed.

ನಿಮಂತ್ರಣ s. n. Invitation, esp. to a śrâddha.

ನಿಮಾಜು. = ನಮಾಜು, q. v.

ನಿಮಾನಿಮಿ h. a. Exact, quite correct; ad. Exactly, etc.

ನಿಮಿತ್ತ, ನಿಮಿತ್ಯ s. n. A mark, aim. 2, sign; omen. 3, cause, motive, reason. -ವಾಗಿ. Because of, on account of. -ಗಾರ. A fortune-teller.

ನಿಮಿರು. = ನಿಗುರು, q. v.

ನಿಮಿರ್ಚು. = ನಿಗುರಿಸು, q. v.

ನಿಮಿಷ s. n. Twinkling, winking; the twinkling of an eye; a moment. 2, a minute.

ನಿಂಬ s. n. The Nimb-tree, Azadirachta indica. -ತರು. The coral tree.

ನಿಂಬೆ (= ಲಿಂಬೆ) k. n. The acid lime, Citrus medica.

ನಿಮ್ಮ 1. (pl. of ನಿನ್ನ) k. pro. Your. -ದು. Yours. Acc. ನಿಮ್ಮನ್ನು. Abl. ನಿಮ್ಮಿಂದ. Dat. ನಿಮಗೆ. Loc. ನಿಮ್ಮಲ್ಲಿ.

ನಿಮ್ನ 2. s. n. Depth; a slope; a gap. a. Deep, low.

ನಿಯತ s. a. Checked; controlled. 2, fixed, permanent. 3, certain. 4, positive. n. Restraint; a religious duty. ನಿಯತಿ. Restraint, restriction; rule. 2, destiny, fate.

ನಿಯತ್ತು (tb. of ನಿಯತ) n. Truthfulness.

ನಿಯಮ (= ನೇಮ) s. n. Ruling. 2, a rule, law, precept; a regular practice; appointment. 3, agreement, contract. 4, any religious observance. -ನಿಷ್ಠೆ. Regular and rigid observance of meritorious rites or works. ನಿಯಮಿತ. Regulated, prescribed; fixed. ನಿಯಮಿಸು (= ನೇಮಿಸು). To restrain, subdue; to lay down a rule; to order; to appoint, fix; to nominate.

ನಿಯಾಮಕ s. n. Guiding, governing. 2, a ruler. 3, a charioteer. 4, a boatman; a pilot. 5, rule, order.

ನಿಯಾಮಿಸು. = ನಿಯಮಿಸು s. ನಿಯಮ, q. v.

ನಿಯುಕ್ತ s. a. Fastened to; appointed; employed; assigned. ನಿಯುಕ್ತಿ. Injunction, order; charge.

ನಿಯುತ s. n. A great number.

ನಿಯೋಗ s. n. Application, use, employment. 2, order, command. 3, trust; business. ನಿಯೋಗಿ. A functionary; a minister; a class of Brâhmaṇas. ನಿಯೋಗಿಸು. To assign; to employ; to command.

ನಿಯೋಜನ s. n. Uniting; ordering; appointing to. ನಿಯೋಜಿಸು. To assign, appoint, etc.

ನಿರ್, ನಿಸ್, ನಿಷ್ (= ನಿಃ) s. pref. Certainty. 2, negation, privation. 3, out, without.

ನಿರಕ್ಷರ s. a. Illiterate. -ಕುಕ್ಷಿ. An illiterate person.

ನಿರಖು h. n. Current price. -ಪಟ್ಟಿ. A price-current.

ನಿರಂಕುಶ s. a. Unchecked, uncontrolled, self-willed.

ನಿರಂಜನ s. a. Unstained, untinged, pure.

ನಿರತ s. a. Engaged or interested in.

ನಿರತೆ (ರ = ಱ) k. n. Beauty, charm, elegance; cf. ನಿರಿ 1.

ನಿರಂತರ s. a. Having no interval; continuous; without interstices, compact, dense; uninterrupted, constant. ad. Continuously.

ನಿರಪರಾಧಿ s. n. A faultless or guiltless person.

ನಿರಪಾಯ s. a. Imperishable; infallible.

ನಿರಪೇಕ್ಷೆ s. n. Absence of desire or expectation.

ನಿರರ್ಥಕ s. a. Nonsensical, useless, unprofitable.

ನಿರವಧಿ s. a. Unlimited, interminable.

ನಿರವಯವ s. n. Without limbs or members.

ನಿರಶನ s. n. Fasting; a fast.

ನಿರಹಂಕಾರ s. n. Absence of selfishness.

ನಿರಹಂಕೃತ s. a. Unselfish.

ನಿರಾಕರಣ s. n. Repudiation, rejection. ನಿರಾಕರಿಸು. To put away, repudiate, etc.

ನಿರಾಕಾಂಕ್ಷೆ s. n. Desirelessness.

ನಿರಾಕಾರ s. a. Formless, shapeless; ugly, also ನಿರಾಕೃತಿ.

ನಿರಾಕ್ಷೇಪ s. a. Unblamable, unobjectionable. -ಣೆ. Unobjectionableness.

ನಿರಾಜಿ h. a. Furnished with kalâbatu, as a cloth.

ನಿರಾಧಾರ s. n. Groundlessness, poorness, etc. ನಿರಾಧಾರಿ. A poor person.

ನಿರಾಯಾಸ s. a. Not causing trouble; not requiring efforts; not fatiguing.

ನಿರಾಶೆ s. n. Hopelessness, despair.

ನಿರಾಶ್ರಯ s. a. Supportless; friendless, destitute.

ನಿರಾಹಾರ s. n. Foodlessness, fasting. ನಿರಾಹಾರಿ. A fasting person.

ನಿರಾಳ (tb. of ನಿರಾಕುಲ) n. Doubtlessness, certainty; calmness. 2, the sky.

ನಿರಿ 1. (ರಿ = ಱಿ) k. v. i. To be arranged, to be ready; cf. ನೆರೆ 3. n. Orderly arrangement.

ನಿರಿ 2., ನಿರಿಗೆ k. n. Foldings: the folds of a garment, as of a dôtra or sîrĕ.

ನಿರಿಸು (ರಿ = ಱಿ. = ಇರಿಸು) a. k. v. t. To put down; to arrange; to adjust. n. Arrangement; display.

ನಿರೀಕ್ಷೆ s. n. Looking towards, expectation, waiting for. ನಿರೀಕ್ಷಣ. Looking at; expecting; a look. ನಿರೀಕ್ಷಿಸು. To look at, gaze at; to behold; to expect.

ನಿರೀಶ್ವರ s. a. Godless, atheistic. -ವಾದ. Atheism. -ವಾದಿ. An atheist.

ನಿರುಕೆ (ರು = ಱು) k. n. Orderly arrangement; properness.

ನಿರುಕ್ತ s. a. Uttered, explained. n. One of the vêdâṅgas.

ನಿರುತ s. a. Undoubted; true. n. Undoubtedness, truth; unfailingness; rectitude. [reposed.

ನಿರುತ್ತರ s. a. Without a reply; silenced,

ನಿರುದ್ಯೋಗ s. a. Inactive, lazy; without employment. ನಿರುದ್ಯೋಗಿ. One who is unemployed.

ನಿರುಪದ್ರ, -ವ s. a. Undisturbed; harmless, inoffensive. n. Undisturbedness.

ನಿರುಪಮ, ನಿರುಪಮಾನ, ನಿರುಪಮಿತ s. a. Matchless, unequalled.

ನಿರುಪಯುಕ್ತ s. a. Useless.

ನಿರುಪಾಧಿ, -ಕ s. a. Free from cares or trouble.

ನಿರುಪಾಯ s. a. Helpless, remediless.

ನಿರೂಢಿ s. n. Fame. 2, skilfulness.

ನಿರೂಪ s. n. An order, command; a written order. -ಣ, -ಣೆ. Representing; investigation; determination, definition; sight; telling, narrating. ನಿರೂಪಿಸು. To order; to make known; to define. ನಿರೂಪ್ಯಮಾನ. Being defined, determined.

ನಿರೋಗ s. a. Free from sickness, healthy, well; also ನೀರೋಗ. ನಿರೋಗಿ. A healthy person; also ನೀರೋಗಿ.

ನಿರೋಧ s. n. Shutting in; check; coercion, restraint; hindrance. ನಿರೋಧಿಸು. To obstruct; to restrain, keep back.

ನಿರೋಪ (tb. of ನಿರೂಪ) n. A message; permission to depart.

ನಿರ್ಗತ s. a. Gone out, disappeared, extinct. 2, freed from. [ty.

ನಿರ್ಗತಿ s. n. Helplessness, misery, pover-

ನಿರ್ಗಮ s. n. Going forth, setting out, receding; departure; also -ನ.

ನಿರ್ಗರ್ವ. = ನಿಗರ್ವ, q. v.

ನಿರ್ಗುಣ s. a. Without qualities. n. The supreme soul.

ನಿರ್ಗುಂಡಿ s. n. A shrub, the five-leaved chaste-tree, *Vitex negundo*.

ನಿರ್ಘೋಷ, -ಣ s. n. A loud sound, noise.

ನಿರ್ಜನ s. a. Unpeopled, uninhabited, desolate. [A god.

ನಿರ್ಜರ s. a. Undecaying, immortal. n.

ನಿರ್ಜಲ s. a. Waterless, dry.

ನಿರ್ಜೀವ s. n. Lifelessness. a. Lifeless, inanimate. ನಿರ್ಜೀವಿ. A lifeless being.

ನಿರ್ಣಯ s. n. Decision, determination; precise definition. 2, sentence, decree, verdict. 3, final settlement. -ಮಾಡು, ನಿರ್ಣಯಿಸು. To settle, decide, come to a decision; to give a verdict; to decree, order. ನೀತಿ-. Justification (*Christ.*). ಅಜ್ಞೆ-. Damnation (*Christ.*).

ನಿರ್ದಯ s. a. Pitiless, unmerciful, unkind. ನಿರ್ದಯೆ. Unmercifulness, cruelty.

ನಿರ್ದಿಷ್ಟ s. a. Assigned; directed; described, ascertained.

ನಿರ್ದುಷ್ಟ s. n. Faultlessness.

ನಿರ್ದೇಶ s. n. Pointing out, denoting; directing; order, command, direction; description. ನಿರ್ದೇಶಿಸು. To point out, show; to specify, *etc*.

ನಿರ್ದೈವ s. a. Luckless.

ನಿರ್ದೋಷ s. a. Faultless; guiltless, innocent. ನಿರ್ದೋಷಿ. A guiltless person.

ನಿರ್ಧನ (= ನಿಧನ) s. a. Poor. n. Poverty.

ನಿರ್ಧರಿಸು s. v. t. To determine, ascertain, settle, make sure.

ನಿರ್ಧಾರ s. n. Particularizing; determining, defining, settling; certainty; judgment; also -ಣ.

ನಿರ್ಧೂತ s. *a.* Shaken off, removed.

ನಿರ್ನಾಮ s. *a.* Nameless. 2, ruined. *n.* Ruin.

ನಿರ್ನಿಮಿತ್ತ s. *a.* Causeless, groundless. *n.* Causelessness. *ad.* Causelessly.

ನಿರ್ಬಂಧ s. *n.* Restraining; hindrance, obstruction; *also* -ನ. 2, force, violence. 3, a rule. -ಗೊಳಿಸು. To use force. ನಿರ್ಬಂಧಿಸು. To restrain, hinder; to urge, force.

ನಿರ್ಬಲ s. *a.* Powerless. *n.* Powerlessness.

ನಿರ್ಬಾಧ s. *n.* Freedom from trouble or annoyance.

ನಿರ್ಬುದ್ಧಿ s. *a.* Senseless, stupid. *n.* Stupidity.

ನಿರ್ಭಯ s. *a.* Fearless; secure. *n.* Fearlessness; freedom from danger.

ನಿರ್ಭಾಗ್ಯ s. *n.* Unluckiness. *a.* Unlucky.

ನಿರ್ಭೀತ s. *a.* Fearless, undaunted. ನಿರ್ಭೀತಿ. Fearlessness.

ನಿರ್ಮದ s. *a.* Sober; humble.

ನಿರ್ಮರಣ s. *a.* Deathless.

ನಿರ್ಮಲ (= ನಿರ್ಮಳ) s. *a.* Spotless, stainless; virtuous; clean, pure, serene; shining; charming. -ಮಾಡು. To clean, *as* a house, *etc.* -ತೆ, -ತ್ವ. Purity, cleanliness.

ನಿರ್ಮಾಂಸ s. *a.* Fleshless, emaciated.

ನಿರ್ಮಾಣ s. *n.* Forming, making, creating; creation. -ಮಾಡು. To produce; to create.

ನಿರ್ಮಾತೃ s. *n.* A maker, creator.

ನಿರ್ಮಾಲ್ಯ s. *n.* Stainlessness, purity; the remains of an offering to an idol, *as* flowers, *etc.*

ನಿರ್ಮಿಸು s. *v. t.* To make, form, fabricate, create.

ನಿರ್ಮುಕ್ತ s. *a.* Set free, liberated.

ನಿರ್ಮೂಲ s. *a.* Rootless; unfounded. *n.* Eradication, extirpation. -ಮಾಡು. To eradicate, extirpate. ನಿರ್ಮೂಲಿಸು. To uproot, pluck out, extirpate.

ನಿರ್ಮೋಹ s. *n.* Absence of love.

ನಿರ್ಯಾಣ s. *n.* Departure. 2, disappearance. 3, separation. 4, death.

ನಿರ್ಯಾಸ s. *n.* Exudation of trees, *as* juice, gum, resin, milk, *etc.*

ನಿರ್ಲಕ್ಷ್ಯ s. *n.* Disregard, contempt.

ನಿರ್ಲಜ್ಜೆ s. *n.* Shamelessness, impudence.

ನಿರ್ಲೇಪ s. *a.* Stainless, spotless. *n.* Spotlessness.

ನಿರ್ಲೋಭ s. *n.* Unavariciousness, unselfishness. ನಿರ್ಲೋಭಿ. Unselfish.

ನಿರ್ವಂಚನೆ s. *n.* Fraudlessness. 2, sincerity; *also* ನಿರ್ವಂಚಕತ್ವ. ನಿರ್ವಂಚಕ. Sincere.

ನಿರ್ವರ್ತಿಸು s. *v. t.* To complete, finish.

ನಿರ್ವಹಿಸು s. *v. t.* To carry out; to accomplish, effect.

ನಿರ್ವಾಣ s. *a.* Extinguished; liberated from existence. *n.* Extinction of life; the delivery of the individual soul from the body and further transmigration. 2, death. 3, highest felicity and reunion with the supreme soul. 4, vacuity. 5, immersion. 6, a kind of penance. 7, nakedness.

ನಿರ್ವಾಹ s. *n.* Extricating one's self out of; a way out, an escape. 2, accomplishment; doing, managing. 3, supporting; subsisting on. 4, sufficiency; competent means of living. -ಮಾಡು, ನಿರ್ವಹಿಸು. To accomplish; to live frugally; to be content with what is absolutely necessary to sustain life. -ಸಾಗಿಸು. To obtain or supply the means of sustenance; to maintain. -ಶಾಲಿ. An accomplisher.

ನಿರ್ವಿಕಲ್ಪ s. *a.* Changeless, unalterable.

ನಿರ್ವಿಕಾರ s. *a.* Unchangeable, immutable.

ನಿರ್ವಿಘ್ನ s. *a.* Unobstructed. *n.* Absence of impediment; *also* -ತೆ. -ನಾಯಕ. Gaṇêśa.

ನಿರ್ವಿವಾದ s. *n.* Absence of contention.

ನಿರ್ವಿಶೇಷ s. *n.* Absence of difference. *a.* Without distinction; indiscriminate.

ನಿರ್ವಿಷ s. *a.* Poisonless, innocuous. *n.* An antidote to poison.

ನಿರ್ವಿಷಯ s. a. Unattached to any object.

ನಿರ್ವೃತಿ (= ನಿವೃತ್ತಿ) s. n. Bliss; final emancipation.

ನಿರ್ವೇಶ s. n. Entering into. 2, expiation, atonement; *also* -ನ.

ನಿರ್ವ್ಯಸನ s. n. Unconcernedness.

ನಿರ್ವ್ಯಾಜ s. a. Without deceit, candid, honest, plain. 2, without a pretext, cause or reason.

ನಿರ್ಹೇತುಕ s. a. Causeless, reasonless.

ನಿಲ (= ನಿಲು) k. n. Standing. 2, the side-post of a door. 3, remainder, balance; *also* -ವಾಟ. -ಕಡೆ, -ಗಡೆ. Attitude; leisure; patience; composure.

ನಿಲಕು. = ನಿಲುಕು, q. v.

ನಿಲಯ s. n. An abode, residence. -ವಾನ್. A householder.

ನಿಲವು (= ನಿಲ) k. n. Standing. 2, position. 3, height. 4, cessation, leisure. 5, a seat, place of abode. *a.* High. ನಿಲವಂಗಿ. A long garment.

ನಿಲಿಸು. = ನಿಲ್ಲಿಸು, q. v.

ನಿಲು. = ನಿಲ, q. v. -ಕಡೆ. = ನಿಲಕಡೆ. Patience; composure; leisure. -ಗಣ್ಣು. A staring eye. -ಗನ್ನಡಿ. A full-length-mirror.

ನಿಲುಕು k. v. t. To stretch one's self. *v. i.* To reach; to stand upon one's tiptoes. 2, to come within reach. 3, to begin.

ನಿಲುಂಬು a. k. v. t. To heap up, amass. *v. i.* To crowd. 2, to jump.

ನಿಲುವಿಕೆ. = ನಿಲವು, q. v.

ನಿಲುವು. = ನಿಲವು, q. v.

ನಿಲ್ಲಿಸು k. v. t. To cause to stand, stop, cease, stay, *etc.*

ನಿಲ್ಲು k. v. i. To stand; to stand up; to stop; to stay; to be; to wait; to remain; to stand or last, *as* colour; to remain without injury; to cease, *as* rain; to rest; to endure, *etc.* *P. ps.* ನಿತ್ತು, ನಿಂತು. ನಿಂತಿತು, ನಿಂತು, ನಿತ್ತಿತು. It stopped, stood. ನಿಂದಿರಿಸು. To cause to stand, place, *etc.* ನಿಂದಿರು. To stand, remain.

ನಿವರು k. v. t. To stroke or rub gently. ನಿವರಿಸು. To cause to stroke.

ನಿವರ್ತನ s. n. Accomplishment; turning back; ceasing. ನಿವರ್ತಿಸು. To turn away, repel; to leave off, remove.

ನಿವಾರಣ s. n. Keeping back or off, warding off; averting; preventing, hindering, checking. *Cpds.:* ಅರಿಷ್ಟ-, ದಾಹ-, ದುಃಖ-, ಶ್ರಮ-. ನಿವಾರಿಸು. To keep back, ward off; to avert.

ನಿವಾಸ s. n. A resting-place, abode, dwelling.

ನಿವಾಸಿ s. n. An inhabitant. -ಸು. To dwell, reside.

ನಿವಾಳಿ f. n. The act of waving a thing in front of a person or idol to remove any evil. -ಮಾಡು, -ಸು. To wave anything to avert any evil.

ನಿವೃತ್ತಿ s. n. Return; disappearance, cessation, inactivity; leaving off, desisting from; abstinence; rest. 2, felicity, bliss.

ನಿವೇದನ s. n. Communication, announcement; information; delivering, offering. ನಿವೇದಿಸು. To make known; to present, offer. ನಿವೇದ್ಯ. An oblation, gift of food to an idol.

ನಿವೇಶ s. n. Entering; a settlement; a house; a camp.

ನಿಶಾ 1. s. n. Night. -ಚರ. Moving about by night; the moon; a thief. -ಟನ. An owl. -ದಿ. Evening. -ನಾಥ, -ಪತಿ. The moon. ನಿಶಾಂತ. Break of day; quiet; a house.

ನಿಶಾ 2. f. n. Intoxication. -ಖೋರ. A man taking intoxicants.

ನಿಶಾನಿ h. n. An ensign, flag, standard.

ನಿಶಾಸ್ತ್ರವಾದ s. n. Deism; natural religion.

ನಿಶಿ 1., ನಿಶೆ (= ನಿಶಾ, q. v.) s. n. Night.

ನಿಶಿ 2. h. ad. Together with, along with.

ನಿಶ್ಚಂಚಲ s. a. Fixed, firm, steady; *also* ನಿಶ್ಚಂಚಲಿತ.

ನಿಶ್ಚಯ (= ನಿಚ್ಚಯ) s. n. Ascertainment; certain knowledge; conviction; certainty; determination, resolution, final decision; design, purpose. -ತಾಂಬೂಲ. The ceremony of betrothal. -ಮಾಡು. To ascertain, arrive at a decision; to resolve; to appoint. ನಿಶ್ಚಯಿಸು. To ascertain; to settle; to determine, resolve; to appoint.

ನಿಶ್ಚಲ s. a. Immovable, invariable. 2, fixed, steady. n. A mountain. 2, an ascetic. 3, the earth.

ನಿಶ್ಚಿತ s. a. Settled, decided, certain. ನಿಶ್ಚಿತಾರ್ಥ. A fixed matter; a certain kind of betrothal.

ನಿಶ್ಚಿಂತ s. a. Thoughtless, careless; unconcerned; free from care or anxiety. ನಿಶ್ಚಿಂತೆ. Thoughtlessness; freedom from anxiety, care.

ನಿಶ್ಚೇಷ್ಟೆ s. n. Motionlessness; want of power.

ನಿಶ್ಚೈತನ್ಯ s. n. Want of strength or power.

ನಿಶ್ವಾಸ s. n. Inspiration, inhaling. ನಿಶ್ವಾಸೋಚ್ಛ್ವಾಸ. Inhaling and exhaling.

ನಿಶ್ಶಂಕೆ. = ನಿಃಶಂಕೆ, q. v.

ನಿಶ್ಶಬ್ದ. = ನಿಃಶಬ್ದ, q. v.

ನಿಶ್ಶೇಷ. = ನಿಃಶೇಷ, q. v.

ನಿಶ್ಶ್ವಾಸ s. n. Breathing out, expiration. 2, = ನಿಶ್ವಾಸ, q. v.

ನಿಷಾದ s. n. N. of a wild aboriginal tribe; a Hŏlĕya.

ನಿಷಿದ್ಧ s. a. Prohibited, forbidden, prevented.

ನಿಷೂದನ s. n. Killing, destroying.

ನಿಷೇಧ s. n. Prohibition, forbidding, hindering; negation, denial. -ರೂಪ. The negative form of a verb. ನಿಷೇಧಿಸು. To forbid.

ನಿಷೇವಣ s. n. Waiting on; service, worship.

ನಿಷ್ಕಪಟ s. a. Guileless. n. Guilelessness; also -ತನ. -ಸ್ಥ, ನಿಷ್ಕಪಟಿ. A guileless, candid person.

ನಿಷ್ಕರುಣ s. a. Pitiless, unmerciful, cruel. ನಿಷ್ಕರುಣಿ. A pitiless, cruel person.

ನಿಷ್ಕರ್ಷೆ s. n. Ascertainment, decision, settlement. ನಿಷ್ಕರ್ಷಿಸು. To determine, settle.

ನಿಷ್ಕಲಂಕ s. a. Stainless, spotless, sinless.

ನಿಷ್ಕಾಪಟ್ಯ s. n. Guilelessness.

ನಿಷ್ಕಾಮ s. a. Desireless, disinterested; unselfish. n. Absence of desire, disinterestedness. ನಿಷ್ಕಾಮಿ. A person free from desire.

ನಿಷ್ಕಾರಣ s. a. Causeless, groundless.

ನಿಷ್ಕುಟ s. n. The hollow of a tree. 2, a garden attached to a house.

ನಿಷ್ಕೃತಿ s. n. Expiation, compensation, discharge of a debt or obligation.

ನಿಷ್ಠ s. a. Staying on, grounded on; devoted to, practising. n. Intention, aim.

ನಿಷ್ಠುರ, ನಿಷ್ಠೂರ (= ನಿಟ್ಟುರ) s. a. Hard, rough; harsh, unkind, cruel, severe. -ತನ, -ತೆ, -ತ್ವ. Harshness, etc., severity, cruelty.

ನಿಷ್ಠೆ s. n. Position; condition. 2, devotedness; uniform practice, religious duty; faith. 3, excellence, perfection. 4, conclusion, the end of a drama, etc. 5, death. 6, certainty. 7, trouble.

ನಿಷ್ಪಕ್ಷಪಾತ s. a. Impartial. n. Impartiality.

ನಿಷ್ಪಾಪ s. a. Sinless, guiltless.

ನಿಷ್ಪೇಷಣ s. n. Grinding, pulverizing.

ನಿಷ್ಪ್ರಯೋಜಕ s. a. Useless; needless.

ನಿಷ್ಪ್ರಯೋಜನ s. a. Causeless, groundless; useless. n. Uselessness.

ನಿಷ್ಫಲ s. a. Fruitless, barren; unprofitable.

ನಿಸರ್ಗ s. n. Relinquishment; evacuation; 2, giving away. 3, the natural state.

ನಿಸಿ k. v. t. To squeeze between fingers.

ನಿಸ್ತರಣ s. n. Going out; crossing over; passing time. ನಿಸ್ತರಿಸು. To spend, pass, as time.

ನಿಸ್ತ್ರಾರ್ತ. *tb. of* ನಿಶ್ಚಿತಾರ್ಥ, *q. v.*

ನಿಸ್ತ್ರಾಣ s. *a.* Weightless, light, pithless, weak. *n.* Weakness.

ನಿಸ್ತೇಜ s. *a.* Devoid of energy; dull; impotent. *n.* Want of brilliancy.

ನಿಸ್ಪೃಹ s. *a.* Desireless; indifferent; content. *n.* Absence of covetousness; *also* -ತೆ.

ನಿಸ್ಸಂಶಯ s. *a.* Undoubted, unerring, certain.

ನಿಸ್ಸಂಗ. = ನಿಃಸಂಗ, *q. v.*

ನಿಸ್ಸತ್ವ s. *a.* Pithless, sapless. *n.* Want of energy; weakness; *also* ನಿಃಸತ್ವ.

ನಿಸ್ಸಂತಾನ s. *a.* Childless, issueless; *also* ನಿಃಸಂತಾನ.

ನಿಸ್ಸಂದೇಹ. = ನಿಃಸಂದೇಹ, *q. v.*

ನಿಸ್ಸಹಾಯ. = ನಿಃಸಹಾಯ, *q. v.*

ನಿಸ್ಸಾರ (= ನಿಃಸಾರ, *q. v.*) s. *a.* Sapless; insipid, pithless; worthless, vain. *n.* Saplessness, insipidity.

ನಿಳ್ಕು. = ನಿಲುಕು, *q. v.*

ನೀ k. *pro.* Thou; *pl.* ನೀವು. *See its declension s.* ನಿನ್.

ನೀಗು k. *v. t.* To quit, leave, abandon, get rid of; to lose; to remove, take away; to squander.

ನೀಚ s. *a.* Low, base, vile, mean. -ತನ. Meanness, vileness.

ನೀಟ k. *n.* Length. -ಸಾಲು. A long row.

ನೀಟು k. *n.* Straightness. 2, properness, neatness, beauty, tidiness. -ಗಾರ. A tidy man; *f.* -ಗಾತಿ.

ನೀಡು k. *v. t.* To extend, stretch out, *as* fingers, arms, *etc.* 2, to offer, present, give; to serve out; to put. *n.* Extension, length. 2, presenting. *ad.* Abundantly, much; further. -ಮಾಡು. To raise.

ನೀತಿ s. *n.* Leading, guidance; moral behaviour; political science, policy, statesmanship; moral philosophy, ethics; prudence; acquisition. 2, righteousness; justification (*Christ.*). -ಗ. A well-conducted, virtuous man. -ಮಾರ್ಗ. Moral conduct. -ವಂತ. A moral, just, prudent man. -ವಿದ್ಯೆ, -ಶಾಸ್ತ್ರ. The science of ethics or morals. -ವಚನ, -ವಾಕ್ಯ, -ಮಾತು. A moral saying.

ನೀನು k. *pro.* Thou.

ನೀರ್. = ನೀರು, *q. v.* ನೀರಡಿಕೆ. Thirst. ನೀರಡಿಸು. To be thirsty. ನೀರಣುಗ. The moon. -ಬೆಕ್ಕು, -ನಾಯಿ. An otter. -ದಾರಿ. ನೀರಬಟ್ಟೆ. A water passage. -ಮಾಡು. To liquefy. ನೀರಾಗು. To melt, *as* metals, sugar, *etc.* ನೀರಾಟ. Sporting in water. ನೀರಾಮೆ. A turtle. ನಿರಾವರಿ, ನೀರಾವರಿಕೆ. Abundance of water; soil fit for wet cultivation. ನೀರುಳ್ಳಿ. The onion. ನೀರೆರೆ. To pour water. ನೀರೆಸರು. A kind of plain pepper-water. ನೀರೊತ್ತು. The tide. ನೀರೋಟ. Stream, current.

ನೀರಜ s. *n.* A lotus. 2, a pearl. 3, the garden plant *Costus speciosus*. *a.* Free from impurity.

ನೀರಂಧ್ರ s. *a.* Coarse, thick.

ನಿರಲು. = ನೇರಲು, *q. v.*

ನಿರಾಂಜನ. = ನೀರಾಂಜನ, *q. v.*

ನೀರು (= ನೀರ್) k. *n.* Water. 2, the lustre of a gem. ನೀರಿನವ. A waterman. -ಕಟ್ಟು. To turn water. -ಕಾಗೆ, -ಗಾಗೆ. A kind of cormorant, shag, diver. -ಕಾಲುವೆ. A channel. -ಕೊಕ್ಕರೆ. A curlew. -ಗಂಗಾಳ. A basin of water. -ಗಣಿಗಿಲು. The water hog-weed, *Barringtonia acutangula*. -ಗಣ್ಣು. A water-spring. -ಕೋಳಿ. A water-fowl. -ಗೋಳಿಗಿಡ. A small potherb, *Portulaca oleracea*. -ಚೀಲ. The bladder. -ತೊಟ್ಟಿ. A water-trough. -ದಗೆ. Thirst. -ದಾರಿ. A water-course. -ನಾಯಿ. The river-otter. -ನೆತ್ತಿ. A water-shed; the crest of a hill adjoining cultivation. -ಬಿಡು. To let water. -ಬೆಕ್ಕು. = ನೀರುನಾಯಿ, *q. v.* -ಬ್ರಹ್ಮಿ. The Thyme-leaved Gratiola, *Herpestis moniera*. -ಮಳೆ. Rain that brings water to fields, tanks, *etc.* -ಸರಿ. Stream, current; water-cess. -ಹಕ್ಕಿ. The Indian or

Siberian crane, *Ardea sibirica*. -ಹಂದಿ. The skate fish. -ಹುಲ್ಲು. The water-reed, *Calamus fasciculatus*. -ಹಾವು. A water-snake. -ಹೊಗೆ. Fog arising from water; steam, vapour.

ನೀರೆ (ರೆ = ಱೆ) a. k. n. A damsel; a gay woman.

ನೀರ್. = ನೀರು, q. v. -ಕುಡಿ, -ಗುಡಿ. Water to drink. -ಗುಳ್ಳೆ. A water-bubble. -ಪಡಿಸು. To soak. -ಸೆಳೆ. To draw water. -ಮಾನಸೆ. A mermaid, nymph. -ಪುಟ್ಟು. A paddle. -ಪೂವು. A lotus, *etc.*

ನೀಲ s. a. Dark-blue or black; dyed with indigo. 2, bad; vile. 3, slow, lazy. n. The sapphire. 2, N. of a monkey attendant on Râma. 3, sin, crime. 4, indigo. -ಕಂಠ, -ಕಂಧರ. A peacock; a quail; Šiva; N. -ಗಾರ. An indigo-dyer. -ಗಿರಿ. The Nilagiri hill. -ಮಣಿ. The sapphire. ನೀಲಾಂಬರಿ. N. of a râga.

ನೀಲಾಂಜನ s. n. A small lamp used for waving before an idol, *etc.*

ನೀಲಿ s. n. An indigo shrub, *Indigofera tinctoria*. 2, indigo, the dye. 3, a female evil spirit that speaks lies. -ಗಣ್ಣು. An eye with a bluish pupil. -ಗಾರ. An indigo-dyer. -ಮಾತು. A falsehood. -ವಾರ್ತೆ. A false report. ನೀಲೋತ್ಪಲ. The blue water-lily, *Nymphaea cyanea;* a blue lotus.

ನೀವಾರ f. n. Rice growing wild.

ನೀವಿ s. n. A cloth worn round a woman's waist. 2, capital, stock. 3, a wager, stake. 4, junction, union.

ನೀವು 1. k. *pro.* (*pl. of* ನೀನು) You. *See its decl. s.* ನಿಮ್ಮ.

ನೀವು 2. k. v. t. To rub softly, stroke down, *as* the hair, cloth, *etc.*

ನೀಸು (*tb. of* ನಯಿಸು) v. t. To manage; to fulfill.

ನೀಳ (= ನೀಡು) k. n. Extension, length, height.

ನೀಳು (*cf.* ನೀಡು) a. k. v. i. To grow long, extend, be stretched out.

ನು s. *int.* Now? what? indeed?

ನುಗಿ (= ನುಗ್ಗು) k. v. t. To powder.

ನುಗಿಲು k. v. i. To slip.

ನುಗ್ಗ. = ನುಗ್ಗೆ, q. v.

ನುಗ್ಗು 1. k. v. i. To force one's self into; to enter without permission, *as* a house, *etc.*; to creep into.

ನುಗ್ಗು 2. (= ನುಗ್ಗಿ, q. v.) k. v. t. To crush, powder, grind. n. Crushed or crumbled state. ನುಗ್ಗಾಗು. To be crushed to pieces, crumble.

ನುಗ್ಗೆ (= ನುಗ್ಗಿ) k. n. The horse-radish, *Moringa pterigosperma*. *Cpds.:* -ಕಾಯಿ, -ಗಿಡ, -ಬೀಜ, ಮರ, -ಸೊಪ್ಪು, *etc.*

ನುಂಗು k. v. t. To swallow; to devour

ನುಚ್ಚು (= ನುಗ್ಗು 2, *etc.*) k. n. Fragments, bits: grits of any grain. 2, wasting away, ruin, *etc.* ನುಚ್ಚಕ್ಕಿ. Broken rice. -ಗಂಜಿ. Ganji made of nuċcu.

ನುಡಿ k. v. t. To utter; to speak; to say. n. A voice; speech; a word; a promise; a language. *Cpds.:* ಎಡೆ-, ಹುಸ್ಸ-, ಜವಳಿ-, ತಪ್ಪು-, ತೊದಲು-, ಬಲು-, ಬಿರು-, ಬಿರುಸು-, ಮರುಳಾಟ-, *etc.* -ಕೊಡು. To promise. -ಮೆಚ್ಚು. Assent by word. -ತ. Speech. -ಸು. To cause to utter, speak, *etc.*; to perform music upon, to play.

ನುಣ್ಪು a. k. n. Smoothness, softness, gentleness; *also* ನುಣುಪು, ನುಣುಪು. -ಗಾರೆ, ನುಣುಗಾರೆ. Fine, smooth plaster. -ಬಗಲಿ. A soft seat. -ಅರಿಸಿನ. Fine turmeric. -ನುಡಿ, ನುಣ್ಣುಡಿ. A gentle word. -ಬೆಳಗು. A delicate lustre. -ಮಣಿ. A delicate gem. -ಮಾತು. = -ನುಡಿ, q. v. -ಮುತ್ತು. A fine pearl. ನುಣ್ಣಗೆ, ನುಣ್ಣನೆ. Smoothness, baldness. a. Smooth; bald. ad. Completely.

ನುಣ್ಪು. = ನುಣುಪು, q. v.

ನುತಿ s. n. Praise, eulogium; worship. -ಸು. To praise, *etc.*

ನುಂದು. = ನೊಂದು, q. v.

ನುರಿ (ರಿ = ಱಿ. = ನುಗ್ಗು 2, q. v.) k. v. i. To be crushed, *etc.* 2, to be harassed; to be inured to; to become familiar with.

ನುರು (ರು = ಱು) k. n. The state of being harassed or exercised. -ಪಡಿ. Familiarity with, etc.

ನುರುಕು (ರು = ಱು) k. v. i. To wane away. v. t. (= ನುಗ್ಗು 2) To reduce to powder, etc.

ನುರುಜು (ರು = ಱು) k. n. Gravel.

ನುಲಿ k. v. t. To twist, as a rope, etc.; to wring, as clothes in washing; to curl, as the whiskers, etc. 2, the intestines to gripe. n. A twist, cord. 2, griping pain in the intestines; also ನುಲಿಕೆ. ನುಲಿಸು. To cause to twist.

ನುಲಿಕೆ, ನುಲಿಗೆ k. n. A twist, cord, thread, twine. -ಮಾಡು. To twist. -ಅಗಣಿ, -ಯುಗಣಿ. The twisting pin that elevates or depresses the shaft of the oil-mill.

ನುಸಿ 1. k. n. Powder, dust.

ನುಸಿ 2. k. n. An insect that destroys cloth, grain, etc. 2, an eye-fly; a gnat.

ನುಸಿ 3. (= ನುಸುಳು) k. v. i. To enter a door, etc. P. ps. ನುಸಿದು, ನುಸ್ತು.

ನುಸುಳು (= ನುಸಿ 3) k. v. i. To enter a door; to get into; to retreat, hide one's self, slink. n. Entering a door. 2, evasion, falsehood.

ನುಸ್ತು. = ನುಸಿದು. P. p. of ನುಸಿ 3.

ನೂಕು k. v. t. To shove, push; to push away or aside; to push on, urge on. 2, to spend, as time. 3, to fare. n. Shoving; a push. ನೂಕಿಸು. To cause to push, etc.

ನೂತನ s. a. New, novel, recent; fresh, young; strange. -ಗಾರ. A schemer.

ನೂತಿ (tb. of ಲೂತಿ) n. A cancerous disease.

ನೂರು (ರು = ಱು) k. a. A hundred. ನೂರನೆಯ. Hundredth. ನೂರಾಐವತ್ತು. 150. ನೂರ್ಇಪ್ಪತ್ತೈದು. 125. ನೂರಾರು. Fully a 100. -ಪಟ್ಟು, -ಮಡಿ. A hundred fold.

ನೂಲು k. n. Yarn, thread. v. t. To make thread, spin. P. p. ನೂತು. -ಕಂಟಿಕೆ, -ಕಂಡಿಕೆ. A ball of thread. -ಬಟ್ಟೆ. Cotton cloth. -ಹುಣ್ಣಿಮೆ. A festival on which the sacred thread is renewed.

ನೂಳದು k. ad. Much, exceedingly.

ನೃ s. n. Man. -ಪ, -ಪತಿ, -ಪಾಲಕ. A king. -ಪವಿದ್ಯೆ. State policy. -ಪೇಂದ್ರ. An excellent king. -ಹರಿ. Vishṇu's incarnation of man-lion; also ನರಸಿಂಹ.

ನೃತ್ಯ s. n. Dancing, pantomime.

ನೆಕ್ಕು (= ನಕ್ಕು) k. v. t. To lick. ನೆಕ್ಕಿಸು. To cause to lick.

ನೆಗಚು (= ನೆಗಸು) a. k. v. t. To cause to jump.

ನೆಗಡಿ k. n. A cold, catarrh. -ಬರು, -ಹಿಡಿ. To catch cold.

ನೆಗತ k. n. Leaping, jumping.

ನೆಗಪು, ನೆಗಹು a. k. v. t. To raise, lift up. n. Lifting up.

ನೆಗಸು. = ನೆಗಚು, q. v.

ನೆಗಳ್ (ಳ್ = ೞ್) a. k. v. t. To undertake; to engage in; to perform, do. v. i. To come; to be used.

ನೆಗಳು 1. (ಳು = ೞು) a. k. v. i. To become manifest, well known, famous; to shine; to appear.

ನೆಗಳು 2., ನೆಗಳೆ k. n. An alligator.

ನೆಗಳ್ತೆ a. k. n. Action; work; conduct. 2, fame, accomplishment.

ನೆಗೆ k. v. i. To be purified, to be clear, to shine. 2, to jump up, to bound. 3, to rise, ascend. v. t. To raise, lift up. P. ps. ನೆಗದು, ನೆಗೆದು. ನೆಗೆತ. Leaping.

ನೆಗ್ಗಲು, ನೆಗ್ಗಿಲು k. n. The small caltrops, *Tribulus lanuginosus*; also -ಮುಳ್ಳು.

ನೆಗ್ಗು 1. k. v. i. To be curved or bent inward; to sink in; to disappear; to get a bruise.

ನೆಗ್ಗು 2. k. v. t. To crush, smash, destroy.

ನೆಚ್ಚು (= ನಚ್ಚು 1, q. v.) k. v. t. To believe, trust; to confide in. n. Confidence, trust, faith, reliance. ನೆಚ್ಚಿಕೆ, -ಗೆ. = ನಚ್ಚಿಗೆ s. ನಚ್ಚು 1, q. v.

ನೆಟ್ಟಗೆ, ನೆಟ್ಟನೆ k. a. Straight, erect. ad. Straightly; orderly, regularly; rightly, distinctly; well, in good health. ನೆಟ್ಟಗಾಗು. To become straight. -ಮಾಡು. To repair; to do well; to arrange.

ನೆಟ್ಟನ್ನ, ನೆಟ್ಟಾನ, ನೆಟ್ಟಾನೆ k. a. Straight, regular, proper, *etc. Cpds.:* -ಗೆರೆ, -ದಾರಿ, -ಮಾತು, *etc.*

ನೆಡು (= ನಡು 2, *etc., q. v.*) k. *v. t.* To fix firmly, plant, *etc. P. p.* ನೆಟ್ಟು.

ನೆಣ k. *n.* Fat, marrow.

ನೆಂಟ (= ನಂಟ, *q. v.*) k. *n.* A kinsman, relative. -ರುಇಷ್ಟರು, ನೆಂಟರಿಷ್ಟರು. Relations and other beloved ones. -ತನ, -ಸ್ತನ, -ಸ್ತಿಕೆ. Relationship.

ನೆಂಟು. = ನಂಟು, *q. v.*

ನೆತ್ತ (*tb. of* ನೇತ್ರ) *n.* The eye. 2, a die; a cowry used in gaming. 3, gambling. -ದ ಹಲಿಗೆ. A play-board. ನೆತ್ತದಾಟ. Playing at backgammon, *etc.* ನೆತ್ತಿಗ. A gambler.

ನೆತ್ತರು (= ನೆತ್ರ) k. *n.* Blood. -ಕುರು. A kind of bleeding boil.

ನೆತ್ತಿ k. *n.* The forehead; the crown of the head. -ಮುತ್ತು. A pearl in the head.

ನೆತ್ರು. = ನೆತ್ತರು, *q. v.*

ನೆನ. = ನೆನದು. *P. p. of* ನೆನೆ 1, *in* ನೆನ ಕೊಳ್ಳು.

ನೆನೆ 1. k. *v. i. & t.* To think, imagine; to think upon; to be mindful of; to wish; to remember; *also* ನೆನಸು. ನೆನಪು, ನೆನವು. Thought, reflection; recollection, remembrance. -ಪು ಇಡು, ನೆನಹಿಡು. To think about, remember. -ಪು ಇರು, ನೆನಪಿರು. To bear in mind. ನೆನವರಿಕೆ. Recollection.

ನೆನೆ 2. k. *v. i.* To become wet. *P. ps.* ನೆನದು, ನೆನೆದು, ನೆಂದು. -ಯುವಿಕೆ. Becoming wet, *etc.* -ಹಾಕು. To put for soaking. -ಅಕ್ಕಿ, ನೆನೆಯಕ್ಕಿ. Soaked rice; a kind of sweetmeat. ನೆನಗಡಲೆ. Soaked kaḍale. -ಸು ನೆನಸು. To make wet, moisten.

ನೆಪ್ಪು (= ನೆನಪು, *etc.*) k. *n.* Recollection. 2, acquaintance.

ನೆಮ್ಮದಿ f. *n.* Serenity; comfort, happiness. -ವಂತ, -ಸ್ತ. A happy man.

ನೆಮ್ಮು a. k. *v. i.* To lean on; to take for one's support. *n.* Leaning upon; a support. -ಗೆ. = ನಂಬಿಕೆ. ನೆಮ್ಮಿಸು. To charge with, attribute.

ನೆಯ್, ನೆಯಿ k. *v. t.* To weave; to entwine; *also* ನೆಯ್ಯು. ನೆಯಿಗೆ. Weaving; a web. -ಗೆಯುವ, -ಕಾರ. A weaver.

ನೆಯ್ದಲೆ, ನೆಯ್ದಿಲೆ k. *n.* A water-lily.

ನೆರ 1. (= ನೆರೆ 1) k. *n.* Nearness; joining; assistance. *a.* Adjoining, coming near (to assist). -ನಾಡು. An adjoining district. -ಮನೆ (= ನೆರೆ-). A neighbouring house: next door. -ಯವ, -ಮನೆಯವ. A neighbour. -ಹೊರೆಯವರು. Next door and other neighbours.

ನೆರ 2. (ರ = ಱ) k. *n.* A vital point or organ; a secret. -ತೆ. Fullness, completeness.

ನೆರಕೆ (= ನೆರಿಕೆ) k. *n.* A fence of bamboos, *etc.*

ನೆರದು. = ನೆರೆದು. *P. p. of* ನೆರೆ, *q. v.*

ನೆರಪು, ನೆರಸು a. k. *v. t.* To bring together, join, collect, convene.

ನೆರವಣಿಗೆ (ರ = ಱ) a. k. *n.* Fullness; accomplishment; nicety; goodness.

ನೆರವಿ k. *n.* A union, mass, crowd, multitude, *etc.* [help.

ನೆರವು 1. k. *n.* A mass. 2, an assistance,

ನೆರವು 2. (ರ = ಱ) k. *n.* Fullness, completeness. -ಏರಿಸು, ನೆರವೇರಿಸು. To fulfil, accomplish. ನೆರವೇರು. To be completed, fulfilled, *as* a word, work, *etc.*

ನೆರವೇರು. *See s.* ನೆರವು 2.

ನೆರಳು k. *n.* Shade; shadow; shelter.

ನೆರಿಕೆ. = ನೆರಕೆ, *q. v.*

ನೆರೆ 1. k. *v. i.* To join; to come together, assemble; to associate with. *P. ps.* ನೆರೆದು, ನೆರದು. *n.* Proximity, neighbourhood; union, company. -ಮನೆ. = ನೆರಮನೆ. -ಯವ. A neighbour. -ಊರು, ನೆರೆಯೂರು. A neighbouring village. -ಹಳ್ಳಿ. A neighbouring hamlet.

ನೆರೆ 2. = ನರೆ, *q. v.*

ನೆರೆ 3. (ರೆ = ಐ⁵) k. v. i. To become entire, full, complete, ready, perfect, mature, sufficient. *P. ps.* ನೆರದು, ನೆರೆದು. *n.* Completeness; maturity, *etc.* 2, a flood. *ad.* Completely, perfectly, fully, exceedingly. -ಜಾಣ. Replete with wisdom.

ನೆಲ k. *n.* Ground, soil; land; floor; a country, kingdom; the earth. ಜವುಗು-. Swampy ground. ತವರು-. Rising ground. -ಕಡಲೆ. The earth-nut. -ಕಲ. A miser. -ಕಂಚಿ, -ನಾರಿಂಗ. A small shrub, *Naregamia alata.* -ಗಟ್ಟು. Pavement. -ಗುಂಬಳ. A creeper, *Ipomaea digitata.* -ಗುಮ್ಮ. A kind of bird. -ಗುಳ್ಳ. A prickly nightshade. -ತಾವರೆ, -ದಾವರೆ. The plant *Hibiscus mutabilis.* -ನೆಲ್ಲಿ. A small herb, *Phyllanthus madraspatensis.* -ಬೇವು. The plant *Gentiana cherayta.* -ಮನೆ. A cellar; a dungeon. -ವಾಳಿಗೆ. A granary. -ವರೆ (-ಅವರೆ). The plant *Cassia aborata.* -ವಾಗು. To take root; to become a protection. -ಸರಿ, -ಸಮಾನ. Level with the ground. -ಸಂಪಿಗೆ. A fragrant garden-flower, *Kaemferia rotunda.* -ಸು. To settle; to stay; to stand. -ಹಲಸು. The ananas. -ದಾರಿ. A land-way. ನೆಲಾವರೆ. The Senna plant.

ನೆಲವು, ನೆಲಹು k. *n.* A net-work of rope in which pots, etc. are suspended.

ನೆಲೆ k. *n.* Standing-place; a place of residence; an apartment of a house; place; ground; footing; basis; certainty; certain knowledge; a mystery. -ಕಟ್ಟು, -ಗಟ್ಟು. = ನೆಲಗಟ್ಟು, *q. v.* -ಗಣ್ಣು. A penetrating eye. -ಗೆಡು. Ground to lose, *etc.* -ಗೊಳ್ಳು. To take footing; to take root, *as* plants, *etc.*; to become settled. -ಗೊಳಿಸು. To place, establish, *etc.* -ಮನೆ. An abode. -ಮಾಡ. An upper story. -ಯಾಗು. To get a firm footing; to be in use.

ನೆಲ್ಲಿ k. *n.* The emblic myrobalan, *Phyllanthus emblica.*

ನೆಲ್ಲು k. *n.* Paddy, rice in its husk. -ಅಕ್ಕಿ, ನೆಲ್ಲಕ್ಕಿ. Rice. -ಗದ್ದೆ. A paddy-field. -ಹುಲ್ಲುಸರವೆ. A band of paddy straw.

ನೆವ, ನೆವನ (*tb. of* ನಿಭ) *n.* A pretence, pretext, plea. -ತೆಗೆ, -ಮಾಡು. To pretend. -ಹೇಳು. To utter a pretext, to plead an excuse.

ನೆಸೆ (= ನೆಗೆ, *q. v.*) k. *v. i.* To jump about, *etc.* 2, to give one's self airs. *P. ps.* ನೆಸದು, ನೆಸೆದು, ನೆಸ್ತು. -ಆಟ, ನೆಸ್ತಾಟ. Jumping about. ನೆಸ್ತಾಡು. To jump about.

ನೆಳಲು (ಳ = ಐ). = ನೆರಳು, *q. v.*

ನೇ. = ನೇಯು, *q. v.*

ನೇಗಲಿ, ನೇಗಲು, ನೇಗಿಲು (*tb. of* ಲಾಂಗಲ) *n.* A plough. -ಈಡು. A plough-shaft. -ಸಾಲು. A furrow. -ಹೂಡು. To yoke oxen to a plough. -ಹೊಡೆ. To plough.

ನೇಗೆ. = ನೇಯಿಗೆ, *etc.*, *q. v.*

ನೇಜಿ k. *n.* Young plants, *esp.* of rice; *also* ನಾಟಿ.

ನೇಟು (= ನೀಟು, *q. v.*) k. *n.* Straightness; truth.

ನೇಣು k. *n.* A cord, rope; a noose. -ಹಾಕಿಕೊಳ್ಳು. To hang one's self.

ನೇತು. *P. p. of* ನೇಲು, *q. v.*

ನೇತ್ರ s. *n.* A leader; leading. 2, the eye. -ತ್ರಯ. Śiva. -ವೈದ್ಯ. An oculist. ನೇತ್ರಾಂಬು. Tears. ನೇತ್ರಾವತಿ. N. of a river in S. Canara.

ನೇಪಾಲ, ನೇಪಾಳ s. *n.* N. of a country, Nepal. 2, = ಜಾಪಾಳ.

ನೇಮ (*tb. of* ನಿಯಮ, *q. v.*) *n.* A rule, order, appointment. -ಕ. Ruling; a rule; an appointment, *etc.* -ತೆಗೆ. To lay down as a rule. -ವಂತ. = ನಿಯಮವಂತ.

ನೇಮಣೂಕ, ನೇಮಣೂಕಿ s. *n.* Appointment; allowance, stipend.

ನೇಮಿ s. *n.* The circumference of a wheel.

ನೇಮಿಸು. *tb. of* ನಿಯಮಿಸು, *q. v.*

ನೇಯಿಗೆ (= ನೆಯಿಗೆ, *q. v.*) k. *n.* Weaving.

ನೇಯು. = ನೆಯ್ಯು, *q. v.*

ನೇರ k. n. Straightness; propriety; harmony; rightness; fitness; order. ನೇರ ನೇರ. rep. Quite proportionate; face to face.

ನೇರಿಮ a. k. n. Propriety, rectitude, etc. ನೇರಿದ. A Brâhmaṇa; f. ನೇರಿದಳ್.

ನೇರಲು, ನೇರಳೆ, ನೇರಿಲು (ರ=ಱ) k. n. A common tree with purple berries, Eugenia jambolana.

ನೇರೆ f. n. A breakfast.

ನೇಲು k. v. i. To be suspended, to hang, swing, dangle. P. p. ನೇತು. ನೇತಾಡು.= ನೇಲು, q. v.

ನೇವರಿಸು k. v. t. To make straight or smooth; to rub gently with the hand.

ನೇವಳ a. k. n. A necklace of silver or gold; a girdle.

ನೇವುರ (tb. of ನೂಪುರ) n. An anklet.

ನೇಸರು (ರು=ಱು) a. k. n. The sun. -ಗಲ್ಲು. Crystal.

ನೇಸ್ತ, ನೇಹ (tb. of ಸ್ನೇಹ) n. Love. -ಗಾರ. A male friend; f. -ಗಾತಿ.

ನೈಚ್ಯ (fr. ನೀಚ) s. n. Lowness; humility.

ನೈಜ (fr. ನಿಜ) s. a. Real. n. Reality, truth.

ನೈಟ್ರೋಜನು e. n. Nitrogen, an element.

ನೈಮಿತ್ತಿಕ s. a. Accidental, occasional.

ನೈಮಿಷ s. a. Momentary. n. N. of a forest.

ನೈಮೇಯ (=ನಿಮಯ) s. n. Barter, exchange.

ನೈಯಾಯಿಕ s. n. A dialectician, logician.

ನೈರುತಿ (tb. of ನೈಋತಿ) n. The south-west quarter.

ನೈಋತ s. a. South-western. n. The ruler of that quarter. ನೈಋತಿ. The south-west quarter.

ನೈರ್ಮಲ್ಯ (fr. ನಿರ್ಮಲ) s. n. Stainlessness, purity.

ನೈಲ್ಯ (fr. ನೀಲ) s. n. Blueness; blackness.

ನೈವೇದ್ಯ (fr. ನಿವೇದ್ಯ) s. n. An offering of eatables to a deity. -ಈ, -ಕೊಡು, -ಮಾಡು. To present a naivêdya.

ನೈಷ್ಠಿಕ (fr. ನಿಷ್ಠೆ) s. a. Steady, firm, devoted. -ತನ. Constancy, steady adherence to rules; firm belief.

ನೊಗ (tb. of ಯುಗ) n. A yoke. -ಕಟ್ಟು, -ಹಾಕು. To yoke.

ನೊಚ್ಚಗೆ k. n. Agreeableness or pleasant feeling when eating, hearing sweet words, etc.

ನೊಣ k. n. A fly. -ಕಸ. A common plant, Plectranthos cordifolius. -ಬ. One of the Kuruba tribe.

ನೊಣೆ k. v. t. To clean the teeth with the tongue. 2, (a. k.) to swallow.

ನೊಂದಿಸು (=ನಂದಿಸು, ನುಂದಿಸು, q. v.) k. v. t. To extinguish, quench. ಬೆಂಕೀ-. To quench fire. ದುಃಖ-. To alleviate sorrow. ದಾಹ-. To slake thirst.

ನೊಂದು (=ನಂದು, ನುಂದು, q. v.) k. v. i. To be extinguished, to go out.

ನೊಯಿಸು.=ನೋಯಿಸು, q. v.

ನೊಯ್ಯು.=ನೋ, q. v. P. p. ನೊಂದು.

ನೊರಜು k. n. A gnat, eye-fly.

ನೊರೆ k. n. Foam, froth. -ಕಟ್ಟು, -ಗಟ್ಟು. Foam to be formed. -ಬಾಯಿ. A frothy mouth. -ಹಾಲು. Frothy milk fresh from the cow. -ಹಪ್ಪಳ. A kind of rice-happaḷa. -ಬೀಳು, -ಸೋರು. To foam at the mouth.

ನೊಸಲು k. n. The forehead. ನೊಸಲಕ್ಕರ, ನೊಸಲಬರಹ. The writ of destiny on the forehead. ನೊಸಲಬೊಟ್ಟು. A sandal mark on the forehead.

ನೋ (=ನೊಯ್ಯು, ನೋಯು) k. v. i. To feel pain, to ache; to be afflicted or grieved. P. p. ನೊಂದು.

ನೋಟ (fr. ನೋಡು) k. n. Viewing, beholding; a sight; a spectacle; a look; appearance; examination. -ಕ, -ಕಾರ, -ಗಾರ. A spectator; an eye-witness; an examiner: a shroff.

ನೋಟೀಸು e. n. Notice; information.

ನೋಡು k. v. t. To look; to view, behold; to look after; to examine; to consider; to take care; to see. ರುಚಿ-. To taste. ವಾಸನೆ-. To smell. ಕೈ-. To feel the pulse. ಹಣಿಕಿ-. To peep. ತಿರುಗಿ-. To look back. ಎದುರು-. To wait, look for. ನೋಡಿಸು. To cause to look, *etc.* -ವಿಕೆ. Looking, *etc.*

ನೋತ (*fr.* ನೋ) k. *n.* Ache, pain.

ನೋನು k. *v. t.* To observe a vow or perform any meritorious act. *P. ps.* ನೋತು, ನೋಂತು.

ನೋಂಪಿ k. *n.* Any meritorious act of devotion, penance, or austerity.

ನೋಯು. = ನೋ, *etc.*, *q. v.* ನೋಯಿಸು. To cause to suffer pain; to pain, afflict.

ನೋರು h. *n.* Fare, freight.

ನೋವು (*fr.* ನೋ) k. *n.* Ache, pain; affliction. -ಕೊಡು, -ಮಾಡು. = ನೋಯಿಸು, *q. v.* ತಲೆ-. Headache. ಹೊಟ್ಟೆ-. Stomach-ache, colic.

ನೌ s. *n.* A ship, boat. -ಕೆ. A small ship.

ನೌಕರ. = ನವುಕರ, *q. v.*

ನೌಲು. = ನವಿಲು, *q. v.*

ನ್ಯಗ್ರೋಧ s. *n.* The Indian fig or banyan tree, *Ficus bengalensis.*

ನ್ಯಾಯ (= ನಾಯ) s. *n.* Method, way, rule, manner, system, plan. 2, fitness, right, justice; law; a lawful act. 3, a lawsuit; dispute. 4, a logical argument; syllogism; logic. 5, an axiom. -ತೀರಿಕೆ. A case; being settled (*also* -ತೀರುವಿಕೆ. Last judgment). -ತೀರಿಸು. To decide a case; to judge. -ತೀರಿಸುವಿಕೆ. Deciding a case. -ದ ಕಟ್ಟು. A system of rules. -ಕಾರ. A quarrelsome man. -ನಿರ್ಣಯ. A sentence or verdict. -ಪ್ರಮಾಣ. A standard of law; decalogue, the ten commandments of God. -ಮಾರ್ಗ. The way of justice. -ವಂತ, -ಸ್ಥ. A just man. -ವಿಚಾರಕ. A judge. -ವಿಚಾರಣೆ. Investigation of a lawsuit. -ವಿಧಾಯಕ. Legislative. -ವಿಧಾಯಕಸಭೆ. Legislative council. -ಸಭೆ. A court of justice. -ಸ್ಥಾನ. A court, cutcherry. ನ್ಯಾಯಾಧಿಪತಿ, ನ್ಯಾಯಾಧೀಶ. A judge. ನ್ಯಾಯಾಸನ. The judgment seat, bench.

ನ್ಯಾಸ s. *n.* Depositing; consigning; a deposit, pledge. 2, certain religious ceremonies.

ನ್ಯೂನ s. *a.* Deficient, defective, wanting. -ತೆ. Deficiency, want.

ಪ್

ಪ್. The thirty-ninth letter of the alphabet.

ಪ k. *A letter used in reiteration, as:* ಆಸ್ತಿ ಪಾಸ್ತಿ, ಕಲ್ಲು ಪಲ್ಲು, ಕಾಯಿ ಪಾಯಿ, ಲೆಕ್ಕ ಪಕ್ಕ, ಸುಳ್ಳು ಪಳ್ಳು, *etc.* 2, a. k., *a letter to form the future tense and the present rel. part., as:* ಇರ್ಪ, ಉದಯಿಪ, ಕಾಪ, ತಾಪ, ಪೋಪ, ಬರ್ಪ, ಮಾಳ್ಪ.

ಪಕಳೆ f. *n.* A petal of a flower.

ಪಕಾರ s. *n.* The letter ಪ.

ಪಕಾಲಿ h. *n.* A double water-skin carried on a bullock.

ಪಕೀರ. = ಫಕೀರ, *q. v.*

ಪಕ್ಕ (*tb. of* ಪಕ್ಷ) *n.* A wing. 2, the flank or side; a side, party, faction. 3, neighbourhood. 4, support. -ವಿ. The flank or side. -ರಕ್ಕೆ, -ರಿಕ್ಕೆ (*tb. of* ಪಕ್ಷರಕ್ಷೆ). The armour of horses or elephants. -ಶೂಲೆ. Pleurisy.

ಪಕ್ಕನೆ (= ಫಕ್ಕನೆ) k. *ad.* Suddenly. -ನಗು. To burst out a laughing.

ಪಕ್ಕಲೆ f. *n.* A kind of vessel.

ಪಕ್ಕಾ (*tb. of* ಪಕ್ವ) *a.* Mature, ripe; perfect; shrewd; accomplished. -ಖರಡೆ. The regular account compiled from the diary. -ಆದವ, -ದವ. A shrewd, cunning man. -ಮಾತು. An apt word.

-ರಂಗು. Lasting colour. -ಸಿಪಾಯಿ. An accomplished soldier. -ಸೇರು. A large measuring sôru.

ಪಕ್ಕಿ f. n. A manner, way, means. 2, = ಹಕ್ಕಿ, q. v.

ಪಕ್ಕೆ 1. a. k. n. Lying down; reposing. 2, a dormitory; the lair of wild beasts; a nest. 3, a cow-pen. 4, closeness, contact.

ಪಕ್ಕೆ 2. = ಪಕ್ಕ, etc., q. v. n. The side. 2, the page of a book.

ಪಕ್ವ (= ಪಕ್ಕಾ, q. v.) s. a. Cooked, baked. 2, mature, ripe. 3, accomplished, perfect, fully developed, ready; shrewd; strong. ಪಕ್ವಾನ್ನ. Cooked food; a dish. -ಮಾಡು. To cook; to make fit. -ಆಗು. To grow ripe or fit for use.

ಪಕ್ಷ (= ಪಕ್ಕ, q. v.) s. n. A wing; a feather. 2, the side of anything; the flank. 3, a side, part; a party, faction. 4, a follower, partisan. 5, partiality. 6, a case; an alternative; supposition (ಆ ಪಕ್ಷದಲ್ಲಿ, in that case, provided). 7, the half of a lunar month. -ಮಾಡು. To be partial. -ಹಿಡಿ. To side with. -ಪಾತ. Partiality. -ಪಾತಿ. A partisan. -ಪ್ರಾಯಶ್ಚಿತ್ತ. An expiatory act performed at the śuklapaksha. -ಭೇದ. Partiality. -ಭೇದಮಾಡು. To be partial, to show partiality. ಪಕ್ಷಾಂತರ. Another way or manner. ಪಕ್ಷಾಪರ-. Siding with another party. ಪ್ರತಿ-. Against, opposite (party).

ಪಕ್ಷಿ s. n. A bird. 2, siding with. -ಗೂಡು. A bird's nest; a bird-cage. -ರಾಜ. Garuḍa. -ವಾಹನ. Vishṇu. -ಸೇರಿಸು. To espouse a side.

ಪಕ್ಷ್ಮ s. n. A wing. 2, an eye-lash. 3, the filament of a flower.

ಪಗಡಿ h. n. A turban.

ಪಗಡೆ 1. k. n. A frequently cultivated tree, *Mimusops elengi*.

ಪಗಡೆ 2. f. n. A mark on a die; a cowry for playing a kind of backgammon. 2, the play itself. -ಯ ಕೋಟೆ. The centre of a dice-cloth. *Cpds.:* -ಯ ಬೀದಿ, -ಯ ಮನೆ, -ಯ ಸಾಲು, *etc.* -ಯಾಟ. The pagaḍě-play.

ಪಗದಸ್ತು f. a. Cautious, *as* in speech; painstaking. -ಗಾರ. A painstaking man.

ಪಗದಿ k. n. Tribute, tax.

ಪಗಲು. = ಹಗಲು, q. v.

ಪಗಾರ f. n. Pay, salary.

ಪಗಿನು. = ಹಗಿನು, q. v.

ಪಗಿಲ್ a. k. v. i. To be sticky, viscid; to adhere. 2, to be afflicted.

ಪಗೆ. = ಹಗೆ, q. v.

ಪಂಕ 1. f. n. A large fan, punka.

ಪಂಕ 2. s. n. Mud, mire. 2, sin. -ಜ, -ಜಾತ. A lotus. -ಜಗರ್ಭ, -ಜನಾಭ. Brahmâ. -ಜವೈರಿ. The moon. -ಜಾಕ್ಷ, -ಜೋದರ. Vishṇu.

ಪಂಕ್ತಿ s. n. A line, range, row, series. 2, a row of people at a meal. 3, a flock, troop; a company. -ಗ್ರೀವ. Râvaṇa. -ಭೇದ. Partiality in serving guests. -ರಥ. Daśaratha. *Cpds.:* ರಾಜ-, ಸಭಾ-, *etc.*

ಪಂಗ k. n. A fork, a forked branch. -ನಾಮ. A large forehead-mark. --ಹಾಕು. To deceive.

ಪಂಗಡ k. a. Apart, distinct. n. A party of people.

ಪಂಗು s. a. Lame, crippled.

ಪಚಗಾರಿಸು. = ಪಚಾರಿಸು, q. v.

ಪಚಡಿ. = ಪಚ್ಚಡಿ, q. v.

ಪಚನ, ಪಚನೆ s. n. Cooking, roasting; maturing; digesting. 2, fire.

ಪಚಾರ f. n. Reproach. ಪಚಾರಿಸು. To reproach, chide, jeer.

ಪಚ್ಚೆ 1. k. n. Greenness; an emerald. -ಕರ್ಪೂರ. Superior camphor. -ನೆ. Greenness.

ಪಚ್ಚೆ 2. (tb. of ಪ್ರಚ್ಛದ) n. Dress, adorning; an ornament. -ಡ, -ವಡ (= ಹಚ್ಚಡ). A large wrapper; a stout cotton cloth used as a cover at night. -ಪಡಿಸು. To decorate, adorn.

ಪಚ್ಚಡಿ (=ಪಚಡಿ) k. n. A kind of pickles made of green vegetables.

ಪಚ್ಚೆ k. n. A precious stone set in gold without soldering.

ಪಚ್ಚೀಸು h. a. Twenty-five. 2, a kind of play.

ಪಚ್ಚುಗೆ k. n. Privacy; consulting in private.

ಪಚ್ಚೆ (=ಪಚ್ಚ) k. n. Greenness. 2, yellowish colour. 3, young sprouts; growing corn, *etc.*, and their colour. 4, freshness, unripeness, rawness. 5, an emerald. 6, N. of a plant with fragrant ears; *also* -ತೆನೆಗಿಡ. 7, any tatooed figure on the skin. -ಕಾಯಿಗಿಡ. A climbing herb, *Cucumis pubescens*. -ತೋರಣ. A festoon of green leaves.

ಪಜೀತಿ. = ಫಜೀತಿ, *q. v.*

ಪಜ್ಜೆ. = ಹೆಜ್ಜೆ, *q. v.*

ಪಂಚ s. a. Five. 2, incomparable. *n.* A jury. -ಕ. Made of five; a pack of five, *as* of paper. -ಕಜ್ಜಾಯ. A sweet meat made of five ingredients, *as* avalakki, ĕḷḷu, kaḍlĕ, kŏbari and bella. -ಕೋಣ. A pentagon. -ಘಾಯ. The five wounds of Christ, *as* of hands, feet and heart. -ಗವ್ಯ. Five things from the cow: milk, curds, ghee, urine and dung. -ಗೌಡ. Brâhmaṇas of Bengal and northern provinces. -ತಂತ್ರ. N. of a collection of stories and fables in five chapters. -ತ್ವ. Fivefoldness; death. -ಪರ್ವ. Five days in a month on which Brâhmaṇas perform special worship. -ಪಾಂಡವ. The five sons of Pâṇḍu, who are worshipped by peasants in the form of stones. -ಪಾತ್ರೆ. A metal vessel. -ಪ್ರಾಣ. The five vital airs. -ಭೂತ. The five elements: earth, fire, water, air and ether. -ಮ. The fifth; a Śûdra; a čâṇḍâla. -ಮಹಾಪಾತಕ, -ಮಹಾಪಾಪ. The five heinous sins: killing a Brâhmaṇa, *etc.* -ಮಹಾಯಜ್ಞ, -ಯಜ್ಞ. Devotional acts performed in reference to the vêda, the gods, the manes of ancestors, men and all beings. -ಮಹಾವಾದ್ಯ. Five musical instruments: a horn, tabor, conch-shell, kettle-drum, and a gong. -ಮಿ. The 5th day of the lunar fortnight; the ablative case. -ಮುದ್ರೆ. Five gestures of fingers made in presenting offerings; five sectarian marks of Śaivas. -ರಂಗು. =-ವರ್ಣ. -ರಾತ್ರ. N. of doctrinal books of Vaishṇava sects. -ರಾಶಿ, -ರಾಶಿಕ. The double rule of three. -ಲೋಹ. An alloy of 5 metals, viz. gold, silver, copper, tin and iron. -ವಕ್ತ್ರ. A lion; Śiva. -ವಟಿ. N. of a place where Râma resided. -ವರ್ಣ. The five colours: white, black, red, yellow, and green; five letters or castes. -ವಾದ್ಯ. The bhêri, śaṅkha, kahaḷĕ, ganṭĕ, and vîṇe. -ವಿಷಯ. The five objects of sense: rasa, rûpa, gandha, śabda, and sparśa.

ಪಂಚಾಂಗ s. n. A calendar or almanac. -ದವ. An astrologer; a poor man. -ಹೇಳು. To tell the things from an almanac; to tell verbosely.

ಪಂಚಾಮೃತ s. n. The five nectarious substances: milk, curds, ghee, honey, and sugar.

ಪಂಚಾಯಿತಿ h. n. An assembly to settle a matter by arbitration; arbitration. -ಪೈಸಲು. An award of arbitrators. ಪಂಚಾಯಿತ. An arbitrator.

ಪಂಚಾಲ s. n. N. of a tribe and their country in the north.

ಪಂಚಾವಸ್ಥೆ s. n. Five states of humanity: childhood, boyhood, youth, manhood, and old age.

ಪಂಚಾಶತ್ s. a. Fifty. -ತಮ. Fiftieth. ಪಂಚಾಶತ್ತಿನ ಹಬ್ಬ. Pentecost; the pouring down of the Holy Spirit on the disciples of Christ.

ಪಂಚಾಳ s. n. One of the five classes of artificers: goldsmiths, carpenters, blacksmiths, braziers and stone-cutters. 2, a goldsmith.

ಪಂಚಿ (= ಪಂಜಿ) f. n. A small dôtra.

ಪಂಚೇಂದ್ರಿಯ s. n. The five organs of sense: the eye, ear, nose, tongue and skin.

ಪಂಛೇರು (fr. ಪಂಚ-ಸೇರು) s. h. n. One-eighth of a maund.

ಪಂಜರ s. n. A cage. 2, a skeleton.

ಪಂಜಾಬು (tb. of ಪಂಚ-ಆಪ) n. The Panjab.

ಪಂಜಿಕೆ f. n. The cotton-ball from which the thread is spun. 2, an almanac. 3, a journal; a register.

ಪಂಜು f. n. A torch.

ಪಂಜೆ 1. k. n. A poor, weak person. -ತನ. Poverty.

ಪಂಜೆ 2. = ಪಂಜ, q. v.

ಪಟ (= ಪಟ್ಟ) s. n. Cloth. 2, fine cloth; = ಪಟವೆ, q. v. 3, a veil, screen. 4, a sheet; an expanse; vastness. 5, a tablet or plate. 6, a thatch, roof. 7, a sail. 8, a paper-kite. 9, a picture. 10, a basin for watering plants. 11, a plat. -ಕ. Cotton cloth; a camp. -ಕಾರ. A weaver; alum. -ಕುಟಿ, -ಗೃಹ, -ವಾಸ. A tent. -ವಾಸಕ. A perfumed powder. -ಸ್ತಂಭ. A mast.

ಪಟಕ (tb. of ಸ್ಫಟಿಕಾ) n. Sulphate of alumina or alum; also ಪಟಿಕಾರ.

ಪಟಕಾರು k. n. Tongs, pincers.

ಪಟಣಿ. tb. of ಪಠನ, q. v.

ಪಟಲ s. n. A roof, thatch. 2, a cover, veil. 3, a basket. 4, tb. of ಪಟೋಲ.

ಪಟವೆ s. n. Silk. -ಕಾರ, -ಗಾರ. A man who dyes silk yarn, makes silk tassels, etc.

ಪಟಾ f. n. A stripe, streak. -ಪಟಿ. Striped. -ಯಿತ. Striped, as a tiger.

ಪಟಾಕಿ, ಪಟಾಕ್ಷಿ h. n. A cracker, squib.

ಪಟಾಟೋಪ s. n. Ostentatious display of one's dress.

ಪಟಾಣ h. n. A Pathân, Afghân.

ಪಟಾಲಮ್ f. n. A battalion, regiment, army.

ಪಟಾವಳಿ s. n. Stripes, lines. 2, woven silk. -ಸೀರೆ. A sīrĕ with coloured stripes.

ಪಟಿಕ. = ಪಟಕ, q. v. 2, tb. of ಸ್ಫಟಿಕ.

ಪಟಿಂಗ f. n. An unprincipled fellow, a lecher; a prodigal; an adulterer. -ತನ. Unprincipledness, profligacy.

ಪಟೀರ s. n. Sandal wood. 2, the belly. 3, bamboo manna.

ಪಟು s. a. Sharp. 2, fierce; pungent; violent; active; strong, great. 3, clever, skilful; crafty. 4, eloquent, talkative. -ಮಾಡು. To kindle. -ತ್ವ. Sharpness; cleverness; eloquence.

ಪಟೇಲ h. n. A village officer.

ಪಟೋಲ s. n. A species of long cucumber, *Trichosanthes dioeca;* the snake-gourd; also ಪಡವಲ.

ಪಟ್ಟ s. n. Cloth; silk. 2, a tablet, plate; a royal edict or grant. 3, a frontlet with which a king is decorated at coronation; royalty; a royal throne; dignity, office. -ಕಟ್ಟು. To invest with dignity or authority. (-ಕ್ಕೆ or) -ದ ಮೇಲೆ ಕುಳಿತುಕೊಳ್ಳು. To come to the throne. -ಕ್ಕೆ ಕೂಡ್ರಿಸು. To place on the throne. -ದಿಂದ ತೆಗದುಹಾಕು, -ದಿಂದ ತಳ್ಳು. To dethrone. -ದರಸಿ, -ದ ರಾಣಿ. The queen. -ಪಣಿ. A throne. -ಆಗು, -ವಾಗು. To be enthroned. -ಏರು, -ವೇರು. To ascend the throne. -ಬದ್ಧ. A king. -ಮಹಿಷಿ. The queen. -ವರ್ಧನ. A vaidika Brâhmaṇa of much reading. -ಶಾಲೆ. A reading hall. ಪಟ್ಟಾಭಿಷೇಕ. The coronation of a king, ordination of a priest.

ಪಟ್ಟಡಿ, ಪಟ್ಟಡೆ k. n. An anvil. -ಮನೆ. A workshop.

ಪಟ್ಟಣ (tb. of ಪತ್ತನ) n. A town, city. ಪಟ್ಟಣಿಗ. A townsman.

ಪಟ್ಟಳೆ s. n. A girth, martingale.

ಪಟ್ಟಾ f. n. A long broad sword; also -ಕತ್ತಿ.

ಪಟ್ಟಾಂಗ f. n. Idle talk.

ಪಟ್ಟಿ s. n. A stripe, line. 2, a strip, slip, strap, as of lace, cloth; a narrow and long piece, as of cloth, leather, metal, wood, etc.; a bar of iron, a rail for a railroad; a piece of timber of a door-frame; a squared rafter, joist; a female's zone; a dog's collar. 3, a roll of betel-leaves. 4, a fold, as of a turban. 5, a bed in gardens or fields. 6, a roll of a general collection; a list of collection, subscription or contribution. 7, pay, salary. 8, a roll or list, as of names, etc. -ಖೋರ. A slanderer. -ವೀಳ್ಯ. = ಪಟ್ಟಿ No. 3. -ಹಾಕು. To collect money by subscription.

ಪಟ್ಟಿಕೆ s. n. A tablet; a kind of necklace. 2, a document. 3, a bandage, ligature. 4, a frontlet.

ಪಟ್ಟು 1. k. v. t. To seize, catch, take hold of. n. Hold; a firm grasp. 2, persistence; resolution; pertinacy. 3, an application to a swelling to allay pain. 4, a callous spot.

ಪಟ್ಟು 2. P. p. of ಪಡು 1, q. v. 2, (fr. ಪಡು 2) lying down. ಪಟ್ಟಿಂಸು. To lay down, place.

ಪಟ್ಟು 3. k. n. So much as; time, repetition.

ಪಟ್ಟೆ 1. k. n. The bark of trees. 2, plantain fibres folded up so as to hold snuff, etc.

ಪಟ್ಟೆ 2. (= ಪಟ್ಟಿ, q. v.) s. n. The pate, i. e. a head without hair. 2, a stripe, as of colour. 3, a broad tape. 4, a strap, girth, girdle. 5, a zone, sash. 6, a plat. 7, the outer iron rim of a wheel. 8, a roll of assessment. -ಕಂಬಳಿ. A striped kambly. -ತಗೆ. To shave the head in stripes. -ಮಂಚ. A cot with tape bottom.

ಪಟ್ಟೆ 3. (= ಪಟ್ಟ No. 1) s. n. Silk; woven silk.

ಪಟ್ಣ. = ಪಟ್ಟಣ, q. v.

ಪಠನ s. n. Reading, reciting. ಪಠನಾಗಾರ. A school. ಪಠಿಸು. To read; to recite; to study.

ಪಡೆ 1. = ಪಡದು, ಪಡೆದು. P. p. of ಪಡೆ, in ಪಡಕೊಳ್ಳು.

ಪಡೆ 2. (tb. of ಪಟ) n. Cloth. 2, a thatch. -ಸಾಲೆ. A veranda, balcony.

ಪಡಗು (= ಹಡಗು, q. v.) a. k. n. A ship, etc.

ಪಡಚ. = ಪಡಚ, q. v.

ಪಡದೆ (= ಪರದೆ) h. n. A curtain; a veil.

ಪಡಪೋಶಿ h. n. Inattention, carelessness.

ಪಡಮ f. n. Coarse cotton used for bags, etc.

ಪಡಲು k. n. A lying or falling down. ಪಡಲಿಡು. To fall down here and there.

ಪಡವಲ. = ಪಟೋಲ, q. v.

ಪಡವಲು. = ಪಡುವ, q. v.

ಪಡಾವು h. n. Wholesale merchandise. -ದಾರ. A wholesale merchant.

ಪಡಿ 1. a. k. n. Manner, way. 2, incurring, obtaining. -ಪಾಟು. Troubles.

ಪಡಿ 2. k. n. A measure of capacity = ½ sheer.

ಪಡಿ 3. k. n. A leaf or panel of a door.

ಪಡಿ 4. k. n. An allowance in food. -ತರ. Daily allowance at a temple.

ಪಡಿ 5. (tb. of ಪ್ರತಿ) n. Equality, likeness, comparison, par. ad. Instead of; beside; against. -ಕಟ್ಟು. To produce equipoise. -ಕಲ್ಲು. A stone used to produce equipoise. -ಗುಂಡು. A round stone used to break another one. -ತೊತ್ತು. An extra servant. -ಮುಖ. tb. of ಪ್ರತಿಮುಖ. -ಮೆಚ್ಚು. Doubt. -ಯಚ್ಚು. A puncheon with which impressions are struck.

ಪಡಿಗ (tb. of ಪ್ರತಿಗ್ರಹ) n. A spitting-pot, spittoon.

ಪಡಿಚ (= ಪಡಚ) h. n. Clearance (of a debt); consumption (of articles or provision); ruin.

ಪಡಿತಳ a. k. n. Effort, exertion. ಪಡಿತಳಿಸು. To make effort.

ಪಡಿಯಾರ (tb. of ಪ್ರತಿಹಾರ) n. A doorkeeper; f. -ತಿ.

ಪಡಿಸು k. v. t. To cause to incur, get, etc. -ವಿಕೆ. Causing to get.

ಪಡು 1. (= ಪಡೆ 1) k. *v. t.* To get, obtain; to catch; to incur, undergo; to experience, feel; to suffer. *Affixed to the infinitive of verbs it gives them a passive signification; as:* ಬರೆಯು-, ಬರೆಯಲ್-. To be written, *etc.*

ಪಡು 2. a. k. *v. i.* To lie down; to go down, set, *as* the sun; to wear away; to die. *n.* Setting: the west. -ಕಡೆ, -ಗಡೆ. The western side. -ವ, -ವಲು. The region of sun-set: the west.

ಪಡೆ 1. (= ಪಡು 1) k. *v. t.* To get; to incur, undergo; to experience; to gain, obtain. 2, to beget; *esp.* to bear, give birth to, *as* a mother. *P. ps.* ಪಡದು, ಪಡೆದು. -ಯುವಿಕೆ, -ವಿಕೆ. Obtaining, incurring; experiencing.

ಪಡೆ 2. k. *n.* A multitude, force, army. -ವಳಿ, -ವಳ್ಳಿ. A general. -ಯಿಲ. A soldier.

ಪಡ್ಡಳ (*tb. of* ಪ್ರತಿಹಾಸ) *n.* The sweet-scented oleander, *Nerium odorum.*

ಪಣ 1. f. *n.* Any tribe; a sectarian division. -ಕಟ್ಟು. Caste rules.

ಪಣ 2. (= ಹಣ) s. *n.* Play, playing for a stake. 2, a stake at play, a wager. 3, wages, hire. 4, a fanam, a small coin. 5, a weight of two tolas. 6, price. 7, money, wealth. 8, business, trade. 9, a shop, stall. -ಕಟ್ಟು. To wager.

ಪಣತೆ (*tb. of* ಪ್ರಣೀತ) *n.* A saucer-shaped lamp-cup.

ಪಣೆ k. *n.* A stick, bat. -ಚೆಂಡು. A play with a bat and ball.

ಪಣೆ. = ಹಣೆ, *q. v.* 2, tillage; a quarry.

ಪಂಡಿತ s. *n.* A Pandit, scholar, learned man, doctor; *f.* -ಳು.

ಪಣ್ಣು 1. a. k. *v. t.* To make ready; to array; to dress; to trim. ಪಣ್ಣಿಕ. Arranging, equipping; an ornamental mark on the forehead. ಪಣ್ಣಿಸು. To cause to make ready.

ಪಣ್ಣು 2. = ಹಣ್ಣು, *q. v.*

ಪಣ್ಣಯ k. *n.* A farm.

ಪಣ್ಯ s. *a.* Saleable, vendible. *n.* An article of trade, wares. 2, a shop.

ಪತಂಗ s. *n.* A bird. 2, a grasshopper. 3, any flying insect, *esp.* a moth. 4, the sun. 5, a sort of paper-kite. 6, an arrow.

ಪತಂಜಲಿ s. *n.* N. of a muni, author of the yôga philosophy.

ಪತನ s. *n.* Falling down.

ಪತಾಕಿ s. *n.* A standard-bearer, an ensign. -ನಿ. An army.

ಪತಾಕೆ s. *n.* A flag, banner.

ಪತಿ s. *n.* A master, owner. 2, a governor, ruler, lord. 3, a husband. -ವ್ರತೆ. A virtuous and faithful wife. -ಪತ್ನಿ. Husband and wife.

ಪತಿತ s. *a.* Fallen; wicked. -ತ್ವ. Wickedness. -ಪಾವನ. Purifier and restorer of the fallen.

ಪತ್ತಲ f. *n.* A lower garment of females.

ಪತ್ತಳಿಕೆ (= ಬತ್ತಳಿಕೆ) s. *n.* A quiver.

ಪತ್ತಾರಿ h. *n.* An examiner of tax money and measurer of public corn.

ಪತ್ತಿ s. *n.* Going, moving. 2, a footman. 3, a share of some joint concern. -ಗ, -ಗಾರ. A partner.

ಪತ್ತಿಗೆ k. *n.* A hold: a wall-shelf. 2, (*tb. of* ಪತ್ರಿಕೆ) a sword-blade; a knife.

ಪತ್ತು 1. (= ಹತ್ತು 1, *q. v.*) a. k. *v. i.* To hold to, stick to, *etc.* *n.* Hold, adhesion. 2, a grapple in fight. 3, friendship. -ವಳಿ. The amount of frauds on government charged to a public functionary.

ಪತ್ತು 2. = ಹತ್ತು 2, *q. v.*

ಪತ್ತು 3. f. *n.* Credit, reputation.

ಪತ್ತೆ h. *n.* Tidings; trace, clue. -ಹಚ್ಚಿಸು, -ಹುಟ್ಟಿಸು. To trace. -ದಾರ. A detective. -ತೋರು. Traces to appear.

ಪತ್ತೇಮಾರಿ f. *n.* A Pattimar.

ಪತ್ನಿ s. *n.* A wife. *Cpds.:* ಗುರು-, ರಾಜ-, *etc.*

ಪತ್ಯ. *tb. of* ಪಥ್ಯ, *q. v.*

ಪತ್ರ s. n. A wing. 2, a vehicle. 3, a leaf. 4, a letter, note; a written paper or deed. 5, the leaf of a book; *also* -ಕ. 6, a knife. -ದ್ವಾರ. By means of a letter. -ಪುಟಿಕೆ. A basket of leaves. ಪತ್ರಾಂಗ. Sappan wood; red sanders. -ವ್ಯವಹಾರ. Correspondence. ಪತ್ರಾವಳಿ. A plate made of leaves.

ಪತ್ರಿ f. n. The coat of the nutmeg, mace. *a.* Having wings or leaves.

ಪತ್ರಿಕೆ s. n. A letter; a leaf. ಜನ್ಮ-. A paper containing the horoscope.

ಪತ್ರೆ. = ಪತ್ರಿ, *q. v.* [traveller.

ಪಥ s. n. A path, way, road. ಪಥಿಕ. A

ಪಥ್ಯ s. *a.* Proper, fit, suitable, as diet. *n.* Diet, dietetics. -ಮಾಡು. To observe dietetical rules. -ಕರ. Wholesome.

ಪದ 1. = ಹದ, *q. v.*

ಪದ 2. s. *n.* A step; footstep; a trace, mark. 2, a verse-line; a verse, stanza. 3, a footing, standpoint, position. 4, an abode. 5, an object. 6, cause. 7, an inflected word. -ಗ. A pedestrian; a foot-soldier. -ಗತಿ. Gait. -ಚ್ಛೇದ. Parsing. -ಪಾಠ. A peculiar method of reading and writing vedic texts. -ಪೂರ. Expletive. -ಪೂರಕ. An expletive. -ವಿಸ್ತೃತಿ. The course of a verse. -ಸಂಧಾನ. Combination of words or composing of verses. ಪದಾದಿ. The beginning of a word. ಪದಾಂತ್ಯ. Final. ಪದಾಂತ್ಯಸಂಧಿ. Euphonic coalition of a final letter with the letter of the next word.

ಪದಕ s. n. An ornamental breast-plate.

ಪದಪು a. k. *n.* Zeal; pleasure; charm.

ಪದರು 1. f. *n.* A fold, *as* of cloth; a division; a thin layer of stone; a coat of an onion; scale of a fish. 2, the lap, as protection, *as:* ಒಬ್ಬನನ್ನು ತನ್ನ ಪದರಿನಲ್ಲಿ ಇಟ್ಟುಕೊಳ್ಳು.

ಪದರು 2. (ರು = ಱು) k. *v. i.* To be overhasty. 2, to blabber. ಪದರಾಡು, ಪದರು. To talk nonsense. ಪದರಾಟ. Loquacity; haste.

ಪದವಿ s. *n.* A path, road. 2, situation, rank, office; wealth. ದಿವ್ಯ-, ಮೋಕ್ಷ-. Heaven. [an.

ಪದಾಜಿ, ಪದಾತಿ s. *n.* A footman, pedestri-

ಪದಾರ್ಥ s. *n.* The meaning of a word. 2, a thing. 3, a head; a category. 4, a dish of any vegetables; curry.

ಪದಿ. = ಹದಿ, *q. v.*

ಪದುಳ (= ಹದುಳ) a. k. *n.* Well-being, welfare; safety. ಪದುಳಿಗ. A happy man. ಪದುಳಿರು. To cheer up. ಪದುಳಿಸು. To become well or happy; to feel refreshed.

ಪದೆ a. k. *v. t.* To desire, wish. *n.* Desire, wish.

ಪದೇ s. *ad.* At a step. -ಪದೇ. At every step, on every occasion.

ಪದ್ಧತಿ s. *n.* A way. 2, manner, mode, usage, custom. *Cpds.:* ಲೋಕ-, ಜನ-, ಶಾಸ್ತ್ರ, *etc.*

ಪದ್ಮ s. *n.* A lotus, *Nelumbium speciosum.* 2, the water-lily. 3, a species of fragrant plant used in medicine. 4, the moon. 5, a particular posture of the body in religious meditation. 6, thousand billions. -ಗರ್ಭ, -ಜ, -ಭವ, -ಸಂಭವ. Brahmâ. -ನಾಭ. Vishṇu -ಪತ್ರ. *Costus speciosus.* -ಪಾಣಿ. Lakshmî; Pârvatî. -ಪುರಾಣ. N. of a Purâṇa. -ಬಂಧು, -ಸಖ. The sun. -ಮುದ್ರೆ. A certain intertwining of the fingers in devotion; a sectarian mark on the forehead. -ರಾಗ. Lotus coloured; a ruby. ಪದ್ಮಾಕ್ಷ. Lotus-eyed; the seed of the lotus. ಪದ್ಮಾವತಿ. N. of a woman; the town Patna. ಪದ್ಮಾಸನ. = ಪದ್ಮ. No. 5, *q. v.*

ಪದ್ಯ s. *n.* A verse; metre; poetry.

ಪನಸ s. *n.* The jack tree.

ಪನಿ. = ಹನಿ, *q. v.*

ಪನಿವಾರ k. *n.* A sweet cake, fritter; *also* ಪನಿಯಾಣ.

ಪನೀರು f. *n.* Cheese.

ಪಂತ 1. (*tb. of* ಪಣಿತ) *n.* A bet, wager. 2, a promise or vow; a challenge. -ಕ

ಟ್ಟು. To bet, wager. -ಮಾಡು, -ಹಾಕು. To challenge, vow. -ಗಾರ. A wagerer.

ಪಂತ 2. s. n. A learned man, Pandit; a schoolmaster.

ಪಂತಿ. tb. of ಪಂಕ್ತಿ, q. v.

ಪಂತು. tb. of ಪಂಥ, q. v.

ಪಂತೋಜಿ f. n. A schoolmaster.

ಪಂಥ s. n. A path, road.

ಪಂದರು, ಪಂದಲ್ k. n. A pandal, shed.

ಪಂದಿ. = ಹಂದಿ, q. v.

ಪಂದೆ (= ಹಂದೆ, q. v.) a. k. n. A coward. -ತನ. Cowardice.

ಪನ್ನ 1. a. k. n. Pride.

ಪನ್ನ 2. h. n. The breadth of cloth.

ಪನ್ನಗ s. n. A snake. -ಭೂಷಣ. Śiva. -ಶಯನ. Vishṇu. ಪನ್ನಗಾಂತಕ, ಪನ್ನಗಾಶನ. Garuḍa.

ಪನ್ನಂಗ (tb. of ಪಲ್ಯಂಕ) n. The canopy over a palanquin or couch; also ಪಲ್ಲಂಗ.

ಪನ್ನತಿಕೆ a. k. n. Valour, courage.

ಪನ್ನಾಡೆ k. n. The web surrounding the lower part of a palm-tree leaf.

ಪನ್ನಿ k. n. Boasting; self-conceit.

ಪನ್ನೀರು k. n. Rose-water; perfumed water.

ಪನ್ನೆ h. n. A funny way of trimming the whiskers.

ಪನ್ನೇರಳು, -ಮರ k. n. A small tree with very fragrant flowers, *Guettarda speciosa*.

ಪಪ್ಪರಿಕೆ. = ಪರ್ಪರಿಕೆ, q. v.

ಪಪ್ಪಳ. = ಹಪ್ಪಳ, q. v.

ಪಪ್ಪಳಿ s. n. A chequered garment; the stuff called "poplin".

ಪಪ್ಪಾಯಿ f. n. The Papaya tree and fruit.

ಪಪ್ಪು k. n. Split pulse, almonds, *etc.*

ಪಪ್ಪುಕ k. n. Beating bushes in hunting.

ಪಂಪ a. k. n. Equal division.

ಪಂಪೆ (= ಹಂಪೆ, q. v.) s. n. The river, lake, or town of Pampā or Hampĕ; also ಪಂಪಾಕ್ಷೇತ್ರ.

ಪಂಬಲ್. = ಹಂಬಲ, q. v.

ಪಯ. = ಪಯಸ್, q. v. ಪಯೋಧರ. A cloud. ಪಯೋಧಿ. The ocean. ಪಯೋನಿಧಿ, ಪಯೋಂಬುಧಿ. The milk-sea.

ಪಯಣ (tb. of ಪ್ರಯಾಣ, q. v.) n. A journey, *etc.*

ಪಯಸ್ s. n. Water. 2, milk.

ಪಯಿರು, ಪಯ್ರು. = ಪೈರು, q. v.

ಪರ s. a. Distant, remote. 2, ulterior, beyond. 3, subsequent, next, future. 4, another, different, foreign, alien. 5, hostile. 6, excellent, best, supreme, chief. 7, intent upon, engrossed in. n. A stranger. 2, final beatitude. -ಕರ್ತೃ. Another agent. -ಕಾಯ. Another body. -ಕೀಯ. Another's; a stranger. -ತಂತ್ರ. Subject to another; dependent on. -ತಂತ್ರತನ. Dependence. -ತೆ, Absoluteness, distinction; priority. -ತ್ರ. Elsewhere, hereafter. -ತ್ವ. = ತೆ. Influence, sway. -ತ್ವದಿಂದ. Through. -ದಾರ. Another's wife. -ದೇಶ. A foreign country. -ದೇಶಸ್ಥ. A man from abroad. -ದೇಶಿ. A foreigner; a poor wanderer; a wretch. -ನಿಂದೆ. Reviling others. -ಪಕ್ಷ. The side of an enemy. -ಪುರುಷ. A stranger. -ಬಲ. A hostile army. -ಬ್ರಹ್ಮ. The supreme soul. -ಭಾಗ. Excellence. -ಭಾಷೆ. Foreign language. -ಮಂಡಲಿಕ. The ruler of another province. -ಮತ. Heterodoxy, heresy. -ರಾಯ. Another or hostile king. -ರಾಷ್ಟ್ರ. A hostile country; another kingdom. -ಲೋಕ. The next world, future state; paradise, heaven. -ವಶ. Subject to another, dependant. -ವಶತೆ. Dependence. -ವಾದಿ. A controversialist, dissenter. -ವಾಸ. A foreign place or abode. -ವಾಸ ಮಾಡು. To stay in a foreign place. -ಸ್ತ್ರೀ. = -ದಾರ. -ಸ್ಥಲ. A foreign place. -ಸ್ಥಾನ. Removing the baggage for a journey on an auspicious day to another house, when it is not convenient to start immediately. -ಸ್ಪರ. One another, each other, mutual; mutually, reciprocally. -ಸ್ವಾಧೀನ. = ಪರಾಧೀನ. -ಹಿಂಸೆ. Injuring others. -ಹಿತ. Benevolent; benevolence. ಪರಾತ್ಪರ. Higher than the highest. ಪರಾರ್ಥ. The profit of another. ಪರಾತ್ರಯ. Dependence. ಪರಾಶ್ರಿತ. Dependant, subject. ಪರಾಹ್ಣ. The afternoon.

ಪರಕಲು (ರ = ಱ) k. n. The state of being emaciated or lean.

ಪರಕಾವಣೆ h. n. Proving coin, shroffing; *also* ಪಾರಕಾವಣೆ.

ಪರಕಾಳೆ f. n. A long cloth.

ಪರಕು 1. = ಪರಕು.

ಪರಕು 2. h. n. Distinction, difference; dissimilitude.

ಪರಕೆ (= ಹರಕೆ, *q. v.*) a. k. n. A benediction. 2, a vow. 3, a broom.

ಪರಗಣೆ h. n. A district.

ಪರಂಗಿ f. n. A Frank; a European.

ಪರಚು (= ಪರಡು) k. v. t. To scratch with the finger nails.

ಪರಜು (*tb. of* ಪರಂಜ) n. The blade of a sword or knife; a sword. 2, a sward-hilt.

ಪರಂಜ್ಯೋತಿ s. n. The supreme light. 2, God.

ಪರಟಿ f. n. A platter, pot; the blade of a hoe. 2, an enclosure around a house.

ಪರಡಿ f. n. A kind of dish. 2, the nape of the neck.

ಪರಡು 1. (= ಹರಡು) a. k. v. t. To spread. 2, to scrape out; to scratch. v. i. To spread, extend.

ಪರಡು 2. a. k. n. The ankle.

ಪರದ. = ಹರದ, *q. v.*

ಪರದೆ (= ಪಡದೆ) h. n. A curtain, veil.

ಪರದೈಸು f. n. Paradise, the garden of Eden; heaven.

ಪರಂತು f. *ad.* But, yet, however.

ಪರಪು a. k. v. t. To spread about. 2, to be divulged.

ಪರಭಾರಿ, ಪರಭಾರೆ f. *ad.* Elsewise, in some other way. n. An assignment, transfer. -ಪತ್ರ. A deed of transfer.

ಪರಮ s. a. Highest, most excellent, best, greatest. 2, extreme. n. The supreme soul. -ಗತಿ. Final beatitude. -ಜ್ಞಾನ. Supreme wisdom; knowledge of salvation (*Christ.*). -ಜ್ಞಾನಿ. A person of superior wisdom. -ತ್ವ. The highest end or aim. -ಪದ. Final beatitude. -ಪುರುಷ. The supreme soul. -ಹಂಸ. An ascetic of the highest order. ಪರಮಾಣು. An atom. ಪರಮಾತ್ಮ. The supreme soul, the soul of the universe; God. ಪರಮಾನಂದ. Supreme felicity. ಪರಮಾನ್ನ. Best food, *as*: rice boiled in milk with sugar. ಪರಮಾರ್ಥ. Reality, truth. ಪರಮಾವಧಿ. Utmost term or limit. ಪರಮೇಶ, ಪರಮೇಶ್ವರ. Supreme lord: Śiva; Vishṇu; Indra.

ಪರಮೆ (ರ = ಱ) a. k. n. A black bee.

ಪರಂಪರ s. a. Successive, repeated. ಪರಂಪರೆ. A series, succession, order; race, lineage.

ಪರವರ್ಷ. *tb. of* ಪರಾಮರ್ಶ, *q. v.*

ಪರವಾ h. n. Care, concern about; anxiety. -ಇಲ್ಲ. Never mind.

ಪರವಾನಾ, ಪರವಾನೆ h. n. An order, pass, commission.

ಪರಶು s. n. An axe. -ಧರ, -ರಾಮ. Râma, the son of Jamadagni.

ಪರಸು. = ಹರಸು, *q. v.*

ಪರಸೆ (= ಪರಿಸೆ. *tb. of* ಪರಿಷದ್) n. People assembled at an idol festival.

ಪರಸ್ಮೈಪದ s. n. The active transitive verb (*g.*).

ಪರಾಕು f. *int.* Attention! take heed! listen! n. Carelessness, inattentiveness, forgetfulness.

ಪರಾಕ್ರಮ s. n. Heroism, valour, courage; power, strength. 2, exertion; effort, enterprise. -ಶಾಲಿ. A valorous man. -ವುಳ್ಳ, ಪರಾಕ್ರಮಿ. Powerful, valorous.

ಪರಾಗ s. n. The pollen of a flower. 2, dust, powder. 3, the nectar or honey of flowers.

ಪರಾಙ್ಮುಖ s. a. Having the face turned away or averted. 2, averse from, regardless of. -ತೆ. Disinclination, aversion.

ಪರಾಚೀನ s. a. Turned away, averted.

ಪರಾಜಯ s. n. Conquest. 2, defeat. 3, loss. -ಪಡು. To be defeated. ಪರಾಜಿತ. Defeated, overcome.

ಪರಾತ, ಪರಾತು f. n. A kind of circular [dish.

ಪರಾಧೀನ s. a. Depending on another, dependant. n. Transfer, alienation.

ಪರಾನ್ನ s. n. Food supplied by another.

ಪರಾಭವ s. n. Passing away. 2, defeat; humiliation. 3, the fortieth year in the cycle of sixty.

ಪರಾಮರಿಕೆ, ಪರಾಂಬರಿಕೆ (tb. of ಪರಾಮರ್ಶ) s. n. Recollection; reflection, thought; discrimination. 2, kindly inquiring into, and relieving the wants of the poor, sick, etc. -ಮಾಡು, ಪರಾಮರ್ಶಿಸು, ಪರಾಂಬರಿಸು, ಪರಾಮರಿಸು, ಪರಾಮ್ಮರಿಸು. To take care of, console; to examine, inquire.

ಪರಾಯಣ s. a. Devoted to, zealously engaged in. n. Principal aim.

ಪರಾಯಿ h. a. Other, foreign; strange.

ಪರಾರಿ f. n. The year before last. 2. = ಫರಾರಿ.

ಪರಿ 1. (= ಹರಿ, q. v.) a. k. v. i. To run, flow, etc. n. Running, flowing. 2, a manner, way; a course. -ಪರಿ. Various ways.

ಪರಿ 2. (ರಿ = ಱ'. = ಹರಿ) a. k. v. t. To tear, rend, break, slit, etc. n. Ornament, decoration.

ಪರಿ 3. s. ad. Round, around, round about; against, towards; beyond; successively; outside of, except; on account of; according to; much. -ಪಾಡು. Fully equal. -ಕ್ರಮ. Walking about for pleasure.

ಪರಿಕರ s. n. Attendants, dependants, retinue; articles used at a pûja.

ಪರಿಕಾಂಕ್ಷೆ s. n. Great desire. ಪರಿಕಾಂಕ್ಷಿತ. Much desired.

ಪರಿಕಾರ 1. s. n. Attendants. 2, seasoning food with salt, pepper, etc.; condiment.

ಪರಿಕಾರ 2. = ಹರಿಕಾರ, q. v.

ಪರಿಕಿಸು. tb. of ಪರೀಕ್ಷಿಸು, q. v.

ಪರಿಖ್ಯಾತಿ s. n. Reputation, fame, celebrity.

ಪರಿಗಣನ s. n. Accurate calculation. 2, deliberate consideration. ಪರಿಗಣಿಸು. To calculate, deliberate.

ಪರಿಗ್ರಹ s. n. Seizing, grasping; taking; acceptance; obtaining; a gift. 2, possession. 3, taking a wife, marrying. 4, a wife. ಪರಿಗ್ರಹಿಸು. To lay hold of, take, receive, accept.

ಪರಿಚಯ s. n. Acquaintance, intimacy.

ಪರಿಚರ s. n. An attendant; a bodyguard. -ಣ. Attendance.

ಪರಿಚರಿಯ (tb. of ಪರಿಚರ್ಯ) n. Waiting upon, attendance, service; worship.

ಪರಿಚಾರ s. n. Attendance, service. 2, attendant, servant; also -ಕ.

ಪರಿಚಿತ s. a. Known, familiar with. ಪರಿಚಿತಿ. = ಪರಿಚಯ, q. v.

ಪರಿಚ್ಛೇದ s. n. Cutting, clipping. 2, a section, chapter. 3, decision, discretion. -ನೆ. Circumcision (with Jews and Mohammadans). ಪರಿಚ್ಛೇದಿಸು. To cut, divide, etc.; to circumcise.

ಪರಿಣತ s. a. Bent, bowed down; changed; ripened, matured; proficient. ಪರಿಣತಿ. Bending; change; ripeness; proficiency.

ಪರಿಣಮಿಸು s. v. i. To bend down. 2, to become changed. 3, to become ripe, to come to perfection, as virtue. 4, to come to its end, as age.

ಪರಿಣಾಮ s. n. Bending. 2, change. 3, expansion. 4, health, ease, welfare. 5, end, conclusion, result, consequence. 6, happy conclusion, as of a work. -ಶೂಲೆ. Flatulence with pain, colic. ಪರಿಣಾಮಿಸು. To be changed; to be healthy; to thrive.

ಪರಿತೋಷ s. n. Gratification, pleasure, delight.

ಪರಿತ್ಯಜನ s. n. Abandoning; giving away. ಪರಿತ್ಯಜಿಸು. To abandon.

ಪರಿತ್ಯಾಗ s. n. Abandoning; rejecting; giving away.

ಪರಿಧಾವಿ s. n. The forty-sixth year of the cycle of sixty.

ಪರಿಧಿ s. n. A halo round the sun or moon. 2, a circle; the circumference of a circle.

ಪರಿನಿರ್ಮಿಸು s. v. t. To make, fabricate.

ಪರಿಪಾಕ s. n. Perfection; cleverness.

ಪರಿಪಾಟಿ s. n. Regular course, order, method.

ಪರಿಪಾತ s. n. Custom; fashion, rule, way.

ಪರಿಪಾಲ s. n. A guardian, protector; *also* -ಕ. -ನೆ. Protecting, nourishing. ಪರಿಪಾಲಿಸು. To protect, guard, *etc.*

ಪರಿಪೂರ್ಣ s. a. Quite full, entire, complete. -ತೆ, -ತ್ವ. Completion, fulness; satisfaction.

ಪರಿಬೋಧಿಸು s. v. t. To take notice or care of.

ಪರಿಭವ s. n. Disregard, contempt, insult, disgrace. ಪರಿಭವಿಸು. To disregard, slight, despise.

ಪರಿಭಾವ. = ಪರಿಭವ, q. v. ಪರಿಭಾವಿಸು, ಪರಿಭವಿಸು. To think, reflect; to consider, mind.

ಪರಿಭಾಷೆ s. n. Speech; definition.

ಪರಿಭ್ರಮಣ s. n. Wandering, roving; wandering (*used also of the mind*).

ಪರಿಮಲ, ಪರಿಮಳ s. n. Fragrance, perfume, fragrant scent. ಪರಿಮಳಿಸು. To be fragrant.

ಪರಿಮಾಣ s. n. Measure; quantity; weight.

ಪರಿಮಿತಿ s. n. Measure, limitation.

ಪರಿಮುಕ್ತ s. a. Unloosened, released, liberated.

ಪರಿಮುಖ s. ad. Round about. -ವಾಗಿ. Through, by means of.

ಪರಿಯಂತ, -ರ. tb. of ಪರ್ಯಂತ, -ರ, q. v.

ಪರಿಯಾಯ. tb. of ಪರ್ಯಾಯ, q. v.

ಪರಿವಟ್ಟ (tb.* of ಪರಿಪಟ) n. A kind of turban.

ಪರಿವರ್ತ, -ನ s. n. Turning round; moving, revolving. 2, change, exchange. ಪರಿವರ್ತಿಸು. To move.

ಪರಿವಾರ s. n. Suite, train, retinue, followers.

ಪರಿವೃತ s. a. Surrounded, encompassed. ಪರಿವೃತ್ತ. Revolved; surrounded, encompassed; exchanged. ಪರಿವೃತ್ತಿ. Revolution; exchange; barter.

ಪರಿವೇಷ s. n. Surrounding; a circle; a wreath. 2, the circumference of a circle. 3, a halo round the sun or moon.

ಪರಿವ್ರಾಜ್ s. n. A mendicant devotee; *also* ಪರಿವ್ರಾಜಕ.

ಪರಿಶಿಷ್ಟ s. a. Left; finished. n. A supplement, appendix.

ಪರಿಶೀಲನ s. n. Fond pursuit of study.

ಪರಿಶುದ್ಧ s. a. Completely cleansed, purified; pure, holy. -ವಂತ. A pure man. -ತ್ವ, -ತನ. Purity, holiness. ಪರಿಶುದ್ಧಿ. Purity. -ನು. The Holy One, Jesus Christ. ಪರಿಶುದ್ಧಾತ್ಮ. The Holy Spirit.

ಪರಿಶೋಧನ s. n. Sifting. 2, searching, enquiry. 3, correction. ಪರಿಶೋಧಕ. A searcher; a corrector. ಪರಿಶೋಧಿಸು. To sift; to scrutinize; to correct.

ಪರಿಶೋಭೆ s. n. Great lustre. ಪರಿಶೋಭಿಸು. To shine brightly.

ಪರಿಶ್ರಮ s. n. Fatigue; distress. -ಮಾಡು. To toil, labour.

ಪರಿಶ್ರಾಂತ s. a. Worn out, wearied. ಪರಿಶ್ರಾಂತಿ. Fatigue, exhaustion.

ಪರಿಷ್ಕಾರ s. n. Ornament, decoration; finishing. ಪರಿಷ್ಕರಿಸು. To prepare; to adorn; to perfect; to finish.

ಪರಿಸೆ. = ಪರಸೆ, q. v.

ಪರಿಸ್ತರಣ s. n. Strewing, *as* the darbhĕ.

ಪರಿಹಾರ s. n. Abandoning, shunning. 2, taking away, removing; remedying, atoning. 3, immunity. ಪಾಪ-. Forgiveness of sin (through Christ's sacrifice by faith; *Christ.* ಪರಿಹರಿಸು. To abandon, leave, reject; to take away, remove, set aside, remedy; to clear off, *as* a debt.

ಪರಿಹಾಸ, ಪರಿಹಾಸ್ಯ s. n. Jesting, joking; a jester, buffoon; *also* -ಕ. 2, mirth, sport; laughter, deriding; mockery.

ಪರೀಕ್ಷೆ s. n. Investigation; examination, test, trial. -ಆಗು. An examination to take place. -ಕೊಡು. To undergo an examination; to pass an examination with success; *also* -ಪಾಸಾಗು. -ಗಾರ. An examiner. -ತೆಗೆ, -ಮಾಡು, ಪರೀಕ್ಷಿಸು. To inspect, examine; to investigate.

ಪರೀಧಾವಿ. = ಪರಿಧಾವಿ, *q. v.*

ಪರುಟವ, -ಣೆ (*tb. of* ಪ್ರಥಿಮನ್) n. Spreading; prolixity; verbosity. ಪರುಟವಿಸು. To spread about; to give details of.

ಪರುವ (*tb. of* ಪರ್ವ) n. A yearly feast at which villagers take a common meal before an idol.

ಪರುಷ s. a. Knotted; rough, rugged; harsh, cruel, stern, rude. n. A touch-stone, the philosopher's stone.

ಪರೆ 1. (= ಹರೆ, *q. v.*) a. k. *v. i.* To spread, disperse. n. Extension, stretch.

ಪರೆ 2. k. n. A scale, coat of an onion; a web on the eye; slough of a snake; a thin layer of stone; a spider's web; scab of a sore; scurf of the head.

ಪರೆ 3. (ರೆ = ಱೆ) a. k. n. A drum. 2, an eyelid. 3, leanness, thinness, feebleness.

ಪರೆಂಗಿ. = ಪರಂಗಿ, *q. v.*

ಪರೆಯ (ರೆ = ಱೆ) k. n. A Pariah.

ಪರೇಶ, ಪರೇಶ್ವರ s. n. The supreme lord.

ಪರೋಕ್ಷ s. a. Invisible, imperceptible; absent. n. Invisibility.

ಪರೋಪಕಾರ s. n. Doing good to others, benevolence, charity. ಪರೋಪಕಾರಿ. A beneficient person.

ಪರ್ಜನ್ಯ s. n. A rain-cloud. 2, Indra. -ಜಪ. A prayer for rain.

ಪರ್ಣ s. n. A leaf. -ಕುಟಿ, -ಶಾಲೆ. A hut made of leaves; a hermitage. -ಭೋಜನ, ಪರ್ಣಾಶನ, ಪರ್ಣಾಹಾರ. Feeding on leaves.

ಪರ್ಪಟ. = ಪಪ್ಪಡ, *q. v.* 2, = -ಕ.

ಪರ್ಪಟಕ s. n. A species of medicinal plant, *Oldenlandia biflora.*

ಪರ್ಪರಿಕೆ (= ಪಪ್ಪರಿಕೆ) a. k. n. Roughness; harshness.

ಪಪ್ಪಾಟಕ f. n. A herb, *Mollugo cerviana.*

ಪರ್ಬು (= ಹಬ್ಬು, *q. v.*) a. k. *v. i.* To spread, *etc.*

ಪರ್ಯಟನ s. n. Roaming, wandering. -ಮಾಡು. To wander about.

ಪರ್ಯಂತ, -ರ s. n. Limit, border, edge, end. *ad.* As far as, until, unto.

ಪರ್ಯಯ s. n. Going round; revolution of time. 2, change, mutation.

ಪರ್ಯವಸಾನ s. n. End, conclusion, issue.

ಪರ್ಯಾಟನ. = ಪರ್ಯಟನ, *q. v.*

ಪರ್ಯಾಪ್ತಿ s. n. Obtaining. 2, end, conclusion. 3, competency. 4, satisfaction.

ಪರ್ಯಾಯ s. n. Revolution, course. 2, repetition. 3, succession, turn. 4, order, method; style; manner. -ನಾಮ. A synonym.

ಪರ್ಯುಷಿತ s. a. Stale, not fresh. -ಭೋಜನ. Eating stale food. ಪರ್ಯುಷಿತಾನ್ನ. Stale rice.

ಪರ್ಯೇಷಣೆ s. n. Search, inquiry. 2, service.

ಪರ್ವ s. n. A knot of a cane. 2, a section, chapter, book. 3, a division of time: the days of the four changes of the moon. 4, a festival. -ಸಂಧಿ. The full and change of the moon.

ಪರ್ವತ s. n. A mountain. -ಕಾಕ. A raven. -ನಾಥ. The Himâlaya. ಪರ್ವತಾರಿ. Indra. ಮೇರು-. N. of a mountain.

ಪರ್ವು. = ಪರ್ಬು, *q. v.*

ಪಲ್. = ಹಲ್ಲು, *q. v.* -ಗಿರಿ. To grin, show the teeth. -ಕಡಿ. To gnash the teeth.

ಪಲ 1, ಪಲವು (= ಹಲವು, *q. v.*) a. k. a. Many, several, various. *Cpds.:* -ದಿವಸ, -ಬಗೆ, -ಮಾತು, -ರೂಪು, *etc.* -ಬರ್, -ವರ್, -ರು. Several persons.

ಪಲ 2. s. n. A particular weight or measure.

ಪಲಗೆ (=ಹಲಗೆ. tb. of ಫಲಕ) n. A plank; a tabor; a shield.

ಪಲಂಗ. tb. of ಪಲ್ಯಂಕ, q. v.

ಪಲಹಾರ, ಪಲಾರ. tb. of ಫಲಾಹಾರ, q. v.

ಪಲಾಯನ s. n. Fleeing, flight; a run. ಪಲಾಯಿತ. Fled.

ಪಲಾವು h. n. The dish called Pulâo.

ಪಲಾಶ s. n. The tree *Butea frondosa*. 2, a leaf.

ಪಲಿತ s. a. Grey haired; old, aged. n. Grey hair; old age.

ಪಲೆಸ್ತೀನು f. n. Palastine, the Holy Land.

ಪಲ್ಯ (=ಪಲ್ಯೆ, ಪಲ್ಲೆ) k. n. Any garden green, any vegetable. 2, a vegetable dish.

ಪಲ್ಯಂಕ s. n. A bedstead. 2, a palanquin.

ಪಲ್ಲ a. k. n. An elephant. 2, the black bee.

ಪಲ್ಲಕ್ಕಿ (tb. of ಪಲ್ಯಂಕ, q. v.) n. A palanquin. 2, =ಪನ್ನಂಗ, q. v.; *also* ಪಲ್ಲಂಗ.

ಪಲ್ಲಟ (tb. of ಪರ್ಯಯ) n. Inversion, irregularity, change, confusion. ಪಲ್ಲಟಿಸು. To change places. 2, to invert.

ಪಲ್ಲವ s. n. A sprout, shoot; young foliage. 2, a vocabulary. 3, a refrain; *also* ಪಲ್ಲ. -ಪಾಣಿ. A hand like fresh shoot. ಪಲ್ಲವಿಸು. To sprout; to spread. ಪಲ್ಲವೋತ್ಸವ. A yearly feast at which young foliage is worshipped in a temple.

ಪಲ್ಲಾ h. n. A measure of capacity of 100 or 120 sêrs.

ಪಲ್ಲಿ (=ಹಲ್ಲಿ, q. v.) k. n. A house-lizard.

ಪಲ್ಲೆ. =ಪಲ್ಯ, *etc.* q. v. 2, =ಹಲ್ಲೆ, q. v.

ಪವಡಿಸು (=ಪವಳಿಸು) f. v. i. To lie down, recline, repose.

ಪವಣು. tb. of ಪ್ರಮಾಣ, q. v. ಪವಣ್ಣರಿ. Exact proof or certainty.

ಪವಣಿಗೆ k. n. Being threaded. ಪವಣಿಸು. To thread, *as* a needle, bead, *etc.*

ಪವನ s. n. Winnowing. 2, wind, air. -ಜ, -ಸುತ. Bhîma; Hanumat.

ಪವಳ. =ಹವಳ, q. v.

ಪವನು e. n. A "pound" in money, gold sovereign.

ಪವಾಡ s. n. A determination to effect an object; fanatical, pompous or marvellous words or acts.

ಪವಿತ್ರ s. a. Pure, clean; sinless, holy. n. The kuśa grass; a ring made of it and put on the fourth finger. 2, the sacrificial thread. 3, the middle finger. -ತೆ, -ತ್ವ. Purity, cleanness; holiness. ಪವಿತ್ರಾತ್ಮ. The Holy Spirit.

ಪವುಜು. =ಫೌಜು, q. v.

ಪವುಂಚಿ h. n. An ornament for the wrist of females.

ಪವುತಿ h. a. Deceased, defunct.

ಪವುಳಿ (=ಪೌಳಿ) f. n. An enclosure; a rampart.

ಪಶು s. n. Cattle; any domestic animal; a brute, beast; an ignorant person; a victim. -ಪತಿ. Śiva; a bull. -ಪಾಲ. -ಪಾಲಕ. A herdsman. -ತನ. Brutishness.

ಪಶ್ಚಾತ್ s. ad. Behind; afterwards. ಪಶ್ಚಾದ್ವಿವೇಕ. Knowledge that comes after an act. ಪಶ್ಚಾತ್ತಾಪ. Sorrow, regret; repentance, remorse. -ಗೊಳ್ಳು, -ಪಡು, -ಹುಟ್ಟು. To repent, regret.

ಪಶ್ಚಿಮ s. a. Hindermost. 2, western. n. The back; the west. -ಗಟ್ಟ. The western ghauts. ಪಶ್ಚಿಮೋತ್ತರ. North-west.

ಪಸದನ. tb. of ಪ್ರಸಾಧನ, q. v.

ಪಸಂದು h. a. Agreeable, comely, pleasing. -ಮಾಡು. To make pretty, nice; to approve.

ಪಸರ. =ಪ್ರಸರ, q. v. ಪಸರಿಸು. To spread, spread abroad.

ಪಸಲೆ k. n. Young, green grass, pasturage.

ಪಸಾಯ, ಪಸಾಯು. tb. of ಪ್ರಸಾದ, q. v.

ಪಸಾರೆ (tb. of ಪ್ರಸಾರ) n. Things spread about; a grocer's shop.

ಪಸಿ. = ಹಸಿ, *q. v.*

ಪಸು a. k. *v. t.* To divide, cut; to share. 2, = ಪಚ್ಚು. -ಗೆ. Division, portion; share; arrangement.

ಪಸುಬೆ (=ಹಸುಬೆ) a. k. *n.* A long bag with an opening in the middle; *also* ಪಸುಂಬೆ. -ಪಳ. A merchant.

ಪಸುರು. = ಹಸರು, *q. v.*

ಪಸುಳೆ (=ಹಸುಳೆ) a. k. *n.* A child. -ತನ. Childhood.

ಪಸೆ (=ಹಸೆ) a. k. *n.* A bed, layer. 2, a meaningless word.

ಪಸ್ಕ f. *n.* Easter, passover; commemoration of the resurrection of Christ; *also* -ಹಬ್ಬ.

ಪಹರೆ (*tb. of* ಪ್ರಹರ) *n.* A period of three hours, watch; a watch or a guard. -ಕಾಯು, -ಕೊಡು. To watch. -ತಿರುಗು. To go about on guard. -ಯವ. A guard, sentinel.

ಪಳ. = ಹಳ, *q. v.*

ಪಳಕ (ಳ=ೞ) k. *n.* Use, practice, habit, custom. ಪಳಕಿಸು. To accustom, habituate, train, practise.

ಪಳಗು (ಳ=ೞ) k. *v. i.* To become used to or familiar with; to be trained. ಪಳಗಿಸು. = ಪಳಕಿಸು, *q. v.*

ಪಳಂಚು a. k. *v. t.* To strike or dash against; *also* ಪಳಂಕು. *n.* Opposition, resistance.

ಪಳದೆ. = ಪಳಿದ್ಯ, *q. v.*

ಪಳಯಿಗೆ, ಪಳವಿಗೆ (ಳ=ೞ. *tb. of* ಪಟಾಕೆ) a. k. *n.* A banner, flag.

ಪಳಯಿಸು, ಪಳವಿಸು (*tb. of* ಪ್ರಲಪಿಸು) *v. i.* To cry, lament.

ಪಳಿ 1. (ಳ=ೞ. = ಹಳಿ) a. k. *v. t.* To revile, scold. *n.* Blame; fault; rebuke.

ಪಳಿ 2. (ಳ=ೞ. *tb. of* ಪ್ರತಿ, *q. v.*) *n.* Equality; counterpart; amends.

ಪಳಿದ್ಯ (= ಪಳದೆ, *q. v.*) *n.* Boiled and seasoned vegetables used as sauce.

ಪಳು (=ಹಳುವ) a. k. *n.* A forest. 2, rubbish; weeds.

ಪಳುಕು (*tb. of* ಸ್ಫಟಿಕ) *n.* Crystal.

ಪಳೆ. = ಹಳೆ, *q. v.*

ಪಳ್ಳ (=ಹಳ್ಳ) a. k. *n.* Depth. 2, a pit. 3, a stream.

ಪಳ್ಳಿ (=ಹಳ್ಳಿ) k. *n.* A hamlet, village.

ಪಾಕ s. *n.* Cooking. 2, maturity; ripeness; completion, accomplishment. 3, syrup. -ಮಾಡು. To cook. -ಶಾಲೆ. A kitchen. -ಶಾಸ್ತ್ರ. A book on cookery; cookery.

ಪಾಕೆ f. *n.* A side of a roof. 2, a cook.

ಪಾಖಂಡಿ (=ಪಾಷಂಡಿ) s. *a.* Heterodox, heretic.

ಪಾಗ (*tb. of* ಪಾದ) *n.* The fourth part of a paṇa: 1 aṇĕ 2 kâsus; *also* ಹಾಗ.

ಪಾಗಾರ (*tb. of* ಪ್ರಾಕಾರ) *n.* An encircling wall, fence, enclosure.

ಪಾಗು h. *n.* A kind of turban.

ಪಾಂಗು a. k. *n.* Manner, form, shape; likeness.

ಪಾಚಕ s. *a.* Cooking; maturing; digestive. *n.* A cook.

ಪಾಚಿ k. *n.* Green stuff on stagnant water. 2, milk, in children's language.

ಪಾಚಿಕೆ s. *n.* A die used in playing.

ಪಾಚ್ಛ h. *n.* A king, Pasha.

ಪಾಜಿ h. *a.* Low, mean. *n.* A scrub.

ಪಾಂಚಾಲ (*fr.* ಪಂಚಾಲ) s. *a.* Belonging to Pañĉâla; the country or ruler of Pañĉâlas. ಪಾಂಚಾಲಿ, ಪಾಂಚಾಲೆ. Draupadî.

ಪಾಟ 1. (*fr.* ಪಾಡು) k. *n.* Singing; a song.

ಪಾಟ 2. s. *n.* Breadth, expanse. 2, *tb. of* ಪಾಠ, *q. v.*

ಪಾಟಲ s. *a.* Pale red. *n.* The trumpet flower, *Bignonia suaveolens.*

ಪಾಟಲಿಪುತ್ರ s. *n.* The capital of Magadha, Palibothra, the modern Patna.

ಪಾಟವ (*fr.* ಪಟು) s. *n.* Sharpness, acuteness, energy; harshness.

ಪಾಟಾ h. *n.* A line, *as* drawn through a letter.

ಪಾಟಿ 1. (= ಪಾಡು) k. *n.* Manner, shape; degree, size; fitness; likeness. 2, downfall, ruin.

ಪಾಟಿ 2. s. n. A gang of workmen.

ಪಾಟು (*fr.* ಪಡು, *q. v.*) k. n. Experiencing, obtaining, undergoing; feeling. 2, (= ಪಾಡು) nature, manner, mode; fitness.

ಪಾಠ s. n. Recitation. 2, reading, study. 3, a lesson. -ಒಪ್ಪಿಸು. To recite a lesson. -ಮಾಡು. To learn by heart; to teach. -ಕ. A reader; a student; a teacher. -ದೋಷ. A false reading. -ಶಾಲೆ. A school, college. ಪಾಠಾಂತರ. A variation of reading. ಪಾಠಿ. One who has read and studied. ಪಾಠಿಸು. To recite; to learn.

ಪಾಡಗ (*tb. of* ಪಾದಕಟಕ) n. An anklet.

ಪಾಡಿ k. n. A hamlet, village.

ಪಾಡು 1. (= ಹಾಡು 1, *q. v.*) k. v. t. To sing. n. Singing; a song.

ಪಾಡು 2. (= ಹಾಡು 2, *q. v.*) k. n. Suffering; trouble; manner, mode; fitness; resemblance.

ಪಾಡ್ಯ (*tb. of* ಪ್ರತಿಪದ್) n. The first day of a lunar fortnight.

ಪಾಣಿ s. n. The hand; holding in hand. -ಗ್ರಹಣ. Marriage. -ಮೂಲ. The wrist.

ಪಾಣಿನಿ s. n. N. of an eminent grammarian. [Pâṇḍu.

ಪಾಂಡವ s. n. A descendant or son of

ಪಾಂಡಿತ್ಯ (*fr.* ಪಂಡಿತ) s. n. Scholarship, learning, erudition; skill.

ಪಾಂಡು s. a. Yellowish white. n. Father of the five Pâṇḍavas. 2, jaundice; *also* -ರೋಗ.

ಪಾಂಡುರ s. a. Pale. n. Jaundice. 2, the white leprosy.

ಪಾಂಡುರಂಗ s. n. N. of Kṛishṇa.

ಪಾಂಡ್ಯ s. n. N. of a country and people in the Dekhan.

ಪಾತ s. n. Falling, fall; a throw; a stroke; an attack; defect, fault. a. Watched, protected.

ಪಾತಕ s. n. Sin, crime. -ಪರಿಹರಿಸು. Sin to be removed. -ತನ. Sinful state. -ಹಿಡಿ. To incur sin. ಪಾತಕಿ. A sinner.

ಪಾತರ (*tb. of* ಪಾತ್ರ, *q. v.*) n. Performing, dancing. -ಗಿತ್ತಿ. A butterfly; a dancing girl; *also* -ದವಳು.

ಪಾತಾಲ, ಪಾತಾಳ s. n. One of the lower regions, the abode of the serpents and demons. -ಗಡ, -ಗರಡಿ, ಗರುಡ, -ಭೇದಿ. A hooked drag to catch things under water.

ಪಾತಿ k. n. A basin round the foot of a tree, *etc.* 2, a garden-bed.

ಪಾತಿವ್ರತ್ಯ (*fr.* ಪತಿವ್ರತಾ) s. n. Loyalty to a husband, conjugal fidelity.

ಪಾತ್ರ (= ಪಾತರ, ಪಾತ್ರೆ) s. n. A drinking vessel; a goblet, cup, *etc.* 2, a vessel in general. 3, a receptacle; a fit or worthy person; a recipient of punishment, blame, *etc.* 4, an actor. 5, a disguise. 6, performing, dancing. a. Fit for. -ತೆ, -ತ್ವ. Fitness, worthiness. -ದವಳು. A dancing girl.

ಪಾತ್ರೆ. = ಪಾತ್ರ, No. 1-2, *q. v.*

ಪಾಥೋದ, ಪಾಥೋಧರ s. n. A cloud.

ಪಾದ s. n. A foot. 2, *an honorific affix to proper names.* 3, the foot of a mountain. 4, the root of a tree. 5, a verse-line. 6, a fourth part. -ಕಾಣಿಕೆ, -ಗಾಣಿಕೆ. A gift placed at the feet of a guru. -ಚಾರಿ. A footman. -ಜ. A Śûdra. -ತೀರ್ಥ, ಪಾದೋದಕ. Water in which the feet have been washed. -ಪದ್ಮ. A lotus-like foot. -ಪೀಠ. A foot-stool. -ಪೂಜೆ. Homage paid to the feet of a guru. -ಪೂರಣ. An expletive. -ರಕ್ಷೆ. A sandal, shoe.

ಪಾದರಸ f. n. Quicksilver, mercury.

ಪಾದರಿ 1. (= ಪಾದ್ರಿ) f. n. A padre or Christian minister or Catholic priest.

ಪಾದರಿ 2. *tb. of* ಪಾಟಲ.

ಪಾದುಕ, ಪಾದುಕೆ s. n. A wooden shoe; *also* ಪಾದು.

ಪಾದೆಮುಳ್ಳುಗಿಡ k. n. A perennial herb, *Polycarpea corymbosa.*

ಪಾದ್ಯ s. n. Water for washing the feet. 2, washing the feet.

ಪಾದ್ರಿ = ಪಾದರಿ, *q. v.*

ಪಾನ s. *n.* Drinking. 2, a drink, beverage. 3, a canal. -ಕ. A draught, beverage; a beverage made of jaggory, sugar, *etc.* -ಗೋಷ್ಠಿ. A drinking party. -ಪಾತ್ರ, -ಭಾಜನ. A drinking vessel. ಅನ್ನ-. Meat and drink.

ಪಾನಿ s. *n.* Water. ಪಾನೀಯ. Drinkable; a drink. ಪಾನೀಯಶಾಲಿಕೆ. A shed on the roadside for providing passengers with drinking water.

ಪಾನು f. *n.* A leaf; the leaf of a book; the leaf of piper betel.

ಪಾಂಥ s. *n.* A traveller; *also* -ಸ್ಥ.

ಪಾಪ 1. k. *n.* A small child. 2, a doll or puppet.

ಪಾಪ 2. s. *a.* Bad, wicked, sinful, *etc.* *n.* Sin, vice, crime, wickedness, guilt. 2, a bad state, misery. ಪಾಪ. O misery! -ಕ್ಷಮಿಸಿ ಬಿಡು, -ಮಾಫು ಮಾಡು. To forgive sin. -ಕರ್ಮ. An evil deed. -ಕ್ಷಯ, -ನಾಶನ. The destruction of sin. -ನಿವಾರಣ. Averting sin. -ನಿಷ್ಕೃತಿ. Atonement for sin. -ವಿಮೋಚನ. Liberation from sin. -ಪರಿಹಾರ. Forgiveness of sin. -ಹೊರು. To bring sin upon one's self. ಪಾಪಾತ್ಮ. A sinner, a wicked person.

ಪಾಪಟಿ, ಪಾಪಡಿ, ಪಾಪರೆ (*tb. of* ಪರ್ಪಟ) *n.* The bitter apple, colocynth.

ಪಾಪಾಸು. = ಪಾಪೋಸು, *q. v.*

ಪಾಪಿ s. *a.* Wicked; sinful. *n.* A sinner, criminal. -ಷ್ಠ. Most wicked; a sinner.

ಪಾಪೆ (= ಪಾಪ 1) k. *n.* A puppet, doll; an ensign; the pupil of the eye.

ಪಾಪೋಸು (= ಪಾಪಾಸು) h. *n.* A shoe or slipper.

ಪಾಮ (*tb.* ಪಾಮೆ) *n.* Herpes, scab.

ಪಾಮರ s. *a.* Low, vulgar; stupid. *n.* A vulgar man; *f.* ಪಾಮರಿ. -ತನ. Lowness, rudeness; heathenism.

ಪಾಯ್ (= ಹಾಯು) k. *v. i.* To jump over; to cross, leap; to step, advance; to butt, gore; to knock against. *n.* Going; course; manner; fitness.

ಪಾಯ (*tb. of* ಪಾದ) *n.* Foot. -ಖಾನೆ. A privy. -ದಳ. Infantry. -ವಟ್ಟ. A badge of honour for the foot.

ಪಾಯಸ (*fr.* ಪಯಸ್) s. *a.* Made of milk. *n.* A dish of milk, rice, sugar, *etc.*

ಪಾಯಾ f. *n.* A foundation.

ಪಾಯಿ. = ಪಾಯ, *q. v.* -ಜಾಮೆ. Trowsers.

ಪಾಯಿದಾ, ಪಾಯಿದೆ h. *n.* Advantage, profit.

ಪಾರ s. *n.* The opposite bank of a river. 2, the limit of anything. *ad.* Across, over, through. -ಗಾಣಿಸು. To cause to look through; to help to cross. -ಗಾಣು. To see the end of. -ಮಾಡು. To help out of. ಪಾರಾಗು. To be saved from, to get out of. -ಗ. Well versed in. -ಗತ, -ಂಗತ. Adept, proficient. -ದರ್ಶಕ. Transparent.

ಪಾರಕಾವಣೆ. = ಪರಕಾವಣೆ, *q. v.*

ಪಾರಜ, ಪಾರದ s. *n.* Quicksilver.

ಪಾರಣ s. *n.* Breakfast.

ಪಾರಮಾರ್ಥಿಕ (*fr.* ಪರಮಾರ್ಥ) s. *a.* Spiritual; real, true; spiritually-minded.

ಪಾರಂಪರ್ಯ (*fr.* ಪರಂಪರಾ) s. *n.* Hereditary succession. 2, tradition.

ಪಾರಲೌಕಿಕ (*fr.* ಪರಲೋಕ) s. *a.* Relating to the next world.

ಪಾರಾ. = ಪಹರೆ, *q. v.*

ಪಾರಾಯಣ s. *n.* Reading through, perusal; study.

ಪಾರಾವತ (= ಪಾರಿವಾಣ, ಪಾರಿವಾಳ, *etc.*) s. *n.* A pigeon, dove.

ಪಾರಾವಾರ s. *n.* The further and nearer bank or shore. 2, the ocean.

ಪಾರಿಖತ್ತು h. *n.* A partition-deed; a deed relinquishing one's claim.

ಪಾರಿಜಾತ, -ಕ s. *n.* The coral tree *Erythrina indica.*

ಪಾರಿತೋಷಿಕ s. *n.* A reward, present.

ಪಾರಿಪ್ಲವ (*fr.* ಪರಿಪ್ಲವ) s. *a.* Moving to and fro, shaking; unsteady.

ಪಾರಿಭಾಷಿಕ (*fr.* ಪರಿಭಾಷಾ) s. *a.* Common. 2, technical, *as* a term.

ಪಾರಿವಾಣ, ಪಾರಿವಾಳ (*tb. of* ಪಾರಾವತ) *n.* A dove.

ಪಾರಿಸಿ h. *a.* Persian. *n.* A Parsee.

ಪಾರು 1. k. *n.* Looking to or after. -ಪತ್ಯ. Local administration, *as* of a temple, alms-house, *etc.* -ಪತ್ಯಗಾರ. An officer in charge of a temple; a subordinate collector and magistrate.

ಪಾರು 2. *tb. of* ಪಾರ, *q. v.*

ಪಾರು 3. (ರು=ಱು. = ಹಾರು, *q. v.*) k. *v. i.* To leap, jump; to run; to fly; to palpitate. *n.* Running, flying; a kind of boat; a flying vehicle.

ಪಾರೆ. = ಹಾರೆ, *q. v.* 2, a crowbar; *also* ಪಾರೆಂಗಿ.

ಪಾರ್ಥ s. *n.* A king. 2, Arjuna.

ಪಾರ್ಥವ s. *n.* Width; greatness, immensity.

ಪಾರ್ಥಿವ s. *n.* A prince, king. 2, the nineteenth year in the cycle of sixty. 3, Śiva. *a.* Terrestrial. 2, ruling or possessing earth.

ಪಾರ್ವಣ (*fr.* ಪರ್ವ) s. *n.* The general funeral ceremony offered to the deceased ancestors.

ಪಾರ್ವತಿ (*fr.* ಪರ್ವತ) s. *n.* The daughter of Himavat, Durgâ. -ನಂದನ. Kârttikêya. -ಈಶ, -ಈಶ್ವರ. Śiva.

ಪಾರ್ಶ್ವ s. *n.* The part of the body below the arm-pit; the side, flank. -ವರ್ತಿ. An attendant. -ವಾಯು. Partial paralysis. -ಶೂಲೆ. Pleurisy. ಎಡ-. The left side. ಬಲ-. The right side.

ಪಾರ್ಷ್ಣಿ s. *n.* The heel. 2, the rear of an army.

ಪಾಲಕ s. *n.* A guardian; a ruler, king; *f.* -ಳು. ದಿಕ್-. The guardian of one of the quarters of the world.

ಪಾಲಕಿ, ಪಾಲಕ್ಕಿ (*tb. of* ಪಲ್ಯಂಕ) *n.* A palanquin. -ಮೆರವಣಿಗೆ. A procession in a palanquin.

ಪಾಲನ, ಪಾಲನೆ s. *n.* Guarding, protecting; keeping. -ಮಾಡು. = ಪಾಲಿಸು, *q. v.*

ಪಾಲಿ s. *n.* A line, row. 2, a dike, bridge. 3, a wall. 4, a part. 5, a margin, edge. 6, beginning. 7, the tip of the ear. 8, the lap. 9, green ginger.

ಪಾಲಿಸು s. *v. t.* To guard, protect, nourish; to rule; to obey; *as* a command; to observe, *as* a rule; to present, give, *as* an order. ದಯ-. To grant, vouchsafe.

ಪಾಲು 1. (= ಹಾಲು) a. k. *n.* Milk. -ಂಡೆ. A kind of sweetmeat. -ಕರೆ. To milk. -ಪಕ್ಕಿ. A small owl.

ಪಾಲು 2. k. *n.* A division; a part, share; joint property. -ಗಾರ. A partner in business; an associate; one who enjoys or suffers with another; *f.* -ಗಾರಳು, -ಗಾತಿ. -ಗಾರಿಕೆ, -ವಂತಿಗೆ. Partnership.

ಪಾಲೆ k. *n.* A large fruit tree, *Mimusops kauki.* 2, the blue jay. 3, the lobe of the ear.

ಪಾವಕ s. *a.* Purifying, pure, clear; apparent, manifest. *n.* Fire; a fire-poker. 2, religious custom.

ಪಾವಟಿಗೆ f. *n.* A step, stair. -ಏರು. To ascend the steps. -ಕಟ್ಟು. To erect steps.

ಪಾವಡ, ಪಾವಡೆ (*tb. of* ಪ್ರಾವೃತ) *n.* Cloth; a girl's petticoat; a woman's garment.

ಪಾವಡಿಗ. = ಹಾವಡಿಗ, *q. v.*

ಪಾವನ s. *a.* Purifying; pure, holy. *n.* A means of purification: penance; cow-dung; fire. -ತೆ, -ತ್ವ. Purification.

ಪಾವಲಿ, ಪಾವಲೆ f. *n.* A quarter of a Rupee.

ಪಾವಸೆ (= ಪಾಸಿ, ಹಾವಸೆ, *q. v.*) k. *n.* Algae produced on stagnant water, *etc.*, lichens upon stones, walls, *etc.*

ಪಾವು 1. = ಹಾವು, *q. v.*

ಪಾವು 2. (*tb. of* ಪಾದ) *n.* A quarter.

ಪಾವುಗೆ, *tb. of* ಪಾದುಕ, *q. v.*

ಪಾವುಡ. = ಪಾವಡ, *q. v.*

ಪಾಶ s. *n.* A tie, cord, rope, fetter; a noose, snare.

ಪಾಶಕ (= ಪಾಚಿಕೆ) s. *n.* = ಪಾಶ, *q. v.* 2. a die used in playing.

ಪಾಶಿ h. *n.* A rope (for the gallows); hanging. -ಕೊಡು, -ಹಾಕು. To hang.

ಪಾಶುಪತ (*fr.* ಪಶುಪತಿ) s. *a.* Relating or sacred to Śiva. *n.* N. of a weapon; *also* ಪಾಶುಪತಾಸ್ತ್ರ.

ಪಾಷಂಡ s. *n.* Heresy. 2, a heretic; *also* ಪಾಷಂಡಿ, ಪಾಷಾಂಡಿ.

ಪಾಷಾಣ s. *n.* A stone, rock. 2, arsenic and other poisons. -ಭೇದಿ. The plant *Plectranthus scutellarioides.*

ಪಾಸ್ e. *n.* A pass. -ಆಗು. To pass. ಪರೀಕ್ಷೆ ಪಾಸಾಗು. To pass an examination. -ಮಾಡು. To make pass.

ಪಾಸಟಿ a. k. *n.* Likeness, resemblance.

ಪಾಸಲೆ h. *n.* Distance.

ಪಾಸೊಲೆ k. *n.* An earthen saucer-like vessel.

ಪಾಸಿ. = ಪಾಚಿ, ಹಾವಸೆ, *q. v.*

ಪಾಸು. = ಹಾಸು, *q. v.*

ಪಾಳ k. *n.* An ingot or a bar of gold or silver.

ಪಾಳತಿ f. *n.* Spying, searching out, lying in wait. -ನೋಡು. To spy, lurk. -ಗಾರ. A spy.

ಪಾಳಿ. = ಪಾಲಿ, *q. v.*

ಪಾಳು. = ಹಾಳು, *q. v.*

ಪಾಳೆ, ಪಾಳೆಯ, ಪಾಳ್ಯ (*tb. of* ಪಾಲಯ) *n.* An encampment, camp; a settlement, hamlet. -ಗಾರ. A Poligar, a feudal chieftain.

ಪಿಕ s. *n.* The cuckoo, *Cuculus indicus.*

ಪಿಕಲಕ್ಕಿ, ಪಿಕಲಾರಿ k. *n.* The Madras bulbul.

ಪಿಕಾಸು e. *n.* A pickaxe.

ಪಿಕ್ಕಾ h. *a.* Faint, pale; weak; pallid; poor.

ಪಿಕ್ಕು. = ಹಿಕ್ಕು, *q. v.*

ಪಿಂಗ s. *a.* Reddish-brown, tawny. -ಳ. N. of a fabulous nâga; the 51st year of the cycle of sixty. -ಲಿ, -ಲೆ. A kind of owl.

ಪಿಂಗಾಣಿ f. *n.* Crockery; porcelain, China ware. -ಬಟ್ಟಲು. A China cup, mug.

ಪಿಂಗು. = ಹಿಂಗು, *q. v.*

ಪಿಚಕಾರಿ h. *n.* A syringe.

ಪಿಚಂಡ s. *n.* The belly. ಪಿಚಂಡಿ. The thigh.

ಪಿಚಂಡಿ, ಪಿಚಾಡಿ h. *n.* The hinder parts; the heel-ropes, *as* of a horse. -ಬಿಗಿ. To pinion, to tie the hands from behind.

ಪಿಚ್ಚಟ f. *a.* Pressed flat. *n.* A cake. 2, an inflammation of the eyes.

ಪಿಚ್ಚೀಸು e. *n.* Peach, a sweet stone-fruit.

ಪಿಚ್ಚು k. *n.* The rheum of the eye.

ಪಿಚ್ಚೆ k. *n.* Deficiency in measure or weight. *Cpds.:* -ಮೊಳ, -ಸೇರು.

ಪಿಚ್ಛಿಲ s. *a.* Slimy, slippery, smeary. *n.* A miry place.

ಪಿಚ್ಛಿಲೆ s. *n.* The silk-cotton tree, *Bombax heptaphyllum.*

ಪಿಚ್ಛೆ f. *n.* Scum of boiled rice, *etc.* 2, the gum of the silk-cotton tree.

ಪಿಂಜ s. *a.* Confused, confounded, bewildered. 2, injured. *n.* Injury. 2, power, might.

ಪಿಂಜರ s. *a.* Tawny. *n.* Gold. 2, yellow orpiment. 3, a cage. 4, a skeleton; *also* ಪಂಜರ.

ಪಿಂಜಾರ h. *n.* A carder or comber of cotton.

ಪಿಂಜಿ s. *n.* A skein of cotton yarn.

ಪಿಂಜು 1. (= ಹಿಂಜು, *q. v.*) a. k. *v. t.* To divide. 2, to card cotton. *v. i.* To go asunder; to be rent *as* cloth.

ಪಿಂಜು 2. k. *n.* A very tender fruit.

ಪಿಟಕ s. *n.* A basket, box; *also* ಪಿಟ. 2, a boil, blister.

ಪಿಟೀಲು e. *n.* A "fiddle", any stringed instrument.

ಪಿಡಗ f. *n.* Trouble, affliction, disease.

ಪಿಡಿ (= ಹಿಡಿ) a. k. *v. t.* & *i.* To seize, catch, grasp, *etc.* 2, to begin, *as* rain, *etc.*; to be required, *as* time, *etc.*; to hold, *as* in a sack, *etc.* *n.* A seizing; hold. 2, a grasp. 3, the fist. 4, a handle, hilt. 5, a female elephant. 6, a broom. -ತ. Seizure.

ಪಿಡುಗು a. k. *n.* A thunderbolt. 2, = ಪಿಡುಗ, ಪಿಡುಗ. A dauntless, bold man.

ಪಿಂಡ s. n. A lump, clod, ball. 2, heap, cluster. 3, a bite, morsel. 4, a ball of boiled rice offered to the manes. -ಕ. Incense, myrrh. -ಜ. Embryo-born: men and beasts. -ಪ್ರದಾನ. The offering of pindas. ಪಿಂಡಾಂಡ. The body considered as identical with ಬ್ರಹ್ಮಾಂಡ. ಪಿಂಡೋತ್ಪತ್ತಿ. The formation of the fetus.

ಪಿಂಡಿ s. n. A bundle, pack, mass. *Cpds.*: -ಕಟ್ಟು, -ಹೊತ್ತುಕೊಳ್ಳು, -ಹೊರು, *etc.* ಕ. A swelling, protuberance.

ಪುಂಡಿಸೊಪ್ಪು k. n. Deckanee hemp, *Hibiscus cannabinus.*

ಪಿಂಡು. *tb. of* ಪಿಂಡ, *q. v.*

ಪಿಣ್ಯಾಕ f. n. An oil-cake. 2, incense.

ಪಿತ, ಪಿತರ. *tb. of* ಪಿತೃ, *q. v.*

ಪಿತರೌ s. n. Mother and father, parents.

ಪಿತಾಮಹ s. n. A paternal grand-father.

ಪಿತೂರಿ h. n. Revolt, plot, perfidy.

ಪಿತೃ (= ಪಿತ, ಪಿತರ) s. n. A father. -ಗಳು. Forefathers, ancestors; the manes of the dead. -ತರ್ಪಣ. Oblations to the manes. -ತಿಥಿ, -ದಿನ. The death-day of a deceased parent. -ತ್ವ. Fatherhood, paternity. -ಮೇಧ, -ಯಜ್ಞ. Obsequial offerings to the manes. -ಧನ. Patrimony. -ಪಕ್ಷ. The dark half of the ಭಾದ್ರಪದ month. -ವನ. A cemetery. -ವಿಯೋಗ. The loss of a father.

ಪಿತ್ತ s. n. Bile. 2, foolishness, irritability of temper. -ಜ್ವರ. Bilious fever. -ಭ್ರಮೆ. Biliousness; madness. -ಲ. Bilious; roguish behaviour. -ಲಾಟ. Trickery, deceit.

ಪಿನೆಫ್ಲೋರು e. n. A pinafore; an apron worn by children to protect the front of the dress.

ಪಿಂತು, ಪಿಂತೆ, ಪಿಂದು, ಪಿಂದೆ (= ಹಿಂದೆ, *q. v.*) a. k. *ad.* Afterwards, backwards, *etc.* 2, formerly.

ಪಿಪೀಲಿಕ s. n. An ant.

ಪಿಪ್ಪಲ s. n. The holy fig-tree, *Ficus religiosa.*

ಪಿಯಾನೋ e. n. A piano, a musical keyed instrument.

ಪಿರಂಗಿ h. n. A great gun or cannon. 2, a Frank or European. -ಗಾಡಿ. A gun-carriage. -ಬಾಯಿ. The muzzle of a gun.

ಪಿರಿ (= ಹಿರಿ, *q. v.*) a. k. n. Largeness; advanced age. -ದು. = ಹಿರಿದು.

ಪಿರಿಕೆ h. n. A range, division, jurisdiction.

ಪಿರಿಯಾದಿ. = ಫಿರ್ಯಾದಿ, *q. v.*

ಪಿರೆ (= ಪಿಱ) k. n. The posteriors.

ಪಿಲ್ಲಿ k. n. A silver ring worn by married women on the toe.

ಪಿಶಾಚ s. n. A fiend, goblin; a devil; the devil. -ಕರ್ಮ, -ಕೆಲಸ. A devilish affair. -ಬುದ್ಧಿ. Devilish mind.

ಪಿಶಿತ s. n. Flesh, meat. ಪಿಶಿತಾಶ, -ನ. Flesh-eating: a râkshasa.

ಪಿಶುನ s. n. A betrayer, tale-bearer, backbiter, slanderer. -ತನ, -ತ್ವ. Slander, scandal.

ಪಿಷ್ಟ s. a. Ground, pounded. n. Flour, meal.

ಪಿಸರು 1. h. n. Foolish pride, arrogance. -ತೆಗೆ. To scold, reprove.

ಪಿಸರು 2. k. n. Filth of the body, rheum of the eye.

ಪಿಸುಕು k. v. t. To squeeze; to knead; to shampoo.

ಪಿಸುರು. = ಪಿಸರು 1, 2, *q. v.*

ಪಿಸ್ತೂಲು e. n. A "pistol".

ಪಿಳಿ. = ಹಿಳಿ, *q. v.*

ಪಿಳುಂಕು a. k. n. The lower part of an arrow; *also* ಪಿಳ್ಕು.

ಪಿಳ್ಳಿ k. n. A sound as that of a pipe. 2, = ಪಿಳ್ಳೆ, *q. v.* ಪಿಳ್ಳಂಗೋವಿ. A pipe or flute.

ಪಿಳ್ಳೆ k. n. A child; the young of animals.

ಪೀಕ h. n. Spittle. -ದಾನಿ. A spittoon.

ಪೀಕು k. v. t. To pull out; to wrest, tear. ಪೀಕಲಾಟ. Trouble.

ಪೀಚು k. v. i. To squirt, syringe. n. Squirting. 2, shortness.

ಪೀಠ s. n. A stool. 2, the pedestal of an idol. 3, a basement. 4, a pulpit. ಪ್ರಸಂಗ-. The Christian pulpit.

ಪೀಠಿಕೆ s. n. An introduction, preface. 2, a seat, bust.

ಪೀಡನ s. n. Squeezing, pressing; vexing, annoying; hurting, injuring.

ಪೀಡಿ h. n. A generation.

ಪೀಡೆ s. n. Pain, torment, affliction, trouble. 2, a plague, pest; devil. -ಪಡು, -ಹತ್ತು. To suffer pain. -ಮಾಡು. To give pain. -ಹೋಗು. To be relieved of pain. ಪೀಡಿಸು. To torment, trouble; to squeeze. ಪೀಡಿತ. Pressed, pained; hurt, injured.

ಪೀತ s. a. Yellow. 2, drunk, imbibed. n. A topaz; also -ಕಾಂತ. -ದಾರು. A species of pine, *Pinus deodora*. ಪೀತಾಂಬರ. Clad in yellow: Vishṇu or Kṛishṇa; a garment of yellow silk.

ಪೀನ s. a. Fat, fleshy; thick, plump; profuse.

ಪೀನಸ s. n. Cough, catarrh; purulent deflection in the nose.

ಪೀಪ, ಪೀಪಾಯಿ, ಪೀಪು f. n. A cask, barrel, tub.

ಪೀಯೂಷ s. n. Cow's milk during the first seven days of its calving. 2, nectar.

ಪೀರು. = ಹೀರು, q. v.

ಪೀಲಿ (= ಹೀಲಿ, q. v.) a. k. n. A peacock's feather.

ಪೀಲು f. n. The tree *Careya arborea*. 2, a flower. 3, an insect. 4, an atom.

ಪೀಳಿಗೆ f. n. A series of generations, pedigree; offspring; also ಪೀಡಿ.

ಪುಂ, ಪುಂಸ s. a. Male, masculine. -ತ್ವ, ಪುಂಸ್ತ್ವ. Manhood, masculine gender.

ಪುಕಸಟೆ. = ಪುಕ್ಕಟೆ, q. v.

ಪುಕಾರು h. n. Loud bawling; crying out.

ಪುಕ್ಕ 1. (tb. of ಪುಚ್ಛ, q. v.) n. The tail of a bird.

ಪುಕ್ಕ 2. k. n. A timid man, coward.

ಪುಕ್ಕಟೆ, ಪುಕ್ಕಸಟೆ, ಪುಕ್ಸಟ್ಟೆ, ಪುಗಟೆ, ಪುಗಸಟೆ, etc. f. ad. For nothing, gratis. a. Free; worthless. -ಬಾಯಿ. A liar. -ಮನುಷ್ಯ. A good-for-nothing fellow. -ಹೋಗು. To go for nothing.

ಪುಕ್ಕು k. n. Fear, timidity. -ತನ. Cowardice; cf. ಪುಕ್ಕ 2.

ಪುಗು (= ಹೊಗು, q. v.) a. k. v. i. To enter in. n. Entering. ಪುಗಿಲ್. Entering; arrival.

ಪುಗುಳು (= ಬುಗುಳು) k. n. A blister, vesicle. 2, a sore in the mouth.

ಪುಗ್ (= ಪುಗುರ್) h. n. Pride, arrogance.

ಪುಂಗವ s. n. A bull. 2, an eminent person.

ಪುಂಗಿ f. n. A sort of musical pipe.

ಪುಚ್ಚ (tb. of ಪುಚ್ಛ) n. A tail.

ಪುಚ್ಚವಣಿ (tb. of ಪರೀಕ್ಷಣ) n. Trial, examination. 2, manliness, valour.

ಪುಚ್ಚಳಿ (ಳ = ಱ) a. k. n. Ruin, destruction.

ಪುಚ್ಛ s. n. A tail; the hinder part.

ಪುಂಜ 1. (= ಹುಂಜ) k. n. A cock.

ಪುಂಜ 2. s. n. A heap, mass, collection. ಪುಂಜಿಸು. To be heaped.

ಪುಟ 1. k. n. Leaping up, jumping. -ಚೆಂಡು. A kind of play. -ನೆಗೆ. To rise with a bounce. -ಹಾರು. To bounce.

ಪುಟ 2. s. n. A fold. 2, a concavity. 3, a cup. 4, a basket made of leaves. 5, a folding. 6, a cover. 7, an eyelid. 8, a single application, as of fire, air etc., as in preparing medicine. 9, a casket. 10, the leaf of a book; a page. 11, a layer of mud in raising a wall. 12, a footprint. -ಕ್ಕೆ ಹಾಕು. To put into a crucible; to refine, as metal.

ಪುಟಾಣಿ f. n. Bengal gram soaked and parched.

ಪುಟಿ k. v. i. To bounce; to spring, ooze in jets, as water. -ಸು. To cause to bounce. -ತ. Clasped, folded; bound together; reduced to powder; contracted, spoken.

ಪುಟ್ಟ k. n. Shortness, littleness; a short man. a. Small. -ಅಡಿ. The small step of children. -ದು. That is small. -ಮಗು. A little child.

ಪುಟ್ಟಿ k. n. A basket. 2, a (honey) comb.

ಪುಟ್ಟು 1. = ಹುಟ್ಟು, q. v.

ಪುಟ್ಟು 2. k. n. Salted dough baked in steam. 2, a wooden ladle.

ಪುಡಿ k. n. Powder; dust; pollen. 2, a small packet of powder. -ಪುಡಿ ಮಾಡು. To reduce to very fine powder.

ಪುಣಜಿ k. n. A dust-like dry soil.

ಪುಣುಗು k. n. Civet. ಪುಣುಗಿನ ಬೆಕ್ಕು. The Indian civet cat.

ಪುಂಡ f. a. Turbulent; refractory. n. A free-booter; a rascal, rogue; a low man. -ಗಾರ. A depraved man. -ತನ, ಪುಂಡಾಟ, ಪುಂಡಾಟಿಕೆ. Refractoriness; lawlessness, brigandage; wickedness.

ಪುಂಡರೀಕ s. n. A white lotus-flower. 2, a sectarial mark on the forehead. ಪುಂಡರೀಕಾಕ್ಷ. Lotus-eyed: Vishṇu or Kṛishṇa.

ಪುಂಡಿ k. n. The Deckanee hemp, *Hibiscus cannabinus;* red sorrel. *Cpds.:* -ಕಡ್ಡಿ, -ನಾರು, -ಸೊಪ್ಪು.

ಪುಂಡು. = ಪುಂಡ, q. v.

ಪುಂಡ್ರ s. n. A red sugarcane. 2, a sectarial mark.

ಪುಣ್ಯ s. a. Fine, bright; good, pure, right, righteous, virtuous, just, holy; prosperous, lucky. n. Virtue, moral merit; religious merit (real or erroneous). 2, a good, meritorious act. 3, purity. 4, fame. -ಕರ್ಮ, -ಕಾರ್ಯ. A virtuous act. -ಕಾಲ. An auspicious time. -ಮಾರ್ಗ. The right way. -ಜೀವಿ, -ಮೂರ್ತಿ. A virtuous man. -ಲೋಕ. Heaven. -ವಂತ. A virtuous or fortunate man; a rich man. -ಶರೀರ. = ಪುಣ್ಯವಂತ. -ಶೀಲ. Good, virtuous. -ಶ್ಲೋಕ. Well spoken of; N. of Nala. -ಹೀನ. Virtueless. -ಸಾಧನೆ ಮಾಡು. To persevere in good works. ಪುಣ್ಯಾತ್ಮ. Righteous, virtuous, pious.

ಪುತ್ತಳಿ (tb. of ಪುತ್ರಿಕೆ) n. A puppet, doll. 2, a gold coin worth about four rupees; pure gold.

ಪುತ್ತು. = ಹುತ್ತು, q. v.

ಪುತ್ರ s. n. A son; a child. -ಜೀವ. The wild olive, *Putranjiva roxburghii.* -ವತಿ. She who has a son. -ವಧು. A son's wife. -ವಂತ. One who has sons. -ವಿರಹಿತ. A sonless man. -ಸಂತಾನ. Male progeny. -ಸ್ವೀಕಾರ. Adoption. ಕ್ರಿಸ್ತನಲ್ಲಿ--. Adoption by God through Christ.

ಪುತ್ರಿ, ಪುತ್ರಿಕೆ (= ಪುತ್ತಳಿ, q. v.) s. n. A daughter. 2, a puppet, doll.

ಪುದಿ (= ಹುದಿ, q. v.) a. k. v. i. To enter into, *etc.*; to combine. 2, to be hidden.

ಪುದಿನ f. n. Mint, *Mentha sativa.*

ಪುಡಿಂಗು e. n. Pudding, a dish of soft consistence, variously made.

ಪುದು (= ಹುದು, q. v.) a. k. n. Union; holding in common. -ವಾಳು. To live together. -ವಾಳ್ತನ. Joint living or concern.

ಪುದುಗು (= ಹುದುಗು, q. v.) a. k. v. i. To enter. v. t. To hide, shelter.

ಪುದೆ a. k. n. A quiver. 2, a cover; a roof, thatch. 3, a bush; *also* ಪೊದೆ.

ಪುದ್ಗಲ s. a. Beautiful. n. The body. 2, the soul or individuality.

ಪುನಃ (= ಪುನರ್, ಪುನಹ, ಪುನಹಾ) s. *ad.* Further; again; back; in return. -ಪುನಹ. Again and again, frequently.

ಪುನರಪಿ s. *ad.* Even again, also.

ಪುನರಾಗಮನ s. n. Returning to the place set out from. 2, second advent of Christ.

ಪುನರುಕ್ತಿ s. n. Reiteration, repetition, tautology. ಪುನರುಕ್ತ. Reiterated; repetition.

ಪುನರುತ್ಥಾನ s. n. Resurrection, *esp.* of Jesus Christ from the dead.

ಪುನರ್ಜನ್ಮ (ಪುನರ್ಜಲ್ಮ) s. n. Regeneration *(Chr.)*; transmigration. ಪುನರ್ಜಾತ. Born again, regenerated.

ಪುನರ್ದರ್ಶನ s. n. Seeing again.

ಪುನರ್ನವ s. n. Becoming new again. 2, a finger-nail.

ಪುನರ್ನವೆ s. n. Hogweed, *Boerhavia procumbens.*

ಪುನರ್ಭವ s. a. Born again. n. New [birth.

ಪುನರ್ಭೂ s. a. Born again. n. A virgin widow re-married.

ಪುನರ್ವಸು s. n. The seventh of the lunar asterisms.

ಪುನರ್ವಿವಾಹ s. n. Re-marriage.

ಪುನಹ, ಪುನಹಾ. *tb. of* ಪುನಃ, *q. v.*

ಪುನೀತ s. a. Made pure or clean.

ಪುನ್ನಪುಂಸಕ s. a. Masculine and neuter.

ಪುನ್ನಾಗ s. n. A distinguished man. 2, a white elephant. 3, a buffalo.

ಪುಬ್ಬೆ (= ಹುಬ್ಬೆ. *tb. of* ಪೂರ್ವೆ) n. The eleventh of the lunar mansions.

ಪುಯ್ಯಲ್ (=ಹುಯ್ಯಲು, *q. v.*) k. n. Lamentation. 2, solicitation. ಪುಯ್ಯಲಿಡು. To lament; to solicit.

ಪುರ 1. k. n. A stream, brook, rivulet.

ಪುರ 2. s. n. A fortress, castle; a town, city. 2, a house. 3, the body. -ದ್ವಾರ. The gate of a city.

ಪುರಃ, ಪುರಸ್ s. *ad.* In front, in the presence of. -ಸರ. Going in advance.

ಪುರಂದರ s. n. Indra; Śiva. -ದಾಸ. N. of a Canarese poet. -ವಿಟ್ಠಲ. N. of Kṛishṇa.

ಪುರಸತ್ತು h. n. Leisure; interval; time, occasion. 2, relief. -ಇರು. To be at leisure.

ಪುರಸ್ಕಾರ s. n. Reverence, honour. ಪುರಸ್ಕರಿಸು. To honour, exalt.

ಪುರಸ್ತಾತ್ s. *ad.* Before, in front of.

ಪುರಾಣ s. a. Ancient, old; worn out. n. Legendary history, legend; a purâṇa, comprising the whole body of Hindu mythology; there are 18 acknowledged purâṇas, *as:* ಅಗ್ನಿ-, ಪದ್ಮ-, ಬ್ರಹ್ಮ-, ಭವಿಷ್ಯತ್, ಲಿಂಗ-, ವಿಷ್ಣು-, ಶಿವ-, *etc.* -ಪುರುಷ. Vishṇu; Râma; Śiva. ಪುರಾಣಿಕ. A man well read in the purâṇas; an expounder of them.

ಪುರಾತನ s. a. Old, ancient. 2, a man of the past age.

ಪುರಿ 1. (= ಹುರಿ) k. v. i. To parch, as grain, pulse, *etc.* 2, to roast, as coffee, *etc.*

ಪುರಿ 2. (= ಹುರಿ) a. k. n. Twist, twine, string.

ಪುರಿ 3. a. k. n. Strength, courage.

ಪುರಿ 4. s. n. A castle; a town, city.

ಪುರುಡು 1. (= ಹುರುಡು, *q. v.*) a. k. n. Rivalry, envy; jealousy, emulation.

ಪುರುಡು 2. k. n. Uncleanness after childbirth.

ಪುರುಷ s. n. Mankind; a man, male; a person; a husband. 2, the soul. 3 Brahmâ. -ತ್ವ. Manhood; valour. -ರತ್ನ. A perennial herb, *Ionidium suffruticosum.* ಪುರುಷಾರ್ಥ. Any of the four objects of man, viz. dharma, artha, kâma, and môksha. ಪುರುಷೋತ್ತಮ. An excellent man. ಯಜ್ಞ-. Christ.

ಪುರುಳಿ a. k. n. A young parrot.

ಪುರುಳು (=ಹುರುಳು) k. n. Fitness; meaning; power, strength.

ಪುರೋಗತಿ s. n. Preceding; precedence.

ಪುರೋಭಾಗ s. n. The front part. 2, forwardness, obtrusiveness.

ಪುರೋಹಿತ s. n. The family-priest.

ಪುರ್ಗು. = ಪುಗ್ಗು, *q. v.*

ಪುರ್ಬು (=ಹುಬ್ಬು. *tb. of* ಭ್ರುವ) n. An eyebrow, brow. ಪುರ್ಬಿಕ್ಕು. To frown.

ಪುಲಕ s. n. Bristling of the hairs occasioned by delight, *etc.* ಪುಲಕಿತ. Thrilling with joy.

ಪುಲಿ (= ಹುಲಿ, *q. v.*) a. k. n. A tiger.

ಪುಲಿಂದ s. n. One of a barbarous tribe; *f.* ಪುಲಿಂದಿನಿ.

ಪುಲ್ಲಿಂಗ s. n. The masculine gender.

ಪುಲ್ಲು. = ಹುಲ್ಲು, *q. v.*

ಪುಲ್ಲೆ (= ಹುಲ್ಲೆ, *q. v.*) a. k. n. A deer.

ಪುವ್ವು (=ಹೂ, ಹೂವು, *q. v.*) a. k. n. A flower. 2, a disease of the eye.

ಪುಷ್ಕರ s. n. A lotus. 2, the leather of a drum. 3, the Indian crane. 4, a sword. 5, the sky. 6, water. -ಮೂಲ. A garden plant, *Costus speciosus.* ಪುಷ್ಕರಿಣಿ. An artificial tank.

ಪುಷ್ಕಲ s. *a.* Much, many, abundant; excellent, best.

ಪುಷ್ಟ s. *a.* Nourished, well-fed; thriving, strong. ಪುಷ್ಟಿ. Fatness, plumpness; growth, thriving; strength, power; nourishment, support; backing, aid. ಪುಷ್ಟಿಕರ. Nourishing, strengthening. ಪುಷ್ಟೀಕರಿಸು. To nourish, strengthen.

ಪುಷ್ಪ s. *n.* A flower, blossom. -ಕ. A flower; calx of brass; heat of the sun; a self-moving aerial car. -ಕೇತನ. Kâma. -ದಂತ. The elephant of the north-west quarter. -ಫಲ. The wood-apple tree, *Feronia elephantum.* -ಮಾಲಿಕೆ, -ಮಾಲೆ. A garland of flowers. -ಮಾಸ. The spring. -ವತ್, -ವಂತ. Flowery. -ವಾಟಿ, -ವಾಟಿಕೆ. A flower garden. -ವಾಸನೆ. The fragrance of flowers -ವೃಷ್ಟಿ. A shower of flowers. ಸಮಯ. The spring. ಪುಷ್ಪಿತ. Flowered, blooming.

ಪುಷ್ಯ s. *n.* Blossom. 2, the 8th lunar mansion. 3, the month pausha (December-January). -ರಾಗ. A topaz.

ಪುಸಲಾಯಿಸು h. *v. t.* To cajole, coax, wheedle, fawn. ಪುಸಲಾಯಿಕೆ. Cajoling, coaxing.

ಪುಸಿ (= ಹುಸಿ, *q. v.*) a. k. *v. i.* To prove false; to lie. *v. t.* To bear no fruit. *n.* A lie. 2, bearing no fruit; not attaining ripeness, *as* fruits. -ಗ. A liar.

ಪುಸ್ತ s. *a.* Smearing, anointing; writing. -ಕ. A book; a volume.

ಪುಸ್ತಿ. *tb. of* ಪುಷ್ಟಿ, *q. v.* 2, a paper of school-boys showing their progress in writing. 3, a book or pack of paper to write upon.

ಪುಳ (ಳ = ೞ). = ಹುಳ, *q. v.*

ಪುಳಿ (= ಹುಳಿ, *q. v.*) a. k. *n.* Acidity.

ಪುಳುಕು (ಳು = ೞು. = ಹುಳುಕು) k. *n.* A pock-mark. 2, decayed state. 3, a sore.

ಪುಳ್ಳಿ (= ಹುಳ್ಳಿ) k. *n.* A small bit of very dry wood. -ಮಾತು. A useless word.

ಪೂ (= ಹೂ, *q. v.*) a. k. *n.* A flower, *etc.* *Cpds.:* -ಗಣ, -ಗುಡಿ. -ತೊಡಂಬೆ, -ತೋಟ, -ದೂಳು, -ಮರ, -ಮಾಲಿಕೆ, -ಮಾಲೆ, *etc.* -ವಾಗು. To blossom.

ಪೂಗ s. *n.* The areca or betel-nut tree, *Areca catechu.* ಪೂಗೀಫಲ. A betel-nut.

ಪೂಜೆ 1. s. *n.* Honour, respect, reverence, adoration, worship. ಪೂಜಕ. A worshipper. ಮೂರ್ತಿಪೂಜಕ. An idolator. ಪೂಜನ. Reverencing; worshipping; worship. ಪೂಜಾರಿ. The officiating Brâhmaṇa or other person of a temple. ಪೂಜಿತ. Honoured; respected, adored. ಪೂಜಿಸು. To honour, revere, worship, adore. ಮೂರ್ತಿ-. Idol-worship. ಸಾಂತ-. Saint-worship.

ಪೂಜಿ, ಪೂಜೆ 2. f. *n.* A dot; the nasal sound; a cipher; *also* ಪೂಜ್ಯ.

ಪೂಜ್ಯ s. *a.* Honourable, respectable, worshipful. -ತೆ. Honourableness, venerableness. ಪೂಜ್ಯಾರ್ಥ. Honorific meaning.

ಪೂಟು 1. h. *n.* A bit, small portion. ಪೂಟಿ ಜರ್. A summary arji.

ಪೂಟು 2. e. *n.* Foot, a ameasure of space.

ಪೂಡು (= ಹೂಡು, *q. v.*) a. k. *v. t.* To unite; to put to, *etc.*

ಪೂಣ್ a. k. *v. t.* To begin. *v. t.* To admit; to promise; to challenge.

ಪೂತ s. *a.* Made pure or clean; threshed, winnowed.

ಪೂತನಿ, ಪೂತನೆ s. *n.* N. of a female demon killed by Kṛishṇa.

ಪೂತಿ s *n.* Purity, purification. 2, stench, fetor; civet.

ಪೂತು a. k. *int.* Bravo! well done!

ಪೂರ (ಪೂರಾ) s. *n.* Making full. 2, a swelling of rivers, flood. *a.* Full, complete, whole. -ಣ. Filling; filling out; completing, accomplishing; fulfilling; completion; fulness, mass; a cake; the ordinal. ಸಂಖ್ಯಾಪೂರಣ. Gradation number.

ಪೂರಯಿಸು, ಪೂರಯ್ಸು s. v. t. To fill; to fill up, complete; to accomplish; to effect; to fulfil; to blow, sound.

ಪೂರಾ (= ಪೂರ) s. ad. Fully, completely; wholly.

ಪೂರಿ f. n. A thin cake of wheat-flour.

ಪೂರಿಸು. = ಪೂರಯಿಸು, q. v.

ಪೂರ್ಣ h. a. Full; full of. 2, fulfilled, finished. 3, complete, all, entire, perfect. 4, strong, able. -ತೆ. Fulness, plenty. -ಪಾತ್ರ. A full cup; a measure of capacity; a ghee-vessel used at a hôma. -ಮಾಸಿ. The day or night of full moon. -ಮೆ. The full moon. -ವಿರಾಮ. A full stop. ಪೂರ್ಣಾಂಕ. An integer.

ಪೂರ್ತ s. a. Full; complete. n. Fulness, completion. 2, satisfaction. ಪೂರ್ತಿ. Fulness; satiety; perfection.

ಪೂರ್ತಿ. tb. of ಪೂರ್ತ, q. v.

ಪೂರ್ವ s. a. Fore, first; previous to, earlier than. 2, former, prior, preceding. 3, initial. 4, ancient. 5, eastern. 6, preceded by. n. An ancestor. 2, an ancient tradition; ancient times; former events. 3, east. -ಕ. Accompanied by, with; as ಮನಃ-, ವಿನಯ-, etc. -ಕಾಲ. Former times. -ಜ. An elder brother; an ancestor. -ಜನ್ಮ. A former birth. -ದೇಶ. An eastern country. -ಪಕ್ಷ. The first part of an argument, proposition, thesis; the first half of a lunar month. -ಪಕ್ಷಸಿದ್ಧಾಂತ. A demonstration that rests only on the proposition. -ಫಲ್ಗುನಿ. The 11th nakshatra. -ರಂಗ. The prelude of a drama. -ರಾತ್ರಿ. The first part of the night. -ವಯಸ್ಸು. Youth. -ವಾಸರ. Yesterday.

ಪೂರ್ವಣಿ s. n. Continuation of a series.

ಪೂರ್ವಾಪರ s. a. Before and behind, antecedent and subsequent. n. Connection.

ಪೂರ್ವಾಭಾದ್ರಪದೆ, ಪೂರ್ವಾಭಾದ್ರೆ s. n. The 25th nakshatra.

ಪೂರ್ವಾಷಾಢೆ s. n. The 20th nakshatra.

ಪೂರ್ವಾಹ್ಣ s. n. The forenoon.

ಪೂರ್ವಿಕ s. a. Previous, former. n. An ancestor, forefather.

ಪೂರ್ವೆ (= ಹುಬ್ಬೆ) s. n. The 11th nakshatra.

ಪೂರ್ವೋಕ್ತ (ಪೂರ್ವ-ಉಕ್ತ) s. a. Aforesaid, before mentioned.

ಪೂರ್ವೋತ್ತರ (ಪೂರ್ವ-ಉತ್ತರ) s. a. North-eastern. 2, antecedent and subsequent.

ಪೂಲ h. n. A bridge.

ಪೂವಡಿಗ, ಪೂವಳ k. n. A florist.

ಪೂಸು (= ಹೂಸು, q. v.) a. k. v. t. To smear, etc. n. An unguent; smearing.

ಪೂಳು. = ಹೂಳು, q. v.

ಪೃಚ್ಛೆ s. n. Asking; a question, inquiry.

ಪೃಥಕ್ s. ad. Separately, singly. postp. Apart from; except, without. -ಕರಣ. Separating. -ತ್ವ. Separateness, diversity; individuality.

ಪೃಥವಿ, ಪೃಥ್ವಿ s. n. The earth. -ಜೆ. Sîtâ. -ಪತಿ, -ಪಾಲ. A king.

ಪೃಥು s. a. Broad, wide, spacious; numerous; important. -ಕ. = ಅವಲಕ್ಕಿ.

ಪೃಷ್ಟ s. a. Asked, questioned.

ಪೃಷ್ಠ s. n. The back. 2, the rear.

ಪೆಗ್ಗ (= ಪೆಂಗ) k. n. A dolt, fool.

ಪೆಗ್ಗಡೆ, ಪೆರ್ಗಡೆ (= ಹೆಗ್ಗಡೆ) k. n. A headman; a chief; a superintendent.

ಪೆಂಗ k. n. A simpleton, fool; also ಪೆಗ್ಗ.

ಪೆಚ್ಚು 1. = ಹೆಚ್ಚು, q. v.

ಪೆಚ್ಚು 2. (= ಹುಚ್ಚು, q. v. tb. of ಪಿತ್ತ) n. Foolishness. -ತನ. = ಹುಚ್ಚುತನ.

ಪೆಟಲುಪ್ಪು k. n. Saltpetre; also ಪೆಟ್ಲುಪ್ಪು.

ಪೆಟಾರಿ f. n. A large box or chest (of rattan).

ಪೆಟ್ಟಣಿಗೆ k. n. A road tamper.

ಪೆಟ್ಟಲು k. n. A popgun.

ಪೆಟ್ಟಿ, ಪೆಟ್ಟಿಗೆ (tb. of ಪೇಟಿಕೆ) n. A box, chest, trunk, etc.

ಪೆಟ್ಟು k. v. t. To beat. n. A blow, stroke; a hurt. -ಕೊಡು, -ಹೊಡೆ. To beat. -ತಾ

ಗು, -ತಿನ್ನು. To be beaten. -ಬೀಳು. Blows to fall upon. -ಮಣೆ. = ಪೆಟ್ಟಣಿಗೆ. -ಹತ್ತು. To be hurt.

ಪೆಟ್ಲುಪ್ಪು k. n. Saltpetre; *also* ಪೆಟ್ಲುಪು.

ಪೆಡ (=ಹೆಡ) a. k. n. The back. *ad.* Backwards. -ಮೆಟ್ಟು. To retreat; the back part.

ಪೆಡಸು k. n. Hardness; stiffness. 2, brittleness. 3, harshness. 4, difficulty. -ಮಾತು. An offensive word.

ಪೆಣಗು (=ಹೆಣಗು) a. k. v. i. To wrangle, fight.

ಪೆಣೆ (=ಹೆಣೆ, q. v.) a. k. v. t. To twist, twine, *etc.* n. Twining; union.

ಪೆಂಟೆ 1. (=ಹೆಂಟೆ) k. n. A clod; a lump.

ಪೆಂಟೆ 2. f. n. A bundle.

ಪೆಂಡ (=ಪೆಂಣ್, ಹೆಂಡ) a. k. n. A female, woman. -ತಿ (=ಹೆಂಡತಿ). A wife.

ಪೆಂಡಾರಿ f. n. A Pindaree, a freebooter, marauder.

ಪೆಂಡಿ. = ಪೆಂಟೆ 2, q. v.

ಪೆಂಡೆಯ f. n. A badge of honour for the [foot.

ಪೆಣ್ಣು. = ಹೆಣ್ಣು, q. v. -ತನ. A feminine character.

ಪೆದ್ದ. = ಹುಚ್ಚ, q. v.; f. ಪೆದ್ದಿ.

ಪೆನಶನು e. n. Pension, an allowance for past services. -ದಾರ. Pensioner.

ಪೆನಸಿಲು e. n. Pencil.

ಪೆಂತೆಕೊಸ್ತು e. n. Pentecost.

ಪೆಂಪು a. k. n. Greatness; abundance; grandeur, sublimity.

ಪೆಬ್ರುವರಿ e. n. February (2nd month of the year).

ಪೆರ (ರ=ಱ. = ಹೆರ) a. k. n. Hind part, backside. *ad.* Backwards. -ಗು. The back side; afterwards.

ಪೆರೆ (ರೆ = ಱೆ. = ಹೆರೆ, q. v.) a. k. n. The crescent moon.

ಪೇರ್ a. k. n. Largeness, greatness. *Cpds.:* -ಗಿಚ್ಚು, -ಗೊನೆ, -ಗೋಣೆ, -ಜ್ವಾಲೆ, -ದೆರೆ, -ನಗೆ, -ನೊರೆ, -ಬಲೆ, -ಮಗ, -ಮಳೆ, *etc.*

ಪೆರ್ಚಿಗೆ, ಪೆರ್ಚು. = ಹೆಚ್ಚಿಗೆ, ಹೆಚ್ಚು, q. v.

ಪೆಸರು (=ಹೆಸರು, q. v.) a. k. n. A name; fame.

ಪೆಳರು a. k. v. i. To tremble. n. Fear, alarm. ಪೆಳರಿಸು. To alarm, frighten.

ಪೇಂಕುಳಿ a. k. n. A demon. 2, madness, fury.

ಪೇಚಾಟ f. n. Trouble, difficulty, strait. -ಪಡು, ಪೇಚಾಡು. To take pains; to be involved in trouble.

ಪೇಟ h. n. A small kind of turban. 2, a basket; *also* -ಳ.

ಪೇಟೆ h. n. A pettah, market-town, bazaar.

ಪೇಡೆ h. n. A sweetmeat of milk and sugar; *also* ಪೇಡೆ.

ಪೇತು k. n. Confusion; a demon.

ಪೇದಾ, ಪೇದೆ (=ಪ್ಯಾದೆ) h. n. A foot-soldier; a peon; a pawn at chess.

ಪೇನು 1. e. n. A pen.

ಪೇನು 2. (=ಹೇನು) a. k. n. A louse.

ಪೇಯ s. a. Drinkable. n. A drink, beverage.

ಪೇರ್. = ಪೆರ್, q. v., *as:* -ಆನೆ, -ಆಲ, -ಆಮೆ, -ಓಟ, -ಓಲಗ, -ಪತ್ತು, *etc.*

ಪೇರಣೆ f. n. A sword-dance. -ಗ. A dancer, actor.

ಪೇರಲ f. n. The guava, *Psidium guvava.*

ಪೇರಿ f. n. Galloping.

ಪೇರು 1. f. n. Difference in scales. -ಕಟ್ಟು. To remove it.

ಪೇರು 2. = ಹೇರು, q. v.

ಪೇಲವ s. a. Delicate, fine, tender, slender.

ಪೇಲಾಗು e. v. i. To fail in an examination.

ಪೇಲೆ f. n. A cup, bowl.

ಪೇಷ್ಕಾರ h. n. A revenue officer.

ಪೇಷ್ವ h. n. The Peshwâ, the head minister of the Mahratta empire; *also* ಪೇಶವೆ.

ಪೇಳು. = ಹೇಳು, q. v.

ಪೈ f. n. A copper coin; a pie.

ಪೈಕ f. n. Money, cash. 2, a division, set.

ಪೈಕಿ f. ad. Of, out of; from amongst.

ಪೈಗಂಬರ h. n. A prophet.

ಪೈಗಸ್ತಿ h. n. A superintendent; a patrole.

ಪೈಗು f. n. Pegu.

ಪೈಂಗಲ (fr. ಪಿಂಗಲ) s. n. The 51st year of the cycle of sixty.

ಪೈಜಣ f. n. A small tinkling ornament for the feet.

ಪೈಜಾರು h. n. A shoe.

ಪೈಟಿ f. n. A summerset.

ಪೈಠಣ f. n. N. of a town. ಪೈಠಣಿ. Manufactured at Paiṭhaṇa. -ಸೀರೆ. A kind of silk garment.

ಪೈತೃಕ s. a. Paternal. -ಧನ. Patrimony.

ಪೈತ್ಯ (tb. of ಪಿತ್ತ) n. Bilious humour; choler; foolishness, madness. -ಗಾರ. A foolish man.

ಪೈಮಾಯಿಷಿ h. n. Surveying and measuring of lands.

ಪೈರು (=ಪಯ್ರು) k. n. Green corn, growing corn; any green, growing crop.

ಪೈಲವಾನ h. n. An athlete, wrestler.

ಪೈವಸ್ತು h. n. Endorsement on a letter specifying the date of its receipt.

ಪೈಶಾಚ (fr. ಪಿಶಾಚ) s. a. Infernal, demoniacal. n. The lowest form of marriage.

ಪೈಶುನ್ಯ (fr. ಪಿಶುನ) s. a. Tale-bearing, backbiting, calumny.

ಪೈಸ f. n. A copper coin, 4 pies, or 1 duḍḍu. 2, money.

ಪೈಸಲು h. n. Decision of a dispute; settlement of a debt; judgment. ಪೈಸಲಾತಿ. Final settlement.

ಪೈಸೊಲು h. n. Crop, harvest.

ಪೊಕ್ಕುಳು. = ಹೊಕ್ಕುಳು, q. v.

ಪೊಗದಿ k. n. Tribute; tax.

ಪೊಗರು a. k. n. Shine, lustre, colour.

ಪೊಗಳು. = ಹೊಗಳು, q. v.

ಪೊಗು. = ಹೊಗು, q. v.

ಪೊಗೆ (= ಹೊಗೆ, q. v.) a. k. n. Smoke. v. i. To smoke.

ಪೊಂ, ಪೊಜ್ a. k. n. Gold, as: -ಕವಚ, -ಕವಡಿಕೆ, -ಕುಪ್ಪಸ, -ಕೊಡ.

ಪೊಂಗಲು k. n. Boiled rice mixed with milk and sugar. -ಹಬ್ಬ. A festival in honour of the sun entering the sign of Capricorn.

ಪೊಂಗು a. k. v. i. To boil over. 2, to expand, blossom; to exult. n. Boiling over.

ಪೊಟ್ಟಣ (= ಪೊಟ್ಲ, ಪೊಟ್ಲ. tb. of ಪುಟ) n. A small cup or packet made of leaves, paper, etc.

ಪೊಟ್ಟರೆ (= ಪೊಟ್ರು) k. n. A hole in a tree.

ಪೊಟ್ಟು (= ಹೊಟ್ಟು) k. a. Empty, useless. n. Chaff, husk.

ಪೊಟ್ಟೆ (= ಹೊಟ್ಟೆ, q. v.) a. k. n. The belly, etc.

ಪೊಟ್ರು. = ಪೊಟ್ಟರೆ, etc., q. v.

ಪೊಟ್ಲ. = ಪೊಟ್ಟಣ, q. v.

ಪೊಡ 1. (tb. of ಪುಟ) n. A hollow formed by joining the palms of the hands. -ಮುಡು, -ವಡು. To salute respectfully. -ವಡಿಕೆ. A respectful salutation.

ಪೊಡ 2. (tb. of ಸ್ಫುಟ) n. Appearance, form, figure. -ಕರಿಸು. To come in sight, appear.

ಪೊಡರು k. v. i. To tremble, throb, quiver; to flash, shine.

ಪೊಡರ್ಪು a. k. n. Glitter, shine; glory; power. -ಗುಂದಿಸು. To cause lustre, etc.; to decrease.

ಪೊಡವಿ (tb. of ಪೃಥ್ವಿ, q. v.) n. The earth. -ಪ, -ಪತಿ, -ಯೊಡೆಯ. A king.

ಪೊಡೆ 1. (=ಹೊಡಿ, ಹೊಡೆ, q. v.) a. k. v. t. To strike, smite, etc.

ಪೊಡೆ 2. = ಪೊಟ್ಟೆ, q. v. 2, a full ear of corn. 3, extension. 4, pregnancy (of beasts). 5, a pouch formed by folding the front part of one's cloth.

ಪೊಣರು a. k. v. i. To join, couple. 2, to fight. n. Union; a couple. 2, a fight. ಪೊಣರ್ಕೆ. Fighting; a fight.

ಪೊಣೆ (= ಹೊಣೆ, q. v.) a. k. n. Bond, bail; a surety.

ಪೊತ್ತು (= ಹೊತ್ತು, q. v.) a. k. v. i. To be kindled. 2, to be burned, as rice, *etc.*; to be overdone. *n.* Flaming. 2, the sun; time. -ಗಳೆ. To spend time.

ಪೊದಕೆ (= ಹೊದಿಕೆ) k. *n.* A cover, wrapper. 2, a roof, thatch.

ಪೊದರು (ರು = ಱು. = ಹೊದರು, *q. v.*) a. k. *n.* A bush, thicket.

ಪೊದೆ 1. = ಹೊದೆ, *q. v.*

ಪೊದೆ 2. k. *n.* A quiver. 2, a thatch. 3, a bush. 4, a bundle.

ಪೊನ್ (= ಪೊಂ, *q. v.*) a. k. *n.* Gold, *as:* -ತಾವರೆ, -ತೆರೆ, -ತೊಡರು, *etc.*

ಪೊಪ್ಪಿಳಿ k. *n.* A diffuse shrub yielding a yellow dye, *Morinda umbellata.*

ಪೊಮ್ (= ಪೊಂ, *q. v.*) a. k. *n.* Gold; *as:* -ಬಿಸಿಲು, -ಬೆಟ್ಟು, -ಬೆತ್ತ, -ಬೆಸೆ, *etc.*

ಪೊಂಪುಳಿ (ಳಿ = ೞ) k. *n.* Increase, growth, greatness.

ಪೊರ (ರ = ಱ. = ಹೊರ, *q. v.*) a. k. *n.* The outside. -ಮಡು. To set out, start; to quit. -ಗು, -ಗೆ. = ಹೊರಗೆ.

ಪೊರಕೆ k. *n.* A broom.

ಪೊರಳು (= ಹೊರಳು, *q. v.*) a. k. *v. i.* To roll, welter.

ಪೊರಿಗೆ (ರಿ = ಱ. = ಹೊರಿಗೆ) a. k. *n.* Burden; business, work; *also* ಪೊರೆ.

ಪೊರು (ರು = ಱು. = ಹೊರು, *q. v.*) a. k. *v. t.* To bear, *as* a burden, *etc.*

ಪೊರೆ 1. (= ಹೊರೆ 1, *q. v.* ರೆ = ಱೆ) a. k. *n.* A load, *etc.*

ಪೊರೆ 2. (= ಹೊರೆ 2) a. k. *v. t.* To nourish, cherish, invigorate, *etc.* 2, to join. *v. i.* To be joined. *n.* Invigoration, refreshment; union.

ಪೊರೆ 3. (= ಹೊರೆ 3) k. *n.* A fold, layer, stratum.

ಪೊರೆ 4. (= ಹೊರೆ 4) a. k. *n.* Choking sensation while eating or drinking. -ಏರು. To feel a choking sensation.

ಪೊರ್ದು (= ಹೊದ್ದು) a. k. *v. i.* To join; to agree; to reach. -ಗೆ (= ಹೊದ್ದಿಕೆ). Joining, contact; harmony, proximity.

ಪೊಲ. = ಹೊಲ, *q. v.*

ಪೊಲಬು (= ಹೊಲಬು) a. k. *n.* A way; a manner.

ಪೊಲಸು. = ಹೊಲಸು, *q. v.*

ಪೊಲೆ. = ಹೊಲೆ, *q. v.* -ಯ. = ಹೊಲೆಯ; *f.* ಪೊಲತಿ.

ಪೊಲ್ಲ (= ಹೊಲ್ಲ, *q. v.*) a. k. *n.* Meanness, *etc.* *Cpds.:* -ಮಾತು, -ಮೊಗ, -ವಾರ್ತೆ.

ಪೊಸ. = ಹೊಸ, *q. v.*

ಪೊಸಯಿಸು, ಪೊಸವಿಸು a. k. *v. t.* To join; to apply to. 2, to churn, shake about.

ಪೊಸೆ (= ಹೊಸೆ, *q. v.*) a. k. *v. i.* To shake; to rub. 2, to twist, plait.

ಪೊಳಪು (= ಹೊಳಪು) a. k. *n.* Radiance, brightness. 2, shaking, rolling; a swing.

ಪೊಳಲು (= ಹೊಳಲು. ಳ = ೞ) a. k. *n.* A dwelling place: a town, city.

ಪೊಳೆ 1. (= ಹೊಳೆ 1, *q. v.*) a. k. *v. i.* To shine. 2, to roll about.

ಪೊಳೆ 2. (ಳೆ = ೞೆ. = ಹೊಳೆ 2) k. *n.* A river. 2, a path, road.

ಪೊಳ್ಳು (= ಹೊಳ್ಳು) k. *n.* Hollowness; emptiness; trash, worthless stuff. -ಕೂಗು. A false report. -ಮಾತು. A vain word. -ಸುದ್ದಿ. A groundless report. -ಹಲ್ಲು. A hollow tooth.

ಪೋಕ, ಪೋಕರಿ k. *n.* A dissolute, profligate fellow, villain, rogue, prodigal. -ತನ. The ways of a ಪೋಕರಿ.

ಪೋಗು. = ಹೋಗು, *q. v.*

ಪೋಟ k. *n.* A coward. 2, = ಪೋಕ, *q. v.* -ತನ. = ಪೋಕತನ.

ಪೋಟಿ k. *n.* Competition, rivalry; *also* ಪೋಟಾ-. -ಗಾರ. A competitor.

ಪೋಟೆ (= ಪೊಟ್ಟರೆ, *q. v.*) k. *n.* A hole in a tree.

ಪೋಡಿ f. *n.* A slice, bit, *as* of a nut, *etc.*

ಪೋಡು k. *n.* Combination. 2, splitting.

ಪೋಣಿಸು k. *v. t.* To couple, unite, string together; to thread, *as* a needle, *etc.*

ಪೋತ, -ಕ s. *n.* The young of any animal.

ಪೋತಕಿ *n.* The potherb *Basella lucida.*

ಪೋತೊಗ್ರಾಫು e. *n.* Photograph (ಚಿತ್ರತೆಗೆಯುವದು).

ಪೋದ. *Rel. p. p. of* ಪೋಗು.

ಪೋಪ. *Rel. pres. p. of* ಪೋಗು.

ಪೋಪನು e. *n.* The Pope, the head of the Roman Catholic Church.

ಪೋರ f. *n.* A child; a little boy. -ತನ. Childhood. ಪೋರಿ. A little girl.

ಪೋರು. = ಹೋರು 1. 2, *q. v.*

ಪೋಲಿ (=ಪೋಲು) k. *n.* Ruin, destruction; waste, stray; profligacy; wickedness. 2, =ಪೋಕರಿ. -ಮಾಡು. To waste. -ದನ. Stray cattle. -ತನ. = ಪೋಕರಿತನ, *q. v.*

ಪೋಲಿಕೆ s. *n.* A flat cake.

ಪೋಲಿಸು. = ಹೋಲಿಸು, *q. v.*

ಪೋಲೀಸು e. *n.* Police. ಪೋಲೀಸಿನವ. A policeman. -ಕೆಲಸ. The duties of the police.

ಪೋಲು (= ಪೋಲಿ) k. *n.* Ruin; wasting, squandering. 2,=ಹೋಲು. -ಮಾಡು. To squander.

ಪೋಲ್ಟೀಸು e. *n.* Poultice, cataplasm, an application to sore part of the body.

ಪೋಷಣ, ಪೋಷಣೆ s. *n.* Nourishing, cherishing, bringing up. ಪೋಷಕ. A nourisher, supporter. ಪೋಷಿತ. Nourished, cherished, fostered. ಪೋಷಿಸು. To nourish, cherish, *etc.*

ಪೋಷಾಕ, ಪೋಷಾಕು h. *n.* Apparel.

ಪೋಸ್ತುಮಾಸ್ತರ್ e. *n.* Postmaster.

ಪೋಳು. = ಹೋಳು, *q. v.*

ಪೌಜು (= ಪವುಜು, ಫೌಜು) h. *n.* An army, *etc.* -ದಾರ. A native commander. -ದಾರಿಕೆ. His office.

ಪೌತಿ h. *n.* Death. -ಆಸಾಮಿ. A deceased person.

ಪೌತ್ರ s. *n.* A grandson; *f.* ಪೌತ್ರಿ.

ಪೌರ (*fr.* ಪುರ) s. *n.* A townsman. 2, a species of fragrant grass.

ಪೌರಾಣ (*fr.* ಪುರಾಣ) s. *a.* Relating to the past; old, ancient. ಪೌರಾಣಿಕ. = ಪುರಾಣಿಕ, *q. v.*

ಪೌರುಷ (*fr.* ಪುರುಷ) s. *a.* Belonging to man. *n.* Manliness, heroism, power, strength, vigour.

ಪೌರೋಹಿತ (*fr.* ಪುರೋಹಿತ) s. *n.* The office of a purôhita; the family priest. ಪೌರೋಹಿತ್ಯ. The office of a family-priest.

ಪೌರ್ಣಮಿ (*fr.* ಪೂರ್ಣಮಾ) s. *n.* A day of full moon.

ಪೌಳಿ s. *n.* A sort of cake made of grain.

ಪ್ಯಾದೆ. = ಪೇದೆ, *q. v.*

ಪ್ರ s. *pref.* Before, forward, in front, forth; pre-eminently, excessively, very, much.

ಪ್ರಕಟ s. *a.* Evident, clear, manifest; public, commonly known; published; notorious; visible. -ಗೊಳಿಸು, -ಪಡಿಸು. To make manifest. -ಮಾಡು. To publish. -ಣೆ, -ನೆ. Notification; *also* -ಪತ್ರ. ಪ್ರಕಟಿಸು. To manifest; to disclose; to publish, proclaim.

ಪ್ರಕರಣ s. *n.* Expounding, discussion, explanation. 2, a subject, department. 3, a section, chapter. 4, occasion. 5, a prologue, prelude. 6, a drama.

ಪ್ರಕಾಂಡ s. *n.* The stem or trunk of a tree. 2, a branch.

ಪ್ರಕಾರ s. *n.* Sort, kind. 2, way, mode, manner. 3, similitude. *ad.* According to, *etc.* ಈ-. Thus, in this way. ಆ-. So, in that way.

ಪ್ರಕಾಶ s. *n.* Brightness, brilliance, lustre, splendour. 2, elucidation; manifestation; fame. -ಗೊಳಿಸು. To illuminate, make bright; to develop. -ಗೊಳ್ಳು. To obtain lustre. ಪ್ರಕಾಶಿತ. Manifest; displayed; enlightened. ಪ್ರಕಾಶಿಸು. To become manifest; to shine forth, be full of lustre.

ಪ್ರಕೃತಿ s. *n.* The original or natural form of anything. 2, nature, character; constitution of the body; temperament. 3, reality. 4, the five elements. 5, the material world; Nature, as opposed to Purusha. 6, work to be done. 7, cause. 8, a pattern, model. 9, the crude form of a word. ಪ್ರಕೃತ. Made, accomplished; original; natural; real; the present moment.

ಪ್ರಕೋಪ s. *n.* Violent anger, rage; provocation.

ಪ್ರಕ್ರಿಯೆ s. *n.* Conduct, manner; a rite. 2, precedence, prerogative, dignity.

ಪ್ರಕ್ಷಾಲ, -ನ s. *n.* Washing, cleansing, bathing. ಪ್ರಕ್ಷಾಲಿಸು. To wash.

ಪ್ರಕ್ಷೇಪಣ s. *n.* Throwing, casting, depositing.

ಪ್ರಖ್ಯಾತ s. *a.* Celebrated, renowned, famous. ಪ್ರಖ್ಯಾತಿ. Celebrity, fame, praise.

ಪ್ರಗಲ್ಭ s. *a.* Bold; resolute. -ತೆ. Boldness; energy; resoluteness.

ಪ್ರಗ್ರಹ s. *n.* Holding forth. 2, a rope, bridle, halter. 3, a captive.

ಪ್ರಚಂಡ s. *a.* Excessively violent, furious; fierce; intolerable; bold.

ಪ್ರಚಾರ s. *n.* Coming forth; becoming public; being in actual use; currency. 2, conduct, behaviour; custom, usage. -ಗೊಳಿಸು. To make public.

ಪ್ರಚುರ s. *a.* Much, many; plenteous; frequent; prevalent. -ತೆ. Increase; prevelance; publicity. -ಪಡಿಸು. To publish.

ಪ್ರಚೋದನ s. *n.* Animating, exciting; directing. ಪ್ರಚೋದಿತ. Impelled; decreed; prescribed, commanded.

ಪ್ರಚ್ಛನ್ನ s. *a.* Covered; hidden; clothed. 2, private, disguised.

ಪ್ರಜಾಗರ s. *n.* Waking, being awake.

ಪ್ರಜೆ s. *n.* Offspring. 2, people, subjects. ಪ್ರಜಾಪತಿ. Lord of creatures; Brahmá; a king; *also* ಪ್ರಜೇಶ್ವರ. ಪ್ರಜೋತ್ಪತ್ತಿ. The raising up of progeny; the fifth year in the cycle of sixty.

ಪ್ರಜ್ಞ s. *a.* Wise, intelligent, learned. ಪ್ರಜ್ಞಾಚಕ್ಷುಸ್. The mental eye. ಪ್ರಜ್ಞಾ, ಪ್ರಜ್ಞೆ. Intellect, wisdom; *also* ಪ್ರಜ್ಞಾನ.

ಪ್ರಜ್ವಲ, -ನ s. *n.* Blazing up, shining; kindling. ಪ್ರಜ್ವಲಿತ. Being in flames, burning, shining. ಪ್ರಜ್ವಲಿಸು. To be in flames; to shine.

ಪ್ರಣತ s. *a.* Bent forward; bowed; humble. 2, skilful. ಪ್ರಣತಿ. Salutation, obeisance.

ಪ್ರಣಮು. = ಪ್ರಣಾಮ, *q. v.*

ಪ್ರಣಯ s. *n.* Confidence, familiarity; friendship, affection, kindness. 2, affectionate solicitation. ಪ್ರಣಯಿ. A friend, lover; a lord; a petitioner; a humble servant.

ಪ್ರಣವ s. *n.* The mystic syllable ôm.

ಪ್ರಣಾದ s. *n.* A loud noise expressing delight.

ಪ್ರಣಾಮ s. *n.* Prostration, obeisance.

ಪ್ರಣಿಧಾನ s. *n.* Respectful conduct or behaviour towards. 2, profound meditation. 3, great effort, energy.

ಪ್ರಣಿಪಾತ s. *n.* Falling at one's feet, salutation, obeisance.

ಪ್ರತಾಪ s. *n.* Splendour; majesty, dignity. 2, ardour, energy, valour. -ನ. Burning; a particular hell.

ಪ್ರತಿ s. *ad.* Towards, to; against; opposite, contra; before; on a par with; as, like; near, by, at, on; in favour of; in each, at every; every, each; with regard to; on account of; according to; back, again, in lieu of; in return for; in the place of, instead of. *n.* A copy. -ಬರೆ, -ಮಾಡು. To copy. -ಒಂದು. Every one, each one. -ಒಬ್ಬ. Every man, each man. -ದಿನ, -ನಿತ್ಯ. Day by day, daily, every day. -ನಿಮಿಷ. Every moment. -ವರ್ಷ. Every year, annually. *For other cpds. see below.*

ಪ್ರತಿಕಾರ s. *n.* Retaliation, retribution; revenge. 2, counteraction, remedy; *also* ಪ್ರತೀಕಾರ.

ಪ್ರತಿಕೂಲ s. *a.* Contrary, adverse; inauspicious. -ತೆ. Opposition; hostility.

ಪ್ರತಿಕೃತಿ s. *n.* Resistance; requital; revenge. 2, an effigy, image.

ಪ್ರತಿಕ್ರಿಯೆ. = ಪ್ರತೀಕಾರ, *q. v.*

ಪ್ರತಿಗ್ರಹ s. *n.* Receiving, accepting; friendly reception; marrying; favour-

ಪ್ರತಿಚ್ಛಾಯೆ s. n. A reflected image, picture; a shadow.

ಪ್ರತಿಜ್ಞೆ s. n. Admission; consent; a solemn declaration; agreement, engagement, vow, promise; a vow; a statement, affirmation; a proposition. -ಗೈಯು, -ಮಾಡು. To make solemn declaration.

ಪ್ರತಿಧ್ವನಿ s. n. An echo. -ಕೊಡು, -ಮಾಡು. To echo.

ಪ್ರತಿನಿಧಿ s. n. A substitute, representative, proxy; a deputy, vice-regent.

ಪ್ರತಿಪಕ್ಷ s. n. The opposite side or party. ಪ್ರತಿಪಕ್ಷಿ. An opponent.

ಪ್ರತಿಪತ್ತು (tb. of ಪ್ರತಿಪದ್) n. The first day of a lunar fortnight.

ಪ್ರತಿಪತ್ತಿ s. n. Perception, knowledge. 2, intellect. 3, statement. 4, assent. 5, action. 6, elevation; reputation.

ಪ್ರತಿಪದ s. n. A synonym; each word.

ಪ್ರತಿಪದಿ s. n. The first day of a lunar fortnight. 2, preferment, regard.

ಪ್ರತಿಪಾದನ s. n. Explaining, declaring. 2, establishing, proving. ಪ್ರತಿಪಾದಿಸು. To declare; to establish; to accuse. ಪ್ರತಿಪಾದ್ಯ. Fit to be explained or proved.

ಪ್ರತಿಪಾಲನ s. n. Protecting, cherishing, nourishing. ಪ್ರತಿಪಾಲಿಸು. To protect, guard; to nourish.

ಪ್ರತಿಫಲ s. n. Reward, remuneration, retribution. 2, reflection. -ಕೊಡು. To remunerate. -ಹೊಂದು. To receive reward. ಪ್ರತಿಫಲಿಸು. To be rewarded.

ಪ್ರತಿಬಂಧ s. n. An obstacle, hinderance, impediment. -ಕ. Obstructive, hindering; an obstacle; a demon, devil. -ನ. Obstructing, impeding. ಪ್ರತಿಬಂಧಿಸು. To hinder, stop.

ಪ್ರತಿಬಿಂಬ s. n. A reflection; an image, a picture; a shadow. ಪ್ರತಿಬಿಂಬಿಸು. To be reflected; to reflect.

ಪ್ರತಿಭಟ s. n. Vying with, rivalling. ಪ್ರತಿಭಟಿಸು. To rival; to oppose.

ಪ್ರತಿಭೂ s. n. A surety, security.

ಪ್ರತಿಮಾನ s. n. A likeness, image, picture.

ಪ್ರತಿಮೆ s. n. A likeness, image; an idol.

ಪ್ರತಿರವ s. n. Echo; *also* ಪ್ರತಿಧ್ವನಿ, ಪ್ರತಿಶಬ್ದ.

ಪ್ರತಿರೂಪ s. n. An image, representation; a picture. a. Similar, corresponding.

ಪ್ರತಿಲೋಮ s. a. Reverse, inverted; hostile; low; left, not right.

ಪ್ರತಿವಚನ, ಪ್ರತಿವಾಕ್ಯ s. n. An answer, reply.

ಪ್ರತಿವಾದ s. n. A counter assertion, contradiction. ಪ್ರತಿವಾದಿ. An opponent; a defendant.

ಪ್ರತಿಶಬ್ದ s. n. Echo; *also* ಪ್ರತಿರವ.

ಪ್ರತಿಷೇಧ s. n. Forbidding, prohibition; denial; negation; the negative mood. -ಕ್ರಿಯೆ. The negative mood (g.). -ವಿಧಿ. The imperative mood of prohibition.

ಪ್ರತಿಷ್ಠಾಲು s. n. An illustrious person.

ಪ್ರತಿಷ್ಠೆ s. n. Setting up; honour, fame; pride; installation, *as* of a king, *etc.*, consecration, *as* of a church, temple, idol, *etc.* -ವಂತ. An illustrious man. ಪ್ರತಿಷ್ಠಿಸು. To establish; to set up, *as* an idol; to install, consecrate.

ಪ್ರತಿಹಸ್ತ s. n. A deputy, substitute, proxy.

ಪ್ರತಿಹಾರ (= ಪ್ರತೀಹಾರ) s. n. Repelling. 2, a door. 3, a porter. 4, juggling, disguise. 5, a place near a town.

ಪ್ರತೀಕಾರ. = ಪ್ರತಿಕಾರ, q. v.

ಪ್ರತೀಕ್ಷೆ s. n. Looking forward to, waiting for, expectation, hope. ಪ್ರತೀಕ್ಷಿಸು. To expect, wait for.

ಪ್ರತೀಚಿ s. n. Western quarter. ಪ್ರತೀಚೀನ, ಪ್ರತೀಚ್ಯ. Western.

ಪ್ರತೀತ s. a. Gone towards; proved; known; convinced; pleased. ಪ್ರತೀತಿ. Going towards; definite perception; knowledge; conviction; faith; fame; delight.

ಪ್ರತೀಹಾರ. = ಪ್ರತಿಹಾರ, q. v.

ಪ್ರತುಮೆ. *tb. of* ಪ್ರತಿಮೆ, *q. v.*

ಪ್ರತ್ಯಕ್ಷ s. *a.* Perceptible to the eye, visible; clear, distinct, evident, real; cognizable by the senses. *n.* Ocular evidence, distinctness. *ad.* Verily; distinctly. -ವಾಗು. To appear. -ಪ್ರಮಾಣ. The evidence of the senses; axiom. -ತೆ. Appearance. -ತೇ ಹಬ್ಬ. Epiphany, in commemoration of the appearance of the star that led the magi to our Saviour at Bethlehem.

ಪ್ರತ್ಯಗಾತ್ಮ s. *n.* The individual soul.

ಪ್ರತ್ಯಂತರ s. *n.* Another copy.

ಪ್ರತ್ಯಯ s. *n.* Belief, conviction, trust, reliance, confidence. 2, certainty. 3, knowledge; apprehension, intellect. 4, idea, notion. 5, motive. 6, an oath, ordeal. 7, a suffix or affix.

ಪ್ರತ್ಯವಾಯ s. *n.* Decrease, privation, harm; separation.

ಪ್ರತ್ಯಹ s. *ad.* Day by day, daily.

ಪ್ರತ್ಯಾಬ್ದಿಕ s. *ad.* Yearly.

ಪ್ರತ್ಯಾಮ್ನಾಯ s. *ad.* Instead of, in lieu of.

ಪ್ರತ್ಯಾಸಕ್ತಿ s. *n.* Great attachment or devotedness.

ಪ್ರತ್ಯಾಸನ್ನ s. *a.* Near, proximate; imminent.

ಪ್ರತ್ಯಾಹಾರ s. *n.* Restraint of the organs of sense.

ಪ್ರತ್ಯುತ್ತರ s. *n.* An answer, reply; *also* ಪ್ರತ್ಯುಕ್ತಿ. -ವಾಗಿ ಹೇಳು. To say in reply.

ಪ್ರತ್ಯುತ್ಥಾನ s. *n.* Rising to welcome a visitor.

ಪ್ರತ್ಯುಪಕಾರ s. *n.* A return of a kindness.

ಪ್ರತ್ಯುಷಸ್ s. *ad.* Every morning.

ಪ್ರತ್ಯೇಕ s. *a.* Separate, different. *ad.* Separately, severally. ಪ್ರತ್ಯೇಕಿಸು. To separate.

ಪ್ರಥಮ s. *a.* First, chief, principal; most, excellent. *n.* The third person (*g.*). ಪ್ರಥಮಾವಿಭಕ್ತಿ. The nominative case. ಪ್ರಥಮೈಕವಚನ. The nominative singular. ಪ್ರಥಮೈಕಾದಶಿ. The ಶುಕ್ಲ ಏಕಾದಶಿ in the month of ಆಷಾಢ.

ಪ್ರದಕ್ಷಿಣ, ಪ್ರದಕ್ಷಿಣೆ s. *n.* Circumambulation of an object (*as* of an idol, person, *etc.*, by way of reverence).

ಪ್ರದರ್ಶಕ s. *a.* Showing, exhibiting; exhibiter. ಪ್ರದರ್ಶನ. Showing, pointing out, exhibiting; an example.

ಪ್ರದಾನ s. *n.* Giving away; an oblation; a gift, present; *also* ಪ್ರದ.

ಪ್ರದೇಶ s. *n.* A place, region; a country, district.

ಪ್ರದೋಷ s. *a.* Corrupt. *n.* Sin, *etc.* 2, the first part of the night; nightfall. 3, a vrata in worship of Śiva.

ಪ್ರಧಾನ s. *a.* Chief, main, principal, pre-eminent. *n.* A chief object. 2, intellect. 3, the minister of a king. 4, the primary member of a compound (*g.*). -ವಾಕ್ಯ. Principal sentence. -ಯಾಜಕ. High priest (*Jewish*).

ಪ್ರಪಂಚ s. *n.* Development, diffusion, display; expansion; expanse. 2, the visible world or universe. 3, the business of life. 4, manifoldness, diversity. 5, error, illusion. -ಮಾಡು. To carry on the business of life. ಪ್ರಪಂಚಿಸು. To spread, develop.

ಪ್ರಪನ್ನ s. *n.* One who seeks for refuge.

ಪ್ರಪಾತ s. *n.* Rushing forwards. 2, a steep rock, cliff, precipice. 3, a waterfall.

ಪ್ರಪಿತಾಮಹ s. *n.* A paternal great-grandfather; *f.* -ಹಿ.

ಪ್ರಪೌತ್ರ s. *n.* A great-grandson.

ಪ್ರಫುಲ್ಲ s. *a.* Blown as a flower; covered with blossoms.

ಪ್ರಬಂಧ s. *n.* A connection. 2, a continuous series. 3, a connected discussion. 4, a literary composition, treatise.

ಪ್ರಬಲ s. *a.* Predominant; strong; abounding with or in. -ಪಡಿಸು, ಪ್ರಬಲಿಸು. To increase greatly.

ಪ್ರಬುದ್ಧ s. *a.* Awake. 2, clever, wise, learned. ಪ್ರಾಯ-. Adult.

ಪ್ರಬೋಧ s. n. Awaking; vigilance; intellect, knowledge; wisdom, intelligence. -ನ. Instructing. ಪ್ರಬೋಧಿಸು. To instruct.

ಪ್ರಭವ s. n. Origin. 2, the first year of the cycle. ಪ್ರಭವಿಸು. To come into being; to become manifest.

ಪ್ರಭಾವ s. n. Strength, power. 2, majesty, glory. 3, splendour.

ಪ್ರಭಾವಳಿ s. n. The halo around an idol.

ಪ್ರಭು s. a. Powerful, mighty. n. A superior, master, lord. -ತೆ, -ತ್ವ. Lordship, supremacy, power, rule.

ಪ್ರಭೂತ s. a. Much, abundant; high, lofty. n. An oblation of rice, *etc.* on the tenth day after the death of a person.

ಪ್ರಭೆ, ಪ್ರಭಾ s. n. Light, splendour, radiance.

ಪ್ರಮತ್ತ s. a. Excited; wanton; drunken; impassioned. 2, careless, negligent.

ಪ್ರಮಥ s. n. An attendant on Śiva.

ಪ್ರಮದ s. n. Joy, rapture. a. Wanton; impassioned; careless. -ವನ. A royal garden.

ಪ್ರಮಾಣ s. n. Measure, scale, standard; quantity; extent; weight; limit. 2, ground of assurance. 3, proof, authority; support; testimony, evidence. 4, an oath. 5, a correct notion. 6, statute, law, *etc.* 7, cause, motive. -ಮಾಡು. To swear. -ವಾಗಿ ಹೇಳು. To tell correctly. -ವಾಕ್ಯ. Authoritative statement; a formula used in taking an oath. ಪ್ರಮಾಣಿಕ. True, fair, equitable. ಪ್ರಮಾಣಿಕತನ. Truthfulness, honesty. ಪ್ರಮಾಣಿಸು. To discern, examine.

ಪ್ರಮಾಥಿ s. n. Stirring about. 2, the 13th year of the cycle.

ಪ್ರಮಾದ s. n. Intoxication, madness; inadvertence, carelessness; a blunder, error; distress, misfortune.

ಪ್ರಮಾದೀಚ s. n. The 47th year of the cycle.

ಪ್ರಮಿತ s. a. Measured; understood; conformed, *as* by some rule. ಪ್ರಮಿತಿ. Measure, true knowledge.

ಪ್ರಮುಖ s. a. First, foremost, chief, principal. 2, *at the end of cpds.:* headed by, accompanied by; and so on. n. A chief; a respectable man.

ಪ್ರಮೇಯ s. a. Demonstrable. n. A subject, topic in general (= ವಿಷಯ).

ಪ್ರಮೋದ s. n. Joy, delight, happiness. 2, the 4th year of the cycle. ಪ್ರಮೋದಿಸು. To rejoice, be delighted.

ಪ್ರಮೋದೂತ. *tb.* of ಪ್ರಮೋದ, *q. v.*

ಪ್ರಯತ್ನ s. n. Great exertion; an effort; an endeavour, essay. 2, difficulty. -ನಡಿಸು, -ಪಡು, -ಮಾಡು, ಪ್ರಯತ್ನಿಸು. To make effort, endeavour, try.

ಪ್ರಯಾಗ s. n. A sacrifice; a celebrated place of pilgrimage at (Allahabad) the confluence of ಗಂಗಾ and ಯಮುನಾ.

ಪ್ರಯಾಣ s. n. Setting out; a journey, march. 2, departure, death. -ಮಾಡು. To start; to journey; to die. -ಸ್ಥ, ಪ್ರಯಾಣಿಕ. A traveller; a voyager.

ಪ್ರಯಾಸ s. n. Effort, exertion, endeavour, labour, pains; difficulty. -ಪಡು. To labour, take pains. -ವಾಗು. To be difficult; to require pains.

ಪ್ರಯುಕ್ತ s. a. Used, employed; connected with; endowed with; occasioned by. *prep.* On account of, *as:* ಊಟದ-, ಕೆಲಸದ-. ಪ್ರಯುಕ್ತಿ. Use, employment; cause; result.

ಪ್ರಯುತ s. n. A million.

ಪ್ರಯೋಗ s. n. Application, employment, use. 2, undertaking, beginning. 3, an order. 4, a design, device, plan. 5, use, usage, practice. 6, ceremonial form. 7, force or usual form (of a word). -ಮಾಡು, ಪ್ರಯೋಗಿಸು. To use, employ; to throw, *as* an arrow.

ಪ್ರಯೋಜಕ s. a. Useful, beneficial. n. A useful man.

ಪ್ರಯೋಜನ s. n. Application, use. 2, cause, motive, origin. 3, purpose, object, intention, design. 4, profit; gain, usefulness, advantage, benefit.

ಪ್ರಲಪನ s. n. Speaking forth; prattling; crying, lamenting. ಪ್ರಲಪಿಸು. To speak; to lament, wail.

ಪ್ರಲಯ (=ಪ್ರಳಯ) s. n. Dissolution, destruction. 2, the destruction of the world at the end of a kalpa. 3, the deluge of the Bible. -ಕಾಲ. The time of universal destruction.

ಪ್ರಲಾಪ s. n. Senseless talk. 2, prattling. 3, lamentation. -ಸನ್ನಿ. A sanni that produces delirium. ಪ್ರಲಾಪಿಸು. To talk incoherently; to lament, wail.

ಪ್ರವರ s. n. A family, lineage. 2, offspring. 3, one of the 49 gôtras. 4, verbosity, prolixity.

ಪ್ರವರ್ತ s. a. Engaged in, occupied in. -ಕ. Setting in motion; promoting; an originator, founder; a promoter; f. -ಕಿ. -ನ, -ನೆ. Moving forwards; activity, action; business; course, proceeding; behaviour; conduct, way, manner. ಪ್ರವರ್ತಿಸು. To proceed, go on; to come to pass; to engage in, be occupied in; to act; to carry on, perform, as a business.

ಪ್ರವರ್ಧ s. n. Increasing; also -ನ. Augmenting, increase. -ಮಾನ. Growing, increasing. ಪ್ರವರ್ಧಿಸು. To grow, increase.

ಪ್ರವಹ s. n. Flowing, streaming. 2, wind. ಪ್ರವಹಿಸು. To flow; to draw, as a carriage.

ಪ್ರವಾದ s. n. Speaking forth, uttering; proclaiming, declaration; discourse; popular talk, rumour, report. -ನೆ. Prophecy. ಪ್ರವಾದಿ. A prophet (one who speaks by God's order). ಪ್ರವಾದಿಸು. To prophesy; also -ನೆ ಹೇಳು.

ಪ್ರವಾಲ s. n. A young shoot. 2, greenness. 3, coral. -ಭಸ್ಮ. Ashes of coral, used medicinally.

ಪ್ರವಾಸ s. n. Sojourning abroad; a temporary sojourn; a foreign abode. -ಮಾಡು. To go abroad. ಪ್ರವಾಸಿ. A sojourner abroad. -ನ. Dwelling abroad; exile, banishment.

ಪ್ರವಾಹ s. n. A stream, current, flow, course. ಪ್ರವಾಹಿಸು. To stream, flow.

ಪ್ರವಿಷ್ಟ s. a. Entered, gone into.

ಪ್ರವೀಣ s. a. Skilful, clever, proficient, conversant with; f. ಪ್ರವೀಣೆ. -ತೆ, -ತ. Skill, proficiency.

ಪ್ರವುಡ. tb. of ಪ್ರೌಢ, q. v.

ಪ್ರವೃತ್ತಿ s. n. Proceeding; purging. 2, progress; advance. 3, active life. 4, prevalence.

ಪ್ರವೃದ್ಧ s. a. Grown up, increased. ಪ್ರವೃದ್ಧಿ. Growth, increase; prosperity.

ಪ್ರವೇಣಿ s. n. A braided hair.

ಪ್ರವೇಶ s. n. Entering into, entrance. 2, commencement. -ಮಾಡು, ಪ್ರವೇಶಿಸು. To enter into, enter, go into; to interfere; as ಮನೆಗೆ-, ಮನೆಯಲ್ಲಿ-, ಮನೆಯನ್ನು-.

ಪ್ರವ್ರಜನ, ಪ್ರವ್ರಜ್ಯೆ s. n. Going abroad, migration, wandering about, esp. as a religious mendicant.

ಪ್ರವ್ರಾಜಕ s. n. A religious mendicant.

ಪ್ರಶಂಸೆ s. n. Praise, eulogy. ಪ್ರಶಂಸಿಸು. To praise, eulogize.

ಪ್ರಶಮ s. n. Calmness, tranquility, peace, composure. ಪ್ರಶಮಿತ. Appeased, quenched.

ಪ್ರಶಸ್ತ s. n. Praised, extolled; commendable; admirable, excellent.

ಪ್ರಶ್ನ s. n. A question, query, interrogation; also ಪ್ರಶ್ನೆ. -ಕೇಳು. To ask a question. -ಮಾಡು, -ಹಾಕು. To question, ask. -ಚಿಹ್ನ. A sign of interrogation (?). ಪ್ರಶ್ನಾರ್ಥಕ. Interrogative. ಪ್ರಶ್ನೋತ್ತರ. Questions and answers: a dialogue, catechism.

ಪ್ರಸಕ್ತಿ s. n. Connection; the topic of conversation; energy, effort. -ತೆಗೆ. To take up, as a topic of conversation.

ಪ್ರಸಂಗ s. n. Connection, intercourse, meeting. 2, topic, a subject of conversation; discussion; a sermon (Chr.). 3, incident, event. 4, the fit time, season; an occasion. -ನಡಿಸು, -ಮಾಡು, -ಗೈಯು, ಪ್ರಸಂಗಿಸು. To discuss; to preach, proclaim. ಪ್ರಸಂಗಿ. A devotee; a discusser; a preacher. -ಪೀಠ. The Christian pulpit.

ಪ್ರಸನ್ನ s. a. Clear, bright; tranquil; soothed, propitiated, pleased; gracious, propitious, kind, pleased with. -ತ. Pleased. -ತೆ, -ತ್ವ, -ಭಾವ. Clearness; favour, kindness, propitiousness.

ಪ್ರಸರ s. n. Spreading; extending, extent; diffusion; dispersion. 2, expansion. 3, flow, current. 4, speed; force. 5, affection. -ಣ. Spreading; surrounding an enemy. -ಣಶೀಲ. Extensible. ಪ್ರಸರಿಸು. To be extended; to be diffused; to spread.

ಪ್ರಸವ s. n. Childbirth. 2, offspring. 3, a flower. 4, fruit. 5, opening, budding. ಪ್ರಸವಿಸು. To beget, bring forth.

ಪ್ರಸಾದ s. n. Clearness; brightness, purity. 2, calmness, repose, composure; good humour. 3, graciousness, propitiousness, favour, kindness. 4, sacrament, a pledge of grace (as the Lord's Supper and baptism). 5, anything presented to an idol. 6, a free gift, gratuity. -ನ. Rendering clear; tranquillizing; gratifying; a gratuity. -ನೆ. Service, worship.

ಪ್ರಸಾದಿ s. a. Calming; showing favour. 2, come from a king, guru, *etc.*, *as* a blessing. -ತ. Purified; worshipped. -ಸು. To grant graciously.

ಪ್ರಸಾರ s. n. Going forth, spreading, extending. -ಣ. Causing to go forwards, spreading, diffusing, expansion, increase; exhibiting; dissemination.

ಪ್ರಸಿದ್ಧ s. a. Accomplished; well known, renowned, famous; celebrated, public; adorned. -ಪಡಿಸು, -ಮಾಡು. To make known, publish. -ತನ, -ತೆ. Celebrity. -ಪತ್ರ. A notification.

ಪ್ರಸಿದ್ಧಿ s. n. Accomplishment; celebrity, fame, publicity. -ಗೆ ಬರು. To come to fame. -ಮಾಡು.=ಪ್ರಸಿದ್ಧ ಮಾಡು, *q. v.*

ಪ್ರಸೂತ s. a. Begotten; born. ಪ್ರಸೂತಿ. Birth; offspring. ಪ್ರಸೂತೆ. A woman in childbed.

ಪ್ರಸ್ತ (*tb. of* ಪ್ರಾಶಿತ) n. An auspicious ceremony, festive occasion, *as:* the ಉಪನಯನ-, ನಾಮಕರಣ-, ವಿವಾಹ-, *etc.*

ಪ್ರಸ್ತಾಪ (*tb. of* ಪ್ರಸ್ತಾವ) n. Speaking, saying; introduction, preface. 2, beginning. 3, introducing a topic for conversation; the conversation on a topic, the topic itself; narration, news; affair, pursuit. 4, occasion, opportunity; a favourable moment. -ನೆ.=ಪ್ರಸ್ತಾವನೆ. ಪ್ರಸ್ತಾಪಿಸು. To introduce a topic and converse on it.

ಪ್ರಸ್ತಾರ s. n. A plain. 2, a jungle.

ಪ್ರಸ್ತಾವ.=ಪ್ರಸ್ತಾಪ, *q. v.* -ನೆ. Introduction, preface; the prologue of a drama; introducing a topic for conversation; the conversation on a topic.

ಪ್ರಸ್ತುತ s. a. Praised; declared, said; ready; proximate. n. A proposition. *ad.* At present.

ಪ್ರಸ್ಥ s. n. Table-land. 2, a measure of four kuḍavas. a. Going forth.

ಪ್ರಸ್ಥಾನ s. n. Going forth; a march; a journey; a method, system.

ಪ್ರಸ್ರವ s. n. A flow, stream; a fall of water; a cascade.

ಪ್ರಹರ s. n. A watch; the eighth part of a day.

ಪ್ರಹಸನ s. n. Hearty laughter; mirth; mocking; sarcasm, satire; a farce.

ಪ್ರಹ್ಲಾದ s. n. Pleasure, gladness, happiness. 2, sound. 3, N. of a daitya persecuted for his devotion to Vishṇu.

ಪ್ರಳಯ.=ಪ್ರಲಯ, *q. v.*

ಪ್ರಾಕ (*tb. of* ಪ್ರಾಚ್) *ad.* Before; formerly. a. Previous, former.

ಪ್ರಾಕಟ್ಯ s. n. Publicity, manifestation.

ಪ್ರಾಕಾರ (=ಪಾಗಾರ, *q. v.*) s. *n.* A rampart, fence, enclosure.

ಪ್ರಾಕೃತ (*fr.* ಪ್ರಕೃತಿ) s. *a.* Original, natural; ordinary, common, uncultivated, vulgar, low, base; vernacular. *n.* Any provincial or vernacular dialect akin to Saṁskṛita.

ಪ್ರಾಕ್ಕು. = ಪ್ರಾಕ್, *q. v. tb. of* ಪ್ರಾಚ್.

ಪ್ರಾಕ್ತನ s. *a.* Former, prior. *n.* Fate, destiny.

ಪ್ರಾಕ್ಪದ s. *n.* The first member of a compound.

ಪ್ರಾಗಾರಭ್ಯ (*fr.* ಪ್ರಾಕ್-ಆರಭ್ಯ) s. *a.* Beginning from the past time.

ಪ್ರಾಗುದಯ s. *a.* Rising in the east.

ಪ್ರಾಚೀನ s. *a.* Former, prior, ancient; eastern. *n.* The doings of former births and their consequences. 2, a hedge, wall.

ಪ್ರಾಜಾಪತ್ಯ (*fr.* ಪ್ರಜಾಪತಿ) s. *n.* A kind of marriage. 2, a mode of penance.

ಪ್ರಾಜ್ಞ s. *a.* Intelligent, wise, clever. *n.* A learned man.

ಪ್ರಾಣ s. *n.* Breath, respiration. 2, air, wind. 3, a vital air. 4, life, vitality. 5, the soul. 6, strength, might. -ಕೊಡು. To offer one's life for the benefit of another; to die. -ಗೆಳೆಯ, -ಮಿತ್ರ. A dearly loved friend. -ತಕ್ಕೊಳ್ಳು (-ತೆಗೆ). To take away life, kill; to commit suicide. -ದಿಂದ ಹೋಗು. To die; to go alive. -ಕಂಟಕ. Danger of life; a dangerous man. -ಕಾಂತ, -ನಾಥ, -ಪತಿ, -ವಲ್ಲಭ. A dearly beloved husband. -ಘಾತಕ. Killing; money. -ತ್ಯಾಗ. Suicide. -ದಾನ. The gift of life. -ನಷ್ಟ, -ಹಾನಿ. Loss of life. -ಪ್ರತಿಷ್ಠೆ. The rite of bringing life to an idol. -ಪ್ರಿಯ. A dearly beloved man. -ಸಂಕಟ. Jeopardy of life, extreme distress. -ಸ್ನೇಹ. Very intimate friendship. -ಹತ್ಯ. Murder. -ಹಿಂಸೆ. Injury to life. ಪ್ರಾಣಾಯಾಮ. Restraint of breath during meditation.

ಪ್ರಾಣಿ s. *n.* Any living creature; an animal; a person. -ಕೋಟಿ. The animal kingdom.

ಪ್ರಾತಃ, ಪ್ರಾತರ್ s. *ad.* At daybreak. ಪ್ರಾತಃಕಾಲ. The early morning. ಪ್ರಾತಃಸ್ನಾನ. Morning ablution. ಪ್ರಾತರ್ಭೋಜನ. Breakfast.

ಪ್ರಾತಿಭಾಸಿಕ (*fr.* ಪ್ರತಿಭಾಸ) s. *a.* Existing only in appearance. 2, looking like.

ಪ್ರಾದೇಶ (*fr.* ಪ್ರದೇಶ) s. *n.* The span of the thumb and forefinger.

ಪ್ರಾಧಾನ್ಯ (*fr.* ಪ್ರಧಾನ) s. *n.* Pre-eminence, supremacy; prevalence, ascendancy.

ಪ್ರಾಂತ, ಪ್ರಾಂತ್ಯ s. *n.* Edge, border; boundary. 2, a country; a region; a place.

ಪ್ರಾಪಂಚಿಕ s. *a.* Worldly, secular.

ಪ್ರಾಪ್ತ s. *a.* Attained to; obtained, got, acquired; fit, proper. ಪ್ರಾಪ್ತಿ. Attaining to; obtaining; acquisition, profit, advantage; lot; good luck. ಪ್ರಾಪ್ತಿಸು. To be obtained; to come to pass, to come to; to meet with.

ಪ್ರಾಬಲ್ಯ s. *n.* Powerfulness; prevalence.

ಪ್ರಾಮಾಣಿಕ (*fr.* ಪ್ರಮಾಣ) s. *a.* Authentic, credible, true, just. *n.* An upright, honest man. -ತನ, -ತೆ, ಪ್ರಾಮಾಣ್ಯ. Authenticity, credibility; truth, veracity, honesty.

ಪ್ರಾಯ s. *n.* Any period of life, age; prime of life. -ತುಂಬು. A period of age to be reached. -ದವ. A young man. -ಸಲ್ಲು. Age to pass, decline. -ಶಃ. Generally, usually; to all appearances. -ಸ್ಥ. A young man; *f.* -ಸ್ಥಳು, -ಸ್ಥೆ.

ಪ್ರಾಯಶ್ಚಿತ್ತ s. *n.* An expiation, atonement, penance, compensation. 2, the atonement Christ made.

ಪ್ರಾರಬ್ಧ s. *a.* Begun. *n.* Fortune, destiny.

ಪ್ರಾರಂಭ s. *n.* Beginning, commencement. ಪ್ರಾರಂಭಿಸು. To begin; to commence.

ಪ್ರಾರ್ಥನೆ s. n. Requesting, begging; a prayer, entreaty, request, application, petition. 2, a vow. -ಕೂಟ. Prayer-union. -ವಾರ. Prayer-week. -ಮಾಡು, ಪ್ರಾರ್ಥಿಸು. To ask for, beg for; to petition anything; to pray to. ಪ್ರಾರ್ಥಿತ. Requested, asked for, prayed for.

ಪ್ರಾವರಣ s. n. A cover, cloak.

ಪ್ರಾಶನ s. n. Eating, feeding upon, drinking. ಪ್ರಾಶಿತ. Eaten, devoured, drunk. ಪ್ರಾಶ್ಯ. Eatable; edible.

ಪ್ರಾಸ s. n. Alliteration.

ಪ್ರಾಸಂಗಿಕ (fr. ಪ್ರಸಂಗ) s. a. Belonging to any topic, relevant; opportune, seasonable; occasional.

ಪ್ರಾಸಾದ (fr. ಪ್ರಸಾದ) s. n. A temple; a palace.

ಪ್ರಾಹ್ಣ s. n. Forenoon.

ಪ್ರಿಯ s. a. Beloved; dear, valued, amiable, agreeable, desirable; loving, kind, affectionate. 2, dear, high in price. n. Favour, love; a husband, lover; f. ಪ್ರಿಯೆ. -ಕರ. Giving pleasure. -ತಮ. Most beloved; a lover. -ವಾದಿ. One who speaks kindly.

ಪ್ರೀತ s. a. Pleased; joyful; dear.

ಪ್ರೀತಿ s. n. Gratification; satisfaction. 2, grace, favour, kindness; affection, love. -ಮಾಡು. To show affection, to love. -ಇಡು. To bestow love upon; *as* ಅವನಲ್ಲಿ or ಅವನ ಮೇಲೆ ಪ್ರೀತಿ ಇಡು. -ವಂತ, -ಶಾಲಿ. A man full of love. -ಸು. To love.

ಪ್ರೇಕ್ಷೆ s. n. Looking at, viewing; *also* ಪ್ರೇಕ್ಷಣ. 2, a public show. 3, conception, intellect.

ಪ್ರೇತ s. a. Deceased. n. A dead person; a corpse. 2, a ghost. -ಕರ್ಮ. Funeral rites. -ಬಲಿ. Food offered to the departed spirit. -ಸಂಸ್ಕಾರ. The cremation of a corpse.

ಪ್ರೇಮ s. n. Love, affection, kindness. 2, joy; pleasure. -ತೋರಿಸು. To show love. ಪ್ರೇಮಿ. Loving, affectionate; a friend.

ಪ್ರೇರಕ s. n. Urging, impelling, inciting; a pusher.

ಪ್ರೇರಣೆ. = ಪ್ರೇರೇಪಣೆ, q. v.

ಪ್ರೇರಿತ s. a. Driven forwards, impelled, instigated, urged.

ಪ್ರೇರಿಸು. = ಪ್ರೇರೇಪಿಸು, q. v.

ಪ್ರೇರೇಪಣೆ s. n. Pushing on, inciting, urging, instigating; direction; impulse. ಪರಿಶುದ್ಧಾತ್ಮ-. The prompting of the Holy Spirit. ಪ್ರೇರೇಪಿಸು. To persuade, impel, urge on, stimulate, instigate.

ಪ್ರೇಷಣ s. n. Commissioning, ordering, directing.

ಪ್ರೇಷಿತ s. a. Commissioned, sent forth; ordered, directed. n. An apostle.

ಪ್ರೇಷ್ಯ s. n. A male servant; a messenger; f. ಪ್ರೇಷ್ಯೆ.

ಪ್ರೋಗ್ರಾಮು e. n. Programme, an outline of the order of a performance or entertainment.

ಪ್ರೊಟೆಸ್ಟಂಟ e. a. Protesting (*against the doctrines and rites of the Church of Rome*); pertaining to Protestantism. n. A Protestant (*opp. to Roman Catholic*). -ಕ್ರೈಸ್ತ. Protestant Christian. -ಸಭೆ. Protestant church.

ಪ್ರೊಸೀಡಿಂಗ್ಸ್ e. n. Proceedings, course of measures or dealing.

ಪ್ರೋಕ್ತ s. a. Announced, declared, said.

ಪ್ರೋಕ್ಷಣ s. n. Sprinkling with water for purification. 2, killing animals in sacrifice. ಪ್ರೋಕ್ಷಿಸು. To sprinkle.

ಪ್ರೋತ್ಸಾಹ s. n. Great effort, zeal, ardour. 2, stimulus. -ಗೊಳಿಸು, -ಪಡಿಸು. To incite, inspirit, encourage. ಪ್ರೋತ್ಸಾಹಿತ. Stimulated, encouraged.

ಪ್ರೌಢ (= ಪ್ರವೃದ್ಧ) s. a. Grown up, fully developed; mature, adult; proficient; grand, mighty, dignified. -ತನ, -ತೆ. Grandeur; maturity, *etc.;* arrogance. ಪ್ರೌಢಿ. Growth; maturity; elevation, grandeur, pomp; proficiency; self-confidence; zeal, enterprise, exertion. ಪ್ರೌಢಿಕೆ, ಪ್ರೌಢಿಮೆ. Grandeur; proficiency.

ಪ್ಲಕ್ಷ s. n. The waved-leaf fig-tree, *Ficus infectoria.*

ಪ್ಲವ s. n. A float, raft. 2, the thirty-fifth year of the cycle of sixty.

ಪ್ಲವಂಗ s. n. The forty-first year of the cycle of sixty.

ಪ್ಲೀಹ s. n. The spleen. 2, disease of the spleen.

ಪ್ಲುತ s. a. Floating; lengthened, protracted, *as* a vowel. *n.* A long vowel.

ಪ್ಲ್ಯಾನಲ್ e. n. Flannel.

ಫ್

ಫ್. The fortieth letter of the alphabet.

ಫಕಾರ s. n. The letter ಫ.

ಫಕೀರ (= ಪಕೀರ) h. n. A Mahommadan mendicant.

ಫಕ್ಕನೆ. = ಪಕ್ಕನೆ, *q. v.*

ಫಜೀತಿ, ಫಜೀತು h. n. Disgrace; annoyance, harassment.

ಫಡಪೋಸಿ. = ಪಡಪೋಸಿ, *q. v.*

ಫಣಿ s. n. The hood of the cobra. ಫಣಾಮಣಿ. A hood-gem.

ಫಣಿ s. n. A snake; a cobra. -ಧರ. Śiva. -ವೇಣಿ. Braided hair resembling a snake.

ಫನ h. n. Annihilation, ruin.

ಫರಮಾನಾ, ಫರಮಾನಾ h. n. A royal mandate, order; a firman.

ಫರಮಾಯಿಶಿ h. a. Made to order. 2, very excellent.

ಫರಮಾಯಿಸು h. v. t. To order, direct, bid.

ಫರಾಮೋಷಿ h. n. Forgetfulness, oversight; negligence.

ಫರಾರಿ h. a. Absconded or emigrated. 2, (f.) a sail.

ಫಲ s. n. Fruit; a fruit. 2, produce, crop; profit, gain, benefit. 3, offspring. 4, recompense, reward. 5, one's own learning or merits. 6, product, quotient. 7, final liberation. 8, a tablet, board; *also* -ಕ. -ಕಾಲ. The fruit-season. -ಕೊಡು. To yield or produce fruit. ಫಲವಾಗು. Fruit or gain to be produced. -ಹಿಡಿ. To bear fruit. -ದಾನ. A present of fruits. -ದಾಯಕ. One who rewards or retributes (*used of God*). -ಪೂರ್ಣ. Full of fruits. -ಭರಿತ, -ವತ್. Laden with fruits, fruitful. -ಪ್ರಾಪ್ತಿ. Advantage, profit. -ಸಿದ್ಧಿ. A prosperous issue.

ಫಲಕ s. n. A board, plank. 2, a slab, tablet. 3, a shield.

ಫಲಾನ, ಫಲಾನೆ h. *pro.* Such a one.

ಫಲಾಫಲ s. n. Profit and loss.

ಫಲಾಹಾರ (= ಪಲಹಾರ) s. n. Feeding on fruits; a slight repast.

ಫಲಿತ s. a. Bearing fruit. ಫಲಿತಾರ್ಥ. Result.

ಫಲಿಸು s. v. i. Fruit to grow; to grow; to bear fruit, become fruitful; to bear good or bad results; *also* ಫಲ-.

ಫಲೋದಯ s. n. Result, recompense, reward.

ಫಲ್ಗುನ s. n. Arjuna.

ಫಸಲಿ f. n. The official revenue-year.

ಫಸಲು h. n. A crop, harvest.

ಫಾಜಿಲ್ h. n. Excess; surplus or spare; extra.

ಫಾಯಿದಾ h. n. Advantage, profit.

ಫಾಯಿಷ್ h. a. Published, proclaimed, notified.

ಫಾಲ್ಗುನ s. n. N. of the twelfth lunar month.

ಫಿದಿವಿ h. *n.* A servant.

ಫಿರಕ h. *n.* A part, sub-division; a department.

ಫಿರಿಯಾದಿ h. *n.* A complaint, suit. -ದಾರ. A plaintiff, complainant. -ಕೊಡು, -ಮಾಡು. To complain; to file a lawsuit.

ಫುರೋಕ್ತು h. *n.* Sale, selling.

ಫುಲ್ಲ s. *a.* Expanded, blown, *as* a flower; *also* ಫುಲ್ಲಿತ. *n.* A full blown flower.

ಫೇಡಾ, ಫೇಣಿ s. *n.* A kind of sweetmeat like vermicelli.

ಫೇನ s. *n.* Foam, froth. ಫೇನಿಲ. Foamy, frothy; the soap plant, *Sapindus detergens.*

ಫೇರಿಸ್ತು h. *n.* A list, catalogue, roll.

ಫೇಲಿ, ಫೇಲಿಕೆ, ಫೇಲೆ s. *n.* Remnants of food, orts.

ಫೌಜು (= ಪೌಜು, *q. v.*) h. *n.* An army, a body of troops.

ಬ್

ಬ್. The forty-first letter of the alphabet.

ಬಕ s. *n.* A heron, crane. 2, a cheat, rogue. 3, N. of a râkshasa. -ಪುಷ್ಪ. The tree *Sesbana grandiflora.* -ವಿಡಂಬನ. Hypocrisy.

ಬಕರೆ, ಬಕ್ಕರೆ 1. k. *n.* A potsherd.

ಬಕರೆ 2. h. *n.* A goat; *also* ಬಕರಾ.

ಬಕಷಿ (= ಬಕ್ಷಿ) h. *n.* A general; the head of a department. -ಗಿರಿ. His employment.

ಬಕಾರ s. *n.* The letter ಬ.

ಬಕಾಸುರ. = ಬಕ No. 3, *q. v.* 2, a voracious eater.

ಬಕಾಳಭಾತು f. *n.* Rice mixed with curds, butter, and milk.

ಬಕುಳ (= ವಕುಲ) s. *n.* The tree *Mimusops elengi.*

ಬಕ್ಕ, ಬಕ್ಕಟ a. k. *n.* Bareness, voidness.

ಬಕ್ಕರಿ f. *n.* Bread. -ಹಂಚು. A platter for baking bread.

ಬಕ್ಕುದಿ, ಬಕ್ಕುದೆ a. k. *n.* Agitation; amazement; alarm; grief.

ಬಕ್ಕೆ k. *n.* Sweetness, goodness.

ಬಕ್ಷಿ. = ಬಕಷಿ, *q. v.*

ಬಕ್ಷೀಸ್ h. *n.* A present, gift.

ಬಖೇಡಿ h. *n.* Contention; a troublesome business.

ಬಗಬಗ k. *n.* Blazing, crackling of flames. -ನೆ ಉರಿ. To blaze with a crackling noise; to burn, *as* the eyes, *etc.*

ಬಗಟು a. k. *v. i.* To open the legs, to straddle.

ಬಗಡೆ f. *n.* Rice roughly cleaned. 2, a species of pulse. -ಯಕ್ಕಿ. An inferior kind of rice.

ಬಗರ h. *prep.* Without. -ಬತ್ತಿ, -ಬದಲಿ, -ರಜಾ, -ಹುಕುಂ, *etc.* Without—.

ಬಗರನೆ a. k. *n.* A temporary well. 2, a kind of vessel.

ಬಗರಿ (= ಬೊಗರಿ, *q. v.*) f. *n.* A boy's spinning top.

ಬಗರು k. *v. t.* To scratch with the nails or claws.

ಬಗಲ h. *n.* An Arab boat.

ಬಗಲು h. *n.* The armpit; a side. -ಚೀಲ. A bag that is put over the shoulder.

ಬಗಸಿಗೆ, ಬಗಸೆ k. *n.* The palms of the hands joined so as to form a cup.

ಬಗಳು. = ಬಗುಳು, *q. v.*

ಬಗಿ k. *v. t.* To separate; to tear; to scratch. 2, to scrape and remove. ಬಗಿಸು. To cause to scratch or scrape.

ಬಗುಳು (= ಬೊಗಳು, *q. v.*) k. *v. i.* To bark. *n.* Barking.

ಬಗೆ 1. k. *v. t. & i.* To think; to consider, mind, think of; to opine, suppose, conjecture; to know. *P. ps.* ಬಗದು, ಬಗೆದು. *n.* Thought; concern, regard; notion, idea; intention, object, aim; the mind. -ಗುಂದು. To get disappointed. -ಗೆಡು. To be bewildered, confused. -ನೋಽ. To grieve. -ವಡೆ. To think, reflect. -ಹರಿ. One's thought or purpose to proceed without any hindrance.

ಬಗೆ 2. (*cf.* ಬಗಿ) k. *n.* A division, kind, sort; a class, caste; a manner, mode, way. -ಬಗೆ, *rep.* Different or various kinds. -ಹರಿ. To be settled. -ಹರಿಸು. To settle.

ಬಗ್ಗ (*tb. of* ವ್ಯಾಘ್ರ) *n.* A tiger.

ಬಗ್ಗಡ k. *n.* Sediment, dregs, mud, mire.

ಬಗ್ಗನೆ k. *ad.* Quickly.

ಬಗ್ಗರಿ k. *n.* The thorax.

ಬಗ್ಗು 1. a. k. *n.* The crying, cooing, chirping, *etc.*, of birds. ಬಗ್ಗಿಸು. To cry, coo, *etc.*

ಬಗ್ಗು 2. k. *v. i.* To bend, bow; to become submissive. ಬಗ್ಗಿಸು. To bend.

ಬಗ್ಗೆ, ಬಗ್ಗೆಯ (*fr.* ಬಗೆ 1, *n.*) k. *n.* The very thought or purpose. *conj.* On account of, for; with regard to, concerning.

ಬಂಕ (*tb. of* ವಕ್ರ) a. k. *n.* N. 2, a bend; a corner. ಬಂಕು. To be crooked, to bend.

ಬಂಕೆ k. *n.* Gum, glue, resin.

ಬಂಗಡಬಳ್ಳಿ k. *n.* The creeper *Ipomaea biloba*.

ಬಂಗಲೆ h. *n.* A bungalow.

ಬಂಗಾರ (= ಭಂಗಾರ. *tb. of* ಭೃಂಗಾರ) *n.* Gold. -ಕಾಯಿಮರ. The Arnotto tree, *Bixa orellana*. -ದ ಮುಲಾಮು. Gilt.

ಬಂಗಾಳ s. *n.* The country Bengal. ಬಂಗಾಳಿ. A Bengalee. ಬಂಗಾಳಿತನ, -ವಿದ್ಯೆ. Trickery.

ಬಂಗಿ 1. (*tb. of* ಭಂಗಿ, *q. v.*) *n.* Appearance; likeness, similarity.

ಬಂಗಿ 2. (*tb. of* ಭಂಗೆ) *n.* Hemp; a potion prepared from it. 2, a crazy person, crack.

ಬಂಗು f. *n.* A disease of the skin.

ಬಚಾವು h. *n.* Protection; deliverance, escape.

ಬಚ್ಚ (*tb. of* ವತ್ಸ) *n.* A young one; a boy. -ಕಾಸೆ. A cloth for boys.

ಬಚ್ಚಲು k. *n.* A drain from the bathroom; the bathing room. -ಕುಣಿ. The bathroom pit. -ಕೋಣೆ, -ಮನೆ. A bathroom.

ಬಚ್ಚಲೆ (ಬಸಲೆ) k. *n.* Spinage. -ಬಳ್ಳಿ. A small annual plant, *Portulaca quadrifida*.

ಬಚ್ಚು 1. ಬಚ್ಚಿಡು k. *v. t.* To deposit; to put aside, conceal, hide, cover.

ಬಚ್ಚು 2. k. *v. i.* To grow lean.

ಬಜಂತರಿ h. *n.* A musical instrument. 2, a bajantari-player.

ಬಜಾಯಿಸು h. *v. t.* To beat, play a musical instrument. 2, to achieve, execute. ಬಜಾವಣೆ. A musical performance.

ಬಜಾರ, ಬಜಾರು h. *n.* A market; the business of a market. ಬಜಾರಿ. Relating to a market; low, disreputable.

ಬಜೆ (*tb. of* ವಚೆ) *n.* An aromatic water-plant, *Acorus calamus*.

ಬಜ್ಜರ. *tb. of* ವಜ್ರ, *q. v.*

ಬಜ್ಜಿ (*tb. of* ಭ್ರಜ್ಜ) *n.* A čaṭni made of roasted brinjals, chillis, *etc.*

ಬಂಜರು h. *n.* Waste land. -ಬೀಳು. To become waste. -ಭೂಮಿ. = ಬಂಜರು.

ಬಂಜೆ (*tb. of* ವಂಧ್ಯೆ) *n.* A childless woman. 2, barrenness, sterility. -ಆಗು. To become barren, unproductive. -ತನ. Barrenness.

ಬಟ (*tb. of* ಭಟ) *n.* A brave warrior. -ತನ. Bravery, valour. -ಮಾನ್ಯ. A free land granted to a Brâhmaṇa.

ಬಟವೆ f. *n.* A draw-purse.

ಬಟಾ (= ಬಟ್ಟ) k. *a.* Void, empty. -ಬಯಲು. A wide, open plain; emptiness.

ಬಟವಾಡೆ h. *n.* Distributing of wages.

ಬಟಾಟೆ e. *n.* A potato.

ಬಟಾಣಿ h. *n.* The common pea, *Pisum sativum*.

ಬಟುವು (*tb.* *of* ವೃತ್ತ) *n.* Roundness; a circle.

ಬಟ್ಟ 1. (=ಬಕ್ಕ, ಬಕ್ಕಟ) k. *n.* Bareness, voidness. -ತಲೆ. A bald head. -ಬಯಲು. = ಬಟಾಬಯಲು. -ನೆ. Whirlingly.

ಬಟ್ಟ 2. (*tb.* of ವೃತ್ತ) *n.* A circle, disk; that is uniform, regular or beautiful. 2, a circular mark on the forehead. *a.* Round, circular. -ಕುದುರೆ. A chestnut horse. -ಗಡಲೆ. The round pea. -ಗೆ. Roundness. -ಗಿವಿ, -ದಲೆ, -ದೆನೆ, -ವುುತ್ತು, -ಮೊಗ, *etc.* A round—. ಬಟ್ಟನ್ನ. Round, circular.

ಬಟ್ಟ 3. (*tb.* *of* ಭಟ್ಟ) *n.* A learned Brâhmaṇa. 2, a pûjâri. 3, a panegyrist, bard.

ಬಟ್ಟಲು (*tb.* *of* ವರ್ತುಲ) *n.* A bowl, cup, basin, goblet.

ಬಟ್ಟಿ 1. k. *n.* A rupture, hernia.

ಬಟ್ಟಿ 2. h. *n.* A kiln, furnace; a spirit-still. -ಇಳಿಸು. To distil.

ಬಟ್ಟು. = ಬಟ್ಟ 2, *q. v.* 2, a round thing used for weighing.

ಬಟ್ಟೆ 1. (*tb.* *of* ವಾಟ) *n.* A path, road, way. -ಗಾಣು. To see a way. -ಗೆಡು. To lose the way.

ಬಟ್ಟೆ 2. (*tb.* *of* ವಸ್ತ್ರ) *n.* Cloth.

ಬಟ್ಲು. = ಬಟ್ಟಲು, *q. v.*

ಬಡ k. *n.* Poorness; weakness; miserableness; humbleness. *a.* Poor, weak; miserable; humble. *Cpds.:* -ಕುಟುಂಬ, -ಕೆಲಸ, -ಗಿತ, -ದನ, -ನಂಟ, -ಪಾಪಿ, -ಬಗ್ಗ, -ಮಂದಿ, *etc.* -ವ. A poor, miserable, weak man; *f.* -ವಳು, -ವೆ. -ತನ, -ಸ್ತನ, -ಸ್ತಿಕೆ. Thinness; poverty. -ಕ, -ಕಲ. A thin, feeble male. -ಕಲು. Weakness, thinness.

ಬಡಗ, ಬಡಗು k. *n.* The north. *ad.* In the north.

ಬಡಗಿ (=ಬಡಾಯಿ, ಬಡಿಗ, ಬಡಿಗಿ, *q. v.* *tb.* *of* ವರ್ಧಕಿ) *n.* A carpenter. -ತನ. Carpentry.

ಬಡತ (=ಬಡಿತ) k. *n.* Beating; a stroke, blow.

ಬಡಬಡ f. *n.* Gabble, prate. -ಮಾತಾಡು. To gabble, prate, babble.

ಬಡಬಾಗ್ನಿ, ಬಡಬಾನಲ. = ವಡವಾಗ್ನಿ, *q. v.*

ಬಡಾಯಿ 1. = ಬಡಗಿ, *q. v.*

ಬಡಾಯಿ 2. h. *n.* Greatness, vain pomp; bragging. -ಖೋರ, -ಗಾರ. A braggart. -ಸು. To become great; to grow; to increase.

ಬಡಿ (=ಬಡೆ) k. *v. t.* To beat, strike, thresh, bang. 2, to sweep away. *n.* Beating; a blow. -ಕೆ. Beating, *etc.*; trouble, *as* that of old age. -ಗ. One who serves up as a meal; one who beats. -ದಾಟ. Fighting, wrangling. -ದಾಡು. To fight, wrangle. -ಗಲ್ಲು. A stone-trap. -ಮಣೆ. A levelling plank. -ಹೋರಿ. A gelded bull.

ಬಡಿಗ, ಬಡಿಗಿ. = ಬಡಗಿ, *q. v.*

ಬಡಿಗೆ k. *n.* A stick, staff, cudgel.

ಬಡಿತ. = ಬಡತ, *q. v.*

ಬಡಿವಾರ f. *n.* Brag, bragging.

ಬಡಿಸು k. *v. t.* To help at meals, serve up or out. 2, to cause to beat, *etc.*

ಬಡೆ 1. = ಬಡಿ, *q. v.* *P. ps.* ಬಡದು, ಬಡೆದು. ಬಡೆದಾಟ. = ಬಡಿದಾಟ. ಬಡೆದಾಡು. = ಬಡಿದಾಡು.

ಬಡೆ 2. k. *n.* A stick, pole.

ಬಡೆ 3. h. *a.* Great, big. -ಸೋಪು. Aniseseed.

ಬಡ್ಡ k. *n.* A blunt, dull fellow.

ಬಡ್ಡಿ (*tb.* *of* ವೃದ್ಧಿ) *n.* Interest on money; usury. -ಏರು, -ಬೆಳೆಯು. Interest to increase. -ಕೊಡು, -ಗೆ ಕೊಡು. To lend money on interest. -ತೀರಿಸು. To pay interest. -ಹಿಡಿಯು. To charge interest.

ಬಡ್ಡು k. *n.* Barrenness, vainness; bluntness; dullness. -ಅರಸು, -ಕತ್ತಿ, -ಕುದುರೆ, -ಮನುಷ್ಯ, -ಹಸು. A dull, stupid —.

ಬಣಗು a. k. *n.* A wretch; a poor person. -ಕವಿ, -ತಪಸಿ, -ದೈವ, -ಭಕ್ತ, -ಮಾನವ. A poor, wretched—. -ತನ. Wretchedness.

ಬಣಜಿಗ, ಬಣಜಿಗ (*tb.* *of* ವಣಿಜಕ) *n.* A merchant: a merchant caste. -ತನ, ಬಣಜತನ. Trade, traffic.

ಬಣಬೆ, ಬಣಂಬೆ, ಬಣವೆ, ಬಣೆವೆ k. n. A stack, rick.

ಬಂಟ 1. (*tb. of* ವಂಠ) *n.* A servant. -ತನ. Servitude.

ಬಂಟ 2. (=ಬಟ. *tb. of* ಭಟ) *n.* A warrior, soldier; a hero. 2, the farmer-caste of the Tuḷu country.

ಬಂಡ 1. k. *n.* Wool.

ಬಂಡ 2. (*fr.* ಬಂಡು) f. *n.* A shameless, dishonourable, profligate man. -ತನ. Shamelessness, profligacy.

ಬಂಡ 3. (=ವಂಡ) s. *a.* Maimed, defective; impotent. *n.* A tailless ox.

ಬಂಡ 4. (*tb. of* ಭಾಂಡ) *n.* Capital, property; wealth.

ಬಂಡಣ (*tb. of* ಭಂಡನ) *n.* A battle; war.

ಬಂಡವಲ, ಬಂಡವಾಲ, ಬಂಡವಾಳ (*tb. of* ಭಾಂಡ) *n.* Capital, funds; stock, store; *cf.* ಬಂಡ 4.

ಬಂಡಾಯ, ಬಂಡಾಯಿ f. *n.* Quarrelling; revolt.

ಬಂಡಾರ. = ಭಂಡಾರ, *q. v.*

ಬಂಡಿ k. *n.* A wheel. 2, a bandy, cart, carriage. -ಯವ, -ಯಾಳು. A driver, cartman.

ಬಂಡು 1. a. k. *n.* Honey. 2, the pollen of flowers.

ಬಂಡು 2. (=ಬಂಡ 2) f. *n.* Shamelessness, impudence, obscenity, lewdness. 2, awkwardness, trouble, disgrace. ಬಂಡಾಟ. A disgraceful position; a very awkward or troublesome affair, *etc.* -ಚಿತ್ರ, -ಪದ, -ಬಾಳು, -ಮಾತು. A shameless or obscene—. -ತನ. = ಬಂಡತನ, *q. v.*

ಬಂಡೆ k. *n.* A rock, block or slab of stone.

ಬಣ್ಣ (*tb. of* ವರ್ಣ) *n.* Colour, paint. -ಹಚ್ಚು, -ಹಿಡು, -ಹಾಕು. To dye, paint. -ಏರು. To become brighter. -ಕಟ್ಟು. To fix a colour. -ಗಾರ. A dyer; a painter. -ಣೆ. = ವರ್ಣನೆ, *q. v.* -ಸರ. A necklace of gold beads, corals, *etc.*

ಬಣ್ಣಿಸು (*tb. of* ವರ್ಣಿಸು) *v. t.* To colour, paint. 2, to describe.

ಬಟನ್ e. *n.* A button; a knob to fasten the dress.

ಬತ್ತ 1. (=ಭತ್ತ) f. *n.* Paddy, rice in the husk. -ಭರಣ. Paddy and other articles of food.

ಬತ್ತ 2. h. *n.* Batta, an allowance beyond pay, extra allowance.

ಬತ್ತಲು (*fr.* ಬತ್ತು) k. *n.* Dried fruit.

ಬತ್ತಲೆ (= ಬೆತ್ತಲೆ) k. *n.* Bareness, nakedness.

ಬತ್ತಳಿಕೆ (= ಪತ್ತಳಿಕೆ, *q. v.*) f. *n.* A quiver.

ಬತಾಸು h. *n.* A kind of sweetmeat.

ಬತ್ತಿ (*tb. of* ವರ್ತಿ) *n.* A wick, the wick of a lamp; a candle; a cigar. -ಕೊಡು. To cheat. -ಸೇದು. To smoke a cigar.

ಬತ್ತು k. *v. i.* To grow dry, *as* a stream; to dry up, *as* water; to grow lean, to fade, wither. *n.* Drying up, *etc.*

ಬತ್ತೇರಿ e. *n.* A battery.

ಬತ್ಲರ್ e. *n.* A butler: a servant who has charge of the table.

ಬದ. = ಬದುವು, *q. v.*

ಬದಕು. = ಬದುಕು, *q. v.*

ಬದಗು k. *n.* Drudgery. ಬದಗ. A servant.

ಬದನಾಮಿ h. *n.* Ignominy, infamy.

ಬದನೆ k. *n.* The brinjal or egg-plant, *Solanum melongena.*

ಬದರಿ s. *n.* The jujube tree, *Jizyphus jujuba.* 2, the cotton plant. -ಕಾಶ್ರಮ. N. of a hermitage in the Himâlaya.

ಬದರಿಕೆ h. *n.* A convoy, guard on the road.

ಬದಲು h. *n.* Changing; change; alteration; exchange; retaliation. *a.* Other. *ad.* Instead of. ಬದಲಾಗು. To change, be changed. -ಕೊಡು. To give in exchange or as a substitute. -ಮಾಡು. To change, alter. -ಮಾತು. A word in reply; a contradiction. -ಹೇಳು. To reply. ಬದಲಾಬದಲಿ, ಬದಲಾವಣೆ. Exchange, interchange. ಬದಲಾಯಿಸು, ಬದಲಿಸು. To change; to alter, make differ. ಬದಲಿ. A substitute.

ಬದಿ 1. h. *n.* Mud, mire, slush.

ಬದಿ 2. k. n. The side, flank; nearness, vicinity. ಬದಿಗೆ ಮಾಡು. To put to one side. -ಎಲು. A rib.

ಬದುಕು (= ಬದಕು) k. v. i. To live, be alive; to subsist; to live by; to revive, return to life. n. Leaving, life; livelihood; property, things, goods. -ಬಾಳು. dpl. -ಮಾಡು. To carry on a business. ಬದುಕಿಸು. To cause to live or subsist; to save from death; to bring to life.

ಬದುವು (= ಬದ) k. n. A raised bank in fields, a low ridge.

ಬದ್ಧ (tb. of ಬದ್ಧ, q. v.) a. Firm, true. ad. Firmly, certainly.

ಬದ್ದಿಕೆ (tb. of ಬಂಧಕ) n. A band, tie. 2, comparing anything with a standard, as weights, etc. ಬದ್ದಿಸು. To compare anything with a standard; to be bound or obstructed.

ಬದ್ದು f. n. A hole in the ground into which children play marbles.

ಬದ್ಧ (= ಬದ್ದ) s. a. Bound, tied, fastened; fettered, checked, connected, confined; constructed, firm, true. -ಪ್ರಕೃತಿ. A constitution subject to costiveness. -ಮುಷ್ಟಿ. Close-fisted; covetous, miserly. -ವಿರುದ್ಧ, -ವೈರ. Deadly hatred.

ಬಧಿರ s. a. Deaf. -ತ್ವ. Deafness.

ಬನ. tb. of ವನ, q. v.

ಬನಪು k. n. A large timber tree, *Terminalia tomentosa*.

ಬನಾತು h. n. Broad-cloth, woollen.

ಬನಾಯಿಸು h. v. t. To make, fabricate. ಬನಾವಣೆ, ಬನಾವು. Making, bringing about. 2, mutual agreement.

ಬನಿ h. n. Substance, as of grain, milk, etc.

ಬನಿಯನ್ h. n. A waistcoat with short sleeves.

ಬಂತು k. (3rd pers. sing. neut. past of ಬರು) v. i. It came.

ಬಂತೆ. = ಬೊಂತೆ, q. v.

ಬಂದ (tb. of ಬಂಧ, q. v.) n. A bond, etc. -ಕಟ್ಟು. Moderateness; caste-rules; security. -ಮಾರ. The wild mangosteen.

ಬಂದಗಿ h. n. Slavery.

ಬಂದಣಿಕೆ (tb. of ವಂದಾಕ) n. The parasitical plant *Epidendrum tesselatum*.

ಬಂದನೆ. tb. of ಬಂಧನೆ, q. v.

ಬಂದರ h. n. A port; a port-town; a landing place.

ಬಂದಿ s. n. A captive or prisoner. 2, an obstacle; stop; confinement. 3, a tie; an armlet; a neck-ornament of females. 4, plunder, booty. -ಯವ, -ವಾನ. A prisoner. -ಖಾನೆ. A prison.

ಬಂದು (tb. of ಬಂಧ) n. Any tie, bond, fetter; confinement. -ಕಟ್ಟು. Well regulated or compact state. -ಮಾಡು. To close, shut.

ಬಂದೂಕು h. n. A musket; a matchlock.

ಬಂದೋಬಸ್ತಿ, ಬಂದೋಬಸ್ತು h. n. Settlement; well-ordered or firm condition; order; security, safety.

ಬಂಧ (= ಬಂದ, ಬಂದು) s. n. Binding; a bond, tie, chain, fetter; imprisonment, check; agreement; a border. -ಕ. A binder; hindrance; a pledge. -ನ. Binding, fastening; confinement, bondage, imprisonment; a bond, chain, fetter. ಬಂಧಿಸು. To bind, tie, fetter, confine; to bind on one's self; to connect; to inflict punishment, chastise.

ಬಂಧು s. n. Connection, relationship. 2, a kinsman, relation, relative. 3, a friend. -ಜನ. Kinsfolk, relations. -ತೆ, -ತ್ವ. Relationship, affinity. -ವರ್ಗ. Kinsfolk.

ಬಂಧುರ s. a. Uneven, wavy. 2, bent, crooked. 3, pleasing, beautiful. n. A goose.

ಬಂಧ್ಯ. = ವಂಧ್ಯ, q. v.

ಬನ್ನ (tb. of ಭಂಗ, q. v.) n. Sufferings, etc. -ಬಡಿಸು. To cause to suffer discomfiture. -ಬಡು. To suffer ruin.

ಬನ್ನಿ 1. Imp. pl. of ಬರು, q. v.

ಬನ್ನಿ 2. k. n. A prickly tree, *Acacia ferruginea*.

ಬಬ್ಬೂಳ (*tb. of* ಬಬೂರ) n. The thorny Babool tree, *Acacia arabica*.

ಬಭ್ರು s. a. Brown. n. A large kind of mungoose. -ವಾಹನ. N. of a son of Arjuna.

ಬಂಪು k. n. A vegetable mucilage used as soap.

ಬಂಬಲ್ a. k. n. A heap, mass, swarm.

ಬಂಬು k. n. A hollow bamboo.

ಬಯ್ 1. (=ಬಯ್ಯು) k. n. The evening. -ತನಕ. Till evening. -ಸಾರಿ. Evening time.

ಬಯ್ 2. = ಬಯ್ಯು, *q. v.*

ಬಯಕೆ (=ಬಯಿಕೆ) k. n. Longing, wish, desire, hope; a desired object. 2, a deposit, trust.

ಬಯಲು, ಬಯ್ಲು k. n. An open space, field or plain. 2, publicity, conspicuousness, distinction; a vacuity; disappearance; vanity; uselessness. ಬಯಲಾಗು, ಬಯಲಿಗೆ ಬರು, ಬಯಲಿಗೆ ಬೀಳು. To come to light; to become public; to become fruitless. -ಪಡಿಸು, ಬಯಲಿಗೆ ಹಾಕು. To make public; ot show. -ಕಡೆ. A public privy. -ಭೂಮಿ. An open plain; a public privy. -ಸೀಮೆ. An open country, a plain.

ಬಯಸು, ಬಯಿಸು k. v. t. To desire, wish; to long for. -ವಿಕೆ. Desiring.

ಬಯಿ k. n. An open spot, a parting. 2, = ಬಯ್ಯು. -ತಲೆ. Parting of the hair between the sides of the head.

ಬಯಿಕೆ, ಬಯ್ಕೆ. = ಬಯಕೆ, *q. v.*

ಬಯ್ಯು (=ಬಯ್ 1) k. n. The evening, evening-twilight.

ಬಯ್ನೆ k. n. The bastard sago tree, *Caryota urens*.

ಬಯ್ಯು k. v. t. To abuse, revile; to use bad language. ಬಯ್ದಾಡು. = ಬಯ್ಯು. ಬಯ್ಗುಳು. Reviling, abuse, bad language, cursing.

ಬಯ್ರಿಗೆ f. n. A kind of gimlet.

ಬಯ್ಲು. = ಬಯಲು, *q. v.*

ಬರ 1. (ರ=ಱ) k. n. Dryness; dearth, famine, drought; scarcity; hollowness; ruin. -ಗಾಲ. A time of famine. -ಬರು, -ಬೀಳು, -ಏರು. A famine to happen.

ಬರ 2. (*tb. of* ವರ) n. Limit. *ad.* Up to, till.

ಬರ 3. = ಬರದು, ಬರೆದು. *P. p. of* ಬರೆ, *as in* ಬರಕೊಳ್ಳು. -ವಣಿಗೆ. Writing. -ಹಕೆ, -ಹ. Writing; writ, scripture, written letters.

ಬರಕತ್ತು h. n. Success; successfulness; overplus.

ಬರಖಾಸ್ತು h. a. Risen, broken up, *as* an assembly.

ಬರಗು k. n. A kind of grain, *Paspalum frumentaceum*. 2, a kind of hill-grass used for writing pens. 3, Indian millet.

ಬರಟಿ (ರ=ಱ) k. n. Dried cow-dung.

ಬರಡು (ರ=ಱ) k. n. Bareness; vainness; barrenness; dullness. -ಕೆಲಸ. Useless work. ಬರಡ. A useless man. ಬರಡೆಮ್ಮೆ. A barren buffalo.

ಬರಣಿ f. n. A small box, casket, China jar.

ಬರತರಫ h. a. Dismissed, discharged. n. Dismissal.

ಬರತಿ. *tb. of* ಭರ್ತಿ, *q. v.*

ಬರದು. = ಬರೆದು. *P. p. of* ಬರೆ, *q. v.*

ಬರಲು (ಬಱಲ್) k. n. A broom. 2, (ರ=ಱ) bareness. -ಮಾಡು. To make bare, *as* trees.

ಬರವಸ. = ಭರವಸ, *q. v.*

ಬರಾಬರ್ h. a. Equal; correct; proper, fit. ಬರಾಬರಿ. Equality; evenness.

ಬರಾಯಿಸು h. v. t. To fill or enter (items into a book).

ಬರಾವರ್ದ್ h. n. A monthly statement of payable amounts. 2, a list of public servants.

ಬರಿ 1. k. n. The side flank.

ಬರಿ 2. = ಬರೆ, *q. v.*

ಬರಿ 3. (ರಿ=ಱಿ) k. n. Bareness; nakedness; emptiness; soleness; worthlessness, uselessness. -ಕಷ್ಟ. Nothing but trouble. -ಕೊಬ್ಬು. Nothing but fat. -ಗಂಟು. An empty bundle. -ಗಾಲು. A naked foot. ಬರಿದು, ಬರಿದು. Empty, vain, idle. -ದು ಮಾಡು. To empty, *as* a box. ಬರಿದೆ. Vainly, for nothing, idly. -ಕರ್ಮ. Mere sin. -ಗುಲ್ಲು. A useless noise. -ಬಾಯಿ. A person who only speaks but does not act. -ಮಾತು. Mere words. -ಮಾಯೆ. Nothing but tricks. -ಸುಳ್ಳ. A barefaced liar. -ಹೊಟ್ಟೆ. An empty stomach.

ಬರಿಸು k. *v. t.* To cause to come, *etc.* 2, to cause to write.

ಬರು k. *v. i.* To come; to arrive. 2, to accrue, fall to one's share; to come into and be in the possession of; to become an acquisition. 3, to be a matter of possibility. 4, to be under control. 5, to be becoming, fit, suitable, useful, proper, or advisable; to be allowed. 6, to suffice for. *P. p.* ಬಂದು. *Imp.* ಬಾ; *pl.* ಬನ್ನಿ, ಬನ್ನಿರಿ, ಬರ್ರಿ. *rel. part.* ಬರುವ, ಬರ್ಪ, ಬಪ್ಪ, ಬಹ. ಬರಗೊಡು. To allow to come. ಬರ ಬರ. More and more, in course of time. ಬರಬರುತ್ತ. In course of time, by and by, *etc.* ಬರಮಾಡು. To make come; to recover, *as* money, *etc.* ಬರೋಣ. Coming, arrival. ಬಂದು ಹೋಗು. To come and go. ಬರುತ್ತಾ ಬರುತ್ತಾ. = ಬರಬರುತ್ತಾ. -ವಿಕೆ, ಬರವು. = ಬರೋಣ. *Neg.* ಬಾರದ, ಬಾರದೆ.

ಬರೆ 1. (= ಬರಿ) k. *v. t.* To write, draw. *P. p.* ಬರದು, ಬರೆದು.

ಬರೆ 2. = ಬರಿ 3, *q. v.* 2, dry soil. -ನೂಲು, -ನೆರೆ, -ಪೆಟ್ಟಿಗೆ, -ಬಯ್ಯು, -ಮಾತು, -ಹಾಲು. A mere —.

ಬರ್ಚಿ h. *n.* A sort of spear.

ಬರ್ದು a. k. *v. i.* To die. *n.* Death. 2, increase, greatness; skill. -ಗ. A proficient man. -ಗೆ. Death.

ಬರ್ಫ h. *n.* Snow; hoar-frost; ice.

ಬರ್ಬರ s. *n.* A man of low origin, a non-Ârya, barbarian. 2, the thorny Babool tree.

ಬಬ್ಬೂರ (= ಬಬ್ಬುಳ) s. *n.* The thorny Babool tree.

ಬರ್ಮ (*tb. of* ಬ್ರಹ್ಮ) *n.* Burma.

ಬಲುಱ. = ಬರಲು, *q. v.*

ಬರ್ಹಿ s. *n.* A peacock; *also* -ಣ. -ಷ್ಠ. A species of fragrant grass, *Andropogon muricatus;* the resin of *Pinus longifolia.*

ಬಲ್ (= ಬಲು, *q. v.*) a. k. *n.* Strength, firmness, greatness. *Cpds.:* -ಅಡವಿ, -ಎತ್ತು, -ಗತ್ತಲೆ, -ಗಿಡ್ಡ, -ಗೆಯ್, -ಬಂಡಿ, -ಬರ, -ಬಲ, -ಬಿಸಿ, -ಮನೆ, -ಮರ, -ಮರೆ, -ಮುಡಿ, -ಮೊನೆ, -ಸೋನೆ, *etc.* -ಬಂಟ, ಬಲ್ಲಳ, ಬಲ್ಲಾಳ. A very valorous man. ಬಲ್ಲಾಳ್ತನ. Great valour.

ಬಲ 1. k. *n.* The right (not the left), right side. *Cpds.:* -ಕಡೆ, -ಗಣ್ಣು, -ಗಾಲು, -ಗೆಯ್, -ತೊಡೆ, -ಪಂಕ, -ಭಾಗ.

ಬಲ 2. s. *n.* Power, strength, might, vigour; force. 2, violence, severity; daring. 3, help, influence. 4, bulkiness. 5, forces, troops, an army. 6, body, form. -ಕರ. Strengthening. -ಗಾರ. A powerful man. -ಗುಂದು. To decrease in strength. -ಗೊಳ್ಳು. To get strength. -ಕಾಯಿಸು, -ಗೊಳಿಸು, -ಪಡಿಸು. To strengthen. -ದೇವ, -ಭದ್ರ, -ರಾಮ. N. of Kṛishṇa's elder brother. -ರಾಕ್ಷಸಿ. An under-shrub, *Pavonia odorata.* -ವಂತ. A powerful, mighty man; force, violence. -ಶಾಲಿ. Strong, vigorous. -ಹೀನ. Weak, infirm. -ಹೀನತೆ, -ಹೀನತ್ವ. Weakness, infirmity. ಬಲಾಢ್ಯ. Strong, powerful. ಬಲಾತ್ಕಾರ. Doing anything by force; force, violence; compulsion. ಬಲಾತ್ಕಾರ ಮಾಡು, ಬಲಾತ್ಕರಿಸು. To do by force, act with violence; to compel. ಬಲಾಬಲ. Strength and weakness; relative; importance and insignificance. ಬಲಿಷ್ಠ. Very strong or powerful.

ಬಲಿ 1. (*cf.* ಬಲ್) k. *v. i.* To increase, grow; to become abundant, strong, big, tight, or full grown. *v. t.* To increase, strengthen, *etc.* *P. ps.* ಬಲಿದು, ಬಲಿತು.

ಬಲಿ 2. s. n. Tax, tribute. 2, an oblation or religious offering. 3, boiled rice. 4, N. of a daitya. 5, a soldier. 6, a crow. -ಇಕ್ಕು, -ಕೊಡು. To present a bali; to sacrifice. -ಗಲ್ಲು. A stone on which a bali is kept. -ತಿನ್ನು. To eat a bali. -ಹಾಕು. To offer a bali. -ಪೀಠ. An altar.

ಬಲು (=ಬಲ್, q. v.) k. n. Strength, firmness, greatness, etc. *Cpds.:* -ಕಲಹ, -ಗುದ್ದು, -ಗೆಲಸ, -ಗೋಪ, -ಜಾಣ, -ತಂತ್ರ, -ದರ್ಪ, -ದೈನ್ಯ, -ಧನ, -ನುಡಿ, -ಬೊಬ್ಬೆ, -ಯೋಚನೆ, -ಸಂತೋಷ, -ಹಾನಿ, *etc.* -ಮೆ, -ಹು. Strength, power, vigour, ability; firmness; force, violence, compulsion; *also* ಬಲ್ಮೆ.

ಬಲೆ k. n. A net. -ಗಾರ. A fisherman.

ಬಲ್ಯ. = ಬಲ್ಲೆ, *q. v.*

ಬಲ್ಲ k. n. A man who possesses ability, skill or erudition; a man who knows. 2, (*used as a rel. pres. p.*) knowiug, *etc.* -ವ, ಬಲ್ಲಾತ. A man who knows. -ತನ, -ಂದ, -ವಿಕೆ. Ability, knowledge; good sense. ಬಲ್ಲಿದ. A man who is strong, able or clever. ಬಲ್ಲೆ. I know.

ಬಲ್ಲೆ, ಬಲ್ಲೆಯ f. n. A spear, lance, javelin.

ಬವ s. n. The first karaṇa of the day.

ಬವಕೆ. = ಬಯಕೆ, *q. v.*

ಬವಣೆ, ಬವಳಿ (*tb. of* ಭ್ರಮಣಿ) n. Vertigo; confusion.

ಬವನಾಸಿ f. n. A mendicant's vessel for receiving alms.

ಬವರ f. n. Battle, war. 2, *tb. of* ಭ್ರಮರ. ಬವರಿಗ. A warrior.

ಬವರಿ (*tb. of* ಭ್ರಮರಿ) n. Turning, swinging; revolving. -ಸು. To move about.

ಬವರು. = ಬೆವರು, *q. v.*

ಬಸದಿ (= ಬಸ್ತಿ. *tb. of* ವಸತಿ) n. A Jaina temple.

ಬಸರಿ k. n. The waved-leaved fig-tree, *Ficus infectoria.*

ಬಸರು. = ಬಸುರು, *q. v.*

ಬಸಲೆ (= ಬಸಳೆ) k. n. The plant *Basella cordifolia.* 2, the plant *Basella lucida.*

ಬಸವ (*tb. of* ವೃಷಭ) n. A bull; its stone-image worshipped by the Lingâytas; Basava. 2, N. of the founder of the Lingâyta sect. 3, a shameless fellow; *f.* ಬಸವಿ. ಬಸವನ (ಕೊಂಬಿನ or ಕೋಡಿನ) ಹುಳ. A snail. ಬಸವೇಶ್ವರ. The bull on which Śiva rides; its stone-image; the founder of the Lingâyta sect.

ಬಸಳೆ (= ಬಸಲೆ) k. n. The Malabar nightshade, *Basella alba.*

ಬಸಿ k. v. i. To drip, trickle, ooze. v. t. To pour off the water from boiled rice; *etc.;* to strain. *P. ps.* ಬಸಿದು, ಬಸ್ತು. ಬಸ್ತ ಗಂಜಿ, ಬಸ್ತ ಸಾರು. Conjee or broth strained from boiled rice or vegetables.

ಬಸುಮ. *tb. of* ಭಸ್ಮ, *q. v.*

ಬಸುರು (= ಬಸರು. ರು = ಱು) k. n. The belly; the womb; pregnancy. -ಕುತ್ತು. Diarrhœa. ಬಸುರಾಗು. To be pregnant. ಬಸುರಿ. A pregnant woman.

ಬಸೆ (*tb. of* ವಶೆ) n. A barren cow. 2, (*tb. of* ವಸೆ) fat. 3, (k.) a stubble.

ಬಸ್ತಿ. = ಬಸದಿ, *q. v.*

ಬಸ್ತು h. n. A bale of goods; a packet of letters.

ಬಹ a. k. *Pres. rel. part. of* ಬರು. ಬಹುದು (= ಬರುವದು). It will come, *etc.;* it is possible, permitted; it may, *etc.*

ಬಹನೆ h. n. A false plea, pretext.

ಬಹಲಿ, ಬಹಲು h. n. Establishment in an office. -ಬರತರಫ. Appointment and dismissal.

ಬಹಳ (= ಬಾಳ. *tb. of* ಬಹುಲ) a. Abundant, copious, much, many. n. Abundance. -ಮಾಡಿ. Usually; likely, probably; almost, nearly.

ಬಹಾದೂರ್ h. n. A title of honour given to the nobles of the court or to persons of respectable station.

ಬಹಿರ್ s. *ad.* Out, outside; out-of-doors; except, apart; *also* ಬಹಿಸ್. ಬಹಿರಂಗ. The outside; publicity; notoriety. ಬಹಿರಂಗಕ್ಕೆ ತರು, ಬಹಿರಂಗ ಪಡಿಸು, -ಮಾಡು. To make public or known. ಬಹಿರಂಗ

ವಾಗು. To become public. -ದೇಶೆ, -ಭೂಮಿ. A public necessary; voiding excrement. -ಮುಖ. Indifferent to, averse from. -ವಾಸ. An upper garment. ಬಹಿಷ್ಕರಿಸು. To expel; to excommunicate. ಬಹಿಷ್ಕಾರ. Expulsion, exclusion (from caste, *etc.*), excommunication.

ಬಹು s. *a.* Much, abundant; many; large, great, mighty. -ತರ. More, very numerous; for the greater part, chiefly, frequently, often. -ತೇಕ. Many a one, several. -ತ್ವ. Abundance; plurality, majority. -ಧಾನ್ಯ. The twelfth year in the cycle of sixty. -ನಾಯಕತ್ವ. Polyarchy. -ಪಾದ. The Indian fig-tree. -ಭಾಷಣ. Talkativeness, garrulity. -ಭಾಷಿ. A great talker. -ಮಾನ. Respectability, dignity; great respect or regard for; honourable reception; a present. -ಮೂತ್ರ. Diabetes. -ವಚನ. The plural number. -ವರ್ಣ. Many coloured. -ವಿಧ. Manifold, various. -ವ್ರೀಹಿ. A relative or adjective compound.

ಬಹುದು (*fr.* ಬಹ) k. *d. v.* It is possible; it is becoming, fit, suitable, or advisable; it is allowed; it may (one may), *e. g.* ಓದ-, ಬರ-, ಮಾಡ-, ಹೇಳ-, ಹೋಗ-, *etc.*

ಬಹುಲ, ಬಹುಳ s. *a.* Abundant, manifold, many; frequent. 2, spacious; ample; comprehensive. *n.* Abundance, frequency; *also* -ತೆ, -ತ್ವ. 2, the dark fortnight of a lunar month.

ಬಹುಶ, ಬಹುಶಾ (*tb. of* ಬಹುಶಸ್) *ad.* Much, generally speaking, for the most part.

ಬಳಕು. = ಬಳುಕು, *q. v.*

ಬಳಕೆ (= ಬಳಿಕೆ. ಳ = ಱ) k. *n.* Use; custom, practice; exercise; familiarity, familiar intercourse.

ಬಳಗ k. *n.* A multitude, troop, *etc.* 2, the family circle, relations.

ಬಳಚು (ಳ = ಱ) k. *v. t.* To cause to smear (a floor, *etc.*, with cow-dung).

ಬಳಪ k. *n.* A whitish pot-stone, *Lapis ollaris*, frequently used (as a substitute for slate pencil, *etc.*) in writing.

ಬಳಲು (ಳ = ಱ) k. *v. i.* To become weary, fatigued; to droop, fade, to be cast down, distressed. 2, to become slack or loose; to dangle, slip. *n.* The state of being loose. ಬಳಲಿಕೆ, ಬಳಲ್ಕೆ. Weariness, fatigue, distress. ಬಳಲಿಸು. To exhaust, weary.

ಬಳಸು 1. a. k. *v. i.* To go round; to wander about; to turn round, *as* in serving dinner. 2, to be wrapped up. 3, to surround. 4, to be in one's company. *n.* Surrounding. 2, circuitousness, *as* of a road. 3, one round or turn, *as* of a rope, dôtra, śîrĕ, *etc.*; a turn in serving up dinner.

ಬಳಸು 2. (ಳ = ಱ) k. *v. t.* To use; to spend, *as* time; *also* ಬಳಿಸು.

ಬಳಿ 1. (ಳ = ೞ) k. *n.* A way, road. 2, a place, spot. 3, vicinity, nearness; company. 4, way, mode, proper course. 5, race, lineage. 6, succeeding time. *prep.* After, afterwards; further, and. -ಗೆ. To, towards, near. ಬಳಿಯ, ಬಳಿಯಲ್ಲಿ. Near, by, beside. -ಸಲು. To follow. -ವಳಿ. Different ways; presents to one's daughter other than those given at the time of marriage.

ಬಳಿ 2. (ಳ = ೞ) k. *n.* A gift, present.

ಬಳಿ 3. (ಳ = ೞ) k. *v. t.* To sweep, wipe off with the hand. 2, to apply, *as* lime, mud, *etc.* to a wall, cow-dung to the floor, ointment to the body, *etc.*; to besmear; to anoint. *P. ps.* ಬಳಿದು, ಬಳದು.

ಬಳಿಕ k. *prep.* After, afterwards, further; *also* ಬಳಿಯ.

ಬಳಿಕೆ. = ಬಳಕೆ, *q. v.*

ಬಳಿದು k. *n.* Slopeness; gradual ascent.

ಬಳುಕು (= ಬಳಕು) k. *v. i.* To shake, tremble; to bend.

ಬಳೆ (= ಬೆಳೆ) 1. a. k. *v. i.* To increase, grow up, prosper.

ಬಳೆ 2. (*tb. of* ವಲಯ) *n.* A ring; an armlet, bracelet, arm-ring. 2, a bangle. -ಗಾರ, -ಯವ. A bracelet-maker or vendor; *f.* -ಗಾತಿ. -ಮಲಾರ. A bundle of glass bangles strung on a string. ಬಳೆಯುಪ್ಪು. A sort of salt.

ಬಳ್ಳ k. *n.* A measure of capacity.

ಬಳ್ಳಿ (*tb. of* ವಲ್ಲಿ) *n.* A creeper, vine. -ಮಾವು. A kind of mango tree. -ಮಿಂಚು. Lightning in zigzag.

ಬಳ್ಳು k. *n.* A jackal.

ಬಾ 1. k. *Imp. sing. of* ಬರು. Come!

ಬಾ 2. (= ಬಾಯು) k. *v. i.* To swell, tumefy. *P. ps.* ಬಾದು, ಬಾತು.

ಬಾಕ (*tb. of* ಧಾರ್ಷ್ಟ) *n.* A glutton; *also* ಹೊಟ್ಟೆ-. -ತನ. Gluttony; *f.* ಬಾಕಿ.

ಬಾಕಿ h. *n.* Remainder; balance; debt. *a.* Remaining. -ದಾರ. One who is in arrears.

ಬಾಕು h. *n.* A dagger. 2, a bend, curve. 3, a bench. -ಡ. The husband of a pariah woman.

ಬಾಕುಳ, ಬಾಕುಳಿ k. *n.* Excessive desire. 2, a covetous person.

ಬಾಗಲ, ಬಾಗಲು. = ಬಾಗಿಲು, *q. v.*

ಬಾಗವಾನ h. *n.* A gardener; a seller of vegetables and flowers.

ಬಾಗಾಯತಿ, ಬಾಗಾಯತು h. *n.* Garden-land; a garden.

ಬಾಗಿ k. *n.* The tree *Calosanthes indica.*

ಬಾಗಿನ (*tb. of* ವಾಯನ) *n.* A present, gift.

ಬಾಗಿಲು (= ಬಾಗಲ, *etc., q. v.*) k. *n.* A door, gate, door-way. ಬಾಗಿಲವ. A doorkeeper, warder. -ವಾಡ. An up-stair-house over a gate; a door-frame.

ಬಾಗು k. *v. i.* To bend, bow, incline, stoop. *n.* A bend, curve; a bow. ಬಾಗಿಸು. To cause to bend, *etc.*

ಬಾಗುಳ. *tb. of* ವ್ಯಾಕುಲ, *q. v.*

ಬಾಗೆ k. *n.* The tree *Acacia seeressa.*

ಬಾಂಕಿ h. *n.* A kind of bugle.

ಬಾಂಗಿ h. *n.* A pole with slings, attached to the ends for carrying packages across the shoulder; the package so carried. 2, the bangy post.

ಬಾಚಣಿಗೆ k. *n.* A comb. -ಹಲ್ಲು. The tooth of a comb.

ಬಾಚಿ 1. k. *n.* A bodice; a coat of mail.

ಬಾಚಿ 2. (*tb. of* ವಾಶಿ) *n.* An adze.

ಬಾಚು 1. k. *v. t.* To comb. ಬಾಚಿಸು. To cause to comb.

ಬಾಚು 2. k. *v. t.* To scrape together with the hand, *etc.,* and gather up, *as* sweepings, *etc.*; to spoliate.

ಬಾಜಾ (*tb. of* ವಾದ್ಯ) *n.* Playing upon musical instruments; instrumental music; a musical instrument. -ಬಜಂತರಿ. Music played upon all instruments. ಬಾಜಿಸು. To sound; to play a musical instrument.

ಬಾಜಾರ, ಬಾಜಾರು (= ಬಜಾರ, *etc., q. v.*) h. *n.* A bazaar, market. ಬಾಜಾರಿ. Of market; a prostitute.

ಬಾಜು h. *n.* A side; either side of the body; verge; party. -ಆಗು. To go aside. -ಬಂದ. A bracelet.

ಬಾಜಿ. = ಬಾಜಾ, *q. v.*

ಬಾಜೀ h. *a.* Miscellaneous. -ಬಾಬು. A miscellaneous head in accounts.

ಬಾಟೆ h. *n.* A road.

ಬಾಡಿಗೆ (*tb. of* ಭಾಟಕ) *n.* Hire; rent; fare. -ಗೆ ಕೊಡು. To hire out. -ಯವ. A man who has hired. -ಎತ್ತು, -ಕುದುರೆ, -ಬಂಡಿ, -ಮನೆ, *etc.* A hired—.

ಬಾಡು 1. k. *v. i.* To wither, fade, *as* shrubs, *etc.*; to grow dry, *as* wounds; to become weak; to pine away; to be downcast or sad. ಬಾಡಿಸು. To cause to fade, *etc.*; to eat any pungent food to excite appetite.

ಬಾಡು 2. k. *n.* Flesh.

ಬಾಣ s. *n.* A shaft, arrow; a rocket. 2, an asura. -ಎಸೆ, -ಬಿಡು, -ಹೊಡೆ. To shoot an arrow. -ಗಾರ. A maker of fireworks; an archer.

ಬಾಣತಿ, ಬಾಣಂತಿ f. *n.* A lying-in-woman.

ಬಾಣಲಿ, ಬಾಣಲೆ (*tb. of* ಭ್ರಾಷ್ಟ್ರ) *n.* A frying pan; *also* ಬಾಳ್ಳಿ.

ಬಾಣಸ (*tb. of* ಮಹಾನಸ) *n.* A kitchen; cookery. ಬಾಣಸಿ, ಬಾಣಸಿಗ. A cook; *f.* -ಗಿತ್ತಿ.

ಬಾಂಡು e. *n.* A bond. 2, a musical band.

ಬಾತಮಿ h. *n.* Intelligence, news. -ದಾರ. An intelligencer, correspondent.

ಬಾತು. = ಬಾದು. *P. p. of* ಬಾ *and* ಬಾಯು, *q. v.*

ಬಾತು f. *n.* A duck; *also* -ಕೋಳಿ.

ಬಾದರಾಯಣ s. *n.* Vyâsa.

ಬಾದಶಹ, ಬಾದಶಾಹ h. *n.* A Mohammadan or foreign king.

ಬಾದಾಮ, ಬಾದಾಮು f. *n.* An almond. ಬಾದಾಮಿ ಎಣ್ಣೆ. Almond-oil.

ಬಾದಿ f. *n.* Weight, load. 2, a patron.

ಬಾದು h. *a.* Deducted. *n.* Deduction.

ಬಾದ್ಧ್ಯ (*tb. of* ಬಾಂಧವ) *n.* A relative, relation. 2, a man who has a right to; an heir. 3, a right to possession. 4, property, inheritance. -ತನ, -ತೆ, -ತ್ವ, -ಸ್ತಿಕೆ. A right or claim to possession; heirship. -ಸ್ಥ. The rightful owner; an heir.

ಬಾಧ. = ಬಾಧೆ, *q. v.* -ಕ. An oppressor, troubler.

ಬಾಧೆ s. *n.* Pain, suffering, grief, sorrow, annoyance, trouble; opposition, hindrance; objection; a contradiction; injury, hurt. -ಪಡಿಸು, ಬಾಧಿಸು. To oppress, harass, pain, torment, trouble, vex. -ಪಡು. To suffer distress, *etc.*

ಬಾನ a. k. *n.* The sky. 2, a pile of earthen pots or of cowdung-cakes. -ಉ. Cloudiness. ಬಾನಿ, ಬಾನೆ. A large earthen pot.

ಬಾಂದಿ h. *n.* A female slave.

ಬಾಂದು f. *n.* A dam; a heap of stones, *etc.* used as a landmark. -ಕಲ್ಲು. A landmark-stone.

ಬಾಪ್ಪ 1. k. *n.* Boiled-rice.

ಬಾಪ್ಪ 2. h. *n.* A father.

ಬಾಪುರಿ, *tb. of* ಬಾಹುಪುರಿ, *q. v.*

ಬಾಬತು h. *n.* An article, item; a point of view.

ಬಾಬು h. *n.* An article, item; *cf.* ಬಾಬತು.

ಬಾಯಾರು. *See s.* ಬಾಯಿ.

ಬಾಯಿ 1. k. *n.* The mouth; the mouth of a vessel, bag, drain, *etc.*, the head of a drum. 2, the edge of any cutting instrument. -ಕಟ್ಟು. To shut the mouth; to restrain the appetite. -ಕೂಡು. The growth of teeth to be complete, as of cattle; to become conformable. -ಗೆ ಕೊಡು. To give something for the mouth, *as* betel-nut, *etc.* -ಗೆಬರು. To come to one's mouth, *as* words in speaking. -ಗೆ ಬಂದ ಹಾಗೆ ಬಯ್ಯು. To abuse inconsiderately. -ಗೆ ಬೀಳು. To fall into the mouth (of people, wild animals, *etc.*). -ಗೆ ಹಾಕು. To put into the mouth; to bribe. -ಜೊಲ್ಲು. Saliva. -ತಪ್ಪು. A slip of the tongue. -ತೆರೆ, -ಬಿಚ್ಚು. To open the mouth. -ಪಾಠ. Learning by heart. -ಪಾಠವಾಗು. To be learned by heart. -ಪಾಠ ಮಾಡಿಕೊಳ್ಳು. To learn by heart. -ಬಡಕ. One who talks much and foolishly; *f.* -ಬಡಕಿ. -ಬಡುಕೊಳ್ಳು. To beat one's mouth from fear or grief. -ಬಿಡು. To open one's mouth; to humble one's self; to speak, beg; to divulge *as* a secret; to crack, burst. -ಮಾಡು. To use abusive language, chide. -ಮಾತು. A mere word; a vain word; an oral tradition. -ಯಿಲ್ಲದವ. A dumb man. ಬಾಯಾರ, ಬಾಯಾರೆ. Much, to one's heart's content, *as in* ಬಾಯಾರ ಮಾತಾಡು. ಬಾಯಾರು. To become thirsty. ಬಾಯಾರಿಕೆ. Thirst. -ಸವಿ. Savouriness. -ಹಾಕು. To put the mouth into anything *as* dogs; to utter, speak.

ಬಾಯಿ 2. f. *n.* A term of respect for one's mother or an elderly female. 2, an affix of respect to names of females.

ಬಾಯು (= ಬಾ 2, *q. v.*) k. *v. i.* To swell.

ಬಾರ k. *Masc. neg. mood of* ಬರು.

ಬಾರಿ 1. (*tb. of* ಭಾರಿ) *n.* Weightiness, importance, greatness, abundance, valuableness.

ಬಾರಿ 2. h. *n.* A time, turn; a season, year. -ಬಾರಿಗೆ. Again and again, repeatedly, frequently.

ಬಾರಿ 3. h. *n.* The slope at the side of a great well for bullocks to run down in drawing up water.

ಬಾರಿಸು 1. k. *v. t.* To cause to tremble; to set in rapid motion.

ಬಾರಿಸು 2. (ರಿ=ಱ. =ಬಾಜಿಸು) k. *v. t.* To sound or play a musical instrument.

ಬಾರಿಸು 3. (=ವಾರಿಸು) f. *v. t.* To ward off, restrain, remove.

ಬಾರು 1. k. *n.* A strap of leather, thong.

ಬಾರು 2. h. *n.* A charge (of a gun). ಬಾರ ಕೋಟು. Infantry barracks. ಬಾರಿನವ. A foot-soldier. -ಮಾಡು. To load a gun.

ಬಾರು 3. *tb. of* ಭಾರ, *q. v.* -ಮಾಡು. To fill into a book (*as* items).

ಬಾರೋಮೆಟರ್ e. *n.* A barometer, an instrument to measure the weight of the atmosphere.

ಬಾರ್ಲಿ e. *n.* Barley.

ಬಾಲ s. *a.* Young, infantine; newly risen, *as* the sun, waxing, *as* the moon, *etc.* 2, childish, ignorant. *n.* A child, infant; a boy. 2, the young of an animal. 3, a colt, foal. 4, a tail. 5, the cuscus grass. -ಕೇಳಿ. Children's play. -ಗೋಪಾಲ. Kṛishṇa. -ಗ್ರಹ. Convulsions of children. -ಚಂದ್ರ. The waxing moon. -ಚುಕ್ಕಿ. A comet. -ತನ, -ತ್ವ. Childhood; boyhood. -ಬಂದು. The Dêvanâgarî character. -ಬೋಧೆ, -ಬೋಧನೆ, ಬಾಲೋಪದೇಶ. Instruction for the young; catechism. -ಭಾಷೆ. Children's language. -ಮೆಣಸು. Cubeb, *Piper cubeba.* -ರಕ್ಷೆ. A preservative or charm for children. -ಲೀಲೆ. Juvenile pastime. -ಶಯ್ಯೆ. A cradle. -ಶಿಕ್ಷೆ. Punishment, or instruction of children. -ಹತ್ಯೆ. Infanticide.

ಬಾಲಕ s. *a.* Young. *n.* A child, infant; a boy; *f.* ಬಾಲಕಿ.

ಬಾಲಿಕೆ, ಬಾಲೆ s. *n.* A girl.

ಬಾಲ್ಯ, ಬಾಲ್ಯಾವಸ್ಥೆ s. *n.* Childhood, infancy, youth.

ಬಾವ ((*tb. of* ಭಾಮ) *n.* A sister's husband. -ನಂಟ. The relative, *as* a sister's husband. ಬಾವಮೈದುನ. A wife's or husband's brother.

ಬಾವಟೆ. = ಬಾವುಟೆ, *q. v.*

ಬಾವನ್ನ a. k. *n.* Sandalwood. 2, (h.) fifty-two.

ಬಾವಲಿ 1. k. *n.* A bat; the flying fox.

ಬಾವಲಿ 2. f. *n.* A gold ornament worn on the tip of the ear. 2, a doll.

ಬಾವಳಿಸು (*tb. of* ವ್ಯಾಕುಲಿಸು) *v. i.* To be confused, bewildered.

ಬಾವಿ (*tb. of* ವಾಪಿ) *n.* A well.

ಬಾವು k. *n.* A swelling, abscess.

ಬಾವುಗ k. *n.* A male cat.

ಬಾವುಟೆ (=ಬಾವಟೆ) h. *n.* A flag.

ಬಾವುಲಿ. = ಬಾವಲಿ, *q. v.*

ಬಾಷ್ಪ s. *n.* Tears; *also* -ಜಲ.

ಬಾಸಣೆ a. k. *n.* Covering. -ಸು. To cover.

ಬಾಸಿಗ f. *n.* A chaplet of flowers; an ornament of pith worn on the forehead of the bridegroom.

ಬಾಸು h. *n.* Stench.

ಬಾಸುಂಡೆ, ಬಾಸುಳ k. *n.* A wale or mark caused by a blow or stroke.

ಬಾಸೆ (*tb. of* ಭಾಷೆ, *q. v.*) *n.* Speech; a promise; an oath. -ಕೊಡು. To promise, swear. -ಗಳ್ಳ, -ಗೆಡುಕ, -ಯಿಲ್ಲದ. A promise-breaker. -ವಂತ. Faithful; one who keeps a promise.

ಬಾಹ. *Pres. rel. part. of* ಬರು, *q. v.*

ಬಾಹಿರ (*fr.* ಬಹಿರ್) s. *a.* Outer, external; excluded from, devoid of. *n.* A foreigner; an outcast; *f.* -ಗಿತ್ತಿ.

ಬಾಹು s. *n.* The arm; the upper arm. -ಜ. A Kshatriya. -ಪುರಿ, ಬಾಪುರಿ. A bracelet. -ಮೂಲ. The armpit. -ಯು

ದ್ಧ. A close fight, wrestling. -ರಕ್ಷೆ. An armour.

ಬಾಹುಲ್ಯ s. n. Abundance, plenty.

ಬಾಹ್ಯ s. a. Outer; external; cf. ಬಹಿರ. n. An outcast.

ಬಾಳ (tb. of ಬಾಲ) n. A boy. 2, the cuscus-grass. 3, (tb. of ಫಾಲ) the forehead.

ಬಾಳ. = ಬಹಳ, q. v.

ಬಾಳಕ (ಳ = ಱ). = ಬಾಳುಕ, q. v.

ಬಾಳಬಂದು. tb. of ಬಾಲಛಂದು.

ಬಾಳು 1. k. n. A sword, knife.

ಬಾಳು 2. (ಳು = ೞು) k. v. i. To live; to be alive; to subsist; to live by; to live happily; to be preserved, as fruit, etc. 2, to be worth, sell for. n. Living; life; livelihood; property. P. p. ಬಾಳಿ, ಬಾಳ್ದು. ಬಾಳಿಕೆ, ಬಾಳುವಿಕೆ, ಬಾಳ್ಕೆ, ಬಾಳ್ತನ, ಬಾಳ್ತೆ, ಬಾಳ್ವಿಕೆ, ಬಾಳ್ವೆ. Living, livelihood; profession; household.

ಬಾಳುಕ (ಳು = ೞು) k. n. Sliced vegetables dried and fried.

ಬಾಳೆ 1. k. n. The plantain or *Banana;* the plantain tree. -ಕಾಯಿ. An unripe plantain. -ಗೊನೆ. A bunch of plantains. -ತೋಟ. A plantain garden. -ಹಣ್ಣು. A ripe plantain.

ಬಾಳೆ 2. a. k. n. A sea-fish.

ಬಿಕ tb. of ಭಿಕ್ಷ, q. v. -ನಾಸಿ. An avaricious person.

ಬಿಕರಿ (tb. of ವಿಕ್ರಯ) n. Selling, sale. -ದಾರ. A seller, vendor.

ಬಿಕನ. tb. of ಭಿಕ್ಷೆ, q. v.

ಬಿಕಾರಿ h. n. A beggar, poor person. -ತನ. Poverty, wretchedness.

ಬಿಕ್ಕಟ್ಟು. = ಇಕ್ಕಟ್ಟು, q. v.

ಬಿಕ್ಕಲು. = ಬಿಕ್ಕು, q. v. ಬಿಕ್ಕಲ. A stammerer, stutterer. -ಮಾತು. A faltering word.

ಬಿಕ್ಕಳಿಕೆ k. n. Hiccough.

ಬಿಕ್ಕು k. v. i. To sigh, pant; to sob in crying; to hiccough; to falter, stammer, stutter. n. Sobbing; stammering; hiccough. 2, the heart.

ಬಿಕ್ಕುಳಿ k. n. Throwing up; vomiting. -ಸು. To throw up, vomit.

ಬಿಕ್ಕೆ 1. k. n. N. of a small forest tree with eatable fruit, *Gardenia gummifera.*

ಬಿಕ್ಕೆ 2. tb. of ಭಿಕ್ಷೆ, q. v.

ಬಿಗಡಾಯಿಸು f. v. i. To be out of order, as one's health; to disagree, as the mind. ಬಿಗಡಾವು. Disagreement.

ಬಿಗಿ k. v. t. To bind, fasten; to tighten; to compress; to restrain, as desire; to amass firmly. v. i. To be tight, stiff or full. 2, to become proud. n. Tightness, tension; firmness; well-ordered condition. 2, a girth for horses. 3, pride. -ಯಾಗು. To become tight. -ಯೊಳಗೆ ಇಡು. To keep under control. -ಮಾಡು. To tighten; to order, enact; to behave arrogantly. -ತ. Tightening; tightness. -ಸು. To cause to fasten, tighten.

ಬಿಗುರ್ a. k. v. i. To be afraid; to get amazed. n. Fear; amazement.

ಬಿಗುವು, ಬಗುಹು (= ಬಿಗಿ, q. v.) k. n. Tightness, etc.

ಬಿಂಕ (cf. ಬಿಗಿ n.) k. n. Pride; pompousness.

ಬಿಂಕು k. n. Dishonesty, guile.

ಬಿಂಗ, ಬಿಂಗು (tb. of ಭೃಂಗ) n. Talc, mica.

ಬಿಚಾನ h. n. A mattress, mat. ಬಿಚಾಯಿಸು. To spread, as a bed, etc.

ಬಿಚ್ಚಣಿಸು, ಬಿಚ್ಚಳಿಸು k. v. t. To extend, spread, amplify.

ಬಿಚ್ಚರಿಕೆ, ಬಿಚ್ಚಳಕೆ a. k. n. Expansion, extension, spreading.

ಬಿಚ್ಚು k. v. t. To loosen, untie, open, undo, as a bundle, etc.; to lay open, as the mind, etc.; to solve; to draw, as a sword. v. i. To become loose or open, as a tie; to be cracked or broken. n. Loosening; unfolding. ಬಿಚ್ಚಿಸು. To cause to loosen, etc. ಬಿಚ್ಚಿ ಹೇಳು. To tell plainly. -ಕತ್ತಿ. A drawn sword. ಬಿಚ್ಚೋಲೆ. A rolled up palmyra-leaf put in the ear-holes of women.

ಬಿಜಯ (*tb. of* ವಿಜಯ) *n.* Going; coming; *also* ಬಿಜ. -ಂಗೆಯ್ಯು, -ಮಾಡು. To walk, to go, to come.

ಬಿಜಾಗರಿ f. *n.* A jointed hinge, jummers.

ಬಿಜ್ಜಣ, ಬಿಜ್ಜಣಿಗೆ (*tb. of* ವ್ಯಜನ) *n.* A fan.

ಬಿಜ್ಜಲ, ಬಿಜ್ಜೆ 1. a. k. *n.* Greatness.

ಬಿಜ್ಜು k. *n.* A voracious bird, *Patta's paradoxurus.* 2, ruin.

ಬಿಜ್ಜೆ 2. (*tb. of* ವಿದ್ಯೆ) *n.* Knowledge, science. -ವಳ. Gaṇêśa. -ವೆಣ್. Sarasvatî.

ಬಿಟ್ಟಿ (*tb. of* ವಿಷ್ಟಿ) *n.* Compulsory and unpaid labour; press-service; *also* -ಕೆಲಸ. -ಗಂಟು. A load carried without hire; that which is worthless; money obtained without labour. -ಮಾಡು. To perform biṭṭi. -ಯೂಟ. A meal obtained gratis. -ಹಿಡಿ. To exact forced labour.

ಬಿಟ್ಟು. *P. p. of* ಬಿಡು, *q. v.*

ಬಿಡಕೆ k. *n.* Interval; space; cessation; leisure.

ಬಿಡದಿ k. *n.* Lodgings provided for visitors.

ಬಿಡಯ 1. = ಬಿಡಿಯ, *q. v.*

ಬಿಡಯ 2. k. *n.* A mass, flock, swarm. 2, anger, wrath.

ಬಿಡವು. = ಬಿಡತೆ, *q. v.*

ಬಿಡಾರ k. *n.* A halting place; a dwelling place; lodgings.

ಬಿಡಿ (= ಬಿಡು, *q. v.*) k. *a.* Loose, separated. -ಕಟ್ಟಿಗೆ. Loose pieces of wood. -ಬಿಡ್ತಲು 1. Looseness, laxity, freedom. -ಹೂ. A plucked flower.

ಬಿಡಿಕು k. *n.* Separation; a crack.

ಬಿಡಿಕೆ k. *n.* Interval.

ಬಿಡಿತೆ. = ಬಿಡತೆ, *q. v.*

ಬಿಡಿಯ (= ಬಿಡಯ, ಬಿಡೆ) f. *n.* Respect, regard, consideration; deference for. 2, shame, bashfulness; *also* -ತನ.

ಬಿಡಿಸು k. *v. t.* To loosen; to cause to leave; to remove; to cast out; to liberate; to pull out or off, pluck; *etc.* ಅರಳೆಯನ್ನು-, ದಾರಿಯನ್ನು-, ದೆವ್ವನ್ನ-, ಹುಚ್ಚು ತಿಳುವಳಿಕೆಯನ್ನು-, ನಾಚಿಕೆಯನ್ನು-, *etc.*

ಬಿಡು k. *v. t.* To let loose; to discharge, throw, *as* an arrow; to emit, *as* breath; to let drop; to let on; to let down, *as* a rope; to let hang down; to set to; to quit, leave; to abandon, give up; to leave out; to set aside; to take off, *as* from the price; to quit, *as* a debt; to leave off, *as* work; to allow, let; to spare or let live; to let grow; to drive, *as* a horse, *etc.*; to send, *as* a servant, *etc.*; to put forth, *as* leaves, flowers, *etc.* *v. i.* To be loosened; to cease, stop; to halt; to settle; to go away. *P. p.* ಬಿಟ್ಟು. ಬಿಡು, *esp. in common language, is often joined to a P. p. to lay stress upon its meaning or to express the completion of an action, e. g.* ಮಾರಿ-, ಹೇಳಿ-, ಹೋಗಿ-, ಮಾಡಿ-, ಹೊಡೆದು-, ಕೊಟ್ಟು-, ಬಿಚ್ಚಿ-, *etc.* *n.* (= ಬಿಡಿ) Loosening; looseness, freedom, *etc.* -ಗಡೆ. Release, freedom, liberty. -ಗಂಡಿ. A flood-gate. -ಗೊಳು. To scatter about. -ತಲೆ, -ದಲೆ. A head of dishevelled hair. -ವಾಯಿ. An open mouth.

ಬಿಡುಕು. = ಬಿಡಿಕು, *q. v.*

ಬಿಡುವು, ಬಿಡುವಿಕೆ, ಬಿಡುಹು k. *n.* Leaving, giving up, *etc.*

ಬಿಡೆ. = ಬಿಡಯ, ಬಿಡಿಯ, *q. v.*

ಬಿಣ್ಪು a. k. *n.* Largeness, stoutness; hugeness; gravity. 2, a metrically long syllable.

ಬಿತ್ತನೆ, ಬಿತ್ತಿಗೆ k. *n.* Sowing seeds.

ಬಿತ್ತರ. *tb. of* ವಿಸ್ತಾರ, *q. v.* ಬಿತ್ತರಿಸು. = ವಿಸ್ತರಿಸು, *q. v.*

ಬಿತ್ತರಿಗೆ f. *n.* A throne.

ಬಿತ್ತಿ. *tb. of* ಭಿತ್ತಿ. 2, support.

ಬಿತ್ತು 1. k. *v. t.* To put seeds, sow. *n.* Seed; a seed. ಬಿತ್ತಿಸು. To cause to sow.

ಬಿತ್ತು 2. *Third p. sing. of the imp. of* ಬೀಳು, *q. v.*

ಬಿತ್ತೆಗ f. n. A clever, well-educated and polite man.

ಬಿದರು (= ಬಿದಿರು) k. n. The bamboo, *Bambusa arundinacea*. -ಅಕ್ಕಿ, ಬಿದರಕ್ಕಿ. Bamboo seed. -ತಟ್ಟಿ. A bamboo-screen.

ಬಿದಿಗೆ (*tb. of* ದ್ವಿತೀಯೆ) n. A crescent new moon; the second day of a lunar fortnight.

ಬಿದಿರು 1. a. k. v. t. To scatter about; to open, *as* the mouth; to unfold, *as* the wings; to loosen, untie; to throw about. v. i. To be spread about.

ಬಿದಿರು 2, ಬಿದುರು. = ಬಿದರು, q. v. -ಗೆಣ್ಣು. A bamboo knot. -ಮೆಳೆ. A bamboo bush. -ಮೊಳೆ. A bamboo shoot.

ಬಿದ್ದಣ, ಬಿದ್ದನ a. k. n. An invitation to dinner; a banquet; a feasting.

ಬಿದ್ದಿನ a. k. n. A guest. 2, a relative.

ಬಿದ್ದು. *P. p. of* ಬೀಳು, q. v.

ಬಿನುಗು k. n. A low, base, mean person. -ನುಡಿ. Whispering words.

ಬಿಂದಿಗೆ f. n. A metal water-vessel.

ಬಿಂದು s. n. A drop. 2, a dot, mark. 3, a cypher or dot.

ಬಿನ್ನ 1. = ಬಿನ್ನಹ, q. v. -ಮಾಡು. To invite (for dinner). -ವತ್ತಳೆ. A petition.

ಬಿನ್ನ 2. *tb. of* ಭಿನ್ನ, q. v.

ಬಿನ್ನಗೆ, ಬಿನ್ನನೆ k. ad. Silently.

ಬಿನ್ನಣ. = ಬಿನ್ನಾಣ, q. v. ಬಿನ್ನಣಿ. A learned man, a proficient.

ಬಿನ್ನಹ, ಬಿನ್ನಪ (*tb. of* ವಿಜ್ಞಾಪನ) n. Respectful petition. -ಮಾಡು, ಬಿನ್ನಯಿಸು, ಬಿನ್ನವಿಸು. To make a humble petition.

ಬಿನ್ನಾಣ (*tb. of* ವಿಜ್ಞಾನ) n. Knowledge; skill, dexterity; art; device. -ಗಾರ. A clever man; *f.* -ಗಾತಿ, ಬಿನ್ನಾಣಿ.

ಬಿಂಬ s. n. A disk, ball. 2, a mirror. 3, a reflection; an image. 4, a rainbow. 5, the fruit of *Momordica monadelpha*. ಬಿಂಬಿಸು. To be reflected.

ಬಿಮ್ಮಗೆ, ಬಿಮ್ಮನೆ k. ad. Firmly, tightly; loudly; powerfully.

ಬಿರ. *P. p. of* ಬಿರಿ, *as in* ಬಿರಕೊಳ್ಳು.

ಬಿರಕು, ಬಿರವು. = ಬಿರಿಕು, q. v.

ಬಿರಡೆ k. n. A peg to tighten the strings of musical instruments; a cork.

ಬಿರತು, ಬಿರದು. *P. p. of* ಬಿರಿ, q. v.

ಬಿರನೆ (ರ = ಐ) k. ad. Swiftly, quickly.

ಬಿರಸು (ರ=ಐ) k. n. Hardness; roughness, coarseness; harshness; briskness. 2, a rocket, cracker. *Cpds.*: -ಗೂಡದಲು, -ಬತ್ತಿ, -ದಾಣ, -ಮನುಷ್ಯ, -ಮಾತು, -ಹುಲ್ಲು, *etc.*

ಬಿರಾಣಿ f. n. A grain, *as* of gunpowder.

ಬಿರಾದಾರಿ h. n. A band, company, herd.

ಬಿರಿ 1. k. v. i. To burst; to be rent asunder; to split open, crack; to break away; to burst forth; to expand, open, blossom, blow. *P. ps.* ಬಿರಿತು, ಬಿರಿದು, ಬಿರತು, ಬಿರದು.

ಬಿರಿ 2. (ರಿ = ಐ) k. n. Firmness; tightness, *as* of a door.

ಬಿರಿಕು (= ಬಿರಕು) k. n. A cleft, fissure, crack.

ಬಿರಿದು. = ಬಿರುದು, q. v.

ಬಿರಿಸು. = ಬಿರಸು, q. v.

ಬಿರು (ರು = ಐು) k. n. Hardness; roughness; vehemence; swiftness. -ಗಾಳಿ. A hurricane. -ನಡೆ. A brisk walk. -ನುಡಿ. A harsh word. -ನೋಟ. An unkind look. -ಮಳೆ. A heavy rain. -ಬಿಸಿಲು. A great heat of the sun.

ಬಿರುದು (*tb. of* ವಿರುದ) n. Praise. 2, a badge of honour. 3, distinction, valour. ಬಿರುದ. A brave man.

ಬಿರುಸು. = ಬಿರಸು, q. v.

ಬಿಲ s. n. A hole, cavity; a gap, chasm.

ಬಿಲಾರ k. n. The Coromandel ebony-tree, *Diospyros melanoxylon*.

ಬಿಲ್ಕುಲ್ f. ad. Never, by no means (*always negat.*). -ಮಾಡ ಬೇಡ. Never do it.

ಬಿಲ್ಲು k. n. A bow. ಬಿಲ್ಲವ. A bow-man; N. of a low caste in Canara; a toddy-drawer. -ಗಾರ. = ಬಿಲ್ಲವ. ಬಿಲ್ಲೆಸಿಗೆ. A bow-shot.

ಬಿಲ್ಲೆ h. n. The breast-plate of a belt, *as* of a peon. -ಯವ. A peon.

ಬಿಲ್ವ s. n. A thorny tree, the Bael tree, *Aegle marmelos*; *also* -ಪತ್ರ.

ಬಿಸವಳ (*tb. of* ವಿಸ್ಮಯ) *n.* Surprise, wonder.

ಬಿಸಲು. = ಬಿಸಿಲು, *q. v.*

ಬಿಸಾಡು k. *v. t.* To throw away. *P. p.* ಬಿಸಾಟು.

ಬಿಸಿ (= ಬಿಸು 1) k. *n.* Heat. *a.* Hot. *Cpds.:* -ಕಾಫಿ, -ಚಾ, -ನೀರು, -ನೆತ್ತರು, -ಬೆಲ್ಲ, -ಮಾಂಸ, *etc.*

ಬಿಸಿಲು k. *n.* The heat and glare of the sun, sunshine. -ಕುದುರೆ, -ತೊರೆ. The mirage. -ಚಪ್ಪರ. A screen to keep off the sun.

ಬಿಸು 1. = ಬಿಸಿ, *q. v.* -ಸುಯ್ಯು. To sigh hotly.

ಬಿಸು 2. (= ಬೆಸೆ) k. *v. t.* To unite firmly, solder. -ಗೆ. Soldering, composition.

ಬಿಸುಡು (*cf.* ಬಿಸಾಡು) k. *v. t.* To throw, fling away carelessly or heedlessly; to leave apruptly. *P. p.* ಬಿಸುಟು.

ಬಿಸ್ಕೀಟು e. *n.* Biscuit, a kind of sweet cake.

ಬಿಳಗಾರ k. *n.* Borax.

ಬಿಳಪು. = ಬಿಳುಪು, *q. v.*

ಬಿಳಲು (ಳ = ಡ) k. *n.* A pendent root, *as* that of the banian tree.

ಬಿಳಿ, ಬಿಳೆ k. *n.* Whiteness. *a.* White; *also* ಬಿಳಿಯ, ಬಿಳೀ. -ಕಾಗದ, -ಗಡ್ಡ, -ಗಂಟಳೆ, -ಗೂದಲು, -ಗೆಣಸು, -ತಾವರೆ, -ಬಣ್ಣ, -ಮೆಣಸು, -ಮೋಡ, *etc.* A white—. -ಗೆಂಪು. Pale red, pink. -ಜಾಲಿ. *Acacia leucophlaea.* -ದು. That which is white; the colour white; *also* ಬಿಳಪು, ಬಿಳುಪು. -ಮತ್ತಿ. The timber tree *Terminalia paniculata.* -ಮಂದಾರ. A flower plant, *Bauhinia acuminata.*

ಬಿಳಿವಾರ k. *n.* A large forest tree, *Albizzia odoratissima.*

ಬೀ a. k. *v. t.* To cease; to fail; to perish. *P. p.* ಬೀತು. -ಕಲ್. Ending.

ಬೀಗ 1. k. *n.* A lock, pad-lock. -ದ ಕೈ. A key. -ದ ಮರ. The tree *Elaeocarpus lanceaefolius.* -ಮುದ್ರೆ. A seal upon a (closed) door.

ಬೀಗ 2. k. *n.* A relative by marriage. -ತನ. A relationship by marriage; *f.* -ತಿ.

ಬೀಗು a. k. *v. i.* To swell. 2, to be elated. 3, to retreat. *n.* A swelling.

ಬೀಜ s. *n.* Seed (of plants, *etc.*), seed-corn, grain. 2, source, origin. 3, algebra. -ಗಾಣು. To be sown with seed. -ವರಿ. The amount of seed required for a land. -ಕೋಶ. The pericarp of a flower. -ಕೋಶಿ. A pod, legume. -ಗಣಿತ. Algebra. -ಪೂರ. The citron. ಬೀಜಾಕ್ಷರ. The principal syllable of a mantra. ಬೀಜಾವಾಪ. Sowing seed.

ಬೀಟೆ, ಬೀಟಿ 1. k. *n.* The blackwood tree, *Dalbergia latifolia.*

ಬೀಟಿ 2. k. *n.* A chink, crack, crevice. -ಬೀಳು. To crack.

ಬೀಡಿ h. *n.* A small shiroot, cigarette.

ಬೀಡು 1. a. k. *n.* Leave; halting. 2, a halting place, camp, abode, house. ಬೀಡಾಗು, -ಗೊಳ್ಳು, -ಬಿಡು. To encamp. ಬೀಡಾರ. A halting place; a house, lodging. ಬೀಡಿಕೆ. Halting; a halting place; a camp.

ಬೀಡು 2. k. *n.* A waste, uncultivated land. 2, a pile, heap. -ಬಿಡು. To let remain waste. ಬೀಡಾಗು, -ಬೀಳು. To become waste.

ಬೀದಿ (*tb. of* ವೀಥಿ) *n.* A street, road. -ಜಗಳ. A street quarrel. -ವರಿ. To run at one's pleasure; a run *ad libitum.*

ಬೀಮು e. *n.* Beam, main timber. 2, (f.) insurance. -ಪತ್ರ. A policy of insurance.

ಬೀಫು e. *n.* Beef, the flesh of an ox.

ಬೀಬಿ h. *n.* A Mussalman lady. -ಸಾಹೇಬ. A lady; a wife.

ಬೀಭತ್ಸ s. *a.* Loathsome, disgusting, hideous, detesting. *n.* Disgust.

ಬೀರ (*tb. of* ವೀರ 1, *q. v.*) *n.* A hero, *etc.*; *f.* ಬೀರಿ. 2, N. 3, heroism.

ಬೀರು 1. e. *n.* A bureau. 2, beer.

ಬೀರು 2. (ರು = ಱು) k. v. t. To fling, throw, *as* a stone, stick, *etc.* 2, to give liberally. *n.* Flinging. 2, spending profusely.

ಬಿಲ್ಲು e. *n.* A bill; an account, note.

ಬೀಸಣಿಗೆ (*fr.* ಬೀಸು) a. k. *n.* A fan.

ಬೀಸಿಗೆ (*tb. of* ವಿಂಶತಿ) *a.* Twenty.

ಬೀಸು k. *v. t.* To swing, whirl, wave; to mill, grind; to cast. *v. i.* To fan; to blow, *as* the wind. *n.* Swinging, *etc.* ಬೀಸಾಡು. To fling, throw. -ವ ಕಲ್ಲು, -ಗಲ್ಲು. A millstone.

ಬೀಳು 1. (ಳು = ೞು) k. *v. i.* To fall; to happen; to turn out; to become; to slip. 2, to go to ruin; to die. *P. p.* ಬಿದ್ದು; *pers. n. sing.* ಬಿತ್ತು. ಜಾರಿ-. To slip. ಉಪಯೋಗಕ್ಕೆ-, ಪ್ರಯೋಜನಕ್ಕೆ-. To be of use. ಹೆಸರು-. To be named; to lose reputation. ಕ್ರಯ-. To cost; to fall in price. ಬಿದ್ದುಕೊಳ್ಳು. To lie down. ಬಿದ್ದು ಬಿದ್ದು ನಗು. To wallow from laughter. ಬೀಳಗೆಡಹು. To fell. ಬೀಳ ಸದೆ, -ಹೊಡೆ. To beat down. ಬೀಳಿಸು. To cause to fall, to knock down. -ವಿಕೆ. Falling; a fall.

ಬೀಳು 2. (ಳು = ೞು. = ಬೀಡು 2, *q. v.*) k. *n.* A waste, *etc.* 2, badness. 3, prostration. 4, leaving. -ಕೆಡವು. To leave fallow. -ಭೂಮಿ. A waste. -ಕೊಡು, ಬೀಳ್ಕೊಡು. To give leave to go. -ಕೊಳ್ಳು, ಬೀಳ್ಕೊಳ್ಳು. To take leave to go.

ಬೀಳಲು, ಬೀೞಲು. = ಬಿಳಲು, *q. v.*

ಬುಕಣಿ h. *n.* Powder.

ಬುಕ್ಕ f. *n.* The heart. 2, a goat; *also* ಬುಕ್ಕೆ. 3, = ಬುಕ್ಕಿ.

ಬುಕ್ಕಿ f. *n.* A fragrant powder; *also* ಬುಕ್ಕಿಟ್ಟು.

ಬುಗಡಿ, ಬುಗುಡಿ f. *n.* A female's ear-ornament.

ಬುಗರಿ (= ಬೊಗರಿ) f. *n.* A spinning top. 2, (k.) the porcher tree, *Hibiscus populneoides.*

ಬುಗುಟು k. *n.* A swelling, protuberance.

ಬುಗ್ಗೆ k. *n.* A spring of water, fountain.

ಬುಜ. *tb. of* ಭುಜ, *q. v.* 2, *tb. of* ಭೂರ್ಜ. -ಪತ್ರೆ. Birch bark.

ಬುಜ್ಜಯಿಸು f. *v. t.* To cajole, flatter, persuade.

ಬುಟಿ h. *n.* A flower or other figure worked or painted. -ದಾರ. Decorated with flowery work.

ಬುಟ್ಟಿ, ಬುಟ್ಟಿ k. *n.* A basket. 2, an untrimmed object.

ಬುಡ (*tb. of* ಬುಧ್ನ) *n.* The bottom of anything; the foot, *as* of a tree; the roof, *as* of the tongue, *etc.* *Cpds.:* ಮರದ-, ಕಿವಿಯ-, ನಾಲಿಗೆಯ-, ಗಿಡದ-, ಸತ್ಯದ-, ಪ್ರೀತಿಯ-, *etc.* -ಕಟ್ಟು. A clan, family.

ಬುಡಮೆ, ಬುಡುಮೆ k. *n.* A sort of cucumber.

ಬುಡುಬುಡಿಕೆ k. *n.* A small rattle-drum. 2, untruth. -ಯವ. A fantastically dressed Mahratta mendicant with a rattle-drum.

ಬುದ್ದಿ k. *n.* An ink-bottle.

ಬುದ್ದು k. *n.* Roundness, curvedness. ಬುದ್ದ. A bandy-legged man; *f.* ಬುದ್ದಿ.

ಬುತ್ತಿ (*tb. of* ಭುಕ್ತಿ) *n.* Food (*prepared for a journey*); travelling provisions. -ಗಂಟು. A bundle of travelling provisions.

ಬುದ್ದಣಿಗೆ, ಬುದ್ದಲಿ f. *n.* A skin bottle for oil, ghee, *etc.*

ಬುಧ s. *a.* Known, understood; wise. *n.* A learned man. 2, Buddha; a Buddhist. ಬುದ್ಧಾವತಾರ. The ninth incarnation of Vishṇu.

ಬುದ್ಧಿ s. *n.* Perception; intelligence, intellect, judgment, wisdom, sense; knowledge; opinion, notion, view, idea; purpose. *int.* (*in accosting*) Well! right! -ಹೇಳು. To advise, instruct, exhort. -ಪೂರ್ವಕ. Purposely. -ಬಲ. The power of intellect. -ವಂತ, -ವಾನ. An intelligent, sensible man; *f.* -ವಂತಳು, -ವಂತೆ. -ವಂತಿಕೆ. = ಬುದ್ಧಿ. -ವಿಕಾರ. Perverseness of intellect. -ಶಾಲಿ. An intelligent person. -ಸಾಮರ್ಥ್ಯ. = ಬುದ್ಧಿ

ಬಲ, *q. v.* -ಹೀನ. Ignorant, foolish, stupid; a stupid man; *f.* -ಹೀನಳು, -ಹೀನೆ. ಬುದ್ಧೀಂದ್ರಿಯ. The perceptive organ of sense, *as:* eye, ear, nose, tongue and skin. ಕಾಕ-. Insolent notions.

ಬುದ್ಬುದ s. *n.* A bubble.

ಬುಧ s. *n.* The planet Mercury. -ವಾರ. Wednesday.

ಬುಧ್ನ. = ಬುಡ, *q. v.*

ಬುದ್ಧ್ಯಾ s. *ad.* Purposely, designedly.

ಬುನಗು, ಬುನುಗು f. *n.* The rear.

ಬುನಾದಿ h. *n.* Foundation, *as* of a building.

ಬುಂದಿ h. *n.* Fried granules of gram-flour. -ಲಡು. Sweetmeat of such granules.

ಬುಂದು h. *n.* A coffee-berry; *also* ಬುನ್ನು.

ಬುಭುಕ್ಷೆ s. *n.* Appetite, hunger. ಬುಭುಕ್ಷಿತ. Hungry; needy.

ಬುರಕಿ h. *n.* A veil; a cloth covering.

ಬುರಗಲು, ಬುರುಗಲು k. *n.* Parched rice.

ಬುರಡೆ, ಬುರುಡೆ (ರ = ಱ) k. *n.* A gourd-bottle, calabash; an inkstand; a snuff-box; the skull; *dim.* ಬುರಡಿ. 2, a lie, untruth. -ಮನುಷ್ಯ. A liar. -ಮಾತು. A lie. -ಹೊಡೆ. To utter lies.

ಬುರುಗು a. k. *n.* Foam, scum.

ಬುರುಜು h. *n.* A bastion. 2, a drawn play at chess.

ಬುರುಡು k. *n.* Roundness. -ಗಾಲು. A round, beautiful heel. -ಮೊಗ. A round, handsome face.

ಬರುದೆ k. *n.* Mud, mire.

ಬುರ್ಮ f. *n.* A gimlet; a small borer.

ಬುನ್ರಾಸು h. *a.* Nasty, worthless. 2, decayed, spoiled. -ಮನುಷ್ಯ. A worthless man.

ಬುನಿಗಸು f. *n.* A kind of felt.

ಬುಲಾಕು h. *n.* A jewel worn by women in the centre of their nostrils.

ಬುಲ್ಬುಲ್ h. *n.* The Indian nightingale, *Pycnonotus jocosus.*

ಬುಲ್ಲಯಿಸು, ಬುಲ್ಲಿಸು h. *v. t.* To coax, beguile; to fondle. *v. i.* To be elated. ಬುಲ್ಲವಣೆ. Flattering, coaxing; elation.

ಬುಸ f. *n.* Chaff; refuse, rubbish.

ಬುಸು k. *n.* Hissing, snoring. -ಗುಟ್ಟು. To puff, hiss.

ಬೂಕು e. *n.* Book. -ಬೈಂಡರ್. The book-binder.

ಬೂಚಿ k. *n.* A worm, insect.

ಬೂಚು f. *n.* A stopple; a cork.

ಬೂಜು, ಬೂಜೆ (= ಬೂಷ್ಟು) k. *n.* Mould, mildew, mustiness. -ಗಟ್ಟು. Mould to form. -ಹಿಡಿ. To be mouldy.

ಬೂಟಕ k. *n.* Trickery, deceit; a lie, falsehood; *also* -ತನ, ಬೂಟಾಟಿ.

ಬೂತ. *tb. of* ಭೂತ, *q. v.* -ಗನ್ನಡಿ. A magnifying glass, microscope.

ಬೂತು a. k. *n.* Obscenity. 2, an obscene man. 3, (e.) a boot. -ಗ. A shameless man.

ಬೂದಿ (*tb. of* ಭೂತಿ) *n.* Ashes; ash-colour. -ಗುಂಬಳ. The white gourd. -ಬಡಕ. A man who smears his body with ashes. -ಗನಕಸ. An ash-coloured herb, *Aerva lanata.* -ಬಣ್ಣ. Ash-colour. -ಬಾಳೆ. A kind of plantain. -ಹುಣ್ಣಿವೆ. The Hôḷi feast.

ಬೂದು. = ಬೂದಿ, *q. v.*

ಬೂಂದು. = ಬುಂದು, *q. v.*

ಬೂಮಿ. *tb. of* ಭೂಮಿ, *q. v.*

ಬೂರಗ, ಬೂರುಗ k. *n.* The silk-cotton tree, *Bombax.*

ಬೂಷ್ಟು. = ಬೂಜು, *q. v.*

ಬೂಸ f. *n.* N. for cerial grains, grasses, and esculent culms.

ಬೃಹತ್ s. *a.* Great, large, vast. -ಕುಕ್ಷಿ. Corpulent. ಬೃಹದಾರಣ್ಯ. A large forest.

ಬೃಹಸ್ಪತಿ s. *n.* The planet Jupiter. -ವಾರ. Thursday.

ಬೆಕ್ಕಸ a. k. *n.* Astonishment, surprise.

ಬೆಕ್ಕು k. *n.* A cat. *Cpds.:* ಕಾಡು-, ಸೀರು-, ಪುಣುಗಿನ-, ಮಂಟ-, *etc.* ಬೆಕ್ಕಿನ ಹೆಜ್ಜೆ. A winding herb, *Ipomaea palmata.* -ಗಣ್ಣು. A cat's eye. -ಮಾಳಿಗೆ. An opening in the màḷigĕ for the egress of smoke.

ಬೆಗಡು a. k. n. Amazement; fear. -ಗೊಳಿಸು. To frighten.

ಬೆಂ (ಬೆನ್) k. n. The back. -ಗಾವಲು. Body-guard. -ಗೊಡು. To flinch, retreat.

ಬೆಂಕಿ k. n. Heat; fire. -ಕಡ್ಡಿ. A match. -ಪೆಟ್ಟಿಗೆ. A match-box. -ಬೀಳು. Fire to fall upon. -ಮಾಡು. To make a fire. -ಯಾಗು. To become very angry. -ಹಚ್ಚು. -ಹತ್ತಿಸು, -ಹಾಕು. To set fire; to kindle. -ಹತ್ತು. Fire to kindle.

ಬೆಚ್ಚಗೆ, ಬೆಚ್ಚನೆ k. n. Heat; warmth. a. Hot, warm. ad. Warmly. -ಮಾಡು. To make warm; to beat soundly; to give a bribe.

ಬೆಚ್ಚರ a. k. n. Haste, speed. 2, bewilderment. 3, straying. ad. Quickly.

ಬೆಚ್ಚು k. v. i. To be frightened, scared; to fear. n. Fear, dread; a scare-crow. -ಬೀಳು. To be seized with alarm.

ಬೆಜ್ಜ (tb. of ವೇಧ) n. A bore, hole, as in a gem, etc.; the eye of a needle, etc.

ಬೆಜ್ಜರ (= ಬೆಚ್ಚರ) k. n. Fear.

ಬೆಂಚು e. n. A bench.

ಬೆಂಚೆ a. k. n. A small pond.

ಬೆಟ್ಟ 1. k. n. A big hill, mountain. -ದ ಕುರುಬ. A class of Kurubas. -ತೊರೆ. A mountain-stream. -ಬೇಗೆ. Wild fire in hills. -ಸೆಲೆ. A rock-snake.

ಬೆಟ್ಟ 2. (= ಬೆಟ್ಟಿ) k. n. Firmness, hardness, as of metal. -ಬೇಸಗೆ. A severe hot season. -ವೆಸಗೆ. A firm soldering or union. -ನೆ. Harshly, fiercely.

ಬೆಟ್ಟಿ (= ಬೆಟ್ಟ 2) k. n. A rude person. a. Hard. -ಚಿನ್ನ. Hard, brittle gold. -ಬಿಸಳ. A kind of crustacean articulate. -ತು. That is hard, firm, etc.

ಬೆಟ್ಟು 1. a. k. v. t. To strike forcibly into; to impress, stamp, coin. n. A tool for making impressions.

ಬೆಟ್ಟು 2. (= ಬಟ್ಟು) f. n. A finger, toe. -ಮುರಿ. To make the finger-joints crack.

ಬೆಟ್ಟೆ. = ಬೆಟ್ಟ 2, q. v. ಬೆಟ್ಟಡಿಕೆ. A hard, round areca-nut. -ಚಿನ್ನ, -ಬೆಳ್ಳಿ. Hard, brittle gold, silver.

ಬೆಡಗು, ಬೆಡಂಗು a. k. n. Novelty, beauty, grace, pleasantness. 2, showiness, airs. ಬೆಡಗ. A showy man.

ಬೆಣಚೆ, ಬೆಣಚು k. n. Quartz, white spar; also -ಕಲ್ಲು.

ಬೆಣೆ k. n. A peg, plug; a cork.

ಬೆಂಡು k. n. The white corky wood of the beṇḍu kasa, cork, pith. ಬೆಂಡಾಗು. To become like mere pith; to faint. -ಕಸ. A tall annual plant, *Aeschynomene indica*. -ಬತ್ತಾಸು. A porous kind of sweetmeat so named.

ಬೆಂಡೆ k. n. The esculent okra or edible Hibiscus, *Hibiscus esculentus; also* -ಕಾಯಿ.

ಬೆಂಡೇಕು k. n. A large timber tree, *Lagerstrœmia lanceolata.*

ಬೆಣ್ಣೆ k. n. Butter. -ಗರುಗಿಡ. A shrubby plant, *Sida rhombifolia*. -ಗಳ್ಳ. Kṛishṇa. -ಗಾರಿಗೆ. A kind of soft cake fried in ghee.

ಬೆತ್ತ (tb. of ವೇತ್ರ) k. n. A cane, rattan.

ಬೆತ್ತಲೆ. = ಬತ್ತಲೆ, q. v.

ಬೆದ k. n. Heat; also ಬೆದೆ. ad. Hotly, fiercely. -ಬೆದ. Very fiercely.

ಬೆದಕು k. v. t. To seek, search for, look for. 2, to strike with the claws. n. Search.

ಬೆದರು (ರು = ಱು) k. v. i. To be agitated, confounded, alarmed, frightened; to fear. n. Alarm; fright. 2, a scare-crow; also ಬೆದರಿಕೆ. ಬೆದರಿಸು. To alarm, frighten. ಬೆದರಿಸುವಿಕೆ. Frightening.

ಬೆದೆ k. n. Sowing, sowing seed; seed. 2, heat. -ಗಾಲ. Sowing season. -ಮಳೆ. Rain at the sowing season.

ಬೆನ್ k. n. The back. ಬೆಂತಟ್ಟು. To pat one's back, encourage, persuade. ಬೆನ್ನಟ್ಟು, ಬೆನ್ಹತ್ತು. To follow, pursue. ಬೆನ್ನಸ್ಥಿ. The back-bone. ಬೆನ್ನೀ. To turn the back, to retreat, flee. ಬೆನ್ನೀಡ. Flight.

ಬೆಂದು. *P. p. of* ಬೇ 1, *q. v.*

ಬೆನ್ನು (= ಬೆನ್) k. *n.* The back. ಬೆನ್ನಾಗು. To become accustomed to carry loads, *as* a bullock, horse, *etc.*; the back to get sore, *as* of an ox, horse, *etc.* ಬೆನ್ನಾಸರೆ. Support, help. ಬೆನ್ನಿನವನು. A younger brother; a follower. -ಕೊಡು. To flee, retreat. -ಬೀಳು. To follow; to take refuge. -ಹಂಚು. A ridge tile. -ಹತ್ತು. To follow, pursue. -ಹುರಿ, ಬೆನ್ನೆಲುಬು. The spine.

ಬೆಪ್ಪ k. *n.* A confused, stupid man. -ಳ. Alarm, fear.

ಬೆಪ್ಪು k. *n.* Wandering of mind, confusion.

ಬೆಬ್ಬಳ, ಬೆಬ್ಬಳೆ a. k. *n.* Alarm. 2, confusion, distress.

ಬೆಮ್. = ಬೆನ್, *q. v.* ಬೆಂಬತ್ತು. (= ಬೆನ್ನತ್ತು) To pursue. -ಬಲ (= ಬೆನ್-ಬಲ). Rear-force: help, aid. -ಬಳಿ. Following; company; association. -ಬಳಿಸು. To follow. -ಭಾಗ. The back part of the body; the ridge of a building. -ಬಿಡಿ (-ಹಿಡಿ). To follow. -ಬಿಡು. To withdraw.

ಬೆಮರು (= ಬೆವರು, *q. v.*) k. *v. i.* To perspire. *n.* Sweat. -ವಿಕೆ. Perspiring.

ಬೆಮೆ. *tb. of* ಭ್ರಮೆ, *q. v.* 2, desire. -ಗೊಳ್ಳು. To become confused. -ಗೊಳಿಸು. To confuse.

ಬೆಯಿಸು. = ಬೇಯಿಸು, *q. v.*

ಬೆರಕೆ (= ಬೆರಿಕೆ *fr.* ಬೆರೆ 1) k. *n.* Mingling, mixture, combination. 2, touch; contamination.

ಬೆರಗು 1. (ರ = ಐ) k. *n.* Amazement, astonishment, alarm. 2, confusion of mind. ಬೆರಗಾಗು. To become amazed.

ಬೆರಗು 2. k. *n.* Haste, speed. 2, rudeness.

ಬೆರಟು, ಬೆರಂಟು k. *v. t.* To scratch with the nails, claws, *etc.*

ಬೆರಲು, ಬೆರಳು k. *n.* A finger; a toe; the tip of an elephant's trunk. ಬೆರಳಾಡಿಸು. To move a finger about. -ಗಿಣ್ಣು. A finger knuckle.

ಬೆರಸು (= ಬೆರಿಸು) k. *v. t.* To mix, mingle, join. *v. i.* To be mixed, united with. *ad.* Together with, combined with, with.

ಬೆರಿಕೆ. = ಬೆರಕೆ, *q. v.* *Cpds.:* -ಜಾತಿ, -ಮಣ್ಣು, -ಮನುಷ್ಯ, -ಹುಲ್ಲು, *etc.*

ಬೆರಿಸು. = ಬೆರಸು, *q. v.*

ಬೆರೆ 1. k. *v. i.* To be joined, mingled, or mixed; to associate, *etc.* *P. ps.* ಬೆರೆದು, ಬೆರಡು, ಬೆರತು.

ಬೆರೆ 2. (ರ = ಐ) k. *v. i.* To become stiff, *as* from cold, pain, death, *etc.* 2, to be proud or conceited. *P. ps.* ಬೆರೆದು, ಬೆರಡು, ಬೆರತು.

ಬೆಲಪತ್ರೆ. *tb. of* ಬಿಲ್ವಪತ್ರೆ, *q. v.*

ಬೆಲೆ k. *n.* Price, cost. -ಕೊಡು. To pay for. -ಗಾಣು. To be sold for. -ತಗ್ಗು. Price to fall. -ಬರು. Price to fetch. -ಬೀಳು. Price to cost; price to fall.

ಬೆಲ್ಲ k. *n.* Coarse, dark sugar, jaggory.

ಬೆಲ್ಲೊಟ್ಟೆ f. *n.* A shrub with yellow flowers, *Mussaenda frondosa.*

ಬೆವರು 1. (= ಬೆಮರು) k. *v. i.* To perspire, sweat. *n.* Perspiration, sweat; *also* -ನೀರು. -ಗುಳ್ಳೆ, -ಸಾಲೆ. The prickly heat.

ಬೆವರು 2. k. *v. t.* To take away, *as* rubbish. 2, to stir a heap of grain, in sifting.

ಬೆವಸಾಯ. *tb. of* ವ್ಯವಸಾಯ, *q. v.*

ಬೆಸ (*tb. of* ವಿಧ) *n.* Making; act of worship; an order, injunction; asking, inquiry. -ಕೈ, -ಗೈ. To perform; to worship; to obey. -ಗೊಳ್ಳು. To ask, demand; to solicit. -ಸು. To order; to declare; to request.

ಬೆಸಗೆ (= ಬೆಸಿಗೆ) k. *n.* Soldering. -ಹಾಕು. To solder.

ಬೆಸದ. = ಬೆಸ್ತ, *q. v.*

ಬೆಸನ (*tb. of* ವಿಧಾನ) *n.* Order, command. 2, *tb. of* ವ್ಯಸನ, *q. v.* ಬೆಸಸೀ. To order.

ಬೆಸಲ್ a. k. *n.* Birth, bringing forth. ಬೆಸಲಾಗು. To bring forth.

ಬೆಸಿ (*tb. of* ವಿಷಮ) *a.* Odd, not even.

ಬೆಸಿಗೆ, ಬೆಸುಗೆ. = ಬೆಸಗೆ, *q. v.*

ಬಿಸಿ 1. k. v. t. To solder; to unite firmly. v. i. To be in use. 2, to be proud. P. ps. ಬಿಸಿದು, ಬಿಸದು, ಬಿಸ್ತು.

ಬಿಸಿ 2. k. n. A stroke with a whip, etc., a blow. 2, a bow for dressing cotton.

ಬಿಸ್ತ k. n. A fisherman.

ಬೆಳ್ (fr. ಬಿಳಿದು) a. k. n. Whiteness. Cpds.: -ಗದಿರು, -ಗಾಡು, -ಗೊಡೆ, -ದಿಂಗಳು (ಬೆಳದಿಂಗಳು moonlight), -ತೊನ್ನು (white leprosy), -ನೊರೆ, -ಮಿಂಚು, -ಮೃಗ, -ಮುಗಿಲು, ಬೆಳ್ಳಕ್ಕಿ (the white heron); ಬೆಳ್ಳಾನೆ, ಬೆಳ್ಳುಳ್ಳಿ (garlic), etc.

ಬೆಳಕು k. n. Light; a lamp. ಬೆಳಕರೆ. To dawn. -ಬಿಡು. To stand out of the light. -ಮಾಡು. To light. ಬೆಳಕಂಡಿ. A window.

ಬೆಳಗು k. v. i. To shine, become bright. v. t. To cause to shine; to manifest; to kindle; to scour, polish. n. Shine, lustre; the dawn. ಬೆಳಗಿಸು. To lighten; to cause to scour. ಬೆಳಗನಕ. Till dawn. ಬೆಳಗಂಜಾವ. The period of dawn. ಬೆಳಗಾಗು. To dawn. ಬೆಳಗಾತ, ಬೆಳಗಾನಾ. At dawn. -ಮುಂಜಾನೆ. At day-break. -ಎಕೆ. Shining.

ಬೆಳತಿಗೆ, ಬೆಳಂತಿಗೆ k. n. Whiteness; brightness. -ಅಕ್ಕಿ. White rice.

ಬೆಳಲ k. n. The wood-apple tree, *Feronia elephantum*.

ಬೆಳವ k. n. A wild pigeon.

ಬೆಳವಲ, ಬೆಳವಲು. = ಬೆಳಲ, q. v.

ಬೆಳವಾರ k. n. An outcast, low man.

ಬೆಳಸು (= ಬೆಳಿಸು, ಬೆಳೆಸು) k. v. t. To cause to grow; to raise, as a crop; to rear, foster; to increase. n. Growth; a crop of corn, etc.

ಬೆಳಗ್ಗೆ, ಬೆಳಗ್ಗೆ (fr. ಬೆಳಗು) k. ad. When it dawns, at dawn.

ಬೆಳಿಸು. = ಬೆಳಸು, q. v.

ಬೆಳೆ k. v. i. To grow, as corn, grass, trees, etc.; to increase. v. t. To grow, raise, as a crop. P. ps. ಬೆಳೆದು, ಬೆಳದು. n. Growing; growth; crop; standing corn, etc. 2, seedlings. -ಗೇಡು. A failure of crops. -ನೆಡು. To plant seedlings. -ಬಿತ್ತು, -ಇಡು. To plant, sow. -ಮಾಡು. To raise a crop. -ಯುಎಕೆ. Growing, etc. ಬೆಳವಣಿಗೆ, ಬೆಳುವಣಿಗೆ, ಬೆಳವಿಗೆ. Growing, growth; increase.

ಬೆಳ್ವು. = ಬಿಳುಪು, q. v.

ಬೆಳ್ಳಗೆ, ಬೆಳ್ಳನ್ನ, ಬೆಳ್ಳಾನೆ k. a. White.

ಬೆಳ್ಳವಾರ, ಬೆಳ್ಳಾರ k. n. A snare, noose.

ಬೆಳ್ಳಿ k. n. Silver.

ಬೇ 1. (= ಬೇಯು) k. v. i. To be burnt; to be cooked, boiled; to burn with a fever, grief, etc. P. p. ಬೆಂದು.

ಬೇ 2. k. v. t. To beg with an humble, pitiable voice. P. p. ಬೇಡು. -ಕರೆ. A crying beggar.

ಬೇ 3. h. pref. Without; dis-, un-; as: -ಅದಬು. Insult. -ಅಬುರು. Defamation, dishonour. -ಖಬರ್. Careless, stupid. -ಚಿರಾಕು. Untenanted, desolate, as a house. -ನಾಮಿ. Nameless, fictitious.

ಬೇಕು (fr. ಬೇಡು) k. 3rd pers. sing. It is wished, desired, requested; it is necessary; it is wanted; it is due, it must; he, she, thou, you, they are desirable, etc. ಬೇಕಿಲ್ಲ, for ಬೇಡ. ಬೇಕಾಗು. To be desired, necessary, etc. ಬೇಕನ್ನು. To say "it is wished or desired", "it is desirable", etc. ನಾನು ಬೇಕೆಂತ (intentionally) ಬಡಿದೆನೋ? ಬೇಕಂತ (purposely) ತಪ್ಪ ಮಾಡಿದನು.

ಬೇಕೂಬ, ಬೇಖೂಬ h. a. Foolish, silly. n. A fool; see s. ಬೇ 3.

ಬೇಗ (tb. of ವೇಗ) n. Speed. ad. Speedily, quickly. -ನೆ. Quickly. -ಮಾಡು. To hasten.

ಬೇಗಡೆ f. n. Talc mineral, mica; a thin plate of tin covered with some colouring substance.

ಬೇಗಾರಿ h. n. Compulsory labour without wages.

ಬೇಗು (= ಬೇಹು, q. v.) k. n. Spying. -ಗಾರ. = ಬೇಹುಗಾರ.

ಬೇಗುದಿ k. n. Affliction, distress.

ಬೇಗೆ k. *n.* Fire; heat; wild fire in jungles. -ಬೀಳು, -ಹತ್ತು. Wild fire to break out.

ಬೇಂಕು e. *n.* A bank, place where money is deposited. ಬೇಂಕಿನವ. A dealer in money.

ಬೇಜಾ h. *a.* Meaningless, groundless, bad.

ಬೇಜಾರು h. *n.* Weariness (from fatigue, pain, *etc.*), annoyance.

ಬೇಟೆ (=ಬೇಂಟೆ) k. *n.* Hunting, the chase. 2, game. -ಯಾಡು. To hunt. -ಗಾರ. A hunter.

ಬೇಡ 1, -ರವ k. *n.* A huntsman; a tribe of forest people living by the chase; *f.* -ತಿ.

ಬೇಡ 2. (*abbr. of* ಬೇಡದು, *neg. of* ಬೇಡು, *contrary of* ಬೇಕು) k. *def. v.* It is not wished, desired, requested; it is not desirable, required or necessary; it is not wanted; it is not due, it must not; he, she, you, they (are) not desirable, *etc. Hon. pl.* ಬೇಡರಿ, ಬೇಡಿ. ಬೇಡನ್ನು, ಬೇಡೆನ್ನು. To forbid, *etc.*; to refuse, *etc.* ಬೇಡಾಗು. To be undesirable, *etc.*

ಬೇಡಿ h. *n.* A chain, fetter.

ಬೇಡು k. *v. t.* To wish; to beg, pray, entreat, request. -ವಿಕೆ, ಬೇಡಿಕೆ. Asking, begging, entreating.

ಬೇಂಟೆ. = ಬೇಟೆ, *q. v.*

ಬೇತಾಳ (*tb. of* ವೇತಾಲ) *n.* A ghost, goblin, demon.

ಬೇತು h. *n.* Plan, scheme; purpose, design.

ಬೇನೆ k. *n.* Pain; sickness, disease. -ಬರು. Pain or disease to be brought on. -ಬೀಳು. To become sick. -ಯುವ. A sick man. *Cpds.*: ಕಾಲು-, ತಲೆ-, ಹೆರುವ-, ಹೊಟ್ಟೇ-.

ಬೇಪಾರ. *tb. of* ವ್ಯಾಪಾರ, *q. v.*

ಬೇಫಾಮು h. *n.* Heedlessness, negligence; indifference.

ಬೇಬಂದು h. *a.* Confused. *n.* Disorder, *etc.*

ಬೇಯು. = ಬೇ, etc. *P. p.* ಬೆಂದು. -ವದು. Boiling. ಬೇಯಿಸು. To boil up; to prepare, *as* food by boiling; to bake, *as* bread; to pain, afflict.

ಬೇರ. *tb. of* ವ್ಯಾಪಾರ, *q. v.* -ಮಾಡು. To traffic.

ಬೇರೀಜು m. *n.* The total assessment of a land, village, *etc.*

ಬೇರು k. *n.* A root. -ಗ. A root seller. -ಕೀಳು, ಬೇರೊಂದಿಗೆ ಕೀಳು. To uproot, eradicate. -ಗೊಲೆ. Utter ruin. ಬೇರೂರು. To take root, be established; to spring up, originate. ಬೇರಿನ ಪಲ್ಲೆ. Roots used for curry. -ಬಿಡು. To begin to root.

ಬೇರೆ (ರೆ=ಱೆ) k. *a.* Separate, apart, different, other, else. *ad.* Separately, further. -ಬೇರೆ. *rep.* Separate, different; one by one; various. --ಇಡು, --ಇರಿಸು. To place separately. -ಮಾಡು. To separate; to change, alter. -ಯಾಗು. To become separate or changed. ಬೇರೊಂದು. Another thing, something else; another. ಬೇರೊಬ್ಬ. Another man; another.

ಬೇರ್ಪಡು (*fr.* ಬೇರೆ) k. *v. i.* To be separated. ಬೇರ್ಪಡಿಸು. To distinguish; to separate.

ಬೇಲ (= ಬೆಳಲ) k. *n.* The wood-apple tree.

ಬೇಲಿ k. *n.* A hedge, fence. -ಕಟ್ಟು, -ನಾಟು, -ಹಾಕು. To put a fence.

ಬೇವಸ (*fr.* ಬೇ) k. *n.* Grief, anxiety.

ಬೇವಾರಸು h. *a.* Without heir or owner, unclaimed.

ಬೇವು k. *n.* The neem tree or margosa tree, *Melia azadirachta.*

ಬೇಷು h. *a.* Good, proper, well.

ಬೇಸಗೆ, = ಬೇಸಿಗೆ, *q. v.*

ಬೇಸತ್ತು. *P. p. of* ಬೇಸರು, *q. v.*

ಬೇಸರ, ಬೇಸರಿಕೆ, ಬೇಸರು (ರ=ಱ) k. *n.* Weariness, fatigue; disgust, vexation. *v. i.* To grow weary or fatigued; to be disgusted. *P. p.* ಬೇಸತ್ತು. -ಗೊಳ್ಳು, -ಪಡು, ಬೇಸರಾಗು. To get tired of, feel dislike, *etc.*

ಬೇಸಾಯ (*tb. of* ವ್ಯವಸಾಯ, *q. v.*) *n.* Agriculture. -ಮಾಡು, -ಸಾಗಿಸು. To cultivate. -ಗಾರ. A farmer.

ಬೇಸಿಗೆ (= ಬೇಸಗೆ. *tb. of* ವೈಶಾಖ) k. *n.* The hot season. -ಕಾಲ. The hot weather.

ಬೇಸು. = ಬೇಯಿಸು, *q. v.*

ಬೇಹು (= ಬೇಗು, *q. v.*) k. *n.* Spying. -ಗಾರ, ಬೇಹವ, ಬೇಹಿನವ. A spy.

ಬೇಹುಷಾರು h. *n.* Want of attention or care. 2, indisposition.

ಬೇಳ್, ಬೇಳುವೆ a. k. *n.* Bewilderment, confusion, madness. ಬೇಳಾಗು. To grow bewildered.

ಬೇಳಂಬ k. *n.* Desire, extreme anxiety.

ಬೇಳು a. k. *v. i.* To offer into fire, *as* ghee, animals, *etc.*

ಬೇಳೆ 1. k. *n.* Split pulse, *as of* ಕಡ್ಲೆ-, ತೊಗರಿ-, ಹೆಸರು-, *etc.* 2, the half of a ಹಾಗ (=).

ಬೇಳೆ 2. k. *n.* A common potherb, *Chenopodium album.*

ಬೈ. = ಬಯ್ಯು, *q. v.*

ಬೈಕ (*tb. of* ಭೈಕ್ಷ) *n.* Charity, alms.

ಬೈಗಳು. = ಬಯ್ಗಳು, *s.* ಬಯ್ಯು, *q. v.*

ಬೈತನಕ k. *ad.* Till evening.

ಬೈಬಲು f. *n.* The Bible, the name given to the book that contains the Christian sacred Scriptures, Word of God.

ಬೈರಾಗಿ (*tb. of* ವೈರಾಗಿ) *n.* One of a class of mendicants.

ಬೈಲು. = ಬಯಲು, *q. v.*

ಬೈಸಿಕಲ್ e. *n.* A bicycle, two-wheeled veloceped.

ಬೈಸಿಕೆ h. *n.* Sitting down and rising in alternation (as an exercise or punishment at school).

ಬೈಸು. = ಬಯಸು, *q. v.*

ಬೊಕ್ಕ 1. k. *ad.* With a turn or bend. -ಬೊರಲು, -ಬೋರಲ. Headlong, flatwise. --ಬೀಳು. To fall headlong.

ಬೊಕ್ಕ 2. (= ಬೊಚ್ಚು 2) f. *n.* A toothless man. *a.* Bare, uncovered. -ಬಾಯಿ. A toothless mouth.

ಬೊಕ್ಕಣ k. *n.* A pocket in a coat; a betel pouch; horse's gram bag. 2, *tb. of* ಭಕ್ಷಣ.

ಬೊಕ್ಕಸ h. *n.* A coffer, treasury (*as* of a king, rich man or temple). -ದ ಮನೆ. A treasury. -ದವನು. A treasurer.

ಬೊಕ್ಕೆ k. *n.* A pimple, blister, boil. 2, any round small hole made by rats, *etc.*

ಬೊಗರಿ (= ಬುಗರಿ) k. *n.* A spinning top.

ಬೊಗಸೆ (= ಬಗಸೆ, *q. v.*) k. *n.* The palms of the hands joined like a cup.

ಬೊಗಳು, ಬೊಗುಳು (= ಬಗುಳು, *q. v.*) k. *v. i.* To bark, clamour.

ಬೊಗ್ಗು (= ಬಗ್ಗು, *q. v.*) k. *v. i.* To bend, stoop. ಬೊಗ್ಗಿ ನೋಡು. To stoop down and look. ಬೊಗ್ಗಿಸು. To cause to bend. ಬೊಗ್ಗಿ ಹಾಕು. To humble.

ಬೊಂಕು k. *v. i.* & *t.* To lie or speak falsely, deny.

ಬೊಚ್ಚು 1. k. *a.* Wool, fine hair, down.

ಬೊಚ್ಚು 2. = ಬೊಕ್ಕ 2, *q. v.*

ಬೊಜ್ಜ (*tb. of* ಭೋಜ್ಯ) *n.* A feast, *etc.* the last śrâddha ceremony performed for a deceased relative.

ಬೊಜ್ಜು k. *n.* A pot-belly.

ಬೊಟ್ಟು (= ಬೆಟ್ಟು, *q. v.*) f. *n.* A finger; a toe. 2, a small quantity, drop. 3, (*tb. of* ವೃತ್ತ) a circular mark (of sandal paste, *etc.*) on the forehead.

ಬೊಡ್ಡಿ, ಬೊಡೆ. = ಬಡಿ, *q. v.*

ಬೊಡ್ಡೆ (*tb. of* ಬುಧ್ನ, *q. v.*) *n.* The trunk of a tree.

ಬೊಂಡುಳ k. *n.* An annual herb, *Physalis indica.*

ಬೊಂತೆ f. *n.* A cloth made of quilted rags. -ಗಳ್ಳಿ. A large leafless shrub, the triangular spurge, *Euphorbia antiquorum.*

ಬೊಬ್ಬಡೆ k. *n.* Rind, bark.

ಬೊಬ್ಬುಳಿ 1. (*tb. of* ಬರ್ಬರ) *n.* The thorny Babool tree, *Acacia arabica.*

ಬೊಬ್ಬುಳಿ 2. a. k. *n.* A bubble.

ಬೊಬ್ಬೆ k. n. An outcry, shout, bawl, yell; a great noise; loud sound. ಬೊಬ್ಬಾಟ. Bawling, etc. -ಕೊಡು, -ಮಾಡು, -ಹಾಕು, -ಹೊಡೆ, ಬೊಬ್ಬಿಡು. To bawl, shout, etc.

ಬೊಂಬೆ (=ಗೊಂಬೆ) k. n. An image, figure, a puppet, doll; an idol. -ಯಾಟ. A puppet-show. -ಕಟ್ಟು. To curse by sorcery.

ಬೊಮ್ಮ. tb. of ಬ್ರಹ್ಮ, q. v.

ಬೊರಲು k. n. A broom.

ಬೊಳ. = ಬಳ 3, q. v.

ಬೋಕೆ k. n. A potsherd.

ಬೋಗ. tb. of ಭೋಗ, q. v.

ಬೋಗಣಿ, ಬೋಗುಣಿ f. n. A metal vessel.

ಬೋಗಾರ (tb. of ವ್ಯೋಕಾರ) n. A blacksmith. 2, a coppersmith.

ಬೋಡ k. n. A toothless man; f. ಬೋಡಿ. ಬೋಡು. Toothlessness.

ಬೋಣಿ, ಬೋಣಿಗೆ h. n. The first sale of goods at dawn; handsel.

ಬೋಂಡಾ f. n. A fried cake made of horse gram, salt, chillies, etc.

ಬೋದಿಗೆ k. n. The cornice or capital of a column or pillar.

ಬೋದು k. n. Luxuriance in growth; rank fruits (as badanŏ, savutĕ, etc.) without substance or taste.

ಬೋದುಗೆ = ಬೋದಿಗೆ, q. v.

ಬೋದೆಹುಲ್ಲು k. n. The Roussa or ginger grass, Andropogon martini.

ಬೋಧ, ಬೋಧೆ s. n. Making known; instruction; awakening. 2, understanding; perception; knowledge. -ಕ. Instructing; an instructor, teacher; preacher; indicating, signifying. -ನ, -ನೆ. Making known, explaining, instructing, teaching; instruction, admonition. ಕ್ರಿಸ್ತ-. Christian teaching. ವಿಶ್ವಾಸ-. Dogmatics. ದುರ್-. Bad advice. ಸು-. Good advice. ಬೋಧಿತ. Explained; instructed. ಬೋಧಿಸು. To make known, explain, teach, instruct.

ಬೋನ 1. k. n. Boiled rice; food. -ಗಿತ್ತಿ. A female cook.

ಬೋನ 2. f. n. A metal vessel for culinary purposes; cf. ಬೋಗಿ.

ಬೋನು k. n. A trap. ಇಲಿ-. A rat-trap.

ಬೋನುಸು e. n. A bonus, an extra dividend to shareholders out of accumulated profits.

ಬೋಯಿ h. n. A class of palanquin-bearers and fishermen.

ಬೋಯಿಲರ್ e. n. Boiler, a vessel in which the steam is generated.

ಬೋರಲ, -ಲು (= ಬೋರ್ಲ) k. ad. Upside down, topsyturvy. -ಬೀಳು. To fall on the face; to be upset. -ಹಾಕು. To put (as a vessel) upside down.

ಬೋರೆ 1. k. n. A hill, hillock; a swelling.

ಬೋರೆ 2. (tb. of ಬದರಿ) n. The jujube-tree and its fruit. 2, chestnut colour. -ಕಾಯಿ. An unripe jujube. -ಹಣ್ಣು. Its fruit.

ಬೋರ್ಲ. = ಬೋರಲ, q. v.

ಬೋವ. = ಬೋಯಿ, q. v. 2, a foreman. -ತನ. Leadership.

ಬೋಸರ f. n. False courtesy, flattery. ಬೋಸರಿಸು. To flatter, coax.

ಬೋಸಿ. = ಬೋನ, q. v.

ಬೋಳ (ಳ = ಱ) k. n. A man with a bald or shaven head. a. Bald, shaven; uncovered. -ಪತ್ರಿ. A roadside plant, Erigeron asteroides. -ತಲೆ, -ಮಂಡೆ. A shaven or bald head. -ಮಾಳಿಗೆ. The flat roof of a house without a balustrade. ಬೋಳಿ. A shaven widow. ಬೋಳಿಸು. To shave (esp. the head). ಬೋಳಿಸಿಕೊಳ್ಳು. To have one's head shaved. ಬೋಳು. A bald, bare, roofless, leafless, treeless state. Cpds.: -ತಲೆ, -ಬೆಟ್ಟ, -ಮನೆ, -ಮರ, -ಮುಂಡೆ, etc.

ಬೋಳಯಿಸು, ಬೋಳಯ್ಸು, ಬೋಳವಿಸು k. v. t. To coax, caress, fondle, court.

ಬೌದ್ಧ (fr. ಬೋಧ, ಬುದ್ಧ) s. a. Relating to intellect. n. A Buddhist; a Buddha. -ಧರ್ಮ. The religion of Buddha. -ಮಾರ್ಗ. The Buddhistic ways.

ಬ್ರಹಸ್ಪತಿ. *tb. of* ಬೃಹಸ್ಪತಿ, *q. v.*

ಬ್ರಹ್ಮ (=ಬೊಮ್ಮ) **s.** *n.* Brahmâ, the first deity of the Hindu triad, the creator. 2, a vedic text. 3, the vedas. 4, religious knowledge. 5, liberation from further existence. 6, the soul of the universe. 7, the supreme soul. 8, a Brâhmaṇa. -ಕಲ್ಪ. The age of Brahmâ. -ಚರ್ಯ. Religious studentship; abstinence; chastity. -ಚಾರಿ. A young Brâhmaṇa student; a bachelor. -ಜ್ಞಾನ. Knowledge of the soul of the universe. -ಜ್ಞಾನಿ. One who possesses that knowledge. -ತಿ.=-ಹತ್ಯ. -ತ್ವ. Brahmanhood. -ದಾರು. The Indian mulberry tree, *Morus indica;* the tree *Ficus religiosa.* -ಪುತ್ರ. N. of a river; a vegetable poison. -ರಂಧ್ರ. An aperture in the crown of the head through which the soul is said to escape at death. -ರಾಕ್ಷಸ. A fiend of the Brâhmaṇas. -ಲೋಕ. The heaven of Brahmâ. -ವರ್ಚಸ. Divine splendour or glory. -ವಿದ್ಯೆ. The vêda and vêdânta. -ವೀಣೆ. A sort of lute. -ವೃಕ್ಷ. The tree *Butea frondosa.* -ಸಾಯುಜ್ಯ. Union with Brahmâ. -ಸೂತ್ರ. The sacrificial thread; the vêdânta sûtra. -ಸ್ವ. Property belonging to Brâhmaṇas. -ಹತ್ಯ. Killing a Brâhmaṇa. ಬ್ರಹ್ಮಾಂಜಲಿ. Joining the hollowed hands in token of homage while repeating the vêda. ಬ್ರಹ್ಮಾಂಡ. The universe; a great quantity, excess. ಬ್ರಹ್ಮಾಂಡ ಪುರಾಣ. N. of a Purâṇa. ಬ್ರಹ್ಮಾಮ್ಲಿಕ. The monkey-bread tree, *Adansonia digitata.* ಬ್ರಹ್ಮಾರ್ಪಣ. Dedicating to Brahmâ, *as* ceremonies of a śrâddha. ಬ್ರಹ್ಮಿ. The plant *Aloe perfoliata.* ಬ್ರಹ್ಮೇತಿ.=ಬ್ರಹ್ಮಹತ್ಯ). ಬ್ರಹ್ಮೇತಿಗಾರ. A killer of a Brâhmaṇa. ಬ್ರಹ್ಮೋಪದೇಶ. Instruction in mantras, *esp.* the gâyatrî.

ಬ್ರಾಂದಿ e. *n.* Brandy.

ಬ್ರಾಹ್ಮ **s.** *a.* Brahmanical. *n.* A Brâhmaṇa. 2, a form of marriage. -ಣ. Brahmanical; a Brâhmaṇa, a priest, *f.* ಬ್ರಾಹ್ಮಣಿ; a portion of the vêda containing the sacrificial ritual with legends and old stories. -ಣತ್ವ, -ಣಿಕೆ, -ಣ್ಯ. Brahmanhood.

ಬ್ರಾಹ್ಮಿ **s.** *n.* The personified energy of Brahmâ. 2, Brahmâ's wife. 3, the moon-plant, *Asclepias acida.* -ಮುಹೂರ್ತ (*tb. of* ಬ್ರಾಹ್ಮ್ಯಮುಹೂರ್ತ). The hour preceding sun-rise, dawn.

ಭ್. The forty-second letter of the alphabet.

ಭಕಾರ **s.** *n.* The letter ಭ.

ಭಕುತಿ. *tb. of* ಭಕ್ತಿ, *q. v.*

ಭಕ್ತ **s.** *a.* Attached to, devoted to. *n.* A follower of, worshipper, votary; *f.* -ಳು, ಭಕ್ತೆ. -ವತ್ಸಲ. Kind to worshippers.

ಭಕ್ತಿ (=ಭಕುತಿ) **s.** *n.* Devotion, devotedness, loyalty, loving faith; love; homage, worship. -ಭಾವ. A devoted mind. -ಮಾರ್ಗ. The way of loving faith. -ರಸ. Sense of devotion. -ವಂತ. A pious, religious man. -ಹೀನ. Devoid of devotion or piety, *etc.*; a man lacking in devotion; *f.* -ಹೀನಳು, -ಹೀನೆ. -ಹೀನತೆ. Devotionlessness, *etc.*

ಭಕ್ಷ **s.** *n.* Eating; an eatable, food; drink. -ಕ. An eater; voracious, gluttonous. -ಕಾರ. A baker. -ಕಾರಿ. A glutton. -ಣ. Eating; an eatable, *esp.* a sweetmeat. ಭಕ್ಷಿಸು. To eat, devour. ಭಕ್ಷ್ಯ. Edible; a cake.

ಭಗ s. n. The sun. 2, fate, good fortune. 3, dignity; glory. 4, strength. 5, effort. 6, radiance. 7, love. 8, knowledge. 9, law; religion. 10, final emancipation. -ನ್ದರ. A carbuncle. -ವತ್. Venerable; a deity. -ವತಿ. Durgâ, Pârvatî. -ವದ್ಗೀತೆ. N. of an episode in the Mahâbhârata. -ವಂತ. A god.

ಭಗಿನಿ s. n. A sister. -ಜ. A sister's son.

ಭಗೀರಥ s. n. N. of a king who brought down the Ganges.

ಭಗೇಂದ್ರ (tb. of ಭಗಂದರ) n. A carbuncle.

ಭಗ್ನ s. a. Broken; defeated; destroyed; disheartened, disappointed. -ಮನಸು. Discouragement, disappointment. -ಮಾನಸ. Discouraged, disappointed.

ಭಂಗ s. n. Breaking. 2, a break. 3, fall, downfall, ruin. 4, defeat, overthrow; distress, trouble. 5, disappointment. 6, flight. 7, bowing; a bend. 8, a wave. 9, falsehood; deceit, fraud. -ಪಡಿಸು. To ruin, defeat, *etc.* -ಪಡು. To be ruined, defeated, troubled, disappointed, *etc.* -ಶ್ಲೇಷ. A kind of pun in rhetoric.

ಭಂಗಾರ. tb. of ಬಂಗಾರ, q. v.

ಭಂಗಿ s. n. Breaking; a wave. 2, irony, wit; pretext, fraud. 3, a way, manner, mode. -ಸು. To break, ruin, destroy.

ಭಂಗುರ s. a. Frail, changeful; variable. 2, crooked. n. A bend.

ಭಂಗೆ (= ಬಂಗಿ, q. v.) s. n. The common hemp plant, *Cannabis sativa.*

ಭಜನ, ಭಜನೆ s. n. Adoring, adoration, worship, devotion. 2, dividing (*arith.*). ಭಜಕ. A worshipper, votary. ಭಜಿಸು. To adore, worship.

ಭಂಜಕ s. n. A breaker, destroyer. ಭಂಜನ. Destroying; routing; afflicting. ಭಂಜಿಸು. To break; to humiliate.

ಭಟ (= ಬಟ) s. n. A warrior, soldier. a hero.

ಭಟ್ಟ (= ಬಟ್ಟ 3) s. n. Any learnedm an, doctor or philosopher; *used also as* a title. 2, a bard; f. ಭಟ್ಟಿನಿ.

ಭಂಟಾಕಿ, ಭಂಡಾಕಿ s. n. The egg-plant, *Solanum melongena.*

ಭಂಡ (= ಬಂಡ 2) s. n. A jester, buffoon; a mimic. 2, N. of a mixed caste. ಭಂಡು. = ಬಂಡು.

ಭಂಡಾರ (tb. of ಭಾಂಡಾಗಾರ, q. v.) n. A store-room, magazine, treasury. ಭಂಡಾರಿ. A treasurer, storekeeper.

ಭಂಡಿ s. n. Bengal madder, *Rubia munjista.*

ಭಂಡಿಲ s. a. Fortunate, prosperous. n. Fortune; welfare. 2, a messenger. 3, an artizan.

ಭದ್ರ s. a. Good, well. 2, favourable, gracious. 3, pleasant. 4, safe, secure; firm, strong, *as* a cloth or rope. n. Happiness, welfare, good fortune. 2, a bull. -ಕಾಲಿ, -ಕಾಳಿ. Pârvatî, Durgâ. -ದಾಯಕ. The bestower of welfare. -ದಾರು. A sort of pine, *Pinus deodora.* -ಪದೆ. N. of the 3rd and 4th asterisms. -ಮಂಟಪ. A nuptial shed. -ಮುಸ್ತಕ, -ಮುಸ್ತೆ. A kind of sedge, *Cyperus hexastachyus.* -ಶ್ರೀ. Sandalwood.

ಭದ್ರಾ s. n. N. of the second, seventh and twelfth days of the lunar fortnight. -ಕರಣ. The act of shaving. ಭದ್ರಾಸನ. A splendid seat; a posture in devotion.

ಭದ್ರಾಕ್ಷ s. n. A kind of seed used as beads.

ಭದ್ರೆ s. n. The 7th astrological division of the day.

ಭಯ s. n. Fear, alarm, dread; dismay; fright, terror; danger, risk. -ಆಸ್ಪದ. Reason for fear. -ಗೊಳ್ಳು. To become afraid, alarmed. -ಗೊಳ್ಳಿಸು, -ಪಡಿಸು. To frighten. -ಂಕರ. Fear-causing; fearful, terrible. -ತಟ್ಟು. Fear to seize. -ಪಡು. To fear, to be alarmed. -ಭಕ್ತಿ. Fear and devotion. -ತ್ರಸ್ತ. Trembling for fear. -ದ್ರುತ. Fleeing for fear. -ಧ್ವನಿ. A voice expressing fear. -ಭ್ರಷ್ಟ. Put to flight in terror. -ಭ್ರಾಂತ. Confused from terror. -ಸ್ಥ.

A man in fear; *f.* -ಸ್ಥೆ, -ಸ್ಥಳು. ಭಯಾನಕ. Fearful, terrible; fear, terror. ಭಯಾತುರ. Alarmed. ಭಯಾತುರ. Alarm.

ಭರ s. *n.* Bearing, upholding, supporting. 2, a burden, load, weight. 3, a large quantity, multitude, plenty. 4, desire. 5, exacerbation. 6, haste. -ಕ್ಕೆ ಬೀಳು. To be irritated. -ಭರನೆ. *rep.* In great haste. -ಣ. Bearing; supporting, maintaining; wages, hire; filling; filling stuff.

ಭರಣಿ. = ಬರಣಿ, *q. v.* 2, the second nakshatra.

ಭರತ s. *n.* An actor, dancer. 2, N. of a muni. 3, N. of one of Daśaratha's sons and Râma's younger brother. 4, N. of a monarch. 5, the flux of the ocean, flow. -ಇಳಿತ. Flow and ebb. -ಖಂಡ, -ವರ್ಷ. India.

ಭರದ್ವಾಜ s. *n.* A sky-lark. 2, N. of a ṛishi.

ಭರವಸ *f. n.* Confidence, trust. 2, quickness. -ಇಡು. To believe, trust.

ಭರಿತ s. *a.* Full, filled, full of.

ಭರ್ತ, ಭರ್ತಾರ. *tb. of* ಭರ್ತೃ, *q. v.*

ಭರ್ತಿ (= ಭರತಿ) s. *n.* Loaded state, *as of* a cart, vessel, bag, *etc.* 2, the flux of the ocean.

ಭರ್ತೃ (= ಭರ್ತ, ಭರ್ತಾರ) s. *n.* A cherisher, supporter; a master; a husband; a chief. -ದಾರಕ. A crown prince; *f.* -ದಾರಿಕೆ.

ಭಲ, ಭಲರೆ, ಭಲಾ *f. int.* Fine! well done! bravo!

ಭಲ್ಲ s. *n.* A kind of pointed arrow.

ಭಲ್ಲಾತಕ s. *n.* The marking-nut tree, *Semecarpus anacardium.*

ಭಲ್ಲುಕ, ಭಲ್ಲೂಕ s. *n.* A bear.

ಭವ s. *n.* Becoming, existing, existence. 2, birth, origin. 3, transmigration. 4, life. 5, the world. 6, welfare. -ದೂರ. Far from the world and its misery. -ಬಂಧನ, -ಪಾಶ. Fetters of worldly existence. -ಸಾಗರ, ಭವಾಬ್ಧಿ. The ocean of transmigration. ಭವಾಂತರ. Another existence.

ಭವತ್ s. *n.* Present time. 2, you, your honour. ಭವತಿ. Your ladyship, lady. ಭವದೀಯ. Your, your honour's.

ಭವನ s. *n.* Existing; production, birth. 2, a house, dwelling, mansion. 3, a field.

ಭವಾನಿ s. *n.* Pârvatî, Śiva's wife.

ಭವಿ s. *n.* Living; a living being. 2, a worldling. -ಸು. To produce.

ಭವಿಷ್ಯ s. *a.* To be about to become, future, imminent. -ತ್. Future; futurity, future time; the future tense. -ಕಾಲ. Future time; the future tense.

ಭಸ್ಮ (= ಬಸುಮ) s. *n.* Ashes; any metallic oxide. -ಪುಟ. Application to fire in order to make ashes. ಭಸ್ಮಾಸುರ. N. of a demon.

ಭಳರೆ, ಭಳಿರೆ. = ಭಲ, *q. v.*

ಭಾಗ s. *n.* A fraction; a part, portion; share; a division. 2, lot, luck. 3, a place, region. ಮುಂ-. The front part. ಹಿಂ-. The hind part. ಭಾಗಾಕಾರ, ಭಾಗಾರ. Division (*arith.*).

ಭಾಗವತ (*fr.* ಭಗವತ್) s. *n.* A whorshipper of Vishṇu or Kṛishṇa. 2, N. of a Purâṇa; *also* -ಪುರಾಣ. 3, the manager of a dramatic performance.

ಭಾಗಿ s. *a.* Having a share. *n.* A partner; a co-heir. 2, a possessor. ಭಾಗಿಸು. To divide (*esp. arith.*).

ಭಾಗೀರಥಿ s. *n.* The Ganges.

ಭಾಗ್ಯ s. *n.* Lot, luck, fate, fortune. 2, good fortune; welfare; riches. -ಲಕ್ಷ್ಮಿ. Goddess of good fortune; welfare, riches. -ವಂತ, -ಶಾಲಿ. A lucky, fortunate or rich man. -ಹೀನ. A luckless or poor man. ದೌರ್-. Ill-luck. ಸೌ-. Good luck.

ಭಾಜಕ s. *n.* A divisor (*arith.*). ಭಾಜನ. Dividing, division; a vessel; a receptacle; a recipient; a fit, clever person. ಭಾಜ್ಯ. The dividend (*arith.*).

ಭಾಣ s. n. A kind of dramatic entertainment.

ಭಾಂಡ s. n. Any vessel, pot, pan, cup, plate, dish, *etc.* 2, any implement, instrument. 3, horse trappings, harness. 4, goods, wares. 5, mimicry, buffoonery. -ಗಾರ (= ಭಂಡಾರ, *q. v.*). A store-room, store-house; a treasury.

ಭಾದ್ರ (*fr.* ಭದ್ರ) s. n. The month Bhâdra (August-September); *also* -ಪದ.

ಭಾನು s. n. Light. 2, the sun. -ಜ. The planet Saturn. -ಭಾಮೆ. The sun's wife. -ಮತ್. Luminous, splendid. -ಮತಿ. Duryôdhana's wife. -ವಾರ. Sunday.

ಭಾಪು h. *int.* Hurrah! well done! -ಭಾಪುರೆ. *rep.*

ಭಾಮ s. n. Passion, anger. 2, splendour; the sun. 3, a sister's husband.

ಭಾಮಿನಿ s. n. A passionate woman; a woman. -ಷಟ್ಪದಿ. N. of a metre.

ಭಾಮೆ s. n. A wife; a woman.

ಭಾಯಿ h. *aff.* Person, fellow, man, chap; brother.

ಭಾರ s. n. Bearing. 2, a burden, load. 3, heaviness, weight. 4, gravity; importance; influence. 5, heavy work, labour, toil. -ಧರಿಸು, -ಹೊತ್ತುಕೊಳ್ಳು. To take up a burden, bear the responsibility.

ಭಾರತ (*fr.* ಭರತ) s. n. A descendant of Bharata. 2, India. 3, N. of the Mahâbhârata in Kannaḍa. -ನಿಘಂಟು. N. of a small vocabulary to it. -ವರುಷ. India.

ಭಾರತಿ s. n. Sarasvatî. 2, one of the styles of dramatic composition. 3, a learned man. -ಕ. An actor.

ಭಾರದ್ವಾಜ (*fr.* ಭರದ್ವಾಜ) s. a. Coming from Bharadvâj. n. N. of a ṛishi. 2, a sky-lark.

ಭಾರಿ s. n. Bearing; a bearer; abundance. a. Heavy. -ಕ. A porter.

ಭಾರ್ಗವ (*fr.* ಭೃಗು) s. a. Coming from Bhṛigu. n. Śukra, the regent of the planet Venus. 2, Paraśurâma. -ವಾರ. Friday.

ಭಾರ್ಯೆ, ಭಾರ್ಯಾ s. n. A wife.

ಭಾವ 1. (*tb. of* ಭಾವು) n. A brother-in-law, sister's husband. -ಮೈದನ, -ಮೈದುನ. A wife's brother.

ಭಾವ 2. s. n. Becoming; existence, appearance. 2, origin. 3, state, condition. 4, truth. 5, manner of being, nature, innate property, temperament, disposition. 6, affection, feeling, emotion, passion. 7, sentiment, idea, thought, supposition, conjecture; intention. 8, meaning, sense. 9, the soul, heart, mind. 10, behaviour, action. 11, an abstract idea. 12, the eighth year in the cycle of sixty. -ಚೇಷ್ಟೆ. Emotion. -ಜ, -ಜಾತ. Kâma; love. -ಜ್ಞ. Knowing the heart or aim of others. -ನ, -ನೆ. Reverencing, treating with respect; imagining, fancying, supposing, thinking; imagination, fancy, reflection; thought; (*in med.*) saturating any powder with fluid. -ಬೋಧಕ. Indicating a feeling or passion. -ವಚನ, -ವಾಚಕ. An abstract verbal noun. -ವಾಡು. = ಭಾವಿಸು. ಭಾವಾರ್ಥ. The simple meaning of a word; the obvious purport of a phrase, letter, affair, *etc.*

ಭಾವಿ s. a. About to come, future. n. The future tense; *also* -ಕಾಲ. -ಕ. Full of feeling or sentiment; a prophet. -ತ. Obtained; manifested; conceived, imagined, thought about, happy, well. -ಸು. To conceive, imagine, fancy; to think, consider; to think of, meditate on (*with acc.*, *as* ದೇವರನ್ನು ಭಾವಿಸು).

ಭಾಷಣ s. n. Speaking; speech, talk.

ಭಾಷಾಂತರ s. n. A translation. -ಮಾಡು, ಭಾಷಾಂತರಿಸು. To translate.

ಭಾಷಿ s. n. A speaker. -ಸು. To speak, talk.

ಭಾಷೆ (=ಬಾಸೆ) s. n. Speech; language; a dialect. 2, a promise; an oath.

-ಅಳಿ, -ಮೀರು. To break a promise. -ಆಡು. To speak a language. -ಇಡು. To swear. -ಈ, -ಕೊಡು, -ನುಡಿ. To promise. -ಕೆಡು, -ಗೆಡು. A promise to be broken. -ಮುಟ್ಟಿಸು, -ಸಲಿಸು. To fulfill a promise. -ವಂತ. Faithful. -ಹಿಡಿ, -ತೋರು. To make a promise.

ಭಾಷ್ಯ s. n. An exposition, gloss, commentary. -ಕಾರ. A commentator, expounder.

ಭಾಸ s. n. Light, lustre. 2, a vulture. 3, a cock. -ಮಾನ. Shining; appearing; lustre, brightness.

ಭಾಸುರ s. a. Shining, splendid. 2, terrible. n. Splendour, beauty. 2, a hero. -ತರ. Uncommonly splendid or beautiful.

ಭಾಸ್ಕರ s. n. The sun. 2, a N.

ಭಿಕ್ಷ, ಭಿಕ್ಷೆ s. n. Begging. 2, alms. 3, wages. 4, service. -ಇಕ್ಕು. To give alms. -ಬೇಡು. To beg. -ಗಾರ. A beggar. ಭಿಕ್ಷಾಟನ. Mendicancy. ಭಿಕ್ಷಿಸು. To beg alms. ಭಿಕ್ಷು. A beggar; a religious mendicant. ಭಿಕ್ಷುಕ. A male mendicant; f. ಭಿಕ್ಷುಕಿ.

ಭಿತ್ತಿ s. n. A bit, fragment, piece. 2, a rent, fissure. 3, a wall, partition. 4, an asylum.

ಭಿಂದಿವಾಲ s. n. A short javelin; also ಭಿಂದಿಪಾಲ.

ಭಿನ್ನ s. a. Broken, split, fractured, torn, rent; disunited; expanded; destroyed. 2, separated, distinct, other, different; deprived of. n. A fragment, bit. -ಕರ್ತೃ, -ಕರ್ತೃಕ. A causative agent. -ಭಾವ. Another mind, incongruity of state. -ಭಿನ್ನ. Various. -ಭೇದ. Difference. -ವೃತ್ತ. A metrical fault. -ಶಬ್ದ. A faulty term. ಭಿನ್ನಾ-. Separate and not separate. ಭಿನ್ನಿಸು. To break, split; to loosen; to alter, change.

ಭಿಲ್ಲ s. n. A wild mountain race.

ಭಿಷಜ್, ಭಿಷಜ s. n. A physician.

ಭೀಕರ s. a. Formidable, terrible.

ಭೀತ s. a. Frightened, alarmed, afraid. ಭೀತಿ. Fear, alarm, apprehension, dread; danger.

ಭೀಮ s. a. Fearful, dreadful. n. Bhîma the second son of Pâṇḍu; also -ಸೇನ. 2, a strong man, hero. -ನದಿ, -ರಥಿ. N. of a river.

ಭೀರು s. a. Timid, cowardly; shy. -ತ್ವ. Timidity, cowardice.

ಭೀಷ್ಮ s. a. Terrible, fearful. n. Fear, horror. 2, the grand-uncle of the Pâṇḍavas. -ಕ. N. of Rukmiṇî's father; Damayanti's father.

ಭುಕ್ತ s. a. Enjoyed; eaten. -ಗೃಹ. A dining-room. ಭುಕ್ತಿ. Enjoyment; fruition, possession; food; the daily motion of a planet. -ಮುಕ್ತಿ. Fruition and final emancipation.

ಭುಜ (=ಬುಜ) s. n. The arm. -ಕೀರ್ತಿ. An epaulet-like ornament for the upper arm. -ಗ, -ಂಗ. A snake. -ಗಶಯನ. Vishṇu. -ಬಲ. Strength of arm. ಭುಜಾಗ್ರ. The shoulder.

ಭುಜಿಸು, ಭುಂಜಿಸು s. v. t. To eat; to enjoy; to suffer, experience.

ಭುವನ s. n. A living creature. 2, the world; the earth. 3, water. 4, the sky. -ಮಾತೆ. Pârvatî, Lakshmî. ಭುವನಾಕ್ಷಿ. The sun.

ಭುವಸ್, ಭುವರ್ s. n. The atmosphere, sky. ಭುವರ್ಲೋಕ. The space between earth and heaven.

ಭೂ s. n. Being. 2, the earth. 3, land, ground; earth, as a substance. 4, a country, district. -ಕಂಪ, -ಕಂಪನ. An earthquake. -ಗತ. Destroyed. -ಗತ ಮಾಡು. To destroy. -ಗೋಲ, -ಗೋಳ. The terrestrial globe, earth. -ಗೋಲವಿದ್ಯೆ, -ಗೋಲಶಾಸ್ತ್ರ. Geography. -ಚಕ್ರ. The earth's orbit; the equator; an umbrella attached to a throne. -ಚರ. Moving on earth; a man. -ಛಾಯೆ. Darkness. -ಜಾತೆ. Sîtâ. -ತಲ. The earth. -ದಾನ. Donation of landed property. -ದೆಸೆ. The regions of the earth. -ದೇವ. A Brâhmaṇa. -ನಾಗ. An earth-worm. -ನಾಥ, -ಪ, -ಪತಿ, -ಪಾಲ, -ಪಾಲಕ, -ಭುಜ್. A king. -ಪ್ರದಕ್ಷಿಣ. Going round the earth. -ಭಾರ. A wicked man. -ರಚನೆ. The composition of a soil. -ರುಹ. A tree. -ಲೋಕ, -ಮಂಡಲ. The terrestrial globe. -ಶಿರ. A cape. -ಸಾರ. The strength of a soil. -ಸುರ. A Brâhmaṇa. -ಸ್ಥಾಪನೆ. Putting in the ground, *as* money. -ಸ್ಥಿತಿ. Landed property.

ಭೂತ s. *a*. Become, produced. 2, past, gone, former. 3, got, obtained. 4, right, fit. *n*. Past time, the past, the past tense. 2, a living being, creature. 3, a goblin, demon; a ghost. 4, an element, *as* earth, water, fire, air, ether. 5, *in law:* fact, matter of fact. -ಕಾಲ, -ಕಾಲಕ್ರಿಯೆ. The past time; past tense. -ಗಣ. The aggregate of beings; a class of demons. -ಗ್ರಹ. The bhûta-imp. -ಚಿಕಿತ್ಸೆ. The science of administering antidotes for demoniacal possessions. -ದಯೆ. Universal benevolence. -ಪಂಚಕ. The aggregate of the five elements. -ಬಲಿ. An offering to demons. -ವಿದ್ಯೆ. Demonology. -ನಾಥ, -ಪತಿ, ಭೂತಾಧಿಪ. Śiva. -ಶಂಕೆ. Doubt arising from demons. -ಸೇವೆ. Demonolatry. ಭೂತಾತ್ಮ. The vital principle; the individual soul. ಭೂತಾರ್ಥ. A matter of fact, fact. ಭೂತಾವೇಶ. A demoniac possession. ಭೂತೇಶ. Lord of beings; Śiva.

ಭೂತಿ s. *n*. Being, existence; birth. 2, well-being; wealth, riches. 3, power, dignity. 4, ashes. -ಕ. The plant *Gentiana chirayta;* lemon grass.

ಭೂಮಿ (= ಬೂಮಿ) s. *n*. The earth. 2, soil, ground; a country; land, estate; a place, site in general. -ಪ, -ಪತಿ, -ಪಾಲ, -ಪಾಲಕ, -ವಲ್ಲಭ, ಭೂಮಿನಾಥ, ಭೂಮೀಶ್ವರ. A king.

ಭೂರಿ s. *a*. Much, many, numerous. *n*. Gold. 2, a gift of money to those present at any festival or funeral; *also* -ದಕ್ಷಿಣೆ.

ಭೂಷಣ s. *n*. Decorating; ornament, decoration, embellishment; a trinket, *etc.* ಭೂಷಿತ. Decorated, adorned. ಭೂಷಿಸು. To decorate, adorn; to praise. ಭೂಷೆ. An ornament, jewel.

ಭ್ರುಕುಟಿ s. *n*. A frown.

ಭೃಗು s. *n*. N. of a ṛishi. 2, Venus. 3, a cliff, slope. -ವಾರ. Friday.

ಭೃಂಗ s. *n*. The large black bee. 2, the bird *Cuculus melanoleucus*. 3, woody Cassia, *Laurus cassia*.

ಭೃಂಗಾರ (= ಭಂಗಾರ) s. *n*. A vase used at a king's inauguration or at a marriage. 2, gold.

ಭೃತ s. *a*. Borne, carried; *also* -ಕ. ಭೃತಿ. Support; wages, hire; capital. ಭೃತ್ಯ. A servant, minister. ಭೃತ್ಯತೆ. Servitude. ಭೃತ್ಯೆ. Service; hire, wages.

ಭೆಟ್ಟಿ = ಭೇಟಿ, *q. v.* -ತಕೊಳ್ಳು. To visit. -ಯಾಗು. To meet, encounter; a visit to take place.

ಭೇಟಿ (= ಭೆಟ್ಟಿ, *q. v.*) h. *n*. Meeting; an interview, visit. -ಗೆ ಬರು. To come to visit. -ಕೊಡು. To favour one with a visit. -ಮಾಡಿಸು. To introduce. -ಮಾಡು. To visit.

ಭೇದ s. *n*. Breaking, dividing. 2, division, separation, portion. 3, discrimination. 4, distinction, difference, variety. 5, change, modification. 6, dissension, disunion, disagreement. 7, creating divisions (among confederates). 8, an opponent. -ಬುದ್ಧಿ. Idea of a difference. -ಕ. Breaking; distinguishing. -ನ. Separating, loosening.

ಭೇದಿ s. *n*. A destroyer; loosening the bowels, purging. -ಕಟ್ಟು. To stop purging. -ಸು. To break, split; to distinguish; to separate; to destroy; to disclose; to be broken, *as* the heart; to separate. ಭೇದ್ಯ. Breakable, frangible, fragile.

ಭೇರಿ s. n. A kettle-drum.

ಭೇಷಜ s. n. A remedy, medicament. 2, (= ವೈಷಿಕ) hypocrisy, deceit. -ಗಾರ. A hypocrite.

ಭೈರವ (fr. ಭೀರು) s. a. Formidable, awful, terrific. n. A form of Śiva. ಭೈರವಿ. N. of a tune.

ಭೋಕ್ತ, ಭೋಕ್ತಾರ (tb. of ಭೋಕ್ತೃ) n. An enjoyer, eater, feeder; enjoying, eating. ಭೋಕ್ತವ್ಯ. Fit to be enjoyed.

ಭೋಗ s. n. Enjoyment; eating; use, application. 2, possessing; protecting. 3, perception of sorrow or joy. 4, pleasure. 5, feasting, a banquet. 6, money, wealth. 7, fullness. -ಸ್ಥಿತಿ, -ಭೂಮಿ. A place of enjoyment. ಭೋಗಿ. Enjoying; using; suffering; an enjoyer; a happy person; a voluptuary; a king; a barber. -ಮಾಡು, ಭೋಗಿಸು. To eat; to enjoy; to experience, feel, suffer. ಭೋಗ್ಯ. Enjoyable. ಭೋಗ್ಯಾಧಿ. A pledge which may be used by the mortgagee until redeemed. ಭೋಗ್ಯಾಧಿ ಪತ್ರ. A mortgage-deed.

ಭೋಜನ s. n. The act of enjoying, eating; a meal; food. -ಮಾಡು. To eat. -ದಕ್ಷಿಣೆ. Money-presents to Brâhmaṇas at a meal. ಭೋಜನಾರ್ಥ. On account of a meal. ಭೋಜನಾರ್ಥಿ. A stranger who asks for a meal. ಭೋಜ್ಯ. Eatable; food; a dainty. ರಾತ್ರಿ-. The Lord's Supper.

ಭೋರನೆ k. ad. Swiftly, quickly.

ಭೋಷ s. n. Decorum, decency, honour.

ಭೌತಿಕ (fr. ಭೂತ) s. a. Relating to existing beings; material.

ಭೌಮ (fr. ಭೂಮಿ) s. a. Earthly, terrestrial. n. The planet Mars. -ವಾರ. Tuesday.

ಭ್ರಂಶ s. n. Falling off, declining; losing; straying from.

ಭ್ರುಕುಟಿ (= ಭೃಕುಟಿ) s. n. A frown.

ಭ್ರಮ, ಭ್ರಮೆ s. n. Roaming about; whirling, going round; a whirl; a whirlpool; giddiness, dizziness: confusion, perplexity, mistake, misconception, delusion. -ಗೊಳ್ಳು. To become confused or bewildered. ಭ್ರಮಿಸು. To roam about, wander; to be confused, perplexed; to act foolishly. ಭ್ರಮಣ, ಭ್ರಮಣೆ. Roaming; whirling; revolution; wavering, staggering, unsteadiness; confusion, giddiness, dizziness.

ಭ್ರಮರ s. n. The large black bee, *Bombinatrix glabra*. 2, giddiness, vertigo.

ಭ್ರಷ್ಟ s. a. Fallen, ruined, lost; strayed from; fallen (*as* from dignity, power, caste, virtue); depraved, vicious. -ತ್ವ, -ತೆ. Depravity, viciousness, wickedness.

ಭ್ರಾತೃ s. n. A brother. -ಜ, -ಪುತ್ರ, -ವ್ಯ. A brother's son. ಭ್ರಾತ್ರೀಯ. Fraternal.

ಭ್ರಾಂತ s. a. Whirled round. 2, confused, perplexed, bewildered. -ತೆ. Confusion, bewilderment. ಭ್ರಾಂತಿ. Roaming, *etc.*; confusion, perplexity, bewilderment; mistake, delusion, false idea. ಭ್ರಾಂತಿಗೊಳ್ಳು, -ಪಡು. To be confused.

ಭ್ರೂ s. n. An eyebrow, the brow. -ಕುಟಿ. = ಭೃಕುಟಿ, *q. v.*

ಮ್

ಮ್. The forty-third letter of the alphabet.

ಮಕರ s. n. A sea-monster (crocodile, shark, *etc.*). 2, tenth sign of the zodiac: *Capricornus*. -ಕುಂಡಲ. A kind of ear-ornament. -ಡಿಪ್ಪಿ. A mortar-piece. -ತೋರಣ. A makara-like festoon carried before idols, gurus, and kings. -ಧ್ವಜ. Kâma. -ಮಾಸ. The tenth solar month. -ಸಂಕ್ರಮಣ, -ಸಂಕ್ರಾಂತಿ. The sun's passage from *Sagittarius* into *Capricornus*.

ಮಕರಂದ s. n. The nectar of flowers; honey.

ಮಕರಿ, -ಕೆ s. n. Figures drawn with fragrant pigments on the breast, arm, neck, *etc.*

ಮಕಾರ s. n. The letter ಮ. 2, dishonour.

ಮಕುಟ (=ಮುಕುಟ) s. n. A crown, crest, diadem. -ವರ್ಧನ. A crowned sovereign.

ಮಕ್ಕ, ಮಕ್ಕಾ f. n. Mecca.

ಮಕ್ಕರಿ k. n. A basket plaited of stout bamboo slits.

ಮಕ್ಕಳು k. n. Children; *pl. of* ಮಗ, ಮಗಳು, ಮಗು, *etc.*, *q. v.* ಮಕ್ಕಳಾಟಿಕೆ, ಮಕ್ಕಳಾಟಿಗೆ. Children's play. -ಮರಿಗಳು. *dpl.* ಮೊಂ-. Grand-children.

ಮಕ್ಕಿ h. n. A copy. -ಕಾಂಮಕ್ಕಿ. An exact copy.

ಮಕ್ಕಿಗದ್ದೆ k. n. Rice-field above the level of a valley.

ಮಕ್ಷಿಕ s. n. A fly; a bee.

ಮಖ s. n. A sacrifice.

ಮಖಮಲ್ಲು h. n. Velvet.

ಮಖೆ. = ಮಘೆ, *q. v.*

ಮಗ k. n. A son; a male; *f.* -ಳು. *Pl.* ಮಕ್ಕಳು. ಮಗನ-, ಮೊಂ-. A grandson. ಸಾಕು-. An adopted son.

ಮಗಚು, ಮಗುಚು k. *v. i.* To turn round; to return (*as in* ಮಗಚಿ ಬಂದನು). 2, to fall upside down. *v. t.* To turn, *as* the leaf of a book. 2, to turn upside down, overthrow. 3, to grind, whet.

ಮಗಟ f. n. A silk or linen cloth with borders worn during pûja or meal and considered ceremonially clean.

ಮಗಧ s. n. N. of South Behâr. 2, its inhabitant.

ಮಗಿಮಾವು s. n. The monkey-bread tree, Baobab, *Adansonia digitata*.

ಮಗು, -ವು (*cf.* ಮಗ) k. n. An infant, child; *pl.* ಮಕ್ಕಳು. -ತನ. Childhood.

ಮಗುಳು (ಳು=ಱು) s. k. *v. i.* To turn round, to be turned upside down; to recede, retreat; to happen. ಮಗುಳೆ. Again. ಮಗುಳೆ ಮಗುಳೆ. *rep.* Again and again.

ಮಗ್ಗ k. n. A weaver's loom. -ದ ಕುಣಿ, -ಗುಂಡಿ. A hole in which a weaver puts his feet when at work. -ದವ. A weaver.

ಮಗ್ಗಲು, ಮಗ್ಗಿಲು (= ಮಗ್ಗುಲು) k. n. Side; the side. ಮಗ್ಗಲುಹಾಸಿಗೆ. A coverlet.

ಮಗ್ಗಾರೆ k. n. The thorny shrub *Vangueria spinosa*.

ಮಗ್ಗಿ k. n. Multiplication-table. -ಗುಣಿತ. Multiplication.

ಮಗ್ಗು s. k. *v. i.* To become pale or sallow; to grow dim, *as* gold; to wither; to vanish away, disappear; to grow dirty or rusty; to perish. 2, to roar. *n.* Subjection, submission.

ಮಗ್ಗುಲು. = ಮಗ್ಗಲು, *q. v.*

ಮಗ್ನ s. *a.* Plunged, immersed; sunk into; absorbed. -ತೆ. The state of absorption, despondency.

ಮಘೆ s. n. The 10th nakshatra.

ಮಂಕಣಿ f. n. A frame-work set on beasts for carrying pitchers, *etc.*

ಮಂಕು k. n. Dimness, want of lustre (*as of* pearls, gold, *etc.*); obscurity of intellect, silliness, stupidity. ಮಂಕ. A stupid fellow; *f.* ಮಂಕಿ. -ಬೀಳು, ಮಂಕಾಗು. To become stupid, *etc.* -ತನ, ಮಂಕಾಟ. Silly behaviour. -ತಪ್ಪು. = -ಹಿಡಿ, *q. v.* -ಬುದ್ಧಿ. A dull understanding. -ಮರುಳು. *dpl.* -ಮಳೆ. A furious, heavy rain. -ಹಿಡಿ. To become perplexed or stupid.

ಮಂಗ (*tb. of* ಮರ್ಕಟ) n. A monkey. -ಚೇಷ್ಟೆ. Apish grimaces. -ಬಾವು. Mumps. -ತನ, -ನಾಟ, ಮಂಗಾಟ. Apish behaviour. ಮಂಗೇಶ. Hanumat; N.

ಮಂಗರಬಳ್ಳಿ, ಮಂಗರೋಳಿ k. n. A climbing shrub with eatable stem, *Vitis quadrangularis*.

ಮಂಗಲ, ಮಂಗಳ s. a. Fortunate, auspicious, prosperous; beautiful, pleasing. n. Good fortune, success, prosperity, welfare, happiness. 2, a good omen; an auspicious prayer; benediction; lines at the opening or end of a poem in praise of a deity. 3, any lucky object. 4, any happy event, as marriage, *etc.* 5, the planet Mars. -ಕಷ್ಟ. Trouble arising from Mars. -ಕಾರ್ಯ. A festive occasion. -ಪ್ರದ. Bestowing welfare or prosperity. -ವಾರ. Tuesday. -ಸೂತ್ರ. A marriage badge worn round the neck by a wife. ಮಂಗಲಾಚರಣ. Benediction; lines at the beginning or close of a poem in praise of a deity. ಮಂಗಳಾರತಿ. Waving of a burning lamp; the lamp so waved. ಮಂಗಳಾಶಾಸನ. Benediction. ಮಂಗಳೂರು. N. of a sea-port in South-Canara.

ಮಂಗಾರೆ k. n. The thorny shrub *Vangueria spinosa*.

ಮಚ್ಚೆ, ಮಚ್ಚೆ k. n. A black speck or scar, mole, freckle. 2, a piece of gold or silver kept for a sample or test.

ಮಚ್ಚರ. tb. of ಮತ್ಸರ, q. v. ಮಚ್ಚರಿಸು. To be envious, jealous, selfish; to grudge.

ಮಚ್ಚು 1. = ಮೆಚ್ಚು, q. v.

ಮಚ್ಚು 2. k. n. A bill-hook for cutting bushes, *etc.; also* -ಕತ್ತಿ.

ಮಜಕೂರು h. a. Above mentioned, current. n. Affair, concern; an oral communication; the contents of an epistle.

ಮಜಬೂತು h. a. Strong, firm, fast.

ಮಜಲು h. n. A stage, halting place; a day's journey. -ಗದ್ದೆ. A paddy-field yielding two crops, generally higher than ಬೈಲುಗದ್ದೆ and lower than ಬೆಟ್ಟುಗದ್ದೆ.

ಮಜಾ, ಮಜಾಕು h. n. Flavour, taste.

ಮಜೂರಿ h. n. The wages of a labourer; his business. -ಆಳು. A hired cooly.

ಮಜ್ಜ s. n. The marrow of bones. 2, the pith of plants. -ಸಾರ, ಮಜ್ಜಾಸಾರ. Pith, substance; that is most important; flatulence.

ಮಜ್ಜನ s. n. Bathing, ablution; water for bathing. -ಗೃಹ, -ಶಾಲೆ. A bathroom.

ಮಜ್ಜಿಗೆ k. n. Buttermilk. 2, whey. -ನೀರು. Buttermilk mixed with water. -ಪಲ್ಯ. The yellow wood-sorrel, *Oxalis corniculata*. -ಪಳದ್ಯ. A kind of sour sauce. -ಹುಲ್ಲು. The lemon grass, *Andropogon schoenanthus*.

ಮಂಚ (fr. ಮಲಗು) k. n. A bedstead, cot, bed. 2, an elevated shed.

ಮಂಚಿಕೆ, ಮಂಚಿಗೆ k. n. A stand in a field, jungle, *etc.*, for watching the crops or the chase, *etc.*

ಮಂಜರಿ s. n. A cluster of blossoms; a flower-bud; a sprout, sprig, stalk; *also* -ಕೆ. ಶಬ್ದ-. A cluster or glossary of words, a dictionary.

ಮಂಜಳ k. n. Indian saffron, turmeric.

ಮಂಜಾಡಿ (tb. of ಮಂಜಿಷ್ಠ) n. The red seeds of the red-wood tree which are used in weighing gold and diamond.

ಮಂಜಿ k. n. The bow-string hemp, *Sanseviera zeylanica*. 2, a coasting boat.

ಮಂಜಿಷ್ಠ s. n. The Bengal madder, *Rubia munjista*.

ಮಂಜೀರ k. n. An anklet. 2, a post round which the string of a churning stick passes.

ಮಂಜು 1. k. n. Dew, fog, coldness, coolness; dimness of sight; obscurity. 2, a N. -ಗಾಲ. The cold season. ಮಂಜ. N. of Śiva or of any male; f. ಮಂಜಿ.

ಮಂಜು 2, ಮಂಜುಲ s. a. Beautiful, lovely, charming, pleasing; sweet, melodious.

ಮಂಜೂರು h. n. Approval, confirmation; sanction. a. Approved, confirmed; -ಮಾಡು. To approve, sanction, confirm.

ಮಟ. *tb. of* ಮಠ, *q. v.*

ಮಟ್ಟ 1. (ಮಟ್ಟಸ) k. *n.* Levelness, equality, regularity, exactness. 2, a carpenter's level. 3, (= ಮಟ್ಟು) measure, extent, limit. -ಗೋಲು. A mason's level. -ಸ. Levelness, evenness, smoothness. -ಸ ಮಾಡು. To make even or smooth. -ಮೊದಲು. At the very beginning. -ಹಲಿಗೆ. A carpenter's ruler.

ಮಟ್ಟ 2. k. *n.* Shortness; abating, *as* wind, rain, fever, price, *etc.*; inferiority. 2, a pony. -ಜಾತಿ. An inferior caste. -ತರ. An inferior kind.

ಮಟ್ಟ 3. k. *n.* Illusion, phantom, ruin. -ಮಾಯ. *reit.* Perfect disappearance.

ಮಟ್ಟಿ (*tb. of* ಮೃದ್) *n.* Earth, clay.

ಮಟ್ಟು (= ಮಟ್ಟ 1, No. 3) k. *n.* Measure; extent, height; bound, limit. ಮಟ್ಟಿಗೆ. Till, until, as far as. ಎಷ್ಟು ಮಟ್ಟಿಗೆ. How far? *Cpds.:* ತಕ್ಕ-, ಕೈಲಾದ-, ಸಾಕಾದ-, *etc.* ಅಷ್ಟು-, ಅಷ್ಟರ-. So far as that. ಇಷ್ಟು-, ಇಷ್ಟರ-. So far as this. ಈ ದಿನದ-. Until this day.

ಮಟ್ಟೆ 1. k. *n.* A bough of the palm, *etc.* 2, the fibrous coat of a cocoanut.

ಮಟ್ಟೆ 2. f. *n.* The bucket of a bullock-draw-well.

ಮಠ s. *n.* A hut, cottage; a hermitage; a residence of a guru; a convent, monastery; a temple; a school. *Cpds.:* ಓದುವ-, ಗುರು-, ಗೋಸಾಯಿ-, ಜಂಗಮ-, ಸನ್ಯಾಸಿ-, *etc.*

ಮಡ. = ಮಡಿ 4, *q. v.*

ಮಡಕಿ f. *n.* A much cultivated annual pulse, *Phaseolus aconitifolius.*

ಮಡಕೆ 1. = ಮಡಿಕೆ 1, *q. v.*

ಮಡಕೆ 2. (= ಮಡಿಕೆ 2) k. *n.* A pot; a water-jar.

ಮಡಗು k. *v. t.* To lay down, place, put (*cf.* ಮಲಗು); to take into one's service; to procure, *as* a horse, *etc.* 2, to hide.

ಮಡತೆ a. k. *n.* Folding; a fold.

ಮಡದಿ k. *n.* A woman. 2, a wife.

ಮಡಪು k. *n.* A fold, as of cloth, betel-leaf, *etc.*

ಮಡಲು k. *n.* Thick foliage; a thicket, bush; a bough of the cocoanut tree. ಮಡಲಿಡು. To spread, run, as a creeper; to prevail, increase.

ಮಡಿ 1. k. *n.* A fold. 2, the pouch-like fold in front part of the garment to put in eatables, *etc.; also* ಮಡಲು. 3, the bed of a garden. 4, fold, times, *as:* ಇಂ-, ಮೂಂ-, ನಾಲ್-, *etc.* *v. t.* To bend; to fold.

ಮಡಿ 2. k. *v. i.* To die, perish.

ಮಡಿ 3. k. *n.* A washed, clean cloth. 2, purity. -ಧೋತ್ರ. A washed, clean dôtra.

ಮಡಿ 4. (= ಮಡ) k. *n.* The heel, *in* ಹಿಮ್ಮಡಿ.

ಮಡಿಕೆ 1. (= ಮಡತೆ 1) k. *n.* A fold; fold, times. 2, the warp ready for the loom. 3, a kind of harrow or rake.

ಮಡಿಕೆ 2. = ಮಡಕೆ 2, *q. v.*

ಮಡಿವಳ, ಮಡಿವಾಳ (*fr.* ಮಡಿ 3) k. *n.* A washerman. -ಗಿತ್ತಿ. A washer-woman. -ಹಾಗಲಬಳ್ಳಿ. A climbing herb, *Momordica dioica; also* ಮಡಿಹಾಗಲಬಳ್ಳಿ.

ಮಡಿಸು (*fr.* ಮಡಿ 1) k. *v. t.* To bend, fold, fold up. ಮಡಿಸಿದ ವಸ್ತ್ರ. A folded cloth.

ಮಡು, ಮಡುವು k. *n.* Deep water; a pool.

ಮಡೆ k. *n.* A small dam or dike.

ಮಡ್ಡ k. *n.* A stupid man. -ತನ. Stupidity.

ಮಡ್ಡಿ 1. (= ಮಡ್ಡು) k. *n.* Dregs, lees, *as* of oil, ghee, *etc.* 2, = ಕಲಗಚ್ಚು.

ಮಡ್ಡಿ 2. k. *n.* A tree yielding a soft gum, *Ailanthus malabarica.*

ಮಡ್ಡಿ 3. k. *n.* A stupid, dull person. 2, awkwardness, rudeness. -ಕಾಗದ. A coarse paper. -ಗಾರೆ. Rough plaster. -ತನ. Stupidity, rudeness.

ಮಡ್ಡು. = ಮಡ್ಡಿ 1, *q. v.*

ಮಣಿ, -ವು (= ಮಣು) f. n. A measure of capacity: a maund, quarter = 28 lbs.

ಮಣಿಕ k. n. A young cow or buffalo. -ನೆ. Quickly.

ಮಣಿಲು. = ಮಳಲು, q. v.

ಮಣಿ 1. k. v. i. To bend, bow; to make obeisance. n. A bend, bow; an obeisance. -ಕಟ್ಟು. The wrist. -ಸು. To cause to bend.

ಮಣಿ 2. s. n. A jewel, gem, precious stone. 2, an ornament in general. 3, a bed. -ತೊಂಡೆ ಬಳ್ಳಿ. A creeping herb, *Bryonia scabrella*. -ಗಾರ. A jeweller. *Cpds.*: -ದರ್ಪಣ, -ದೋಷ, -ಪೀಠಿಕೆ, *etc.* -ಶಿಲೆ. A reddish mineral used for medicinal purposes.

ಮಣಿಯ k. n. Superintendence of temples, maṭhas, palaces, *etc.* -ಗಾರ. A maṇiya-officer, superintendent.

ಮಣು, -ವು. = ಮಣಿ, q. v.

ಮಣೆ k. n. A stool, low bench, seat.

ಮಣೆಯ. = ಮಣಿಯ, q. v. 2, a religious performance or vow. -ಕಟ್ಟಿಸು, -ಹಾಕಿಸು. To have this maṇeya performed. -ಗಾರ. = ಮಣಿಗಾರ, q. v.

ಮಂಟ. = ಮಟಿ, q. v. -ಬೆಕ್ಕು. A wild cat, tree-cat.

ಮಂಟಪ s. n. A halting place for travellers; a temporary shed erected on festive occasions (*as* marriage, muñji, *etc.*); a sacrificial shed; a structure for carrying about an idol.

ಮಂಡ s. n. The scum on the surface of any liquid; cream, barm, gruel. 2, the castor-oil plant. 3, the head.

ಮಂಡಕ. = ಮಂಡಿಗೆ, q. v.

ಮಂಡನ s. n. Adorning; ornament.

ಮಂಡಪ. = ಮಂಟಪ, q. v. ಮಂಡಪಿಗೆ. A small shed, shop.

ಮಂಡಲ s. n. A disk (of the sun or moon); a circle, globe, ball, orb; a halo. 2, the visible horizon. 3, a district, territory; an empire. 4, a multitude, group, body, society. 5, a period of forty-eight days. -ಹಾವು. A kind of snake. -ಕ. White leprosy.

ಮಂಡಲಿ, ಮಂಡಳಿ s. n. A circle, orb. 2, a multitude, company, congregation. 3, whirling. 4, a kind of snake. -ಸು. To whirl, turn round; to be amassed. -ಕ, ಮಂಡಲೇಶ್ವರ. A ruler, prefect, superintendent.

ಮಂಡಿ 1. k. n. The knee. -ಇಡು, -ಊರು, -ಹಾಕು, -ಹೂಡು. To kneel. -ಕಾಲು. = ಮಂಡಿ 1.

ಮಂಡಿ 2. h. n. A wholesale shop, warehouse.

ಮಂಡಿ 3. f. n. Gout or rheumatism of the thigh.

ಮಂಡಿಗೆ (*tb. of* ಮಂಡಕ) n. A sugared cake of wheaten flour.

ಮಂಡಿಸು k. v. i. To sit down; to be set or turned towards, *as* the eye.

ಮಂಡೂಕ s. n. A frog. -ಪರ್ಣಿ. Bengal madder, *Rubia munjista*.

ಮಂಡೂರ s. n. Rust of iron, scoriae. -ಭಸ್ಮ. Calcined iron.

ಮಂಡೆ (*tb. of* ಮಂಡ) n. The head. -ನೋವು. Headache. -ಸುತ್ತು. A turban.

ಮಣ್ಣು k. n. Earth, clay, mud, soil, ground. ಮಣ್ಣಡಿಕೆ. The Sepistan plum, *Cordia myxa*. ಮಣ್ಣಾಗು. To become earth, be soiled; to be ruined. ಮಣ್ಣಾಶೆ. Desire after landed property. -ಕೂಡಿಸು, -ಕೊಡು. To bury. -ಗಡ್ಡೆ. A clod of earth. -ಗೋಡೆ. A mud wall. -ಪಾತ್ರೆ. An earthen vessel. -ಪಾಲು. Destruction, death. -ಬೀಳು. To get disappointed. -ಮಾಡು. To bury. -ಹಾಕು. To put earth (into a person's mouth, *i. e.* to deceive and ruin him). -ಹುಳ, ಮಣ್ಣುಣಿ. An earth-worm.

ಮತ s. a. Thought, considered, intended. n. A thought, idea; an opinion, view; a doctrine, creed, sect; design. -ದ್ವೇಷ. Sectarian enmity. -ಭ್ರಷ್ಟ. Fallen from one's creed; an apostate. -ವಿಚಾರ. Examination of a creed. -ಸಿದ್ಧಾಂತ. The dogma of a sect. -ಸ್ಥ. A man belonging to a sect. ಮತಾ

ಚಾರ. The customs of a sect. ಕ್ರೈಸ್ತ-. Christianity. ಹಿಂದು-. Hinduism.

ಮತಲಬು h. n. Purpose; purport, *as* of a document.

ಮತಾಪು, ಮತಾಬು h. n. A kind of firework.

ಮತಿ s. n. Mind; understanding, intellect, will, judgment. 2, thought, idea, opinion. 3, counsel, advice. 4, wish, inclination, purpose. -ಗೆಡು. To lose one's wits; to be perplexed; to become stupid. -ಭ್ರಷ್ಟ. Devoid of sense; foolish. -ವಂತ, -ವಾನ್. A sensible, clever man. -ಶೂನ್ಯ, -ಹೀನ. Stupid.

ಮತ್ಕುಣ s. n. A bug; a flea.

ಮತ್ತ 1. s. a. Intoxicated, drunk. 2, mad, furious. 3, lustful, wanton. 4, delighted. 5, proud. -ತ್ವ. Intoxication; *also* -ತೆ.

ಮತ್ತ 2, ಮತ್ತಂ (= ಮತ್ತೂ, ಮತ್ತೆಯೂ) a. k. *conj*. Again, further, moreover, and.

ಮತ್ತಿ 1. k. n. A freckle, mark.

ಮತ್ತಿ 2. k. n. N. of several species of timber trees of the genus *Terminalia*.

ಮತ್ತು 1. k. *conj*. Other, again, further, besides, and. ಮತ್ತಿನ. Of another, different. ಮತ್ತಿಷ್ಟು. Twice as much. ಮತ್ತೂ. = ಮತ್ತ 2. ಮತ್ತೆಲ್ಲಿ. Where else? anywhere else. ಮತ್ತೆಲ್ಲಿಯೂ. At or to any other place. ಮತ್ತೇನು. What else? what more? ಮತ್ತೇನೂ. Any other thing. ಮತ್ತೊಂದು, *etc*. *See s.* ಮತ್ತೆ. ಮತ್ತ್ಯಾಕೆ. For what other reason? ಮತ್ತ್ಯಾರು. Who else? who more? ಮತ್ತ್ಯಾವ. What other thing? *etc*. ಮತ್ತ್ಯಾವಾಗಾದರೂ. At any other time.

ಮತ್ತು 2. (*tb. of* ಮತ್ತ, ಮದ) n. Intoxication; pride.

ಮತ್ತೆ (= ಮತ್ತು, q. v.) k. *ad*. Other, else, again, further, besides, afterwards, and. ಮತ್ತೊಂದು. Another—, a different—; another thing, *etc*. ಮತ್ತೊಬ್ಬ. Another one; *f*. ಮತ್ತೊಬ್ಬಳು. ಮತ್ತೊಮ್ಮೆ. Another time, once more.

ಮತ್ಯ s. n. Exercise of knowledge. ಏಕ-. Concord.

ಮತ್ಸರ (= ಮಚ್ಚರ, q. v.) s. a. Envious, grudging, jealous. 2, selfish, greedy. n. Envy, grudge; jealousy, hostility; greediness; anger; *also* -ಭಾವ, -ಬುದ್ಧಿ. -ಗೊಳ್ಳು, -ಪಡು, ಮತ್ಸರಿಸು. To be envious.

ಮತ್ಸ್ಯ s. n. A fish. -ಧ್ವಜ. Kâma. -ಪುರಾಣ. One of the 18 purâṇas. -ಸಂಘಾತ. A shoal of young fry. ಮತ್ಸ್ಯಾವತಾರ. N. of Vishṇu's first incarnation.

ಮಥನ s. n. Stirring; churning; rubbing, friction; crushing; injury, trouble. ಮಥನಿಸು, ಮಥಿಸು. To churn; to discuss; to quarrel.

ಮದ 1. (= ಮದಿವೆ, ಮದುವೆ, q. v.) k. n. A wedding, marriage. -ಮಕ್ಕಳು. The bride and bridegroom. -ಮಗ, -ಲಿಗ, -ಲಿಂಗ, -ವಣಿಗ, -ವಳಿಗ. A bridegroom. -ಮಗಳು, -ಲಗಿತ್ತಿ, -ವಣಿಗಿತ್ತಿ, -ವಳಿಗೆ. A bride. -ವನ. A husband.

ಮದ 2. s. n. Intoxication. 2, madness. 3, ardent passion, love, lust; lasciviousness. 4, delight. 5, pride, conceit. 6, bloom of youth. 7, honey. 8, musk. *Cpds*.: ಅನ್ನ-, ಅರ್ಥ-, ಧನ-, ಯೌವನ-, ವಿದ್ಯಾ-, *etc*. -ಏರಿಸು, -ವೇರಿಸು. To raise intoxication, *etc*. -ಏರು. To be intoxicated; to be ruttish, proud or furious. -ಗಜ. An elephant in rut. ಮದಾಂಧ, ಮದಾಂಧಕ. Blinded by passion. ಮದೋನ್ಮತ್ತ. Intoxicated with passion or pride.

ಮದಗ, ಮದಗು k. n. A sluice, flood-gate.

ಮದಡು k. n. Dullness, stupidity. ಮದಡ. A stupid man.

ಮದತ (= ಮದ್ದತು) h. n. Aid, help.

ಮದನ (= ಮದ 2, q. v.) s. a. Intoxicating; exhilerating. n. Passion, lust. 2, an intoxicated, mad, haughty man. 3, Kâma. 4, the thorn-apple, *Datura metel*. 5, bees' wax. -ಕೈ. Ornamental supports of the eaves of a house; a crutch-like stand. -ವೈರಿ. Śiva.

ಮದರಂಗ, -ಗಿ s. n. The Henna plant, *Lawsonia alba*.

ಮದರಿ (*tb. of* ಮಧುರೆ) n. N. of a town in the Tamil country where red cloths are made. -ರುಮಾಲು. A red turban.

ಮದಿಪು (*fr.* ಮತಿ) s. n. Estimation, valuation, rating.

ಮದಿರೆ, ಮದಿರಾ s. n. Spirituous liquor. ಮದಿರಾಗೃಹ. A tavern.

ಮದಿವೆ, ಮದುವೆ k. n. Wedding, marriage. -ಮಾಡಿ ಕೊಡು. To give away as wife. -ಮಾಡಿ ಕೊಳ್ಳು. To marry. -ಮಾಡಿಸು. To cause to be married. -ಮಾಡು. To perform a marriage. -ಆಗು, -ಯಾಗು. To be married. *Cpds.:* -ಚಪ್ಪರ, -ಮನೆ, -ನಿಬ್ಬಣ.

ಮದಿಸು (*fr.* ಮದ) s. v. i. To be proud. 2, to grow fat or plump.

ಮದು. = ಮದ 1, *q. v.*

ಮದುರೆ. *tb. of* ಮಧುರೆ, *q. v.*

ಮದೋದ್ಧತ s. a. Arrogant, haughty.

ಮದ್ದತು, ಮದ್ದತ್ತು (= ಮದತು) h. n. Aid, help; succour.

ಮದ್ದಲೆ, ಮದ್ದಳೆ (*tb. of* ಮರ್ದಲ) n. A kind of drum, a tabor.

ಮದ್ದು 1. (= ಮದ್ದು) k. n. Any drug, medicine, whether a powder, pill, or fluid; a remedy. 2, gunpowder. ಮದ್ದಿನ ಚೀಲ. A powder bag.

ಮದ್ದು 2. (*tb. of* ಮತ್ತು) f. n. Intoxication, madness; an intoxicant. -ಗುಣಿಕೆ. The thorn-apple. ಮದ್ದಾನೆ. An elephant in rut.

ಮದ್ಯ s. a. Intoxicating, gladdening. n. Any intoxicating drink, spirituous liquor. -ಪ, -ಪಾನಿ. A drinker. -ಪಾನ. Drinking of intoxicating liquor.

ಮದ್ರಾಸು f. n. Madras.

ಮಧು s. a. Sweet; pleasant. n. Honey; the nectar of flowers. 2, ambrosia, milk. 3, mead, spirituous liquor. 4, liquorice. 5, the black bee. 6, spring, the vernal season. -ಕ, -ವಲ್ಲಿ. The liquorice root. -ಪರ್ಕ. A mixture of honey, and milk; the ceremony of receiving a guest. -ಪರ್ಣೀ. The creeper *Cocculus cordifolius*. -ಪಾನ. Spirituous liquor, sipping it. -ಪ್ರಿಯ. The black bee; a voluptuary. -ಮಿತ್ರ, -ಪ. A bee. -ರ. Sweet; pleasant, pleasing; melodious; sweetness; a kind of sugar; the red sugar-cane. -ರತ್ವ. Sweetness. -ರಸ. Honey.

ಮಧುರೆ s. n. Madura in the Tamil country. 2, the plant *Anethum sowa*. -ರಂಗು. A purple colour from that town.

ಮಧ್ಯ s. a. Middle, central; intermediate. 2, middling. 3, right, just. n. The middle, midst, centre. 2, the waist. -ರಾತ್ರಿ, -ರಾತ್ರೆ. Midnight. -ರೇಖೆ, -ರೇಷೆ. The equator. -ವರ್ತಿ. A mediator. -ಸ್ತ, -ಸ್ಥ. Central; mediation; a mediator, arbitrator; *also* -ಸ್ತಗಾರ. -ಸ್ಥಾನ. A middle place; the waist. -ಸ್ತಿಕೆ. Mediation, mediatorship (*Christ in the work of redemption*).

ಮಧ್ಯಮ s. a. Middle, central; intermediate; middling; moderate. n. A middle condition or quality, mediocrity. 2, the waist. 3, the second person; *also* -ಪುರುಷ.

ಮಧ್ಯಾಹ್ನ s. n. Midday, noon. -ಮಲ್ಲಿಗೆ. The marvel of Peru or four-o'clock flower, *Mirabilis jalappa*.

ಮನ (= ಮನಸು, ಮನಸ್ಸು, *q. v. tb. of* ಮನಸ್) n. Mind, *etc.* -ಕೆ ತರು. To take to heart. -ಕೆ ಬರು. To enter the mind; to be agreeable. -ಕ್ಲೇಶ. Mental affliction. -ಗಾಣು. To observe, apprehend. -ಗುಂದು. To grieve; grief, sorrow. -ಗೆಡಿಸು. To spoil the intentions (of another). -ಗೆಡು. The mind to be spoiled or altered. -ಗೊಡು. To pay attention. -ಂಗೊಳಿಸು. To fascinate, charm. -ಂಗೊಳ್ಳು. To be fascinated, charmed. -ತಟ್ಟು, -ದಟ್ಟು. To touch the mind, be known. -ದೊಳಗೆ ಇಡು. To consider and remember. -ಮಿಗು. To be baffled, disappointed. -ಮುಟ್ಟು. To apply one's (whole) mind to. -ಮುರಿ. Inclination to disappear. -ವರಿ. To know the mind. -ವರಿಕೆ. Knowledge. -ವಾರೆ. With one's whole mind. -ವಿಡು. To feel a desire for. -ಎಳಿ. To be discouraged, humbled. -ವುಕ್ಕು. To be elated. -ವೆರಗು. To make hearty obeisance. -ವೊಲಿ. To rejoice; to long for. -ವೊಲಿಸು. To gain one's favour. -ಸೋಲು. To suffer a mental defeat. -ಸಾರಿ. A fool. ಮನಃಪೂರ್ವಕ. With the whole mind or heart; deliberately. ಮನಃಶುದ್ಧಿ. Sincerity. ಮನಃಸಾಕ್ಷಿ (= ಮನಸ್ಸಾಕ್ಷಿ). Conscience. ಮನೋಗತ. Notion, wish. ಮನೋಗತಿ. The heart's desire; the speed of thought. ಮನೋಜಯ. Conquering the mind; pleasing, agreeable. ಮನೋಜ್ಞ. Pleasing, lovely, charming; a wise man; *f.* ಮನೋಜ್ಞೆ. ಮನೋದುಃಖ. Heart-ache, anguish. ಮನೋದೃಢ. Firm in mind; firmness of mind. ಮನೋಧರ್ಮ. A faculty of the mind, *as* thought, memory, *etc.* ಮನೋನಿಗ್ರಹ. Restraining and governing the mind. ಮನೋರಂಜಕ. Pleasing, lovely. ಮನೋರಂಜನ. Pleasantness; diversion, sport. ಮನೋರಥ. A wish, desire, purpose; a desired object. -ಸಿದ್ಧಿ. The fulfilment of a wish. ಮನೋರಮ. Attractive, pleasing, agreeable. ಮನೋವಾಕ್ಕಾಯ. Mind, word and body. ಮನೋವಿಕಾರ. Passion or emotion of the mind, bewilderment, *etc.* ಮನೋವೃತ್ತಿ. = ಮನೋಧರ್ಮ, *q. v.* ಮನೋವೇಗ. The speed of thought. ಮನೋವ್ಯಥೆ. Mental pain, anguish. ಮನೋವ್ಯಾಪಾರ. Mental operation. ಮನೋಹರ. Captivating, attractive, delightful, charming, beautiful.

ಮನನ s. *a.* Thoughtful, careful. *n.* Thought; understanding; knowledge; meditation.

ಮನವಿ, ಮನವೆ s. *n.* A petition, request, solicitation.

ಮನಸು, ಮನಸ್ಸು (=ಮನ, *q. v. tb. of* ಮನಸ್) *n.* Mind, intellect, conscience, will; the mind; the heart. 2, intention, design, purpose; will, wish; desire; liking, choice. ಮನಸಿಗಾಗು. To be suitable for one's mind. ಮನಸಿಗೆ ತರು. = ಮನಕೆ ತರು. ಮನಸಿಗೆ ಬರು. = ಮನಕೆ ಬರು. ಮನಸಿನಲ್ಲಿಟ್ಟುಕೊಳ್ಳು. To keep in mind, remember, *etc.* ಮನಸಿಗೆ ಹತ್ತು. To remain in the mind. ಮನಸಿಗೆ ಹಿಡಿ. To touch the mind; to retain in the mind. ಮನಸಿಡು. = ಮನವಿಡು. ಮನಸಿನ ಮೇಲೆ ತಕ್ಕೊಳ್ಳು. To mind, attend to diligently. ಮನಸಿನೊಳಗೆ ಬರು. To enter the mind. -ಕರಗು. The heart to melt. -ಕೂಡು. Opinions to agree. -ಕೊಡು, -ಗೊಡು. = ಮನಗೊಡು. -ತಿರುಗಿಸು. To change the mind, repent. -ನೋಯು. The mind to be pained. -ನೋಯಿಸು. To pain the mind. -ಬರು. To desire, list. -ಬಂದ ಹಾಗೆ ಮಾಡು. To do as one pleases, *etc.* -ಬಿಚ್ಚು. To open ones mind. -ಬಿಚ್ಚಿ ಮಾತಾಡು. To speak out one's thoughts. -ಮಾಡು. To make up one's mind; to resolve. -ಹಾಕು. To engage in. -ಹೇಸು. The mind to feel disgust. ಮನಸ್ಕರಿಸು. To be inclined, to will. ಮನಸ್ಕಾರ. Full perception; perfect consciousness. ಮನಸ್ತಾಪ. Mental pain, agony; remorse, regret.

ಮನಸ್ವಿ s. *a.* According to one's inclination. 2, capricious, fanciful.

ಮನು s. *n.* Man, mankind; the father of mankind; one of the 14 successive progenitors or sovereigns of the earth, to the 1st of them is ascribed the code of Manu. -ಜ. A man; *f.* -ಜೆ. -ಸ್ಮೃತಿ. The code of Manu.

ಮನುಷ್ಯ s. *n.* A man; *f.* ಮನುಷ್ಯಳು, ಮನುಷ್ಯೆ. -ತ್ವ. Manhood. -ಧರ್ಮ. The duty of man. -ಮಾತ್ರ. A mere man.

ಮನೆ k. *n.* A habitation, abode; a house; an apartment, room. *Cpds.:* ಚಪ್ಪಿಗರ-, ದೀವಿಗೆ-, ಮಲಗುವ-, ಮಾಯುವ-, ಸೆಜ್ಜೆಯ-, ಹೆತ್ತ-, *etc.* -ಕೆಲಸ. Domestic work. -ಖರ್ಚು. Household expenses. -ತನ. Household, household-life. -ತನ ಮಾಡು. To keep house, to support a family. -ತನದವ, -ತನಸ್ಥ. A householder; a worthy, honourable man. -ತೊತ್ತು. A house-maid. -ದೇವ, -ದೈವ. A household deity. -ಬದುಕು, -ವಾರ್ತೆ. Household affairs; domestic property. -ಮಾಡಿಕೊಳ್ಳು. To settle. -ಮಾಡು. To build a house. -ಮಾರು. *redt.* House and its appendages. -ಮುಟ್ಟು. To reach the house; the furniture of a house. -ಮುರುಕ. One who ruins a house. -ಮುರುಕತನ. Ruining a house. -ಯಜಮಾನ. The master of a house, *f.* -ಯಜಮಾನಳು, -ಯಜಮಾನಿ. -ಯವ. An inmate of a house; *f.* -ಯವಳು; *pl.* -ಯವರು; *also* the master of a house (*in the wife's language*); *f.* -ಯವಳು, -ಯಾಕೆ. -ಯಾಳು. A domestic servant.

ಮಂತನ, ಮಂಥಾನ. = ಮನೆತನ, *q. v.*

ಮಂತರ. *tb. of* ಮಂತ್ರ, *q. v.*

ಮಂತು (*tb. of* ಮಂಥ) *n.* Churning. 2, a churning-stick. 3, a fault, an offence.

ಮಂತ್ರ s. *n.* A vedic verse of prayer. 2, a magical formula, incantation, charm, spell. 3, secret consultation; counsel; secret plan. -ಗಾರ, -ವಾದಿ. A magician, conjurer. -ಜ್ಞ. A learned Brahmana, a priest; a secret agent. -ತಂತ್ರ. Spells and devices. -ಭೇದ. Breach of counsel; a particular magical incantation. -ವಾದಿ. A magician, conjurer. -ಶಾಸ್ತ್ರ. Magical science. ಮಂತ್ರಾಕ್ಷತೆ. Akshatĕ consecrated by mantras. ಮಂತ್ರಾಲೋಚಕ. A councillor. ಮಂತ್ರಾಲೋಚನ. A private consultation. ಮಂತ್ರಾಲೋಚನ ಸಭೆ. A council.

ಮಂತ್ರಿ s. *n.* A king's councillor, minister. 2, a conjurer. -ಕ. A magician. -ತನ, -ತ್ವ. Ministership. -ಸು. To counsel, advice; to enchant with spells or charms.

ಮಂಥ (= ಮಂತು) s. *n.* Churning, agitating, kindling; a churning-stick; *also* -ದಂಡ. -ನ. Churning; kindling fire by friction.

ಮಂದ s. *a.* Slow, idle, lazy, apathetic. 2, dull, heavy, stupid, silly, foolish. 3, little; dim, faint, *as* light, *etc.*; mild, *as* a smile; low, *as* a tone; gentle, *as* breeze; feeble, *as* digestion; thick, *as* a cloth, plank, wall, cords, *etc.* *n.* Indigestion. 2, the planet Saturn. -ಕಾರಿ. Causing indigestion. -ಗತಿ. A slow motion; *also* -ಗಮನ. -ಗಾಮಿ. Marching slowly. -ಜ. A lotus. -ತ್ವ. Slowness, dulness, stupidity. -ಬುದ್ಧಿ, -ಮತಿ. Stupidity, dulness. -ಮಾರುತ. A gentle breeze; *also* ಮಂದಾನಿಲ. ಮಂದಾಕ್ಷ. Weak-eyed; bashfulness. -ಸ್ಮಿತ, -ಹಾಸ. A smile. ಮಂದಾಗ್ನಿ. Weakness of digestion. ಮಂದಾಸನ. A wooden chest. ಮಂದೋಷ. Lukewarm, tepid; gentle heat.

ಮಂದಟ್ಟು (*fr.* ಮನ-ತಟ್ಟು) k. *n.* Knowledge.

ಮಂದರ s. *n.* N. of a mountain with which the ocean was churned by the gods and asuras; *also* ಮಂದರಾಚಲ. *a.* Large, bulky; thick.

ಮಂದಾಕಿನಿ s. *n.* The Ganges.

ಮಂದಾರ s. *n.* The Coral tree, *Erythrina indica.* 2, a white species of swallow-wort, *Calotropis gigantea.*

ಮಂದಿ k. *n.* Persons, people. *Cpds.:* ಅನೇಕ-, ಒಳ್ಳೇ-, ಬಹು-, ಸಾವಿರ-, ಹೆಚ್ಚು-. -ವಾಳ. Impertinence, arrogance.

ಮಂದಿರ s. *n.* A habitation, house. ದೇವ-. A temple. ರಾಜ-. A palace.

ಮಂದು k. *n.* A hamlet of the Todas on the Nilagiri.

ಮಂದೆ s. *n.* A flock of sheep or goats, herd of cattle. 2, a fold, pen.

ಮಂದೈಸು f. *v. i.* To thicken, coagulate, to form a mass; to become pleasing.

ಮನ್ನ f. *n.* Manna, the (bread-like) food miraculously supplied to the Israelites in the wilderness.

ಮನ್ನಣೆ (*tb. of* ಮಾನನ) *n.* Veneration, reverence. ಮನ್ನಿಸು. To honour, reverence; to show kindness, treat kindly.

ಮನ್ನಾ h. *a.* Forbidden, stopped. *n.* Prohibition, stoppage. -ಆಗು. To be stopped, to cease. -ಮಾಡು. To stop, prohibit.

ಮನ್ನಿಸು (*fr.* ಮನ್ನಾ) h. *v. t.* To bear with, overlook, excuse, pardon.

ಮನ್ಮಥ s. *n.* Love; Kâma. 2, the wood-apple tree, *Feronia elephantum.*

ಮನ್ಯು s. *n.* Anger, wrath, fury. 2, sorrow, distress.

ಮನ್ಯೆ s. *n.* The nape of the neck.

ಮನ್ವಂತರ (*fr.* ಮನು) s. *n.* A Manu's age comprising 71 great yugas.

ಮಬ್ಬು k. *n.* Darkness; gloom; dimness; drowsiness; dulness, stupidity. -ಕಣ್ಣು. Dim sight. -ಗತ್ತಲೆ. Sable darkness. ಮಬ್ಬಿಗ. An Asura, Râkshasa.

ಮಮ s. *pro.* Of me, mine. -ಕಾರ. Attachment, love; selfishness. -ತೆ. Love, tenderness, affection; selfishness; pride, arrogance.

ಮಮ್ಮು k. *n.* Food (*in children's language*).

ಮಯ್, ಮಯಿ (= ಮೈ, *q. v.*) k. *n.* The body. -ಗತ, -ಸಾಲ. Money lent without document or interest.

ಮಯ s. *a.* Made of, consisting of, full of. *n.* N. of an asura.

ಮಯಿದುನ. = ಮಯ್ದುನ, *q. v.*

ಮಯೂರ s. *n.* A peacock. 2, a species of flower, cock's comb, *Celosia cristata; also* -ಶಿಖೆ. -ಕ, -ಕಂಠ, -ತುತ್ಥ. Blue vitriol. -ಗಮನ, -ಧ್ವಜ. Shaṇmukha.

ಮಯ್ದುನ (= ಮಯಿದುನ, ಮೈದುನ) k. *n.* A husband's or wife's brother; a sister's husband; a maternal uncle's son.

ಮಯ್ಲಿ (= ಮೈಲಿ) h. *n.* Impurity, dirt. 2, pox (the small-, chicken-, vaccine-). -ಏಳು. Pox to break out. -ತೆಗಿಸು. To have (a person) vaccinated. -ತೆಗೆ. To vaccinate. -ಹಾಲು. Vaccine matter. -ಗೆ, ಮಯ್ಲು, ಮಯ್ಲೆ. Impurity, dirt, dirtiness; a dirty thing.

ಮರ k. *n.* A tree; wood, timber. -ಅವುಡಲ. A hedge-shrub, *Jatropha curcas.* -ಕಟ್ಟು. To draw toddy. -ಕಬ್ಬು. A hard kind of sugar-cane. -ಕಾಲು, -ಗಾಲು. A stilt; a wooden leg; a corn or salt measure. -ಕುಟಕ, -ಕುಟಿವಕ್ಕಿ, -ಕುಟಿಗ, -ಗಡಕ. The wood-pecker. -ಕೆಲಸ. Carpentry. -ಗಾಣ. A wooden oil-mill. -ಗಿಣಿ. A tree parrot which cannot talk. -ಗೊರಡು. A log of wood. -ದಣಬೆ. A tree-mushroom. -ದರಸಿನ, -ದರಿಸಿನ. A species of Curcuma. -ಪಟ್ಟಿ. A carpenter's work-board. -ಬೆಕ್ಕು. The Bondar, *Paradoxurius bondar.* -ಮೆಣಸು. The *Pimento* tree, *Pimenta acris.* -ಹುಣಿಸೆ. The hog-plum, *Spondias mangifera.*

ಮರ. = ಮರು 1, *q. v.*

ಮರಕತ s. *n.* An emerald.

ಮರಕಳಿಸು (ರ = ಱ) k. *v. i.* To ruminate, chew the cud, *as* an animal.

ಮರಗ f. *n.* Mint, *Mentha sativa.*

ಮರಗಿ, ಮರಗೆ k. *n.* A wooden basin; a sort of bucket.

ಮರಗು. = ಮರುಗು, *q. v.*

ಮರಣ s. *n.* Dying, death. -ಕಾಲ. The time of death. -ಪಡಿಸು. To kill. -ಪಡು, -ವಾಗು, -ಹೊಂದು. To die. -ವೇದನೆ, -ಸಂಕಟ. The agony of death. -ಶಾಸನ. A last will. ಮರಣಾಂತ. Ending in death.

ಮರತು, ಮರದು. = ಮರೆದು (ರ = ಱ). *P. p. of* ಮರೆ, *q. v.* ಮರಪು. = ಮರವು, *q. v.*

ಮರಲು 1. k. *v. i.* To turn; to retreat, return; to occur or do again. ಮರಳಿ. Again, back.

ಮರಲು 2. k. *n.* Sand, gravel. 2. flower.

ಮರವಳಿ k. *n.* The produce of trees. -ಗುತ್ತಿಗೆ. Renting such produce.

ಮರವು 1, ಮರವೆ 1. s. k. *n.* Intoxication, madness; bewilderment, torpor. ಮರಸು. To become furious.

ಮರವು 2, ಮರವೆ 2. (ರ = ಱ) k. *n.* Hiding; secrecy; forgetting; forgetfulness, oblivion. ಮರಸು (= ಮರಿಸು). To veil, hide, conceal; to cause to forget.

ಮರಸುತ್ತು f. n. A screw.

ಮರಹಮ್ಮತು. = ಮರಾಮತ್, q. v.

ಮರಳು 1. = ಮರಲು 1, q. v.

ಮರಳು 2. = ಮರಲು 2, q. v.

ಮರಳು 3. k. v. i. To bubble up, boil fiercely. ಮರಳಿಸು. To cause to bubble up, etc.

ಮರಳು 4. = ಮರುಳು, q. v.

ಮರಾಟ (tb. of ಮಹಾರಾಷ್ಟ್ರ) n. Mahratta; a Mahratta man. ಮರಾಟಿ. Belonging to Mahratta; a Mahratta person; also ಮರಾಟಿಯವ; f. ಮರಾಟಿಯವಳು.

ಮರಾಮತ್ h. n. Repairs, as of roads, houses, tanks, etc. -ಇಲಾಖೆ. The public works department.

ಮರಾಲ, ಮರಾಳ s. n. A flamingo; a goose. a. Soft, tender.

ಮರಿ (ರಿ = ಱಿ) s. n. The young of any animal; a young child; a pupil; a shoot, sapling. -ಕೋಳೀ. A chicken. -ಈ, -ಕೊಡು, -ಹಾಕು. To bring forth young, to yean. -ಗುದುರೆ. A colt. -ಗೋಗಿಲೆ. A young cuckoo. -ಜೇಡ ಹುಳ. A young spider. -ಮಕ್ಕಳು (pl. of ಮರಿಮಗ). Great grand-children. -ಮಗ. A great grand-son. -ಮಗಳು. A great grand-daughter. -ಮಾಡು. To hatch, as fowls.

ಮರಿಸು. = ಮರಸು, q. v.

ಮರಿಗೆ. = ಮರಗೆ, q. v.

ಮರಿಯಾದೆ. tb. of ಮರ್ಯಾದೆ, q. v.

ಮರೀಚಿಕೆ s. n. Mirage.

ಮರು 1. (ರು = ಱು) k. a. Other; next, following, second; again; opposite. n. Forgetfulness. -ಕಳಿಸು. To return, as fever. -ಚಲ. A third or last born child. -ದಿನ, -ದಿವಸ. The next day. -ಮಾತು. An answer. -ವಸಲ. An antagonist, enemy.

ಮರು 2. s. n. A sandy desert. -ಭೂಮಿ. = ಮರು.

ಮರುಕ (ರ = ಱ) k. n. Sorrow, grief; affection, love; allurement, infatuation.

ಮರುಕುಳಿ k. n. Bewilderment. 2, a forgetful man.

ಮರುಗ (tb. of ಮರುವಕ) n. A kind of Ocimum. 2, sweet marjoram.

ಮರುಗು (ರು = ಱು) k. v. i. To burn, be very hot; to fret, grieve; to be distressed.

ಮರುತ, ಮರುತ್ತು (tb. of ಮರುತ್) n. Wind. 2, the god of the wind.

ಮರುವ, -ಕ. = ಮರುಗ, q. v.

ಮರುಳ (ಜಡೆ) k. n. A kind of plant. 2, a mad, foolish man; f. ಮರುಳಿ.

ಮರುಳು (=ಮರಳು) k. n. Bewilderment, confusion, foolishness, stupidity; fury, madness, frenzy. ಮರುಳ. A fool. ಮರುಳಾಗು. To become mad, confused. ಮರುಳಾಟ. Confusion, madness, etc. -ಗೊಳ್ಳು. To become mad, etc. Cpds.: -ನಾಯಿ, -ನುಡಿ, -ಮಾತು, etc. -ತನ. Madness, frenzy.

ಮರೆ (ರೆ = ಱೆ) k. v. t. & v. i. To forget. 2, to be forgotten. P. ps. ಮರತು, ಮರದು, ಮರೆದು. n. Disappearance; secrecy, concealment; cover, veiling; a screen; shelter, refuge. -ಬಿಡು. To stand out of one's light. -ಬೀಳು. To take refuge, to seek shelter. -ಮಾಡು. To hide. -ಮೊಗ. A veiled face. -ಯಾಗು, -ಗೊಳ್ಳು. To disappear. -ಹೊಗು. To resort to, to go for protection.

ಮರ್ಕಟ s. n. A monkey, ape. ಮರ್ಕಟಿ. The Molucca bean; cowhage.

ಮರ್ಜಿ h. n. Will, pleasure, opinion; disposition; manner, way.

ಮರ್ಡಿ k. n. A hill.

ಮರ್ತಬಾ h. n. Rank, station, dignity.

ಮರ್ತ್ಯ s. n. A mortal, man. a. Mortal. -ಲೋಕ. The earth.

ಮರ್ದನ s. n. Crushing, grinding, pounding; rubbing; pressing. -ಮಾಡು, ಮರ್ದಿಸು. To crush, grind, pound; to rub; to destroy.

ಮರ್ದಲ. = ಮದ್ದಳೆ, q. v.

ಮರ್ದು. = ಮದ್ದು, q. v.

ಮರ್ಮ s. n. A vital part. 2, a secret, mystery; secret meaning; secret purpose; a secret quality. -ತಿಳಿ, -ಹಿಡಿ, -ಸಿಕ್ಕು. To find out a secret. -ಜ್ಞ. A discerning man. ಮರ್ಮಿ. A mysterious person.

ಮರ್ಮರ s. n. A rustling sound, murmur.

ಮರ್ಯಾದೆ (= ಮರಿಯಾದೆ) s. n. A limit, border. 2, the bounds of morality, moral law; rule of decency; propriety of conduct; reverential demeanour, respect, civility. -ಮಾಡು, -ತೋರಿಸು, -ಕೊಡು. To show respect, *etc.* *Cpds.:* ಕುಲದ-, ಗ್ರಾಮ-, ದೇಶದ-.

ಮಲ 1. (= ಮರು, *q. v.*) k. *a.* Other; next, second, *etc.* -ಚಲ. A third or last child. -ತಂದೆ. A step-father. -ತಮ್ಮ. A step-mother's son. -ತಾಯಿ. A step-mother. -ಮಾಸ. An intercalary month.

ಮಲ 2. = ಮಲೆ 1, *q. v.* -ನಾಡು. A hilly country. -ವಾರು, -ಯಾಳ. Malabar.

ಮಲ 3. s. n. Excretions of the body; dirt, filth, excrement, *etc.*; dregs, dross of metal. 2, moral impurity, sin. 3, original sin. -ಕಟ್ಟು, -ಬದ್ಧ. Constipation. -ನಾಗರು, -ರೋಗ. Epilepsy. -ಪೃಷ್ಠ. The fly-leaf of a book. -ವಿಸರ್ಜನೆ, -ಶುದ್ಧಿ, -ಶೋಧನೆ. Evacuation of the bowels; a purgative. -ತೆ, -ತ್ವ. Dirtiness, impurity.

ಮಲಕು 1. k. n. A round ornament of glass beads, corals, *etc.* 2, a kind of necklace.

ಮಲಕು 2. k. n. Bringing up again in rumination. -ಹಾಕು. To chew the cud.

ಮಲಗು k. v. i. To recline, lie down, repose, rest. 2, to incline, bend, *as* paddy-ears, *etc.* n. A pillow, cushion. ಮಲಗಿಸು. To cause to lie down, or recline, to place; to lay down, *etc.*

ಮಲಪೂಪ h. n. Enclosure, *as* of a letter.

ಮಲಮಲು h. n. Muslin.

ಮಲಯ s. n. N. of a hill-range in Malabar; Malabar country. -ಪರ್ವತ. Malabar mountain. -ಪವನ. Malabar air. ಮಲಯಾಳ. The Malayâlam country.

ಮಲರ್ (= ಮರಲು 2, *q. v.*) Sand. 2, a flower. -ಪುಡಿ. The pollen of flowers.

ಮಲಾಮತು h. n. A difficulty, strait; trouble.

ಮಲಾಮು h. n. Ointment, plaster.

ಮಲಾರ s. n. A cluster or string of glass bracelets.

ಮಲಿನ (*fr.* ಮಲ 3) s. *a.* Dirty, filthy, unclean. 2, sinful, vile. 3, dark, obscure (*as* the intellect); dull, rusty (*as* learning, *etc.*). -ಚಿತ್ತ, -ಬುದ್ಧಿ. A depraved or dull mind. -ತೆ, ತ್ವ. Filthiness, impurity.

ಮಲುಕು. = ಮಲಕು, *q. v.*

ಮಲೆ 1. (= ಮಲ 2, ಮಲಯ) k. n. A mountain. -ಯಾಳ. = ಮಲಯಾಳ, *q. v.*

ಮಲೆ 2. a. k. v. t. To oppose, fight against. *v. i.* To be refractory; to be haughty, insolent. ಪಾರ್-. To rebel.

ಮಲ್ಲ k. n. A wrestler, boxer; an athlete. *a.* Strong, stout; good. -ಯುದ್ಧ. A wrestling match. -ರಂಗ. A palaestra. ಮಲ್ಲಾಡು. To struggle or strive. ಮಲ್ಲಾಟ. Mutual strife.

ಮಲ್ಲಳಿ (ಳಿ = ಱು) a. k. n. Turning round. 2, bewilderment, alarm, fear. 3, the black bee. 4, a crowd.

ಮಲ್ಲಿ 1, ಮಲ್ಲಿಗೆ (*tb. of* ಮಲ್ಲಿಕಾ) n. A cultivated flower shrub, *Jasminum sambac.* *Varieties:* ಅಡವಿಯ-, ಕದರು-, ಕಸ್ತೂರಿ-, ಕೋಲು-, ದುಂಡು-, ಸಂಜೆ-, ಹಸರು-.

ಮಲ್ಲಿ 2. s. n. A female image of metal with a lamp-cup; *also* ದೀಪದ-.

ಮಲ್ಲಿಕಾರ್ಜುನ s. n. N. of Śiva and of a linga.

ಮವುಜು h. n. A plantain.

ಮವುಜೆ h. n. A village.

ಮಶಕ s. n. A gnat, musquito; a bug.

ಮಶೀನು e. n. A machine (ಯಂತ್ರ).

ಮಶೀತಿ, ಮಶೀದಿ (= ಮಸೀದಿ) h. n. A mosque.

ಮಷಾಲು h. n. A torch. ಮಷಾಲ್ಜಿ. A torch-bearer; a menial servant of an office.

ಮಷಿ. = ಮಸಿ, q. v.

ಮಷ್ಕರಿ h. n. Obstinacy, stubbornness.

ಮಷ್ಟು. = ಮಡ್ಡಿ 1, q. v.

ಮಸಕ 1. a. k. n. Great agitation, passion; wrath, rage.

ಮಸಕ 2, ಮಸಕು (= ಮಸ್ಕು) k. n. Duskiness; a dusky colour, etc.; impurity.

ಮಸಗು a. k. v. i. To expand, develop; to be displayed, agitated; enraged. v. t. To display, exhibit. 2, to rub, whet.

ಮಸಣ, ಮಸಾಣ (tb. of ಶ್ಮಶಾನ, q. v.) n. A cemetry; also -ಗಾಡು, -ವಟ್ಟಿಗೆ, -ವಟ್ಟಿ.

ಮಸರು. = ಮೊಸರು, q. v.

ಮಸಲತು h. n. Planning, scheming; a plan, plot; counsel; clever contrivance.

ಮಸಾರೆ (ಭೂಮಿ) f. n. A kind of good red soil.

ಮಸಾಲಾ, ಮಸಾಲೆ f. n. Seasoning drugs; spicery. -ವಡೆ. A kind of spiced cake.

ಮಸಿ (= ಮಷಿ) s. n. Ink; soot, lamp-black; charcoal. -ಕುಡಿಕೆ, -ಪಾತ್ರೆ. An inkstand. -ಬಟ್ಟೆ. A rag used in lifting pots from the fire. -ಯಾಗು. To become charcoal (*said of buried money*).

ಮಸೀದಿ. = ಮಶೀತಿ, etc., q. v.

ಮಸುಕು. = ಮಸಕು, q. v.

ಮಸುಳು a. k. v. i. To grow dim, faint, to become pale, etc. ಮಸುಳಿಸು. To cause to grow dim, etc.

ಮಸೂದೆ h. n. A sketch; a draft.

ಮಸೂರ, ಮಸೂರಿ h. n. A sort of pulse or lentil, *Ervum hirsutum*. ಮಸೂರಿಕೆ. Pustules, small-pox; a musquito-curtain; a cushion.

ಮಸೆ k. n. Whetting, sharpness. 2, a slight wound. 3, lustre, shine. v. t. To rub; to grind, whet, sharpen; to rub off. P. ps. ಮಸದು, ಮಸೆದು, ಮಸ್ತು.

ಮಸ್ಕೀರಿ h. n. A good-for-nothing fellow.

ಮಸ್ಕು. = ಮಸಕ 2, q. v.

ಮಸ್ತಕ s. n. The head, skull; the top of anything.

ಮಸ್ತಿ h. n. Intoxication; pride. 2, fatness, rut. ಮಸ್ತು. Intoxicated; fat, bulky; abundant, plentiful; intoxication; abundance, plenty.

ಮಸ್ತಿಷ್ಕ s. n. The brain.

ಮಸ್ಲತು. = ಮಸಲತು, q. v.

ಮಸ್ಲೀನು h. n. Muslin; also ಮಲಮಲು.

ಮಹ. = ಮಹಾ, q. v.

ಮಹಜರು h. n. A general affidavit; a certificate signed by all present at a transaction.

ಮಹತ್ (= ಮಹಾ) s. a. Great, mighty, strong, big, large. 2, abundant, much. 3, high, lofty, noble; excellent. -ತಮ. Greatest, mightiest. -ತರ. Greater; the oldest; most respectable. ಮಹತ್ವ, ಮಹತ್ವತೆ. Greatness, majesty, mightiness, etc. ಮಹರ್ಷಿ. A great ṛishi.

ಮಹತಾಪು, ಮಹತಾಬು (= ಮತಾಪು) f. n. A kind of fire-work.

ಮಹತ್ತು. tb. of ಮಹತ್, q. v.

ಮಹಂತ. tb. of ಮಹತ್, q. v.

ಮಹಮದ, ಮಹಮ್ಮದ h. n. Mahomed; a Mahomedan.

ಮಹಲು. = ಮಹಾಲು, q. v.

ಮಹಸೂಲು h. n. Public revenue; private income from land. -ದಾರ. A receiver of taxes.

ಮಹಳ. tb. of ಮಹಾಲಯ, q. v.

ಮಹಾ (= ಮಹ, ಮಹತ್ತು, ಮಹತ್, q. v.) s. a. Great, mighty. -ಕಾಲ. Śiva; a fierce man. -ಕಾಳಿ, -ಕಾಳಿ. Durgâ. -ಖರ್ವ. Ten kharvas. -ಜನ. The populace; respectable men. -ತಲ. The 6th of the lower worlds. -ದಾನ. N. of certain valuable gifts to priests. -ದೇವ. Śiva; f. -ದೇವಿ. -ನಶ. A large kettle-drum. -ನವಮಿ. The 9th or last day of the navarâtri festival. -ನುಭಾವ. Worthy, pre-eminent; a gentleman. -ಪದ್ಮ. Ten padmas, a million of millions. -ಪಾತಕ. A heinous crime. -ಪುರುಷ. An eminent personage. -ಪ್ರಲಯ. The total annihilation of the universe. -ಪ್ರಾಣ. An aspirate; a vital air. -ಫಲ. Great fruit; the citron. -ಭಾರತ. N. of a great epic poem. -ಭಾಷ್ಯ. Patañjali's great commentary on Pâṇini's grammar. -ಭೂತ. A primary element. -ಮನಸ್. High-minded, liberal, magnanimous. -ಮಾಯೆ. Great illusion: Durgâ. -ಮೇರು. The great Mêru. -ರಥ. A great chariot; great warrior. -ರಾಜ. An emperor; a word of respectful compellation. -ರಾಣಿ. An empress. -ರಾಷ್ಟ್ರ. A great realm; the Mahratta country. -ರೌರವ. One of the 21 hells. -ಬುರ್ದ. Ten arbudas. -ಲಕ್ಷ್ಮಿ. The Śakti or wife of Nârâyaṇa. -ಶಯ. The ocean; an honorific title; high-minded, magnanimous. -ಸಾಗರ. The great ocean.

ಮಹಾತ್ಮ s. a. High-souled; noble-minded, generous; eminent, mighty. n. A noble-minded man. ಮಹಾತ್ಮೆ. Noble-mindedness; a noble-minded woman.

ಮಹಾಂತ s. n. Abundance. 2, an eminent man.

ಮಹಾಲಯ (= ಮಹಲು) s. n. A great dwelling, palace, temple. 2, (= ಮಹಳ) the latter fortnight of the bhâdrapada month; the śrâddha performed at that time.

ಮಹಾಲು (= ಮಹಲು, ಮಹಾಲಯ) h. n. A palace, hall. 2, a subdivision of a talook or district.

ಮಹಿ s. a. Great, large. n. Greatness. 2, the earth; soil. -ತಲ. The earth's surface. -ಧರ. A mountain. -ಕಾಂತ, -ಪ, -ಪತಿ, -ಪಾಲ, -ಭುಜ. -ರಮಣ. A king. -ಮಂಡಲ. The whole earth.

ಮಹಿಮೆ s. n. Greatness, grandeur, majesty, glory; might, power, energy. -ಪಡಿಸು. To glorify, magnify. -ಕೊಡು. To give glory, etc. ಮಹಿಮಾಕರ. A mine of glory; glorious.

ಮಹಿಷ s. n. A male buffalo. ಮಹಿಷಿ. A buffalo-cow. ಮಹಿಷಾಸುರ. N. of an asura slain by Durgâ.

ಮಹೇಂದ್ರ s. n. Great Indra; regent of the east quarter. -ಜಾಲ. Indra's net: trick; cheating; illusion; jugglery, sorcery.

ಮಹೇಶ, ಮಹೇಶ್ವರ s. n. A great lord; Śiva; f. ಮಹೇಶ್ವರಿ.

ಮಹೋತ್ಪಾತ s. n. A meteor, comet.

ಮಹೋತ್ಸವ s. n. A great festival.

ಮಹೋತ್ಸಾಹ s. n. Great effort. a. Very energetic, persevering.

ಮಹೋದಯ s. n. Great happiness. 2, a very auspicious day.

ಮಹೋದರ s. n. Dropsy.

ಮಹೋನ್ನತ s. a. Very high, lofty.

ಮಹೋಪದ್ರವ s. n. Great distress.

ಮಹೋಲ್ಲಾಸ s. n. Great delight.

ಮಹೌಷಧ s. n. A very efficacious remedy.

ಮಳಲು k. n. Sand, gravel. ಮಳಲೇರಿ. A sand-bank.

ಮಳಿಗೆ f. n. A warehouse, shop.

ಮಳೆ (ಳೆ = ಱು) k. n. Rain. -ಕಾಲ, -ಗಾಲ. The rainy season. -ಗರೆ, -ಸುರಿ. To rain. -ಗುರುತು. Signs of rain. -ನೀರು. Rain-water. -ಬಿಡು. Rain to cease. -ಬಿಲ್ಲು. A rainbow. -ಹನಿ. A rain-drop. -ಹಿಡಿ. Rain to set in.

ಮಾ 1. tb. of ಮಹಾ, q. v. -ಗೆಲಸ. Great work. -ಕಾಳಿ, -ತಾಯಿ. Durgâ.

ಮಾ 2. k. n. Great emotion. -ಮಸಕ. Great agitation or activity.

ಮಾಂಸ s. n. Flesh, meat; the pulp of fruit. -ಗ್ರಂಥಿ. A gland, wen. -ಜೀವಿ, -ಭಕ್ಷಕ, ಮಾಂಸಾಹಾರಿ. Carnivorous; a flesh-eater. ಮಾಂಸಲ. Fleshy, lusty, muscular; strong. ಮಾಂಸಾಹಾರ. Animal food. ಮಾಂಸಿಕ. A butcher. -ಚಕ್ಕಲಿ. A cannibal. ಗೋ-. Beef.

ಮಾಕರಿಸು k. v. i. To reveal secrets.

ಮಾಗಣೆ 1. k. n. A garden-herb, *Coleus barbatus*.

ಮಾಗಣೆ 2. h. n. A division of a talook.

ಮಾಗಧ (fr. ಮಗಧ) s. a. Relating to Magadha. n. A bard, minstrel. ಮಾಗಧಿ. The Magadha language; a sort of jasmin, *Jasminum auriculatum*.

ಮಾಗಾಯಿ k. n. A small ear-ornament of females.

ಮಾಗಿ, ಮಾಗೆ (tb. of ಮಾಘ) n. The cold season; *also* -ಕಾಲ.

ಮಾಗು k. v. i. To ripen fully, *as* fruit; to be mature, *as* a medicine. ಮಾಗಿಸು. To cause to ripen, *etc.*

ಮಾಘ (= ಮಾಗಿ, ಮಾಗೆ) s. n. The 11th lunar month (January-February). -ಸ್ನಾನ. A bath in that month.

ಮಾಂಗಲ್ಯ (fr. ಮಂಗಲ) s. a. Auspicious. n. An auspicious or festive ceremony. 2, prosperity, welfare. -ಸೂತ್ರ. = ಮಂಗಲಸೂತ್ರ.

ಮಾಚಿ k. n. A species of plant. -ಪತ್ರಿ, ಪತ್ರೆ. A common weed, *Artemisia maderaspatana*.

ಮಾಜಿ h. a. Gone by, passed away; late; former.

ಮಾಜು k. v. t. To cause to disappear; to hide, conceal, efface. n. Dissimulation, deceit, fraud.

ಮಾಜುಂ h. n. An intoxicating preparation of the hemp plant.

ಮಾಟ (fr. ಮಾಡು) k. n. Making; doing; a work, business, undertaking. 2, a manner, way. 3, handsomeness, beauty. 4, trickery; jugglery, magic, sorcery. -ಕೂಟ. Good execution, finish. -ಗಾರ. A sorcerer; f. -ಗಾತಿ. -ಗಾರಿಕೆ. Sorcery.

ಮಾಡ 1. (= ಮಾಡು 2) k. n. A hole or niche in a wall. 2, a kind of litter.

ಮಾಡ 2. (= ಮಾಡು 3; cf. ಮಾಳಿಗೆ) f. n. A large building. 2, an upstair house; *also* ಮಾಡಿ. 3, a gable roof. -ಹಾಗಲಬಳ್ಳಿ. A climbing herb, *Momordica dioica*.

ಮಾಡು 1. k. v. t. To do, make, perform, accomplish, effect, prepare, construct, build, execute; to cultivate, *as* a field, *etc.* P. p. ಮಾಡಿ. *Cpds.:* ಅಡಿಗೆ-, ಅವಮಾನ-, ಆರಿಕೆ-, ಉಪವಾಸ-, ಕೆಲಸ-, ಕೇಡು-, ಜೀವನ-, ದಾನ-, ಪಕ್ವ-, ಪರೀಕ್ಷೆ-, ಪೂಜೆ-, ಪ್ರೀತಿ-, ಮೋಸ-, ಯುದ್ಧ-, ವರ್ತಕತನ-, ವಶ-, ಸೇವೆ-, ಸ್ತೋತ್ರ-, ಸ್ನಾನ-, ಸ್ನೇಹ-, ಹಗೆ-, *etc.* ಮಾಡಗೊಡು. To allow to do, *etc.* ಮಾಡೇ-. *rep.* To do certainly. ಮಾಡುವಿಕೆ. Doing, *etc.* ಮಾಡಿಸು. To cause to make, do, perform, *etc.* ಮಾಡಿಸುವಿಕೆ. Causing to make, *etc.*

ಮಾಡು 2. = ಮಾಡ 1, q. v.

ಮಾಡು 3. = ಮಾಡ 2, q. v.

ಮಾಣಿಕ (tb. of ಮಾಣಿಕ್ಯ) n. A ruby. 2, redness.

ಮಾಣು k. v. i. To stop, cease, subside, be checked; to desist, cease from, give over. 2, to be healed, cured. P. p. ಮಾಣ್ದು. ಮಾಣಿಸು. To cause to stop, *etc.*

ಮಾಂಡಲಿಕ s. a. Provincial. n. The governor of a province.

ಮಾತಂಗ s. n. A man of the lowest rank; an outcast; f. ಮಾತಂಗಿ.

ಮಾತಾಮಹ s. n. A maternal grandfather; f. ಮಾತಾಮಹಿ.

ಮಾತು 1. k. n. A word; a saying; a language; a promise, slander, rumour. ಮಾತಾಟ. Talking; talk, garrulity. ಮಾತಾಡು. To speak, converse. ಮಾತಾಳಿ. A talkative man. -ಕೊಡು. To promise. -ಗಳ್ಳ. A cheat, liar. -ಕೇಳು. To listen to words. -ತಪ್ಪಿಸು, -ತಿರಿಗಿಸು, -ಮುರಿ. To break a promise. -ತಪ್ಪು. A promise to be broken. -ಮಾಡು. To make an oral agreement. -ಹಿಡಿ. To lay hold of a word; to catch one by his word. -ಹೊರಿಸು. To accuse. -ಗ, -ಗಾರ. A talkative man. -ಗಾರತನ, -ಗಾರಿಕೆ. Talkativeness.

ಮಾತು 2. *tb. of* ಮಾತೃ, *q. v.* -ಶ್ರೀ. A word of respect for one's mother or an elderly female. -ಉ. A thorn-apple; a maternal uncle. -ಳಾನಿ. His wife.

ಮಾತುಬರಿ h. *a.* Respectable, trustworthy, honest. *n.* Trustworthiness, respectability.

ಮಾತುಲಂಗ, ಮಾತುಲುಂಗ s. *n.* The citron.

ಮಾತೃ (= ಮಾತು 2, *q. v.*, ಮಾದಿರಿ, *etc.*) s. *n.* A measurer. 2, a mother; *also* ಮಾತೆ. -ಕ. Maternal, fostered. -ಕೆ. A mother; the original of a copy. -ವಿಯೋಗ. The separation from a mother. -ಷ್ವಸೃ. A maternal aunt. -ಸೇವೆ. Waiting on a mother. -ಹತ್ಯೆ. Matricide.

ಮಾತ್ರ s. *n.* Measure, quantity, size, bulk. 2, the whole; the only thing. 3, a minute portion, particle. 4, a prosodical instant. *ad.* As much as; nothing but, mere, only, none but. *Cpds.*: ಅದು-, ಇದು-, ಇಷ್ಟು-, ನೀನು-, ಅವನು-, ಒಂದು-, ಹದಗ-. Only that, *etc.* ಸ್ವಲ್ಪ-. Just a little.

ಮಾತ್ರೆ (= ಮಾತ್ರ *n.*, *q. v.*) s. *n.* Measure, *etc.* 2, a pill.

ಮಾತ್ಸರ್ಯ (*fr.* ಮತ್ಸರ) s. *n.* Envy, jealousy, malice.

ಮಾದ s. *n.* Drunkenness, stupor. 2, joy, delight. 3, pride, passion. 4, *tb. of* ಮಹಾದೇವ.

ಮಾದಲ, ಮಾದಾಳ (*tb. of* ಮಾತುಲಂಗ) *n.* The citron tree, *Citrus medica.*

ಮಾದಿಗ (*tb. of* ಮಾತಂಗ) *n.* A cobbler, chuckler; an outcast.

ಮಾದಿರಿ, ಮಾದ್ರಿ (*tb. of* ಮಾತೃಕೆ) *n.* The original. 2, a pattern, specimen, sample.

ಮಾದೇವ. *tb. of* ಮಹಾದೇವ, *q. v.*

ಮಾದೃಶ s. *ad.* Like me, resembling me.

ಮಾಧವ (*fr.* ಮಧು) s. *a.* Sweet. *n.* Honey; mead. 2, the month vaiśâkha (April-May). 3, spring. 4, Vishṇu.

ಮಾಧುರ್ಯ s. *n.* Sweetness; pleasantness. 2, kindness, amiability.

ಮಾಧ್ವ s. *a.* Belonging to Madhva's doctrine; *n.* An adherent of Madhva; sweetness.

ಮಾನ 1. s. *n.* Measure, dimension; a measure; rule, standard. 2, half a sêru. 3, likeness, resemblance. -ಅಕ್ಕಿ, ಮಾನಕ್ಕಿ. A measure of rice.

ಮಾನ 2. s. *n.* Opinion; conception. 2, conceit, arrogance, pride. 3, regard for others; honour, respect, reverence; dignity, respectability. 4, indignation; caprice. -ಕಳೆ, -ತೆಗೆ. To disgrace. -ಕಾಯು. To protect honour. -ಕೊಡು, -ಮಾಡು. To honour. -ಗೇಡಿ. A dishonourable person. -ಗೇಡಿತನ. Disgracefulness. -ಗೇಡು. Disgrace. -ತೋರಿಸು. To show respect. -ನಷ್ಟ. Defamation. -ಹೊಂದು. To receive honour. -ಭಂಗ. Loss of honour, humiliation. -ಮರ್ಯಾದೆ. Reputation, respect, regard. -ವಂತ, -ಸ್ಥ. A respectable man. *f.* -ವತಿ, -ವಂತಿ. -ಸ್ಥಾನ. The private parts. -ಹಾನಿ. Dishonour. -ಹೀನ. Disgraceful.

ಮಾನವ s. *a.* Human. *n.* A man. ಮಾನವಿ. A woman; human.

ಮಾನಸ (*fr.* ಮನಸ್) s. *a.* Mental; ideal. *n.* The mental powers, the mind. 2, N. of a lake. ಮಾನಸಾಂತರ. Change of mind, repentance (*for sins, Chr.*). ಮಾನಸಿಕ. Mental.

ಮಾನನಿಕ (*fr.* ಮಾಣು) k. *n.* Stopping, cessation.

ಮಾನಾಯ s. *n.* Fees in grain given to a measurer of a village produce.

ಮಾನಿ s. *n.* A respectable person; *f.* -ನಿ. -ಷ್ಠ. Very highly honoured. -ಸು. To honour.

ಮಾನುಷ, ಮಾನುಷ್ಯ s. *a.* Human. *n.* Humanity.

ಮಾನೆ (= ಮಾನ 1) s. *n.* A copy to write from a model. -ತಿದ್ದು. To draw the pen over the mânĕ as an exercise.

ಮಾಂತ್ರಿಕ (*fr.* ಮಂತ್ರ) s. *n.* An enchanter, conjurer, sorcerer.

ಮಾಂದು k. *v. t.* To stop, ward off, check.

ಮಾಂದ್ಯ (*fr.* ಮಂದ) s. *n.* Slowness; laziness. 2, torpor; apathy; weakness. 3, indisposition, apepsy.

ಮಾನ್ಯ s. *a.* Respectable, honourable; acceptable. *n.* A ruler. 2, honour; a privilege. 3, land either liable to a trifling quit-rent or free from tax. 4, a complimentary form of address in letters. -ಗಾರ. One holding a mânya; an incumbent.

ಮಾಪ f. *n.* Measure. -ಣ, ಮಾಪಿ. Measuring. ಮಾಪಿ ಜೀನಸು. Articles of capacity.

ಮಾಫಕು h. *a.* Conformable, suitable.

ಮಾಫ, ಮಾಫಿ h. *a.* Pardoned; gratis. *n.* Remission (as of tax, *etc.*); pardon, excusing.

ಮಾಮಲ, ಮಾಮಲೆ h. *n.* The office of a Mâmaledâra. -ದಾರ. A subordinate collector of the revenues of a talook.

ಮಾಮಸಕ k. *n.* Bustling activity, great zeal, ardour.

ಮಾಮೂಲು h. *a.* Usual, ordinary. *n.* Custom, usage, prescription. -ಪ್ರಕಾರ ನಡೆ. To act according to an established custom.

ಮಾಯ (*tb. of* ಮಾಯೆ, *q. v.*) *n. Also:* disappearance, vanishing. -ಕ. = ಮಾಯಿಕ. -ಕ ಮಾಡು. To conceal; to cheat. -ವಾಗು. To vanish. -ಕಾರ, -ಗಾರ. A deceiver; a juggler. -ಪಾಶ. The fetters of illusion. -ವಾದ. Falsehood. -ವಾದಿ. A liar. -ವಿದ್ಯೆ. Jugglery, witchcraft. ಮಾಯಾದೇವಿ. Buddha's mother; Durgâ. ಮಾಯಾವಿ. Illusory, magical; a conjurer, juggler.

ಮಾಯಿ 1. s. *a.* Illusory, unreal, deceptive. *n.* A juggler, a cheat. 2, deceit. -ಕ. Illusory, deceitful; a juggler.

ಮಾಯಿ 2. h. *n.* A mother.

ಮಾಯು 1. k. *v. i.* To be healed. *P. p.* ಮಾದು. ಮಾಯಿಸು. To heal.

ಮಾಯು 2. s. *n.* Sounding, crying. 2, gall, bile.

ಮಾಯೆ (= ಮಾಯ) s. *n.* Art. 2, illusion, trick, deceit, deception, fraud; jugglery, sorcery. 3, phantasm, phantom. 4, idealism, unreality.

ಮಾರ, ಮಾರಣ s. *n.* Killing, slaughter; destruction. 2, a magical ceremony for the purpose.

ಮಾರನೆ (ರ = ಱ) k. *a.* Other, following, next. -ದಿನ, -ದಿವಸ. The next day.

ಮಾರಾಟ. *See s.* ಮಾರು 2.

ಮಾರಾಮಾರಿ h. *n.* Mutual fighting or beating.

ಮಾರಿ (*cf.* ಮಾರ) s. *n.* Killing. 2, a plague, epidemic, pestilence; the cholera. 3, the goddess of death; Durgâ; *also* -ಅಮ್ಮ. -ಕುತ್ತ, -ಜಡ, -ರೋಗ. The cholera. -ಕಾ. A plague, pestilence, *etc.*

ಮಾರೀಚ s. *n.* N. of a râkshasa.

ಮಾರೀಫತ್ತು h. *n.* Trust, charge; instrumentality. *prep.* By means of, through.

ಮಾರು 1. k. *n.* A fathom.

ಮಾರು 2. (ರು = ಱು) k. *v. t.* To barter, sell. *v. i.* To be sold; to be exchanged. *P. p.* ಮಾರಿ. ಮಾರಾಟ. Exchange, barter, sale. ಮಾರಾಡು. To sell.

ಮಾರು 3. (ರು = ಱು) k. *n.* The state of being other, different, next; change; exchange, barter; sale. 2, hostility. ಮಾರಡಿ. An opponent, enemy. ಮಾರನೆ. Following, subsequent. ಮಾರನೆ ದಿನ. The next day. ಮಾರವ. A seller. ಮಾರುತ್ತರ. A reply. ಮಾರುತ್ತರ ಕೊಡು. To reply. ಮಾರುಳಿ. Another affair.

ಮಾರ್. = ಮಾರು 3, *q. v.* -ಕಟ್ಟೆ. A markét. -ದನಿ. An echo. -ನುಡಿ. To answer; a reply. -ಪಡೆ. Equality, likeness; another force. -ಪೊಡಪು, -ಪೊಳಪು. A reflection. -ಪೊಳೆ. To be reflected. -ಬಡ್ಡಿ. Compound interest. -ಬಲ. An opposing force. -ಮಲೆ. To oppose, rebel.

ಮಾರ್ಗ (*fr.* ಮೃಗ) s. *n.* Search. 2, a road, way, track. 3, a channel, canal. 4, mode, manner; usage, custom; style. -ಕ್ರಮಣ. Journeying. -ವಿದ. A knower of the right way. -ಶೀರ್ಷ. N. of the 9th lunar month. ಅಡ್ಡ-. A cross road. ದುರ್-, ದುರ್ಮಾರ್ಗತನ. Immorality, wickedness. ಸನ್-. Good conduct. ಸನ್ಮಾರ್ಗಕ್ಕೆ ಬರು. To reform. -ಕಾಣು. To find the road. -ಸ್ಥ, ಮಾರ್ಗಿಗ. A traveller.

ಮಾರ್ಚ್ e. *n.* March (*3rd month of the year*).

ಮಾರ್ಜಿನ್ e. *n.* Margin.

ಮಾರ್ಜನ s. *n.* Cleansing, scouring, washing. ಮಾರ್ಜನಿ. A broom.

ಮಾರ್ಜಾರ s. *n.* A cat; *also* ಮಾರ್ಜಾಲ.

ಮಾರ್ತಂಡ, ಮಾರ್ತಾಂಡ s. *n.* The sun.

ಮಾರ್ಪು (*cf.* ಮಾರು 3, *q. v.*) k. *n.* Exchange, change. ಮಾರ್ಪಾಟು. Change. ಮಾರ್ಪಾಗು, ಮಾರ್ಪಾಟವಾಗು. To change.

ಮಾಲವ (= ಮಾಳವ) s. *n.* N. of a country, Malva.

ಮಾಲಾ. = ಮಾಲಿ, *q. v.* -ಕಾರ. A florist.

ಮಾಲಿ s. *n.* Wearing a garland. 2, a gardener. -ಕ. A florist; *f.* -ನಿ. -ಕೆ. A garland; a necklace; a collection of things arranged, *as* ನವ-, ಪುಷ್ಪ-, ರಾಗ-.

ಮಾಲಿನ್ಯ (*fr.* ಮಲಿನ) s. *n.* Uncleanness, impurity, sinfulness. 2, obscurity.

ಮಾಲಿಸು k. *v. i.* To look obliquely, to leer. *v. t.* To bend to one side, *as* a post, *etc.*

ಮಾಲೀಕ k. *n.* An owner, master.

ಮಾಲೀಸು h. *n.* Grooming (of a horse).

ಮಾಲು 1. k. *v. t.* To bend. *n.* Sloping; a slope, descent. -ಕಣ್ಣು. A squint-eye.

ಮಾಲು 2. h. *n.* Property; goods, wares. -ದಾರ. A man of property, an owner.

ಮಾಲೂರ f. *n.* The bael tree, *Aegle marmelos.* 2, the wood-apple tree, *Feronia elephantum.*

ಮಾಲೆ s. *n.* A wreath, garland; a chaplet; a necklace; a rosary. 2, a row; a series. -ಗಾರ. A florist; *f.* -ಗಾತಿ. ಜಪ-. A rosary. ಮುತ್ತು-. A pearl necklace. ಹೂ-. A wreath of flowers.

ಮಾವ (*tb. of* ಮಾಮ) *n.* A father-in-law. ಸೋದರ-. A maternal uncle.

ಮಾವಟಿಗ, ಮಾವತ, ಮಾವಂತ s. *n.* An elephant driver, mahaut.

ಮಾವಿ h. *a.* Yellowish green.

ಮಾವು k. *n.* The mango; the mango tree, *Mangifera indica.* *Cpds.:* ಮಾವಿನಕಾಯಿ, ಮಾವಿನಗಿಡ, ಮಾವಿನ ಹಣ್ಣು, *etc.*

ಮಾವುತ. = ಮಾವಟಿಗ, *q. v.*

ಮಾಷ s. *n.* A bean; a kind of pulse, *Phaseolus radiatus.* 2, a weight of gold = 11 grs. troy.

ಮಾಸ s. *n.* The moon; a month of thirty days. -ಗಟ್ಲೆ. A monthly practice; monthly. -ಮಾಸ. Every month.

ಮಾಸರ s. *n.* A meal of parched barley soaked with sour milk. 2, rice gruel.

ಮಾಸವಳ, ಮಾಸವಳ್ಳ, ಮಾಸಾಳು (*tb. of* ಮಹಸ್) *n.* A great man, hero, leader.

ಮಾಸಿಕ (*fr.* ಮಾಸ) s. *a.* Monthly. -ಶ್ರಾದ್ಧ. A monthly śrâddha.

ಮಾಸು (= ಮಾಜು, *q. v.*) k. *v. i.* To grow dim; to become dusky, foul, dirty. *v. t.* To dirty, soil. *n.* Filth, dirt. ಮಾಸಲು. Impurity, dirtiness.

ಮಾಹಾತ್ಮ್ಯ (*fr.* ಮಹಾತ್ಮ) s. *n.* High-mindedness. 2, greatness, majesty, dignity. 3, a legend.

ಮಾಹಿೀತು h. *n.* Experience, observation; knowledge.

ಮಾಹೆ h. *n.* A month. -ವಾರಿ. A monthly settlement; monthly accounts.

ಮಾಹೇಶ, ಮಹೇಶ್ವರ s. *n.* Relating to Śiva. ಮಾಹೇಶ್ವರಿ. Pârvatî, Durgâ.

ಮಾಳ f. *n.* A plain, a tract of ground. 2, a bed of the sea.

ಮಾಳವ. = ಮಾಲವ, *q. v.*

ಮಾಳಿ f.*n.* A washerman. 2, a female gardener.

ಮಾಳಿಗೆ (*tb. of* ಮಾಲಿಕೆ) *n.* An upstair house with a flat roof; a flat roof. -ಮನೆ. A house with a flat roof.

ಮಿಕ್ಕು 1. *P. p. of* ಮಿಗು, *q. v.*

ಮಿಕ್ಕು 2. (= ಮಿಗು) k. *v. i.* To increase, exceed; to remain. *n.* Excess; remainder, rest. ಮಿಕ್ಕಾಗು. To remain.

ಮಿಗ. *tb. of* ಮೃಗ, *q. v.*

ಮಿಗು (= ಮಿಕ್ಕು 1) k. *v. i.* To grow great, abundant, to exceed; to be in excess; to remain; to go beyond, surpass. *P. p.* ಮಿಕ್ಕಿ, ಮಿಕ್ಕು. -ತೆ, ಮಿಗತೆ. Surplus; remnant, rest. ಮಿಗಲು, ಮಿಗಿಲು. Greatness; abundance; excellence, excess; remainder, rest. ಮಿಗಿಲಾಗು. To surpass; excel; to remain. ಮಿಗಿಸು. To cause to be left or remain.

ಮಿಗೆ a. k. *ad.* Abundantly, much; further; well.

ಮಿಜಾಕು h. *n.* Airs and affectation, high notions and fancies.

ಮಿಂಚು 1. (= ಮಿಗು, *etc.*, *q. v.*) k. *v. i.* To become great; to excel, exceed; to expire, *as* a period; to pass beyond reach; to behave proudly.

ಮಿಂಚು 2. k. *v. i.* To shine, sparkle, glitter; to flash, lighten. *n.* Shine, lustre, brightness; lightning. -ಗಲ್ಲು. Talc. -ಬಳ್ಳಿ. The heart-pea. -ಮಾಡು, ಮಿಂಚಿಸು. To cause to shine; to furbish, polish. -ಹುಳ. A glow-worm.

ಮಿಟುಕಿಸು, ಮಿಟುಕು k. *v. i.* To twinkle, blink; to stare.

ಮಿಟಲ (= ಮಿಟ್ಲೆ) k. *n.* N. of a plant.

ಮಿಟಿ k. *n.* Blinking; staring. -ನೋಡು. To look at in a blinking and inquisitive manner. -ಮಿಟಿ ಸ್ವರ್ಗ. A svarga without attractions and happiness.

ಮಿಟ್ಟನೆ (*fr.* ಮಿಡುಕು) k. *ad.* In a sorrowful manner. -ಮಿಡುಕು. To be greatly grieved.

ಮಿಟ್ಟೆ k. *n.* Jutting out; rising ground; a hill. -ತಗ್ಗು. Hills and dales. -ನೆಲ. Rising ground.

ಮಿಟ್ಲೆ (= ಮಿಟಲ) k. *n.* -ಗಿಡ. A small craggy tree with rough leaves, *Epicarpurus orientalis.*

ಮಿಠಾಯಿ h. *n.* Sweetmeat. -ಗಾರ. A confectioner.

ಮಿಡಿ 1. (= ಮೀಟು) k. *v. i.* To strike, fillip. 2, to toss up with the thumb, *as* a Rupee.

ಮಿಡಿ 2. a. k. *v. i.* To leap, bounce, hop; to move about rapidly; to shed, as tears. *n.* Springing, bouncing, hopping.

ಮಿಡಿ 3. k. *n.* A very young and unripe fruit. -ಕಾಯಿ. An unripe fruit.

ಮಿಡಿಚೆ, ಮಿಡಿತೆ k. *n.* A grasshopper, locust.

ಮಿಡುಕು a. k. *v. i.* To grieve, *etc.* 2, to become conscious, lively or vigorous, be alive. 3, to move. 4, to urge on. *n.* Grieving. 2, animation, liveliness; activity; strength, vigour.

ಮಿಣುಕು, ಮಿಣುಕು (= ಮಿಂಚು 2, *q. v.*) k. *v. i.* To glitter. *n.* Glittering. -ಹುಳ. A glow-worm.

ಮಿಣಿ k. *n.* A rope of twisted leather straps.

ಮಿಂಡ k. *n.* A paramour, lover. 2, a hero; *f.* ಮಿಂಡಿ.

ಮಿಣ್ಣೆ k. *n.* A small wooden or metal spoon. 2, a small drinking vessel.

ಮಿತ s. *a.* Measured; limited; moderate; scanty, frugal; sparing; brief.

ಮಿತಿ s. *n.* Measure; limit; moderation; accurate knowledge. -ಮೀರಿ. *dpl.* -ತಪ್ಪಿ ಹರಿ. To overflow its bounds, *as* a river. -ತಪ್ಪಿ ಹೋಗು. To go beyond limits. -ಇಲ್ಲದ. Boundless, immeasurable.

ಮಿತ್ರ s. *n.* A friend, associate. 2, an ally. 3, the sun; *f.* ಮಿತ್ರಳು, ಮಿತ್ರೆ. -ಘ್ನ. Treacherous. -ಜ್ಞ. Thankful to a friend. -ತ್ವ. Friendship, intimacy. -ದ್ರೋಹ. Betrayal of a friend. -ದ್ರೋಹಿ. A treacherous friend. -ಭೇದ. Breach of friendship. -ಲಾಭ. Acquisition of friends.

ಮಿಥುನ s. *n.* A pair, couple. 2, the sign of the zodiac *Gemini.*

ಮಿಥ್ಯಾ (= ಮಿಥ್ಯೆ) s. ad. Falsely; untruly, *etc.* a. False, sham, untrue. -ತ್ವ. Falsity, untruth. -ದೃಷ್ಟಿ. Heresy. -ಪವಾದ. A false accusation. -ಮತಿ. A false opinion. -ವಾದಿ. A liar.

ಮಿಥ್ಯೆ (= ಮಿಥ್ಯಾ) s. n. Untruth, falsehood, fraud.

ಮಿದಿ k. v. t. To pound; to kill; to rub, grind. -ಸು. To cause to pound, *etc.*

ಮಿದು. *tb. of* ಮೃದು, *q. v.*

ಮಿದುಗು, ಮಿದುಳು (*tb. of* ಮೇದಸ್) n. Marrow; the brain.

ಮಿನಹು h. *ad.* Till, until.

ಮಿನಾಹಿ h. n. Dismissing, discharging; abolishing.

ಮಿನಿಕೆ k. n. A climbing herb, the melon vine, ***Cucumis melo.***

ಮಿನುಕು, ಮಿನುಗು (= ಮಿಣುಕು, *q. v.*) k. v. t. To glitter, shine. 2, to murmur. n. Glitter, lustre.

ಮಿಂದು. *P. p. of* ಮೀಯು, *q. v.*

ಮಿರಾಸಿ h. n. A hereditary title to periodical gifts of money, corn, *etc.* -ದಾರ. A holder of a mirâsi title.

ಮಿರುಗು (ರ = ಐ. = ಮಿನುಕು, *q. v.*) k. v. i. To glitter, flash, sparkle, shine. n. Glitter, shine, lustre.

ಮಿಲನ s. n. Mixing with, union, contact. ಮಿಲಾಕತ್ತು. Mingling, mixing; a meeting, interview. ಮಿಲಾಯಿಸು. To mix, mingle; to join; to introduce. ಮಿಲಾವಣೆ. Mixing. ಮಿಲಿತ, ಮಿಳಿತ. Mixed, united, combined.

ಮಿಲ್ಲ್ಯನ್ e. n. A million, 10 times 100,000.

ಮಿಶ್ರ s. a. Mixed, mingled; combined; manifold, diverse. n. Mixture. -ಣ. Mixing, union, combination. ಮಿಶ್ರಿತ. Mixed, blended.

ಮಿಶ್ಯನ್ e. n. Mission; propagation of the Gospel. -ಕಾರ್ಯ, -ಕೆಲಸ. M. work. -ವಾರ್ತೆ, -ವರ್ತಮಾನ. M. news. -ಸಂಘ. M. society, *as* Basle German Mission, London Mission, Church Mission, *etc.* -ಸೂತ್ರ. M. policy. -ನವರು. Protestant Christians. ಮಿಶ್ನೇರಿ. A missionary; *also* ಮಿಷನೇರಿ.

ಮಿಸಕು. = ಮಿಸುಕು, *q. v.*

ಮಿಸಲು f. n. Official inspection (*as* of troops, peons, horses, *etc.*).

ಮಿಸಿ e. n. Miss, an unmarried lady; *also* -ಯವರು, -ಯಮ್ಮನವರು.

ಮಿಸುಕು k. v. i. To move, stir; to quiver, throb, swing, *etc.* -ಆಡು, ಮಿಸುಕಾಡು. To move, stir about.

ಮಿಸುನಿ a. k. n. Gold.

ಮಿಹಿರ s. n. The sun.

ಮಿಳಿ k. n. A leather rope; a strap.

ಮಿಳಿರು a. k. v. i. To move about, swing, wave, roll, *etc.* 2, to prosper, flourish. n. Moving to and fro.

ಮಿಳ್ಳಿ, ಮಿಳ್ಳೆ (= ಮಿಣ್ಣೆ, *q. v.*) k. n. A small drinking vessel made of any metal.

ಮೀ. = ಮಿಯು, *q. v.*

ಮೀಟು 1. k. v. t. To strike the wires of a lute or guitar with the finger. 2, to raise with a lever. n. Eminence, greatness, excess; beauty.

ಮೀಟು 2. f. n. Salt. -ಮೋರಿ. A salt manufactory.

ಮೀಣಿ k. n. Bathing, bath.

ಮೀಂಟು. = ಮೀಟು 1, *q. v.*

ಮೀನ s. n. A fish. 2, the *Pisces* of the zodiac. -ಕಂಡ, -ಗಂಡ. The calf of the leg.

ಮೀನು (*tb. of* ಮೀನ) n. A fish. 2, a star. *Varieties:* ಕರಿಯ-, ಕರು-, ಕೆಂಪು-, ಕೇರೆ-, ಚಳಿಯ-, ಜೊರ-, ಬಳ್ಳಿ-, ಹಾವು-, ಹುಲ್ಲು-, *etc.* -ಬೇಟೆ. Fishing. -ಗಾರ. A fisherman. ಮೀನಾಕ್ಷಿ. A fish-eyed woman; N.

ಮೀಮಾಂಸ (*tb. of* ಮೀಮಾಂಸೆ) n. Reflection, examination, discussion. 2, a philosophical system.

ಮೀಯು (= ಮೀ) k. v. i. To take a bath, to bathe. *P. ps.* ಮಿಂದು, ಮಿಾದು. ಮೀಯಿಸು. To bathe.

ಮೀರು (ರು = ಱು) k. v. i. To transgress; to surpass, exceed; to elapse; to move out of reach, *etc.*; to be elated, lofty; to act proudly. *P. ps.* ಮಿಾರಿ, ಮಿಾರ್ದು. ಆಣೆ-. To violate an oath. ಮಿತಿ-. To exceed the limits. ಹೊತ್ತು-. Time to pass.

ಮಿಾಸ e. *n.* Mass, re-sacrificing of Christ in the Roman Catholic Church.

ಮಿಾಸಲು k. *n.* Anything set apart for a purpose; anything untouched or undefiled, dedicated or vowed. -ಕಾಣಿಕೆ. A present for a particular purpose. *Cpds.:* -ನೀರು, -ಹಸು, -ಹಾಲು, -ಎಮ್ಮೆ, *etc.* -ಕಟ್ಟು. To set apart.

ಮಿಾಸೆ f. *n.* A mustache, the mustaches. -ತಿದ್ದು, -ತಿಕ್ಕು. To trim the mustaches. -ಕಟ್ಟು. To defy, challenge.

ಮುಕ್ k. *a.* Three. ಮುಕ್ಕಟ್ಟು. Three obstacles or ties. ಮುಕ್ಕಣ್ಣ. (Three-eyed) Śiva. ಮುಕ್ಕಂಡಿ. A cow that calves every third year. ಮುಕ್ಕಾಣಿ. Three-sixty-fourths. ಮುಕ್ಕಾಲು. Three feet; a tripod; three-fourths; a copper coin worth three kâsus.

ಮುಕುಟ s. *n.* A crown; crest, diadem.

ಮುಕುತಿ. *tb. of* ಮುಕ್ತಿ, *q. v.*

ಮುಕುಂದ s. *n.* Vishṇu.

ಮುಕುರ s. *n.* A mirror.

ಮುಕುಲ s. *n.* An opening bud.

ಮುಕ್ಕ (*tb. of* ಮೂರ್ಖ) *n.* A common word of abuse; *f.* ಮುಕ್ಕಿ.

ಮುಕ್ಕಳಿಸು. = ಮುಕ್ಕುಳಿಸು, *q. v.*

ಮುಕ್ಕು 1. k. *v. i.* To eat voraciously, greedily; to gobble. ಮುಕ್ಕ. A gobbler.

ಮುಕ್ಕು 2. k. *n.* A small break; a small fragment. 2, pride, arrogance.

ಮುಕ್ಕುರಿ k. *n.* Straining in pain or distress.

ಮುಕ್ಕುರು a. k. *v. i.* To come upon, to inclose. *n.* Coming or falling upon, covering.

ಮುಕ್ಕುಳಿ k. *n.* A mouthful for rinsing. -ಸು. To rinse the mouth with water; to spit out, throw away, abandon.

ಮುಕ್ತ s. *a.* Loosened, let loose, set free; quitted; released, liberated, emancipated. ಮುಕ್ತಾಫಲ. A pearl. ಮುಕ್ತಾವಲಿ. A pearl necklace.

ಮುಕ್ತಾಯ s. *n.* Completing; conclusion, end. -ಗೊಳಿಸು, -ಮಾಡು. To complete, finish, execute.

ಮುಕ್ತಿ s. *n.* Release, setting free. 2, freedom. 3, final liberation, final beatitude. 4, salvation (*Chr.*). -ಪಥ, -ಮಾರ್ಗ. The way to emancipation. -ಸಾಧನೆ. A means of obtaining mukti.

ಮುಖ (= ಮೊಗ) s. *n.* The mouth. 2, the face; a direction, quarter; facing. 3, the fore-part, front. 4, the head, tip of anything. 5, edge; surface. 6, opening; entrance; beginning. 7, means, expedient. *a.* Chief, best. -ಚಪ್ಪಡಿಸು, -ತಿರುವು. To frown. -ದಾಕ್ಷಿಣ್ಯ. Kindness, *etc.*, shown in a person's presence. -ಭಂಗಿತ. Putting to shame. -ಭಾವ. The expression of the countenance. -ಮಜ್ಜನ, -ಮಾರ್ಜನ. Washing the face. -ಲೋಮಿ. A cockroach. -ವೀಣೆ. A kind of pipe. -ಸ್ತುತಿ. Flattery. ಮುಖಾಮುಖಿ. Face to face. -ಬಿಚ್ಚಿ ಮಾತಾಡು. To speak out openly. -ದಿಂದ, ಮುಖಾಂತರ, ಮುಖಾಂತ್ರ. By means of, through.

ಮುಖಮಲು h. *n.* Valvet.

ಮುಖರ s. *a.* Garrulous, noisy. -ತೆ. Garrulity.

ಮುಖ್ಯ s. *a.* Principal, chief, primary; first, eminent; first-rate, most excellent. *n.* The chief; a leader, guide. 2, a principal thing. -ತೆ, -ತ್ವ. Preeminence, superiority. -ಪ್ರಾಣ. Hanumat. -ಮುಖ್ಯ. The various, chief. -ಸ್ಥ. A leader, chief; *f.* ಮುಖ್ಯಸ್ಥಳು.

ಮುಗಸು. = ಮುಗಿಸು, *q. v.*

ಮುಗಳು. = ಮುಗುಳು, *q. v.*

ಮುಗಿ k. *v. i.* To contract or close, *as* a flower. 2, to end, terminate, to be completed, accomplished. *v. t.* To join the open hands (in saluting).

P. ps. ಮುಗದು, ಮುಗಿದು. -ಯುವಿಕೆ. Closing, joining; ending. -ಸು. To finish, close.

ಮುಗಿಲು k. n. A cloud; the sky.

ಮುಗು. = ಮೂಗು, *q. v.* -ದಾರ. The cord put through an ox's nose.

ಮುಗುವಳಿ k. n. A settlement about salary, rent, *etc.*

ಮುಗುಳು (*tb. of* ಮುಕುಲ) *v. i.* To bud, sprout. *n.* A bud, opening bud. ಮುಗುಳಾಗು. To bud.

ಮುಗುಳಿ k. n. A thorny tree, the *Acacia suma.*

ಮುಗ್ಗರಿಸು, ಮುಗ್ರಿಸು k. *v. i.* To stumble, [trip.

ಮುಗ್ಗು 1. k. *v. i.* To be interrupted in going, to stumble; to fall; to sink. *n.* A pitfall, *as in* ತಗ್ಗು-.

ಮುಗ್ಗು 2. k. *v. i.* To be musty or mouldy. *n.* An offensive smell, mouldiness, mustiness. -ನಾತ. A mouldy smell. -ಹಿಡಿ. To become musty. ಮುಗ್ಗಲು. Mustiness, mouldiness.

ಮುಗ್ಧ s. *a.* Perplexed; stupid, ignorant; foolish, silly; artless, innocent. -ತನ, -ಭಾವ. Stupidity, simplicity. ಮುಗ್ಧೆ. An artless woman.

ಮುಂ, ಮುಚ್ (= ಮುಂದು, ಮುನ್ನು, *etc., q. v.*) k. *n.* That which is before, in front of, or preceding, following, *etc.* -ಕೊಳ್ಳು. To move on, advance. -ಗಟ್ಟು. An offset at the foot of a wall. -ಗಡ. Advance in money or kind. -ಗಡೆ. The front side, *etc.* -ಗತ್ತಲೆ. The darkness just after sunset or just before sunrise. -ಗಾಣು. To have foresight. -ಗಾರು, -ಗಾರೆ ಮಳೆ. The first rains. -ಗಾರು ಬೆಳೆ. The first crop. -ಗಾಲು. The fore legs (of quadrupeds); the upper part of the foot. -ಗುರುತು. Foreboding, prognosis. -ಗುರುಳು. A front lock. -ಗೆಡೆ. To fall on the face. -ಗೈ. The forearm. -ಗೋಪ. Momentary anger.

ಮುಂಗಿ, ಮುಂಗಿಲಿ, ಮುಂಗುಲಿ k. *n.* The mungoose.

ಮುಚ್. = ಮು, *q. v.* ಮುಚ್ಚಂಜೆ. Dawn, noon and evening.

ಮುಚ್ಚಳಿಕೆ h. *n.* A final agreement in writing.

ಮುಚ್ಚಲು k. *n.* A winnowing fan, used by children as a toy. 2, = ಮುಚ್ಚಳ, *see s.* ಮುಚ್ಚು.

ಮುಚ್ಚು k. *v. t.* To close, shut; to shut up; to cover; to conceal. *v. i.* To close, shut (*as in* ಮುಚ್ಚಿಕೊಳ್ಳು). *n.* Shutting, closing. -ಗಲ್ಲು. The stone cover of a gutter. -ಮರೆ. Secrecy. ಮುಚ್ಚಳ. A cover, lid. ಮುಚ್ಚಿಕೆ. Shutting, closing; ceiling.

ಮುಚ್ಚೆ. *tb. of* ಮೂರ್ಛೆ, *q. v.*

ಮುಜರಾ h. *n.* Deduction, remission. 2, respect, bow or salâm. -ಮಾಡು. To make all allowance.

ಮುಜಾಂಕು h. *n.* Matter, consequence.

ಮುಂ, ಮುನ್. = ಮುಹ್. ಮುಂಚಿತ. Beforehand, previous. ಮುಂಚು. To precede; to exceed; to outdo, surpass, excel; the preceding, previous or prior state; former time, *etc.* ಮುಂಚೆ. Previously, formerly, first; before, earlier than, ere. ಮುಂಜಾನೆ, ಮುಂಜಾವು. Early morning.

ಮುಂಜ, ಮುಂಜಿ s. *n.* A sort of grass, *Saccharum munja.* 2, the investiture of a boy with the sacred thread.

ಮುಟ್ಟಾಮುಟ್ಟಿ. *tb. of* ಮುಷ್ಟಾಮುಷ್ಟಿ, *q. v.*

ಮುಟ್ಟಿ. *tb. of* ಮುಷ್ಟಿ, *q. v.*

ಮುಟ್ಟಿಸು k. *v. t.* To cause to touch; to apply to; to cause to reach, deliver, *as* a letter, *etc.*; to apply or lay out, *etc.*; to kindle, *as* a light.

ಮುಟ್ಟು 1. k. *v. t.* To touch; to come in contact with. *v. i.* To reach, arrive, *as* a letter, place (*with Dat.*); to be laid out, expended, *as* money, *etc.* *n.* Touch, contact. 2, hindrance. ಮುಟ್ಟ. As far as, till, up to. ಬೇರು ಮುಟ್ಟ ಕೀಳು. To pluck up by the root. ಕಡೆ ಮುಟ್ಟ ಮಾಡು. To finish completely.

ತಲೆ ಮುಳ್ಳ ಮುಣುಗು. To immerse completely. ಮುಟ್ಟಿಗೋಲು. A stoppage-pole, total pillage. ಮುಟ್ಟಗೋಲು ಹಾಕು. To pillage.

ಮುಟ್ಟು 2. k. n. An implement, tool; utensils, furniture.

ಮುಟ್ಟುವಳಿ k. n. Expenses, outlay, *as* of money, grain, *etc.*

ಮುಡಿ 1. k. v. i. To bind or tie the hair of the head; to fasten in it, *as* flowers. n. A knot, bundle; a braid of hair. 2, unshaved hair on account of a vow to an idol. 3, a hollow ring of brass used as a charm. 4, a kind of crown for idols. -ಕಟ್ಟು. To tie up in a bundle of straw; hair braided round the head. -ಬಳೆ. = ಮುಡಿ 2. -ದಾಳ, -ವಾಳ. A kind of fragrant grass, *Andropogon schoenanthus.* -ಸು. To fasten in the hair-knot, *as* flowers.

ಮುಡಿ 2. a. k. v. i. To end, come to an end. n. End. [ಹೂವು-.

ಮುಡು. *P. p. of* ಮುಡಿ 1, *in* ಮುಡುಕೊಳ್ಳು, *as*

ಮುಡುಕು, ಮುಡುಗು k. v. i. To bend, shrink, become crooked, distorted. v. t. To bend, distort. n. Bending, distorting; a curve, an angle.

ಮುಡುಪು k. n. A bundle, money-bag, *as* one dedicated to an idol.

ಮುಡುಹು a. k. n. The shoulder, shoulder-blade.

ಮುಣಗು, ಮುಣೆಗು, ಮುಳುಗು k. v. i. To sink, to be drowned; to dip, bathe; to set, *as* the sun; to be ruined. n. An immersion, dip. ಮುಣಗಿಸು, ಮುಣೆಗಿಸು, ಮುಣುಗಿಸು. To immerse, dip, plunge; to drown; to ruin.

ಮುಂಡ s. a. Shaved, bald. 2, hornless. 3, blunt. 4, mean. n. The trunk of a lopped tree, pollard. 2, a headless body. 3, a bald head. 4, a barber. 5, myrrh. -ಕ. The lopped trunk of a tree; the head. -ನ. Tonsure, shaving. -ಮೋಹು. To cover the head, *as* a widow

ಮುಂಡಾಸ, ಮುಂಡಾಸು h. n. A turban. -ಸುತ್ತು. To wind a turban.

ಮುಂಡಿ s. a. Shaven, bald, shorn. n. A barber. 2, a pestle without a ferrule.

ಮುಂಡಿಗೆ (*tb. of* ಮುಂಡಕ) n. A stem, post, pillar. 2, a wooden bar.

ಮುಂಡು 1. k. n. Kissing, fondling. ಮುಂಡಾಡು. To kiss, fondle.

ಮುಂಡು 2. k. n. A short cloth, used as a garment.

ಮುಂಡು 3. (*tb. of* ಮುಂಡ) n. A headless body. -ಗಳ್ಳಿ. The leafless milk-hedge, *Euphorbia antiquorum;* the triangular spurge. -ಮುಳುಕ. The Bengal kite; a kind of duck.

ಮುಂಡೆ k. n. A widow. -ಮುಸುಕು. A widow's veil.

ಮುತ್ತಗ, ಮುತ್ತಲ, ಮುತ್ತುಗ k. n. The bastard teak, *Butea frondosa.*

ಮುತ್ತಂದೆ, ಮುತ್ತಾತ. *See s.* ಮುತ್ತು 2.

ಮುತ್ತಿಗೆ k. n. Covering; surrounding; a siege, blockade. -ಇಕ್ಕು. = -ಹಾಕು. -ತೆಗೆ. To raise a siege. -ಹಾಕು. To lay siege to; to besiege. -ಬೀಳು. To be besieged.

ಮುತ್ತು 1. k. v. t. To inclose; to cover; to encompass, surround, shut in; to besiege; to attack. v. i. To swarm, *as* bees, *etc.*

ಮುತ್ತು 2. (= ಮುದಿ) k. n. Old age, oldness. ಮುತ್ತಜ್ಜ, ಮುತ್ತಂದೆ, ಮುತ್ತಪ್ಪ, ಮುತ್ತಾತ. A great grandfather. ಮುತ್ತಜ್ಜಿ, ಮುತ್ತಮ್ಮ, ಮುತ್ತವ್ವ. A great grandmother. ಮುತ್ತೈದೆ. A respectable woman whose husband is alive. ಮುತ್ತೈದೆತನ. Being a muttaidĕ. ಮುತ್ತಯ್ಯ. = ಮುತ್ತಜ್ಜ.

ಮುತ್ತು 3. (= ಮುದ್ದು, *q. v.*) k. n. A kiss. -ಇಡು, ಮುತ್ತಿಡು, -ಕೊಡು. To kiss.

ಮುತ್ತು 4. (*tb. of* ಮುಕ್ತಾ) n. A pearl. ಮುತ್ತಿನ ಚಿಪ್ಪು. An oyster.

ಮುತ್ಸದ್ದಿ h. n. An accountant, clerk.

ಮುದ s. n. Joy, pleasure, delight.

ಮುದಕ (= ಮುದುಕ, *q. v.*) k. n. An old man; *f.* ಮುದಕಿ.

ಮುಪಡು. = ಮುದುಡು, *q. v.*

ಮುದಿ (= ಮುತ್ತು2, ಮುದು, *q. v.*) k. *a.* Old. *n.* Advanced age, *etc.* -ಎತ್ತು, -ಕಾಗಿ, -ಗೂಬೆ, -ಡೊಂಬ, *etc.* An old—. -ತನ. Old age. -ತಿ. An old woman.

ಮುದು. = ಮುತ್ತು2, ಮುದಿ, *q. v.* -ಕ. = ಮುದಕ.

ಮುದುಡು, ಮುದುರು (= ಮುದಡು) k. *v. i.* To bend; to shrink, contract, shrivel up, *as* flowers, *etc.*; to wrinkle, *as* hide, skin, *etc.* *v. t.* To bend; to draw in, *as* a limb; to crumple, *as* cloth, paper; to fold, *as* a mat; to pull up; to draw aside.

ಮುದ್ಗರ s. *n.* A mace, rod.

ಮುದ್ದತು, ಮುದ್ದತ್ತು h. *n.* A space of time, term.

ಮುದ್ದಾಮ್, ಮುದ್ದಾಮು h. *ad.* Expressly, positively. *a.* Own. -ಆಳು, -ಮನುಷ್ಯ. Own servant.

ಮುದ್ದು (= ಮುತ್ತು3, *q. v.*) k. *n.* A kiss, love, affection; an object of love. *a.* Dear, affectionate. ಮುದ್ದಾಡು. To kiss mutually. ಮುದ್ದಿಕ್ಕು, ಮುದ್ದಿಡು, -ಕೊಡು. To kiss. -ಗೂಸು, -ಮಗು. A dear child. -ತನ. Pleasantness, charm. -ಮಗ. A dear son. -ಮೊಗ. A sweet face. -ಗೈಯು, -ಮಾಡು. To fondle, caress. -ನುಡಿ, -ಮಾತು. A fondle, pleasant, sweet word.

ಮುದ್ದೆ k. *n.* A ball, roundish lump; a clod. 2, râgi-porridge. 3, a weaver's pegstand. -ಪಲ್ಲೆ. Vegetable porridge. -ಬೆಲ್ಲ. A lump of jaggory.

ಮುದ್ದೈ h. *n.* A plaintiff, complainant, prosecutor (*law*). -ಅಲೆ. A defendant.

ಮುದ್ರೆ s. *n.* A seal, signet, seal-ring. 2, a stamp, print; a seal of lac. 3, a coin. 4, stamp, cast, air. -ಕೋಲು. A wooden seal. -ಯುಂಗರ. A seal-ring. -ಒತ್ತು, -ಮಾಡು, -ಹಾಕು. To seal. -ಕೀಳು, -ಬಿಚ್ಚು, -ಯೊಡೆ. To unseal. ಮುದ್ರಾಕ್ಷರ. Type, print. ಮುದ್ರಾಕ್ಷರಶಾಲೆ. A printing office. ಮುದ್ರಾಂಕಿತ, ಮುದ್ರಿತ. Stamped, printed. ಮುದ್ರಿಕೆ. A seal, seal-ring; an impress; dedication to a deity at the end of a poem or book. ಮುದ್ರಿಸು. To seal; to stamp; to print; to coin; to seal up.

ಮುನ್ (= ಮುಂ, *q. v.*) k. *a.* Three. *n.* That which is before. *ad.* Before. -ತಿಳುಹು. To inform beforehand. -ದಲೆ. The forehead. -ದರಿ. To proceed. -ದೋರು. To appear or show beforehand; to show the way. -ನೀರು. The ocean. -ನೂರು. 300. -ನೇಸರು. The dawn.

ಮುನಸೀಫ಼ h. *n.* A native, subordinate civil judge.

ಮುನಾಸಬು h. *a.* Right, proper, fit, due. *n.* Discretion.

ಮುನಿ 1. k. *v. i.* To become angry, to be displeased. *n.* Anger; *also* -ಪು, -ಸು.

ಮುನಿ 2. s. *n.* An ascetic; a sage, saint; a devotee; a monk; a Buddha. 2, a male devil. ಮುನೀಂದ್ರ, ಮುನೀಶ್ವರ. A great sage.

ಮುನಿಷಿ h. *n.* A writer. 2, a teacher of language.

ಮುನಿಸು s. *n.* Anger, wrath, passion, rage, enmity. -ತಿಳಿ. Anger to calm down. -ಹರಿ. Anger to cease. -ಗಾರ. An angry man.

ಮುಂತು. = ಮುಂದು, *q. v.* ಮುಂತಾಗು. To be the first of a series. ಮುಂತೆ. = ಮುಂದೆ, *q. v.* ಮುಂತಾದ. Etc. ಮುಂತಿಟ್ಟು. In the presence of.

ಮುಂದು (= ಮುಂತು) k. *n.* The front part or side; following, succeeding; the state of being first, before, or future. ಮುಂದಕ್ಕೆ ಮಾಡು. To shut, *as* a door. ಮುಂದಕ್ಕೆ ಹಾಕು. To place in front; to put off, delay. ಮುಂದರಿ. To go before; to surpass; to go forward; to know beforehand, to be far-seeing. ಮುಂದಾಗು. To go to the front, excel. ಮುಂದಿಕ್ಕು, ಮುಂದಿಡು, ಮುಂದಿರಿಸು. To put in front; to put forward, extend. -ಗಡೆ. The front; in front; to the front, forwards. -ಗೆಡು. Prospects to be ruined; to be at a loss, to despair.

-ಗೊಳ್ಳು. To take the lead; to remember. -ಮಾಡು. To put to the front, to bring forward. -ವರಿ. To rush forward; to advance. ಮುಂದೊಟೆ. A leather rope for cart. ಮುಂದೆ (=ಮುಂತೆ). Before, in front of; forward; first, in the first instance; further; thereafter, hereafter, in future. ಮುಂದೆ ಬರು. To come or arrive first; to happen in future.

ಮುಂಡೆ k. n. A jar-like brass vessel.

ಮುಂದೋರು. *See s.* ಮುನ್.

ಮುನ್ನ (= ಮುನ್, ಮುಂದು, *q. v.*). ಮುನ್ನರಿ. To know beforehand. ಮುನ್ನಾದಿನ, ಮುನ್ನಾದಿವಸ. The day before. ಮುನ್ನೋರ್ವ. A predecessor.

ಮುನ್ನೀರು (-ಬು). *See s.* ಮುನ್.

ಮುಪ್. = ಮು, *q. v.* ಮುಪ್ಪಾಗ. Three-fourths of a paṇa (2 aṇōs and 6 kâsus).

ಮುಪ್ಪು k. n. Old age.

ಮುಮ್. = ಮುನ್, *q. v.* -ಬಾಗಲು. The front door. -ಬೆಳಕು. Moon's light in the śukla paksha before it is full. -ಭಾರ. Weight in the front part (of a cart). -ಮಡಿ. Threefold; three times. -ಮಡಿಸು. To treble; to do thrice as much.

ಮುಮುಕ್ಷು s. a. Desirous of freeing. n. A person desirous of mukti.

ಮುಯಿಬು k. n. Return, recompense; retaliation, punishment. 2, a gift, present. -ಮಾಡು. To present an object at a marriage. -ಗೆ ಮುಯಿಕೊಡು, -ಗೆ ಮುಯಿ ತೀರಿಸು. To repay (*in a good or bad sense*); to revenge.

ಮುರ 1. = ಮುರವು, *q. v.*

ಮುರ 2. s. a. Encompassing, surrounding. n. A daitya slain by Kṛishṇa. -ರಿಪು, ಮುರಾರಿ. Vishṇu, Kṛishṇa.

ಮುರಕ, ಮುರಕು. = ಮುರುಕು, *q. v.*

ಮುರದಾರಸಿಂಗಿ h. n. Sulphate of copper; or semi-vitrified oxide of lead.

ಮುರಲಿ, ಮುರಳಿ k. n. A flute, pipe. -ಧರ. Kṛishṇa as flute-bearer.

ಮುರವು (= ಮುರ, ಮುರುವು) k. n. An ear- or nose-ring.

ಮುರಿ 1. k. v. i. To bend, be bent; to grow crooked; to turn; to wind; to stretch one's self (with windings of the limbs). n. A bend, curve, winding. 2, a ring worn on the wrist. 3, a pad of wool laid under the saddle of an ox.

ಮುರಿ 2. (ರಿ = ಱಿ) k. n. A fragment, piece. v. t. To break; to break off; to crush; to break down, defeat, destroy; to break up; to do away. v. i. To break; to lose strength; to be impaired, *etc.* *P. ps.* ಮುರದು, ಮುರಿದು. -ಸು. To cause to break, crush; to get changed *as* a coin. -ಯುವಿಕೆ. Breaking.

ಮುರಿಕೆ, ಮುರಿಗೆ, ಮುರಿವು k. n. Bending, twisting. -ಬಳೆ. A twisted bracelet.

ಮುರು (= ಮುರವು 2) k. n. Turning, a turn. -ದೆಲೆ. The turning point in a cross-road. -ವು. = ಮುರವು.

ಮುರುಕು (ರು=ಱು) k. n. A fragment, bit, *as* of bread, sweetmeat, *etc.* 2, frowning, making grimaces; foppishness; showiness.

ಮುರುಟು (= ಮುದುಡು, *q. v.*) k. v. i. To be bent, shrink, shrivel. n. Shrinking, shrivelling.

ಮುರುಡಿ k. n. A shrub or small tree, *Helicteres isora.*

ಮುರುಡು (= ಮೊರಡು) k. n. Roughness, ruggedness, unevenness. ಮುರಡಿಸು. To pluck out by twisting.

ಮುರುವ (ರು = ಱು) k. n. A maimed or imbecile man.

ಮುರುವು. = ಮುರವು, *q. v.*

ಮುರ್ಗಿನಹುಳಿ k. n. The mate mangosteen, *Garcinia purpurea.*

ಮುಲಾಜು, ಮುಲಾಜಿ h. n. Respect, regard for.

ಮುಲಾಮು. = ಮಲಾಮು, *q. v.* 2, a gilding or plating.

ಮುಲುಕು k. v. i. To groan, *as* when lifting a heavy load; to strain. 2, to feel disgust. n. Straining.

ಮುಲ್ಕಿ f. n. Revenue. a. Relating to revenue. 2, native, indigenous.

ಮುಲ್ಲ h. n. A Mahomedan jurist or theologian; a schoolmaster. -ಶಾಸ್ತ್ರ. The Koran.

ಮುಲ್ಲಂಗಿ. = ಮೂಲಂಗಿ, q. v.

ಮುವ್ವತ್ತು k. n. Thirty. ಮುವ್ವರು. Three persons.

ಮುಶಲ s. n. A pestle, club.

ಮುಷ್ಕರ k. n. Stubbornness, obstinacy, insolence. -ಹಿಡಿ. To be obstinate.

ಮುಷ್ಕೀಲು h. a. Difficult, hard. n. A difficulty.

ಮುಷ್ಟಿ s. n. The closed hand, fist. 2, a hilt or handle of a sword, etc. -ಗೆಯ್ಯು, -ಹಿಡಿ. To clench the fist. -ಬಂಧ. Clenching the fist; a handful. -ಯುದ್ಧ. A fight with fists. ಮುಷ್ಟಾ-. Fisticuffs.

ಮುಸಕು. = ಮುಸುಕು, q. v.

ಮುಸಡಿ, ಮುಸಡು. = ಮುಸುಡಿ, q. v.

ಮುಸರೆ k. n. Boiled rice considered to be unclean. -ಗಡಿಗೆ, -ಪಾತ್ರೆ. A pot in which anything has been boiled.

ಮುಸಲ, -ಮಾನ h. n. A Mussulmân. -ಮತ. Mohammedanism.

ಮುಸಾಫರ h. n. A traveller. ಮುಸಾಫರಿ. Relating to travellers. -ಬಂಗಲೆ. A travellers' bangalow.

ಮುಸಿ s. n. A crucible.

ಮುಸು k. n. A black ape; also -ವ.

ಮುಸುಕು (= ಮುಸಕು) k. v. t. To cover; to hide; to veil, shroud. v. i. To come or fall upon, as flies, etc.; to swarm. n. Covering; a cover; a veil. -ಇಡು, -ಹಾಕು. To put on a veil.

ಮುಸುಕೆ h. n. The elephant-creeper, *Argyreia speciosa*.

ಮುಸುಡಿ, ಮುಸುಡು (= ಮುಸಡಿ, q. v.) k. n. The face; the snout, muzzle.

ಮುಸುಂಡಿ k. n. A crooked, rude person; a coward. -ತನ. Crookedness; cowardice.

ಮುಸುರು (ರು=ಱು) k. v. t. To cover; to hide; to swarm, crowd. n. A cover, veil. -ಗಟ್ಟು. A cover to form.

ಮುಸುವ k. n. A large and black kind of ape; also ಮುಸು.

ಮುಸ್ತ s. n. A species of grass, *Cyperus rotundus*; also ಮುಸ್ತೆ.

ಮುಸ್ತಾಭ s. n. The grass, *Cyperus hexastachyus*.

ಮುಸ್ತೈದು h. a. Prepared, ready. ಮುಸ್ತೈದೆ. Preparation; things prepared.

ಮುಹುರ್, ಮುಹುಸ್ s. ad. In or for a moment, repeatedly, again and again.

ಮುಹೂರ್ತ 1. s. n. A moment, instant. 2, the fit time. 3, the twelfth part of a day and night. ಮುಹೂರ್ತಿಕ. An astrologer.

ಮುಹೂರ್ತ 2. (tb. of ಮೂರ್ತ) n. A sitting posture. -ಗೊಳ್ಳು. To sit down.

ಮುಳಗು. = ಮುಳುಗು, q. v.

ಮುಳಿ 1. k. v. i. To grow passionate, angry, etc. -ಯಿಸು. To enrage. -ಸು. Anger, passion.

ಮುಳಿ 2. k. n. A cause.

ಮುಳುಗು (ಳು=ೞು. = ಮುೞುಗು, ಮುಳಗು, etc.) k. v. i. To sink under water; to sink; to immerse one's self, dive; to set as the sun, etc.; to be ruined. ಮುಳುಗಿಸು. To immerse; to dip, plunge; to bathe; to ruin.

ಮುಳುವು a. k. n. Ruin, loss.

ಮುಳ್ಳು k. n. A thorn; a pointed thing, a sting, spur; the hand of a clock; the tongue of a balance, etc. ಮುಳ್ಳೇಳು. Horripilation to take place. -ಕಲ್ಲು. Thorns and stones. -ಗಳ್ಳಿ. The prickly pear, *Opuntia dillenii*. -ಗೆಣಸು. A prickly kind of yam, *Dioscorea tomentosa*. -ಗೋರಟೆ, -ಗೋರಂಟೆ. A small prickly shrub, *Barleria prionitis*. -ಬೇಲಿ. A thorny hedge. -ಮುತ್ತಗ. The tree *Andersonia rohitaka*. -ಮುಸ್ತು. A spinous shrub, *Canthium parviflorum*. -ಮೊನೆ. The point of a thorn. -ಮೋರೆ. A pock-marked face. -ಸವುತೆ. The common cucumber, *Cucumis sativus*. -ಸೇವಂತಿಗೆ. A kind of white rose, *Rosa glandulifera*. -ಹಂದಿ, ಮುಳ್ಳಿಕ್ಕ. A porcupine. -ಕಂತು, -ಚುಚ್ಚು, -ನಾಟು, -ಬಯ್ಯು. A thorn to prick.

ಮೂ (= ಮೂರು) k. *a*. Three. *Cpds.*: -ಗಾವುದ, -ಜಗ, -ಲೋಕ, -ದಲೆ. -ನೂರು. 300. -ವತ್ತು. 30. -ವತ್ತೊಂದು. 31. -ವರು. Three persons.

ಮೂಕ s. *a*. Dumb; speechless, silent, mute. *n*. A dumb man; *f*. ಮೂಕಿ. -ತೆ. Dumbness, silence.

ಮೂಕಾಂಬೆ k. *n*. N. of Śiva's śakti.

ಮೂಕೆ k. *n*. The taper pole or shaft of a carriage.

ಮೂಕುತಿ. = ಮೂಗುತಿ, *q. v.*

ಮೂಗ. *tb. of* ಮೂಕ, *q.v.* -ತನ, -ತೆ. Dumbness.

ಮೂಗು k. *n*. The nose; a forepart; a bill or beak; the nozzle of a vessel. ಮೂಗ್ಗುರಕ. A man whose nose is cut off; *f*. ಮೂಗ್ಗುರಕಿ. ಮೂಗಿಲಿ. A musk-rat. -ದಾಣ, -ದಾರ, -ನೇಣು, ಮೂದಾಣ. The cord put through an ox's nose. -ಕಟ್ಟು, -ಮುಚ್ಚು. To stop the nose. ಮೂಗಿನ ರಂಧ್ರ, ಮೂಗಿನ ಸೊಳ್ಳೆ, ಮೂಗಿನ ಹೊಳ್ಳೆ. The nostril. -ತಿ, -ಬೊಟ್ಟು. A nose-jewel.

ಮೂಜುವರಿ, ಮೂಜೂರಿ h. *n*. Refractoriness.

ಮೂಟೆ k. *n*. A bundle of grain, cloth, *etc.*; a pack, bale.

ಮೂಡ, ಮೂಡಲು, ಮೂಡ್ಲ (= ಮೂಡು) k. *n*. The east. -ಗಡೆ. Eastward. ಮೂಡಣ. Eastern. -ಗಿರಿ. N. of a mountain or person. ಮೂಡಲ್ಲರಿ. To dawn.

ಮೂಡಿಗೆ k. *n*. A quiver.

ಮೂಡು k. *v. i.* To rise; to originate; to be born; to become visible; to come about. ಮೂಡಿಸು. To cause to rise, *etc.*

ಮೂಡೆ (= ಮುಡಿ) k. *n*. A straw-bundle containing rice, pulse or râgi.

ಮೂಢ s. *a*. Perplexed; stupid, dull, silly, foolish, ignorant; gone astray. *n*. An ignorant man, fool, *etc.* -ತನ, -ತ್ವ, -ತೆ. Stupidity, folly, ignorance. -ಜನ. Ignorant people. -ಭಕ್ತಿ. A blind faith. ಮೂಢಾತ್ಮ. A foolish, ignorant person.

ಮೂತಿ k. *n*. The face, mouth, snout, beak.

ಮೂತ್ರ s. *n*. Urine. -ಕಟ್ಟು, -ಕೃಚ್ಛ್ರ, -ಬಂಧ. Stoppage of urine, strangury. -ಶಂಕೆ. Making water. ಬಹು-. Diabetes. ಮೂತ್ರಿಸು. To discharge urine.

ಮೂದಲೆ k. *n*. Confronting and upbraiding, taunt. ಮೂದಲಿಸು. To confront, and upbraid, taunt.

ಮೂಬದಲು, ಮೂಬದಲೆ f. *n*. Exchange, barter; sums lent and paid on running accounts.

ಮೂರು (ರು = ಱು) k. *a*. Three. ಮೂರಕಣ್ಣ. Agni. ಮೂರನೆಯ. Third. ಮೂರನೆಯವ. A third man. ಮೂರವಸರ. = -ಹೊತ್ತು. -ನಾಮ. Three sectarian marks of a Vaishṇava's forehead. -ನಾಲ್ಕು. Three or four. - ಮೂರು. Three and three, each three. -ಮೂರ್ತಿ. = ತ್ರಿಮೂರ್ತಿ, *q. v.* -ಲೋಕ. The three worlds. -ವರ್ಣ. Three letters or colours, *etc.* ಮೂರುವರೆ. Three and a half. -ಸಂಜೆ. Evening-twilight, nightfall. -ಹೊತ್ತು. Morning, noon, and evening. ಮೂರೂ ಕಾಲು. Three and a quarter.

ಮೂರ್ಖ s. *a*. Stupid, foolish, silly, ignorant. *n*. A fool, blockhead. -ತನ, -ತೆ, -ತ್ವ. Stupidity, foolishness, ignorance.

ಮೂರ್ಛನ s. *n*. Stupefying. 2, fainting, stupor. 3, vehemence. 4, rising of sounds, intonation. 5, a semi-tone in the musical scale. ಮೂರ್ಛಿತ. Stupefied, fainted, fainting. ಮೂರ್ಛಿಸು. To faint away, swoon. ಮೂರ್ಛೆ. Fainting, loss of consciousness; swoon; hallucination. ಮೂರ್ಛೆಗೊಳ್ಳು, -ಬೀಳು, -ಹಿಡಿ, -ಹೊಂದು. To faint away. -ತಿಳಿ. To recover from fainting. -ರೋಗ. Epilepsy.

ಮೂರ್ತ. = ಮುಹೂರ್ತ 2, *q. v.*

ಮೂರ್ತಿ s. *n.* A solid body; a material form, visible shape; matter, substance; embodiment, incarnation. 2, an image, idol, figure, form. -ಗೊಳ್ಳು. To assume a form; to sit down. -ಪೂಜಕ. An idol-worshipper. -ಪೂಜೆ. Idol-worship. -ಮತ್. Material, embodied, corporeal, personified.

ಮೂರ್ಧ s. *n.* The forehead; the head. -ನ್ಯ. Cerebral, *as* a letter. ಮೂರ್ಧಾಭಿಷಿಕ್ತ. Inaugurated, installed; a consecrated king; a Kshatriya.

ಮೂಲ s. *n.* The basis, ground-work, beginning. 2, root, origin; cause, means. 3, the original. 4, capital, stock. 5, the 19th lunar asterism. 6, termination, ruin. -ಕಾರಣ. The first cause. -ಗಾರ. The proprietor of a land. -ಗಂಟು, -ಧನ, -ಬಂಡವಲ. Capital, principal. -ಗೇಣಿ. Permanent rent or tenancy. -ನಿವಾಸಿ. An aboriginal. -ಬಲ. An original force. -ರೋಗ, -ವ್ಯಾಧಿ. Piles. -ಸ್ಥಾನ. The place of origin. -ಸ್ಥಾಪಕ. The founder. ಮೂಲಿವರ್ಗ. Proprietary right of a land.

ಮೂಲಕ (= ಮುಲ್ಲಂಗಿ, ಮೂಲಂಗಿ) s. *a.* Rooted in springing from. *prep.* On account of. *n.* An esculent root, radish.

ಮೂಲಂಗಿ (*tb. of* ಮೂಲಕ) *n.* The radish, *Raphanus sativus.*

ಮೂಲಿಕ s. *a.* Primary. ಮೂಲಿಕೆ. A root; Ceylon leadwort. ಮೂಲಿಗ. A vendor of medicinal roots.

ಮೂಲೆ k. *n.* A corner; an angle; a point of the compass. -ಗೆ ಮುಟ್ಟಾಗಿ ಹೋಗು. To be ruined.

ಮೂವತ್ತು k. *a.* Thirty.

ಮೂಷಕ s. *n.* A thief; a mouse; a rat; *also* ಮೂಷಿಕ.

ಮೂಸು k. *v. t.* To smell. ಮೂಸಿ ನೋಡು. To test by the smell.

ಮೂಸೆ (*tb. of* ಮೂಷಾ) *n.* A crucible. 2, a mould.

ಮೂಳ (ಳ = ೞ) k. *n.* An earless man. 2, a man who has lost any limb; a fool, brute; *f.* ಮೂಳಿ; *also* a widow.

ಮೂಳೆ k. *n.* A bone.

ಮೃಗ (= ಮಿಕ, ಮಿಗ) s. *n.* A wild beast. 2, any animal in general, *as* a cow. 3, a deer, antelope; game in general. -ಜಲ, -ತೃಷ್ಣೆ. Mirage. -ಶಿರ, -ಶಿರಸ್, -ಶೀರ್ಷ. The fifth lunar mansion. -ಪತಿ, ಮೃಗೇಂದ್ರ. A lion; a tiger. -ತನ, -ಭಾವ. Brutishness.

ಮೃಜೆ s. *n.* Wiping, cleansing.

ಮೃತ s. *a.* Dead, deceased; mortal. *n.* Death; *also* ಮೃತಿ. -ವಾಗು. To die. -ತಿಥಿ. The death-day on which śrâddha is performed. -ಪತ್ರ. A written will. -ಸಂಸ್ಕಾರ. Obsequies. -ಸಂಜೀವ. Revival of the dead; N. of a plant. -ಸ್ನಾನ. Ablution after a funeral.

ಮೃತ್ತಿಕೆ s. *n.* Earth, clay.

ಮೃತ್ಯು s. *n.* Death. 2, Yama. ಮೃತ್ಯುಂಜಯ. Overcoming death; Śiva.

ಮೃದಂಗ s. *n.* A sort of tabour.

ಮೃದು (= ಮಿದು, ಮೆದು, *q. v.*) s. *a.* Soft, tender, flexible, pliant. 2, mild, gentle; weak; slow. *n.* Softness, mildness, gentleness. -ತರ. Uncommonly mild. -ಯಾನ. Slow walk. -ವಾಕ್ಯ, -ಶಬ್ದ, ಮೃದೂಕ್ತಿ. A gentle word. -ಸ್ಮಿತ. A gentle smile.

ಮೃನ್ಮಯ s. *a.* Earthen.

ಮೃಷೆ s. *n.* Untruth. ಮೃಷಾ. Falsely; uselessly.

ಮೃಷ್ಟ s. *a.* Clean, pure; dressed, savoury. ಮೃಷ್ಟಾನ್ನ. Delicate food, dainties.

ಮೆಕ್ಕಾ. = ಮಕ್ಕಾ, *q. v.*

ಮೆಕ್ಕೆ k. *n.* A climbing herb, *Cucumis trigonus.*

ಮೆಚ್ಚು k. *v. t.* To assent, agree to, approve, be pleased with; to like. *n.* Assent, approbation; what is pleasant; satisfaction, pleasure. -ವಣಿಗೆ. What is praiseworthy. ಮೆಚ್ಚಿಕೆ, ಮೆಚ್ಚು

ಗೆ, ಮೆಚ್ಚುವಿಕೆ. Assent, approbation, approval, liking, pleasure. ಮೆಚ್ಚಿಸು. To cause to assent, *etc.*; to please.

ಮೆಜಿಸ್ತ್ರೇಟು e. *n.* Magistrate, a justice of the peace.

ಮೆಟ್ಟಿಗೆ (=ಮೆಟ್ಲು) k. *n.* A step, stair; steps, stairs.

ಮೆಟ್ಟು 1. k. *v. t.* To step, pace, walk; to tread or trample on; to put on, *as* slippers. ಮೆಟ್ಟಿಸು. To cause to step, *etc.*

ಮೆಟ್ಟು 2. k. *n.* A step of the foot. 2, a step of a stringed instrument. 3, a sandal, shoe. 4, the step of a stair. ಮೆಟ್ಟಕ್ಕಿ. A platter filled with rice on which the bridegroom has to stand at a certain part of the marriage ceremonies. -ಗಲ್ಲು. A stair.

ಮೆಟ್ರಿ k. *n.* The throat. -ಗಟ್ಟು. Glandular swelling of the throat.

ಮೆಟ್ಲು k. *n.* A step, stair.

ಮೆಣಸು k. *n.* Black pepper, chilli. ಮೆಣಸಿನ ಕಾಯಿ. Chilli, Cayenne pepper. ಮೆಣಸಿನ ಬಳ್ಳಿ. The black pepper vine. ಮೆಣಸಿನ ಕಾಳು. A corn of black pepper.

ಮೆತ್ತಗೆ, ಮೆತ್ತಿಗೆ (*tb. of* ಮೃದು) *n.* Softness. *a.* Soft, pliant, *etc.* *ad.* Softly; slowly. ಮೆತ್ತನೆ, ಮೆತ್ತನ್ನ, ಮೆತ್ತಾನೆ. Soft, *etc.*

ಮೆತ್ತು k. *v. t.* To coat walls with chunam or mud; to plaster, lay on, press into. ಮೆತ್ತಿಗೆ, ಮೆತ್ತನೆ. Plastering; plaster. -ಹಾಕು. To plaster.

ಮೆತ್ತೆ k. *n.* Bedding; a mattress.

ಮೆದಗು, ಮೆದಳು, ಮೆದುಳು (*tb. of* ಮೇದಸ್) *n.* Marrow; the brain.

ಮೆದು. *tb. of* ಮೃದು, *q. v.*

ಮೆದೆ k. *n.* A heap, pile, stack, *esp. of* straw. 2, silliness. -ಒಟ್ಟು, -ಯೊಟ್ಟು, -ಹಾಕು. To pile, stack.

ಮೆಂತೆ (*tb. of* ಮಂಥೆ) *n.* Fenugreek, *Trigonella foenum graecum.*

ಮೆಯ್ (=ಮೈ, *q. v.*) k. *n.* The body; side, part, place. -ಕಟ್ಟು. The form of the body. -ಕೆಡು. The body to be wasted away. -ಕೊಡು. To present one's self, to apply the body (or shoulders) to. -ಗರೆ. To hide one's self. -ಗಲಿ. A valiant person. -ಗಳ್ಳ (=ಮೈಗಳ್ಳ). A lazy man. -ಗಳ್ಳತನ. Laziness. -ಗಾವಲು. A body-guard. -ಗುಂದು. To become lean or emaciated. -ಜೋಡು. A coat of mail. -ತಡವು. To stroke the body, caress. -ತುಂಬ. All over the body; through the whole body. -ತುಂಬು. The body to become stout and strong. -ತೊಡಿಗೆ. Apparel of the body. -ದೋರು. To appear one's self; to show; to exhibit valour. -ನೋತ, -ನೋವು. Pain in the body. -ಬರು. To become stout and strong. -ಬೊಗ್ಗು. To bend the body, *as* in work. -ಮರವು, -ಮರವೆ. Unconsciousness; swoon; inadvertence. -ಮರೆ. To swoon, faint; to be careless. -ಮೇಲೆ ಬರು. To fall upon; to attack. -ಮೇಲೆ ಹಾಕು. To put upon; to burden on. -ಮೇಲೆ ಹೋಗು. To attack. -ವುರಿ. The body to burn; burning heat of the body. -ಯಾರೈಕೆ. Taking care of one's body. -ಯಿಕ್ಕು. To make obeisance, to prostrate; salutation, obeisance. -ಯುಣ್ಣು. To imbibe, absorb. -ಸಾಲ. A loan without pledge or mortgage. -ಸಾಲಪತ್ರ. A simple bond. -ಸಿರಿ. Beauty, comeliness. -ಹತ್ತು. To act upon the body, *as* food, medicine, *etc.*

ಮೆರವಣಿಗೆ (ರ=ಱ) k. *n.* A great display; a public procession.

ಮೆರುಗು k. *n.* Shine, lustre.

ಮೆರೆ 1. (ರೆ=ಱೆ) k. *v. i.* To shine; to gleam, glitter; to appear. 2, to display, exhibit, parade. *P. ps.* ಮೆರದು, ಮೆರೆದು. *n.* Shine, lustre; ostentation. ಮೆರಸು, ಮೆರಿಸು. To cause to shine; to display; to exhibit.

ಮೆರೆ 2. k. *v. i.* To wander, roam about. ಮೆರಸು. To spread abroad, *as* a secret.

ಮೆಲ್, ಮೆಲು (*tb. of* ಮೃದು) k. *a.* Soft, tender, gentle, mild, *etc.* ಮೆಲ್ನಗೆ. A smile.

ಮೆಲ್ನಡೆ. A slow pace. ಮೆಲ್ನುಡಿ. A gentle voice or word.

ಮೆಲಕು, ಮೆಲುಕು (fr. ಮೆಲ್ಲು) k. n. Rumination. 2, the lower jaw. -ಹಾಕು, ಮೆಲಕಾಡು, ಮೆಲಕಾಡಿಸು. To chew the cud.

ಮೆಲು. = ಮೆಲ್ಲು, q. v.

ಮೆಲ್ಲ, ಮೆಲ್ಲಕೆ, ಮೆಲ್ಲಗೆ, ಮೆಲ್ಲನೆ (fr. ಮೆಲ್. tb. of ಮೃದು) ad. Gently; slowly; deliberately. ಮೆಲ್ಲ-. Very gently or slowly.

ಮೆಲ್ಲು (=ಮೆಲು) k. v. t. To chew, masticate, mumble, eat. P. p. ಮೆದ್ದು.

ಮೆಹರ್ಬಾನಿ h. n. Condescension, favour.

ಮೆಳೆ k. n. A bush, clump, thicket.

ಮೆಳ್ಳೆ k. n. Rolling; looking obliquely, squinting. -ಗಣ್ಣು. A squint-eye. ಮೆಳ್ಳ. A squint-eyed man. -ನೋಟ. Oblique vision.

ಮೆಸ್ಸೀಯಾ e. n. Messiah, the Anointed One or Christ, the Saviour.

ಮೇ 1. = ಮೇಯು, q. v.

ಮೇ 2. e. n. May (the 5th month of the year).

ಮೇ 3. = ಮೇಲೆ, q. v. -ಗಡೆ. The upper side. -ಗಾಟು. The main guard. -ಗಾಲು. The instep. -ಗಾವಲು. Guard, supervision. -ಗೈ. The back of the hand.

ಮೇಕು 1. k. n. Rivalry.

ಮೇಕು 2. h. n. A peg, tent-pin, nail.

ಮೇಕೆ k. n. A she-goat.

ಮೇಖಲೆ s. n. A girdle, zone. 2, a sword-belt.

ಮೇಗು, ಮೇಗೆ k. n. The upper side, surface. ad. Upwards.

ಮೇಘ s. n. A cloud. -ಗರ್ಜನೆ, -ಘೋಷ, -ಧ್ವನಿ, -ನಾದ. Thunder. -ಜ್ಯೋತಿ, -ವಹ್ನಿ. Lightning. -ದ್ವಾರ. The sky. -ಮಂಡಲ. The atmosphere. -ಕವಿ, -ಮುಸುಕು, -ಮುಚ್ಚು. Clouds to collect and overspread. -ವರ್ಣ. Ash-colour.

ಮೇಚಕ s. a. Dark-blue. n. Dark-blue-colour.

ಮೇಜು h. n. A table; dinner. ಮೇಜವಾನಿ. Entertaining, receiving hospitably.

ಮೇಜೋಡು k. n. A pair of stockings.

ಮೇಟಿ 1. k. n. A chief, head. 2, a head-servant. 3, the plough-tail.

ಮೇಟಿ 2. (tb. of ಮೇಥಿ) n. A pillar, post.

ಮೇಡು k. n. Height; a hillock.

ಮೇಣ (tb. of ಮದನ) n. Bees' wax, oily dirt; gum, resin. -ದ ಬತ್ತಿ. A wax-candle. -ದ ಗೊಂಬೆ. A wax-doll.

ಮೇಣಿ (=ಮೇಟಿ) k. n. The plough-tail. -ಪಾಲು. The share of the crop given to the person who assisted in ploughing.

ಮೇಣು k. ad. Upwards; further; besides.

ಮೇದ 1, ಮೇದರ k. n. A basket- and mat-maker.

ಮೇದ 2. = ಮೇದಸ್, q. v.

ಮೇದಕ s. n. Spirituous liquor.

ಮೇದಸ್ (= ಮಿದುಡು, ಮಿದುಳು) s. n. Fat, marrow, brain.

ಮೇದಿನಿ s. n. The earth, land. -ಪಾಲ, ಮೇದಿನೀಶ. A king.

ಮೇಧ s. n. A sacrifice (as ಅಶ್ವ-, ನರ-, ಪಶು-). -ವಾನ್. An intelligent, wise man. ಮೇಧಾವಿ. Intelligent, wise; a learned man.

ಮೇನ f. n. A kind of palankeen.

ಮೇಯು (= ಮೇ 1) k. v. i. To graze, eat grass, feed. P. p. ಮೇದು. ಮೇಯಿಸು. To graze, feed.

ಮೇರು s. n. N. of a fabulous mountain said to be in the middle of Jambudvîpa.

ಮೇರೆ (tb. of ಮರ್ಯಾದೆ) n. A boundary, limit, verge; an end; the bounds of propriety; manner; extent, rate. 2, sphere, region. 3, devotion. ಈ-, ಇದೇ-. In this manner. -ಕಟ್ಟು. To fix boundaries. -ಕಲ್ಲು. A boundary-stone. -ತಪ್ಪು, -ದಾಟು, -ಮೀರು. To exceed bounds. -ಒತ್ತು. To encroach upon another's boundary. ಮಿತಿ ಮೇರೆ ಇಲ್ಲದ. Immoderate.

ಮೇಲ್ (= ಮೇಲು, q. v.) k. In comp. ಮೇಲಾಗು, -ಪಡು. To become higher, superior, *etc.* -ಉಡೆ. The upper garment. -ಕಟ್ಟು. An awning, a canopy. -ಕಡೆ. On the top; above, upon. -ಗಾವಲಿ. Control, superintendence. -ತರ. A superior kind. -ದವಡೆ. The upper jaw. -ಬರಹ. A superscription. -ಬೀಳು. To rush upon. -ಭಾಗ. The upper part. -ಮಾಡು. To turn upwards. -ಮಾಳಿಗೆ. An upper story. -ಮುಚ್ಚಳ, -ಮುಚ್ಚಿಗೆ. A lid; a thatch, roof. -ಮೇಲೆ. One upon or after the other. -ಲೋಕ. Heaven. -ವಟ್ಟ. An awning. -ವರಿ. To rush upon. -ವಿಚಾರಕ. An overseer, superintendent. -ವಿಚಾರಣೆ. Overseership, superintendence. -ಸೀಮೆ. The country on the Ghauts. -ಸೆರಗು. The skirts of a woman's garment.

ಮೇಲ (= ಮೇಳ) s. n. Meeting, assembly, *etc.* 2, a set of singers. 3, a concourse of people; a fair.

ಮೇಲು k. n. That which is above, top-part, upper part; the surface; superior position. *a.* Future, following. *prep.* Over, above, on. *ad.* Upwards; afterwards; after, farther. ಯಾತರ ಮೇಲಿಂದ? On what account? why? ಮೇಲಾಟ. Outbidding. ಮೇಲಾಡು. To outbid. ಮೇಲಿನ ದಿನ. The next day. ಮೇಲಿಂದ ಮೇಲೆ. One after the other, again and again, continually. -ಗೊಳ್ಳು, -ಪಡು. To be successful. -ಜಾತಿ. A high caste. -ತುಟಿ. The upper lip. -ನೋಟ. A fine sight. -ಪಂಕ್ತಿ. An upper line. -ಬರು. To prosper. -ಬೀಳು. To outbid; to fall upon. -ಮಾಡು. To turn upward; to do a kindness. -ಮಾಳಿಗೆ. = ಮೇಲ್ಮಾಳಿಗೆ, *q. v.* -ಮುದ್ದೆ. The earth put on a ceiling or a flat roof. -ವಿಳಾಸ. The address on a letter. -(ಉ)ಸುರು. A pant. -ಹೊದಿಕೆ. An upper garment. ಮೇಲೋಗರ. Vegetables; vegetable sauce.

ಮೇಲೆ k. *prep.* Above; over; on, upon. *ad.* Upwards; afterwards; more; farther; for, toward; on account of. -ಇಡು. To put upon. -ಕೆಳಗೆ ಆಗು. To move up and down. -ಬೀಳು. To fall upon; to begin to quarrel; to compete with impertinence. -ಹಾರಿಸು. To toss up. ಮೇಲೆತ್ತು, ಮೇಲೆಬ್ಬಿಸು. To lift up. ಮೇಲೇರು. To ascend, mount. ಆ-. After that. ಇನ್ನು-. Hereafter.

ಮೇವು k. n. Grazing; pasturage, feed.

ಮೇಷ s. n. A ram. 2, the sign of the zodiac *Aries*.

ಮೇಸು. = ಮೇಯಿಸು, *q. v.*

ಮೇಸ್ತ್ರಿ f. n. A head workman.

ಮೇಹ s. n. Urine. 2, urinary disease; *also* -ರೋಗ.

ಮೇಹನತು h. n. Exertion, pains. -ಮಾಡು. To take pains.

ಮೇಳ. = ಮೇಲ, *q. v.* k. n. 4, mirth, merriment, jest, sport, fun. 5, a musical instrument. 6, a band of musicians. -ಗಾರ, -ದವ. A musician. -ಯಿಸು, -ವಿಸು, ಮೇಳಿಸು. To meet, combine; to join, assemble. -ನ, -ವ. Union, harmony, chorus. -ವಣಿ. A chorus; a dance with music. ಮೇಳಿಗೆ. An assembly.

ಮೈ (= ಮಯಿ, *q. v.*) k. n. The body, *etc.* -ಗಳ್ಳ. A lazy man, sluggard. -ಗಳ್ಳತನ. Laziness. -ಸಾಲ. *See* s. ಮಯಿ.

ಮೈತ್ರ (*fr.* ಮಿತ್ರ) s. a. Friendly. n. Friendship, goodwill; intimacy. 2, a friend; *also* ಮೈತ್ರ್ಯ.

ಮೈದಾನ h. n. A plain, a level tract.

ಮೈನ h. n. The Goravaṅka, a kind of jay.

ಮೈನಾಕ s. n. N. of a mountain.

ಮೈಲಿ, ಮೈಲಿಗೆ, ಮೈಲೆ (= ಮಯ್ಲಿ, *q. v.*) f. n. Filth, pollution, dirtiness.

ಮೈಲು e. n. A mile. -ಕಲ್ಲು. A milestone.

ಮೊಕ. *tb. of* ಮುಖ, *q. v.*

ಮೊಕದ್ದಮೆ h. n. An affair, matter; a case, civil or criminal.

ಮೊಕರರು, ಮೊಕರರೂರು h. a. Settled, fixed, certain. n. An appointment. -ಮಾಡು. To appoint.

ಮೊಕಾಬಿಲೆ (= ಮುಖಾಬಿಲೆ) h. n. Comparison, collation.

ಮೊಕಾಮು, ಮೊಕ್ಕಾಮು h. n. A stage; encamping; a place of residence.

ಮೊಕೋಬಿ h. n. A kind of scented snuff.

ಮೊಕ್ಕಳ a. k. n. A heap, mass, assemblage.

ಮೊಖ್ತಾ (tb. of ಮುಖತಾ) prep. In front, before, face to face.

ಮೊಖ್ತಿಯಾರ್ h. a. Absolute, free. n. Independence; an agent, attorney. -ನಾಮೆ. A power of attorney.

ಮೊಖ್ತೇಸರ h. n. A headman; a chief officer; a trustee, as of a temple.

ಮೊಗ. tb. of ಮುಖ, q. v. -ಗೆಡಿಸು. To put to shame in a person's front. -ಗೊಡು. To turn the face towards one. -ಚಿಟ್ಲಿಸು, -ಸಿಂಡ್ರಿಸು. To frown. -ವಡ, -ವಾಡ. A head-stall for horses; a mask; a muzzle. -ವರಿಕೆ. Aquaintance, intimacy. -ಸಾಲೆ. A front verandah, portico.

ಮೊಗಚು. = ಮಗಚು, q. v.

ಮೊಗಲ h. n. A Mogul.

ಮೊಗಸು k. v. i. To exert one's self. v. t. To cover; to attack. n. Desire.

ಮೊಗಳು k. n. The ridge of a roof.

ಮೊಗು. = ಮುಗು, q. v.

ಮೊಗುಮ್ h. a. General, undefined; implied.

ಮೊಗೆ 1. k. v. t. To take (water with a vessel out of a tank, etc.). 2, to lade out, scoop, bale.

ಮೊಗೆ 2. k. n. A small earthen vessel.

ಮೊಗ್ಗರ (= ಮೊಕ್ಕಳ, q. v.) a. k. n. A mass, heap; a body, force.

ಮೊಗ್ಗು, ಮೊಗ್ಗೆ k. n. A bud, blossom.

ಮೊಚ್ಚೆ f. n. A shoe.

ಮೊಟಕು k. n. A bit, piece, as of a pencil, etc. -ಬೆರಳು. A little finger. -ಹಾದಿ. A short road.

ಮೊಟ್ಟು k. v. t. To rap one's head with the knukles of the fist. n. A rap with the knuckles of the fist.

ಮೊಟ್ಟೆ 1. k. n. An egg.

ಮೊಟ್ಟೆ 2. k. n. A bundle, bale, burden, load.

ಮೊಡವಿ, ಮೊಡವೆ k. n. A small pimple in the face.

ಮೊಣ (= ಮೊಳ) k. n. A projecting joint. -ಕಾಲು. The knee. -ಕಾಲುಕಣ್ಣು. The hollow on each side of the knee. -ಕಾಲುಚಿಪ್ಪು. The knee-pan. -ಕಾಲು ಊರು, -ಕಾಲು ಬಗ್ಗಿಸು. To kneel. -ಕೈ, -ಗೈ. The elbow.

ಮೊಂಡ. tb. of ಮುಂಡ, q. v. -ಕೈ. A maimed hand. -ಕತ್ತಿ, -ಗತ್ತಿ, -ಚೂರಿ. A blunt knife. -ಗುದ್ದಲಿ. A blunt hoe. -ಬೀಳು, -ಹೋಗು. To be obstinate, refractory.

ಮೊಂಡು k. n. Stupid obstinacy, esp. in dunning; also ಮೊಂಡಾಟ, ಮೊಂಡುತನ. ಮೊಂಡ. An obstinate man.

ಮೊತ್ತ k. n. A heap, mass; a multitude, flock, etc.; a collection.

ಮೊದಲು k. n. The state of being first, preceding, prior; the chief thing; the beginning; the base; the principal or capital. ad. At the beginning, first, etc.; for the first time. -ಕಾರಣ. The first cause. -ಗೊಳ್ಳು. To begin. -ತರ. The best sort. -ಮಾಡು. To begin. ಮೊದಲನೇ. First, etc. ಮೊದಲನೇದು. That which is the first, the first. ಮೊದಲನೆಯವ. The first. ಮೊದಲಾಗು. To become first of a series. ಮೊದಲಿಗ. A headman. ಮೊದಲಿನ. Preceding, prior. ಮೊದಲಿನಷ್ಟು. As much as in former times. ಮೊದಲಿನಂತೆ. As before. ಮೊದಲೆ. At first; first of all. -ಹಿಡಿದು ಮಾತಾಡು. To speak out fully.

ಮೊದ್ದು k. n. A block, log of wood. 2, stupidity; bluntness. ಮೊದ್ದ. A male blockhead; f. ಮೊದ್ದಿ.

ಮೊನೆ 1. k. n. A point; an extremity, end; sharpness. 2, courage. -ಗಾರು. A tongue used to make wire. -ಕೆಡು, -ಗೆಡು. To become blunt. -ಮಾಡು, -ತಿವಿ, -ಮಾಡು. To make pointed. -ಗಾರ. A bold man.

ಮೊನೆ 2. a. k. n. A fight, battle. -ಸಾಗಿಸು. To carry on warfare.

ಮೊನ್ನೆ k. *ad.* The day before yesterday; the other day; lately. -ಮೊನ್ನೆ. *rep.* Lately.

ಮೊಬಲಗು h. *n.* Sum; money.

ಮೊಬ್ಬು. = ಮಬ್ಬು, *q. v.*

ಮೊಮ್ಮಗ k. *n.* A grand-son. ಮೊಮ್ಮಗಳು. A grand-daughter. ಮೊಮ್ಮಕ್ಕಳು. Grand-children.

ಮೊರ (ರ = ಐ) k. *n.* A bamboo fan used for winnowing corn, *etc.*

ಮೊರಡಿ, ಮೊರಡು 1. k. *n.* A hill, hillock.

ಮೊರಡು 2. = ಮುರುಟು, *q. v.*

ಮೊರಲೆ, ಮೊರವೆ (ರ = ಐ) k. *n.* A large tree, bearing a kind of almonds, *Buchanania latifolia.*

ಮೊರೆ 1. (ರೆ = ಱೆ) k. *v. i.* To roar, *as* the sea, tiger, *etc.*; to clamour, bawl, complain. *n.* Roaring; wailing, lamentation. 2, complaint. -ಇಡು, -ಇಟ್ಟುಕೊಳ್ಳು. To cry loud; to wail; to complain; to beseech fervently. ಮೊರತ. Roar- ing, *etc.*

ಮೊರೆ 2. k. *v. i.* To hum, buzz; to sound; to murmur; to bubble. *n.* Humming.

ಮೊಲ k. *n.* A hare; a rabbit.

ಮೊಲೆ k. *n.* The female breast. -ಕುನ್ನಿ, -ಗುನ್ನಿ. A puppy. -ಕೂಸು, -ಗೂಸು, -ಮೊಗು. A suckling. -ತುದಿ, -ತೊಟ್ಟು. The nipple. -ಉಣ್ಣು, -ತಿನ್ನು. To suck the breast. -ಕೊಡು, -ಊಡು. To suckle, give the breast. -ಬಿಡಿಸು. To wean.

ಮೊಲ್ಲೆ k. *n.* A kind of jasmine, *Jasminum multiflorum.*

ಮೊಸರು k. *n.* Curds. -ಕಡೆ. To churn the turned milk. -ಸೋಸು. To strain curds. ಮೊಸರನ್ನ. Boiled rice mixed with curds.

ಮೊಸಳೆ k. *n.* An alligator, crocodile. -ಮಡುವು. A lake abounding with alligators.

ಮೊಹತರ್ಫ f. *n.* A tax on artizans.

ಮೊಹರ, ಮೊಹರಿ 1. h. *n.* A gold coin, mohur.

ಮೊಹರಮ್ h. *n.* An annual Mussulman festival commemorating the death of two heroes, called *Hassan* and *Hoossein,* Moharam.

ಮೊಹರಾ h. *n.* A leader, chief; *cf.* ಮೊಹರ.

ಮೊಹರಿ 2. h. *n.* A little channel to carry off water.

ಮೊಹರು h. *n.* A seal; a seal-ring.

ಮೊಹಸಲೆ h. *n.* Restraint put on a person to prevent his escape or to enforce the payment of a demand; arrest.

ಮೊಳ (= ಮೊಣ. ಳ = ಐ) k. *n.* A projecting joint; a cubit. -ಕಾಲು (= ಮೊಣಕಾಲು). The knee. -ಕೈ (= ಮೊಣಕೈ). The elbow.

ಮೊಳಕೆ, ಮೊಳಿಕೆ k. *n.* A germ, bud, sprout.

ಮೊಳಗು (ಳ = ಐ) a. k. *v. i.* To sound; to roar; to thunder. *n.* Thunder. 2, the plant *Mursilea quadrifolia.*

ಮೊಳಸು k. *n.* Germination, *etc.*

ಮೊಳೆ k. *v. i.* To grow, shoot forth, sprout, bud, shoot; to appear. *P. ps.* ಮೊಳತು, ಮೊಳೆತು. *n.* A germ, bud, sprout. 2, a pin, nail, spike, wedge, peg, stake. 3, the core of a boil. 4, piles. ಕಬ್ಬಿಣದ-. An iron nail. ಮರದ-. A wooden peg.

ಮೋಕ್ಷ (= ಮುಕ್ತಿ 1) s. *n.* Liberation, deliverance, release. 2, liberation from individual existence (*Hindu*); salvation, final beatitude (*Chr.*). 3, death. -ಕಾಲ. The time of liberation. -ಧರ್ಮ. Law of emancipation. *Cpds.*: -ಪದವಿ, -ಮಾರ್ಗ, -ಶಾಸ್ತ್ರ, *etc.* -ಸಾಧನ. Means of emancipation. -ಕರ್ತ, -ನಾಯಕ, ಪ್ರಭು. Jesus Christ.

ಮೋಕೂಫು h. *n.* Abolishment, cessation; adjournment or recess, *as* of a court.

ಮೋಚಕ s. *n.* Final emancipation. -ಕ. A deliverer, liberator.

ಮೋಚಿ h. *n.* A shoemaker.

ಮೋಚು k. *v. i.* To become a widow.

ಮೋಚೆ, ಮೋಜಾ (= ಬೂಟ್ಸ್) h. *n.* A boot.

ಮೋಜು h. n. Play, sport. -ಗಾರ. A sportive man.

ಮೋಟನ s. n. Crushing. 2, disgrace.

ಮೋಟು k. n. Stumpiness, maimedness; the stump of a tree; stubbles. ಮೋಟ. An armless or dwarfish man; f. ಮೋಟಿ. -ಮರ. A branchless trunk. -ಕಿವಿ, -ಕೈ. A maimed ear, arm. -ಬಾಲ. A stumpy tail. ಮೋಟಗಾರ, ಮೋಟು ಮನುಷ್ಯ. A foolish man.

ಮೋಡ k. n. A cloud; a cloudy weather. -ಕಟ್ಟು, -ಕವಿ, -ಮುಸುಕು, -ಹಾಗು. To be cloudy or lowering.

ಮೋಡಿ 1. k. n. A kind of craft or enchantment to try the ability of another. -ಗಾರ. A performer of môḍi. ರಾಜ-. Royal grandeur.

ಮೋಡಿ 2. f. n. A running hand; the business character, as in Marâṭṭi. 2, a kind of drug. 3, a style, fashion (of speech, etc.).

ಮೋತಿ 1. k. n. The face, snout.

ಮೋತಿ 2. (tb. of ಮುಕ್ತಾ) n. A pearl.

ಮೋತಿ 3. h. n. A petty grocer. -ಖಾನೆ. A granary.

ಮೋತೆ k. n. The leaf-like spathe over the flowers of the plantain, the cocoanut, etc.

ಮೋದ s. n. Delight, gladness. 2, fragrance. -ಕ. Causing delight; a small, round sweetmeat. ಮೋದಿಸು. To rejoice.

ಮೋದಂಡ s. n. Undefined state.

ಮೋದು a. k. v. t. To strike, beat, smite. n. A swelling caused by a blow; a hard boil.

ಮೋನ (tb. of ಮೌನ) n. Silence. 2, asceticism.

ಮೋಪು k. n. Heaviness, as of a load; severeness, as of a wound; firmness, as of grasping. 2, timber of a building, as beams, rafters, pillars, doors, etc.

ಮೋರಿ f. n. A little water channel.

ಮೋರೆ (ರೆ=ಱೆ) k. n. The face. -ಗಂಟು. A frown. -ಗಂಟಿಡು, -ಗಂಟು ಹಾಕು. To frown. -ತಪ್ಪಿಸಿಕೊಳ್ಳು. To abscond. -ತೋರಿಸು. To show one's self. -ತಗ್ಗಿಸು, -ಬಗ್ಗಿಸು. To hang down the face.

ಮೋರ್ಚಾ h. n. Fortifications.

ಮೋರ್ಚಿಂಗು h. n. A jew's-harp.

ಮೋಷ s. n. Robbery, theft. -ಕ. A robber, thief.

ಮೋಸ k. n. Deceit, fraud, trick, duping; hypocrisy; blunder, fault; danger, peril; loss. ಅವನ ಪ್ರಾಣಕ್ಕೆ ಮೋಸ ವಿಲ್ಲ. There is no danger to his life. -ಗೊಳಿಸು, -ಮಾಡು. To cheat, deceive. -ಗೊಳ್ಳು, -ಬೀಳು, -ಹೋಗು. To be deceived. -ಗಾರ. A deceiver; f. -ಗಾತಿ.

ಮೋಸಬೆ, ಮೋಸಮೆ h. n. Responsibility.

ಮೋಸಲೆ. = ಮೊಸಲೆ, q. v.

ಮೋಹ s. n. Delusion, bewilderment; ignorance, folly; enamoured state; fascination. 2, affection, fondness, love. 3, a magical art. -ಗೊಳಿಸು. To bewilder; to fascinate, charm. -ಗೊಳ್ಳು. To become stupefied; to be fascinated, etc. -ನ. Bewildering; charming, fascinating; temptation, seduction.

ಮೋಹರ a. k. n. A mass, host, army. ಮೋಹರಿಸು. To become plentiful; to array, as troops.

ಮೋಹಿ s. a. Fascinating, charming. -ತ. Deluded, beguiled, fascinated. -ನಿ. A fascinating woman. -ಸು. To faint; to be fascinated; to love; to desire.

ಮೋಹು. = ಮೋದು, q. v.

ಮೋಳೆ k. n. A small hole in the banks of rice-fields; a fissure. 2, a pile, heap (of salt-earth).

ಮೌಂಜಿ s. n. The Brahmanical girdle made of muṅja grass. -ಬಂಧನ. Investiture with it.

ಮೌಢ್ಯ (fr. ಮೂಢ) s. n. Stupidity, folly.

ಮೌನ (fr. ಮುನಿ) s. n. Silence; stillness. -ಗೊಳ್ಳು. To become silent. -ಗೊಳಿಸು.

To silence. -ತ್ವ. Silence. -ವ್ರತ. A vow of silence. ಮೌನಿ (=ಮುನಿ). A silent person.

ಮೌರಿ s. n. A clarionet.

ಮೌಲವಿ h. n. A Mussalman priest.

ಮೌಲಿ, ಮೌಳಿ s. n. The head, top. 2, a crown, crest.

ಮೌಲ್ಯ s. n. Price, value, cost.

ಮ್ಲಾನ s. a. Withered, faded; languid; feeble, weak; dejected, melancholy. -ತೆ. Witheredness; languor.

ಮ್ಲೇಚ್ಛ, ಮ್ಲೇಂಛ s. n. A non-Aryan, barbarian, outcast. -ದೇಶ. A foreign or barbarous country.

ಯ್

ಯ್. The forty-fourth letter of the alphabet. *For words beginning with* ಯ *not found here, see s.* ಎ.

ಯಕಾರ s. n. The letter ಯ.

ಯಕ್ಕು. = ಎಕ್ಕು, *q. v.*; *also:* to beat soundly.

ಯಕ್ಷ s. n. N. of certain demi-gods attending on Kubêra; *f.* ಯಕ್ಷಿಣಿ. -ಗಾನ. A kind of dramatic composition. -ಧೂಪ. The resin of *Shorea robusta.* -ಪ, -ರಾಜ್. Kubêra. ಯಕ್ಷಿಣಿ (= ಜಕ್ಕಣಿ). A female Yaksha; Kubêra's wife; a female fiend; sorcery done with that fiend's help. ಯಕ್ಷಿಣಿಗಾರ. A sorcerer. ಯಕ್ಷಿಣಿವಿದ್ಯೆ. Sorcery.

ಯಕ್ಷ್ಮರೋಗ. = ಕ್ಷಯರೋಗ, *q. v.*

ಯಜಮಾನ (= ಎಜಮಾನ) s. n. A householder; the master of a house; the head of a family, caste, *etc.*; a respectable, elderly man. (*pl.*) -ರು. A wife's name for her husband. -ತನ. ಯಜಮಾನಿಕೆ. The position of a Yajamâna. -ಗಿತ್ತಿ, -ತಿ, ಯಜಮಾನಿ. A mistress; a wife.

ಯಜು. *tb. of* ಯಜುಸ್, *q. v.*

ಯಜುಸ್ s. n. A sacrificial prayer or formula. 2, the yajurvêda. ಯಜುರ್ವೇದ. The sacrificial vêda.

ಯಜ್ಞ s. n. A sacrifice. -ಮಾಡು. To sacrifice; to kill; to beat soundly. -ಕುಂಡ. A hole for the sacrificial fire. -ದೀಕ್ಷೆ. Initiation into sacrificial rites. -ಪಶು. A sacrificial victim. -ಪುರುಷ, ಯಜ್ಞೇಶ್ವರ. Fire, Agni; Vishṇu. -ಸೂತ್ರ, ಯಜ್ಞೋಪವೀತ. A sacrificial thread. -ಪುರುಷ. Agni; Jesus Christ.

ಯತನ. = ಯತ್ನ, *q. v.*

ಯತಿ s. n. Restraint, control. 2, an ascetic, devotee; a religious mendicant. 3, a pause (*in music*). 4, caesura (*in prosody*). ಯತೀಂದ್ರ. A great ascetic.

ಯತ್ಕಿಂಚಿತ್, ಯತ್ಕಿಂಚಿತ s. *ad.* Whatsoever, somewhat.

ಯತ್ನ (= ಎತ್ನ, ಯತನ) s. n. Effort, exertion; energy, diligence, perseverence; pains, care; effort for; eagerness; help. -ನಡಿಸು, -ಮಾಡು, ಯತ್ನಯಿಸು, ಯತ್ನಿಸು, ಯತ್ನೈಸು. To make effort, take pains.

ಯಥಾ s. *ad.* In which manner, as, like as, like. -ಕಾಮ. At pleasure. -ಕಾಲ. In due time. -ಗತಿ. As usual, as before. -ಪೂರ್ವ, -ಪ್ರಕಾರ. As before, as previously. -ಪ್ರತಿ. A true copy. -ಪ್ರಯೋಗ. Common usage or custom. -ಮತಿ. According to opinion; to the best of one's judgment. -ಯುಕ್ತ. Properly, suitably; by degrees. -ಯೋಗ್ಯ. Rightly, suitably. -ವತ್. Becomingly, properly, truly. -ವಿಧಿ. According to precept, duly, fitly. -ಶಕ್ತಿ. To the utmost of one's power. -ಶಾಸ್ತ್ರ. According to law. -ಸ್ಥಾನ. Proper place; in regular order, properly, suitably. -ಸ್ಥಿತಿ. As usual, as on previous occasions.

ಯಥಾರ್ಥ s. a. True, real, genuine, right. *ad.* Truly, justly, suitably. *n.* Truth, *etc.* -ತ್ವ. Truthfulness, veracity, propriety.

ಯಥೇಚ್ಛ (*fr.* ಯಥಾ-ಇಚ್ಛ) s. *ad.* According to wish or desire; plentifully, copiously. ಯಥೇಚ್ಛೆ. A suitable wish or desire. = ಯಥೇಚ್ಛ.

ಯದಾ s. *ad.* When; since, as.

ಯದು s. *n.* N. of an ancient hero and his race.

ಯದೃಚ್ಛೆ s. *n.* Self-will, wilfulness, independence; accident, chance.

ಯದ್ವಾ s. *conj.* Or, else, whether. -ತದ್ವಾ. Disorderly; disorder, confusion.

ಯಂತ್ರ s. *n.* Any instrument, machine, engine, apparatus. 2, a band, fastening. 3, restraint. 4, an amulet, charm; a diagram of a mystical or astrological nature. -ಕಟ್ಟು. To tie an amulet. -ಕ. A machinist. -ಕಲೆ. The mechanical art.

ಯಮ s. *n.* Keeping in check; restraint; self-control. 2, the god of the infernal regions, punisher of the dead. 3, a pair; a twin. 4, the south-quarter. -ನಿಯಮ. Self-imposed restraint. -ದಿಕ್ಕು. The south. -ದೂತ, ಯಮನಾಳು. Messenger of death. -ಪಟ್ಣ, -ಪುರ, -ಪುರಿ, -ಲೋಕ. Yama's region, hell. -ಬಾಧೆ, -ಯಾತನೆ. The torture inflicted by Yama, hell-torments.

ಯಮಕ s. *n.* Restraint; a religious obligation. 2, a twin, pair. 3, a kind of play upon words or paronomasia. *a.* Two-fold, doubled.

ಯಮಲ s. *n.* A pair. 2, twin; *also* ಯಮಳಿ. 3, the number two.

ಯಮುನೆ s. *n.* N. of a river.

ಯಯಾತಿ s. *n.* N. of the fifth monarch of the lunar race.

ಯವ s. *n.* Barley, *Hordeum hexastichon*; *also* -ಕ. -ಕ್ಷಾರ. Saltpetre, nitre, nitrate of potash.

ಯವನ s. *n.* A Greek; a Mahomedan; a foreigner. -ದೇಶ. Bactria; Turkisthân, Arabia.

ಯವಾರ (*tb. of* ವ್ಯವಹಾರ) *n.* A law-suit; quarrel.

ಯವೆ. *tb. of* ಯವ, *q. v.*

ಯವ್ವನ. *tb. of* ಯೌವನ, *q. v.*

ಯಶ, ಯಶಸ್ (*tb.* ಯಶಸ್ಸು) s. *n.* Honour, glory, fame, reputation; beauty, splendour. ಯಶಸ್ಕರ, ಯಶಸ್ವಿ. Famous, glorious. ಯಶೋವಂತ. A famous man.

ಯಶೋದೆ s. *n.* Kṛishṇa's foster-mother. 2, N. of a female.

ಯಾ (= ವಾ, *q. v.*) s. *conj.* Or.

ಯಾಕೆ k. *pro.* Why? wherefore? ಯಾಕಾಗವಲ್ಲದು? (*i. e.* ಯಾಕೆ ಆಗ ಒಲ್ಲದು?)

ಯಾಗ s. *n.* A sacrifice; *also* ಯಜ್ಞ.

ಯಾಗಪ್ಪ f. *n.* A stone cutter's chisel.

ಯಾಚನೆ, ಯಾಚ್ಞೆ s. *n.* A petition, request; begging. ಯಾಚಕ, ಯಾಚನಕ. A petitioner, beggar. ಯಾಚಿಸು. To ask, beg, request.

ಯಾಜಕ s. *n.* A sacrificer; a priest. ಪ್ರಧಾನ-. A high priest. ಮಹಾ ಪ್ರಧಾನ-. Christ. ಯಾಜನ. Assisting at a sacrifice.

ಯಾಜ್ಞವಲ್ಕ್ಯ s. *n.* N. of the author of a code of law.

ಯಾತ 1. (= ಏತ) k. *n.* A picotta.

ಯಾತ 2. s. *n.* The driving of an elephant with a goad. 2, going, motion.

ಯಾತಕ್ಕೆ k. *pro.* Why? for what?

ಯಾತನ, ಯಾತನೆ s. *n.* Requital, retaliation. 2, acute pain, torment, anguish, agony, pain, *as* of hell.

ಯಾತರ k. *pro.* Of what? ಯಾತರಿಂದ. From what? ಯಾತರದು. Of what it (is). ಯಾತರವ. Of what (is) he?

ಯಾತು s. *n.* A traveller, wayfarer. 2, an evil spirit, demon. 3, witchcraft, torture.

ಯಾತ್ರೆ (= ಜಾತ್ರೆ, *q. v.*) s. *n.* Going, travel; expedition. 2, going on a pilgrimage, pilgrimage. 3, a car-festival; a festive procession. 4, support of life, maintenance. ಕಾಶಿ-, ತಿರುಪತಿ-, ಶ್ರೀರಂಗ-, ಸೇತು-. Pilgrimage to Benares, Tirupati, Shrîrangam, Râmêśvaram, *etc.*

ಯಾದ (*tb. of* ಯಾದಸ್) *n.* A large aquatic animal, sea-monster.

ಯಾದವ (*fr.* ಯದು) s. *n.* A descendant of Yadu; Kṛishṇa.

ಯಾದಾಸ್ತು h. *n.* A memorandum, rough note. [scrap.

ಯಾದಿ h. *n.* Remembrance; a memo-

ಯಾದೃಶ s. *pro. (int.)* Which or what like? which? what?

ಯಾನ s. *n.* Going. 2, a conveyance or vehicle of any kind.

ಯಾನೆ f. *a.* Another. *conj.* Alias, or.

ಯಾಂತ್ರಿಕ s. *a.* Relating to instruments or machines.

ಯಾಪನ s. *n.* Delay, procrastination; loitering. 2, maintenance, support.

ಯಾಪಾರ (*tb. of* ವ್ಯಾಪಾರ, *q. v.*) *n.* Trade, traffic.

ಯಾಮ (= ಜಾವ) s. *n.* Going; motion, course. 2, a night-watch, eighth part of a day.

ಯಾಯಾವರ (*tb.* ಯಾಯುವಾರ) *n.* Wandering; a vagrant mendicant; alms.

ಯಾರು k. *pro.* (*pl. of* ಯಾವ, *q. v.*) Who?

ಯಾಲಕ್ಕಿ (= ಏಲಕ್ಕಿ, *q. v.*) f. *n.* Cardamoms.

ಯಾವ k. (*int.*) *pro.* What? which? ಯಾವ್ಯಾವ (= ಯಾವ ಯಾವ). Whichever. -ನು. Who? which man? -ಲ್ಲಿ. Where? whither? -ಳು, ಯಾವಾಕೆ. Which woman? ಯಾವಾಗ, ಯಾವಾಗ್ಗೆ. When? ಯಾವಾಗಲಾದರೂ. At any time, whensoever. ಯಾವಾಗಲು, ಯಾವಾಗಲೂ, ಯಾವಾಗ್ಯೂ. Always, ever.

ಯಾವಜ್ಜೀವ s. *ad.* Throughout life.

ಯಾವತ್ತು (*tb. of* ಯಾವತ್) *n.* All, the whole.

ಯಾವಾಗ, ಯಾವಾಗ್ಗೆ. *See s.* ಯಾವ.

ಯು, ಯೂ. *For Kannaḍa words with these initials, see s.* ಇ *and* ಈ.

ಯುಂಗಡಿಸು. = ಎಂಗಡಿಸು, *q. v.*

ಯುಕುತಿ. *tb. of* ಯುಕ್ತಿ, *q. v.*

ಯುಕ್ತ s. *a.* Yoked, endowed with, having, possessed of, adopted, fitted, fit, suitable, right; moderate; intent on; engaged in; proved, inferred; *f.* ಯುಕ್ತೆ, ಯುಕ್ತಳು. ಯುಕ್ತಾಯುಕ್ತ. Suitable and unsuitable.

ಯುಕ್ತಿ (= ಯುಕುತಿ) s. *n.* Combination, union. 2, application, practice. 3, appliance, means, plan, scheme, expedient, trick, contrivance, device, ingenuity. 4, skill, art, tact. 5, suitableness, propriety, fitness; the secret, key, *etc.* 6, argument, inference. 7, connection of events in a plot (*in drama*). -ತೆಗೆ. To take hold of a device. -ಹುಡುಕಿ ತೆಗೆ. To make an invention. -ವಂತ, -ಶಾಲಿ. An ingenious or clever man. -ಸಾಧ್ಯ. Attainable by expedients, *etc.* -ಸಾಮರ್ಥ್ಯ. The power of expedients, *etc.* ಕಪಟ-, ಕು-. A sly scheme.

ಯುಗ (= ನೊಗ) s. *n.* A yoke. 2, a pair, couple. 3, a lustrum. 4, the period of a year (*see* ಯುಗಾದಿ). 5, one of the 4 ages of the world. ಯುಗಾದಿ. The beginning of a year, a new year's first day (its feast); *also* ಯುಗಾದಿಹಬ್ಬ.

ಯುಗಲ, ಯುಗ್ಮ s. *n.* A pair, couple.

ಯುದ್ಧ s. *n.* A war, battle, fight, combat. -ನಡೆ. A war to happen. -ಮಾಡು. To make war; to fight. -ಭೂಮಿ, -ರಂಗ. A battle-field. ದಂಡ-. A fight with cudgels. ಮಲ್ಲ-. Boxing. -ಸ್ಥ. A warrior.

ಯುಧಿಷ್ಠಿರ s. *n.* N. of the eldest of the Pâṇḍu princes.

ಯುವ s. *a.* Young, youthful. *n.* A youth, young man; *f.* -ತಿ. 2, the ninth year in the Hindu cycle. -ರಾಜ. An heir apparent, crown prince.

ಯೂಥ s. n. A flock, herd; a troop. -ನಾಥ, -ಪ. The leader of a herd, *as* of elephants.

ಯೂಪ s. n. A post to which the sacrificial victim is tied; *also* -ಸ್ತಂಭ. 2, a column erected in honour of a victory.

ಯೆಂಗಿ. *tb. of* ವ್ಯಂಗ್ಯ. -ಹಾಕು. To cheat.

ಯೆಹೂದ್ಯ f. n. A Jew, Hebrew or Israelite.

ಯೆಹೋವ f. n. Jehovah, God as revealed to men by His Word (*lit.* the Self-existent and Eternal). -ದಯ. The grace of Jehovah.

ಯೇಸು f. n. Jesus, the Saviour of the world. -ವಿನ ಶಿಷ್ಯ. A Christian. -ವಿತ. A Jesuit, one to counterinfluence the Reformation; a crafty person. -ವಿತರ ಬೋಧನೆ. The teachings of the Jesuits.

ಯೋಗ s. n. Yoking, union, contact; connection; mixture; arrangement; manner, means; an expedient, plan; charm, magic. 2, work, business; performance. 3, fitness, propriety. 4, accession of property. 5, conjunction (of stars); an auspicious moment; good luck. 6, a period of time. 7, a constellation. 8, etymology. 9, construction. 10, an aphorism. 11, abstract contemplation, meditation. 12, N. of a system of philosophy. 13, the body. 14, a remedy. -ಕ್ಷೇಮ. Well-being, welfare. -ಧ್ಯಾನ. Contemplation (of the Deity). -ನಿದ್ರೆ. A state between sleep and wakefulness. -ವಂತ, -ಶಾಲಿ. A lucky man. -ವಾಹ. A letter on the top of another. ಯೋಗಾಕ್ಷರ. A compound consonant. ಯೋಗಾಭ್ಯಾಸ. Practice of the yôga.

ಯೋಗಿ (=ಜೋಗಿ) s. n. A yôgi; an ascetic; a devotee; *f.* -ನಿ.

ಯೋಗ್ಯ s. n. Useful, serviceable, fit, suitable, proper; able. *n.* A useful, worthy man; *f.* -ಳು. -ತನ, -ತೆ. Suitableness, fitness; ability.

ಯೋಚನ, ಯೋಚನೆ (*tb. of* ಯೋಜನ) *n.* Application of the mind, consideration, reflection, (sorrowful) thought. ಯೋಚಿಸು. To deliberate, reflect, think; to consider, ponder; to ascertain.

ಯೋಜನ (=ಯೋಚನ) s. n. Junction; application. 2, a measure of distance (= about 9 English miles). 3, grammatical construction (*g.*). 4, abstraction. ಯೋಜಿಸು. To deliberate; to approve, assent.

ಯೋಧಕ s. n. A warrior, soldier.

ಯೋನಿ s. n. The womb; birth, origin; family, race. -ಜ. Viviparous.

ಯೌವನ (*fr.* ಯುವ. =ಜವ್ವನ, ಯುವ್ವನ) s. n. Youth; prime of life, manhood. *a.* Juvenile. -ಸ್ಥ. A young man; *f.* ಯೌವನಿ. ಯೌವನಾವಸ್ಥೆ. Youthfulness.

ರ

ರ. The forty-fifth letter of the alphabet.

ರಕಮು h. n. An item; an amount; a dose; a piece. -ವಾರು. Piece by piece.

ರಕಾರ s. n. The letter ರ.

ರಕ್ಕಸ. *tb. of* ರಾಕ್ಷಸ, *q. v.* *f.* ರಕ್ಕಸಿ. *tb. of* ರಾಕ್ಷಸಿ.

ರಕ್ಕೆ. *tb. of* ರಕ್ಷೆ, *q. v.*

ರಕ್ತ s. a. Coloured, dyed. 2, red; loving, dear, lovely. *n.* Blood. 2, saffron. 3, vermilion. -ಕಮಲ. A red lotus-flower. -ಕಾಸ. Cough with hemoptysis. -ಕುಷ್ಠ. Red leprosy. -ಚಂದನ. Red sandal, *Pterocarpus santolinus.*

-ತೆ. Redness. -ಪವಳ, -ಬಾಳ. Gum-myrrh; aloes. -ಪುಷ್ಪ. A red flower. -ಭೇದಿ, ರಕ್ತಾತಿಸಾರ. The dysentery. -ಮಂಡಲ. A red-ringed snake.

ರಕ್ತಾಕ್ಷಿ s. n. A buffalo. 2, the fifty-eighth year in the cycle of sixty.

ರಕ್ಷ್, ರಕ್ಷಕ s. n. A guardian, protector, saviour. 2, the only Saviour Jesus Christ. ರಕ್ಷಣ, ರಕ್ಷಣೆ. Watching, tending, protecting, preserving, saving; salvation in Christ. ರಕ್ಷಾಪತ್ರ. A book-cover. ರಕ್ಷಾಬಂಧ. The binding of thread around the wrist as a preservative (against evil spirits, *etc.*). ರಕ್ಷಿಸು. To guard, protect, preserve, save, keep, tend; to save (*from sin by Christ's atonement).*

ರಕ್ಷಸ್. = ರಾಕ್ಷಸ, *q. v.*

ರಕ್ಷೆ s. n. Protecting, protection, care; a preservative; a mark of ashes on the forehead; a charm, amulet. -ಕಟ್ಟು, -ಗಟ್ಟು. To tie an amulet. -ಬಳೆ. An amulet-ring. ಅಂಗ-. A coat. ಪಾದ-. A sandal. ತಲೆ-. A turban. ರಕ್ಷ್ಯ. Proper to be guarded, protected, *etc.*

ರಗಡ h. n. Abundance, profusion, masses, lots, heaps; throng.

ರಗಡೆ f. n. A grinding stone.

ರಗಳೆ (*tb. of* ರಥೋದ್ಧತ) n. Vain words, gabble. 2, a never-ending business; prolixity.

ರಘು s. n. N. of an ancient king. -ವಂಶ. His race or family, *also* -ಕುಲ; N. of a poem (by Kâḷidâsa). -ನಂದನ, -ನಾಥ, -ರಾಮ, -ವರ, -ವೀರ, -ಸುತ. Râma.

ರಂಕ s. a. Indigent, poor. n. A beggar.

ರಂಗ (= ರಂಗು, *q. v.*) s. n. Colour, paint, hue. 2, a stage, arena, circus. 3, a place of assembly; an assemblage of spectators. 4, a battle-field. 5, dancing, acting; fun. 6, splendour, glow. -ನಾಥ. Vishṇu. -ಭೂಮಿ. An arena, theatre. -ವಲಿ, -ವಲ್ಲಿ. Ornamental lines and figures drawn with various powders on the floor. -ಸ್ವಾಮಿ. Vishṇu; N. ರಣ-, ಯುದ್ಧ-. The battle-field. ರಂಗಿಸು. To be coloured; to be excited.

ರಂಗಳಿಸು f. v. t. To press and rub fine, *as* small articles.

ರಂಗಾರೆ h. n. A dyer.

ರಂಗು. *tb. of* ರಂಗ, *q. v.* -ಮಹಲು. A saloon, drawing-room.

ರಂಗೋಲೆ. *tb. of* ರಂಗವಲಿ, *q. v.*

ರಚನೆ s. n. Making, forming, formation, creation, arranging; arrangement, disposition, performance; embellishment; composition; a literary production. ರಚಿತ. Made, formed, produced, planned, composed, *etc.* ರಚಿಸು. To make, form, construct, compose, array, *etc.*

ರಚ್ಚೆ (= ರಚ್ಚು 2) k. n. Crying aloud (of children), noisy clamour. 2, report, publication.

ರಜ. = ರಜಸ್, *q. v.* -ವಂದಿ. Acceptable; a compromise, composition deed.

ರಜಕ s. n. A washerman; *f.* ರಜಕಿ.

ರಜತ s. a. White, silver-coloured; pure. -ಗಿರಿ, -ಪರ್ವತ, -ಶೈಲ, ರಜತಾಚಲ, ರಜತಾದ್ರಿ. N. of a mountain. -ಭಸ್ಮ. Calcined silver.

ರಜನಿ s. n. Night. 2, Durgâ. -ಕರ, -ಚರ, -ಪತಿ, -ಪಾಲ. The moon.

ರಜಪುತ್ರ, ರಜಪೂತ (*tb. of* ರಾಜಪುತ್ರ, *q. v.*) n. A Rajpoot.

ರಜಸ್, ರಜಸ್ಸು (= ರಜ, *q. v.*) s. n. Gloom, dimness. 2, dust, powder. 3, the pollen of flowers. 4, passion, foulness.

ರಜಾ h. n. Leave, permission. 2, leave of absence.

ರಜ್ಜು s. n. A rope, cord, string.

ರಂಜಕ s. a. Colouring. 2, gladdening, rejoicing, pleasing (*see* ಮನೋ-). 3, powder. 4, the train of powder to a mine. ರಂಜನ. Colouring; delighting, rejoicing. ರಂಜಿಸು. To shine;

to appear; to be beautiful; to be affected, excited; to be pleased.

ರಟ್ಟು 1. k. n. A coarse, thick cloth. 2, the cover of a book; its binding.

ರಟ್ಟು 2. = ರಟ್ಟೆ, q. v.

ರಡ್ಡಿ tb. n. A Roḍḍi: a title of a caste of Telugu cultivators.

ರಣ s. n. Noise. 2, battle, war, combat. 3, joy, delight. -ಗಲಿ. A hero in war. -ಗಾಳೆ. A war-trumpet. -ಹದ್ದು. A vulture. -ಹೇಡಿ. A coward in battle. -ಭೂಮಿ, -ಮಂಡಲ, -ರಂಗ. A battle-field. -ಭೇರಿ. A war-drum. -ವಾದ್ಯ. Martial music. -ವೀರ, -ಶೂರ. A warrior. ರಣಾಗ್ರ. The front of a battle. ರಣಾಂಗಣ. A battle-field; war, battle.

ರಂಟೆ k. n. A small plough.

ರಂಡೆ k. n. A widow. 2, the plant *Salvinia cucullata*. -ತನ. Widowhood.

ರತ s. a. Pleased, satisfied; delighted with; intent on; devoted to, engaged in. n. Pleasure.

ರತಿ 1. s. n. Pleasure. 2, love, affection. 3, Kâma's wife; *also* -ದೇವಿ.

ರತಿ 2. f. n. A small weight.

ರತ್ನ s. n. A jewel, gem, precious stone; a pearl. 2, any precious thing. -ಕಂಬಲ, -ಗಂಬಳಿ. A figured carpet. -ಗಂಧಿ. A shrub with showy flowers, the peacock's pride, *Calesalpinia pulcherrima*. -ನಗರಿ, -ಪುರಿ. N. of a town. -ಪರೀಕ್ಷೆ. Jewel-testing. -ಗರ್ಭ. The sea; Kubêra. -ಗರ್ಭೆ. The earth. -ಮಾಲೆ. A jewel necklace; N. of a work.

ರಥ s. n. A carriage, car, chariot. 2, a warrior. 3, the body. 4, the foot. 5, a limb, member. 6, pleasure, desire. -ಶಾಲೆ. A carriage-shed. -ಸಪ್ತಮಿ. A feast on the 7th day of the eleventh lunar month. ರಥಾರೋಹ, ರಥಾರೋಹಣ. Mounting a chariot; the ceremony of placing an idol on a car. ರಥಿಕ. The owner of a carriage; a charioteer. ರಥೋತ್ಸವ. A car-festival. ಮನೋ-. Wish, desire; object.

ರದ್ದು h. a. Null and void, cancelled, repealed. -ಮಾಡು. To repeal, cancel. -ಆಗು, -ಪಡು. To be repealed.

ರಂಧ್ರ s. n. A split, fissure, opening, hole, cavity; a defect, fault, flaw. ರಂಧ್ರಿಸು. To bore a hole.

ರನ್ನ. tb. of ರತ್ನ, q. v. Cpds.: -ಗನ್ನಡಿ, -ಗಲಿ, -ದೊಡವು, -ವಲ್ಲಿಕೆ, -ವಣೆ, etc.

ರಪಣ s. n. A kind of weapon.

ರಫು, ರಪ್ಫು h. n. Darning. -ಗಾರ. A darner. -ಮಾಡು. To darn.

ರಪ್ತು f. n. Exportation. -ಆಗು. To be exported.

ರಭಸ s. n. Violence, vehemence, haste, speed. 2, passion, anger. 3, pleasure. 4, a loud cry, clamour.

ರಮಣ s. a. Pleasing, agreeable, delightful. n. A lover; a husband; pleasure. ರಮಣಿ. A wife. ರಮಣೀಯ. Pleasing, agreeable, delightful, lovely. ರಮಾ-. Vishṇu.

ರಮಾ, ರಮೆ s. n. A wife; a woman; Lakshmî. ರಮಾಧವ, ರಮಾಪತಿ. Vishṇu. ರಮಿಸು. To rejoice, play.

ರಂಪ k. n. Clamour.

ರಂಪಿಗೆ k. n. A shoemaker's awl.

ರಂಬೆ k. n. A twig, small bough.

ರಂಭೆ s. n. The plantain tree, *Musa sapientum*. 2, N. of an Apsaras.

ರಮ್ಯ s. a. Enjoyable, pleasant, delightful, beautiful.

ರಯತ, ರಯಿತ (= ರೈತ) h. n. A subject; a tenant; a ryot. ರಯತಾಪಿ. Peasantry.

ರವ s. n. A cry, shriek, yell, howl, roar; sound, noise. -ಣ. Crying, sounding; jesting; a camel. ರವಿಸು. To cry, *etc.*

ರವಳಿ a. k. n. Cry, clamour. -ಗೆ. A small bamboo basket. -ಸು. To vociferate.

ರವಾನೆ h. n. Despatch; a pass, permit, passport. -ಮಾಡು, ರವಾನಿಸು. To send on, despatch, transmit.

ರವಿ s. n. The sun. 2, a mountain. 3, wealth. -ಕಾಂತ. A sort of crystal. -ಕುಲ. The solar race of kings. -ವಾರ. Sunday.

ರವೆ (tb. of ಲವ) n. A grain, granule; a particle of anything; hail; grits. -ಅಷ್ಟು, ರವಷ್ಟು. A little, trifle.

ರಶೀತಿ, ರಶೀದಿ e. n. A receipt.

ರಶ್ಮಿ s. n. A rope. 2, a ray of light. 3, an eyelash.

ರಸ s. n. The sap or juice of plants; syrup. 2, essence. 3, any liquid. 4, ghee; water; milk, *etc.* 5, sauce, seasoning. 6, quicksilver. 7, resin. 8, constituent fluid of the body. 9, taste, savour, relish. 10, passion, desire. 11, pleasure, charm, grace, sweetness, spirit, wit, joy, *etc.* 12, style. 13, sentiment, feeling, pathos. -ಕರ್ಪೂರ. Sublimate of mercury. -ಘುಟಿಕೆ. A pill made with quicksilver. -ಜ್ಞ. An alchemist. -ದಾಳಿ. A fine sort of sugarcane. -ದಾಳೆ. A plantain of a sweet flavour. -ಭಸ್ಮ. Calx or oxide of mercury. -ವತ್, -ವತ್ತು. Tasteful, well-flavoured; tasty. -ವರ್ಗ. All condiments (*as* pepper, salt, *etc.*). -ವಾದ. Metallurgy; alchemy. -ವಾದಿ. An alchemist. -ಸಿದ್ಧಿ. Skill in alchemy. -ಸಿಂದೂರ. A sort of factitious cinnabars. ನವ-. The nine sentiments of poetry, *as* ಶೃಂಗಾರ, love; ವೀರ, heroism; ಕರುಣ, tenderness; ಅದ್ಭುತ, surprise; ಹಾಸ್ಯ, mirth; ಭಯಾನಕ, terror; ಬೀಭತ್ಸ, disgust; ರೌದ್ರ, anger; ಶಾಂತ, tranquillity.

ರಸಾತಲ s. n. The lower world; one of the 7 regions under the earth.

ರಸಾಭಾಸ s. n. The unsuitable manifestation of a sentiment. 2, disorder, confusion.

ರಸಾಯನ s. n. An elixir; any medicinal compound. 2, alchemy, chemistry. 3, boiled fruit-juice mixed with sugar, milk, *etc.* -ಶಾಸ್ತ್ರ, -ವಿದ್ಯೆ. Chemistry.

ರಸಾಲ s. n. The mango tree. 2, the sugarcane; *also* ರಸದಾಳಿ.

ರಸಿಕ s. a. Tasty, savoury. 2, graceful, elegant. 3, spirited, witty. 4, having a liking for. -ತನ, -ತ್ವ. Tastefulness, sapidity; affection; taking pleasure in.

ರಸುಮೆ. tb. of ರಶ್ಮಿ, q. v.

ರಸ್ತಾಳಿ (tb. of ರಸದಾಳಿ) n. A fine sort of sugarcane.

ರಸ್ತು h. n. Grain stored up for an army.

ರಸ್ತೆ h. n. A road, way.

ರಹ (= ರಹಸ್) s. n. Wonderfulness, a marvel. 2, way, method.

ರಹಣಿ s. n. Dancing, pantomime; manner.

ರಹದಾರಿ h. n. Passage to and fro; traffic; a passport.

ರಹಸ್ (= ರಹ) s. n. Solitude, privacy; a secret, mystery. ರಹಸ್ಯ. Secret, private, mysterious; a secret, a mystery.

ರಹಾಟ. = ರಾಟಣ, q. v.

ರಹಿತ s. a. Left, abandoned. 2, deprived of, void or destitute of, without. -ತೆ. The state of being without.

ರಾಕಟಿ f. n. A golden circular ornament worn by females on their hairtresses.

ರಾಕಾ, ರಾಕೆ s. n. The full moon.

ರಾಕ್ಷಸ (= ರಕ್ಕಸ, q. v.) s. n. An evil being or demon; a goblin. 2, a form of marriage. -ಕೃತ್ಯ. A cruel deed. -ವೈದ್ಯ. Harsh medical treatment. ರಾಕ್ಷಸಿ (= ರಕ್ಕಸಿ). A female demon.

ರಾಗ s. n. Colour, hue. 2, affection, emotion, feeling. 3, love, sympathy, joy, pleasure. 4, greediness, envy. 5, anger. 6, loveliness. 7, a musical note; a tune, music. -ತೆಗೆ. To begin to sing. -ದ್ವೇಷ. Hatred from anger or envy. -ನುಡಿಸು. To make music. -ಮಾಡು, -ಹಾಡು, -ಹೇಳು. To sing a tune. -ಮಾಲಿಕೆ, -ಮಾಲೆ. A piano, harmonium; *also* -ಮಾಲಿಕೆ ಪೆಟ್ಟಿಗೆ.

ರಾಗಟಿ. = ರಾಕಟಿ, *q. v.*

ರಾಗಿ 1. k. *n.* Raggy, a sort of grain, *Eleusine coracana*. -ಯಂಬಲಿ. Raggy gruel. -ರೊಟ್ಟಿ. R. bread. -ಹಿಟ್ಟು. R. meal; its porridge.

ರಾಗಿ 2. s. *a.* Coloured; red; given up to passion; full of love; fond of. *n.* A painter; a lover. -ಸು. To be coloured; to be very fond of.

ರಾಘವ (*fr.* ರಘು) s. *n.* A descendant of Raghu. 2, Râmačandra; *also* ರಾಘವೇಂದ್ರ.

ರಾಜ (=ಅರಸು, ರಾಯ, *q. v.*) s. *n.* A king, sovereign, prince, chief; an excellent man; a master. 2, a Kshatriya. -ಕ. A petty king; what comes from a king. -ಕನ್ನಿಕೆ. A (virgin) princess. -ಕಾರ್ಯ. State affairs. -ಕೀಯ. Royal, kingly. -ಕುಮಾರ. A prince. -ಕುರು. A carbuncle. -ಕುಲ. A royal family. -ಗೃಹ, -ಭವನ, -ಮಂದಿರ. A palace. -ಚಿಹ್ನ, -ಚಿಹ್ನೆ, -ಲಕ್ಷಣ, -ಸದನ. Insignia of royalty. -ಚೂಡಾಮಣಿ. The best of kings. -ತ್ವ. Kingship, royalty. -ತರು. The tree *Cassia fistula*; the plant *Pterospermum acerifolium*. -ಧರ್ಮ. A king's duties; a virtue fit for a king. -ಧಾನಿ. A capital. -ನೀತಿ. Royal politics. -ಪಟ್ಟ. A royal tiara. -ಪತ್ನಿ. A queen. -ಪದವಿ. Kingship. -ಪುತ್ರ. A prince; a Rajpoot. -ಪೂಜಿತ. Excellent (*an honorific term*). -ಬೀದಿ, -ಬಾಟೆ, -ಮಾರ್ಗ. A high road, main road. -ಮರ್ಯಾದೆ. Respect shown to a king or to superiors. -ಮಾನ್ಯ. Excellent. -ಮುದ್ರೆ. A royal signet. -ಯೋಗ. An easy mode of meditation. -ಯೋಗ್ಯ. Princely. -ಋಷಿ. A royal saint. -ವಂಶ. A royal family. -ವಿದ್ಯೆ. State policy. -ವೈದ್ಯ. A royal physician; an excellent practice of medicine. -ಶಾಸನ. A royal edict. -ಶಿಖಾಮಣಿ, -ಶಿರೋಮಣಿ. The first of kings. -ಶೇಖರ. The chief of kings; Šiva; N. of a king. -ಶೇಖರವಿಲಾಸ. N. of a Kannaḍa poem. -ಶ್ರೀ. A term of courtesy. -ಸಭೆ. A royal assembly, a court of justice. -ಸೂಯ. A great sacrifice at a king's coronation. -ಸೇವೆ. King's service. -ಹಂಸ. A flamingo. -ಹುಣ್ಣು. Scrofula. ರಾಜಾಜ್ಞೆ. A royal decree. ರಾಜಾಧಿರಾಜ. A king of kings.

ರಾಜಿ 1. s. *n.* A strip, line, row.

ರಾಜಿ 2. h. *a.* Willing, ready. *n.* Full consent, willingness, agreement, content. -ನಾಮೆ. A deed of resignation (of an office, claim, *etc.*), an acquittance. -ಮಾಡು. To bring to terms. -ಯಾಗು. To consent, acquiesce.

ರಾಜಿಕ, ರಾಜೀಕ s. *a.* Relating to a king. *n.* A lord, noble person.

ರಾಜಿತ s. *a.* Illuminated; adorned.

ರಾಜಿಸು s. *v. i.* To shine, glitter. *v. t.* To make radiant.

ರಾಜೀವ s. *n.* A species of fish. 2, a lotus. 3, water. -ನೇತ್ರ. Vishṇu. -ಮಿತ್ರ, -ಸಖ. The sun.

ರಾಜೇಂದ್ರ s. *n.* A king of kings.

ರಾಜ್ಞಿ (= ರಾಣಿ) s. *n.* A queen.

ರಾಜ್ಯ s. *n.* A kingdom, empire, country, government. 2, administration of government. 3, kingship. -ಗೆಯ್ಯು, -ಮಾಡು, -ವಾಳು. To rule. -ಭಾರ. Rule, reign. -ಭಾರ ಮಾಡು. To exercise government. -ಶ್ರೀ. An empire; an honorific term. ರಾಜ್ಯಾಧಿಪತಿ. A ruler, king. ರಾಜ್ಯಾಭಿಷೇಕ. Coronation.

ರಾಟಣ, ರಾಟವಾಣ, ರಾಟವಾಳ, ರಾಟೆ, ರಾಟ್ಟ (*tb. of* ಅರಘಟ್ಟ) *n.* A machine for drawing water; a spinning wheel; a wheel of any machine. 2, a whirling machine. ರಾಟಿಸು. To wind upon a reel.

ರಾಡಿ s. *n.* A mass of mud. *a.* Foul, turbid.

ರಾಣಿ (*tb. of* ರಾಜ್ಞಿ) *n.* A queen. 2, a wife. -ರಾಜ್ಯ. A queen's government. -ವಾಸ. A queen's apartment.

ರಾತಲು h. n. A weight of 12 or 16 ounces, a pound.

ರಾತೀಪ್ತ, ರಾತೀಬು h. n. A nutritive and fattening diet; a regular quantity of food.

ರಾತ್ರಿ s. n. Night. -ಕಾಲ. Night-time. -ಪತಿ, -ಮಣಿ, ರಾತ್ರೀಶ. The moon. ಅರ್ಧ-, ಸಮ-, ನಡು-, ಮಧ್ಯ-. Midnight. ಶಿವ-. An annual festival in honour of Śiva's birth. -ಭೋಜನ. The Lord's Supper instituded by Christ.

ರಾದಾರಿ. = ರಹದಾರಿ, q. v.

ರಾದ್ಧ s. a. Accomplished; prepared; obtained. ರಾದ್ಧಾಂತ. A demonstrated truth, dogma.

ರಾಧೆ s. n. N. of the foster-mother of Karṇa. 2, N. of Kṛishṇa's favourite wife.

ರಾಪ f. n. Astringent property, as juice of fruits.

ರಾಪ್ತಿ h. n. Custom, usage. -ಬೀಳು. To become familiar.

ರಾಮ s. a. Pleasing; lovely, charming. 2, white, pure. n. N. of Vishṇu's 7th incarnation; also -ಚಂದ್ರ. -ಗುಳ್ಳ. The plant Solanum jacquini. -ತುಳಸಿ. The herb Ocimum album. -ದೂತ. Hanumat. -ಪುರ. N. of several places. -ಫಲ. The bullock's heart (a fruit). -ಸೇತು. Adam's bridge. ಪರಶು-. Vishṇu's 6th incarnation. ಬಲ-. Kṛishṇa's elder brother. ರಾಮಾನುಜ. A Vaishṇava teacher of the twelfth century. ರಾಮಾಯಣ. An epic poem by Vâlmîki describing the adventures of Râma. ರಾಮಾಯಣಪಾರಾಯಣ. Reading the Râmâyaṇa. ರಾಮೇಶ್ವರ. N. of a place between Ceylon and Coromandel coast.

ರಾಯ. tb. of ರಾಜ, q. v. -ಬಹಾದರ್. A title of honour. -ಭಾರಿ. An embassador. -ಭಾರ, -ಭಾರಿಕೆ. Government, ruling; ambassadorship. -ಚೋರೆ. A large shrub, Webera corymbosa.

ರಾಯಸ s. n. Secretaryship in native government. 2, a letter from a superior (guru, etc.). -ದವ. A clerk.

ರಾವಣ s. n. Roaring; N. of the ruler of Laṅkâ (Ceylon) slain by Râma.

ರಾವು (tb. of ರಾಹು) n. The daitya Râhu. 2, a startle. -ಗಣ್ಣು. The evil eye. -ತಟ್ಟು, -ಬಡಿ. A horror to touch. -ತೆಗೆ. To wave an offering before a person to remove evil influences.

ರಾವುತ (tb. of ರಾಹುತ) n. A horseman.

ರಾಶಿ s. n. A heap, mass, pile, quantity. 2, a sign of the zodiac. a. Exceedingly much. -ಚಕ್ರ. An astrological diagram. -ಮಾಡು, -ಹಾಕು. To pile, heap up.

ರಾಷ್ಟ್ರ s. n. A kingdom, realm, empire; a district. ಮಹಾ-. The Mahratta country.

ರಾಸ s. n. Uproar, noise. 2, a rustic dance, as of Kṛishṇa and gôpis; also -ಕ್ರೀಡೆ.

ರಾಸಿ. tb. of ರಾಶಿ, q. v. -ಮಸಕ. Excessive passion. -ಮಾಡು. To heap up.

ರಾಸ್ನೆ s. n. The thorny shrub Mimosa octandra.

ರಾಹು s. n. N. of a demon supposed to swallow the sun and moon and thus cause eclipses. 2, the ascending node of the moon. 3, a startling event, as an eclipse, etc.

ರಾಹುತ. = ರಾವುತ, q. v.

ರಾಳ f. n. Resin in general. -ದ ಮರ. The white dammer tree, Vateria indica.

ರಿಕಾಪು h. n. A stirrup.

ರಿಕಾಮಿ f. n. Empty, vacant, unemployed.

ರಿಕಾರ್ಡು e. n. Record.

ರಿಕ್ಕಟ k. n. Silence. ad. Silently.

ರಿಕ್ತ s. a. Empty; poor; vain, worthless. ರಿಕ್ತೆ. A poor woman.

ರಿಖಾನೆ h. n. A column in a form. -ಭರಾಯಿಸು. To fill up the columns of a tabular form.

ರಿಂಗಣ s. n. Crawling, creeping. 2, dancing. 3, slipping; deviating.

ರಿಜಿಸ್ತ್ರಾರು e. n. A registrar, as of assurances, etc. ರಿಜಿಸ್ತ್ರಿ. Registry.

ರಿಣ. *tb. of* ಋಣ, *q. v.*

ರಿಪು s. *n.* An enemy, foe.

ರಿಯಾಯತಿ h. *n.* Protection; leniency, indulgence. -ಮಾಡು. To make an exception, treat leniently.

ರಿವಾಜು h. *n.* Usage, custom.

ರಿಸಾಲು h. *n.* A troop of horses.

ರೀತಿ s. *n.* A course. 2, way, method, mode, manner, fashion; usage. 3, style, diction.

ರೀಪು f. *n.* A wooden lath, reeper.

ರುಕ್ಮ s. *a.* Bright, radiant. *n.* Gold. -ಕಾರಕ. A goldsmith. ರುಕ್ಮಾಂಗದ. N. of a king.

ರುಕ್ಮಿಣಿ s. *n.* N. of a daughter of king Bhishmaka and wife of Kṛishṇa.

ರುಚಕ s. *a.* Agreeable, pleasing. 2, tonic, stomachic. *n.* The citron.

ರುಚಿ s. *n.* Light, lustre. 2, wish, will; taste for. 3, taste, flavour, relish, savour, appetite. -ಕಾಣು, -ನೋಡು. To taste, try. -ಹತ್ತು. To be tasty or agreeable. -ಕರ. Savoury, tasty. -ಕೊಡು. To impart a flavour. -ಸು. To be savoury or tasty; to be agreeable, *as* a word.

ರುಚಿರ s. *a.* Bright, beautiful; sweet, pleasant, nice.

ರುಜನ s. *n.* Sickness; toil, fatigue; *cf.* ರೋಗ-.

ರುಜು h. *n.* Signature; proof. -ಮಾಡು. To sign; to prove. -ವಾತು. Proved; proof, evidence. ಕೇಳಿಕೇ ರುಜುವಾತು. Hearsay evidence. ಸಂಗತ್ಯಾನುಸಾರ ರುಜುವಾತು. Circumstantial evidence.

ರುಣ. *tb. of* ಋಣ, *q. v.*

ರುಂಡ s. *n.* A headless trunk; a skull. -ಮಾಲೆ. A wreath of skulls.

ರುತು. *tb. of* ಋತು, *q. v.*

ರುದ್ರ s. *n.* Crying, howling. 2, N. of the god of tempests. 2, Śiva. -ಗಂಟು. A peculiar knot of a Śaiva's sacrificial thread. -ಭೂಮಿ. A place of burial or cremation. -ಮಂತ್ರ, -ಸೂಕ್ತ. N. of a ṛigvêda hymn. -ವೀಣೆ. A kind of lute. ರುದ್ರಾಭಿಷೇಕ. Anointing a liṅga reciting -ಸೂಕ್ತ. ರುದ್ರಾವತಾರ. Śiva's incarnation; excitement, rage, fury. ರುದ್ರಾಕ್ಷ, ರುದ್ರಾಕ್ಷಿ. The berry of *Elaeocarpus ganitrus* tree.

ರುಧಿರೋದ್ಗಾರಿ s. *n.* Spitting blood; the fifty-seventh year in the cycle of sixty.

ರುಪಾಯಿ. = ರೂಪಾಯಿ, *q. v.*

ರುಬರೂಬು. = ರೂಬರೂ, *q. v.*

ರುಬ್ಬು k. *v. t.* To grind. *n.* Grinding.

ರುಮಾಲ, ರುಮಾಲು h. *n.* A turban. 2, a handkerchief; *also* ಕೈ-.

ರುವಿ, ರುವ್ವಿ (*tb. of* ರೂಪ) *n.* A pie, kâsu.

ರುಷಿ. *tb. of* ಋಷಿ, *q. v.*

ರುಷಿತ s. *a.* Enraged, angry.

ರುಸುಮು h. *n.* Fees, dues, commission.

ರುಳಿ f. *n.* A silver chain worn on the legs by women.

ರೂ k. *n.* Repetition of words and sentences. -ಹಾಕು. To repeat them frequently, to commit them to memory.

ರೂಕ್ಷ s. *n.* Emaciation; harshness, cruelty.

ರೂಡಿ. *tb. of* ರೂಢಿ, *q. v.*

ರೂಢ s. *a.* Commonly known, popular, conventional. -ನಾಮ. A common noun.

ರೂಢಿ (= ರೂಡಿ) s. *n.* Rise; origin. 2, custom, usage, common currency, general use; a popular use of words (*opposed to etymological meaning*). -ಬೀಳು, -ಯಾಗು. To become common. -ಮಾಡು. To practice. -ಮಾತು, -ಶಬ್ದ. A common word.

ರೂಢಿಸು s. *v. i.* To be commonly known and used; to become famous. 2, to improve, accumulate.

ರೂಪ (= ರೂಪು, ರೂಹು) s. *n.* Any form, figure, shape; an image. 2, an inflected form (*g.*). 3, shapeliness, beauty. 4, feature, character. 5, kind, sort. 6, a single specimen, type, pattern. 7, mode. -ವಂತ. A handsome man; *f.* -ವಂತಳು, -ವಂತೆ, -ವತಿ. -ಹೀನ. Ugly. ರೂಪಾಂತರ. A change of form, transfiguration, *as* of Christ. -ತಕ್ಕೊಳ್ಳು, -ಧರಿಸು, -ಮಾಡಿಕೊಳ್ಳು. To assume a form. ರೂಪಿಸು. To form, mould, figure; to represent, show, point out.

ರೂಪಕ s. *a.* Figurative. *n.* A metaphor. 2, a form, figure, image. 3, a drama, play; a dramatic composition or performance.

ರೂಪಾಯಿ (*tb. of* ರೂಪ್ಯ) s. *n.* A rupee. -ತೂಕ. A rupee's weight, tola.

ರೂವು. *tb. of* ರೂಪ, *q. v.*

ರೂಪ್ಯ s. *a.* Handsome. 2, stamped. *n.* A stamped coin; silver.

ರೂಬರೂ, ರೂಬರೂಬು h. *ad.* Face to face.

ರೂಲು e. *n.* A rule; a line.

ರೂಹು. *tb. of* ರೂಪ, *q. v.*

ರೆಕ್ಕೆ (ರೆ = ಱ) k. *n.* A wing. -ಯಿರುವೆ. A winged ant. -ಬಡಿ, -ಯಾಡಿಸು. To shake the wings.

ರೆಟ್ಟೆ (ರೆ = ಱ) k. *n.* The arm; the upper part of the arm; *also* ರಟ್ಟೆ.

ರೆಪ್ಪೆ (ರೆ = ಱ) k. *n.* An eyelid. -ಹಾಕು. The twinkling of an eye. -ಬಡಿ, -ಹಾಕು. To wink.

ರೆಂಬೆ (= ರಂಬೆ) k. *n.* A twig.

ರೆಳ್ಳು k. *n.* A reed used to write with, *Saccharum sara.*

ರೇಕ f. *n.* Emptying, evacuating, leaving; purging. 2, doubt.

ರೇಕು k. *n.* A thin plate of metal. 2, the petal of a flower.

ರೇಕೆ (*tb. of* ರೇಖೆ, *q. v.*) *n.* A line.

ರೇಖೆ (= ರೇಕೆ) s. *n.* A line; a streak, stripe; a row; drawing. 2, the first meridian. 3, a small quantity. ರೇಖಾಂತ. Longitude. ರೇಖಾಗಣಿತ. Geometry.

ರೇಗು k. *v. i.* To be aroused, excited; to become angry. ರೇಗಿಸು. To irritate, excite, make angry.

ರೇಚಕ s. *n.* Purging; expiration. 2, a purge.

ರೇಜಿಗೆ f. *n.* Disgust.

ರೇಜು. = ರೇತಿ, *q. v.*

ರೇಣು s. *n.* Dust. 2, the pollen of a flower. -ಕ. A Yaksha. -ಕೆ. The mother of Paraśurâma.

ರೇತಿ h. *n.* Sand. -ದಾನಿ. A sandbox.

ರೇಫ s. *n.* A burr: the letter ೯. 2, passion. *a.* Low, vile.

ರೇವಡಿ f. *n.* A kind of sweetmeat. 2, discomfiture. -ಗಿಡ. A wiry thorny shrub, *Capparis divaricata.*

ರೇವತಿ s. *n.* N. of the twenty-seventh nakshatra. 2, N. of Balarâma's wife.

ರೇವಲ್ಚಿನ್ನಿ f. *n.* The perennial plant *Rhubarb, Rheum palmatum.*

ರೇವು k. *n.* A landing place, beach, port.

ರೇವೆ f. *n.* Fine gravel; the grit of sugar.

ರೇಶ್ಮಿ, ರೇಸ್ಮೆ, ರೇಶಿಮೆ, *etc.* h. *n.* Silk. *a.* Silken. -ಹುಳ. The silk-worm.

ರೈ s. *n.* Wealth; gold; lustre. -ವತ. Rich, wealthy; N. of a king or a mountain.

ರೈಟರ್ e. *n.* A writer.

ರೈತ. = ರಯತ, *q. v.*

ರೊಕ್ಕ f. *n.* Cash, ready money; change; money in general. ಚಿಲ್ಲರೆ-. Small change.

ರೊಚ್ಚು, ರೊಚ್ಚೆ, ರೊಜ್ಜು k. *n.* Mud, mire, foul water.

ರೊಟ್ಟಿ f. *n.* Bread; a cake of bread. -ಗಿಡ. A spreading herb, *Malva rotundifolia.*

ರೊಗ್ಗ k. *n.* The left. -ಕೈ. The left hand.

ರೊಂಡಿ k. *n.* The haunch.

ರೊಂಡೆ k. *n.* Mud.

ರೊಪ್ಪ (ರೊ = ಱೊ) k. *n.* A fold.

ರೊಷ್ಟು k. *n.* Teasing, annoying. 2, (e.) roast.

ರೋಕ s. n. Light. 2, a hole, cavity. 3, buying for cash.

ರೋಗ s. n. Sickness, disease, malady; cf. ರುಜನ. -ದಲ್ಲಿ ಬೀಳು. To fall sick. -ಚಿಹ್ನೆ, -ಲಕ್ಷಣ. The symptoms of a disease. -ಪರೀಕ್ಷೆ. Examination of a disease. -ರಾಜ. Consumption. -ರುಜನ. dpl. -ಶಾಂತಿ. Cure of a malady. -ಸ್ಥ. A sick man. -ಹರ. Curative. -ಹಾರಿ. Curing, curative; a physician. ರೋಗಿ. Sick, ill; a sick person. ರೋಗಿಷ್ಠ. One who is sickly.

ರೋಚಕ s. a. Sapid, tasty, savoury. n. A stimulant, stomachic. 2, hunger, appetite.

ರೋಜ಼ 1. e. n. A rose.

ರೋಜ 2, ರೋಜಾ h. n. Fast, a fast.

ರೋಜು h. n. A day; service, work; a day's wages. -ಗಾರ. A workman, servant. -ಗಾರಿ, -ಗಾರಿಕೆ. Work; wages; earning. -ನಾಮು. A diary, ledger-book.

ರೋಡ್ e. n. A road.

ರೋಡು (ರೂ = ಜೋ) s. v. i. To be foolish. ರೋಡಾಡು. To laugh at with grimaces; to deride.

ರೋತೆ (= ರೋಸು, q. v.) k. n. Dirt, filth, any nasty thing.

ರೋದನ s. n. Weeping, wailing. ರೋದಿಸು. To weep, wail.

ರೋಧ s. n. Checking; restraint, obstruction, prohibiting. See ನಿ-, ವಿ-, etc.

ರೋಮ (= ರೋವು) s. n. The hair on the body; wool, down, bristles, feathers. -ಕೂಪ. A pore of the skin. -ರಾಜಿ. A row of hair. -ವಿಕಾರ, -ಹರ್ಷ. Horripilation; bristling of hair; thrill, shudder; also ರೋಮಾಂಚ.

ರೋಮನ್ e. a. Pertaining to Rome. -ಕಥೋಲಿಕ. Roman Catholic. -ಕಥೋಲಿಕ ಮತ. Roman Catholicism. -ಕಥೋಲಿಕ ಆಚಾರ. R. Catholic ceremonies.

ರೋಷ s. n. Anger, rage, wrath. -ಣ. Angry, passionate.

ರೋಷನ್ h. n. Lighting, illumination.

ರೋಸು (= ರೋತೆ) k. n. Dirt, filth. v. i. To feel disgusted.

ರೋಹಣ s. n. Rising, ascending; see ಆ-.

ರೋಹಿಣಿ s. n. Rising. 2, N. of the fourth or ninth nakshatra. 3, N. of Daksha's daughter, Balarâmâ's mother. 4, a young girl. -ಸುತ. The planet Mercury; Balarâma.

ರೋಹಿತ s. a. Red. n. A kind of deer.

ರೌದ್ರ (fr. ರುದ್ರ) s. a. Rudra-like; violent, terrible, formidable. n. Ardour, passion, anger, fury. -ತೆ. Fierceness, formidableness.

ರೌದ್ರಿ s. n. The fifty-fourth year of the cycle of sixty.

ರೌರವ (fr. ರುರು) s. a. Dreadful, terrible. n. One of the hells; also -ನರಕ.

ೞ

ೞ. The forty-sixth letter of the alphabet; *now out of use and represented by* ಳ.

ಲ

ಲ. The forty-seventh letter of the alphabet.

ಲಕಡಿ h. n. Wood.

ಲಕಲಕ f. n. Glitter, flash. *ad.* Brightly, brilliantly.

ಲಕಾರ s. n. The letter ಲ.

ಲಕುಚ s. n. A kind of bread-fruit tree, *Artocarpus lacucha*.

ಲಕೋಟು, ಲಕೋಟೆ h. n. The envelope of a letter; a closed letter.

ಲಕ್ಕಾ f. n. A kind of pigeon.

ಲಕ್ಕಿ k. n. The shrub *Vitex negundo*; *also* -ಲಿ.

ಲಕ್ಷ s. n. A mark, sign, token. 2, a butt, aim. 3, appearance, show, pretence. 4, a lac, one hundred thousand. 5, (= ಲಕ್ಷ್ಯ n. No. 2) attention, regard, consideration. -ಕೊಡು. To give heed, pay attention to, to mind, aim at. -ಗಟ್ಟಲೆ. By lacs. -ದೊಳಗೆ ಇಡು. To consider, regard. -ದೊಳಗೆ ಬರು. To come under observation, to be perceived. ಲಕ್ಷಾಧಿಕಾರಿ, ಲಕ್ಷಾಧಿಪತಿ, ಲಕ್ಷೇಶ್ವರ. A millionaire. ಲಕ್ಷಾಂತರ. A lac and more, very much. ಲಕ್ಷಾವಧಿ. By lacs, very much, very many. ಲಕ್ಷಿಸು, ಲಕ್ಷೀಕರಿಸು. To distinguish; to aim at; to consider, regard; to behold, notice, know.

ಲಕ್ಷಣ s. n. A distinctive mark, token, characteristic; character, attribute. 2, a favourable sign; handsomeness. 3, a symptom, *as* of a disease. 4, a definition. 5, aim, scope, object. -ಗೇಡಿ. An unlucky person. -ವಂತ. A lucky or handsome man. ಲಕ್ಷಣೆ. An ellipsis, metonymy.

ಲಕ್ಷ್ಮಣ s. a. Having signs. 2, lucky, fortunate. n. N. of Râma's younger brother. 2, the male Indian crane; *f.* ಲಕ್ಷ್ಮಣೆ.

ಲಕ್ಷ್ಮೀ s. n. Good fortune, prosperity, wealth, happiness. 2, beauty, loveliness. 3, N. of the goddess of fortune and beauty, Vishṇu's wife. -ಕರ. Causing prosperity. -ಕಾಂತ, -ಪತಿ, -ರಮಣ, -ವಲ್ಲಭ, -ವರ. Vishṇu. -ವಂತ. A wealthy man.

ಲಕ್ಷ್ಯ s. a. To be marked; to be aimed at. n. An aim, object, butt, a feature. 2, attention, consideration, regard, care for. -ಕೊಡು. = ಲಕ್ಷಕೊಡು. -ಮಾಡು, -ಕ್ಕೆ ತರು. To mark, mind. -ದಲ್ಲಿ ಇಡು. = ಲಕ್ಷದೊಳಗೆ ಇಡು. -ಸಿದ್ಧಿ. Proof derived from examples.

ಲಗಡಿಸು h. v. t. To beat, flog.

ಲಗತ h. n. Enclosure, appendage. -ಮಾಡು. To append, enclose. ಲಗತಿ. Adjoining.

ಲಗಬಗಿ f. n. Haste, bustle. ಲಗಬಗೆ, ಲಗೆಬಗೆ. Hastily.

ಲಗಾಂ (= ಲಗಾಮು) h. n. The bit of a bridle; a bridle.

ಲಗಾಟೆ s. n. A wicked woman.

ಲಗಾಡಿ. = ಲಿಗಾಡು, *q. v.*

ಲಗಾಮು. = ಲಗಾಂ, *q. v.*

ಲಗಾವು f. n. Union, connection. 2, application. -ಮಾಡು. To make applicable to, *as* provisions of law. ಲಗಾಯಿಸು. To join; to beat; to eat.

ಲಗು (*tb. of* ಲಘು, *q. v.*) a. Light. n. Alleviation. *ad.* Quickly, swiftly. -ಬಿಗು. The state of being easy or difficult. -ಲಗು. Very quickly.

ಲಗ್ಗೆ (*tb. of* ಲಂಘ) n. Ascending, scaling; an assault, attack. -ಆಗು. To be scaled. -ಮಾಡು, -ಹತ್ತು, -ಹೋಗು. To scale.

ಲಗ್ನ s. n. Attached; joined, united; auspicious. n. The time of the sun's entrance into a zodiacal sign; an auspicious moment; time for action; *also* ಸು-, ಶುಭ-. 2, marriage. 3, the rising of the sun, planets, *etc.* -ಕಾಲ. An auspicious moment; the marriage-time. ಜನ್ಮ-. A natal star. -ಪತ್ರಿಕೆ. A paper on which the time of celebrating a wedding is noted down; a letter of invitation for a wedding. ಮದುವೆ-. A marriage ceremony.

ಲಘಿಮೆ s. *n.* Lightness. 2, smallness. 3, frivolousness. 4, meanness. ಲಘಿಷ್ಠ. Lightest, smallest.

ಲಘು (=ಲಗು) s. *a.* Quick, swift, fleet. 2, light, easy. 3, little, small, slight, trivial, trifling, insignificant. 4, weak, low; mean, frivolous. 5, soft, gentle. *ad.* Quickly. -ಕೆಲಸ. A trifling business. -ತ್ವ. Quickness; lightness; levity; incivility, disrespect; frivolity. -ಶಂಕೆ. Making water. -ಹಸ್ತ. Light-handed, expert.

ಲಂಕಿಣಿ s. *n.* A female demon of Lanka.

ಲಂಕೆ, ಲಂಕಾ s. *n.* The capital of Râvaṇa in Ceylon; Ceylon.

ಲಂಗ h. *n.* A skirt.

ಲಂಗರು, ಲಂಗರ h. *n.* An anchor. -ಬಿಡು. To cast anchor. -ಎತ್ತು. To weigh anchor.

ಲಂಗೋಟಿ h. *n.* A piece of cloth covering the privities.

ಲಂಘನ s. *n.* Jumping; leaping over, crossing. 2, transgression; offence. 3, ascending; assaulting; capture. 4, fasting, abstinence. ಲಂಘಿಸು. To leap, spring; to overstep; to ascend, *etc.*

ಲಜ್ಜೆ, ಲಜ್ಜಾ s. *n.* Shame, bashfulness; perplexity. ಲಜ್ಜಾವತಿ. A modest woman; a prickly shrub *Mimosa pudica*. ಲಜ್ಜಾಳು, ಲಜ್ಜಾಶೀಲ, ಲಜ್ಜಿತ. Bashful, modest, shameful. ಲಜ್ಜಾಹೀನ. Shameless, impudent.

ಲಂಚ, ಲಂಚೆ s. *n.* A present, bribe. ಲಂಚ ಗಿಂಚ, -ಪಂಚ. *redt.* -ಕೊಡು, -ಹಾಕು. To bribe. -ತಿನ್ನು, -ತೆಗೆ. To take bribes. -ಖೋರ, -ಗಾರ, -ಗುಳಿ. A receiver of bribes.

ಲಟಕಟಿಸು f. *v. i.* To grow agitated; to be restless; to be alarmed.

ಲಟಾಪಟ f. *n.* Altercation, coming to blows.

ಲಟ್ಟ h. *n.* A stick; a club. *a.* Stout, thick. -ಣಿಗೆ. A roller; a rolling-pin. ಲಟ್ಟಿಸು. To roll out, *as* dough.

ಲಡಾಯಿ h. *n.* Fighting; a fight; war.

ಲಡಿ h. *n.* A string, *as* of pearls.

ಲಡ್ಡ s. *n.* A wretch, villain.

ಲಡ್ಡು 1. k. *n.* Pithlessness, weakness. -ಆಗು, ಲಡ್ಡಾಗು. To become pithless, *as* wood. -ಸವುದೆ. Pithless firewood.

ಲಡ್ಡು 2. f. *n.* A sweetmeat-ball; *also* ಲಡ್ಡುಕ, ಲಡ್ಡಿಗೆ, ಲಡ್ಡುಗೆ.

ಲಂಡ. *tb. of* ಲಡ್ಡ. 2, (=ಲದ್ದಿ) excrement.

ಲತೆ s. *n.* A creeper. 2, a plant in general. 2, a branch. ಲತಾಗೃಹ. A creeper-house, arbour. ಲತಾಂಗಿ. A woman of delicate form. ಲತಿಕೆ. A small creeper.

ಲತ್ತೆ f. *n.* A kick; a blow. -ಕೊಡು, -ಹಾಕು. To kick; to give a blow.

ಲದ್ದಿ h. *n.* The dung of elephants, horses, camels, *etc.*

ಲಪನ s. *n.* Speaking, talk. 2, the mouth. ಲಪಿತ. Spoken, said; speech.

ಲಪ್ಪಟ್ಟಿ s. *n.* A cloth for wrapping round the head.

ಲಬ್ಧ s. *a.* Obtained, got, gained, acquired. 2, obtained, *as* a quotient. -ನಾಶ. Loss of any thing acquired.

ಲಬ್ಧಿ s. *n.* Gaining, acquisition. 2, gain, profit. 3, quotient (*arith.*).

ಲಬ್ಬೆ h. *n.* A caste of Mahomedans.

ಲಭ್ಯ s. *a.* Acquirable, obtainable; attainable. 2, suitable, proper, fit. ಲಭಿಸು. To be gained or obtained, *etc.*

ಲಂಪಟ s. *a.* Covetous, greedy; desirous; addicted to. -ತನ, -ತೆ. Greediness; lewdness.

ಲಂಪಟಿ k. *n.* Weariness, fatigue.

ಲಂಬ s. *a*. Hanging down, pendulous, dangling. 2, hanging upon. 3, long; spacious. *n*. Length. 2, a perpendicular (*geom*.). -ನ. Hanging down; a necklace.

ಲಂಬಾಡಿ, ಲಂಬಾಣಿ h. *n*. A Lumbadee, a migratory caste trading in salt, grain, *etc*.

ಲಂಬಿ s. *a*. Hanging down, pendent; resting on. -ಸು. To hang down or from, to dangle. *v. t*. To lengthen, expand (*as* words, time, *etc*.).

ಲಂಬೋದರ s. *a*. Pot-bellied. *n*. Gaṇêśa.

ಲಯ s. *n*. Clinging, adherence. 2, a dwelling; rest, repose. 3, melting away; dissolution; extinction, destruction; disappearing. 4, time or pause in music. -ನ. Rest, repose; a place of rest.

ಲಲನ s. *n*. Playing, sporting. 2, lolling the tongue.

ಲಲನೆ s. *n*. A woman, wife. 2, the tongue.

ಲಲಾಟ s. *n*. The forehead. -ರೇಖೆ. Destiny written on the forehead. ಲಲಾಟಾಕ್ಷ. Śiva.

ಲಲಾಮ s. *n*. A mark; sign. 2, a banner, flag. 3, greatness, dignity. 4, beauty. 5, an ornament. 6, an eminent person. 7, a horse.

ಲಲಿತ s. *a*. Sported; wanton, voluptuous; lovely, beautiful; simple; soft, gentle; pleasant, sweet. *n*. Sport; beauty, grace. 2, simplicity, artlessness. -ವೃತ್ತ, ಲಲಿತೆ. One of the ragaḷĕ metres.

ಲಲ್ಲೆ s. *n*. Caressing; love, affection; a kiss. -ಗೆಯ್ಯು. To caress; to kiss; *also* ಲಲ್ಲಯಿಸು.

ಲವ s. *n*. Cutting; plucking. 2, a fragment, piece, bit, a little. 3, a moment, instant. 4, wool, hair. 5, N. of a son of Râma.

ಲವಂಗ s. *n*. The clove tree, *Myristica cariophyllata*, cloves. -ಚಕ್ಕೆ. Cinnamon. -ದಾನಿ. A clove-box. -ಪತ್ರೆ. The leaves of *Laurus cassia*. -ವಾಸರಿ ಹುಲ್ಲು. A grass with fragrant roots, *Pancicum cimicinum*.

ಲವಡಿ h. *n*. A female slave; a strumpet.

ಲವಣ s. *n*. Salt. 2, N. of a Daitya. *a*. Saline, briny, salt. -ಭಸ್ಮ. Calcined salt. -ಸಮುದ್ರ, ಲವಣೋದಧಿ. Ocean.

ಲವಣಿ s. *n*. Stooping, bending, winding. 2, flash, shine. ಲವಣಿಸು. To wind; to shine, flash.

ಲವಲವಿಕೆ f. *n*. Ardent desire, longing. ಲವಲವಿಸು. To desire ardently.

ಲವುಡಿ. = ಲವಡಿ, *q. v*. 2, an iron club.

ಲಶುನ s. *n*. Garlic.

ಲಷ್ಕರು h. *n*. An army; a cantonment. 2, a lascar.

ಲಸಿತ s. *a*. Shining, glittering; skilful, clever. -ವಚನ. A clever word. ಲಸಿತ. Played, sported; come to light; skilled.

ಲಹರಿ 1. s. *n*. A large wave, billow; a waving line.

ಲಹರಿ 2. h. *n*. Intoxication.

ಲಳಿ s. *n*. Liveliness; enthusiasm, animation, cheerfulness; dexterity.

ಲಳಿಗೆ. = ನಳಿಗೆ, *q. v*.

ಲಳ್ಳಿ (= ನಳ್ಳಿ, *q. v*.) k. *n*. A crab.

ಲಾಕ್ಷ, ಲಾಕ್ಷೆ s. *n*. Lac, sealing wax.

ಲಾಕ್ಷಣಿಕ (*fr*. ಲಕ್ಷಣ) s. *a*. Distinguished, characteristic; technical. *n*. A distinguished teacher.

ಲಾಖಿ h. *a*. Red, crimson.

ಲಾಗ f. *n*. A summerset. -ಹಾಕು, -ಹೊಡೆ. To make a summerset, to tumble.

ಲಾಗವತು, ಲಾಗವಾಡು f. *n*. Expense, cost.

ಲಾಗಾಯಿತು h. *n*. Beginning, commencement. *a*. From the beginning.

ಲಾಗು (= ಲಾಗ) f. *n*. A leap, jump; a summerset. 2, excess. 3, catch, hold; an aim.

ಲಾಘವ (*fr*. ಲಘು) s. *n*. Quickness, swiftness; lightness, levity; dexterity, ease; littleness; delicacy; slight.

ಲಾಂಗಲ s. n. A plough. 2, the palm tree.

ಲಾಂಗೂಲ s. n. A tail.

ಲಾಚಾರು h. a. Helpless, poor. -ತನ, ಲಾಚಾರಿ. Helplessness.

ಲಾಜ, ಲಾಜೆ s. n. Parched grain.

ಲಾಂಛನ s. n. A mark, sign; a stain, stigma. ಲಾಂಛಿತ. Furnished with; marked, characterised.

ಲಾಟ s. a. Old, worn, spoiled. n. N. of a people. 2, repetition of words in the same sense.

ಲಾಟನು e. n. A lantern.

ಲಾಟು e. n. A lot.

ಲಾಡಿ f. n. A cord. 2, a strap. 3, a tape.

ಲಾಡು. = ಲಡ್ಡು 2, q. v.

ಲಾತು. = ಲತ್ತೆ, q. v.

ಲಾಂದರ. = ಲಾಟನು, q. v.

ಲಾಭ s. n. Gain, advantage, profit; emolument. -ನಷ್ಟ. Profit and loss. ಲಾಭಿಸು. To gain, to profit.

ಲಾಮಚ, ಲಾಮಂಚ (tb. of ಲಾಮಜ್ಜ) n. The cuscus-grass, *Andropogon muricatus*.

ಲಾಯ (fr. ಲಯ) s. n. A stable.

ಲಾಯಖ್ h. a. Fit, proper; merited, qualified; excellent. ನಾ-. Unfit, *etc.*

ಲಾಲನ, ಲಾಲನೆ s. n. Caressing, fondling, dandling. ಲಾಲಿತ. Caressed, fondled, *etc.* ಲಾಲಿಸು. To caress, fondle; to listen kindly, accept favourably; to attend to.

ಲಾಲಸ s. n. Longing, ardent desire. a. Ardently desirous.

ಲಾಲಾ, ಲಾಲಾಜಲ s. n. Saliva, spittle.

ಲಾಲಿ k. n. A lullaby sung to children. -ಹಾಡು. To sing lullaby.

ಲಾಳೆ. = ಲಾಲಾ, q. v.

ಲಾವ s. n. Cutting; plucking. 2, a sort of quail. -ಕ್ಕಿ. The red spur-fowl.

ಲಾವಕ s. n. A reaper. 2, a snake-catcher and exhibiter. 3, a quail. -ತನ. Tale-bearing.

ಲಾವಂಚ. = ಲಾಮಚ, q. v.

ಲಾವಣಿ f. n. A list of soldiers or public servants.

ಲಾವಣಿ f. n. A ballad. 2, a collection, throng.

ಲಾವಣ್ಯ (fr. ಲವಣ) s. n. Saltness. 2, beauty, loveliness, charm. -ವಂತ. A handsome man; f. -ವಂತಳು, -ವತಿ, -ವಂತೆ.

ಲಾವಿಗೆ, ಲಾವುಗೆ. = ಲಾವಕ, q. v.

ಲಾಳ (tb. of ನಾಲ) n. A tube; a stalk. 2, a kind of reed used for pens. 3, (= ನಾಲ 1) a horse shoe.

ಲಾಳಿ (=ನಾಳಿ, *etc.*) f. n. A weaver's shuttle.

ಲಿಖಿತ s. a. Written, drawn. n. Writing, a document or composition. ಲಿಖಿಸು. To write.

ಲಿಗಾಡು f. n. A trouble, perplexity. 2, compensation for damages.

ಲಿಂಗ s. n. A mark, sign, emblem; a characteristic. 2, a proof, evidence. 3, Śiva, *as* worshipped. 4, an idol. 5, gender (*g.*). -ತೊಂಡೆಬಳ್ಳಿ. A climbing herb, *Bryonia laciniosa*. -ಪ್ಪ. N.; f. -ವ್ವ. -ತ್ರಯ. The three genders (*g.*). -ಧಾರಕ, -ವಂತ, -ಧಾರಿ. A Liṅgavanta. -ಧರಿಸು, -ಕಟ್ಟಿಕೊಳ್ಳು. To put on the liṅga. ಗುರು-. A spiritual guide. -ಜಂಗಮ. A mendicant Liṅgâita priest. ಲಿಂಗಾಯತ, ಲಿಂಗಾಯಿತ.=ಲಿಂಗಧಾರಕ, q. v. ಲಿಂಗಾನುಶಾಸನ. The rules of grammatical gender. ಲಿಂಗಿ. An ascetic; a Liṅgavanta.

ಲಿಪಿ s. n. Smearing; painting, drawing, writing. 2, written characters, the letters. 3, a writing, document, letter. -ಕ, -ಕಾರ. A writer, scribe. ಲಿಪ್ತ. Smeared; stained; poisoned.

ಲಿಫಾಫೆ h. n. An envelope, cover.

ಲಿಂಬೆ (tb. of ನಿಂಬೆ) n. The acid lime, *etc.*

ಲೀನ s. a. Clung to, attached to; resting on, entered into. 2, dissolved, melted; absorbed; united with. 3, vanished. -ತೆ. The state of being hidden, absorbed, united, *etc.*

ಲೀಲಾವತಿ s. n. A beautiful woman. 2, N. of a treatise.

ಲೀಲೆ, ಲೀಲಾ s. n. Play, sport, amusement, pastime. 2, wanton sport. 3, sportive appearance, sham, child's play. 4, air, mien. 5, grace, beauty. 6, a story about a deity's sports. *Cpds.*: ಕೃಷ್ಣ-, ದೇವರ-, ಶಿವ-, ಬಾಲ-, *etc.*

ಲುಕಸಾನು, ಲುಕ್ಸಾನು h. n. Loss; damage. -ಆಗು, -ಬೀಳು. To suffer damage or loss.

ಲುಂಗಿ h. n. A cloth tied by males round the loins.

ಲುಚ್ಚಾ f. n. Dissolute, mean, base, low. -ಗಿರಿ, -ತನ. Dissoluteness, meanness. -ಮನುಷ್ಯ. A base fellow.

ಲುಟಾಯಿಸು f. v. t. To plunder, pillage.

ಲುಪ್ತ s. a. Broken; deprived of; omitted; elided; obsolete.

ಲುಬ್ಧ s. a. Desiring; covetous, greedy. -ಕ. A miser; the sixth nakshatra. -ತ್ವ. Avariciousness.

ಲುಳಿ a. tb. n. Agility, briskness, quick motion.

ಲೂಟಿ f. n. Robbing; booty, spoil. 2, misbehaviour, mischief. -ಗಾರ. A mischievous fellow.

ಲೂತಿ, ಲೂತೆ s. n. A cutaneous disease.

ಲೆಕ್ಕ (tb. of ಲೇಖಾ) n. Reckoning, numbering, calculation; arithmetic; a sum; an account; a number. 2, estimation, regard. -ಇಡು. To keep account. -ಕೊಡು. To give an account. -ಮಾಡು. To count, reckon up. -ನೋಡು, -ಸರಿನೋಡು. To examine an account. ಲೆಕ್ಕಾಚಾರ (= ಲೆಕ್ಕ). Accounts, transaction. ಲೆಕ್ಕಿಸು. To count, reckon up; to esteem, regard.

ಲೆಕ್ಕಣಿ, ಲೆಕ್ಕಣಿಗೆ. tb. of ಲೇಖನಿ, q. v.

ಲೆತ್ತ. = ನೆತ್ತ, q. v. -ಪಗಡೆ. Lĕtta and pagaḍĕ.

ಲೇಖ s. n. A writing, writ, letter, document, *etc.* -ಕ. A writer, copyist; a clerk. -ನ. Writing, copying. -ವಾಹಕ. A letter-carrier. ಲೇಖಾಮುಂಡಲಿಕ. An accountant general. -ನಿ, -ನಿಕೆ (= ಲೆಕ್ಕಣಿ). A reed-pen, pen. ಲೇಖಿಸು. To write.

ಲೇಖೆ (= ರೇಖೆ, q. v.) s. n. A scratch. 2, a writ.

ಲೇಡಿ e. n. A lady.

ಲೇಣಾ, ಲೇಣಿ h. n. Borrowing. ಲೇಣಿದಾರ. A borrower. -ದೇಣಿ. Borrowing and lending.

ಲೇಪ, ಲೇಪನ s. n. Besmearing, daubing. 2, salve; plaster, mortar, chunam, white-wash, *etc.* ಲೇಪಿಸು. To smear, besmear, anoint, *etc.*

ಲೇಪು f. n. A mattress, bed.

ಲೇವಡಿ h. n. Derision, mockery.

ಲೇವಾ. = ಲೇಣಾ, q. v. -ದೇವಿ. Borrowing and lending.

ಲೇವ್ಯ f. n. A Levite, one of the tribe of Levi (*Jewism*).

ಲೇಶ s. n. A particle, atom, bit, small quantity; smallness. -ಮಾತ್ರ. Only a little.

ಲೇಸು k. n. Goodness, excellence; well-being, welfare; pleasantness; beauty; propriety, fitness; reality.

ಲೇಹ s. n. Licking, tasting, sipping. 2, a lambative, linctus. -ನ. Licking. ಲೇಹ್ಯ. A lambative, emulsion.

ಲೈಲಾಮ್ h. n. Auction. -ಗಾರ, -ದಾರ. Auctioneer.

ಲೈಸೆನ್ಸ್ e. n. License, permission.

ಲೊಚಗುಟ್ಟು k. v. i. To lap, *as* dogs, *etc.*; to smack in tasting.

ಲೊಟಕಲೆ, ಲೊಟಗರೆ k. n. Gabbling, jabbering. v. t. To gabble, jabber.

ಲೊಟಕು k. v. t. To scold.

ಲೊಟ್ಟೆ k. n. A smack with the tongue. 2, emptiness, hollowness. 3, a lie, fib. -ಹೊಡೆ. To smack the tongue; to lie.

ಲೊಡ್ಡು. = ಲಡ್ಡು, q. v.

ಲೊಡಳೆ, ಲೊಡ್ಲೆ k. n. Saliva.

ಲೊಲ್ಲೊಟ್ಟೆ k. n. Nothing.

ಲೋಕ s. n. The wide world, sky; the world; any place, region, country. 2, mankind, folk, man, people. 3, common life or practice. 4, sight, regard. -ಕರ್ತ. The Creator of the world. -ತ್ರಯ. The three worlds: heaven, earth, and lower regions. -ದವ. An inhabitant of the world; a worldling. -ನಾಥ. Lord of lords; a king. -ನೇತ್ರ. The sun, moon. ಪರ-, ಸ್ವರ್ಗ-. Heaven, the place of the ransomed souls. ಇಹ-, ಈ-. This world. *Cpds.:* -ನಡತೆ, -ಪದ್ಧತಿ, -ಪಾಲ, -ಪ್ರಸಿದ್ಧಿ, -ರಕ್ಷಕ, -ರೀತಿ, -ರೂಢಿ, -ಮರ್ಯಾದೆ, -ವಾದ, -ವಿರುದ್ಧ, -ವ್ಯವಹಾರ, ಲೋಕಾಚಾರ. -ನ. Seeing, viewing. ಲೋಕಾಂತರ. Another world; a future life. ಲೋಕಾಲೋಕ. The visible and invisible world. ಲೋಕೋಪಕಾರ. A public charity.

ಲೋಚನ s. n. The eye. -ಗೋಚರ. Perceptible.

ಲೋಟಾ h. n. An earthen pot.

ಲೋಟು f. n. Pushing, disturbance, annoyance.

ಲೋಡು f. n. A long bolster to recline upon.

ಲೋಪ s. n. Cutting off; deprivation, want; ellipsis. 2, omission, dropping or falling out; annulling; elision (*g.*), *as:* ಅಕ್ಷರ-, ಪದ-, ಪ್ರತ್ಯಯ-, ವಿಭಕ್ತಿ-, ವಾಕ್ಯ-. The dropping of—, *etc.* ಲೋಪಿಸು. To omit, drop, elide.

ಲೋಬಾನ h. n. Frankincense, olibanum.

ಲೋಭ s. n. Eager desire, cupidity, avarice, greed; *also* -ತ್ವ. 2, affection, favour. ಲೋಭಿ. Greedy, covetous, avaricious; a greedy, *etc.* person. -ತನ, -ತ್ವ. Greediness, stinginess.

ಲೋಮ s. n. The hair of the body. -ಶ. Hairy. -ಹರ್ಷ, -ಹರ್ಷಣ. The bristling of the hair, horripilation.

ಲೋಲಿ. = ಲೋಳೆ, *q. v.*

ಲೋಲ s. a. Moving hither and thither, shaking; agitated, alarmed; unsteady, restless; changeable, fickle. 2, longing for. *n.* Joy. -ತೆ. Fickleness; cupidity. ಲೋಲುಪ. Very eager, greedy after, covetous. ಲೋಲಾಪ್ತಿ, ಲೋಲುಪತೆ, ಲೋಲುಪತ್ವ, ಲೋಲುಪ್ತಿ. Eager desire; greediness, desire, lust.

ಲೋವೆ k. n. A sloping fixture to a flat roof.

ಲೋಷ್ಟ s. n. A lump, clod; *also* -ಕ.

ಲೋಹ s. n. Any metal; iron; copper. 2, a weapon. 3, aloe wood. -ಕಾಂತ. A loadstone, magnet. -ಕಾರ. A blacksmith. -ಕಿಟ್ಟ. Rust of iron. -ದ್ರುತಿ. Steel drops. -ಭಸ್ಮ. Calcined metal. -ಮಂಡೂರ. Manganese. -ಮಾರ್ಗ. A railway. ಲೋಹಾಭಿಸಾರ, ಲೋಹಾಭಿಹಾರ. Lustration of arms.

ಲೋಹಿತ s. a. Red. *n.* The colour red.. 2, blood. 3, copper. 4, anger. 5, an axe. -ಕ. A ruby. -ಚಂದನ, Saffron.

ಲೋಳಿ, ಲೋಳು k. n. Mucilage, mucus. albumen, gelatine; *also* ಲೋಳೆ. -ಸರ. The aloe, *Aloe litoralis* or *perfoliata.*

ಲೋಳೆ k. n. Saliva; tenacious mucus, phlegm.

ಲೌಕಿಕ (*fr.* ಲೋಕ) s. a. Worldly, mundane; popular, general; vulgar, common; secular, not sacred. *n.* A man of the world; a secular business. -ವ್ಯಾಪಾರ. Common practice.

ಲೌಕೀಕ. *tb. of* ಲೌಕಿಕ, *q. v.* -ಕೆಲಸ. A secular business.

ಲಾಭ್ಯ (*fr.* ಲೋಭ) s. n. Cupidity, avarice.

ವ್

ವ್. The forty-eighth letter of the alphabet.

ವ k. *A syllable used to form the pres. or fut. rel. part. and future tense, as:* ಮಾಡುವ, ಹೇಳುವ, ಇಡುವ, *etc.* ಮಾಡುವನು, ಇಡುವನು, ಕೊಡುವನು, *etc.*

ವಂಶ s. n. A bamboo. 2, a flute. 3, the spine. 4, a lineage, race, family; a dynasty. 5, an assemblage. 6, the Sal tree, *Shorea robusta.* -ಜ. Belonging to the family of. -ನಾಶಕ, ವಂಶಾಂತಕ. The last of a family, or race. -ಪರಂಪರೆ. Lineage, descent; progeny. -ವೃಕ್ಷ. Genealogical tree. -ಸ್ಥ. One of a (good) family. ವಂಶಾವಳಿ. The line of a family, genealogy, pedigree. ವಂಶೋದ್ಧಾರಕ. A deliverer or preserver of a family.

ವಕಾರ s. n. The letter ವ.

ವಕಾಲತ್ತು h. n. The duties of a Vakil. -ನಾಮೆ. A power of attorney.

ವಕೀಲ h. n. A lawyer, pleader; an envoy.

ವಕುಲ, ವಕುಳ (= ಬಕುಳ) s. n. The tree *Mimusops elengi.*

ವಕ್ಕಣೆ (*tb. of* ವ್ಯಾಖ್ಯಾನ) n. Comment; statement. 2, the address to a letter or petition. ಚಮತ್ಕಾರದ-. A subtle style. ವಕ್ಕಣಿಸು. To explain, state.

ವಕ್ತವ್ಯ s. a. Proper to be said; blamable; accountable, responsible; dependent, subject. n. A precept, sentence; speaking, censure.

ವಕ್ತಾರ (*tb. of* ವಕ್ತೃ) n. A speaker; an orator. a. Eloquent, loquacious.

ವಕ್ತ್ರ s. n. The mouth; the face.

ವಕ್ರ s. a. Crooked, winding, curved, bent, curly; retrograde. 2, cunning, dishonest; evasive, ambiguous. 3, cruel. -ಗತಿ. Crooked course. -ತೆ, -ತ್ವ. Crookedness, meander; retrograde motion. -ನಾಸಿಕ. An owl. -ಬುದ್ಧಿ. A crooked mind. -ಭಾವ. Crookedness; cunning. -ರೇಖೆ. A curved line. ವಕ್ರೋಕ್ತಿ. Indirect speech, evasive reply; insinuation; sarcasm.

ವಕ್ಷ (*tb. of* ವಕ್ಷಸ್) n. The breast; *also* -ಸ್ಥಳ.

ವಗೈರೆ h. *prep. Et caetera,* and the rest.

ವಗ್ರಹ, ವಗ್ರಾಹ (*tb. of* ಅವಗ್ರಾಹ) n. Drought.

ವಂಕ. *tb. of* ವಕ್ರ, *q. v.* ವಂಕಿ. A kind of curved armlet; a hook.

ವಂಕುಡಿ k. n. A dagger.

ವಂಗ s. n. Bengal proper; its inhabitant. 2, tin. 3, lead. -ಭಸ್ಮ. Calx of tin.

ವಂಗಡ a. k. n. An assemblage, multitude.

ವಚನ s. n. Speaking. 2, a speech, word, expression, utterance, sentence; a promise. 3, a text, aphorism, rule. 4, grammatical number (*g.*). -ಕೊಡು. To promise. -ಕಡೆಗಾಣಿಸು, -ನೆರವೇರಿಸು. To fulfil a promise. -ತ್ರಯ. The three numbers (*g.*): singular, dual, and plural. -ದೋಷ. A slip of the tongue. -ಭ್ರಷ್ಟ. One who has broken his promise. -ಸ್ಥ. A trustworthy man. ವಚನೀಯ. Fit or proper to be spoken. ವಚನೀಯತೆ. Rumour, report, scandal.

ವಜೆ. = ಬಜೆ, *q. v.*

ವಜನು h. n. Weight. -ದಾರ. Weighty; influential; an influential man. ವಜನಿ. Of weight.

ವಜಾ h. n. Subtracted. n. Subtraction; deduction; removal. -ಮಾಡು. To subtract, *etc.* -ವಟ್ಟು. Making up and settling of accounts.

ವಜೀರ h. n. A vizier, prime minister.

ವಜ್ರ s. a. Adamantine, hard; severe. n. A thunderbolt; a discus. 2, a diamond. 3, a strong glue. -ಕಾಯ, -ದೇಹ. One who has a very robust and hardy body. -ಗಾರೆ. A durable plaster. -ಜ್ವಾಲೆ. Lightning. -ಪಾಣಿ. Indra. -ಮುಷ್ಟಿ. A hard fist; a weapon of the athlete. -ತುಂಟ. A stupid man.

ವಂಚಕ s. a. Deceitful, crafty. n. A deceiver, rogue, cheat. -ತ್ವ. Fraud. ವಂಚನ, ವಂಚನೆ. Cheating, tricking, defrauding; fraud, deceit; illusion. ವಂಚಿಸು. To deceive, cheat.

ವಟ s. n. The banyan or Indian fig-tree, *Ficus indica*. 2, (= ಬಡೆ) a kind of fried cake; *also* -ಕ.

ವಟಾರ (= ಬಟಾರ) f. n. The compound round a house. 2, a lodge, room.

ವಟು s. n. A boy, lad. 2, a Brahmachâri, a religious student.

ವಟ್ಟ (= ಬಟ್ಟ, q. v.) h. n. Discount: a deduction made by money-changers or money-lenders in their own favour.

ವಡಬಾಗ್ನಿ, ವಡವಾಗ್ನಿ s. n. Submarine fire; *also* ವಡಬಾಗ್ನಿ, ವಡವಾನಲ, ವಡವಾಮುಖ.

ವಡವೆ. = ಒಡವೆ, q. v.

ವಡಿ k. n. Heat.

ವಡಿಗ k. *An affix of nouns to intimate a person's trade or employment, as:* ಹೂ-. A florist.

ವಡೆ (tb. of ವಟ) n. A fried cake made of pulse.

ವಣಿಗ k. *An affix of masc. nouns to express fondness or habit, as:* ಲಂಚ-. A person fond of bribes. ಮಾತು-. A talkative person. ವಣಿಗೆ, *neut.*, *as* ಮರ-, ಬೆಳೆ-, *etc.*

ವಣಿಜ s. n. A merchant, trader. 2, trade, merchandise.

ವತನ h. n. A hereditary estate. -ದಾರ. Its holder.

ವತಿ (= ವಂತೆ) s. *fem. affix.* She who possesses. n. Asking, begging.

ವತ್ಸ s. n. A calf; a child, boy; a son; f. ವತ್ಸೆ. 2, a year (= -ರ). -ಕ. A little calf; the medicinal plant, *Wrightia antidysenterica*.

ವತ್ಸನಾಭಿ s. n. A strong poison taken from aconite.

ವತ್ಸರ s. n. A year.

ವತ್ಸಲ s. a. Affectionate, kind, loving; fond of. -ತೆ, -ತ್ವ. Affection, tenderness.

ವದ s. n. Speaking. 2, speaking well or sensibly. ವದಾನ್ಯ. Eloquent; affable; liberal. ವದಾವದ. Talkative; eloquent.

ವದನ s. n. Speaking. 2, the mouth, face.

ವಧ. = ವಧೆ, q. v.

ವಧು, ವಧೂ s. n. A bride, young wife. ವಧೂವರ. Bride and bridegroom.

ವಧೆ s. n. Slaughter, murder. ವಧಿಸು. To kill, slay.

ವನ (= ಬನ) s. n. A wood, forest; a garden. 2, a residence. -ಗಜ. A wild elephant. -ಚರ. Living in a forest. -ದೇವತೆ. A sylvan deity. -ಧಿ, -ನಿಧಿ. The ocean. -ಪಶು. A wild beast. -ಪಾಲ, -ಪಾಲಕ. A gardener. -ಪ್ರಿಯ. The cuckoo. -ಪ್ರಸ್ಥ (cf. ವಾನಪ್ರಸ್ಥ). Retiring into a forest, living as an anchorite. -ಮಲ್ಲಿಕೆ. Wild jasmine. -ವಾಸ. Living in a wood. -ವಾಸಿ, -ಸ್ಥ. A hermit, ascetic. ವನಸ್ಪತಿ. A large tree bearing fruit but apparently having no blossoms; any tree; vegetable kingdom. ವನಾಂತರ. The interior of a forest; a forest.

ವನಾಶ್ರಯ s. n. Living in a forest.

ವನಿತೆ s. n. A wife. 2, a woman in general.

ವಂತ. tb. of ವತ್. *An affix used to form masc. derivatives, as:* ಬುದ್ಧಿ-, ಧನ-, ಧರ್ಮ-; f. ವಂತೆ, ವಂತಳು.

ವಂತಿ (= ಬಂತು, q. v.) k. n. A turn, time.

ವಂತಿಗೆ s. n. A public subscription. -ಎತ್ತು, -ಹಾಕು. To subscribe.

ವಂತೆ (tb. of ವತಿ) Fem. affix. of ವಂತ, q. v.

ವಂದನ, ವಂದನೆ s. n. Soliciting. 2, praising. 3, obeisance, reverence, worship, adoration. 4, a festoon. -ಗೆಯ್ಯು. To reverence, salute respectfully.

ವಂದಿ s. n. A praiser, bard. ವಂದಿತ. Praised, extolled. -ಸು. To praise, eulogise; to show honour; to worship. ವಂದ್ಯ. Laudable, praiseworthy; adorable.

ವಂದಿ. = ಬಂದಿ, q. v.

ವಪನ s. n. Sowing seed. 2, shaving.

ವಪುಸ್ s. n. A form, figure; body.

ವಪೆ s. n. A hollow. 2, fat, marrow.

ವಪ್ರ s. n. A sown field. 2, a rampart, mudwall, mound; a bank; a ditch.

ವಮನ s. n. Vomiting. 2, an emetic.

ವಯ, ವಯಸು, ವಯಸ್ಸು (tb. of ವಯಸ್) n. Youth, prime of life. 2, age, time of life. ವಯೋಽಧಿಕ. An old man. ವಯೋಽವೃದ್ಧ. Advanced in age.

ವಯಿನ (tb. of ವಚನ) n. A way, means.

ವಯ್ಯಾರ (tb. of ವಿಹಾರ. = ಒಯ್ಯಾರ, q. v.) n. Parade, showiness, dandyism, coquetry; also ವಯ್ಯಾರಿ. A showy person.

ವಯ್ಯಾಳಿ (tb. of ವಾಹ್ಯಾಳಿ) n. An excursion on horseback, ride; a procession of idols carried by people.

ವಯ್ವಾಟ f. n. Administration; despatch; business; use; practice; also ವಹಿವಾಟು.

ವರ s. n. Choice, election. 2, a boon, blessing, favour; talent; a gift; a reward. 3, a dowry. 4, charity. 5, a lover, bridegroom; a husband. a. Desirable; valuable, best, most excellent. -ಕವಿ. A gifted poet. -ದಕ್ಷಿಣೆ. A present made to the bridegroom on account of the bride. -ಪ್ರಸಾದ. An eminent favour. -ಸಾಮ್ಯ. Likeness (in form) of the bride to the bridegroom. -ಕೇಳು. To entreat a favour. -ಕೊಡು. To confer a boon.

ವರಕು h. n. A thin plate of metal, tinsel.

ವರಂಡ s. n. A veranda, portico. 2, (e.) warrant, right authority to do a certain act.

ವರದಿ (tb. of ವಾರ್ತಾ; cf. ವರ್ತಮಾನ) n. Tidings, report, intelligence. -ಕೊಡು. To report.

ವರಸೆ (= ವರಿಸೆ) k. n. A line, row; lineage, race, family.

ವರಹ, ವರಹಾ (tb. of ವರಾಹ) n. A boar. 2, a gold coin with a boar-stamp, a pagoda. -ಕಟ್ಟು, -ಕೂರ್ಚ. A brush, made of a hog's bristles.

ವರಾಟ s. n. A cowry, *Cypraea moneta* (used as a coin, $\frac{1}{80}$ of a paṇa).

ವರಾಡ f. n. A public subscription; tax. -ಎತ್ತು, -ಹಾಕಿಕೊಳ್ಳು. To make a subscription.

ವರಾತ, ವರಾತು h. n. Urging for payment.

ವರಿ 1. (fr. ವರ) s. n. Tax, cess; levy. -ಎತ್ತು, -ತೆಗೆ. To raise taxes. -ಕೊಡು, -ತೆರು. To pay taxes.

ವರಿ 2. (= ವರೆ) k. n. Limit. -ಗೆ. Up to, till, until; as far as. ಈ-. Up to this.

ವರಿಸು s. v. t. To choose, espouse, elect, desire, claim; also ವರಯಿಸು.

ವರಿಸೆ. = ವರಸೆ, q. v.

ವರುಣ s. n. N. of the god of heavens and waters. 2, the regent of the western quarter.

ವರುಷ. tb. of ವರ್ಷ, q. v. -ವರುಷ, ವರುಷಾನು-. rep. Every year, for years.

ವರೂಥ s. n. Protection; armour; shield. 2, a multitude, assemblage, army. 3, a chariot.

ವರೆ (= ವರಿ) f. n. Limit, boundary. prep. Until, as far as. -ಗೆ. Until, as far as, up to.

ವರ್ಗ s. n. A division, class, tribe, society, family. 2, any classified group of words or consonants; heading, category. 3, a section, chapter. 4, a sphere, province. 5, a school-class. 6, the square of a number. 7, transfer, *as* of officers, *etc.* 8, a ledger. -ಪ್ರಾಸ. A kind of alliteration. -ಮೂ

ಲ. Square root. ವರ್ಗಾಕ್ಷರ. A classified consonant. ವರ್ಗೀಯ. Belonging to a class of consonants.

ವರ್ಚಸ್ s. n. Vigour. 2, lustre, brilliancy. 3, form, figure, shape. ವರ್ಚಸ್ವಿ. Full of lustre.

ವರ್ಜ, -ನ s. n. Excluding, avoiding, leaving; exclusion. 2, hurting, injury. ವರ್ಜನೀಯ, ವರ್ಜ್ಯ. Avoidable; improper. ವರ್ಜಿತ. Excluded, avoided. ವರ್ಜಿಸು. To avoid, leave, abandon, *etc.*

ವರ್ಣ s. n. Exterior, form, figure. 2, colour, hue, dye, paint; lustre. 3, dress. 4, gold. 5, a sort, kind, class, race, tribe, caste. 6, a letter of the alphabet. 7, property, quality. 8, a musical mode. -ಕ. A mask; colour; a syllable; a bard; a poetical diction. -ನ, -ನೆ. Description, explanation, pointing out qualities; praise, panegyric. -ನೆ ಮಾಡು. To describe, *etc.* -ಮಾಲೆ. The alphabet. -ಸಂಕರ. A mixture of castes. ವರ್ಣಾಶ್ರಮ. Caste and order. ವರ್ಣಾಶ್ರಮಧರ್ಮ. Their duties. ವರ್ಣಿಸು. To depict, delineate, write, describe; to praise.

ವರ್ತಕ s. n. A trader, merchant. -ತನ. Traffic, trade. -ಮಾಡು. To trade.

ವರ್ತನ, ವರ್ತನೆ s. n. Moving about. 2, proceeding, conduct; practice, employment, use. 3, abiding; living. 4, living on; livelihood, subsistance; earnings, wages. 5, occupation, profession; commerce. 6, appointment.

ವರ್ತಮಾನ s. a. Present, existing. n. The present tense. 2, news, tidings, notice. -ಕಾಲ. The present time, present tense; *also* -ಕ್ರಿಯೆ. -ಪತ್ರ. A newspaper.

ವರ್ತಿ s. n. Moving, going; behaving, acting. 2, the wick of a lamp; *also* -ಕೆ. 3, a swelling, rupture. -ಸು. To move, go; to conduct one's self; to take place, occur; to enter upon; to stay; abide.

ವರ್ತುಲ s. a. Round, circular. n. A circle. 2, a kind of pulse, pea.

ವರ್ಧ s. n. Increasing, augmenting. -ಕ. Increasing, strengthening; cutting. -ಕಿ. A carpenter. -ನ. Increasing, growing; increase, growth; prosperity; success; strengthening; a restorative; cutting. -ನಿ. A broom, brush. ವರ್ಧಂತಿ. (= ಬಡ್ಡಂತಿ, q. v.) A birthday, nativity. -ಮಾನ. Increasing, growing, thriving; prosperous; the castor-oil plant; Burdwan. ವರ್ಧಿತ. Grown, *etc.* ವರ್ಧಿಸು. To increase, grow, thrive.

ವರ್ಮ s. n. A coat of mail. 2, a bulwark, shelter, defence. 3, = ಮರ್ಮ.

ವರ್ಯ s. a. Eligible; eminent, best.

ವರ್ವರ. = ಬರ್ಬರ, q. v.

ವರ್ಷ (= ಬರುಷ, ವರುಷ, *etc.*, q. v.) s. n. Rain. 2, a year. -ಕಾಲ, -ಋತು. The rainy season. -ಗಂತಿ. (A cow, *etc.*) calving yearly. -ಣ. Raining. -ಧಾರೆ. A stream of rain. ವರ್ಷಾವಧಿ. Yearly. ವರ್ಷಾಋತು, ವರ್ಷಾಕಾಲ. = -ಕಾಲ. ವರ್ಷಾಂತರ. Another year; some years. ವರ್ಷಾಶನ. Annual allowance.

ವಲಯ s. n. A bracelet, armlet; a girdle, zone. 2, a circle, boundary; enclosure.

ವಲಸೆ (= ಬಲಸೆ, q. v.) k. n. Flight, emigration. -ತೆಗೆ. (People) to leave a village *en masse*.

ವಲೀಕ s. n. The eaves of a roof.

ವಲ್ಕಲ s. n. A garment made of bark.

ವಲ್ಮೀಕ s. n. An ant-hill. 2, swelling.

ವಲ್ಲಭ s. n. A lover, husband, friend; f. ವಲ್ಲಭೆ. A wife, beloved female.

ವಶ s. n. Subdued, tamed. n. Power, control, charge, custody, subjection, submission. -ಆಗು. To become subject to. -ಮಾಡು, ವಶೀಕರಿಸು. To subdue. ವಶಂವದ. Submissive, compliant. ವಶೀಕರಣ. Subjugating, enchanting.

ವಶ್ಯ. Controllable, subdued; docile, humble, tame; a decoy.

ವಸಡಿ, ವಸಡು (=ಒಸಡು, q. v.) k. n. The gums.

ವಸತಿ s. n. Dwelling; a dwelling place, house, abode. 2, comfort, commodity, convenience.

ವಸನ s. n. Clothing, clothes, dress. 2, a dwelling, residence.

ವಸಂತ s. n. Spring. 2, a kind of râga. 3, (=ಓಕುಳಿ) saffron water. -ಕಾಲ, -ಋತು. The vernal season. -ದೂತ. The cuckoo. -ದೂತಿ, -ದೂತಿಕೆ. The creeper *Gaertnera racemosa*. -ಮಂಟಪ. A shed erected for recreation during the hot season. ವಸಂತೋತ್ಸವ. A festive occasion on which vasanta (ôkaḷi) is sprinkled.

ವಸಲೀನು e. n. Vasaline.

ವಸಾರೆ h. n. A veranda. 2, a perfume.

ವಸಿಷ್ಠ s. n. N. of a ṛishi.

ವಸಿಸು s. v. i. To dwell, live, abide.

ವಸೀಲು h. n. Support, patronage. -ದಾರ. A patron.

ವಸು s. a. Good; wealthy; chief. n. Excellence. 2, light; fire, agni. 3, wealth; a gem, *etc.* 4, N. of a deity. -ಕಾಂತಿ. The moon-plant *Asclepias acida*. -ಧೆ, -ಮತಿ. The earth.

ವಸೂಲು h. n. Collection; revenue; *also* ವಸೂಲಾತಿ. -ಮಾಡು. To collect, *as* revenue, *etc.* -ಬಾಕಿ. A balance of revenue due.

ವಸೆ s. n. The marrow of the flesh.

ವಸ್ತಾದ h. n. A teacher of wrestling, dancing, *etc.*

ವಸ್ತಿ s. n. Abiding, staying; an abode; the people, population. 2, the abdomen. 3, the ends or skirt of a cloth.

ವಸ್ತು s. n. A real substance. 2, object; a thing in general; an article, substance, wealth, goods. 3, essential property. -ಕ. Real, faithful. ವಸ್ತ್ಯ. An abode, house.

ವಸ್ತ್ರ s. n. Cloth, clothes, garment, dress; a cloth. -ಗಾಯು. Sifting through a cloth. -ಗಲಿತ, -ಗಾಲಿತ. Strained through a cloth. -ದಾನ. A gift of clothes. -ಹೀನ. Destitute of or without clothes.

ವಹ, ವಹನ s. n. Bearing, carrying, conveying. 2, any vehicle or means of conveyance. 3, a road, way. 4, a raft.

ವಹವಾ. = ವಾಹವಾ, q. v.

ವಹಿ f. n. A stitched book. -ಕ. A bearer.

ವಹಿಲ s. n. Quickness, agility. *ad.* Quickly.

ವಹಿವಾಟು. = ವಯ್ವಾಟ, q. v.

ವಹಿಸು s. v. t. To bear, sustain; to carry; to appropriate to one's self; to proceed; to become current.

ವಹ್ನಿ s. n. Fire. 2, lead-wort, *Plumbago zeylanica.*

ವಳ k. *An affix of nouns implying profession: e. g.* ತೋಟ-. A gardener. ಮಡಿ-. A washerman. ಅಡು-. A cook.

ವಳಿ 1. k. *An affix for forming neuter nouns: e. g.* ನಡ-, ಸಲು-, ಹುಟ್ಟು-, *etc.*

ವಳಿ 2. s. n. A wave; a wrinkle.

ವಳಿತ s. n. A circle, district, dependency.

ವಳ್ತಿ k. *Fem. form of* ವಳ.

ವಾ *conj.* s. Or.

ವಾಃ. = ವಾಹವಾ, q. v.

ವಾಕರಿ. = ಓಕರಿ, *etc.*, q. v.

ವಾಕ್. = ವಾಕ್ಕು, ವಾಚ್. -ಕಲಹ. Quarrel, dispute. -ಚಾತುರ್ಯ. Cleverness of speech. -ಚಾಪಲ್ಯ. Rattle, gabble. -ಪಟುತ್ವ. Eloquence. -ಪರಿಣತ, -ಪ್ರೌಢ. Proficient in speech or language. -ಪೌರುಷ. Power in using big words.

ವಾಕಿ f. n. A wrist ornament.

ವಾಕ್ಕು (*tb. of* ವಾಕ್) n. Speech; language. 2, Sarasvatî.

ವಾಕ್ಯ s. n. Speech, saying; a word. 2, a sentence; 3, a rule, precept. -ಖಂಡ. Syntax. -ದೋಷ. Faulty poetical composition. -ಮಾಲೆ. A sentence. ವಾಕ್ಯಾನ್ವಯ. The connection of words in a sentence. ವಾಕ್ಯಾರ್ಥ. The meaning of a sentence; a lecture. ವಾಕ್ಯಾಲಂಕಾರ. An expletive.

ವಾಗ್. = ವಾಕ್, *q. v.* ವಾಗಾಡಂಬರ. A vain display of words. ವಾಗೀಶ. A master of language; an eloquent man. ವಾಗೀಶ್ವರ. Brahmâ. ವಾಗೀಶ್ವರಿ. Sarasvatî. ವಾಗ್ಜಾಲ. Prate, gabble; eloquence. ವಾಗ್ದತ್ತ, ವಾಗ್ದಾನ. A promise. ವಾಗ್ದೇವತೆ, ವಾಗ್ದೇವಿ. Sarasvatî, muse. ವಾಗ್ಧೋರಣೆ. Good style of composition. ವಾಗ್ಬಲ. The power of speech. ವಾಗ್ವಾದ. Quarrel, dispute. ವಾಙ್ಮಾಧುರ್ಯ. Sweetness of speech. ವಾಙ್ಮೂಲ. Deposition.

ವಾಗ್ಮಿ s. *a.* Loquacious, talkative, eloquent. *n.* An eloquent man.

ವಾಚ್ (= ವಾಕ್, ವಾಗ್) s. *n.* Speech; language; discourse; a word. 2, Sarasvatî. ವಾಚಕ. Reading; declaratory; verbal; a speaker, reader. ವಾಚಕಶಕ್ತಿ. Reading power. ವಾಚಾಟ, ವಾಚಾಲ. Talkative, loquacious; wrangle.

ವಾಚಿ s. *a.* Speaking, uttering; a word, an attribute. 2, a speaker, minister. -ಕ. Verbal, oral; news, tidings. -ಸು. To speak, say, *etc.*

ವಾಚ್ಯ s. *a.* To be spoken; blamable, censurable. 2, attributive, declinable. *n.* A predicate (*g.*). 2, the voice of a verb (*g.*). ವಾಚ್ಯಾವಾಚ್ಯ. Proper and improper to be said.

ವಾಜ s. *n.* Strength, energy. 2, speed. 3, vegetable food. 4, ghee.

ವಾಜಿ s. *a.* Strong, powerful; swift. *n.* A horse. -ತರ. A mule. -ನಿ. A mare.

ವಾಜಿಬಿ, ವಾಜಿಮಿ h. *a.* Fit, proper, right.

ವಾಂಛೆ s. *n.* Wish, desire. ವಾಂಛಿತ. Wished, desired, longed for. ವಾಂಛಿಸು. To wish, desire.

ವಾಟ 1. = ಓಟ, *q. v.*

ವಾಟ 2. k. *n.* A slope, incline.

ವಾಟ 3. s. *n.* An enclosure; a court-yard; a compound, garden. 2, a road, way. 3, course, procedure.

ವಾಡಬ, ವಾಡವ s. *n.* Submarine fire. 2, the lower regions. ವಾಡಬಾನಲ, ವಾಡವಾಗ್ನಿ, ವಾಡವಾನಲ. The fire of the lower regions.

ವಾಡಿಕೆ k. *n.* Usage, custom, practice.

ವಾಡೆ. = ಒಡೆ, *q. v.*

ವಾಣಿ s. *n.* Sound, speech; voice. 2, Sarasvatî. 3, a Banyan. 4, an oilman. 5, weaving; a weaver's loom. -ಜ. A merchant, Banyan. -ಜ್ಯ, -ಜತನ. Traffic, trade. -ನಿ. A shrewd or passionate woman.

ವಾತ s. *n.* Wind, air, breeze. 2, rheumatism, gout. -ಗುಲ್ಮ. Acute gout. -ಧಾತು, -ನಾಡಿ. One of the (three) arteries near the wrist. -ರೋಗ. = ವಾತ No. 2. ವಾತಾಶನ, ವಾತಾಹಾರಿ. A serpent; a tiger.

ವಾತ್ಸಲ್ಯ (*fr.* ವತ್ಸಲ) s. *n.* Tender fondness, love. *Cpds.:* ಜಾತಿ-, ಮತ-, ಧನ-, ದೇಶ-.

ವಾದ s. *n.* Talking. 2, sound; playing on a musical instrument. 3, discourse. 4, disputation, debate, dispute; controversy. 5, explanation. 6, a plaint. 7, report. -ವಿವಾದ. Argument and disputation. ವಾದಿ. A disputant; a plaintiff; an expounder. ವಾದಿಪ್ರತಿವಾದಿ. A plaintiff and a defendant. -ಸು. To dispute; to debate.

ವಾದ್ಯ s. *n.* Any musical instrument. -ಬಾರಿಸು. To play upon it.

ವಾನ (*fr.* ವನ) s. *a.* Relating to a forest. -ಪ್ರಸ್ಥ. A Brâhmaṇa of the third order: a hermit, anchorite.

ವಾನರ s. *n.* A monkey.

ವಾಂತಿ s. *n.* Vomiting; an emetic. -ಭೇದಿ, -ಭ್ರಾಂತಿ. Cholera.

ವಾಪಸು h. *ad.* Back, in return.

ವಾಪಿ s. *n.* A sowing machine. 2, a well.

ವಾಮ s. *ad.* Beautiful, pleasing, lovely. *a.* Reverse, adverse, opposite. 2, left, not right. 3, crooked. 4, short.

ವಾಮಾಂಗಿ. A wife (who is the left side of her husband).

ವಾಮನ s. a. Short, dwarfish. n. A dwarf. 2, Vishṇu in his 5th incarnation. -ಪುರಾಣ. A purâṇa about this incarnation. ವಾಮನಾವತಾರ. = ವಾಮನ No. 2.

ವಾಯ (tb. of ವ್ಯಾಜ) n. Deceit, lie; pretext. 2, (s.) wearing; sewing.

ವಾಯನ s. n. Presents of cocoanuts, sweetmeats, etc. offered to a deity by a Brâhmaṇa married woman.

ವಾಯವ್ಯ s. a. Windy. n. The north-west quarter.

ವಾಯಸ s. n. A crow. ವಾಯಸಿ. The plant *Solanum indicum*.

ವಾಯಿದೆ h. n. Period; a term fixed for payment; instalment. -ಚೀಟು. Notice of demand of the assessment to be paid within a given time. -ಗೇಣಿ. Tenancy for a stipulated period.

ವಾಯು s. n. Wind, air; the god of wind. 2, a vital air. 3, flatulence, rheumatism, gout. -ಪಂಚಕ. The set of five vital airs. -ನಂದನ, -ಪುತ್ರ, -ಸುತ. Bhîma; Hanumat. -ವಿಳಂಗ. A plant of which the seed is used as a vermifuge, *Erycibe paniculata*. -ವೇಗ. The velocity of wind. -ಸಖ, -ಸಖಿ. Fire.

ವಾರ 1. k. n. A landlord's half share of the produce of a field as rent. 2, = ಓರ.

ವಾರ 2. s. n. A turn, time. 2, a day of the week; a recurring day for furnishing a meal to poor males. 3, a moment, occasion. -ದನ್ನ. Food obtained by poor males in rotation. -ಶೂಲೆ. Unpropitious day for a journey, etc. ಶ್ರೀ-. Good-Friday.

ವಾರಗಿತ್ತಿ. = ಓರಗಿತ್ತಿ, q. v.

ವಾರಣ s. n. Warding off, keeping off; removing; protecting; resisting; opposition. 2, armour. 3, an elephant. 4, an embankment. -ಮಾಡು. To ward off, remove, as fear.

ವಾರಣಾಸಿ, ವಾರಾಣಸಿ s. n. The town Benares.

ವಾರವಾಣ s. n. A bodice; a quilted jacket; armour.

ವಾರಸು h. n. Heritage; the proprietorship of it; claim, title. -ದಾರ. An inheritor, heir. -ಪತ್ರ. An assignment. ಬೇ-. Ownerless, unclaimed.

ವಾರಿ 1. f. prep. By; according to; for; also ವಾರು.

ವಾರಿ 2. s. n. Water. -ಚರ. Aquatic. -ಜ. A lotus. -ಜರಿಪು, -ಜವೈರಿ. The moon. -ಜಭವ, -ಜಾಸನ. Brahmâ. -ಜಾಕ್ಷ. Vishṇu. -ಧಿ. The ocean. -ಧಿಕನ್ಯೆ. Lakshmî. -ವಾಹ. A cloud.

ವಾರಿಸು 1. s. v. t. To ward off, keep back, stop, remove.

ವಾರಿಸು 2. = ವಾರಸು, q. v.

ವಾರು. = ವಾರಿ 1, q. v.

ವಾರುಣ (fr. ವರುಣ) s. a. Of Varuṇa. ವಾರುಣಿ. The west.

ವಾರೆ (= ಓರೆ, q. v.) k. n. Declivity, sloping.

ವಾರ್ತ s. n. Welfare. 2, chaff. 3, (= ವಾರ್ತೆ) news. ವಾರ್ತಿಕ. A reporter, teacher; a critical gloss.

ವಾರ್ತೆ s. n. Livelihood; profession. 2, tidings, rumour, news, intelligence. 3, knowledge. 4, meanness. *Cpds.*: ಮನೆ-, ಮಿಶನ್-, ಶಾಲೆ-.

ವಾರ್ಧಕ (fr. ವೃದ್ಧಿ) s. n. Increase. 2, old age; also ವಾರ್ಧಕ್ಯ. -ಷಟ್ಪದಿ. N. of a metre.

ವಾರ್ಯ s. a. To be warded off. 2, eligible, desirable.

ವಾರ್ಷಿಕ (fr. ವರ್ಷ) s. a. Annual.

ವಾಲ s. n. Hair. 2, tail. 3, the cuscus-grass. -ಖಿಲ್ಯ. A certain divine personage.

ವಾಲಕ s. n. A bracelet. 2, a finger-ring. 3, the cuscus-grass. 4, a tail.

ವಾಲಗ (= ಓಲಗ, q. v. tb. of ವಾಲಕ) n. Service, etc. 2, a hautboy.

ವಾಲಿ s. n. N. of a monkey. -ಜ. Aṅgada.

ವಾಲೀ h. n. A protector, patron; a master.

ವಾಲು (= ಮಾಲು 1) k. v. i. To bend; to slope.

ವಾಲುಕ s. n. Sand, gravel. 2, a species of cucumber. ವಾಲುಕಾಸ್ತಂಭ. A cloud of drifting sand.

ವಾಲೆ. = ಓಲೆ, q. v.

ವಾಲ್ಮೀಕ, ವಾಲ್ಮೀಕಿ s. n. N. of the author of the Râmâyaṇa.

ವಾವಿ, ವಾವೆ (tb. of ಜಾಮಿ) n. Affinity, relationship.

ವಾಶಿ s. n. Singing, crying; a war-cry; voice. 2, an adze.

ವಾಸ s. n. Dwelling; a dwelling-place, habitation; site, abode. 2, (= -ನೆ) scent, trace. 3, dress, clothes; as in ಕಟ್ಟು-, ಪಟ್ಟ-. -ಯೋಗ್ಯ. Fit to reside in. -ಸ್ಥಲ, -ಸ್ಥಾನ. A place of residence.

ವಾಸನೆ s. n. Smell, odour, scent; fragrance, flavour. 2, inclination, desire. -ನೋಡು. To smell. ದುರ್-. A stink. ಸು-. Aroma.

ವಾಸರ 1. = ಓಸರ, q. v.

ವಾಸರ 2. s. n. A day. -ಪತಿ, -ಮಣಿ. The sun.

ವಾಸಿ 1. s. n. An inhabitant. a. Abiding, dwelling; clothed, as: ಗ್ರಾಮ-, ನಗರ-, ವನ-, ಸಹ-.

ವಾಸಿ 2. (tb. of ವಾಟ) n. The state of being so and so much; as: ಅರ-, ಕಾಲು-, ಮುಕ್ಕಾಲು-, etc. 2, an improved state (as of health, etc.), relief, ease; superiority, preference; as in ಕಾಯಿಗ-, ಹೆಸರು-, etc. 3, moderation (in price, etc.), as in ಧಾರಣೆ-. 4, excess, interest, as in ತಲ-.

ವಾಸಿತ s. a. Perfumed, scented.

ವಾಸಿಸು s. v. i. To dwell, reside. 2, to smell, be fragrant, be perfumed. v. t. To smell.

ವಾಸುಕಿ s. n. N. of a serpent.

ವಾಸುದೇವ s. n. N. of Vishṇu or Kṛishṇa.

ವಾಸ್ತವ, ವಾಸ್ತವಿಕ (fr. ವಸ್ತು) s. a. Substantial; real, true; substantiated, demonstrated. ವಾಸ್ತವ್ಯ. Real, true; fit for habitation; an inhabitant.

ವಾಸ್ತು s. n. The site or foundation of a house. 2, a habitation. -ಪುರುಷ. The tutelary deity of a house. -ಶಾಂತಿ. = ಗೃಹಶಾಂತಿ. -ಪೂಜೆ. The ceremony before beginning to build a house.

ವಾಹ s. n. Bearing, conveying, carrying; as in ಪ್ರ-, ವಿ-. 2, a porter, carrier. 3, a vehicle. -ಕ. Bearing, conveying; a porter; a driver; a horseman. -ನ. A vehicle, chariot, carriage.

ವಾಹವಾ h. int. Bravo! capital! excellent!

ವಾಹಿ s. n. Bearing, carrying. -ನಿ. A river; an army. -ನೀಪತಿ. A general. -ಸು. To cause to bear.

ವಾಳ s. n. A tail. 2, a tumour. 3, aff. = ವಳ.

ವಿ s. pref. Apart from, asunder; off; away; various; manifold.

ವಿಂಶತಿ s. a. Twenty.

ವಿಕಟ s. a. Large; formidable, hideous, ugly; horrible; crooked, perverse.

ವಿಕರಾಲ s. a. Very terrible; hideous.

ವಿಕರಿಸು s. v. t. To alter, change (arith.).

ವಿಕಲ s. a. Defective, incomplete. 2, decayed, impaired. 3, confused, confounded. -ತೆ, -ತ್ವ. Confusion, agitation; sorrow.

ವಿಕಲ್ಪ s. n. Alternative, option. 2, uncertainty; indecision, doubt. 3, error. 4, suspicion; an evil thought. ವಿಕಲ್ಪಿಸು. To form differently.

ವಿಕಸನ s. n. Bursting, blossoming, expanding; cf. ವಿಕಾಸ.

ವಿಕಾರ s. n. Change, modification, abnormity. 2, change for the worse, disease. 3, perturbation, passion, excitement. Cpds.: ಧ್ವನಿ-, ನಿದ್ರಾ-, ಮುಖ-, ರೋಮ-, etc. ಮನೋ-, ಬುದ್ಧಿ-. Perversion of understanding. ವಿಕಾರಿ. Changing; an ugly person; the thirty-third year in the cycle of sixty.

ವಿಕಾಶ, ವಿಕಾಸ s. n. Opening, expanding, blowing, budding. 2, expanse, sky. 3, appearance, display, manifestation.

ವಿಕಿರ, ವಿಕೀರಣ s. n. Scattering about (*as* boiled rice at a śrâddha).

ವಿಕೀರ್ಣ s. a. Scattered, dispersed; spread about; filled with; famous.

ವಿಕೃತ s. a. Changed; disfigured, ugly; afflicted; unnatural; estranged; strange. n. Change; a disorder. ವಿಕೃತಿ. Change from a natural or healthy state. 2, the twenty-fourth year in the cycle of sixty.

ವಿಕ್ರಮ s. n. Stepping or going beyond; a step, stride. 2, heroism, prowess. 3, = ವಿಕ್ರಮಾದಿತ್ಯ, q. v. 4, the fourteenth year in the cycle of sixty. -ಶಕ. The era of Vikramâditya. -ಶಾಲಿ. A valorous person. ವಿಕ್ರಮಾದಿತ್ಯ, ವಿಕ್ರಮಾರ್ಕ. N. of a king of Ujjayini.

ವಿಕ್ರಯ s. n. Sale, selling. ವಿಕ್ರಯಿಸು. To sell, vend. ವಿಕ್ರೀತ. Sold. ವಿಕ್ರೇಯ. Saleable.

ವಿಕ್ಷಿಪ್ತ s. a. Thrown away; scattered; bewildered.

ವಿಕ್ಷೇಪ s. n. Throwing away; rejecting; scattering; confusion; a side-glance.

ವಿಖ್ಯಾತ s. a. Renowned, famous, celebrated. ವಿಖ್ಯಾತಿ. Fame, celebrity.

ವಿಖ್ಯಾಪನ s. n. Making known, announcing, publishing; acknowledging, confessing; exposition.

ವಿಗಡ. *tb. of* ವಿಕಟ, q. v.

ವಿಗತ s. a. Gone, departed, disappeared, devoid of, obscured.

ವಿಗಲಿತ, ವಿಗಳಿತ s. a. Flowed away, trickled; dropped, fallen; liquefied.

ವಿಗ್ರಹ s. n. Shape, form; an image, idol. 2, the body. 3, separation, analysis; a division, portion. 4, encounter, conflict, war. ವಿಗ್ರಹಾರಾಧಕ. An idolator. ವಿಗ್ರಹಾರಾಧನೆ. Idol-worship. ವಿಗ್ರಹಿಸು. To oppose. -ಕ್ಕೆ ಪ್ರಾಣಪ್ರತಿಷ್ಠೆ ಮಾಡು. To perform the rite of bringing life into an idol.

ವಿಘಟಿಕೆ s. n. The sixtieth part of a ghaṭikâ.

ವಿಘಾತ, ವಿಘಾತಿ s. n. Destruction; a blow; opposition, prevention, obstacle.

ವಿಘ್ನ s. n. An obstacle, impediment, hindrance, opposition. 2, any trouble. -ರಾಜ, ವಿಘ್ನೇಶ್ವರ. Gaṇêśa.

ವಿಂಗಡ (*tb. of* ವಿಘಟ) n. Separating, disuniting; separation, parting. ವಿಂಗಡಿಸು. To separate; to disunite.

ವಿಚಕ್ಷಣ s. a. Far-sighted, discerning, wise, clever. ವಿಚಕ್ಷಣೆ. A clever woman; cleverness, skill.

ವಿಚಲ s. a. Moving about, unsteady.

ವಿಚಾರ s. n. Deliberation, consideration, examination, trial. 2, discrimination, judgment, decision. 3, subject, topic. 4, doubt; perplexity, anxiety, trouble. -ಕ. An investigator, judge. -ಗೇಡಿ. A fool. -ಗೇಡಿತನ. Foolishness. -ಮಾಡು. To inquire into; to reflect. -ಪರ. Thoughtful, inquisitive. -ವಂತ. A thoughtful or considerate man; *also* ವಿಚಾರಿ. -ಣೆ. Deliberation, examination, investigation; the exercise of judgment. ನ್ಯಾಯ-. The trial of a lawsuit. -ಣೆಯಾಗು, -ಣೆ ನಡೆ. A trial to take place. -ಣೆಕರ್ತ. A judge; a manager, superintendent. -ಣೆ ಮಾಡು, ವಿಚಾರಿಸು. To examine, try, inquire; to ask; to reflect.

ವಿಚಿತ್ರ s. a. Variegated; wonderful, surprising.

ವಿಚ್ಛಿತ್ತಿ s. n. Separating; cutting off; interruption, cessation; destruction, loss; pause in a verse; limit.

ವಿಚ್ಛಿನ್ನ s. a. Cut asunder, severed, divided; broken off; interrupted; violated; destroyed; variegated.

ವಿಚ್ಛೇದ s. n. Separation; cutting off; interruption, termination, disappearance; a section; dissension.

ವಿಜನ s. a. Lonely, solitary.

ವಿಜಯ s. n. Conquest, victory. 2, the twenty-seventh year of the cycle of sixty. -ದಶಮಿ. The tenth day of dasarâ festival. -ನಗರ. N. of a town. -ರಾಘವ. Râma. -ಲಕ್ಷ್ಮಿ, -ಶ್ರೀ.= ಜಯಲಕ್ಷ್ಮಿ.

ವಿಜಾತ s. a. Of a mixed origin; generated; wild, refractory. ವಿಜಾತಿ. A different kind or caste; a low caste. ವಿಜಾತೀಯ. Of a different kind, of mixed origin.

ವಿಜಾಪುರ s. n. N. of a town.

ವಿಜೃಂಭಣ s. n. Gaping; expanding, exhibiting; displaying, budding; pastime, sport; extravagance. ವಿಜೃಂಭಿಸು. To gape; to expand, display, *etc.*

ವಿಜ್ಞಪ್ತಿ. = ವಿಜ್ಞಾಪನೆ, *q. v.*

ವಿಜ್ಞಾನ s. n. Understanding; discerning; intelligence, knowledge, science, learning. ವಿಜ್ಞಾನಿ. Learned, proficient.

ವಿಜ್ಞಾಪನೆ s. n. A petition, solicitation, representation, humble intimation; application. -ಮಾಡು, ವಿಜ್ಞಾಪಿಸು. To request, state respectfully; to represent, submit.

ವಿಟ s. n. A libertine; a rogue, cheat. -ಚೇಷ್ಟೆ, -ತನ, -ತ್ವ. Lewdness.

ವಿಟಂಕ s. n. A dove-cot.

ವಿಟ್ಠಲ, ವಿಠಲ s. n. Vishṇu as worshipped at Paṇḍharapur.

ವಿಡಂಗ. = ವಾಯುವಿಳಂಗ, s. ವಾಯು, *q. v.*

ವಿಡಂಬನ s. n. Imitation, copying, disguise, masquerade; simulation; imposture, deception, fraud. 2, displaying, showing. 3, ridiculing, mocking. 4, vexation.

ವಿಡಾಯ, ವಿಡಾಯಿ s. n. Grand display, pomp.

ವಿಡೂರ, ವಿಡ್ಡೂರ f. n. Enmity, annoyance.

ವಿತಂಡ, ವಿತಂಡೆ s. n. Cavil, frivolous argument; criticism.

ವಿತತ s. a. Broad, wide; expanded; accomplished, celebrated. n. A stringed instrument. ವಿತತಿ. Stretching out; extension; a collection, multitude; a cluster.

ವಿತರಣ s. n. A gift, donation. 2, giving up. 3, liberality.

ವಿತರ್ಕ s. n. Argument, discussion, conjecture; opinion; deliberation; doubt.

ವಿತಲ s. n. The second of the seven lower regions.

ವಿತಾನ s. n. Stretching out, expansion. 2, an awning, canopy.

ವಿತ್ತ s. a. Known. 2, found, gained, acquired. n. Property, wealth. 2, power. -ವಣಿಜ. A shroff. ವಿತ್ತೇಷಣ. Desire of wealth.

ವಿದ s. n. Knowing; a knower.

ವಿದರ್ಭ s. n. N. of a district in Bengal, the modern Berar proper. -ಜೆ. Damayanti; Rukmiṇi.

ವಿದಲ s. a. Split, rent; opened, blown (as a flower). n. Cuttings, chips.

ವಿದಾರಣ s. n. Splitting, rending, killing; war.

ವಿದಾರಿ s. n. Tearing asunder. 2, the plant *Batatas paniculata*. -ಸು. To split, rend.

ವಿದಿಕ್ಕು (*tb. of* ವಿದಿಶ್) n. An intermediate point of the compass.

ವಿದಿತ s. a. Known, understood; informed; represented. n. Knowledge; information; thought.

ವಿದುರ s. a. Knowing, intelligent. n. N. of the younger brother of Dhṛitarâshṭra and Pâṇḍu.

ವಿದುಷ s. n. A wise man; a scholar; *f.* ವಿದುಷಿ.

ವಿದೂರ s. n. Remote; devoid of, without.

ವಿದೂಷಕ s. n. An abuser; a jester, buffoon.

ವಿದೇಶ s. n. Foreign country.

ವಿದೇಹ s. a. Bodiless. n. Mithilâ, Tirhut; its people.

ವಿದ್ದೆ. = ವಿದ್ಯೆ, *q. v.*

ವಿದ್ದ್ಯ. *tb. of* ವಿದ್ಯೆ, *q. v.*

ವಿದ್ಯಮಾನ s. a. Being known, existing; actual, real.

ವಿದ್ಯಾ (= ವಿದ್ಯೆ, q. v.) s. n. Knowledge, etc. -ಗುರು, -ದಾತೃ. A teacher. -ದಾನ. Giving of knowledge, teaching. -ಧನ. Wealth of learning. -ಧರ. Knowledge-holder; a genius; a N.; f. -ಧರಿ. -ಭ್ಯಾಸ. Study. -ಲಯ, -ಶಾಲೆ. A school. -ವಂತ. A learned man; f. -ವಂತಳು, -ವಂತೆ. -ಶಾಲಿ. A learned person. -ಸಾಧನೆ. Acquisition of knowledge. -ಸಾಫಲ್ಯ. Profit of knowledge. -ಹೀನ. Ignorant, uninstructed. -ರ್ಥಿ. A student, pupil, disciple.

ವಿದ್ಯುತ್ s. n. Lightning.

ವಿದ್ಯುಲ್ಲತೆ s. n. Zigzag lightning.

ವಿದ್ಯೆ (= ವಿದ್ಯ, ವಿದ್ಯಾ) s. n. Knowledge, learning, science; an art; magical skill. ದೇವ-. Theology. ಕ್ರಿಸ್ತ-. Christology. ಶಿಲ್ಪ-. Architecture.

ವಿದ್ರಧಿ s. n. An internal abscess.

ವಿದ್ರವ, ವಿದ್ರಾವ s. n. Flight, retreat; panic; liquefaction.

ವಿದ್ವತ್, ವಿದ್ವತ್ವ s. n. Learning, erudition. ವಿದ್ವಜ್ಜನ. A scholar, philosopher. ವಿದ್ವತ್ಸಭೆ, ವಿದ್ವತ್ಸಮೂಹ. An assembly of scholars.

ವಿದ್ವಾನ್. = ವಿದ್ವಾಂಸ, q. v.

ವಿದ್ವಾಂಸ (tb. of ವಿದ್ವಸ್) a. Learned. n. A wise man, scholar.

ವಿದ್ವೇಷ s. n. Enmity, hatred; contempt. ವಿದ್ವೇಷಿ. An enemy.

ವಿಧ s. n. Form, manner, kind, sort; fold. -ವಿಧ. rep. -ವಿಧವಾಗಿ. Variously.

ವಿಧವತೆ s. n. Widowhood. ವಿಧವಾ, ವಿಧವೆ. A widow.

ವಿಧಾನ s. n. Arranging, disposing; arrangement; action. 2, a rule, precept; a law, ordinance; a regulation, sacred text. 3, a rite, ceremony. 4, a form, mode, manner. -ಪೂರ್ವಕ. According to rule.

ವಿಧಾಯಕ s. a. Disposing, arranging. n. A precept. 2, a ruler, leader.

ವಿಧಿ s. n. A rule, formula, precept, injunction; a vedic text. 2, an order, ordinance, statute. 3, a rite, ceremony. 4, a method, manner. 5, fate, destiny. -ಕ್ರಿಯೆ, -ರೂಪ. The imperative (g.). -ಪ್ರಕಾರ. According to rule. -ವತ್. In due form. ವಿಧಿಸು. To prescribe, order, ordain, appoint, allot.

ವಿಧುರ s. a. Separated. 2, agitated, troubled; adverse. n. Separation; adversity. 2, a widower.

ವಿಧೃತ s. a. Kept apart. 2, seized, held; taken, assumed.

ವಿಧೆ. = ವಿಧ, q. v.

ವಿಧೇಯ s. a. Arrangeable; governable; submissive, obedient. -ತೆ, -ತ್ವ. Obedience, docility.

ವಿಧ್ಯರ್ಥ s. n. The imperative (g.).

ವಿಧ್ವಂಸ s. n. Ruin, destruction. 2, aversion, enmity. 3, insult, offence.

ವಿನತ, ವಿನಮಿತ s. a. Bowed down; humble, modest. ವಿನತಿ. Bowing down; humility, modesty.

ವಿನಮತ್ s. a. Bending down, bowing. ವಿನಮಿಸು. To make obeisance. ವಿನಮ್ರ. Humble, modest.

ವಿನಯ s. n. Leading, guidance; gentlemanlike bearing, good behaviour; condescension, humility; reverence, courtesy. ಠಕ್ಕು-, ನಕ್ಕ-. Pretended modesty. -ವಾಗಿ ನಡೆ. To behave modestly. -ಪೂರ್ವಕ. With reverence, etc. ವಿನಯಿತ. A well-behaved man.

ವಿನಹ, ವಿನಹಾ (tb. of ವಿನಾ) ad. Without, except.

ವಿನಾಡಿ s. n. A period of twenty-four seconds.

ವಿನಾಯಕ s. n. Gaṇêśa. 2, a leader. a. Anarchical.

ವಿನಾಯಿತಿ h. n. Exemption, as from passing an examination. ವಿನಾಯಿಸು. To except, exempt. v. i. To be exempted.

ವಿನಾಶ, ವಿನಾಶನ s. n. Perdition, ruin, destruction, extinction.

ವಿನಿಮಯ s. n. Exchange, barter. 2, deposit, security.

ವಿನಿಯೋಗ s. n. Unyoking. 2, assignment, distribution (as of eatables). 3, application, use, employment. 4, a business. ವಿನಿಯೋಗಿಸು. To assign; to use.

ವಿನೀತ s. a. Well-trained, educated, well-behaved; modest, gentle; lovely, handsome. ವಿನೀತಿ. Good behaviour.

ವಿನುತಿ s. n. Praise. ವಿನುತ, ವಿನೂತ. Praised.

ವಿನೋದ s. n. Diversion, sport, play. 2, interesting pursuit, pleasure. 3, jesting, joking. -ಗಾರ. A playful man; one fond of jesting. ವಿನೋದಿಸು. To play, sport; to be delighted.

ವಿಂಧ್ಯ, ವಿಂಧ್ಯಾಚಲ, ವಿಂಧ್ಯಾದ್ರಿ s. n. N. of a mountain range.

ವಿನ್ಯಾಸ s. n. Depositing; a deposit; arranging, distributing; disposition; a receptacle. 2, gesticulation.

ವಿಪಕ್ಷ s. n. An opponent, adversary, enemy; a rival. 2, a syllogism.

ವಿಪತ್ಕಾಲ s. n. Adversity.

ವಿಪತ್ತಿ, ವಿಪತ್ತು (tb. of ವಿಪದ್) n. Adversity, calamity, misfortune, disaster.

ವಿಪರೀತ s. a. Reversed, adverse, contrary; uncommon, unusual; different; disagreeable. -ಕೆಲಸ. An unusual act. -ಕಾಲ. An adverse time.

ವಿಪರ್ಯಯ, ವಿಪರ್ಯಾಯ s. n. Reverse, contrariety; perverseness; opposition; misfortune; exchange, barter; error, mistake; also ವಿಪರ್ಯಾಸ.

ವಿಪಲ s. n. A moment, instant.

ವಿಪಾಕ s. n. Cooking; ripening, maturity; result; calamity, distress.

ವಿಪಿನ s. n. A wood, forest, grove.

ವಿಪುಲ s. a. Large, great, broad, wide; spacious; ample; profound.

ವಿಪ್ಪತ್ತು. = ವಿಪತ್ತಿ, q. v.

ವಿಪ್ರ s. n. A poet. 2, a Brâhmaṇa.

ವಿಪ್ರತಿಷಿದ್ಧ s. a. Contradicted; prohibited.

ವಿಪ್ರತಿಸಾರ s. n. Repentance.

ವಿಪ್ರಯೋಗ s. n. Disjunction, separation.

ವಿಪ್ರಲಬ್ಧ s. a. Cheated; hurt; afflicted.

ವಿಪ್ರಲಾಪ s. n. Prattling; wrangling, quarrel.

ವಿಫಲ s. a. Fruitless, useless.

ವಿಬುಧ s. n. A learned or wise man.

ವಿಬೋಧ s. n. Awaking; intelligence; wisdom. 2, absence of mind.

ವಿಭಕ್ತ s. a. Divided. 2, parted separated. -ಕುಟುಂಬ. A divided family. ಸಹೋದರರು. Divided brothers.

ವಿಭಕ್ತಿ s. n. A division, partition. 2, a portion, part. 3, inflection of the cases of a noun or pronoun. -ಮಾಲೆ. A table of inflection of cases.

ವಿಭಜನ s. n. Division (arith.), separation, partition. ವಿಭಜಿಸು. To divide (arith.).

ವಿಭವ s. n. Display; greatness, glory, dignity; power; wealth; magnanimity. 2, the second year in the cycle of sixty.

ವಿಭಾಗ s. n. Division, separation; partition, part, share; distribution. -ಪತ್ರ, -ಸಾಧನ. A deed of partition. ವಿಭಾಗಿಸು. To divide, distribute. ವಿಭಾಜ್ಯ. Divisible, portionable.

ವಿಭಾವ s. n. Discrimination, judgment. 2, a friend. -ನ. Clear perception, discrimination.

ವಿಭಾಷೆ s. n. A foreign language. 2, an alternative, option.

ವಿಭಾಸೆ s. n. Light, lustre.

ವಿಭೀತ, -ಕ s. a. Fearless. n. The tree *Terminalia bellerica*.

ವಿಭೀಷಣ s. a. Terrifying, formidable. n. N. of Râvaṇa's younger brother.

ವಿಭು s. a. Omnipresent; excellent, eminent, supreme. n. A master, lord, ruler. -ತ್ವ. Might, power; ownership.

ವಿಭೂತಿ s. n. Great power; might, dominion; dignity; great success, prosperity, welfare; glory. 2, the ashes.

-ಧರಿಸು, -ಹಚ್ಚು. To put ashes on the forehead.

ವಿಭೂಷಣ s. n. Decoration; an ornament. ವಿಭೂಷಿತ. Adorned, decorated.

ವಿಭೇದ s. n. Breaking asunder, separating; a variety, kind. ವಿಭೇದಿಸು. To divide, pierce; to become different; to alter.

ವಿಭ್ರಮ, -ಣ s. n. Roaming about; error, doubt, apprehension; hurry, confusion, bewilderment, flurry. ವಿಭ್ರಮಿಸು. To be confused, bewildered.

ವಿಭ್ರಾಂತಿ s. n. Confusion, bewilderment; hurry, flurry.

ವಿಮತ s. a. Disagreed; dissenting. n. A different religion. -ಸ್ಥ. A man of a different religion.

ವಿಮನಸ್ s. a. Displeased; sad, heartbroken; perplexed. -ಕ. Sad, melancholy.

ವಿಮಯ (ವಿಮೇಯ) s. n. Exchange, barter.

ವಿಮರ್ದ s. n. Grinding, pounding; trituration; also -ನ.

ವಿಮರ್ಶ, ವಿಮರ್ಶೆ s. n. Investigation, inquiry.

ವಿಮಲ s. a. Stainless, spotless, pure. -ತ್ವ. Stainlessness, purity. -ಮತಿ. Pure-minded.

ವಿಮಾತೃ s. n. A step-mother. -ಜ. Her son.

ವಿಮಾನ s. n. A measure. 2, a chariot of the gods going through the skies; a baloon.

ವಿಮುಕ್ತ s. a. Let loose, liberated. ವಿಮುಕ್ತಿ. Liberation, release; final emancipation.

ವಿಮುಖ s. a. Averted; turned away from; disinclined.

ವಿಮೆ h. n. Insurance. -ಕೂಟ. I. company. -ಪತ್ರ. I. policy.

ವಿಮೋಕ್ಷ s. n. Liberation, release; final emancipation.

ವಿಮೋಚನ, ವಿಮೋಚನೆ s. n. Liberating; escape, liberation, release; salvation. ಋಣ-. Paying off debts. ಪಾಪ-. Forgiveness of sin (through Christ). ವಿಮೋಚಿಸು. To liberate, set free; to save.

ವಿಯೋಗ s. n. Separation, disunion; loss, death. Cpds.: ಪಿತೃ-, ಮಾತೃ-, ಭಾರ್ಯಾ-, etc.

ವಿರಕ್ತ s. a. Disaffected, indifferent. 2, free from passion or affection. n. One who is free from worldly affections or passions. ವಿರಕ್ತಿ. Absence of affections or passions, indifference, apathy. ವಿರಕ್ತಿ ಪಡು, -ಬರು, -ಹುಟ್ಟು. To be indifferent.

ವಿರಚನೆ s. n. Arrangement; compiling; contrivance; composition. ವಿರಚಿಸು. To arrange, construct, compile, etc.

ವಿರಂಚಿ, ವಿರಿಂಚಿ s. n. Brahmâ.

ವಿರತ s. a. Stopped, ceased, rested. ವಿರತಿ. Cessation, end; indifference.

ವಿರಲ s. a. Thin, delicate; loose; wide, apart; rare, scarce; remote. -ತೆ, -ತ್ವ. Rareness, etc.

ವಿರಸ s. a. Juiceless, sapless, tasteless, insipid; unenergetic. -ಮಾಡು. To offend. -ಹುಟ್ಟು. To become offended.

ವಿರಹ s. n. Separation; loneliness; want of; abandonment, cessation. -ಅಗ್ನಿ, -ಜ್ವರ, -ತಾಪ, -ವೇದನೆ. Ardour of love in separated lovers.

ವಿರಹಿತ s. a. Absent from, bereft of, deserted, devoid of, destitute of, free from, without.

ವಿರಳ. = ವಿರಲ, q. v.

ವಿರಾಗ s. n. Passionlessness.

ವಿರಾಜ s. n. Shining; splendour, beauty. -ಮಾನ. Shining, splendid, handsome. ವಿರಾಜಿಸು. To shine, be brilliant, etc.

ವಿರಾಟ, -ಪುರುಷ s. n. The first progeny of Brahmâ; also ವಿರಾಟ್ಪುರುಷ.

ವಿರಾಮ s. n. Cessation, rest; stoppage, pause. 2, end, conclusion. -ಚಿಹ್ನೆ. A sign of pause.

ವಿರುದ್ಧ s. a. Opposed, hindered, obstructed; contrary, opposite; reverse; hostile, adverse; disagreeable; prohibited. *n.* Opposition, hostility. ವಿರುದ್ಧಾರ್ಥ. Contrary meaning.

ವಿರೂಪ s. *a.* Deformed, misshapen, ugly, monstrous. *n.* Deformity; *also* -ತೆ. ವಿರೂಪಾಕ್ಷ. Śiva.

ವಿರೇಕ, ವಿರೇಚನ s. *n.* Purging of the bowels. 2, a purgative.

ವಿರೋಚನ s. *n.* Shining. 2, the sun; the moon; the fire. 3, Bali's father.

ವಿರೋಧ s. *n.* Opposition, obstruction, hindrance; restraint; contradiction, contrariety, contrast; inconsistency; hostility, enmity. ಮತ-. Opposed to a religious sect. ಶಾಸ್ತ್ರ-. Opposed to scripture. ವಿರೋಧಿ. An enemy, opponent; the twenty-third year of the cycle of sixty. ವಿರೋಧಿಕೃತ್. The forty-fifth year of the cycle. ವಿರೋಧಿಸು. To oppose, hinder, obstruct; to hate. *v. i.* To be opposed.

ವಿಲಕ್ಷಣ s. *a.* Other, different; extraordinary, strange, odd, novel. *n.* Oddness, strangeness.

ವಿಲಂಬ s. *a.* Hanging down; pendulous. *n.* Slowness, delay; *also* -ನ.

ವಿಲಂಬಿ s. *a.* Depending; pendulous; slow. *n.* The thirty-second year of the cycle of sixty. -ಸು. To hang down; to protract.

ವಿಲಯ s. *n.* Dissolution; destruction.

ವಿಲಸತ್ s. *a.* Flashing, shining, brilliant, splendid. ವಿಲಸಿತ. Shining; sportive; a gleam, flash; sport.

ವಿಲಾಪ s. *n.* Lamentation, crying, weeping.

ವಿಲಾಯಿತಿ h. *n.* Europe; a foreign country. *a.* Foreign, European.

ವಿಲಾಸ s. *n.* A label, address on a letter; *also* ಮೇಲ್ವಿಲಾಸ. 2, sport, pastime, amusement; coquetry. 3, grace, elegance, charm. -ವಾಸ. A pleasure-house. ವಿಲಾಸಿ. Sportive, playful; a sensualist. ವಿಲಾಸಿನಿ. A coquettish woman.

ವಿಲೆ h. *n.* A class, head, order, arrangement. -ವಾರಿ. Assorting; classifying; distribution; settlement. - - ಮಾಡು. To order.

ವಿಲೇಪನ s. *n.* Besmearing, anointing. ವಿಲೇಪಿತ. Smeared over. ವಿಲೇಪಿಸು. To smear over, *etc.*

ವಿಲೋಚನ s. *n.* The eye.

ವಿಲೋಭನ s. *a.* Beguiling; allurement, attraction, temptation. ವಿಲೋಭಿಸು. To allure, tempt.

ವಿಲೋಮ s. *a.* Reverse, contrary, opposite. *n.* Reverse order.

ವಿಲೋಲ s. *a.* Shaking, tremulous, fickle, unsteady. *n.* Tremor; rolling. -ತೆ. Tremulousness.

ವಿವಕ್ಷೆ s. *n.* Meaning, sense; intention, purpose, wish. ವಿವಕ್ಷಿಸು. To wish to say; to intend.

ವಿವರ s. *n.* Expansion; specification, detailed account, particulars. 2, an interval; a breach. -ಣೆ. Explanation, exposition, interpretation; description, detail. -ಪತ್ರಿಕೆ. A statement of particulars. ವಿವರಿಸು. To explain, interpret; to detail, specify.

ವಿವರ್ಜಿಸು s. *v. t.* To leave, abandon.

ವಿವರ್ಣ s. *a.* Colourless; pale, pallid; ignorant.

ವಿವರ್ಧನ s. *n.* Increase, growth.

ವಿವಾದ s. *n.* A dispute, quarrel, controversy, debate, contest, contention.

ವಿವಾಹ s. *n.* Marriage, matrimony. -ಮಾಡಿಕೊಳ್ಳು. To marry. -ವಾಗು. To become married. -ಮಾಡಿಕೊಡು. To give away in marriage. ಪುನರ್-. Widow-marriag.

ವಿವಿಧ s. *a.* Diverse, manifold, various.

ವಿವೇಕ s. *n.* Discrimination, discernment, judgment; *also* -ತೆ. 2, true knowledge. 3, discretion. 4, discussion, investigation. ವಿವೇಕಿ. Discriminating, prudent; a discriminator. ವಿವೇಕಿಸು. To discriminate, decide.

ವಿವೇಚನೆ s. *n.* Discriminating. *n.* Investigation.

ವಿಶಂಕೆ s. *n.* Suspicion, doubt, fear.

ವಿಶದ s. *a.* Clear, pure, bright; white; evident, obvious. -ತ್ವ. Clearness. ವಿಶದೀಕರಿಸು. To clear, explain.

ವಿಶಾಖೆ s. n. The sixteenth lunar asterism.

ವಿಶಾರದ s. a. Skilled in, conversant with. 2, confident, bold.

ವಿಶಾಲ s. a. Large, wide, broad, extensive. -ತೆ. Expansion, magnitude.

ವಿಶಿಷ್ಟ s. a. Distinguished; endowed with; superior, excellent. 2, without a rest, all.

ವಿಶುದ್ಧ s. a. Clean; pure; pious; rectified, accurate. ವಿಶುದ್ಧಿ. Purity; rectitude.

ವಿಶೇಷ s. n. Discrimination. 2, difference, distinction, speciality, peculiarity; particularity. 3, a defining word (*g.*). 4, a sort, variety, species, kind, *etc.* 5, peculiar merit. *a.* Extraordinary, singular, much, more. -ಧೂಪ. Resin of *Boswellia thurifera*. -ಕ. Distinguishing, characteristic; an attribute, predicate. -ಣ. Distinguishing, discriminative; distinction; discrimination; an attribute, adjective (*g.*). -ವಾಗಿ. Especially. ವಿಶೇಷಿಸು. To distinguish; to particularise, specify. ವಿಶೇಷ್ಯ. Distinguished; a noun; the subject of a predicate (*g.*); *also* -ಪದ.

ವಿಶ್ರಮ, -ಣ s. n. Rest, repose; pause, stop; *also* ವಿಶ್ರಾಮ. ವಿಶ್ರಮಿಸು. To rest, repose.

ವಿಶ್ರಾಂತ s. a. Rested, reposed; calm, composed.

ವಿಶ್ರಾಂತಿ s. n. Rest, repose. -ಆರಿಸಿಕೊಳ್ಳು, -ಗೊಳ್ಳು, -ತೀರಿಸು. To take rest. -ದಿವಸ. The Sabbath-day.

ವಿಶ್ರುತ s. a. Renowned, famous.

ವಿಶ್ವ s. a. All, every; much, many. *n.* The universe, world. -ಕರ್ತ. The creator. -ಕರ್ಮ. The architect of the gods; a minister. -ದಾತ. The giver of all. -ನಾಥ, -ಪತಿ, ವಿಶ್ವೇಶ್ವರ. Śiva; a N. ವಿಶ್ವಂಭರ. Supporting the universe; Vishṇu. -ರೂಪ. Universal, omnipresent. ವಿಶ್ವಾತ್ಮ. The universal soul.

ವಿಶ್ವಸನ (= ವಿಶ್ವಾಸ) s. n. Trusting, confiding. ವಿಶ್ವಸನೀಯ. Trustworthy. ವಿಶ್ವಸಿಸು. = ವಿಶ್ವಾಸಿಸು, *q. v.*

ವಿಶ್ವಾಮಿತ್ರ s. n. N. of a Kshatriya who became a Brâhmaṇa.

ವಿಶ್ವಾವಸು s. n. N. of one of the gandharvas. 2, the thirty-ninth year in the cycle of sixty.

ವಿಶ್ವಾಸ s. n. Trust, confidence, faith, reliance; hope; affection, love. 2, a secret. ಕ್ರೈಸ್ತರ-. The faith of Christians. -ಪ್ರಮಾಣ. The creed. -ಬೋಧನ. Dogmatics. -ಇಡು. To believe, place confidence in. -ಘಾತ, -ಘಾತಕ. Breach of trust. -ಘಾತಕ. A traitor; *f.* -ಘಾತಕಿ. -ತನ. Trustworthiness. ವಿಶ್ವಾಸಿ. Trusting, confiding; trustworthy, honest; a trustworthy person. ಅವಿಶ್ವಾಸಿ. An unbeliever. ವಿಶ್ವಾಸಿಸು. To trust, believe, confide in; to love.

ವಿಷ s. n. Poison, venom; anything bitter; bitterness. 2, intoxication. -ಇಕ್ಕು. To administer poison. -ಇಳಿಸು. To dispel poison. -ಏರು. Poison to take effect. -ಕಾರಕ. Poisonous. -ಜತ. An ichneumon. -ಪ. Elephantiasis. -ಪುಚ್ಛ. A scorpion. -ಬ್ರಧ್ನ. A cloud; a forest; a snake. -ಭಿಷಜ್, -ವೈದ್ಯ. A poison-doctor. -ಹರ. Antidotal.

ವಿಷಮ s. a. Uneven, rough. 2, unequal, irregular. 3, odd. 4, different. 5, coarse, cross. 6, disagreeable, troublesome. 7, unusual. 8, adverse. *n.* Unevenness, *etc.* -ಜ್ವರ, -ಶೀತಜ್ವರ. An unremittent fever. -ಬುದ್ಧಿ. A crooked mind. -ಸಂಖ್ಯೆ. An odd number. ವಿಷಮಿಸು. To become abnormal, *as* a fever.

ವಿಷಯ s. n. An object or organ of sense; any thing perceptible by the senses. 2, an affair, business. 3, concern, respect, regard, reference; subject, subject-matter. 4, a region; field, sphere; scope, range, reach. ವಿಷಯಾಂತರ. A different topic. ವಿಷಯಿ. A man of the world; a materialist. -ದಲ್ಲಿ, -ವಾಗಿ, -ಕ್ಕೆ. Respecting, concerning, about. -ಲಂಪಟ. Addicted to worldly objects.

ವಿಷಾದ s. n. Dejection, despondency, lassitude; sadness; fear.

ವಿಷು s. a. Various, manifold. n. The fifteenth year in the cycle of sixty. 2, = ವಿಷುವ, q. v.

ವಿಷುವ, -ತ್ s. n. The equinox.

ವಿಷೂಚಿ s. n. A kind of spasmodic cholera.

ವಿಷ್ಣು s. n. The second deity of the Hindu triad. -ಕ್ರಾಂತಿ. A small creeping herb, *Evolvulus alsinoides*. -ಪದ. The sky. -ಪದಿ. The Ganges. -ರಥ, -ವಾಹನ. Garuḍa.

ವಿಸಂವಾದ s. n. False assertion; deception; disagreement.

ವಿಸಂಧಿ s. n. Absence of euphony.

ವಿಸರ್ಗ s. n. Emission; dismissal, getting rid of; separation; the aspirate marked by two dots (ಃ).

ವಿಸರ್ಜನೆ s. n. Sending forth, letting go; relinquishing; abandoning, getting rid of; voiding; donation, gift. ವಿಸರ್ಜಿಸು. To get rid of, reject, relinquish.

ವಿಸರ್ಪ s. n. Erysipelas; a kind of itch; elephantiasis. -ಣ. Spreading, itching.

ವಿಸೃಷ್ಟ s. a. Let go; emanated, created.

ವಿಸ್ತರ, ವಿಸ್ತಾರ s. n. Spreading; extension, diffuseness; prolixity; minute detail. 2, vastness, expanse. 3, a layer; a seat. 4, abundance. ವಿಸ್ತರಿಸು, ವಿಸ್ತಾರಿಸು. To spread out, extend, amplify, detail.

ವಿಸ್ತೀರ್ಣ s. a. Spread about; expanded; broad; large, vast; roomy, wide. n. Extent; area.

ವಿಸ್ಮಯ s. n. Wonder, surprise, amazement. -ಗೊಳ್ಳು, -ಪಡು, ವಿಸ್ಮಯಿಸು. To be astonished, surprised, *etc.* ವಿಸ್ಮಿತ. Surprised, astonished, perplexed.

ವಿಸ್ಮರಣ s. n. Forgetting, oblivion. ವಿಸ್ಮೃತಿ. Forgetfulness, oblivion, unmindfulness.

ವಿಸ್ರಾವ s. n. Floating forth, trickling.

ವಿಹರಣ s. n. Going about. 2, pastime, pleasure.

ವಿಹಾರ s. n. Walking for pleasure, taking an airing, roaming. 2, sporting, pastime, pleasure. 3, a Buddhist or Jaina temple. 4, a pleasure-garden. ವಿಹರಿಸು, ವಿಹಾರಿಸು. To take away; to ramble, roam; to sport, play.

ವಿಹಿತ s. a. Regulated, settled; suitable, fit, proper.

ವಿಹೀನ s. a. Destitute; devoid of, free from, without. *Cpds.*: ಕುಲ-, ಗತಿ-, ನೀತಿ-, ರಸ-, *etc.* -ತೆ, -ತ್ವ. Being wholly free from.

ವಿಹ್ವಲ s. a. Agitated, alarmed, confused; distressed.

ವಿಳಂಗ. = ವಿಡಂಗ, q. v.

ವೀಕ್ಷೆ s. n. Looking at, sight. ವೀಕ್ಷಿಸು. To see, behold, observe.

ವೀಜ. = ಬೀಜ, q. v. 2, a king's attendant.

ವೀಜನ s. n. Fanning; a fan.

ವೀಟ. = ವೀಳೆ, *etc.*, q. v.

ವೀಣೆ s. n. The Indian lute. -ಗಾರ. A lutanist.

ವೀತ s. a. Gone, accepted, liked; quiet, tame. 2, set free, exempted. -ರಾಗ. Free from passions; calm. -ಶೋಕ. Free from sorrow.

ವೀಥಿ (= ಬೀದಿ, q. v.) s. n. A row, line. 2, a road, street.

ವೀರ s. a. Heroic, mighty, robust. n. A hero, warrior, champion; prowess; valour. -ಕಂಕಣ. A warrior's wrist ornament. -ಕೆಲಸ, -ಗೆಲಸ. A heroic act. -ತನ, -ತ್ವ. Heroism, prowess. -ಭದ್ರ. N. of a great hero. -ರಾಘವ. Râmachandra; N. -ಲಕ್ಷ್ಮಿ, -ಶ್ರೀ. The glory of valour. -ವೈಷ್ಣವ. A follower of Râmânuja. -ಸೇನ. N. of Nala's father. -ಶೈವ. A Lingavanta. ವೀರಾಸನ. Kneeling on one knee.

ವೀರಣೆ k. n. A double drum used at weddings, *etc.* 2, (s.) a fragrant grass.

ವೀರ್ಯ s. n. Vigour, strength, energy. 2, heroism, prowess, courage. -ವಂತ, -ಶಾಲಿ. A vigorous man.

ವೀಸ k. n. A sixteenth, $\frac{1}{16}$ of a haṇa. -ಬಡ್ಡಿ. Interest at one-sixteenth.

ವೀಳೆ, ವೀಳೆಯ, ವೀಳ್ಯ, ವೀಳ್ಯೆ (*tb. of* ವೀಟಿ, *q. v.*) n. The betel plant, *Piper betel;* the leaf of *Piper betel.*

ವು, ವೂ. *For Kannaḍa words with these initials see s.* ಉ, ಊ.

ವೃಕ s. n. A wolf. 2, a jackal. ವೃಕೋದರ. Bhīma.

ವೃಕ್ಷ s. n. A tree; a shrub. -ಭೇದಿ. A hatchet. -ರುಹೆ, ವೃಕ್ಷಾದನಿ. A parasitical plant. ವೃಕ್ಷಾಮ್ಲ. The hog-plum, *Spondias mangifera.*

ವೃಜಿನ s. a. Crooked, curved. 2, wicked; wrong. 3, sin, vice. 4, distress.

ವೃತ್ತ s. a. Turned. 2, round, circular. 3, existed; happened; past; gone, done; fixed. n. Event, news. 2, practice, occupation. 3, action; conduct. 4, a circle, circumference. 5, metre; a verse. -ಶಾಲಿ, -ಸಂಪನ್ನ, ಸು-. Well-behaved; a man of good conduct. ವೃತ್ತಾಂತ. Occurrence, event; tidings, rumour, report; a tale, story; a subject.

ವೃತ್ತಿ s. n. State, condition. 2, course, conduct, practice, profession, employment; livelihood, maintenance; inâm land. 3, use, currency. 4, style in composition. 5, comment, exposition, gloss. 6, a hedge. *Cpds.:* ಅಕ್ಷರ-, ಅರ್ಥ-, ನಿ-, ಪರಿ-, ಪ್ರ-, ಮನೋ-, *etc.*

ವೃತ್ರ s. n. Darkness. 2, N. of a demon.

ವೃಥಾ s. ad. Unnecessarily, uselessly, fruitlessly. a. Vain, useless.

ವೃದ್ಧ s. a. Grown up. 2, old, aged, ancient. 3, large. 4, wise. n. An old man; *f.* ವೃದ್ಧೆ. -ತ್ವ, ವೃದ್ಧಾಪ್ಯ. Old age.

ವೃದ್ಧಿ s. n. Increase, increment, growth. 2, an assemblage. 3, prosperity, success, advancement. 4, profit, gain. 5, money-lending, usury, interest (= ಬಡ್ಡಿ). 6, lengthening of a vowel, augment (*g.*). -ಜೀವ. A usurer. -ಜೀವನ. Living by usury.

ವೃಂದ s. n. A multitude, flock. ವೃಂದಾವನ. A little tower-form erection of clay or stone in which Kṛishṇa's worshippers plant and preserve the tulasi.

ವೃಶ್ಚಿಕ s. n. A scorpion. 2, the zodiacal sign *Scorpio.* -ಮಾಸ. The month when the sun is in *Scorpio.*

ವೃಷ s. n. A rainer. 2, a bull; the sign *Taurus.* -ಕೇತು. Karṇa's son. -ಧ್ವಜ. Śiva; Gaṇapati.

ವೃಷಭ s. n. A bull. 2, the zodiacal sign *Taurus.* -ಧ್ವಜ, -ವಾಹನ. Śiva. -ಮಾಸ. The month when the sun is in *Taurus.*

ವೃಷಿ s. n. A seat of a religious student or ascetic.

ವೃಷ್ಟಿ s. n. Rain, shower.

ವೆಕ್ಕಸ a. k. n. Roughness; harshness; unkindness, unpleasantness.

ವೆಕ್ತ. *tb. of* ವ್ಯಕ್ತ, *q. v.*

ವೆಗ್ಗಳ a. k. n. Abundance, excess. -ತನ, ವೆಗ್ಗಳಿಕೆ. Excessiveness, muchness. ವೆಗ್ಗಳಿಸು. To become much, to increase; to be actuated by impulse.

ವೆಂಕ, ವೆಂಕಟ s. n. N. of an idol of Vishṇu on the hill at Tirupati. -ಗಿರಿ, ವೆಂಕಟಾಚಲ. A fort on that hill. ವೆಂಕಪ್ಪ, ವೆಂಕಟೇಶ. N. ವೆಂಕಟರಮಣ. Vishṇu.

ವೆಂಗ್ಯ (*tb. of* ವ್ಯಂಗ್ಯ) n. Crookedness; perverseness.

ವೆಚ್ಚ (*tb. of* ವ್ಯಯ) n. Spending, expenditure, outlay, disbursement. -ಮಾಡು, ವೆಚ್ಚಿಸು. To spend. -ವಾಗು. To be spent. -ಹತ್ತು, -ಹಿಡಿ. Expense to be required.

ವೆಟ್ಟ k. n. Heat.

ವೆತ್ಯಾಸ. *tb. of* ವ್ಯತ್ಯಾಸ, *q. v.*

ವೆವಸಾಯ. *tb. of* ವ್ಯವಸಾಯ, *q. v.*

ವೆವಹಾರ. *tb. of* ವ್ಯವಹಾರ, *q. v.*

ವೆಸನ. *tb. of* ವ್ಯಸನ, *q. v.*

ವೇಗ (= ಬೇಗ, *q. v.*) s. *n.* Impetus. 2, speed, quickness; velocity. 3, activity, energy, force. -ತನ, -ತ್ವ. Haste, violence. -ಶಾಲಿ. An active person. ವೇಗಾಯಿಲ. A courier, an express; *also* ವೇಗಿ.

ವೇಡೆ, ವೇಡೆಯ (*tb. of* ವೇಷ್ಟ) *n.* Enclosing, surrounding; an enclosure, fence. ವೇಡಯಿಸು. To surround, enclose.

ವೇಣಿ s. *n.* A braid of hair. 2, conflux of rivers. 3, a stream, current.

ವೇಣು s. *n.* A bamboo. 2, a flute, fife. -ಗೋಪಾಲ. Kṛishṇa playing a flute.

ವೇತನ, ವೇತಿ s. *n.* Wages; livelihood.

ವೇತಾಲ s. *n.* A goblin, demon.

ವೇತ್ತ (*tb. of* ವೇತ್ತೃ) s. *n.* A knower, sage. -ತಿ. Knowledge.

ವೇದ s. *n.* Knowledge. 2, the vêda, the three vêdas: ṛigvêda, yajurvêda, and sâmavêda. -ಪಾರಾಯಣ. Reciting the vêda. -ಬಾಹ್ಯ. Not founded on the vêda. -ಮೂರ್ತಿ. An honorific title prefixed to a learned Brâhmaṇa's name. -ವಿತ್, -ವಿದ್. Conversant with the vêda. -ವ್ಯಾಸ. N. of Bâdarâyaṇa. -ಶಾಸ್ತ್ರಸಂಪನ್ನ. Versed in the vêdas and śâstras; an epithet of a learned Brâhmaṇa; *also* -ಪಾರಗ. ವೇದಾಂಗ. N. of certain works which are auxiliary to or part of the vêdas. ವೇದಾಂತ. An Upanishad; N. of a philosophical system. ವೇದಾಂತಶಾಸ್ತ್ರ. The vêdânta philosophy. ವೇದಾಧ್ಯಾಸ. Study of the vêda. ವೇದೋಕ್ತ. Declared in the vêdas. ವೇದೋಕ್ತ ಆಶೀರ್ವಾದ. A mode of blessing in a letter from a Brâhmaṇa. ಸದ್ವೇದ. The Bible.

ವೇದನೆ s. *n.* Knowledge, perception. 2, pain, torment, agony.

ವೇದಿ 1. s. *n.* A learned Brâhmaṇa; a teacher.

ವೇದಿ 2, ವೇದಿಕೆ s. *n.* A raised place prepared for sacrifice; an altar, pulpit.

ವೇದಿಸು s. *v. t.* To make known. 2, to afflict, trouble.

ವೇದೆ. = ವೇದನೆ, *q. v.*

ವೇದ್ಯ s. *a.* Known.

ವೇಧ (*tb. of* ವೇಧಸ್) *n.* An arranger; Brahmâ. 2, boring a hole.

ವೇಲೆ. = ವೇಳೆ, *q. v.*

ವೇಶ s. *n.* Entrance, ingress. 2, an abode. 3, dress; disguise. -ನ. Access. ವೇಶ್ಯೆ. A harlot; *also* -ಸ್ತ್ರೀ, ವೇಶ್ಯಾಸ್ತ್ರೀ.

ವೇಷ s. *n.* Dress, apparel. 2, disguise; hypocrisy, falsity. 3, ornament. -ಗಾರ. A masquerader; a hypocrite. -ಧಾರಿ. One who is disguised; a hypocrite. -ಸ್ತ್ರೀ. The guise of a woman. -ಧರಿಸು, -ಹಾಕು. To disguise one's self.

ವೇಷ್ಟನ s. *n.* Surrounding; a wrapper; a turban, diadem; a girdle; a cover.

ವೇಷ್ಟಿ s. *n.* A dôtra. -ತ. Surrounded, wrapped up. -ಸು. To surround, encircle, wrap round.

ವೇಸ. *tb. of* ವೇಷ, *q. v.*

ವೇಳೆ, ವೇಳ್ಯ (*tb. of* ವೇಲೆ, *q. v.*) *n.* Time; season. 2, opportunity, leisure; convenience. 3, tide. -ಕಳೆ. To spend time. -ಯಾಳು. A watchman.

ವೈಕಲ್ಯ s. *n.* Imperfection, deficiency, defect (*as:* ಅಂಗ-, ಇಂದ್ರಿಯ-, ಬುದ್ಧಿ-); incompetency; agitation, flurry.

ವೈಕುಂಠ s. *n.* Vishṇu or Kṛishṇa. 2, the heaven of Vishṇu. -ಯಾತ್ರೆ. Death.

ವೈಖರಿ s. *n.* Articulate utterance; the faculty of speech.

ವೈಖಾನಸ s. *n.* A Brâhmaṇa of the third order, a hermit. 2, N. of a sect of Vaishṇavas. -ಸೂತ್ರ. Their scriptures.

ವೈಚಕ್ಷಣ್ಯ (*fr.* ವಿಚಕ್ಷಣ) s. *n.* Proficiency, skill.

ವೈಚಿತ್ರ್ಯ (*fr.* ವಿಚಿತ್ರ) s. *n.* Variety; manifoldness; surprise.

ವೈಜಯಂತಿ s. *n.* A banner, flag.

ವೈಡೂರ್ಯ s. n. A gem of a dark colour, *Lapis lazuli*.

ವೈಣಿಕ s. n. A flutist.

ವೈತರಣಿ s. n. The river of hell.

ವೈದಗ್ಧ್ಯ (fr. ವಿದಗ್ಧ) s. n. Cleverness, skill, wit; cunning.

ವೈದಿಕ (fr. ವೇದ) s. a. Vedic, scriptural, sacred. n. A religious mendicant. -ಜೀವನ, -ವೃತ್ತಿ. Living as a religious mendicant.

ವೈದೀಕ. tb. of ವೈದಿಕ, q. v. 2, the day of performing a śrâddha.

ವೈದೇಹ, -ಕ s. n. A trader, merchant.

ವೈದ್ಯ (fr. ವೇದ) s. a. Vedic. 2, medical. n. A doctor, physician; medical practice. -ತನ. Medical science. -ನಾಥ. Śiva; N. of a poet. -ಶಾಸ್ತ್ರ. The science of medicine. -ಮಾಡು. To practice as a doctor.

ವೈಧವ್ಯ s. n. Widowhood.

ವೈಧೇಯ (fr. ವಿಧೇಯ) s. a. Foolish, ignorant.

ವೈನತೇಯ s. n. Garuḍa.

ವೈಪರೀತ್ಯ (fr. ವಿಪರೀತ) s. n. Contrariety, adverseness, reverse.

ವೈಭವ, ವೈಭೋಗ s. n. Power, greatness, grandeur, glory, wealth.

ವೈಮನಸ್ಯ (fr. ವಿಮನಸ್) s. n. Great sadness or sorrow. 2, hostility of feeling towards.

ವೈಮಲ್ಯ s. n. Spotlessness, purity.

ವೈಮೇಯ (fr. ವಿಮಯ) s. n. Barter, exchange.

ವೈಯಾಕರಣ s. a. Grammatical. ವೈಯಾಕರಣಿ. A grammarian.

ವೈಯಾರ. = ವಯ್ಯಾರ, q. v.

ವೈರ (fr. ವೀರ) s. n. Heroism. 2, enmity, malice, spite. -ತನ, -ತ್ವ. Enmity, hostility. ವೈರಿ. An enemy, foe.

ವೈರಾಗ್ಯ s. n. Passionlessness; absence of worldly desires. ವೈರಾಗಿ. An ascetic or devotee.

ವೈಲಕ್ಷಣ್ಯ (fr. ವಿಲಕ್ಷಣ) s. n. Contrariety, disparity, difference. 2, novelty, strangeness.

ವೈವರ್ತ (fr. ವಿವರ್ತ) s. n. Revolution, change of existence.

ವೈವಸ್ವತ (fr. ವಿವಸ್ವತ) s. n. Vivasvat's son Yama. 2, the Manu of the present period. 3, the present period.

ವೈವಾಹ, ವೈವಾಹಿಕ (fr. ವಿವಾಹ) s. a. Relating to marriage.

ವೈಶಂಪಾಯನ s. n. N. of a sage; Vyâsa.

ವೈಶಾಖ s. n. The second month of the lunar year (April-May).

ವೈಶೇಷಿಕ (fr. ವಿಶೇಷ) s. a. Particular, characteristic. n. N. of a philosophical system founded by Kaṇâda.

ವೈಶ್ಯ s. n. A man of the third caste; f. ವೈಶ್ಯೆ.

ವೈಶ್ವದೇವ s. n. A daily offering to all deities.

ವೈಶ್ವಾನರ s. n. Agni, fire.

ವೈಷಮ್ಯ s. n. Inequality, oddness. 2, calamity, distress. 3, injustice.

ವೈಷ್ಣವ s. n. Relating to Vishṇu. n. A follower of Vishṇu.

ವೈಸಿಕ (tb. of ವೈಶಿಕ) n. Deceit, fraud.

ವೈಹಾಸಿಕ (fr. ವಿಹಾಸ) s. n. A comic actor, buffoon.

ವೊ & ವೋ k. *For Kannaḍa words with these initials not found below, see s.* ಒ & ಓ.

ವ್ಯಕ್ತ s. a. Manifest, apparent, clear, evident; specific. -ಪಡಿಸು. To make clear, show. -ತರ. Very plain. ವ್ಯಕ್ತಿ. Clearness, distinctness, discrimination; indication; individuality; an individual; an entity.

ವ್ಯಗ್ರ s. a. Distracted, perplexed, agitated. 2, zealous, occupied. -ತೆ. Perplexity, confusion; zeal.

ವ್ಯಂಗ s. a. Limbless; deformed, crippled.

ವ್ಯಂಗ್ಯ s. a. Sarcastic, allusive. n. Sarcasm; insinuation; crookedness, perversity, impropriety. ವ್ಯಂಗ್ಯಾರ್ಥ. A covert meaning. ವ್ಯಂಗ್ಯೋಕ್ತಿ. Covert language; improper speech.

ವ್ಯಂಜನ s. n. A consonant. 2, a mark, sign. 3, seasoning, condiment. -ಸಂಧಿ. Euphony of consonants (*g.*).

ವ್ಯತಿ s. a. Different. -ಕ್ರಮ. Transgressing, violating; reverse; opposition; crime, sin; misfortune. -ರಿಕ್ತ. Surpassing; separate; different from; without, except; withdrawn. -ರೇಕ. Separateness, difference, distinction; exception; contrast; negative inference. -ಹಾರ. Barter, exchange; reciprocity.

ವ್ಯತೀತ s. a. Passed away, gone.

ವ್ಯತೀಪಾತ s. n. Deviation from right; any portent or prodigy indicating calamity, *as* a comet, *etc.*; one of the astronomical yôgas.

ವ್ಯತ್ಯಾಸ (=ವೆತ್ಯಾಸ) s. n. Reverse order; variation; difference. ವ್ಯತ್ಯಸ್ತ. Reversed; contrary.

ವ್ಯಥೆ s. n. Disquietude, perturbation; pain, agony; sorrow; distress; anguish, alarm, fear. ವ್ಯಥಿತ. Distressed, afflicted; troubled. ವ್ಯಥಿಸು. To be afflicted.

ವ್ಯಭಿಚಾರ s. n. Going astray; following improper courses; profligacy; adultery; anomaly. -ಮಾಡು. To commit adultery. ವ್ಯಭಿಚರಿಸು. To go astray; to adulterate. ವ್ಯಭಿಚಾರಸ್ಥ, ವ್ಯಭಿಚಾರಿ. An adulterer; *f.* ವ್ಯಭಿಚಾರಳು, ವ್ಯಭಿಚಾರಿಣಿ.

ವ್ಯಯ s. n. Decay; decline. 2, spending, expense, outlay; squandering, waste. 3, the twentieth year of the cycle of sixty.

ವ್ಯರ್ಥ s. a. Useless, unprofitable, fruitless; vain; unmeaning.

ವ್ಯವಕಲನ s. n. Subtraction, deduction.

ವ್ಯವಧಾನ s. n. Intervention, separation; a screen, partition; interval; space, covering; leisure.

ವ್ಯವಸಾಯ s. n. Resolve. 2, endeavour, exertion, activity, energy, industry, perseverance. 3, a trade, business. 3, cultivation, agriculture. -ಗಾರ. A farmer. -ಮಾಡು. To cultivate, farm. ವ್ಯವಸಾಯಿ. A diligent man.

ವ್ಯವಸ್ಥೆ s. n. Adjusting; arrangement. 2, settlement, decision, decree, rule. 3, an affirmation; a state, course, condition. -ಮಾಡು. To lay down a law.

ವ್ಯವಹಾರ s. n. Conduct; action; process; procedure; affair; work, business; dealing, traffic, commerce; a lawsuit; quarrel; usage, habit, custom; *also* ವ್ಯವಹರಣ. -ಕಾಲ. A mundane period. ವ್ಯವಹಾರಿ. A trader; litigant. ವ್ಯವಹಾರಿಕ. Customary, usual, common. ವ್ಯವಹರಿಸು. To be in use; to deal in, to traffic, trade; to litigate, contend. ವ್ಯವಹರ್ತೃ. A plaintiff, litigant.

ವ್ಯಷ್ಟಿ s. n. Individuality.

ವ್ಯಸನ (=ವೆಸನ) s. n. Violation; ill-luck. 2, a vice, vicious habit. 3, grief, sorrow. -ಕರ. Grievous. -ಪಡು. To grieve. ವ್ಯಸನಿ. Addicted to a vice, of vicious habits; a sorrowful person.

ವ್ಯಸ್ತ s. a. Separated, divided; dispersed. 2, different, various. 3, troubled, confused; deranged. -ಪದ. A simple word (*g.*).

ವ್ಯಾಕರಣ s. n. Grammar; grammatical analysis. -ಕಾರ, -ಜ್ಞ. A grammarian.

ವ್ಯಾಕುಲ s. a. Confounded, perplexed; troubled. *n.* Anxious thought, grief. -ತೆ. Perplexity; grief. ವ್ಯಾಕುಲಿತ. Perplexed; grieved. ವ್ಯಾಕುಲಿಸು. To be perplexed; to grieve.

ವ್ಯಾಕೃತಿ s. n. Analysing. 2, grammar. 3, change of form. 4, a way, form.

ವ್ಯಾಖ್ಯಾನ (=ವಕ್ಕಣೆ) s. n. Explanation, exposition; comment, interpretation; description; *also* ವ್ಯಾಖ್ಯೆ. ವ್ಯಾಖ್ಯಾನಿ. A commentator, annotator, *as.:* ಬೈಬಲ್ ವ್ಯಾಖ್ಯಾನಿ, ಶಾಸ್ತ್ರ-.

ವ್ಯಾಘಾತ s. n. Contradiction; inconsistency.

ವ್ಯಾಘ್ರ s. n. A tiger.

ವ್ಯಾಜ s. n. Deceit, fraud, craft; disguise; pretence. -ನಿಂದೆ. Disguised reproach.

ವ್ಯಾಜ್ಯ s. n. A contest, quarrel; dispute, a law-suit. -ಗಾರ. A litigant, a party in a suit (*law*). -ತೀರಿಸು. To settle a dispute. -ಮಾಡು, -ಹಾಡು. To quarrel; to litigate, sue. -ದ ಹೇತು. The cause of action (*law*).

ವ್ಯಾಧ s. n. A hunter, fowler.

ವ್ಯಾಧಿ s. n. Sickness, disease. -ತ. Sick, [ill.

ವ್ಯಾನ s. n. One of the vital airs.

ವ್ಯಾಪಕ s. a. Pervading, diffusive, widely spreading. n. An intimate associate. ಸರ್ವ-. All-pervading. ವ್ಯಾಪನ. Pervading, penetrating. ವ್ಯಾಪಿಸು. To reach through, pervade, cover, fill.

ವ್ಯಾಪಾರ s. n. Occupation, business, trade, profession. 2, exertion, practice. 3, work, affair, operation, transaction. 4, trade, traffic. -ಸಾಪಾರ. *redl.* -ನಡಿಸು, -ಮಾಡು. To do a work; to trade. -ಗಾರ, -ಸ್ಥ, ವ್ಯಾಪಾರಿ. A tradesman, dealer, merchant. ಮನೋ-. Mental operation. ಸದ್-. An excellent practice.

ವ್ಯಾಪ್ತಿ s. n. Pervasion, permeation. 2, universality. 3, obtaining, acquiring. 4, occupation, work. ವ್ಯಾಪ್ತ. Pervaded, pervading; filled up, full; overspread.

ವ್ಯಾಮ s. n. A fathom. 2, sickliness.

ವ್ಯಾಮೋಹ s. n. Bewilderment. 2, inordinate affection, carnal desire.

ವ್ಯಾಯಾಮ s. n. Athletic exercise, exercise of the body in general.

ವ್ಯಾಲ s. n. A snake. 2, a beast of prey. 3, a villain, rogue. -ಗ್ರಾಹಿ. A snake-catcher. -ಶಾಯಿ. Vishṇu.

ವ್ಯಾವಹಾರಿಕ (*fr.* ವ್ಯವಹಾರ) s. a. Practical, active, judicial, legal; customary. n. Use.

ವ್ಯಾವೃತ್ತಿ s. n. Separation from. 2, exception, removal. 3, turning away. 4, repetition.

ವ್ಯಾಸ s. n. Distribution, severality, detail; diffusion, extension; the diameter of a circle. 2, Vyâsa, the original arranger of the vêdas. -ಪೀಠ. A kind of stool for placing a reading book.

ವ್ಯಾಸಂಗ s. n. Assiduous application to.

ವ್ಯಾಹಾರ s. n. Utterance, speech, a word; a humorous speech.

ವ್ಯುತ್ಕ್ರಮ s. n. Transgression; disorder, confusion.

ವ್ಯುತ್ಪತ್ತಿ s. n. Production, origin; derivation, etymology. 2, scholarship, proficiency, learning. ಕಾವ್ಯ-. Proficiency in poetry. ಶಾಸ್ತ್ರ-. Proficiency in śâstras.

ವ್ಯುತ್ಪನ್ನ s. a. Produced, derived; taught; quite proficient in; learned.

ವ್ಯುತ್ಪಾದನ s. n. Tracing (words) back to a root. ವ್ಯುತ್ಪಾದಿಸು. To derive from a root.

ವ್ಯೂಹ s. n. A mass, flock; an army; military array. -ಕಟ್ಟು, -ಮಾಡು. To array.

ವ್ಯೋಕಾರ s. n. A blacksmith. 2, a coppersmith.

ವ್ಯೋಮ s. n. The sky, ether, atmosphere. -ಕೇಶ. Śiva. -ಗಂಗೆ, The heavenly Ganges.

ವ್ರಜ s. n. A road. 2, a flock, herd. 3, a cowpen, cattle-shed.

ವ್ರಣ s. n. A wound, sore, boil, bruise.

ವ್ರತ s. n. Rite, observance. 2, any religious act; a vow. -ಭಂಗ. The breach of a vow. -ಭ್ರಷ್ಟ. Deviated from one's vow. -ಸ್ಥ. One who keeps a vow. -ಹೀನ. One who neglects his vow. ವ್ರತಿ. An ascetic. ಪತಿವ್ರತೆ. A chaste woman.

ವ್ರಯ (*tb. of* ವ್ಯಯ) n. Expenditure, [outlay.

ವ್ರಾತ್ಯ s. n. One of the three first classes who has lost caste through non-observance of the saṁskâras; an outcast; an illiterate, ill-bred man. -ತನ. Wickedness.

ಶ್

ಶ್. The forty-ninth letter of the alphabet. *It does not occur in pure Kannaḍa.*

ಶಂಸನ s. n. Saying, reciting; praising. ಶಂಸಿತ. Said; praised. ಶಂಸೆ. Speech. praise; *cf.* ಪ್ರ-.

ಶಕ s. n. An era, epoch. -ವರುಷ, ಶಕಾಬ್ದ. A year of the śaka year, *esp.* of ಶಾಲಿವಾಹನ.

ಶಕಟ (= ಬಕ್ಕಡಿ) s. n. A cart, waggon.

ಶಕಾರ s. n. The letter ಶ್.

ಶಕುನ s. n. A bird. 2, an omen, prognostic. ಅಪ-, ಕೆಟ್ಟ-, ದುಃ-. A bad omen. ಶುಭ-. A good omen. -ನೋಡು. To consult an omen. ಶಕುನಿ. A bird; a kite; N. of the maternal uncle of the Kauravas.

ಶಕುಂತಲೆ s. n. N. of the daughter of an Apsaras, the heroine of a celebrated drama.

ಶಕ್ತಿ s. n. Strength, power; ability, capacity, faculty; regal power; the energy of a deity personified as his wife. ಬಿಂಬ-, ವಿಗ್ರಹ-. The inherent power of an idol. -ಉಪದ್ರ, -ಕಾಟ, -ಬೇನೆ. A plague occasioned by a village goddess. -ಪೂಜೆ. Śakti-worship. *Cpds.:* ಔಷಧ-, ಜ್ಞಾನ-, ಬುದ್ಧಿ-, ವಿಶ್ವಾಸ-, *etc.* -ಮಾನ, -ವಂತ. Strong, mighty, able. -ಹೀನ. Powerless, impotent. ಶಕ್ತ. Strong, mighty; able, capable; clever, intent.

ಶಕ್ಯ s. a. Able, possible, practicable; ಶಕ್ಯಾರ್ಥ. Admissible meaning; meaning conveyed by a word.

ಶಕ್ರ s. a. Powerful, strong. n. Indra. 2, Vishṇu. -ಚಾಪ, -ಧನುಸ್, -ಶರಾಸನ. The rainbow.

ಶಂಕರ s. a. Causing happiness. n. Śiva; a N. ಶಂಕರಾಚಾರ್ಯ. N. of a celebrated scholar.

ಶಂಕು s. n. A pin, peg; a stake, post, pillar. 2, a dart. 3, the trunk of a lopped tree. 4, the pin of a dial. 5, a surveyor's compass. -ಯಂತ್ರ. A sun-dial.

ಶಂಕೆ s. n. Doubt, uncertainty, scruple, suspicion, misgiving, fear, alarm. 2, presumption. ಗಾಳಿ-, ದೆವ್ವ-, ಭೀತಿ-, ಭೂತ-, ವಾಯು-. An evil spirit. ಅಲ್ಪ-, ಜಲ-, ಮೂತ್ರ-. Making water. ಶಂಕಿಸು. To doubt, hesitate; to fear; to suspect. ಶಂಕಿತ. Doubted; doubtful; alarmed; scrupulous; suspicious.

ಶಂಖ s. n. A shell, conch-shell. 2, the cheek-bone. 3, one of Kubêra's treasures. -ಪಾಲ. N. of a serpent. -ಪಾಷಾಣ. White oxide of arsenic. -ಪುಷ್ಪಬಳ್ಳಿ. A climbing herb with blue or white flowers, *Clitoria ternatea.* -ಮುದ್ರೆ. The seal of a conch. -ವಾದ್ಯ. A conch-shell blowing as a horn.

ಶಚಿ s. n. N. of Indra's wife; *also* -ದೇವಿ. -ಪತಿ, -ಪಾಲ. Indra.

ಶಠ s. a. Wicked, bad, dishonest. n. A rogue, knave; a fool; roguery. -ತ್ವ. Wickedness, roguery; foolishness.

ಶತ s. n. A hundred. -ಕೋಟಿ. A hundred crores. -ಘ್ನಿ. A cannon. -ತಮ. The hundredth. -ದ್ರು. The river Sutlej. -ದ್ರೋಹಿ. One who is guilty of a hundred acts of treason. -ಧಾರ. A thunder-bolt. -ಪದಿ. A centipede. -ತಾರೆ, -ಭಿಷಜ್, -ಭಿಷೆ. N. of a nakshatra. -ಮಾನ. A century; a hundred-fold. -ಮೂಲಿಕೆ, ಶತಾವರಿ. The shrub *Asparagus racemosus.*

ಶತ್ರು s. n. An enemy, foe, adversary. -ಘ್ನ. N. of Râma's youngest brother. -ತನ, -ತ್ವ, -ಭಾವ. Enmity.

ಶನಿ s. n. The planet Saturn. 2, a wicked person. -ಗ್ರಹ, ಶನೀಶ್ವರ, ಶನೈ

ಶ್ಚರ. The planet Saturn. -ವಾರ. Saturday.

ಶಪಥ s. n. An imprecation, curse. 2, an oath, ordeal, swearing.

ಶಪನ s. n. Cursing. 2, an oath. ಶಪಿಸು. To curse; to abuse.

ಶಬ (tb. of ಶವ, q. v.) n. A corpse. 2, clothes. 3, all sorts of beasts.

ಶಬಗಸ್ತು h. n. Nocturnal procession.

ಶಬರ s. n. N. of a wild mountaineer tribe; f. ಶಬರಿ. 2, a sort of deer. 3, N. of a demon. -ಶಂಕರ. Šiva.

ಶಬ್ದ s. n. Sound, noise. 2, a word. -ಖಂಡ. A chapter on words. -ಖಂಡನ. Verbal criticism. -ಚೋರ. A plagiarist. -ಜ್ಞ. A philologist, grammarian. -ಮಂಜರಿ. N. of a Kannaḍa vocabulary. -ಮಣಿದರ್ಪಣ. N. of a Kannaḍa grammar. -ಶಾಸ್ತ್ರ. A grammar. -ಸಂಗ್ರಹ. A vocabulary. ಶಬ್ದಾನುಶಾಸನ. N. of a Kannaḍa grammar in Sanskrit. ಶಬ್ದಾರ್ಥ. The meaning of a word. ಶಬ್ದಾಲಂಕಾರ. Rhetorical use of words. ಶಬ್ದಾವಯವ. The component parts of a term. ನಿಶ್ಶಬ್ದ. Noiseless, still.

ಶಮ s. n. Quiet, tranquillity, rest, calm. 2, quietude, stillness, absence of passion. -ದಮ. Quietism and self-command. -ಥ. Quiet, tranquillity. -ನ. Appeasing, tranquilizing, soothing; tranquillity; cessation, end. *Cpds.:* ತಾಪ-, ದುಃಖ-, ದಾಹ-, ರೋಗ-, *etc.* ಶಮಿತ. Appeased, allayed, calmed. ಶಮಿಸು. To be appeased, alloyed, calmed; to cease; to appease, pacify, soothe, *etc.*

ಶಮಿ s. n. A legume, pod. 2, the tree *Mimosa suma*. 3, calm, tranquil.

ಶಂಬರ s. n. N. of a demon and of a daitya. 2, water. 2, a cloud.

ಶಂಬಲ (= ಸಂಬಳ) s. n. Provisions for a journey.

ಶಂಭು s. a. Causing happiness. n. A happy, prosperous man. 2, Brahmâ. 3, Vishṇu. 4, Šiva.

ಶಯನ s. n. Lying down, reposing, sleeping. 2, sleep. 3, a couch, bed. -ಗೃಹ, -ಸ್ಥಾನ, ಶಯ್ಯಾಗೃಹ. A dormitory. ಶಯನಿಸು. To lie down, repose, sleep. ಶಯಾಲು. Sleepy, slothful. ಶಯ್ಯೆ. A couch, bed; sleeping, sleep.

ಶರ s. n. A sort of reed or grass *Saccharum sara*. 2, an arrow. 3, cream. 4, water; a lake. 5, sound, noise.

ಶರಣ s. n. A protector, preserver. 2, protection, help, refuge. 3, a refuge, asylum. 4, a house. 5, a devotee. ಶರಣಾಗತ. Come for protection; a refugee. ಶರಣಾಗತಿ. Coming for protection. ಶರಣಾರ್ಥ. A person seeking protection; a form of salutation. ಶರಣು ಬೀಳು. To take refuge. ಶರಣು ಹೋಗು. To seek refuge. ಶರಣ್ಯ. Dependent; poor, helpless; protection, defence; a protector.

ಶರತ್ಕಾಲ, ಶರದ್, ಶರದೃತು, ಶರದೆ s. n. [Autumn.

ಶರಧಿ s. n. The ocean.

ಶರಭ s. n. A fabulous animal.

ಶರಾರತ್ h. n. Wickedness, outrage. ಶರಾರು. Hurtful, mischievous.

ಶರೀರ s. n. The body. -ತ್ಯಾಗ. Suicide. -ದಂಡನೆ. Corporal punishment. -ಧರ್ಮ. The functions of the body. -ಪ್ರಕೃತಿ, -ಗುಣ. Constitution of the body. -ಸಂಬಂಧ. Affinity. ಶರೀರಾಂತ, ಶರೀರಾವಸಾನ. Death. ಪುಣ್ಯ-. A blessed body. ಸ್ಥೂಲ-. The gross material body. ಸೂಕ್ಷ್ಮ-. The atomic body. ಪಿತ್ತ-. A bilious habit. ಸ್ವರ್ಗೀಯ-. A glorified body. -ಸಂಬಂಧಿ. A relative. -ದಂಡಿಸಿ ತಿನ್ನು. To live by hard labour. ಶರೀರಿ. Embodied, a sentient being.

ಶರೆ. = ಸೆರೆ, q. v.

ಶರ್ಕರೆ s. n. A potsherd. 2, a pebble, gravel. 3, candied sugar.

ಶರ್ಮ s. n. Happiness, delight. 2, refuge. 3, an ending of a Brâhmaṇa's name.

ಶರ್ವರಿ s. n. Night. -ಶಪತಿ. The moon.

ಶಲ s. n. A porcupine's quill; *also* ಶಲಲ.

ಶಲಭ s. n. A grasshopper; a locust.

ಶಲಾಕೆ s. n. A dart, spike, shaft, a thin bar.

ಶಲ್ಯ 1. s. n. A stake, pin, splinter. 2, a dart, javelin; a pike; an arrow. 3, N. of the maternal uncle of Pâṇḍavas.

ಶಲ್ಯ 2, ಶಲ್ಲೆ (tb. of ಚೇಲ) n. Thin muslin cloth; a shawl.

ಶವ s. n. A corpse. -ಸಂಸ್ಕಾರ. Cremation or interment of a corpse.

ಶಶ, -ಕ s. n. A hare, rabbit. -ಧರ, ಶಶಾಂಕ. The moon.

ಶಶಿ s. n. The moon. -ಕಲೆ, -ಖಂಡ, -ರೇಖೆ, -ಲೇಖೆ. The digit of the moon. -ಕಾಂತ. The moon-stone.

ಶಸ್ತ s. a. Said. 2, praised. 3, best; happy. 4, struck.

ಶಸ್ತ್ರ s. n. A weapon; a sword, knife. 2, steel. -ಜೀವಿ, -ಧಾರಿ, ಶಸ್ತ್ರಜೀವಿ. A soldier. -ಯುದ್ಧ. A sword-fight. -ವಿದ್ಯೆ. The science of arms. -ವೈದ್ಯ. A surgeon; surgery. ಶಸ್ತ್ರಾಭ್ಯಾಸ. Military exercise. ಶಸ್ತ್ರಾಸ್ತ್ರ. Arms and missile weapons.

ಶಹಬಾಸು (=ಶಾಬಾಸು) h. int. Bravo! well done!

ಶಹರ, ಶಹರು h. n. A city or large town.

ಶಹಾಣೆ h. a. Sagacious, clever.

ಶಹಾಮೃಗ h.-s. n. An ostrich.

ಶಾಕ s. n. Any vegetable; vegetable food. 2, power, strength.

ಶಾಕಿನಿ s. n. A female demon attendant on Durgâ.

ಶಾಕ್ತ, ಶಾಕ್ತೇಯ s. a. Relating to śakti. n. A worshipper of śakti.

ಶಾಕ್ಯ s. n. Buddha; also -ಮುನಿ, -ಸಿಂಹ.

ಶಾಖಾ, ಶಾಖೆ s. n. The branch of a tree, etc., branch in general. 2, an arm. 3, a section of a book. 4, a sect, party. ಶಾಖಾಚರ, ಶಾಖಾಮೃಗ. A monkey. -ನಗರ. A suburb.

ಶಾಟಿ, ಶಾಟೆ f. n. Cloth, garment; a petticoat. ಸ್ನಾನ-. A bathing cloth.

ಶಾಠ್ಯ s. n. Villainy, dishonesty, deceit.

ಶಾಣ 1. f. n. A clever man; f. ಶಾಣೆ.

ಶಾಣ 2. s. n. Sharpening, whetting. 2, a whetstone.

ಶಾಣ 3. s. a. Hempen. ಶಾಣಿ. A hempen garment.

ಶಾತ s. a. Whetted, sharp. 2, thin; weak. n. Happiness. -ಕುಂಭ. Gold.

ಶಾದಿ h. n. Marriage.

ಶಾನಭವ, ಶಾನಭಾಗ, ಶಾನಭೋಗ f. n. A village clerk. -ತನ. The business of a village clerk.

ಶಾನೆ (tb. of ಸೇನೆ) a. Much; many.

ಶಾಂತ s. a. Appeased, calmed, hushed; tranquil, calm, satisfied; extinguished; mild, gentle; meek. -ಮನುಷ್ಯ. A meek man. -ತನ, -ತೆ, -ತ್ವ. Calmness, meekness. -ಪಡಿಸು. To pacify, etc.

ಶಾಂತನವ s. n. Bhîshma, son of Śantanu.

ಶಾಂತಿ s. n. Quietness, calmness, peace; serenity; mildness; quietism, stoicism; rest, repose; appeasing, soothing; any expiatory or propitiatory rite for averting evil. ತಾಪ-. Allaying of distress. ದಾಹ-. Quenching thirst. ರೋಗ-. The curing of a disease. -ಕಾಯಿ. The nut of Termalia belerica. -ಪಡಿಸು. To appease, etc. -ಪರ್ವ. N. of the 12th book of the Mahâbhârata.

ಶಾಪ s. n. Curse, cursing. 2, abuse. 3, an oath. -ಕೊಡು, ಶಾಪಿಸು (= ಶಪಿಸು). To curse. -ಗ್ರಸ್ತ. Seized by a curse. -ರಹಿತ. Void of curse. -ಮುಕ್ತಿ, -ಮೋಕ್ಷ, -ವಿಮುಕ್ತಿ, -ವಿಮೋಚನೆ. Deliverance from a curse.

ಶಾಬಾಸು. = ಶಹಬಾಸು, q. v.

ಶಾಬ್ದ s. a. Sounding; verbal, oral. ಶಾಬ್ದಿಕ. Wordy; a philologist, grammarian.

ಶಾಮ. tb. of ಶ್ಯಾಮ, q. v.

ಶಾಮಕ s. a. Appeasing, curing.

ಶಾಮಿಲು h. a. Including, extending to. ಶಾಮಿಲಾತು. A tract of land attached to an estate.

ಶಾಯಿ h. n. Ink. -ದಾನಿ, -ದವತಿ, -ಬರುಡೆ. An inkstand.

ಶಾಯಿದಿ h. n. A witness at law; witness, deposition.

ಶಾರದ s. a. Autumnal. 2, fresh, new. 3, able, clever. ಶಾರದಾ, ಶಾರದೆ. Sarasvati; intelligence.

ಶಾರೀರ, ಶಾರೀರಕ s. a. Corporeal, bodily; embodied. ಶಾರೀರಾಗ್ನಿ. The gastric-juice.

ಶಾರ್ಙ್ಗ s. n. A bow. -ಧನ್ವ, -ಧರ. Vishṇu.

ಶಾರ್ದೂಲ s. n. A tiger.

ಶಾರ್ವರಿ s. n. The thirty-fourth year of the cycle of sixty.

ಶಾಲಗ್ರಾಮ s. n. A black stone worshipped as sacred to Vishṇu.

ಶಾಲಿ s. a. Endowed with, possessing, having, as: ಗುಣ-, ಜಯ-, ಬುದ್ಧಿ-, ಧೈರ್ಯ-, ಯುದ್ಧ-, etc.

ಶಾಲಿವಾಹನ s. n. N. of an ancient king and institutor of the era so called. -ಶಕ. The era of Šâlivâhana.

ಶಾಲು, ಶಾಲುವೆ h. n. A woollen shawl. -ಜೋಡು, -ಜೋಡಿ. A pair of shawls. ಕಾಶ್ಮೀರ-. Cashmere shawl. ಶಲಬಳೀ.-.= ಶಾಲು.

ಶಾಲೆ s. n. A hall; a room; a house. 2, a school. ಅಶ್ವ-. A horse-stable. ಆಯುಧ-. An arsenal, armoury. ಪಾಕ-. A kitchen. ಪಾಠ-. A school. ವಿದ್ಯಾ-. A college, etc.

ಶಾಲ್ಮಲಿ s. n. The silk-cotton tree.

ಶಾವಿಗೆ.= ಸಾವಿಗೆ, q. v.

ಶಾಶ್ವತ s. a. Eternal, perpetual, permanent. -ಕೆಲಸ. A lasting work. -ಬೇರೀಜು. A permanent assessment.

ಶಾಸನ s. n. Ruling, government, training; punishing. 2, discipline. 3, an order; a precept. 4, a charter, edict; a deed. -ಮಾಡು. To punish.

ಶಾಸ್ತ್ರ s. n. An order, rule. 2, a religious or scientific treatise; scripture, institutes of a religion. 3, a book. -ಜ್ಞ. A scientist. Cpds.: ಕ್ರೈಸ್ತ-, ಗಣಿತ-, ಧರ್ಮ-, ವೇದಾಂತ-, -ಪದ್ಧತಿ, -ಪಾಠ, -ವಿಧಿ, -ಸಿದ್ಧಿ, -ಸಿದ್ಧಾಂತ, etc. -ವ್ಯುತ್ಪತ್ತಿ. Perfect conversancy with the šâstras. ನೀತಿ-. The sience of ethicks. ಸೂಪ-. A work on cookery. ಶಾಸ್ತ್ರಿ. A learned man; a teacher of the Šâstras. ಶಾಸ್ತ್ರೋಕ್ತ. Declared by the Šâstras.

ಶಿಂಶಪೆ, ಶಿಂಶುಪೆ f. n. The tree *Dalbergia sisu*.

ಶಿಕಸ್ತು h. a. Folding, as of paper.

ಶಿಕಾರಿ h. n. Hunting, the chase. -ಮಾಡು, -ಹೋಗು. To hunt. -ಗಾರ, -ಯವ. A hunter.

ಶಿಕ್ಯ.= ಸಿಕ್ಕ, q. v.

ಶಿಕ್ಷಕ s. n. A teacher, instructor.

ಶಿಕ್ಷಣ s. n. Learning, knowledge. 2, training.

ಶಿಕ್ಷೆ, ಶಿಕ್ಷಾ s. n. Study. 2, teaching, instruction. 3, punishment. -ಅನುಭೋಗಿಸು, -ತಾಳು, -ತಿನ್ನು. To suffer punishment. -ಕೊಡು, -ಮಾಡು. To punish. -ರಕ್ಷೆ. Chastising and protecting. ಶಿಕ್ಷಿಸು. To teach; to check, discipline; to chastise, punish.

ಶಿಖಂಡಿ s. n. A peacock. 2, N. of a son of Drupada born as a female. 3, an hermaphrodite.

ಶಿಖರ s. n. A point, top, summit; the peak of a mountain. ಶಿಖರಿ. Pointed; a mountain; a cover; a forest.

ಶಿಖಿ s. a. Crested, tufted. n. A peacock. 2, a comet. 3, a crest, helmet. 4, a lock of hair. -ಪಿಂಛ. A peacock's feather.

ಶಿಖೆ, ಶಿಖಾ s. n. A point, peak, top. 2, a crest, tuft, plume; a lock of hair on the head; the acme. 3, a flame; a ray of light. ಶಿಖಾಮಣಿ. A crest-gem; pre-eminent (*at the end of Cpds.*).

ಶಿತಾರು h. n. A cithara; a stringed instrument.

ಶಿಥಿಲ s. a. Loose, lax, not rigid; out of repair. 2, inert, feeble. n. Looseness, laxity. -ತೆ, -ತ್ವ. Laxity; languor.

ಶಿಪಾರಸು h. n. Recommendation; patronage.

ಶಿಪಿ s. n. A ray of light. -ವಿಷ್ಟ. Leprosy.

ಶಿಬಿಕೆ.= ಶಿವಿಕೆ, q. v.

ಶಿಂಬೆ f. n. A legume, pod.

ಶಿರ, ಶಿರಸ್ (= ಶಿರಸ್ಸು) s. n. The head, skull. ಶಿರದಲಿ ಧರಿಸು, ಶಿರಸಾವಹಿಸು. To accept with pleasure; to honour highly. ಶಿರಚ್ಛೇದ. Decapitation. ಶಿರಸ್ತ್ರ, ಶಿರಸ್ತ್ರಾಣ. A helmet. -ಸ್ನಾನ. A bath of the whole body. ಶಿರೋಭ್ರಮಣ. Vertigo, giddiness. ಶಿರೋಮಣಿ. A crest-jewel; a distinguished person. ಶಿರೋರೋಗ, ಶಿರೋವೇದನೆ, ಶಿರೋವ್ಯಥೆ, ಶಿರೋವ್ಯಾಧಿ. Headache.

ಶಿರಸ್ತೆದಾರ h. n. The native head clerk in a collector's office or in a court.

ಶಿರಸ್ಸು (tb. of ಶಿರಸ್). = ಶಿರ, q. v.

ಶಿಲುಕು h. n. Balance in hand. -ಬಾಕಿ. Balance left.

ಶಿಲೆ, ಶಿಲಾ s. n. A stone; a rock. ಶಿಲಾಜತು, ಶಿಲಾಜತ್, ಶಿಲಾಧಾತು. Bitumen; red chalk, *etc.* ಶಿಲಾವರ್ಷ, ಶಿಲಾವೃಷ್ಟಿ. Hail. ಶಿಲಾಶಾಸನ. An edict or inscription on a stone.

ಶಿಲುಬೆ (= ಸಿಲುಬೆ, q.v.) f. n. A cross. 2, sorrow, grief. -ಕರ್ತ, -ಸ್ವಾಮಿ. Jesus Christ. ಶಿಲುಬಿಸು. To crucify; *also* ಶಿಲುಬೆಗೆ ಹಾಕು, ಶಿಲುಬೆಯಲ್ಲಿ ಜಡಿ.

ಶಿಲ್ಪ s. n. An art, any manual or mechanical art. -ಕೆಲಸ. Artisanship. -ಕ, -ಗಾರ. An artisan, mechanic. -ವಿದ್ಯೆ. Handicraft, art. -ಶಾಲೆ. A workshop. -ಶಾಸ್ತ್ರ. Mechanics. ಶಿಲ್ಪಿ. An artificer, artist, artisan; *also* ಶಿಲ್ಪಿಕ, ಶಿಲ್ಪಿಗ.

ಶಿವ s. a. Auspicious, happy. n. Bliss, happiness. 2, Śiva. 3, virtue, *etc.* -ಕ. A post, peg. -ಕಾರಿ. One who causes happiness. -ಗಣ. Śiva's followers. -ದಾನ. Buttermilk. -ಗಂಗೆ. N. of a village in Mysore. -ಪುರ. Kailâsa. -ಪ್ರಾಣಿ, -ಭಕ್ತ. A Lingavanta. -ರಕ್ತಬಳ್ಳಿ, -ಶಕ್ತಿಬಳ್ಳಿ. A scandent plant, *Gloriosa superba.* -ರಾತ್ರಿ, -ರಾತ್ರೆ. A festival held in honour of Śiva. -ಶರಣ. A Jangama; a Lingavanta. *Other cpds.:* -ಮೂರ್ತಿ, -ಯೋಗ, -ಲಿಂಗ, -ಲೀಲೆ, -ಲೋಕ, -ಸೂತ್ರ. ಶಿವಾಲಯ. A temple dedicated to Śiva.

ಶಿವಾಯಿ h. *ad.* Besides; except; extra.

ಶಿವಿಕೆ (= ಶಿಬಿಕೆ) f. n. A palanquin, litter.

ಶಿಶಿರ s. a. Cool, cold. n. Coolness, cold. 2, the cold season; *also* -ಋತು. -ಕರ. The moon. ಶಿಶಿರೋಪಚಾರ. Kind treatment with cooling articles.

ಶಿಶು s. n. A child, infant; the young of any animal. -ತ್ವ. Infancy, childhood.

ಶಿಷ್ಟ s. a. Disciplined, trained; obedient; learned; eminent, noble. 2, remaining. n. A learned man. 2, remainder. -ಪಾಲಕ. A guardian of the virtuous. ಶಿಷ್ಟಾಚಾರ. The custom of good people.

ಶಿಷ್ಯ s. n. A pupil, disciple. -ತನ, -ತ್ವ. Pupilage. ಕ್ರಿಸ್ತನ-. A disciple of Christ.

ಶಿಸ್ತು h. n. Aim. 2, assessment, tax. 3, decoration. -ಗಾರ. A fop; a lewd man; f. -ಗಾತಿ. -ಗಾರಿಕೆ. Lewdness.

ಶೀ. = ಸೀ, q. v.

ಶೀಘ್ರ s. a. Quick, speedy. ಶೀಘ್ರಂ. Quickly, swiftly. -ಗಾಮಿ. A camel.

ಶೀತ s. a. Cold, chilly. 2, idle, lazy. 3, damp. n. Cold; dampness. -ಕರ, -ರಶ್ಮಿ. The moon. -ಜ್ವರ. Ague. -ಶಿವ. A kind of fennel.

ಶೀತಲ s. a. Cold, chilly, cool.

ಶೀತಲೆ s. n. Small-pox.

ಶೀಮೆ. = ಸೀಮೆ, q. v.

ಶೀರೆ. = ಸೀರೆ, q. v.

ಶೀರ್ಣ s. a. Withered; rotten; slender; shattered, injured.

ಶೀರ್ಷ (= ಶಿರಸ್, q. v.) s. n. The head. -ಕ. A helmet, turban.

ಶೀಲ s. n. Disposition, character; habit. 2, practice, conduct. 3, good disposition or character, good nature, *etc.*, virtue; *also* -ಸ್ವಭಾವ. 4, form, beauty. *At the end of cpds.:* possessed of, disposed to, *as:* ಕಾರ್ಯ-, ಧರ್ಮ-, ಗುಣ-, ವಿವೇಕ-, ಬುದ್ಧಿ-, *etc.* -ವಂತ, ಸು-. A man of good conduct. -ವೃದ್ಧ. Very virtuous. ದುಶ್ಶೀಲ. Ill-natured.

ಶೀಳು. = ಸೀಳು, *q. v.*

ಶುಕ s. *n.* A parrot. 2, a mango tree. 3, a son of Vyâsa. 4, an ascetic. -ಪಂಜರ. A parrot's cage. -ವಾಣಿ. The prate of a parrot.

ಶುಕ್ತ s. *a.* Acid; harsh. *n.* Sour gruel.

ಶುಕ್ತಿ s. *n.* An oyster-shell. -ಜ. A pearl.

ಶುಕ್ರ s. *a.* Bright; white. *n.* The planet Venus. -ವಾರ. Friday. ಶುಕ್ರಾಚಾರ್ಯ. The preceptor of the Asuras.

ಶುಕ್ಲ (= ಶುಕ್ರ) s. *a.* Bright; white. *n.* The light half of a solar month. 2, the third year in the cycle of sixty. -ತ್ವ. Whiteness. -ಪಕ್ಷ. = ಶುಕ್ಲ *n.* No. 1. -ಪಾಡ್ಯ. The first day of -ಪಕ್ಷ.

ಶುಚಿ s. *a.* Clean, pure. 2, virtuous, innocent; honest, true; accurate. *n.* Purity, virtue, *etc.* -ಕರ. Purifying. -ತನ, -ತ್ವ. Cleanness, purity.

ಶುಂಠ f. *n.* A blockhead, dolt.

ಶುಂಠಿ s. *n.* Dry ginger.

ಶುಂಡ, ಶುಂಡೆ (= ಸುಂಡಿಲು) s. *n.* An elephant's trunk, proboscis.

ಶುದ್ಧ s. *a.* Purified, clean, pure. 2, stainless, true, fair, honest, holy. 3, correct, right. 4, simple, mere, only, alone. *ad.* Nothing but; wholly. *n.* Purity, *etc.* -ಕಳ್ಳ. A downright thief. -ಗೊಳಿಸು, ಶುದ್ಧೀಕರಿಸು. To purify. -ಪಡವಲು. Due west. -ಮಾಡು. To make clean. -ಲೋಭಿ. A complete miser. -ಸುಳ್ಳು. A pure lie. -ತೆ, -ತ್ವ. Purity, *etc.* -ಪತ್ರಿಕೆ.=ಶುದ್ಧಿಪತ್ರ. -ಪ್ರತಿ. A fair copy. -ಭಕ್ತಿ. True devotion. -ಮನಸ್ಸು. A pure mind. ಶುದ್ಧಾಚಾರ. Virtuous conduct. ಶುದ್ಧಾಶುದ್ಧ. Pure and impure.

ಶುದ್ಧಿ s. *n.* Purity, cleanness, holiness. 2, purification, cleansing. 3, goodness; clearance; correction; accuracy; truth. -ಪತ್ರ. An errata list.

ಶುಭ s. *a.* Bright. 2, auspicious, lucky, right, virtuous. *n.* Good luck; welfare, hail, joy. -ಕರ್ಮ, -ಕಾರ್ಯ. An auspicious ceremony. -ಕೃತ್. The thirty-sixth year in the cycle of sixty. -ನಕ್ಷತ್ರ. A favourable star. ಶುಭಮಸ್ತು. May it be auspicious. -ವಾರ್ತೆ. Good news, gospel. -ಶಕುನ. A good omen. ಶುಭಾಚಾರ. Good conduct.

ಶುಭ್ರ s. *a.* Shining, bright. 2, white. -ವಸ್ತ್ರ. A white cloth.

ಶುಲ್ಕ (= ಸುಂಕ) s. *n.* Toll, duty. 2, a dower. 3, gain. ಕನ್ಯಾ-. The price given for a wife. ವಿದ್ಯಾ-. The teacher's fee.

ಶುಶ್ರೂಷಣೆ, ಶುಶ್ರೂಷೆ s. *n.* Service; reverence.

ಶುಷ್ಕ s. *a.* Dried, dry; shriveled; useless; fruitless, vain. -ವಾದ. Useless talk. ಶುಷ್ಕೋಪಚಾರ. Vain compliments.

ಶೂಕ s. *n.* The awn of barley. -ಧಾನ್ಯ. Bearded grain.

ಶೂಕರ. = ಸೂಕರ, *q. v.*

ಶೂದ್ರ s. *n.* A man of the fourth caste; *f.* ಶೂದ್ರಳು, ಶೂದ್ರಿ, ಶೂದ್ರೆ. -ತ್ವ. The state or condition of a śûdra.

ಶೂನ್ಯ (=ಸೊನ್ನೆ) s. *a.* Empty, void, hollow; vacant. 2, utterly destitute, without. 3, ruined. 4, bare. *n.* A void, blank; a cypher; a desert. 2, a zero. 3, the anusvâra. 4, vacuity. 5, sorcery. -ಮಾಡು. To injure by sorcery. -ಕೀಳು, -ತೆಗೆ. To remove the effects of sorcery. -ಗಾರ. A sorcerer; *f.* -ಗಾತಿ. -ವಾದಿ. An atheist; a Buddhist. -ದ ಬೊಂಬೆ. An effigy.

ಶೂರ s. *n.* A hero, warrior, mighty man. -ತನ, -ತೆ, -ತ್ವ. Heroism, *etc.*

ಶೂರಣ (= ಸೂರಣ) s. *n.* An esculent root, *Amorphophallus campanulatus,* Telinga potato.

ಶೂರ್ಪ s. *n.* A van; a sifting fan. -ಕರಣ. Winnowing, sifting. -ಕರ್ಣ. An elephant; Gaṇêśa. -ಣಖಿ, -ಣಖೆ. N. of the sister of Râvaṇa; any monstrous female.

ಶೂಲ s. n. A spear, pike, lance; the trident of Śiva; also ತ್ರಿ-. 2, any acute pain, colic.

ಶೂಲೆ (= ಶೂಲ No. 2) s. n. A sharp pain, colic, headache. ಹೊಟ್ಟೆ-. The colic. ಪಕ್ಕ-, ಪಾರ್ಶ್ವ-. Pain in the sides; pleurisy. ಹೃದಯ-, ಎದೆ-. An aching heart.

ಶೃಂಖಲ s. n. A chain, fetter. 2, a girdle, zone.

ಶೃಂಗ s. n. A horn, a mountain peak; height, supremacy. 2, N. of a ṛishi. ಶೃಂಗಿ. Horned; peaked; a mountain; a deer.

ಶೃಂಗಾರ s. n. Decoration, embellishment; beauty. -ಮಾಡು, ಶೃಂಗರಿಸು, ಶೃಂಗಾರಿಸು. To ornament, decorate.

ಶೃಂಗೇರಿ s. n. N. of a village and maṭha on the ghâts.

ಶೆಟ್ಟಿ. = ಸೆಟ್ಟಿ, q. v.

ಶೆರೆ. = ಸೆರೆ, q. v.

ಶೇಕದಾರ h. n. The native collector of the revenue of a division of villages.

ಶೇಖರ s. n. A chaplet, crest, diadem. 2, a chief.

ಶೇಲೆ (= ಸೇಲೆ. tb. of ಚೇಲ) n. Cloth; a garment.

ಶೇದು. = ಸೇದು, q. v.

ಶೇರು. = ಸೇರು, q. v.

ಶೇರುವೆ. = ಸೇರುವೆ, q. v.

ಶೇಷ s. n. Remaining. 2, remainder, rest. 2, N. of the thousand-headed serpent. -ಗಿರಿ. N. ಶೇಷೆ. Rice thrown on the heads of a wedding couple as an auspicious rite.

ಶೈತ್ಯ (fr. ಶೀತ) s. n. Coldness, coolness; dampness; chilliness. -ಪದಾರ್ಥ. A cooling thing, as an orange, etc. ಶೈತೋಪಚಾರ. Presenting a tired guest with cool drinks.

ಶೈಲ s. a. Stony, rocky. n. A mountain.

ಶೈವ (fr. ಶಿವ) s. a. Relating to Śiva. n. A worshipper of Śiva. -ಪುರಾಣ. N. of Śiva purâṇa.

ಶೋಕ s. n. Sorrow, grief, mourning. -ಪಡು, -ಮಾಡು, ಶೋಕಿಸು. To mourn, lament. ಶೋಕಾಗ್ನಿ. Deep sorrow or distress.

ಶೋಧ s. n. Search, inquiry, scrutiny. -ಕ. Purificatory; a purifier, refiner; an inquirer, seeker, searcher, examiner, scrutinizer; a tempter. -ನ, -ನೆ. Search, research, examination; cleaning, cleansing, purifying; trial, temptation, correction, clearing away faults; the refining of metals. ಶೋಧಿತ. Cleansed, etc. ಶೋಧಿಸು. To purify, cleanse; to correct; to strain, sift, filter; to refine, clean; to examine, investigate, search.

ಶೋಫ s. n. Swelling, tumefaction.

ಶೋಭಕೃತ್ s. n. The thirty-seventh year in the cycle of sixty.

ಶೋಭೆ s. n. Brilliance, lustre. -ನ. Handsome; auspicious; lustre, brilliance; any auspicious ceremony, as a marriage; also -ನಪ್ರಸ್ಥ. ಶೋಭಾಯಮಾನ. Beautiful, splendid. ಶೋಭಿಸು. To shine, be splendid, look beautiful. ಶೋಭೆ. Light, lustre, splendour; beauty, elegance, comeliness.

ಶೋಷಣ s. n. Drying up; draining; withering; exhaustion. ಶೋಷಿತ. Dried up, exhausted. ಶೋಷಿಸು. To dry up; to become dry; to make dry.

ಶೌಚ (fr. ಶುಚಿ) s. n. Purification. 2, easing nature. 3, evacuation; excrement. ಶೌಚಾಚಾರ. Practice of purification. -ಕ್ಕೆ ಹೋಗು. To go to stool.

ಶೌರ್ಯ (fr. ಶೂರ) s. n. Heroism, prowess, might, courage; also -ತೆ. -ವಂತ. A hero, valiant man.

ಶ್ಮಶಾನ (= ಮಸಣ) s. n. A cemetery, burning or burial ground; also -ಭೂಮಿ. ಶ್ಮಶಾನಿ. Kâli or Durgâ.

ಶ್ಯಾನಭೋಗ. = ಶಾನಭೋಗ, q. v.

ಶ್ಯಾಮ (= ಶಾಮ) s. a. Dark-blue. -ತೆ. Blackness. -ಕ, ಶ್ಯಾಮಾಕ (= ಸಾಮೆ). A kind of edible grain, *Panicum frumentaceum*; also -ಅಕ್ಕಿ.

ಶ್ರದ್ಧೆ. ಶ್ರದ್ಧಾ s. n. Faith, belief, trust, confidence. 2, reverence; hope; wish. ಶ್ರದ್ಧಾಭಕ್ತಿ. Faith and devotion. ಶ್ರದ್ಧಾಳು. Faithful.

ಶ್ರಮ, ಶ್ರಮೆ s. n. Exertion, labour, toil, taking pains. 2, exercise, drill. 3, weariness, fatigue. 4, distress; annoyance. 5, penance. -ಗೊಳಿಸು. To fatigue, annoy. -ಗೊಳ್ಳು. To be fatigued, wearied. -ತೆಗೆದುಕೊಳ್ಳು. To take pains. -ಪಡಿಸು. To weary. -ಪಡು, -ಬೀಳು. To be wearied; to suffer. -ಗಾರ. A hard working man. ಕ್ರಿಸ್ತನ-. Christ's passion. -ವಾರ. Week of passions of Christ. -ಣ. Labouring; an ascetic; a Buddhist mendicant.

ಶ್ರಯ (tb. of ಶ್ರಾಯ) n. Improvement of land by cultivation. -ಸಾಗುವಳಿ. Farming land on a rent less than its original value. -ಪಟ್ಟೆ. -ಚೀಟು. A lease on such terms.

ಶ್ರವ s. n. Hearing, listening. 2, the ear. -ಣ. Hearing; the ear; the twenty-second lunar asterism; a goldsmith's pincers. ಶ್ರವಣೇಂದ್ರಿಯ. The organ of hearing.

ಶ್ರಾದ್ಧ (fr. ಶ್ರದ್ಧಾ) s. n. An anniversary ceremony performed to the manes of the nearest relatives. -ಕರ್ತೃ. Its performer. -ದೇವ. Yama.

ಶ್ರಾಂತ s. a. Tired, fatigued, exhausted. 2, calm, tranquil. ಶ್ರಾಂತಿ. Fatigue, exhaustion.

ಶ್ರಾವಕ s. n. A hearer; a pupil. 2, a particular class of Jainas.

ಶ್ರಾವಣ s. a. Audible. n. N. of the fifth lunar month.

ಶ್ರೀ s. n. Prosperity, well-being; success; wealth, riches. 2, dignity, majesty, fame. 3, beauty, loveliness; splendour, lustre. 4, Lakshmî, the wife of Vishṇu. 5, any virtue or excellence. 6, decoration. 7, an honorific prefix. -ಗಂಧ. Sandalwood. -ತಾಳಿ, -ತಾಳೆ. The talipot or fan-palm, *Corypha umbraculifera*. -ತುಳಸಿ. The holy basil. -ಧರ. Vishṇu or Kṛishṇa. -ನಿವಾಸ. Vishṇu. -ಪತಿ. A king. -ಪರ್ಣ. The shrub *Gmelina arborea*. -ಮತ್, -ಮತು. Prosperous, famous; an honorific title. -ಮಂತ. A nobleman, rich man. -ಮಂತರಾಜಶ್ರೀ. A general term of courtesy. -ಮುಖ. The seventh year in the cycle of sixty. -ಮುದ್ರೆ. The five seals used by Mâdhvas. -ರಂಗ. Kṛishṇa; N. of a town near Trichinopoly. -ರಂಗಪಟ್ಟಣ. N. of a town near Mysore. -ವೈಷ್ಣವ. A Vaishṇava of the Viśishṭhâdvaita sect. -ಶುಕ್ರವಾರ. Good-Friday. -ಹರ್ಷ. N. of a Saṁskṛita poet.

ಶ್ರುತ s. a. Heard; reported; understood. n. Traditional learning, a śâstra, the vêda. -ಪಡಿಸು. To let know, tell. ಶ್ರುತಿ. Hearing; an ear; oral account, news; the vêda; any vedic text; a sort of drone. ಶ್ರುತಿಕಷ್ಟ. Harsh to the ear. -ಗಾರ. A drone-player. ಶ್ರುತಿಬಾಹ್ಯ. Contrary to vêdas. ಶ್ರುತಿಶಿರಸ್. The vêdânta.

ಶ್ರೇಣಿ s. n. A line, row, range. 2, a multitude, troop.

ಶ್ರೇಯಸ್ s. a. Best, preferable. n. Virtue, moral merit. 2, good fortune, bliss. 3, final beatitude. ಶ್ರೇಯೋವಂತ, ಶ್ರೇಯಸ್ಕ. A prosperous man.

ಶ್ರೇಷ್ಠ s. a. Best, excellent, very eminent, far better; most prosperous; senior. -ತನ, -ತೆ, -ತ್ವ. Superiority, excellence. ಶ್ರೇಷ್ಠಿ (= ಸೆಟ್ಟಿ). The head of a tribe or company.

ಶ್ರೋತ್ರ s. n. The ear; *also* ಶ್ರೋತ್ರೇಂದ್ರಿಯ.

ಶ್ರೋತ್ರಿಯ s. n. A Brâhmaṇa versed in the vêdas.

ಶ್ಲಾಘನೆ, ಶ್ಲಾಘೆ s. n. Flattery; praise; boasting. -ಮಾಡು, ಶ್ಲಾಘಿಸು. To praise. ಶ್ಲಾಘ್ಯ. Praiseworthy, respectable.

ಶ್ಲೇಷ s. n. A figure of speech in rhetoric, connecting words of a double meaning, pun; *also* ಶ್ಲೇಷಾಲಂಕಾರ.

ಶ್ಲೇಷ್ಮ s. n. Phlegm, rheum. -ರೋಗ. A phlegmatic disease. -ಶರೀರ. A phlegmatic constitution.

ಶ್ಲೋಕ s. n. Any verse or stanza. 2, a kind of metre. 3, celebrity, fame. ಪುಣ್ಯ-, ಉತ್ತಮ-. Well-spoken of; a famous person.

ಶ್ವಪಚ s. n. A man of low caste; a Caṇḍâla.

ಶ್ವಶುರ s. n. A father-in-law; *f.* ಶ್ವಶ್ರು.

ಶ್ವಸನ s. n. Breathing, respiration.

ಶ್ವಾನ s. n. A dog.

ಶ್ವಾಪದ s. n. A beast of prey.

ಶ್ವಾಸ s. n. Breath, respiration; air, wind; hard breathing. -ಆಡಿಸು. To breathe. -ಎಳೆ. To inhale. -ಧಾರಣೆ. Suspension of breath. -ಬಿಡು. To exhale.

ಶ್ವೇತ s. a. White. n. Silver. -ಕುಷ್ಠ. White leprosy. -ಕೇತು. N. of a sage and of a king. -ರೋಗ. A kind of venereal affection.

ಷ್

ಷ್. The fiftieth letter of the alphabet. *It does not occur in pure Kannaḍa.*

ಷಕಾರ s. n. The letter ಷ.

ಷಕ್ಕು h. n. Doubt, suspicion; blemish, [fault.

ಷಟ್, ಷಡ್ s. a. Six. ಷಟ್ಕರ್ಮ. The six duties of a Brâhmaṇa, *as:* ಯಜನ, sacrificing; ಯಾಜನ, officiating at sacrifices made by others; ಅಧ್ಯಯನ, studying the vêdas; ಅಧ್ಯಾಪನ, teaching vêdas; ದಾನ, bestowing alms; ಪ್ರತಿಗ್ರಹ, receiving alms. ಷಟ್ಕೋಣ. A hexagon. ಷಟ್ಪದಿ. N. of a Kannaḍa metre. ಷಡಂಗ. Six-membered; the six vedâṅgas. ಷಡಂಗಕಷಾಯ. A decoction of six medicinal ingredients. ಷಡರಿ. Six enemies: ಕಾಮ, ಕ್ರೋಧ, ಲೋಭ, ಮೋಹ, ಮದ, ಮತ್ಸರ. ಷಡಿಂದ್ರಿಯ. The six indriyas. ಷಡ್ವಿಷಯ. The six objects of sense, *as:* ಶಬ್ದ, ಸ್ಪರ್ಶ, ರೂಪ, ರಸ, ಗಂಧ, ಜ್ಞಾನ. ಷಡ್ಗುಣ. Sixfold; an aggregate of six qualities.

ಷಡ್ಜ s. a. Six-born. n. N. of the fourth note of music.

ಷಡ್ದರ್ಶನ s. n. The six recognised systems of philosophy: mîmâmsâ (by Jaimini), vêdânta (by Bâdarûyaṇa), nyâya (by Gautama), vaiśêshika (by Kaṇâda), sâṅkhya (by Kapila), and yôga by Patañjali).

ಷಡ್ರಸ s. n. The six tastes: madhura, kaṭu, amla, tuvara, tikta, and lavaṇa.

ಷಡ್ವರ್ಗ, ಷಡ್ವೈರಿ. = ಷಡರಿ, q. v.

ಷಂಡ s. n. A multitude, collection, group, heap, flock. -ಕ. A eunuch.

ಷರತ್ h. n. A wager, bet. 2, agreement, condition.

ಷರಬತ್ h. n. A sweet drink so called.

ಷರಾ h. n. Remark; *nota-bene.*

ಷರಾಬು h. n. Spirituous liquor.

ಷರಾಯಿ h. n. Trousers.

ಷಷ್ಟ s. a. Sixtieth. 2, = ಷಷ್ಠ. ಷಷ್ಟಿ. Sixty; = ಷಷ್ಠಿ.

ಷಷ್ಠ s. a. Sixth. ಷಷ್ಠಿ. The sixth day of a lunar fortnight.

ಷಾಪ್ e. n. A shop.

ಷಾಲು. = ಶಾಲು, q. v.

ಷಿಕಮಿ h. n. A subordinate tenure whose revenue is paid through the proprietor.

ಷುರು h. a. Begun. n. Beginning, commencement.

ಷೋಕಿ, ಷೋಕು f. n. Voluptuousness. -ದಾರ. A voluptuous man.

ಷೋಡಶ s. a. Sixteenth. 2, sixteen. ಷೋಡಶೋಪಚಾರ. Sixteen ways of doing homage (to idols) or civility (to men). -ಸಂಸ್ಕಾರ. Sixteen ceremonies to be performed from birth to death.

ಸ್

ಸ್. The fifty-first letter of the alphabet.

ಸಂ. = ಸಮ್, *q. v.*

ಸಂಯಮ s. *n.* Restraint, check. 2, humanity, forbearance. 3, a religious vow. -ನ. Restraining, checking. ಸಂಯಮಿ. An ascetic.

ಸಂಯುಕ್ತ s. *a.* United; attached; blended; endowed with.

ಸಂಯೋಗ s. *n.* Connection, junction; union, association; conjunction. ಸಂಯೋಗಿಸು. To join, mix.

ಸಂರಕ್ಷಕ s. *n.* A guardian. ಸಂರಕ್ಷಣೆ. Protecting, guarding, preserving; saving. ಸಂರಕ್ಷಿಸು. To guard, protect, save.

ಸಂಲಾಪ s. *n.* Talking, friendly conversation, chat.

ಸಂವತ್ಸರ s. *n.* A year. ಚಾಂದ್ರಮಾನ-. The lunar year. ಸೌರಮಾನ-. The solar year.

ಸಂವರಣೆ (*tb. of* ಸಂಭರಣ) *n.* Preparing, preparation, procuring. ಸಂವರಿಸು. To make ready, prepare.

ಸಂವಾದ s. *n.* Conversation, dialogue; discussion; communication, report. ಸಂವಾದಿಸು. To speak with, converse; to discuss.

ಸಂವಿಧಾನ s. *n.* Disposition; performance; plan; minding.

ಸಂವೇದ s. *n.* Perception, consciousness, understanding. ಸಂವೇದಿಸು. To know, learn.

ಸಂಶಯ s. *n.* Uncertainty, doubt, scruple, suspicion. 2, difficulty, risk. -ಗೊಳ್ಳು, -ತಕ್ಕೊಳ್ಳು, -ತೆಗೆ. To waver, to become suspicious. -ಪಡು, -ಬೀಳು, -ಮಾಡು, ಸಂಶಯಿಸು. To doubt, suspect.

ಸಂಶ್ರಯ s. *n.* Refuge, shelter, protection. 2, league. -ಕೊಡು. To shelter.

ಸಂಸರ್ಗ s. *n.* Close union; close contact; association; intercourse; acquaintance.

ಸಂಸಾರ s. *n.* Secular life; the affairs of life; worldly illusion; a household; a family; a wife. -ತಾಪತ್ರಯ. Family-cares. -ನಡಿಸು, -ಮಾಡು, -ಸಾಗಿಸು. To manage the affairs of life; to keep house. -ಭಾರ. The weight of affairs of life. -ವಿಮೋಚನ. Emancipation from the world. ಸಂಸಾರಿ. Worldly secular. ಸಂಸಾರಿಕ. One who has a family.

ಸಂಸಿದ್ಧಿ s. *n.* Complete accomplishment, perfection. 2, nature.

ಸಂಸೃಷ್ಟ s. *a.* Conjoined, united, common to all; re-united (*as* kinsmen). ಸಂಸೃಷ್ಟಿ. Union, combination; a re-united kinsman, co-partner.

ಸಂಸಿ. *tb. of* ಸಂಶಯ, *q. v.*

ಸಂಸ್ಕಾರ s. *n.* Refinement. 2, conception, idea. 3, any faculty, instinct. 4, preparation; consecration, dedication. 5, a sanctifying or purificatory rite or ceremony, *as:* ಗರ್ಭಾಧಾನ, ಜಾತಕರ್ಮ, ನಾಮಕರಣ, ಚೌಲ, ಉಪನಯನ, ವಿವಾಹ, *etc.* 6, funeral obsequies. ಸಂಸ್ಕರಿಸು. To prepare, refine; to sanctify, consecrate. ಸಂಸ್ಕೃತ. Refined, polished; consecrated; the Saṁskṛita language.

ಸಂಸ್ತುತ s. *a.* Praised; lauded. ಸಂಸ್ತುತಿ. Praise, eulogy.

ಸಂಸ್ಥಾನ s. *n.* A collection; conformation. 2, any place, a station, presidency. 3, a royal city; a capital; a state, government. ಸಂಸ್ಥಾನಿಕ, ಸಂಸ್ಥಾನಾಧಿಪತಿ. A ruler, chief.

ಸಂಸ್ಥಾಪನ s. *n.* Confirming, establishing; establishment; a regulation.

ಸಂಸ್ಥಿತಿ s. n. Standing with; contiguity; duration. 2, abiding; situation, condition. 3, standing still; death.

ಸಂಸ್ಪರ್ಶ s. n. Mutual contact. 2, perception, sense.

ಸಂಸ್ಮರಣ, ಸಂಸ್ಮರಣೆ s. n. Remembering, recollecting.

ಸಂಹತಿ s. n. Close combination; compactness; an assemblage.

ಸಂಹರ s. n. Destroying, destruction. ಸಂಹರಿಸು. To destroy, annihilate.

ಸಂಹರ್ಷ s. n. Thrill of delight, joy, pleasure.

ಸಂಹಾರ s. n. Destruction, annihilation; cf. ಸಂಹರ. ಸಂಹಾರಿಸು. = ಸಂಹರಿಸು, q. v.

ಸಂಹಿತೆ s. n. A compilation, compendium. 2, any arranged collection of texts; the hymnical text of the vêdas.

ಸಕತಿ. tb. of ಶಕ್ತಿ, q. v.

ಸಕರ್ಮಕ s. n. Transitive. n. The transitive verb.

ಸಕಲ s. a. All, whole, entire. n. Every thing; the whole.

ಸಕಲಾತಿ h. n. European woollen cloth.

ಸಕಾರ s. n. The letter ಸ್.

ಸಕಾಲ s. n. Good time. a. Seasonable. ad. Betimes.

ಸಕುಟುಂಬ s. a. With family or wife. 2, all sorts together

ಸಕೇಶ s. a. Having hair, hairy. ಸಕೇಶಿ. An unshaven widow.

ಸಕ್ಕರೆ (tb. of ಶರ್ಕರೆ) n. Sugar. ಕಲ್ಲು-, ಖಂಡ-. Sugar-candy. -ಕಂಚಿ. The large citron. -ಕಡ್ಡಿ. A sugar stick.

ಸಕ್ತ s. a. Attached to; diligent, attentive. ಸಕ್ತಿ. Attachment, contact; severity. ಸಕ್ತು. Hard; harsh; oppressive.

ಸಕ್ರೆ. = ಸಕ್ಕರೆ, q. v.

ಸಖ, ಸಖಿ s. n. An associate, companion. ಸಖಿತ್ವ, ಸಖ್ಯ. Friendship, intimacy.

ಸಗಟು f. n. The whole in a lump; an average.

ಸಗಣಿ, ಸಗಣೆ s. n. Cowdung.

ಸಗಾಟ, ಸಗಾಟಿಕೆ s. n. Great friendship.

ಸಗುಣ s. a. Virtuous; worldly.

ಸಗೋತ್ರ s. n. A kinsman. 2, race, lineage.

ಸಗ್ಗ. tb. of ಸ್ವರ್ಗ, q. v.

ಸಗ್ಗಿಗ (tb. of ಸ್ವರ್ಗಿ) n. A deity.

ಸಂಕ f. n. A bridge.

ಸಂಕಟ s. a. Narrow, strait. n. A strait, difficulty, trouble, hardship; affliction, distress. -ಗೊಳ್ಳು, -ಪಡು, -ಬೀಳು, -ವಾಗು. To suffer distress. ಪ್ರಾಣ-. The agony of death; any great difficulty. Other cpds.: ಅನ್ನ-, ದಾಹ-, ಜನ-, ಮರಣ-.

ಸಂಕರ s. n. Union; confusion; unlawful mixture. 2, a mixed caste; also ಜಾತಿ-. 3, sweepings, dust. 4, a double sack. 5, tb. of ಶಂಕರ.

ಸಂಕರ್ಷಣ s. n. Contracting, shortening, attracting. 2, Baladêva.

ಸಂಕಲನ s. n. Addition (arith.). ಸಂಕಲಿತ. Added; addition (arith.).

ಸಂಕಲಿಕೆ s. n. A pair of wedding garments.

ಸಂಕಲೆ (tb. of ಶೃಂಖಲೆ) n. A chain, fetter.

ಸಂಕಲ್ಪ s. n. Will, volition, purpose, resolution, vow. 2, wish. 3, thought, fancy; consideration. 4, mind, soul. 5, declaration of purpose. ದೇವರ-. The will of God. -ಮಾಡು, ಸಂಕಲ್ಪಿಸು. To will, purpose, resolve; to wish for.

ಸಂಕೀರ್ತನ, ಸಂಕೀರ್ತನೆ s. n. Lauding, praising; glorification.

ಸಂಕುಚಿತ s. a. Contracted, shrivelled up, wrinkled.

ಸಂಕುಲ s. a. Crowded together; confused; filled with. n. A crowd, throng. -ತೆ. Confusion, perplexity.

ಸಂಕೇತ s. n. Gesture, hint, a sign, token, symbol; convention; engagement. -ಸ್ಥಲ. An appointed place. ಸಂಕೇತಾಕ್ಷರ. A secret writing. Cpds.: ಕೈ-, ಬಾಯಿ-.

ಸಂಕೋಚ s. n. Shrinking, contraction; abridgment, diminution. 2, reserve;

repression. -ಪಡು, ಸಂಕೋಚಿಸು. To shrink, close; to hesitate, doubt. -ಮಾಡು. To abridge. -ಗಾರ. A hesitator.

ಸಂಕೋಲೆ (*tb. of* ಶೃಂಖಲ, *q. v.*) *n.* A chain. -ಬೀಳು. To be fettered. -ಹಾಕು. To fetter.

ಸಂಕ್ರಮಣ s. *n.* Transition, progress; passage. 2, the sun's passage from one sign of the zodiac to another. 3, the day on which the sun so passes; *also* ಸಂಕ್ರಾಂತಿ.

ಸಂಕ್ರಾಮ s. *n.* Difficult passage. 2, a causeway.

ಸಂಕ್ಲೇಶ s. *n.* Affliction, pain, torment.

ಸಂಕ್ಷಿಪ್ತ s. *a.* Abridged, abbreviated; concise, compact.

ಸಂಕ್ಷೇಪ s. *n.* Abridgment, abbreviation; conciseness, brevity; an epitome. ಸಂಕ್ಷೇಪವಾಗಿ. Briefly. ಸಂಕ್ಷೇಪಿಸು. To abridge, shorten.

ಸಂಖ್ಯೆ, ಸಂಖ್ಯಾ s. *n.* Numeration. 2, an account, sum. 3, number; a numeral. ಸಂಖ್ಯಾತ. Reckoned, numbered. ಅಸಂಖ್ಯಾತ. Innumerable. ಸಂಖ್ಯಾಪೂರಣ. Ordinal number. ಸಂಖ್ಯಾವಾಚಕ, ಸಂಖ್ಯಾವಾಚಿ. A numeral.

ಸಂಗ s. *n.* Union, contact; intercourse, association. -ಮಾಡು. To associate with. ದುರ್ಜನ-, ದುಃ-. Bad company. ಸಜ್ಜನ-, ಸತ್-. Good company. ನಿಃ-. Absence of attachment.

ಸಂಗಡ (*tb. of* ಸಂಘಾತ) *prep.* Together with, with; by, in presence. -ಕರಕೊಂಡು ಹೋಗು, -ತಕ್ಕೊಳ್ಳು, -ತೆಗೆದುಕೊಂಡು ಹೋಗು. To take (somebody or something) with (one's self). ಸಂಗಡಿ, ಸಂಗಡಿಗ. A companion, friend. ಸಂಗಡಿಸು. To assemble; to crowd, *etc.*

ಸಂಗತ s. *a.* Joined, united; assembled. 2, proper, seasonable, applicable; fitted for. *n.* Union; association.

ಸಂಗತಿ s. *n.* Union; association, company. 2, occurrence, affair; matter, subject, business. -ಗೆ ಬೀಳು. To fall into society. -ಒಡಿ. To keep company with. ಸಂಗತ್ಯಾನುಸಾರ. According to circumstances.

ಸಂಗಮ s. *n.* Meeting; union, junction; association, intercourse. 2, the confluence of two rivers.

ಸಂಗರ s. *n.* Agreement, assent. 2, a day and night. 3, devouring. 4, war, battle. 5, trouble, pain.

ಸಂಗಳಿಸು s. *v. i.* To be joined, mixed. 2, to be brought about; to come to pass, occur.

ಸಂಗಾತ (*tb. of* ಸಂಘಾತ) *n.* Union, company. *prep.* With, together with. ಸಂಗಾತಿ. A companion, friend. -ಬಿಡು. To give up connection with a person.

ಸಂಗೀತ s. *a.* Sung together. *n.* Symphony; a concert, chorus. -ಗಾರ. A singer, a music-master. -ವಿದ್ಯೆ, -ಶಾಸ್ತ್ರ. The science of music. -ಸ್ವರ. The notes of the musical scale.

ಸಂಗ್ರಹ s. *n.* Seizing, grasp, taking hold of. 2, reception; gathering, collection, heap, store; a compilation; a totality. 3, an abridgment, summary. 4, a catalogue. 5, a storeroom. -ಮಾಡು. To collect, lay up in store. ಸಂಗ್ರಹಿಸು. To gather, acquire, amass; to abridge; to include, comprehend ಮದುವೆಗೆ ಸಂಗ್ರಹ ಮಾಡು. To provide necessaries for a wedding.

ಸಂಗ್ರಾಮ s. *n.* A battle, war, fighting.

ಸಂಘ s. *n.* A combination, gathering, multitude, crowd, group; a commitee.

ಸಂಘಟನ, ಸಂಘಟನೆ, ಸಂಘುಟ್ಟನ s. *n.* Union; junction; being effected; collision; friction. ಸಂಘಟಿಸು. To occur, happen; to be effected; to strike against.

ಸಂಘರ್ಷ, ಸಂಘರ್ಷಣ s. *n.* Rubbing, grinding, friction, collision, emulation.

ಸಂಘಾತ (= ಸಂಗಡ, ಸಂಗಾತ, *q. v.*) s. *n.* Union, association. 2, a mass, heap, assemblage, cluster. ಸಂಘಾತಿ. A companion.

ಸಚರಾಚರ s. a. Animate and inanimate; universal. n. The universe.

ಸಚಿವ s. n. A companion. 2, a counsellor, minister.

ಸಚೇತನ s. a. Sentient, animate, living.

ಸಚೇಲ s. a. Clothed, dressed. -ಸ್ನಾನ. Ablution in one's garments.

ಸಚ್ಚಿದಾನಂದ s. n. Existence, thought and joy (*of the universal soul—vedantic*).

ಸಜಾ h. n. Punishment.

ಸಜಾತಿ, ಸಜಾತೀಯು s. a. Of the same caste or tribe.

ಸಜೀವ s. a. Alive, animate.

ಸಜ್ಜ s. a. Covered. 2, trimmed. 3, prepared, ready. 4, armed. n. Equipment, harness.

ಸಜ್ಜನ s. a. Respectable; virtuous, good. n. A good or virtuous man. -ಸಂಗ. Good company. ಸಜ್ಜನಿಕೆ. Goodness. = ಸೌಜನ್ಯ.

ಸಜ್ಜರಸ. *tb. of* ಸರ್ಜರಸ, *q. v.*

ಸಜ್ಜೆ, ಸಜ್ಜು. *tb. of* ಸಜ್ಜ, *q. v.*

ಸಜ್ಜಿಗೆ (= ಸೊಜ್ಜಿಗ, ಸೋಜ) f. n. Wheaten flour, rolong. 2, a dish made of it.

ಸಜ್ಜೀಕಾರ (*tb. of* ಸರ್ಜಿಕಾಕ್ಷಾರ) n. Country alkali, carbonate of soda.

ಸಜ್ಜೆ 1. k. n. The grain *Holcus spicatus*.

ಸಜ್ಜೆ 2. (*tb. of* ಶಯ್ಯೆ) n. A place of rest. 2, an upper story. -ಮನೆ. A sleeping apartment.

ಸಂಚ 1. = ಸಂಚು, *q. v.*

ಸಂಚ 2. (*tb. of* ಸಂಚಯ) n. That is accumulated or saved (*as* money, grain, *etc.*).

ಸಂಚಕಾರ (*tb. of* ಸತ್ಯಂಕಾರ) n. Advance, earnest money, pledge, deposit.

ಸಂಚಯು s. n. Heaping up, collection, heap, store, quantity. -ನ. Putting up or saving; taking the ashes of a cremated body and throwing in a river. -ಮಾಡು, ಸಂಚಯ್ಸು. To collect, put up.

ಸಂಚರ, ಸಂಚರಣ s. n. Travelling, going about; motion. ಸಂಚರಿಸು. To walk or move about, roam, wander. ಸಂಚಾರ. Roaming, wandering; passage, progress, course; a passage. ಸಂಚಾರ ಮಾಡು. = ಸಂಚರಿಸು, *q. v.* ಸಂಚಾರಿ. A wanderer, traveller. ದೇಶ-, ಭೂ-. Foreign travel.

ಸಂಚಿ f. n. A sack, bag.

ಸಂಚಿಕೆ f. n. A section or part of a book.

ಸಂಚಿತ s. a. Heaped up, amassed, collected, saved. 2, filled with. *Cpds.*: -ಕರ್ಮ, -ದ್ರವ್ಯ, -ಪುಣ್ಯ.

ಸಂಚು k. n. An expedient, means; an artifice; a trick, intrigue; skill. ಒಳ-. A secret plot, intrigue. -ನಡಿಸು, -ಮಾಡು. To intrigue. -ಗಾರ. A spy; *f.* -ಗಾತಿ, -ಗಾತಿಗ.

ಸಂಜೀವನ s. n. Remaining alive. 2, bringing to life; an animating process; an elixir. ಸಂಜೀವಿನಿ. A plant that restores to life. ಸಂಜೀವಿಸು. To remain alive, to resuscitate.

ಸಂಜೆ (*tb. of* ಸಂಧ್ಯೆ) n. Evening. -ಗತ್ತಲೆ, -ಹೊತ್ತು. Evening twilight.

ಸಂಜ್ಞಾ, ಸಂಜ್ಞೆ s. n. Sense; knowledge, thought, mind. 2, a sign, token, signal, symbol, gesture, hint. 3, a title, term. ಸಂಜ್ಞಾಕ್ಷರ. An initial letter.

ಸಟುಕ. = ಸಟ್ಟುಗ, *q. v.*

ಸಟೆ (*tb. of* ಶಠ) n. Falsehood, lying, cheating; villainy; *also* -ಪಟೆ. *reit.* -ಮಾತು, -ಪಟೆಮಾತು. A lie. -ಗಾರ. A liar.

ಸಟ್ಟುಗ k. n. A spoon, ladle.

ಸಡಗರ k. n. Agitation; eagerness; joy; festivity; festive display. 2, excellence, beauty. ಸಡಗರಿಸು. To grow agitated, elated or joyful; to adorn.

ಸಡಲು, ಸಡಿಲು (= ಸಡ್ಲ, *q. v.*) k. a. Loose, slack, relaxed or lax. ಸಡಲಾಗು. To become lax. -ಮಾಡು, ಸಡಿಲಿಸು. To slacken, loosen. -ಬಿಡು. To relax; to give liberty.

ಸಡ್ಡಕ f. n. A brother-in-law, the husband of a man's wife's sister.

ಸಡ್ಡೆ 1. f. n. A sowing machine used with the hand.

ಸಡ್ಡೆ 2. (*tb. of* ಶ್ರದ್ಧೆ) n. Respect, honour, esteem; attention, heed. -ಮಾಡು. To respect, *etc.*; *cf.* ಅ-.

ಸಡ್ಲು. = ಸಡಲು, *q. v.*

ಸಣಬು (*tb. of* ಶಣ) n. Hemp, *Cannabis sativa.*

ಸಂಡಿಗೆ (*tb. of* ಷಡಂಕ) n. A thin crisp cake made of the flour of any grain mixed with or without chillies, salt, *etc.*, dried and roasted or fried.

ಸಣ್ಣ (*tb. of* ಸನ್ನ) a. Small, little, tiny, fine, thin, delicate, slender. *Cpds.*: -ಅಕ್ಕಿ, -ಇರಿವೆ, -ಕೆರೆ, -ಗೋದಿ, -ನೆಗ್ಗಿಲು, -ಹನಿ, -ಹುಡುಗ, -ಹುಡುಗಿ, *etc.* -ದೊಡ್ಡ. Small and big. -ದು. That is small; a small thing. -ಧ್ವನಿ. A low voice. -ನಡು. A slender waist. -ಮಾತು. An insignificant or mean word. -ಮೋರೆ. A dejected face. -ವ. A boy; *f.* -ವಳು. -ಗೆ, -ನೆ. Small, fine, *etc.* ಸಣ್ಣಾಗು. To be small, low.

ಸಣ್ಣೆ f. n. A garment of coarse silk.

ಸತ್ (= ಸದು, *etc.*) s. a. Being; real, true. 2, virtuous, good; right; excellent. -ಕರ್ಮ, -ಕಾರ್ಯ. A good or virtuous action. -ಕೀರ್ತಿ. Great fame. -ಕುಲ. A good family. -ಕೃತಿ, -ಕ್ರಿಯೆ. A good composition; a virtuous act. -ಕ್ರೈಸ್ತ. A true Christian. -ಪಾತ್ರ. A worthy or virtuous person. -ಪುಣ್ಯ. A real merit. -ಪುತ್ರ. A virtuous son. -ಪುರುಷ. A virtuous man; a respectable person. -ವಿಶ್ವಾಸ. True, living faith. -ಸಂಗ, -ಸಹವಾಸ. Good company.

ಸತತ s. a. Constant, perpetual, eternal. *ad.* Always.

ಸತವು (*tb. of* ಸತ್ವ) n. Strength; firmness.

ಸತಿ s. n. A faithful wife. 2, a wife.

ಸತುವು (*tb. of* ಸತ್ವ) n. Strength, *etc.* 2, pewter, zinc.

ಸತ್ಕಾರ s. n. Hospitality; respect; care, attention. -ಮಾಡು, ಸತ್ಕರಿಸು. To receive hospitably; to treat kindly; to welcome.

ಸತ್ತಾ (= ಸತ್ತೆ 2) s. n. Existence; authority, sway; power, might.

ಸತ್ತಿಗೆ (*tb. of* ಛತ್ರಿಕೆ) n. An umbrella.

ಸತ್ತು. *P. p. of* ಸಾಯು.

ಸತ್ತೆ 1. k. n. Rubbish, dirt, stuff, trash.

ಸತ್ತೆ 2. = ಸತ್ತಾ, *q. v.*

ಸತ್ಯ s. a. True, real, sincere, honest, truthful, faithful. n. Truth, sincerity, reality; a fixed rule. 2, a promise, oath. -ತನ, -ತೆ, -ತ್ವ. Truth; sincerity, veracity. -ಪ್ರತಿಜ್ಞೆ, -ಪ್ರಮಾಣ. A sincere vow or oath. -ವಚನ. A true word; a sincere promise. -ಲೋಕ. The highest of the seven worlds. -ಯುಗ. The first of the four yugas. -ವಂತ, -ಶಾಲಿ. A faithful, honest man. -ವಾದಿ. A truth-speaking man. ಸತ್ಯಾಚರಣೆ. Observance of truth. ಸತ್ಯಾನೃತ. Truth and lie; commerce.

ಸತ್ರ s. n. A sacrifice; an oblation; liberality; wealth. 2, a place of refuge. -ಶಾಲೆ. An alms-house.

ಸತ್ವ s. n. Essence, life. 2, breath; mind. 3, a substance. 4, nature. 5, goodness; truth; strength, energy, power. -ಗುಣ. The quality of purity or goodness; generosity; valour. -ವಂತ, -ಶಾಲಿ. A powerful man. -ಹೀನ. A weak man.

ಸತ್ವರ s. a. Quick, speedy.

ಸದ್. = ಸತ್, *q. v.* -ಗತಿ. Felicity, fortune. -ಗುಣ. A good quality. -ಗುರು. A true guru. -ಧರ್ಮ. A good religion, justice, virtue. -ಭಕ್ತ. A true devotee. -ಭಕ್ತಿ. True devotion. -ಭಾವ. Reality; goodness, amiability. -ವೃತ್ತಿ. Good conduct. -ವ್ಯವಹಾರ, -ವ್ಯಾಪಾರ. Good occupation or transaction.

ಸದನ s. n. A seat. 2, an abode, house. 3, exhaustion.

ಸದಮಲ s. a. True and pure; truly pure. -ಭಕ್ತಿ. Truly pure devotedness.

ಸದರ್ h. *n.* The highest court of law. 2, a state-room. -ಅದಾಲತ್. A zillah court. -ಅಮೀನ. A subordinate judge.

ಸದರ f. *n.* Familiarity, friendliness; facility.

ಸದರಹು, ಸದರಿ h. *a.* Afore-said, above-mentioned.

ಸದರು. = ಸದರ್, *q. v.*

ಸದಸ್ (*tb.* ಸದಸ್ಸು) s. *n.* An assembly, meeting. 2, a set. ಸದಸ್ಯ. An assessor, member.

ಸದಾ s. *ad.* Always, at all times, continually, ever; *also* -ಕಾಲ. -ಚರಣ, -ಚಾರ. Good manners; a good custom. -ಚಾರಿ. A virtuous person. -ನಂದ, -ಶಿವ. Always happy; N. of Śiva.

ಸದಾಪ, ಸದಾಬು f. *n.* The strong-smelling rue, *Ruta graveolens.*

ಸದೃಶ s. *a.* Like, similar, same; fit, proper. -ತೆ, -ತ್ವ. Likeness, similarity.

ಸದೆ a. k. *v. t.* To bruise, crush; to strike, beat. *v. i.* To be reduced to powder. *n.* Trash, rubbish, stuff.

ಸದ್ದು 1. k. *v. i.* To cease, stop (*used only in the imperative*).

ಸದ್ದು 2. *tb. of* ಶಬ್ದ, *q. v.*

ಸದ್ಯ, ಸದ್ಯಾ (*tb. of* ಸದ್ಯಸ್) *ad.* Today, this moment, now; at once, on the spot, presently.

ಸನ್ h. *n.* An age or period, year; *anno* [*Domini.*

ಸನಕ, ಸನತ್ಕುಮಾರ, ಸನತ್ಸುಜಾತ s. *n.* Ns. of Brahmâ's sons.

ಸನದು s. *n.* A grant, diploma, charter, patent. ಸನದಿ. Held by a grant.

ಸನಾತನ s. *a.* Eternal; ancient. *n.* A hautboy.

ಸನಾಥ s. *a.* Having a master. 2, possessing, having.

ಸನಾದಿ h. *n.* A clarion, hautboy.

ಸನಿ. *tb. of* ಶನಿ, *q. v.*

ಸನೀನು h. *n.* A bayonet.

ಸಂತ (*fr.* ಸತ್. = ಶಾಂತ) s. *n.* A saint. *a.* Venerable, respected. 2, gentle, calm, soft. -ಆರಾಧನೆ, -ಸೇವೆ. Saints' worship. -ಯಿಸು. -ಯ್ಸು, -ಎಸು. To appease, allay, pacify, calm, soothe, comfort, console.

ಸಂತತ s. *a.* Continuous, lasting, eternal.

ಸಂತತಿ s. *n.* Lineage; offspring, progeny. ಸ್ತ್ರೀ-. The female line. ಪುರುಷ-. The male line.

ಸಂತಪ್ತ s. *a.* Inflamed, hot, glowing; [burnt up.

ಸಂತರ್ಪಣೆ s. *n.* A sumptuous meal.

ಸಂತಸ. *tb. of* ಸಂತೋಷ, *q. v.*

ಸಂತಾನ (= ಸಂತತಿ) s. *n.* Progeny, offspring; a child. -ಸಮೃದ್ಧಿ. Increase of progeny. -ಅಳಿದು ಹೋಗು, ನಿಸ್ಸಂತಾನವಾಗು. A generation to perish to be childless.

ಸಂತಾಪ s. *n.* Great heat. 2, affliction, pain, anguish, distress. 3, remorse, penitence; resentment. -ಪಡಿಸು. To afflict, torment. -ಪಡು, ಸಂತಾಪಿಸು. To be distressed or afflicted.

ಸಂತು k. *3rd pers. sing. of the imperf. of* ಸಲ್ಲು.

ಸಂತುಷ್ಟ s. *a.* Satisfied, contented, well-pleased, delighted. ಸಂತುಷ್ಟಿ. Satisfaction, contentment.

ಸಂತೃಪ್ತಿ s. *n.* Complete satisfaction, satiety.

ಸಂತೆ 1. (*tb. of* ಸಂಸ್ಥಾ) *n.* A mass, crowd. 2, a fair or market. -ಕಟ್ಟು, -ಕೂಡು, -ನೆರೆ. A market to convene. -ಹರಿ. A market to disperse.

ಸಂತೆ 2. f. *n.* A lesson. -ಹೇಳು. To tell a santĕ repeatedly.

ಸಂತೋಷ (= ಸಂತಸ) s. *n.* Satisfaction. 2, happiness, delight, joy, pleasure. -ಕೊಡು. To give joy. -ಗೊಳಿಸು, -ಪಡಿಸು. To please, gladden, gratify. -ಪಡು, ಸಂತೋಷಿಸು. To feel happy or glad. -ಕರ. Causing joy, *etc.*, pleasing. -ಪುರುಷ. A cheerful man. -ಬಾಷ್ಪ. Tears of joy. -ಇಂದಿರು, -ದಲ್ಲಿರು. To be pleased, cheerful.

ಸಂದಣಿ (*tb. of* ಸಂಧಾನ) *n.* A collection, crowd, flock, throng. -ಸು (*v. i.*). To collect, meet, crowd, flock.

ಸಂದರ್ಭ s. n. Convenience, opportunity, leisure. 2, affair, matter. -ಆಗು, -ಬೀಳು, ಸಂದರ್ಭಿಸು. To be opportune or convenient.

ಸಂದರ್ಶನ s. n. Seeing, sight, vision; meeting; an interview, visit. -ಕೊಡು, -ತೆಗೆದುಕೊಳ್ಳು. To visit.

ಸಂದಾಯ k. n. Payment of what is due. -ಆಗು. To be paid up. -ಮಾಡು. To pay.

ಸಂಡಿ. = ಸಂದು 2, q. v.

ಸಂದಿಗ್ಧ s. a. Obscure; dubious, doubtful, uncertain.

ಸಂದಿಸು s. v. t. To join; to fasten; to tie; to fix. v. i. To associate one's self to. 2, to occur, happen.

ಸಂದು 1. P. p. of ಸಲ್ಲು, q. v. -ಹೋಗು. To die.

ಸಂದು 2. (= ಸಂದಿ. tb. of ಸಂಧಿ) n. Juncture; a joint; a nook, corner; a lane; a cleft, gap, crack, opening. -ಕಟ್ಟು. Opportunity, convenience; a junction of two roads. -ಕೂಡಿಸು. Tor abbet. -ಬಳ್ಳಿ. A climbing herb, *Vitis quadrangularis.* -ವಾತ. Rheumatism of the joints. -ಬಿಡು. To leave a space. -ಬೀಳು. To crack; to be patched. -ಹಾಕು. To patch. -ಸೇರುವೆ. Exact joinery.

ಸಂದೂಕ, ಸಂದೂಕು h. n. A large box, chest.

ಸಂದೇಶ s. n. Information, tidings; a [message.

ಸಂದೇಹ s. n. Doubt, uncertainty; scruple; risk, danger. -ಗೊಳ್ಳು, -ಪಡು, ಸಂದೇಹಿಸು. To doubt, suspect. -ತೀರಿಸು. To remove a doubt.

ಸಂಧಾನ (= ಸಂದಣಿ, q. v.) s. n. Junction; combination; alliance, league; peace; reception. ಲಾಕೇಶ-. Bribe.

ಸಂಧಿ (= ಸಂದಿ, ಸಂದು, q. v.) s. n. Conjunction, union. 2, alliance, peace. 3, euphonic junction of letters (g.). 4, a joint. 5, a critical juncture. 6, a breach, gap, hole; a chapter. 7, an interval. -ವಾತ (= ಸಂದುವಾತ). Rheumatism. -ಸೂಚನೆ. Contents of a chapter. ಸಂಧ್ಯಕ್ಷರ. A diphthong.

ಸಂಧ್ಯಾಕಾಲ. Evening time, evening. ಸಂಧ್ಯಾರಾಗ. Twilight; evening. ಸಂಧ್ಯಾವಂದನ. Morning and evening adoration. ಸಂಧ್ಯೆ. = ಸಂಜೆ, *etc.*, q. v.

ಸನ್ನದ್ಧ s. a. Armed; arrayed, prepared; provided, ready.

ಸನ್ನಹ, ಸನ್ನಾಹ s. n. Preparation, military array. 2, armour, mail.

ಸನ್ನಿ. tb. of ಸನ್ನಿಪಾತ, q. v.

ಸನ್ನಿಕರ್ಷ, -ಣೆ s. n. Approximation, nearness, vicinity.

ಸನ್ನಿಧ s. n. Proximity, vicinity, nearness. ಸನ್ನಿಧಾನ, ಸನ್ನಿಧಿ. Proximity, nearness, presences; *Cpds.:* ಸಾಹೇಬರ-, ದೇವರ-, ದೊರೆಗಳ-, *etc.*

ಸನ್ನಿಪಾತ s. n. Falling down; collision. 2, combined derangement of the three humours (wind, bile, and phlegm).

ಸನ್ನೆ 1. (tb. of ಸಂಜ್ಞೆ, q. v.) n. A sign, hint.

ಸನ್ನೆ 2, -ಕೋಲು k. n. A lever.

ಸನ್ನ್ಯಾಸ s. n. Laying aside, resignation, abandonment of all worldly possessions and earthly affections, asceticism. ಸನ್ನ್ಯಾಸಿ. An ascetic, religious mendicant.

ಸನ್ಮತ s. n. Approbation, sanction. ಸನ್ಮತಿ. A good understanding.

ಸನ್ಮಾನ s. n. Respect, honour. -ಮಾಡು. To honour. ಸನ್ಮಾನಿಸು. To respect, honour.

ಸನ್ಮಾರ್ಗ s. n. The right way; a virtuous conduct. -ಸ್ಥ. A man of good conduct.

ಸನ್ಯಾಸ, ಸನ್ಯಾಸಿ. tb. of ಸನ್ನ್ಯಾಸ, ಸನ್ನ್ಯಾಸಿ, q. v.

ಸಪಾಯಿ h. n. Polish, gloss; smoothness; cleanness, neatness, elegance.

ಸಪಿಂಡ s. n. A kinsman. ಸಪಿಂಡಿ. Offering of a ball of rice to a deceased relative. ಸಪಿಂಡೀಕರಣ. Performing the said rite for a deceased relative.

ಸಪ್ತ s. a. Seven. -ಋಷಿ, ಸಪ್ತರ್ಷಿ. The constellation *Ursa major;* seven great ṛishis. -ದಶ. The seventeenth. *Cpds.:* -ದ್ವೀಪ, -ಧಾತು, -ನಾದ, -ಸ್ವರ, -ಲೋಕ. -ತಿ.

Seventy. -ಮ. The seventh. ಸಪ್ತಮಿ. The seventh case, locative; the seventh day of the lunar fortnight. -ವಿಧವಿಭಕ್ತಿ. The seven kinds of case-terminations.

ಸಪ್ಪಗೆ, ಸಪ್ಪನೆ (= ಚಪ್ಪಗೆ, q. v.) k. n. Flatness; dulness; insipidness. a. Flat; dull; effectless. ad. Flatly, insipidly.

ಸಪ್ಪಂಗ f. n. The suppan or brasiletto, *Caesalpinia sappan.*

ಸಪ್ಪಳ k. n. A sound, noise. -ಮಾಡು. To make a sound or noise.

ಸಪ್ಪು (= ಸೊಪ್ಪು, q. v.) k. n. Foliage, leaves.

ಸಪ್ಪೆ (= ಚಪ್ಪೆ, q. v.) k. a. Insipid, dull, dejected, inert. n. Flatness, insipidness, spiritlessness. -ಪಥ್ಯ. Diet without salt and acids.

ಸಫಲ s. a. Fruitful, productive, successful. -ತೆ, -ತ್ವ. Fruitfulness, productiveness.

ಸಫೇದು h. a. White.

ಸಬಕಾರ (ಸಬ್ಬು) f. n. Soap.

ಸಬಗ. = ಸೊಬಗ, q. v.

ಸಬಬು h. n. Cause, reason, motive.

ಸಬರ k. n. A pack-saddle for bullocks.

ಸಬಲ s. a. Powerful, strong.

ಸಬಳ s. n. A spear, lance, pike.

ಸಬ್ಬಕ್ಕಿ, ಸಬ್ಬು f. n. Sago.

ಸಬ್ಬತು f. n. Sabbath, day of rest and Divine worship.

ಸಬ್ಬವ s. n. Mirth, jest, fun. -ಕಾರ. A jester, buffoon.

ಸಬ್ಬಸಿಗೆ f. n. A sort of fennel, *Anethum panmorium.*

ಸಬ್ಬಿಗೆ, ಸಬ್ಬೆ k. n. A slender branch of a tree.

ಸಬ್ಬು (= ಸಬಕಾರ) f. n. Soap. 2, sago.

ಸಭೆ s. n. An assembly, congregation, meeting; a company; a community. ಕ್ರೈಸ್ತ-. The Christian church. -ಮಾಡು. To constitute an assembly. -ಕೂಡು. An assembly to meet. *Cpds.:* ಧರ್ಮ-, ನ್ಯಾಯ-, ರಾಜ-, ವಿದ್ಯಾ-. ಸಭಾಕಂಪ. Bashfulness in the public assembly. ಸಭಾಜನ. Courtesy, politeness, civility; persons of an assembly. ಸಭಾಧ್ಯಕ್ಷ, ಸಭಾನಾಯಕ, ಸಭಾಪತಿ. The president or chairman of an assembly. ಸಭಾಮನೆ. A meeting house. ಸಭಾಪರ್ವ. N. of the 2nd book of the Mahâbhârata. ಸಭಾಮಂಟಪ. An audience hall, council-chamber. ಸಭಾಸದ. A member of any society.

ಸಭ್ಯ s. n. Fit or suitable for an assembly; well-bred, decent, civilized; gentle. n. A polite man. -ತನ, -ತ್ವ. Politeness, refinement.

ಸಮ್ s. prep. Con, with, along with. *ad.* Greatly, thoroughly, well.

ಸಮ s. a. Even, level, flat. 2, same, equal; like, similar. 3, straight; upright; honest, just; good; fit, proper, right; perfect. n. Identity of objects compared. -ಗೊಳಿಸು. To put in order. -ಮಾಡು. To make even or equal; to put in order; to make proper. -ಕಾಲ. The same time; simultaneous. -ಚಿತ್ತ. Even-minded; indifferent. -ಚ್ಛೇದ. Common denominator (*arith.*). -ಜಾತಿ. Homogeneous. -ತೆ, -ತ್ವ. Evenness, equality; fairness; justness. -ದೃಷ್ಟಿ. Impartiality. -ಭಾಗ. An equal share. -ಭಾವ. Of like nature; sameness, equability. -ಭೂಮಿ. Level ground. -ರಾತ್ರಿ. Midnight. -ರೇಖೆ. A straight line.

ಸಮಗ್ರ s. a. All, entire, whole. a. Totality; *also* -ತೆ, -ತ್ವ.

ಸಮಜಾಯಿಷಿ, ಸಮದಾಯಿಷಿ h. n. Persuading, appeasing; peace. ಸಮಜಾಯಿಸು, ಸಮದಾಯಿಸು. To persuade, satisfy, appease, calm, quiet.

ಸಮನಿಸು a. k. v. i. To be acquired, found, or got; to come about; to occur. v. t. To prepare.

ಸಮಂತ s. a. Universal; entire. n. Limit, term. ಸಮಂತಾತ್. All round.

ಸಮಂತು s. ad. In that way, so, thus.

ಸಮಭಿಹಾರ s. n. Repetition, reiteration

ಸಮಯ s. n. Proper time, opportunity, occasion; time; leisure. 2, conventional usage. -ಸಂದುಕಟ್ಟು. A difficulty. -ತಪ್ಪಿ ಹೋಗು. An opportunity to be lost. -ಕ್ಕೆ ಬರು. To come in time; to be opportune. ಸಮಯಾ. In due time or season. ಸಮಯಾಧೀನ. Dependant on circumstances. ಸಮಯೋಚಿತ. Seasonable, opportune.

ಸಮರ s. n. Conflict, battle, war. -ರಂಗ, ಸಮರಂಗ. A battle-field. ಸಮರೋಚಿತ. Fit for war.

ಸಮರು (ರು=ಱು) k. v. t. To trim; to adjust the contents of a corn-measure.

ಸಮರ್ಥ s. a. Proper, fit; capable, competent. 2, strong, powerful, able. 3, having the same sense. -ತೆ, -ತ್ವ, -ನ. Adequacy; capability, ability. ಸಮರ್ಥಿಸು. To make fit or ready.

ಸಮರ್ಪಕ s. a. Suiting; worthy of, conformable.

ಸಮರ್ಪಣ, ಸಮರ್ಪಣೆ s. n. Presenting, offering. ಸಮರ್ಪಿಸು. To present, offer; to deliver.

ಸಮಲ s. a. Dirty, impure. n. Ordure.

ಸಮವಾಯ s. n. Close union; intimate relation. ಸಮವಾಯಿ. Closely connected; inseparable cause. ಸಮವಾಯಿ ಕಾರಣ. Material cause.

ಸಮಷ್ಟಿ s. n. Totality.

ಸಮಸು (= ಸಮಿಸು) k. v. t. To make wear away.

ಸಮಸ್ತ s. a. All, whole, entire. n. The whole.

ಸಮಸ್ಯೆ s. n. Giving part of a stanza by a person to be completed by another as a trial of skill.

ಸಮಾಖ್ಯೆ, ಸಮಾಜ್ಞೆ s. n. Report; fame, renown. 2, a term. 3, a document of convention signed by all concerned.

ಸಮಾಗಮ s. n. Meeting, encounter; union, junction; company.

ಸಮಾಚಾರ s. n. Upright conduct, usage. 2, news, accounts, intelligence. -ತೆಗೆ. To inquire about. -ಪತ್ರ. A newspaper.

ಸಮಾಜ s. n. A meeting, assembly, congregation; a society, club.

ಸಮಾಧಾನ s. n. Satisfaction; relief, calm, peace. 2, removal of an objection. -ಗೊಳಿಸು, -ಪಡಿಸು, -ಮಾಡು. To satisfy; to comfort, appease, *etc.* -ದಿಂದ ಇರು. To be contented. ಜಗಳ ಸಮಾಧಾನವಾಗು. A quarrel to be appeased. ಜ್ವರ ಸಮಾಧಾನವಾಗು. Fever to abate.

ಸಮಾಧಿ s. n. A grave, tomb. 2, deep meditation; silence. -ಸ್ಥ. Absorbed in meditation.

ಸಮಾನ s. a. Same, alike, similar, uniform. 2, common. n. An equal, a friend. 2, one of the vital airs. -ಕಾಲಿಕ, -ಕಾಲೀನ. Contemporaneous, simultaneous. -ತ್ವ. Sameness, likeness. -ಸ್ಥ. An equal.

ಸಮಾಪನ, ಸಮಾಪ್ತಿ s. n. Accomplishment, completion, conclusion, finish, end. ಸಮಾಪ್ತ. Finished, *etc.* -ಮಾಡು. To finish.

ಸಮಾರಂಭ s. n. Enterprise, beginning. 2, a festival.

ಸಮಾರಾಧನೆ s. n. Worship, service. 2, a festive or religious entertainment to Brâhmaṇas. ಸಮಾರಾಧಿಸು. To worship, serve.

ಸಮಾವರ್ತನೆ s. n. Completing, fulfilling. 2, (the ceremony of) a student's returning home after finishing his religious studies.

ಸಮಾಸ s. n. Composition of words; a compound word. 2, whole, totality. 3, contraction, abridgment, brevity. ಸಮಾಸಿಸು. To compound.

ಸಮಾಹೃತ s. a. Compiled; contracted. 2, accepted, received. ಸಮಾಹೃತಿ. Compilation, abridgment.

ಸಮಾಳಿಸು f. v. t. To manage, control.

ಸಮಿತ s. a. Limited; met. n. Conflict. ಸಮಿತಿ. Meeting; conflict; sameness.

ಸಮಿಧ್ s. n. Fuel; *also (tb.)* ಸಮಿಧ.

ಸಮಿಸು. = ಸಮಸು, *q. v.*

ಸಮೀಕರಣ s. n. Reducing of fractions to a common denominator, equation. ಸಮೀಕರಿಸು. To equalise.

ಸಮೀಪ s. a. Near, close by, at hand. n. Proximity, vicinity. ಸಮೀಪಿಸು. To come near, approach.

ಸಮುಖ s. a. Talkative; eloquent.

ಸಮುಚಿತ s. a. Suitable, proper, appropriate, worthy.

ಸಮುಚ್ಚಯ s. n. Accumulation, aggregation. 2, conjunction of words or sentences (g.). ಸಮುಚ್ಚಯಿಸು. To join words or sentences. ಸಮುಚ್ಚಾಯಕ. Conjoining. ಸಮುಚ್ಚಾಯಕಾವ್ಯಯ. A conjunction (g.).

ಸಮುದಯ, ಸಮುದಾಯ s. n. Rise, ascent. 2, a collection, mass, multitude, quantity. 3, the whole; totality. 4, combination.

ಸಮುದ್ರ s. n. The sea, ocean. -ದ ಉಪ್ಪು, -ಲವಣ. Sea-salt. -ಫಲ. An evergreen tree, *Baringtonia racemosa*. -ವಹ್ನಿ. Submarine fire.

ಸಮೂಲ s. a. Along with the root. -ವಾಗಿ. With the roots, completely.

ಸಮೂಹ s. n. A collection, assemblage, multitude, quantity. -ಗೊಳ್ಳು. To be assembled.

ಸಮೃದ್ಧ s. n. Thriving, prospering. 2, rich, full. 3, complete. ಸಮೃದ್ಧಿ. Increase; profusion; plenty, wealth.

ಸಮೆ 1. = ಸವೆ, q. v.

ಸಮೆ 2. f. n. A lamp-stand.

ಸಮೇತ s. a. Come together; united with, furnished with, having.

ಸಂಪಗೆ (= ಸಂಪಿಗೆ. tb. of ಚಂಪಕ) n. A tall flower-tree, *Michelia champaca*, bearing fragrant flowers.

ಸಂಪತ್ತಿ, ಸಂಪತ್ತು, ಸಂಪದ (tb. of ಸಂಪದ್) n. Prosperity, welfare; luck; wealth, riches; excess, abundance.

ಸಂಪನ್ನ s. a. Prosperous, accomplished; acquired; possessed of, endowed with. -ಗೃಹಸ್ಥ. A worthy householder. -ತೆ. Prosperity; accomplishment, attainment, ability.

ಸಂಪರ್ಕ s. n. Mixing together, union; contact, touch.

ಸಂಪಾದನೆ s. n. Gaining, acquiring, getting, attaining; gain; acquisition. ಸಂಪಾದಿಸು. To acquire, obtain, get. ಸಂಪಾದ್ಯ. Gain, acquisition.

ಸಂಪಿಗೆ. = ಸಂಪಗೆ, q. v. -ಮರ. The sampigĕ tree. -ಹೂ. A s. flower.

ಸಂಪೀಡನ s. n. Compression; paining, punishment; pain.

ಸಂಪು. = ಸೊಂಪು, q. v.

ಸಂಪುಟ s. n. A casket, box; *also* -ಕ.

ಸಂಪೂರ್ಣ s. a. Full; complete; all, whole, entire. -ತನ, -ತೆ, -ತ್ವ, ಸ್ಂಪೂರ್ತಿ. Perfection, completeness.

ಸಂಪ್ರತಿ s. n. The present time. *ad.* Now, at present.

ಸಂಪ್ರದಾನ s. n. Gift, donation. 2, the dative case.

ಸಂಪ್ರದಾಯ s. n. Tradition, traditional belief or usage; custom, usage. ಸಂಪ್ರದಾಯಿ. A member of a sect.

ಸಂಪ್ರಾಪ್ತಿ s. n. Attainment, acquisition; gaining. -ಸು. To be got, found. ಅ-. Failure, missing.

ಸಂಬಂಧ (=ಸಮ್ಮಂಧ, q. v.) s. n. Connection; relationship, relation; a relation, relative. 2, the genitive case. -ಕ, ಸಂಬಂಧಿ, ಸಂಬಂಧೀಕ. A relation; a friend. ಸಂಬಂಧಿಸು. To be related; to join.

ಸಂಬರ (= ಸಂಬಾರ, q. v. tb. of ಸಂಭಾರ) n. Seasoning ingredients, *as* pepper, cloves, nutmeg, *etc.* -ಕಾಗೆ. The crow pheasant.

ಸಂಬಳ s. n. Pay, salary. -ಕ್ಕೆ ಇಡು. To take (any body) into one's employ for pay. -ತಕ್ಕೊಳ್ಳು. To receive pay. -ನಿಷ್ಕರ್ಷೆ ಮಾಡು, -ಗೊತ್ತುಮಾಡು ಮಾಡು. To fix a salary. -ದವ. A paid servant; a retainer; *also* -ಗಾರ.

ಸಂಬಾರ. = ಸಂಬರ, q. v.

ಸಂಬಾಳಿಸು s. v. t. To manage. 2, to support, to take care of. 3, to last.

ಸಂಬುದ್ಧಿ s. n. Perfect knowledge. 2, calling to; the vocative case.

ಸಂಬೆ k. n. The sword-bean, *Canavalia ensiformis*. -ನೆಲ್ಲು. A superior kind of rice.

ಸಂಬೋಧನ s. n. The vocative case. 2, instructing, addressing. ಸಂಬೋಧಿಸು. To instruct, advise.

ಸಂಬ್ರಾಣಿ f. n. The Java almond, *Canarium commune*.

ಸಂಭವ s. n. Birth, origin. 2, cause; possibility, probability. ಸಂಭವಿಸು. To occur; to take place, happen.

ಸಂಭಾರ s. n. Preparation, provision; apparatus, necessaries; ingredient; wealth.

ಸಂಭಾವನೆ s. n. Fitness, adequacy, ability. 2, idea, fancy. 3, regard, esteem. 4, worship, honour. 5, a present. 6, value, price. ಸಂಭಾವಿತ. Esteemed, honourable; a respectable man. ಸಂಭಾವಿಸು. To honour, esteem, greet. ಸಂಭಾವ್ಯ. Suitable; possible, probable; respectable.

ಸಂಭಾಷಣೆ s. n. Conversation, discourse, conference; *also* ಸಂಭಾಷೆ. -ಮಾಡು. To converse with.

ಸಂಭೋಗ s. n. Enjoyment, pleasure, delight; fruition. ಸಂಭೋಗಿ. A sensualist. -ಮಾಡು, ಸಂಭೋಗಿಸು. To enjoy.

ಸಂಭ್ರಮ s. n. Whirling about; hurry; confusion; zeal; rapture, pleasure; grandeur, pomp. ಸಂಭ್ರಮಿಸು. To be confused; to be in rapture.

ಸಮ್ಮ. *tb. of* ಚರ್ಮ, *q. v.* -ಗಾರ. A shoemaker; *f.* -ಗಾತಿ.

ಸಮ್ಮತ *a.* Agreed, assented to; esteemed; considered. *n.* Consent; approval. 2, opinion. ಸಮ್ಮತಿ. Agreement, permission, consent, assent, approval; esteem; regard; order. ಸಮ್ಮತಿಸು. To agree, consent to.

ಸಮ್ಮತು h. n. The division of a talook.

ಸಮ್ಮಂಧ. *tb. of* ಸಂಬಂಧ, *q. v.*

ಸಮ್ಮಾನ (=ಸನ್ಮಾನ, *q. v.*) s. n. Honour. ಸಮ್ಮಾನಿಸು. To honour.

ಸಮ್ಮಾರ್ಜನ, ಸಮ್ಮಾರ್ಜನೆ s. n. Cleaning, scouring, sweeping; purefying. 2, smearing with cow-dung. ಸಮ್ಮಾರ್ಜನಿ. A brush, broom. ಸಮ್ಮಾರ್ಜಿಸು. To clean, sprinkle; to smear with cow-dung.

ಸಮ್ಮಿಶ್ರ s. a. Commingled, mixed, blended.

ಸಮ್ಮುಖ s. n. Facing; confronting, meeting; presence. *ad.* In front of.

ಸಮ್ಮೇಲ s. n. Union; a large concourse of people. 2, a double drum. -ನ. Coming together; mixure.

ಸಮ್ರಾಜ್ s. n. A sovereign lord.

ಸಯ್ 1. (=ಸೈ) k. n. Straightness, rectitude, propriety. *v. i.* To cease; to be quieted.

ಸಯ್ 2, ಸಯಿ 1. k. *int.* Indeed, aye, of course, well said, correct.

ಸಯಿ 2. h. (=ಸಹಿ) n. Signature. -ಹಾಕು. To sign.

ಸಯಿಸು. = ಸಹಿಸು, *q. v.*

ಸಯ್ತು, ಸಯ್ಪು s. k. n. Cessation, rest, quiet, silence. 2, rectitude, propriety,

ಸಯ್ರಣೆ (=ಸೈರಣೆ. *tb. of* ಸಹನ) n. Patience, endurance, bearing. ಸಯ್ರಿಸು. (=ಸೈರಿಸು, ಸಹಿಸು). To suffer, endure; to be patient, to put up with.

ಸರ್ h. *pref.* The chief, principal, superintendent.

ಸರ 1. (*tb. of* ಸ್ವರ, *q. v.*) n. Sound, *etc.*

ಸರ 2. (=ಸರಸ್) s. n. A lake, pond, pool.

ಸರ 3. s. n. A string. 2, a piece of timber put across a roof.

ಸರ 4. f. n. A sudden rush; a fit of delirium. -ತಪ್ಪು. Many mistakes. -ಬಟ್ಟೆ. Disorderliness; falsehood, lie. -ಮಗ್ಗಿ. A chief multiplication-table.

ಸರಕಾರ h. n. The government of a state; the supreme power; the state. -ಖಾತೆ. Public department. -ದವರು. Government officers. -ದ ಹಣ. Public money.

ಸರಕು 1. h. v. i. To move on, slip aside; to give place, yield. ಸರಿಸು. To push aside.

ಸರಕು 2. k. n. Goods, things, commodities, cargo; valuable articles, as cloths, rice, etc.

ಸರಗಸ್ತು. = ಶಬಗಸ್ತು, q. v.

ಸರಗುಣಿಕೆ k. n. A loop with a running knot, a noose.

ಸರಂಜಾಮು h. n. Materials, apparatus, tools, etc.

ಸರತಿ, ಸರದಿ (= ಸತಿಕ, q. v. tb. ಸರತ್) n. A time; a turn, rotation. -ಯ ಮೇಲೆ. By turns.

ಸರದಾರ h. n. A chieftain; a prince or leader; an officer.

ಸರದಿ h. n. Coldness, dampness (as of climate, air, etc.); morbid cold.

ಸರದು. P. p. of ಸರಿ 1, q. v.

ಸರಪಣಿ, ಸರಪಳಿ (tb. of ಸರ್ಪಣ) n. A chain. 2, a necklace.

ಸರಫರಾಜು f. n. The regard or kindness shewn by a superior to an inferior.

ಸರಬರಾಯಿ h. n. Providing supplies for a journey; supplies.

ಸರಲ (= ಸರಳ) s. a. Straight, right; honest, sincere, simple, upright. -ಬಡ್ಡಿ. Simple interest. -ತೆ, -ತ್ವ. Straightness; honesty.

ಸರಸ್ (= ಸರಸಿ) s. n. A lake, pond.

ಸರಸ s. a. Succulent, juicy; fresh; tasty; spirited, piquant, witty; charming. 2, cheap. n. Piquancy, wit, fun, joke. ಗಂಡಹೆಂಡರ-. Dalliance of husband and wife. -ಆಡು, -ವಾಡು. To sport. -ಕೇಲಿ. Jocose play. -ಮಾತು, ಸರಸೋಕ್ತಿ. A jocose expression. -ಗಾರ, ಸರಸಿ. A jocose person.

ಸರಸಿ s. n. A pond. -ಜ. A lotus. -ಜಮಿತ್ರ, -ಜಸಖ. The sun. -ಜಾತ, -ರುಹ. A lotus.

ಸರಸ್ವತಿ s. n. The goddess of speech and eloquence and wife of Brahmâ. 2, speech. 3, a river. -ಪೂಜೆ. The worship of Sarasvatî. -ವೀಣೆ. A kind of lute.

ಸರಹದ್ದು f. n. Frontier, boundary.

ಸರಳ. = ಸರಲ, q. v.

ಸರಳು k. n. An iron rod, bar. 2, an arrow.

ಸರಳೆ f. n. The notes of the gamut.

ಸರಾಗ f. a. Unobstructed, easy. -ಮಾರ್ಗ. An easy road.

ಸರಾಫ h. n. A shroff, banker; a cashkeeper.

ಸರಾಯಿ, ಸರಾಯು f. n. Spirituous liquor. -ಬಟ್ಟಿ. A spirit-still.

ಸರಾಸರಿ h. ad. Anyhow; on an average; approximately. n. Average.

ಸರಾಳ (fr. ಸರಲ) s. n. Going uninterruptedly, without difficulty.

ಸರಿ 1. k. v. i. To move, go; to move aside; to slide, slip; to run over. v. t. To shove in. 2, to put in proper order. n. Sliding; a precipice, ravine.

ಸರಿ 2. k. n. Fitness, propriety, rightness; correctness; evenness; similarity. a. Fit, proper, right, correct, even, reasonable. ad. Indeed, in truth. -ಕತನ, Equality of position. -ಕ, -ವಕ. -ಗ. A man of equal position. -ಗಟ್ಟು. To make equal. -ಗೂಡು. To agree with. -ಗೆ ಸರಿ ಮಾಡು. To requite, repay. -ನೋಡು. To compare; to examine. -ಬರು. To become right; to suit. -ಬೀಳು. To become right; to agree with, suit. -ಬೆಸ. Even and odd. -ಮಗ. A grown up son; f. -ಮಗಳು. -ಮಾಡು. To adjust; to compare; to make even. -ಮಾಡಿ ನೋಡು. To compare. -ಯಾಗು. To become equal, fit or right. -ರಾತ್ರಿ. Midnight. ಸರಿಯಾಗಿ. Properly, rightly, correctly. -ಯೇ ಸರಿ. Very proper indeed. -ಸಮ, -ಸಮಾನ. Quite equal. -ಹಗಲು. Noon. -ಹೊತ್ತು. Exact time. -ಹೊಂದು. To become fit or equal. -ಹೋಲುವಿಕೆ. Resemblance.

ಸರಿ 3. a. k. n. Rain. 2, a heap.

ಸರಿ 4. (ರಿ=ಱ) k. n. Paste, gum, glue.

ಸರಿಗೆ f. n. A necklace of females. 2, a wire. 3, = ಜರಿ 2, q. v.

ಸರಿಸ a. k. n. Straightness; exactness; measure; equality.

ಸರಿಸು k. v. t. To move aside. ಸರಿಸಾಡು. To move about.

ಸರುಕಂ. = ಸರಕು 2, q. v.

ಸರೆ. = ಸರಾಯಿ, q. v. -ಗಾರ. A liquor-manufacturer.

ಸರೋಜ s. n. A lotus. -ರಿಪು. The moon. -ಸಖ. The sun.

ಸರೋವರ s. n. A lake, pond.

ಸರ್ಕಾರ. = ಸರಕಾರ, q. v.

ಸರ್ಗ s. n. Abandonment. 2, creation. 3, the universe. 4, a chapter, section.

ಸರ್ಜ s. n. A timber tree, *gatica robusta*. -ರಸ. Resin.

ಸರ್ತಿ, ಸರ್ದಿ. = ಸರತಿ, q. v.

ಸರ್ಪ s. n. A snake, serpent. -ಯಾಗ. Serpent-sacrifice. -ರಾಜ. Vâsuki. ಸರ್ಪಾರಿ. A peacock; Garuḍa. ನಾಗ-. A hooded serpent.

ಸರ್ಲೆ, -ಹಕ್ಕಿ k. n. A water-fowl, the teal.

ಸರ್ವ s. a. All, every; whole, entire, complete. -ಗತ. All-pervading, omnipresent. -ಜಿತ್, -ಜಿತು. All-conquering; the 21st year of the cycle. -ಜ್ಞ. All-knowing, all-wise. -ಜ್ಞತೆ, -ಜ್ಞತ್ವ. Omniscience. -ತ್ರಾಣಿ. Almighty. -ಧಾರಿ. The 22nd year of the cycle. -ನಾಮ. A pronoun. -ನಿಯಾಮಕ. All-controlling. -ಪ್ರಕಾರ. Every way. -ಭಕ್ಷಕ. Omnivorous. -ಮಂಗಲ. All-auspicious. -ಮಂಗಲೆ. Durgâ, Pârvati. -ಮಯ. Universal. -ಲೋಕ. The universe. -ವ್ಯಾಪಕ. All-pervading. -ಶಕ್ತಿ. All might; almighty. -ಸಾಧಾರಣ. Common to all. -ಸಾಮರ್ಥ್ಯ. All power. -ಸಿದ್ಧಿ. Universal success. -ಸ್ವತಂತ್ರ. Free, unrestrained. ಸರ್ವಾಂಗ. The whole body. ಸರ್ವಾಧಿಕಾರ. Universal rule. ಸರ್ವಾಪರಾಧ. All offences. ಸರ್ವಾಪರಾಧಿ. One who is guilty of all sorts of transgressions. ಸರ್ವಾರ್ಥ. All matters; all objects. ಸರ್ವಾರ್ಥಸಿದ್ಧಿ. Universal success. ಸರ್ವೇಶ. Lord of all; the universal monarch.

ಸರ್ವತ್ರ s. ad. Everywhere; always. 2, all.

ಸರ್ವಥಾ s. ad. In all ways, by all means; entirely, wholly; assuredly, certainly; exceedingly; at all times.

ಸರ್ವದಾ s. ad. Always, at all times.

ಸರ್ವಸ್ವ s. n. The whole of one's property.

ಸಲ k. n. A time.

ಸಲಗ k. n. The leader of a herd.

ಸಲವು k. n. Cause, account. ಸಲವಾಗಿ. On account of, for.

ಸಲವೆ k. n. Washing and bleaching new cotton cloth.

ಸಲಹಾ, ಸಲಹೆ (= ಸಲ್ಲಾ, q. v.) h. n. Counsel.

ಸಲಹು k. v. t. To foster, preserve, bring up, take care of. -ವಿಕೆ. Fostering.

ಸಲಾದು f. n. Salad, raw herbs dressed with vinegar, oil, *etc.* -ಎಣ್ಣೆ. S. oil.

ಸಲಾಮ್, ಸಲಾಮು h. n. Safety, peace. 2, a mode of salutation expressive of respects or thanks. -ಮಾಡು. To salute, complement; to greet. -ಹೇಳು. To tell one's compliments or thanks.

ಸಲಾಕಿ, ಸಲಾಕೆ (*tb. of* ಶಲಾಕೆ) n. An iron rod or bar.

ಸಲಿಕೆ 1. (*fr.* ಸಲು, q. v.) k. n. Paying, payment.

ಸಲಿಕೆ 2. = ಸಲಾಕಿ, q. v. n. A crowbar; a kind of spade.

ಸಲಿಗೆ k. n. Familiarity; freedom, indulgence.

ಸಲು. = ಸಲ್ಲು, q. v. ಸಲಿಸು. = ಸಲ್ಲಿಸು, q. v.

ಸಲುವಳಿ k. n. Fitness, propriety; currency. -ಕ್ರಯ. A just price. -ಮಾತು. A proper word.

ಸಲುವಾಗಿ. = ಸಲವಾಗಿ, q. v.

ಸಲೆ 1. k. *ad.* Currently; constantly; properly; well.

ಸಲೆ 2. (= ಸಲಿಕೆ, *q. v.*) k. *n.* Payment. 2, product. -ಮಾಡು. To find an area. -ಯಡಿ. A cubic foot.

ಸಲ್ಲಾ (= ಸಲಹಾ, *etc., q. v.*) h. *n.* Counsel. 2, peace, truce.

ಸಲ್ಲಾಪ (= ಸಂಲಾಪ) s. *n.* Conversation, familiar discourse. ಸಲ್ಲಾಪಿಸು. To discourse.

ಸಲ್ಲಿಸು k. *v. t.* To fulfil; to give, grant; to show; to pay; to spend.

ಸಲ್ಲು k. *v. i.* To accrue; pass, be current (*as* money, *etc.*); to be in use; to pass by general consent, be valid or fit; to depart from life; to be given, be paid or liquidated. 2, to be famous. *P. p.* ಸಂದು. ಸಲ್ಲದು. It is unfit, improper, *etc.* ಸಲ್ಲದವ. A useless man.

ಸವ. *tb. of* ಸಮ, *q. v.* -ನು. To be equal. -ನೆ. Quite equal; in the very same manner.

ಸವಟು (= ಸೌಟು) k. *n.* A ladle, spoon. *v. t. & i.* To dirty, or be dirty, *as* clothes.

ಸವಣ f. *n.* Pincers.

ಸವಣಿಸು (= ಸವರಿಸು. *tb. of* ಸಂವರಿಸು) *v. t.* To prepare, get ready, arrange. ಮೀಸೆ ಸವಣಿಸಿಕೊಳ್ಳು. To trim one's mustaches.

ಸವತಿ (*tb. of* ಸಪತ್ನಿ) *n.* A second or rival wife. -ತಾಯಿ. A step-mother. -ಮಗ. A step-son. -ಮತ್ಸರ. Jealousy between rival wives.

ಸವದೆ. = ಸವುದೆ, ಸೌದೆ, *q. v.*

ಸವನಿಸು k. *v. i.* To be acquired; to occur.

ಸವಯಸ್ಸ s. *n.* Coeval, contemporary. *n.* A coeval; a contemporary, friend.

ಸವರಿಸು. = ಸವಣಿಸು, *q. v.*

ಸವರು 1. k. *v. t.* To cut off branches of a tree, *etc.* 2, to chip. ಸವರಿಸು. To cause to cut off branches; to cause to chip.

ಸವರು 2. k. *v. t.* To rub in or apply to, *as* water, oil, *etc.* ಸವರಿಸು. To have applied to.

ಸವರು 3. (ರು = ಱು) k. *v. t.* To trim (*as* the hair *etc.*); to measure even with the striker.

ಸವರ್ಣ s. *n.* The letter ಸ. 2, the homogen. *a.* Belonging to the same class of letters; homogeneous.

ಸವಾ h. *a.* One and a quarter. -ಸೇರು. $1\frac{1}{4}$ sheer.

ಸವಾರ h. *n.* A man on horseback, horseman, rider.

ಸವಾರಿ h. *n.* Riding upon the back of any animal or in a carriage, riding. *Cpds.:* -ಎತ್ತು, -ಕುದುರೆ, -ಬಂಡಿ, *etc.*; ಕುದುರೇ-, ಬಂಡೀ-, *etc.*

ಸವಾಲು h. *n.* A question, inquiry.

ಸವಿ 1. (= ಸವೆ) k. *v. i.* To wear away; to pass, *as* time.

ಸವಿ 2. k. *v. t.* To taste; to eat. *a.* Savoury, sweet or nice. *n.* Taste; sweetness; ambrosia. -ಗಾಣು, -ತಕ್ಕೊಳ್ಳು, -ನೋಡು. To taste; to be pleased. -ಗಾರ. A witty man. *Cpds.:* -ತುಟಿ, -ತುತ್ತು, -ನೀರು, -ನೋಟ, -ನುಡಿ, -ಮಾತು, -ಮಾವು, -ಹಣ್ಣು. *etc.* -ಯೂಟ. A delicious meal. -ಹತ್ತು. To have a pleasing taste.

ಸವಿಸ್ತಾರ s. *a.* Detailed. *ad.* Minutely.

ಸವುಟು (= ಸೌಟು) k. *n.* A spoon, ladle.

ಸವುತೆ (= ಸೌತೆ) k. *n.* A kind of cucumber, *Cucumis utilissimus; also* -ಕಾಯಿ.

ಸವುದೆ (= ಸವದೆ, ಸೌದೆ) f. *n.* Firewood. fuel.

ಸವುಳು (= ಸೌಳು) k. *n.* Brackishness. *a.* Brackish. *Cpds.:* -ನೀರು, -ನೆಲ, -ಪದಾರ್ಥ, -ಮಣ್ಣು.

ಸವೆ (= ಸಮೆ) k. *v. i.* To be spent; to wear away, be wasted; to pass away. 2, to be made ready.

ಸವ್ಯ s. *a.* Left. 2, southern. 3, reversed, contrary. -ವಹಾರ. Intercourse.

ಸಸನೆ k. *a.* Still, motionless.

ಸಸಿ 1. (*tb. of* ಸಸ್ಯ) *n.* Corn; a young, plant.

ಸಸಿ 2. k. *v. t.* To pull out, *as* corn. 2, to dress cotton.

ಸಸಿನ a. k. *n.* Straightness, rectitude. ಸಸಿನೆ. Straightly, properly, nicely.

ಸಸ್ಯ s. *n.* Corn, grain; fruit. ಸಸ್ಯಾವಳಿ. All sorts of corn or grain.

ಸಹ s. *ad.* With, together; also, too; *also* ಸಹಾ. -ಕಾರ. Acting with, co-operation; assistance. -ಕಾರಿ. One who co-operates with another; an assistant, associate. -ಗಮನ, -ಮರಣ. A woman's burning herself with her husband's dead body. -ಚರಿ, -ಚಾರಿ. A wife. -ಜಾತ. A brother; innate. -ದೇವ. The youngest of the Pâṇḍava princes; *f.* -ದೇವಿ, *also* the ash-coloured flea-bane. -ಧರ್ಮಿಣಿ. A lawful wife. -ಭೋಜನ. Eating together. ಸಹಾಧ್ಯಾಯಿ. A fellow-student.

ಸಹಜ s. *a.* Innate; inherent; natural. 2, true, proper. -ಗುಣ. Inherent nature. -ದೋಷ. An offence easily accounted for.

ಸಹನ, ಸಹನೆ s. *n.* Enduring, endurance, patience, toleration. -ಶೀಲ. Of a patient disposition.

ಸಹವಾಸ s. *n.* Companionship; intercourse. ಸಹವಾಸಿ. A companion, friend.

ಸಹಸಾ s. *ad.* On a sudden, suddenly; at once. 2, by no means.

ಸಹಸಿ s. *a.* Powerful, strong, mighty. -ಗ. A powerful man.

ಸಹಸ್ರ s. *n.* A thousand. -ಕಾಲ. Many years. -ನಾಮ. The thousand names of any deity. -ಕರ, -ಕಿರಣ, -ಪಾದ. The sun. ಸಹಸ್ರಾಧಿಪತಿ. A chief of a district. ಸಹಸ್ರಾವಧಿ. By thousands.

ಸಹಾಯ s. *n.* Aid, help, assistance, succour. -ಕೊಡು, -ಮಾಡು. To help, aid. -ಗಾರ. A helper.

ಸಹಿ (= ಸಯಿ, *q. v.*) h. *n.* Signature.

ಸಹಿತ s. *a.* Accompanied by, possessed of; along with, with.

ಸಹಿಸು (= ಸಯ್ರಿಸು, *q. v.*) s. *v. t.* To bear, endure, *etc.*

ಸಹೃದಯ s. *a.* Good-hearted, amiable; sincere.

ಸಹೋದರ s. *n.* A brother; *f.* ಸಹೋದರಿ.

ಸಹ್ಯ s. *a.* Endurable, sufferable. *n.* Health; a healthy man. 2, wish. 3, adequacy.

ಸಾಂಯಾತ್ರಿಕ s. *n.* A merchant trading by sea.

ಸಾಂವತ್ಸರ, ಸಾಂವತ್ಸರಿಕ (*fr.* ಸಂವತ್ಸರ) s. *a.* Yearly, annual. *n.* An astrologer.

ಸಾಂಸರ್ಗಿಕ (*fr.* ಸಂಸರ್ಗ) s. *a.* Contagious (*as* a disease).

ಸಾಂಸಾರಿಕ (*fr.* ಸಂಸಾರ) s. *a.* Worldly.

ಸಾಂಸಿದ್ಧಿಕ s. *a.* Natural, innate.

ಸಾಕಲ್ಯ (*fr.* ಸಕಲ) s. *n.* Totality, completeness; all. -ವಚನ. A complete perusal.

ಸಾಕಾರ s. *a.* Having form, figurate. *n.* A definite shape.

ಸಾಕು 1. k. *v. t.* To bring up, foster, rear, feed, protect, preserve. *n.* Bringing up, fostering. -ತಂದೆ. A foster-father. -ತಾಯಿ. A foster-mother. -ತೆಗೆ. To adopt. -ಮಗ, ಸಾಕಿದ ಮಗ. A foster or adopted son. ಸಾಕಿದ ಕುರಿ ಮರಿ. A foster lamb. ಸಾಕುವ ದಾದಿ. A wet nurse. ಸಾಕಿಸು. To cause to bring up, *etc.*

ಸಾಕು 2. k. *n.* Sufficiency. *a.* Sufficient, enough. *int.* Enough! *v. i.* It is enough (*imperat. only*). ಸಾಕಾಗು. To become sufficient; to become disgustful. -ಮಾಡು. To make sufficient; to give up with disgust. ಸಾಕಷ್ಟು. As much as is wanted.

ಸಾಕ್ಷಾತ್ s. *ad.* Visibly, evidently, manifestly, openly; truly, certainly. ಸಾಕ್ಷಾತ್ಕರಿಸು. To see with one's own eyes. ಸಾಕ್ಷಾತ್ಕಾರ. Perception with one's own eyes. -ಕೃತ್. Made manifest.

ಸಾಕ್ಷಿ s. *n.* Evidence, testimony. 2, an eye-witness; a witness. -ಯವನು,

-ಗಾರ, -ದಾರ. A witness. -ದಾಖಿತೆ, -ಪಟ್ಟಿ. A list of witnesses. -ವಾಙ್ಮೂಲ. A deposition of a witness. ಅಪ-, ಅಬದ್ಧ-, ಕಳ್ಳ-, ತಪ್ಪು-, ಸುಳ್ಳು-. A false witness. ಕರ್ಮ-, ಲೋಕ-. The sun. ಮನಃ-, ಅಂತರಾತ್ಮ-. Conscience.

ಸಾಗ. = ಸಾಗು, *q. v.*

ಸಾಗಡೆ k. *n.* The forest tree *Sleichera trijuga.*

ಸಾಗರ 1. k. *n.* Extending and bending forwards. -ಬೀಳು. To extend and bend forwards.

ಸಾಗರ 2. s. *n.* The ocean.

ಸಾಗವಳಿ. = ಸಾಗುವಳಿ, *q. v.*

ಸಾಗಿಸು k. *v. t.* To carry on, perform; to conduct (*as* affairs); to manage (*as* a household); to convey; to nourish (*as* the belly). 2, to cultivate.

ಸಾಗು 1. k. *v. i.* To move forward (*as* a ship, person, *etc.*); to proceed, advance (*as* work, *etc.*); to continue in time; to be brought about. ಸಾಗ ಕಳುಹಿಸು. To send on, to accompany a short distance. ಸಾಗ ಹಾಕು. To carry on; to send on.

ಸಾಗು 2. k. *n.* Cultivation, tillage. -ಆಗು. Cultivation to take place. -ಬೀಳು. Cultivation to be abandoned. -ಮಾಡು. To cultivate.

ಸಾಗು 3. k. *v. i.* To lengthen, extend. ಸಾಗ ಬಡಿ. To elongate (*as* iron by hammering).

ಸಾಗುವಳಿ (= ಸಾಗವಳಿ) k. *n.* Cultivation. -ಮಾಡು. To cultivate. -ಯಾಗು. To be cultivated.

ಸಾಂಕ್ರಾಮಿಕ (*fr.* ಸಂಕ್ರಾಮ) s. *a.* Contagious (*as* disease).

ಸಾಂಖ್ಯ (*fr.* ಸಂಖ್ಯಾ) s. *a.* Relating to number or calculation; deliberating, reasoning. *n.* N. of a philosophical system; *also* -ಶಾಸ್ತ್ರ.

ಸಾಂಗ (*fr.* ಸ-ಅಂಗ) s. *a.* Having members; complete, finished, perfect. ಸಾಂಗೋಪಾಂಗ. With all members and parts.

ಸಾಂಗ್ರಾಣಿ s. *n.* A flat circular stone with a hole in the middle used in gymnastic exercises.

ಸಾಂಚಾ h. *a.* True, real. 2, a mould or matrice.

ಸಾಜ. *tb. of* ಸಹಜ, *q. v.*

ಸಾಟಿ k. *n.* Likeness. *a.* Like, equal.

ಸಾಟೀನ. = ಸಾತೀನು, *q. v.*

ಸಾಟಿ h. *n.* Exchange, barter. -ವ್ಯಾಪಾರ. Bartered merchandise.

ಸಾಣ, ಸಾಣಿ (*tb. of* ಶಾಣ) *n.* A grindstone, whet-stone; *also* -ಕಲ್ಲು. -ಗೊಡು, -ಹಿಡಿ. To grind, sharpen, *as* a knife. -ಗ, -ಗಾರ. A sharpener of tools.

ಸಾಣಿಗೆ f. *n.* A sieve, strainer. -ಹಾಕು. To sift, strain. [cloth.

ಸಾತೀನು e. *n.* Satin, a species of silk

ಸಾತ್ವಿಕ, ಸಾತ್ತ್ವಿಕ s. *a.* Real, substantial, natural, genuine, true; honest, sincere, good, amiable, gentle. -ತನ, -ತ್ವ. Honesty, sincerity, *etc.*

ಸಾದರ s. *n.* Respect; love.

ಸಾದರು h. *a.* Arrived, come; issued.

ಸಾದಾ. = ಸಾಧಾ, *q. v.*

ಸಾದಿಲವಾರು h. *n.* Any contingent charge (*as* of an office, stationery).

ಸಾದು 1. k. *n.* The black colour with which females mark their foreheads.

ಸಾದು 2. = ಸಾಧು, *q. v.*

ಸಾದೃಶ್ಯ s. *n.* Likeness, resemblance; a protrait; a likeness.

ಸಾಧಕ s. *n.* Exercise, practice. 2, a skilful man; a practiser. -ಮಾಡು, To practice. ಗರಡೀ-. Practice in arms generally. ಕತ್ತೀ-. Sword exercise.

ಸಾಧನ, ಸಾಧನೆ s. *n.* A means, expedient; an instrument, agent; an implement, utensil, ingredient. 2, exercise, practice. 3, a document. -ಸಂಪತ್ತು. Materials and means. -ಮಾಡು. To practice; to recover.

ಸಾಧಾ (= ಸಾದಾ) s. *a.* Plain, simple; mere, pure, *etc.* -ಉಡುಗೆ. A plain dress. -ಬಟ್ಟೆ. A plain cloth. -ಬಡತನ. Mere poverty.

ಸಾಧಾರಣ s. a. Common, general, universal. 2, middling, ordinary. n. The forty-fourth year of the cycle. -ತಃ. Generally. -ರೀತಿ. Ordinary manner.

ಸಾಧಿತ s. a. Accomplished, succeeded; recovered; subdued. 2, derivative.

ಸಾಧಿಸು s. v. t. To effect, perform, do, complete, settle; to substantiate, prove. 2, to recover. 3, to obtain; to acquire. 4, to subdue; to master. 5, to charge (upon another). ತಪ್ಪು-. To prove an offence. ವಿದ್ಯೆ-. To master an art or science.

ಸಾಧು s. a. Virtuous; mild, tame or gentle (*used also of beasts*). 2, fit, right. n. A good or honest man; a saint. -ಜನ. A good person.

ಸಾಧ್ಯ s. a. Practicable, feasible, possible. 2, subduable. 3, curable. n. Accomplishment. 2, a thing to be proved.

ಸಾಧ್ವಿ s. n. A chaste or virtuous woman; a faithful wife.

ಸಾನಂದ s. a. Delighted. n. Joy, happiness.

ಸಾನಿ h. n. A companion, colleague; *also a fem. affix, e. g.* ದೊರೆ-, ನಾಯಕ-, *etc.*

ಸಾನು f. n. A table-land. 2, a summit.

ಸಾನುಕೂಲ s. a. Suitable, favourable.

ಸಾನುನಯ s. a. Courteous, kind, polite.

ಸಾನುಭವ s. n. Fruition, experience.

ಸಾನುಮತ, ಸಾನುಮತಿ s. n. Approbation, assent.

ಸಾಂತ 1. = ಸಂತ, q. v.

ಸಾಂತ 2. *tb. of* ಶಾಂತ, q. v. -ಪ್ಪ. N. of a man; *f.* -ಮ್ಮ, -ವ್ವ.

ಸಾಂತ್ವ s. n. Consolation, comforting; conciliation. -ನ. Consoling; friendly salutation and enquiry.

ಸಾನ್ನಿಧ್ಯ (*fr.* ಸನ್ನಿಧ) s. n. Nearness, vicinity; presence.

ಸಾಫ. = ಸಾಫು, q. v.

ಸಾಫಲ್ಯ s. n. Fruitfulness, profit; success.

ಸಾಫು h. a. Clean; pure; smooth; plain, clear; simple. n. Utter ruin.

ಸಾಬ. = ಸಾಹೇಬ, q. v.

ಸಾಬೀತು, ಸಾಬೂತು h. a. Proved, established.

ಸಾಮ s. n. Calming, soothing; conciliation; gentleness. 2, negotiation. -ವೇದ. N. of one of the four vêdas.

ಸಾಮಗ್ರಿ s. n. Wholeness. 2, a collection of materials, apparatus, goods, effects. -ಸನ್ನಾಹ. Preparation of materials.

ಸಾಮತಿ (*tb. of* ಸಾಮ್ಯತೆ) n. Likeness; a comparison, simile.

ಸಾಮಂತ s. a. Neighbouring. n. A neighbour. 2, a feudatory chief; a leader.

ಸಾಮರ್ಥ್ಯ s. n. Force, capacity, power, ability, capability, strength, energy. ಬುದ್ಧಿ-. Intellectual power. ವಿದ್ಯಾ-. Distinction in science.

ಸಾಮಾಜಿಕ s. a. Relating to an assembly. n. A member of an assembly.

ಸಾಮಾನ, ಸಾಮಾನು h. n. Instruments; apparatus, furniture; goods, things, articles. ಅಡಿಗೇ-. Materials for cooking; cooking utensils. ಕಬ್ಬಿಣದ-, ಕಮ್ಮಾರ-. A smith's tools.

ಸಾಮಾನ್ಯ s. a. Common, general. 2, vulgar, ordinary, low. n. Generality. 2, kind, sort. -ಗುಣ. A common temper. -ಧರ್ಮ. A general duty.

ಸಾಮಿಪ್ಯ s. n. Nearness.

ಸಾಮು h. n. Gymnastics, feats of strength.

ಸಾಮುದ್ರಿಕೆ s. n. Palmistry.

ಸಾಮೆ (*tb. of* ಶ್ಯಾಮಕ, q. v.) *see s.* ಶ್ಯಾಮ.

ಸಾಮೋಪಚಾರ s. n. A mild, conciliating measure.

ಸಾಮೋಪಾಯ s. n. A mild remedy, gentle means. 2, negotiation.

ಸಾಂಪ್ರತ s. n. The present time. *ad.* At present, now.

ಸಾಂಪ್ರದಾಯ (*fr.* ಸಂಪ್ರದಾಯ) s. n. Custom, practice, tradition. ಸಾಂಪ್ರದಾಯಕ. Traditionary.

ಸಾಂಬ (*fr.* ಸ-ಅಂಬ) s. n. Śiva. -ಶಿವ. Śiva along with Amba.

ಸಾಂಬ್ರಾಜ್ಯ. *tb. of* ಸಾಮ್ರಾಜ್ಯ, *q. v.*

ಸಾಂಬ್ರಾಣಿ. *tb. of* ಸಾಮ್ರಾಣಿ, *q. v.*

ಸಾಮ್ಯ s. n. Likeness; a comparison, simile, harmony. 2, (*tb. of* ಸ್ವಾಮ್ಯ) fees paid for the performance of some ceremonies. -ತೆ. Equality, sameness.

ಸಾಮ್ರಾಜ್ಯ s. n. Universal sovereignty, empire.

ಸಾಮ್ರಾಣಿ (= ಸಾಂಬ್ರಾಣಿ) s. n. Benzoin. 2, a kind of perfume.

ಸಾಯ. *tb. of* ಸಹಾಯ, *q. v.*

ಸಾಯಂ, -ಕಾಲ s. n. Evening, eventide.

ಸಾಯರು h. n. Excise, custom.

ಸಾಯು k. v. i. To die, decease, depart from life. *P. p.* ಸತ್ತು. 2, power to be lost, *as* that of a limb, *etc.* ಸತ್ತು ಸತ್ತು ಉಳಿ, ಸತ್ತು ಸತ್ತು ಬದುಕು. To recover from a dangerous illness.

ಸಾಯುಜ್ಯ s. n. Intimate union, absorption into the divine essence.

ಸಾರ 1. k. n. Scaffolding.

ಸಾರ 2. s. n. Essence, substance; the essential part of anything; the matter of a speech, *etc.*; real truth. 2, marrow; pith. 3, the sap of trees; nectar. 4, strength, power; vigour. 5, a summary, epitome. 6, a verdict. *a.* Excellent; real; sound. ಸಾರಾ-. Real and vain. ಅ-, ನಿಃ-. Pithless, juiceless. ಭೂ-. The strength of a soil.

ಸಾರಕ s. a. Cathartic, laxative. ಉತ್-. Expelling.

ಸಾರಗ, ಸಾರಂಗ s. n. The spotted antelope; a deer. 2, the čātaka bird. 3, a large bee.

ಸಾರಂಗಿ f. n. A kind of fiddle.

ಸಾರಟಿ s. n. A chariot, gig.

ಸಾರಣಿ s. n. A drain, channel.

ಸಾರಣಿಗೆ (*tb. of* ಚಾಲನಿ) n. A sieve, strainer.

ಸಾರಣೆ k. n. Smearing, smoothing (with cow-dung, *etc.*); *also* ಸಾರವಣೆ. *Cpds.:* ಕೋಟೆ-, ಗೋಡೆ-, ಮನೆ-, ಶಾಲಾ-, ಸಗಣೆ-.

ಸಾರಥಿ s. n. A coachman. -ತನ, ಸಾರಥ್ಯ. Charioteering, driving.

ಸಾರವಾನ h. n. A camel-driver. 2, (s.) a scholar.

ಸಾರಸ (*fr.* ಸರಸ್) s. n. The Indian crane. 2, a goose. 3, a lotus. 4, Yama. 5, a mountain. 6, weariness. 7, a sharp man. 8, a girdle or zone.

ಸಾರಾಂಶ s. n. Essence, substance; scope, purport; an abstract, epitome.

ಸಾರಾಯ, ಸಾರಾಯಿ (= ಸರಾಯ, *etc.*, *q. v.*) k. n. Spirituous liquor, gin. -ಅಂಗಡಿ. A gin shop. -ಗುತ್ತಿಗೆ. A tax levied on the sale of spirituous liquors; a liquor shop.

ಸಾರಿ, ಸಾರೆ k. n. A time, turn; time.

ಸಾರಿಗೆ k. n. A piece of land.

ಸಾರಿಸು k. v. t. To smear, smooth, clean.

ಸಾರು 1. (ರ = ಱ) k. v. t. To cry out, proclaim, publish. ಸಾರಿಸು. To cause to proclaim, publish.

ಸಾರು 2. (ರ = ಱ) k. n. Sauce, broth, pepper-water. *Cpds.:* ಬೇಳೆ-, ಮೆಣಸು-, ತಿಳಿ-, ಸಪ್ಪೆ-, ಹುಣಿಸೇ-.

ಸಾರೂಪ್ಯ s. n. Sameness, resemblance, conformity.

ಸಾರ್ (*fr.* ಸಾರಿಸು) k. v. i. To go near, approach. 2, to apply to, to put.

ಸಾರ್ಥ (*fr.* ಸ-ಅರ್ಥ) s. a. Significant, important, useful; wealthy. *n.* A caravan. -ಕ. Important, useful, advantageous; fruitful.

ಸಾರ್ವ s. a. Relating to all, general. -ಕಾಲ. Continually. -ಜನಿಕ. Universal, public. -ತ್ರಿಕ. Suited to all places, general. -ಭೌವು. Comprising the whole world; a universal monarch, emperor.

ಸಾಲ್, ಸಾಲು h. n. A year. -ಗುಜಸ್ತಾ. The past year. -ಮಜಕೂರು. The present year. -ವಾರ್. Annual.

ಸಾಲ k. n. Debt. -ಕೇಳು. To ask for a loan; to demand payment of a debt. -ಕೊಡು. To lend. -ತೀರಿಸು. To discharge a debt. -ತೆಗೆದುಕೊಳ್ಳು, -ಮಾಡು. To borrow. -ಬಿಡು. To quit a debt. -ಬಡಕ, -ವಣಿಗ. A contractor of debts. ಮೈ-. A loan without security. ಬಡ್ಡೀ-. A loan on interest. -ತೀರಿಸು, -ಮುಟ್ಟಿಸು, -ಸಲ್ಲಿಸು, -ಪರಿಹರಿಸು. To pay a debt. -ಗಾರ. A creditor; a debtor.

ಸಾಲಗ್ರಾಮ. = ಶಾಲಗ್ರಾಮ, q. v.

ಸಾಲದು (neg. of ಸಾಲು) k. v. i. It is not enough; it is insufficient. ಸಾಲದೆ ಬರು. To be deficient. ಸಾಲದೆ ಹೋಗು. To be insufficient.

ಸಾಲಾಮಿಸ್ರಿ f. n. Salep, the tubers of *Orchis mascula*.

ಸಾಲಾವಳಿ k. n. Fitness, suitableness.

ಸಾಲಿಗ k. n. A debtor. 2, a creditor. 3, (fr. ಸಾಲೆ) a weaver.

ಸಾಲಿಗ್ರಾಮ. = ಶಾಲಗ್ರಾಮ, q. v.

ಸಾಲು 1. k. v. i. To be sufficient or enough, suffice.

ಸಾಲು 2. k. n. A line, row, range; a furrow. -ಇಡು, -ಕಟ್ಟು. To put in rows; to arrange. ಸಾಲಾಗಿ. In a row.

ಸಾಲು 3. = ಸಾಲ್, q. v.

ಸಾಲೆ (tb. of ಶಾಲೆ, q. v.) n. A school. -ಗೆ ಹಾಕು. To put to school, -ಬರೆ. To study at school. -ಸ್ಥಾಪಿಸು, -ಹಾಕು. To establish a school. ಧರ್ಮ-. An alms-house. ಪಡ-. An (inclosed) veranda; an out-house.

ಸಾಲೋಕ್ಯ s. n. Abiding in the same heaven with the deity.

ಸಾವಕಾರ (= ಸಾವುಕಾರ) h. n. A banker, merchant; a rich man. -ಕೆ, ಸಾವಕಾರಿಕೆ. The business of a merchant.

ಸಾವಕಾಶ f. n. Leisure, an interval; slowness. a. Leisurely, slow. -ಗತಿ. Slow manner.

ಸಾವಧಾನ (fr. ಸ-ಅವಧಾನ) s. n. Attention, carefulness, due heed. a. Attentive, careful, cautious.

ಸಾವಂತ. = ಸಾಮಂತ, q. v.

ಸಾವಂತಿಗೆ f. n. The garden-flower, *Chrysanthemum indicum*.

ಸಾವಯವ (fr. ಸ-ಅವಯವ) s. a. Composed of parts.

ಸಾವರಿಸು f. v. t. To recruit one's spirits.

ಸಾವಿಗೆ (tb. of ಶಾವಿಗೆ) n. Macaroni, vermicelli.

ಸಾವಿತ್ರಿ s. n. A cluster of solar rays. 2, a N. of Brahmâ's wife. 3, N. of Umâ.

ಸಾವಿರ (tb. of ಸಹಸ್ರ, q. v.) n. A thousand. ಸಾವಿರಾರು. A great number, thousands.

ಸಾವು k. n. Death. 2, a corpse. -ನೋವು. Death-pangs. -ಹುಟ್ಟು. Death and birth.

ಸಾವುಕಾರ. = ಸಾವಕಾರ, ಸಾಹುಕಾರ, q. v.

ಸಾವೆ (tb. of ಶ್ಯಾಮಕ) n. The grain *Panicum frumentaceum*.

ಸಾವೇರಿ s. n. N. of a tune.

ಸಾಷ್ಟಾಂಗ (fr. ಸ-ಅಷ್ಟ-ಅಂಗ) s. n. A mode of humble prostration by which eight parts of the body, viz. the hands, breast, forehead, knees and feet are made to touch the ground. -ನಮಸ್ಕಾರ, -ಪ್ರಣಾಮ. Such a salutation. -ಎರಗು, -ಬೀಳು, -ಮಾಡು. To prostrate as above.

ಸಾಸ. tb of ಸಾಹಸ, q. v.

ಸಾಸವಿ, ಸಾಸವೆ, ಸಾಸಿವೆ, ಸಾಸುವೆ (tb. of ಸರ್ಷಪ) n. Mustard, *Sinapis dichotoma*. -ಕಾಳು. Mustard seed.

ಸಾಸಿಗ. tb. of ಸಾಹಸಿಗ, q. v.

ಸಾಸಿರ. tb. of ಸಹಸ್ರ, q. v.

ಸಾಹಜಿಕ (fr. ಸಹಜ) s. a. Natural, coexistent.

ಸಾಹಸ s. n. Boldness, daring, courage, effort, valour, power. -ಗಾರ, -ವಂತ, ಸಾಹಸಿಗ. A bold, daring, *etc.*, man. ಸಾಹಸಿ. Bold, daring.

ಸಾಹಿತ್ಯ s. n. Association. 2, literary composition, poetry. 3, a collection of materials or implements.

ಸಾಹುಕಾರ. = ಸಾವಕಾರ, q. v.

ಸಾಹೇಬು (=ಸಾಬ್) h. n. A lord or master; a gentleman, sir, etc.

ಸಾಳೇರಿಮೃಗ s. n. A porcupine.

ಸಿಂಹ s. n. A lion. 2, the sign of the zodiac *Leo*. 3, a hero. -ನಾದ. A war-cry. -ಲ. Ceylon. ಸಿಂಹಾಸನ. A throne. ಸಿಂಹಿ. A lioness.

ಸಿಕತ s. n. Sand; a sand-bank; *also* ಸಿಕತೆ.

ಸಿಕಾರ, ಸಿಕಾರಿ (= ಶಿಕಾರಿ, q. v.) h. n. Hunting, game. -ಖಾನೆ. A menagerie, aviary.

ಸಿಕ್ಕೆ h. n. The royal seal; a coining die.

ಸಿಕ್ಕಟಿ, ಸಿಕ್ಕಣಿಗೆ k. n. A comb.

ಸಿಕ್ಕು k. v. i. To be caught; to fall into the hands of; to get among; to be found; to be obtained or got. 2, to insert. n. Entanglement, intricacy; impediment, obstacle, trouble. -ಬಿಡಿಸು. To disentangle. -ಬೀಳು, ಸಿಕ್ಕಿಬೀಳು, ಸಿಕ್ಕಿಕೊಳ್ಳು. To fall into a snare; to be caught. ಸಿಕ್ಕಿಸು. To insert; to cause to be caught; to entangle. ಸಿಕ್ಕಿಸಿಕೊಳ್ಳು. To hold or tuck anything under the arms, *etc.*

ಸಿಗಿ k. v. t. To split; to tear or rend. ಸಿಗಸು, ಸಿಗಿಸು. To get split.

ಸಿಗು. = ಸಿಕ್ಕು, q. v.

ಸಿಗುರು a. k. n. A splinter, shiver, rind.

ಸಿಗ್ಗು k. n. Shame, decency, modesty; timidity; disgust. ಸಿಗ್ಗಾಗು. To feel ashamed. ಸಿಗ್ಗಾಳಿ. A bashful person.

ಸಿಂಗ. tb. of ಸಿಂಹ, q. v.

ಸಿಂಗರ, ಸಿಂಗಾರ. tb. of ಶೃಂಗಾರ, q. v.

ಸಿಂಗಲೀಕ k. n. A black monkey.

ಸಿಟ್ಟು k. n. Anger, passion, wrath, rage. ಸಿಟ್ಟಾಗು. To get angry, *etc.* ಸಿಟ್ಟೆಗೆಬ್ಬಿಸು. To provoke to wrath. -ಇಳಿ. Anger, *etc.* to abate. -ಗೊಳ್ಳು. To become angry. -ತೀರಿಸು. To revenge one's self. -ತಡೆಕೊಳ್ಳು, -ನುಂಗು. To keep down or suppress one's anger. -ಬರು. Anger, *etc.* to come. -ಬಿಡು. To forsake anger. -ಮಾಡು. To become angry with. -ಹಿಡಿ. To grow angry. -ಗಾರ. A passionate or angry man. ಸಿಟ್ಟೆಬ್ಬಿಸು. To enrage; *cf.* ಸಿಟ್ಟೆಗೆಬ್ಬಿಸು.

ಸಿಡಿತ (*fr.* ಸಿಡಿ 2.) k. n. Headache. 2, jumping about from pride.

ಸಿಡಿ 1. k. a. Small, fine. -ಮಳೆ, -ಸೋನೆ. Drizzling rain.

ಸಿಡಿ 2. k. n. A hook-machine on which men are suspended in the air by a hook passed through the sinews of the back. -ಪೂಜೆ, -ಹಬ್ಬ. The swinging feast.

ಸಿಡಿ 3. k. v. i. To fly about; to be spattered, *as* mud, *etc.*; to snap, *as* parched grain; to start; to bounce. n. Scattering, spattering. 2, a spring trap. 3, fear, perplexity. -ಮಿಡಿ. Alarm, consternation. -ಸು. To spatter, bespatter.

ಸಿಡಿ 4. h. n. A ladder; a staircase.

ಸಿಡಿಲು, ಸಿಡ್ಲು k. n. A thunder-bolt, shaft of lightning.

ಸಿಡುಕು k. v. t. To chide, scold. n. Peevishness, wrath. -ಮೋರೆ. A peevish face. ಸಿಡುಕ. A peevish man; *f.* ಸಿಡುಕಿ.

ಸಿಡುಬು k. n. The small-pox. -ಹಾಕು, -ಹಾಕು. To vaccinate. -ಮೋರೆ. A pock-marked face.

ಸಿಂಡು k. n. A fetid smell.

ಸಿಂಡ್ರಿಸು k. v. i. To frown.

ಸಿತ s. a. White. n. Whiteness. -ಶೂಕ. Barley. ಸಿತಾಬ್ಜ, ಸಿತಾಂಬುಜ. A white lotus.

ಸಿದ್ದ. tb. of ಸಿದ್ಧ, q. v.

ಸಿದ್ದಾಯ s. n. Tribute; revenue.

ಸಿದ್ದಿ f. n. An Abyssinian.

ಸಿದ್ದಿಗೆ, ಸಿದ್ದೆ f. n. A leather-bottle.

ಸಿದ್ಧ s. a. Accomplished, finished, perfected. 2, successful. 3, established, demonstrated, proved. 4, valid; primitive (*g*.). 5, ready; decided, settled. 5, thoroughly prepared; dressed; matured; ripened. 6, sanctified; emancipated; eminent. *n*. A semi-divine being; an inspired sage or seer; a saint. -ಮಾಡಿಸು. To have made ready. -ಮಾಡು. To prove; to decide; to prepare. -ತೆ. Perfection; validity (*as* of a rule). -ಧಾತು. Ore; a primitive verbal theme (*g*.). -ರಸ. Quicksilver. ಸಿದ್ಧಾನ್ನ. Cooked food.

ಸಿದ್ಧಾಂತ s. *n*. Established truth, conclusion, dogma, axiom; a theorem. -ಮಾಡು. To prove, demonstrate. ಸಿದ್ಧಾಂತಿ. An astrologer or astronomer.

ಸಿದ್ಧಾರ್ಥಿ s. *n*. N. of the fifty-third year in the cycle of sixty.

ಸಿದ್ಧಿ s. *n*. Accomplishment, fulfilment, perfection. 2, success. 3, proof; validity. 4, certainty; determination. 5, solution of a problem. 6, preparation; readiness. 7, a supernatural faculty. 8, good effect; advantage. -ಗೆ ಒಯ್ಯು, -ಗೆ ತರು. To bring to completion, to accomplish. -ಗೆ ಹೋಗು. To be fulfilled. -ಸು. To be accomplished; to prepare.

ಸಿದ್ಧೇಶ, ಸಿದ್ಧೇಶ್ವರ s. *n*. N. of Śiva.

ಸಿಧ್ಮ s. *n*. A kind of leprosy; *also* -ಆ.

ಸಿಂದೂರ s. *n*. Red lead, minium.

ಸಿಂಧು s. *n*. The river Indus. 2, the sea, ocean. -ದೇಶ. The country of Sindh. -ನದಿ. The river Indus. -ಲವಣ. Rock-salt.

ಸಿಪಾಯಿ h. *n*. A native soldier; a policeman, a belted peon.

ಸಿಪ್ಪು (= ಚಿಪ್ಪು) k. *n*. An oyster-shell.

ಸಿಪ್ಪೆ k. *n*. The skin of fruits and vegetables.

ಸಿಬಂದಿ, ಸಿಬ್ಬಂದಿ h. *n*. An establishment of clerks, peons and servants.

ಸಿಬ್ಮ. = ಸಿಧ್ಮ, *q. v.*

ಸಿಂಪಡಿಸು (= ಸಿಂಬಡಿಸು) s. *v. t.* To sprinkle, besprinkle.

ಸಿಂಪಿ s. *n*. An oyster-shell.

ಸಿಂಪಿಗ. (= ಚಿಪ್ಪಿಗ *fr.* s. ಸಿವ್) *n*. A tailor. -ನಹುಲ್ಲು. A common grass, *Panicum cruscorvi.*

ಸಿಂಬಡಿಸು. = ಸಿಂಪಡಿಸು, *q. v.*

ಸಿಂಬಳ k. *n*. The mucus of the nose. -ತೆಗೆ. To blow the nose.

ಸಿಂಬಿ k. *n*. A coil of straw for setting a vessel on the ground. 2, the coil of a snake. -ಸುತ್ತು. To coil.

ಸಿರಿ. *tb. of* ಶ್ರೀ, *q. v.* -ಕನ್ನೆ. The sunflower. -ಕಾಳಗಿಡ. A strong smelling herb, *Gynandropsis pentaphylla.* -ವಂತ. A wealthy man.

ಸಿರ್ಕಾ h. *n*. Vinegar.

ಸಿರ್ಕೆ. = ಸಿಕ್ಕು, *q. v.*

ಸಿಲುಕು 1. (= ಸಿಕ್ಕು, *q. v.*) k. *v. i.* To be entangled, caught. *n*. Troublesomeness; *also* ಸಿಲ್ಕು.

ಸಿಲುಕು 2. h. *n*. Balance in hand; *also* ಸಿಲ್ಕು.

ಸಿಲುಬೆ (= ಶಿಲುಬೆ) h. *n*. A crucifix, cross.

ಸಿಲುವು k. *n*. Thin, *as* boards, paper; transparent, *as* water.

ಸಿವಂಗಿ k. *n*. The hyena.

ಸಿವಡು k. *n*. A bundle of straw or grass. 2, a pad put under a load or vessel; *also* ಸಿವುಡಿ.

ಸಿವಿಲ್ e. *a*. Civil.

ಸಿಹಿ. = ಸೀ, *q. v.*

ಸಿಳ್ಳು 1. k. *n*. Whistling. -ಹಾಕು. To whistle.

ಸಿಳ್ಳು 2. k. *n*. Rheum of the eye.

ಸಿಳ್ಳೆ k. *n*. A bifurcation, fork.

ಸೀ 1. k. *n*. Sweetness. -ಕರಣೆ. The pulp of ripe mangoes mixed with sugar. -ಗೆಣಸು. The Goa potato, *Dioscorea aculeata.* -ನೀರು. Drinking water. -ಪಲ್ಯ, -ಸಾರು. A vegetable dish without tamarind. -ಮೊಸರು. Fresh curds.

ಸೀ 2. k. *v. i.* To be scorched, burnt, parched. *P. p.* ಸೀದು. -ತೆನೆ. A parched ear of corn. -ಕರಿ. Parched, or burnt state. -ಕು. Anything burnt in the bottom of a vessel in cooking.

ಸೀಕು e. a. Sick. -ಮನೆ. A sick house.

ಸೀಗಡಿ f. n. A very small kind of fish.

ಸೀಗೆ k. n. A climbing prickly shrub, *Acacia concinna*, the pods of which are used like soap. -ಕಾಯಿ. Its pod. -ಬಳ್ಳಿ. Its creeper.

ಸೀಂಟು k. v. i. To slide along on the posteriors.

ಸೀತಳ f. n. Combined derangement of the three humours.

ಸೀತಾಫಲ f. n. The custard-apple.

ಸೀತಾಳ, -ಳೆ f. n. The chicken-pox.

ಸೀತೆ s. n. N. of the wife of Râma. ಸೀತಾಪತಿ, ಸೀತಾರಾಮ. Râma.

ಸೀನು k. n. Sneering; a sneer. v. i. To sneeze. P. p. ಸೀತು.

ಸೀಪು (= ಚೀಪು 1) k. v. t. To suck.

ಸೀಬಿ h. n. The guava. -ಹಣ್ಣು. Its fruit.

ಸೀಬು k. n. The bamboo-slit. 2, bamboo twigs put on roofs of houses.

ಸೀಮಂತ s. n. Parting of hair on each side of the head. 2, a ceremony performed during the time of a woman's first pregnancy. -ಪುತ್ರ. A first-born son; f. -ಪುತ್ರಿ.

ಸೀಮೆ s. n. A boundary, frontier, landmark. 2, a country. -ಕೋಳಿ. A duck; a goose. -ಯಕ್ಕಿ. Sago. -ಯಗಸೆ. The ring-worm shrub, *Cassia alata*. -ಯೆಣ್ಣೆ. Kerosene oil. -ಸುಣ್ಣ. Chalk.

ಸೀಯಾಳ k. n. A tender cocoa-nut.

ಸೀರ (ರ = ಱ) k. n. A streak, stripe.

ಸೀರಣಿ k. n. A small chisel.

ಸೀರಣಿಗೆ k. n. A comb.

ಸೀರು 1. k. v. t. To louse. n. A nit.

ಸೀರು 2. (ರು = ಱು) a. k. v. i. To become angry. n. Raging, fierceness. ಸೀರನಾಯಿ. A wild dog.

ಸೀರೆ (tb. of ಚೀರ) n. A female's garment.

ಸೀವನ್ನಿ. tb. of ಶ್ರೀವರ್ಣಿ, q. v.

ಸೀವರಿಸು a. k. v. i. To hiss, puff; to show disgust.

ಸೀಸ, ಸೀಸು s. n. Lead.

ಸೀಸೆ h. n. A bottle, flagon.

ಸೀಳು k. v. i. To split, to be cleft, to be rent. v. t. To split, rend. n. A split, fragment, piece.

ಸು s. pref. *implying* good, well, excellent, excellently; excessive, excessively, much, readily, *etc.* -ಕರ. Practicable, feasible; doing well. -ಕಾಲ. A time of plenty. -ಕೀರ್ತಿ. Good report. -ಕುಮಾರ. A beautiful youth (f. -ಕುಮಾರಿ); tender, delicate. -ಕೃತ. Well made; virtuous, pious; a virtuous act; virtue; fortune; auspiciousness; reward. -ಕ್ಷೇಮ. Perfect health. -ಗತಿ. A fine gait; a good condition. -ಗಂಧ. Fragrant; fragrance. -ಗಂಧತೈಲ. Scented oil. -ಗಂಧಮುಸ್ತೆ. Indian spikenard. -ಗಂಧರಾಜ. The tuberose, *Polianthes tuberosa*. -ಗಂಧಿ. Sweet-smelling; a kind of fragrant flower-grass. -ಗಂಧಿಬೇರು. The country sarsaparilla. -ಗಮ. Easy, practicable; plain, intelligible. -ಗುಣ. A good quality. -ಗುಣಿ. A person of good qualities. -ಚರಿತ. Well conducted, well behaved. -ಚಿತ್ತ. Good mind. -ಜನ. A gentleman. -ಜನತೆ, -ಜನತ್ವ. Gentlemanliness. -ಜ್ಞಾನ. Understanding, knowledge. -ಜ್ಞಾನಿ. A wise person. -ತಲ. One of the lower regions. -ದರ್ಶನ. Good looking; Vishṇu's discus. -ದಿನ. An auspicious day. -ದೇಶ. A good country. -ಧರ್ಮ. Justice, virtue. -ನಾಮ. A good name. -ನೀತ. Well-behaved, polite. -ನೀತಿ. Good manners, good policy. -ಪರ್ಣ. Garuḍa. -ಪ್ರತಿಷ್ಠೆ. Installation, consecration. -ಪ್ರಭಾತ. An auspicious dawn; a morning prayer. -ಪ್ರಲಾಪ. Eloquence. -ಪ್ರಸನ್ನ. Well-pleased, gracious. -ಪ್ರಸಾದ. Great propitiousness. -ಫಲ. Very fertile, profitable; good fruit; good reward. -ಬುದ್ಧಿ. Good understanding. -ಬೋ

ಧನೆ. Good instruction. -ಭಗ. Very fortunate, prosperous; amiable. -ಭಟ. A valiant man; a good servant. -ಭಾನು. The 17th year of the cycle. -ಭಾಷಿತ. Well-spoken, eloquent; an elegant composition. -ಭಿಕ್ಷ. Abundance of food or provisions. -ಮಂಗಲ. Very auspicious. -ಮಂಗಲಿ. A woman whose husband is alive. -ಮತಿ. Benevolence, kindness; kindly disposed. -ಮನ. Very charming; one who has a good mind. -ಮನಸ್. Good-minded; well-pleased; a learned man. -ಮಾನ, ಸುಮ್ಮಾನ. Joy, delight. -ಮಿತ್ರ. A good friend; N. -ಮಿತ್ರೆ. Lakshmaṇa's mother. -ಮುಖ. A handsome face; lovely, pleasing. -ಮೇರು. The mountain Mêru. -ರಕ್ಷಿತ. Safe and sound. -ರಸ. Juicy, sweet. -ಲಕ್ಷಣ. An auspicious mark; a grace; fortunate. -ಲಗ್ನ. An auspicious time. -ಲಲಿತ. Very pleasing, pure. -ಲಾಲಿಸು. To listen to very kindly. -ಲೋಚನ. Fine-eyed; spectacles. -ವರ್ಣ. Gold; a gold coin. -ವರ್ಣಕಾರ. A goldsmith. -ವಾರ್ತೆ. Good news, gospel. -ವಾಸ, -ವಾಸನೆ. Fragrance -ವಾಸಿನಿ. A term of courtesy for a respectable woman whose husband is alive (*cf.* -ಮಂಗಲಿ). -ವಿಚಾರ. Good thoughts. -ವಿಶೇಷ. Good tidings, news. -ವ್ರತ. Strict in observing a vow. -ವ್ರತೆ. A virtuous wife. -ಶಿಕ್ಷಿತ. Well-trained, disciplined, skilful. -ಶಿಕ್ಷೆ. Good training. -ಶೀಲ. Well-disposed; good temper. -ಶೀಲೆ. A good-tempered female; N. -ಶೀಲತೆ. Good morals; amiability. -ಶ್ರುತ. Well heard. -ಷಿರ. Perforated, hollow; a hole; a wind-instrument. -ಷುಪ್ತಿ. Deep sleep. -ಸಾಧ್ಯ. Easily attainable. -ಸೂತ್ರ. Easily, without obstruction. -ಸ್ಥಲ. An excellent place. -ಸ್ಥಿತಿ. Good condition; well-being, welfare. -ಸ್ಥಿರ. Very firm or steady. -ಸ್ವಪ್ನ. A lucky dream. -ಸ್ವರ. A pleasant note; well sounding, melodious. -ಹಿತ. Salutary, beneficial, satisfied. -ಹೃದ್. Cordial, friendly; a good man. -ಹೃದಯ. Goodhearted, well-disposed.

ಸುಕಾಣಿ. = ಚುಕಾಣಿ, *q. v.*

ಸುಕ್ಕು k. *n.* Shrinkage; a wrinkle, fold. *v. i.* To shrink, shrivel.

ಸುಖ s. *n.* Happiness, pleasure, delight, joy, comfort, ease. *a.* Happy, joyful; agreeable, suitable. -ಕರ. Causing happiness; done easily. -ಕೊಡು. To give pleasure. -ದಿಂದ ಇರು. To be happy. -ಪಡಿಸು. To make happy. -ಗೊಳ್ಳು, -ಪಡು, -ಭೋಗಿಸು. To feel happy. -ದ, -ಪ್ರದ. Giving happiness. -ದುಃಖ. Pleasure and pain. -ರೂಪ. Well, happy. ಸುಖಾಸನ. A comfortable seat. ಸುಖಿ. Happy, joyful, comfortable; a happy man. ಸುಖಿಸು. To feel pleasure.

ಸುಗಿ a. k. *v. i.* To tear off; to plunder.

ಸುಗ್ಗಿ k. *n.* Harvest, *esp.* the time of reaping the corn and grain. 2, plenty. -ಕಾಲ. The season of gathering crop.

ಸುಗ್ಗು k. *n.* Rice parched, ground and mixed with jaggory and cocoanut. ಸುಗ್ಗಿನುಂಡೆ. A ball of ಸುಗ್ಗು.

ಸುಗ್ರೀವ s. *n.* N. of a monkey-king.

ಸುಂಕ (*tb. of* ಶುಲ್ಕ) *n.* Toll, duty, customs. -ದವ. A publican; *also* ಸುಂಕಿಗ.

ಸುಂಕು 1. a. k. *n.* A fold, curl. 2, = ಸೊಂಕು, *q. v.*

ಸುಂಕು 2. (*tb. of* ಶೂಕ) *n.* An awn.

ಸುಚಿ. *tb. of* ಶುಚಿ, *q. v.*

ಸುಟ್ಟಿ k. *a.* Clever, able, powerful.

ಸುಟ್ಟು k. *P. p. of* ಸುಡು, *q. v.* -ರೆ. A whirlwind; *also* -ರೆ ಗಾಳಿ.

ಸುಡು k. *v. t.* To burn; to roast; to bake; to fire off; to consume. *v. i.* To burn; to be very hot; to feel heated; to be consumed. *P. p.* ಸುಟ್ಟು. *n.* Burning. ಸುಟ್ಟ ಬೂದಿ. Burnt ashes. ಸುಟ್ಟ ಮಾಂಸ. Roast meat. ಸುಟ್ಟು ಹಾಳು ಮಾಡಿಬಿಡು.

To destroy by fire. -ಗರ. *Ignis fatuus.* -ಗಾಡು. A cemetery. -ಗಾಡು ಮಾತು. A disagreeable word.

ಸುಂಟರ, ಸುಂಟ್ಳುರ k. *n.* A cyclone, hurricane; *also* -ಗಾಳಿ.

ಸುಂಟಿ (*tb. of* ಶುಂಠಿ) *n.* Dry ginger, the common ginger. [ಸುಂಡಿಲಿ.

ಸುಂಡ (*tb. of* ಶುಂಡ) *n.* A musk rat; *also*

ಸುಂಡಲು, ಸುಂಡಿಲು (= ಸೊಂಡಲು, *etc. tb. of* ಶುಂಡಾರ) *n.* An elephant's trunk.

ಸುಂಡು k. *v. i.* To evaporate. ಸುಂಡಿಸು. To cause to evaporate.

ಸುಣ್ಣ (*tb. of* ಚೂರ್ಣ) *n.* Chunam, lime, quicklime. -ದ ಗೂಡು. A lime-kiln. -ಪಾದ. The basement of a pillar.

ಸುತ s. *a.* Begotten. *n.* A son; *f.* ಸುತೆ.

ಸುತರಾಮ್ s. *ad.* Altogether; utterly; never.

ಸುತ್ತ, ಸುತ್ತಲು, ಸುತ್ತಮುತ್ತಲು (*cf.* ಸುತ್ತು) k. *prep.* About, round about, surrounding; all around. -ಬರು. To come round about. -ನೋಡಿ ಕಾರ್ಯ ಮಾಡು. To do a thing with circumspection. ಸುತ್ತಾಲೆ. The surrounding wall of a temple.

ಸುತ್ತಿಗೆ k. *n.* A hammer.

ಸುತ್ತು k. *v. t.* To surround, put around, inwrap; to roll up, wrap up. *v. i.* To go around; to walk about. *n.* Enclosure; expansion; a coil, roll, cheeroot; a walk round; a turn. *a.* Circuitous, round. -ಅಳತೆ, ಸುತ್ತಳತೆ. Compass, circumference. -ಮುತ್ತಲು. = ಸುತ್ತ, *q. v.* ಸುತ್ತಿಕೊಂಡು ಹೋಗು. To wind up; to go round about. ಸುತ್ತಿ ಕೊಂಡು ಬೀಳು. To reel and fall. ಸುತ್ತಿ ನೋಡು. To go round and look. ತಲೆ-. To feel giddy. -ಹಾಕು. To surround. -ಎಳೆ. Turning round. ಸುತ್ತಿಸು. To cause to roll or wind.

ಸುದಾ s. *ad.* Along with, also, even; *also* ಸುಧಾ.

ಸುದಾಮ s. *n.* A liberal man. 2, N. of a poor Brâhmaṇa.

ಸುದ್ದಿ (*tb. of* ಶುದ್ಧಿ) *n.* News, tidings, intelligence, rumour, talk.

ಸುಧಾರಣೆ s. *n.* A civilized or enlightened state; revising, *as* a work. 2, rest, forbearance, shift.

ಸುಧಾರಿಸು s. *v. t.* To adjust; to train; to finish; to polish; to civilise, enlighten. 2, to rest; to manage or get through. *v. i.* To be civilised or enlightened.

ಸುಧೆ (ಸುಧಾ) s. *n.* Nectar, ambrosia; milk; juice. 2, lime, mortar. 3, the emblic myrobalan.

ಸುನತಿ h. *n.* Circumcision.

ಸುನಾಯಾಸ s. *ad.* Without trouble or difficulty, easily.

ಸುನಾವಣೆ h. *n.* Reading and explaining. ಸುನಾಯಿಸು. To explain, tell.

ಸುಂದರ s. *a.* Beautiful, handsome, charming, agreeable. -ತೆ. Beauty.

ಸುಪ್ತ s. *a.* Slept, asleep; numbed. ಸುಪ್ತಿ. Sleep; numbness.

ಸುಪ್ಪತ್ತಿಗೆ f. *n.* A sleeping mattress.

ಸುಬೆ h. *n.* A province. -ದಾರ. The chief native officer of a talook.

ಸುಬ್ಬ (*tb. of* ಶುಭ್ರ) *n.* The serpent âdiśêsha. 2, N. -ರಾಯ. N.

ಸುಬ್ಬಲು k. *n.* Roughness.

ಸುಬ್ರಹ್ಮಣ್ಯ s. *n.* Kârttikêya; N. of a place of pilgrimage in S. Canara.

ಸುಭದ್ರೆ (ಸುಭದ್ರಾ) s. *n.* N. of Kṛishṇa's sister and Arjuna's wife.

ಸುಮಾರ, ಸುಮಾರು h. *n.* Conjecture or guess. 2, nearness, aboutness. 3, moderateness, tolerableness. *a.* Middling, ordinary. *ad.* About.

ಸುಂಬಳ 1. = ಸಿಂಬಳ, *q. v.*

ಸುಂಬಳ 2. f. *n.* White arsenic; *also* -ಕಾರ.

ಸುಮ್ಮಗೆ, ಸುಮ್ಮನೆ k. *ad.* Quietly, silently; causelessly, for nothing, uselessly. *a.* Quiet, silent. -ಕೊಡು. To give gratis. -ಬರು. To come without any particular business; to come often. -ಇರಿಸು, ಸುಮ್ಮನಿರಿಸು. To silence. ಸುಮ್ಮಗಿರು, ಸುಮ್ಮನಿರು. To be silent; (*imp. 2nd pers.*) be silent.

ಸುಯಿ k. *v. i.* To breathe; to sigh. *n.* Breath; a sigh; *also* -ಲು.

ಸುರ s. n. A god, deity. -ಗಿರಿ. The mountain Mêru. -ಗುರು. Bṛihaspati. -ಚಾಪ, -ಧನು. A rainbow. -ಪ, -ಪತಿ, -ರಾಜ, -ವರ. Indra. -ಪುರ. Indra's capital. -ರಿಪು, ಸುರಾರಿ. A god's enemy.

ಸುರಗಿ k. n. N. of a tree with very fragrant flowers. 2, (tb. of ಕ್ಷುರಿಕೆ) a sword.

ಸುರಂಗ f. n. A hole made by burglars in a house-wall, etc.; a mine.

ಸುರಟಿ s. n. N. of a tune.

ಸುರಣ f. n. An esculent root *Arum campanulatum.*

ಸುರತ s. n. N. of Surat. a. Playful; tender.

ಸುರಪರ್ಣ s. n. The tree *Rottleria tinctoria; also* ಸುರಹೊನ್ನೆ.

ಸುರಭಿ s. a. Agreeable. 2, fragrant. n. The cow of plenty. 2, a wise man. 3, mint, *Mentha sativa.*

ಸುರಮ. = ಸುರುಮ, q. v.

ಸುರಳಿ (= ಸುರುಳಿ) k. n. A coil, roll. ಮಾತಿನ-. Many words.

ಸುರಳಿತ f. a. Straight and smooth; fair and flowing; plain.

ಸುರಿ 1. k. v. i. To flow, pour, drop, *as* tears, blood, rain, *etc.* v. t. To pour, drop, shoot out, *etc.* ಸುರಿಸು. To cause to flow, *etc.* -ಯುವಿಕೆ. Flowing, *etc.* -ವು. To pour.

ಸುರಿ 2. (ರಿ = ಱ) k. v. i. To drink with a supping noise.

ಸುರು. = ಶುರು, q. v.

ಸುರುಟು k. v. i. To become shrivelled; to coil or roll up.

ಸುರುಮ h. n. A collyrium for the eyes. 2, sulphuret of antimony.

ಸುರುಳಿ. = ಸುರಳಿ, q. v.

ಸುರೆ (ಸುರಾ) s. n. Spirituous liquor, toddy. ಸುರಾಪಾನ. Drinking of spirituous liquor.

ಸುಕ್ಕು k. v. i. To shrivel, contract; to curl. n. Shrivelling, shrinking; a wrinkle; a curl. -ಸುರು (-ಉಸುರು). Suppressed breath.

ಸುಲಂಗಿ (tb. of ಶಲಾಕೆ) n. A mining crowbar. 2, a spike for peeling cocoanuts.

ಸುಲತಾನ h. n. A sultan. ಸುಲತಾನಿ. Relating to a sultan. ಸುಲತಾನಿ ಹಣ. A kind of coin.

ಸುಲಭ s. a. Easy, attainable, feasible. -ಬೀಳು. To be easy.

ಸುಲಾವಣೆ. = ಸುನಾವಣೆ, q. v.

ಸುಲಿ k. v. t. To strip off; to peel; to skin. 2, to plunder, rob. *P. ps.* ಸುಲದು, ಸುಲಿದು. -ಗೆ. Plundering, robbery, pillage, booty. -ಗೆ ಮಾಡು, ಸುಲುಕೊಳ್ಳು. To plunder, rob.

ಸುವ್ವಿ k. n. A chorus used by women at marriages, when pounding rice, *etc.*

ಸುಸ್ತಿ, ಸುಸ್ತು h. n. Slowness, delay; laziness. -ಮಾಡು. To delay, loiter. -ಗಾರ. A lazy man.

ಸುಳಿ (ಳಿ = ೞ) k. v. i. To turn round, whirl, revolve, to curl; to wander, roam; to move; to walk; to be unsteady, to waver, flicker. n. Whirling, waving, motion; a whirl-pool. 2, the tender leaf of a plantain, cocoa or areca-nut tree. 3, deception, fraud. -ದಾಡು, (-ದು ಆಡು). To move about. -ಗುಂಡಿ. A whirl-pool. -ನೆತ್ತಿ. The fontanelle.

ಸುಳಿವು, ಸುಳುವು (ಳಿ, ಳು = ೞ, ೞು) k. n. Motion, waving. 2, a glimpse, slight notice or sign.

ಸುಳುವು (tb. of ಸುಲಭ) n. Facility; fine workmanship; ingenuity; cheapness.

ಸುಳ್ಳು k. n. Falsehood, untruth, lie; *also* -ಮಾತು. ಸುಳ್ಳ. A liar. ಸುಳ್ಳಾಡು. To lie. ಸುಳ್ಳಾಸೆ. False hopes. -ಕಥೆ. A fable. -ಗಾರ. A liar. -ಚಾಡಿ. Calumny, false accusation. -ತನ. Falsification. -ನಿಮಿತ್ತ, -ನೆವನ. A false plea. -ಮನುಷ್ಯ. A fraudulent man. -ಮುಚ್ಚು. To hide a lie. -ಸಾಕ್ಷಿ. A false witness. -ಹೇಳು. To lie.

ಸೂಕ್ತ s. n. A vedic hymn. 2, a good word. a. Well spoken.

ಸೂಕ್ಷ್ಮ s. a. Subtile, minute, atomic, small, thin, fine, sharp; subtle, artful, sly. *n.* An atom. -ಕಾರ್ಯ, -ಕೆಲಸ. A delicate work. -ದೃಷ್ಟಿ. Sharp sight. -ಬುದ್ಧಿ. Acute intellect. -ಶರೀರ. The subtile body.

ಸೂಚನೆ s. *n.* Indication, intimation, hinting. 2, hint, information. 3, an index, summary. -ಆಗಿ ಹೇಳು. To tell briefly. ಸೂಚಿಸು. To point out, indicate, intimate, hint; to show.

ಸೂಚಿ (*tb.* ಶೂಚಿ) s. *n.* A needle. 2, a bristle, quill. 3, an index, list.

ಸೂಜಿ. *tb. of* ಶೂಚಿ, *q. v.* -ಕಣ್ಣು. The eye of a needle. -ಕಲ್ಲು. A magnet. -ತೂತು, -ತೂಬು. = ಸೂಜಿಕಣ್ಣು.

ಸೂಟಿ k. *n.* Smartness, quickness.

ಸೂಟೆ f. *n.* A torch of wisps, *etc.*

ಸೂಡಿ k. *n.* A sheaf or bundle of grass; *also* ಸೂಡು *n.*, *q. v.*

ಸೂಡು a. k. *v. t.* To put on the head, *etc., as* flowers, *etc.*; to receive. *n.* A bundle; *also* ಸೂಡಿ, *q. v.*

ಸೂತ s. *n.* A charioteer. 2, a bard.

ಸೂತಕ s. *n.* Impurity from childbirth, menses or death.

ಸೂತಿ s. *n.* Birth; offspring, progeny.

ಸೂತ್ರ s. *n.* A thread, string. 2, a precept, rule, law, canon, decree. 3, art, spring (*as* of a piece of mechanism). -ಧಾರ. A stage-director; *also* -ಧಾರಕ, -ಧಾರಿ.

ಸೂದ s. *n.* Cooking; a cook. ಸೂದಾಗಾರ. A kitchen.

ಸೂನಗಿ, ಸೂನಂಗಿ (*tb. of* ಶೂಲಿಕೆ) *n.* A spike for peeling cocoanuts; *also* ಸುಲಂಗಿ.

ಸೂನು s. *n.* A son; a child.

ಸೂಪ s. *n.* Soup, broth, sauce. 2, a cook. -ಕಾರ. A cook. -ಶಾಸ್ತ್ರ. Cookery; a book on cookery.

ಸೂರಣ. = ಸುರಣ, *q. v.*

ಸೂರು. = ಚೂರು, *q. v.*

ಸೂರುಳು a. k. *n.* An oath. *v. i.* To swear; *also* ಸೂರುಳಿಸು.

ಸೂರೆ (ರೆ = ಱೆ) k. *n.* Plundering, pillaging; plunder, spoil. -ಕೊಡು. To lavish, squander. -ಗಾರ. A plunderer. -ಮಾಡು. To plunder. -ಯಾಗು, -ಹೋಗು. To be plundered.

ಸೂರ್ಯ s. *n.* The sun. -ಕಾಂತ. Crystal. -ಕಾಂತಿ. Sun-shine; the sun-flower. -ಗ್ರಹಣ. A solar eclipse. -ಬಿಂಬ, -ಮಂಡಲ. The disk of the sun. -ವಂಶ. The solar race. ಸೂರ್ಯಾಸ್ತ, ಸೂರ್ಯಾಸ್ತಮಯ, ಸೂರ್ಯಾಸ್ತಮಾನ. Sun-set. ಸೂರ್ಯೋದಯ. Sun-rise. -ಸಂಕ್ರಮಣ. The sun's passage from one sign of the zodiac to another.

ಸೂಲ (*tb. of* ಸೂತ) *n.* Child-bearing; bringing forth. -ಗಾತಿ, -ಗಿತ್ತಿ. A midwife.

ಸೂಸಕ a. k. *n.* A forehead-jewel, trinket.

ಸೂಸಲು k. *n.* A kind of dish; *also* -ಕಡುಬು.

ಸೂಸು a. k. *v. i.* To issue, *as* breath, *etc.*; to flow, drop, shower, *as* water, rain. *v. t.* To spread, scatter or sprinkle about, *as* water, *etc.* *n.* Sprinkling.

ಸೂಳು 1. a. k. *n.* A loud sound, noise.

ಸೂಳು 2. (ಳು = ೞು) a. k. *n.* A time, turn; a season. ಸೂಳಾಯ್ತ. A herald.

ಸೂಳೆ (*tb. of* ಶೂಲಿ) *n.* A harlot, whore. -ಗಾರ. A whoremonger. -ಗಾರಿಕೆ. Whoredom.

ಸೃಜಿಸು. = ಸೃಷ್ಟಿಸು, *q. v.* 2, to let go.

ಸೃಷ್ಟ s. *a.* Created, made. -ಕೆ, -ನೆ. Making, fabrication, forgery, falsehood. -ನೆಪತ್ರ. A forged document. ಸೃಷ್ಟಿ. Creation; emanation; nature; natural property. ಸೃಷ್ಟಿಕರ್ತ. A creator. ವ್ಯಷ್ಟಿಸೃಷ್ಟಿ. A creation in which the deity is inherent in all the parts. ಸೃಷ್ಟಿಸು. To create, produce, make.

ಸೆಕೆ, ಸೆಖೆ (*tb. of* ಶಿಖಿ) *n.* Heat. -ನಾಡು. A hot country.

ಸೆಜ್ಜೆ 1. k. *n.* A cultivated grass, *Holcus spicatus.*

ಸೆಜ್ಜೆ 2. (= ಸಜ್ಜೆ. *tb. of* ಶಯ್ಯೆ) *n.* A bed.

ಸೆಟೆ k. *v. i.* To bend.

ಸೆಟ್ಟಿ (*tb. of* ಶ್ರೇಷ್ಠಿ) *n.* A title for a banker, merchant; the head of a caste.

ಸಡೆ k. v. i. To grow bulky; to get puffed up. 2, to become stiff, *as* limbs, *etc.* 3, to bend, shrink. 4, to fear. ಸೆಡಕು. Pride, haughtiness. ಸೆಡವು. The state of being crooked or bent; pride.

ಸೆಣಸು a. k. v. i. To be envious or jealous. *n.* Anger, wrath.

ಸೆರಗು (ರ=ಱ) k. n. The loose end of a garment; cover, protection. ಸೆರಗೊಡ್ಡು. To stretch the end of one's garment as a sign of humble petition.

ಸೆರೆ 1. k. n. The hollowed palm of the hand; a handful.

ಸೆರೆ 2. (ರೆ=ಱೆ) k. n. Confinement, captivity; a prison, hold. -ಬಿಡಿಸು. To release from prison. -ಯಾಗು. To become a prisoner. -ಹಾಕು. To imprison. -ಹಿಡಿ. To take prisoner.

ಸೆರ್ಟಿಫಿಕೇಟು e. n. A certificate, testimonial.

ಸೆಲೆ a. k. n. Sound; echo. 2, a spring, fountain.

ಸೆಳೆ 1. a. k. n. A twig, stick, rod.

ಸೆಳೆ 2. k. v. t. To cane, beat or flog.

ಸೆಳೆ 3. k. v. t. To draw, drag, pull. *v. i.* To draw up, *as* a limb. *n.* Pulling the current of a stream; *also* -ತ, ಸೆಳವು.

ಸೇಕ (= ಸೆಕೆ, *q. v.*) f. n. Heat. 2, fomentation. 3, sprinkling, effusion.

ಸೇಕಡಾ h. a. Per hundred.

ಸೇಗುಡಿ k. n. N. of a medicinal plant.

ಸೇಚನ s. n. Sprinkling, shedding; effusion. 2, a bucket.

ಸೇಡು k. n. Bending, shrinking, contraction.

ಸೇಡು (= ಸಿಟ್ಟು, *q. v.*) k. n. Anger, *etc.*

ಸೇತು, ಸೇತುವೆ s. n. A bridge; a mound, dike.

ಸೇದು k. v. t. To draw up water; to pull in (a string); to snuff; to draw in (*as* breath); to smoke (as a pipe, cheroot). *v. i.* To suffer spasms; to throb and pain; to be contracted.

ಸೇನ h. n. A revenue officer of a village. -ಬೋವ (= ಶಾನಭಾಗ). A village clerk.

ಸೇನಾ, ಸೇನೆ s. n. A host, army. ಸೇನಾಧಿಪತಿ, ಸೇನಾನಾಯಕ, ಸೇನಾನಿ, ಸೇನಾಪತಿ. A commander, general.

ಸೇಬು h. n. An apple.

ಸೇರು. k. v. i. To go to; to approach, to reach; to belong to; to enter; to be included; to join, to meet; to agree to; to be in harmony; to agree with, *as* food; to be agreeable. *P. p.* ಸೇರಿ. *n.* Meeting, *etc.* -ವಿಕೆ. Joining, *etc.* ಸೇರಿಸು. To join; to put together; to put into; to make enter; to insert; to assemble.

ಸೇರು 2. f. n. A seer, a measure of weight or capacity.

ಸೇರುವೆ, ಸೇರ್ವೆ k. n. Connection, company, a herd of cattle. -ಗಾರ. One in charge of a cattle-pound.

ಸೇಲೆ. *tb. of* ಚೇಲ, *q. v.*

ಸೇವಗೆ, ಸೇವಿಗೆ k. n. Macaroni.

ಸೇವಂತಿಗೆ s. n. A kind of jasmine, *Jasminum auriculatum.*

ಸೇವೆ s. n. Service, attendance, worship, homage; devotion; use, practice. -ಮಾಡು. To serve. ಸೇವಕ. A servant, attendant; a worshipper; *f.* ಸೇವಕಳು. ಸೇವನೆ. Service; devotion; using, taking, enjoying. ಸೇವನ ಮಾಡು. To use, enjoy, take. ಸೇವಿಸು. To serve, honour, worship; to enjoy, use. ಸೇವಾವೃತ್ತಿ. The functions of service. *Cpds.:* ಅತ್ತೆ-, ದೇವರ-, ಭೂತದ-, ಮಾಂಸದ-, ಮೂರ್ತಿ-, ಸೈತಾನನ-, *etc.*

ಸೇಸೆ (*tb. of* ಶೇಷ) n. The remains of flowers, raw rice and other offerings made to an idol. 2, raw rice thrown on the heads of a married couple.

ಸೈ (= ಸಯ್, *q. v.*) k. n. Straightness; rectitude; propriety.

ಸೈತಾನ h. n. Satan, the devil. -ಬುದ್ಧಿ, -ಭಾವ. Devilish disposition.

ಸೈತ್ಯ (*tb. of* ಶೈತ್ಯ) n. Catarrh.

ಸೈನಿಕ s. a. Military. n. A soldier.

ಸೈಂಧವ (*fr.* ಸಿಂಧು) s. *n.* A native of Sindh. 2, a kind of rock-salt. *a.* Marine, aquatic.

ಸೈನ್ಯ (*fr.* ಸೇನಾ) s. *n.* An army.

ಸೈರಣೆ, ಸೈರಿಸು. = ಸಯ್ರಣೆ, ಸಯ್ರಿಸು, *q. v.*

ಸೈರಂಧ್ರಿ (*tb.* ಸ್ವೈರೇಂದ್ರಿ) s. *n.* A female attendant; a toilet woman.

ಸೊಕ್ಕು k. *v. i.* To become mad or intoxicated, to get bewildered or confused; to be proud or arrogant. *n.* Infatuation; stupefaction; pride, arrogance. ಸೊಕ್ಕಳಿ. To be humbled. ಸೊಕ್ಕೇರು. Pride to arise.

ಸೊಗಡು a. k. *n.* A sharp smell. 2, touch.

ಸೊಗಯಿಸು, ಸೊಗಸು k. *v. i.* To shine, look beautiful, be pleasant. ಸೊಗಸು. Shine; beauty; charm; happiness, pleasure, delight; glee, gaiety. -ಗಾರ. A beau, gay man. -ಗುಂದು. Pleasure to be less.

ಸೊಂಕು a. k. *v. i.* To touch, come near; to infect, taint. *n.* Touch, contact, infection. -ರೋಗ. An infectious disease.

ಸೊಟ್ಟ, ಸೊಟ್ಟು k. *n.* Crookedness, curvedness. -ಗಾಲು. A bandy-leg. -ಗೈ. A crump hand. -ಬಾಯಿ, -ಮೋರೆ. A wry mouth or face. ಸೊಟ್ಟಗೆ. Crookedly.

ಸೊಡರು, ಸೊಡಲು k. *n.* A lamp.

ಸೊಣೆ k. *v. i.* To point at a person, as a sign of mockery.

ಸೊಂಟ k. *n.* The hip, loins, waist.

ಸೊಂಡಲು, ಸೊಂಡಿಲು, ಸೊಂಡ್ಲು (= ಸುಂಡಲು, *q. v. tb. of* ಶುಂಡಾರ) *n.* An elephant's trunk.

ಸೊಂಡಿಲಿ (*tb. of* ಶುಂಡ) *n.* The musk shrew; *also* ಸುಂಡಿಲಿ.

ಸೊಂಡೆ k. *n.* The plant *Solanum pubescens.*

ಸೊತ್ತು 1. (= ಸೊಟ್ಟ) k. *n.* Crookedness.

ಸೊತ್ತು 2. (*tb. of* ಸ್ವತ್ವ) *n.* Property, goods.

ಸೊನೆ k. *n.* The juice that exudes from a stalk, twig, etc.

ಸೊನ್ನ (*tb. of* ಸ್ವರ್ಣ) *n.* Gold. -ಗಾರ. A goldsmith. ಸೊನ್ನಾರ. Gilt, gilding.

ಸೊನ್ನೆ (*tb. of* ಶೂನ್ಯ) *n.* The anusvâra. 2, a cypher or zero. 3, (*tb. of* ಸ್ವರ್ಣ) Gold. -ವರದ. A dealer in gold.

ಸೊಪ್ಪು 1. k. *n.* Slackness; weakness. *v. t.* To repress, check. ಸೊಪ್ಪಾಗು. To slacken (*as* cloth, lips, *etc.*); to pine; grow weak.

ಸೊಪ್ಪು 2. k. *n.* Foliage; a vegetable, herb, greens. -ಗುಟ್ಟು. To beat the bush for game. -ಸದೆ. Leaves and litter.

ಸೊಪ್ಪೆ k. *n.* The straw of millet.

ಸೊಬಗು (*tb. of* ಸುಭಗ) *n.* Beauty, charm, loveliness, *etc.* ಸೊಬಗ. A beautiful man; *f.* ಸೊಬಗಿ.

ಸೊಂಪು (= ಸಂಪು) k. *n.* Beauty, elegance, charm, grace. ಸೊಂಪಗೆ. Nicely, beautifully.

ಸೊರಗು k. *v. i.* To wither, languish; to grow lean or meagre.

ಸೊರಟು k. *n.* The state of being contracted; shrivelled *as* a leaf, or crooked *as* a bamboo.

ಸೊರೆ 1. = ಸೋರೆ, *q. v.*

ಸೊರೆ 2. k. *n.* The milk collected in the udder of a cow or buffalo. -ಬಿಡು. To let down that milk.

ಸೊರ್ಕು. = ಸೊಕ್ಕು, *q. v.*

ಸೊಲಗೆ, ಸೊಲಿಗೆ k. *n.* A measure of capacity $= \frac{1}{4}$ of a kuḍava or balla.

ಸೊಲ್ಲು k. *v. i.* To say, speak. *n.* A word. ಸೊಲ್ಲಿಸು. To be said.

ಸೊಸೆ (*tb. of* ಸ್ನುಷೆ) *n.* A daughter-in-law.

ಸೊಳ್ಳೆ k. *n.* A nostril. 2, a musquito. ಮೂಗಿನ-. A nostril. ಕಣ್ಣು-. An eye-fly.

ಸೋ (= ಸೋವು) k. *v. t.* To drive off, scare away.

ಸೋಕು. = ಸೊಂಕು, *q. v.*

ಸೋಗು (*tb. of* ಯೋಗ) *n.* A disguise, mask. -ತೆಗೆದು ಕೊಳ್ಳು, -ಮಾಡು. To assume a disguise. -ಹಾಕು. To disguise one's self.

ಸೋಗೆ k. *n.* The peculiar leaf of palms, sugar-cane, *etc.* 2, a peacock's tail.

3, a rudder. *Cpds.*: ಅವಿಕೆ-, ಕಬ್ಬಿನ-, ತಾಳೆ-, ತೆಂಗಿನ-.

ಸೋಜಿ f. *n.* Meal ground coarse, grits of wheat, rolong.

ಸೋಜಿಗ (= ಚೋಜಿಗ, *q. v. tb. of* ಚೋದ್ಯ) *n.* Surprise, wonder; a wonder.

ಸೋಟೆ k. *n.* The lower part of the cheek. -ಸುಲಿ. To pinch it.

ಸೋಡ f. *n.* Letting go freely, acquittance. -ಪತ್ರ. A bill of divorce.

ಸೋಡಿ f. *n.* Remission of a debt, *etc.*; the sum remitted. 2, release from bondage, freedom.

ಸೋತು. *P. p. of* ಸೋಲು, *q. v.*

ಸೋದರ s. *a.* Co-uterine. *n.* An own brother. -ಅತ್ತೆ, ಸೋದರತ್ತೆ. A father's sister; a mother's brother's wife. -ಮಾವ. A maternal uncle. -ಅಳಿಯ. A nephew, sister's son.

ಸೋನೆ a. k. *n.* An incessant drizzle.

ಸೋಪಸ್ಕರ s. *n.* Materials, provision. ಸೋಪಸ್ಕಾರ. A measure or means.

ಸೋಪಾನ s. *n.* Stairs, steps. -ಕಟ್ಟು. A staircase.

ಸೋಪು k. *n.* Anise-seed, *Pimpinella anisum.*

ಸೋಬತಿ f. *n.* A companion, fellow. ಸೋಬತು. Company, society.

ಸೋಬಾನೆ (*tb. of* ಶೋಭನ) *n.* A festive song.

ಸೋಮ s. *n.* A climbing plant, *Sarcostema viminalis;* its juice. 2, nectar. 3, the moon. 4, Śiva. -ನಾಥ. Śiva; N. -ಣ್ಣ, -ಪ್ಪ, -ಯ್ಯ. N. -ಯಾಗ. A sôma sacrifice. -ಯಾಜಿ. A sôma sacrificer; a title among Brâhmaṇas. -ವಂಶ. The lunar dynasty. -ವಾರ. Monday. -ಸೂತ್ರ. A sluice for conveying the water bathed to an idol or liṅga. ಸೋಮೇಶ, ಸೋಮೇಶ್ವರ. Śiva or his representation; N. of a Kannaḍa poet.

ಸೋಮಾರಿ k. *n.* A sluggard, idler. -ತನ. Laziness. -ಕೆಲಸ. Lazy work.

ಸೋಯಿ f. *n.* Opportuneness of circumstances.

ಸೋರು k. *v. i.* To drop, drip, trickle, ooze, flow; to leak (*P. p.* ಸೋರಿ). *n.* Dropping, leaking. ಸೋರುವ ಮನೆ. A leaking house. ಸೋರಿಸು. To cause to drop or flow.

ಸೋರುಪ್ಪು f. *n.* Nitre, saltpetre.

ಸೋರೆ (= ಸೊರೆ 1) k. *n.* The bottle gourd. *Cpds.*: ಕೈ-, ಶೀ-, ಹಾಲು-; -ಬುಳ್ಳಿ, -ಬುರುಡೆ. A calabash.

ಸೋಲು k. *v. i.* To be defeated or overcome; to lose, forfeit, fail. 2, to be captivated allured. (*P. p.* ಸೋತು). *n.* Defeat, loss; *also* ಸೋಲುವಿಕೆ, ಸೋಲ, ಸೋಲುವೆ. -ಗೆಲವು. Defeat and success. ಸೋಲಿಸು. To defeat, vanquish.

ಸೋಲೆ k. *n.* The slough of a snake; coa of an onion.

ಸೋವು 1. (= ಸೋ, *q. v.*) a. k. *v. t.* To drive off, *etc.*

ಸೋವು 2. k. *n.* Trace, mark, sign.

ಸೋಸು 1. *tb. of* ಶೋಧಿಸು, *q. v.*

ಸೋಸು 2. (*tb. of* ಸಹಿಸು) *v. t.* To endure, bear, suffer.

ಸೌಕರ್ಯ (*fr.* ಸುಕರ) s. *n.* Easiness of performance.

ಸೌಖ್ಯ (*fr.* ಸುಖ) s. *n.* Pleasure, happiness, ease, comfort, enjoyment. -ದಿಂದಇರು. To be happy, *etc.*

ಸೌಗಂಧ (*fr.* ಸುಗಂಧ) s. *a.* Sweet-scented, fragrant.

ಸೌಜನ್ಯ (*fr.* ಸುಜನ) s. *n.* Goodness, generosity, kindness, benevolence; friendship.

ಸೌಜ್ಞೆ. *tb. of* ಸಂಜ್ಞೆ.

ಸೌದೆ (= ಸವದೆ, ಸವುದೆ, *q. v.*) f. *n.* Firewood. -ಒಟ್ಟು. A stack of wood. -ಹೊರೆ. A faggot.

ಸೌಧ (*fr.* ಸುಧಾ) s. *n.* A plastered mansion; a palace.

ಸೌಂದರ, ಸೌಂದರ್ಯ (*fr.* ಸುಂದ) s. *n.* Beauty, loveliness, elegance. -ಶಾಲಿ. A beautiful person.

ಸೌಭದ್ರ (*fr.* ಸುಭದ್ರಾ) s. *n.* Abhimanyu, son of Subhadrâ.

ಸೌಭಾಗ್ಯ (*fr.* ಸುಭಗ) s. *n.* Good fortune, good luck; blessedness; beauty, charm; the state of wifehood. -ವತಿ. A married and unwidowed woman.

ಸೌಮ್ಯ (*fr.* ಸೋಮ) s. *a.* Handsome, pleasing, mild, calm, gentle. *n.* The planet Mercury. 2, the 43rd year of the cycle. -ರೂಪ. A pleasing form. -ವಾರ. Wednesday.

ಸೌರ (*fr.* ಸೂರ) s. *n.* The planet Saturn. 2, a solar month. *a.* Solar. -ಮಾನ. A solar measurement of time. -ಮಾಸ. A solar month. -ಮಾನವರ್ಷ. A solar year.

ಸೌರಾಷ್ಟ್ರ (*fr.* ಸುರಾಷ್ಟ್ರ) s. *a.* Relating to Surat. *n.* Surat. 2, N. of a tune.

ಸೌಲಭ್ಯ (*fr.* ಸುಲಭ) s. *n.* Easiness of acquisition; facility.

ಸೌಳು. = ಸವುಳು, *q. v.*

ಸ್ಕಂದ s. *n.* Kârttikêya, the god of war. 2, a learned man. -ಪುರಾಣ. N. of a purâṇa.

ಸ್ಕಂಧ s. *n.* The shoulder. 2, a large branch. 3, a section, chapter. 4, a troop. 5, a prince; a wise man.

ಸ್ಖಲನ s. *n.* Slipping, tripping, tottering; falling or deviating from; an error, mistake, blunder; dropping; shock, collision. ಸ್ಖಲಿತ. Stumbled; unsteady; erring.

ಸ್ತನ s. *n.* The breast of a woman, udder. -ಪ, -ಂಧಯ. A male infant.

ಸ್ತನಯಿತ್ನು, ಸ್ತನಿತ s. *n.* Thunder.

ಸ್ತಬಕ s. *n.* A cluster, bunch. 2, quantity, multitude.

ಸ್ತಬ್ಧ s. *a.* Fixed, stiff, rigid; immovable, motionless, numb, paralyzed; senseless, dull. -ತ್ವ. Fixedness, immobility.

ಸ್ತಂಬ. *tb. of* ಸ್ತಂಭ, *q. v.*

ಸ್ತಂಭ s. *n.* Fixedness, stiffness. 2, a pillar, column, post; a stem, trunk. 3, numbness, stupor; paralysis; stupidity. 4, stoppage. -ನ. Fixing firmly, paralysing, stunning; arresting, stopping, *etc.* ಸ್ತಂಭಿಸು. To fix firmly, stop.

ಸ್ತವ, ಸ್ತವನ s. *n.* Praising; praise, a hymn. ಸ್ತವನೀಯ. Praiseworthy.

ಸ್ತಿಮಿತ s. *a.* Still, motionless, steady, fixed, immovable. 2, tender; wet, moist.

ಸ್ತುತಿ s. *n.* Praise, eulogy; commendation, adulation. ಆತ್ಮ.- Self-praise. ಮುಖ-. Flattery, ಸ್ತುತ್ಯ. Laudable, praiseworthy. -ಪಾಠಕ. A panegyrist, bard. -ಸು. To praise, laud; to praise in song.

ಸ್ತೂಪ s. *n.* A heap or pile of earth; a Buddhist monument.

ಸ್ತೇಯ s. *n.* Theft, robbery. ಸ್ತೇಯಿ. A thief, robber.

ಸ್ತೋಕ s. *a.* Little, small. *n.* A tail. 2, offspring. -ಕ. The châtaka bird.

ಸ್ತೋತ್ರ s. *n.* Praise, eulogium; a hymn of praise, ode.

ಸ್ತೋಮ s. *n.* Praise. 2, an oblation. 3, a multitude; a heap, collection, mass.

ಸ್ತೌತ್ಯ (*fr.* ಸ್ತುತಿ) s. *n.* Praise, *etc.* 2, prayer.

ಸ್ತ್ರೀ s. *n.* A woman, female. -ಜಾತಿ. The female sex. -ಬುದ್ಧಿ. A fickle, effeminate mind. -ಲಿಂಗ. The feminine gender. -ವಾಚಕ. A feminine noun.

ಸ್ಥಲ, ಸ್ಥಳ s. *n.* Ground, land. 2, a place, spot, site, locality. 3, stead, place, lieu. 4, station. -ಪಲ್ಲಟ. Transfer; confusion of places. -ವಂತಿಗ, ಸ್ಥಲೀಕ. A resident. -ವಾರ (= ತಳವಾರ). A watchman, beadle. -ವಾಸ. Place of residence.

ಸ್ಥಾನ s. *n.* Standing; state; a place, spot, site. 2, situation, position; office, rank. 3, an abode, house. 4, an object. -ಭ್ರಷ್ಟ. Displaced, out of place. ಸ್ಥಾನಾಂತರ. Another place. ಸ್ಥಾನಿಕ. Local; a paid-servant in a temple who assists the pûjâri. ಸ್ಥಾನೀಯ. Local.

ಸ್ಥಾಪಕ s. *n.* An establisher, founder. ಸ್ಥಾಪನ, ಸ್ಥಾಪನೆ. Establishing, founding, instituting; appointing. ಪುನಃಸ್ಥಾಪನ. The Reformation. ಸ್ಥಾಪನೆ ಮಾಡು. To establish. ಸ್ಥಾಪಿತ. Established, founded. ಸ್ಥಾಪಿಸು. To establish, set up, found, institute; to place, set, lay.

ಸ್ಥಾಯಿ s. a. Situated; fixed, stationary, enduring, constant, lasting; steady, firm. -ಭಾವ. A fixed condition of mind or body.

ಸ್ಥಾಲಿ s. n. A pot, pan, kettle, boiler.

ಸ್ಥಾವರ s. a. Standing still, fixed, stationary, firm, immovable, real. -ಸೊತ್ತು. Real estate. -ಜಂಗಮ. Immovable and movable.

ಸ್ಥಿತಿ s. n. Situation, state, position, condition; good condition; station, rank; good manners; property, wealth. -ಗತಿ. State and course of life. -ವಂತ. A wealthy man. -ಸ್ಥಾಪಕ. Elastic; elasticity. ಸ್ಥಿತ. Situated; fixed, settled, steady.

ಸ್ಥಿರ s. a. Firm, steady; permanent, durable, lasting; immovable, still; constant, faithful, certain, sure; firm, strong. -ಗೊಳಿಸು, -ಪಡಿಸು. To confirm, strengthen. -ಂಜೀವಿ. Long-lived. -ತನ, -ತೆ, -ತ್ವ. Firmness, stability, steadfastness. -ಬುದ್ಧಿ. Steadiness of mind. -ವಾರ. Saturday. ಸ್ಥಿರಾಯು. Long-lived.

ಸ್ಥೂಲ s. a. Stout, bulky; thick, fat, corpulent; clumsy, coarse; stupid. -ದೇಹ, -ಶರೀರ. The material body. -ಬುದ್ಧಿ. Dulness. -ಸೂಕ್ಷ್ಮ. Mighty and subtile.

ಸ್ಥೈರ್ಯ (fr. ಸ್ಥಿರ) s. n. Firmness, steadiness; resolution, constancy; hardness, solidity, calmness, patience.

ಸ್ನಾತ s. a. Bathed; immersed; deeply engaged. n. An initiated householder; also -ಕ.

ಸ್ನಾನ s. n. Bathing, ablution. 2, baptism. -ಮಾಡು. To bathe. ಕಂಠ-. Bathing all but the head. ಆತ್ಮ-. Receiving the Holy Spirit. ಜ್ಞಾನ-. Receiving knowledge, baptism.

ಸ್ನಾಯು s. n. A sinew, tendon, muscle.

ಸ್ನಿಗ್ಧ s. a. Oily, greasy, fat, sticky, viscid; smooth; moist; cooling; tender. 2, attached, lovely.

ಸ್ನೇಹ s. n. Tenderness, love, affection, fondness, friendship. -ಬೆಳೆ. Friendship to originate. -ಮಾಡು. To court friendship; to love. ಸ್ನೇಹಿಸು. To love. ಸ್ನೇಹಿತ. A friend; f. -ಳು.

ಸ್ಪಂದ, -ನ s. n. Throbbing, moving, motion.

ಸ್ಪರ್ಧೆ s. a. Rivalry; envy, jealousy; competition. ಸ್ಪರ್ಧಿಸು. To rival, envy.

ಸ್ಪರ್ಶ s. n. Touching, touch, contact; the sense of touch. -ಮಾಡು, ಸ್ಪರ್ಶಿಸು. To touch.

ಸ್ಪಷ್ಟ s. a. Distinct, clear, plain, intelligible; true, real.

ಸ್ಪೃಹತೆ, ಸ್ಪೃಹೆ s. n. Desire, wish; envy. ನಿ-. Freedom from desire or envy.

ಸ್ಫಟಿಕ s. n. Crystal; quartz. ಸ್ಫಟಿಕೆ. Alum.

ಸ್ಫುಟ s. a. Burst open; clear, plain, evident.

ಸ್ಫುರಣ s. n. Trembling, vibration, rising to mind, suggesting itself. ಸ್ಫುರಿಸು. To rise to mind, suggest itself.

ಸ್ಫೋಟ, ಸ್ಫೋಟಕ s. n. A swelling, boil, tumour, pimple; small-pox. ಸ್ಫೋಟನ. Breaking; cracking; disclosing.

ಸ್ಮರಣ s. n. Recollection, reminiscence; remembrance; memory. 2, tradition. ಸ್ಮರಿಸು. To remember, recollect, bear in mind, be mindful of; to call upon God.

ಸ್ಮಾರ್ತ (fr. ಸ್ಮೃತಿ) s. a. Relating to memory. 2, recorded in the smṛiti. n. A Brâhmaṇa belonging to the advaita vêdânta creed. 2, any act enjoined by the smṛiti.

ಸ್ಮೃತಿ s. n. Remembrance, memory, recollection. 2, the body of traditional law; any particular law-book. -ಕರ್ತ. A legislator.

ಸ್ಮೇರ s. n. A smile, gentle laugh.

ಸ್ಯಂದನ s. n. A car. 2, water. 3, a river. 4, air, wind.

ಸ್ಯಾಲ s. n. A wife's brother.

ಸ್ರಜ s. n. A chaplet, garland.

ಸ್ರವ (= ಶ್ರವ, q. v.) s. n. Flowing, streaming, trickling. 2, a spring, fountain; *also* -ಣ.

ಸ್ವ s. a. Own, one's own. 2, native, natural, proper. n. Self. *Cpds.:* -ಕಾರ್ಯ, -ಕ್ಷೇತ್ರ, -ಗ್ರಾಮ, -ಜನ, -ಜಾತಿ, -ದೇಶ, -ಧರ್ಮ, -ಪ್ರಯೋಜನ, -ಬುದ್ಧಿ, -ರೂಪ, -ಹೀನ, -ಹಸ್ತ, *etc.*

ಸ್ವಕೀಯ s. a. Own, one's own; belonging to one's self. -ಜನ. A relative; own persons.

ಸ್ವಚ್ಛ s. a. Pellucid; white; pure; clear. -ತನ, -ತೆ. Purity, clearness.

ಸ್ವಚ್ಛಂದ s. n. One's own will, own choice. a. Self-willed; spontaneous. ಸ್ವಚ್ಛಂದಿ. Self-willed, wilful.

ಸ್ವತಃ (*tb. of* ಸ್ವತಸ್) *ad.* By one's self, of one's own accord. -ಪ್ರಮಾಣ. Self-evident.

ಸ್ವತಂತ್ರ s. n. Self-dependence; independence, freedom. a. Independent, free; self-willed, unruly. -ದಿಂದ ಇರು. To be independent. -ತನ, -ತ್ವ. Independence.

ಸ್ವತಾ. = ಸ್ವತಃ, *q. v.*

ಸ್ವತೇವ s. a. Of one's self; by itself.

ಸ್ವಧಾ, ಸ್ವಧೆ s. n. One's own condition or nature. 2, custom, usage. 3, oblation offered to pitṛis.

ಸ್ವದನ s. n. Tasting, eating.

ಸ್ವತ್ತು (*tb. of* ಸ್ವತ್ವ) n. Property, wealth.

ಸ್ವಂತ (*tb. of* ಸ್ವ, *q. v.*) a. Own; proper, peculiar, *etc.* -ಗಾರ. A proprietor.

ಸ್ವಪ್ನ s. n. Sleep. 2, a dream, dreaming. ಒಳ್ಳೇ-, ಸು-. A pleasant dream. ಕೆಟ್ಟ-, ದುಃ-. A bad dream.

ಸ್ವಭಾನು s. n. The 47th year of the cycle. a. Selfish.

ಸ್ವಭಾವ s. n. Natural state, natural temper, nature; innate disposition. *Cpds.:* -ಗುಣ, -ಸತತೆ, -ಬುದ್ಧಿ, -ಲಕ್ಷಣ, *etc.* ಸ್ವಭಾವಿಕ. = ಸ್ವಾಭಾವಿಕ, *q. v.*

ಸ್ವಯಂ s. n. Self. a. Of one's own self. -ವರ. The election of a husband by a virgin girl who was not married in time. -ಕೃತ. Self-made, natural, spontaneous. -ಪಾಕ. Cooking for one's self. -ಪಾಕಿ. A cook. -ಭೂ. Selfexistent; Brahmâ. ಸ್ವಯಮೇವ. Of one's own accord.

ಸ್ವಯಾರ್ಜಿತ. = ಸ್ವಾರ್ಜಿತ, *q. v.*

ಸ್ವಯಿರ. *tb. of* ಸ್ವೈರ, *q. v.*

ಸ್ವರ s. n. Sound, noise; voice. 2, tone, music; a note of the musical scale. 3, a vowel. 4, an accent. -ಧಾತು. A verbal theme ending in a vowel. -ಭಂಗ. Hoarseness. -ಸಂಧಿ. Junction of vowels.

ಸ್ವರೂಪ s. n. One's own form, features; natural state or appearance. a. Similar, like, identical. -ನಾಶನ, -ಭಂಗ. Disgrace.

ಸ್ವರ್ಗ s. n. Heaven, paradise. 2, happiness, joy. -ಲೋಕ. The celestial region. -ಸ್ಥ. A deity; dead. ಸ್ವರ್ಗೀಯ. Heavenly, celestial.

ಸ್ವರ್ಣ s. n. Gold; a gold coin. -ಮಯ. Consisting of gold.

ಸ್ವಲ್ಪ (*its tb.* ಸ್ವಲ್ಪು) s. a. Very small; little, minute, trifling; very few. -ಸ್ವಲ್ಪ. *rep.* -ದಿವಸ. A few days. -ದೂರ. Not far. -ಹೊತ್ತು. A little while.

ಸ್ವಸ್ತಿ s. n. Welfare, health, blessing. *int.* May it be well! hail! -ವಾಚನ. Invocation of blessings.

ಸ್ವಸ್ಥ s. a. Well, healthy, comfortable. n. Well-being, health; *also* -ತೆ. *ad.* At ease, in health.

ಸ್ವಹಸ್ತ s. n. One's own hand. 2, handwriting, signature.

ಸ್ವಾಗತ s. n. Welcome, welcoming. a. Come of one's self.

ಸ್ವಾತಂತ್ರ್ಯ (*fr.* ಸ್ವತಂತ್ರ) s. *n.* Independence; free will.

ಸ್ವಾತಿ s. *n.* The star *Arcturus.*

ಸ್ವಾದ s. *n.* Taste, flavour; liking, relishing, enjoyment. ಸ್ವಾದಿಸು. To be pleasant to the taste, to taste.

ಸ್ವಾಧೀನ s. *a.* Self-dependent; independent. 2, in one's own power or subjection. 3, at the control of, under. -ಮಾಡು. To subject; to take possession of; to control; *also* -ಮಾಡಿಕೊಳ್ಳು.

ಸ್ವಾಧ್ಯಾಯ s. *n.* Repeating to one's self.

ಸ್ವಾನುಭವ s. *n.* One's own personal experience.

ಸ್ವಾಭಾವಿಕ (*fr.* ಸ್ವಭಾವ) s. *a.* Natural, peculiar, constitutional; spontaneous.

ಸ್ವಾಮಿ s. *n.* A proprietor, owner. 2, a master, lord, sovereign; a guru; a learned Brâhmaṇa. -ತನ, -ತ್ವ. Lordship, ownership. -ದ್ರೋಹ. Treachery to a master. -ದ್ರೋಹಿ. A traitor. -ಭಕ್ತಿ. Devotedness to a master. ರಕ್ಷಾ-, ಕ್ರಿಸ್ತ-. Christ.

ಸ್ವಾಮ್ಯ s. *n.* Supremacy, dominion.

ಸ್ವಾರಸ್ಯ (*fr.* ಸ್ವರಸ) s. *n.* Possession of natural pathos, fire, *etc.*; goodness.

ಸ್ವಾರ್ಜಿತ s. *a.* Self-acquired; *also* ಸ್ವಯಾರ್ಜಿತ.

ಸ್ವಾರ್ಥ s. *n.* One's own advantage or interest, self-interest; selfishness. -ಪರ. Self-interested, selfish. -ಬುದ್ಧಿ. Selfishness.

ಸ್ವಾಶ್ರಿತ s. *a.* Self-dependent.

ಸ್ವಾಸ್ತ್ಯ (*fr.* ಸ್ವ-ಅಸ್ತಿ) s. *n.* Land exempt from tax or liable for a trifling quit-rent.

ಸ್ವಾಸ್ಥ್ಯ (*fr.* ಸ್ವಸ್ಥ) s. *n.* Self-reliance, resoluteness, firmness. 2, sound state, of health, prosperity, happiness. 3, contentment.

ಸ್ವಾಹಾ s. *n.* Agni's wife. *int.* An exclamation made at oblations: Hail! blessing!

ಸ್ವೀಕರಿಸು s. *v. t.* To make one's own, adopt, accept; to embrace, *as* a faith; to admit, assume.

ಸ್ವೀಕಾರ s. *n.* Making one's own, appropriation; taking, adoption. ಪುತ್ರ-. Adoption of a son.

ಸ್ವೀಯ s. *a.* Own, peculiar, characteristic.

ಸ್ವೇಚ್ಛಾ, ಸ್ವೇಚ್ಛೆ s. *n.* One's own wish or will; self-will, wilfulness.

ಸ್ವೇದ s. *n.* Sweat, perspiration. -ಜ. Insects, vermin, *etc.* produced by sweat.

ಸ್ವೈರ (= ಸ್ವಯಿರ) s. *a.* Self-willed, wilful. *n.* Wilfulness, self-will.

ಹ

ಹ್ The fifty-second letter of the alphabet.

ಹಂಸ s. *n.* A goose, swan, flamingo. -ಕ. An anklet. -ಪಾದ. A caret. -ರಥ, -ವಾಹನ. Brahmâ.

ಹಕಾರ s. *n.* The letter ಹ.

ಹಕೀಕತು h. *n.* Account, statement; affairs, facts.

ಹಕೀಮ h. *n.* A physician.

ಹಕ್ಕರಿಕೆ (ರಿ = ಱಿ) k. *n.* The plant *chrysopogon aciculatus.*

ಹಕ್ಕಲ, ಹಕ್ಕಲು k. *n.* Gleanings (of corn). ಹಕ್ಕಲಾಯು, ಹಕ್ಕಲಾರಿಸು. To glean.

ಹಕ್ಕಳೆ k. *n.* An incrustation or scab.

ಹಕ್ಕಿ (*tb. of* ಪಕ್ಷಿ) *n.* A bird. -ಕೂದಲು. The plumage of a bird. -ಗರಿ. The quill. -ಗೂಡು. A bird's nest.

ಹಕ್ಕಿಬಿಕ್ಕಿ f. *n.* Sleight of hand.

ಹಕ್ಕು 1. k. n. Dry mucus or rheum; a scab.

ಹಕ್ಕು 2. h. n. Right, title; a just right or claim. -ದಾರ. The holder of a right. -ದಾರಿ, -ದಾರಿಕೆ. = ಹಕ್ಕು.

ಹಕ್ಕೆ k. n. A place for reposing, *etc.*; a bed.

ಹಗ. = ಹಗೆಯು, *q. v.*

ಹಗರ. = ಹಗುರ, *q. v.*

ಹಗರಣ k. n. Vain talk, chatter, babble. -ಗಾರ. A babbler.

ಹಗರು k. n. The dandruff of the head. 2, a split of a bamboo.

ಹಗಲು k. n. The daytime; a day. *ad.* By day. -ಗಳ್ಳ. A day-robber. -ರಾತ್ರಿ, -ಇರುಳು. Day and night. -ಬತ್ತಿ. A kind of firework.

ಹಗಿನು k. n. Gum, resin.

ಹಗುರ, ಹಗುರು k. a. Light; easy; mean. -ಮಾಡು. To make light. -ತನ. Lightness.

ಹಗೆ k. n. Hatred, enmity. -ತೀರಿಸು, -ಸಾಧಿಸು. To revenge one's self. -ಗೊಳ್ಳು, -ಮಾಡು. To hate. -ಗಾರ, -ಯುವ. An enemy. -ತನ. Hatred.

ಹಗೆಯು, ಹಗೇವು (= ಹಗ) k. n. A subterraneous granary.

ಹಗ್ಗ (*tb. of* ಪ್ರಗ್ರಹ) n. A rope or cord. *Cpds.*: ನೂಲಿನ-, ನಾರಿನ-, *etc.*

ಹಗ್ಗು k. n. Low ground.

ಹಂಕಾರ. *tb. of* ಅಹಂಕಾರ, *q. v.*

ಹಂಗಣ. = ಹಂಗು, *q. v.*

ಹಂಗರಲು, ಹಂಗರು k. n. An evergreen shrub, *Dodonaea viscosa*.

ಹಂಗಾಮಿ h. a. Temporary. ಹಂಗಾಮು. The season, time, *as* for business or anything. -ಉದ್ಯೋಗ. A temporary employment.

ಹಂಗಾಮು h. n. Uproar, tumult, riot; an assault. -ಮಾಡು, -ನಡಿಸು. To make an assault.

ಹಂಗು k. n. An obligation, indebtedness; regard. ಹಂಗಾಳು, ಹಂಗಿಗ. A man under obligation. ಹಂಗಿಸು. To remind a person of neglecting his obligation.

ಹಂಗುಳಿ, -ಗೆ k. n. A stool.

ಹಚ್ಚನೆ (= ಪಚ್ಚನೆ) k. n. Greenness. *a.* Green; yellowish. *ad.* Greenly.

ಹಚ್ಚಡ (= ಪಚ್ಚಡ, *q. v.*) k. n. A stout cotton cloth; a bed sheeting.

ಹಚ್ಚು k. v. t. To apply to; to put to; to join, affix, attach; to fix. 2, to use or employ. 3, to kindle, light. 4, to mince; *cf.* ಕೊಚ್ಚು. ಬೆಂಕಿ-. To set fire to. ಹಚ್ಚಿಸು. To kindle, light; to cause to apply to; to have planted; to put or join to.

ಹಚ್ಚೆ k. n. Cane or ratan; tattoo. 2, a bamboo split. -ಚುಚ್ಚು. To tattoo. -ತಿಲಕ, -ಬೊಟ್ಟು. A tattooed mark on the forehead.

ಹಜಂ h. n. Concealment. 2, digestion.

ಹಜಾಮು h. n. A barber. -ತ್. Shaving.

ಹಜಾರ h. n. A hall, pavilion.

ಹಜೂರು h. n. The presence of a superior authority, *as* collector, judge, *etc.* 2, the principal collector's office; *also* -ಕಚೇರಿ.

ಹಂಚಿಕೆ 1. k. n. Sharing, dividing, distributing. -ಗಾರ, ಹಂಚಿಗ. A divider.

ಹಂಚಿಕೆ 2. k. n. A means, plan, expedient. -ತೆಗೆ, -ಮಾಡು. To devise a plan. -ಗಾರ. A contriver, *etc.*

ಹಂಚು 1. k. v. t. To divide, share, distribute.

ಹಂಚು 2. k. n. A tile. 2, a potsherd. ಬೆನ್ನು-. A ridge tile. ಹಂಚಿನ ಮನೆ. A house with a tiled roof.

ಹಂಜರ 1. (= ಪಂದರು, ಹಂದರ) k. n. A pandal.

ಹಂಜರ 2. (ರ = ಱ) k. n. A bamboo split.

ಹಂಜಿ (= ಪಂಜಿಕೆ, *q. v.*) f. n. A roll of cotton.

ಹಟ (*tb. of* ಹಠ) n. Obstinacy, stubbornness; obstinate insisting upon. -ಗಾರ, -ಮಾರಿ, -ವಾದಿ. An obstinate person. -ತಟಿ. Importunity. -ವಾಗಿರು, -ಹಿಡಿ. To be obstinate. -ಸಾಧಿಸು. To persevere in obstinacy.

ಹಟ್ಟಿ k. n. A fold, cow-pen. -ಕಾರ. A herdsman.

ಹಟ್ಟೆ (tb. of ಪಟ್ಟೆ) n. Woven silk. -ಗಾರ. A silk-weaver.

ಹಠ (= ಹಟ, q. v.) s. n. Violence, force. 2, obstinacy. -ಯೋಗ. A mode of contemplation. ಹಠಾತ್. By force, forcibly, suddenly. ಹಠಾತ್ಕಾರ. Suddenness.

ಹಡಗ, ಹಡಗು k. n. A ship, sailing vessel. -ದ (ಹಡಗಿನ) ಠೇವು. A harbour. -ನಡಿಸು. To steer a vessel. -ದವರು, ಹಡಗಿನವರು. Mariners, sailors.

ಹಡದಿ, ಹಡದೆ k. n. An annual allowance of grain or money to washermen, barbers, etc.

ಹಡಪ k. n. A betel-nut pouch. 2, a barber's bag. -ಗಾರ. A barber; also ಹಡಪಿಗ.

ಹಡಲಗೆ, ಹಡಲಿಗೆ (= ಅಡ್ಲಗೆ) k. n. A flat round basket.

ಹಡಿ. = ಹಡೆ, q. v.

ಹಡಿಕೆ k. n. A disagreeable smell, stench. -ನಾತ. Stench. -ನಾರು. To stink.

ಹಡುಕು (= ಹಡಿಕೆ) k. n. A bad smell.

ಹಡೆ (=ಪಡೆ, q. v.) k. v. t. To get, obtain, etc.; to bear, give birth to.

ಹಡ್ಲು k. n. Mud. a. Uncultivated. -ಗದ್ದೆ. An uncultivated paddy-field.

ಹಣ (tb. of ಪಣ 2.) n. Money; wealth. 2, an old coin equal to As. 4-8. -ಗಾರ, -ವಂತ, -ವುಳ್ಳವ. A rich man. -ದ ನೋಟ. Shroffing. -ಕಟ್ಟು. To pay taxes. -ಮಾರಿಸು, -ಮುರಿಸು. To change money.

ಹಣಕು k. v. i. To look slyly, pry, peep; also ಹಣಕಿನೋಡು.

ಹಣತೆ (tb. of ಪ್ರಣೀತ). = ಪಣತೆ, q. v.

ಹಣಾ k. n. Beating. -ಹಣಿ. Mutual beating. -ಹಣಿಜಗಳ. A quarrel with mutual beating.

ಹಣಿ k. v. t. To beat thin, sharpen by beating, as a sickle. -ತ. Beating; a blow.

ಹಣಿಕು. = ಹಣಕು, q. v.

ಹಣಿಗೆ k. n. A comb. 2, one of the clusters of fruits, as of plantains.

ಹಣೆ k. n. The forehead. 2, the lair of wild beasts. -ಗೆ ಗಟ್ಟಿಸಿ ಕೊಳ್ಳು, -ಗೆ ಬಡ ಕೊಳ್ಳು. To affix to one's forehead, i. e. to use (said contemptuously). -ಬರಹ. Destiny, fortune.

ಹಂಡಬಂಡ reit. n. A certain colour of a pigeon.

ಹಂಡಾ, ಹಂಡೆ f. n. A large metal pot or boiler.

ಹಣ್ಣೆ, ಹಣ್ಣ k. n. The sunflower, *Heliotropium indicum*.

ಹಣ್ಣು k. n. A ripe fruit; ripeness. -ಗಾಯಿ. A ripe pod vegetable. -ಮುದುಕ. A very old man; f. -ಮುದುಕಿ. -ಹಂಪಲ. reit. -ಸಿಪ್ಪೆ. The rind or peel of a fruit. ಹಣ್ಣಿನ ರುಚಿ. The taste of a fruit.

ಹಣ್ಣೆ. = ಹಣ್ಣ 2, q. v. 2, the kitchen herb *Celosia albida*.

ಹತ್ interj. for angry reproof.

ಹತ s. a. Struck; killed; wounded; ruined; disappointed. -ಕ. Miserable. -ವಾಗಿ ಹೋಗು. To die, perish. ಹತಾಹತಿ. Mutual striking.

ಹತ್ತ k. a. Close. 2, all. ad. Closely. 2, together. -ಕಟ್ಟು. To tie tightly, as a necklace, etc. -ಕಾಸು. To heat thoroughly. -ಬಡಿ. To beat all (fruits) off (from a tree). -ಸೇದು. To draw tightly.

ಹತ್ತಡಿ (=ಹತ್ರಿ) k. n. A carpenter's plane.

ಹತ್ತರ k. n. Nearness, proximity. ad. Near, close by, by; also ಹತ್ತಿರ, ಹತ್ತಿರೆ.

ಹತ್ತಿ k. n. Cotton in the pod; cotton in general. -ಕಾಯಿ. An unripe cotton pod. -ಕಾಳು, -ಬೀಜ. Cotton seed. -ಬಿಡಿಸು. To pluck cotton; to dress cotton. -ಬೆಳೆ. A cotton crop.

ಹತ್ತು 1. k. v. i. To stick to; to join; to apply to; to touch; to reach, as a shore. 2, to be reached, arrived at, found as a road, etc. 3, to be required; to suffice. 4, to begin. 5, to take root. 6, to ascend, climb, mount. n. Joining, etc.; climbing, scaling. ಹತ್ತಗೊಡು. To let mount. ಹತ್ತಿಸು. To apply; to cause to climb; to kindle, light, *as* fire, a light. ಹತ್ತಿಸರಿಗೆ ಬರು. To be nearly done up, *as* rice in cooking; to be on death-bed. ಹತ್ತೊತ್ತು. To press firmly; to suppress, *as* laughter.

ಹತ್ತು 2. k. *a.* Ten. -ಅವತಾರ. Vishṇu's ten incarnations. ಹತ್ತೊಂಬತ್ತು. 19.

ಹತ್ತು 3. (= ಹೊತ್ತು) k. *v. i.* To be kindled. 2, to be burnt in cooking.

ಹತ್ಯ s. *n.* Killing, slaying; murder.

ಹತ್ಯಾರ h. *n.* A weapon, instrument.

ಹತ್ರ = ಹತ್ತರ, *q. v.*

ಹತ್ರಿ = ಹತ್ತದಿ, *q. v.*

ಹದ k. *n.* Properness, proper way; the tempered state, *as* of any food, *etc.*; sharpness; *also* -ನ. -ಕೆಡು, -ಗೆಡು. To lose the proper state, *etc.* (*used of food, rain, crop, etc.*). -ಗೆಯ್ಯು, -ಮಾಡು. To make fit for use, *etc.* -ಇಡು. To temper, sharpen. -ಎಳಸು. To reduce to proper state.

ಹದಿ 1. k. *v. t.* To lay stone or brick (*P. ps.* ಹದಿದು, ಹದ್ದು). *n.* A layer of stone or brick.

ಹದಿ 2. (= ಹತ್ತು, *q. v.*) k. *a.* Ten. -ನಾರು. Sixteen. -ನಾಲ್ಕು. Fourteen. -ನೆಂಟು. Eighteen. -ನೇಳು. Seventeen. -ನೈದು. Fifteen. -ಮೂರು. Thirteen.

ಹದಿರು k. *n.* An unripe fruit. 2, way, manner.

ಹದುಗು k. *v. i.* To bend.

ಹದುಳ (= ಪದುಳ, *q. v.*) a. k. *n.* Well-being; steadiness. ಹದುಳಿಗ. A happy man. ಹದುಳಿಸು. To be well; to be soothed; to feel refreshed.

ಹದ್ದು 1. k. *n.* A kite; a hawk; a vulture.

ಹದ್ದು 2. h. *n.* A limit, border. -ತಪ್ಪು, -ಕೆಡು. To violate borders. -ಬಸ್ತು. Demarcation of boundaries.

ಹದ್ದು 3. *P. p. of* ಹದಿ, *q. v.*

ಹನ್ k. *a.* Ten. ಹನ್ನೆರಡು. Twelve. ಹನ್ನೊಂದು. Eleven.

ಹನನ s. *n.* Slaughter, destruction; hurting, injuring.

ಹನಿ k. *n.* A drop. *v. i.* To fall in drops. -ಸು. To pour, *as* water, *etc.*

ಹನುಮ, ಹನುಮಂತ (*tb. of* ಹನುಮತ್) *n.* N. of a monkey-chief, the ally of Râmaćandra.

ಹಂತ k. *n.* A stair, step; a flight of steps.

ಹಂತಿ (*tb. of* ಪಂಕ್ತಿ) *n.* A line, row.

ಹಂದರ (= ಹಂಜರ, *q. v.*) k. *n.* A pandal, temporary shed.

ಹಂದಿ k. *n.* A pig, hog, swine. ಕಾಡು-. A wild hog. -ಕೇರ. The small screech-owl. -ಕೋರೆ. A boar's tusk. -ತನ. Piggishness.

ಹಂದು k. *v. i.* To move shake. ಹಂದಾಡು. To move about.

ಹಂದೆ k. *n.* A coward.

ಹಪ್ತಾ h. *n.* An instalment. 2, a week.

ಹಪ್ಪಳ (= ಪಪ್ಪಳ) f. *n.* A very thin cake.

ಹಬಶಿ h. *n.* An Abyssinian.

ಹಬೆ (= ಹವೆ, *q. v.*) f. *n.* Vapour, heat. 2, *tb. of* ಪ್ರಭೆ.

ಹಬ್ಬ (*tb. of* ಪರ್ವ) *n.* A festival, feast, holiday. -ಆಚರಿಸು, -ಮಾಡು. To celebrate a feast. -ಗುಳ್ಳ. The Indian night-shade, *Solanum indicum.*

ಹಬ್ಬು k. *v. i.* To spread, extend, *etc.*; to spread, *as* a creeper. *n.* The state of being spread. -ಗೆ, -ವಿಕೆ. Spreading, extention, vastness. ಹಬ್ಬಿಸು. To cause to spread.

ಹಬ್ಬೆ k. *n.* Cane, ratan, *Calamus rotang.*

ಹಮಾಮು h. *a.* All, together. -ಜೀನಸು. All kinds of articles.

ಹಮಾಲ h. *n.* A bearer (of a palanquin, *etc.*); a porter.

ಹಮೀರ (= ಅಮೀರ, *q. v.*) h. *n.* An emir, nobleman. *a.* Excellent.

ಹಮೇಷಾ h. *ad.* Always, ever.

ಹಂಬಲ, ಹಂಬಲು k. *n.* Ardent desire; look-out; solicitous thought. ಹಂಬಲಿಸು. To desire, to long for, crave for; to mind, heed.

ಹಂಬು k. *n.* A creeper.

ಹಮ್ಮದ a. k. n. Fainting, stupor, torpor. ಹಮ್ಮಯಿಸು. To faint, swoon.

ಹಮ್ಮಿಣಿ (=ಹಿಮ್ಮಣಿ) n. A long and narrow money-bag.

ಹಮ್ಮು k. n. Pride, conceit. -ಗಾರ. A proud man.

ಹಯ s. n. A horse. -ಗ್ರೀವ, -ವದನ. N. of a form of Vishṇu. -ಜ್ಞತೆ. Horsemanship. -ಪ್ರಾಸ. A kind of alliteration.

ಹಯನು, ಹಯ್ನು, ಹಯ್ಯು s. n. Milk and all that is made of milk, as curds, butter, etc.

ಹಯಿಲು k. n. Bewilderment.

ಹರ 1. k. n. Broadness, breadth. 2, spreading. 3, flying, etc. -ಗಲ, -ಗೋಲು. A basket-boat lined with leather; also ಹರಿಗೋಲು.

ಹರ 2. s. n. Conveying, carrying; seizing; removing; a seizer, etc. 2, Śiva. Cpds.: ಪ್ರಾಣ-; ಮನೋ-; ವಾತಾರ್ಶ-; etc.

ಹರಕತ್ತು h. n. Opposition, hindrance.

ಹರಕಾರ. = ಹರಿಕಾರ, q. v.

ಹರಕು (= ಹರುಕು. ರ = ಱ) k. n. A tatter, rag. a. Torn, rent; old. -ಅರಿವೆ, -ಬಟ್ಟೆ, -ವಸ್ತ್ರ. A rag. -ಪುಸ್ತಕ. A torn book. -ಮಾತು. An incoherent speech. ಹರಕ. A man in rags.

ಹರಕೆ k. n. A blessing. 2, a vow. -ಕೊಡು. To bless. -ಮಾಡು, -ಹರಸು. To vow. -ತೀರಿಸು, -ಸಲ್ಲಿಸು. To fulfil a vow. -ಮುರಿ, -ತಪ್ಪಿಸು. To break a vow.

ಹರಗು k. v. t. To clean (a field) by removing the grass, weeds, etc. ಹರಗಣೆ. Removing superfluous standing corn.

ಹರಟೆ k. n. Idle talk, jabber, babble. -ಕೋರ, -ಗಾರ. A babbler. ಹರಟು. To talk idly, prate, blabber.

ಹರಡಿ, ಹರಡು 1. k. n. The ankle; the wrist. 2, a wrist-bracelet of gold and coral beads.

ಹರಡು 2. k. v. t. To spread; to scratch, claw. v. i. To spread.

ಹರಡೆ k. n. The ink-nut.

ಹರಣ 1. s. n. Taking, removing. 2, stealing; withholding.

ಹರಣ 2. tb. of ಪ್ರಾಣ, q. v. -ಕೊಡು, -ಎರೆಯು. To restore life. -ಪಡೆ. To obtain life.

ಹರತಾಳ. tb. of ಹರಿತಾಲ, q. v.

ಹರತ (ರ = ಱ) k. n. Sharpness.

ಹರದ a. k. n. A trader, merchant. ಹರದಿಕೆ, ಹರದು. Trade, traffic.

ಹರದಾರಿ (fr. ಹರಿ 1) k. n. A distance of three English miles.

ಹರದು. P. p. of ಹರೆ 1, q. v.

ಹರವರಿ k. n. Manifestation; display.

ಹರವಸ (tb. of ಪರವಶ) n. Loss of self-control.

ಹರವಿ (= ಹರಿವಿ) k. n. An earthen water-vessel.

ಹರವು, ಹರಹು k. v. i. To spread. v. t. To spread out. n. Spreading, extension.

ಹರಸು (= ಹರಿಸು, q. v.) k. v. t. To bless. 2, to make a vow.

ಹರಳು k. n. A pebble, stone, grit. 2, the castor-oil plant, Palma christi. ಹರಳೆಣ್ಣೆ. Castor-oil.

ಹರಾಮು h. a. Unlawful; wicked, wrong; vile. -ಕುದುರೆ. A restive horse.

ಹರಿ 1. k. v. i. To run; to flow; to creep, proceed; to disappear, as trouble. n. A run, flowing; cf. ಹರ 1. -ಕಾರ. A runner, courier; a hawker; a spy. -ಗಲು, -ಗೋಲು. A wicker boat lined with leather. -ವು. Streaming; current. ಹರಿದಾಡು. To creep or move about. ಹರಿದಾರಿ. = ಹರದಾರಿ, q. v. -ನಾಳ, -ನಾಳಿಗೆ. A gutter, channel.

ಹರಿ 2. (ರಿ = ಱ) k. v. t. To tear, rend, break, slit, etc.; to pluck. v. i. To cut, as a knife. 2, to be torn or rent. n. Tearing. -ಗಲ್ಲು. A split stone.

ಹರಿ 3. a. k. *v. i.* To spread, disperse.

ಹರಿ 4. s. *a.* Green; yellow. *n.* The sun. 2, the moon. 3, Indra. 4, Vishṇu, Kṛishṇa. 5, Brahmâ. 6, a lion. -ಕಥೆ. Any puranic story related with music and singing. -ದಾಸ. One who relates such a story. -ದ್ವಾರ. A place of pilgrimage on the Ganges. -ನಾಮ. Vishṇu's name. -ನೀಲ. Sapphire. -ವಂಶ. Kṛishṇa's family. -ವಾಸ. Vishṇu's day: the eleventh lunar day; a day of fasting. -ಪೀಠ, -ವಿಷ್ಟರ. A throne. -ಉವ್ವ. A ceremony on the fourth day of a marriage. -ಭಕ್ತ. A worshipper of Vishṇu. ಹರಿಶ್ಚಂದ್ರ. N. of a king of the solar dynasty. -ಹರ. Śiva.

ಹರಿಕಾರ. *See s.* ಹರಿ 1.

ಹರಿಕೆ. = ಹರಕೆ, *q. v.*

ಹರಿಣ s. *n.* A deer, antelope. ಹರಿಣಿ. A doe.

ಹರಿತಾಲ (= ಹರತಾಳ, ಅರದಳ) s. *n.* Sulphuret of arsenic, yellow orpiment.

ಹರಿಬ k. *n.* A host, assemblage. 2, business, affair, concern.

ಹರಿಯಣ, ಹರಿಯಾಣ, ಹರಿವಾಣ k. *n.* A metal dish of any kind.

ಹರಿವಿ. = ಹರವಿ, *q. v.*

ಹರಿವೆ (ರಿ = ಱ) k. *n.* A common potherb, *Amarantus oleraceus.*

ಹರಿಸು 1. (= ಹರಸು, *q. v.*) k. *v. t.* To [bless.

ಹರಿಸು 2. s. *v. t.* To take away, divide.

ಹರೀತಕಿ s. *n.* The yellow myrobalan tree, *Terminalia chebula.*

ಹರುಕು. = ಹರಕು, *q. v.*

ಹರುವು k. *n.* A way, means, expedient.

ಹರುಷ. *tb. of* ಹರ್ಷ, *q. v.*

ಹರೆ 1. (= ಪರೆ, ಹರಿ) k. *v. i.* To spread; to disperse. *P. ps.* ಹರದು, ಹರೆದು.

ಹರೆ 2. k. *v. i.* To begin to shine, dawn. *n.* Dawn. ಮೂಡಲ-. (The sun) to dawn in the east.

ಹರೆಯ (*tb. of* ಪ್ರಾಯ) *n.* The time of youth, prime of life. ಹರೇತನ. Youth. -ದವ, ಹರೇದವ. A young man; *f.* -ದವಳು, ಹರೇದವಳು.

ಹರ್ಷ s. *n.* Bristling, thrilling. 2, rapture, delight, joy, pleasure, gladness. -ದ. Gladdening, delightful. ಹರ್ಷಾಶ್ರು. Tears of joy. ಹರ್ಷೋತ್ಸವ. Abundance of joy. ಹರ್ಷಿಸು. To rejoice, exult, be glad or pleased.

ಹಲ್ 1. (= ಹಲ್ಲು, *q. v.*) k. *n.* A tooth. -ಕಡಿ. To gnash the teeth. -ಕುರು. A gumboil.

ಹಲ್ 2. s. *n.* A consonant. ಹಲಂತ. Ending in a consonant. -ಸಂಧಿ. Euphony of consonants.

ಹಲ 1. = ಪಲ 1, ಹಲವು, *q. v.* -ಬರು, -ವರು. Many or several persons.

ಹಲ 2. (= ಪಲ 2, *q. v.*) s. *n.* A particular weight.

ಹಲ 3. s. *n.* A plough. -ದಂಡ. The shaft of a plough.

ಹಲಕು k. *n.* The lower part of the cheek. 2, a kind of harrow. *v. t.* To climb a tree.

ಹಲಗೆ (*tb. of* ಫಲಕ) *n.* A plank, board. 2, a shield. -ಸೇರುವೆ. A ceiling of boards.

ಹಲಚೆ f. *n.* Flatness. -ಮೂಗಿನವ. A flat-nosed man.

ಹಲದಿ. = ಹಳದಿ, *q. v.*

ಹಲವು k. *a.* Much, many; some. -ಕೆಲವು. Some, several. -ಪ್ರಕಾರ, -ಬಗೆ. Various kinds. -ಮಕ್ಕಳು. Many children. -ಮಕ್ಕಳ ತಾಯಿ, -ಮಕ್ಕಳ ಬಳ್ಳಿ. The shrub *Asparagus sarmentosus.* -ನುಡಿ, -ಮಾತು. Very verbose.

ಹಲಸಂದಿ. = ಅಲಸಂದಿ, *q. v.*

ಹಲಸು (*tb. of* ಪನಸ) *n.* The jack tree; *also* ಹಲಸಿನ ಮರ. ಹಲಸಿನ ಹಣ್ಣು. A jack fruit.

ಹಲಾಕು h. *a.* Oppressed, overcome, ruined, lost.

ಹಲಾಯಿಸು h. *v. t.* To shake, agitate.

ಹಲಾಯುಧ s. *n.* N. of Balarâma. 2, Râmačandra.

ಹಲಾಲ್ಖೋರ h. *n.* A sweeper, scavenger.

ಹಲಾಹಲ s. *n.* A deadly poison.

ಹಲಿಗೆ. = ಹಲಗೆ, *q. v.*

ಹಲಿವೆ, ಹಲುಬೆ, ಹಲುವೆ k. *n.* A kind of rake or harrow.

ಹಲುಬು a. k. *v. i.* To lament.

ಹಲ್ಕಾ h. *a.* Light; unimportant, trifling, inferior, vulgar; *also* ಹಲ್ಕಿ.

ಹಲ್ಲಕಲ್ಲೋಲ. = ಅಲ್ಲಕಲ್ಲೋಲ, *q. v.*

ಹಲ್ಲಣಿಸು a. k. *v. i.* To go on, advance.

ಹಲ್ಲಾ h. *n.* An attack, onset; scaling a fort. -ಏರು, -ಹತ್ತು. To scale, *as* a fort.

ಹಲ್ಲಿ k. *n.* The small house-lizard, *Lacerta gecko.*

ಹಲ್ಲು (= ಹಲ್) k. *n.* A tooth, a step of a ladder; a spoke of a wheel. -ಕಡಿ, -ತಿನ್ನು. To gnash the teeth. -ಕಡ್ಡಿ. A tooth-pick. -ಕಿರಿ. To grin. -ಕುರು. A gumboil. -ನೋವು, -ಬೇನೆ, -ಶೂಲೆ. The toothache. -ಪುಡಿ. Tooth-powder. ಹಾಲ-, ಮೊಳೆ-. Milk teeth. -ಪೊಳವು. The lacker of the teeth.

ಹಲ್ಲೆ 1. k. *n.* The lobe of the ear. 2, a horse or bullock-shoe.

ಹಲ್ಲೆ 2. k. *n.* The seed or pod of the climbing shrub *Entada monastachya*.

ಹಲ್ಲೆಲೂಯಾ f. *int.* Halelujah (*Hebr.*): 'Praise ye the Lord'. *n.* A song of praise.

ಹಲ್ಲೋಲಕಲ್ಲೋಲ (= ಅಲ್ಲೋಲಕಲ್ಲೋಲ, *q. v.*) k. *n.* Tumult; tossing, *as* the sea, waves, *etc.*

ಹವಣು (*tb. of* ಪ್ರಮಾಣ, *q. v.*) *n.* Measure, proper measure, fitness, *etc.*; making ready, preparing. ಹವಣಿಕೆ. Due consideration; contemplation; thought; desire. ಹವಣಿಸು. To make ready, prepare, arrange; to think; to desire.

ಹವನ s. *n.* An oblation, sacrifice.

ಹವಳ (*tb. of* ಪ್ರವಾಲ) *n.* Coral. -ಕ್ರಿಮಿ, -ದ ಹುಳ. The coral polyp. -ಬಂಡೆ. A coral rock. -ಸರಗಂಧಕ. A kind of sulphur.

ಹವಾ. = ಹವೆ, *q. v.* [debt.

ಹವಾಲತೆ, ಹವಾಲ್ತೆ h. *n.* Transfer, *as* of a

ಹವಾಲು, ಹವಾಲೆ h. *n.* Charge, trust, care. ಹವಾಲದಾರ, ಹವಾಲುದಾರ, ಹವಾಲ್ದಾರ. A native officer in the army.

ಹವಿಸ್ಸು s. *n.* Any thing offered as oblation.

ಹವೀಕ. = ಹೈಗ, *q. v.*

ಹವುದಾ. = ಹೌದಾ, *q. v.*

ಹವುದು (= ಅಹುದು, ಹೌದು, *q. v.*) k. ((*v. i.*) *ad.* Yes; it is so.

ಹವುರ. = ಹೌರ, *q. v.*

ಹವೆ h. *n.* Air, wind; weather; climate; *also* ಹವಾ.

ಹವೇಲಿ h. *n.* A large house, villa.

ಹವ್ಯ s. *n.* Oblation. *a.* Fit for oblation. -ಕವ್ಯ. Oblations to the gods and the manes of ancesters.

ಹವ್ಯಾಸ h. *n.* Desire, lust.

ಹವ್ವ, ಹವ್ವನೆ k. *ad.* Suddenly.

ಹಸ 1. (*tb. of* ಪಶು) *n.* A cow. -ಕರ. A cow and a calf.

ಹಸ 2, ಹಸತೆ s. *n.* Laughing, smiling; a laugh; *also* ಹಸನ. ಹಸನ್ಮುಖ. A smiling face.

ಹಸನ, ಹಸನು k. *n.* Good state or order; tillage; purity. -ಗೆಡು. Beauty to be lost. -ಮಾಡು. To till; to clean.

ಹಸರ್, ಹಸರು (= ಹಸುರು) k. *n.* Green colour, greenness; freshness; tenderness; young, green grass. -ಕಾಯಿ. An unripe fruit. -ಬಣ್ಣ. Green colour. -ರತ್ನ. Emerald. -ಹಾವು. A kind of green snake. -ವಾಣಿ, ಹಸರ್ವಾಣಿ, ಹಸರಾಣಿ. Vegetables of trade.

ಹಸಿ 1. k. *n.* Greenness; freshness, rawness. *a.* Green, fresh, moist, *etc.* -ಅಕ್ಕಿ, -ಯಕ್ಕಿ. Raw rice. -ಕಟ್ಟಿಗೆ. Green wood. -ಹಿಟ್ಟು, ಹಸಿಟ್ಟು. Raw flour of râgi. -ಬಿಸಿ. Slightly boiled. -ಮಾಂಸ. Raw flesh. -ಕಾಯಿ. A green unripe fruit.

ಹಸಿ 2. k. *v. i.* To hunger, crave food. *P. p.* ಹಸಿದು, ಹಸ್ತು. -ವು, -ವೆ. Hunger.

ಹಸಿ 3. = ಅಸಿ 2, *q. v.* -ಕಲ್ಲು. The lower part of a grinding-stone.

ಹಸಿಗೆ 1. f. *n.* A toll (*as* of vegetable, *etc.*) exacted by officials from the vendors.

ಹಸಿಗೆ 2. k. n. Sharing of the produce between the landlord and cultivator.

ಹಸಿಬೆ, ಹಸುಬೆ (= ಪಸುಬೆ, q. v.) k. n. A long bag with an opening in the middle, carried on the shoulder or on a beast; a wallet.

ಹಸು 1. k. a. Young, fresh, tender. -ಗೂಸು. A tender infant. -ಮಕ್ಕಳು. Young children.

ಹಸು 2. (= ಹಸ 1, q. v. tb. of ಪಶು) n. A cow.

ಹಸುಕು k. n. A sharp smell.

ಹಸುಬೆ. = ಹಸಿಬೆ, q. v.

ಹಸುರು. = ಹಸರು, q. v.

ಹಸುಳ, ಹಸುಳೆ (= ಪಸುಳೆ, q. v.) k. n. A child. -ತನ. Childhood.

ಹಸೆ (= ಪಸೆ, q. v.) k. n. A bed; a decorated seat or place.

ಹಸ್ತ s. n. The hand. 2, an elephant's trunk. 3, a cubit. -ಕ. A mate, associate. -ಕಂಕಣ, -ಕಡಗ. A bracelet. -ಕೌಶಲ, -ಕೌಶಲ್ಯ, -ಲಾಘವ. Sleight of hand, legerdemain. -ಗತ. Come to hand, procured, obtained. -ಗುಣ. Luck. -ದೋಷ. A slip of the hand. -ಪರೀಕ್ಷೆ. Examination (of the lines on the palms) of the hand. -ಲಾಘವ. Dexterity; sleight of hand. ಹಸ್ತಾಕ್ಷರ. Autograph signature, handwriting. ಹಸ್ತಾಂತರ. That is in hand, *as* capital; a treasury. ಹಸ್ತೋದಕ. Water poured upon the hand prior to a meal.

ಹಸ್ತಿ s. n. An elephant. -ದಂತ. Ivory. -ನಾಪುರ. The ancient Delhi.

ಹಳ (ಳ = ೞ) k. a. Old. n. Oldness. 2, weeds. -ಗನ್ನಡ. = ಹಳೆಗನ್ನಡ, s. ಹಳೆ, q. v. -ಬ. An old man; an old servant.

ಹಳಚು a. k. v. t. To strike against.

ಹಳತು, ಹಳದು (ಳ = ೞ) k. n. That is old.

ಹಳದಿ f. a. Yellow, greenish, yellow. n. Turmeric, *Curcuma longa*.

ಹಳಮೆ (ಳ = ೞ) k. n. Antiquity; a tradition.

ಹಳವಂಡ, ಹಳಹಳಿ f. n. Inquietude; painful restlessness. ಹಳವಳಿಸು. To become unquiet and anxious.

ಹಳಸು (ಳ = ೞ) k. v. i. To spoil, become old. ಹಳಸಲು. That which is spoiled.

ಹಳಿ 1, **ಹಳುಕು** k. n. A bit, piece, lump.

ಹಳಿ 2. (= ಪಳಿ 1. ಳಿ = ೞಿ) k. v. t. To revile, scold, rebuke, scorn. n. Blame, rebuke, calumny; *also* -ವು.

ಹಳುವು (ಳು = ೞು) k. n. A forest, jungle.

ಹಳೆ (= ಹಳ) k. a. Old, ancient, antique. -ಕನ್ನಡ, -ಗನ್ನಡ, -ಕರ್ಣಾಟಕ. Ancient Kannaḍa. -ಚಿಂದಿ. An old rag. -ದು. That is old. -ನೀರು. Stale water. -ಬ. = ಹಳಬ s. ಹಳ. -ಪೈಕ. One of a class of Shûdras. -ಮಗ. A house slave. -ಮಾತು, -ವಾತು. A tradition, legend. -ನಾಣ್ಯ. An ancient coin.

ಹಳ್ಳ (= ಪಳ್ಳ) k. n. Depth; a pit, hole in the ground; low ground; a stream, rivulet.

ಹಳ್ಳಿ k. n. A hamlet, village. -ಗಾಡಿನವ. A rustic. -ಗಾಡು. A hamlet without civilisation. -ಗಾರ. A villager.

ಹಾಕು k. v. t. To put; to put on; to lay out, plan, plant; to sow; to pour; to cast or throw; to bring forth; to apply, perform; *used also pleonastically, as:* ಕಟ್ಟಿ-, ತಿಂದು-, ಬಡಿದು-, *etc.* ಕಿತ್ತು-. To pluck out. ಕೊಯಿದು-. To cut off. ಚೀಟು-. To cast lots. ತೆಗೆದು-. To take out. ದೊಬ್ಬಿ-. To push away. ಹಾಕಿಸು. To cause to put, *etc.* -ವಿಕೆ. Putting, throwing.

ಹಾಗ f. n. One aṇĕ and two kâsus; one-fourth. ಹಾಗೂವೀಸ. 1 aṇe 5½ kâsus.

ಹಾಗಲ k. n. A winding plant with bitter fruit, *Momordica charantia; cf.* ಮಡ-. -ವಾಡಿ. N. of a place.

ಹಾಗೆ k. ad. In that manner, thus, so; like; as; likewise; so that; for nothing. ಹಾಗೂ. So also; likewise, also. ಹಾಗೇ, ಹಾಗೆಯೇ. Even so.

ಹಾಂಗೆ. = ಹಾಗೆ, q. v.

ಹಾಜರ್, ಹಾಜರು h. a. Present; ready. ಹಾಜರು. Presence. -ಜವಾಬು. A ready answer, a repartee. -ಜಾಮೀನು. A bail for presenting a person. -ಪಟ್ಟಿ.

A muster roll. ಗೈರ-. Absent.

ಹಾಗು k. v. t. & v. i. To sing. n. Singing (*also* ಹಾಡಿಕೆ); a song. -ಗಾರ. A singer, minstrel. ಧ್ವನಿ ಎತ್ತಿ-. To sing aloud. ಸ್ವರ ತಗ್ಗಿಸಿ-. To sing lowly. -ಹಾಡು. To sing a song.

ಹಾಗು 2. k. n. Manner, mode. 2, suffering, trouble.

ಹಾಣಾಹಾಣಿ k. n. Mutual beating.

ಹಾತು f. n. A hand. -ಬೇಡಿ. A handcuff.

ಹಾದರ k. n. Adultery; fornication. -ಗಳ್ಳ. An adulterer. -ಗಿತ್ತಿ. An adulteress. -ತನ. Adultery.

ಹಾದಿ k. n. A road, way. -ಕಾರ. A traveller. -ಖರ್ಚು. Travelling expenses. -ನಡೆ. To walk on a road. -ನೋಡು. To look out for, wait for. -ದಾಸ. A beggar at the roadside. -ಯುವ, -ಹೋಕ. A wayfarer. -ತಪ್ಪಿ ಹೋಗು. To go astray.

ಹಾದು. *P. p. of* ಹಾಯು, *q. v.*

ಹಾನಿ s. n. Loss; decrease; damage, harm, destruction, hurt. -ಹೊಂದು. To suffer loss.

ಹಾಯ್, ಹಾಯಿ k. n. A sail. 2, crossing; course, way. *a.* Nice, pleasant. -ಗತ. A fording place. -ದೋರು. To be agreeable.

ಹಾಯು (= ಪಾಯ್, *q. v.*) k. v. t. To assault; to butt. *v. i.* To step or pass over; to cross, leap; to go, flow. *P. ps.* ಹಾಯಿದು, ಹಾದು. ಹಾಹಾಟ. Mutual butting; fording. ಹಾದಾಡು. To butt with horns; to cross.

ಹಾರ s. n. A string of pearls; a necklace. 2, taking, conveying; captivating, charming; *also* -ಕ.

ಹಾರಯಿಸು (= ಆರಯಿಸು, *q. v.*) k. v. t. To look for; to desire; *also* ಹಾರಯ್ಸು. ಹಾರಯ್ಕೆ. Wish, desire.

ಹಾರವಾಣ (*tb. of* ಪಾರಾವತ) n. A dove, *etc.*

ಹಾರು 1. k. v. t. To look for. 2, to desire. ಹಾರವ, ಹಾರುವ, ಹಾರ್ವ. A Brâhmaṇa; *f.* -ವಗಿತಿ, ಹಾರ್ವತಿ.

ಹಾರು 2. (ರು = ಱು) k. v. i. To leap up; to jump, spring; to run; to fly; to fly about; to cross by jumping. ಹಾರ ತೆಗೆ, ಹಾರ ಬಡಿ. To open (a door) completely. ಹಾರಾಡು, ಹಾರ್ಯಾಡು. To fly about, run about. ಹಾರಿಸು. To cause to jump, *etc.* -ವಿಕೆ, ಹಾರಿಕೆ. Jumping. ಹಾರಿ ಹಾರಿ ಬೀಳು. To fall upon in a passion.

ಹಾರೆ f. n. A crowbar -ಕಾಲು. The spoke of a wheel.

ಹಾಲವಕ್ಕಿ f. n. A small bird the cry of which is said to be ominous.

ಹಾಲಹವಾಲು h. n. Distressful condition; fatigue, humour, *etc.;* a grievance.

ಹಾಲಿ f. *ad.* At present, now; current.

ಹಾಲಿವಾಣ f. n. The coral tree. 2, a dove.

ಹಾಲು 1. k. n. Milk; the white juice of a cocoanut or any plant. 2, (e.) a hall. -ಅನ್ನ, ಹಾಲನ್ನ. Milk and boiled rice. ಹಾಲಿನವ. A milkman. ಹಾಲುಣ್ಣೆ. A wart. -ತೆನೆ. The cream of milk. -ಬೆಳ್ಳಿ. Pure silver. -ವಕ್ಕಿ. = ಹಾಲವಕ್ಕಿ. ಮೊಲೇ-. Breast-milk. -ಮೊಸರು. Excellent curds. ಹಾಲೋಗರ. Rice boiled with milk.

ಹಾಲು 2. = ಹಾಲಿ, *q. v.*

ಹಾಲುವಾಣ. = ಹಾಲಿವಾಣ, *q. v.*

ಹಾಲೆ k. n. The tree *Mimusops kauki.* 2, the lobe of the ear.

ಹಾವ f. n. Gestures; dalliance; airs. -ಭಾವ. Gesticulation.

ಹಾವಸೆ k. n. The aquatic plant, *Vallisneria octandra.*

ಹಾವಳಿ k. n. Trouble, harass, annoyance, molestation; havoc.

ಹಾವಿಗೆ (*tb. of* ಪಾದುಕೆ) n. A wooden shoe.

ಹಾವು k. n. A snake, serpent. -ಗಾರ. = ಹಾವಡಿಗ, ಹಾವಾಡಿಗ. A snake-charmer. ಹೆಬ್ಬಾವು. A boa. ಪೊರೆ ತೆಗೆದ-. A serpent which has cast its slough. ಹಾವಿನ ದಾಡೆ. A serpent's fang. -ಮೀನು. A kind of muscle shell. -ಮೆಕ್ಕೆ. Colocynth, *Cucumis colocynthis.* -ರಾಣಿ. A kind of skink.

ಹಾವುಗೆ. = ಹಾವಿಗೆ, *q. v.*

ಹಾಸ s. *n.* Laughing, laughter, derision. -ಕ. A laugher, buffoon; *cf.* ಹಾಸ್ಯ.

ಹಾಸರ. = ಹೇಸರ, *q. v.*

ಹಾಸಲ್ ಕಲಂ h. *n.* Essence; abstract. *ad.* Briefly, shortly.

ಹಾಸಲು, ಹಾಸಿಲು h. *n.* Postage; custom, toll, duty.

ಹಾಸು 1. k. *v. t.* To spread; to lay. *n.* A bed. 2, the warp. 3, a chequered cloth. -ಗಲ್ಲು. A slab; *also* ಹಾಸಿ ಗಲ್ಲು. ಹಾಸಿಕ್ಕು. To prepare the warp. -ಗೆ. That is spread; a bed, cover; *also* ಹಾಸಿಕೆ.

ಹಾಸು 2. *tb. of* ಪಾಶ, *q. v.*

ಹಾಸೆ k. *n.* A beautiful seat.

ಹಾಸ್ಯ s. *n.* Laughter; jest, amusement. 2, ridicule, derision. *a.* Laughable, ridiculous. -ಗಾರ. A gester, buffoon. -ರಸ. Sense of humour. ಹಾಸ್ಯಾಸ್ಪದ. A laughing-stock.

ಹಾಹಾ s. *int.* of grief, surprise, pain. -ಕಾರ, -ರವ. A general lamentation.

ಹಾಳ k. *n.* A sheet of glass. 2, a division of paddy land.

ಹಾಳತ, ಹಾಳಿತ (ಳ, ಳಿ = ೞ, ೞಿ) k. *n.* Propriety, fitness; due proportion.

ಹಾಳು (ಳು = ೞು) k. *n.* Ruin; desolation; destruction; a waste. ಹಾಳ. A miserable being. -ಬೀಳು, ಹಾಳಾಗು. To go to ruin; to be destroyed. -ಗೋಡೆ. A dilapidated wall. -ಬಾವಿ. An unused well. -ಭೂಮಿ. Waste land. -ಮಣ್ಣು. A sterile soil. -ಮನೆ. A house in ruins. -ಮಾಡು. To ruin; to destroy; to waste. -ಸ್ಥಲ. A desolate place. -ಹರಟೆ. Idle, useless talk. ಹಾಳೂರು. A deserted village.

ಹಿಂಸೆ, ಹಿಂಸೆ s. *n.* Injury, hurt. 2, molesting, tormenting. 3, killing, slaughter. ಜೀವ-, ಪ್ರಾಣ-. Murder; a violent assault. ಹಿಂಸಕ. A murderer, persecutor; injurious, hurtful, savage. ಹಿಂಸಕ ಪ್ರಾಣಿ. A beast of prey. ಹಿಂಸಿಸು. To hurt, harm, wound, injure; to kill, slay, destroy.

ಹಿಕಮತ್ತು h. *n.* Skill, cunning; art, trick. -ಗಾರ. A clever or cunning man.

ಹಿಕ್ಕಟ್ಟು k. *n.* The backside, *as* of a ship; lateness, *as* of rain.

ಹಿಕ್ಕಲು k. *n.* A small branch-channel in gardens.

ಹಿಕ್ಕು k. *v. t.* To comb.

ಹಿಕ್ಕೆ k. *n.* The dung of goats, sheep, *etc.* 2, (f.) hiccough.

ಹಿಗ್ಗಾಮುಗ್ಗಾ h. *ad.* Backwards and forwards.

ಹಿಗ್ಗು k. *v. i.* To separate, extend. 2, to grow elated, begin to rejoice. ಹಿಗ್ಗಲಿಸು, ಹಿಗ್ಗಿಸು. To separate, straddle; to open, *as* the mouth of a bag; to slacken.

ಹಿಂ, ಹಿಮ್ k. *ad.* Behind, after. -ಗಟ್ಟು, -ಗಡೆ. The backside, place behind. -ಗತ್ತಲೆ. The early dawn; darkness after moonset. -ಗಾರಿ, -ಗಾರು. The latter rain; *also* -ಗಾರ ಮಳೆ. -ಗಾರು ಪೈರು. The second crop. -ಗಾಲು. The hind leg of a quadruped.

ಹಿಂಗು 1. (= ಪಿಂಗು) k. *v. i.* To go back, retreat; to fail. 2, to be imbibed.

ಹಿಂಗು 2. s. *n.* Asafoetida.

ಹಿಂಗುಲ, ಹಿಂಗೂಲಕ (= ಇಂಗಲಿಕ) s. *n.* Vermilion.

ಹಿಜರಿ h. *n.* The Mahomedan era.

ಹಿಂಚು k. *v. i.* To be behind. *ad.* Behind. -ಮುಂಚು. = ಹಿಂದು ಮುಂದು.

ಹಿಂಚೆ. = ಹಿಂದೆ, *q. v.*

ಹಿಂಜರಿ k. *v. i.* To retreat, withdraw, recoil; to backslide.

ಹಿಂಜು k. *v. t.* To separate, disentangle.

ಹಿಟ್ಟು (*tb. of* ಪಿಷ್ಟ) *n.* Flour, meal. 2, porridge. 3, food. -ಬಟ್ಟೆ. Food and raiment. -ಬಳಪ. A soft kind of potstone. -ಬೀಸು. To grind flour. -ಗಾಳಿಸು. To sift flour. -ಕುಟ್ಟು. To beat flour. -ಕಲಸು. To mix flour. ಹಿಟ್ಟಡಿಗೆ. A cake.

ಹಿಡಿ. *P. p. of* ಹಿಡಿ. -ಕೊಳ್ಳು. To seize, lay hold on. -ತ. Grasping, seizing; parsimony.

ಹಿಡಿ 1. (= ಪಿಡಿ, *q. v.*) k. *v. t.* To seize, catch, take hold of; to hold, take possession, *as* of a country. 2, to restrain, *as* the breath, *etc.* 3, to undertake, begin. 4, to find out, discover. 5, to stop, *as* pay. ' *v. i.* To be attacked by insects. 2, to cost. 3, to fit, suit. 4, to be possessed by evil spirits. 5, to be absorbed, *as* colours. 6, to be affected by disease or pain. 7, to take up time. ಅಮಲು-. To be intoxicated. ಉಳುಕು-. To be sprained. ಬೂಜು-, ಬೂಷ್ಟು-. To grow mouldy. ದಾರಿ-. To take a road; begone! ಕೈ-. To marry; to uphold. -ದು ಕೊಂಡು ಬರು. To bring by force. -ಕೊಂಡು ಹೋಗು. To take away by force. -ತ. = ಹಿಡಿತ, *q. v.* -ಸು. To cause to seize, *etc.*

ಹಿಡಿ 2. k. *n.* A hold; a handful, grasp. 2, a handle, hilt. 3, a broom. -ಕಿ, -ಕೆ. A handle, hilt; the fist. -ಗಲು. A broom. -ತುಂಬ. A handful. -ಯಾಳು. A captive.

ಹಿಡಿಂಬ s. *n.* N. of a râkshasa slain by Bhîma.

ಹಿಡುವಳಿ k. *n.* Possession, ownership (of land). -ದಾರ. A possessor.

ಹಿಣಿ, ಹಿಣಿಲು k. *n.* A bullock's hump. 2, a bow-string. 3, a braid of hair.

ಹಿಂಟೆ (= ಹೆಂಟೆ) k. *n.* A lump, clod.

ಹಿಂಡಿ k. *n.* The refuse of oil-seed, an oil-cake. 2, a chutney of *Emblic myrobalan.*

ಹಿಂಡು 1. k. *v. t.* To press, squeeze out; to wring, *as* a wet cloth; to pinch, *as* the ears; to extract, *as* milk; to harass.

ಹಿಂಡು 2. (*tb. of* ಪಿಂಡ) *n.* A multitude, flock, herd. *Cpds.:* ಆನೆಗಳ-, ಕುರಿಗಳ-, ಪಶುಗಳ-, *etc.* -ಗಟ್ಟು, -ಗೂಡು. To form a herd, to come together in crowds.

ಹಿತ s. *a.* Suitable; advantageous, beneficial, useful; salutary, wholesome, agreeable. 2, friendly, kind. *n.* Advantage, profit, benefit, welfare. -ಕರ, -ಕಾರಕ. Beneficial. -ಕಾರಿ. Doing services, befriending. -ವಂತ, -ವಾದಿ. A benefactor, friend. -ಶತ್ರು. A secret enemy. -ಶತ್ರುತ್ವ. Secret enmity. ಹಿತಾವಹ. Salutary, salubrious. ಹಿತೋಪದೇಶ. Friendly advice, good counsel; N. of a popular work.

ಹಿತ್ತಲು k. *n.* A back-yard.

ಹಿತ್ತಳೆ, ಹಿತ್ತಾಳಿ, ಹಿತ್ತಾಳೆ k. *n.* Brass.

ಹಿದುಕು k. *v. t.* To peel soaked pulse.

ಹಿಂ, ಹಿನ್. = ಹಿಂದೆ, *q. v.* -ತಿರುಗು, -ದಿರುಗು. To turn back; to return. -ತಿರುಗಿಸು (*v. t.*). To turn back, *etc.* -ತೆಗೆ, -ದೆಗೆ. To draw back, flinch.

ಹಿಂದ. = ಹಿಂದು, *q. v.* -ಗಡೆ. Afterwards.

ಹಿಂದಟ್ಟು k. *v. t.* To follow, pursue.

ಹಿಂದು 1. k. *n.* That which is behind, (*in place*), back, previous or past; past time. *ad.* Behind, *etc.* ಹಿಂದಕ್ಕೆ ಮುಂದಕ್ಕೆ. Backwards and forwards. ಹಿಂದಟ್ಟು. To follow, pursue. ಹಿಂದಾಗು. To be behind, flinch. ಹಿಂದಾಡು. To speak behind a person. -ಗಡೆ. A place that is behind; subsequent time. -ಗಳೆ. To flinch; to transgress. -ಗೊಳ್ಳು. To follow. -ಮುಂದು. That is behind and in front. -ಮುಂದು ನೋಡು. To be cautious; to hesitate.

ಹಿಂದು 2. (*tb. of* ಸಿಂಧು) *n.* A Hindoo. -ಜನ. Hindoos. -ದೇಶ, -ಸ್ಥಾನ. India. -ಸ್ಥಾನಿ. The Hindustani language.

ಹಿಂದೆ (= ಹಿಂ, ಹಿಂದು 1, *q. v.*) k. *n.* Past time. *prep.* Behind, after, at the back, backwards; in former times, ago; later on, afterwards. -ಬೀಳು. To lag behind; to be less in use. -ಆಡು, -ಯಾಡು. To backbite. -ಹತ್ತು, -ಹೋಗು. To follow.

ಹಿಂದೋಲ s. *n.* A swing, hammock.

ಹಿಪ್ಪಲಿ (*tb. of* ಪಿಪ್ಪಲಿ) *n.* Long pepper, *Piper longum.* -ನೇರಳೆ. The mulberry, *Morus indica.*

ಹಿಪ್ಪಿ, ಹಿಪ್ಪೆ k. *n.* The refuse after the juice has been squeezed out.

ಹಿಂ, ಹಿಮ್.=ಹಿಂದು 1, *q. v.* ಹಿಂಬಲ. Help, refuge. -ಬಳೆ. A wrist-ornament worn behind the kaḍaga. -ಬಳಿ. The rear. -ಬಾರ. Weight in the back part (of a cart). -ಬಾಲ. The tail, hind part, following. -ಬಾಲ ಮಾಡು, -ಬಾಲಿಸು. To follow. -ಭಾಗ. The back part. -ಮಡಿ. The heel. -ಮೆಟ್ಟು. To step backwards.

ಹಿಮ s. *a.* Cold, frosty. *n.* Frost, ice, snow, dew, cold. -ಕರ, -ಕಿರಣ. The moon. -ವತ್. Snowy, icy. -ಗಿರಿ, -ವತ್, ಹಿಮಾಚಲ, ಹಿಮಾದ್ರಿ, ಹಿಮಾಲಯ. The Himâlaya mountain.

ಹಿಮ್ಮಣಿ.=ಹಮ್ಮಣಿ, *q. v.*

ಹಿಮ್ಮತ್ತು h. *n.* Protection, patronage, aid.

ಹಿಯ್ಯಾಳಿ.=ಹೀಯಾಳಿ, *q. v.*

ಹಿರಣ್ಯ s. *n.* Gold. 2, wealth, riches. ಹಿರಣ್ಮಯ. Golden. -ಕಶಿಪು. N. of a daitya king killed by Narasiṁha. -ಗರ್ಭ. Brahmâ. ಹಿರಣ್ಯಾಕ್ಷ. Brother of ಹಿರಣ್ಯಕಶಿಪು.

ಹಿರಿ 1. k. *a.* Great, elder, senior. -ತನ. Dignity, greatness. -ದು. That is big, older, superior, *etc.* -ಮಗ. The eldest son. -ಯ. An elder, senior. -ಯರು. Elders, ancesters.

ಹಿರಿ 2. k. *v. t.* To break up, pull to pieces; to pull out of; to unsheathe. *v. i.* To be broken; to fall out of.

ಹಿರೆ.=ಹಿರಿ 1, *q. v.*

ಹಿಸಕು, ಹಿಸಿಕು, ಹಿಸುಕು k. *v. t.* To squeeze, press, *as* a fruit; to knead; to shampoo.

ಹಿಸಾಬು h. *n.* Calculation; an account. 2, practical arithmetic.

ಹಿಸಿ k. *v. i.* To burst (*as* a jack fruit); to crack (*as* a wall).

ಹಿಸ್ಸೆ h. *n.* A share, part. -ದಾರ. A shareholder.

ಹಿಳಲು (=ಹಿಣಿಲು) k. *n.* A bullock's hump.

ಹಿಳಿಗೆ (*tb. of* ಪಿಟಕ) *n.* A basket; *cf.* [ಹೆಡಗೆ.

ಹಿಳ್ಳು, ಹಿಳ್ಳೆ k. *n.* A shoot, rootlet. -ಯೊಡೆ. Shoots to break forth.

ಹೀಗಳಿ, ಹೀಗಳೆ k. *v. t.* To scoff, revile. -ಯುವಿಕೆ. Scoffing.

ಹೀಗೆ, ಹೀಂಗೆ k. *ad.* In this manner, thus, so, like. -ಯು. Even in this manner. -ಯೇ. In this very manner. ಹೀಗಿರಲಿಕ್ಕೆ, ಹೀಗಿರುವಲ್ಲಿ. While, thus.

ಹೀಚು (=ಪಿಂಚು 2, *q. v.*) k. *n.* A fruit newly come out of blossom; *also* ಈಚು.

ಹೀಜು.=ಈಚು, *q. v.*

ಹೀನ s. *a.* Deprived of, devoid of, without; bereft of; deficient, faulty; mean, base, vile, low. -ಕೆಲಸ. A base act. *Cpds.:* ಕುಲ-, ಜಾತಿ-, ಬುದ್ಧಿ-, ಭಾಗ್ಯ-, ಮತಿ-, ಮಾನ-, ರಾಜ್ಯ-, ಲಜ್ಜಾ-, *etc.* -ಜಾತಿ. Low-born; a low caste. -ತನ, -ತೆ, -ತ್ವ. Baseness; meanness. -ದಶೆ. Miserable state. -ಸ್ವರ. A bad voice. ಹೀನಾಯ. Want; dishonour. -ಯಿಸು, -ಯ್ಸು, ಹೀನೈಸು. To despise, degrade, disesteem.

ಹೀಬ್ರು f *n.* A Jew. 2, the Hebrew language.

ಹೀಯಾಳಿ (=ಹಿಯ್ಯಾಳಿ) k. *n.* Scoffing, sneer; rough or cruel treatment; a despicable person. -ಸು. To scoff, sneer; to upbraid; *cf.* ಹೀಗಳಿ.

ಹೀರು k. *v. t.* To suck up, absorb, *as* water, *etc.*; to drink. *P. p.* ಹೀರಿ.

ಹೀರೆ k. *n.* The vegetable *Luffa acutangula.* -ಕಾಯಿ. Its fruit.

ಹೀಲಿ s. k. *n.* A peacock's tail.

ಹುಕುಂ, ಹುಕ್ಕುಂ h. *n.* A command, order. -ನಾಮೆ. A written order, decree.

ಹುಕ್ಕಾ h. *n.* A smoking apparatus, hooka. -ಕುಡಿ, -ಸೇದು. To smoke the hooka.

ಹುಗಳು.=ಹುಗುಳು, *q. v.*

ಹುಗಿ k. *v. t.* To inter, bury. ಹುಗಿತ. Burying. ಹುಗಿಸು. To cause to bury.

ಹುಗುಳು (=ಪುಗುಳು, ಹುಗಳು) k. *n.* A blister, boil, sore.

ಹುಗ್ಗಿ k. *n.* Boiled rice mixed with any split pulse and salted or sweetened to taste, *as:* ಹೆಸರುಬೇಳೆ-, ತೊಗರಿಬೇಳೆ-.

ಹುಚ್ಚು (= ಪೆಚ್ಚು, q. v. tb. of ಪಿತ್ತ) n. Foolishness, folly, madness. ಹುಚ್ಚ. A fool; f. ಹುಚ್ಚಿ. ಹುಚ್ಚಾಟ. Silly conduct. Cpds.: -ಕೆಲಸ, -ಕೋಪ, -ಗಾಳಿ, -ತಿಳುವಳಿ, -ನಾಯಿ, -ಪ್ರೀತಿ, -ಬುದ್ಧಿ, -ಮಳೆ, etc. -ಹತ್ತು. Foolishness to seize. -ಮಾಡು. To make a fool of. -ಮೋರೆ ಮಾಡು. To put on a frightful look. ಹುಚ್ಚೋಟ. A rash run. -ತನ. Madness.

ಹುಜತ್ತು h. n. Perverse wrangling, objecting or making difficulties. -ಗಾರ, ಹುಜತ್ತಿನವ. A perverse objector.

ಹುಂಜ 1, ಹುಂಜು k. n. A cock. -ದಡಿ. A kind of border of a cloth.

ಹುಂಜ 2. f. n. A quantity of cotton yarn. -ಕೋಡು. A twist, skein.

ಹುಟ್ಟ 1. (= ಹುಟ್ಟು 1, n. q. v.) ಹುಟ್ಟಾ. From one's very birth. ಹುಟ್ಟಾವಳಿ. = ಹುಟ್ಟುವಳಿ, q. v.

ಹುಟ್ಟ 2. k. n. A (honey) comb.

ಹುಟ್ಟಿಸು k. v. t. To create, produce, originate.

ಹುಟ್ಟು 1. k. v. i. To arise, originate, come into existence, be born, be produced. n. Birth, origin; produce; family. -ಕುರುಡ. A male born blind; f. -ಕುರುಡಿ. -ಗುಣ. A natural disposition. -ಬುದ್ಧಿ. Instinct. -ಮನೆ. The house in which one has been born. ಹುಟ್ಟುವಳಿ (=ಹುಟ್ಟಾವಳಿ). Produce, as of a garden, field, etc.; the amount of an assessment. -ವಿಕೆ. Coming into existence. ಹುಟ್ಟೂರು. A birth-place.

ಹುಟ್ಟು 2. k. n. A wooden spoon; a paddle.

ಹುಡಕು. = ಹುಡುಕು, q. v.

ಹುಡಗ. = ಹುಡುಗ, q. v. ಹುಡಗಿ. = ಹುಡುಗಿ, q. v.

ಹುಡಿ (= ಪುಡಿ) k. n. Powder; dust; snuff. -ಮಣ್ಣು. Fine earth, dust. -ಮಾಡು. To reduce to powder. -ಯಾಗು. To be powdered.

ಹುಡಿಗಿ. = ಹುಡುಗಿ, q. v.

ಹುಡುಕು (= ಹುಡಕು) k. v. t. To seek, seek for, search for, try to find. 2, to search, examine.

ಹುಡುಗ (= ಹುಡಗ) k. n. A boy. 2, a child. -ತನ, ಹುಡುಗು. Childhood; boyishness, childishness; also ಹುಡುಗಾಟ, ಹುಡುಗಾಟಿಕೆ.

ಹುಡುಗಿ k. n. A girl. -ತನ. Girlhood.

ಹುಡುಗು k. v. t. To sweep n. Sweeping. -ಮಾಡು. To sweep.

ಹುಣಸೆ, ಹುಣಿಸಿ, ಹುಣಿಸೆ k. n. The tamarind, Tamarindus indica. Cpds.: -ಕಾಯಿ, -ಗಿಡ, -ಬೀಜ, -ಮರ, -ಹಣ್ಣು, -ಹುಳಿ. -ಬೀಜದ ಹುರಕು. A fried preparation of tamarind seeds.

ಹುಣಿಮೆ. = ಹುಣ್ಣಿಮೆ, q. v.

ಹುಂಡಿ 1. k. n. A hamlet.

ಹುಂಡಿ 2. f. n. A bill of exchange; also -ಕಾಗದ, -ಚೀಟು.

ಹುಣ್ಣಮೆ, ಹುಣ್ಣಿವೆ (tb. of ಪೂರ್ಣಿಮಾ) n. Full moon.

ಹುಣ್ಣು k. n. A sore, ulcer, abscess. ಅರಸ-, ರಾಜ-. A carbuncle. -ಒಡಿ, -ಹತ್ತು. A sore to break out. ಹುಣ್ಣಿನಲ್ಲಿ ಕೀವು ಸೋರು. An ulcer to discharge matter.

ಹುತ್ತ, ಹುತ್ತು k. n. A white-ant hill. -ಗಾಲು. A kind of elephantiasis.

ಹುದುಗ k. n. A cover. ಹುದುಗು. To be covered; to hide, conceal one's self.

ಹುದ್ದೆ h. n. An office, post. -ದಾರ. An officer. -ದಾರಿ. The business of an officer.

ಹುನ್ನರ f. n. An art; power of skill, scheme.

ಹುಬ್ಬು (tb. of ಭ್ರೂ) n. The eye-brow. -ಗಂಟು. A frown. -ಗಂಟಿಕ್ಕು, -ಗಂಟು ಹಾಕು. To frown.

ಹುಬ್ಬೆ (tb. of ಪೂರ್ವೆ) n. The eleventh of the lunar mansions.

ಹುಮ್ಮಸ f. n. Pride, arrogance.

ಹುಯಿ k. v. t. To beat. P. p. ಹುಯಿದು, ಹೂದು.

ಹುಯಿಲು, ಹುಯ್ಲು k. n. Vociferation. -ಇಡು, ಹುಯಿಲಿಡು, ಹುಯ್ಲಿಕ್ಕು. To roar out.

ಹುರ. = ಹುರಿ 1, q. v. 2, (= ಹುರು) roughness. -ಬರಕ. Roughness. -ಕಲು.

Parched corn or pulse. -ಹುರುಕು. Roughness of the skin; a kind of herpes; itches. -ವಳಿಸು. To be parched.

ಹುರಮುಂಜಿ. = ಹುರುಮಂಜಿ, *q. v.*

ಹುರಳಿ (= ಹುಳಿ) k. *n.* Horse-gram, *Dolichos uniflorus.* -ಕಟ್ಟು ತಿನ್ನಿಸು. To give (a horse) gram.

ಹುರಿ 1. (= ಉರಿ 1) k. *v. t.* To roast, parch, *as* grain, pulse, *etc.* *n.* Parching. -ಯಕ್ಕಿ, ಹುರ್ಯಕ್ಕಿ. Parched rice. -ಗಡಲೆ, -ಗಡ್ಲೆ. Parched (Bengal) gram. -ಸಕ್ಕರೆ. A kind of sugar.

ಹುರಿ 2. k. *n.* Twist, cord, twine; a twisting. -ಕಳಚು, -ಬಿಚ್ಚು. To untwist a thread. ಮಾಡು. To twist.

ಹುರಿ 3. k. *n.* Strength, courage, valour. 2, the spine. -ಗೊಡಿಸು, -ಗೊಳಿಸು, -ದುಂಬಿಸು, -ಮಾಡು. To encourage. -ದುಂಬು. To be courageous; to encourage.

ಹುರುಕು. = ಹುರಕು, *q. v.*

ಹುರುಡು k. *n.* Rivalry; envy, jealousy, emulation. -ಮಾಡು, ಹುರುಡಿಸು. To rival, envy. ಹುರುಡಿಗ. An envious man.

ಹುರುಮಂಜಿ (= ಹುರಮಂಜಿ) h. *n.* A particular kind of red ochre.

ಹುರುಳಿ, ಹುರ್ಳಿ. = ಹುರಳಿ, *q. v.*

ಹುರುಳು (= ಪುರುಳು, *q. v.*) k. *n.* Meaning; power; use; service. ಇದರಲ್ಲಿ ಏನು ಹುರುಳಿಲ್ಲ. There is no use in this, *etc.*

ಹುಲಬು, ಹುಲುಬು k. *v. i.* To come to light, to be detected.

ಹುಲಸು. = ಹುಲಿಸು, *q. v.*

ಹುಲಿ k. *n.* A tiger. -ಯುಗುರು. A tiger's claws; a scandant plant, *Gloriosa superba* (= ಕೋಳಿಕುಟುಮ). -ಯ ಚರ್ಮ, -ಯತೊಗಲು. A tiger's skin. ಹೆಣ್ಣು-. A tigress. ಹೆಬ್ಬುಲಿ. A royal tiger.

ಹುಲಿಗಿಲಿ, ಹುಲಿಗಿಲು k. *n.* The Indian beech, *Pongamia glabra.*

ಹುಲಿವೆ k. *n.* The timber tree, *Terminalia paniculata.*

ಹುಲಿಸು, ಹುಲುಸು k. *v. i.* To increase, thrive, grow. *n.* Increase in bulk, richness, *as* of a crop.

ಹುಲ್ಲು k. *n.* Grass; straw, hay. -ಕಡ್ಡಿ. A piece of straw. -ಗದ್ದೆ. A paddy-field overgrown with grass. -ಗಾವಲು. Pasture land. -ತುಳಿಸು. To tread out corn with oxen. -ಬಡಿ. To thrash corn. -ಬಣವೆ, -ಮೆದೆ. A stack of straw. -ಮೇಯು. To eat grass, graze *as* cattle. -ಚಾಪೆ. A grass mat. -ಮನೆ. A thatched house. -ಮೂಟೆ, ಹುಲ್ಲಡಕ. A heap of straw. ಹುಲ್ಲೊಕ್ಕಲ್. Bullocks treading thrashed straw.

ಹುಲ್ಲೆ k. *n.* An antelope or deer.

ಹುವ್ವು (= ಹೂ, ಹೂವು, *q. v.*) k. *n.* A flower.

ಹುಷಾರ, ಹುಷಾರು h. *a.* Smart, sharp; attentive, alert, watchful; fresh. ಹುಷಾರಿ. Smartness, intelligence. -ಇರು. To be alert.

ಹುಸಿ (= ಪುಸಿ) k. *v. i.* To become untrue or false. *n.* A falsehood, lie; *also* -ನುಡಿ, -ಮಾತು. -ಗಾಯಿ. An unripe fruit. -ಗುಂಡು. A missed shot. -ನಗೆ. A pretended or gentle smile. -ಹೂ. A flower that drops without producing fruit.

ಹುಳ (ಳ = ೞ) k. *n.* A worm, insect in general. -ಕು. = ಹುಳುಕು, *q. v.*

ಹುಳಿ 1. k. *n.* Acidity, sourness. 2, leaven. *a.* Sour, acid. *v. i.* To be sour. *Cpds.:* -ನೀರು, -ಪದಾರ್ಥ, -ಪಲ್ಯ, -ಮರ, -ಮಾವು, -ರಸ, -ಸೊಪ್ಪು, -ಹಣ್ಣು, *etc.* -ಹಿಡಿ. To turn sour.

ಹುಳಿ 2. (ಳ = ೞ) k. *v. i.* To get worm-eaten, rot, decay.

ಹುಳು (= ಹುಳ. ಳು = ೞು) -ಕಲು. Decayed state. -ಕು (= ಹುಳಕು). Decay, rottenness; decayed; unsound, corrupt. -ಕು ನೀತಿ. Base precepts. -ಕು ಮನಸ್ಸು. A corrupt mind. -ಕು ಮರ. A rotten tree. -ಕು ಮೋರೆ. A pock-marked face. -ಕು ಹಲ್ಲು. A carious tooth.

ಹೂ 1. (= ಹುವ್ವು) k. *n.* A flower, blossom. -ಗಣ್ಣು. Albugo. -ಗಾಯ. A slight wound. -ಚೆಂಡು. A bouquet. -ದಿಂಗಣ. The Indian shot, *Canna indica.* -ದೋಟ. A flower-garden. -ಬಣ್ಣ. Any light colour. -ಬಾಣ. A kind of firework. -ಬಿಡು. To begin to blossom. -ಬಿಸಲು. A moderate evening sunshine. -ಗಾರ, -ವಡಿಗ, -ವಾಡಿಗ. A florist. -ಮಾಲೆ. A chaplet or garland of flowers; *also* -ಹಾರ.

ಹೂ 2. k. *A particle expressing consent or assent:* yes, well.

ಹೂಂ s. *int.* of reproach, menace, *etc.* -ಕರಿಸು. To cry out angrily.

ಹೂಜ, ಹೂಜೆ 1. (=ಕೂಜೆ, *q. v.*) h. *n.* A goglet, jug.

ಹೂಜೆ 2. k. *n.* Envy, jealousy. -ಗಾರ. A jealous man; *f.* -ಗಾತಿ.

ಹೂಟ k. *n.* A plan, means, expedient, scheme. 2, yoking. -ಗಾರ. A schemer; contriver.

ಹೂಡು k. *v. t.* To join, unite; to yoke; to put oxen, horses, *etc.* to carts or plough; to arrange, make ready.

ಹೂಡೆ k. *n.* A circular bastion-like structure of stones for defence.

ಹೂಣ s. *n.* A barbarian, Hun; a European. *Cpds.:* -ಭಾಷೆ, -ತನ.

ಹೂಣಿಗ a. k. *n.* A bold man. -ತನ. Bravery.

ಹೂಣು k. *v. t.* To bury; *also* ಹೂಣಿಸು. ಹೂಣುವ ಸ್ಥಳ. A burial ground.

ಹೂನು, ಹೂಂಡು. = ಹೂ 2, *q. v.*

ಹೂರಣ, ಹೂರ್ಣ (*tb. of* ಪೂರ್ಣ) *n.* The stuffing of cakes. -ಹೋಳಿಗೆ. A stuffed cake.

ಹೂಲಿ 1. k. *n.* N. of a straggling shrub.

ಹೂಲಿ 2. f. *n.* A commotion, alarm. -ಎಬ್ಬಿಸು. To raise an alarm.

ಹೂವು. = ಹೂ, *q. v.*

ಹೂಸು k. *v. t.* To daub, smear. 2, to break wind downwards. *n.* A fart.

ಹೂಳು (ಳು = ಯು) k. *v. t.* To cover; to bury; *also* ಹೂಣು. *v. i.* To sink into, *as* a foot, *etc.* -ವ ಭೂಮಿ, -ವ ಸ್ಥಳ. A burial place.

ಹೃದ್ (ಹೃತ್) s. *n.* The heart, mind. -ರೋಗ, ಹೃಚ್ಛೋಕ. Heart-ache. -ಕಂಪ. Heart-throb; anxiety. -ತಾಪ. Mental distress. -ಗತ. Conceived; believed, cherished. ಹೃದಯ. The heart; the mind, soul, seat of thought and feeling; breast, chest, bosom. ಹೃದಯ ಭೇದಕ. Heart-rending. ಹೃದಯಾಳು. Kind, affectionate.

ಹೆಕ್ಕತ್ತು k. *n.* The nape of the neck.

ಹೆಕ್ಕಳ a. k. *n.* Abundance. 2, conceit, pride; *cf.* ಹಗ್ಗಳ. ಹೆಕ್ಕಳಿಸು. To get proud.

ಹೆಕ್ಕು k. *v. t.* To pick up, take up one by one. 2, to comb.

ಹೆಗ್ k. *n.* Largeness. -ಗಟ್ಟು. A strong band or knot. ಹೆಗ್ಗಡೆ. A headman, chief; *f.* -ಗಡತಿ. -ಗಣ. A very large rat, bandicoot. -ಗಣಬೋನು. A bandicoot trap. -ಗ್ಗತ್ತು. = ಹೆಕ್ಕತ್ತು, *q. v.* -ಗಾಡು (-ಕಾಡು). A thick forest. -ಗಾಣ. A large oil-mill of stone. -ಗುಂಟೆ. A weeding plough. -ಗುರುತು. A prominent mark. -ಗೊಂಬೆ. A main branch of a tree. -ಗೋರಟೆ. Globe amaranth, *Gomphrena globosa.*

ಹೆಗಲು k. *n.* The shoulder. -ಬಡಿಕ. A ruthless man.

ಹೆಗ್ಗು (= ಎಗ್ಗು, *q. v.*) k. *n.* Blame, fault, censure, *etc.*

ಹೆಂ. = ಹೆಣ್ಣು, *q. v.* -ಗೂಸು (-ಕೂಸು). A female child.

ಹೆಂಗಸು (*fr.* ಹೆಂ-ಕೂಸು) k. *n.* A female; a woman. 2, a wife; *pl.* ಹೆಂಗಸರು.

ಹೆಂಗೆ. = ಹ್ಯಾಗೆ, *q. v.*

ಹೆಚ್ಚರ. = ಎಚ್ಚರ, *q. v.*

ಹೆಚ್ಚಳ k. *n.* Pride, conceit, elation; excess. -ಗೊಳ್ಳು, -ಪಡು, ಹೆಚ್ಚಳಿಸು. To become elated, to rejoice.

ಹೆಚ್ಚಿಗೆ 1. k. *n.* Increase, growth; excess, superfluity. *a.* Extra, beyond what is expected. *ad.* Greatly, much, more. -ತೆಗೆದುಕೊಳ್ಳು. To take more than is due. -ಮಾಡು. To increase; exalt.

ಹೆಚ್ಚಿಗೆ 2. k. *n.* A small flat basket.

ಹೆಚ್ಚು 1. k. *v. i.* To become more, increase, thrive, grow, swell. *n.* Increase, growth; largeness; excess;

superfluity, surplus, excess, *etc.* *a.* More, excessive. ಹೆಚ್ಚಿಸು. To cause to increase, *etc.*, to multiply, increase. -ಕಡಿಮೆ. Difference; variation; more or less, about. -ಆಗು. To augment, increase; to abound, become too much. -ಗಾರಿಕೆ. Exaltation. -ಗುಣಿಸು. To multiply. -ಗೆ (= ಹೆಚ್ಚಿಗೆ). Increase, growth. -ಗೊಳ್ಳು. To increase. -ಮಾಡು. To increase (*v. t.*). -ವಿಕೆ. Increasing. -ಹೆಚ್ಚು. More and more.

ಹೆಚ್ಚು 2. k. *v. t.* To mince, *as* vegetables, *etc.*

ಹೆಚ್ಚೆ. = ಹಜ್ಜೆ, *q. v.*

ಹೆಜ್ (= ಹೆಗ್) k. *n.* Largeness. -ಜೇನು. Superior honey.

ಹೆಜ್ಜೆ. (= ಪಜ್ಜೆ) k. *n.* A foot-step; a foot-print, track. 2, the foot. -ಇಡು, -ಹಾಕು. To walk. -ಯ ಹಿಡಿ. To track, follow by the foot-steps.

ಹೆಂಚು (= ಹಂಚು, *q. v.*) k. *n.* A tile.

ಹೆಟ್ಟ k. *n.* A bush-harrow. 2, dregs of castor-oil. 3, a clod.

ಹೆಟ್ಟಿಗೆ k. *n.* A stout beam. 2, (f.) a dovecot.

ಹೆಟ್ಟು (= ಪೆಟ್ಟು, *q. v.*) k. *v. t.* To beat, box, give a blow. 2, to insert, put, *as* a morsel into the mouth.

ಹೆಟ್ಟೆ k. *n.* A lump of earth, clod.

ಹೆಡ k. *n.* The back, rear. -ಕಟ್ಟು. Hind-binding; to pinion; *also* -ಗುಡಿ ಕಟ್ಟು. -ತಲೆ. The back of the head. -ಮುರಿಕೆ, -ಮುರಿಗೆ. Pinioning. -ಮುರಿಗೆ ಕಟ್ಟು. To pinion.

ಹೆಡಕಲು k. *n.* The back of the neck.

ಹೆಡಗೆ, ಹೆಡಿಗೆ (*tb. of* ಪಿಟಕ) *n.* A basket.

ಹೆಡೆ (*tb. of* ಸ್ಫಟ) *n.* The expanded hood of a serpent.

ಹೆಡ್ಡ k. *n.* A dull, stupid man, fool. *a.* Dull, foolish. -ತನ, ಹೆಡ್ಡು. Stupidity. ಹೆಡ್ಡಾಳು. A stupid, foolish person.

ಹೆಣ k. *n.* A corpse; a carcass. -ದತ್ತ, -ಮೋರೆ. A good-for-nothing fellow; a coward. -ಹೂಳು. To bury a corpse. -ಗಾಡು. A cemetery.

ಹೆಣಗು k. *v. i.* To wrangle, quarrel, fight, strive. ಹೆಣಗಾಟ. Quarrel, fight. ಹೆಣಗಾಡು. = ಹೆಣಗು, *q. v.* ಹಣಗಿಸು. To cause to fight.

ಹೆಣಿಗೆ k. *n.* Plaiting; that is plaited.

ಹೆಣೆ k. *v. t.* To intertwine, plait, *as* mats, *etc.*; to braid, *as* the hair; to knit, *as* nets; to rattan, *as* a chair. *n.* Joining together; plait, braid. -ಕೊಳ್ಳು. To intertwine; to plait. -ಕಟ್ಟು. To tie cattle in a row for treading corn.

ಹೆಂಟೆ k. *n.* A lump of earth, a clod. 2, an unburnt brick. 3, a bush-harrow.

ಹೆಂಡ 1. k. *n.* A female; a wife, *also* -ತಿ. *Pl.* ಹೆಂಡರು, ಹೆಂಡಂದಿರು, ಹೆಂಡಿರು. ಹೆಂಡರು ಮಕ್ಕಳು. Wife and children.

ಹೆಂಡ 2. k. *n.* Spirituous liquor, toddy. ಈಚಲು-. Date toddy. ತೆಂಗಿನ-. Cocoa-nut toddy. ತಾಳೇ-. Palmyra toddy.

ಹೆಂಡೆ k. *n.* Cowdung. 2, = ಹೆಂಟೆ.

ಹೆಣ್ಣಗ k. *n.* A coward. -ತನ. Cowardice.

ಹೆಣ್ಣು k. *n.* A female; a woman. *a.* Female, feminine. *Cpds.*: -ಆಡು, -ಆಳು, -ಒಂಟೆ, -ಕಪ್ಪೆ, -ಕರ, -ಕರಡಿ, -ಕುದುರೆ (mare), -ಕೂಸು, -ಕೋಳಿ (hen), -ಗುಬ್ಬಿ (hen-sparrow), -ಚಿಗರಿ -ತೋಳ, -ದೇವತೆ, -ನರಿ, -ನಾಯಿ (bitch), -ಸಿಂಹ (lioness), -ಹಂದಿ (sow), -ಹುಲಿ (tigress). -ಮಕ್ಕಳು. Female children; women. ಹೆಣ್ಣಾನೆ, ಹೆಣ್ಣಾಳು, ಪೆಣ್ಣೊಂಟೆ. A female goat, *etc.*

ಹೆತ್ತಪ್ಪ, ಹೆತ್ತಯ್ಯ, ಹೆತ್ತಾತ k. *n.* A grandfather. ಹೆತ್ತಮ್ಮ. A grandmother.

ಹೆತ್ತು. *P. p. of* ಹೆರು.

ಹೆದ್ k. *a.* Large, big. -ದನಿ. A loud voice. -ದಳೆ. An extensive barren tract. -ದಾರಿ. A high-road. -ದಿಂಡಿ (-ತಿಂಡಿ), -ದೀನಿ (-ತೀನಿ). Much food; an omnivorous person. -ದೀನಿ ಉಣ್ಣು. To eat voraciously. -ದೀನಿ ಉಣ್ಣುವವ. A glutton.

ಹೆದರು (ರು = ಱು) k. v. i. To be alarmed or frightened, to fear. n. Fear, alarm, fright. ಹೆದರದವ. A courageous man. ಹೆದರಿಕೆ. Fear. ಹೆದರಿಸು. To frighten.

ಹೆದೆ a. k. n. A bow-string.

ಹೆದ್ದ k. n. A lever used in moving a car.

ಹೆಪ್ಪು 1. k. n. Any thing put into milk to cause it to turn or curdle. -ಗಟ್ಟು, ಹೆಪ್ಪಾಗು. To be turned, as milk. -ಇಡು, -ಕೊಡು, -ಹಾಕು. To curdle or turn milk.

ಹೆಪ್ಪು 2. k. n. Sod, sward, grass, turf.

ಹೆಬ್ k. a. Large, big. -ಬಲಸು (-ಹಲಸು). The jungle jack, *Artocarpus pubescence*. -ಬಾಗಿಲು. The principal gate or door. -ಬಾರ, -ಬಾರುವ (-ಹಾರ, -ಹಾರುವ). The head Brâhmaṇa of a caste. -ಬಾವು (-ಹಾವು). The boa. -ಬುಲಿ (-ಹುಲಿ). The royal tiger. -ಬೆಟ್ಟು, -ಬೆರಳು, -ಬೊಟ್ಟು. The thumb; the great toe.

ಹೆಮ್ k. a. Large, big. -ಮರ. A large tree; a lofty tree producing a fragrant resin, *Ailanthus malabarica*. -ಮಾರಿ. A wicked woman; Durga. -ಮುಗುಳು. A garden plant, *Spilanthes acmella*.

ಹೆಮ್ಮೆ k. n. Greatness, etc.; pride, vanity. -ಗಾರ. A proud man. -ಗೊಳಿಸು (-ಕೊಳಿಸು). To elate.

ಹೆರ (ರ = ಱ) k. pro. Another, other. -ಗೆ. Outside. -ರು. Others.

ಹೆರಲು, ಹೆರಳು k. n. A braid of hair. -ಹಾಕು. To braid the hair.

ಹೆರು 1. (ರು = ಱು) k. v. t. To bear, bring forth, give birth to. P. p. ಹೆತ್ತು. ಹೆತ್ತವರು. Parents. ಹೆರಿಗೆ, ಹೆರುವಿಕೆ. Bringing forth, delivery.

ಹೆರು 2. (ರು = ಱು) k. v. i. To thicken, congeal, as clarified butter. P. p. ಹೆತ್ತು. ಹೆತ್ತುಪ್ಪ. Congealed ghee.

ಹೆರೆ 1. k. v. t. To scrape, as a fruit, the floor, etc.; to shave; to grub, as grass.

ಹೆರೆ 2. k. n. The slough of a serpent.

ಹೆರೆ 3. (ರೆ = ಱೆ) a. k. n. The crescent, the moon.

ಹೆಸರು 1. k. n. A name; fame, celebrity. -ಗೊಳ್ಳು, -ಪಡು, -ಸಂಪಾದಿಸು, -ಹೊಂದು, ಹೆಸರಾಗು, ಹೆಸರಿಗೆ ಬರು. To get a name, become famous. ಹೆಸರಿಗೆ ಮಾತ್ರ. In name only. -ಇಡು, ಹೆಸರಿಡು. To name. -ಪಡೆ. To get a name. -ವಾಸಿ. Fame, reputation. -ಹೋಗು. A name to go; to become noted.

ಹೆಸರು 2. (ರು = ಱು) k. n. Green gram, *Phaseolus mungo*.

ಹೆಳಲು (= ಹೆರಳು) k. n. A braid of hair.

ಹೆಳವ (ಳ = ೞ) k. n. A lame man, cripple; f. ಹೆಳವಿ.

ಹೇ s. *A voc. particle*: Oh! ho! -ಕರಿಸು. To neigh.

ಹೇಗೆ k. ad. How?

ಹೇಟಿ, ಹೇಂಟೆ k. n. A hen.

ಹೇಡಿ k. n. A timid person, coward. -ತನ. Cowardice. ರಣ-. A coward in battle.

ಹೇತಿ s. n. A weapon. 2, light; flame.

ಹೇತು s. n. Motive; cause, ground, reason, purpose; proof; logic; sophistry. -ಕ. Causal, instrumental; cause. ಜಗಳಕ್ಕೆ-, ವ್ಯಾಜ್ಯಕ್ಕೆ-, ಸಾವಿಗೆ-, etc. The cause of a quarrel, etc.

ಹೇನು k. n. A louse. -ಸೀರು. A nit. -ಎತ್ತು. To pick out lice.

ಹೇಮ 1. s. n. Gold.

ಹೇಮ 2. s. n. Winter; also ಹೇಮಂತ. -ಪರ್ವತ, ಹೇಮಾದ್ರಿ. The mountain Mêru.

ಹೇಯ s. a. To be gone; to be avoided. n. Dislike.

ಹೇರಳ k. n. Largeness, greatness, abundance. a. Much, many; also ಹೇರಾಳ.

ಹೇರಾಸಿ k. n. Abundance.

ಹೇರು (ರು = ಱು) k. v. t. To lift up and put upon; to load, lade; to pile up. n. A load; a bullock-load.

ಹೇರುಳ k. n. A kind of bitter orange.

ಹೇಲು k. v. i. To void excrements, cack (P. p. ಹೇತು). n. Ordure. 2, the dung of men, dogs, *etc.* -ಮನುಷ್ಯ. A filthy man. -ಮಾತು. A loathsome word.

ಹೇವ a. k. *n.* Disgust, repugnance. 2, shame, modesty. ಹೇವರಿಸು. To recoil, shrink.

ಹೇವಿಲಂಬಿ (*tb. of* ಹೇಮಲಂಬ) *n.* N. of the thirty-first year of the cycle.

ಹೇಷ, ಹೇಷಾ s. *n.* Neighing, braying.

ಹೇಷ್ಯ (*tb. of* ಐಷ್ಯತ್) *n.* A portent, an ill-omen.

ಹೇಸರ (*tb. of* ವೇಸರ) *n.* A mule.

ಹೇಸು k. *v. i.* To feel aversion, have a dislike, to recoil. *n.* = ಹೇಸಿಕೆ. -ತನ. Nastiness. ಹೇಸಿ. A disgustful female. ಹೇಸಿಕೆ, ಹೇಸಿಗೆ. Aversion, disgust; nastiness; a nasty, disagreeable object; filthy, nasty, loathsome. ಹೇಸಿಕೆಗಿಡ. A prickly shrub, *Lantana aculeata.* ಹೇಸಿಕೆಗೊಳಿಸು, ಹೇಸಿಕೆ ಮಾಡು. To soil, dirty.

ಹೇಳಿಗೆ (= ಪೇಳಿಗೆ. *tb. of* ಪೇಟಕಾ) *n.* A basket; a snake-basket.

ಹೇಳು (ಳು = ಱು) k. *v. t. & v. i.* To say, speak; to name; to mention; to narrate, relate; to tell; to order, command. ಹೇಳಿ ಕಳಿಸು, ಹೇಳಿ ಕಳುಹಿಸು. To send word, to let know. ಹೇಳ ಕೂಡದ ಕೆಲಸ. A shameful business. ಹೇಳಿಕೊಡು. To instruct, communicate. ಹೇಳಿ ತೀರದ. Unspeakable. ಹೇಳಿಕೊಟ್ಟ ಮಾತು. A communicated word. ಊಟಕ್ಕೆ-. To invite to a meal. ಹೇಳಿಸು. To cause to say, *etc.* -ವಿಕೆ, ಹೇಳಿಕೆ, ಹೇಳ್ತಿಕೆ. Saying, telling. ಹೇಳಿಕೇ ಮಾತು. Rumour, hearsay.

ಹೈಗ (*tb. of* ವೈದ್ಯಕ) *n.* A class of Smârta Brâhmaṇas.

ಹೈಡ್ರೊಜಿನ್ e. *n.* Hydrogen, a highly inflammable gas.

ಹೈನು. = ಹಯ್ನು, *q. v.*

ಹೈಮಂತ (*fr.* ಹೇಮಂತ) s. *a.* Wintery, cold. *n.* The winter season.

ಹೈರಾನು h. *n.* Distressful condition, bewilderment, confusion, trouble, harass. -ಮಾಡು. To trouble, dun.

ಹೈರೊಗ್ಲಿಫಿಕ್ಸ್ e. *n.* Hieroglyphics; the symbolic writing of the ancient Egyptians and Mexicans.

ಹೈರೋಡ್ e. *n.* A high-road.

ಹೊ. = ಹೋ 2, *q. v.*

ಹೊಕ್ಕಳು, ಹೊಕ್ಕುಳು (ಳು = ಱು) k. *n.* The navel. 2, the perpendicular dash put under a letter to make it aspirate. -ಮಾಡು, -ಸೀಳು. To make this dash, *as* ದ *into* ಧ.

ಹೊಕ್ಕು k. *n.* A boil. 2, the woof of a [loom.

ಹೊಕ್ಕು. *P. p. of* ಹೊಗು, *q. v.* -ಬಳಕೆ. Familiar intercourse.

ಹೊಗರು a. k. *n.* Shine, lustre, effulgence.

ಹೊಗಳು (= ಪೊಗಳು. ಳು = ಱು) k. *v. t.* To praise. *n.* Praise, renown. ಹೊಗಳಿಕೆ. Praise; flattery. ಹೊಗಳಿಸು. To cause to praise.

ಹೊಗು k. *v. i.* To enter. *P. p.* ಹೊಕ್ಕು. ಹೊಗಿಸು. To cause to enter. ಹೊಗಗೊಡು, ಹೊಗಗೊಡಿಸು. To allow to enter.

ಹೊಗೆ k. *v. i.* To smoke. 2, to look sullen. *n.* Smoke; steam, vapour. -ಕಟ್ಟು. Soot. -ಕೊಡು. To apply smoke to; to give a thin coating of gold or silver. -ಬಂಡಿ. A railway carriage. -ಬತ್ತಿ, -ಸುತ್ತು. A cheeroot, cigar. -ಸೊಪ್ಪು. Tobacco. -ಹಡಗ. A steam-ship. -ಹಾಕು. To smoke, produce smoke. -ಯೇರು, -ಯಿಡಿ. To become black from smoke.

ಹೊಂ, ಹೊಜ್ k. *n.* Gold. -ಗಟ್ಟು (-ಕಟ್ಟು). A golden ferrule. -ಗರಿ. A gold-coloured feather. -ಗಲಸ (-ಕಲಸ). A gold penacle. -ಗೆಲಸ (-ಕೆಲಸ). Work in gold.

ಹೊಂಗರ, ಹೊಂಗರಕ k. *n.* The Indian coral tree, *Erythrina indica.*

ಹೊಂಗು a. k. *v. i.* To swell, rise up, *as* the sea; to be elated; to exult.

ಹೊಂಗೆ k. *n.* The Indian beech, *Bongamia glabra.*

ಹೊಚ್ಚು k. *v. t.* To put on, *as* tiles; to cover. ಹೊಚ್ಚಿಸು. To cause to put on.

ಹೊಂಚು k. v. i. To look after; to spy, lurk; to lie in wait, be on the look-out. n. Lying hid. -ಗಾರ. A spy. -ಜಾಗ. An ambush. -ಎಕೆ. Being on the look-out for, lurking.

ಹೊಟ್ಟು k. n. Chaff; husk of rice or corn; a pod without its contents. -ಕೇರು. To winnow. -ಗುಟ್ಟು (-ಕುಟ್ಟು). To speak nonsense.

ಹೊಟ್ಟೆ k. n. The belly; the body of a vessel. ಡೊಳ್ಳು-. Potbellied. -ಉರಿ, -ಕಿಚ್ಚು, ಹೊಟ್ಟುರಿ. Envy. -ಕಟ್ಟು. To restrain the appetite; to live frugally; to be constipated. -ಕಳತ. Purging. -ಕಳೆ, -ಝಾಡಿಸು. The bowels to purge. -ಖರ್ಚು. Expense for food. -ಗೆ ಹಾಕು. To give to eat. -ತುಂಬು. To fill the belly. -ನೋವು, -ಬೇನೆ, -ಶೂಲೆ. Colic. -ಬಾಕ. A glutton. -ಬಾಕತನ. Gluttony. -ಯ ಮೇಲೆ ಬಡಿ. To take away the means of sustenance. -ಯೊಳಗೆ ಬೆಂಕಿ ಬೀಳು. Envy or sorrow to be produced. -ಯೊಳಗೆ ಹಾಕು. To keep to one's self, conceal and forgive. -ಯೊಳಗಿನ ಮಾತು. A covert expression. -ಹೊರೆ. To support life.

ಹೊಡ. = ಹೊಡದು, ಹೊಡೆದು. P. p. of ಹೊಡೆ, in ಹೊಡಕೊಳ್ಳು.

ಹೊಡಕೆ k. n. The elephant grass.

ಹೊಡಗು k. n. A hole.

ಹೊಡಿ, ಹೊಡೆ 1. k. v. t. To strike, beat, lash, flog, smite; to cast, as a stone; to shoot, as an arrow; to drive cattle, cart, etc.; to drive away, beat off; to devour. P. ps. ಹೊಡದು, ಹೊಡೆದು. ಕೊಳ್ಳೆ-. To sack, plunder. ಗಂಟೆ-. To strike the hour, ring a bell. ಘಾಳಿ-. The wind to blow. ಗುಡಾರಾ-. To pitch a tent. ತಲೇ-. To behead. ಮಳೆ-. Rain to fall. ಹೊಡತ. Beating; a stroke, blow. ಹೊಡತಾ-. To beat severely. ಹೊಡದಾಟ. Beating. ಹೊಡ ದಾಡು. To beat mutually.

ಹೊಡೆ 2. k. n. The principal top-beam in a roof.

ಹೊಡೆ 3. k. n. An ear of corn. 2, the calyx of the kêdagĕ.

ಹೊಣೆ k. n. Bond, bail; a bondsman, surety. -ಕೊಡು. To give bail. -ಗಾರ. A surety. -ಬೀಳು, -ಯಾಗು. To stand security for.

ಹೊಂಡ k. n. A pit, hole; a pond.

ಹೊಂಡೆ f. n. The small tree, *Cerbera-odollam*.

ಹೊತ್ತಾರೆ k. n. Day-break. ad. At day-break.

ಹೊತ್ತಗೆ, ಹೊತ್ತಿಗೆ. tb. of ಪುಸ್ತಕ, q. v.

ಹೊತ್ತು 1. (=ಹತ್ತು 3) k. v. i. To be kindled, catch fire. 2, to be burnt at the bottom of a cooking vessel. ಹೊತ್ತಿಸು. To kindle, light.

ಹೊತ್ತು 2. k. n. The sun; time; a time of the day. -ಆಗು. To be time. -ಕಳೆ. To spend time. -ಗೊತ್ತು ಮಾಡು. To fix a time. -ಮಾಡು. To delay. -ಮೀರು. Time to be passed. -ಮುಳುಗು. The sun to set. -ಮೂಡು, -ಹುಟ್ಟು. The sun to rise. -ಸಾಧಿಸು. To await an opportunity. -ಹೋಗು. Time to pass. -ಹೊತ್ತಿಗೆ. From time to time. ಹೊತ್ತುಂಟಲೆ. At day-break, early.

ಹೊತ್ತು 3. k. P. p. of ಹೊರು, q. v.

ಹೊದಕೆ k. n. A cover, covering, wrapper. 2, a thatch, roof.

ಹೊದರು 1. k. n. The hollow of a tree.

ಹೊದರು 2. (ರು=ಱು) k. n. A bush. 2, a mass; a host; a herd.

ಹೊದಿ. = ಹೊದೆ, q. v. -ಸು. To put on, cover, etc. -ಕೆ. = ಹೊದಕೆ, q. v.

ಹೊದೆ 1. (= ಹೊದಿ) k. v. t. To put on; to put over; to wrap round; to cover. P. ps. ಹೊದದು, ಹೊದೆದು, ಹೊದ್ದು. ಹೊದ್ದುಕೊಳ್ಳು. To put on one's self. ಹೊದ್ದಿಸು. To put on.

ಹೊದೆ 2. = ಪೊದೆ, q. v.

ಹೊದ್ದಿಕೆ k. n. Union; concord. 2, a cover, wrapper; cf. ಹೊದಕೆ.

ಹೊದ್ದು a. k. v. i. To join; to go near.

ಹೊನಲು a. k. n. A stream.

ಹೊಂತ (tb. of ಪಂಥ) n. A path, way. -ಗಾರ. A clever, able man.

ಹೊಂದಿಕೆ k. n. Fitness; intimacy, attachment, friendship.

ಹೊಂದಿಸು k. v. t. To join (as limbs for greeting); to attach; to collect; to make fit, as price.

ಹೊಂದು k. v. t. To obtain, get, procure, acquire; to experience; to suffer. v. i. To touch; to go nigh, approach; to join; to agree, befit, suit.

ಹೊನ್ನು, (ಹೊನ್) k. n. Gold; a gold coin; ½ of a varaha. ಹೊನ್ನಗನ್ನೆ. A common weed, used as a potherb, *Alternanthera sessilis*.

ಹೊನ್ನೆ k. n. The tree *Terminalia tomentosa*. 2, a large timber-tree yielding a red dye.

ಹೊಪ್ಪೆ k. n. A natural division in some fruits. 2, a large timber tree yielding a red dye.

ಹೊಮ್. = ಹೊನ್ನು. -ಬಳಿ. To gild. -ಬಾಳೆ. A kind of plantain.

ಹೊಮಿಯೊಪಥಿ f. n. Homoeopathy.

ಹೊಮ್ಮು k. v. i. To rise, break out, run over, come forth. 2, to be thick, rank.

ಹೊಯಿ (= ಹೊಯ್ಯು, q. v.) k. v. t. To beat, cast; to pour. n. Beating; a stroke, blow. -ಗಡುಬು. A cake made by pouring the dough into a vessel. -ಸು. To cause to beat, cast or pour. -ದಾಟ. Mutual beating. -ದಾಡು. To beat mutually. -ತ, -ಲು, ಹೊಯ್ಲು. Beating; a stroke, blow.

ಹೊಯಿಗೆ k. n. Sand.

ಹೊಯಿಲು, ಹೊಯ್ಲು (= ಹುಯಿಲು) k. n. Calling out. 2, the current of a stream.

ಹೊಯ್ಯು (= ಹೊಯಿ, q. v.) k. v. t. To beat, strike, smite; to kill; to cast, pour; to drive (as: ಕೈ-, ತಲೆ-, ನೀರು-), etc. n. A stroke, blow. ಉಚ್ಚೆ-. To void urine.

ಹೊರ 1. (ರ = ಱ) k. n. The outside. a. Outside, outer. ad. To the outside. -ಕಡೆ, -ಗಡೆ. The outside; a public privy; evacuation of bowels. -ಗು. The outside. -ಗೆ. Outside, without. -ಗಾಗು. To be excluded. -ಗಿಕ್ಕು, -ಗಿಡು. To put outside. -ಬರು. To come out. -ಮಾಡು. To expel. -ತರು. To divulge, bring out. -ಚೆಲ್ಲು. To pour out; to be spilt. -ನೂಕು. To push out. -ಪಡಿಸು. To make public. -ಪಡು. To become public. -ಬೀಳು. To come out; to become public. -ಮಗ್ಗಲು. The outside. -ಮೈ. The outside. -ವಡು. To set out, start. -ಹೊಮ್ಮು. To rise; to come forth. -ಹೊರಡು. To go forth.

ಹೊರ 2. P. p. of ಹೊರೆ, in ಹೊರಕೊಳ್ಳು. -ಕ. One who nourishes, as ಹೊಟ್ಟೆ ಹೊರಕ.

ಹೊರಜಿ k. n. A stout long rope.

ಹೊರಡು (fr. ಹೊರ. ರ = ಱ) k. v. i. To go out; to come forth; to set out, sally forth; to start. P. p. ಹೊರಟು. ಹೊರಡಿಸು. To cause to start. ಹೊರಡುವಿಕೆ. Starting. ಹೊರಟು ಹೋಗು. To set out.

ಹೊರತು (fr. ಹೊರ. ರ = ಱ) k. prep. Except, without. -ಮಾಡು. To except, exempt.

ಹೊರಸು k. n. A cot, couch. 2, a kind of pigeon.

ಹೊರಳಿ a. k. n. A heap, mass.

ಹೊರಳು k. v. i. To roll; to wallow, welter. ನಾಲಿಗೆ-, ಮಾತು-. To be retracted, as a word or promise. ಹೊರಳಾಡು. To roll about. ಹೊರಳಿಸು. To cause to roll, etc.; to roll about.

ಹೊರಳೆ k. n. A nostril. 2, money [illegible] counts transferred from one [illegible] another.

ಹೊರಿಕೆ k. n. [illegible] of an onion, a la[illegible]

ಹೊರಿಗೆ (ರ = [illegible]k.

ಹೊರಿಸು k. v. [illegible]e [illegible]self nourished. n[illegible]use to nourish; cf. ಹೊರಿಸು [illegible]

ಹೊರು (ರು = [illegible] To bear, carry on the he[illegible] upon one's self; to impute[illegible]me. P. p. ಹೊತ್ತು.

ಹೊತ್ತುಕೊಳ್ಳು. To take upon one's self; to put on. ಹೊತ್ತುಕೊಂಡು ಹೋಗು. To carry, bear, sustain. ಸಾಲಾ-. To be in debt. ಹೊರೆ-. To carry a load. ಹೊರಿಸು. To put on; to cause to carry; to lay on, impose; to impute; *as:* ಅಪರಾಧ-, ತಪ್ಪು-, ದೋಷ-, *etc.*

ಹೊರೆ 1. (*fr.* ಹೊರು. ರೆ = ಱೆ) k. *n.* A load, burden. -ಗಾರ, -ಯಾಳು. A porter, carrier. ಸವುದೆ-. A faggot. ಹುಲ್ಲು-. A bundle of grass.

ಹೊರೆ 2. k. *v. t.* To nourish, invigorate, foster, support, preserve. *n.* Spirit, courage. ಹೊಟ್ಟೆ-. To sustain the belly.

ಹೊರೆ 3. k. *n.* The slough of a serpent; a coat of a plantain tree; a fold. 2, a web of cloth. 3, neighbourhood, vicinity, *as in* ನೆರೆ-.

ಹೊರೆ 4. (= ಪೊರೆ 4) k. *n.* Choking sensation. -ಹೋಗು. To feel a choking sensation.

ಹೊರ್ತು. = ಹೊರತು, *q. v.*

ಹೊಲ k. *n.* A plough-field; a corn-field. -ಬಿತ್ತು. To sow a field. -ಮಾಡು. To till the ground. -ದ ಪೈರು, -ದ ಬೆಳೆ. A crop. -ಹರಗು. To weed a field.

ಹೊಲಗೆ. = ಹೊಲಿಗೆ, *q. v.*

ಹೊಲತಿ k. *n.* A low-caste woman.

ಹೊಲಬು a. k. *n.* A way; a manner, mode. -ಗೆಡು. To become bewildered.

ಹೊಲಸು k. *n.* Nastiness; nasty matter, filth; dirtiness. *a.* Nasty. -ತನ. Nastiness, obscenity. -ನುಡಿ, -ಮಾತು. [illegible]n obscene word.

[illegible] *v. t.* To sew, stitch. -ಗೆ. Sewing; [illegible]work. -ಗೆ ಬಿಚ್ಚು. To open a [illegible]ut a seam.

ಹೊ[illegible]efilement; impu[illegible]-ಗೇರಿ. A place where [illegible]yas live. ಹೊಲೆಯ. A l[illegible]n, a Hŏlĕya; *f.* ಹೊಲತಿ. -ಚ[illegible]w-caste servant. -ಗೆ ಹೋಗು. Ob[illegible]course.

ಹೊಲ್ಲ a. k. *n.* [illegible]impropriety. *a.* Wicked; b[illegible]d.

ಹೊಸ k. *a.* New, novel; fresh, recent. *Cpds.:* -ಹುಪ್ಪ, -ನೀರು, -ಬೆಣ್ಣೆ, -ರೊಟ್ಟಿ, -ವರ, -ಹುಣುಮೆ, *etc.* -ತು, -ದು. That which is new, fresh, *etc.* -ಬ. A new man; *f.* -ಬಳು. -ತಾಗಿ, ಹೊಸ್ತಾಗಿ. Newly, recently.

ಹೊಸಕು, ಹೊಸಗು k. *v. t.* To rub anything between the hands or with the foot.

ಹೊಸಗೆ, ಹೊಸಿಗೆ k. *n.* Report, news, tidings. 2, joy. -ಹೇಳು. To relate news.

ಹೊಸತಿಲು, ಹೊಸ್ತಿಲು k. *n.* A threshold. -ದಾಟು. To cross the threshold.

ಹೊಸೆ (= ಪೊಸೆ) k. *v. t.* To twist, plait, make rope. 2, To churn.

ಹೊಸ್ತು. = ಹೊಸತು, *q. v.*

ಹೊಳಕು a. k. *v. i.* To appear, be manifest.

ಹೊಳಪು, ಹೊಳವು k. *n.* Radiance, lustre, brightness. ಹೊಳಪಿಸು. To furbish, scour.

ಹೊಳಲು (= ಪೊಳಲು. ಳ = ೞ) k. *n.* A town.

ಹೊಳೆ 1. k. *v. i.* To be radiant or bright; to shine, glitter. ಹೊಳಸು. = ಹೊಳಪಿಸು, *q. v.*

ಹೊಳೆ 2. (ಳೆ = ೞೆ) k. *n.* A river. -ಹಳ್ಳ, *dupl.* -ಗೆ ಕಟ್ಟು. A water-dam. -ದಾಟು, -ಹಾಯು. To cross a river.

ಹೊಳ್ಳು. = ಪೊಳ್ಳು, *q. v.*

ಹೊಳ್ಳು (= ಹೊರಳು, *q. v.*) k. *v. i.* To roll, *etc.* ಹೊಳ್ಳಿಸು. To cause to roll; to roll.

ಹೊಳ್ಳೆ (= ಸೊಳ್ಳೆ) k. *n.* A nostril.

ಹೋ 1. k. *int.* *A particle used in stopping, rejoicing or in sorrow.*

ಹೋ 2. k. *abbr. of* ಹೋಗುವ. -ಕ. Goer, *as* ದಾರಿಹೋಕ, ಹಾದಿಹೋಕ, *etc.* -ಗಾಲ. going time; death.

ಹೋ 3. k. *n.* *A particle of calling or surprise.*

ಹೋಕು k. *n.* A defect, fault, flaw. -ಮಾಡು. To maim. -ಹೋಗು. To be frustrated.

ಹೋಕೆ k. n. A way, passage. 2, impudence; hypocrisy. 3, debauchery.

ಹೋಗು k. v. i. To go, go off or away, proceed. 2, to be lost, disappear; to die. *P. p.* ಹೋಗಿ. *Rel. p. p.* ಹೋದ. -ಗೊಡು, -ಬಿಡು. To allow to go. ಹೋಗಿ ಬರು. To go and come. ಹೋಗಿಬಿಡು. To go away. ಕೊಂಡು-, ತೆಗೆದು ಕೊಂಡು-. To carry off. ಹೋಗಲಾಡಿಸು, ಹೋಗಾಡಿಸು. To make away with; to dissipate, destroy. ಹೋಗಲಾಡು. To let go; to lose. ಹೋಗಾಡು. To throw away, dissipate, squander; to quit. -ವಿಕೆ. Going, exit. ಹೋಯಿತು. *3rd pers. sing. imp. of* ಹೋಗು.

ಹೋಟೆ a. k. n. The hollow of a tree; emptiness.

ಹೋತ, ಹೋತು k. n. A he-goat.

ಹೋತೃ s. n. An offerer of an oblation.

ಹೋಬಳಿ k. n. A division of a talook. -ದಾರ. A chief of armed peons. -ಶಾನ ಭೋಗ. A village accountant.

ಹೋಮ s. n. A burnt-offering; a sacrifice. -ಕುಂಡ. A fireplace prepared for an oblation; *also* -ಶಾಲೆ. ಹೋಮಾಗ್ನಿ. A sacrificial fire.

ಹೋರಿ k. n. A young bull; a he-buffalo. -ಕರ. A he-calf. ಬೀಜದ-, ಕಾಯಿ-. An uncastrated bull. ಬೀಜ ಒಡದ-. A castrated bull.

ಹೋರು 1. k. v. t. To wrestle; to fight; to altercate. ಹೋರಾಟ. Mutual fight, strife, altercation. ಹೋರಾಡು. To wrestle, fight, wrangle.

ಹೋರು 2. k. n. A hole.

ಹೋರೆ (ರ = ಱ) k. n. Business, work.

ಹೋಲು k. v. i. To be like, resemble. -ವಿಕೆ, -ವೆ, ಹೋಲಿಕೆ. Resemblance, likeness, similarity. ಹೋಲಿಕೆ ಮಾಡು, ಹೋಲಿಸು. To make analogous; to compare.

ಹೋಹ (= ಹೋಗುವ) a. k. *Rel. pres. part. of* ಹೋಗು.

ಹೋಳಿ f. n. The hôḷi festival in desecration of cupid when his effigy is burnt; *also* -ಹಬ್ಬ.

ಹೋಳಿಗೆ (*tb. of* ಪೋಲಿಕಾ) n. A cake in general.

ಹೋಳು (ಳು = ೞು) k. n. A split, piece, slice.

ಹೌದಾ (=ಹವುದಾ, *q. v.*) f. n. An uncovered chair upon an elephant. 2, a reservoir.

ಹೌದು (= ಹವುದು, *q. v.*) k. *ad.* Yes. ಹೌದೇ, ಹೌದೇನೇ. Is it so? ಹೌದೇನೋ. Whether is it so? ಹೌದೋ ಅಲ್ಲವೋ. Is it or is it not?

ಹೌರ. = ಹವುರ, *q. v.*

ಹೌಸ h. n. Ambition, lust.

ಹ್ಯಾಗೆ, ಹ್ಯಾಂಗೆ k. *ad.* In what manner? how? ಹ್ಯಾಗಂದರೆ. That is to say, namely. ಹ್ಯಾಗಾದರೂ, ಹ್ಯಾಗೂ, ಹ್ಯಾಂಗಾದರೂ, ಹ್ಯಾಂಗೂ. Somehow; in one way or another, however, at all events.

ಹ್ರಸ್ವ s. *a.* Short, small. *n.* A short vowel.

ಹ್ರಾಸ s. n. Loss, detriment. 2, decrease, decline.

క్ష

క్ష The fifty-third letter of the alphabet.

ఱ

ఱ The fifty-fourth letter of the alphabet. ***At present it is obsolete and represented by ర.***